W9-ACC-544

JAMES FENIMORE COOPER

JAMES FENIMORE COOPER

THE LEATHERSTOCKING TALES

VOLUME I

The Pioneers, or the Sources of the Susquehanna; A Descriptive Tale

The Last of the Mohicans; A Narrative of 1757

The Prairie; A Tale

THE LIBRARY OF AMERICA

Distributed to the trade in the United States
and Canada by the Viking Press.

Published outside North America by the Press Syndicate of the
University of Cambridge,
The Pitt Building, Trumpington Street, Cambridge CB2 1RP, England.
ISBN 0 521 30096 7

Library of Congress Catalog Card Number: 84–25060
For Cataloging in Publication Data, see end of *Notes* section.
ISBN 0–940450–20–8

First Printing

Manufactured in the United States of America

BLAKE NEVIUS

WROTE THE NOTES AND SELECTED THE TEXTS FOR THIS VOLUME

The texts in this volume are from The Writings of James Fenimore Cooper, edited by James Franklin Beard, Editor-in-Chief, and James P. Elliott, Chief Textual Editor, sponsored by Clark University and the American Antiquarian Society, and published by the State University of New York Press. The text of The Pioneers was edited by Lance Schachterle and Kenneth M. Andersen, Jr.; the text of The Last of the Mohicans was edited by James A. Sappenfield and E. N. Feltskog; the text of The Prairie was edited by James P. Elliott.

Grateful acknowledgement is made to the National Endowment for the Humanities and the Ford Foundation for their generous financial support of this series.

Contents

Readers who wish to follow the chronological order of Natty Bumppo's career should read The Leatherstocking Tales in the following sequence: The Deerslayer, The Last of the Mohicans, The Pathfinder, The Pioneers, and The Prairie.

THE PIONEERS

or the Sources of the Susquehanna
A Descriptive Tale

"Extremes of habits, manners, time and space,
Brought close together, here stood face to face,
And gave at once a contrast to the view,
That other lands and ages never knew."

Paulding, *The Backwoodsman*, II, 571–4.

TO

Jacob Sutherland,

of Blenheim, Schoharie,

ESQUIRE.

The length of our friendship would be a sufficient reason for prefixing your name to these pages; but your residence so near the scene of the tale, and your familiarity with much of the character and kind of life that I have attempted to describe, render it more peculiarly proper. You, at least, dear Sutherland, will not receive this dedication as a cold compliment, but as an evidence of the feeling that makes me,

Warmly and truly,
Your friend,

——— ———.

Preface

TO MR. CHARLES WILEY, *Bookseller.*

Every man is, more or less, the sport of accident; nor do I know that authors are at all exempted from this humiliating influence. This is the third of my novels, and it depends on two very uncertain contingencies, whether it will not be the last;—the one being the public opinion, and the other mine own humour. The first book was written, because I was told that I could not write a grave tale; so, to prove that the world did not know me, I wrote one that was so grave nobody would read it; wherein I think that I had much the best of the argument. The second was written to see if I could not overcome this neglect of the reading world. How far I have succeeded, Mr. Charles Wiley, must ever remain a secret between ourselves. The third has been written, exclusively, to please myself; so it would be no wonder if it displeased every body else; for what two ever thought alike, on a subject of the imagination!

I should think criticism to be the perfection of human acquirements, did there not exist this discrepancy in taste. Just as I have made up my mind to adopt the very sagacious hints of one learned Reviewer, a pamphlet is put into my hands, containing the remarks of another, who condemns all that his rival praises, and praises all that his rival condemns. There I am, left like an ass between two locks of hay; so that I have determined to relinquish my animate nature, and remain stationary, like a lock of hay between two asses.

It is now a long time, say the wise ones, since the world has been told all that is new and novel. But the Reviewers (the cunning wights!) have adopted an ingenious expedient, to give a freshness to the most trite idea. They clothe it in a language so obscure and metaphysical, that the reader is not about to comprehend their pages without some labour. This is called a great "range of thought;" and not improperly, as I can testify; for, in my own case, I have frequently ranged the universe of ideas, and come back again in as perfect ignorance of their meaning as when I set out. It is delightful, to see the literati of a circulating library get hold of one of these difficult periods! Their praise of the performance is exactly commensurate with its obscurity. Every body knows that to seem wise is the first requisite in a great man.

A common word in the mouths of all Reviewers, readers of magazines, and young ladies, when speaking of novels, is "*keeping*;" and yet there are but few who attach the same meaning to it. I belong, myself, to the old school, in this particular, and think that it applies more to the subject in hand, than to any use of terms, or of cant expressions. As a man might just as well be out of the world as out of "keeping," I have endeavoured to confine myself, in this tale, strictly to its observance. This is a formidable curb to the imagination, as, doubtless, the reader will very soon discover; but under its influence I have come to the conclusion, that the writer of a tale, who takes the earth for the scene of his story, is in some degree bound to respect human nature. Therefore I would advise any one, who may take up this book, with the expectation of meeting gods and goddesses, spooks or witches, or of feeling that strong excitement that is produced by battles and murders, to throw it aside at once, for no such interest will be found in any of its pages.

I have already said, that it was mine own humour that suggested this tale; but it is a humour that is deeply connected with feeling. Happier periods, more interesting events, and, possibly, more beautiful scenes, might have been selected, to exemplify my subject; but none of either that would be so dear to me. I wish, therefore, to be judged more by what I have done, than by my sins of omission. I have introduced one battle, but it is not of the most Homeric kind. As for murders, the population of a new country will not admit of such a waste of human life. There might possibly have been one or two hangings, to the manifest advantage of the "settlement;" but then it would have been out of "keeping" with the humane laws of this compassionate country.

The "Pioneers" is now before the world, Mr. Wiley, and I shall look to you for the only true account of its reception. The critics may write as obscurely as they please, and look much wiser than they are; the papers may puff or abuse, as their changeful humours dictate; but if you meet me with a smiling face, I shall at once know that all is essentially well.

If you should ever have occasion for a preface, I beg you will let me hear from you, in reply.

Yours, truly,

THE AUTHOR.

New-York, January 1st, 1823.

Introduction

As this work professes, in its title page, to be a descriptive tale, they who will take the trouble to read it, may be glad to know how much of its contents is literal fact, and how much is intended to represent a general picture. The author is very sensible, that had he confined himself to the latter, always the most effective, as it is the most valuable mode of conveying knowledge of this nature, he would have made a far better book. But, in commencing to describe scenes, and perhaps he may add characters, that were so familiar to his own youth, there was a constant temptation to delineate that which he had known rather than that which he might have imagined. This rigid adhesion to truth, an indispensable requisite in history and travels, destroys the charm of fiction, for all that is necessary to be conveyed to the mind by the latter had better be done by delineations of principles and of characters in their classes, than by a too fastidious attention to originals.

New-York having but one county of Otsego, and the Susquehannah but one proper source, there can be no mistake as to the site of the Tale. The history of this district of Country, so far as it is connected with civilized man, is soon told.

Otsego, in common with most of the interior of the Province of New-York, was included in the county of Albany, previously to the war of the separation. It then became, in a subsequent division of territory, a part of Montgomery; and, finally, having obtained a sufficient population of its own, it was set apart as a county by itself, shortly after the peace of 1783. It lies among those low spurs of the Alleganies which cover the midland counties of New-York, and it is a little east of a meridional line drawn through the centre of the state. As the waters of New-York either flow southerly into the Atlantic, or northerly into Ontario and its outlet, Otsego Lake, being the source of the Susquehannah, is, of necessity, among its highest lands. The face of the country, the climate as it was found by the whites, and the manners of the settlers, are described with a minuteness for which the author has no other apology than the force of his own recollections.

Otsego is said to be a word compounded of Ot, a place of meeting, and Sego, or Sago, the ordinary term of salutation, used by the Indians of this region. There is a tradition which says, that the neighbouring tribes were accustomed to meet on the banks of the lake, to make their treaties, and otherwise to strengthen their alliances, and which refers the name to this practice. As the Indian Agent of New-York had a log dwelling at the foot of the lake, however, it is not impossible that the appellation grew out of the meetings that were held at his "Council Fires." The war drove off the agent, in common with the other officers of the crown, and his rude dwelling was soon abandoned. The author remembers it, a few years later, reduced to the humble office of a smoke-house.

In 1779, an expedition was sent against the hostile Indians who dwelt, about a hundred miles west of Otsego, on the banks of the Cayuga. The whole country was then a wilderness, and it was necessary to transport the baggage of the troops, by means of the rivers, a devious but practicable route. One brigade ascended the Mohawk, until it reached the point nearest to the sources of the Susquehannah, whence it cut a lane through the forest to the head of the Otsego. The boats and baggage were carried over this 'portage,' and the troops proceeded to the other extremity of the lake, where they disembarked and encamped. The Susquehannah, a narrow though rapid stream at its source, was much filled with "flood wood," or fallen trees, and the troops adopted a novel expedient to facilitate their passage. The Otsego is about nine miles in length, varying in breadth, from half a mile to a mile and a half. The water is of great depth, limpid, and supplied from a thousand springs. At its foot, the banks are rather less than thirty feet high, the remainder of its margin being in mountains, intervals, and points. The outlet, or the Susquehannah, flows through a gorge, in the low banks just mentioned, which may have a width of two hundred feet. This gorge was dammed, and the waters of the lake collected. The Susquehannah was converted into a rill. When all was ready, the troops embarked, the dam was knocked away, the Otsego poured out its torrent, and the boats went merrily down with the current.

Gen. James Clinton, the brother of George Clinton, then

Governor of New-York, and the father of De Witt Clinton, who died Governor of the same state in 1827, commanded the brigade employed on this duty. During the stay of the troops at the foot of the Otsego, a soldier was shot for desertion. The grave of this unfortunate man was the first place of human interment that the author ever beheld, as the smoke-house was the first ruin! The swivel, alluded to in this work, was buried, and abandoned by the troops, on this occasion, and it was subsequently found in digging the cellars of the author's paternal residence.

Soon after the close of the war, Washington, accompanied by many distinguished men, visited the scene of this tale, it is said with a view to examine the facilities for opening a communication by water, with other points of the Country. He staid but a few hours.

In 1785, the author's father, who had an interest in extensive tracts of land in this wilderness, arrived with a party of Surveyors. The manner in which the scene met his eye is described by Judge Temple. At the commencement of the following year, the settlement began, and from that time to this, the county has continued to flourish. It is a singular feature in American life, that, at the beginning of this century, when the proprietor of the estate, had occasion for settlers, on a new settlement and in a remote county, he was enabled to draw them from among the increase of the former colony.

Although the settlement of this part of Otsego a little preceded the birth of the author, it was not sufficiently advanced to render it desirable that an event, so important to himself, should take place in the wilderness. Perhaps his mother had a reasonable distrust of the practice of Dr. Todd, who must then have been in the noviciate of his experimental acquirements. Be that as it may, the author was brought an infant into this valley and all his first impressions were here obtained. He has inhabited it, ever since, at intervals, and he thinks he can answer for the faithfulness of the picture he has drawn.

Otsego has now become one of the most populous districts of New-York. It sends forth its emigrants like any other old region, and it is pregnant with industry and enterprise. Its manufactures are prosperous, and, it is worthy of remark, that one of the most ingenious machines known in European art, is derived from the keen ingenuity which is exercised in this remote region.

In order to prevent mistake, it may be well to say that the incidents of this tale are purely a fiction. The literal facts are chiefly connected with the natural and artificial objects, and the customs of the inhabitants. Thus the Academy, and Court house, and gaol, and inn, and most similar things are tolerably exact. They have all, long since, given place to other buildings of a more pretending character. There is also some liberty taken with the truth in the description of the principal dwelling: the real building had no "firstly" and "lastly." It was of bricks and not of stones, and its roof exhibited none of the peculiar beauties of the "composite order." It was erected in an age too primitive for that ambitious school of architecture. But the author indulged his recollections freely, when he had fairly entered the door. Here all is literal, even to the severed arm of Wolfe and the urn which held the ashes of Queen Dido.*

The author has elsewhere said that the character of the Leather Stocking is a creation, rendered probable by such auxiliaries as were necessary to produce that effect. Had he drawn still more upon fancy, the lovers of fiction would not have so much cause for their objections to his work. Still the picture would not have been in the least true, without some substitutes for most of the other personages. The great Proprietor resident on his lands, and giving his name to instead of receiving it from his estates, as in Europe, is common over the whole of New York. The physician, with his theory rather obtained than corrected by experiments on the human constitution, the pious, self-denying, laborious, and ill paid missionary, the half-educated, litigious, envious and disreputable lawyer with his counterpoise, a brother of the profession of better origin and of better character, the shiftless, bargaining,

*Though forests still crown the mountains of Otsego, the bear, the wolf and the panther are nearly strangers to them. Even the innocent deer is rarely seen bounding beneath their arches, for the rifle and the activity of the settlers have driven them to other haunts. To this change, which in some particulars is melancholy to one who knew the country in its infancy, it may be added that the Otsego is beginning to be a niggard of its treasures.

discontented seller of his "betterments," the plausible carpenter, and most of the others are more familiar to all who have ever dwelt in a new Country.

From circumstances, which, after this introduction, will be obvious to all, the author has had more pleasure in writing The Pioneers, than the book will probably ever give any of its readers. He is quite aware of its numerous faults, some of which he has endeavoured to repair in this edition, but as he has, in intention at least, done his full share in amusing the world, he trusts to its good nature for overlooking this attempt to please himself.

Paris, March, 1832.

Chapter I

"See, Winter comes, to rule the varied year,
Sullen and sad, with all his rising train;
Vapours, and clouds, and storms—"
Thomson, *The Seasons*, "Winter," 1–3.

NEAR THE CENTRE of the State of New-York lies an extensive district of country, whose surface is a succession of hills and dales, or, to speak with greater deference to geographical definitions, of mountains and valleys. It is among these hills that the Delaware takes its rise; and flowing from the limpid lakes and thousand springs of this region, the numerous sources of the Susquehanna meander through the valleys, until, uniting their streams, they form one of the proudest rivers of the United States. The mountains are generally arable to the tops, although instances are not wanting, where the sides are jutted with rocks, that aid greatly in giving to the country that romantic and picturesque character which it so eminently possesses. The vales are narrow, rich, and cultivated; with a stream uniformly winding through each. Beautiful and thriving villages are found interspersed along the margins of the small lakes, or situated at those points of the streams which are favourable to manufacturing; and neat and comfortable farms, with every indication of wealth about them, are scattered profusely through the vales, and even to the mountain tops. Roads diverge in every direction, from the even and graceful bottoms of the valleys, to the most rugged and intricate passes of the hills. Academies, and minor edifices of learning, meet the eye of the stranger, at every few miles, as he winds his way through this uneven territory; and places for the worship of God, abound with that frequency which characterises a moral and reflecting people, and with that variety of exterior and canonical government which flows from unfettered liberty of conscience. In short, the whole district is hourly exhibiting how much can be done, in even a rugged country, and with a severe climate, under the dominion of mild laws, and where every man feels a direct interest in the prosperity of a commonwealth, of which he knows himself to form a part. The expedients of the pioneers who first broke ground in the settlement of this country, are succeeded by the permanent improvements of the yeoman, who intends to leave his remains to moulder under the sod which he tills, or, perhaps, of the son, who, born in the land, piously wishes to linger around the grave of his father.——Only forty years* have passed since this territory was a wilderness.

Very soon after the establishment of the independence of the States by the peace of 1783, the enterprise of their citizens was directed to a development of the natural advantages of their widely extended dominions. Before the war of the revolution, the inhabited parts of the colony of New-York were limited to less than a tenth of its possessions. A narrow belt of country, extending for a short distance on either side of the Hudson, with a similar occupation of fifty miles on the banks of the Mohawk, together with the islands of Nassau and Staten, and a few insulated settlements on chosen land along the margins of streams, composed the country, which was then inhabited by less than two hundred thousand souls. Within the short period we have mentioned, the population has spread itself over five degrees of latitude and seven of longitude, and has swelled to a million and a half of inhabitants†, who are maintained in abundance, and can look forward to ages before the evil day must arrive, when their possessions shall become unequal to their wants.

Our tale begins in 1793, about seven years after the commencement of one of the earliest of those settlements, which have conduced to effect that magical change in the power and condition of the state, to which we have alluded.

It was near the setting of the sun, on a clear, cold day in December, when a sleigh was moving slowly up one of the mountains in the district we have described. The day had been fine for the season, and but two or three large clouds, whose colour seemed brightened by the light reflected from the mass of snow that covered the earth, floated in a sky of the purest blue. The road wound along the brow of a precipice, and on one side was upheld by a foundation of logs,

*The book was written in 1821–22.

†The population of New York is now (1831) quite 2,000,000.

piled one upon the other, while a narrow excavation in the mountain, in the opposite direction, had made a passage of sufficient width for the ordinary travelling of that day. But logs, excavation, and every thing that did not reach several feet above the earth, lay alike buried beneath the snow. A single track, barely wide enough to receive the sleigh*, denoted the route of the highway, and this was sunk nearly two feet below the surrounding surface. In the vale, which lay at a distance of several hundred feet lower, there was what in the language of the country was called a *clearing*, and all the usual improvements of a new settlement: these even extended up the hill to the point where the road turned short and ran across the level land, which lay on the summit of the mountain; but the summit itself remained in forest. There was a glittering in the atmosphere, as if it were filled with innumerable shining particles, and the noble bay horses that drew the sleigh were covered, in many parts, with a coat of hoar frost. The vapour from their nostrils was seen to issue like smoke; and every object in the view, as well as every arrangement of the travellers, denoted the depth of a winter in the mountains. The harness, which was of a deep dull black, differing from the glossy varnishing of the present day, was ornamented with enormous plates and buckles of brass, that shone like gold in those transient beams of the sun, which found their way obliquely through the tops of the trees. Huge saddles, studded with nails, and fitted with cloths that served as blankets to the shoulders of the animals, supported four high, square-topped turrets, through which the stout reins led from the mouths of the horses to the hands of the driver, who was

*Sleigh is the word used in every part of the United States to denote a traineau. It is of local use in the west of England, whence it is most probably derived by the Americans. The latter draw a distinction between a sled, or sledge, and a sleigh; the sleigh being shod with metal. Sleighs are also subdivided into two-horse and one-horse sleighs. Of the latter, there are the cutter, with thills so arranged as to permit the horse to travel in the side track; the "pung," or "tow-pung," which is driven with a pole, and the "jumper," a rude construction used for temporary purposes, in the new countries.

Many of the American sleighs are elegant, though the use of this mode of conveyance is much lessened with the melioration of the climate, consequent on the clearing of the forests.

a negro, of apparently twenty years of age. His face, which nature had coloured with a glistening black, was now mottled with the cold, and his large shining eyes filled with tears; a tribute to its power, that the keen frosts of those regions always extracted from one of his African origin. Still there was a smiling expression of good humour in his happy countenance, that was created by the thoughts of home, and a Christmas fire-side, with its Christmas frolics. The sleigh was one of those large, comfortable, old-fashioned conveyances, which would admit a whole family within its bosom, but which now contained only two passengers besides the driver. The colour of its outside was of a modest green, and that of its inside a fiery red. The latter was intended to convey the idea of heat in that cold climate. Large buffalo skins, trimmed around the edges with red cloth, cut into festoons, covered the back of the sleigh, and were spread over its bottom, and drawn up around the feet of the travellers—one of whom was a man of middle age, and the other a female, just entering upon womanhood. The former was of a large stature; but the precautions he had taken to guard against the cold, left but little of his person exposed to view. A great-coat, that was abundantly ornamented by a profusion of furs, enveloped the whole of his figure, excepting the head, which was covered with a cap of marten skins, lined with morocco, the sides of which were made to fall, if necessary, and were now drawn close over the ears, and fastened beneath his chin with a black ribbon. The top of the cap was surmounted with the tail of the animal whose skin had furnished the rest of the materials, which fell back, not ungracefully, a few inches behind the head. From beneath this masque were to be seen part of a fine manly face, and particularly a pair of expressive, large blue eyes, that promised extraordinary intellect, covert humour, and great benevolence. The form of his companion was literally hid beneath the garments she wore. There were furs and silks peeping from under a large camblet cloak, with a thick flannel lining, that, by its cut and size, was evidently intended for a masculine wearer. A huge hood of black silk, that was quilted with down, concealed the whole of her head, except at a small opening in front for breath, through which occasionally sparkled a pair of animated jet-black eyes.

Both the father and daughter (for such was the connexion between the two travellers) were too much occupied with their reflections to break a stillness, that received little or no interruption from the easy gliding of the sleigh, by the sound of their voices. The former was thinking of the wife that had held this their only child to her bosom, when, four years before, she had reluctantly consented to relinquish the society of her daughter, in order that the latter might enjoy the advantages of an education, which the city of New York could only offer at that period. A few months afterwards death had deprived him of the remaining companion of his solitude; but still he had enough of real regard for his child, not to bring her into the comparative wilderness in which he dwelt, until the full period had expired, to which he had limited her juvenile labours. The reflections of the daughter were less melancholy, and mingled with a pleased astonishment at the novel scenery she met at every turn in the road.

The mountain on which they were journeying was covered with pines, that rose without a branch some seventy or eighty feet, and which frequently doubled that height, by the addition of the tops. Through the innumerable vistas that opened beneath the lofty trees the eye could penetrate, until it was met by a distant inequality in the ground, or was stopped by a view of the summit of the mountain which lay on the opposite side of the valley to which they were hastening. The dark trunks of the trees, rose from the pure white of the snow, in regularly formed shafts, until, at a great height, their branches shot forth horizontal limbs, that were covered with the meager foliage of an evergreen, affording a melancholy contrast to the torpor of nature below. To the travellers there seemed to be no wind; but these pines waved majestically at their topmost boughs, sending forth a dull, plaintive sound, that was quite in consonance with the rest of the melancholy scene.

The sleigh had glided for some distance along the even surface, and the gaze of the female was bent in inquisitive, and, perhaps, timid glances, into the recesses of the forest, when a loud and continued howling was heard, pealing under the long arches of the woods, like the cry of a numerous pack of hounds. The instant the sound reached the ears of the gentleman, he cried aloud to the black—

"Hold up, Aggy; there is old Hector; I should know his bay among ten thousand. The Leather-stocking has put his hounds into the hills this clear day, and they have started their game. There is a deer-track a few rods ahead;—and now, Bess, if thou canst muster courage enough to stand fire, I will give thee a saddle for thy Christmas dinner."

The black drew up, with a cheerful grin upon his chilled features, and began thrashing his arms together, in order to restore the circulation to his fingers, while the speaker stood erect, and, throwing aside his outer covering, stept from the sleigh upon a bank of snow, which sustained his weight without yielding.

In a few moments the speaker succeeded in extricating a double-barrelled fowling piece from amongst a multitude of trunks and bandboxes. After throwing aside the thick mittens which had encased his hands, that now appeared in a pair of leather gloves tipped with fur, he examined his priming, and was about to move forward, when the light bounding noise of an animal plunging through the woods was heard, and a fine buck darted into the path, a short distance ahead of him. The appearance of the animal was sudden, and his flight inconceivably rapid; but the traveller appeared to be too keen a sportsman to be disconcerted by either. As it came first into view he raised the fowling piece to his shoulder, and, with a practised eye and steady hand, drew a trigger. The deer dashed forward undaunted, and apparently unhurt. Without lowering his piece, the traveller turned its muzzle towards his victim, and fired again. Neither discharge, however, seemed to have taken effect.

The whole scene had passed with a rapidity that confused the female, who was unconsciously rejoicing in the escape of the buck, as he rather darted like a meteor, than ran across the road, when a sharp, quick sound struck her ear, quite different from the full, round reports of her father's gun, but still sufficiently distinct to be known as the concussion produced by fire-arms. At the same instant that she heard this unexpected report, the buck sprang from the snow, to a great height in the air, and directly a second discharge, similar in sound to the first, followed, when the animal came to the earth, falling headlong, and rolling over on the crust with its own velocity. A loud shout was given by the unseen marksman, and a couple of men instantly appeared from behind the trunks of two of the pines, where they had evidently placed themselves in expectation of the passage of the deer.

"Ha! Natty, had I known you were in ambush, I should not have fired," cried the traveller, moving towards the spot where the deer lay—near to which he was followed by the delighted black, with his sleigh; "but the sound of old Hector was too exhilarating to be quiet; though I hardly think I struck him either."

"No—no—Judge," returned the hunter, with an inward chuckle, and with that look of exultation, that indicates a consciousness of superior skill; "you burnt your powder, only to warm your nose this cold evening. Did ye think to stop a full grown buck, with Hector and the slut open upon him, within sound, with that pop-gun in your hand? There's plenty of pheasants amongst the swamps; and the snow birds are flying round your own door, where you may feed them with crumbs, and shoot them at pleasure, any day; but if you're for a buck, or a little bear's meat, Judge, you'll have to take the long rifle, with a greased wadding, or you'll waste more powder than you'll fill stomachs, I'm thinking."

As the speaker concluded he drew his bare hand across the bottom of his nose, and again opened his enormous mouth with a kind of inward laugh.

"The gun scatters well, Natty, and it has killed a deer before now," said the traveller, smiling good humouredly. "One barrel was charged with buck shot; but the other was loaded for birds only.—Here are two hurts; one through the neck, and the other directly through the heart. It is by no means certain, Natty, but I gave him one of the two."

"Let who will kill him," said the hunter, rather surlily, "I suppose the cretur is to be eaten." So saying, he drew a large knife from a leathern sheath, which was stuck through his girdle or sash, and cut the throat of the animal. "If there is two balls through the deer, I would ask if there wasn't two rifles fired—besides, who ever saw sich a ragged hole from a smooth-bore, as this through the neck?—and you will own yourself, Judge, that the buck fell at the last shot, which was sent from a truer and a younger hand, than your'n or mine 'ither; but for my part, although I am a poor man, I can live without the venison, but I don't love to give up my lawful dues in a free country.—Though, for the matter of that, might often makes right here, as well as in the old country, for what I can see."

An air of sullen dissatisfaction pervaded the manner of the hunter during the whole of this speech; yet he thought it prudent to utter the close of the sentence in such an under tone, as to leave nothing audible but the grumbling sounds of his voice.

"Nay, Natty," rejoined the traveller, with undisturbed good humour, "it is for the honour that I contend. A few dollars will pay for the venison; but what will requite me for the lost honour of a buck's tail in my cap? Think, Natty, how I should triumph over that quizzing dog, Dick Jones, who has failed seven times already this season, and has only brought in one wood-chuck and a few grey squirrels."

"Ah! the game is becoming hard to find, indeed, Judge, with your clearings and betterments," said the old hunter, with a kind of compelled resignation. "The time has been, when I have shot thirteen deer, without counting the fa'ns, standing in the door of my own hut;—and for bear's meat, if one wanted a ham or so, he had only to watch a-nights, and he could shoot one by moonlight, through the cracks of the logs; no fear of his over-sleeping himself, n'ither, for the howling of the wolves was sartin to keep his eyes open. There's old Hector,"—patting with affection a tall hound, of black and yellow spots, with white belly and legs, that just then came in on the scent, accompanied by the slut he had mentioned; "see where the wolves bit his throat, the night I druve them from the venison that was smoking on the chimbly top—that dog is more to be trusted than many a Christian man; for he never forgets a friend, and loves the hand that gives him bread."

There was a peculiarity in the manner of the hunter, that attracted the notice of the young female, who had been a close and interested observer of his appearance and equipments, from the moment he came into view. He was tall, and so meager as to make him seem above even the six feet that he actually stood in his stockings. On his head, which was thinly covered with lank, sandy hair, he wore a cap made of fox-skin, resembling in shape the one we have already described, although much inferior in finish and ornaments. His face was skinny, and thin almost to emaciation; but yet it bore no signs of disease;—on the contrary, it had every indication of the most robust and enduring health. The cold and the exposure had, together, given it a colour of uniform red; his grey eyes were glancing under a pair of shaggy brows, that overhung them in long hairs of grey mingled with their natural hue; his scraggy neck was bare, and burnt to the same tint with his face; though a small part of a shirt collar, made of the country check, was to be seen above the over-dress he wore. A kind of coat, made of dressed deer-skin, with the hair on, was belted close to his lank body, by a girdle of coloured worsted. On his feet were deer-skin moccasins, ornamented with porcupines' quills, after the manner of the Indians, and his limbs were guarded with long leggings of the same material as the moccasins, which, gartering over the knees of his tarnished buck-skin breeches, had obtained for him, among the settlers, the nick name of Leather-stocking. Over his left shoulder was slung a belt of deer-skin, from which depended an enormous ox horn, so thinly scraped, as to discover the powder it contained. The larger end was fitted ingeniously and securely with a wooden bottom, and the other was stopped tight by a little plug. A leathern pouch hung before him, from which, as he concluded his last speech, he took a small measure, and, filling it accurately with powder, he commenced re-loading the rifle, which, as its butt rested on the snow before him, reached nearly to the top of his fox-skin cap.

The traveller had been closely examining the wounds during these movements, and now, without heeding the ill humour of the hunter's manner, he exclaimed—

"I would fain establish a right, Natty, to the honour of this death; and surely if the hit in the neck be mine, it is enough; for the shot in the heart was unnecessary—what we call an act of supererogation, Leather-stocking."

"You may call it by what larned name you please, Judge," said the hunter, throwing his rifle across his left arm, and knocking up a brass lid in the breech, from which he took a small piece of greased leather, and wrapping a ball in it, forced them down by main strength on the powder, where he continued to pound them while speaking. "It's far easier to call names, than to shoot a buck on the spring; but the cretur come by his end from a younger hand than 'ither your'n or mine, as I said before."

"What say you, my friend," cried the traveller, turning pleasantly to Natty's companion; "shall we toss up this dollar for the honour, and you keep the silver if you lose—what say you, friend?"

"That I killed the deer," answered the young man, with a little haughtiness, as he leaned on another long rifle, similar to that of Natty's.

"Here are two to one, indeed," replied the Judge, with a smile; "I am out-voted—over-ruled, as we say on the bench. There is Aggy, he can't vote, being a slave; and Bess is a minor—so I must even make the best of it. But you'll sell me the venison; and the deuce is in it, but I make a good story about its death."

"The meat is none of mine to sell," said Leather-stocking, adopting a little of his companion's hauteur; "for my part, I have known animals travel days with shots in the neck, and I'm none of them who'll rob a man of his rightful dues."

"You are tenacious of your rights, this cold evening, Natty," returned the Judge, with unconquerable good nature; "but what say you, young man, will three dollars pay you for the buck?"

"First let us determine the question of right to the satisfaction of us both," said the youth, firmly but respectfully, and with a pronunciation and language vastly superior to his appearance; "with how many shot did you load your gun?"

"With five, sir," said the Judge, a little struck with the other's manner; "are they not enough to slay a buck like this?"

"One would do it; but," moving to the tree from behind which he had appeared, "you know, sir, you fired in this direction—here are four of the bullets in the tree."

The Judge examined the fresh marks in the bark of the pine, and, shaking his head, said, with a laugh—

"You are making out the case against yourself, my young advocate—where is the fifth?"

"Here," said the youth, throwing aside the rough over-coat that he wore, and exhibiting a hole in his under garment, through which large drops of blood were oozing.

"Good God!" exclaimed the Judge, with horror; "have I been trifling here about an empty distinction, and a fellow creature suffering from my hands without a murmur? But hasten—quick—get into my sleigh—it is but a mile to the village, where surgical aid can be obtained;—all shall be done at my expence, and thou shalt live with me until thy wound is healed—aye, and for ever afterwards."

"I thank you for your good intention, but I must decline your offer. I have a friend who would be uneasy were he to hear that I am hurt and away from him. The injury is but slight, and the bullet has missed the bones; but I believe, sir, you will now admit my title to the venison."

"Admit it!" repeated the agitated Judge; "I here give thee a right to shoot deer, or bears, or any thing thou pleasest in my woods, forever. Leather-stocking is the only other man that I have granted the same privilege to; and the time is coming when it will be of value. But I buy your deer—here, this bill will pay thee, both for thy shot and my own."

The old hunter gathered his tall person up into an air of pride, during this dialogue, but he waited until the other had done speaking.

"There's them living who say, that Nathaniel Bumppo's right to shoot on these hills, is of older date than Marmaduke Temple's right to forbid him," he said. "But if there's a law about it at all, though who ever heard of a law, that a man should'nt kill deer where he pleased!—but if there is a law at all, it should be to keep people from the use of smooth-bores. A body never knows where his lead will fly, when he pulls the trigger of one of them uncertain fire-arms."

Without attending to the soliloquy of Natty, the youth bowed his head silently to the offer of the bank note, and replied—

"Excuse me; I have need of the venison."

"But this will buy you many deer," said the Judge; "take it I entreat you," and lowering his voice to a whisper, he added—"it is for a hundred dollars."

For an instant only, the youth seemed to hesitate, and then, blushing even through the high colour that the cold had given to his cheeks, as if with inward shame at his own weakness, he again declined the offer.

During this scene the female arose, and, regardless of the cold air, she threw back the hood which concealed her features, and now spoke, with great earnestness—

"Surely, surely—young man—sir—you would not pain my father so much, as to have him think that he leaves a fellow creature in this wilderness, whom his own hand has injured. I entreat you will go with us, and receive medical aid."

Whether his wound became more painful, or there was something irresistible in the voice and manner of the fair pleader for her father's feelings, we know not, but the distance of the young man's manner was sensibly softened by this appeal, and he stood, in apparent doubt, as if reluctant to comply with, and yet unwilling to refuse her request. The Judge, for such being his office, must, in future, be his title, watched, with no little interest, the display of this singular contention in the feelings of the youth, and advancing, kindly took his hand, and, as he pulled him gently towards the sleigh, urged him to enter it.

"There is no human aid nearer than Templeton," he said, "and the hut of Natty is full three miles from this;—come—come, my young friend, go with us, and let the new doctor look to this shoulder of thine. Here is Natty will take the tidings of thy welfare to thy friend; and should'st thou require it, thou shalt return home in the morning."

The young man succeeded in extricating his hand from the warm grasp of the Judge, but he continued to gaze on the face of the female, who, regardless of the cold, was still standing with her fine features exposed, which expressed feelings that eloquently seconded the request of her father. Leather-stocking stood, in the mean time, leaning upon his long rifle, with his head turned a little to one side, as if engaged in sagacious musing; when, having apparently satisfied his doubts, by revolving the subject in his mind, he broke silence—

"It may be best to go, lad, after all; for if the shot hangs under the skin, my hand is getting too old to be cutting into human flesh, as I once used to could. Though some thirty years agone, in the old war, when I was out under Sir William, I travelled seventy miles alone in the howling wilderness, with a rifle bullet in my thigh, and then cut it out with my own jack-knife. Old Indian John knows the time well. I met him with a party of the Delawares, on the trail of the Iroquois, who had been down and taken five scalps on the Schoharie. But I made a mark on the red-skin that I'll warrant he carried to his grave. I took him on his posterum, saving the lady's presence, as he got up from the amboosh, and rattled three buck shot into his naked hide, so close, that you might have laid a broad joe upon them all—" here Natty stretched out his long neck, and straightened his body, as he opened his mouth, which exposed a single tusk of yellow bone, while his eyes, his face, even his whole frame, seemed to laugh, although no sound was emitted, except a kind of thick hissing, as he inhaled his breath in quavers. "I had lost my bullet mould in crossing the Oneida outlet, and had to make shift with the buck shot; but the rifle was true, and didn't scatter like your two legged thing there, Judge, which don't do, I find, to hunt in company with."

Natty's apology to the delicacy of the young lady was unnecessary, for, while he was speaking, she was too much employed in helping her father to remove certain articles of baggage to hear him. Unable to resist the kind urgency of the travellers any longer, the youth, though still with an unaccountable reluctance, suffered himself to be persuaded to enter the sleigh. The black with the aid of his master threw the buck across the baggage, and entering the vehicle themselves, the Judge invited the hunter to do so likewise.

"No—no—" said the old man, shaking his head; "I have work to do at home this Christmas eve—drive on with the boy, and let your doctor look to the shoulder; though if he will only cut out the shot, I have yarbs that will heal the wound quicker than all his foreign 'intments." He turned and was about to move off, when, suddenly recollecting himself, he again faced the party, and added—"If you see any thing of Indian John about the foot of the lake, you had better take him with you, and let him lend the doctor a hand; for, old as he is, he is curous at cuts and bruises, and it's likelier than not he'll be in with brooms to sweep your Christmas ha'arths."

"Stop—stop," cried the youth, catching the arm of the black as he prepared to urge his horses forward; "Natty—you need say nothing of the shot, nor of where I am going—remember, Natty, as you love me."

"Trust old Leather-stocking," returned the hunter, significantly; "he has'nt lived fifty years in the wilderness, and not larnt from the savages how to hold his tongue—trust to me, lad; and remember old Indian John."

"And, Natty," said the youth, eagerly, still holding the black by the arm, "I will just get the shot extracted, and bring you up, to-night, a quarter of the buck, for the Christmas dinner."

He was interrupted by the hunter, who held up his finger with an expressive gesture for silence. He then moved softly along the margin of the road, keeping his eyes steadfastly fixed on the branches of a pine. When he had obtained such a position as he wished, he stopped, and cocking his rifle, threw one leg far behind him, and stretching his left arm to its utmost extent along the barrel of his piece, he began slowly to raise its muzzle in a line with the straight trunk of the tree. The eyes of the group in the sleigh naturally preceded the movement of the rifle, and they soon discovered the object of Natty's aim. On a small dead branch of the pine, which, at the distance of seventy feet from the ground, shot out horizontally, immediately beneath the living members of the tree, sat a bird, that in the vulgar language of the country, was indiscriminately called a pheasant or a partridge. In size, it was but little smaller than a common barn-yard fowl. The baying of the dogs, and the conversation that had passed near the root of the tree on which it was perched, had alarmed the bird, which was now drawn up near the body of the pine, with a head and neck so erect, as to form nearly a straight line with its legs. As soon as the rifle bore on the victim, Natty drew his trigger, and the partridge fell from its height with a force that buried it in the snow.

"Lie down, you old villain," exclaimed Leather-stocking, shaking his ramrod at Hector as he bounded towards the foot of the tree, "lie down, I say." The dog obeyed, and Natty proceeded with great rapidity, though with the nicest accuracy, to reload his piece. When this was ended, he took up his game, and showing it to the party without a head, he cried—"Here is a tit bit for an old man's Christmas—never mind the venison, boy, and remember Indian John; his yarbs are better than all the foreign 'intments. Here, Judge," holding up the bird again, "do you think a smooth-bore would pick game off their roost, and not ruffle a feather?" The old man gave another of his remarkable laughs, which partook so largely of exultation, mirth, and irony, and shaking his head, he turned, with his rifle at a trail, and moved into the forest with steps that were between a walk and a trot. At each movement he made, his body lowered several inches, his knees yielding with an inclination inward; but as the sleigh turned at a bend in the road, the youth cast his eyes in quest of his old companion, and he saw that he was already nearly concealed by the trunks of the trees, while his dogs were following quietly in his footsteps, occasionally scenting the deer track, that they seemed to know instinctively was now of no farther use to them. Another jerk was given to the sleigh, and Leather-stocking was hid from view.

Chapter II

"All places that the eye of Heaven visits,
Are to a wise man ports and happy havens:—
Think not the king did banish thee;
But thou the king.—"

Richard II, I.iii.275–76, 279–80.

An ancestor of Marmaduke Temple had, about one hundred and twenty years before the commencement of our tale, come to the colony of Pennsylvania, a friend and co-religionist of its great patron. Old Marmaduke, for this formidable prenomen was a kind of appellative to the race, brought with him to that asylum of the persecuted, an abundance of the good things of this life. He became the master of many thousands of acres of uninhabited territory, and the supporter of many a score of dependents. He lived greatly respected for his piety, and not a little distinguished as a sectary; was entrusted by his associates with many important political stations; and died, just in time to escape the knowledge of his own poverty. It was his lot to share the fortune of most of those, who brought wealth with them into the new settlements of the middle colonies.

The consequence of an emigrant into these provinces was generally to be ascertained by the number of his white servants or dependents, and the nature of the public situations that he held. Taking this rule as a guide, the ancestor of our Judge must have been a man of no little note.

It is, however, a subject of curious inquiry at the present day, to look into the brief records of that early period, and observe how regular, and with few exceptions how inevitable, were the gradations, on the one hand, of the masters to poverty, and on the other, of their servants to wealth. Accustomed to ease, and unequal to the struggles incident to an infant society, the affluent emigrant was barely enabled to maintain his own rank, by the weight of his personal superiority and acquirements; but the moment that his head was laid in the grave, his indolent, and comparatively uneducated offspring, were compelled to yield precedency to the more active energies of a class, whose exertions had been stimulated by necessity. This is a very common course of things, even in the present state of the Union; but it was peculiarly the fortunes of the two extremes of society, in the peaceful and unenterprising colonies of Pennsylvania and New-Jersey.

The posterity of Marmaduke did not escape the common lot of those, who depend rather on their hereditary possessions than on their own powers; and in the third generation, they had descended to a point, below which, in this happy country, it is barely possible for honesty, intellect, and sobriety, to fall. The same pride of family, that had, by its self-satisfied indolence, conduced to aid their fall, now became a principle to stimulate them to endeavour to rise again. The feeling, from being morbid, was changed to a healthful and active desire to emulate the character, the condition, and, peradventure, the wealth, of their ancestors also. It was the father of our new acquaintance, the Judge, who first began to re-ascend in the scale of society; and in this undertaking he was not a little assisted by a marriage, which aided in furnishing the means of educating his only son, in a rather better manner than the low state of the common schools in Pennsylvania could promise; or than had been the practice in the family, for the two or three preceding generations.

At the school where the reviving prosperity of his father was enabled to maintain him, young Marmaduke formed an intimacy with a youth, whose years were about equal to his own. This was a fortunate connexion for our Judge, and paved the way to most of his future elevation in life.

There was not only great wealth, but high court interest, amongst the connexions of Edward Effingham. They were one of the few families, then resident in the colonies, who thought it a degradation to its members, to descend to the pursuits of commerce; and who never emerged from the privacy of domestic life, unless to preside in the councils of the colony, or to bear arms in her defence. The latter had, from youth, been the only employment of Edward's father. Military rank, under the crown of Great Britain, was attained with much longer probation, and by much more toilsome services, sixty years ago, than at the present time. Years were passed, without murmuring, in the subordinate grades of the service;

and those soldiers who were stationed in the colonies, felt, when they obtained the command of a company, that they were entitled to receive the greatest deference from the peaceful occupants of the soil. Any one of our readers, who has occasion to cross the Niagara, may easily observe, not only the self-importance, but the real estimation enjoyed by the humblest representative of the Crown, even in that polar region of royal sunshine. Such, and at no very distant period, was the respect paid to the military in these States, where now, happily, no symbol of war is ever seen, unless at the free and fearless voice of their people. When therefore, the father of Marmaduke's friend, after forty years' service, retired with the rank of Major, maintaining in his domestic establishment a comparative splendour, he became a man of the first consideration in his native colony—which was that of New-York. He had served with fidelity and courage, and, having been, according to the custom of the provinces, entrusted with commands much superior to those to which he was entitled by rank, with reputation also. When Major Effingham yielded to the claims of age, he retired with dignity, refusing his half-pay or any other compensation for services, that he felt he could no longer perform. The ministry proffered various civil offices, which yielded not only honour but profit; but he declined them all, with the chivalrous independence and loyalty, that had marked his character through life. The veteran soon caused this act of patriotic disinterestedness, to be followed by another of private munificence, that, however little it accorded with prudence, was in perfect conformity with the simple integrity of his own views. The friend of Marmaduke was his only child; and to this son, on his marriage with a lady to whom the father was particularly partial, the Major gave a complete conveyance of his whole estate, consisting of moneys in the funds, a town and country residence, sundry valuable farms in the old parts of the colony, and large tracts of wild land in the new;—in this manner throwing himself upon the filial piety of his child for his own future maintenance. Major Effingham, in declining the liberal offers of the British ministry, had subjected himself to the suspicion of having attained his dotage, by all those who throng the avenues to court patronage, even in the remotest corners of that vast empire; but, when he thus voluntarily stript himself of his great personal wealth, the remainder of the community seemed instinctively to adopt the conclusion also, that he had reached a second childhood. This may explain the fact of his importance rapidly declining; and, if privacy was his object, the veteran had soon a free indulgence of his wishes. Whatever views the world might entertain of this act of the Major, to himself and to his child, it seemed no more than a natural gift by a father, of those immunities which he could no longer enjoy or improve, to a son, who was formed, both by nature and education, to do both. The younger Effingham did not object to the amount of the donation; for he felt, that while his parent reserved a moral controul over his actions, he was relieving himself from a fatiguing burthen; such, indeed, was the confidence existing between them, that to neither did it seem any thing more, than removing money from one pocket to another.

One of the first acts of the young man, on coming into possession of his wealth, was to seek his early friend, with a view to offer any assistance, that it was now in his power to bestow.

The death of Marmaduke's father, and the consequent division of his small estate, rendered such an offer extremely acceptable to the young Pennsylvanian: he felt his own powers, and saw, not only the excellencies, but the foibles, in the character of his friend. Effingham was by nature indolent, confiding, and at times impetuous and indiscreet; but Marmaduke was uniformly equable, penetrating, and full of activity and enterprise. To the latter, therefore, the assistance, or rather connexion, that was proffered to him, seemed to produce a mutual advantage. It was cheerfully accepted, and the arrangement of its conditions was easily completed. A mercantile house was established in the metropolis of Pennsylvania, with the avails of Mr. Effingham's personal property; all, or nearly all, of which was put into the possession of Temple, who was the only ostensible proprietor in the concern, while in secret, the other was entitled to an equal participation in the profits. This connexion was thus kept private for two reasons; one of which, in the freedom of their intercourse, was frankly avowed to Marmaduke, while the other continued profoundly hid in the bosom of his friend. The last was nothing more than pride. To the descendant of a line of soldiers, commerce, even in that indirect manner, seemed a degrading pursuit;—but an insuperable obstacle to the disclosure existed in the prejudices of his father.

We have already said that Major Effingham had served as a soldier, with reputation. On one occasion, while in command on the western frontier of Pennsylvania, against a league of the French and Indians, not only his glory, but the safety of himself and his troops were jeoparded, by the peaceful policy of that colony. To the soldier, this was an unpardonable offence. He was fighting in their defence—he knew that the mild principles of this little nation of practical christians, would be disregarded by their subtle and malignant enemies; and he felt the injury the more deeply, because he saw that the avowed object of the colonists, in withholding their succours, would only have a tendency to expose his command, without preserving the peace. The soldier succeeded, after a desperate conflict, in extricating himself with a handful of his men, from their murderous enemy; but he never forgave the people who had exposed him to a danger, which they left him to combat alone. It was in vain to tell him, that they had no agency in his being placed on their frontier at all; it was evidently for their benefit that he had been so placed, and it was their "religious duty," so the Major always expressed it, "it was their religious duty to have supported him."

At no time was the old soldier an admirer of the peaceful disciples of Fox. Their disciplined habits, both of mind and body, had endowed them with great physical perfection, and the eye of the veteran was apt to scan the fair proportions and athletic frames of the colonists, with a look that seemed to utter volumes of contempt for their moral imbecility. He was also a little addicted to the expression of a belief, that, where there was so great an observance of the externals of religion, there could not be much of the substance.—It is not our task to explain what is, or what ought to be, the substance of christianity, but merely to record in this place the opinions of Major Effingham.

Knowing the sentiments of the father, in relation to this people, it was no wonder that the son hesitated to avow his connexion with, nay, even his dependence on the integrity of, a quaker.

It has been said that Marmaduke deduced his origin from the cotemporaries and friends of Penn. His father had married without the pale of the church to which he belonged, and had, in this manner, forfeited some of the privileges which would have descended to his offspring. Still, as young Marmaduke was educated in a colony and society, where even the ordinary intercourse between friends, was tinctured with the aspect of this mild religion, his habits and language were somewhat marked by its peculiarities. His own marriage at a future day with a lady without, not only the pale, but the influence of this sect of religionists, had a tendency, it is true, to weaken his early impressions; still he retained them, in some degree, to the hour of his death, and was observed uniformly, when much interested or agitated, to speak in the language of his youth——But this is anticipating our tale.

When Marmaduke first became the partner of young Effingham, he was quite the quaker in externals; and it was too dangerous an experiment for the son to think of encountering the prejudices of the father on this subject. The connexion, therefore, remained a profound secret to all but those who were interested in it.

For a few years, Marmaduke directed the commercial operations of his house with a prudence and sagacity, that afforded rich returns. He married the lady we have mentioned, who was the mother of Elizabeth, and the visits of his friend were becoming more frequent. There was a speedy prospect of removing the veil from their intercourse, as its advantages became each hour more apparent to Mr. Effingham, when the troubles that preceded the war of the revolution, extended themselves to an alarming degree.

Educated in the most dependent loyalty, Mr. Effingham had, from the commencement of the disputes between the colonists and the crown, warmly maintained, what he believed to be, the just prerogatives of his prince; while, on the other hand, the clear head and independent mind of Temple had induced him to espouse the cause of the people. Both might have been influenced by early impressions; for, if the son of the loyal and gallant soldier bowed in implicit obedience to the will of his sovereign, the descendant of the persecuted follower of Penn, looked back, with a little bitterness, to the unmerited wrongs that had been heaped upon his ancestors.

This difference in opinion had long been a subject of amicable dispute between them, but, latterly, the contest was getting to be too important to admit of trivial discussions on the part of Marmaduke, whose acute discernment was already catching faint glimmerings of the important events that were in embryo. The sparks of dissension soon kindled into a blaze; and the colonies, or, rather, as they quickly declared themselves, THE STATES, became a scene of strife and bloodshed for years.

A short time before the battle of Lexington, Mr. Effingham, already a widower, transmitted to Marmaduke for safe keeping, all his valuable effects and papers; and left the colony without his father. The war had, however, scarcely commenced in earnest, when he re-appeared in New-York, wearing the livery of his king, and in a short time, he took the field at the head of a provincial corps. In the mean time, Marmaduke had completely committed himself in the cause, as it was then called, of the rebellion: of course all intercourse between the friends ceased—on the part of Col. Effingham, it was unsought, and on that of Marmaduke, there was a cautious reserve. It soon became necessary for the latter to abandon the capital of Philadelphia; but he had taken the precaution to remove the whole of his effects, beyond the reach of the royal forces, including the papers of his friend also. There he continued serving his country during the struggle, in various civil capacities, and always with dignity and usefulness. While, however, he discharged his functions with credit and fidelity, Marmaduke never seemed to lose sight of his own interests; for, when the estates of the adherents of the crown fell under the hammer, by the acts of confiscation, he appeared in New-York, and became the purchaser of extensive possessions, at, comparatively, low prices.

It is true that Marmaduke, by thus purchasing estates that had been wrested by violence from others, rendered himself obnoxious to the censures of that sect, which, at the same time that it discards its children from a full participation in the family union, seems ever unwilling to abandon them entirely to the world. But either his success, or the frequency of the transgression in others, soon wiped off this slight stain from his character; and although there were a few, who, dissatisfied with their own fortunes, or conscious of their own demerits, would make dark hints concerning the sudden prosperity of the unportioned quaker, yet his services, and possibly his wealth, soon drove the recollection of these vague conjectures from men's minds.

When the war ended, and the independence of the states was acknowledged, Mr. Temple turned his attention from the pursuit of commerce, which was then fluctuating and uncertain, to the settlement of those tracts of land which he had purchased. Aided by a good deal of money, and directed by the suggestions of a strong and practical reason, his enterprise throve to a degree, that the climate and rugged face of the country which he selected, would seem to forbid. His property increased in a tenfold ratio, and he was already ranked among the most wealthy and important of his countrymen. To inherit this wealth he had but one child—the daughter whom we have introduced to the reader, and whom he was now conveying from school, to preside over a household that had too long wanted a mistress.

When the district in which his estates lay, had become sufficiently populous to be set off as a county, Mr. Temple had, according to the custom of the new settlements, been selected to fill its highest judicial station. This might make a Templar smile, but in addition to the apology of necessity, there is ever a dignity in talents and experience, that is commonly sufficient, in any station, for the protection of its possessor; and Marmaduke, more fortunate in his native clearness of mind, than the judge of king Charles, not only decided right, but was generally able to give a very good reason for it. At all events, such was the universal practice of the country and the times; and Judge Temple, so far from ranking among the lowest of his judicial cotemporaries in the courts of the new counties, felt himself, and was unanimously acknowledged to be, among the first.

We shall here close this brief explanation of the history and character of some of our personages, leaving them in future to speak and act for themselves.

Chapter III

"All that thou see'st, is nature's handy work:
Those rocks, that upward throw their mossy brows,
Like castled pinnacles of elder times!
These venerable stems, that slowly rock
Their tow'ring branches in the wintry gale!
That field of frost, which glitters in the sun,
Mocking the whiteness of a marble breast!—
Yet man can mar such works with his rude taste,
Like some sad spoiler of a virgin's fame."

Duo.

SOME LITTLE TIME elapsed ere Marmaduke Temple was sufficiently recovered from his agitation, to scan the person of his new companion. He now observed, that he was a youth of some two or three and twenty years of age; and rather above the middle height. Further observation was prevented by the rough over-coat, which was belted close to his form by a worsted sash, much like the one worn by the old hunter. The eyes of the Judge, after resting a moment on the figure of the stranger, were raised to a scrutiny of his countenance. There had been a look of care, visible in the features of the youth, when he first entered the sleigh, that had not only attracted the notice of Elizabeth, but which she had been much puzzled to interpret. His anxiety seemed the strongest when he was enjoining his old companion to secrecy; and even when he had decided, and was, rather passively, suffering himself to be conveyed to the village, the expression of his eyes by no means indicated any great degree of self-satisfaction at the step. But the lines of an uncommonly prepossessing countenance were gradually becoming composed; and he now sat silent, and apparently musing. The Judge gazed at him for some time with earnestness, and then smiling, as if at his own forgetfulness, he said—

"I believe, my young friend, that terror has driven you from my recollection—your face is very familiar, and yet for the honour of a score of bucks'-tails in my cap, I could not tell your name."

"I came into the county but three weeks since," returned

the youth coldly, "and, I understand you have been absent twice that time."

"It will be five to-morrow. Yet your face is one that I have seen; though it would not be strange, such has been my affright, should I see thee in thy winding-sheet, walking by my bedside, to-night. What say'st thou, Bess? Am I compos mentis or not?—Fit to charge a grand jury, or, what is just now of more pressing necessity, able to do the honours of a Christmas-eve, in the hall of Templeton?"

"More able to do either, my dear father," said a playful voice from under the ample enclosures of the hood, "than to kill deer with a smooth-bore." A short pause followed; and the same voice, but in a different accent continued—"We shall have good reasons for our thanksgiving to-night, on more accounts than one."

The horses soon reached a point, where they seemed to know by instinct that the journey was nearly ended, and, bearing on the bits, as they tossed their heads, they rapidly drew the sleigh over the level land, which lay on the top of the mountain, and soon came to the point where the road descended suddenly, but circuitously, into the valley.

The Judge was roused from his reflections, when he saw the four columns of smoke, which floated above his own chimneys. As house, village, and valley burst on his sight, he exclaimed cheerfully to his daughter—

"See, Bess, there is thy resting-place for life! And thine too, young man, if thou wilt consent to dwell with us."

The eyes of his auditors involuntarily met; and if the colour, that gathered over the face of Elizabeth, was contradicted by the cold expression of her eye, the ambiguous smile that again played about the lips of the stranger, seemed equally to deny the probability of his consenting to form one of this family group. The scene was one, however, which might easily warm a heart less given to philanthropy than that of Marmaduke Temple.

The side of the mountain, on which our travellers were journeying, though not absolutely perpendicular, was so steep as to render great care necessary in descending the rude and narrow path, which, in that early day, wound along the precipices. The Negro reined in his impatient steeds, and time was given Elizabeth to dwell on a scene which was so rapidly altering under the hands of man, that it only resembled, in its outlines, the picture she had so often studied, with delight, in childhood. Immediately beneath them lay a seeming plain, glittering, without inequality, and buried in mountains. The latter were precipitous, especially on the side of the plain, and chiefly in forest. Here and there the hills fell away in long, low points, and broke the sameness of the outline; or setting to the long and wide field of snow, which, without house, tree, fence, or any other fixture, resembled so much spotless cloud settled to the earth. A few dark and moving spots were, however, visible on the even surface, which the eye of Elizabeth knew to be so many sleighs going their several ways, to or from the village. On the western border of the plain, the mountains, though equally high, were less precipitous, and as they receded, opened into irregular valleys and glens, or were formed into terraces and hollows that admitted of cultivation. Although the evergreens still held dominion over many of the hills that rose on this side of the valley, yet the undulating outlines of the distant mountains, covered with forests of beech and maple, gave a relief to the eye, and the promise of a kinder soil. Occasionally, spots of white were discoverable amidst the forests of the opposite hills, which announced, by the smoke that curled over the tops of the trees, the habitations of man, and the commencement of agriculture. These spots were, sometimes, by the aid of united labour, enlarged into what were called settlements; but more frequently were small and insulated; though so rapid were the changes, and so persevering the labors of those who had cast their fortunes on the success of the enterprise, that it was not difficult for the imagination of Elizabeth to conceive they were enlarging under her eye, while she was gazing, in mute wonder, at the alterations that a few short years had made in the aspect of the country. The points on the western side of this remarkable plain, on which no plant had taken root, were both larger and more numerous than those on its eastern, and one in particular thrust itself forward in such a manner, as to form beautifully curved bays of snow on either side. On its extreme end an oak stretched forward, as if to overshadow, with its branches, a spot which its roots were forbidden to enter. It had released itself from the thraldom, that a growth of centuries had imposed on the branches of the surrounding forest trees, and threw its gnarled and fantastic arms abroad, in the wildness of liberty. A dark spot of a few acres in extent at the southern extremity of this beautiful flat, and immediately under the feet of our travellers, alone showed, by its rippling surface, and the vapors which exhaled from it, that what at first might seem a plain, was one of the mountain lakes, locked in the frosts of winter. A narrow current rushed impetuously from its bosom at the open place we have mentioned, and was to be traced, for miles, as it wound its way towards the south through the real valley, by its borders of hemlock and pine, and by the vapour which arose from its warmer surface into the chill atmosphere of the hills. The banks of this lovely basin, at its outlet, or southern end, were steep but not high, and in that direction the land continued, far as the eye could reach, a narrow but graceful valley, along which the settlers had scattered their humble habitations, with a profusion that bespoke the quality of the soil, and the comparative facilities of intercourse. Immediately on the bank of the lake and at its foot, stood the village of Templeton. It consisted of some fifty buildings, including those of every description, chiefly built of wood, and which, in their architecture, bore no great marks of taste, but which also, by the unfinished appearance of most of the dwellings, indicated the hasty manner of their construction. To the eye, they presented a variety of colours. A few were white in both front and rear, but more bore that expensive color on their fronts only, while their economical but ambitious owners had covered the remaining sides of the edifices, with a dingy red. One or two were slowly assuming the russet of age; while the uncovered beams that were to be seen through the broken windows of their second stories, showed, that either the taste, or the vanity of their proprietors, had led them to undertake a task, which they were unable to accomplish. The whole were grouped in a manner that aped the streets of a city, and were evidently so arranged, by the directions of one, who looked to the wants of posterity, rather than to the convenience of the present incumbents. Some three or four of the better sort of buildings, in addition to the uniformity of their colour, were fitted with green blinds, which, at that season at least, were rather strangely contrasted to the chill aspect of the lake, the mountains, the forests, and the wide fields of snow. Before the doors of these pretending dwellings, were placed a few saplings either without branches, or possessing only the feeble shoots of one or two summers' growth, that looked not unlike tall grenadiers on post, near the threshold of princes. In truth, the occupants of these favoured habitations were the nobles of Templeton, as Marmaduke was its king. They were the dwellings of two young men who were cunning in the law; an equal number of that class who chaffered to the wants of the community, under the title of store-keepers; and a disciple of Æsculapius, who, for a novelty, brought more subjects into the world than he sent out of it. In the midst of this incongruous group of dwellings, rose the mansion of the Judge, towering above all its neighbours. It stood in the centre of an enclosure of several acres, which were covered with fruit-trees. Some of the latter had been left by the Indians, and began already to assume the moss and inclination of age, therein forming a very marked contrast to the infant plantations that peer'd over most of the picketed fences of the village. In addition to this show of cultivation, were two rows of young Lombardy poplars, a tree but lately introduced into America, formally lining either side of a path-way, which led from a gate, that opened on the principal street, to the front door of the building. The house itself had been built entirely under the superintendence of a certain Mr. Richard Jones, whom we have already mentioned, and who, from his cleverness in small matters, and an entire willingness to exert his talents, added to the circumstance of their being sisters' children, ordinarily superintended all the minor concerns of Marmaduke Temple. Richard was fond of saying, that this child of his invention, consisted of nothing more nor less, than what should form the ground work of every clergyman's discourse; viz. a firstly, and a lastly. He had commenced his labours in the first year of their residence, by erecting a tall, gaunt edifice of wood, with its gable towards the highway. In this shelter, for it was little more, the family resided three years. By the end of that period, Richard had completed his design. He had availed himself, in this heavy undertaking, of the experience of a certain wandering, eastern mechanic, who, by exhibiting a few soiled plates of English architecture, and talking learnedly of friezes, entablatures, and particularly of the composite order, had obtained a very undue influence over Richard's taste, in every thing that pertained to that branch of the fine arts. Not that Mr. Jones did not affect to consider Hiram Doolittle a perfect empyric in his profession; being in the constant habit of listening to his treatises on architecture, with a kind of indulgent smile, yet, either from an inability to oppose them by any thing plausible from his own stores of learning, or from secret admiration, Richard generally submitted to the arguments of his co-adjutor. Together, they had not only erected a dwelling for Marmaduke, but they had given a fashion to the architecture of the whole county. The composite order, Mr. Doolittle would contend, was an order composed of many others, and was intended to be the most useful of all, for it admitted into its construction such alterations, as convenience or circumstances might require. To this proposition, Richard usually assented; and when rival geniuses, who monopolise not only all the reputation, but most of the money of a neighbourhood, are of a mind, it is not uncommon to see them lead the fashion, even in graver matters. In the present instance, as we have already hinted, the castle, as Judge Temple's dwelling was termed in common parlance, came to be the model, in some one or other of its numerous excellencies, for every aspiring edifice within twenty miles of it.

The house itself, or the lastly, was of stone; large, square, and far from uncomfortable. These were four requisites, on which Marmaduke had insisted with a little more than his ordinary pertinacity. But every thing else was peaceably assigned to Richard and his associate. These worthies found the material a little too solid for the tools of their workmen, which, in general, were employed on a substance no harder than the white pine of the adjacent mountains, a wood so proverbially soft, that it is commonly chosen by the hunters for pillows. But for this awkward dilemma, it is probable that the ambitious tastes of our two architects would have left us much more to do in the way of description. Driven from the faces of the house by the obduracy of the material, they took refuge in the porch and on the roof. The former, it was decided, should be severely classical, and the latter a rare specimen of the merits of the composite order.

A roof, Richard contended, was a part of the edifice that the ancients always endeavoured to conceal, it being an excrescence in architecture that was only to be tolerated on account of its usefulness. Besides, as he wittily added, a chief merit in a dwelling was to present a front, on whichever side it might happen to be seen; for as it was exposed to all eyes in all weathers, there should be no weak flank, for envy or unneighbourly criticism to assail. It was, therefore, decided, that the roof should be flat, and with four faces. To this arrangement, Marmaduke objected the heavy snows that lay for months, frequently covering the earth to a depth of three or four feet. Happily, the facilities of the composite order presented themselves to effect a compromise, and the rafters were lengthened, so as to give a descent that should carry off the frozen element. But unluckily, some mistake was made in the admeasurement of these material parts of the fabric, and as one of the greatest recommendations of Hiram, was his ability to work by the "square rule," no opportunity was found of discovering the effect, until the massive timbers were raised, on the four walls of the building. Then, indeed, it was soon seen, that, in defiance of all rule, the roof was by far the most conspicuous part of the whole edifice. Richard and his associate consoled themselves with the belief, that the covering would aid in concealing this unnatural elevation; but every shingle that was laid only multiplied objects to look at. Richard essayed to remedy the evil with paint, and four different colours were laid on by his own hands. The first, was a sky-blue, in the vain expectation that the eye might be cheated into the belief, it was the heavens themselves that hung so imposingly over Marmaduke's dwelling: the second was, what he called, a cloud-colour, being nothing more nor less than an imitation of smoke: the third was what Richard termed an invisible green, an experiment that did not succeed against a back-ground of sky. Abandoning the attempt to conceal, our architects drew upon their invention for means to ornament the offensive shingles. After much deliberation, and two or three essays by moonlight, Richard ended the affair by boldly covering the whole beneath a colour that he christened "sunshine," a cheap way, as he assured his cousin, the Judge, of always keeping fair weather over his head. The platform, as well as the eaves of the house, were surmounted by gaudily painted railings, and the genius of Hiram was exerted in the fabrication of divers urns and mouldings, that were scattered profusely around this part of their labours. Richard had originally a cunning expedient, by which the chimneys were intended to be so low, and so situated, as to resemble ornaments on the balustrades; but comfort required that the chimneys should rise with the roof, in order that the smoke might be carried off, and they thus became four extremely conspicuous objects in the view.

As this roof was much the most important architectural undertaking in which Mr. Jones was ever engaged, his failure produced a correspondent degree of mortification. At first, he whispered among his acquaintances, that it proceeded from ignorance of the square rule on the part of Hiram, but as his eye became gradually accustomed to the object, he grew better satisfied with his labours, and instead of apologizing for the defects, he commenced praising the beauties of the mansion house. He soon found hearers; and, as wealth and comfort are at all times attractive, it was, as has been said, made a model for imitation on a small scale. In less than two years from its erection, he had the pleasure of standing on the elevated platform, and of looking down on three humble imitators of its beauty.—Thus it is ever with fashion, which even renders the faults of the great, subjects of admiration.

Marmaduke bore this deformity in his dwelling with great good nature, and soon contrived, by his own improvements, to give an air of respectability and comfort to his place of residence; still there was much of incongruity, even immediately about the mansion-house. Although poplars had been brought from Europe to ornament the grounds, and willows and other trees were gradually springing up nigh the dwelling, yet many a pile of snow betrayed the presence of the stump of a pine; and even, in one or two instances, unsightly remnants of trees that had been partly destroyed by fire, were seen rearing their black, glistening columns twenty or thirty feet above the pure white of the snow. These, which in the language of the country are termed stubbs, abounded in the open fields adjacent to the village, and were accompanied, occasionally, by the ruin of a pine or a hemlock that had been stripped of its bark, and which waved in melancholy grandeur its naked limbs to the blast, a skeleton of its former glory. But these and many other unpleasant additions to the view were unseen by the delighted Elizabeth, who, as the horses moved down the side of the mountain, saw only in gross, the cluster of houses that lay like a map at her feet; the fifty smokes that were curling from the valley to the clouds; the frozen lake, as it lay embedded in mountains of evergreen, with the long shadows of the pines on its white surface, lengthening in the setting sun; the dark ribband of water, that gushed from the outlet, and was winding its way towards the distant Chesapeake—the altered, though still remembered, scenes of her childhood.

Five years had wrought greater changes, than a century would produce in countries, where time and labour have given permanency to the works of man. To the young hunter and the Judge the scene had less novelty; though none ever emerge from the dark forests of that mountain, and witness the glorious scenery of that beauteous valley, as it bursts unexpectedly upon them, without a feeling of delight. The former cast one admiring glance from north to south, and sunk his face, again, beneath the folds of his coat; while the latter contemplated, with philanthropic pleasure, the prospect of affluence and comfort, that was expanding around him; the result of his own enterprise, and, much of it, the fruits of his own industry.

The cheerful sound of sleigh bells, however, attracted the attention of the whole party, as they came jingling up the sides of the mountain, at a rate that announced a powerful team and a hard driver. The bushes which lined the highway interrupted the view, and the two sleighs were close upon each other before either was seen.

Chapter IV

"How now? whose mare's dead? what's the matter?"
2 *Henry IV*, II.i.43–44.

A LARGE LUMBER-SLEIGH, drawn by four horses, was soon seen dashing through the leafless bushes, which fringed the road. The leaders were of gray, and the pole-horses of a jet black. Bells, innumerable, were suspended from every part of the harness, where one of the tinkling balls could be placed, while the rapid movement of the equipage, in defiance of the steep ascent, announced the desire of the driver to ring them to the utmost. The first glance at this singular arrangement acquainted the Judge with the character of those in the sleigh. It contained four male figures. On one of those stools that are used at writing desks, lashed firmly to the sides of the vehicle, was seated a little man, enveloped in a great coat fringed with fur, in such a manner that no part of him was visible excepting a face, of an unvarying red colour. There was an habitual upward look about the head of this gentleman, as if dissatisfied with its natural proximity to the earth, and the expression of his countenance was that of busy care. He was the charioteer, and he guided the mettled animals along the precipice, with a fearless eye, and a steady hand. Immediately behind him, with his face toward the other two, was a tall figure, to whose appearance not even the duplicate over-coats which he wore, aided by the corner of a horse blanket, could give the appearance of strength. His face was protruding from beneath a woollen night-cap, and when he turned to the vehicle of Marmaduke as the sleighs approached each other, it seemed formed by nature to cut the atmosphere with the least possible resistance. The eyes alone appeared to create an obstacle, for from either side of his forehead their light, blue, glassy balls projected. The sallow of his countenance was too permanent to be affected even by the intense cold of the evening. Opposite to this personage, sat a solid, short, and square figure. No part of his form was to be discovered, through his over dress, but a face that was illuminated by a pair of black eyes, that gave the lie to every demure feature in his countenance.—A fair, jolly wig furnished a neat and rounded outline to his visage, and he, as well as the other two, wore marten-skin caps. The fourth, was a meek-looking, long-visaged man, without any other protection from the cold than that which was furnished by a black surtout, made with some little formality, but which was rather thread bare and rusty. He wore a hat of extremely decent proportions, though frequent brushing had quite destroyed its nap. His face was pale, and withal a little melancholy, or what might be termed of a studious complexion. The air had given it, just now, a slight and somewhat feverish flush. The character of his whole appearance, especially contrasted to the air of humour in his next companion, was that of habitual mental care. No sooner had the two sleighs approached within speaking distance, than the driver of this fantastic equipage shouted aloud—

"Draw up in the quarry—draw up, thou king of the Greeks; draw into the quarry, Agamemnon, or I shall never be able to pass you. Welcome home, cousin 'duke—welcome, welcome, black-eyed Bess. Thou seest, Marmaduke, that I have taken the field with an assorted cargo, to do thee honour. Monsieur Le Quoi has come out with only one cap; Old Fritz would not stay to finish the bottle; and Mr. Grant has got to put the lastly to his sermon, yet. Even all the horses would come—by-the-by, Judge, I must sell the blacks for you, immediately; they interfere, and the nigh one is a bad goer in double harness. I can get rid of them to——"

"Sell what thou wilt, Dickon," interrupted the cheerful voice of the Judge, "so that thou leavest me my daughter and my lands. Ah! Fritz, my old friend, this is a kind compliment, indeed, for seventy to pay to five and forty. Monsieur Le Quoi, I am your servant. Mr. Grant," lifting his cap, "I feel indebted to your attention. Gentlemen, I make you acquainted with my child. Yours are names with which she is very familiar."

"Velcome, velcome, Tchooge," said the elder of the party, with a strong German accent. "Miss Petsy vilt owe me a kiss."

"And cheerfully will I pay it, my good sir," cried the soft voice of Elizabeth; which sounded in the clear air of the hills, like tones of silver, amid the loud cries of Richard. "I have always a kiss for my old friend, Major Hartmann."

By this time the gentleman in the front seat, who had been addressed as Monsieur Le Quoi, had arisen with some difficulty, owing to the impediment of his over coats, and steadying himself by placing one hand on the stool of the charioteer, with the other, he removed his cap, and bowing politely to the Judge, and profoundly to Elizabeth, he paid his compliments.

"Cover thy poll, Gaul, cover thy poll," cried the driver, who was Mr. Richard Jones; "cover thy poll, or the frost will pluck out the remnant of thy locks. Had the hairs on the head of Absalom been as scarce as thine, he might have been living to this day." The jokes of Richard never failed of exciting risibility, for he uniformly did honor to his own wit; and he enjoyed a hearty laugh on the present occasion, while Mr. Le Quoi resumed his seat with a polite reciprocation in his mirth. The clergyman, for such was the office of Mr. Grant, modestly, though quite affectionately, exchanged his greetings with the travellers also, when Richard prepared to turn the heads of his horses homewards.

It was in the quarry alone that he could effect this object, without ascending to the summit of the mountain. A very considerable excavation had been made in the side of the hill, at the point where Richard had succeeded in stopping the sleighs, from which the stones used for building in the village, were ordinarily quarried, and in which he now attempted to turn his team. Passing itself, was a task of difficulty, and frequently of danger, in that narrow road; but Richard had to meet the additional risk of turning his four-in-hand. The black civilly volunteered his services to take off the leaders, and the Judge very earnestly seconded the measure, with his advice. Richard treated both proposals with great disdain—

"Why, and wherefore, cousin 'duke," he exclaimed a little angrily; "the horses are gentle as lambs. You know that I broke the leaders myself, and the pole-horses are too near my whip to be restive. Here is Mr. Le Quoi, now, who must know something about driving, because he has rode out so often with me; I will leave it to Mr. Le Quoi whether there is any danger."

It was not in the nature of the Frenchman to disappoint expectations so confidently formed; although he sat looking down the precipice which fronted him, as Richard turned his leaders into the quarry, with a pair of eyes that stood out like those of lobsters. The German's muscles were unmoved, but his quick sight scanned each movement. Mr. Grant placed his hands on the side of the sleigh, in preparation for a spring, but moral timidity deterred him from taking the leap, that bodily apprehension strongly urged him to attempt.

Richard, by a sudden application of the whip, succeeded in forcing the leaders into the snow bank that covered the quarry; but the instant that the impatient animals suffered by the crust, through which they broke at each step, they positively refused to move an inch further in that direction. On the contrary, finding that the cries and blows of their driver, were redoubled at this juncture, the leaders backed upon the pole-horses, who, in their turn, backed the sleigh. Only a single log lay above the pile which upheld the road, on the side toward the valley, and this was now buried in the snow. The sleigh was easily forced across so slight an impediment, and before Richard became conscious of his danger, one half of the vehicle was projected over a precipice, which fell, perpendicularly, more than a hundred feet. The Frenchman, who, by his position, had a full view of their threatened flight, instinctively threw his body as far forward as possible, and cried, "Ah! Mon cher monsieur Deeck! mon Dieu! que faites vous!"

"Donner and blitzen, Richart," exclaimed the veteran German, looking over the side of the sleigh with unusual emotion, "put you will preak ter sleigh and kilt ter horses."

"Good Mr. Jones," said the clergyman, "be prudent, good sir—be careful."

"Get up, obstinate devils," cried Richard, catching a bird's-eye view of his situation, and, in his eagerness to move forward, kicking the stool on which he sat,—"Get up, I say—Cousin 'duke, I shall have to sell the grays too; they are the worst broken horses—Mr. Le Quaw!" Richard was too much agitated to regard his pronunciation, of which he was commonly a little vain, "Monsieur Le Quaw, pray get off my leg;

you hold my leg so tight that it's no wonder the horses back."

"Merciful Providence!" exclaimed the Judge, "they will be all killed!"

Elizabeth gave a piercing shriek, and the black of Agamemnon's face changed to a muddy white.

At this critical moment, the young hunter, who, during the salutations of the parties, had sat in rather sullen silence, sprang from the sleigh of Marmaduke to the heads of the refractory leaders. The horses, who were yet suffering under the injudicious and somewhat random blows of Richard, were dancing up and down with that ominous movement, that threatens a sudden and uncontrollable start, still pressing backward. The youth gave the leaders a powerful jerk, and they plunged aside, and re-entered the road in the position in which they were first halted. The sleigh was whirled from its dangerous position, and upset with the runners outwards. The German and the divine, were thrown rather unceremoniously into the highway, but without danger to their bones. Richard appeared in the air, describing the segment of a circle, of which the reins were the radii, and landed at the distance of some fifteen feet, in that snow bank which the horses had dreaded, right end uppermost. Here, as he instinctively grasped the reins, as drowning men seize at straws, he admirably served the purpose of an anchor. The Frenchman, who was on his legs in the act of springing from the sleigh, took an aerial flight also, much in the attitude which boys assume when they play leap-frog, and flying off in a tangent to the curvature of his course, came into the snow bank head foremost, where he remained, exhibiting two lathy legs on high, like scare-crows waving in a corn field. Major Hartmann, whose self-possession had been admirably preserved during the whole evolution, was the first of the party that gained his feet and his voice.

"Ter deyvel, Richart," he exclaimed, in a voice half serious, half comical, "Put you unloat your sleigh very hantily."

It may be doubtful, whether the attitude in which Mr. Grant continued for an instant after his overthrow, was the one into which he had been thrown, or was assumed, in humbling himself before the power that he reverenced, in thanksgiving at his escape. When he rose from his knees, he began to gaze about him, with anxious looks, after the welfare of his companions, while every joint in his body trembled with nervous agitation. There was some confusion in the faculties of Mr. Jones, also; but as the mist gradually cleared from before his eyes, he saw that all was safe, and with an air of great self-satisfaction, he cried, " well—that was neatly saved, any how——It was a lucky thought in me to hold on the reins, or the fiery devils would have been over the mountain by this time. How well I recovered myself, 'duke; another moment would have been too late—But I knew just the spot where to touch the off-leader; that blow under his right flank, and the sudden jerk I gave the rein, brought them round quite in rule, I must own myself."

The spectators, from immemorial usage, have a right to laugh at the casualties of a sleigh-ride; and the Judge was no sooner certain that no harm was done, than he made full use of the privilege.

"Thou jerk! thou recover thyself, Dickon!" he said; "but for that brave lad yonder, thou and thy horses, or rather mine, would have been dashed to pieces—But where is Monsieur Le Quoi?"

"Oh! mon cher Juge! Mon ami!" cried a smothered voice, "praise be God I live; vill-a you, Mister Agamemnon, be pleas come down ici, and help-a me on my leg?"

The divine and the negro seized the incarcerated Gaul by his legs, and extricated him from a snow-bank of three feet in depth, whence his voice had sounded as from the tombs. The thoughts of Mr. Le Quoi, immediately on his liberation, were not extremely collected; and when he reached the light, he threw his eyes upwards, in order to examine the distance he had fallen. His good humour returned however, with a knowledge of his safety, though it was some little time before he clearly comprehended the case.

"What, monsieur," said Richard, who was busily assisting the black in taking off the leaders; "are you there? I thought I saw you flying towards the top of the mountain just now."

"Praise be God, I no fly down into de lake," returned the Frenchman, with a visage that was divided between pain, occasioned by a few large scratches that he had received in forcing his head through the crust, and the look of complaisance that seemed natural to his pliable features; "ah! mon cher Mister Deeck, vat you shall do next?—dere be noting you no try."

"The next thing, I trust, will be to learn to drive," said the Judge, who had busied himself in throwing the buck, together with several other articles of baggage, from his own sleigh into the snow; "here are seats for you all, gentlemen; the evening grows piercingly cold, and the hour approaches for the service of Mr. Grant: we will leave friend Jones to repair the damages, with the assistance of Agamemnon, and hasten to a warm fire. Here, Dickon, are a few articles of Bess's trumpery, that you can throw into your sleigh when ready, and there is also a deer of my taking, that I will thank you to bring—Aggy! remember there will be a visit from Santaclaus* to-night."

The black grinned, conscious of the bribe that was offered him for silence on the subject of the deer, while Richard, without, in the least, waiting for the termination of his cousin's speech, began his reply—

"Learn to drive, sayest thou, cousin 'duke? Is there a man in the county who knows more of horse-flesh than myself? Who broke in the filly, that no one else dare mount; though your coachman did pretend that he had tamed her before I took her in hand, but any body could see that he lied—he was a great liar, that John—what's that, a buck?"—Richard abandoned the horses, and ran to the spot where Marmaduke had thrown the deer; "It is a buck! I am amazed! Yes, here are two holes in him; he has fired both barrels, and hit him each time. Ecod! how Marmaduke will brag! he is a prodigious bragger about any small matter like this now; well, to think that 'duke has killed a buck before christmas! There will be no such thing as living with him—they are both bad shots though, mere chance—mere chance;—now, I never fired twice at a cloven hoof in my life;—it is hit or miss with me—dead or runaway:—had it been a bear, or a wild-cat, a man

*The periodical visits of St. Nicholas, or Santaclaus as he is termed, were never forgotten among the inhabitants of New York, until the emigration from New England brought in the opinions and usages of the puritans. Like the "bon homme de Noël," he arrives at each Christmas.

might have wanted both barrels. Here! you Aggy! how far off was the Judge when this buck was shot?"

"Eh! Massa Richard, may be a ten rod," cried the black, bending under one of the horses, with the pretence of fastening a buckle, but in reality to conceal the grin that opened a mouth from ear to ear.

"Ten rod!" echoed the other; " why, Aggy, the deer I killed last winter was at twenty—yes! if any thing it was nearer thirty than twenty. I wouldn't shoot at a deer at ten rod: besides, you may remember, Aggy, I only fired once."

"Yes, Massa Richard, I 'member 'em! Natty Bumppo fire t'oder gun. You know, sir, all 'e folk say, Natty kill 'em."

"The folks lie, you black devil!" exclaimed Richard in great heat. "I have not shot even a gray squirrel these four years, to which that old rascal has not laid claim, or some one else for him. This is a damn'd envious world that we live in—people are always for dividing the credit of a thing, in order to bring down merit to their own level. Now they have a story about the Patent*, that Hiram Doolittle helped to plan the steeple to St. Paul's; when Hiram knows that it is entirely mine; a little taken from a print of its namesake in London, I own; but essentially, as to all points of genius, my own."

"I don't know where he come from," said the black, losing every mark of humour in an expression of admiration, "but eb'ry body say, he wonnerful hansome."

"And well they may say so, Aggy," cried Richard, leaving the buck, and walking up to the negro with the air of a man who has new interest awakened within him. "I think I may say, without bragging, that it is the handsomest and the most scientific country church in America. I know that the Connecticut settlers talk about their Wethersfield meeting-house: but I never believe more than half what they say, they are such unconscionable braggers. Just as you have got a thing

*The grants of land, made either by the crown or the state, were by letters patent under the great seal, and the term "patent" is usually applied to any district of extent, thus conceded. Though under the crown, manorial rights being often granted with the soil, in the older counties, the word "manor" is frequently used. There are many "manors" in New York, though all political and judicial rights have ceased.

done, if they see it likely to be successful they are always for interfering, and then it is ten to one but they lay claim to half, or even all of the credit. You may remember, Aggy, when I painted the sign of the bold dragoon for Capt. Hollister, there was that fellow, who was about town laying brick dust on the houses, came one day and offered to mix what I call the streaky black, for the tail and mane, and then, because it looks like horse hair, he tells every body that the sign was painted by himself and Squire Jones. If Marmaduke don't send that fellow off the Patent, he may ornament his village with his own hands, for me." Here Richard paused a moment, and cleared his throat by a loud hem, while the negro, who was all this time busily engaged in preparing the sleigh, proceeded with his work in respectful silence. Owing to the religious scruples of the Judge, Aggy was the servant of Richard, who had his services for a *time**, and who, of course, commanded a legal claim to the respect of the young negro. But when any dispute between his lawful and his real master occurred, the black felt too much deference for both to express any opinion. In the mean while, Richard continued watching the negro as he fastened buckle after buckle, until, stealing a look of consciousness toward the other, he continued, "Now, if that young man, who was in your sleigh, is a real Connecticut settler, he will be telling every body how he saved my horses, when, if he had let them alone for half-a-minute longer, I would have brought them in much better, without upsetting, with the whip and rein—it spoils a horse to give him his head. I should not wonder if I had to sell the whole team, just for that one jerk he gave them." Richard paused, and hemmed, for his conscience smote him a little, for censuring a man who had just saved his life—" who

*The manumission of the slaves in New York has been gradual. When public opinion became strong in their favour, then grew up a custom of buying the services of a slave, for six or eight years, with a condition to liberate him at the end of the period. Then the law provided that all born after a certain day should be free, the males at twenty-eight, and the females at twenty-five. After this the owner was obliged to cause his servants to be taught to read and write before they reached the age of eighteen, and, finally, the few that remained were all unconditionally liberated in 1826, or after the publication of this tale. It was quite usual for men more or less connected with the quakers, who never held slaves, to adopt the first expedient.

is the lad, Aggy—I don't remember to have seen him before?"

The black recollected the hint about Santaclaus, and while he briefly explained how they had taken up the person in question on the top of the mountain, he forbore to add any thing concerning the accident of the wound, only saying, that he believed the youth was a stranger. It was so usual for men of the first rank to take into their sleighs any one they found toiling through the snow, that Richard was perfectly satisfied with this explanation. He heard Aggy, with great attention, and then remarked, "Well, if the lad has not been spoiled by the people in Templeton, he may be a modest young man, and as he certainly meant well, I shall take some notice of him,—perhaps he is land-hunting—I say, Aggy—may be he is out hunting?"

"Eh! yes, massa Richard," said the black, a little confused; for as Richard did all the flogging, he stood in great terror of his master, in the main—"yes, sir, I b'lieve he be."

"Had he a pack and an ax?"

"No, sir, only he rifle."

"Rifle!" exclaimed Richard, observing the confusion of the negro, which now amounted to terror. "By Jove! he kill'd the deer—I knew that Marmaduke couldn't kill a buck on the jump—How was it, Aggy; tell me all about it, and I'll roast 'duke quicker than he can roast his saddle—How was it, Aggy? the lad shot the buck, and the Judge bought it, ha! and he is taking the youth down to get the pay?"

The pleasure of this discovery had put Richard in such a good humour, that the negro's fears in some measure vanished, and he remembered the stocking of Santaclaus. After a gulp or two he made out to reply.

"You forgit a two shot, Sir."

"Don't lie, you black rascal," cried Richard, stepping on the snow bank to measure the distance from his lash to the negro's back; "speak truth, or I trounce you." While speaking, the stock was slowly rising in Richard's right hand, and the lash drawing through his left, in the scientific manner with which drummers apply the cat, and Agamemnon, after turning each side of himself towards his master, and finding both equally unwilling to remain there, fairly gave in. In a very few words he made his master acquainted with the truth, at the same time earnestly conjuring Richard to protect him from the displeasure of the Judge.

"I'll do it, boy, I'll do it," cried the other, rubbing his hands with delight; "say nothing, but leave me to manage 'duke—I have a great mind to leave the deer on the hill, and to make the fellow send for his own carcass: but no, I will let Marmaduke tell a few bouncers about it before I come out upon him—Come, hurry in, Aggy, I must help to dress the lad's wound; this Yankee* Doctor knows nothing of surgery—I had to hold old Milligan's leg for him, while he cut it off." Richard was now seated on the stool again, and the black taking the hind seat, the steeds were put in motion towards home. As they dashed down the hill, on a fast trot, the driver occasionally turned his face to Aggy, and continued speaking; for, notwithstanding their recent rupture, the most perfect cordiality was again existing between them. "This goes to prove that I turned the horses with the reins, for no man who is shot in the right shoulder, can have strength enough to bring round such obstinate devils—I knew I did it from the first; but I did not want to multiply words with Marmaduke about it—Will you bite? you villain!—hip, boys, hip—Old Natty too, that is the best of it—Well, well—'duke will say no more about my deer—and the Judge fired both barrels, and hit nothing but a poor lad, who was behind a pine tree—I must help that quack to take out the buck shot for the poor fellow." In this manner Richard descended the mountain; the bells ringing and his tongue going, until they entered the village, when the whole attention of the driver was devoted to a display of his horsemanship, to the admiration of all the gaping women and children, who thronged the windows, to witness the arrival of their landlord and his daughter.

*In America the term Yankee is of local meaning. It is thought to be derived from the manner in which the Indians of New England pronounced the word "English" or "Yengeese." New York being originally a Dutch province, the term of course was not known there, and further south different dialects among the natives, themselves, probably produced a different pronunciation. Marmaduke and his cousin being Pennsylvanians by birth were not Yankees in the American sense of the word.

Chapter V

"Nathaniel's coat, sir, was not fully made,
And Gabriel's pumps were all unfinish'd i' th' heel;
There was no link to colour Peter's hat,
And Walter's dagger was not come from sheathing:
There were none fine, but Adam, Ralph and Gregory."
The Taming of the Shrew, IV.i.132–36.

AFTER WINDING along the side of the mountain, the road, on reaching the gentle declivity which lay at the base of the hill, turned at a right angle to its former course, and shot down an inclined plane, directly into the village of Templeton. The rapid little stream that we have already mentioned, was crossed by a bridge of hewn timber, which manifested, by its rude construction, and the unnecessary size of its framework, both the value of labour, and the abundance of materials. This little torrent, whose dark waters gushed over the limestones that lined its bottom, was nothing less than one of the many sources of the Susquehanna; a river, to which the Atlantic herself, has extended an arm in welcome. It was at this point, that the powerful team of Mr. Jones, brought him up to the more sober steeds of our travellers. A small hill was risen, and Elizabeth found herself, at once, amid the incongruous dwellings of the village. The street was of the ordinary width, notwithstanding the eye might embrace in one view, thousands, and tens of thousands of acres, that were yet tenanted only by the beasts of the forest. But such had been the will of her father, and such had also met the wishes of his followers. To them, the road, that made the most rapid approaches to the condition of the old, or, as they expressed it, the *down* countries, was the most pleasant; and surely nothing could look more like civilization, than a city, even if it lay in a wilderness! The width of the street, for so it was called, might have been one hundred feet; but the track for the sleighs was much more limited. On either side of the highway, were piled huge heaps of logs that were daily increasing rather than diminishing in size, notwithstanding the enormous fires that might be seen through every window.

The last object at which Elizabeth gazed when they renewed their journey, after the rencontre with Richard, was the sun, as it expanded in the refraction of the horizon, and over whose disk, the dark umbrage of a pine was stealing, while it slowly sunk behind the western hills. But its setting rays darted along the openings of the mountain she was on, and lighted the shining covering of the birches, until their smooth and glossy coats, nearly rivalled the mountain-sides in colour. The outline of each dark pine was delineated far in the depths of the forest; and the rocks, too smooth and too perpendicular to retain the snow that had fallen, brightened, as if smiling at the leave-taking of the luminary. But at each step, as they descended, Elizabeth observed that they were leaving the day behind them. Even the heartless, but bright rays of a December sun, were missed, as they glided into the cold gloom of the valley. Along the summits of the mountains in the eastern range, it is true, the light still lingered, receding step by step from the earth into the clouds that were gathering, with the evening mist, about the limited horizon; but the frozen lake lay without a shadow on its bosom; the dwellings were becoming already gloomy and indistinct; and the woodcutters were shouldering their axes, and preparing to enjoy, throughout the long evening before them, the comforts of those exhilarating fires that their labour had been supplying with fuel. They paused only to gaze at the passing sleighs, to lift their caps to Marmaduke, to exchange familiar nods with Richard, and each disappeared in his dwelling. The paper curtains dropped behind our travellers in every window, shutting from the air even the fire-light of the cheerful apartments; and when the horses of her father turned, with a rapid whirl, into the open gate of the mansion-house, and nothing stood before her but the cold, dreary stone-walls of the building, as she approached them through an avenue of young and leafless poplars, Elizabeth felt as if all the loveliness of the mountain-view had vanished like the fancies of a dream. Marmaduke had retained so much of his early habits as to reject the use of bells, but the equipage of Mr. Jones came dashing through the gate after them, sending its jingling sounds through every cranny of the building, and in a moment the dwelling was in an uproar.

On a stone platform, of rather small proportions, considering the size of the building, Richard and Hiram had, conjointly, reared four little columns of wood, which in their turn supported the shingled roofs of the portico—this was the name that Mr. Jones had thought proper to give to a very plain, covered, entrance. The ascent to the platform was by five or six stone steps, somewhat hastily laid together, and which the frost had already begun to move from their symmetrical positions. But the evils of a cold climate, and a superficial construction, did not end here. As the steps lowered, the platform necessarily fell also, and the foundations actually left the superstructure suspended in the air, leaving an open space of a foot between the base of the pillars and the stones on which they had originally been placed. It was lucky for the whole fabric, that the carpenter, who did the manual part of the labour, had fastened the canopy of this classic entrance so firmly to the side of the house, that, when the base deserted the superstructure in the manner we have described, and the pillars, for the want of a foundation, were no longer of service to support the roof, the roof was able to uphold the pillars. Here was indeed an unfortunate gap left in the ornamental part of Richard's column; but, like the window in Aladdin's palace, it seemed only left in order to prove the fertility of its master's resources. The composite order again offered its advantages, and a second edition of the base was given, as the booksellers say, with additions and improvements. It was necessarily larger, and it was properly ornamented with mouldings; still the steps continued to yield, and, at the moment when Elizabeth returned to her father's door, a few rough wedges were driven under the pillars to keep them steady, and to prevent their weight from separating them from the pediment which they ought to have supported.

From the great door, which opened into the porch, emerged two or three female domestics, and one male. The latter was bare-headed, but evidently more dressed than usual, and on the whole, was of so singular a formation and attire, as to deserve a more minute description. He was about five feet in height, of a square and athletic frame, with a pair of shoulders that would have fitted a grenadier. His low stature was rendered the more striking by a bend forward that he was in the habit of assuming, for no apparent reason, unless it might be to give greater freedom to his arms, in a particularly sweeping swing, that they constantly practised when their master was in motion. His face was long, of a fair complexion, burnt to a fiery red; with a snub nose, cocked into an inveterate pug; a mouth of enormous dimensions, filled with fine teeth; and a pair of blue eyes, that seemed to look about them, on surrounding objects, with habitual contempt. His head composed full one fourth of his whole length, and the queue that depended from its rear occupied another. He wore a coat of very light drab cloth, with buttons as large as dollars, bearing the impression of a foul anchor. The skirts were extremely long, reaching quite to the calf, and were broad in proportion. Beneath, there were a vest and breeches of red plush, somewhat worn and soiled. He had shoes with large buckles, and stockings of blue and white stripes.

This odd-looking figure reported himself to be a native of the county of Cornwall, in the island of Great Britain. His boyhood had passed in the neighbourhood of the tin mines, and his youth, as the cabin-boy of a smuggler, between Falmouth and Guernsey. From this trade he had been impressed into the service of his king, and, for the want of a better, had been taken into the cabin, first as a servant, and finally as steward to the captain. Here he acquired the art of making chowder, lobskous, and one or two other sea-dishes, and, as he was fond of saying, had an opportunity of seeing the world. With the exception of one or two out-ports in France, and an occasional visit to Portsmouth, Plymouth, and Deal, he had in reality seen no more of mankind, however, than if he had been riding a donkey in one of his native mines. But, being discharged from the navy at the peace of '83, he declared, that, as he had seen all the civilized parts of the earth, he was inclined to make a trip to the wilds of America. We will not trace him in his brief wanderings, under the influence of that spirit of emigration, that sometimes induces a dapper Cockney to quit his home, and lands him, before the sound of Bow-bells is out of his ears, within the roar of the cataract of Niagara, but shall only add, that, at a very early day, even before Elizabeth had been sent to school, he had found his way into the family of Marmaduke Temple, where, owing to a combination of qualities that will be developed in the course of the tale, he held, under Mr. Jones, the office of major-domo. The name of this worthy was Benjamin Penguillan, according to his own pronunciation; but, owing to a marvellous tale that he was in the habit of relating, concerning the length of time he had to labour to keep his ship from sinking after Rodney's victory, he had universally acquired the nickname of Ben Pump.

By the side of Benjamin, and pressing forward as if a little jealous of her station, stood a middle-aged woman, dressed in calico, rather violently contrasted in colour, with a tall, meager, shapeless figure, sharp features, and a somewhat acute expression of her physiognomy. Her teeth were mostly gone, and what did remain were of a light yellow. The skin of her nose was drawn tightly over the member, to hang in large wrinkles in her cheeks and about her mouth. She took snuff in such quantities, as to create the impression, that she owed the saffron of her lips and the adjacent parts, to this circumstance; but it was the unvarying colour of her whole face. She presided over the female part of the domestic arrangements, in the capacity of housekeeper, was a spinster, and bore the name of Remarkable Pettibone. To Elizabeth she was an entire stranger, having been introduced into the family since the death of her mother.

In addition to these, were three or four subordinate menials, mostly black, some appearing at the principal door, and some running from the end of the building, where stood the entrance to the cellar-kitchen.

Besides these, there was a general rush from Richard's kennel, accompanied with every canine tone, from the howl of the wolf-dog to the petulant bark of the terrier. The master received their boisterous salutations with a variety of imitations from his own throat, when the dogs, probably from shame at being outdone, ceased their outcry. One stately, powerful mastiff, who wore around his neck a brass collar, with "M. T." engraved in large letters on the rim, alone was silent. He walked majestically, amid the confusion, to the side of the Judge, where, receiving a kind pat or two, he turned to Elizabeth, who even stooped to kiss him, as she called him kindly by the name of "Old Brave." The animal seemed to know her, as she ascended the steps, supported by Monsieur

Le Quoi and her father, in order to protect her from falling on the ice, with which they were covered. He looked wistfully after her figure, and when the door closed on the whole party, he laid himself in a kennel that was placed nigh by, as if conscious that the house contained something of additional value to guard.

Elizabeth followed her father, who paused a moment to whisper a message to one of his domestics, into a large hall, that was dimly lighted by two candles, placed in high, old-fashioned, brass candlesticks. The door closed, and the party were at once removed from an atmosphere that was nearly at zero, to one of sixty degrees above. In the centre of the hall stood an enormous stove, the sides of which appeared to be quivering with heat; from which a large, straight pipe, leading through the ceiling above, carried off the smoke. An iron basin, containing water, was placed on this furnace, for such only it could be called, in order to preserve a proper humidity in the apartment. The room was carpeted, and furnished with convenient, substantial furniture; some of which was brought from the city, and the remainder having been manufactured by the mechanics of Templeton. There was a sideboard of mahogany, inlaid with ivory, and bearing enormous handles of glittering brass, and groaning under the piles of silver plate. Near it stood a set of prodigious tables, made of the wild cherry, to imitate the imported wood of the sideboard, but plain, and without ornament of any kind. Opposite to these stood a smaller table, formed from a lighter coloured wood, through the grains of which the wavy lines of the curled-maple of the mountains were beautifully undulating. Near to this, in a corner, stood a heavy, old-fashioned, brass-faced clock, encased in a high box, of the dark hue of the black-walnut from the seashore. An enormous settee, or sofa, covered with light chintz, stretched along the walls for near twenty feet on one side of the hall, and chairs of wood, painted a light yellow, with black lines that were drawn by no very steady hand, were ranged opposite, and in the intervals between the other pieces of furniture. A Fahrenheit's thermometer, in a mahogany case, and with a barometer annexed, was hung against the wall, at some little distance from the stove, which Benjamin consulted, every half-hour, with prodigious exactitude. Two small glass chandeliers were suspended at equal distances between the stove and the outer doors, one of which opened at each end of the hall, and gilt lustres were affixed to the frame-work of the numerous side doors, that led from the apartment. Some little display in architecture had been made in constructing these frames and casings, which were surmounted with pediments, that bore each a little pedestal in its centre. On these pedestals were small busts in blacked plaster of Paris. The style of the pedestals, as well as the selection of the busts, were all due to the taste of Mr. Jones. On one stood Homer, a most striking likeness, Richard affirmed, "as any one might see, for it was blind." Another bore the image of a smooth visaged gentleman, with a pointed beard, whom he called Shakspeare. A third ornament, was an urn, which, from its shape, Richard was accustomed to say, intended to represent itself as holding the ashes of Dido. A fourth was certainly old Franklin, in his cap and spectacles. A fifth as surely bore the dignified composure of the face of Washington. A sixth was a non-descript, representing "a man with a shirt-collar open," to use the language of Richard, " with a laurel on his head;—it was Julius Cæsar or Dr. Faustus; there were good reasons for believing either."

The walls were hung with a dark, lead-coloured English paper, that represented Britannia weeping over the tomb of Wolfe. The hero himself stood at a little distance from the mourning goddess, and at the edge of the paper. Each width contained the figure, with the slight exception of one arm of the General, which ran over on to the next piece, so that when Richard essayed, with his own hands, to put together this delicate outline, some difficulties occurred, that prevented a nice conjunction, and Britannia had reason to lament, in addition to the loss of her favourite's life, numberless cruel amputations of his right arm.

The luckless cause of these unnatural divisions now announced his presence in the hall by a loud crack of his whip.

"Why, Benjamin! you Ben Pump! is this the manner in which you receive the heiress?" he cried. "Excuse him, cousin Elizabeth. The arrangements were too intricate to be trusted to every one; but now I am here, things will go on better.

Come, light up, Mr. Penguillan, light up, light up, and let us see one another's faces. Well, 'duke, I have brought home your deer; what is to be done with it, ha?"

"By the Lord, Squire," commenced Benjamin in reply, first giving his mouth a wipe with the back of his hand, "if this here thing had been ordered sum'at earlier in the day, it might have been got up, d'ye see, to your liking. I had mustered all hands, and was exercising candles, when you hove in sight; but when the women heard your bells, they started an end, as if they were riding the boatswain's colt; and, if-so-be there is that man in the house, who can bring up a parcel of women when they have got headway on them, until they've run out the end of their rope, his name is not Benjamin Pump. But Miss Betsy here, must have altered more than a privateer in disguise, since she has got on her woman's duds, if she will take offence with an old fellow, for the small matter of lighting a few candles."

Elizabeth and her father continued silent, for both experienced the same sensation on entering the hall. The former had resided one year in the building before she left home for school, and the figure of its lamented mistress was missed by both husband and child.

But candles had been placed in the chandeliers and lustres, and the attendants were so far recovered from surprise as to recollect their use: the oversight was immediately remedied, and in a minute the apartment was in a blaze of light.

The slight melancholy of our heroine and her father was banished by this brilliant interruption, and the whole party began to lay aside the numberless garments they had worn in the air.

During this operation, Richard kept up a desultory dialogue with the different domestics, occasionally throwing out a remark to the Judge concerning the deer; but as his conversation at such moments was much like an accompaniment on a piano, a thing that is heard without being attended to, we will not undertake the task of recording his diffuse discourse.

The instant that Remarkable Pettibone had executed her portion of the labour in illuminating, she returned to a position near Elizabeth, with the apparent motive of receiving the clothes that the other threw aside, but in reality to examine, with an air of curiosity—not unmixed with jealousy,—the appearance of the lady who was to supplant her in the administration of their domestic economy. The housekeeper felt a little appalled, when, after cloaks, coats, shawls and socks had been taken off in succession, the large black hood was removed, and the dark ringlets, shining like the raven's wing, fell from her head, and left the sweet but commanding features of the young lady exposed to view. Nothing could be fairer and more spotless than the forehead of Elizabeth, and preserve the appearance of life and health. Her nose would have been called Grecian, but for a softly rounded swell, that gave in character to the feature what it lost in beauty. Her mouth, at first sight, seemed only made for love, but the instant that its muscles moved, every expression that womanly dignity could utter, played around it, with the flexibility of female grace. It spoke not only to the ear, but to the eye. So much, added to a form of exquisite proportions, rather full and rounded for her years, and of the tallest medium height, she inherited from her mother. Even the colour of her eye, the arched brows, and the long silken lashes, came from the same source; but its expression was her father's. Inert and composed, it was soft, benevolent, and attractive; but it could be roused, and that without much difficulty. At such moments it was still beautiful, though it was a little severe. As the last shawl fell aside, and she stood, dressed in a rich blue riding-habit, that fitted her form with the nicest exactness; her cheeks burning with roses, that bloomed the richer for the heat of the hall, and her eyes slightly suffused with moisture, that rendered their ordinary beauty more dazzling, and with every feature of her speaking countenance illuminated by the lights that flared around her, Remarkable felt that her own power had ended.

The business of unrobing had been simultaneous. Marmaduke appeared in a suit of plain neat black; Monsieur Le Quoi, in a coat of snuff-colour, covering a vest of embroidery, with breeches, and silk stockings, and buckles—that were commonly thought to be of paste. Major Hartmann wore a coat of sky-blue, with large brass buttons, a club wig, and boots; and Mr. Richard Jones had set off his dapper little form in a frock of bottle-green, with bullet buttons; by one of which the sides were united over his well-rounded waist, opening above, so as to show a jacket of red cloth, with an under vest of flannel, faced with green velvet, and below, so as to exhibit a pair of buckskin breeches, with long, soiled, white-top boots, and spurs; one of the latter a little bent, from its recent attacks on the stool.

When the young lady had extricated herself from her garments, she was at liberty to gaze about her, and to examine not only the household over which she was to preside, but also the air and manner in which their domestic arrangements were conducted. Although there was much incongruity in the furniture and appearance of the hall, there was nothing mean. The floor was carpeted, even in its remotest corners. The brass candlesticks, the gilt lustres, and the glass chandeliers, whatever might be their *keeping* as to propriety and taste, were admirably kept as to all the purposes of use and comfort. They were clean, and glittering in the strong light of the apartment. Compared with the chill aspect of the December night without, the warmth and brilliancy of the apartment produced an effect that was not unlike enchantment. Her eye had not time to detect in detail the little errors, which, in truth, existed, but was glancing around her in delight, when an object arrested her view, that was in strong contrast to the smiling faces and neatly attired personages who had thus assembled to do honour to the heiress of Templeton.

In a corner of the hall, near the grand entrance, stood the young hunter, unnoticed, and for the moment apparently forgotten. But even the forgetfulness of the Judge, which, under the influence of strong emotion, had banished the recollection of the wound of this stranger, seemed surpassed by the absence of mind in the youth himself. On entering the apartment he had mechanically lifted his cap, and exposed a head, covered with hair that rivalled in colour and gloss the locks of Elizabeth. Nothing could have wrought a greater transformation, than the single act of removing the rough fox-skin cap. If there was much that was prepossessing in the countenance of the young hunter, there was something even noble in the rounded outlines of his head and brow. The very air and manner with which the member haughtily maintained itself over the coarse, and even wild attire, in which the rest of his frame was clad, bespoke not only familiarity with a splendour that in those new settlements was thought to be unequalled, but something very like contempt also.

The hand that held the cap, rested lightly on the little ivory-mounted piano of Elizabeth, with neither rustic restraint, nor obtrusive vulgarity. A single finger touched the instrument, as if accustomed to dwell on such places. His other arm was extended to its utmost length, and the hand grasped the barrel of his long rifle, with something like convulsive energy. The act and the attitude were both involuntary, and evidently proceeded from a feeling much deeper than that of vulgar surprise. His appearance, connected as it was with the rough exterior of his dress, rendered him entirely distinct from the busy group that were moving across the other end of the long hall, occupied in receiving the travellers, and exchanging their welcomes; and Elizabeth continued to gaze at him in wonder. The contraction of the stranger's brows increased, as his eyes moved slowly from one object to another. For moments the expression of his countenance was fierce, and then again it seemed to pass away in some painful emotion. The arm, that was extended, bent, and brought the hand nigh to his face, when his head dropped upon it, and concealed the wonderfully speaking lineaments.

"We forget, dear sir, the strange gentleman," (for her life Elizabeth could not call him otherwise,) "whom we have brought here for assistance, and to whom we owe every attention."

All eyes were instantly turned in the direction of those of the speaker, and the youth, rather proudly, elevated his head again, while he answered—

"My wound is trifling, and I believe that Judge Temple sent for a physician the moment we arrived."

"Certainly," said Marmaduke; "I have not forgotten the object of thy visit, young man, nor the nature of my debt."

"Oh!" exclaimed Richard, with something of a waggish leer, "thou owest the lad for the venison, I suppose, that thou killed, cousin 'duke! Marmaduke! Marmaduke! That was a marvellous tale of thine about the buck! Here, young man, are two dollars for the deer, and Judge Temple can do no less than pay the Doctor. I shall charge you nothing for my services, but you shall not fare the worse for that. Come, come, 'duke, don't be down-hearted about it; if you missed the buck, you contrived to shoot this poor fellow through a pine tree. Now I own that you have beat me; I never did such a thing in all my life."

"And I hope never will," returned the Judge, "if you are to experience the uneasiness that I have suffered. But be of good cheer, my young friend, the injury must be small, as thou movest thy arm with apparent freedom."

"Don't make the matter worse, 'duke, by pretending to talk about surgery," interrupted Mr. Jones, with a contemptuous wave of the hand; "it is a science that can only be learnt by practice. You know that my grandfather was a doctor, but you haven't got a drop of medical blood in your veins; these kind of things run in families. All my family by the father's side had a knack at physic. There was my uncle that was killed at Brandywine, he died as easy again as any other man in the regiment, just from knowing how to hold his breath naturally. Few men know how to breathe, naturally."

"I doubt not, Dickon," returned the Judge, meeting the bright smile, which, in spite of himself, stole over the stranger's features, "that thy family thoroughly understood the art of letting life slip through their fingers."

Richard heard him quite coolly, and, putting a hand in either pocket of his surtout, so as to press forward the skirts, began to whistle a tune; but the desire to reply overcame his philosophy, and with great heat he exclaimed—

"You may affect to smile, Judge Temple, at hereditary virtues, if you please; but there is not a man on your Patent who don't know better.—Here, even this young man, who has never seen any thing but bears, and deer, and wood-chucks, knows better, than to believe virtues are not transmitted in families. Don't you, friend?"

"I believe that vice is not," said the stranger abruptly, his eye glancing from the father to the daughter.

"The Squire is right, Judge," observed Benjamin, with a knowing nod of his head towards Richard, that bespoke the cordiality between them. "Now, in the old-country, the King's Majesty touches for the evil, and that is a disorder that the greatest doctor in the fleet, or, for the matter of that,

Admiral either, can't cure; only the King's Majesty, or a man that's been hanged. Yes, the Squire is right, for if-so-be that he wasn't, how is it that the seventh son always is a doctor, whether he ships for the cock-pit or not? Now when we fell in with the mounsheers, under De Grasse, d'ye see, we had aboard of us a doctor"——

"Very well, Benjamin," interrupted Elizabeth, glancing her eyes from the hunter to Monsieur Le Quoi, who was most politely attending to what fell from each individual in succession, "you shall tell me of that, and all your entertaining adventures together; just now, a room must be prepared, in which the arm of this gentleman can be dressed."

"I will attend to that myself, cousin Elizabeth," observed Richard, somewhat haughtily.—"The young man shall not suffer, because Marmaduke chooses to be a little obstinate. Follow me, my friend, and I will examine the hurt myself."

"It will be well to wait for the physician," said the hunter coldly; "he cannot be distant."

Richard paused, and looked at the speaker, a little astonished at the language, and a good deal appalled at the refusal. He construed the latter into an act of hostility, and, placing his hands in the pockets again, he walked up to Mr. Grant, and putting his face close to the countenance of the divine, said in an under tone—

"Now mark my words: there will be a story among the settlers, that all our necks would have been broken, but for that fellow—as if I did not know how to drive. Why you might have turned the horses yourself, sir; nothing was easier; it was only pulling hard on the nigh rein, and touching the off flank of the leader. I hope, my dear sir, you are not at all hurt by the upset the lad gave us?"

The reply was interrupted by the entrance of the village physician.

Chapter VI

"———And about his shelves,
A beggarly account of empty boxes,
Green earthen pots, bladders, and musty seeds,
Remnants of pack-thread, and old cakes of roses,
Were thinly scattered to make up a show."
Romeo and Juliet, V.i.44–48.

DOCTOR ELNATHAN TODD, for such was the name of the man of physic, was commonly thought to be, among the settlers, a gentleman of great mental endowments; and he was assuredly of rare personal proportions. In height he measured, without his shoes, exactly six feet and four inches. His hands, feet, and knees, corresponded in every respect with this formidable stature; but every other part of his frame appeared to have been intended for a man several sizes smaller, if we except the length of the limbs. His shoulders were square, in one sense at least, being in a right line from one side to the other; but they were so narrow, that the long, dangling arms they supported, seemed to issue out of his back. His neck possessed, in an eminent degree, the property of length to which we have alluded, and it was topped by a small bullet-head, that exhibited, on one side, a bush of bristling brown hair, and on the other, a short, twinkling visage, that appeared to maintain a constant struggle with itself in order to look wise. He was the youngest son of a farmer in the western part of Massachusetts, who, being in somewhat easy circumstances, had allowed this boy to shoot up to the height we have mentioned, without the ordinary interruptions of field-labour, wood-chopping, and such other toils as were imposed on his brothers. Elnathan was indebted for this exemption from labour, in some measure, to his extraordinary growth, which, leaving him pale, inanimate, and listless, induced his tender mother to pronounce him "a sickly boy, and one that was not equal to work, but who might arn a living, comfortably enough, by taking to pleading law, or turning minister, or doctoring, or some sitch-like easy calling." Still there was great uncertainty which of these vocations the youth was best endowed to fill; but, having no other employment, the stripling was constantly lounging about the "homestead," munching green apples, and hunting for sorrel; when the same sagacious eye, that had brought to light his latent talents, seized upon this circumstance, as a clue to his future path through the turmoils of the world. "Elnathan was cut out for a doctor," she knew, "for he was for ever digging for yarbs, and tasting all kinds of things that grow'd about the lots. Then again he had a naateral love for doctor-stuff, for when she had left the bilious pills out for her man, all nicely covered with maple sugar, just ready to take, Nathan had come in, and swallowed them, for all the world as if they were nothing, while Ichabod (her husband) could never get one down without making sitch desperate faces, that it was awful to look on."

This discovery decided the matter. Elnathan, then about fifteen, was, much like a wild colt, caught and trimmed, by clipping his bushy locks; dressed in a suit of homespun, died in the butternut bark; furnished with a "New Testament," and a "Webster's Spelling-Book," and sent to school. As the boy was by nature quite shrewd enough, and had previously, at odd times, laid the foundations of reading, writing, and arithmetic, he was soon conspicuous in the school for his learning. The delighted mother had the gratification of hearing, from the lips of the master, that her son was a "prodigious boy, and far above all his class." He also thought that "the youth had a natural love for doctoring, as he had known him frequently advise the smaller children against eating too much, and once or twice, when the ignorant little things had persevered in opposition to Elnathan's advice, he had known her son empty the school-baskets with his own mouth, to prevent the consequences."

Soon after this comfortable declaration from his schoolmaster, the lad was removed to the house of the village doctor, a gentleman whose early career had not been unlike that of our hero, where he was to be seen, sometimes watering a horse, at others watering medicines, blue, yellow and red; then again he might be noticed, lolling under an apple tree, with Ruddiman's Latin Grammar in his hand, and a corner of Denman's Midwifery sticking out of a pocket;—for his instructor held it absurd to teach his pupil how to despatch a patient regularly from this world, before he knew how to bring him into it.

This kind of life continued for a twelvemonth, when he suddenly appeared at meeting in a long coat (and well did it deserve the name) of black homespun, with little bootees, bound with uncoloured calf-skin, for the want of red morocco.

Soon after, he was seen shaving with a dull razor. Three or four months had scarce elapsed before several elderly ladies were observed hastening towards the house of a poor woman in the village, while others were running to and fro in great apparent distress. One or two boys were mounted, bareback, on horses, and sent off at speed in various directions. Several indirect questions were put, concerning the place where the physician was last seen; but all would not do; and at length Elnathan was seen issuing from his door, with a very grave air, preceded by a little white-headed boy, out of breath, trotting before him. The following day the youth appeared in the street, as the highway was called, and the neighbourhood was much edified by the additional gravity of his air. The same week he bought a new razor; and the succeeding Sunday he entered the meeting-house with a red silk handkerchief in his hand, and with an extremely demure countenance. In the evening he called upon a young woman of his own class in life, for there were no others to be found, and, when he was left alone with the fair, he was called, for the first time in his life, Doctor Todd, by her prudent mother. The ice once broken in this manner, Elnathan was greeted from every mouth with his official appellation.

Another year passed under the superintendence of the same master, during which the young physician had the credit of "riding with the old doctor," although they were generally observed to travel different roads. At the end of that period, Dr. Todd attained his legal majority. He then took a jaunt to Boston, to purchase medicines, and, as some intimated, to walk the hospital; we know not how the latter might have been, but if true, he soon walked through it, for he returned within a fortnight, bringing with him a suspicious-looking box, that smelt powerfully of brimstone.

The next Sunday he was married; and the following

morning he entered a one-horse sleigh with his bride, having before him the box we have mentioned, with another filled with home-made household linen, a paper-covered trunk, with a red umbrella lashed to it, a pair of quite new saddle-bags, and a band-box. The next intelligence that his friends received of the bride and bridegroom was, that the latter was "settled in the new-countries, and well to do as a doctor, in Templetown, in York state."

If a templar would smile at the qualifications of Marmaduke to fill the judicial seat he occupied, we are certain that a graduate of Leyden or Edinburgh would be extremely amused with this true narration of the servitude of Elnathan in the temple of Æsculapius. But the same consolation was afforded to both the jurist and the leech; for Dr. Todd was quite as much on a level with his compeers of the profession, in that country, as was Marmaduke with his brethren on the bench.

Time and practice did wonders for the physician. He was naturally humane, but possessed of no small share of moral courage; or, in other words, he was chary of the lives of his patients, and never tried uncertain experiments on such members of society as were considered useful; but once or twice, when a luckless vagrant had come under his care, he was a little addicted to trying the effects of every vial in his saddle-bags on the stranger's constitution. Happily their number was small, and in most cases their natures innocent. By these means Elnathan had acquired a certain degree of knowledge in fevers and agues, and could talk with much judgment concerning intermittents, remittents, tertians, quotidians, &c.—In certain cutaneous disorders, very prevalent in new settlements, he was considered to be infallible; and there was no woman on the Patent, but would as soon think of becoming a mother without a husband, as without the assistance of Dr. Todd. In short, he was rearing, on this foundation of sand, a superstructure, cemented by practice, though composed of somewhat brittle materials. He, however, occasionally renewed his elementary studies, and, with the observation of a shrewd mind, was comfortably applying his practice to his theory.

In surgery, having the least experience, and it being a business that spoke directly to the senses, he was most apt to distrust his own powers; but he had applied oils to several burns, cut round the roots of sundry defective teeth, and sewed up the wounds of numberless wood-choppers, with considerable eclat, when an unfortunate jobber* suffered a fracture of his leg, by the tree that he had been felling. It was on this occasion that our hero encountered the greatest trial his nerves and moral feeling had ever sustained. In the hour of need, however, he was not found wanting. Most of the amputations in the new settlements, and they were quite frequent, were performed by some one practitioner, who, possessing originally a reputation, was enabled by this circumstance to acquire an experience that rendered him deserving of it; and Elnathan had been present at one or two of these operations. But on the present occasion the man of practice was not to be obtained, and the duty fell, as a matter of course, to the share of Mr. Todd. He went to work with a kind of blind desperation, observing, at the same time, all the externals of decent gravity and great skill. The sufferer's name was Milligan, and it was to this event that Richard alluded, when he spoke of assisting the Doctor, at an amputation—by holding the leg! The limb was certainly cut off, and the patient survived the operation. It was, however, two years before poor Milligan ceased to complain that they had buried the leg in so narrow a box, that it was straitened for room; he could feel the pain shooting up from the inhumed fragment into the living members. Marmaduke suggested that the fault might lie in the arteries and nerves, but Richard, considering the amputation as part of his own handy-work, strongly repelled the insinuation, at the same time declaring, that he had often heard of men who could tell when it was about to rain, by the toes of amputated limbs. After two or three years, notwithstanding Milligan's complaints gradually diminished, the leg was dug up, and a larger box furnished, and from that hour no one had heard the sufferer utter another complaint on the subject. This gave the public great confidence in Doctor Todd, whose reputation was hourly increasing, and, luckily for his patients, his information also.

*People who clear land by the acre or job, are thus called.

Notwithstanding Mr. Todd's practice, and his success with the leg, he was not a little appalled, on entering the hall of the mansion-house. It was glaring with the light of day; it looked so splendid and imposing, compared with the hastily built and scantily furnished apartments which he frequented in his ordinary practice, and contained so many well-dressed persons, and anxious faces, that his usually firm nerves were a good deal discomposed. He had heard from the messenger who summoned him, that it was a gun-shot wound, and had come from his own home, wading through the snow, with his saddle-bags thrown over his arm, while separated arteries, penetrated lungs, and injured vitals, were whirling through his brain, as if he were stalking over a field of battle, instead of Judge Temple's peaceable enclosure.

The first object that met his eye, as he moved into the room, was Elizabeth, in her riding-habit, richly laced with gold cord, her fine form bending towards him, and her face expressing deep anxiety in every one of its beautiful features. The enormous bony knees of the physician struck each other with a noise that was audible, for in the absent state of his mind, he mistook her for a general officer, perforated with bullets, hastening from the field of battle to implore assistance. The delusion, however, was but momentary, and his eye glanced rapidly from the daughter to the earnest dignity of the father's countenance; thence to the busy strut of Richard, who was cooling his impatience at the hunter's indifference to his assistance, by pacing the hall and cracking his whip; from him to the Frenchman, who had stood for several minutes unheeded with a chair for the lady; thence to Major Hartmann, who was very coolly lighting a pipe three feet long by a candle in one of the chandeliers; thence to Mr. Grant, who was turning over a manuscript with much earnestness at one of the lustres; thence to Remarkable, who stood, with her arms demurely folded before her, surveying with a look of admiration and envy the dress and beauty of the young lady; and from her to Benjamin, who, with his feet standing wide apart, and his arms a-kimbo, was balancing his square little body, with the indifference of one who is accustomed to wounds and bloodshed. All of these seemed to be unhurt, and the operator began to breathe more freely; but before he had time to take a second look, the Judge, advancing, shook him kindly by the hand, and spoke.

"Thou art welcome, my good sir, quite welcome, indeed; here is a youth, whom I have unfortunately wounded in shooting a deer this evening, and who requires some of thy assistance."

"Shooting at a deer, 'duke," interrupted Richard,—"Shooting at a deer. Who do you think can prescribe, unless he knows the truth of the case? It is always so, with some people; they think a doctor can be deceived, with the same impunity as another man."

"Shooting at a deer truly," returned the Judge, smiling, "although it is by no means certain that I did not aid in destroying the buck; but the youth is injured by my hand, be that as it may; and it is thy skill, that must cure him, and my pocket shall amply reward thee for it."

"Two ver good tings to depend on," observed Monsieur Le Quoi, bowing politely, with a sweep of his head, to the Judge and the practitioner.

"I thank you, Monsieur," returned the Judge; "but we keep the young man in pain. Remarkable, thou wilt please to provide linen, for lint and bandages."

This remark caused a cessation of the compliments, and induced the physician to turn an inquiring eye in the direction of his patient. During the dialogue, the young hunter had thrown aside his over coat, and now stood clad in a plain suit of the common, light-coloured homespun of the country, that was evidently but recently made. His hand was on the lapels of his coat, in the attitude of removing the garment, when he suddenly suspended the movement, and looked towards the commiserating Elizabeth, who was standing in an unchanged posture, too much absorbed with her anxious feelings to heed his actions. A slight colour appeared on the brow of the youth.

"Possibly the sight of blood may alarm the lady; I will retire to another room, while the wound is dressing."

"By no means," said Doctor Todd, who, having discovered that his patient was far from being a man of importance, felt much emboldened to perform the duty.—"The strong light of these candles is favourable to the operation, and it is seldom that we hard students enjoy good eyesight."

While speaking, Elnathan placed a pair of large, iron-rimmed spectacles on his face, where they dropped, as it were by long practice, to the extremity of his slim, pug nose; and if they were of no service as assistants to his eyes, neither were they any impediment to his vision; for his little, gray organs were twinkling above them, like two stars emerging from the envious cover of a cloud. The action was unheeded by all but Remarkable, who observed to Benjamin—

"Doctor Todd is a comely man to look on, and disp'ut pretty. How well he seems in spectacles. I declare, they give a grand look to a body's face. I have quite a great mind to try them myself."

The speech of the stranger recalled the recollection of Miss Temple, who started, as if from deep abstraction, and, colouring excessively, she motioned to a young woman, who served in the capacity of maid, and retired, with an air of womanly reserve.

The field was now left to the physician and his patient, while the different personages who remained, gathered around the latter, with faces expressing the various degrees of interest, that each one felt in his condition. Major Hartmann alone retained his seat, where he continued to throw out vast quantities of smoke, now rolling his eyes up to the ceiling, as if musing on the uncertainty of life, and now bending them on the wounded man, with an expression, that bespoke some consciousness of his situation.

In the mean time, Elnathan, to whom the sight of a gun-shot wound was a perfect novelty, commenced his preparations, with a solemnity and care that were worthy of the occasion. An old shirt was procured by Benjamin, and placed in the hands of the other, who tore divers bandages from it, with an exactitude, that marked both his own skill, and the importance of the operation.

When this preparatory measure was taken, Dr. Todd selected a piece of the shirt with great care, and, handing it to Mr. Jones, without moving a muscle, said—

"Here, Squire Jones, you are well acquainted with these things; will you please to scrape the lint? It should be fine, and soft, you know, my dear sir; and be cautious that no cotton gets in, or it may p'ison the wownd. The shirt has been made with cotton thread, but you can easily pick it out."

Richard assumed the office, with a nod at his cousin, that said, quite plainly, "you see, this fellow can't get along without me;" and began to scrape the linen on his knee, with great diligence.

A table was now spread, with vials, boxes of salve, and divers surgical instruments. As the latter appeared, in succession, from a case of red morocco, their owner held up each implement, to the strong light of the chandelier, near to which he stood, and examined it, with the nicest care. A red silk handkerchief was frequently applied to the glittering steel, as if to remove from the polished surfaces, the least impediment, which might exist, to the most delicate operation. After the rather scantily furnished pocket-case, which contained these instruments, was exhausted, the physician turned to his saddle-bags, and produced various vials, filled with liquids, of the most radiant colours. These were arranged, in due order, by the side of the murderous saws, knives, and scissors, when Elnathan stretched his long body to its utmost elevation, placing his hand on the small of his back, as if for support, and looked about him, to discover what effect this display of professional skill, was likely to produce on the spectators.

"Upon my wort, toctor," observed Major Hartmann, with a roguish roll of his little black eyes, but with every other feature of his face in a state of perfect rest, "put you have a very pretty pocket-pook of tools tere, and your toctor-stuff glitters, as if it was petter for ter eyes as for ter pelly."

Elnathan gave a hem,—one that might have been equally taken, for that kind of noise, which cowards are said to make, in order to awaken their dormant courage, or for a natural effort, to clear the throat: if for the latter, it was successful; for, turning his face to the veteran German, he said—

"Very true, Major Hartmann, very true, sir; a prudent man will always strive to make his remedies agreeable to the eyes, though they may not altogether suit the stomach. It is no small part of our art, sir," and he now spoke with the confidence of a man who understood his subject, "to reconcile the patient to what is for his own good, though, at the same time, it may be unpalatable."

"Sartain! Doctor Todd is right," said Remarkable, "and has scripter for what he says. The Bible tells us, how things mought be sweet to the mouth, and bitter to the inwards."

"True, true," interrupted the Judge, a little impatiently; "but here is a youth who needs no deception to lure him to his own benefit. I see, by his eye, that he fears nothing more than delay."

The stranger had, without assistance, bared his own shoulder, when the slight perforation, produced by the passage of the buck-shot, was plainly visible. The intense cold of the evening, had stopped the bleeding, and Dr. Todd, casting a furtive glance at the wound, thought it by no means so formidable an affair as he had anticipated. Thus encouraged, he approached his patient, and made some indication of an intention to trace the route that had been taken by the lead.

Remarkable often found occasions, in after days, to recount the minutiæ of that celebrated operation; and when she arrived at this point, she commonly proceeded as follows:—"And then the Doctor tuck out of the pocket-book a long thing, like a knitting-needle, with a button fastened to the end on't; and then he pushed it into the wownd; and then the young man looked awful; and then I thought I should have swan'd away—I felt in sitch a disp'ut taking; and then the Doctor had run it right through his shoulder, and shoved the bullet out on t'other side; and so Doctor Todd cured the young man—of a ball that the Judge had shot into him, for all the world, as easy as I could pick out a splinter, with my darning-needle."

Such were the impressions of Remarkable on the subject; and such, doubtless, were the opinions of most of those, who felt it necessary to entertain a species of religious veneration for the skill of Elnathan; but such was far from the truth.

When the physician attempted to introduce the instrument, described by Remarkable, he was repulsed by the stranger, with a good deal of decision, and some little contempt, in his manner.

"I believe, sir," he said, "that a probe is not necessary; the shot has missed the bone, and has passed directly through the arm, to the opposite side, where it remains, but skin-deep, and whence, I should think, it might be easily extracted."

"The gentleman knows best," said Dr. Todd, laying down the probe, with the air of a man who had assumed it merely in compliance with forms; and, turning to Richard, he fingered the lint, with the appearance of great care and foresight. "Admirably well scraped, Squire Jones! it is about the best lint I have ever seen. I want your assistance, my good sir, to hold the patient's arm, while I make an incision for the ball. Now, I rather guess, there is not another gentleman present, who could scrape the lint so well as Squire Jones."

"Such things run in families," observed Richard, rising with alacrity, to render the desired assistance; "my father, and my grandfather before him, were both celebrated for their knowledge of surgery; they were not, like Marmaduke here, puffed up with an accidental thing, such as the time when he drew in the hip-joint of the man, who was thrown from his horse; that was the fall before you came into the settlement, Doctor; but they were men who were taught the thing regularly, spending half their lives in learning those little niceties; though, for the matter of that, my grandfather was a college-bred physician, and the best in the colony, too—that is, in his neighbourhood."

"So it goes with the world, Squire," cried Benjamin; "if-so-be a man want to walk the quarter-deck with credit, d'ye see, and with regular-built swabs on his shoulders, he mus'nt think to do it, by getting in at the cabin-windows. There are two ways to get into a top, besides the lubber-holes. The true way to walk aft, is to begin forrard; tho'f it be only in a humble way, like myself, d'ye see, which was, from being only a hander of top-gallant-sails, and a stower of the flying-jib, to keeping the key of the Captain's locker."

"Benjamin speaks quite to the purpose," continued Richard. "I dare say, that he has often seen shot extracted, in the different ships in which he has served; suppose we get him to hold the basin; he must be used to the sight of blood."

"That he is, Squire, that he is," interrupted the ci-devant steward; "many's the good shot, round, double-headed, and grape, that I've seen the doctors at work on. For the matter of that, I was in a boat, alongside the ship, when they cut out the twelve-pound shot from the thigh of the Captain of the Foody-rong, one of Mounsheer Ler Quaw's countrymen!"*

"A twelve-pound ball, from the thigh of a human being!" exclaimed Mr. Grant, with great simplicity, dropping the sermon he was again reading, and raising his spectacles to the top of his forehead.

"A twelve-pounder!" echoed Benjamin, staring around him, with much confidence; "a twelve-pounder! ay! a twenty-four pound shot can easily be taken from a man's body, if-so-be a doctor only knows how. There's Squire Jones, now, ask him, sir; he reads all the books; ask him, if he never fell in with a page, that keeps the reckoning of such things."

"Certainly, more important operations than that have been performed," observed Richard; "the Encyclopædia mentions much more incredible circumstances than that, as, I dare say, you know, Doctor Todd."

"Certainly, there are incredible tales told in the Encyclopædias," returned Elnathan, "though I cannot say, that I have ever seen, myself, any thing larger than a musket bullet extracted."

During this discourse, an incision had been made, through the skin of the young hunter's shoulder, and the lead was laid bare. Elnathan took a pair of glittering forceps, and was in the act of applying them to the wound, when a sudden motion of the patient, caused the shot to fall out of itself. The long arm and broad hand of the operator were now of singular service; for the latter expanded itself, and caught the lead, while at the same time, an extremely ambiguous motion was made, by its brother, so as to leave it doubtful to the spectators, how great was its agency in releasing the shot. Richard, however, put the matter at rest, by exclaiming—

"Very neatly done, Doctor! I have never seen a shot more neatly extracted; and, I dare say, Benjamin will say the same."

"Why, considering," returned Benjamin, "I must say, that it was ship-shape, and Brister-fashion.—Now all that the Doctor has to do, is to clap a couple of plugs in the holes,

*It is possible that, the reader may start at this declaration of Benjamin, but those who have lived in the new settlements of America, are too much accustomed to hear of these European exploits, to doubt it.

and the lad will float in any gale, that blows in these here hills."

"I thank you, sir, for what you have done," said the youth, with a little distance: "But here is a man, who will take me under his care, and spare you all, gentlemen, any further trouble on my account."

The whole group turned their heads, in surprise, and beheld, standing at one of the distant doors of the hall, the person of Indian John.

Chapter VII

"From Susquehanna's utmost springs,
Where savage tribes pursue their game,
His blanket tied with yellow strings,
The shepherd of the forest came."
Freneau, "The Indian Student," ll. 1–4.

BEFORE THE EUROPEANS, or, to use a more significant term, the Christians, dispossessed the original owners of the soil, all that section of country, which contains the New-England States, and those of the Middle which lie east of the mountains, was occupied by two great nations of Indians, from whom had descended numberless tribes. But, as the original distinctions between these nations, were marked by a difference in language, as well as by repeated and bloody wars, they never were known to amalgamate, until after the power and inroads of the whites had reduced some of the tribes to a state of dependence, that rendered not only their political, but, considering the wants and habits of a savage, their animal existence also, extremely precarious.

These two great divisions consisted, on the one side, of the Five, or, as they were afterwards called, the Six Nations, and their allies; and, on the other, of the Lenni Lenape, or Delawares, with the numerous and powerful tribes, that owned that nation as their Grandfather. The former were generally called, by the Anglo-Americans, Iroquois, or the Six Nations, and sometimes Mingoes. Their appellation, among their rivals, seems generally to have been the Mengwe, or Maqua. They consisted of the tribes, or, as their allies were fond of asserting, in order to raise their consequence, of the several nations, of the Mohawks, the Oneidas, the Onondagas, Cayugas, and Senecas; who ranked, in the confederation, in the order in which they are named. The Tuscaroras were admitted to this union, near a century after its formation, and thus completed the number to six.

Of the Lenni Lenape, or, as they were called by the whites, from the circumstance of their holding their great council-fire on the banks of that river, the Delaware nation, the principal tribes, besides that which bore the generic name, were, the Mahicanni, Mohicans, or Mohegans, and the Nanticokes, or Néntigoes. Of these, the latter held the country along the waters of the Chesapeake, and the seashore; while the Mohegans occupied the district between the Hudson and the ocean, including much of New-England: of course, these two tribes were the first who were dispossessed of their lands by the Europeans.

The wars of a portion of the latter, are celebrated among us, as the wars of King Philip; but the peaceful policy of William Penn, or Miquon, as he was termed by the natives, effected its object, with less difficulty, though not with less certainty. As the natives gradually disappeared from the country of the Mohegans, some scattering families sought a refuge around the council-fire of the mother tribe, or the Delawares.

This people had been induced to suffer themselves to be called *women*, by their old enemies, the Mingoes, or Iroquois, after the latter, having in vain tried the effects of hostility, had recourse to artifice, in order to prevail over their rivals.—According to this declaration, the Delawares were to cultivate the arts of peace, and to intrust their defence, entirely, to the *men*, or warlike tribes of the Six nations.

This state of things continued until the war of the revolution, when the Lenni Lenape formally asserted their independence, and fearlessly declared, that they were again men. But, in a government, so peculiarly republican as the Indian polity, it was not, at all times, an easy task, to restrain its members within the rules of the nation. Several fierce and renowned warriors, of the Mohegans, finding the conflict with the whites to be in vain, sought a refuge with their Grandfather, and brought with them the feelings and principles, that had so long distinguished them in their own tribe. These chieftains kept alive, in some measure, the martial spirit of the Delawares; and would, at times, lead small parties against their ancient enemies, or such other foes as incurred their resentment.

Among these warriors, was one race, particularly famous for their prowess, and for those qualities that render an Indian hero celebrated. But war, time, disease, and want, had conspired to thin their number; and the sole representative of this once renowned family, now stood in the hall of Marmaduke Temple. He had, for a long time, been an associate of the white-men, particularly in their wars; and, having been, at a season when his services were of importance, much noticed and flattered, he had turned Christian, and was baptized by the name of John. He had suffered severely, in his family, during the recent war, having had every soul to whom he was allied, cut off by an inroad of the enemy; and when the last, lingering remnant of his nation, extinguished their fires, amongst the hills of the Delaware, he alone had remained, with a determination of laying his bones in that country, where his fathers had so long lived and governed.

It was only, however, within a few months, that he had appeared among the mountains that surrounded Templeton. To the hut of the old hunter, he seemed peculiarly welcome; and, as the habits of the "Leather-stocking," were so nearly assimilated to those of the savages, the conjunction of their interests excited no surprise. They resided in the same cabin, ate of the same food, and were chiefly occupied in the same pursuits.

We have already mentioned the baptismal name of this ancient chief; but in his conversation with Natty, held in the language of the Delawares, he was heard uniformly to call himself Chingachgook, which, interpreted, means the "Great Snake." This name he had acquired in youth, by his skill and prowess in war; but when his brows began to wrinkle with time, and he stood alone, the last of his family, and his particular tribe, the few Delawares, who yet continued about the head-waters of their river, gave him the mournful appellation of Mohegan. Perhaps there was something of deep feeling, excited in the bosom of this inhabitant of the forest, by the sound of a name, that recalled the idea of his nation in ruins, for he seldom used it himself—never, indeed, excepting on the most solemn occasions; but the settlers had united, according to the Christian custom, his baptismal with his national name, and to them, he was generally known as John Mohegan, or, more familiarly, as Indian John.

From his long association with the white-men, the habits of Mohegan, were a mixture of the civilized and savage states, though there was certainly a strong preponderance in favour of the latter. In common with all his people, who dwelt within the influence of the Anglo-Americans, he had acquired new wants, and his dress was a mixture of his native and European fashions. Notwithstanding the intense cold without, his head was uncovered; but a profusion of long, black, coarse hair, concealed his forehead, his crown, and even hung about his cheeks, so as to convey the idea, to one who knew his present and former conditions, that he encouraged its abundance, as a willing veil, to hide the shame of a noble soul, mourning for glory once known. His forehead, when it could be seen, appeared lofty, broad, and noble. His nose was high, and of the kind called Roman, with nostrils, that expanded, in his seventieth year, with the freedom that had distinguished them in youth. His mouth was large, but compressed, and possessing a great share of expression and character, and, when opened, it discovered a perfect set of short, strong, and regular teeth. His chin was full, though not prominent; and his face bore the infallible mark of his people, in its square, high cheek-bones. The eyes were not large, but their black orbs glittered in the rays of the candles, as he gazed intently down the hall, like two balls of fire.

The instant that Mohegan observed himself to be noticed by the group, around the young stranger, he dropped the blanket, which covered the upper part of his frame, from his shoulders, suffering it to fall over his leggins, of untanned deer-skin, where it was retained by a belt of bark, that confined it to his waist.

As he walked slowly down the long hall, the dignified and deliberate tread of the Indian, surprised the spectators. His shoulders, and body, to his waist, were entirely bare, with the exception of a silver medallion of Washington, that was suspended from his neck by a thong of buck-skin, and rested on his high chest, amidst many scars. His shoulders were rather broad and full; but the arms, though straight and graceful, wanted the muscular appearance, that labour gives to a race of men. The medallion was the only ornament he wore, although enormous slits, in the rim of either ear, which suffered the cartilages to fall two inches below the members, had evidently been used for the purposes of decoration, in other days. In his hand, he held a small basket, of the ash-wood slips, coloured in divers fantastical conceits, with red and black paints mingled with the white of the wood.

As this child of the forest approached them, the whole party stood aside, and allowed him to confront the object of his visit. He did not speak, however, but stood, fixing his glowing eyes on the shoulder of the young hunter, and then turning them intently on the countenance of the Judge. The latter was a good deal astonished, at this unusual departure from the ordinarily subdued and quiet manner of the Indian; but he extended his hand, and said—

"Thou art welcome, John. This youth entertains a high opinion of thy skill, it seems, for he prefers thee, to dress his wound, even to our good friend Dr. Todd."

Mohegan now spoke, in tolerable English, but in a low, monotonous, guttural tone:—

"The children of Miquon do not love the sight of blood; and yet, the Young Eagle has been struck, by the hand that should do no evil!"

"Mohegan! old John!" exclaimed the Judge, "thinkest thou, that my hand has ever drawn human blood willingly? For shame! for shame, old John! thy religion should have taught thee better."

"The evil spirit sometimes lives in the best heart," returned John, "but my brother speaks the truth; his hand has never taken life, when awake; no! not even when the children of the great English Father, were making the waters red with the blood of his people."

"Surely, John," said Mr. Grant, with much earnestness, "you remember the divine command of our Saviour, 'judge not, lest ye be judged.' What motive could Judge Temple have, for injuring a youth like this; one to whom he is unknown, and from whom he can receive neither injury nor favour?"

John listened respectfully to the divine, and when he had concluded, he stretched out his arm, and said with energy—

"He is innocent—my brother has not done this."

Marmaduke received the offered hand of the other, with a smile, that showed, however he might be astonished at his suspicion, he had ceased to resent it; while the wounded youth stood, gazing from his red friend to his host, with interest powerfully delineated in his countenance. No sooner was this act of pacification exchanged, than John proceeded to discharge the duty, on which he had come. Dr. Todd was far from manifesting any displeasure at this invasion of his rights, but made way for the new leech, with an air that expressed a willingness to gratify the humours of his patient, now that the all-important part of the business was so successfully performed, and nothing remained to be done, but what any child might effect. Indeed, he whispered as much to Monsieur Le Quoi, when he said—

"It was fortunate that the ball was extracted before this Indian came in; but any old woman can dress the wound. The young man, I hear, lives with John and Natty Bumppo, and it's always best to humour a patient, when it can be done discreetly—I say, discreetly, Mounsheer."

"Certainement," returned the Frenchman; "you seem ver happy, Mister Toad, in your practeece. I tink de elder lady might ver well finish, vat you so skeelfully begin."

But Richard had, at the bottom, a great deal of veneration for the knowledge of Mohegan, especially in external wounds; and retaining all his desire for a participation in glory, he advanced nigh the Indian, and said—

"Sago, sago, Mohegan! sago, my good fellow! I am glad you have come; give me a regular physician, like Doctor Todd, to cut into flesh, and a native to heal the wound. Do you remember, John, the time when I and you set the bone of Natty Bumppo's little finger, after he broke it, by falling from the rock, when he was trying to get the partridge that fell on the cliffs. I never could tell yet, whether it was I or Natty, who killed that bird: he fired first, and the bird stooped, but then it was rising again as I pulled trigger. I should have claimed it, for a certainty, but Natty said the hole was too big for shot, and he fired a single ball from his rifle; but the piece I carried then, didn't scatter, and I have known it to bore a hole through a board, when I've been shooting at a mark, very much like rifle-bullets. Shall I help you, John? You know I have a knack at these things."

Mohegan heard this disquisition quite patiently, and when Richard concluded, he held out the basket, which contained his specifics, indicating, by a gesture, that he might hold it. Mr. Jones was quite satisfied with this commission; and, ever after, in speaking of the event, was used to say, that "Doctor Todd and I cut out the bullet, and I and Indian John dressed the wound."

The patient was much more deserving of that epithet, while under the hands of Mohegan, than while suffering under the practice of the physician. Indeed, the Indian gave him but little opportunity for the exercise of a forbearing temper, as he had come prepared for the occasion. His dressings were soon applied, and consisted only of some pounded bark, moistened with a fluid, that he had expressed from some of the simples of the woods.

Among the native tribes of the forest, there were always two kinds of leeches to be met with. The one placed its whole dependence on the exercise of a supernatural power, and was held in greater veneration than their practice could at all justify; but the other was really endowed with great skill, in the ordinary complaints of the human body, and was, more particularly, as Natty had intimated, "curous in cuts and bruises."

While John and Richard were placing the dressings on the wound, Elnathan was acutely eyeing the contents of Mohegan's basket, which Mr. Jones, in his physical ardour, had transferred to the Doctor, in order to hold, himself, one end of the bandages. Here he was soon enabled to detect sundry fragments of wood and bark, of which he, quite coolly, took possession, very possibly without any intention of speaking at all upon the subject; but when he beheld the full, blue eye of Marmaduke, watching his movements, he whispered to the Judge—

"It is not to be denied, Judge Temple, but what the savages are knowing, in small matters of physic. They hand these things down in their traditions. Now, in cancers, and hydrophoby, they are quite ingenous. I will just take this bark home, and analyze it; for, though it can't be worth sixpence to the young man's shoulder, it may be good for the toothache, or rhoomatis, or some of them complaints. A man should never be above larning, even if it be from an Indian."

It was fortunate for Dr. Todd, that his principles were so

liberal, as, coupled with his practice, they were the means by which he acquired all his knowledge, and by which he was gradually qualifying himself for the duties of his profession. The process to which he subjected the specific, differed, however, greatly from the ordinary rules of chemistry; for, instead of separating, he afterwards united the component parts of Mohegan's remedy, and thus was able to discover the tree, whence the Indian had taken it.

Some ten years after this event, when civilization and its refinements had crept, or rather rushed, into the settlements among these wild hills, an affair of honour occurred, and Elnathan was seen to apply a salve to the wound received by one of the parties, which had the flavour that was peculiar to the tree, or root, that Mohegan had used. Ten years later still, when England and the United States were again engaged in war, and the hordes of the western parts of the state of New-York, were rushing to the field, Elnathan, presuming on the reputation obtained by these two operations, followed in the rear of a brigade of militia, as its surgeon!

When Mohegan had applied the bark, he freely relinquished to Richard the needle and thread, that were used in sewing the bandages, for these were implements of which the native but little understood the use; and, stepping back, with decent gravity, awaited the completion of the business by the other.

"Reach me the scissors," said Mr. Jones, when he had finished, and finished for the second time, after tying the linen in every shape and form that it could be placed; "reach me the scissors, for here is a thread that must be cut off, or it might get under the dressings, and inflame the wound. See, John, I have put the lint I scraped, between two layers of the linen; for though the bark is certainly best for the flesh, yet the lint will serve to keep the cold air from the wound. If any lint will do it good, it is this lint; I scraped it myself, and I will not turn my back, at scraping lint, to any man on the Patent. I ought to know how, if any body ought, for my grandfather was a doctor, and my father had a natural turn that way."

"Here, Squire, is the scissors," said Remarkable, producing from beneath her petticoat of green moreen, a pair of dull-looking shears; "well, upon my say so, you *have* sewed on the rags, as well as a woman."

"As well as a woman!" echoed Richard, with indignation; "what do women know of such matters? and you are proof of the truth of what I say. Who ever saw such a pair of shears used about a wound? Dr. Todd, I will thank you for the scissors from the case. Now, young man, I think you'll do. The shot has been very neatly taken out, although, perhaps, seeing I had a hand in it, I ought not to say so; and the wound is admirably dressed. You will soon be well again; though the jerk you gave my leaders, must have a tendency to inflame the shoulder, yet, you will do, you will do. You were rather flurried, I suppose, and not used to horses; but I forgive the accident, for the motive;—no doubt, you had the best of motives;—yes, now you will do."

"Then, gentlemen," said the wounded stranger, rising, and resuming his clothes, "it will be unnecessary for me to trespass longer on your time and patience. There remains but one thing more to be settled, and that is, our respective rights to the deer, Judge Temple."

"I acknowledge it to be thine," said Marmaduke; "and much more deeply am I indebted to thee, than for this piece of venison. But in the morning, thou wilt call here, and we can adjust this, as well as more important matters. Elizabeth,"—for the young lady, being apprized that the wound was dressed, had re-entered the hall,—"thou wilt order a repast, for this youth, before we proceed to the church; and Aggy will have a sleigh prepared, to convey him to his friend."

"But, sir, I cannot go, without a part of the deer," returned the youth, seemingly struggling with his own feelings: "I have already told you, that I needed the venison for myself."

"Oh! we will not be particular," exclaimed Richard; "the Judge will pay you, in the morning, for the whole deer; and, Remarkable, give the lad all the animal excepting the saddle: so, on the whole, I think, you may consider yourself as a very lucky young man;—you have been shot, without being disabled; have had the wound dressed in the best possible manner, here in the woods, as well as it would have been done in the Philadelphia hospital, if not better; have sold your deer at a high price, and yet can keep most of the carcass, with the skin in the bargain. 'Marky, tell Tom to give him the skin too; and in the morning, bring the skin to me, and I will give you half-a-dollar for it, or at least, three-and-sixpence. I want just such a skin, to cover the pillion that I am making for cousin Bess."

"I thank you, sir, for your liberality, and, I trust, am also thankful for my escape," returned the stranger; "but you reserve the very part of the animal that I wish for my own use. I must have the saddle myself."

"Must!" echoed Richard; "must is harder to be swallowed than the horns of the buck."

"Yes, must," repeated the youth; when, turning his head proudly around him, as if to see who would dare to controvert his rights, he met the astonished gaze of Elizabeth, and proceeded more mildly—"that is, if a man is allowed the possession of that which his hand hath killed, and the law will protect him in the enjoyment of his own."

"The law will do so," said Judge Temple, with an air of mortification, mingled with surprise. "Benjamin, see that the whole deer is placed in the sleigh; and have this youth conveyed to the hut of Leather-stocking. But, young man, thou hast a name, and I shall see you again, in order to compensate thee for the wrong I have done thee?"

"I am called Edwards," returned the hunter, "Oliver Edwards. I am easily to be seen, sir, for I live nigh by, and am not afraid to show my face, having never injured any man."

"It is we, who have injured you, sir," said Elizabeth; "and the knowledge, that you decline our assistance, would give my father great pain. He would gladly see you in the morning."

The young hunter gazed at the fair speaker, until his earnest look brought the blood to her temples; when, recollecting himself, he bent his head, dropping his eyes to the carpet, and replied—

"In the morning, then, will I return, and see Judge Temple; and I will accept his offer of the sleigh, in token of amity."

"Amity!" repeated Marmaduke; "there was no malice in the act that injured thee, young man; there should be none in the feelings which it may engender."

"Forgive us our trespasses, as we forgive those who trespass against us," observed Mr. Grant, "is the language used by our Divine Master himself, and it should be the golden rule of us, his humble followers."

The stranger stood a moment, lost in thought, and then, glancing his dark eyes, rather wildly, around the hall, he bowed low to the divine, and moved from the apartment, with an air that would not admit of detention.

"'Tis strange, that one so young should harbour such feelings of resentment," said Marmaduke, when the door closed behind the stranger; "but while the pain is recent, and the sense of the injury so fresh, he must feel more strongly than in cooler moments. I doubt not, we shall see him, in the morning, more tractable."

Elizabeth, to whom this speech was addressed, did not reply, but moved slowly up the hall, by herself, fixing her eyes on the little figure of the English ingrained carpet, that covered the floor; while, on the other hand, Richard gave a loud crack with his whip, as the stranger disappeared, and cried—

"Well, 'duke, you are your own master, but I would have tried law for the saddle, before I would have given it to the fellow. Do you not own the mountains, as well as the valleys? are not the woods your own? what right has this chap, or the Leather-stocking, to shoot in your woods, without your permission? Now, I have known a farmer, in Pennsylvania, order a sportsman off his farm, with as little ceremony as I would order Benjamin to put a log in the stove. By-the-by, Benjamin, see how the thermometer stands. Now, if a man has a right to do this, on a farm of a hundred acres, what power must a landlord have, who owns sixty thousand—ay! for the matter of that, including the late purchases, a hundred thousand? There is Mohegan, to-be-sure, he may have some right, being a native; but it's little the poor fellow can do now with his rifle. How is this managed in France, Monsieur Le Quoi? do you let every body run over your land, in that country, helter-skelter, as they do here, shooting the game, so that a gentleman has but little or no chance with his gun?"

"Bah! diable, no, Meester Deeck," replied the Frenchman; "we give, in France, no liberty, except to de ladi."

"Yes, yes, to the women, I know," said Richard; "that is

your Sallick law. I read, sir, all kinds of books; of France, as well as England; of Greece, as well as Rome. But if I were in 'duke's place, I would stick up advertisements, to-morrow morning, forbidding all persons to shoot, or trespass, in any manner, on my woods. I could write such an advertisement myself, in an hour, as would put a stop to the thing at once."

"Richart," said Major Hartmann, very coolly knocking the ashes from his pipe into the spitting-box by his side, "now listen: I have livet seventy-five years on ter Mohawk, and in ter woots.—You hat petter mettle as mit ter deyvel, as mit ter hunters. Tey live mit ter gun, and a rifle is petter as ter law."

"A'nt Marmaduke a Judge?" said Richard, indignantly; "where is the use of being a Judge or having a Judge, if there is no law? Damn the fellow, I have a great mind to sue him in the morning myself, before Squire Doolittle, for meddling with my leaders. I am not afraid of his rifle. I can shoot too. I have hit a dollar, many a time, at fifty rods."

"Thou hast missed more dollars than ever thou hast hit, Dickon," exclaimed the cheerful voice of the Judge.—"But we will now take our evening's repast, which, I perceive by Remarkable's physiognomy, is ready. Monsieur Le Quoi, Miss Temple has a hand at your service. Will you lead the way, my child?"

"Ah! ma chère Mam'selle, comme je suis enchanté!" said the Frenchman. "Il ne manque que les dames de faire un paradis de Templeton."

Mr. Grant and Mohegan, continued in the hall, while the remainder of the party withdrew to an eating parlour, if we except Benjamin, who civilly remained, to close the rear after the clergyman, and to open the front door, for the exit of the Indian.

"John," said the divine, when the figure of Judge Temple disappeared, the last of the group, "to-morrow is the festival of the nativity of our blessed Redeemer, when the church has appointed prayers and thanksgivings, to be offered up by her children, and when all are invited to partake of the mystical elements. As you have taken up the cross, and become a follower of good, and an eschewer of evil, I trust I shall see you before the altar, with a contrite heart, and a meek spirit."

"John will come," said the Indian, betraying no surprise, though he did not understand all the terms used by the other.

"Yes," continued Mr. Grant, laying his hand gently on the tawny shoulder of the aged chief, "but it is not enough to be there in the body; you must come in the spirit, and in truth. The Redeemer died for all, for the poor Indian, as well as for the white man. Heaven knows no difference in colour; nor must earth witness a separation of the church. It is good and profitable, John, to freshen the understanding, and support the wavering, by the observance of our holy festivals; but all form is but stench, in the nostrils of the Holy One, unless it be accompanied by a devout and humble spirit."

The Indian stepped back a little, and, raising his body to its utmost powers of erection, he stretched his right arm on high, and dropped his fore-finger downward, as if pointing from the heavens, then striking his other hand on his naked breast, he said, with energy—

"The eye of the Great Spirit can see from the clouds;—the bosom of Mohegan is bare."

"It is well, John, and I hope you will receive profit and consolation, from the performance of this duty. The Great Spirit overlooks none of his children; and the man of the woods, is as much an object of his care, as he who dwells in a palace. I wish you a good night, and pray God to bless you."

The Indian bent his head, and they separated—the one to seek his hut, and the other to join the party at the supper-table. While Benjamin was opening the door, for the passage of the chief, he cried, in a tone that was meant to be encouraging—

"The parson says the word that is true, John. If-so-be, that they took count of the colour of the skin in heaven, why, they might refuse to muster on their books, a christian-born, like myself, just for the matter of a little tan, from cruising in warm latitudes; though, for the matter of that, this damned nor-wester is enough to whiten the skin of a blackamoor. Let the reef out of your blanket, man, or your red hide will hardly weather the night, without a touch from the frost."

Chapter VIII

"For here the exile met from every clime,
And spoke, in friendship, every distant tongue."
Campbell, *Gertrude of Wyoming*, I.iv.3–4.

WE HAVE MADE our readers acquainted with some variety in character and nations, in introducing the most important personages of this legend to their notice: but in order to establish the fidelity of our narrative, we shall briefly attempt to explain the reason why we have been obliged to present so motley a dramatis personæ.

Europe, at the period of our tale, was in the commencement of that commotion, which afterwards shook her political institutions to the centre. Louis the Sixteenth had been beheaded, and a nation, once esteemed the most refined amongst the civilized people of the world, was changing its character, and substituting cruelty for mercy, and subtlety and ferocity for magnanimity and courage. Thousands of Frenchmen were compelled to seek protection in distant lands. Among the crowds who fled from France and her islands, to the United States of America, was the gentleman whom we have already mentioned as Monsieur Le Quoi. He had been recommended to the favour of Judge Temple, by the head of an eminent mercantile house in New-York, with whom Marmaduke was in habits of intimacy, and accustomed to exchange good offices. At his first interview with the Frenchman, our Judge had discovered him to be a man of breeding, and one who had seen much more prosperous days, in his own country. From certain hints that had escaped him, Monsieur Le Quoi was suspected of having been a West-India planter, great numbers of whom had fled from St. Domingo and the other islands, and were now living in the Union, in a state of comparative poverty, and some in absolute want. The latter was not, however, the lot of Monsieur Le Quoi. He had but little, he acknowledged, but that little was enough to furnish, in the language of the country, an "assortment for a store."

The knowledge of Marmaduke was eminently practical, and

there was no part of a *settler's* life with which he was not familiar. Under his direction, Monsieur Le Quoi made some purchases, consisting of a few cloths; some groceries, with a good deal of gunpowder and tobacco; a quantity of iron-ware, among which was a large proportion of Barlow's jack-knives, potash-kettles, and spiders; a very formidable collection of crockery, of the coarsest quality, and most uncouth forms; together with every other common article, that the art of man has devised for his wants, not forgetting the luxuries of looking-glasses and Jew's-harps. With this collection of valuables, Monsieur Le Quoi had stepped behind a counter, and, with a wonderful pliability of temper, had dropped into his assumed character, as gracefully as he had ever moved in any other. The gentleness and suavity of his manners, rendered him extremely popular; besides this, the women soon discovered that he had a taste; his calicoes were the finest, or, in other words, the most showy, of any that were brought into the country; and it was impossible to look at the prices, asked for his goods, by "so pretty a spoken man." Through these conjoint means, the affairs of Monsieur Le Quoi were again in a prosperous condition, and he was looked up to by the settlers as the second best man on the "Patent."

This term, "Patent," which we have already used, and for which we may have further occasion, meant the district of country that had been originally granted to old Major Effingham, by the "King's letters patent," and which had now become, by purchase under the act of confiscation, the property of Marmaduke Temple. It was a term in common use, throughout the *new* parts of the state, and was usually annexed to the landlord's name, as, "Temple's, or Effingham's Patent."

Major Hartmann was the descendant of a man, who, in company with a number of his countrymen, had emigrated, with their families, from the banks of the Rhine, to those of the Mohawk. This migration had occurred as far back as the reign of Queen Anne; and their descendants were now living, in great peace and plenty, on the fertile borders of that beautiful stream.

The Germans, or "High Dutchers," as they were called, to distinguish them from the original, or Low Dutch colonists, were a very peculiar people. They possessed all the gravity of the latter, without any of their phlegm; and, like them, the "High Dutchers" were industrious, honest, and economical.

Fritz, or Frederick Hartmann, was an epitome of all the vices and virtues, foibles and excellencies, of his race. He was passionate, though silent, obstinate, and a good deal suspicious of strangers; of immoveable courage, inflexible honesty, and undeviating in his friendships. Indeed, there was no change about him, unless it were from grave to gay. He was serious by months, and jolly by weeks. He had, early in their acquaintance, formed an attachment for Marmaduke Temple, who was the only man, that could not speak High Dutch, that ever gained his entire confidence. Four times in each year, at periods equi-distant, he left his low stone dwelling, on the banks of the Mohawk, and travelled thirty miles, through the hills, to the door of the mansion-house in Templeton. Here he generally staid a week, and was reputed to spend much of that time in riotous living, greatly countenanced by Mr. Richard Jones. But every one loved him, even to Remarkable Pettibone, to whom he occasioned some additional trouble, he was so frank, so sincere, and, at times, so mirthful. He was now on his regular Christmas visit, and had not been in the village an hour, when Richard summoned him to fill a seat in the sleigh, to meet the landlord and his daughter.

Before explaining the character and situation of Mr. Grant, it will be necessary to recur to times, far back in the brief history of the settlement.

There seems to be a tendency in human nature, to endeavour to provide for the wants of this world, before our attention is turned to the business of the other. Religion was a quality but little cultivated, amid the stumps of Temple's Patent, for the first few years of its settlement; but as most of its inhabitants were from the moral states of Connecticut and Massachusetts, when the wants of nature were satisfied, they began seriously to turn their attention to the introduction of those customs and observances, which had been the principal care of their forefathers. There was certainly a great variety of opinions, on the subject of grace and free-will, amongst the tenantry of Marmaduke; and, when we take into consideration the variety of religious instruction which they received, it can easily be seen, that it could not well be otherwise.

Soon after the village had been formally laid out, into the streets and *blocks* that resembled a city, a meeting of its inhabitants had been convened, to take into consideration the propriety of establishing an Academy. This measure originated with Richard, who, in truth, was much disposed to have the institution designated a University, or at least a College. Meeting after meeting was held, for this purpose, year after year. The *resolutions* of these assemblages, appeared in the most conspicuous columns of a little, blue-looking newspaper, that was already issued weekly from the garret of a dwelling-house in the village, and which the traveller might as often see, stuck into the fissure of a stake, erected at the point where the footpath from the log cabin of some settler entered the highway, as a post-office for an individual. Sometimes the stake supported a small box, and a whole neighbourhood received a weekly supply, for their literary wants, at this point, where the man who "rides post," regularly deposited a bundle of the precious commodity. To these flourishing resolutions, which briefly recounted the general utility of education, the political and geographical rights of the village of Templeton, to a participation in the favours of the regents of the university, the salubrity of the air, and wholesomeness of the water, together with the cheapness of food, and the superior state of morals in the neighbourhood, were uniformly annexed, in large Roman capitals, the names of Marmaduke Temple, as chairman, and Richard Jones, as secretary.

Happily for the success of this undertaking, the regents were not accustomed to resist these appeals to their generosity, whenever there was the smallest prospect of a donation to second the request. Eventually, Judge Temple concluded to bestow the necessary land, and to erect the required edifice at his own expense. The skill of Mr., or, as he was now called, from the circumstance of having received the commission of a justice of the peace, Squire Doolittle, was again put in requisition, and the science of Mr. Jones was once more resorted to.

We shall not recount the different devices of the architects on the occasion; nor would it be decorous so to do, seeing that there was a convocation of the society of the ancient and honourable fraternity "of the free and accepted masons," at the head of whom was Richard, in the capacity of master, doubtless to approve or reject such of the plans as, in their wisdom, they deemed to be for the best. The knotty point was, however, soon decided; and, on the appointed day, the brotherhood marched, in great state, displaying sundry banners and mysterious symbols, each man with a little mimic apron before him, from a most cunningly contrived apartment in the garret of the "Bold Dragoon," an inn, kept by one Captain Hollister, to the site of the intended edifice. Here Richard laid the corner-stone, with suitable gravity, amidst an assemblage of more than half the men, and all the women, within ten miles of Templeton.

In the course of the succeeding week, there was another meeting of the people, not omitting swarms of the gentler sex, when the abilities of Hiram, at the "square rule," were put to the test of experiment. The frame fitted well; and the skeleton of the fabric was reared without a single accident, if we except a few falls from horses, while the labourers were returning home in the evening. From this time, the work advanced with great rapidity, and in the course of the season, the labour was completed; the edifice standing, in all its beauty and proportions, the boast of the village, the study of young aspirants for architectural fame, and the admiration of every settler on the Patent.

It was a long, narrow house, of wood, painted white, and more than half windows; and when the observer stood at the western side of the building, the edifice offered but a small obstacle to a full view of the rising sun. It was, in truth, but a very comfortless, open place, through which the daylight shone with natural facility. On its front were divers ornaments, in wood, designed by Richard, and executed by Hiram; but a window in the centre of the second story, immediately over the door, or grand entrance, and the "steeple," were the pride of the building. The former was, we believe, of the composite order, for it included in its composition a multitude of ornaments, and a great variety of proportions. It consisted of an arched compartment in the centre, with a square and small division on either side, the whole encased in heavy frames, deeply and laboriously moulded in pine wood, and lighted with a vast number of blurred and green-looking glass, of those dimensions which are commonly called "eight by ten." Blinds, that were intended to be painted green, kept the window in a state of preservation, and probably might have contributed to the effect of the whole, had not the failure in the public funds, which seems always to be incidental to any undertaking of this kind, left them in the sombre coat of lead-colour with which they had been originally clothed. The "steeple" was a little cupola, reared on the very centre of the roof, on four tall pillars of pine, that were fluted with a gouge, and loaded with mouldings. On the tops of the columns was reared a dome, or cupola, resembling in shape an inverted tea-cup without its bottom, from the centre of which projected a spire, or shaft of wood, transfixed with two iron rods, that bore on their ends the letters N. S. E. and W., in the same metal. The whole was surmounted by an imitation of one of the finny tribe, carved in wood, by the hands of Richard, and painted, what he called, a "scale-colour." This animal Mr. Jones affirmed to be an admirable resemblance of a great favourite of the epicures in that country, which bore the title of "lake-fish;" and doubtless the assertion was true; for, although intended to answer the purposes of a weather-cock, the fish was observed invariably to look, with a longing eye, in the direction of the beautiful sheet of water that lay imbedded in the mountains of Templeton.

For a short time after the charter of the regents was received, the trustees of this institution employed a graduate of one of the eastern colleges, to instruct such youth as aspired to knowledge, within the walls of the edifice which we have described. The upper part of the building was in one apartment, and was intended for gala-days and exhibitions; and the lower contained two rooms, that were intended for the great divisions of education, viz. the Latin and the English scholars. The former were never very numerous; though the sounds of "nominative, *pennaa*; genitive, *penny*," were soon heard to issue from the windows of the room, to the great delight and manifest edification of the passengers.

Only one labourer in this temple of Minerva, however, was known to get so far as to attempt a translation of Virgil. He, indeed, appeared at the annual exhibition, to the prodigious exultation of all his relatives, a farmer's family in the vicinity, and repeated the whole of the first eclogue from memory, observing the intonations of the dialogue with much judgment and effect. The sounds, as they proceeded from his mouth, of

"Titty-ree too patty-lee ree-coo-bans sub teg-mi-nee faa-gy
Syl-ves-trem ten-oo-i moo-sam med-i-taa-ris aa-ve-ny"—

were the last that had been heard in that building, as probably they were the first that had ever been heard, in the same language, there or any where else. By this time, the trustees discovered, that they had anticipated the age, and the *instructor*, or *principal*, was superseded by a *master*, who went on to teach the more humble lesson, of "the more haste the worse speed," in good, plain English.

From this time until the date of our incidents, the Academy was a common country school; and the great room of the building was sometimes used as a court-room, on extraordinary trials; sometimes for conferences of the religious, and the morally disposed, in the evening; at others for a ball in the afternoon, given under the auspices of Richard; and on Sundays, invariably, as a place of public worship.

When an itinerant priest, of the persuasion of the Methodists, Baptists, Universalists, or of the more numerous sect of the Presbyterians, was accidentally in the neighbourhood, he was ordinarily invited to officiate, and was commonly rewarded for his services by a collection in a hat, before the congregation separated. When no such regular minister offered, a kind of colloquial prayer or two was made, by some of the more gifted members, and a sermon was usually read, from Sterne, by Mr. Richard Jones.

The consequence of this desultory kind of priesthood was, as we have already intimated, a great diversity of opinion, on the more abstruse points of faith. Each sect had its adherents, though neither was regularly organized and disciplined. Of the religious education of Marmaduke, we have already written, nor was the doubtful character of his faith completely removed by his marriage. The mother of Elizabeth was an Episcopalian, as, indeed, was the mother of the Judge himself;

and the good taste of Marmaduke revolted at the familiar colloquies which the leaders of the conferences held with the Deity, in their nightly meetings. In form, he was certainly an Episcopalian, though not a sectary of that denomination. On the other hand, Richard was as rigid in the observance of the canons of his church, as he was inflexible in his opinions. Indeed, he had once or twice essayed to introduce the Episcopal form of service, on the Sundays that the pulpit was vacant; but Richard was a good deal addicted to carrying things to an excess, and then there was something so papal in his air, that the greater part of his hearers deserted him on the second Sabbath—on the third, his only auditor was Ben Pump, who had all the obstinate and enlightened orthodoxy of a high-churchman.

Before the war of the revolution, the English church was supported, in the colonies, with much interest, by some of its adherents in the mother country, and a few of the congregations were very amply endowed. But, for a season, after the independence of the states was established, this sect of Christians languished, for the want of the highest order of its priesthood. Pious and suitable divines were at length selected, and sent to the mother country, to receive that authority, which, it is understood, can only be transmitted directly from one to the other, and thus obtain, in order to preserve, that unity in their churches, which properly belonged to a people of the same nation. But unexpected difficulties presented themselves, in the oaths with which the policy of England had fettered their establishment, and much time was spent, before a conscientious sense of duty would permit the prelates of Britain to delegate the authority so earnestly sought. Time, patience, and zeal, however, removed every impediment, and the venerable men, who had been set apart by the American churches, at length returned to their expecting dioceses, endowed with the most elevated functions of their earthly church. Priests and Deacons were ordained; and missionaries provided, to keep alive the expiring flame of devotion, in such members as were deprived of the ordinary administrations, by dwelling in new and unorganized districts.

Of this number was Mr. Grant. He had been sent into the county of which Templeton was the capital, and had been kindly invited by Marmaduke, and officiously pressed by Richard, to take up his abode in the village. A small and humble dwelling was prepared for his family, and the divine had made his appearance in the place, but a few days before the time of his introduction to the reader. As his forms were entirely new to most of the inhabitants, and a clergyman of another denomination had previously occupied the field, by engaging the academy, the first Sunday after his arrival was suffered to pass in silence; but now that his rival had passed on, like a meteor, filling the air with the light of his wisdom, Richard was empowered to give notice, that "Public worship, after the forms of the Protestant Episcopal Church, would be held, on the night before Christmas, in the long-room of the academy in Templeton, by the Rev. Mr. Grant."

This annunciation excited great commotion among the different sectaries. Some wondered as to the nature of the exhibition; others sneered; but a far greater part, recollecting the essays of Richard in that way, and mindful of the liberality, or rather laxity, of Marmaduke's notions on the subject of sectarianism, thought it most prudent to be silent.

The expected evening was, however, the wonder of the hour; nor was the curiosity at all diminished, when Richard and Benjamin, on the morning of the eventful day, were seen to issue from the woods in the neighbourhood of the village, each bearing on his shoulders a large bunch of evergreens. This worthy pair was observed to enter the academy, and carefully to fasten the door, after which their proceedings remained a profound secret to the rest of the village; Mr. Jones, before he commenced this mysterious business, having informed the schoolmaster, to the great delight of the white-headed flock he governed, that there could be no school that day. Marmaduke was apprized of all these preparations, by letter, and it was especially arranged, that he and Elizabeth should arrive in season, to participate in the solemnities of the evening.

After this digression, we shall return to our narrative.

Chapter IX

"Now all admire, in each high-flavour'd dish,
The capabilities of flesh—fowl—fish;
In order due each guest assumes his station,
Throbs high his breast with fond anticipation,
And prelibates the joys of mastication."

Heliogabaliad.

THE APARTMENT to which Monsieur Le Quoi handed Elizabeth, communicated with the hall, through the door that led under the urn which was supposed to contain the ashes of Dido. The room was spacious, and of very just proportions; but in its ornaments and furniture, the same diversity of taste, and imperfection of execution, were to be observed, as existed in the hall. Of furniture, there were a dozen green, wooden arm-chairs, with cushions of moreen, taken from the same piece as the petticoat of Remarkable. The tables were spread, and their materials and workmanship could not be seen; but they were heavy, and of great size. An enormous mirror, in a gilt frame, hung against the wall, and a cheerful fire, of the hard or sugar-maple, was burning on the hearth. The latter was the first object that struck the attention of the Judge, who, on beholding it, exclaimed, rather angrily, to Richard—

"How often have I forbidden the use of the sugar-maple, in my dwelling. The sight of that sap, as it exudes with the heat, is painful to me, Richard. Really, it behooves the owner of woods so extensive as mine, to be cautious what example he sets his people, who are already felling the forests, as if no end could be found to their treasures, nor any limits to their extent. If we go on in this way, twenty years hence, we shall want fuel."

"Fuel in these hills, cousin 'duke!" exclaimed Richard, in derision—"fuel! why, you might as well predict, that the fish will die, for the want of water in the lake, because I intend, when the frost gets out of the ground, to lead one or two of the springs, through logs, into the village. But you are always a little wild on such subjects, Marmaduke."

"Is it wildness," returned the Judge, earnestly, "to condemn a practice, which devotes these jewels of the forest, these precious gifts of nature, these mines of comfort and wealth, to the common uses of a fire-place? But I must, and will, the instant the snow is off the earth, send out a party into the mountains, to explore for coal."

"Coal!" echoed Richard; "who the devil do you think will dig for coal, when in hunting for a bushel, he would have to rip up more roots of trees, than would keep him in fuel for a twelvemonth? Poh! poh! Marmaduke, you should leave the management of these things to me, who have a natural turn that way. It was I that ordered this fire, and a noble one it is, to warm the blood of my pretty cousin Bess."

"The motive, then, must be your apology, Dickon," said the Judge.—"But, gentlemen, we are waiting. Elizabeth, my child, take the head of the table; Richard, I see, means to spare me the trouble of carving, by sitting opposite to you."

"To be sure I do," cried Richard; "here is a turkey to carve, and I flatter myself that I understand carving a turkey, or, for that matter, a goose, as well as any man alive. Mr. Grant! where's Mr. Grant? will you please to say grace, sir? Every thing is getting cold. Take a thing from the fire, this cold weather, and it will freeze in five minutes. Mr. Grant! we want you to say grace. 'For what we are about to receive, the Lord make us thankful.' Come, sit down, sit down. Do you eat wing or breast, cousin Bess?"

But Elizabeth had not taken her seat, nor was she in readiness to receive either the wing or breast. Her laughing eyes were glancing at the arrangements of the table, and the quality and selection of the food. The eyes of the father soon met the wondering looks of his daughter, and he said, with a smile—

"You perceive, my child, how much we are indebted to Remarkable, for her skill in housewifery; she has indeed provided a noble repast; such as well might stop the cravings of hunger."

"Law!" said Remarkable, "I'm glad if the Judge is pleased; but I'm notional that you'll find the sa'ce overdone. I thought, as Elizabeth was coming home, that a body could do no less than make things agreeable."

"My daughter has now grown to woman's estate, and is

from this moment mistress of my house," said the Judge; "it is proper, that all, who live with me, address her as Miss Temple."

"*Do* tell!" exclaimed Remarkable, a little aghast; " well who ever heerd of a young woman's being called Miss? If the Judge had a wife now, I shouldn't think of calling her any thing but Miss Temple; but—"

"Having nothing but a daughter, you will observe that style to her, if you please, in future," interrupted Marmaduke.

As the Judge look'd seriously displeased, and, at such moments, carried a particularly commanding air with him, the wary housekeeper made no reply; and, Mr. Grant entering the room, the whole party were soon seated at the table. As the arrangements of this repast were much in the prevailing taste of that period and country, we shall endeavour to give a short description of the appearance of the banquet.

The table-linen was of the most beautiful damask, and the plates and dishes of real china, an article of great luxury at this early period in American commerce. The knives and forks were of exquisitely polished steel, and were set in unclouded ivory. So much being furnished by the wealth of Marmaduke, was not only comfortable, but even elegant. The contents of the several dishes, and their positions, however, were the result of the sole judgment of Remarkable. Before Elizabeth, was placed an enormous roasted turkey, and before Richard, one boiled. In the centre of the table, stood a pair of heavy silver castors, surrounded by four dishes; one a fricassee, that consisted of gray squirrels; another of fish fried; a third of fish boiled; the last was a venison steak. Between these dishes and the turkeys, stood, on the one side, a prodigious chine of roasted bear's meat, and on the other a boiled leg of delicious mutton. Interspersed among this load of meats, was every species of vegetables that the season and country afforded. The four corners were garnished with plates of cake. On one was piled certain curiously twisted and complicated figures, called "nut-cakes." On another were heaps of a black-looking substance, which, receiving its hue from molasses, was properly termed "sweet-cake;" a wonderful favourite in the coterie of Remarkable. A third was filled, to use the language of the housekeeper, with "caards of gingerbread;" and the last held a "plum-cake," so called from the number of large raisins that were showing their black heads, in a substance of a suspiciously similar colour. At each corner of the table, stood saucers, filled with a thick fluid, of somewhat equivocal colour and consistence, variegated with small dark lumps of a substance that resembled nothing but itself, which Remarkable termed her "sweet-meats." At the side of each plate, which was placed bottom upwards, with its knife and fork most accurately crossed above it, stood another, of smaller size, containing a motley-looking pie, composed of triangular slices of apple, mince, pumpkin, craneberry, and *custard*, so arranged as to form an entire whole. Decanters of brandy, rum, gin, and wine, with sundry pitchers of cider, beer, and one hissing vessel of "flip," were put wherever an opening would admit of their introduction. Notwithstanding the size of the tables, there was scarcely a spot where the rich damask could be seen, so crowded were the dishes, with their associated bottles, plates and saucers. The object seemed to be profusion, and it was obtained entirely at the expense of order and elegance.

All the guests, as well as the Judge himself, seemed perfectly familiar with this description of fare, for each one commenced eating, with an appetite that promised to do great honour to Remarkable's taste and skill. What rendered this attention to the repast a little surprising, was the fact, that both the German and Richard had been summoned from another table, to meet the Judge; but Major Hartmann both ate and drank without any rule, when on his excursions; and Mr. Jones invariably made it a point, to participate in the business in hand, let it be what it would. The host seemed to think some apology necessary, for the warmth he had betrayed on the subject of the firewood, and when the party were comfortably seated, and engaged with their knives and forks, he observed—

"The wastefulness of the settlers, with the noble trees of this country, is shocking, Monsieur Le Quoi, as doubtless you have noticed. I have seen a man fell a pine, when he has been in want of fencing-stuff, and roll his first cuts into the gap, where he left it to rot, though its top would have made rails enough to answer his purpose, and its butt would have sold in the Philadelphia market for twenty dollars."

"And how the devil—I beg your pardon, Mr. Grant," interrupted Richard; "but how is the poor devil to get his logs to the Philadelphia market, pray? put them in his pocket, ha! as you would a handful of chestnuts, or a bunch of chickerberries? I should like to see you walking up High-street, with a pine log in each pocket.—Poh! poh! cousin 'duke, there are trees enough for us all, and some to spare. Why I can hardly tell which way the wind blows, when I'm out in the clearings, they are so thick, and so tall;—I couldn't at all, if it wasn't for the clouds, and I happen to know all the points of the compass, as it were, by heart."

"Ay! ay! Squire," cried Benjamin, who had now entered, and taken his place behind the Judge's chair, a little aside withal, in order to be ready for any observation like the present; "look aloft, sir, look aloft. The old seamen say, 'that the devil wouldn't make a sailor, unless he look'd aloft.' As for the compass, why, there is no such thing as steering without one. I'm sure I never lose sight of the main-top, as I call the Squire's look-out on the roof, but I set my compass, d'ye see, and take the bearings and distance of things, in order to work out my course, if-so-be that it should cloud up, or the tops of the trees should shut out the light of heaven. The steeple of St. Paul's, now that we have got it on end, is a great help to the navigation of the woods, for, by the Lord Harry, as I was"—

"It is well, Benjamin," interrupted Marmaduke, observing that his daughter manifested displeasure at the major-domo's familiarity; "but you forget there is a lady in company, and the women love to do most of the talking themselves."

"The Judge says the true word," cried Benjamin, with one of his discordant laughs: "now here is Mistress Remarkable Prettybones; just take the stopper off her tongue, and you'll hear a gabbling, worse like than if you should happen to fall to leeward, in crossing a French privateer, or some such thing, mayhap, as a dozen monkeys stowed in one bag."

It were impossible to say, how perfect an illustration of the truth of Benjamin's assertion the housekeeper would have furnished, if she had dared; but the Judge looked sternly at her, and, unwilling to incur his resentment, yet unable to contain her anger, she threw herself out of the room, with a toss of the body, that nearly separated her frail form in the centre.

"Richard," said Marmaduke, observing that his displeasure had produced the desired effect, "can you inform me of any thing concerning the youth, whom I so unfortunately wounded? I found him on the mountain, hunting in company with the Leather-stocking, as if they were of the same family; but there is a manifest difference in their manners. The youth delivers himself in chosen language; such as is seldom heard in these hills, and such as occasions great surprise to me, how one so meanly clad, and following so lowly a pursuit, could attain. Mohegan also knew him. Doubtless he is a tenant of Natty's hut. Did you remark the language of the lad, Monsieur Le Quoi?"

"Certainement, Monsieur Templ'," returned the Frenchman, "he deed, conevairse in de excellent Anglaise."

"The boy is no miracle," exclaimed Richard; "I've known children that were sent to school early, talk much better, before they were twelve years old. There was Zared Coe, old Nehemiah's son, who first settled on the beaver-dam meadow, he could write almost as good a hand as myself, when he was fourteen; though it's true, I helped to teach him a little, in the evenings. But this shooting gentleman ought to be put in the stocks, if he ever takes a rein in his hand again. He is the most awkward fellow about a horse I ever met with. I dare say, he never drove any thing but oxen in his life."

"There I think, Dickon, you do the lad injustice," said the Judge; "he uses much discretion in critical moments.—Dost thou not think so, Bess?"

There was nothing in this question particularly to excite blushes, but Elizabeth started from the reverie into which she had fallen, and coloured to her forehead, as she answered—

"To me, dear sir, he appeared extremely skillful, and prompt, and courageous; but perhaps cousin Richard will say, I am as ignorant as the gentleman himself."

"Gentleman!" echoed Richard; "do you call such chaps gentlemen, at school, Elizabeth?"

"Every man is a gentleman, who knows how to treat a woman with respect and consideration," returned the young lady, promptly, and a little smartly.

"So much for hesitating to appear before the heiress in his shirt sleeves," cried Richard, winking at Monsieur Le Quoi, who returned the wink with one eye, while he rolled the other, with an expression of sympathy, towards the young lady.—"Well, well, to me he seemed any thing but a gentleman. I must say, however, for the lad, that he draws a good trigger, and has a true aim. He's good at shooting a buck, ha! Marmaduke?"

"Richart," said Major Hartmann, turning his grave countenance towards the gentleman he addressed, with much earnestness, "ter poy is goot. He savet your life, and my life, and ter life of Tominie Grant, and ter life of ter Frenchman; and, Richart, he shall never vant a pet to sleep in, vile olt Fritz Hartmann hast a shingle to cover his het mit."

"Well, well, as you please, old gentleman," returned Mr. Jones, endeavouring to look indifferent; "put him into your own stone house, if you will, Major. I dare say, the lad never slept in any thing better than a bark shanty in his life, unless it was some such hut as the cabin of Leather-stocking. I prophesy, you will soon spoil him; any one could see how proud he grew, in a short time, just because he stood by my horses' heads, while I turned them into the highway."

"No, no, my old friend," cried Marmaduke, "it shall be my task, to provide in some manner for the youth: I owe him a debt of my own, besides the service he has done me, through my friends. And yet I anticipate some little trouble, in inducing him to accept of my services. He showed a marked dislike, I thought, Bess, to my offer of a residence within these walls for life."

"Really, dear sir," said Elizabeth, projecting her beautiful under-lip, "I have not studied the gentleman so closely, as to read his feelings in his countenance. I thought he might very naturally feel pain from his wound, and therefore pitied him; but"—and as she spoke, she glanced her eye, with suppressed curiosity, towards the major-domo—"I dare say, sir, that Benjamin can tell you something about him. He cannot have been in the village, and Benjamin not have seen him often."

"Ay! I have seen the boy before," said Benjamin, who wanted little encouragement to speak: "he has been backing and filling in the wake of Natty Bumppo, through the mountains, after deer, like a Dutch long-boat in tow of an Albany sloop. He carries a good rifle too. The Leather-stocking said, in my hearing, before Betty Hollister's bar-room fire, no later than the Tuesday night, that the younker was certain death to the wild beasts. If-so-be he can kill the wild cat, that has been heard moaning on the lake-side, since the hard frosts and deep snows have driven the deer to herd, he will be doing the thing that is good. Your wild cat is a bad shipmate, and should be made to cruize out of the track of christian-men."

"Lives he in the hut of Bumppo?" asked Marmaduke, with some interest.

"Cheek by jowl: the Wednesday will be three weeks since he first hove in sight, in company with Leather-stocking. They had captured a wolf between them, and had brought in his scalp for the bounty. That Mister Bump-ho has a handy turn with him, in taking off a scalp; and there's them, in this here village, who say he larnt the trade by working on christian-men. If-so-be that there is truth in the saying, and I commanded along shore here, as your honour does, why d'ye see, I'd bring him to the gangway for it, yet. There's a very pretty post rigged alongside of the stocks, and for the matter of a cat, I can fit one with my own hands; ay! and use it too, for the want of a better."

"You are not to credit the idle tales you hear of Natty: he has a kind of natural right to gain a livelihood in these mountains; and if the idlers in the village take it into their heads to annoy him, as they sometimes do reputed rogues, they shall find him protected by the strong arm of the law."

"Ter rifle is petter as ter law," said the Major, sententiously.

"That for his rifle!" exclaimed Richard, snapping his fingers; "Ben is right, and I"—He was stopped by the sounds of a common ship-bell, that had been elevated to the belfry of the academy, which now announced, by its incessant ringing, that the hour for the appointed service had arrived. " 'For this, and every other instance of his goodness'—I beg pardon, Mr. Grant; will you please to return thanks, sir? it is time we should be moving, as we are the only Episcopalians in the neighbourhood; that is, I, and Benjamin, and Elizabeth; for I count half-breeds, like Marmaduke, as bad as heretics."

The divine arose, and performed the office, meekly and fervently, and the whole party instantly prepared themselves for the church—or rather academy.

Chapter X

> "And calling sinful man to pray,
> Loud, long, and deep the bell had toll'd."
> Bürger, "The Wild Huntsman," ll. 11–12 (tr. Scott).

WHILE RICHARD and Monsieur Le Quoi, attended by Benjamin, proceeded to the academy, by a foot-path through the snow, the Judge, his daughter, the Divine, and the Major, took a more circuitous route to the same place by the streets of the village.

The moon had risen, and its orb was shedding a flood of light over the dark outline of pines, which crowned the eastern mountain. In many climates, the sky would have been thought clear and lucid for a noontide. The stars twinkled in the heavens, like the last glimmerings of distant fire, so much were they obscured by the overwhelming radiance of the atmosphere; the rays from the moon striking upon the smooth white surfaces of the lake and fields, reflecting upwards a light that was brightened by the spotless colour of the immense bodies of snow.

Elizabeth employed herself with reading the signs, one of which appeared over almost every door, while the sleigh moved, steadily and at an easy gait, along the principal street. Not only new occupations, but names that were strangers to her ears, met her gaze at every step they proceeded. The very houses seemed changed. This had been altered by an addition; that had been painted; another had been erected on the site of an old acquaintance, which had been banished from the earth, almost as soon as it made its appearance on it. All were, however, pouring forth their inmates, who uniformly held their way towards the point where the expected exhibition, of the conjoint taste of Richard and Benjamin, was to be made.

After viewing the buildings, which really appeared to some advantage, under the bright but mellow light of the moon, our heroine turned her eyes to a scrutiny of the different figures that they passed, in search of any form that she knew. But all seemed alike, as, muffled in cloaks, hoods, coats, or tippets, they glided along the narrow passages in the snow, which led under the houses, half hid by the bank that had been thrown up in excavating the deep path in which they trod. Once or twice she thought there was a stature, or a gait, that she recollected, but the person who owned it instantly disappeared behind one of those enormous piles of wood, that lay before most of the doors. It was only as they turned from the main street into another that intersected it at right angles, and which led directly to the place of meeting, that she recognised a face and building that she knew.

The house stood at one of the principal corners in the village, and, by its well-trodden doorway, as well as the sign, that was swinging, with a kind of doleful sound, in the blasts that occasionally swept down the lake, was clearly one of the most frequented inns in the place. The building was only of one story, but the dormer windows in the roof, the paint, the window-shutters, and the cheerful fire that shone through the open door, gave it an air of comfort, that was not possessed by many of its neighbours. The sign was suspended from a common alehouse post, and represented the figure of a horseman, armed with sabre and pistols, and surmounted by a bear-skin cap, with the fiery animal that he bestrode "rampant." All these particulars were easily to be seen, by the aid of the moon, together with a row of somewhat illegible writing, in black paint, but in which Elizabeth, to whom the whole was familiar, read with facility, "The Bold Dragoon."

A man and a woman were issuing from the door of this habitation, as the sleigh was passing. The former moved with a stiff, military step, that was a good deal heightened by a limp in one leg; but the woman advanced with a measure and an air, that seemed not particularly regardful of what she might encounter. The light of the moon fell directly upon her full, broad, and red visage; exhibiting her masculine countenance, under the mockery of a ruffled cap, that was intended to soften the lineaments of features that were by no means squeamish. A small bonnet, of black silk, and of a slightly formal cut, was placed on the back of her head, but not so as to shade her visage in the least. Her face, as it encountered the rays of the moon from the east, seemed not unlike a sun rising in the west. She advanced, with masculine strides, to intercept the sleigh, and the Judge, directing the namesake of the Grecian king, who held the lines, to check his horses, the parties were soon near to each other.

"Good luck to ye, and a wilcome home, Jooge," cried the female, with a strong Irish accent; "and I'm sure it's to me that ye'r always wilcome. Sure! and there's Miss 'Lizzy, and a fine young woman is she grown. What a heart-ach would she be giving the young men now, if there was sich a thing as a rigiment in the town. Och! but it's idle to talk of sich vanities, while the bell is calling us to mating, jist as we shall be call'd away unexpictedly, some day, when we are the laist calkilating. Good even, Major; will I make the bowl of gin-toddy the night?—or it's likely ye'll stay at the big house, the Christmas eve, and the very night of ye'r getting there."

"I am glad to see you, Mrs. Hollister," returned Elizabeth. "I've been trying to find a face that I knew, since we left the door of the mansion-house, but none have I seen except your own. Your house, too, is unaltered, while all the others are so changed, that, but for the places where they stand, they would be utter strangers. I observe you also keep the dear sign, that I saw cousin Richard paint, and even the name at the bottom, about which, you may remember, you had the disagreement."

"Is it the bould dragoon ye mane? and what name would he have, who niver was known by any other, as my husband here, the Captain, can tistify. He was a pleasure to wait upon, and was iver the foremost in need. Och! but he had a sudden ind! But it's to be hoped, that he was justified by the cause. And it's not Parson Grant there, who'll gainsay that same.—Yes, yes—the Squire would paint, and so I thought that we might have *his* face up there, who had so often shared good and evil wid us. The eyes is no so large nor so fiery as the Captain's own, but the whiskers and the cap is as like as two paas. Well, well——I'll not keep ye in the cowld, talking, but will drop in, the morrow, after sarvice, and ask ye how ye do. It's our bounden duty to make the most of this present, and to go to the house which is open to all: so God bless ye, and keep ye from evil.—Will I make the gin-twist the night, or no, Major?"

To this question the German replied, very sententiously, in

the affirmative; and, after a few words had passed between the husband of this fiery-faced hostess and the Judge, the sleigh moved on. It soon reached the door of the academy, where the party alighted and entered the building.

In the mean time, Mr. Jones and his two companions, having a much shorter distance to journey, had arrived before the appointed place several minutes sooner than the party in the sleigh. Instead of hastening into the room, in order to enjoy the astonishment of the settlers, Richard placed a hand in either pocket of his surtout, and affected to walk about, in front of the academy, like one to whom the ceremonies were familiar.

The villagers proceeded uniformly into the building, with a decorum and gravity that nothing could move, on such occasions; but with a haste, that was probably a little heightened by curiosity. Those who came in from the adjacent country, spent some little time in placing certain blue and white blankets over their horses, before they proceeded to indulge their desire to view the interior of the house. Most of these men Richard approached, and inquired after the health and condition of their families. The readiness with which he mentioned the names of even the children, showed how very familiarly acquainted he was with their circumstances; and the nature of the answers he received, proved that he was a general favourite.

At length one of the pedestrians from the village stopped also, and fixed an earnest gaze at a new brick edifice, that was throwing a long shadow across the fields of snow, as it rose, with a beautiful gradation of light and shade, under the rays of a full moon. In front of the academy was a vacant piece of ground, that was intended for a public square. On the side opposite to Mr. Jones, the new, and as yet unfinished, church of St. Paul's was erected. This edifice had been reared, during the preceding summer, by the aid of what was called a subscription; though all, or nearly all, of the money, came from the pocket of the landlord. It had been built under a strong conviction of the necessity of a more seemly place of worship than "the long-room of the academy," and under an implied agreement, that, after its completion, the question should be fairly put to the people, that they might decide to what denomination it should belong. Of course, this expectation kept alive a strong excitement, in some few of the sectaries who were interested in its decision; though but little was said openly on the subject. Had Judge Temple espoused the cause of any particular sect, the question would have been immediately put at rest, for his influence was too powerful to be opposed; but he declined interference in the matter, positively refusing to lend even the weight of his name on the side of Richard, who had secretly given an assurance to his Diocesan, that both the building and the congregation would cheerfully come within the pale of the Protestant Episcopal Church. But when the neutrality of the Judge was clearly ascertained, Mr. Jones discovered that he had to contend with a stiff-necked people. His first measure was to go among them, and commence a course of reasoning, in order to bring them round to his own way of thinking. They all heard him patiently, and not a man uttered a word in reply, in the way of argument: and Richard thought, by the time that he had gone through the settlement, the point was conclusively decided in his favour. Willing to strike while the iron was hot, he called a meeting, through the newspaper, with a view to decide the question, by a vote, at once. Not a soul attended, and one of the most anxious afternoons that he had ever known, was spent by Richard in a vain discussion with Mrs. Hollister, who strongly contended that the Methodist (her own) church was the best entitled to, and most deserving of, the possession of the new tabernacle. Richard now perceived that he had been too sanguine, and had fallen into the error of all those who, ignorantly, deal with that wary and sagacious people. He assumed a disguise himself, that is, as well as he knew how, and proceeded step by step to advance his purpose.

The task of erecting the building had been unanimously transferred to Mr. Jones and Hiram Doolittle. Together they had built the mansion-house, the academy, and the jail; and they alone knew how to plan and rear such a structure as was now required. Early in the day, these architects had made an equitable division of their duties. To the former was assigned the duty of making all the plans, and to the latter, the labour of superintending the execution.

Availing himself of this advantage, Richard silently determined that the windows should have the Roman arch; the first positive step in effecting his wishes. As the building was made of bricks, he was enabled to conceal his design, until the moment arrived for placing the frames: then, indeed, it became necessary to act. He communicated his wishes to Hiram, with great caution; and without in the least adverting to the spiritual part of his project, he pressed the point a little warmly, on the score of architectural beauty. Hiram heard him patiently, and without contradiction; but still Richard was unable to discover the views of his coadjutor, on this interesting subject. As the right to plan was duly delegated to Mr. Jones, no direct objection was made in words, but numberless unexpected difficulties arose in the execution. At first, there was a scarcity in the right kind of material necessary to form the frames; but this objection was instantly silenced, by Richard running his pencil through two feet of their length at one stroke. Then the expense was mentioned; but Richard reminded Hiram that his cousin paid, and that *he* was his treasurer. This last intimation had great weight, and, after a silent and protracted, but fruitless opposition, the work was suffered to proceed on the original plan.

The next difficulty occurred in the steeple, which Richard had modelled after one of the smaller of those spires that adorn the great London Cathedral. The imitation was somewhat lame, it is true, the proportions being but indifferently observed; but, after much difficulty, Mr. Jones had the satisfaction of seeing an object reared, that bore, in its outlines, a striking resemblance to a vinegar-cruet. There was less opposition to this model than to the windows, for the settlers were fond of novelty, and their steeple was without a precedent.

Here the labour ceased for the season, and the difficult question of the interior remained for further deliberation. Richard well knew, that when he came to propose a reading-desk and a chancel, he must unmask; for these were arrangements, known to no church in the country, but his own. Presuming, however, on the advantages he had already obtained, he boldly styled the building St. Paul's, and Hiram prudently acquiesced in this appellation, making, however, the slight addition of calling it "*New* St. Paul's," feeling less aversion to a name taken from the English Cathedral, than from the saint.

The pedestrian, whom we have already mentioned, as pausing to contemplate this edifice, was no other than the gentleman so frequently named as Mr., or Squire Doolittle. He was of a tall, gaunt formation, with rather sharp features, and a face that expressed formal propriety, mingled with low cunning. Richard approached him, followed by Monsieur Le Quoi and the Major-Domo.

"Good evening, Squire," said Richard, bobbing his head, but without moving his hands from his pockets.

"Good evening, Squire," echoed Hiram, turning his body, in order to turn his head also.

"A cold night, Mr. Doolittle, a cold night, sir."

"Coolish; a tedious spell on't."

"What, looking at our church, ha! it looks well by moonlight; how the tin of the cupola glistens. I warrant you, the dome of the other St. Paul's never shines so in the smoke of London."

"It is a pretty meeting-house to look on," returned Hiram, "and I believe that Monshure Ler Quow and Mr. Penguilliam will allow it."

"Sairtainlee!" exclaimed the complaisant Frenchman, "it ees ver fine."

"I thought the Monshure would say so. The last molasses that we had was excellent good. It isn't likely that you have any more of it on hand?"

"Ah! oui; ees, sair," returned Monsieur Le Quoi, with a slight shrug of his shoulder, and a trifling grimace, "dere is more. I feel ver happi dat you love eet. I hope dat Madame Dooleet' is in good 'ealth."

"Why, so as to be stirring," said Hiram.—"The Squire hasn't finished the plans for the inside of the meeting-house yet?"

"No—no—no," returned Richard, speaking quickly, but making a significant pause between each negative—"it requires reflection. There is a great deal of room to fill up, and I am afraid we shall not know how to dipsose of it to advantage. There will be a large vacant spot around the pulpit, which I do not mean to place against the wall, like a sentry-box stuck up on the side of a fort."

"It is ruleable to put the deacons' box under the pulpit,"

said Hiram; and then, as if he had ventured too much, he added, "but there's different fashions in different countries."

"That there is," cried Benjamin; "now, in running down the coast of Spain and Portingal, you may see a nunnery stuck out on every head-land, with more steeples and outriggers, such as dog-vanes and weather-cocks, than you'll find aboard of a three-masted schooner. If-so-be that a well-built church is wanting, Old England, after all, is the country to go to, after your models and fashion-pieces. As to Paul's, thof I've never seen it, being that it's a long way up town from Rad-cliffe-highway and the docks, yet every body knows that it's the grandest place in the world. Now, I've no opinion but this here church over there, is as like one end of it, as a grampus is to a whale; and that's only a small difference in bulk. Mounsheer Ler Quaw here, has been in foreign parts, and thof that is not the same as having been at home, yet he must have seen churches in France too, and can form a small idee of what a church should be: now, I ask the Mounsheer to his face, if it is not a clever little thing, taking it by and large?"

"It ees ver apropos of saircumstonce," said the Frenchman—"ver judgement—but it is in de Catholique country dat dey build de—vat you call—ah-a-ah-ha—la grande cathédrale—de big church. St. Paul Londre, is ver fine; ver bootiful; ver grand—vat you call beeg; but, Monsieur Ben, pardonnez moi, it is no vort so much as Notre Dame"—

"Ha! Mounsheer, what is that you say?" cried Benjamin—"St. Paul's Church not worth so much as a damn! mayhap you may be thinking, too, that the Royal Billy isn't so good a ship as the Billy de Paris; but she would have lick'd two of her, any day, and in all weathers."

As Benjamin had assumed a very threatening kind of attitude, flourishing an arm, with a bunch at the end of it, that was half as big as Monsieur Le Quoi's head, Richard thought it time to interpose his authority.

"Hush, Benjamin, hush," he said; "you both misunderstand Monsieur Le Quoi, and forget yourself.—But here comes Mr. Grant, and the service will commence. Let us go in."

The Frenchman, who received Benjamin's reply with a well-bred good humour, that would not admit of any feeling but pity for the other's ignorance, bowed in acquiescence, and followed his companion.

Hiram and the Major-Domo brought up the rear, the latter grumbling, as he entered the building—

"If-so-be that the King of France had so much as a house to live in, that would lay alongside of Paul's, one might put up with their jaw. It's more than flesh and blood can bear, to hear a Frenchman run down an English church in this manner. Why, Squire Doolittle, I've been at the whipping of two of them in one day—clean built, snug frigates, with standing-royals and them new-fashioned cannonades on their quarters—such as, if they had only Englishmen aboard of them, would have fout the devil."

With this ominous word in his mouth, Benjamin entered the church!

Chapter XI

"And fools, who came to scoff, remain'd to pray."
Goldsmith, "The Deserted Village," l. 179.

NOTWITHSTANDING the united labours of Richard and Benjamin, the "long-room" was but an extremely inartificial temple. Benches, made in the coarsest manner, and entirely with a view to usefulness, were arranged in rows, for the reception of the congregation, while a rough, unpainted box, was placed against the wall, in the centre of the length of the apartment, as an apology for a pulpit. Something like a reading-desk was in front of this rostrum, and a small mahogany table, from the mansion-house, covered with a spotless damask cloth, stood a little on one side, by the way of an altar. Branches of pines and hemlocks were stuck in each of the fissures that offered, in the unseasoned, and hastily completed wood-work, of both the building and its furniture; while festoons and hieroglyphics met the eye, in vast profusion, along the brown sides of the scratch-coated walls. As the room was only lighted by some ten or fifteen miserable candles, and the windows were without shutters, it would have been but a dreary, cheerless place for the solemnities of a Christmas-eve, had not the large fire, that was crackling at each end of the apartment, given an air of cheerfulness to the scene, by throwing an occasional glare of light through the vistas of bushes and faces.

The two sexes were separated by an area in the centre of the room, immediately before the pulpit, and a few benches lined this space, that were occupied by the principal personages of the village and its vicinity. This distinction was rather a gratuitous concession, made by the poorer and less polished part of the population, than a right claimed by the favoured few. One bench was occupied by the party of Judge Temple, including his daughter; and, with the exception of Dr. Todd, no one else appeared willing to incur the imputation of pride, by taking a seat in what was, literally, the high place of the tabernacle.

Richard filled the chair, that was placed behind another

table, in the capacity of clerk; while Benjamin, after heaping sundry logs on the fires, posted himself nigh by, in reserve for any movement that might require co-operation.

It would greatly exceed our limits, to attempt a description of the congregation, for the dresses were as various as the individuals. Some one article of more than usual finery, and perhaps the relic of other days, was to be seen about most of the females, in connexion with the coarse attire of the woods. This, wore a faded silk, that had gone through at least three generations, over coarse, woolen, black stockings; that, a shawl, whose dies were as numerous as those of the rainbow, over an awkwardly-fitting gown, of rough, brown " woman's-wear." In short, each one exhibited some favourite article, and all appeared in their best, both men and women; while the ground-works in dress, in either sex, were the coarse fabrics manufactured within their own dwellings. One man appeared in the dress of a volunteer company of artillery, of which he had been a member, in the "down-countries," precisely for no other reason, than because it was the best suit he had. Several, particularly of the younger men, displayed pantaloons of blue, edged with red cloth down the seams, part of the equipments of the "Templeton Light Infantry," from a little vanity to be seen in "boughten clothes." There was also one man in a "rifle frock," with its fringes and folds of spotless white, striking a chill to the heart with the idea of its coolness; although the thick coat of brown "home-made," that was concealed beneath, preserved a proper degree of warmth.

There was a marked uniformity of expression in countenance, especially in that half of the congregation, who did not enjoy the advantages of the polish of the village. A sallow skin, that indicated nothing but exposure, was common to all, as was an air of great decency and attention, mingled, generally, with an expression of shrewdness, and, in the present instance, of active curiosity. Now and then a face and dress were to be seen, among the congregation, that differed entirely from this description. If pock-marked, and florid, with gaitered legs, and a coat that snugly fitted the person of the wearer, it was surely an English emigrant, who had bent his steps to this retired quarter of the globe. If hard-featured, and without colour, with high cheek-bones, it was a native of

Scotland, in similar circumstances. The short, black-eyed man, with a cast of the swarthy Spaniard in his face, who rose repeatedly, to make room for the belles of the village, as they entered, was a son of Erin, who had lately left off his pack, and become a stationary trader in Templeton. In short, half the nations in the north of Europe had their representatives in this assembly, though all had closely assimilated themselves to the Americans, in dress and appearance, except the Englishman. He, indeed, not only adhered to his native customs, in attire and living, but usually drove his plough, among the stumps, in the same manner as he had before done, on the plains of Norfolk, until dear-bought experience taught him the useful lesson, that a sagacious people knew what was suited to their circumstances, better than a casual observer; or a sojourner, who was, perhaps, too much prejudiced to compare, and, peradventure, too conceited to learn.

Elizabeth soon discovered that she divided the attention of the congregation with Mr. Grant. Timidity, therefore, confined her observation of the appearances which we have described, to stolen glances; but, as the stamping of feet was now becoming less frequent, and even the coughing, and other little preliminaries of a congregation settling themselves down into reverential attention, were ceasing, she felt emboldened to look around her. Gradually all noises diminished, until the suppressed cough denoted, that it was necessary to avoid singularity, and the most profound stillness pervaded the apartment. The snapping of the fires, as they threw a powerful heat into the room, was alone heard, and each face, and every eye, were turned on the divine.

At this moment, a heavy stamping of feet was heard in the passage below, as if a new comer was releasing his limbs from the snow, that was necessarily clinging to the legs of a pedestrian. It was succeeded by no audible tread; but directly Mohegan, followed by the Leather-stocking and the young hunter, made his appearance. Their footsteps would not have been heard, as they trod the apartment in their moccasins, but for the silence which prevailed.

The Indian moved with great gravity, across the floor, and, observing a vacant seat next to the Judge, he took it, in a manner that manifested his sense of his own dignity. Here, drawing his blanket closely around him, so as partly to conceal his countenance, he remained during the service, immoveable, but deeply attentive. Natty passed the place, that was so freely taken by his red companion, and seated himself on one end of a log, that was lying near the fire, where he continued, with his rifle standing between his legs, absorbed in reflections, seemingly, of no very pleasing nature. The youth found a seat, among the congregation, and another silence prevailed.

Mr. Grant now arose, and commenced his service, with the sublime declaration of the Hebrew prophet—"The Lord is in his holy temple; let all the earth keep silence before him." The example of Mr. Jones was unnecessary, to teach the congregation to rise: the solemnity of the divine, effected this as by magic. After a short pause, Mr. Grant proceeded with the solemn and winning exhortation of his service. Nothing was heard but the deep, though affectionate, tones of the reader, as he slowly went through this exordium; until, something unfortunately striking the mind of Richard as incomplete, he left his place, and walked on tip-toe from the room.

When the clergyman bent his knees in prayer and confession, the congregation so far imitated his example, as to resume their seats; whence no succeeding effort of the divine, during the evening, was able to remove them in a body. Some rose, at times, but by far the larger part continued unbending; observant, it is true, but it was the kind of observation that regarded the ceremony as a spectacle, rather than a worship in which they were to participate. Thus deserted by his clerk, Mr. Grant continued to read; but no response was audible. The short and solemn pause, that succeeded each petition, was made; still no voice repeated the eloquent language of the prayer.

The lips of Elizabeth moved, but they moved in vain; and, accustomed, as she was, to the service in the churches of the metropolis, she was beginning to feel the awkwardness of the circumstance most painfully, when a soft, low, female voice repeated after the priest, "We have left undone those things which we ought to have done." Startled, at finding one of her own sex in that place, who could rise superior to natural timidity, Miss Temple turned her eyes in the direction of the penitent. She observed a young female, on her knees, but a short distance from her, with her meek face humbly bent over her book. The appearance of this stranger, for such she was, entirely, to Elizabeth, was light and fragile. Her dress was neat and becoming; and her countenance, though pale, and slightly agitated, excited deep interest, by its sweet, and melancholy expression. A second and third response were made by this juvenile assistant, when the manly sounds of a male voice, proceeded from the opposite part of the room. Miss Temple knew the tones of the young hunter instantly, and, struggling to overcome her own diffidence, she added her low voice to the number.

All this time, Benjamin stood thumbing the leaves of a prayer-book with great industry, but some unexpected difficulties prevented his finding the place. Before the divine reached the close of the confession, however, Richard re-appeared at the door, and, as he moved lightly across the room, he took up the response, in a voice that betrayed no other concern than that of not being heard. In his hand he carried a small open box, with the figures of "8 by 10" written, in black paint, on one of its sides; which having placed in the pulpit, apparently as a footstool for the divine, he returned to his station, in time to say, sonorously, "amen." The eyes of the congregation, very naturally, were turned to the windows, as Mr. Jones entered with this singular load, and then, as if accustomed to his "general agency," were again bent on the priest, in close, and curious attention.

The long experience of Mr. Grant admirably qualified him to perform his present duty. He well understood the character of his listeners, who were mostly a primitive people in their habits; and who, being a good deal addicted to subtleties and nice distinctions in their religious opinions, viewed the introduction of any such temporal assistance as form, into their spiritual worship, not only with jealousy, but frequently with disgust. He had acquired much of his knowledge, from studying the great book of human nature, as it lay open in the world; and, knowing how dangerous it was to contend with ignorance, uniformly endeavoured to avoid dictating, where his better reason taught him it was the most prudent to attempt to lead. His orthodoxy had no dependence on his cassock; he could pray, with fervour and with faith, if circumstances required it, without the assistance of his clerk; and he had even been known to preach a most evangelical sermon, in the winning manner of native eloquence, without the aid of a cambric handkerchief!

In the present instance he yielded, in many places, to the prejudices of his congregation; and when he had ended, there was not one of his new hearers, who did not think the ceremonies less papal and offensive, and more conformant to his or her own notions of devout worship, than they had been led to expect from a service of forms. Richard found in the divine, during the evening, a most powerful co-operator in his religious schemes. In preaching, Mr. Grant endeavoured to steer a middle course, between the mystical doctrines of those sublimated creeds, which daily involve their professors in the most absurd contradictions, and those fluent rules of moral government, which would reduce the Saviour to a level with the teacher of a school of ethics. Doctrine it was necessary to preach, for nothing less would have satisfied the disputatious people who were his listeners, and who would have interpreted silence on his part, into a tacit acknowledgment of the superficial nature of his creed. We have already said that, amongst the endless variety of religious instructors, the settlers were accustomed to hear every denomination urge its own distinctive precepts; and to have found one indifferent to this interesting subject, would have been destructive to his influence. But Mr. Grant so happily blended the universally received opinions of the Christian faith, with the dogmas of his own church, that, although none were entirely exempt from the influence of his reasons, very few took any alarm at the innovation.

"When we consider the great diversity of the human character, influenced as it is by education, by opportunity, and by the physical and moral conditions of the creature, my dear hearers," he earnestly concluded, "it can excite no surprise, that creeds, so very different in their tendencies, should grow out of a religion, revealed, it is true, but whose revelations are obscured by the lapse of ages, and whose doctrines were, after the fashion of the countries in which they were first promulgated, frequently delivered in parables, and in a language abounding in metaphors and loaded with figures. On points where the learned have, in purity of heart, been compelled to differ, the unlettered will necessarily be at variance. But, happily for us, my brethren, the fountain of divine love flows from a source, too pure to admit of pollution in its course; it extends, to those who drink of its vivifying waters, the peace of the righteous, and life everlasting; it endures through all time, and it pervades creation. If there be mystery in its workings, it is the mystery of a Divinity. With a clear knowledge of the nature, the might, and majesty of God, there might be conviction, but there could be no faith. If we are required to believe in doctrines, that seem not in conformity with the deductions of human wisdom, let us never forget, that such is the mandate of a wisdom that is infinite. It is sufficient for us, that enough is developed to point our path aright, and to direct our wandering steps to that portal, which shall open on the light of an eternal day. Then, indeed, it may be humbly hoped, that the film, which has been spread by the subtleties of earthly arguments, will be dissipated, by the spiritual light of heaven; and that our hour of probation, by the aid of divine grace, being once passed in triumph, will be followed by an eternity of intelligence, and endless ages of fruition. All that is now obscure, shall become plain to our expanded faculties; and what, to our present senses, may seem irreconcilable to our limited notions of mercy, of justice, and of love, shall stand, irradiated by the light of truth, confessedly the suggestions of Omniscience, and the acts of an All-powerful Benevolence.

"What a lesson of humility, my brethren, might not each of us obtain, from a review of his infant hours, and the recollection of his juvenile passions. How differently do the same acts of parental rigour appear, in the eyes of the suffering child, and of the chastened man. When the sophist would supplant, with the wild theories of his worldly wisdom, the positive mandates of inspiration, let him remember the expansion of his own feeble intellects, and pause—let him feel the wisdom of God, in what is partially concealed, as well as in that which is revealed;—in short, let him substitute humility for pride of reason—let him have faith, and live!

"The consideration of this subject is full of consolation, my hearers, and does not fail to bring with it lessons of humility and of profit, that, duly improved, would both chasten the heart, and strengthen the feeble-minded man in his course. It is a blessed consolation, to be able to lay the misdoubtings of our arrogant nature at the threshold of the dwelling-place of the Deity, from whence they shall be swept away, at the great opening of the portal, like the mists of the morning before the rising sun. It teaches us a lesson of humility, by impressing us with the imperfection of human powers, and by warning us of the many weak points, where we are open to the attacks of the great enemy of our race; it proves to us, that we are in danger of being weak, when our vanity would fain soothe us into the belief that we are most strong; it forcibly points out to us the vain-glory of intellect, and shows us the vast difference between a saving faith, and the corollaries of a philosophical theology; and it teaches us to reduce our self-examination to the test of good works. By good works must be understood, the fruits of repentance, the chiefest of which is charity. Not that charity only, which causes us to help the needy and comfort the suffering, but that feeling of universal philanthropy, which, by teaching us to love, causes us to judge with lenity, all men; striking at the root of self-righteousness, and warning us to be sparing of our condemnation of others, while our own salvation is not yet secure.

"The lesson of expediency, my brethren, which I would gather from the consideration of this subject, is most strongly inculcated by humility. On the leading and essential points of our faith, there is but little difference, amongst those classes of Christians, who acknowledge the attributes of the Saviour, and depend on his mediation. But heresies have polluted every church, and schisms are the fruits of disputation. In order to arrest these dangers, and to insure the union of his followers, it would seem, that Christ had established his visible church, and delegated the ministry. Wise and holy men, the fathers of our religion, have expended their labours, in clearing what was revealed from the obscurities of language; and the results of their experience and researches have been embodied in the form of evangelical discipline. That this discipline must be salutary, is evident, from the view of the weakness of human nature, that we have already taken: and that it may be profitable to us, and all who listen to its precepts and its liturgy, may God, in his infinite wisdom, grant.—And now to," &c.

With this ingenious reference to his own forms and ministry, Mr. Grant concluded the discourse. The most profound attention had been paid to the sermon during the whole of its delivery, although the prayers had not been received with so perfect a demonstration of respect. This was by no means an intended slight of that liturgy, to which the divine alluded, but was the habit of a people, who owed their very existence, as a distinct nation, to the doctrinal character of their ancestors. Sundry looks of private dissatisfaction were exchanged between Hiram and one or two of the leading members of the *conference*, but the feeling went no farther at that time; and the congregation, after receiving the blessing of Mr. Grant, dispersed in silence, and with great decorum.

Chapter XII

"Your creeds, and dogmas of a learned church,
May build a fabric, fair with moral beauty;
But it would seem, that the strong hand of God
Can, only, 'rase the devil from the heart."

Duo.

WHILE THE CONGREGATION was separating, Mr. Grant approached the place where Elizabeth and her father were seated, leading the youthful female, whom we have mentioned in the preceding chapter, and presented her as his daughter. Her reception was as cordial and frank, as the manners of the country, and the value of good society, could render it; the two young women feeling, instantly, that they were necessary to the comfort of each other. The Judge, to whom the clergyman's daughter was also a stranger, was pleased to find one, who, from habits, sex, and years, could probably contribute largely to the pleasures of his own child, during her first privations, on her removal from the associations of a city to the solitude of Templeton; while Elizabeth, who had been forcibly struck with the sweetness and devotion of the youthful suppliant, removed the slight embarrassment of the timid stranger, by the ease of her own manners. They were at once acquainted, and, during the ten minutes while the "academy" was clearing, engagements were made between the young people, not only for the succeeding day, but they would probably have embraced in their arrangements half of the winter, had not the divine interrupted them, by saying—

"Gently, gently, my dear Miss Temple, or you will make my girl too dissipated. You forget that she is my housekeeper, and that my domestic affairs must remain unattended to, should Louisa accept of half the kind offers you are so good as to make her."

"And why should they not be neglected entirely, sir?" interrupted Elizabeth. "There are but two of you, and certain I am that my father's house will not only contain you both, but will open its doors spontaneously, to receive such guests.

Society is a good, not to be rejected on account of cold forms, in this wilderness, sir; and I have often heard my father say, that hospitality is not a virtue in a new country, the favour being conferred by the guest."

"The manner in which Judge Temple exercises its rites, would confirm this opinion; but we must not trespass too freely. Doubt not that you will see us often, my child particularly, during the frequent visits, that I shall be compelled to make, to the distant parts of the county. But to obtain an influence with such a people," he continued, glancing his eyes towards the few, who were still lingering, curious observers of the interview, "a clergyman must not awaken envy or distrust, by dwelling under so splendid a roof as that of Judge Temple."

"You like the roof, then, Mr. Grant," cried Richard, who had been directing the extinguishment of the fires, and other little necessary duties, and who approached, in time, to hear the close of the divine's speech—"I am glad to find one man of taste at last. Here's 'duke now, pretends to call it by every abusive name he can invent; but though 'duke is a very tolerable judge, he is a very poor carpenter, let me tell him.—Well, sir, well, I think we may say, without boasting, that the service was as well performed this evening as you often see; I think, quite as well as I ever knew it to be done in old Trinity—that is, if we except the organ. But there is the schoolmaster, leads the psalm with a very good air. I used to lead myself, but latterly I have sung nothing but bass. There is a good deal of science to be shown in the bass, and it affords a fine opportunity to show off a full, deep voice. Benjamin, too, sings a good bass, though he is often out in the words. Did you ever hear Benjamin sing the 'Bay of Biscay, O?' "

"I believe he gave us part of it this evening," said Marmaduke, laughing.—"There was, now and then, a fearful quaver in his voice, and it seems that Mr. Penguillian, like most others who do one thing particularly well, knows nothing else. He has, certainly, a wonderful partiality to one tune, and he has a prodigious self-confidence in that one, for he delivers himself like a north-wester sweeping across the lake.—But come, gentlemen, our way is clear, and the sleigh waits.—Good evening, Mr. Grant. Good night, young lady. Remember that you dine beneath the Corinthian roof to-morrow, with Elizabeth."

The parties separated, Richard holding a close dissertation with Mr. Le Quoi, as they descended the stairs, on the subject of psalmody, which he closed by a violent eulogium on the air of the "Bay of Biscay, O," as particularly connected with his friend Benjamin's execution.

During the preceding dialogue, Mohegan retained his seat, with his head shrouded in his blanket, as seemingly inattentive to surrounding objects, as the departing congregation was, itself, to the presence of the aged chief. Natty, also, continued on the log, where he had first placed himself, with his head resting on one of his hands, while the other held the rifle, which was thrown carelessly across his lap. His countenance expressed uneasiness, and the occasional unquiet glances, that he had thrown around him, during the service, plainly indicated some unusual causes for unhappiness. His continuing seated was, however, out of respect to the Indian chief, to whom he paid the utmost deference, on all occasions, although it was mingled with the rough manner of a hunter.

The young companion of these two ancient inhabitants of the forest, remained, also, standing before the extinguished brands, probably from an unwillingness to depart without his comrades. The room was now deserted by all but this group, the divine and his daughter. As the party from the Mansion-House disappeared, John arose, and dropping the blanket from his head, he shook back the mass of black hair from his face, and approaching Mr. Grant, he extended his hand, and said, solemnly—

"Father, I thank you. The words that have been said, since the rising moon, have gone upward, and the Great Spirit is glad. What you have told your children, they will remember, and be good." He paused a moment, and then elevating himself with the grandeur of an Indian chief, he added—"If Chingachgook lives to travel towards the setting sun, after his tribe, and the Great Spirit carries him over the lakes and mountains, with the breath in his body, he will tell his people the good talk he has heard; and they will believe him, for who can say that Mohegan has ever lied?"

"Let him place his dependence on the goodness of Divine mercy," said Mr. Grant, to whom the proud consciousness of the Indian sounded a little heterodox, "and it never will desert him. When the heart is filled with love to God, there is no room for sin.—But, young man, to you I owe not only an obligation, in common with those you saved this evening, on the mountain, but my thanks, for your respectful and pious manner, in assisting in the service, at a most embarrassing moment. I should be happy to see you sometimes, at my dwelling, when, perhaps, my conversation may strengthen you in the path which you appear to have chosen. It is so unusual to find one of your age and appearance, in these woods, at all acquainted with our holy liturgy, that it lessens at once the distance between us, and I feel we are no longer strangers. You seem quite at home in the service: I did not perceive that you had even a book, although good Mr. Jones had laid several in different parts of the room."

"It would be strange, if I were ignorant of the service of our church, sir," returned the youth, modestly, "for I was baptized in its communion, and I have never yet attended public worship, elsewhere. For me, to use the forms of any other denomination, would be as singular as our own have proved, to the people here this evening."

"You give me great pleasure, my dear sir," cried the divine, seizing the other by the hand, and shaking it cordially.—"You will go home with me now—indeed you must—my child has yet to thank you for saving my life. I will listen to no apologies. This worthy Indian, and your friend there, will accompany us.—Bless me! to think, that he has arrived at manhood, in this country, without entering a dissenting* meeting-house!"

"No, no," interrupted the Leather-stocking, "I must away to the wigwam: there's work there, that mus'nt be forgotten, for all your churchings and merry-makings. Let the lad go with you in welcome; he is used to keeping company with ministers, and talking of such matters; so is old John, who was christianized by the Moravians, about the time of the old

*The divines of the Protestant Episcopal Church of the United States, commonly call other denominations *Dissenters*, though there never was an established church in their own country!

war. But I am a plain, unlarned man, that has sarved both the king and his country, in his day, ag'in the French and savages, but never so much as looked into a book, or larnt a letter of scholarship, in my born days. I've never seen the use of sich in-door work, though I've lived to be partly bald, and in my time, have killed two hundred beaver in a season, and that without counting the other game. If you mistrust what I'm telling you, you can ask Chingachgook there, for I did it in the heart of the Delaware country, and the old man is knowing to the truth of every word I say."

"I doubt not, my friend, that you have been both a valiant soldier and skilful hunter, in your day," said the divine; "but more is wanting, to prepare you for that end which approaches.—You may have heard the maxim, that 'young men *may* die, but that old men *must*.' "

"I'm sure I never was so great a fool as to expect to live for ever," said Natty, giving one of his silent laughs: "no man need do that, who trails the savages through the woods, as I have done, and lives, for the hot months, on the lake-streams. I've a strong constitution, I must say that for myself, as is plain to be seen, for I've drunk the Onondaga water a hundred times, while I've been watching the deer-licks, when the fever-an-agy seeds was to be seen in it, as plain and as plenty as you can see the rattle-snakes on old Crumhorn. But then, I never expected to hold out for ever; though there's them living, who have seen the Garman Flats a wilderness, ay! and them that's larned, and acquainted with religion too; though you might look a week now, and not find even the stump of a pine on them; and that's a wood, that lasts in the ground the better part of a hundred years after the tree is dead."

"This is but time, my good friend," returned Mr. Grant, who began to take an interest in the welfare of his new acquaintance, "but I would have you prepare for eternity. It is incumbent on you to attend places of public worship, as I am pleased to see that you have done this evening. Would it not be heedless in you to start on a day's toil of hard hunting, and leave your ramrod and flint behind?"

"It must be a young hand in the woods," interrupted Natty, with another laugh, "that didn't know how to dress a rod out of an ash sapling, or find a fire-stone in the mountains. No, no, I never expected to live for ever; but I see, times be altering in these mountains from what they was thirty years ago, or for that matter, ten years. But might makes right, and the law is stronger than an old man, whether he is one that has much larning, or only one like me, that is better now at standing at the passes than in following the hounds, as I once used to could.—Heigh-ho! I never know'd preaching come into a settlement, but it made game scearce, and raised the price of gun-powder; and that's a thing that's not as easily made as a ramrod, or an Indian flint."

The divine, perceiving that he had given his opponent an argument, by his own unfortunate selection of a comparison, very prudently relinquished the controversy; although he was fully determined to resume it, at a more happy moment. Repeating his request to the young hunter, with great earnestness, the youth and Indian consented to accompany him and his daughter to the dwelling, that the care of Mr. Jones had provided for their temporary residence. Leather-stocking persevered in his intention of returning to the hut, and at the door of the building they separated.

After following the course of one of the streets of the village a short distance, Mr. Grant, who led the way, turned into a field, through a pair of open bars, and entered a foot-path, of but sufficient width to admit one person to walk in it, at a time. The moon had gained a height, that enabled her to throw her rays perpendicularly on the valley; and the distinct shadows of the party flitted along on the banks of the silvery snow, like the presence of aerial figures, gliding to their appointed place of meeting. The night still continued intensely cold, although not a breath of wind was felt. The path was beaten so hard, that the gentle female, who made one of the party, moved with ease along its windings; though the frost emitted a low creaking, at the impression of even her light footsteps.

The clergyman, in his dark dress of broadcloth, with his mild, benevolent countenance occasionally turned towards his companions, expressing that look of subdued care, which was its characteristic, presented the first object in this singular group. Next to him moved the Indian, his hair falling about his face, his head uncovered, and the rest of his form concealed beneath his blanket. As his swarthy visage, with its muscles fixed in rigid composure, was seen under the light of the moon, which struck his face obliquely, he seemed a picture of resigned old age, on whom the storms of winter had beaten in vain, for the greater part of a century; but when, in turning his head, the rays fell directly on his dark, fiery eyes, they told a tale of passions unrestrained, and of thoughts free as air. The slight person of Miss Grant, which followed next, and which was but too thinly clad for the severity of the season, formed a marked contrast to the wild attire, and uneasy glances of the Delaware chief; and more than once, during their walk, the young hunter, himself no insignificant figure in the group, was led to consider the difference in the human form, as the face of Mohegan, and the gentle countenance of Miss Grant, with eyes that rivalled the soft hue of the sky, met his view, at the instant that each turned, to throw a glance at the splendid orb which lighted their path. Their way, which led through fields, that lay at some distance in the rear of the houses, was cheered by a conversation, that flagged or became animated with the subject. The first to speak was the divine.

"Really," he said, "it is so singular a circumstance, to meet with one of your age, that has not been induced, by idle curiosity, to visit any other church than the one in which he has been educated, that I feel a strong curiosity to know the history of a life so fortunately regulated.—Your education must have been excellent; as indeed is evident from your manners and language. Of which of the states are you a native, Mr. Edwards? for such, I believe, was the name that you gave Judge Temple."

"Of this——"

"Of this! I was at a loss to conjecture, from your dialect, which does not partake, particularly, of the peculiarities of any country with which I am acquainted. You have, then, resided much in the cities, for no other part of this country is so fortunate, as to possess the constant enjoyment of our excellent liturgy."

The young hunter smiled, as he listened to the divine, while he so clearly betrayed from what part of the country he had come himself; but, for reasons, probably, connected with his present situation, he made no answer.

"I am delighted to meet with you, my young friend, for I think an ingenuous mind, such as I doubt not yours must be, will exhibit all the advantages of a settled doctrine and devout liturgy. You perceive how I was compelled to bend to the humours of my hearers this evening. Good Mr. Jones wished me to read the communion, and, in fact, all the morning service; but, happily, the canons do not require this of an evening. It would have wearied a new congregation; but to-morrow I propose administering the sacrament—do you commune, my young friend?"

"I believe not, sir," returned the youth, with a little embarrassment, that was not at all diminished by Miss Grant's pausing involuntarily, and turning her eyes on him in surprise—"I fear that I am not qualified; I have never yet approached the altar; neither would I wish to do it, while I find so much of the world clinging to my heart."

"Each must judge for himself," said Mr. Grant; "though I should think, that a youth who had never been blown about by the wind of false doctrines, and who has enjoyed the advantages of our liturgy for so many years, in its purity, might safely come. Yet, sir, it is a solemn festival, which none should celebrate, until there is reason to hope it is not mockery. I observed, this evening, in your manner to Judge Temple, a resentment, that bordered on one of the worst of human passions.—We will cross this brook on the ice: it must bear us all, I think, in safety.—Be careful not to slip, my child." While speaking, he descended a little bank, by the path, and crossed one of the small streams that poured their waters into the lake; and, turning to see his daughter pass, observed that the youth had advanced, and was kindly directing her footsteps. When all were safely over, he moved up the opposite bank, and continued his discourse:—"It was wrong, my dear sir, very wrong, to suffer such feelings to rise, under any circumstances, and especially in the present, where the evil was not intended."

"There is good in the talk of my father," said Mohegan, stopping short, and causing those who were behind him to pause also; "It is the talk of Miquon. The white man may do as his fathers have told him; but the 'Young Eagle' has the blood of a Delaware chief in his veins: it is red, and the stain it makes, can only be washed out with the blood of a Mingo."*

Mr. Grant was surprised by the interruption of the Indian, and, stopping, faced the speaker. His mild features were confronted to the fierce and determined looks of the chief, and expressed the horror he felt, at hearing such sentiments, from one who professed the religion of his Saviour. Raising his hands to a level with his head, he exclaimed—

"John, John! is this the religion that you have learned from the Moravians? But no—I will not be so uncharitable as to suppose it. They are a pious, a gentle, and a mild people, and could never tolerate these passions. Listen to the language of the Redeemer—'But I say unto you, love your enemies, bless them that curse you; do good to them that hate you; pray for them that despitefully use you and persecute you.'—This is the command of God, John, and without striving to cultivate such feelings, no man can see him."

The Indian heard the divine with attention; the unusual fire of his eye gradually softened, and his muscles relaxed into their ordinary composure; but, slightly shaking his head, he motioned with dignity for Mr. Grant to resume his walk, and followed himself in silence. The agitation of the divine caused him to move with unusual rapidity along the deep path, and the Indian, without any apparent exertion, kept an equal pace; but the young hunter observed the female to linger in her steps, until a trifling distance intervened between the two former and the latter. Struck by the circumstance, and not perceiving any new impediment to retard her footsteps, the youth made a tender of his assistance.

"You are fatigued, Miss Grant," he said: "the snow yields to the foot, and you are unequal to the strides of us men. Step on the crust, I entreat you, and take the help of my arm. Yonder light is, I believe, the house of your father; but it seems yet at some distance."

"I am quite equal to the walk," returned a low, tremulous voice, "but I am startled by the manner of that Indian. Oh!

*His enemy.

his eye was horrid, as he turned to the moon, in speaking to my father.—But I forget, sir; he is your friend, and, by his language, may be your relative; and yet, of you I do not feel afraid."

The young man stepped on the bank of snow, which firmly sustained his weight, and by a gentle effort, induced his companion to follow. Drawing her arm through his own, he lifted his cap from his head, allowing the dark locks to flow in rich curls over his open brow, and walked by her side, with an air of conscious pride, as if inviting an examination of his inmost thoughts. Louisa took but a furtive glance at his person, and moved quietly along, at a rate that was greatly quickened by the aid of his arm.

"You are but little acquainted with this peculiar people, Miss Grant," he said, "or you would know that revenge is a virtue with an Indian. They are taught, from infancy upward, to believe it a duty, never to allow an injury to pass unrevenged; and nothing but the stronger claims of hospitality, can guard one against their resentments, where they have power."

"Surely, sir," said Miss Grant, involuntarily withdrawing her arm from his, "you have not been educated with such unholy sentiments."

"It might be a sufficient answer, to your excellent father, to say that I was educated in the church," he returned; "but to you I will add, that I have been taught deep and practical lessons of forgiveness. I believe that, on this subject, I have but little cause to reproach myself; it shall be my endeavour, that there yet be less."

While speaking, he stopped, and stood with his arm again proffered to her assistance. As he ended, she quietly accepted his offer, and they resumed their walk.

Mr. Grant and Mohegan had reached the door of the former's residence, and stood waiting near its threshold, for the arrival of their young companions. The former was earnestly occupied, in endeavouring to correct, by his precepts, the evil propensities, that he had discovered in the Indian, during their conversation; to which the latter listened in profound, but respectful attention. On the arrival of the young hunter and the lady, they entered the building.

The house stood at some distance from the village, in the

centre of a field, surrounded by stumps, that were peering above the snow, bearing caps of pure white, nearly two feet in thickness. Not a tree nor a shrub was nigh it; but the house, externally, exhibited that cheerless, unfinished aspect, which is so common to the hastily-erected dwellings of a new country. The uninviting character of its outside was, however, happily relieved by the exquisite neatness, and comfortable warmth, within.

They entered an apartment, that was fitted as a parlour, though the large fire-place, with its culinary arrangements, betrayed the domestic uses to which it was occasionally applied. The bright blaze from the hearth, rendered the light that proceeded from the candle Louisa produced, unnecessary; for the scanty furniture of the room was easily seen and examined, by the former. The floor was covered, in the centre, by a carpet made of rags, a species of manufacture that was, then, and yet continues to be, much in use, in the interior; while its edges, that were exposed to view, were of unspotted cleanliness. There was a trifling air of better life, in a tea-table and work-stand, as well as in an old-fashioned mahogany book-case; but the chairs, the dining-table, and the rest of the furniture, were of the plainest and cheapest construction. Against the walls were hung a few specimens of needle-work and drawing, the former executed with great neatness, though of somewhat equivocal merit in their designs, while the latter were strikingly deficient in both.

One of the former represented a tomb, with a youthful female weeping over it, exhibiting a church with arched windows, in the back-ground. On the tomb were the names, with the dates of the births and deaths, of several individuals, all of whom bore the name of Grant. An extremely cursory glance at this record, was sufficient to discover to the young hunter the domestic state of the divine. He there read, that he was a widower, and that the innocent and timid maiden, who had been his companion, was the only survivor of six children. The knowledge of the dependence, which each of these meek christians had on the other, for happiness, threw an additional charm around the gentle, but kind attentions, which the daughter paid to the father.

These observations occurred while the party were seating

themselves before the cheerful fire, during which time, there was a suspension of discourse. But when each was comfortably arranged, and Louisa, after laying aside a thin coat of faded silk, and a Gipsy hat, that was more becoming to her modest, ingenuous countenance, than appropriate to the season, had taken a chair between her father and the youth, the former resumed the conversation.

"I trust, my young friend," he said, "that the education you have received, has eradicated most of those revengeful principles, which you may have inherited by descent; for I understand, from the expressions of John, that you have some of the blood of the Delaware tribe. Do not mistake me, I beg, for it is not colour, nor lineage, that constitutes merit; and I know not, that he, who claims affinity to the proper owners of this soil, has not the right to tread these hills with the lightest conscience."

Mohegan turned solemnly to the speaker, and, with the peculiarly significant gestures of an Indian, he spoke:—

"Father, you are not yet past the summer of life; your limbs are young. Go to the highest hill, and look around you. All that you see, from the rising to the setting sun, from the head-waters of the great spring, to where the 'crooked river'* is hid by the hills, is his. He has Delaware blood, and his right is strong. But the brother of Miquon is just: he will cut the country in two parts, as the river cuts the low-lands, and will say to the 'Young Eagle,' Child of the Delawares! take it—keep it—and be a chief in the land of your fathers."

"Never!" exclaimed the young hunter, with a vehemence that destroyed the rapt attention with which the divine and his daughter were listening to the Indian—"The wolf of the forest is not more rapacious for his prey, than that man is greedy of gold; and yet his glidings into wealth are subtle as the movements of a serpent."

"Forbear, forbear, my son, forbear," interrupted Mr. Grant.—"These angry passions must be subdued. The accidental injury you have received from Judge Temple, has heightened the sense of your hereditary wrongs. But remem-

*The Susquehannah means crooked river, "hannah," or hannock, meant "river," in many of the native dialects. Thus we find Rappehannock, as far south as Virginia.

ber, that the one was unintentional, and that the other is the effect of political changes, which have, in their course, greatly lowered the pride of kings, and swept mighty nations from the face of the earth. Where now are the Philistines, who so often held the children of Israel in bondage! or that city of Babylon, which rioted in luxury and vice, and who styled herself the Queen of Nations, in the drunkenness of her pride? Remember the prayer of our holy litany, where we implore the Divine power—'That it may please thee to forgive our enemies, persecutors, and slanderers, and to turn their hearts.' The sin of the wrongs which have been done to the natives, are to be alleged against Judge Temple, only, in common with a whole people, and your arm will speedily be restored to its strength."

"This arm!" repeated the youth, pacing the floor in violent agitation; "think you, sir, that I believe the man a murderer?—oh, no! he is too wily, too cowardly, for such a crime. But, let him and his daughter riot in their wealth—a day of retribution will come. No, no, no," he continued, as he trod the floor more calmly—"it is for Mohegan to suspect him of an intent to injure me; but the trifle is not worth a second thought."

He seated himself, and hid his face between his hands, as they rested on his knees.

"It is the hereditary violence of a native's passion, my child," said Mr. Grant, in a low tone, to his affrighted daughter, who was clinging, in terror, to his arm. "He is mixed with the blood of the Indians, you have heard; and neither the refinements of education, nor the advantages of our excellent liturgy, have been able entirely to eradicate the evil. But care and time will do much for him yet."

Although the divine spoke in a low tone, yet what he uttered was heard by the youth, who raised his head, with a smile of indefinite expression, and spoke more calmly:—

"Be not alarmed, Miss Grant, at either the wildness of my manner, or that of my dress. I have been carried away by passions, that I should struggle to repress. I must attribute it, with your father, to the blood in my veins, although I would not impeach my lineage willingly; for it is all that is left me to boast of. Yes! I am proud of my descent from a Delaware chief, who was a warrior that ennobled human nature. Old Mohegan, was his friend, and will vouch for his virtues."

Mr. Grant here took up the discourse, and, finding the young man more calm, and the aged chief attentive, he entered into a full and theological discussion of the duty of forgiveness. The conversation lasted for more than an hour, when the visiters arose, and, after exchanging good wishes with their entertainers, they departed. At the door they separated, Mohegan taking the direct route to the village, while the youth moved towards the lake. The divine stood at the entrance of his dwelling, regarding the figure of the aged chief, as it glided, at an astonishing gait, for his years, along the deep path; his black, straight hair, just visible over the bundle formed by his blanket, which was sometimes blended with the snow under the silvery light of the moon. From the rear of the house was a window, that overlooked the lake; and here Louisa was found by her father, when he entered, gazing, intently on some object, in the direction of the eastern mountain. He approached the spot, and saw the figure of the young hunter, at the distance of half a mile, walking with prodigious steps, across the wide fields of frozen snow, that covered the ice, towards the point, where he knew the hut inhabited by the Leather-stocking was situated, on the margin of the lake, under a rock, that was crowned by pines and hemlocks. At the next instant, the wildly looking form entered the shadow, cast from the overhanging trees, and was lost to view.

"It is marvellous, how long the propensities of the savage continue, in that remarkable race," said the good divine; "but if he persevere, as he has commenced, his triumph shall yet be complete. Put me in mind, Louisa, to lend him the homily 'against peril of idolatry,' at his next visit."

"Surely, father, you do not think him in danger of relapsing into the worship of his ancestors!"

"No, my child," returned the clergyman, laying his hand affectionately on her flaxen locks, and smiling, "his white blood would prevent it; but there is such a thing as the idolatry of our passions."

Chapter XIII

"And I'll drink out of the quart pot,
Here's a health to the barley mow."
Anon., "The Barley-Mow."

On one of the corners, where the two principal streets of Templeton intersected each other, stood, as we have already mentioned, the inn called the "Bold Dragoon." In the original plan, it was ordained that the village should stretch along the little stream, that rushed down the valley, and the street which led from the lake to the academy, was intended to be its western boundary. But convenience frequently frustrates the best regulated plans. The house of Mr., or as, in consequence of commanding the militia of that vicinity, he was called, Captain Hollister, had, at an early day, been erected directly facing the main street, and ostensibly interposed a barrier to its further progress. Horsemen, and subsequently teamsters, however, availed themselves of an opening, at the end of the building, to shorten their passage westward, until, in time, the regular highway was laid out along this course, and houses were gradually built, on either side, so as effectually to prevent any subsequent correction of the evil.

Two material consequences followed this change in the regular plans of Marmaduke. The main street, after running about half its length, was suddenly reduced to precisely that difference in its width; and the "Bold Dragoon" became, next to the Mansion-house, by far the most conspicuous edifice in the place.

This conspicuousness, aided by the characters of the host and hostess, gave the tavern an advantage over all its future competitors, that no circumstances could conquer. An effort was, however, made to do so; and, at the corner diagonally opposite, stood a new building, that was intended, by its occupants, to look down all opposition. It was a house of wood, ornamented in the prevailing style of architecture, and about the roof and balustrades, was one of the three imitators of the Mansion-House. The upper windows were filled with rough boards, secured by nails, to keep out the cold air; for the edifice was far from finished, although glass was to be seen in the lower apartments, and the light of the powerful fires, within, denoted that it was already inhabited. The exterior was painted white, on the front, and on the end which was exposed to the street; but in the rear, and on the side which was intended to join the neighbouring house, it was coarsely smeared with Spanish brown. Before the door stood two lofty posts, connected at the top by a beam, from which was suspended an enormous sign, ornamented around its edges, with certain curious carvings, in pine boards, and on its faces, loaded with masonic emblems. Over these mysterious figures, was written, in large letters, "The Templetown Coffee-House, and Traveller's Hotel," and beneath them, "By Habakkuk Foote and Joshua Knapp." This was a fearful rival to the "Bold Dragoon," as our readers will the more readily perceive, when we add, that the same sonorous names were to be seen over the door of a newly-erected store in the village, a hatter's shop, and the gates of a tan-yard. But, either because too much was attempted to be executed well, or that the "Bold Dragoon" had established a reputation which could not be easily shaken, not only Judge Temple and his friends, but most of the villagers also, who were not in debt to the powerful firm we have named, frequented the inn of Captain Hollister, on all occasions where such a house was necessary.

On the present evening, the limping veteran, and his consort, were hardly housed, after their return from the academy, when the sounds of stamping feet at their threshold announced the approach of visiters, who were probably assembling, with a view to compare opinions, on the subject of the ceremonies they had witnessed.

The public, or, as it was called, the "bar-room," of the "Bold Dragoon," was a spacious apartment, lined on three sides with benches, and on the fourth by fire-places. Of the latter, there were two, of such size as to occupy, with their enormous jambs, the whole of that side of the apartment where they were placed, excepting room enough for a door or two, and a little apartment in one corner, which was protected by miniature pallisadoes, and profusely garnished with bottles and glasses. In the entrance to this sanctuary, Mrs. Hollister was seated, with great gravity in her air, while her husband occupied himself with stirring the fires; moving the logs with a large stake, burnt to a point at one end.

"There, Sargeant dear," said the landlady, after she thought the veteran had got the logs arranged in the most judicious manner, "give over poking, for it's no good yee'll be doing, now that they burn so convaniently. There's the glasses on the table there, and the mug that the Doctor was taking his cider and ginger in, before the fire here,—jist put them in the bar, will ye? for we'll be having the Joodge, and the Major, and Mr. Jones, down the night, widout reckoning Benjamin Poomp, and the Lawyers: so yee'll be fixing the room tidy; and put both flip-irons in the coals; and tell Jude, the lazy, black baste, that if she's no be claning up the kitchen, I'll turn her out of the house, and she may live wid the jontlemen that kape the 'Coffee-house,' good luck to 'em. Och! Sargeant, sure it's a great privilege to go to a mateing, where a body can sit asy, widout joomping up and down so often, as this Mr. Grant is doing that same."

"It's a privilege at all times, Mistress Hollister, whether we stand or be seated; or, as good Mr. Whitefield used to do, after he had made a wearisome day's march, get on our knees and pray, like Moses of old, with a flanker to the right and left, to lift his hands to heaven," returned her husband, who composedly performed what she had directed to be done. "It was a very pretty fight, Betty, that the Israelites had, on that day, with the Amalekites. It seems that they fout on a plain, for Moses is mentioned, as having gone on to the heights, to overlook the battle, and wrestle in prayer; and if I should judge, with my little larning, the Israelites depended mainly on their horse, for it is written, that Joshua cut up the enemy with the edge of the *sword*: from which I infar, not only that they were horse, but well disciplyn'd troops. Indeed, it says as much, as that they were chosen men; quite likely volunteers; for raw dragoons seldom strike with the *edge* of their swords, particularly if the weapon be any way crooked."

"Pshaw! why do ye bodder yourself wid taxts, man, about so small a matter," interrupted the landlady; "sure it was the Lord who was wid 'em; for he always sided wid the Jews, before they fell away; and it's but little matter what kind of men Joshua commanded, so that he was doing the right bidding. Aven them cursed millishy, the Lord forgi'e me for swearing, that was the death of him, wid their cowardice, would have carried the day in old times. There's no rason to be thinking that the soldiers was used to the drill."

"I must say, Mrs. Hollister, that I have not often seen raw troops fight better than the left flank of the militia, at the time you mention. They rallied handsomely, and that without beat of drum, which is no easy thing to do under fire, and were very steady till he fell. But the scriptures contain no unnecessary words; and I will maintain, that horse, who know how to strike with the *edge* of the sword, must be well disciplyn'd. Many a good sarmon has been preached about smaller matters than that one word. If the text was not meant to be particular, why wasn't it written, with the sword, and not with the edge? Now, a back-handed stroke, on the edge, takes long practice. Goodness! what an argument would Mr. Whitefield make of that word edge!—As to the Captain, if he had only called up the guard of dragoons, when he rallied the foot, they would have shown the inimy what the edge of a sword was; for, although there was no commissioned officer with them, yet I think I may say,"—the veteran continued, stiffening his cravat about the throat, and raising himself up, with the air of a drill-sergeant,—"they were led by a man, who know'd how to bring them on, in spite of the ravine."

"Is it lade on ye would?" cried the landlady, "when ye know yourself, Mr. Hollister, that the baste he rode was but little able to joomp from one rock to another, and the animal was as spry as a squirrel? Och! but it's useless to talk, for he's gone this many a year. I would that he had lived to see the true light; but there's mercy for a brave sowl, that died in the saddle, fighting for the liberty. It's a poor tomb-stone they have given him, any way, and many a good one that died like himself: but the sign is very like, and I will be kapeing it up, while the blacksmith can make a hook for it to swing on, for all the 'coffee-houses' betwane this and Albany."

There is no saying where this desultory conversation would have led the worthy couple, had not the men who were stamping the snow off their feet, on the little platform before the door, suddenly ceased their occupation, and entered the bar-room.

For ten or fifteen minutes, the different individuals, who intended either to bestow or receive edification, before the fires of the "Bold Dragoon," on that evening, were collecting, until the benches were nearly filled with men of different occupations. Dr. Todd, and a slovenly-looking, shabby genteel young man, who took tobacco profusely, wore a coat of imported cloth, cut with something like a fashionable air, frequently exhibited a large, French, silver watch, with a chain of woven hair and a silver key, and who, altogether, seemed as much above the artisans around him, as he was himself inferior to the real gentlemen, occupied a high-back, wooden settee, in the most comfortable corner in the apartment.

Sundry brown mugs, containing cider or beer, were placed between the heavy andirons, and little groups were formed among the guests, as subjects arose, or the liquor was passed from one to the other. No man was seen to drink by himself, nor in any instance was more than one vessel considered necessary, for the same beverage; but the glass, or the mug, was passed from hand to hand, until a chasm in the line, or a regard to the rights of ownership, would regularly restore the dregs of the potation to him who defrayed the cost.

Toasts were uniformly drunk; and occasionally, some one, who conceived himself peculiarly endowed by nature to shine in the way of wit, would attempt some such sentiment as "hoping that he" who treated "might make a better man than his father;" or "live till all his friends wished him dead;" while the more humble pot-companion contented himself by saying, with a most imposing gravity in his air, "come, here's luck," or by expressing some other equally comprehensive wish. In every instance, the veteran landlord was requested to imitate the custom of the cup-bearers to kings, and taste the liquor he presented, by the invitation of "after you is manners;" with which request he ordinarily complied, by wetting his lips, first expressing the wish of "here's hoping," leaving it to the imagination of the hearers to fill the vacuum by whatever good each thought most desirable. During these movements, the landlady was busily occupied with mixing the various compounds required by her customers, with her own hands, and occasionally exchanging greetings and inquiries concerning the conditions of their respective families, with such of the villagers as approached "the bar."

At length, the common thirst being in some measure assuaged, conversation of a more general nature became the order of the hour. The physician, and his companion, who was one of the two lawyers of the village, being considered the best qualified to maintain a public discourse with credit, were the principal speakers, though a remark was hazarded, now and then, by Mr. Doolittle, who was thought to be their inferior, only in the enviable point of education. A general silence was produced on all but the two speakers, by the following observation from the practitioner of the law:—

"So, Doctor Todd, I understand that you have been performing an important operation, this evening, by cutting a charge of buck-shot from the shoulder of the son of Leather-stocking?"

"Yes, sir," returned the other, elevating his little head, with an air of importance. "I had a small job, up at the Judge's, in that way: it was, however, but a trifle to what it might have been, had it gone through the body. The shoulder is not a very vital part; and I think the young man will soon be well. But I did not know that the patient was a son of Leather-stocking: it is news to me, to hear that Natty had a wife."

"It is by no means a necessary consequence," returned the other, winking, with a shrewd look around the bar-room; "there is such a thing, I suppose you know, in law, as a 'filius nullius.' "

"Spake it out, man," exclaimed the landlady, "spake it out in king's English; what for should ye be talking Indian, in a room full of Christian folks, though it is about a poor hunter, who is but a little better in his ways than the wild savages themselves? Och! it's to be hoped that the missionaries will, in his own time, make a convarsion of the poor divils; and then it will matter little of what colour is the skin, or wedder there be wool or hair on the head."

"Oh! it is Latin, not Indian, Miss Hollister," returned the lawyer, repeating his winks and shrewd looks; "and Dr. Todd understands Latin, or how would he read the labels on his gallipots and drawers? No, no, Miss Hollister, the Doctor understands me; don't you, Doctor?"

"Hem—why I guess I am not far out of the way," returned Elnathan, endeavouring to imitate the expression of the other's countenance, by looking jocular; "Latin is a queer language, gentlemen;—now, I rather guess there is no one in the room, except Squire Lippet, who can believe that 'Far. Av.' means oatmeal, in English."

The lawyer, in his turn, was a good deal embarrassed by this display of learning; for although he actually had taken his first degree at one of the eastern universities, he was somewhat puzzled with the terms used by his companion. It was dangerous, however, to appear to be outdone in learning in a public bar-room, and before so many of his clients; he therefore put the best face on the matter, and laughed knowingly, as if there were a good joke concealed under it, that was understood only by the physician and himself. All this was attentively observed by the listeners, who exchanged looks of approbation; and the expressions of "tonguey man," and "I guess Squire Lippet knows, if any body doos," were heard in different parts of the room, as vouchers for the admiration of his auditors. Thus encouraged, the lawyer rose from his chair, and, turning his back to the fire, and facing the company, he continued—

"The son of Natty, or the son of nobody, I hope the young man is not going to let the matter drop. This is a country of laws; and I should like to see it fairly tried, whether a man who owns, or says he owns, a hundred thousand acres of land, has any more right to shoot a body, than another. What do you think of it, Dr. Todd?"

"Oh! sir, I am of opinion that the gentleman will soon be well, as I said before; the wownd isn't in a vital part, and as the ball was extracted so soon, and the shoulder was what I call well attended to, I do not think there is as much danger as there might have been."

"I say, Squire Doolittle," continued the attorney, raising his voice, "you are a magistrate, and know what is law, and what is not law. I ask you, sir, if shooting a man is a thing that is to be settled so very easily? Suppose, sir, that the young man had a wife and family; and suppose that he was a mechanic, like yourself, sir; and suppose that his family depended on him for bread; and suppose that the ball, instead of merely going through the flesh, had broken the shoulder-blade, and crippled him for ever;—I ask you all, gentlemen, supposing this to be the case, whether a jury wouldn't give what I call handsome damages?"

As the close of this supposititious case was addressed to the company, generally, Hiram did not, at first, consider himself called on for a reply; but finding the eyes of the listeners bent on him in expectation, he remembered his character for judicial discrimination, and spoke, observing a due degree of deliberation and dignity.

"Why, if a man should shoot another," he said, "and if he should do it on purpose, and if the law took notice on't, and if a jury should find him guilty, it would be likely to turn out a state-prison matter."

"It would so, sir," returned the attorney.—"The law, gentlemen, is no respecter of persons, in a free country. It is one of the great blessings that has been handed down to us from our ancestors, that all men are equal in the eye of the law, as they are by nater. Though some may get property, no one knows how, yet they are not privileged to trangress the laws, any more than the poorest citizen in the state. This is my notion, gentlemen; and I think that if a man had a mind to bring this matter up, something might be made out of it, that would help pay for the salve—ha! Doctor?"

"Why, sir," returned the physician, who appeared a little uneasy at the turn the conversation was taking, "I have the promise of Judge Temple, before men—not but what I would take his word as soon as his note of hand—but it was before men. Let me see—there was Mounshier Ler Quow, and Squire Jones, and Major Hartmann, and Miss Pettibone, and one or two of the blacks by, when he said that his pocket would amply reward me for what I did."

"Was the promise made before or after the service was performed?" asked the attorney.

"It might have been both," returned the discreet physician, "though I'm certain he said so, before I undertook the dressing."

"But it seems that he said his pocket should reward you, Doctor," observed Hiram; "now I don't know that the law will hold a man to such a promise: he might give you his pocket with sixpence in't, and tell you to take your pay out on't."

"That would not be a reward in the eye of the law," interrupted the attorney—"not what is called a 'quid pro quo;' nor is the pocket to be considered as an agent, but as part of a man's own person, that is, in this particular. I am of opinion that an action would lie on that promise, and I will undertake to bear him out, free of costs, if he don't recover."

To this proposition the physician made no reply, but he was observed to cast his eyes around him, as if to enumerate the witnesses, in order to substantiate this promise also, at a future day, should it prove necessary. A subject so momentous, as that of suing Judge Temple, was not very palatable to the present company, in so public a place; and a short silence ensued, that was only interrupted by the opening of the door, and the entrance of Natty himself.

The old hunter carried in his hand his never-failing companion, the rifle; and, although all of the company were uncovered, excepting the lawyer, who wore his hat on one side, with a certain dam'me air, Natty moved to the front of one of the fires, without in the least altering any part of his dress or appearance. Several questions were addressed to him, on the subject of the game he had killed, which he answered readily, and with some little interest; and the landlord, between whom and Natty there existed much cordiality, on account of their both having been soldiers in youth, offered him a glass of a liquid, which, if we might judge from its reception, was no unwelcome guest. When the forester had gotten his potation also, he quietly took his seat on the end of one of the logs, that lay nigh the fires, and the slight interruption, produced by his entrance, seemed to be forgotten.

"The testimony of the blacks could not be taken, sir," continued the lawyer, "for they are all the property of Mr. Jones, who owns their time. But there is a way by which Judge Temple, or any other man, might be made to pay for shooting another, and for the cure in the bargain.—There is a way, I say, and that without going into the 'court of errors' too."

"And a mighty big error ye would make of it, Mister Todd," cried the landlady, "should ye be putting the matter into the law at all, with Joodge Temple, who has a purse as long as one of them pines on the hill, and who is an asy man to dale wid, if yees but mind the humour of him. He's a good man is Joodge Temple, and a kind one, and one who will be no the likelier to do the pratty thing, bekaase ye would wish to tarrify him wid the law. I know of but one objaction to the same, which is an over carelessness about his sowl. It's nather a Methodie, nor a Papish, nor a Prasbetyrian, that he is, but jist nothing at all; and it's hard to think that he 'who will not fight the good fight, under the banners of a rig'lar church, in this world, will be mustered among the chosen in heaven,' as my husband, the Captain there, as ye call him, says—though there is but one captain that I know, who desaarves the name. I hopes, Lather-stocking, ye'll no be foolish, and putting the boy up to try the law in the matter; for 'twill be an evil day to ye both, when ye first turn the skin of so paceable an animal as a sheep into a bone of contention. The lad is wilcome to his drink for nothing, until his shouther will bear the rifle ag'in."

"Well, that's gin'rous," was heard from several mouths at once, for this was a company in which a liberal offer was not thrown away; while the hunter, instead of expressing any of that indignation which he might be supposed to feel, at hearing the hurt of his young companion alluded to, opened his mouth, with the silent laugh for which he was so remarkable; and after he had indulged his humour, made this reply—

"I know'd the Judge would do nothing with his smoothbore, when he got out of his sleigh. I never see'd but one smooth-bore, that would carry at all, and that was a French ducking-piece, upon the big lakes: it had a barrel half as long ag'in as my rifle, and would throw fine shot into a goose, at a hundred yards; but it made dreadful work with the game, and you wanted a boat to carry it about in. When I went with Sir William ag'in the French, at Fort Niagara, all the rangers used the rifle; and a dreadful weepon it is, in the hands of one who knows how to charge it, and keeps a steady aim. The Captain knows, for he says he was a soldier in Shirley's, and though they were nothing but baggonet-men, he must know how we cut up the French and Iroquois in the skrimmages, in that war. Chingachgook, which means 'Big Sarpent' in English, old John Mohegan, who lives up at the hut with me, was a great warrior then, and was out with us; he can tell all about it, too; though he was overhand for the tomahawk, never firing more than once or twice, before he was running in for the scalps. Ah! times is dreadfully altered since then. Why, Doctor, there was nothing but a foot-path, or at the most a track for pack-horses, along the Mohawk, from the Garman Flats up to the forts. Now, they say, they talk of running one of them wide roads with gates on't, along the river; first making a road, and then fencing it up! I hunted one season back of the Kaatskills, nigh-hand to the settlements, and the dogs often lost the scent, when they com'd to them highways, there was so much travel on them; though I can't say that the brutes was of a very good breed.—Old Hector will wind a deer in the fall of the year, across the broadest place in the Otsego, and that is a mile and a half, for I paced it myself on the ice, when the tract was first surveyed under the Indian grant."

"It sames to me, Natty, but a sorry compliment, to call your cumrad after the evil one," said the landlady; "and it's no much like a snake that old John is looking now. Nimrood would be a more besaming name for the lad, and a more Christian too, seeing that it comes from the Bible. The Sargeant read me the chapter about him, the night before my christening, and a mighty asement it was, to listen to any thing from the book."

"Old John and Chingachgook were very different men to look on," returned the hunter, shaking his head at his melancholy recollections.—"In the 'fifty-eight war,' he was in the middle of manhood, and taller than now by three inches. If you had seen him, as I did, the morning we beat Dieskau, from behind our log walls, you would have called him as comely a red-skin as ye ever set eyes on. He was naked, all to his breech-cloth and leggens; and you never seed a creater so handsomely painted. One side of his face was red, and the other black. His head was shaved clean, all to a few hairs on the crown, where he wore a tuft of eagle's feathers, as bright as if they had come from a peacock's tail. He had coloured his sides, so that they looked like an atomy, ribs and all; for Chingachgook had a great taste in such things: so that, what with his bold, fiery countenance, his knife and his tomahawk,

I have never seed a fiercer warrior on the ground. He played his part, too, like a man; for I seen him next day, with thirteen scalps on his pole. And I will say this for the 'Big Snake,' that he always dealt fair, and never scalped any that he didn't kill with his own hands."

"Well, well," cried the landlady, "fighting is fighting, any way, and there's different fashions in the thing; though I can't say that I relish mangling a body after the breath is out of it; neither do I think it can be uphild by doctrine. I hopes, Sargeant, ye niver was helping in sich evil worrek."

"It was my duty to keep my ranks, and to stand or fall by the baggonet or lead," returned the veteran. "I was then in the fort, and seldom leaving my place, saw but little of the savages, who kept on the flanks, or in front, skrimmaging. I remember, howsomever, to have heard mention made of the 'Great Snake,' as he was called, for he was a chief of renown; but little did I ever expect to see him enlisted in the cause of Christianity, and civilized, like old John."

"Oh! he was christianized by the Moravians, who was always over intimate with the Delawares," said Leather-stocking. "It's my opinion, that had they been left to themselves, there would be no such doings now, about the head-waters of the two rivers, and that these hills mought have been kept as good hunting-ground, by their right owner, who is not too old to carry a rifle, and whose sight is as true as a fish-hawk, hovering—"

He was interrupted by more stamping at the door, and presently the party from the Mansion-house entered, followed by the Indian himself.

Chapter XIV

"There's quart pot, pint pot, half-pint,
Gill pot, half-gill, nipperkin,
And the brown bowl.—
Here's a health to the barley mow,
My brave boys,
Here's a health to the barley mow."
Anon., "The Barley-Mow."

SOME LITTLE COMMOTION was produced by the appearance of the new guests, during which the lawyer slunk from the room. Most of the men approached Marmaduke, and shook his offered hand, hoping "that the Judge was well;" while Major Hartmann, having laid aside his hat and wig, and substituted for the latter a warm, peaked, woollen night-cap, took his seat very quietly, on one end of the settee which was relinquished by its former occupants. His tobacco-box was next produced, and a clean pipe was handed him by the landlord. When he had succeeded in raising a smoke, the Major gave a long whiff, and turning his head towards the bar, he said—

"Petty, pring in ter toddy."

In the mean time, the Judge had exchanged his salutations with most of the company, and taken a place by the side of the Major, and Richard had bustled himself into the most comfortable seat in the room. Mr. Le Quoi was the last seated, nor did he venture to place his chair finally, until, by frequent removals, he had ascertained that he could not possibly intercept a ray of heat from any individual present. Mohegan found a place on an end of one of the benches, and somewhat approximated to the bar. When these movements had subsided, the Judge remarked, pleasantly—

"Well, Betty, I find you retain your popularity, through all weathers, against all rivals, and amongst all religions.—How liked you the sermon?"

"Is it the sarmon?" exclaimed the landlady. "I can't say but it was rasonable; but the prayers is mighty unasy. It's no so small a matter for a body, in their fifty-nint' year, to be moving so much in church. Mr. Grant sames a godly man, any way, and his garrel is a hoomble one, and a devout.—Here, John, is a mug of cider lac'd with whisky. An Indian will drink cider, though he niver be athirst."

"I must say," observed Hiram, with due deliberation, "that it was a tonguey thing; and I rather guess that it gave considerable satisfaction. There was one part, though, which might have been left out, or something else put in; but then, I s'pose that, as it was a written discourse, it is not so easily altered, as where a minister preaches without notes."

"Ay! there's the rub, Joodge," cried the landlady; "how can a man stand up and be praching his word, when all that he is saying is written down, and he is as much tied to it as iver a thaving dragoon was to the pickets?"

"Well, well," cried Marmaduke, waving his hand for silence, "there is enough said; as Mr. Grant told us, there are different sentiments on such subjects, and in my opinion he spoke most sensibly.—So, Jotham, I am told you have sold your betterments to a new settler, and have moved into the village and opened a school. Was it cash or dicker?"

The man who was thus addressed, occupied a seat immediately behind Marmaduke; and one who was ignorant of the extent of the Judge's observation, might have thought he would have escaped notice. He was of a thin, shapeless figure, with a discontented expression of countenance, and with something extremely shiftless in his whole air. Thus spoken to, after turning and twisting a little, by way of preparation, he made a reply.

"Why, part cash, and part dicker. I sold out to a Pumfret-man, who was so'thin forehanded. He was to give me ten dollars an acre for the clearin, and one dollar an acre over the first cost, on the wood-land: and we agreed to leave the buildins to men. So I tuck Asa Mountagu, and he tuck Absalom Bement, and they two tuck old Squire Naphtali Green. And so they had a meetin, and made out a vardict of eighty dollars for the buildins. There was twelve acres of clearin, at ten dollars, and eighty-eight at one, and the whull came to two hundred and eighty-six dollars and a half, after paying the men."

"Hum," said Marmaduke; "what did you give for the place?"

"Why, besides what's comin to the Judge, I gi'n my brother Tim, a hundred dollars for his bargain; but then there's a new house on't, that cost me sixty more, and I paid Moses a hundred dollars, for choppin', and loggin, and sowin; so that the whull stood me in about two hundred and sixty dollars. But then I had a great crop off on't, and as I got twenty-six dollars and a half more than it cost, I conclude I made a pretty good trade on't."

"Yes, but you forgot that the crop was yours without the trade, and you have turned yourself out of doors for twenty-six dollars."

"Oh! the Judge is clean out," said the man, with a look of sagacious calculation; "he turned out a span of horses, that is wuth a hundred and fifty dollars of any man's money, with a bran new wagon; fifty dollars in cash; and a good note for eighty more; and a side-saddle, that was valood at seven and a half—so there was jist twelve shillings betwixt us. I wanted him to turn out a set of harness, and take the cow and the sap-troughs. He wouldn't—but I saw through it; he thought I should have to buy the tacklin afore I could use the wagon and horses; but I know'd a thing or two myself: I should like to know of what use is the tacklin to him! I offered him to trade back ag'in, for one hundred and fifty-five. But my woman said she wanted a churn, so I tuck a churn for the change."

"And what do you mean to do with your time, this winter? you must remember that time is money."

"Why, as the master is gone down country, to see his mother, who, they say, is going to make a die on't, I agreed to take the school in hand, till he comes back. If times doosn't get wuss in the spring, I've some notion of going into trade, or maybe I may move off to the Genessee; they say they are carryin on a great stroke of business that-a-way. If the wust comes to the wust, I can but work at my trade, for I was brought up in a shoe manufactory."

It would seem, that Marmaduke did not think his society of sufficient value, to attempt inducing him to remain where he was; for he addressed no further discourse to the man, but turned his attention to other subjects.—After a short pause, Hiram ventured a question:—

"What news doos the Judge bring us from the legislater? it's not likely that congress has done much this session; or maybe the French haven't fit any more battles lately?"

"The French, since they have beheaded their king, have done nothing but fight," returned the Judge. "The character of the nation seems changed. I knew many French gentlemen, during our war, and they all appeared to me to be men of great humanity and goodness of heart; but these Jacobins are as blood-thirsty as bull-dogs."

"There was one Roshambow wid us, down at Yorrek-town," cried the landlady; "a mighty pratty man he was too; and their horse was the very same. It was there that the Sargeant got the hurt in the leg, from the English batteries, bad luck to 'em."

"Ah! mon pauvre Roi!" murmured Monsieur Le Quoi.

"The legislature have been passing laws," continued Marmaduke, "that the country much required. Among others, there is an act, prohibiting the drawing of seines, at any other than proper seasons, in certain of our streams and small lakes; and another, to prohibit the killing of deer in the teeming months. These are laws that were loudly called for, by judicious men; nor do I despair of getting an act, to make the unlawful felling of timber a criminal offence."

The hunter listened to this detail with breathless attention, and when the Judge had ended, he laughed in open derision.

"You may make your laws, Judge," he cried, "but who will you find to watch the mountains through the long summer days, or the lakes at night? Game is game, and he who finds may kill; that has been the law in these mountains for forty years, to my sartain knowledge; and I think one old law is worth two new ones. None but a green-one would wish to kill a doe with a fa'n by its side, unless his moccasins was getting old, or his leggins ragged, for the flesh is lean and coarse. But a rifle rings amongst them rocks along the lake shore, sometimes, as if fifty pieces was fired at once; it would be hard to tell where the man stood who pulled the trigger."

"Armed with the dignity of the law, Mr. Bumppo," returned the Judge, gravely, "a vigilant magistrate can prevent much of the evil that has hitherto prevailed, and which is already rendering the game scarce. I hope to live to see the day, when a man's rights in his game shall be as much respected as his title to his farm."

"Your titles and your farms are all new together," cried Natty; "but laws should be equal, and not more for one than another. I shot a deer, last Wednesday was a fortnight, and it floundered through the snow-banks till it got over a brush fence; I catch'd the lock of my rifle in the twigs, in following, and was kept back, until finally the creater got off. Now I want to know who is to pay me for that deer; and a fine buck it was. If there hadn't been a fence, I should have gotten another shot into it; and I never draw'd upon any thing that hadn't wings, three times running, in my born days.—No, no, Judge, it's the farmers that makes the game scearce, and not the hunters."

"Ter teer is not so plenty as in ter olt war, Pumppo," said the Major, who had been an attentive listener, amidst clouds of smoke; "put ter lant is not mate, as for ter teer to live on, put for Christians."

"Why, Major, I believe you're a friend to justice and the right, though you go so often to the grand house; but it's a hard case to a man, to have his honest calling for a livelihood stopt by laws, and that too when, if right was done, he mought hunt or fish on any day in the week, or on the best flat in the Patent, if he was so minded."

"I unterstant you, Letter-stockint," returned the Major, fixing his black eyes, with a look of peculiar meaning, on the hunter; "put you tidn't use to pe so prutent, as to look ahet mit so much care."

"Maybe there wasn't so much 'casion," said the hunter, a little sulkily; when he sunk into a silence, from which he was not roused for some time.

"The Judge was saying so'thin about the French," Hiram observed, when the pause in the conversation had continued a decent time.

"Yes, sir," returned Marmaduke, "the Jacobins of France seem rushing from one act of licentiousness to another. They continue those murders, which are dignified by the name of executions. You have heard, that they have added the death of their Queen to the long list of their crimes."

"Les monstres!" again murmured Monsieur Le Quoi, turning himself suddenly in his chair, with a convulsive start.

"The province of La Vendée is laid waste by the troops of the republic, and hundreds of its inhabitants, who are royalists in their sentiments, are shot at a time.—La Vendée is a district in the south-west of France, that continues yet much attached to the family of the Bourbons: doubtless Monsieur Le Quoi is acquainted with it, and can describe it more faithfully."

"Non, non, non, mon cher ami," returned the Frenchman, in a suppressed voice, but speaking rapidly, and gesticulating with his right hand, as if for mercy, while with his left he concealed his eyes.

"There have been many battles fought lately," continued Marmaduke, "and the infuriated republicans are too often victorious. I cannot say, however, that I am sorry they have captured Toulon from the English, for it is a place to which they have a just right."

"Ah—ha!" exclaimed Monsieur Le Quoi, springing on his feet, and flourishing both arms with great animation; "ces Anglais!"

The Frenchman continued to move about the room with great alacrity for a few minutes, repeating his exclamations to himself; when, overcome by the contradictory nature of his emotions, he suddenly burst out of the house, and was seen wading through the snow towards his little shop, waving his arms on high, as if to pluck down honour from the moon. His departure excited but little surprise, for the villagers were used to his manner; but Major Hartmann laughed outright, for the first time during his visit, as he lifted the mug, and observed—

"Ter Frenchman is mat—put he is goot as for notting to trink; he is trunk mit joy."

"The French are good soldiers," said Captain Hollister; "they stood us in hand a good turn, down at York-town; nor do I think, although I am an ignorant man about the great movements of the army, that his Excellency would have been able to march against Cornwallis, without their reinforcements."

"Ye spake the trut', Sargeant," interrupted his wife, "and I would iver have ye be doing the same. It's varry pratty men is the French; and jist when I stopt the cart, the time when ye was pushing on in front it was, to kape the rig'lars in, a rigiment of the jontlemen marched by, and so I dealt them out to their liking. Was it pay I got? sure did I, and in good, solid crowns; the divil a bit of continental could they muster among them all, for love nor money. Och! the Lord forgive me for swearing and spakeing of sich vanities; but this I will say for the French, that they paid in good silver; and one glass would go a great way wid 'em, for they gin'rally handed it back wid a drop in the cup; and that's a brisk trade, Joodge, where the pay is good, and the men not over partic'lar."

"A thriving trade, Mrs. Hollister," said Marmaduke. "But what has become of Richard? he jumped up as soon as seated, and has been absent so long that I am fearful he has frozen."

"No fear of that, cousin 'duke," cried the gentleman himself; "business will sometimes keep a man warm, the coldest night that ever snapt in the mountains. Betty, your husband told me, as we came out of church, that your hogs were getting mangy, so I have been out to take a look at them, and found it true. I stepped across, Doctor, and got your boy to weigh me out a pound of salts, and have been mixing it with their swill. I'll bet a saddle of venison against a gray squirrel, that they are better in a week. And now, Mrs. Hollister, I'm ready for a hissing mug of flip."

"Sure, I know'd yee'd be wanting that same," said the landlady; "it's mixt and ready to the boiling. Sargeant dear, be handing up the iron, will ye?—no the one in the far fire, it's black, ye will see.—Ah! you've the thing now; look if it's not as red as a cherry."

The beverage was heated, and Richard took that kind of draught which men are apt to indulge in, who think that they have just executed a clever thing, especially when they like the liquor.

"Oh! you have a hand, Betty, that was formed to mix flip," cried Richard, when he paused for breath. "The very iron has a flavour in it. Here, John; drink, man, drink. I and you and Dr. Todd, have done a good thing with the shoulder of that lad, this very night. 'Duke, I made a song while you were gone; one day when I had nothing to do; so I'll sing you a verse or two, though I haven't really determined on the tune yet.

What is life but a scene of care,
  Where each one must toil in his way?
Then let us be jolly, and prove that we are
A set of good fellows, who seem very rare,
  And can laugh and sing all the day.
    Then let us be jolly,
    And cast away folly,
  For grief turns a black head to gray.

There, 'duke, what do you think of that? There is another verse of it, all but the last line; I haven't got a rhyme for the last line yet.—Well, old John, what do you think of the music? as good as one of your war-songs, ha!"

"Good," said Mohegan, who had been sharing deeply in the potations of the landlady, besides paying a proper respect to the passing mugs of the Major and Marmaduke.

"Pravo! pravo! Richart," cried the Major, whose black eyes were beginning to swim in moisture; "pravissimo! it is a goot song; put Natty Pumppo hast a petter. Letter-stockint, vilt sing? say, olt poy, vilt sing ter song, as apout ter woots?"

"No, no, Major," returned the hunter, with a melancholy shake of the head, "I have lived to see what I thought eyes could never behold in these hills, and I have no heart left for singing. If he, that has a right to be master and ruler here, is forced to squinch his thirst, when a-dry, with snow-water, it ill becomes them that have lived by his bounty to be making merry, as if there was nothing in the world but sunshine and summer."

When he had spoken, Leather-stocking again dropped his head on his knees, and concealed his hard and wrinkled features with his hands. The change from the excessive cold without to the heat of the bar-room, coupled with the depth and frequency of Richard's draughts, had already levelled whatever inequality there might have existed between him and the other guests, on the score of spirits; and he now held out a pair of swimming mugs of foaming flip towards the hunter, as he cried—

"Merry! ay! merry Christmas to you, old boy! Sunshine

and summer! no! you are blind, Leather-stocking, 'tis moonshine and winter;—take these spectacles, and open your eyes.

So let us be jolly,
And cast away folly,
For grief turns a black head to gray.

Hear how old John turns his quavers. What damned dull music an Indian song is, after all, Major. I wonder if they ever sing by note?"

While Richard was singing and talking, Mohegan was uttering dull, monotonous tones, keeping time by a gentle motion of his head and body. He made use of but few words, and such as he did utter were in his native language, and consequently, only understood by himself and Natty. Without heeding Richard, he continued to sing a kind of wild, melancholy air, that rose, at times, in sudden and quite elevated notes, and then fell again into the low, quavering sounds, that seemed to compose the character of his music.

The attention of the company was now much divided, the men in the rear having formed themselves into little groups, where they were discussing various matters, among the principal of which were, the treatment of mangy hogs, and Parson Grant's preaching; while Dr. Todd was endeavouring to explain to Marmaduke the nature of the hurt received by the young hunter. Mohegan continued to sing, while his countenance was becoming vacant, though, coupled with his thick bushy hair, it was assuming an expression very much like brutal ferocity. His notes were gradually growing louder, and soon rose to a height that caused a general cessation in the discourse. The hunter now raised his head again, and addressed the old warrior, warmly, in the Delaware language, which, for the benefit of our readers, we shall render freely into English.

"Why do you sing of your battles, Chingachgook, and of the warriors you have slain, when the worst enemy of all is near you, and keeps the Young Eagle from his rights? I have fought in as many battles as any warrior in your tribe, but cannot boast of my deeds at such a time as this."

"Hawk-eye," said the Indian, tottering with a doubtful step from his place, "I am the Great Snake of the Delawares; I can track the Mingoes, like an adder that is stealing on the whip-poor-will's eggs, and strike them, like the rattle-snake, dead at a blow. The white man made the tomahawk of Chingachgook bright as the waters of Otsego, when the last sun is shining; but it is red with the blood of the Maquas."

"And why have you slain the Mingo warriors? was it not to keep these hunting-grounds and lakes to your father's children? and were they not given in solemn council to the Fire-eater? and does not the blood of a warrior run in the veins of a young chief, who should speak aloud, where his voice is now too low to be heard?"

The appeal of the hunter seemed, in some measure, to recall the confused faculties of the Indian, who turned his face towards the listeners, and gazed intently on the Judge. He shook his head, throwing his hair back from his countenance, and exposed eyes, that were glaring with an expression of wild resentment. But the man was not himself. His hand seemed to make a fruitless effort to release his tomahawk, which was confined by its handle to his belt, while his eyes gradually became vacant. Richard at that instant thrusting a mug before him, his features changed to the grin of idiocy, and seizing the vessel with both hands, he sunk backward on the bench, and drunk until satiated, when he made an effort to lay aside the mug, with the helplessness of total inebriety.

"Shed not blood!" exclaimed the hunter, as he watched the countenance of the Indian in its moment of ferocity—"but he is drunk, and can do no harm. This is the way with all the savages; give them liquor, and they make dogs of themselves. Well, well—the time will come when right will be done, and we must have patience."

Natty still spoke in the Delaware language, and of course was not understood. He had hardly concluded, before Richard cried—

"Well, old John is soon sowed up. Give him a berth, Captain, in the barn, and I will pay for it. I am rich to-night, ten times richer than 'duke, with all his lands, and military lots, and funded debts, and bonds, and mortgages.

Come let us be jolly,
And cast away folly,
For grief—

Drink, King Hiram—drink, Mr. Doo-nothing—drink, sir, I say. This is a Christmas eve, which comes, you know, but once a year."

"He! he! he! the Squire is quite moosical to-night," said Hiram, whose visage began to give marvellous signs of relaxation. "I rather guess we shall make a church on't yet, Squire?"

"A church, Mr. Doolittle! we will make a cathedral of it! bishops, priests, deacons, wardens, vestry and choir; organ, organist and bellows! By the Lord Harry, as Benjamin says, we will clap a steeple on the other end of it, and make two churches of it. What say you, 'duke, will you pay? ha! my cousin Judge, wilt pay?"

"Thou makest such a noise, Dickon," returned Marmaduke, "it is impossible that I can hear what Dr. Todd is saying. I think thou observed, it is probable the wound will fester, so as to occasion danger to the limb, in this cold weather?"

"Out of nater, sir, quite out of nater;" said Elnathan, attempting to expectorate, but succeeding only in throwing a light, frothy substance, like a flake of snow, into the fire—"quite out of nater, that a wownd so well dressed, and with the ball in my pocket, should fester. I s'pose, as the Judge talks of taking the young man into his house, it will be most convenient if I make but one charge on't."

"I should think one would do," returned Marmaduke, with that arch smile that so often beamed on his face; leaving the beholder in doubt whether he most enjoyed the character of his companion, or his own covert humour.

The landlord had succeeded in placing the Indian on some straw, in one of his out-buildings, where, covered with his own blanket, John continued for the remainder of the night.

In the mean time, Major Hartmann began to grow noisy and jocular; glass succeeded glass, and mug after mug was introduced, until the carousal had run deep into the night, or rather morning; when the veteran German expressed an inclination to return to the Mansion-house. Most of the party had already retired, but Marmaduke knew the habits of his friend too well to suggest an earlier adjournment. So soon, however, as the proposal was made, the Judge eagerly availed himself of it, and the trio prepared to depart. Mrs. Hollister attended them to the door in person, cautioning her guests as to the safest manner of leaving her premises.

"Lane on Mister Jones, Major," said she, "he's young, and will be a support to ye. Well, it's a charming sight to see ye, any way, at the Bould Dragoon; and sure it's no harm to be kaping a Christmas-eve wid a light heart, for it's no telling when we may have sorrow come upon us. So good night Joodge, and a merry Christmas to ye all, to-morrow morning."

The gentlemen made their adieus as well as they could, and taking the middle of the road, which was a fine, wide, and well-beaten path, they did tolerably well until they reached the gate of the Mansion-house; but on entering the Judge's domains, they encountered some slight difficulties. We shall not stop to relate them, but will just mention that, in the morning, sundry diverging paths were to be seen in the snow; and that once during their progress to the door, Marmaduke, missing his companions, was enabled to trace them by one of these paths to a spot, where he discovered them with nothing visible but their heads; Richard singing in a most vivacious strain,

"Come let us be jolly,
And cast away folly,
For grief turns a black head to gray."

Chapter XV

"As she lay, on that day, in the Bay of Biscay, O!"
Anon., "The Bay of Biscay, O." ll. 15–16.

PREVIOUSLY TO the occurrence of the scene at the "Bold Dragoon," Elizabeth had been safely reconducted to the Mansion-house, where she was left, as its mistress, either to amuse or employ herself during the evening, as best suited her own inclinations. Most of the lights were extinguished; but as Benjamin adjusted, with great care and regularity, four large candles, in as many massive candlesticks of brass, in a row on the sideboard, the hall possessed a peculiar air of comfort and warmth, contrasted with the cheerless aspect of the room she had left, in the academy.

Remarkable had been one of the listeners to Mr. Grant, and returned with her resentment, which had been not a little excited by the language of the Judge, somewhat softened by reflection and the worship. She recollected the youth of Elizabeth, and thought it no difficult task, under present appearances, to exercise that power indirectly, which hitherto she had enjoyed undisputed. The idea of being governed, or of being compelled to pay the deference of servitude, was absolutely intolerable; and she had already determined within herself, some half-dozen times, to make an effort, that should at once bring to an issue the delicate point of her domestic condition. But as often as she met the dark, proud eye of Elizabeth, who was walking up and down the apartment, musing on the scenes of her youth, and the change in her condition, and perhaps the events of the day, the housekeeper experienced an awe, that she would not own to herself could be excited by any thing mortal. It, however, checked her advances, and for some time held her tongue-tied. At length she determined to commence the discourse, by entering on a subject that was apt to level all human distinctions, and in which she might display her own abilities.

"It was quite a wordy sarmont that Parson Grant give us to-night," said Remarkable.—"Them church ministers be commonly smart sarmonizers; but they write down their idees, which is a great privilege. I don't think that by nater they are as tonguey speakers for an off-hand discourse, as the standing-order ministers."

"And what denomination do you distinguish as the standing-order?" inquired Miss Temple, with some surprise.

"Why, the Presbyterans, and Congregationals, and Baptists too, for-ti-'now, and all sich as don't go on their knees to prayer."

"By that rule, then, you would call those who belong to the persuasion of my father, the sitting-order," observed Elizabeth.

"I'm sure I've never heer'n 'em spoken of by any other name than Quakers, so called," returned Remarkable, betraying a slight uneasiness. "I should be the last to call them otherwise, for I never in my life used a disparaging tarm of the Judge, or any of his family. I've always set store by the Quakers, they are so pretty-spoken, clever people; and it's a wonderment to me, how your father come to marry into a church family, for they are as contrary in religion as can be. One sits still, and for the most part, says nothing, while the church folks practyse all kinds of ways, so that I sometimes think it quite moosical to see them; for I went to a church-meeting once before, down country."

"You have found an excellence in the church liturgy, that has hitherto escaped me. I will thank you to inquire whether the fire in my room burns; I feel fatigued with my journey, and will retire."

Remarkable felt a wonderful inclination to tell the young mistress of the mansion, that by opening a door she might see for herself; but prudence got the better of resentment, and after pausing some little time, as a salve to her dignity, she did as desired. The report was favourable, and the young lady, wishing Benjamin, who was filling the stove with wood, and the housekeeper, each a good night, withdrew.

The instant the door closed on Miss Temple, Remarkable commenced a sort of mysterious, ambiguous discourse, that was neither abusive nor commendatory of the qualities of the absent personage; but which seemed to be drawing nigh, by regular degrees, to a most dissatisfied description. The Major-domo made no reply, but continued his occupation with great industry, which being happily completed, he took a look at the thermometer, and then, opening a drawer of the sideboard, he produced a supply of stimulants, that would have served to keep the warmth in his system, without the aid of the enormous fire he had been building. A small stand was drawn up near the stove, and the bottles and the glasses necessary for convenience, were quietly arranged. Two chairs were placed by the side of this comfortable situation, when Benjamin, for the first time, appeared to observe his companion.

"Come," he cried, "come, Mistress Remarkable, bring yourself to an anchor in this chair. It's a peeler without, I can tell you, good woman; but what cares I, blow high or blow low, d'ye see, it's all the same thing to Ben. The niggers are snug stowed below, before a fire that would roast an ox whole. The thermometer stands now at fifty-five, but if there's any vartue in good maple wood, I'll weather upon it, before one glass, as much as ten points more, so that the Squire, when he comes home from Betty Hollister's warm room, will feel as hot as a hand that has given the rigging a lick with bad tar. Come, Mistress, bring up in this here chair, and tell me how you like our new heiress."

"Why, to my notion, Mr. Penguillum—"

"Pump—Pump," interrupted Benjamin, "it's Christmas-eve, Mistress Remarkable, and so d'ye see, you had better call me Pump. It's a shorter name, and as I mean to pump this here decanter till it sucks, why you may as well call me Pump."

"Did you ever!" cried Remarkable, with a laugh that seemed to unhinge every joint in her body; "You're a moosical creater, Benjamin, when the notion takes you. But as I was saying, I rather guess that times will be altered now in this house."

"Altered!" exclaimed the Major-domo, eyeing the bottle, that was assuming the clear aspect of cut glass with astonishing rapidity; "it don't matter much, Mistress Remarkable, so long as I keep the keys of the lockers in my pocket."

"I can't say," continued the housekeeper, "but there's good eatables and drinkables enough in the house for a body's content—a little more sugar, Benjamin, in the glass—for Squire

Jones is an excellent provider. But new lords, new laws; and I shouldn't wonder if you and I had an unsartain time on't in footer."

"Life is as unsartain as the wind that blows," said Benjamin with a moralizing air; "and nothing is more varible than the wind, Mistress Remarkable, unless you happen to fall in with the trades, d'ye see, and then you may run for the matter of a month at a time, with studding-sails on both sides, alow and aloft, and with the cabin-boy at the wheel."

"I know that life is disp'ut unsartain," said Remarkable, compressing her features to the humour of her companion; "but I expect there will be great changes made in the house to rights; and that you will find a young man put over your head, as there is one that wants to be over mine; and after having been settled as long as you have, Benjamin, I should judge that to be hard."

"Promotion should go according to length of sarvice," said the Major-domo, "and if-so-be that they ship a hand for my berth, or place a new steward aft, I shall throw up my commission in less time than you can put a pilot-boat in stays. Thof Squire Dickens"—this was a common misnomer with Benjamin—"is a nice gentleman, and as good a man to sail with as heart could wish, yet I shall tell the Squire, d'ye see, in plain English, and that's my native tongue, that if-so-be he is thinking of putting any Johnny-raw over my head, why I shall resign. I began forrard, Mistress Pretty-bones, and worked my way aft, like a man. I was six months aboard a Garnsey lugger, hauling in the slack of the lee-sheet, and coiling up rigging. From that I went a few trips in a fore-and-after, in the same trade, which after all, was but a blind kind of sailing in the dark, where a man larns but little, excepting how to steer by the stars. Well! then d'ye see, I larnt how a topmast should be slushed, and how a top-gallant-sail was to be becketted; and then I did small jobs in the cabin, sich as mixing the skipper's grog. 'Twas there I got my taste, which you must have often seen, is excellent.—Well, here's better acquaintance to us."

Remarkable nodded a return to the compliment, and took a sip of the beverage before her; for, provided it was well sweetened, she had no objection to a small potation now and then. After this observance of courtesy between the worthy couple, the dialogue proceeded.

"You have had great experunces in life, Benjamin; for, as the scripter says, 'they that go down to the sea in ships see the works of the Lord.' "

"Ay! for that matter, they in brigs and schooners too; and it mought say the works of the devil. The sea, Mistress Remarkable, is a great advantage to a man, in the way of knowledge, for he sees the fashions of nations, and the shape of a country. Now, I suppose, for myself here, who is but an unlarned man to some that follows the seas, I suppose that, taking the coast from Cape Ler-Hogue as low down as Cape Finish-there, there isn't so much as a head-land, or an island, that I don't know either the name of it, or something more or less about it. Take enough, woman, to colour the water. Here's sugar. It's a sweet tooth, that fellow that you hold on upon yet, Mistress Pretty-bones. But as I was saying, take the whole coast along, I know it as well as the way from here to the Bold Dragoon; and a devil of an acquaintance is that Bay of Biscay. Whew! I wish you could but hear the wind blow there. It sometimes takes two to hold one man's hair on his head. Scudding through the Bay is pretty much the same thing as travelling the roads in this country, up one side of a mountain, and down the other."

"Do tell!" exclaimed Remarkable, "and doos the sea run as high as mountains, Benjamin?"

"Well I will tell; but first let's taste the grog.—Hem! it's the right kind of stuff, I must say, that you keeps in this country; but then you're so close aboard the West Indees, you make but a small run of it. By the Lord Harry, woman, if Garnsey only lay somewhere between Cape Hatteras and the Bite of Logann, but you'd see rum cheap. As to the seas, they runs more in lippers in the Bay of Biscay, unless it may be in a sow-wester, when they tumble about quite handsomely; thof it's not in the narrow sea that you are to look for a swell; just go off the Western Islands, in a westerly blow, keeping the land on your larboard hand, with the ship's head to the south'ard, and bring to, under a close-reef'd topsail; or mayhap a reef'd foresail, with a fore-topmast staysail; and mizzen staysail, to keep her up to the sea, if she will bear it; and lay there for the matter of two watches, if you want to see mountains. Why, good woman, I've been off there in the Boadishey frigate, when you could see nothing but some such matter as a piece of sky, mayhap, as big as the mainsail; and then again, there was a hole under your lee-quarter, big enough to hold the whole British navy."

"Oh! for massy's sake! and wa'nt you afeard, Benjamin? and how did you get off?"

"Afeard! who the devil do you think was to be frightened at a little salt water tumbling about his head? As for getting off, when we had enough of it, and had washed our decks down pretty well, we called all hands, for d'ye see, the watch below was in their hammocks, all the same as if they were in one of your best bed-rooms; and so we watched for a smooth time; clapt her helm hard a-weather, let fall the foresail, and got the tack aboard; and so, when we got her afore it, I ask you, Mistress Pretty-bones, if she didn't walk? didn't she! I'm no liar, good woman, when I say that I saw that ship jump from the top of one sea to another, just like one of these squirrels, that can fly, jumps from tree to tree."

"What, clean out of the water!" exclaimed Remarkable, lifting her two lank arms, with their bony hands spread in astonishment.

"It was no such easy matter to get out of the water, good woman, for the spray flew so that you couldn't tell which was sea and which was cloud. So there we kept her afore it, for the matter of two glasses. The First Lieutenant he cun'd the ship himself, and there was four quarter-masters at the wheel, besides the master, with six forecastle men in the gun-room, at the relieving tackles. But then she behaved herself so well! Oh! she was a sweet ship, mistress! That one frigate was well worth more, to live in, than the best house in the island. If I was King of England, I'd have her hauled up above Lon'on bridge, and fit her up for a palace; because why? If any body can afford to live comfortably, his majesty can."

"Well! but Benjamin," cried the listener, who was in an ecstasy of astonishment, at this relation of the steward's dangers, "what *did* you do?"

"Do! why we did our duty, like hearty fellows. Now, if the countrymen of Mounsheer Ler Quaw had been aboard of her, they would have just struck her ashore on some of them small islands; but we run along the land until we found her dead to leeward off the mountains of Pico, and dam'me if I know to this day how we got there, whether we jumped over the island, or hauled round it: but there we was, and there we lay, under easy sail, fore-reaching, first upon one tack and then upon t'other, so as to poke her nose out now and then, and take a look to wind'ard, till the gale blow'd its pipe out."

"I wonder now!" exclaimed Remarkable, to whom most of the terms used by Benjamin were perfectly unintelligible, but who had got a confused idea of a raging tempest; "it must be an awful life, that going to sea! and I don't feel astonishment that you're so affronted with the thoughts of being forced to quit a comfortable home like this. Not that a body cares much for't, as there's more housen than one to live in. Why, when the Judge agreed with me to come and live with him, I'd no more notion of stopping any time, than any thing. I happened in, just to see how the family did, about a week after Miss Temple died, thinking to be back home agin night; but the family was in sich a distressed way, that I couldn't but stop awhile and help 'em on. I thought the sitooation a good one, seeing that I was an unmarried body, and they was so much in want of help; so I tarried."

"And a long time have you left your anchors down in the same place, mistress; I think you must find that the ship rides easy."

"How you talk, Benjamin! there's no believing a word you say. I must say that the Judge and Squire Jones have both acted quite clever, so long; but I see that now we shall have a spicimin to the contrary. I heer'n say that the Judge was gone a great 'broad, and that he meant to bring his darter hum, but I didn't calcoolate on sich carrins on. To my notion, Benjamin, she's likely to turn out a disp'ut ugly gall."

"Ugly!" echoed the Major-domo, opening eyes, that were beginning to close in a very suspicious sleepiness, in wide amazement; "by the Lord Harry, woman, I should as soon think of calling the Boadishey a clumsy frigate. What the devil would you have? arn't her eyes as bright as the morning and evening stars! and isn't her hair as black and glistening as rigging that has just had a lick of tar! doesn't she move as stately as a first-rate in smooth water, on a bow line! Why, woman, the figure-head of the Boadishey was a fool to her, and that, as I've often heard the captain say, was an image of a great Queen; and arn't Queens always comely, woman? for who do you think would be a King, and not choose a handsome bed-fellow?"

"Talk decent, Benjamin," said the housekeeper, "or I won't keep your company. I don't gainsay her being comely to look on, but I will maintain that she's likely to show poor conduct. She seems to think herself too good to talk to a body. From what Squire Jones had tell'd me, I some expected to be quite captivated by her company. Now, to my reckoning, Lowizy Grant is much more pritty behaved than Betsy Temple. She wouldn't so much as hold discourse with me, when I wanted to ask her how she felt, on coming home and missing her mammy."

"Perhaps she didn't understand you, woman; you are none of the best linguister, and then Miss Lizzy has been exercising the King's English under a great Lon'on lady, and, for that matter, can talk the language almost as well as myself, or any native born British subject. You've forgot your schooling, and the young mistress is a great scollard."

"Mistress!" cried Remarkable; "don't make one out to be a nigger, Benjamin. She's no mistress of mine, and never will be. And as to speech, I hold myself as second to nobody out of New-England. I was born and raised in Essex county, and I've always heer'n say, that the Bay State was provarbal for pronounsation."

"I've often heard of that Bay of State," said Benjamin, "but can't say that I've ever been in it, nor do I know exactly where away it is that it lays; but I suppose there's good anchorage in it, and that it's no bad place for the taking of ling; but for size, it can't be so much as a yawl to a sloop of war, compared with the Bay of Biscay, or mayhap, Tor-bay. And as for language, if you want to hear dictionary overhauled, like a log-line in a blow, you must go to Wapping, and listen to the Lon'oners, as they deal out their lingo. Howsomever, I see no such mighty matter that Miss Lizzy has been doing to you, good woman, so take another drop of your brew, and forgive and forget, like an honest soul."

"No, indeed! and I shan't do sich a thing, Benjamin. This treatment is a newity to me, and what I won't put up with. I have a hundred and fifty dollars at use, besides a bed and twenty sheep, to good; and I don't crave to live in a house where a body musn't call a young woman by her given name to her face. I *will* call her Betsy as much as I please; it's a free country, and no one can stop me. I did intend to stop while summer, but I shall quit to-morrow morning; and I will talk just as I please."

"For that matter, Mistress Remarkable," said Benjamin, "there's none here who will contradict you, for I'm of opinion that it would be as easy to stop a hurricane with a Barcelony hankerchy, as to bring up your tongue, when the stopper is off. I say, good woman, do they grow many monkeys along the shores of that Bay of State?"

"You're a monkey yourself, Mr. Penguillum," cried the enraged housekeeper, "or a bear! a black, beastly bear! and an't fit for a decent woman to stay with. I'll never keep your company agin, sir, if I should live thirty years with the Judge. Sitch talk is more befitting the kitchen than the keeping-room of a house of one who is well to do in the world."

"Look you, Mistress Pitty—Patty—Pretty-bones, mayhap I'm some such matter as a bear, as they will find who come to grapple with me; but dam'me if I'm a monkey—a thing that chatters without knowing a word of what it says—a parrot, that will hold dialogue, for what an honest man knows, in a dozen languages; mayhap in the Bay of State lingo; mayhap in Greek or High Dutch. But dost it know what it means itself? canst answer me that, good woman? Your Midshipman can sing out, and pass the word, when the Captain gives the order, but just set him adrift by himself, and let him work the ship of his own head, and, stop my grog, if you don't find all the Johnny-raws laughing at him."

"Stop your grog indeed!" said Remarkable, rising with great indignation, and seizing a candle; "you're groggy now, Benjamin, and I'll quit the room before I hear any misbecoming words from you."

The housekeeper retired, with a manner but little less dignified, as she thought, than the air of the heiress, muttering, as she drew the door after her, with a noise like the report of a musket, the opprobrious terms of "drunkard," "sot," and "beast."

"Who's that you say is drunk?" cried Benjamin, fiercely, rising and making a movement towards Remarkable. "You talk of mustering yourself with a lady! you're just fit to grumble and find fault. Where the devil should you larn behaviour and dictionary? in your damn'd Bay of State, ha!"

Benjamin here fell back in his chair, and soon gave vent to certain ominous sounds, which resembled, not a little, the growling of his favourite animal, the bear itself. Before, however, he was quite locked, to use the language that would suit the Della-cruscan humour of certain refined minds of the present day, "in the arms of Morpheus," he spoke aloud, observing due pauses between his epithets, the impressive terms of "monkey," "parrot," "pic-nic," "tar-pot," and "linguisters."

We shall not attempt to explain his meaning, nor connect his sentences, and our readers must be satisfied with our informing them, that they were expressed with all that coolness of contempt that a man might well be supposed to feel for a monkey.

Nearly two hours passed in this sleep, before the Major-domo was awakened by the noisy entrance of Richard, Major Hartmann, and the master of the mansion. Benjamin so far rallied his confused faculties, as to shape the course of the two former to their respective apartments, when he disappeared himself, leaving the task of securing the house to him who was most interested in its safety. Locks and bars were but little attended to, in the early day of that settlement; and so soon as Marmaduke had given an eye to the enormous fires of his dwelling, he retired. With this act of prudence closes the first night of our tale.

Chapter XVI

"*Watch.* (*aside.*) Some treason, masters—
Yet stand close."
Much Ado about Nothing, III.iii.106–7.

IT WAS FORTUNATE for more than one of the bacchanalians, who left the "Bold Dragoon" late in the evening, that the severe cold of the season was becoming, rapidly, less dangerous, as they threaded the different mazes, through the snow-banks, that led to their respective dwellings. Thin, driving clouds began, towards morning, to flit across the heavens, and the moon set behind a volume of vapour, that was impelled furiously towards the north, carrying with it the softer atmosphere from the distant ocean. The rising sun was obscured by denser and increasing columns of clouds, while the southerly wind that rushed up the valley, brought the never-failing symptoms of a thaw.

It was quite late in the morning, before Elizabeth, observing the faint glow which appeared on the eastern mountain, long after the light of the sun had struck the opposite hills, ventured from the house, with a view to gratify her curiosity with a glance by daylight at the surrounding objects, before the tardy revellers of the Christmas-eve should make their appearance at the breakfast-table. While she was drawing the folds of her pelisse more closely around her form, to guard against a cold that was yet great, though rapidly yielding, in the small enclosure that opened in the rear of the house on a little thicket of low pines, that were springing up where trees of a mightier growth had lately stood, she was surprised at the voice of Mr. Jones.

"Merry Christmas, merry Christmas to you, cousin Bess," he shouted. "Ah, ha! an early riser, I see; but I knew I should steal a march on you. I never was in a house yet, where I didn't get the first Christmas greeting on every soul in it, man, woman and child; great and small; black, white and yellow. But stop a minute, till I can just slip on my coat; you are about to look at the improvements, I see, which no one can explain so well as I, who planned them all. It will be an hour before 'duke and the Major can sleep off Mrs. Hollister's confounded distillations, and so I'll come down and go with you."

Elizabeth turned, and observed her cousin in his night-cap, with his head out of his bed-room window, where his zeal for pre-eminence, in defiance of the weather, had impelled him to thrust it. She laughed, and promising to wait for his company, re-entered the house, making her appearance again, holding in her hand a packet that was secured by several large and important seals, just in time to meet the gentleman.

"Come, Bessy, come," he cried, drawing one of her arms through his own; "the snow begins to give, but it will bear us yet. Don't you snuff old Pennsylvania in the very air? This is a vile climate, girl; now at sunset last evening it was cold enough to freeze a man's zeal, and that, I can tell you, takes a thermometer near zero for me; then about nine or ten it began to moderate; at twelve it was quite mild, and here all the rest of the night I have been so hot as not to bear a blanket on the bed.—Holla! Aggy!—merry Christmas, Aggy—I say, do you hear me, you black dog! there's a dollar for you; and if the gentlemen get up before I come back, do you come out and let me know. I wouldn't have 'duke get the start of me for the worth of your head."

The black caught the money from the snow, and promising a due degree of watchfulness, he gave the dollar a whirl of twenty feet in the air, and catching it as it fell, in the palm of his hand, he withdrew to the kitchen, to exhibit his present, with a heart as light as his face was happy in its expression.

"Oh, rest easy, my dear coz," said the young lady; "I took a look in at my father, who is likely to sleep an hour; and by using due vigilance you will secure all the honours of the season."

"Why, 'duke is your father, Elizabeth, but 'duke is a man who likes to be foremost, even in trifles. Now, as for myself, I care for no such things, except in the way of competition; for a thing which is of no moment in itself, may be made of importance in the way of competition. So it is with your father, he loves to be first; but I only struggle with him as a competitor."

"It's all very clear, sir," said Elizabeth; "you would not care a fig for distinction, if there were no one in the world but yourself; but as there happen to be a great many others, why you must struggle with them all—in the way of competition."

"Exactly so; I see you are a clever girl, Bess, and one who does credit to her masters. It was my plan to send you to that school; for when your father first mentioned the thing, I wrote a private letter for advice to a judicious friend in the city, who recommended the very school you went to. 'Duke was a little obstinate at first, as usual, but when he heard the truth, he was obliged to send you."

"Well, a truce to 'duke's foibles, sir; he is my father; and if you knew what he has been doing for you while we were in Albany, you would deal more tenderly with his character."

"For me!" cried Richard, pausing a moment in his walk to reflect. "Oh! he got the plans of the new Dutch meeting-house for me, I suppose; but I care very little about it, for a man, of a certain kind of talent, is seldom aided by any foreign suggestions; his own brain is the best architect."

"No such thing," said Elizabeth, looking provokingly knowing.

"No! let me see—perhaps he had my name put in the bill for the new turnpike, as a director?"

"He might possibly; but it is not to such an appointment that I allude."

"Such an appointment!" repeated Mr. Jones, who began to fidget with curiosity; "then it is an appointment. If it is in the militia, I won't take it."

"No, no, it is not in the militia," cried Elizabeth, showing the packet in her hand, and then drawing it back, with a coquettish air; "it is an office of both honour and emolument."

"Honour and emolument!" echoed Richard, in painful suspense; "show me the paper, girl. Say, is it an office where there is any thing to *do*?"

"You have hit it, cousin Dickon; it is the executive office of the county; at least so said my father, when he gave me this packet to offer you as a Christmas box—'Surely, if any thing will please Dickon,' he said, 'it will be to fill the executive chair of the county.' "

"Executive chair! what nonsense!" cried the impatient gentleman, snatching the packet from her hand; "there is no such office in the county. Eh! what! it is, I declare, a commission, appointing Richard Jones, Esquire, Sheriff of the county. Well, this is kind in 'duke, positively. I must say 'duke has a warm heart, and never forgets his friends. Sheriff! High Sheriff of—! It sounds well, Bess, but it shall execute better. 'Duke is a judicious man, after all, and knows human nature thoroughly. I'm sure I'm much obliged to him," continued Richard, using the skirt of his coat, unconsciously, to wipe his eyes; "though I would do as much for him any day, as he shall see, if I can have an opportunity to perform any of the duties of my office on him. It shall be well done, cousin Bess—it shall be well done I say.—How this cursed south wind makes one's eyes water."

"Now, Richard," said the laughing maiden, "now I think you will find something to do. I have often heard you complain of old, that there was nothing to do in this new country, while to my eyes, it seemed as if every thing remained to be done."

"Do!" echoed Richard, who blew his nose, raised his little form to its greatest elevation, and looked serious. "Every thing depends on system, girl. I shall sit down this afternoon, and systematize the county. I must have deputies, you know. I will divide the county into districts, over which I will place my deputies; and I will have one for the village, which I will call my home department. Let me see—oh! Benjamin! yes, Benjamin will make a good deputy; he has been naturalized, and would answer admirably, if he could only ride on horseback."

"Yes, Mr. Sheriff," said his companion, "and as he understands ropes so well, he would be very expert, should occasion happen for his services, in another way."

"No," interrupted the other, "I flatter myself that no man could hang a man better than—that is—ha—oh! yes, Benjamin would do extremely well, in such an unfortunate dilemma, if he could be persuaded to attempt it. But I should despair of the thing. I never could induce him to hang, or teach him to ride on horseback. I must seek another deputy."

"Well, sir, as you have abundant leisure for all these important affairs, I beg that you will forget that you are High

Sheriff, and devote some little of your time to gallantry. Where are the beauties and improvements which you were to show me?"

"Where! why every where. Here I have laid out some new streets; and when they are opened, and the trees felled, and they are all built up, will they not make a fine town? Well, 'duke is a liberal-hearted fellow, with all his stubbornness.—Yes, yes, I must have at least four deputies, besides a jailer."

"I see no streets in the direction of our walk," said Elizabeth, "unless you call the short avenues through these pine bushes by that name. Surely you do not contemplate building houses, very soon, in that forest before us, and in those swamps."

"We must run our streets by the compass, coz, and disregard trees, hills, ponds, stumps, or, in fact, any thing but posterity. Such is the will of your father, and your father, you know—"

"Had you made Sheriff, Mr. Jones," interrupted the lady, with a tone that said very plainly to the gentleman, that he was touching a forbidden subject.

"I know it, I know it," cried Richard; "and if it were in my power, I'd make 'duke a king. He is a noble-hearted fellow, and would make an excellent king; that is, if he had a good prime minister.—But who have we here? voices in the bushes;—a combination about mischief, I'll wager my commission. Let us draw near, and examine a little into the matter."

During this dialogue, as the parties had kept in motion, Richard and his cousin advanced some distance from the house, into the open space in the rear of the village, where, as may be gathered from the conversation, streets were planned and future dwellings contemplated; but where, in truth, the only mark of improvement that was to be seen, was a neglected clearing along the skirt of a dark forest of mighty pines, over which the bushes or sprouts of the same tree had sprung up, to a height that interspersed the fields of snow with little thickets of evergreen. The rushing of the wind, as it whistled through the tops of these mimic trees, prevented the footsteps of the pair from being heard, while the branches concealed their persons. Thus aided, the listeners drew nigh to a spot where the young hunter, Leather-stocking and the

Indian chief were collected in an earnest consultation. The former was urgent in his manner, and seemed to think the subject of deep importance, while Natty appeared to listen with more than his usual attention, to what the other was saying. Mohegan stood a little on one side, with his head sunken on his chest, his hair falling forward, so as to conceal most of his features, and his whole attitude expressive of deep dejection, if not of shame.

"Let us withdraw," whispered Elizabeth; "we are intruders, and can have no right to listen to the secrets of these men."

"No right!" returned Richard, a little impatiently, in the same tone, and drawing her arm so forcibly through his own as to prevent her retreat; "you forget, cousin, that it is my duty to preserve the peace of the county, and see the laws executed. These wanderers frequently commit depredations; though I do not think John would do any thing secretly. Poor fellow! he was quite boozy last night, and hardly seems to be over it yet. Let us draw nigher, and hear what they say."

Notwithstanding the lady's reluctance, Richard, stimulated doubtless by his nice sense of duty, prevailed; and they were soon so near as distinctly to hear sounds.

"The bird must be had," said Natty, "by fair means or foul. Heigho! I've known the time, lad, when the wild turkeys wasn't over scarce in the country; though you must go into the Virginy gaps, if you want them now. To be sure, there is a different taste to a partridge, and a well-fatted turkey; though, to my eating, beaver's tail and bear's hams makes the best of food. But then every one has his own appetite. I gave the last farthing, all to that shilling, to the French trader, this very morning, as I come through the town, for powder; so, as you have nothing, we can have but one shot for it. I know that Billy Kirby is out, and means to have a pull of the trigger at that very turkey. John has a true eye for a single fire, and somehow, my hand shakes so, whenever I have to do any thing extrawnary, that I often lose my aim. Now when I killed the she-bear this fall, with her cubs, though they were so mighty ravenous, I knocked them over one at a shot, and loaded while I dodged the trees in the bargain; but this is a very different thing, Mr. Oliver."

"This," cried the young man, with an accent that sounded as if he took a bitter pleasure in his poverty, while he held a shilling up before his eyes—"this is all the treasure that I possess—this and my rifle! Now, indeed, I have become a man of the woods, and must place my sole dependence on the fruits of the chase. Come, Natty, let us stake the last penny for the bird; with your aim, it cannot fail to be successful."

"I would rather it should be John, lad; my heart jumps into my mouth, because you set your mind so much on't; and I'm sartain that I shall miss the bird. Them Indians can shoot one time as well as another; nothing ever troubles them. I say, John, here's a shilling; take my rifle, and get a shot at the big turkey they've put up at the stump. Mr. Oliver is over anxious for the creater, and I'm sure to do nothing when I have over anxiety about it."

The Indian turned his head gloomily, and after looking keenly for a moment, in profound silence, at his companions, he replied—

"When John was young, eyesight was not straighter than his bullet. The Mingo squaws cried out at the sound of his rifle. The Mingo warriors were made squaws. When did he ever shoot twice! The eagle went above the clouds, when he passed the wigwam of Chingachgook; his feathers were plenty with the women.—But see," he said, raising his voice from the low, mournful tones in which he had spoken, to a pitch of keen excitement, and stretching forth both hands—"they shake like a deer at the wolf's howl. Is John old? When was a Mohican a squaw, with seventy winters! No! the white man brings old age with him—rum is his tomahawk!"

"Why then do you use it, old man?" exclaimed the young hunter; "why will one so noble by nature, aid the devices of the devil, by making himself a beast!"

"Beast! is John a beast?" replied the Indian, slowly; "yes; you say no lie, child of the Fire-eater! John is a beast. The smokes were once few in these hills. The deer would lick the hand of a white man, and the birds rest on his head. They were strangers to him. My fathers came from the shores of the salt lake. They fled before rum. They came to their grandfather, and they lived in peace; or when they did raise the hatchet, it was to strike it into the brain of a Mingo. They gathered around the council-fire, and what they said was done. Then John was the man. But warriors and traders with light eyes followed them. One brought the long knife, and one brought rum. They were more than the pines on the mountains; and they broke up the councils, and took the lands. The evil spirit was in their jugs, and they let him loose.—Yes, yes—you say no lie, Young Eagle, John is a Christian beast."

"Forgive me, old warrior," cried the youth, grasping his hand; "I should be the last to reproach you. The curses of Heaven light on the cupidity that has destroyed such a race. Remember, John, that I am of your family, and it is now my greatest pride."

The muscles of Mohegan relaxed a little, and he said more mildly—

"You are a Delaware, my son; your words are not heard.—John cannot shoot."

"I thought that lad had Indian blood in him," whispered Richard, "by the awkward way he handled my horses, last night. You see, coz, they never use harness. But the poor fellow shall have two shots at the turkey, if he wants it, for I'll give him another shilling myself; though, perhaps, I had better offer to shoot for him. They have got up their Christmas sports, I find, in the bushes yonder, where you hear the laughter;—though it is a queer taste this chap has for turkey; not but what it is good eating too."

"Hold, cousin Richard," exclaimed Elizabeth, clinging to his arm, " would it be delicate to offer a shilling to that gentleman?"

"Gentleman again! do you think a half-breed, like him, will refuse money? No, no, girl; he will take the shilling; ay! and even rum too, notwithstanding he moralizes so much about it.—But I'll give the lad a chance for his turkey, for that Billy Kirby is one of the best marksmen in the country; that is, if we except the—the gentleman."

"Then," said Elizabeth, who found her strength unequal to her will, "then, sir, I will speak."—She advanced, with an air of determination, in front of her cousin, and entered the little circle of bushes that surrounded the trio of hunters. Her appearance startled the youth, who at first made an unequivocal motion towards retiring, but, recollecting himself, bowed, by lifting his cap, and resumed his attitude of leaning on his rifle. Neither Natty nor Mohegan betrayed any emotion, though the appearance of Elizabeth was so entirely unexpected.

"I find," she said, "that the old Christmas sport of shooting the turkey is yet in use among you. I feel inclined to try my chance for a bird. Which of you will take this money, and, after paying my fee, give me the aid of his rifle?"

"Is this a sport for a lady!" exclaimed the young hunter, with an emphasis that could not well be mistaken, and with a rapidity that showed he spoke without consulting any thing but feeling.

"Why not, sir? If it be inhuman, the sin is not confined to one sex only. But I have my humour as well as others. I ask not your assistance; but"—turning to Natty, and dropping a dollar in his hand—"this old veteran of the forest will not be so ungallant, as to refuse one fire for a lady."

Leather-stocking dropped the money into his pouch, and throwing up the end of his rifle, he freshened his priming; and, first laughing in his usual manner, he threw the piece over his shoulder, and said—

"If Billy Kirby don't get the bird before me, and the Frenchman's powder don't hang fire this damp morning, you'll see as fine a turkey dead, in a few minutes, as ever was eaten in the Judge's shanty. I have know'd the Dutch women on the Mohawk and Scoharie count greatly on coming to the merry-makings; and so, lad, you shouldn't be short with the lady. Come, let us go forward, for if we wait, the finest bird will be gone."

"But I have a right before you, Natty, and shall try my own luck first. You will excuse me, Miss Temple; I have much reason to wish that bird, and may seem ungallant, but I must claim my privileges."

"Claim any thing that is justly your own, sir," returned the lady; "we are both adventurers, and this is my knight. I trust my fortune to his hand and eye. Lead on, Sir Leather-stocking, and we will follow."

Natty, who seemed pleased with the frank address of the young and beauteous Elizabeth, who had so singularly intrusted him with such a commission, returned the bright smile with which she had addressed him, by his own peculiar mark of mirth, and moved across the snow, towards the spot whence the sounds of boisterous mirth proceeded, with the long strides of a hunter. His companions followed in silence, the youth casting frequent and uneasy glances towards Elizabeth, who was detained by a motion from Richard.

"I should think, Miss Temple," he said, so soon as the others were out of hearing, "that if you really wished a turkey, you would not have taken a stranger for the office, and such a one as Leather-stocking. But I can hardly believe that you are serious, for I have fifty at this moment shut up in the coops, in every stage of fat, so that you might choose any quality you pleased. There are six that I am trying an experiment on, by giving them brick-bats with—"

"Enough, cousin Dickon," interrupted the lady; "I do wish the bird, and it is because I so wish, that I commissioned this Mr. Leather-stocking."

"Did you ever hear of the great shot that I made at the wolf, cousin Elizabeth, who was carrying off your father's sheep?" said Richard, drawing himself up into an air of displeasure.—"He had the sheep on his back; and had the head of the wolf been on the other side, I should have killed him dead; as it was—"

"You killed the sheep,—I know it all, dear coz. But would it have been decorous, for the High Sheriff of—— to mingle in such sports as these?"

"Surely you did not think I intended actually to fire with my own hands?" said Mr. Jones.—"But let us follow, and see the shooting. There is no fear of any thing unpleasant occurring to a female, in this new country, especially to your father's daughter, and in my presence."

"My father's daughter fears nothing, sir, more especially, when escorted by the highest executive officer in the county."

She took his arm, and he led her through the mazes of the bushes, to the spot where most of the young men of the village were collected for the sports of shooting a Christmas match, and whither Natty and his companions had already preceded them.

Chapter XVII

"I guess, by all this quaint array,
The burghers hold their sports to-day."
Scott, *The Lady of the Lake*, V.xx.31–32.

THE ANCIENT amusement of shooting the Christmas turkey, is one of the few sports that the settlers of a new country seldom or never neglect to observe. It was connected with the daily practices of a people, who often laid aside the axe or the sithe, to seize the rifle, as the deer glided through the forests they were felling, or the bear entered their rough meadows, to scent the air of a clearing, and to scan, with a look of sagacity, the progress of the invader.

On the present occasion, the usual amusement of the day had been a little hastened, in order to allow a fair opportunity to Mr. Grant, whose exhibition was not less a treat to the young sportsmen, than the one which engaged their present attention. The owner of the birds was a free black, who had prepared for the occasion a collection of game, that was admirably qualified to inflame the appetite of an epicure, and was well adapted to the means and skill of the different competitors, who were of all ages. He had offered to the younger and more humble marksmen divers birds of an inferior quality, and some shooting had already taken place, much to the pecuniary advantage of the sable owner of the game. The order of the sports was extremely simple, and well understood. The bird was fastened by a string to the stump of a large pine, the side of which, towards the point where the marksmen were placed, had been flattened with an axe, in order to serve the purpose of a target, by which the merit of each individual might be ascertained. The distance between the stump and shooting-stand was one hundred measured yards; a foot more or a foot less being thought an invasion of the rights of one of the parties. The negro affixed his own price to every bird, and the terms of the chance; but when these were once established, he was obliged, by the strict principles of public justice that prevailed in the country, to admit any adventurer who chose to offer.

The throng consisted of some twenty or thirty young men, most of whom had rifles, and a collection of all the boys in the village. The little urchins, clad in coarse but warm garments, stood gathered around the more distinguished marksmen, with their hands stuck under their waistbands, listening eagerly to the boastful stories of skill that had been exhibited on former occasions, and were already emulating in their hearts these wonderful deeds in gunnery.

The chief speaker was the man who had been mentioned by Natty, as Billy Kirby. This fellow, whose occupation, when he did labour, was that of clearing lands, or chopping jobs, was of great stature, and carried, in his very air, the index of his character. He was a noisy, boisterous, reckless lad, whose good-natured eye contradicted the bluntness and bullying tenor of his speech. For weeks he would lounge around the taverns of the county, in a state of perfect idleness, or doing small jobs for his liquor and his meals, and cavilling with applicants about the prices of his labour; frequently preferring idleness to an abatement of a tittle of his independence, or a cent in his wages. But when these embarrassing points were satisfactorily arranged, he would shoulder his axe and his rifle, slip his arms through the straps of his pack, and enter the woods with the tread of a Hercules. His first object was to learn his limits, round which he paced, occasionally freshening, with a blow of his axe, the marks on the boundary trees. Then he would proceed, with an air of great deliberation, to the centre of his premises, and throwing aside his superfluous garments, measure, with a knowing eye, one or two of the nearest trees, that were towering apparently into the very clouds, as he gazed upward. Commonly selecting one of the most noble, for the first trial of his power, he approached it with a listless air, whistling a low tune; and wielding his axe, with a certain flourish not unlike the salutes of a fencing-master, he would strike a light blow into the bark, and measure his distance. A pause of a moment was ominous of the fall of the forest, which had flourished there for centuries. The heavy and brisk blows that he struck, were soon succeeded by the thundering report of the tree, as it came, first cracking and threatening, with the separation of its own last ligaments, then threshing and tearing with its branches the tops of its surrounding brethren, and finally meeting the ground, with a shock but little inferior to an earthquake. From that moment, the sounds of the axe were ceaseless, while the falling of the trees was like a distant cannonading; and the daylight broke into the depths of the woods, with the suddenness of a morning in winter.

For days, weeks, nay, months, Billy Kirby would toil, with an ardour that evinced his native spirit, and with an effect that seemed magical; until, his chopping being ended, his stentorian lungs could be heard, emitting sounds, as he called to his patient oxen, which rung through the hills like the cries of an alarm. He had been often heard, on a mild summer's evening, a long mile across the vale of Templeton; the echoes from the mountains taking up his cries, until they died away in feeble sounds, from the distant rocks that overhung the lake. His piles, or, to use the language of the country, his logging, ended, with a despatch that could only accompany his dexterity and Herculean strength, the jobber would collect together his implements of labour, light the heaps of timber, and march away, under the blaze of the prostrate forest, like the conqueror of some city, who, having first prevailed over his adversary, applies the torch as the finishing blow to his conquest. For a long time Billy Kirby would then be seen, sauntering around the taverns, the rider of scrub-races, the bully of cock-fights, and, not unfrequently, the hero of such sports as the one in hand.

Between him and the Leather-stocking there had long existed a jealous rivalry, on the point of skill with the rifle. Notwithstanding the long practice of Natty, it was commonly supposed that the steady nerves and quick eye of the woodchopper, rendered him his equal. The competition had, however, been confined, hitherto, to boastings, and comparisons made from their success in various hunting excursions; but the present occasion was the first time that they had ever come in open collision. A good deal of higgling, about the price of a shot at the choicest bird, had taken place between Billy Kirby and its owner, before Natty and his companions rejoined the sportsmen. It had, however, been settled at one shilling* a shot, which was the highest sum ever exacted, the black taking care to protect himself from losses, as much as possible, by the conditions of the sport. The turkey was already fastened at the "mark," its body being entirely hid by the surrounding snow, nothing being visible but its red, swelling head, and long neck. If the bird was injured by any bullet that struck beneath the snow, it was to continue the property of its present owner; but if a feather was touched in a visible part, the animal became the prize of the successful adventurer.

These terms were loudly proclaimed by the negro, who was seated in the snow, in a somewhat hazardous vicinity to his favourite bird, when Elizabeth, and her cousin approached the noisy sportsmen. The sounds of mirth and contention sensibly lowered at this unexpected visit, but after a moment's pause, the curious interest exhibited in the face of the young lady, together with her smiling air, restored the freedom of the morning; though it was somewhat chastened, both in language and vehemence, by the presence of such a spectator.

"Stand out of the way there, boys," cried the wood-chopper, who was placing himself at the shooting-point—"stand out of the way, you little rascals, or I will shoot through you. Now, Brom, take leave of your turkey."

"Stop!" cried the young hunter; "I am a candidate for a chance. Here is my shilling, Brom; I wish a shot too."

"You may wish it in welcome," cried Kirby; "but if I ruffle the gobbler's feathers, how are you to get it? is money so plenty in your deer-skin pocket, that you pay for a chance you may never have?"

"How know you, sir, how plenty money is in my pocket?" said the youth, fiercely. "Here is my shilling, Brom, and I claim a right to shoot."

"Don't be crabbed, my boy," said the other, who was very coolly fixing his flint. "They say you have a hole in your left shoulder, yourself; so I think Brom may give you a fire for

*Before the revolution each province had its own money of account, though neither coined any but copper pieces. In New York the Spanish dollar was divided into eight shillings, each of the value of a fraction more than sixpence sterling. At present the Union has provided a decimal system, and coins to represent it.

half-price. It will take a keen one to hit that bird, I can tell you, my lad, even if I give you a chance, which is what I have no mind to do."

"Don't be boasting, Billy Kirby," said Natty, throwing the breech of his rifle into the snow, and leaning on its barrel; "you'll get but one shot at the creater, for if the lad misses his aim, which wouldn't be a wonder if he did, with his arm so stiff and sore, you'll find a good piece and an old eye comin a'ter you. Maybe it's true, that I can't shoot as I used to could, but a hundred yards is a short distance for a long rifle."

"What, old Leather-stocking, are you out this morning?" cried his reckless opponent. "Well, fair play's a jewel. I've the lead of you, old fellow; so here goes, for a dry throat or a good dinner."

The countenance of the negro evinced not only all the interest which his pecuniary adventure might occasion, but also the keen excitement that the sport produced in the others, though certainly with a very different wish as to the result. While the wood-chopper was slowly and steadily raising his rifle, he bawled—

"Fair play, Billy Kirby—stand back—make 'em stand back, boys—gib a nigger fair play—poss up, gobbler; shake a head, fool; don't a see 'em taking aim?"

These cries, which were intended as much to distract the attention of the marksman, as for any thing else, were fruitless. The nerves of the wood-chopper were not so easily shaken, and he took his aim with the utmost deliberation. Stillness prevailed for a moment, and he fired. The head of the turkey was seen to dash on one side, and its wings were spread in momentary fluttering; but it settled itself down, calmly, into its bed of snow, and glanced its eyes uneasily around. For a time long enough to draw a deep breath, not a sound was heard. The silence was then broken, by the noise of the negro, who laughed, and shook his body, with all kinds of antics, rolling over in the snow in the excess of delight.

"Well done a gobbler," he cried, jumping up, and affecting to embrace his bird; "I tell 'em to poss up, and you see 'em dodge. Gib anoder shillin, Billy, and hab anoder shot."

"No—the shot is mine," said the young hunter; "you have my money already. Leave the mark, and let me try my luck."

"Ah! it's but money thrown away, lad," said Leather-stocking. "A turkey's head and neck is but a small mark for a new hand and a lame shoulder. You'd best let me take the fire, and maybe we can make some sittlement with the lady about the bird."

"The chance is mine," said the young hunter. "Clear the ground, that I may take it."

The discussions and disputes concerning the last shot were now abating, it having been determined, that if the turkey's head had been any where but just where it was at the moment, the bird must certainly have been killed. There was not much excitement produced by the preparations of the youth, who proceeded in a hurried manner to take his aim, and was in the act of pulling the trigger, when he was stopped by Natty.

"Your hand shakes, lad," he said, "and you seem over eager. Bullet wownds are apt to weaken flesh, and, to my judgment, you'll not shoot so well as in common. If you will fire, you should shoot quick, before there is time to shake off the aim."

"Fair play," again shouted the negro; "fair play—gib a nigger fair play. What right a Natty Bumppo advise a young man? Let 'em shoot—clear a ground."

The youth fired with great rapidity; but no motion was made by the turkey; and when the examiners for the ball returned from the "mark," they declared that he had missed the stump.

Elizabeth observed the change in his countenance, and could not help feeling surprise, that one evidently so superior to his companions, should feel a trifling loss so sensibly. But her own champion was now preparing to enter the lists.

The mirth of Brom, which had been again excited, though in a much smaller degree than before, by the failure of the second adventurer, vanished, the instant Natty took his stand. His skin became mottled with large brown spots, that fearfully sullied the lustre of his native ebony, while his enormous lips gradually compressed around two rows of ivory, that had hitherto been shining in his visage, like pearls set in jet. His nostrils, at all times the most conspicuous features of his face, dilated, until they covered the greater part of the diameter of his countenance; while his brown and bony hands unconsciously grasped the snow-crust near him, the excitement of the moment completely overcoming his native dread of cold.

While these indications of apprehension were exhibited in the sable owner of the turkey, the man who gave rise to this extraordinary emotion was as calm and collected, as if there was not to be a single spectator of his skill.

"I was down in the Dutch settlements on the Scoharie," said Natty, carefully removing the leathern guard from the lock of his rifle, "jist before the breaking out of the last war, and there was a shooting-match amongst the boys; so I took a hand. I think I opened a good many Dutch eyes that day, for I won the powder-horn, three pounds of lead, and a pound of as good powder as ever flashed in pan. Lord! how they did swear in Garman! They did tell of one drunken Dutchman, who said he'd have the life of me, before I got back to the lake ag'in. But if he had put his rifle to his shoulder, with evil intent, God would have punished him for it; and even if the Lord didn't, and he had missed his aim, I know one that would have given him as good as he sent, and better too, if good shooting could come into the 'count."

By this time the old hunter was ready for his business, and, throwing his right leg far behind him, and stretching his left arm along the barrel of his piece, he raised it towards the bird. Every eye glanced rapidly from the marksman to the mark; but at the moment when each ear was expecting the report of the rifle, they were disappointed by the ticking sound of the flint.

"A snap—a snap," shouted the negro, springing from his crouching posture, like a madman, before his bird. "A snap good as fire—Natty Bumppo gun he snap—Natty Bumppo miss a turkey."

"Natty Bumppo hit a nigger," said the indignant old hunter, "if you don't get out of the way, Brom. It's contrary to the reason of the thing, boy, that a snap should count for a fire, when one is nothing more than a fire-stone striking a steel pan, and the other is sudden death; so get out my way, boy, and let me show Billy Kirby how to shoot a Christmas turkey."

"Gib a nigger fair play," cried the black, who continued resolutely to maintain his post, and making that appeal to the justice of his auditors, which the degraded condition of his caste so naturally suggested. "Ebbery body know dat snap as good as fire. Leab it to Massa Jone—leab it to young lady."

"Sartain," said the wood-chopper; "it's the law of the game in this part of the country, Leather-stocking. If you fire ag'in, you must pay up the other shilling. I b'lieve I'll try luck once more myself; so, Brom, here's my money, and I take the next fire."

"It's likely you know the laws of the woods better than I do, Billy Kirby!" returned Natty. "You come in with the settlers, with an ox goad in your hand, and I come in with moccasins on my feet, and with a good rifle on my shoulders, so long back as afore the old war; which is likely to know best! I say, no man need tell me that snapping is as good as firing, when I pull the trigger."

"Leab it to Massa Jone," said the alarmed negro; "he know ebbery ting."

This appeal to the knowledge of Richard was too flattering to be unheeded. He therefore advanced a little from the spot whither the delicacy of Elizabeth had induced her to withdraw, and gave the following opinion, with the gravity that the subject and his own rank demanded:—

"There seems to be a difference in opinion," he said, "on the subject of Nathaniel Bumppo's right to shoot at Abraham Freeborn's turkey, without the said Nathaniel paying one shilling for the privilege." This fact was too evident to be denied, and after pausing a moment, that the audience might digest his premises, Richard proceeded:—"It seems proper that I should decide this question, as I am bound to preserve the peace of the county; and men with deadly weapons in their hands, should not be heedlessly left to contention, and their own malignant passions. It appears that there was no agreement, either in writing or in words, on the disputed point; therefore we must reason from analogy, which is, as it were, comparing one thing with another. Now, in duels, where both parties shoot, it is generally the rule that a snap is a fire; and if such is the rule, where the party has a right to fire back again, it seems to me unreasonable, to say that a man may stand snapping at a defenceless turkey all day. I therefore am of opinion, that Nathaniel Bumppo has lost his chance, and must pay another shilling before he renews his right."

As this opinion came from so high a quarter, and was delivered with effect, it silenced all murmurs, for the whole of the spectators had begun to take sides with great warmth, except from the Leather-stocking himself.

"I think Miss Elizabeth's thoughts should be taken," said Natty. "I've known the squaws give very good counsel, when the Indians have been dumb-foundered. If she says that I ought to lose, I agree to give it up."

"Then I adjudge you to be a loser, for this time," said Miss Temple; "but pay your money, and renew your chance; unless Brom will sell me the bird for a dollar. I will give him the money to save the life of the poor victim."

This proposition was evidently but little relished by any of the listeners, even the negro feeling the evil excitement of the chances. In the mean while, as Billy Kirby was preparing himself for another shot, Natty left the stand, with an extremely dissatisfied manner, muttering—

"There hasn't been such a thing as a good flint sold at the foot of the lake, sin' the Indian traders used to come into the country;—and if a body should go into the flats or along the streams in the hills, to hunt for such a thing, it's ten to one but they be all covered up with the plough. Heigho! it seems to me, that just as the game grows scarce, and a body wants the best of ammunition, to get a livelihood, every thing that's bad falls on him, like a judgment. But I'll change the stone, for Billy Kirby hasn't the eye for such a mark, I know."

The wood-chopper seemed now entirely sensible that his reputation depended on his care; nor did he neglect any means to insure success. He drew up his rifle, and renewed his aim, again and again, still appearing reluctant to fire. No sound was heard from even Brom, during these portentous movements, until Kirby discharged his piece, with the same want of success as before. Then, indeed, the shouts of the negro rung through the bushes, and sounded among the trees of the neighbouring forest, like the outcries of a tribe of Indians. He laughed, rolling his head, first on one side, then on the other, until nature seemed exhausted with mirth. He danced, until his legs were wearied with motion, in the snow;

and, in short, he exhibited all that violence of joy that characterizes the mirth of a thoughtless negro.

The wood-chopper had exerted all his art, and felt a proportionate degree of disappointment at the failure. He first examined the bird with the utmost attention, and more than once suggested that he had touched its feathers; but the voice of the multitude was against him, for it felt disposed to listen to the often repeated cries of the black, to "gib a nigger fair play."

Finding it impossible to make out a title to the bird, Kirby turned fiercely to the black, and said—

"Shut your oven, you crow. Where is the man that can hit a turkey's head at a hundred yards? I was a fool for trying. You needn't make an uproar, like a falling pine tree, about it. Show me the man who can do it."

"Look this a-way, Billy Kirby," said Leather-stocking, "and let them clear the mark, and I'll show you a man who's made better shots afore now, and that when he's been hard pressed by the savages and wild beasts."

"Perhaps there is one whose right comes before ours, Leather-stocking," said Miss Temple; "if so, we will waive our privilege."

"If it be me that you have reference to," said the young hunter, "I shall decline another chance. My shoulder is yet weak, I find."

Elizabeth regarded his manner, and thought that she could discern a tinge on his cheek, that spoke the shame of conscious poverty. She said no more, but suffered her own champion to make a trial.

Although Natty Bumppo had certainly made hundreds of more momentous shots, at his enemies or his game, yet he never exerted himself more to excel. He raised his piece three several times; once to get his range; once to calculate his distance; and once because the bird, alarmed by the death-like stillness, turned its head quickly, to examine its foes. But the fourth time he fired. The smoke, the report, and the momentary shock, prevented most of the spectators from instantly knowing the result; but Elizabeth, when she saw her champion drop the end of his rifle in the snow, and open his mouth in one of its silent laughs, and then proceed, very coolly, to re-load his piece, knew that he had been successful. The boys rushed to the mark, and lifted the turkey on high, lifeless, and with nothing but the remnant of a head.

"Bring in the creater," said Leather-stocking, "and put it at the feet of the lady. I was her deputy in the matter, and the bird is her property."

"And a good deputy you have proved yourself," returned Elizabeth—"so good, cousin Richard, that I would advise you to remember his qualities." She paused, and the gayety that beamed on her face gave place to a more serious earnestness. She even blushed a little, as she turned to the young hunter, and, with the charm of a woman's manner, added—"But it was only to see an exhibition of the far-famed skill of Leather-stocking, that I tried my fortunes. Will you, sir, accept the bird, as a small peace-offering, for the hurt that prevented your own success?"

The expression with which the youth received this present was indescribable. He appeared to yield to the blandishment of her air, in opposition to a strong inward impulse to the contrary. He bowed, and raised the victim silently from her feet, but continued silent.

Elizabeth handed the black a piece of silver, as a remuneration for his loss, which had some effect in again unbending his muscles, and then expressed to her companion her readiness to return homeward.

"Wait a minute, cousin Bess," cried Richard; "there is an uncertainty about the rules of this sport, that it is proper I should remove.—If you will appoint a committee, gentlemen, to wait on me this morning, I will draw up, in writing, a set of regulations——" He stopped, with some indignation, for at that instant a hand was laid familiarly on the shoulder of the High Sheriff of——.

"A merry Christmas to you, cousin Dickon," said Judge Temple, who had approached the party unperceived: "I must have a vigilant eye to my daughter, sir, if you are to be seized daily with these gallant fits. I admire the taste, which would introduce a lady to such scenes!"

"It is her own perversity, 'duke," cried the disappointed Sheriff, who felt the loss of the first salutation as grievously as many a man would a much greater misfortune; "and I must say that she comes honestly by it. I led her out to show her the improvements, but away she scampered, through the snow, at the first sound of fire-arms, the same as if she had been brought up in a camp, instead of a first-rate boarding-school. I do think, Judge Temple, that such dangerous amusements should be suppressed by statute; nay, I doubt whether they are not already indictable at common law."

"Well, sir, as you are Sheriff of the county, it becomes your duty to examine into the matter," returned the smiling Marmaduke. "I perceive that Bess has executed her commission, and I hope it met with a favourable reception."

Richard glanced his eye at the packet, which he held in his hand, and the slight anger produced by disappointment vanished instantly.

"Ah! 'duke, my dear cousin," he said, "step a little on one side; I have something I would say to you." Marmaduke complied, and the Sheriff led him to a little distance in the bushes, and continued—"First, 'duke, let me thank you for your friendly interest with the Council and the Governor, without which, I am confident that the greatest merit would avail but little. But we are sisters' children—we are sisters' children; and you may use me like one of your horses; ride me or drive me, 'duke, I am wholly yours.—But in my humble opinion, this young companion of Leather-stocking requires looking after. He has a very dangerous propensity for turkey."

"Leave him to my management, Dickon," said the Judge, "and I will cure his appetite by indulgence. It is with him that I would speak. Let us rejoin the sportsmen."

Chapter XVIII

> "Poor wretch! the mother that him bare,
> If she had been in presence there,
> In his wan face, and sun-burn'd hair,
> She had not known her child."
> Scott, *Marmion*, I.xxviii.13–16.

IT DIMINISHED, in no degree, the effect produced by the conversation which passed between Judge Temple and the young hunter, that the former took the arm of his daughter, and drew it through his own, when he advanced from the spot whither Richard had led him, to that where the youth was standing, leaning on his rifle, and contemplating the dead bird at his feet. The presence of Marmaduke did not interrupt the sports, which were resumed, by loud and clamorous disputes concerning the conditions of a chance, that involved the life of a bird of much inferior quality to the last. Leather-stocking and Mohegan had alone drawn aside to their youthful companion; and, although in the immediate vicinity of such a throng, the following conversation was heard only by those who were interested in it.

"I have greatly injured you, Mr. Edwards," said the Judge; but the sudden and inexplicable start with which the person spoken to received this unexpected address, caused him to pause a moment. As no answer was given, and the strong emotion exhibited in the countenance of the youth gradually passed away, he continued—"But, fortunately, it is in some measure in my power to compensate you for what I have done. My kinsman, Richard Jones, has received an appointment that will, in future, deprive me of his assistance, and leaves me, just now, destitute of one who might greatly aid me with his pen. Your manner, notwithstanding appearances, is a sufficient proof of your education, nor will thy shoulder suffer thee to labour, for some time to come." (Marmaduke insensibly relapsed into the language of the Friends as he grew warm.) "My doors are open to thee, my young friend, for in this infant country, we harbour no suspicions; little offering to tempt the cupidity of the evil disposed. Become my assistant, for at least a season, and receive such compensation as thy services will deserve."

There was nothing in the manner or the offer of the Judge, to justify the reluctance, amounting nearly to loathing, with which the youth listened to his speech; but, after a powerful effort, for self-command, he replied—

"I would serve you, sir, or any other man, for an honest support, for I do not affect to conceal that my necessities are very great, even beyond what appearances would indicate; but I am fearful that such new duties would interfere too much with more important business; so that I must decline your offer, and depend on my rifle, as before, for subsistence."

Richard here took occasion to whisper to the young lady, who had shrunk a little from the foreground of the picture—

"This, you see, cousin Bess, is the natural reluctance of a half-breed to leave the savage state. Their attachment to a wandering life is, I verily believe, unconquerable."

"It is a precarious life," observed Marmaduke, without hearing the Sheriff's observation, "and one that brings more evils with it than present suffering. Trust me, young friend, my experience is greater than thine, when I tell thee, that the unsettled life of these hunters is of vast disadvantage for temporal purposes, and it totally removes one from the influence of more sacred things."

"No, no, Judge," interrupted the Leather-stocking; who was hitherto unseen, or disregarded; "take him into your shanty in welcome, but tell him truth. I have lived in the woods for forty long years, and have spent five at a time without seeing the light of a clearing, bigger than a wind-row in the trees, and I should like to know where you'll find a man, in his sixty-eighth year, who can get an easier living, for all your betterments, and your deer-laws; and, as for honesty, or doing what's right between man and man, I'll not turn my back to the longest winded deacon on your Patent."

"Thou art an exception, Leather-stocking," returned the Judge, nodding good-naturedly at the hunter; "for thou hast a temperance unusual in thy class, and a hardihood exceeding thy years. But this youth is made of materials too precious to be wasted in the forest. I entreat thee to join my family, if it be but till thy arm be healed. My daughter here, who is mistress of my dwelling, will tell thee that thou art welcome."

"Certainly," said Elizabeth, whose earnestness was a little checked by female reserve. "The unfortunate would be welcome at any time, but doubly so, when we feel that we have occasioned the evil ourselves."

"Yes," said Richard, "and if you relish turkey, young man, there are plenty in the coops, and of the best kind, I can assure you."

Finding himself thus ably seconded, Marmaduke pushed his advantage to the utmost. He entered into a detail of the duties that would attend the situation, and circumstantially mentioned the reward, and all those points which are deemed of importance among men of business. The youth listened in extreme agitation. There was an evident contest in his feelings; at times he appeared to wish eagerly for the change, and then again, the incomprehensible expression of disgust would cross his features, like a dark cloud obscuring a noon-day sun.

The Indian, in whose manner the depression of self-abasement was most powerfully exhibited, listened to the offers of the Judge, with an interest that increased with each syllable. Gradually he drew nigher to the group, and when, with his keen glance, he detected the most marked evidence of yielding in the countenance of his young companion, he changed at once from his attitude and look of shame, to the front of an Indian warrior, and moving, with great dignity, closer to the parties, he spoke—

"Listen to your Father," he said; "his words are old. Let the Young Eagle and the Great Land Chief eat together; let them sleep, without fear, near each other. The children of Miquon love not blood; they are just, and will do right. The sun must rise and set often, before men can make one family: it is not the work of a day, but of many winters. The Mingoes and the Delawares are born enemies; their blood can never mix in the wigwam; it never will run in the same stream in the battle. What makes the brother of Miquon and the Young Eagle foes! they are of the same tribe; their fathers and mothers are one. Learn to wait, my son: you are a Delaware, and an Indian warrior knows how to be patient."

This figurative address seemed to have great weight with

the young man, who gradually yielded to the representations of Marmaduke, and eventually consented to his proposal. It was, however, to be an experiment only; and if either of the parties thought fit to rescind the engagement, it was left at his option so to do. The remarkable and ill-concealed reluctance of the youth, to accept of an offer, which most men in his situation would consider as an unhoped for elevation, occasioned no little surprise in those to whom he was a stranger; and it left a slight impression to his disadvantage. When the parties separated, they very naturally made the subject the topic of a conversation, which we shall relate; first commencing with the Judge, his daughter, and Richard, who were slowly pursuing the way back to the Mansion-house.

"I have surely endeavoured to remember the holy mandates of our Redeemer, when he bids us 'love them who despitefully use you,' in my intercourse with this incomprehensible boy," said Marmaduke. "I know not what there is in my dwelling, to frighten a lad of his years, unless it may be thy presence and visage, Bess."

"No, no," said Richard, with great simplicity; "it is not cousin Bess. But when did you ever know a half-breed, 'duke, who could bear civilization? for that matter, they are worse than the savages themselves. Did you notice how knock-kneed he stood, Elizabeth, and what a wild look he had in his eyes?"

"I heeded not his eyes, nor his knees, which would be all the better for a little humbling. Really, my dear sir, I think you did exercise the Christian virtue of patience to the utmost. I was disgusted with his airs, long before he consented to make one of our family. Truly, we are much honoured by the association. In what apartment is he to be placed, sir, and at what table is he to receive his nectar and ambrosia?"

"With Benjamin and Remarkable," interrupted Mr. Jones; "you surely would not make the youth eat with the blacks! He is part Indian, it is true, but the natives hold the negroes in great contempt. No, no—he would starve before he would break a crust with the negroes."

"I am but too happy, Dickon, to tempt him to eat with ourselves," said Marmaduke, "to think of offering even the indignity you propose."

"Then, sir," said Elizabeth, with an air that was slightly affected, as if submitting to her father's orders in opposition to her own will, "it is your pleasure that he be a gentleman."

"Certainly; he is to fill the station of one; let him receive the treatment that is due to his place, until we find him unworthy of it."

"Well, well, 'duke," cried the Sheriff, "you will find it no easy matter to make a gentleman of him. The old proverb says, 'that it takes three generations to make a gentleman.' There was my father, whom every body knew; my grandfather was an M.D.; and his father a D.D.; and his father came from England. I never could come at the truth of his origin, but he was either a great merchant, in London, or a great country lawyer, or the youngest son of a bishop."

"Here is a true American genealogy for you," said Marmaduke, laughing. "It does very well, till you get across the water, where, as every thing is obscure, it is certain to deal in the superlative. You are sure that your English progenitor was great, Dickon, whatever his profession might have been?"

"To be sure I am," returned the other; "I have heard my old aunt talk of him by the month. We are of a good family, Judge Temple, and have never filled any but honourable stations in life."

"I marvel that you should be satisfied with so scanty a provision of gentility, in the olden time, Dickon. Most of the American genealogists commence their traditions, like the stories for children, with three brothers, taking especial care that one of the triumvirate shall be the progenitor of any of the same name who may happen to be better furnished with worldly gear than themselves. But, here, all are equal who know how to conduct themselves with propriety; and Oliver Edwards comes into my family, on a footing with both the High Sheriff and the Judge."

"Well, 'duke, I call this democracy, not republicanism; but I say nothing; only let him keep within the law, or I shall show him, that the freedom of even this country is under wholesome restraint."

"Surely, Dickon, you will not execute till I condemn! But what says Bess to the new inmate. We must pay a deference to the ladies, in this matter, after all."

"Oh! sir," returned Elizabeth, "I believe I am much like a certain Judge Temple, in this particular; not easily to be turned from my opinion. But, to be serious, although I must think the introduction of a demi-savage into the family a somewhat startling event, whomsoever you think proper to countenance, may be sure of my respect."

The Judge drew her arm more closely in his own, and smiled, while Richard led the way through the gate of the little court-yard in the rear of the dwelling, dealing out his ambiguous warnings, with his accustomed loquacity.

On the other hand, the foresters, for the three hunters, notwithstanding their difference in character, well deserved this common name, pursued their course along the skirts of the village in silence. It was not until they had reached the lake, and were moving over its frozen surface, towards the foot of the mountain, where the hut stood, that the youth exclaimed—

"Who could have foreseen this, a month since! I have consented to serve Marmaduke Temple! to be an inmate in the dwelling of the greatest enemy of my race! yet what better could I do? The servitude cannot be long, and when the motive for submitting to it ceases to exist, I will shake it off, like the dust from my feet."

"Is he a Mingo, that you will call him enemy?" said Mohegan. "The Delaware warrior sits still, and waits the time of the Great Spirit. He is no woman, to cry out like a child."

"Well, I'm mistrustful, John," said Leather-stocking, in whose air there had been, during the whole business, a strong expression of doubt and uncertainty. "They say that there's new laws in the land, and I am sartain that there's new ways in the mountains. They alter the country so much, one hardly knows the lakes and streams. I must say I'm mistrustful of such smooth speakers, for I've known the whites talk fair, when they wanted the Indian lands most. This I will say, though I'm white myself, and was born nigh York, and of honest parents too."

"I will submit," said the youth; "I will forget who I am. Cease to remember, old Mohegan, that I am the descendant of a Delaware chief, who once was master of these noble hills, these beautiful vales, and of this water, over which we tread.

Yes, yes——I will become his bondsman—his slave! Is it not an honourable servitude, old man?"

"Old man!" repeated the Indian, solemnly, and pausing in his walk, as usual when much excited—"yes; John is old. Son of my brother! if Mohegan was young, when would his rifle be still? where would the deer hide, and he not find him? But John is old; his hand is the hand of a squaw; his tomahawk is a hatchet; brooms and baskets are his enemies—he strikes no other. Hunger and old age come together.—See, Hawk-eye! when young, he would go days, and eat nothing; but should he not put the brush on the fire now, the blaze would go out. Take the son of Miquon by the hand, and he will help you."

"I'm not the man I was, I'll own, Chingachgook," returned the Leather-stocking; "but I can go without a meal now, on occasion. When we tracked the Iroquois through the 'Beech-woods,' they druv the game afore them, for I hadn't a morsel to eat from Monday morning, come Wednesday sundown; and then I shot as fat a buck, on the Pennsylvany line, as ever mortal laid eyes on. It would have done your heart good to have seen the Delaware eat,—for I was out scouting and scrimmaging with their tribe, at the time. Lord! the Indians, lad, lay still, and just waited till Providence should send them their game; but I foraged about, and put a deer up, and put him down too, 'fore he had made a dozen jumps. I was too weak, and too ravenous to stop for his flesh; so I took a good drink of his blood, and the Indians eat of his meat raw. John was there, and John knows. But then starvation would be apt to be too much for me now, I will own, though I'm no great eater at any time."

"Enough is said, my friends," cried the youth; "I feel that everywhere the sacrifice is required at my hands, and it shall be made; but say no more, I entreat you; I cannot bear this subject now."

His companions were silent, and they soon reached the hut, which they entered, after removing certain complicated and ingenious fastenings, that were put there, apparently, to guard a property of but very little value. Immense piles of snow lay against the log walls of this secluded habitation, on one side, while fragments of small trees, and branches of oak and chestnut, that had been torn from their parent stems by the winds, were thrown into a pile, on the other. A small column of smoke rose through a chimney of sticks, cemented with clay, along the side of the rock; and had marked the snow above with its dark tinges, in a wavy line, from the point of emission to another where the hill receded from the brow of a precipice, and held a soil that nourished trees of a gigantic growth, that overhung the little bottom beneath.

The remainder of the day passed off as such days are commonly spent, in a new country.—The settlers thronged to the academy again, to witness the second effort of Mr. Grant; and Mohegan was one of his hearers. But, notwithstanding the divine fixed his eyes intently on the Indian, when he invited his congregation to advance to the table, the shame of last night's abasement was yet too keen in the old chief to suffer him to move.

When the people were dispersing, the clouds, that had been gathering all the morning, were dense and dirty; and before half of the curious congregation had reached their different cabins, that were placed in every glen and hollow of the mountains, or perched on the summits of the hills themselves, the rain was falling in torrents. The dark edges of the stumps began to exhibit themselves, as the snow settled rapidly; the fences of logs and brush, which before had been only traced by long lines of white mounds, that ran across the valley and up the mountains, peeped out from their covering; and the black stubs were momentarily becoming more distinct, as large masses of snow and ice fell from their sides, under the influence of the thaw.

Sheltered in the warm hall of her father's comfortable mansion, Elizabeth, accompanied by Louisa Grant, looked abroad with admiration at the ever varying face of things without. Even the village, which had just before been glittering with the colour of the frozen element, reluctantly dropped its mask, and the houses exposed their dark roofs and smoked chimneys. The pines shook off the covering of snow, and every thing seemed to be assuming its proper hue, with a transition that bordered on the supernatural.

Chapter XIX

"And yet, poor Edwin was no vulgar boy."
Beattie, *The Minstrel*, I.xvi.1.

THE CLOSE of Christmas day, A.D. 1793, was tempestuous, but comparatively warm. When darkness had again hid the objects in the village from the gaze of Elizabeth, she turned from the window, where she had remained while the least vestige of light lingered over the tops of the dark pines, with a curiosity that was rather excited than appeased by the passing glimpses of woodland scenery that she had caught during the day.

With her arm locked in that of Miss Grant, the young mistress of the mansion walked slowly up and down the hall, musing on scenes that were rapidly recurring to her memory, and possibly dwelling, at times, in the sanctuary of her thoughts, on the strange occurrences that had led to the introduction to her father's family of one, whose manners so singularly contradicted the inferences to be drawn from his situation. The expiring heat of the apartment, for its great size required a day to reduce its temperature, had given to her cheeks a bloom that exceeded their natural colour, while the mild and melancholy features of Louisa were brightened with a faint tinge, that, like the hectic of disease, gave a painful interest to her beauty.

The eyes of the gentlemen, who were yet seated around the rich wines of Judge Temple, frequently wandered from the table, that was placed at one end of the hall, to the forms that were silently moving over its length. Much mirth, and that, at times, of a boisterous kind, proceeded from the mouth of Richard; but Major Hartmann was not yet excited to his pitch of merriment, and Marmaduke respected the presence of his clerical guest too much, to indulge in even the innocent humour that formed no small ingredient in his character.

Such were, and such continued to be, the pursuits of the party, for half an hour after the shutters were closed, and candles were placed in various parts of the hall, as substitutes for the departing daylight. The appearance of Benjamin, staggering under the burthen of an armful of wood, was the first interruption to the scene.

"How now, Master Pump!" roared the newly appointed Sheriff; "is there not warmth enough in 'duke's best Madeira, to keep up the animal heat through this thaw? Remember, old boy, that the Judge is particular with his beech and maple, beginning to dread, already, a scarcity of the precious articles. Ha! ha! ha! 'duke, you are a good, warm-hearted relation, I will own, as in duty bound, but you have some queer notions about you, after all. 'Come let us be jolly, and cast away folly.' "—

The notes gradually sunk into a hum, while the Major-domo threw down his load, and turning to his interrogator with an air of earnestness, replied—

"Why, look you, Squire Dickens, mayhap there's a warm latitude round about the table there, thof it's not the stuff to raise the heat in my body neither; the raal Jamaiky being the only thing to do that, beside good wood, or some such matter as Newcastle coal. But if I know any thing of weather, d'ye see, it's time to be getting all snug, and for putting the ports in, and stirring the fires abit. Mayhap I've not followed the seas twenty-seven years, and lived another seven in these here woods, for nothing, gemmen."

"Why, does it bid fair for a change in the weather, Benjamin?" inquired the master of the house.

"There's a shift of wind, your honour," returned the steward; "and when there's a shift of wind, you may look for a change, in this here climate. I was aboard of one of Rodney's fleet, d'ye see, about the time we licked De Grasse, Mounsheer Ler Quaw's countryman, there; and the wind was here at the south'ard and east'ard; and I was below, mixing a toothful of hot-stuff for the Captain of marines, who dined, d'ye see, in the cabin, that there very same day; and I suppose he wanted to put out the Captain's fire with a gun-room ingyne: and so, just as I got it to my own liking, after tasting pretty often, for the soldier was difficult to please, slap come the foresail ag'inst the mast, and whiz went the ship round on her heel, like a whirlygig. And a lucky thing was it that our helm was down; for as she gathered starnway she payed off, which was more than every ship in the fleet did, or could do. But she strained herself in the trough of the sea, and she shipped a deal of water over her quarter. I never swallowed so much clear water at a time, in my life, as I did then, for I was looking up the after-hatch at the instant."

"I wonder, Benjamin, that you did not die with a dropsy!" said Marmaduke.

"I mought, Judge," said the old tar, with a broad grin; "but there was no need of the med'cine chest for a cure; for, as I thought the brew was spoilt for the marine's taste, and there was no telling when another sea might come and spoil it for mine, I finished the mug on the spot. So then all hands was called to the pumps, and there we began to ply the pumps—"

"Well, but the weather?" interrupted Marmaduke; "what of the weather without doors?"

"Why, here the wind has been all day at the south, and now there's a lull, as if the last blast was out of the bellows; and there's a streak along the mountains, to the north'ard, that, just now, wasn't wider than the bigness of your hand; and then the clouds drive afore it as you'd brail a mainsail, and the stars are heaving in sight, like so many lights and beacons, put there to warn us to pile on the wood; and, if-so-be that I'm a judge of weather, it's getting to be time to build on a fire; or you'll have half of them there porter-bottles, and them dimmy-johns of wine, in the locker here, breaking with the frost, afore the morning watch is called."

"Thou art a prudent sentinel," said the Judge. "Act thy pleasure with the forests, for this night at least."

Benjamin did as he was ordered; nor had two hours elapsed, before the prudence of his precautions became very visible. The south wind had, indeed, blown itself out, and it was succeeded by the calmness that usually gave warning of a serious change in the weather. Long before the family retired to rest, the cold had become cuttingly severe; and when Monsieur Le Quoi sallied forth, under a bright moon, to seek his own abode, he was compelled to beg a blanket, in which he might envelope his form, in addition to the numerous garments that his sagacity had provided for the occasion. The divine and his daughter remained, as inmates of the Mansion-house, during the night, and the excess of last night's merriment induced the gentlemen to make an early retreat to their several apartments. Long before midnight, the whole family were invisible.

Elizabeth and her friend had not yet lost their senses in sleep, when the howlings of the northwest wind were heard around the buildings, and brought with them that exquisite sense of comfort, that is ever excited under such circumstances, in an apartment where the fire has not yet ceased to glimmer, and curtains, and shutters, and feathers, unite to preserve the desired temperature. Once, just as her eyes had opened, apparently in the last stage of drowsiness, the roaring winds brought with them a long and plaintive howl, that seemed too wild for a dog, and yet resembled the cries of that faithful animal, when night awakens his vigilance, and gives sweetness and solemnity to his alarms. The form of Louisa Grant instinctively pressed nearer to that of the young heiress, who, finding her companion was yet awake, said, in a low tone, as if afraid to break a charm with her voice—

"Those distant cries are plaintive, and even beautiful. Can they be the hounds from the hut of Leather-stocking?"

"They are wolves, who have ventured from the mountain, on the lake," whispered Louisa, "and who are only kept from the village by the lights. One night, since we have been here, hunger drove them to our very door. Oh! what a dreadful night it was! But the riches of Judge Temple have given him too many safeguards, to leave room for fear in this house."

"The enterprise of Judge Temple is taming the very forests!" exclaimed Elizabeth, throwing off the covering, and partly rising in the bed. "How rapidly is civilization treading on the footsteps of nature!" she continued, as her eye glanced over not only the comforts, but the luxuries of her apartment, and her ear again listened to the distant, but often repeated howls from the lake. Finding, however, that the timidity of her companion rendered the sounds painful to her, Elizabeth resumed her place, and soon forgot the changes in the country, with those in her own condition, in a deep sleep.

The following morning, the noise of the female servant, who entered the apartment to light the fire, awoke the females. They arose, and finished the slight preparations of their toilettes in a clear, cold atmosphere, that penetrated through all the defences of even Miss Temple's warm room. When

Elizabeth was attired, she approached a window and drew its curtain, and, throwing open its shutters, she endeavoured to look abroad on the village and the lake. But a thick covering of frost, on the glass, while it admitted the light, shut out the view. She raised the sash, and then, indeed, a glorious scene met her delighted eye.

The lake had exchanged its covering of unspotted snow, for a face of dark ice, that reflected the rays of the rising sun, like a polished mirror. The houses were clothed in a dress of the same description, but which, owing to its position, shone like bright steel; while the enormous icicles that were pendent from every roof, caught the brilliant light, apparently throwing it from one to the other, as each glittered, on the side next the luminary, with a golden lustre, that melted away, on its opposite, into the dusky shades of a back-ground. But it was the appearance, of the boundless forests, that covered the hills, as they rose, in the distance, one over the other, that most attracted the gaze of Miss Temple. The huge branches of the pines and hemlocks bent with the weight of the ice they supported, while their summits rose above the swelling tops of the oaks, beeches, and maples, like spires of burnished silver issuing from domes of the same material. The limits of the view, in the west, were marked by an undulating outline of bright light, as if, reversing the order of nature, numberless suns might momentarily be expected to heave above the horizon. In the foreground of the picture, along the shores of the lake, and near to the village, each tree seemed studded with diamonds. Even the sides of the mountains, where the rays of the sun could not yet fall, were decorated with a glassy coat, that presented every gradation of brilliancy, from the first touch of the luminary to the dark foliage of the hemlock, glistening through its coat of crystal. In short, the whole view was one scene of quivering radiancy, as lake, mountains, village, and woods, each emitted a portion of light, tinged with its peculiar hue, and varied by its position and its magnitude.

"See!" cried Elizabeth—"see, Louisa; hasten to the window, and observe the miraculous change."

Miss Grant complied; and, after bending for a moment in silence from the opening, she observed, in a low tone, as if afraid to trust the sound of her voice—

"The change is indeed wonderful! I am surprised that he should be able to effect it so soon."

Elizabeth turned in amazement, to hear so sceptical a sentiment from one educated like her companion; but was surprised to find that, instead of looking at the view, the mild, blue eyes of Miss Grant were dwelling on the form of a well-dressed young man, who was standing before the door of the building, in earnest conversation with her father. A second look was necessary, before she was able to recognise the person of the young hunter, in a plain, but, assuredly, the ordinary garb of a gentleman.

"Every thing in this magical country seems to border on the marvellous," said Elizabeth; "and among all the changes, this is certainly not the least wonderful. The actors are as unique as the scenery."

Miss Grant coloured, and drew in her head.

"I am a simple country girl, Miss Temple, and I am afraid you will find me but a poor companion," she said. "I—I am not sure that I understand all you say. But I really thought that you wished me to notice the alteration in Mr. Edwards. Is it not more wonderful, when we recollect his origin? They say he is part Indian."

"He is a genteel savage; but let us go down, and give the Sachem his tea;—for I suppose he is a descendant of King Philip, if not a grandson of Pocahontas."

The ladies were met in the hall by Judge Temple, who took his daughter aside, to apprize her of that alteration in the appearance of their new inmate, with which she was already acquainted.

"He appears reluctant to converse on his former situation," continued Marmaduke; "but I gather from his discourse, as is apparent from his manner, that he has seen better days; and I really am inclining to the opinion of Richard, as to his origin; for it was no unusual thing for the Indian Agents to rear their children in a very laudable manner, and——"

"Very well, my dear sir," interrupted his daughter, laughing, and averting her eyes; "it is all well enough, I dare say; but as I do not understand a word of the Mohawk language, he must be content to speak English; and as for his behaviour, I trust to your discernment to control it."

"Ay! but, Bess," said the Judge, detaining her gently, with his hand, "nothing must be said to him of his past life. This he has begged particularly of me, as a favour. He is, perhaps, a little soured, just now, with his wounded arm; the injury seems very light, and another time he may be more communicative."

"Oh! I am not much troubled, sir, with that laudable thirst after knowledge, that is called curiosity. I shall believe him to be the child of Corn-stalk, or Corn-planter, or some other renowned chieftain; possibly of the Big Snake himself; and shall treat him as such, until he sees fit to shave his good-looking head, borrow some half-dozen pair of my best ear-rings, shoulder his rifle again, and disappear as suddenly as he made his entrance. So come, my dear sir, and let us not forget the rites of hospitality, for the short time he is to remain with us."

Judge Temple smiled, at the playfulness of his child, and taking her arm, they entered the breakfast parlour, where the young hunter was seated, with an air that showed his determination to domesticate himself in the family, with as little parade as possible.

Such were the incidents that led to this extraordinary increase in the family of Judge Temple, where, having once established the youth, the subject of our tale requires us to leave him, for a time, to pursue with diligence and intelligence the employments that were assigned him by Marmaduke.

Major Hartmann made his customary visit, and took his leave of the party, for the next three months. Mr. Grant was compelled to be absent much of his time, in remote parts of the country, and his daughter became almost a constant visiter at the Mansion-house. Richard entered, with his constitutional eagerness, on the duties of his new office; and, as Marmaduke was much employed, with the constant applications of adventurers, for farms, the winter passed swiftly away. The lake was a principal scene for the amusements of the young people; where the ladies, in their one-horse cutter, driven by Richard, and attended, when the snow would admit of it, by young Edwards, on his skates, spent many hours, taking the benefit of exercise in the clear air of the hills. The reserve of the youth gradually gave way to time and his situation, though it was still evident, to a close observer, that he had frequent moments of bitter and intense feeling.

Elizabeth saw many large openings appear in the sides of the mountains, during the three succeeding months, where different settlers had, in the language of the country, "made their pitch;" while the numberless sleighs that passed through the village, loaded with wheat and barrels of pot-ashes, afforded a clear demonstration that all these labours were not undertaken in vain. In short, the whole country was exhibiting the bustle of a thriving settlement, where the highways were thronged with sleighs, bearing piles of rough household furniture, studded, here and there, with the smiling faces of women and children, happy in the excitement of novelty; or with loads of produce, hastening to the common market at Albany, that served as so many snares, to induce the emigrants to enter into those wild mountains in search of competence and happiness.

The village was alive with business, the artisans increasing in wealth with the prosperity of the country, and each day witnessing some nearer approach to the manners and usages of an old-settled town. The man who carried the mail, or "the post," as he was called, talked much of running a stage, and once or twice, during the winter, he was seen taking a single passenger in his cutter, through the snow-banks towards the Mohawk, along which a regular vehicle glided, semi-weekly, with the velocity of lightning, and under the direction of a knowing whip from the "down countries." Towards spring, divers families, who had been into the "old states," to see their relatives, returned, in time to save the snow, frequently bringing with them whole neighbourhoods, who were tempted by their representations to leave the farms of Connecticut and Massachusetts, to make a trial of fortune in the woods.

During all this time, Oliver Edwards, whose sudden elevation excited no surprise in that changeful country, was earnestly engaged in the service of Marmaduke, during the days; but his nights were often spent in the hut of Leather-stocking. The intercourse between the three hunters was maintained with a certain air of mystery, it is true, but with much zeal and apparent interest to all the parties. Even Mohegan seldom came to the Mansion-house, and Natty, never; but Edwards sought every leisure moment to visit his former abode, from which he would often return in the gloomy hours of night, through the snow, or, if detained beyond the time at which the family retired to rest, with the morning sun. These visits certainly excited much speculation in those to whom they were known, but no comments were made, excepting occasionally in whispers from Richard, who would say—

"It is not at all remarkable;—a half-breed can never be weaned from the savage ways—and for one of his lineage, the boy is much nearer civilisation than could, in reason, be expected."

Chapter XX

"Away! nor let me loiter in my song,
For we have many a mountain path to tread."
Byron, *Childe Harold's Pilgrimage*, II.xxxv.1–2.

AS THE SPRING gradually approached, the immense piles of snow, that, by alternate thaws and frosts, and repeated storms, had obtained a firmness which threatened a tiresome durability, begun to yield to the influence of milder breezes and a warmer sun. The gates of Heaven, at times, seemed to open, and a bland air diffused itself over the earth, when animate and inanimate nature would awaken, and, for a few hours, the gayety of spring shone in every eye, and smiled on every field. But the shivering blasts from the north would carry their chill influence over the scene again, and the dark and gloomy clouds that intercepted the rays of the sun, were not more cold and dreary, than the re-action. These struggles between the seasons became, daily, more frequent, while the earth, like a victim to contention, slowly lost the animated brilliancy of winter, without obtaining the aspect of spring.

Several weeks were consumed, in this cheerless manner, during which the inhabitants of the country gradually changed their pursuits from the social and bustling movements of the time of snow, to the laborious and domestic engagements of the coming season. The village was no longer thronged with visiters; the trade, that had enlivened the shops for several months, begun to disappear; the highways lost their shining coats of beaten snow in impassable sloughs, and were deserted by the gay and noisy travellers who, in sleighs, had, during the winter, glided along their windings; and, in short, every thing seemed indicative of a mighty change, not only in the earth, but in those who derived their sources of comfort and happiness from its bosom.

The younger members of the family in the Mansion-house, of which Louisa Grant was now habitually one, were by no means indifferent observers of these fluctuating and tardy changes. While the snow rendered the roads passable, they had partaken largely in the amusements of the winter, which included not only daily rides over the mountains, and through every valley within twenty miles of them, but divers ingenious and varied sources of pleasure, on the bosom of their frozen lake. There had been excursions in the equipage of Richard, when, with his four horses, he had outstripped the winds, as it flew over the glassy ice which invariably succeeded a thaw. Then the exciting and dangerous "whirligig" would be suffered to possess its moment of notice. Cutters, drawn by a single horse, and hand-sleds, impelled by the gentlemen, on skates, would each in turn be used; and, in short, every source of relief against the tediousness of a winter in the mountains, was resorted to by the family. Elizabeth was willing to acknowledge to her father, that the season, with the aid of his library, was much less irksome than she had anticipated.

As exercise in the open air was, in some degree necessary to the habits of the family, when the constant recurrence of frosts and thaws rendered the roads, which were dangerous, at the most favourable times, utterly impassable for wheels, saddle-horses were used as substitutes for other conveyances. Mounted on small and sure-footed beasts, the ladies would again attempt the passages of the mountains, and penetrate into every retired glen, where the enterprise of a settler had induced him to establish himself. In these excursions they were attended by some one or all of the gentlemen of the family, as their different pursuits admitted. Young Edwards was hourly becoming more familiarized to his situation, and not unfrequently mingled in the parties, with an unconcern and gayety, that, for a short time, would expel all unpleasant recollections from his mind. Habit, and the buoyancy of youth, seemed to be getting the ascendency over the secret causes of his uneasiness; though there were moments, when the same remarkable expression of disgust, would cross his intercourse with Marmaduke, that had distinguished their conversations in the first days of their acquaintance.

It was at the close of the month of March, that the Sheriff succeeded in persuading his cousin and her young friend to accompany him in a ride to a hill, that was said to overhang the lake, in a manner peculiar to itself.

"Besides, cousin Bess," continued the indefatigable Richard, " we will stop and see the 'sugar bush' of Billy Kirby: he is on the east end of the Ransom lot, making sugar for Jared Ransom. There is not a better hand over a kettle in the county, than that same Kirby. You remember, 'duke, that I had him his first season, in our own camp; and it is not a wonder that he knows something of his trade."

"He's a good chopper, is Billy," observed Benjamin, who held the bridle of the horse while the Sheriff mounted; "and he handles an axe, much the same as a forecastle-man does his marling-spike, or a tailor his goose. They say he'll lift a potash kettle off the arch alone, thof I can't say that I've ever seen him do it with my own eyes; but that is the say. And I've seen sugar of his making, which, maybe, wasn't as white as an old top-gallantsail, but which my friend Mistress Prettybones, within there, said, had the true molasses smack to it; and you are not the one, Squire Dickens, to be told that Mistress Remarkable has a remarkable tooth for sweet things in her nut-grinder."

The loud laugh that succeeded the wit of Benjamin, and in which he participated, with no very harmonious sounds, himself, very fully illustrated the congenial temper which existed between the pair. Most of its point was, however, lost on the rest of the party, who were either mounting their horses, or assisting the ladies at the moment. When all were safely in their saddles, they moved through the village in great order. They paused for a moment, before the door of Monsieur Le Quoi, until he could bestride his steed, and then, issuing from the little cluster of houses, they took one of the principal of those highways, that centered in the village.

As each night brought with it a severe frost, which the heat of the succeeding day served to dissipate, the equestrians were compelled to proceed singly, along the margin of the road, where the turf, and firmness of the ground, gave the horses a secure footing. Very trifling indications of vegetation were to be seen, the surface of the earth presenting a cold, wet, and cheerless aspect, that chilled the blood. The snow yet lay scattered over most of those distant clearings that were visible in different parts of the mountains; though here and there an opening might be seen, where, as the white covering yielded to the season, the bright and lively green of the wheat served to enkindle the hopes of the husbandman. Nothing could be more marked, than the contrast between the earth and the heavens; for, while the former presented the dreary view that we have described, a warm and invigorating sun was dispensing his heats, from a sky that contained but a solitary cloud, and through an atmosphere, that softened the colours of the sensible horizon, until it shone like a sea of blue.

Richard led the way, on this, as on all other occasions, that did not require the exercise of unusual abilities; and as he moved along, he essayed to enliven the party with the sounds of his experienced voice.

"This is your true sugar weather, 'duke," he cried; "a frosty night, and a sunshiny day. I warrant me that the sap runs like a mill-tail up the maples, this warm morning. It is a pity, Judge, that you do not introduce a little more science into the manufacture of sugar, among your tenants. It might be done, sir, without knowing as much as Dr. Franklin—it might be done, Judge Temple."

"The first object of my solicitude, friend Jones," returned Marmaduke, "is to protect the sources of this great mine of comfort and wealth, from the extravagance of the people themselves. When this important point shall be achieved, it will be in season to turn our attention to an improvement in the manufacture of the article. But thou knowest, Richard, that I have already subjected our sugar to the process of the refiner, and that the result has produced loaves as white as the snow on yon fields, and possessing the saccharine quality in its utmost purity."

"Saccharine, or turpentine, or any other -ine, Judge Temple, you have never made a loaf larger than a good sized sugar-plum," returned the Sheriff. "Now, sir, I assert, that no experiment is fairly tried, until it be reduced to practical purposes. If, sir, I owned a hundred, or, for that matter, two hundred thousand acres of land, as you do, I would build a sugar-house in the village; I would invite learned men to an investigation of the subject,—and such are easily to be found, sir; yes, sir, they are not difficult to find,—men who unite theory with practice; and I would select a wood of young and thrifty trees; and, instead of making loaves of the size of a lump of candy, dam'me, 'duke, but I'd have them as big as a hay-cock."

"And purchase the cargo of one of those ships that, they say, are going to China," cried Elizabeth; "turn your potash-kettles into tea-cups, the scows on the lake into saucers; bake your cake in yonder lime-kiln, and invite the county to a tea-party. How wonderful are the projects of genius! Really, sir, the world is of opinion that Judge Temple has tried the experiment fairly, though he did not cause his loaves to be cast in moulds of the magnitude that would suit your magnificent conceptions."

"You may laugh, cousin Elizabeth—you may laugh, madam," retorted Richard, turning himself so much in his saddle as to face the party, and making dignified gestures with his whip; "but I appeal to common sense, good sense, or, what is of more importance than either, to the sense of taste, which is one of the five natural senses, whether a big loaf of sugar is not likely to contain a better illustration of a proposition, than such a lump as one of your Dutch women puts under her tongue when she drinks her tea. There are two ways of doing every thing; the right way, and the wrong way. You make sugar now, I will admit, and you may, possibly, make loaf-sugar; but I take the question to be, whether you make the best possible sugar, and in the best possible loaves."

"Thou art very right, Richard," observed Marmaduke, with a gravity in his air, that proved how much he was interested in the subject. "It is very true that we manufacture sugar, and the inquiry is quite useful, how much? and in what manner? I hope to live to see the day, when farms and plantations shall be devoted to this branch of business. Little is known concerning the properties of the tree itself, the source of all this wealth; how much it may be improved by cultivation, by the use of the hoe and plough."

"Hoe and plough!" roared the Sheriff;—"would you set a man hoeing round the root of a maple like this,"—pointing to one of the noble trees, that occur so frequently in that part of the country.—"Hoeing trees! are you mad, 'duke? This is next to hunting for coal! Poh! poh! my dear cousin, hear reason, and leave the management of the sugar-bush to me. Here is Mr. Le Quoi, he has been in the West-Indies, and has seen sugar made. Let him give an account of how it is made there, and you will hear the philosophy of the thing.—Well, Monsieur, how is it that you make sugar in the West-Indies; any thing in Judge Temple's fashion?"

The gentleman to whom this query was put, was mounted on a small horse, of no very fiery temperament, and was riding with his stirrups so short, as to bring his knees, while the animal rose a small ascent in the wood-path they were now travelling, into a somewhat hazardous vicinity to his chin. There was no room for gesticulation or grace in the delivery of his reply, for the mountain was steep and slippery; and although the Frenchman had an eye of uncommon magnitude on either side of his face, they did not seem to be half competent to forewarn him of the impediments of bushes, twigs, and fallen trees, that were momentarily crossing his path. With one hand employed in averting these dangers, and the other grasping his bridle, to check an untoward speed that his horse was assuming, the native of France responded as follows:—

"Sucre! dey do make sucre in Martinique: mais—mais ce n'est pas, one tree;—ah—ah—vat you call—Je voudrois que ces chemins fussent au diable—vat you call—steeck pour le promenade."

"Cane," said Elizabeth, smiling at the imprecation which the wary Frenchman supposed was understood only by himself.

"Oui, Mam'selle, cane."

"Yes, yes," cried Richard, "cane is the vulgar name for it, but the real term is saccharum officinarum: and what we call the sugar, or hard maple, is acer saccharinum. These are the learned names, Monsieur, and are such as, doubtless, you well understand."

"Is this Greek or Latin, Mr. Edwards?" whispered Elizabeth to the youth, who was opening a passage for herself and her companions through the bushes—"or perhaps it is a still more learned language, for an interpretation of which we must look to you."

The dark eye of the young man glanced towards the speaker, but its resentful expression changed, in a moment.

"I shall remember your doubts, Miss Temple, when next I visit my old friend Mohegan, and either his skill, or that of Leather-stocking, shall solve them."

"And are you, then, really ignorant of their language?"

"Not absolutely; but the deep learning of Mr. Jones is more familiar to me, or even the polite masquerade of Monsieur Le Quoi."

"Do you speak French?" said the lady, with quickness.

"It is a common language with the Iroquois, and through the Canadas," he answered, smiling.

"Ah! but they are Mingoes, and your enemies."

"It will be well for me, if I have no worse," said the youth, dashing ahead with his horse, and putting an end to the evasive dialogue.

The discourse, however, was maintained with great vigour by Richard, until they reached an open wood on the summit of the mountain, where the hemlocks and pines totally disappeared, and a grove of the very trees that formed the subject of debate, covered the earth with their tall, straight trunks and spreading branches, in stately pride. The underwood had been entirely removed from this grove, or bush, as, in conjunction, with the simple arrangements for boiling, it was called, and a wide space of many acres was cleared, which might be likened to the dome of a mighty temple, to which the maples formed the columns, their tops composing the capitals, and the heavens the arch. A deep and careless incision had been made into each tree, near its root, into which little spouts, formed of the bark of the alder, or of the sumach, were fastened; and a trough, roughly dug out of the linden, or bass-wood, was lying at the root of each tree, to catch the sap that flowed from this extremely wasteful and inartificial arrangement.

The party paused a moment, on gaining the flat, to breathe their horses, and, as the scene was entirely new to several of their number, to view the manner of collecting the fluid. A fine, powerful voice aroused them from their momentary silence, as it rung under the branches of the trees, singing the following words of that inimitable doggrel, whose verses, if extended, would reach from the waters of the Connecticut to the shores of Ontario. The tune was, of course, that familiar air, which, although it is said to have been first applied to his nation in derision, circumstances have since rendered so glorious, that no American ever hears its jingling cadence, without feeling a thrill at his heart.

"The Eastern States be full of men,
  The Western full of woods, sir;
The hills be like a cattle pen,
  The roads be full of goods, sir,
    Then flow away, my sweety sap,
      And I will make you boily;
    Nor catch a woodman's hasty nap,
      For fear you should get roily.

"The maple tree's a precious one,
  'Tis fuel, food, and timber;
And when your stiff day's work is done,
  Its juice will make you limber.
    Then flow away, &c.

"And what's a man without his glass,
  His wife without her tea, sir?
But neither cup nor mug would pass,
  Without this honey-bee, sir.
    Then flow away," &c.

During the execution of this sonorous doggrel, Richard kept time with his whip on the mane of his charger, accompanying the gestures with a corresponding movement of his head and body. Towards the close of the song, he was overheard humming the chorus, and at its last repetition, to strike in at "sweety sap," and carry a second through, with a prodigious addition to the "effect" of the noise, if not to that of the harmony.

"Well done us!" roared the Sheriff, on the same key with the tune; "a very good song, Billy Kirby, and very well sung. Where got you the words, lad? is there more of it, and can you furnish me with a copy?"

The sugar-boiler, who was busy in his "camp," at a short distance from the equestrians, turned his head with great indifference, and surveyed the party, as they approached, with admirable coolness. To each individual, as he or she rode close by him, he gave a nod, that was extremely good-natured and affable, but which partook largely of the virtue of equality, for not even to the ladies did he in the least vary his mode of salutation, by touching the apology for a hat that he wore, or by any other motion than the one we have mentioned.

"How goes it, how goes it, Sheriff?" said the wood-chopper; "what's the good word in the village?"

"Why, much as usual, Billy," returned Richard. "But how is this! where are your four kettles, and your troughs, and your iron coolers? Do you make sugar in this slovenly way! I thought you were one of the best sugar-boilers in the county."

"I'm all that, Squire Jones," said Kirby, who continued his occupation; "I'll turn my back to no man in the Otsego hills, for chopping and logging; for boiling down the maple sap; for tending brick-kiln; splitting out rails; making potash, and parling too; or hoeing corn. Though I keep myself, pretty much, to the first business, seeing that the axe comes most nateral to me."

"You be von Jack All-trade, Mister Beel," said Monsieur Le Quoi.

"How?" said Kirby, looking up, with a simplicity which, coupled with his gigantic frame and manly face, was a little ridiculous—"if you be for trade, Mounsher, here is some as good sugar as you'll find the season through. It's as clear from dirt as the Jarman Flats is free from stumps, and it has the raal maple flavour. Such stuff would sell in York for candy."

The Frenchman approached the place where Kirby had deposited his cakes of sugar, under the cover of a bark roof, and commenced the examination of the article, with the eye of one who well understood its value. Marmaduke had dismounted, and was viewing the works and the trees very closely, and not without frequent expressions of dissatisfaction, at the careless manner in which the manufacture was conducted.

"You have much experience in these things, Kirby," he said; "what course do you pursue in making your sugar? I see you have but two kettles."

"Two is as good as two thousand, Judge; I'm none of your polite sugar-makers, that boils for the great folks; but if the raal sweet maple is wanted, I can answer your turn. First, I choose, and then I tap my trees; say along about the last of February, or, in these mountains, maybe not afore the middle of March; but any way, just as the sap begins to cleverly run——"

"Well, in this choice," interrupted Marmaduke, "are you governed by any outward signs, that prove the quality of the tree?"

"Why, there's judgment in all things," said Kirby, stirring the liquor in his kettles briskly. "There's something in knowing when and how much to stir the pot. It's a thing that must be larnt. Rome wasn't built in a day, nor, for that matter, Templetown 'ither, though it may be said to be a quick-growing place. I never put my axe into a stunty tree, or one that hasn't a good, fresh-looking bark; for trees have disorders like creaturs; and where's the policy of taking a tree that's sickly, any more than you'd choose a foundered horse to ride post, or an overheated ox to do your logging——"

"All this is true; but what are the signs of illness? how do you distinguish a tree that is well from one that is diseased?"

"How does the doctor tell who has fever, and who colds?" interrupted Richard—"by examining the skin, and feeling the pulse, to be sure."

"Sartain," continued Billy; "the Squire a'nt far out of the way. It's by the look of the thing, sure enough.—Well, when the sap begins to get a free run, I hang over the kettles, and set up the bush. My first boiling I push pretty smart, till I get the vartoo of the sap; but when it begins to grow of a molasses nater, like this in the kettle, one musn't drive the fires too hard, or you'll burn the sugar; and burny sugar is bad to the taste, let it be never so sweet. So you ladle out from one kettle into the other, till it gets so, when you put the stirring-stick into it, that it will draw into a thread; when it takes a kerful hand to manage it. There is a way to drain it off, after it has grained, by putting clay into the pans; but it isn't always practysed: some doos, and some doosn't.——Well, Mounsher, be we likely to make a trade?"

"I vill give you, Mister Beel, for von pound——dix sous."

"No; I expect cash for't; I never dicker my sugar. But, seeing that it's you, Mounsher," said Billy, with a coaxing smile, "I'll agree to receive a gallon of rum, and cloth enough for two shirts, if you will take the molasses in the bargain. It's raal good. I wouldn't deceive you or any man; and to my drinking, it's about the best molasses that come out of a sugar-bush."

"Mr. Le Quoi has offered you ten pence," said young Edwards.

The manufacturer stared at the speaker, with an air of great freedom, but made no reply.

"Oui," said the Frenchman, "ten penny. Je vous remercie, Monsieur; ah! mon Anglois! je l'oublie toujours."

The wood-chopper looked from one to the other, with some displeasure; and evidently imbibed the opinion that they were amusing themselves at his expense. He seized the enormous ladle, which was lying in one of his kettles, and began to stir the boiling liquid with great diligence. After a moment, passed in dipping the ladle full, and then raising it on high, as the thick, rich fluid fell back into the kettle, he suddenly gave it a whirl, as if to cool what yet remained, and offered the bowl to Mr. Le Quoi, saying—

"Taste that, Mounsher, and you will say it is worth more than you offer. The molasses itself would fetch the money."

The complaisant Frenchman, after several timid efforts to trust his lips in contact with the bowl of the ladle, got a good swallow of the scalding liquid. He clapped his hand on his breast, and looked most piteously at the ladies, for a single instant, and then, to use the language of Billy, when he afterwards recounted the tale, "no drum-sticks ever went faster on the skin of a sheep, than the Frenchman's legs, for a round or two: and then, such swearing and spitting, in French, you never seen. But it's a knowing one, from the old countries, that thinks to get his jokes smoothly over a wood-chopper."

The air of innocence with which Kirby resumed the occupation of stirring the contents of his kettle, would have completely deceived the spectators, as to his agency in the temporary suffering of Mr. Le Quoi, had not the reckless fellow thrust his tongue into his cheek, and cast his eyes over the party, with a simplicity of expression that was too exquisite to be natural. Mr. Le Quoi soon recovered his presence of mind, and his decorum; he briefly apologized to the ladies for one or two very intemperate expressions, that had escaped him in a moment of extraordinary excitement, and remounting his horse, he continued in the back-ground during the remainder of the visit, the wit of Kirby putting a violent termination, at once, to all negotiations on the subject of trade. During all this time, Marmaduke had been wandering about the grove, making observations on his favourite trees, and the wasteful manner in which the wood-chopper conducted his manufacture.

"It grieves me to witness the extravagance that pervades this country," said the Judge, " where the settlers trifle with the blessings they might enjoy, with the prodigality of successful adventurers. You are not exempt from the censure yourself, Kirby, for you make dreadful wounds in these trees, where a small incision would effect the same object. I earnestly beg you will remember, that they are the growth of centuries, and when once gone, none living will see their loss remedied."

"Why, I don't know, Judge," returned the man he addressed: "It seems to me, if there's a plenty of any thing in this mountaynous country, it's the trees. If there's any sin in chopping them, I've a pretty heavy account to settle; for I've chopped over the best half of a thousand acres, with my own hands, counting both Varmount and York states; and I hope to live to finish the whull, before I lay up my axe. Chopping comes quite nateral to me, and I wish no other employment; but Jared Ransom said that he thought the sugar was likely to be scurce this season, seeing that so many folks was coming into the settlement, and so I concluded to take the 'bush' on sheares, for this one spring. What's the best news, Judge, concarning ashes? do pots hold so that a man can live by them still? I s'pose they will if they keep on fighting across the water."

"Thou reasonest with judgment, William," returned Marmaduke. "So long as the old world is to be convulsed with wars, so long will the harvest of America continue."

"Well, it's an ill wind, Judge, that blows nobody any good. I'm sure the country is in a thriving way; and, though I know you kalkilate greatly on the trees, setting as much store by them as some men would by their children, yet, to my eyes, they are a sore sight at any time, unless I'm privileged to work my will on them; in which case, I can't say but they are more to my liking. I have heern the settlers from the old countries say, that their rich men keep great oaks and elms, that would make a barrel of pots to the tree, standing round their doors and humsteads, and scattered over their farms, just to look at. Now, I call no country much improved, that is pretty well covered with trees. Stumps are a different thing, for they don't shade the land; and besides, if you dig them, they make a fence that will turn any thing bigger than a hog, being grand for breachy cattle."

"Opinions on such subjects vary much, in different countries," said Marmaduke; "but it is not as ornaments that I value the noble trees of this country; it is for their usefulness. We are stripping the forests, as if a single year would replace what we destroy. But the hour approaches, when the laws will take notice of not only the woods, but the game they contain also."

With this consoling reflection, Marmaduke remounted, and the equestrians passed the sugar-camp, on their way to the promised landscape of Richard. The wood-chopper was left alone, in the bosom of the forest, to pursue his labours. Elizabeth turned her head, when they reached the point where they were to descend the mountain, and thought that the slow fires, that were glimmering under his enormous kettles, his little brush shelter, covered with pieces of hemlock bark, his gigantic size, as he wielded his ladle with a steady and knowing air, aided by the back-ground of stately trees, with their spouts and troughs, formed, altogether, no unreal picture of human life in its first stages of civilization. Perhaps whatever the scene possessed of a romantic character was not injured by the powerful tones of Kirby's voice, ringing through the woods, as he again awoke his strains to another tune, which was but little more scientific than the former. All that she understood of the words, were—

"And when the proud forest is falling,
To my oxen cheerfully calling,
From morn until night I am bawling,
    Woe, back there, and hoy and gee;
Till our labour is mutually ended,
By my strength and cattle befriended,
And against the musquitoes defended,
    By the bark of the walnut tree.—

"Away! then, you lads who would buy land,
Choose the oak that grows on the high land,
Or the silvery pine on the dry land,
    It matters but little to me."

Chapter XXI

"Speed! Malise, speed! such cause of haste
Thine active sinews never brac'd."
Scott, *The Lady of the Lake*, III.xiii.3–4.

THE ROADS of Otsego, if we except the principal highways, were, at the early day of our tale, but little better than wood-paths. The high trees that were growing on the very verge of the wheel-tracks, excluded the sun's rays, unless at meridian, and the slowness of the evaporation, united with the rich mould of vegetable decomposition, that covered the whole country, to the depth of several inches, occasioned but an indifferent foundation for the footing of travellers. Added to these were the inequalities of a natural surface, and the constant recurrence of enormous and slippery roots, that were laid bare by the removal of the light soil, together with stumps of trees, to make a passage not only difficult, but dangerous. Yet the riders, among these numerous obstructions, which were such as would terrify an unpractised eye, gave no demonstrations of uneasiness, as their horses toiled through the sloughs, or trotted with uncertain paces along the dark route. In many places, the marks on the trees were the only indications of a road, with, perhaps, an occasional remnant of a pine, that, by being cut close to the earth, so as to leave nothing visible but its base of roots, spreading for twenty feet in every direction, was apparently placed there as a beacon, to warn the traveller that it was the centre of a highway.

Into one of these roads the active Sheriff led the way, first striking out of the footpath, by which they had descended from the sugar-bush, across a little bridge, formed of round logs laid loosely on sleepers of pine, in which large openings, of a formidable width, were frequent. The nag of Richard, when it reached one of these gaps, laid its nose along the logs, and stepped across the difficult passage with the sagacity of a man; but the blooded filly which Miss Temple rode disdained so humble a movement. She made a step or two with an unusual caution, and then, on reaching the broadest opening, obedient to the curb and whip of her fearless mistress, she bounded across the dangerous pass, with the activity of a squirrel.

"Gently, gently, my child," said Marmaduke, who was following in the manner of Richard——"this is not a country for equestrian feats. Much prudence is requisite, to journey through our rough paths with safety. Thou mayst practise thy skill in horsemanship on the plains of New-Jersey, with safety, but in the hills of Otsego, they must be suspended for a time."

"I may as well, then, relinquish my saddle at once, dear sir," returned his daughter; "for if it is to be laid aside until this wild country be improved, old age will overtake me, and put an end to what you term my equestrian feats."

"Say not so, my child," returned her father; "but if thou venturest again, as in crossing this bridge, old age will never overtake thee, but I shall be left to mourn thee, cut off in thy pride, my Elizabeth. If thou hadst seen this district of country, as I did, when it lay in the sleep of nature, and had witnessed its rapid changes, as it awoke to supply the wants of man, thou wouldst curb thy impatience for a little time, though thou shouldst not check thy steed."

"I recollect hearing you speak of your first visit to these woods, but the impression is faint, and blended with the confused images of childhood. Wild and unsettled as it may yet seem, it must have been a thousand times more dreary then. Will you repeat, dear sir, what you then thought of your enterprise, and what you felt?"

During this speech of Elizabeth, which was uttered with the fervour of affection, young Edwards rode more closely to the side of the Judge, and bent his dark eyes on his countenance, with an expression that seemed to read his thoughts.

"Thou wast then young, my child, but must remember when I left thee and thy mother, to take my first survey of these uninhabited mountains," said Marmaduke. "But thou dost not feel all the secret motives that can urge a man to endure privations in order to accumulate wealth. In my case they have not been trifling, and God has been pleased to smile on my efforts. If I have encountered pain, famine, and disease, in accomplishing the settlement of this rough territory, I have not the misery of failure to add to the grievances."

"Famine!" echoed Elizabeth; "I thought this was the land of abundance! had you famine to contend with?"

"Even so, my child," said her father. "Those who look around them now, and see the loads of produce that issue out of every wild path in these mountains, during the season of travelling, will hardly credit that no more than five years have elapsed, since the tenants of these woods were compelled to eat the scanty fruits of the forest to sustain life, and, with their unpractised skill, to hunt the beasts as food for their starving families."

"Ay!" cried Richard, who happened to overhear the last of this speech, between the notes of the wood-chopper's song, which he was endeavouring to breathe aloud; "that was the starving-time*, cousin Bess. I grew as lank as a weasel that fall, and my face was as pale as one of your fever-and-ague visages. Monsieur Le Quoi, there, fell away like a pumpkin in drying; nor do I think you have got fairly over it yet, Monsieur. Benjamin, I thought, bore it with a worse grace than any of the family, for he swore it was harder to endure than a short allowance in the calm latitudes. Benjamin is a sad fellow to swear, if you starve him ever so little. I had half a mind to quit you then, 'duke, and to go into Pennsylvania to fatten; but, damn it, thinks I, we are sisters' children, and I will live or die with him, after all."

"I do not forget thy kindness," said Marmaduke, "nor that we are of one blood."

"But, my dear father," cried the wondering Elizabeth, "was there actual suffering? where were the beautiful and fertile vales of the Mohawk? could they not furnish food for your wants?"

*The author has no better apology for interrupting the interest of a work of fiction by these desultory dialogues, than that they have reference to facts. In reviewing his work, after so many years, he is compelled to confess it is injured by too many allusions to incidents that are not at all suited to satisfy the just expectations of the general reader. One of these events is slightly touched on, in the commencement of this chapter.

More than thirty years since, a very near and dear relative of the writer, an elder sister and a second mother, was killed by a fall from a horse, in a ride among the very mountains mentioned in this tale. Few of her sex and years were more extensively known, or more universally beloved, than the admirable woman who thus fell a victim to the chances of the wilderness.

"It was a season of scarcity; the necessities of life commanded a high price in Europe, and were greedily sought after by the speculators. The emigrants, from the east to the west, invariably passed along the valley of the Mohawk, and swept away the means of subsistence, like a swarm of locusts. Nor were the people on the Flats in a much better condition. They were in want themselves, but they spared the little excess of provisions, that nature did not absolutely require, with the justice of the German character. There was no grinding of the poor. The word speculator was then unknown to them. I have seen many a stout man, bending under the load of the bag of meal, which he was carrying from the mills of the Mohawk, through the rugged passes of these mountains, to feed his half-famished children, with a heart so light, as he approached his hut, that the thirty miles he had passed seemed nothing. Remember, my child, it was in our very infancy: we had neither mills, nor grain, nor roads, nor often clearings; —we had nothing of increase, but the mouths that were to be fed; for, even at that inauspicious moment, the restless spirit of emigration was not idle; nay, the general scarcity, which extended to the east, tended to increase the number of adventurers."

"And how, dearest father, didst thou encounter this dreadful evil?" said Elizabeth, unconsciously adopting the dialect of her parent, in the warmth of her sympathy. "Upon thee must have fallen the responsibility, if not the suffering."

"It did, Elizabeth," returned the Judge, pausing for a single moment, as if musing on his former feelings. "I had hundreds, at that dreadful time, daily looking up to me for bread. The sufferings of their families, and the gloomy prospect before them, had paralysed the enterprise and efforts of my settlers; hunger drove them to the woods for food, but despair sent them, at night, enfeebled and wan, to a sleepless pillow. It was not a moment for inaction. I purchased cargoes of wheat from the granaries of Pennsylvania; they were landed at Albany, and brought up the Mohawk in boats; from thence it was transported on pack-horses into the wilderness, and distributed amongst my people. Seines were made, and the lakes and rivers were dragged for fish. Something like a miracle was wrought in our favour, for enormous shoals of herrings were discovered to have wandered five hundred miles, through the windings of the impetuous Susquehanna, and the lake was alive with their numbers. These were at length caught, and dealt out to the people, with proper portions of salt; and from that moment, we again began to prosper."*

"Yes," cried Richard, "and I was the man who served out the fish and the salt. When the poor devils came to receive their rations, Benjamin, who was my deputy, was obliged to keep them off by stretching ropes around me, for they smelt so of garlic, from eating nothing but the wild onion, that the fumes put me out, often, in my measurement. You were a child then, Bess, and knew nothing of the matter, for great care was observed to keep both you and your mother from suffering. That year put me back, dreadfully, both in the breed of my hogs, and of my turkeys."

"No, Bess," cried the Judge, in a more cheerful tone, disregarding the interruption of his cousin, "he who hears of the settlement of a country, knows but little of the toil and suffering by which it is accomplished. Unimproved and wild as this district now seems to your eyes, what was it when I first entered the hills! I left my party, the morning of my arrival, near the farms of the Cherry Valley, and, following a deer-path, rode to the summit of the mountain, that I have since called Mount Vision; for the sight that there met my eyes seemed to me as the deceptions of a dream. The fire had run over the pinnacle, and, in a great measure, laid open the view. The leaves were fallen, and I mounted a tree, and sat for an hour looking on the silent wilderness. Not an opening was to be seen in the boundless forest, except where the lake lay, like a mirror of glass. The water was covered by myriads of the wild-fowl that migrate with the changes in the season; and, while in my situation on the branch of the beech, I saw a bear, with her cubs, descend to the shore to drink. I had met many deer, gliding through the woods, in my journey; but not the vestige of a man could I trace, during my progress, nor from my elevated observatory. No clearing, no hut, none of the winding roads that are now to

*All this was literally true.

be seen, were there; nothing but mountains rising behind mountains, and the valley, with its surface of branches, enlivened here and there with the faded foliage of some tree, that parted from its leaves with more than ordinary reluctance. Even the Susquehanna was then hid, by the height and density of the forest."

"And were you alone?" asked Elizabeth;—"passed you the night in that solitary state?"

"Not so, my child," returned her father. "After musing on the scene for an hour, with a mingled feeling of pleasure and desolation, I left my perch, and descended the mountain. My horse was left to browse on the twigs that grew within his reach, while I explored the shores of the lake, and the spot where Templeton stands. A pine of more than ordinary growth stood where my dwelling is now placed; a wind-row had been opened through the trees from thence to the lake, and my view was but little impeded. Under the branches of that tree I made my solitary dinner; I had just finished my repast as I saw a smoke curling from under the mountain, near the eastern bank of the lake. It was the only indication of the vicinity of man that I had then seen. After much toil, I made my way to the spot, and found a rough cabin of logs, built against the foot of a rock, and bearing the marks of a tenant, though I found no one within it.—"

"It was the hut of Leather-stocking," said Edwards, quickly.

"It was; though I, at first, supposed it to be a habitation of the Indians. But while I was lingering around the spot, Natty made his appearance, staggering under the carcass of a buck that he had slain. Our acquaintance commenced at that time; before, I had never heard that such a being tenanted the woods. He launched his bark canoe, and set me across the foot of the lake, to the place where I had fastened my horse, and pointed out a spot where he might get a scanty browsing until the morning; when I returned and passed the night in the cabin of the hunter."

Miss Temple was so much struck by the deep attention of young Edwards, during this speech, that she forgot to resume her interrogatories; but the youth himself continued the discourse, by asking—

"And how did the Leather-stocking discharge the duties of a host, sir?"

"Why, simply but kindly, until late in the evening, when he discovered my name and object, and the cordiality of his manner very sensibly diminished, or, I might better say, disappeared. He considered the introduction of the settlers as an innovation on his rights, I believe; for he expressed much dissatisfaction at the measure, though it was in his confused and ambiguous manner. I hardly understood his objections myself, but supposed they referred chiefly to an interruption of the hunting."

"Had you then purchased the estate, or were you examining it with an intent to buy?" asked Edwards, a little abruptly.

"It had been mine for several years. It was with a view to people the land that I visited the lake. Natty treated me hospitably, but coldly, I thought, after he learnt the nature of my journey. I slept on his own bear-skin, however, and in the morning joined my surveyors again."

"Said he nothing of the Indian rights, sir? The Leather-stocking is much given to impeach the justice of the tenure by which the whites hold the country."

"I remember that he spoke of them, but I did not clearly comprehend him, and may have forgotten what he said; for the Indian title was extinguished so far back as the close of the old war; and if it had not been at all, I hold under the patents of the Royal Governors, confirmed by an act of our own State Legislature, and no court in the country can affect my title."

"Doubtless, sir, your title is both legal and equitable," returned the youth, coldly, reining his horse back, and remaining silent till the subject was changed.

It was seldom Mr. Jones suffered any conversation to continue, for a great length of time, without his participation. It seems that he was of the party that Judge Temple had designated as his surveyors; and he embraced the opportunity of the pause that succeeded the retreat of young Edwards, to take up the discourse, and with it a narration of their further proceedings, after his own manner. As it wanted, however, the interest that had accompanied the description of the

Judge, we must decline the task of committing his sentences to paper.

They soon reached the point where the promised view was to be seen. It was one of those picturesque and peculiar scenes, that belong to the Otsego, but which required the absence of the ice, and the softness of a summer's landscape, to be enjoyed in all its beauty. Marmaduke had early forewarned his daughter of the season, and of its effect on the prospect, and after casting a cursory glance at its capabilities, the party returned homeward, perfectly satisfied that its beauties would repay them for the toil of a second ride, at a more propitious season.

"The spring is the gloomy time of the American year," said the Judge; "and it is more peculiarly the case in these mountains. The winter seems to retreat to the fastnesses of the hills, as to the citadel of its dominion, and is only expelled, after a tedious siege, in which either party, at times, would seem to be gaining the victory."

"A very just and apposite figure, Judge Temple," observed the Sheriff; "and the garrison under the command of Jack Frost make formidable sorties—you understand what I mean by sorties, Monsieur; sallies, in English—and sometimes drive General Spring and his troops back again into the low countries."

"Yes, sair," returned the Frenchman, whose prominent eyes were watching the precarious footsteps of the beast he rode, as it picked its dangerous way among the roots of trees, holes, log-bridges, and sloughs, that formed the aggregate of the highway. "Je vous entend; de low countrie is freeze up for half de year."

The error of Mr. Le Quoi was not observed by the Sheriff; and the rest of the party were yielding to the influence of the changeful season, which was already teaching the equestrians that a continuance of its mildness was not to be expected for any length of time. Silence and thoughtfulness succeeded the gayety and conversation that had prevailed during the commencement of the ride, as clouds began to gather about the heavens, apparently collecting from every quarter, in quick motion, without the agency of a breath of air.

While riding over one of the cleared eminences that

occurred in their route, the watchful eye of Judge Temple pointed out to his daughter the approach of a tempest. Flurries of snow already obscured the mountain that formed the northern boundary of the lake, and the genial sensation which had quickened the blood through their veins, was already succeeded by the deadening influence of an approaching *northwester*.

All of the party were now busily engaged in making the best of their way to the village, though the badness of the roads frequently compelled them to check the impatience of their horses, which often carried them over places that would not admit of any gait faster than a walk.

Richard continued in advance, followed by Mr. Le Quoi; next to whom rode Elizabeth, who seemed to have imbibed the distance which pervaded the manner of young Edwards, since the termination of the discourse between the latter and her father. Marmaduke followed his daughter, giving her frequent and tender warnings as to the management of her horse. It was, possibly, the evident dependence that Louisa Grant placed on his assistance, which induced the youth to continue by her side, as they pursued their way through a dreary and dark wood, where the rays of the sun could but rarely penetrate, and where even the daylight was obscured and rendered gloomy by the deep forests that surrounded them. No wind had yet reached the spot where the equestrians were in motion, but that dead stillness that often precedes a storm, contributed to render their situation more irksome than if they were already subjected to the fury of the tempest. Suddenly the voice of young Edwards was heard shouting, in those appalling tones that carry alarm to the very soul, and which curdle the blood of those that hear them—

"A tree! a tree! whip—spur for your lives! a tree! a tree!"

"A tree! a tree!" echoed Richard, giving his horse a blow, that caused the alarmed beast to jump nearly a rod, throwing the mud and water into the air, like a hurricane.

"Von tree! von tree!" shouted the Frenchman, bending his body on the neck of his charger, shutting his eyes, and playing on the ribs of his beast with his heels, at a rate that caused him to be conveyed, on the crupper of the Sheriff, with a marvellous speed.

Elizabeth checked her filly, and looked up, with an unconscious but alarmed air, at the very cause of their danger, while she listened to the crackling sounds that awoke the stillness of the forest; but, at the next instant, her bridle was seized by her father, who cried—

"God protect my child!" and she felt herself hurried onward, impelled by the vigour of his nervous arm.

Each one of the party bowed to his saddle-bows, as the tearing of branches was succeeded by a sound like the rushing of the winds, which was followed by a thundering report, and a shock that caused the very earth to tremble, as one of the noblest ruins of the forest fell directly across their path.

One glance was enough to assure Judge Temple that his daughter, and those in front of him, were safe, and he turned his eyes, in dreadful anxiety, to learn the fate of the others. Young Edwards was on the opposite side of the tree, his form thrown back in his saddle to its utmost distance, his left hand drawing up his bridle with its greatest force, while the right grasped that of Miss Grant, so as to draw the head of her horse under its body. Both the animals stood shaking in every joint with terror, and snorting fearfully. Louisa herself had relinquished her reins, and with her hands pressed on her face, sat bending forward in her saddle, in an attitude of despair mingled strangely with resignation.

"Are you safe?" cried the Judge, first breaking the awful silence of the moment.

"By God's blessing," returned the youth; "but if there had been branches to the tree we must have been lost—"

He was interrupted by the figure of Louisa, slowly yielding in her saddle; and but for his arm, she would have sunken to the earth. Terror, however, was the only injury that the clergyman's daughter had sustained, and, with the aid of Elizabeth, she was soon restored to her senses. After some little time was lost in recovering her strength, the young lady was replaced in her saddle, and, supported on either side, by Judge Temple and Mr. Edwards, she was enabled to follow the party in their slow progress.

"The sudden falling of the trees," said Marmaduke, "are the most dangerous accidents in the forest, for they are not to be foreseen, being impelled by no winds, nor any extraneous or visible cause, against which we can guard."

"The reason of their falling, Judge Temple, is very obvious," said the Sheriff. "The tree is old and decayed, and it is gradually weakened by the frosts, until a line drawn from the centre of gravity falls without its base, and then the tree comes of a certainty; and I should like to know, what greater compulsion there can be for any thing, than a mathematical certainty. I studied mathe——"

"Very true, Richard," interrupted Marmaduke; "thy reasoning is true, and, if my memory be not over treacherous, was furnished by myself, on a former occasion. But how is one to guard against the danger? canst thou go through the forests, measuring the bases, and calculating the centres of the oaks? answer me that, friend Jones, and I will say thou wilt do the country a service."

"Answer thee that, friend Temple!" returned Richard; "a well-educated man can answer thee any thing, sir. Do any trees fall in this manner, but such as are decayed? Take care not to approach the roots of a rotten tree, and you will be safe enough."

"That would be excluding us entirely from the forests," said Marmaduke. "But, happily, the winds usually force down most of these dangerous ruins, as their currents are admitted into the woods by the surrounding clearings, and such a fall as this has been is very rare."

Louisa, by this time, had recovered so much strength, as to allow the party to proceed at a quicker pace; but long before they were safely housed, they were overtaken by the storm; and when they dismounted at the door of the Mansion-house, the black plumes of Miss Temple's hat were drooping with the weight of a load of damp snow, and the coats of the gentlemen were powdered with the same material.

While Edwards was assisting Louisa from her horse, the warm-hearted girl caught his hand with fervour, and whispered—

"Now, Mr. Edwards, both father and daughter owe their lives to you."

A driving, north-westerly storm succeeded; and before the

sun was set, every vestige of spring had vanished; the lake, the mountains, the village, and the fields, being again hid under one dazzling coat of snow.

Chapter XXII

"Men, boys, and girls,
Desert th' unpeopled village; and wild crowds
Spread o'er the plain, by the sweet frenzy driven."
Somerville, *The Chace*, II.197–99.

FROM THIS time to the close of April, the weather continued to be a succession of great and rapid changes. One day, the soft airs of spring seemed to be stealing along the valley, and, in unison with an invigorating sun, attempting, covertly, to rouse the dormant powers of the vegetable world; while on the next, the surly blasts from the north would sweep across the lake, and erase every impression left by their gentle adversaries. The snow, however, finally disappeared, and the green wheat fields were seen in every direction, spotted with the dark and charred stumps that had, the preceding season, supported some of the proudest trees of the forest. Ploughs were in motion, wherever those useful implements could be used, and the smokes of the sugar-camps were no longer seen issuing from the woods of maple. The lake had lost the beauty of a field of ice, but still a dark and gloomy covering concealed its waters, for the absence of currents left them yet hid under a porous crust, which, saturated with the fluid, barely retained enough strength to preserve the contiguity of its parts. Large flocks of wild geese were seen passing over the country, which hovered, for a time, around the hidden sheet of water, apparently searching for a resting-place; and then, on finding themselves excluded by the chill covering, would soar away to the north, filling the air with discordant screams, as if venting their complaints at the tardy operations of nature.

For a week, the dark covering of the Otsego was left to the undisturbed possession of two eagles, who alighted on the centre of its field, and sat eyeing their undisputed territory. During the presence of these monarchs of the air, the flocks of migrating birds avoided crossing the plain of ice, by turning into the hills, apparently seeking the protection of the forests, while the white and bald heads of the tenants of the lake were turned upward, with a look of contempt. But the time had come, when even these kings of birds were to be dispossessed. An opening had been gradually increasing, at the lower extremity of the lake, and around the dark spot where the current of the river prevented the formation of ice, during even the coldest weather; and the fresh southerly winds, that now breathed freely upon the valley, made an impression on the waters. Mimic waves begun to curl over the margin of the frozen field, which exhibited an outline of crystallizations, that slowly receded towards the north. At each step the power of the winds and the waves increased, until, after a struggle of a few hours, the turbulent little billows succeeded in setting the whole field in motion, when it was driven beyond the reach of the eye, with a rapidity, that was as magical as the change produced in the scene by this expulsion of the lingering remnant of winter. Just as the last sheet of agitated ice was disappearing in the distance, the eagles rose, and soared with a wide sweep above the clouds, while the waves tossed their little caps of snow into the air, as if rioting in their release from a thraldom of five months' duration.

The following morning Elizabeth was awakened by the exhilarating sounds of the martins, who were quarreling and chattering around the little boxes suspended above her windows, and the cries of Richard, who was calling, in tones animating as the signs of the season itself—

"Awake! awake! my fair lady! the gulls are hovering over the lake already, and the heavens are alive with pigeons. You may look an hour before you can find a hole, through which, to get a peep at the sun. Awake! awake! lazy ones! Benjamin is overhauling the ammunition, and we only wait for our breakfasts, and away for the mountains and pigeon-shooting."

There was no resisting this animated appeal, and in a few minutes Miss Temple and her friend descended to the parlour. The doors of the hall were thrown open, and the mild, balmy air of a clear spring morning was ventilating the apartment, where the vigilance of the ex-steward had been so long maintaining an artificial heat, with such unremitted diligence. The gentlemen were impatiently waiting for their morning's repast, each equipt in the garb of a sportsman. Mr. Jones made many visits to the southern door, and would cry—

"See, cousin Bess! see, 'duke! the pigeon-roosts of the south have broken up! They are growing more thick every instant. Here is a flock that the eye cannot see the end of. There is food enough in it to keep the army of Xerxes for a month, and feathers enough to make beds for the whole country. Xerxes, Mr. Edwards, was a Grecian king, who—no, he was a Turk, or a Persian, who wanted to conquer Greece, just the same as these rascals will overrun our wheat-fields, when they come back in the fall.——Away! away! Bess; I long to pepper them."

In this wish both Marmaduke and young Edwards seemed equally to participate, for the sight was exhilarating to a sportsman; and the ladies soon dismissed the party, after a hasty breakfast.

If the heavens were alive with pigeons, the whole village seemed equally in motion, with men, women, and children. Every species of fire-arms, from the French ducking-gun, with a barrel near six feet in length, to the common horseman's pistol, was to be seen in the hands of the men and boys; while bows and arrows, some made of the simple stick of a walnut sapling, and others in a rude imitation of the ancient cross-bows, were carried by many of the latter.

The houses, and the signs of life apparent in the village, drove the alarmed birds from the direct line of their flight, towards the mountains, along the sides and near the bases of which they were glancing in dense masses, equally wonderful by the rapidity of their motion, and their incredible numbers.

We have already said, that across the inclined plane which fell from the steep ascent of the mountain to the banks of the Susquehanna, ran the highway, on either side of which a clearing of many acres had been made, at a very early day. Over those clearings, and up the eastern mountain, and along the dangerous path that was cut into its side, the different individuals posted themselves, and in a few moments the attack commenced.

Amongst the sportsmen was the tall, gaunt form of Leather-stocking, walking over the field, with his rifle hanging on his arm, his dogs at his heels; the latter now scenting the dead or wounded birds, that were beginning to tumble from the flocks, and then crouching under the legs of their master, as if they participated in his feelings, at this wasteful and unsportsmanlike execution.

The reports of the fire-arms became rapid, whole volleys rising from the plain, as flocks of more than ordinary numbers darted over the opening, shadowing the field, like a cloud; and then the light smoke of a single piece would issue from among the leafless bushes on the mountain, as death was hurled on the retreat of the affrighted birds, who were rising from a volley, in a vain effort to escape. Arrows, and missiles of every kind, were in the midst of the flocks; and so numerous were the birds, and so low did they take their flight, that even long poles, in the hands of those on the sides of the mountain, were used to strike them to the earth.

During all this time, Mr. Jones, who disdained the humble and ordinary means of destruction used by his companions, was busily occupied, aided by Benjamin, in making arrangements for an assault of a more than ordinarily fatal character. Among the relics of the old military excursions, that occasionally are discovered throughout the different districts of the western part of New-York, there had been found in Templeton, at its settlement, a small swivel, which would carry a ball of a pound weight. It was thought to have been deserted by a war-party of the whites, in one of their inroads into the Indian settlements, when, perhaps, convenience or their necessity induced them to leave such an encumbrance behind them in the woods. This miniature cannon had been released from the rust, and being mounted on little wheels, was now in a state for actual service. For several years, it was the sole organ for extraordinary rejoicings used in those mountains. On the mornings of the Fourths of July, it would be heard ringing among the hills, and even Captain Hollister, who was the highest authority in that part of the country on all such occasions, affirmed that, considering its dimensions, it was no despicable gun for a salute. It was somewhat the worse for the service it had performed, it is true, there being but a trifling difference in size between the touch-hole and the muzzle. Still, the grand conceptions of Richard had suggested the importance of such an instrument, in hurling death at his nimble enemies. The swivel was dragged by a horse into a part of the open space, that the Sheriff thought most eligible for planting a battery of the kind, and Mr. Pump proceeded to load it. Several handfuls of duck-shot were placed on top of the powder, and the Major-domo announced that his piece was ready for service.

The sight of such an implement collected all the idle spectators to the spot, who, being mostly boys, filled the air with cries of exultation and delight. The gun was pointed high, and Richard, holding a coal of fire in a pair of tongs, patiently took his seat on a stump, awaiting the appearance of a flock worthy of his notice.

So prodigious was the number of the birds, that the scattering fire of the guns, with the hurling of missiles, and the cries of the boys, had no other effect than to break off small flocks from the immense masses that continued to dart along the valley, as if the whole of the feathered tribe were pouring through that one pass. None pretended to collect the game, which lay scattered over the fields in such profusion, as to cover the very ground with the fluttering victims.

Leather-stocking was a silent, but uneasy spectator of all these proceedings, but was able to keep his sentiments to himself until he saw the introduction of the swivel into the sports.

"This comes of settling a country!" he said—"here have I known the pigeons to fly for forty long years, and, till you made your clearings, there was nobody to skear or to hurt them. I loved to see them come into the woods, for they were company to a body; hurting nothing; being, as it was, as harmless as a garter-snake. But now it gives me sore thoughts when I hear the frighty things whizzing through the air, for I know it's only a motion to bring out all the brats in the village. Well! the Lord won't see the waste of his creaters for nothing, and right will be done to the pigeons, as well as others, by-and-by.——There's Mr. Oliver, as bad as the rest of them, firing into the flocks as if he was shooting down nothing but Mingo warriors."

Among the sportsmen was Billy Kirby, who, armed with an old musket, was loading, and, without even looking into the air, was firing, and shouting as his victims fell even on his own person. He heard the speech of Natty, and took upon himself to reply—

"What! old Leather-stocking," he cried, "grumbling at the loss of a few pigeons! If you had to sow your wheat twice, and three times, as I have done, you wouldn't be so massyfully feeling'd to'ards the divils.—Hurrah, boys! scatter the feathers. This is better than shooting at a turkey's head and neck, old fellow."

"It's better for you, maybe, Billy Kirby," replied the indignant old hunter, "and all them that don't know how to put a ball down a rifle-barrel, or how to bring it up ag'in with a true aim; but it's wicked to be shooting into flocks in this wastey manner; and none do it, who know how to knock over a single bird. If a body has a craving for pigeon's flesh, why! it's made the same as all other creater's, for man's eating, but not to kill twenty and eat one. When I want such a thing, I go into the woods till I find one to my liking, and then I shoot him off the branches without touching a feather of another, though there might be a hundred on the same tree. You couldn't do such a thing, Billy Kirby—you couldn't do it if you tried."

"What's that, old corn-stalk! you sapless stub!" cried the wood-chopper. "You've grown wordy, since the affair of the turkey; but if you're for a single shot, here goes at that bird which comes on by himself."

The fire from the distant part of the field had driven a single pigeon below the flock to which it belonged, and, frightened with the constant reports of the muskets, it was approaching the spot where the disputants stood, darting first from one side, and then to the other, cutting the air with the swiftness of lightning, and making a noise with its wings, not unlike the rushing of a bullet. Unfortunately for the wood-chopper, notwithstanding his vaunt, he did not see this bird until it was too late to fire as it approached, and he pulled his trigger at the unlucky moment when it was darting immediately over his head. The bird continued its course with the usual velocity.

Natty lowered the rifle from his arm, when the challenge was made, and, waiting a moment, until the terrified victim had got in a line with his eye, and had dropped near the bank of the lake, he raised it again with uncommon rapidity, and fired. It might have been chance, or it might have been skill, that produced the result; it was probably a union of both; but the pigeon whirled over in the air, and fell into the lake, with a broken wing. At the sound of his rifle, both his dogs started from his feet, and in a few minutes the "slut" brought out the bird, still alive.

The wonderful exploit of Leather-stocking was noised through the field with great rapidity, and the sportsmen gathered in to learn the truth of the report.

"What," said young Edwards, "have you really killed a pigeon on the wing, Natty, with a single ball?"

"Haven't I killed loons before now, lad, that dive at the flash?" returned the hunter. "It's much better to kill only such as you want, without wasting your powder and lead, than to be firing into God's creaters in this wicked manner. But I come out for a bird, and you know the reason why I like small game, Mr. Oliver, and now I have got one I will go home, for I don't relish to see these wasty ways that you are all practysing, as if the least thing was not made for use, and not to destroy."

"Thou sayest well, Leather-stocking," cried Marmaduke, "and I begin to think it time to put an end to this work of destruction."

"Put an ind, Judge, to your clearings. An't the woods his work as well as the pigeons? Use, but don't waste. Wasn't the woods made for the beasts and birds to harbour in? and when man wanted their flesh, their skins, or their feathers, there's the place to seek them. But I'll go to the hut with my own game, for I wouldn't touch one of the harmless things that kiver the ground here, looking up with their eyes on me, as if they only wanted tongues to say their thoughts."

With this sentiment in his mouth, Leather-stocking threw his rifle over his arm, and, followed by his dogs, stepped across the clearing with great caution, taking care not to tread on one of the wounded birds in his path. He soon entered the bushes on the margin of the lake, and was hid from view.

Whatever impression the morality of Natty made on the Judge, it was utterly lost on Richard. He availed himself of the gathering of the sportsmen, to lay a plan for one "fell swoop" of destruction. The musketmen were drawn up in battle array, in a line extending on each side of his artillery, with orders to await the signal of firing from himself.

"Stand by, my lads," said Benjamin, who acted as an aide-de-camp, on this occasion, "stand by, my hearties, and when Squire Dickens heaves out the signal to begin the firing, d'ye see, you may open upon them in a broadside. Take care and fire low, boys, and you'll be sure to hull the flock."

"Fire low!" shouted Kirby—"hear the old fool! If we fire low, we may hit the stumps, but not ruffle a pigeon."

"How should you know, you lubber?" cried Benjamin, with a very unbecoming heat, for an officer on the eve of battle—"how should you know, you grampus? Havn't I sailed aboard of the Boadishy for five years? and wasn't it a standing order to fire low, and to hull your enemy? Keep silence at your guns, boys, and mind the order that is passed."

The loud laughs of the musketmen were silenced by the more authoritative voice of Richard, who called for attention and obedience to his signals.

Some millions of pigeons were supposed to have already passed, that morning, over the valley of Templeton; but nothing like the flock that was now approaching had been seen before. It extended from mountain to mountain in one solid blue mass, and the eye looked in vain over the southern hills to find its termination. The front of this living column was distinctly marked by a line, but very slightly indented, so regular and even was the flight. Even Marmaduke forgot the morality of Leather-stocking as it approached, and, in common with the rest, brought his musket to a poise.

"Fire!" cried the Sheriff, clapping a coal to the priming of the cannon. As half of Benjamin's charge escaped through the touch-hole, the whole volley of the musketry preceded the report of the swivel. On receiving this united discharge of small-arms, the front of the flock darted upward, while, at the same instant, myriads of those in the rear rushed with amazing rapidity into their places, so that when the column of white smoke gushed from the mouth of the little cannon, an accumulated mass of objects was gliding over its point of direction. The roar of the gun echoed along the mountains, and died away to the north, like distant thunder, while the whole flock of alarmed birds seemed, for a moment, thrown into one disorderly and agitated mass. The air was filled with their irregular flight, layer rising above layer, far above the tops of the highest pines, none daring to advance beyond the dangerous pass; when, suddenly, some of the leaders of the feathered tribe shot across the valley, taking their flight directly over the village, and hundreds of thousands in their rear followed the example, deserting the eastern side of the plain to their persecutors and the slain.

"Victory!" shouted Richard, "victory! we have driven the enemy from the field."

"Not so, Dickon," said Marmaduke; "the field is covered with them; and, like the Leather-stocking, I see nothing but eyes, in every direction, as the innocent sufferers turn their heads in terror. Full one half of those that have fallen are yet alive: and I think it is time to end the sport; if sport it be."

"Sport!" cried the Sheriff; "it is princely sport. There are some thousands of the blue-coated boys on the ground, so that every old woman in the village may have a pot-pie for the asking."

"Well, we have happily frightened the birds from this side of the valley," said Marmaduke, "and the carnage must of necessity end, for the present.——Boys, I will give thee sixpence a hundred for the pigeons' heads only; so go to work, and bring them into the village."

This expedient produced the desired effect, for every urchin on the ground went industriously to work to wring the necks of the wounded birds. Judge Temple retired towards his dwelling with that kind of feeling, that many a man has experienced before him, who discovers, after the excitement of the moment has passed, that he has purchased pleasure at the price of misery to others. Horses were loaded with the dead; and, after this first burst of sporting, the shooting of pigeons became a business, with a few idlers, for the remainder of the season. Richard, however, boasted for many a year, of his shot with the "cricket;" and Benjamin gravely asserted, that he thought they killed nearly as many pigeons on that day, as there were Frenchmen destroyed on the memorable occasion of Rodney's victory.

Chapter XXIII

"Help, masters, help; here's a fish hangs in the net, like a poor man's right in the law."

Pericles, II.i.116–17.

THE ADVANCE of the season now became as rapid, as its first approach had been tedious and lingering. The days were uniformly mild, while the nights, though cool, were no longer chilled by frosts. The whip-poor-will was heard whistling his melancholy notes along the margin of the lake, and the ponds and meadows were sending forth the music of their thousand tenants. The leaf of the native poplar was seen quivering in the woods; the sides of the mountains began to lose their hue of brown, as the lively green of the different members of the forest blended their shades with the permanent colours of the pine and hemlock; and even the buds of the tardy oak were swelling with the promise of the coming summer. The gay and fluttering blue-bird, the social robin, and the industrious little wren, were all to be seen, enlivening the fields with their presence and their songs; while the soaring fish-hawk was already hovering over the waters of the Otsego, watching, with native voracity, for the appearance of his prey.

The tenants of the lake were far-famed for both their quantities and their quality, and the ice had hardly disappeared, before numberless little boats were launched from the shores, and the lines of the fishermen were dropped into the inmost recesses of its deepest caverns, tempting the unwary animals with every variety of bait, that the ingenuity or the art of man had invented. But the slow, though certain adventures with hook and line were ill-suited to the profusion and impatience of the settlers. More destructive means were resorted to; and, as the season had now arrived when the bass-fisheries were allowed by the provisions of the law, that Judge Temple had procured, the Sheriff declared his intention by availing himself of the first dark night, to enjoy the sport in person—

"And you shall be present, cousin Bess," he added, when he announced this design, "and Miss Grant, and Mr. Edwards; and I will show you what I call fishing—not nibble, nibble, nibble, as 'duke does, when he goes after the salmon-trout. There he will sit, for hours, in a broiling sun, or, perhaps, over a hole in the ice, in the coldest days in winter, under the lee of a few bushes, and not a fish will he catch, after all this mortification of the flesh. No, no—give me a good seine, that's fifty or sixty fathoms in length, with a jolly parcel of boatmen to crack their jokes, the while, with Benjamin to steer, and let us haul them in by thousands; I call that fishing."

"Ah! Dickon," cried Marmaduke, "thou knowest but little of the pleasure there is in playing with the hook and line, or thou wouldst be more saving of the game. I have known thee to leave fragments enough behind thee, when thou hast headed a night-party on the lake, to feed a dozen famishing families."

"I shall not dispute the matter, Judge Temple: this night will I go; and I invite the company to attend, and then let them decide between us."

Richard was busy, during most of the afternoon, making his preparations for the important occasion. Just as the light of the setting sun had disappeared, and a new moon had begun to throw its shadows on the earth, the fishermen took their departure in a boat, for a point that was situated on the western shore of the lake, at the distance of rather more than half a mile from the village. The ground had become settled, and the walking was good and dry. Marmaduke, with his daughter, her friend, and young Edwards, continued on the high, grassy banks, at the outlet of the placid sheet of water, watching the dark object that was moving across the lake, until it entered the shade of the western hills, and was lost to the eye. The distance round by land, to the point of destination, was a mile, and he observed—

"It is time for us to be moving; the moon will be down ere we reach the point, and then the miraculous hauls of Dickon will commence."

The evening was warm, and, after the long and dreary winter from which they had just escaped, delightfully invigorating. Inspirited by the scene, and their anticipated amusement, the youthful companions of the Judge followed his steps, as he led them along the shores of the Otsego, and through the skirts of the village.

"See!" said young Edwards; "they are building their fire already; it glimmers for a moment, and dies again, like the light of a fire-fly."

"Now it blazes," cried Elizabeth; "you can perceive figures moving around the light. Oh! I would bet my jewels against the gold beads of Remarkable, that my impatient cousin Dickon had an agency in raising that bright flame;—and see; it fades again, like most of his brilliant schemes."

"Thou hast guessed the truth, Bess," said her father; "he has thrown an armful of brush on the pile, which has burnt out as soon as lighted. But it has enabled them to find a better fuel, for their fire begins to blaze with a more steady flame. It is the true fisherman's beacon now; observe how beautifully it throws its little circle of light on the water."

The appearance of the fire urged the pedestrians on, for even the ladies had become eager to witness the miraculous draught. By the time they reached the bank which rose above the low point, where the fishermen had landed, the moon had sunk behind the tops of the western pines, and, as most of the stars were obscured by clouds, there was but little other light than that which proceeded from the fire. At the suggestion of Marmaduke, his companions paused to listen to the conversation of those below them, and examine the party, for a moment, before they descended to the shore.

The whole group were seated around the fire, with the exception of Richard and Benjamin; the former of whom occupied the root of a decayed stump, that had been drawn to the spot as part of their fuel, and the latter was standing, with his arms a-kimbo, so near to the flame, that the smoke occasionally obscured his solemn visage, as it waved around the pile, in obedience to the night-airs, that swept gently over the water.

"Why, look you, Squire," said the Major-domo, "you may call a lake-fish that will weigh twenty or thirty pounds a serious matter; but to a man who has hauled in a shovel-nosed shirk, d'ye see, it's but a poor kind of fishing, after all."

"I don't know, Benjamin," returned the Sheriff; "a haul of one thousand Otsego bass, without counting pike, pickerel, perch, bull-pouts, salmon-trouts, and suckers, is no bad fishing, let me tell you. There may be sport in sticking a shark, but what is he good for after you have got him? Now any one of the fish that I have named is fit to set before a king."

"Well, Squire," returned Benjamin, "just listen to the philosophy of the thing. Would it stand to reason, that such fish should live and be catched in this here little pond of water, where it's hardly deep enough to drown a man, as you'll find in the wide ocean, where, as every body knows, that is, every body that has followed the seas, whales and grampuses are to be seen, that are as long as one of them pine trees on yonder mountain?"

"Softly, softly, Benjamin," said the Sheriff, as if he wished to save the credit of his favourite; " why some of the pines will measure two hundred feet, and even more."

"Two hundred or two thousand, it's all the same thing," cried Benjamin, with an air which manifested that he was not easily to be bullied out of his opinion, on a subject like the present—"Haven't I been there, and haven't I seen? I have said that you fall in with whales as long as one of them there pines; and what I have once said I'll stand to!"

During this dialogue, which was evidently but the close of a much longer discussion, the huge frame of Billy Kirby was seen extended on one side of the fire, where he was picking his teeth with splinters of the chips near him, and occasionally shaking his head, with distrust of Benjamin's assertions.

"I've a notion," said the wood-chopper, "that there's water in this lake to swim the biggest whale that ever was invented; and, as to the pines, I think I ought to know so'thing consarning them; I have chopped many a one that was sixty times the length of my helve, without counting the eye; and I b'lieve, Benny, that if the old pine that stands in the hollow of the Vision Mountain, just over the village,—you may see the tree itself by looking up, for the moon is on its top yet;—well, now I b'lieve, if that same tree was planted out in the deepest part of the lake, there would be water enough for the biggest ship that ever was built to float over it, without touching its upper branches, I do."

"Did'ee ever see a ship, Master Kirby?" roared the steward—"did'ee ever see a ship, man? or any craft bigger than a lime-scow, or a wood-boat, on this here small bit of fresh water?"

"Yes, I have," said the wood-chopper, stoutly; "I can say that I have, and tell no lie."

"Did'ee ever see a British ship, Master Kirby? an English line-of-battle ship, boy? Where away did'ee ever fall in with a regular-built vessel, with starn-post and cutwater, garboard streak and plank-shear, gangways and hatchways, and waterways, quarter-deck and forecastle, ay, and flush-deck?—tell me that, man, if you can; where away did'ee ever fall in with a full-rigged, regular-built, decked vessel?"

The whole company were a good deal astounded with this overwhelming question, and even Richard afterwards remarked, that it "was a thousand pities that Benjamin could not read, or he must have made a valuable officer to the British marine. It is no wonder that they overcome the French so easily on the water, when even the lowest sailor so well understood the different parts of a vessel." But Billy Kirby was a fearless wight, and had great jealousy of foreign dictation; he had arisen on his feet, and turned his back to the fire, during the voluble delivery of this interrogatory, and when the steward ended, contrary to all expectation, he gave the following spirited reply:—

"Where! why on the North River, and maybe on Champlain. There's sloops on the river, boy, that would give a hard time on't to the stoutest vessel King George owns. They carry masts of ninety feet in the clear, of good, solid pine, for I've been at the chopping of many a one in Varmount state. I wish I was captain in one of them, and you was in that Board-dish that you talk so much about, and we'd soon see what good Yankee stuff is made on, and whether a Varmounter's hide an't as thick as an Englishman's."

The echoes from the opposite hills, which were more than half a mile from the fishing point, sent back the discordant laugh that Benjamin gave forth at this challenge; and the woods that covered their sides, seemed, by the noise that issued from their shades, to be full of mocking demons.

"Let us descend to the shore," whispered Marmaduke, "or there will soon be ill blood between them. Benjamin is a fearless boaster, and Kirby, though good-natured, is a careless son of the forest, who thinks one American more than a match for six Englishmen. I marvel that Dickon is silent, where there is such a trial of skill in the superlative!"

The appearance of Judge Temple and the ladies produced, if not a pacification, at least a cessation of hostilities. Obedient to the directions of Mr. Jones, the fishermen prepared to launch their boat, which had been seen in the back-ground of the view, with the net carefully disposed on a little platform in its stern, ready for service. Richard gave vent to his reproaches at the tardiness of the pedestrians, when all the turbulent passions of the party were succeeded by a calm, as mild and as placid as that which prevailed over the beautiful sheet of water, that they were about to rifle of its best treasures.

The night had now become so dark as to render objects, without the reach of the light of the fire, not only indistinct, but, in most cases, invisible. For a little distance the water was discernible, glistening, as the glare from the fire danced over its surface, touching it, here and there, with red, quivering streaks; but at a hundred feet from the shore, there lay a boundary of impenetrable gloom. One or two stars were shining through the openings of the clouds, and the lights were seen in the village, glimmering faintly, as if at an immeasurable distance. At times, as the fire lowered, or as the horizon cleared, the outline of the mountain, on the other side of the lake, might be traced, by its undulations; but its shadow was cast, wide and dense, on the bosom of the water, rendering the darkness, in that direction, trebly deep.

Benjamin Pump was invariably the cockswain and net-caster of Richard's boat, unless the Sheriff saw fit to preside in person; and, on the present occasion, Billy Kirby, and a youth of about half his strength, were assigned to the oars. The remainder of the assistants were stationed at the drag ropes. The arrangements were speedily made, and Richard gave the signal to "shove off."

Elizabeth watched the motion of the batteau, as it pulled from the shore, letting loose its rope as it went, but it very soon disappeared in the darkness, when the ear was her only guide to its evolutions. There was great affectation of stillness, during all these manœuvres, in order, as Richard assured them, "not to frighten the bass, who were running into the shoal waters, and who would approach the light, if not disturbed by the sounds from the fishermen."

The hoarse voice of Benjamin was alone heard, issuing out of the gloom, as he uttered, in authoritative tones, "pull larboard oar," "pull starboard," "give way together, boys," and such other dictative mandates as were necessary for the right disposition of his seine. A long time was passed in this necessary part of the process, for Benjamin prided himself greatly on his skill in throwing the net, and, in fact, most of the success of the sport depended on its being done with judgment. At length a loud splash in the water, as he threw away the "staff," or "stretcher," with a hoarse call from the steward, of "clear," announced that the boat was returning; when Richard seized a brand from the fire, and ran to a point, as far above the centre of the fishing ground, as the one from which the batteau had started was below it.

"Stick her in dead for the Squire, boys," said the steward, "and we'll have a look at what grows in this here pond."

In place of the falling net, were now to be heard the quick strokes of the oars, and the noise of the rope, running out of the boat. Presently the batteau shot into the circle of light, and in an instant she was pulled to shore. Several eager hands were extended, to receive the line, and, both ropes being equally well manned, the fishermen commenced hauling in, with slow and steady drags, Richard standing in the centre, giving orders, first to one party and then to the other, to increase or slacken their efforts, as occasion required. The visiters were posted near him, and enjoyed a fair view of the whole operation, which was slowly advancing to an end.

Opinions, as to the result of their adventure, were now freely hazarded by all the men, some declaring that the net came in as light as a feather, and others affirming that it seemed to be full of logs. As the ropes were many hundred feet in length, these opposing sentiments were thought to be of little moment by the Sheriff, who would go first to one line and then to the other, giving each a small pull, in order to enable him to form an opinion for himself.

"Why, Benjamin," he cried, as he made his first effort in this way, "you did not throw the net clear. I can move it with my little finger. The rope slackens in my hand."

"Did you ever see a whale, Squire?" responded the steward: "I say that if that there net is foul, the devil is in the lake in the shape of a fish, for I cast it as fair as ever rigging was rove over the quarter-deck of a flag-ship."

But Richard discovered his mistake, when he saw Billy Kirby before him, standing with his feet in the water, at an angle of forty-five degrees, inclining shorewards, and expending his gigantic strength in sustaining himself in that posture. He ceased his remonstrances, and proceeded to the party at the other line.

"I see the 'staffs,' " shouted Mr. Jones;—"gather in, boys, and away with it; to shore with her—to shore with her."

At this cheerful sound, Elizabeth strained her eyes, and saw the ends of the two sticks on the seine, emerging from the darkness, while the men closed near to each other, and formed a deep bag of their net. The exertions of the fishermen sensibly increased, and the voice of Richard was heard, encouraging them to make their greatest efforts, at the present moment.

"Now's the time, my lads," he cried; "let us get the ends to land, and all we have will be our own—away with her!"

"Away with her it is," echoed Benjamin—"hurrah! ho-a-hoy, ho-a-hoy, ho-a!"

"In with her," shouted Kirby, exerting himself in a manner that left nothing for those in his rear to do, but to gather up the slack of the rope which passed through his hands.

"Staff, ho!" shouted the steward.

"Staff, ho!" echoed Kirby, from the other rope.

The men rushed to the water's edge, some seizing the upper rope, and some the lower, or lead-rope, and began to haul with great activity and zeal. A deep semicircular sweep, of the little balls that supported the seine in its perpendicular position, was plainly visible to the spectators, and, as it rapidly lessened in size, the bag of the net appeared, while an occasional flutter on the water, announced the uneasiness of the prisoners it contained.

"Haul in, my lads," shouted Richard—"I can see the dogs kicking to get free. Haul in, and here's a cast that will pay for the labour."

Fishes of various sorts were now to be seen, entangled in

the meshes of the net, as it was passed through the hands of the labourers, and the water, at a little distance from the shore, was alive with the movements of the alarmed victims. Hundreds of white sides were glancing up to the surface of the water, and glistening in the fire-light, when, frightened at the uproar and the change, the fish would again dart to the bottom, in fruitless efforts for freedom.

"Hurrah!" shouted Richard; "one or two more heavy drags, boys, and we are safe."

"Cheerily, boys, cheerily!" cried Benjamin; "I see a salmon-trout that is big enough for a chowder."

"Away with you, you varmint!" said Billy Kirby, plucking a bull-pout from the meshes, and casting the animal back into the lake with contempt. "Pull, boys, pull; here's all kinds, and the Lord condemn me for a liar, if there an't a thousand bass!"

Inflamed beyond the bounds of discretion at the sight, and forgetful of the season, the wood-chopper rushed to his middle into the water, and begun to drive the reluctant animals before him from their native element.

"Pull heartily, boys," cried Marmaduke, yielding to the excitement of the moment, and laying his hands to the net, with no trifling addition to the force. Edwards had preceded him, for the sight of the immense piles of fish, that were slowly rolling over on the gravelly beach, had impelled him also to leave the ladies, and join the fishermen.

Great care was observed in bringing the net to land, and, after much toil, the whole shoal of victims was safely deposited in a hollow of the bank, where they were left to flutter away their brief existence, in the new and fatal element.

Even Elizabeth and Louisa were greatly excited and highly gratified, by seeing two thousand captives thus drawn from the bosom of the lake, and laid as prisoners at their feet. But when the feelings of the moment were passing away, Marmaduke took in his hands a bass, that might have weighed two pounds, and, after viewing it a moment, in melancholy musing, he turned to his daughter, and observed—

"This is a fearful expenditure of the choicest gifts of Providence. These fish, Bess, which thou seest lying in such piles before thee, and which, by to-morrow evening, will be rejected food on the meanest table in Templeton, are of a quality and flavour that, in other countries, would make them esteemed a luxury on the tables of princes or epicures. The world has no better fish than the bass of Otsego: it unites the richness of the shad* to the firmness of the salmon."

"But surely, dear sir," cried Elizabeth, "they must prove a great blessing to the country, and a powerful friend to the poor."

"The poor are always prodigal, my child, where there is plenty, and seldom think of a provision against the morrow. But if there can be any excuse for destroying animals in this manner, it is in taking the bass. During the winter, you know, they are entirely protected from our assaults by the ice, for they refuse the hook; and during the hot months, they are not seen. It is supposed they retreat to the deep and cool waters of the lake, at that season; and it is only in the spring and autumn, that, for a few days, they are to be found, around the points where they are within the reach of a seine. But, like all the other treasures of the wilderness, they already begin to disappear, before the wasteful extravagance of man."

"Disappear, 'duke! disappear!" exclaimed the Sheriff; "if you don't call this appearing, I know not what you will. Here are a good thousand of the shiners, some hundreds of suckers, and a powerful quantity of other fry. But this is always the way with you, Marmaduke; first it's the trees, then it's the deer, after that it's the maple sugar, and so on to the end of the chapter. One day, you talk of canals, through a country where there's a river or a lake every half-mile, just because the water won't run the way you wish it to go; and the next, you say something about mines of coal, though any man who has good eyes, like myself—I say with good eyes—can see more wood than would keep the city of London in fuel for fifty years;—wouldn't it, Benjamin?"

"Why, for that, Squire," said the steward, "Lon'on is no small place. If it was stretched an end, all the same as a town on one side of a river, it would cover some such matter as this here lake. Thof I dar'st to say, that the wood in sight

*Of all the fish the writer has ever tasted, he thinks the one in question the best.

might sarve them a good turn, seeing that the Lon'oners mainly burn coal."

"Now we are on the subject of coal, Judge Temple," interrupted the Sheriff, "I have a thing of much importance to communicate to you; but I will defer it until to-morrow. I know that you intend riding into the eastern part of the Patent, and I will accompany you, and conduct you to a spot, where some of your projects may be realized. We will say no more now, for there are listeners; but a secret has this evening been revealed to me, 'duke, that is of more consequence to your welfare, than all your estate united."

Marmaduke laughed at the important intelligence, to which in a variety of shapes he was accustomed, and the Sheriff, with an air of great dignity, as if pitying his want of faith, proceeded in the business more immediately before them. As the labour of drawing the net had been very great, he directed one party of his men to commence throwing the fish into piles, preparatory to the usual division, while another, under the superintendence of Benjamin, prepared the seine for a second haul.

Chapter XXIV

"While from its margin, terrible to tell!
Three sailors with their gallant boatswain fell."
Falconer, *The Shipwreck*, II.354–55.

WHILE THE fishermen were employed in making the preparations for an equitable division of the spoil, Elizabeth and her friend strolled a short distance from the group, along the shore of the lake. After reaching a point, to which even the brightest of the occasional gleams of the fire did not extend, they turned, and paused a moment, in contemplation of the busy and lively party they had left, and of the obscurity, which, like the gloom of oblivion, seemed to envelope the rest of the creation.

"This is indeed a subject for the pencil," exclaimed Elizabeth. "Observe the countenance of that wood-chopper, while he exults in presenting a larger fish than common to my cousin Sheriff; and see, Louisa, how handsome and considerate my dear father looks, by the light of that fire, where he stands viewing the havoc of the game. He seems melancholy, as if he actually thought that a day of retribution was to follow this hour of abundance and prodigality! Would they not make a picture, Louisa?"

"You know that I am ignorant of all such accomplishments, Miss Temple."

"Call me by my christian name," interrupted Elizabeth; "this is not a place, neither is this a scene, for forms."

"Well, then, if I may venture an opinion," said Louisa, timidly, "I should think it might indeed make a picture. The selfish earnestness of that Kirby over his fish, would contrast finely with the—the—expression of Mr. Edwards' face. I hardly know what to call it; but it is—a—is—you know what I would say, dear Elizabeth."

"You do me too much credit, Miss Grant," said the heiress; "I am no diviner of thoughts, or interpreter of expressions."

There was certainly nothing harsh, or even cold, in the manner of the speaker, but still it repressed the conversation, and they continued to stroll still further from the party, retaining each other's arm, but observing a profound silence. Elizabeth, perhaps conscious of the improper phraseology of her last speech, or perhaps excited by the new object that met her gaze, was the first to break the awkward cessation in the discourse, by exclaiming—

"Look, Louisa! we are not alone; there are fishermen lighting a fire on the other side of the lake, immediately opposite to us: it must be in front of the cabin of Leather-stocking!"

Through the obscurity, which prevailed most, immediately under the eastern mountain, a small and uncertain light was plainly to be seen, though, as it was occasionally lost to the eye, it seemed struggling for existence. They observed it to move, and sensibly to lower, as if carried down the descent of the bank to the shore. Here, in a very short time, its flame gradually expanded, and grew brighter, until it became of the size of a man's head, when it continued to shine, a steady ball of fire.

Such an object, lighted as it were by magic, under the brow of the mountain, and in that retired and unfrequented place, gave double interest to the beauty and singularity of its appearance. It did not at all resemble the large and unsteady light of their own fire, being much more clear and bright, and retaining its size and shape with perfect uniformity.

There are moments when the best regulated minds are, more or less, subjected to the injurious impressions, which few have escaped in infancy, and Elizabeth smiled at her own weakness, while she remembered the idle tales, which were circulated through the village, at the expense of the Leather-stocking. The same ideas seized her companion, and at the same instant, for Louisa pressed nearer to her friend, as she said, in a low voice, stealing a timid glance towards the bushes and trees that overhung the bank near them—

"Did you ever hear the singular ways of this Natty spoken of, Miss Temple? They say that, in his youth, he was an Indian warrior, or, what is the same thing, a white man leagued with the savages; and it is thought he has been concerned in many of their inroads, in the old wars."

"The thing is not at all improbable," returned Elizabeth: "he is not alone in that particular."

"No, surely; but is it not strange, that he is so cautious

with his hut? He never leaves it, without fastening it in a remarkable manner; and, in several instances, when the children, or even the men of the village have wished to seek a shelter there from the storms, he has been known to drive them from his door, with rudeness and threats. That surely is singular in this country."

"It is certainly not very hospitable; but we must remember his aversion to the customs of civilized life. You heard my father say, a few days since, how kindly he was treated by him, on his first visit to this place." Elizabeth paused, and smiled, with an expression of peculiar archness, though the darkness hid its meaning from her companion, as she continued:—"Besides, he certainly admits the visits of Mr. Edwards, whom we both know to be far from a savage."

To this speech Louisa made no reply, but continued gazing on the object which had elicited her remarks. In addition to the bright and circular flame, was now to be seen a fainter, though a vivid light, of an equal diameter to the other at the upper end, but which, after extending, downward, for many feet, gradually tapered to a point at its lower extremity. A dark space was plainly visible between the two, and the new illumination was placed beneath the other, the whole forming an appearance not unlike an inverted note of admiration. It was soon evident that the latter was nothing but the reflection from the water of the former, and that the object, whatever it might be, was advancing across, or rather over the lake, for it seemed to be several feet above its surface, in a direct line with themselves. Its motion was amazingly rapid, the ladies having hardly discovered that it was moving at all, before the waving light of a flame was discerned, losing its regular shape, while it increased in size, as it approached.

"It appears to be supernatural!" whispered Louisa, beginning to retrace her steps towards the party.

"It is beautiful!" exclaimed Elizabeth.

A brilliant, though waving flame was now plainly visible, gracefully gliding over the lake, and throwing its light on the water, in such a manner as to tinge it slightly; though, in the air, so strong was the contrast, the darkness seemed to have the distinctness of material substances, as if the fire were embedded in a setting of ebony. This appearance, however, gradually wore off, and the rays from the torch struck out, and enlightened the atmosphere in front of it, leaving the background in a darkness that was more impenetrable than ever.

"Ho! Natty, is that you?" shouted the Sheriff—"paddle in, old boy, and I'll give you a mess of fish that is fit to place before the Governor."

The light suddenly changed its direction, and a long and slightly-built boat hove up out of the gloom, while the red glare fell on the weather-beaten features of the Leather-stocking, whose tall person was seen erect in the frail vessel, wielding, with the grace of an experienced boatman, a long fishing-spear, which he held by its centre, first dropping one end and then the other into the water, to aid in propelling the little canoe of bark, we will not say through, but over the water. At the farther end of the vessel, a form was faintly seen, guiding its motions, and using a paddle with the ease of one who felt there was no necessity for exertion. The Leather-stocking struck his spear lightly against the short staff which upheld, on a rude grating framed of old hoops of iron, the knots of pine that composed the fuel; and the light, which glared high, for an instant fell on the swarthy features, and dark, glancing eyes of Mohegan.

The boat glided along the shore until it arrived opposite the fishing-ground, when it again changed its direction, and moved on to the land, with a motion so graceful, and yet so rapid, that it seemed to possess the power of regulating its own progress. The water, in front of the canoe, was hardly ruffled by its passage, and no sound betrayed the collision, when the light fabric shot on the gravelly beach, for nearly half its length, Natty receding a step or two from its bow, in order to facilitate the landing.

"Approach, Mohegan," said Marmaduke; "approach, Leather-stocking, and load your canoe with the bass. It would be a shame to assail the animals with the spear, when such multitudes of victims lie here, that will be lost as food, for the want of mouths to consume them."

"No, no, Judge," returned Natty, his tall figure stalking over the narrow beach, and ascending to the little grassy bottom where the fish were laid in piles; "I eat of no man's wasty ways. I strike my spear into the eels, or the trout, when I crave the creaters, but I wouldn't be helping to such a sinful kind of fishing, for the best rifle that was ever brought out from the old countries. If they had fur, like a beaver, or you could tan their hides, like a buck, something might be said in favour of taking them by the thousands with your nets; but as God made them for man's food, and for no other disarnable reason, I call it sinful and wasty to catch more than can be eat."

"Your reasoning is mine: for once, old hunter, we agree in opinion; and I heartily wish we could make a convert of the Sheriff. A net of half the size of this would supply the whole village with fish, for a week, at one haul."

The Leather-stocking did not relish this alliance in sentiment, and he shook his head doubtingly, as he answered—

"No, no; we are not much of one mind, Judge, or you'd never turn good hunting grounds into stumpy pastures. And you fish and hunt out of rule; but to me, the flesh is sweeter, where the creater has some chance for its life; for that reason, I always use a single ball, even if it be at a bird or a squirrel; besides, it saves lead, for, when a body knows how to shoot, one piece of lead is enough for all, except hard-lived animals."

The Sheriff heard these opinions with great indignation, and when he completed the last arrangement for the division, by carrying, with his own hands, a trout of a large size, and placing it on four different piles in succession, as his vacillating ideas of justice required, he gave vent to his spleen.

"A very pretty confederacy, indeed! Judge Temple, the landlord and owner of a township, with Nathaniel Bumppo, a lawless squatter, and professed deer-killer, in order to preserve the game of the county! But, 'duke, when I fish, I fish; so, away, boys, for another haul, and we'll send out wagons and carts, in the morning, to bring in our prizes!"

Marmaduke appeared to understand that all opposition to the will of the Sheriff would be useless, and he strolled from the fire, to the place where the canoe of the hunters lay, whither the ladies and Oliver Edwards had already preceded him.

Curiosity induced the females to approach this spot, but it was a different motive that led the youth thither. Elizabeth examined the light ashen timbers and thin bark covering of the canoe, in admiration of its neat but simple execution, and with wonder, that any human being could be so daring as to trust his life in so frail a vessel. But the youth explained to her the buoyant properties of the boat, and its perfect safety, when under proper management, adding, in such glowing terms, a description of the manner in which the fish were struck with the spear, that she changed, suddenly, from an apprehension of the danger of the excursion, to a desire to participate in its pleasures. She even ventured a proposition to that effect to her father, laughing, at the same time, at her own wish, and accusing herself of acting under a woman's caprice.

"Say not so, Bess," returned the Judge; "I would have you above the idle fears of a silly girl. These canoes are the safest kind of boats, to those who have skill and steady nerves. I have crossed the broadest part of the Oneida in one much smaller than this."

"And I the Ontary," interrupted the Leather-stocking; "and that with squaws in the canoe, too. But the Delaware women are used to the paddle, and are good hands in a boat of this nater. If the young lady would like to see an old man strike a trout for his breakfast, she is welcome to a seat. John will say the same, seeing that he built the canoe, which was only launched yesterday; for I'm not over curous at such small work as brooms, and basket-making, and other like Indian trades."

Natty gave Elizabeth one of his significant laughs, with a kind nod of the head, when he concluded his invitation; but Mohegan, with the native grace of an Indian, approached, and taking her soft, white hand into his own swarthy and wrinkled palm, said—

"Come, grand-daughter of Miquon, and John will be glad. Trust the Indian: his head is old, though his hand is not steady. The Young Eagle will go, and see that no harm hurts his sister."

"Mr. Edwards," said Elizabeth, blushing slightly, "your friend Mohegan has given a promise for you. Do you redeem the pledge?"

"With my life, if necessary, Miss Temple," cried the youth,

with fervour. "The sight is worth some little apprehension, for of real danger there is none. I will go with you and Miss Grant, however, to save appearances."

"With me!" exclaimed Louisa; "no, not with me, Mr. Edwards; nor surely do you mean to trust yourself in that slight canoe."

"But I shall, for I have no apprehensions any longer," said Elizabeth, stepping into the boat, and taking a seat where the Indian directed. "Mr. Edwards, you may remain, as three do seem to be enough for such an egg-shell."

"It shall hold a fourth," cried the young man, springing to her side, with a violence that nearly shook the weak fabric of the vessel asunder;—"pardon me, Miss Temple, that I do not permit these venerable Charons to take you to the shades, unattended by your genius."

"Is it a good or evil spirit?" asked Elizabeth.

"Good to you."

"And mine," added the maiden, with an air that strangely blended pique with satisfaction. But the motion of the canoe gave rise to new ideas, and fortunately afforded a good excuse to the young man to change the discourse.

It appeared to Elizabeth, that they glided over the water by magic, so easy and graceful was the manner in which Mohegan guided his little bark. A slight gesture with his spear, indicated the way in which the Leather-stocking wished to go, and a profound silence was preserved by the whole party, as a precaution necessary to the success of their fishery. At that point of the lake, the water shoaled regularly, differing, in this particular, altogether, from those parts, where the mountains rose, nearly in perpendicular precipices, from the beach. There, the largest vessels could have lain, with their yards interlocked with the pines; while here, a scanty growth of rushes lifted their tops above the lake, gently curling the waters, as their bending heads waved with the passing breath of the night air. It was at the shallow points, only, that the bass could be found, or the net cast with success.

Elizabeth saw thousands of these fish, swimming in shoals along the shallow and warm waters of the shore; for the flaring light of their torch laid bare the mysteries of the lake, as plainly as if the limpid sheet of the Otsego was but another atmosphere. Every instant she expected to see the impending spear of Leather-stocking darting into the thronging hosts that were rushing beneath her, where it would seem that a blow could not go amiss; and where, as her father had already said, the prize that would be obtained was worthy any epicure. But Natty had his peculiar habits; and, it would seem, his peculiar tastes also. His tall stature, and his erect posture, enabled him to see much further than those who were seated in the bottom of the canoe; and he turned his head warily, in every direction, frequently bending his body forward, and straining his vision, as if desirous of penetrating the water, that surrounded their boundary of light. At length his anxious scrutiny was rewarded with success, and, waving his spear from the shore, he said, in a cautious tone—

"Send her outside the bass, John; I see a laker there, that has run out of the school. It's sildom one finds such a creater in shallow water, where a spear can touch it."

Mohegan gave a wave of assent with his hand, and in the next instant the canoe was without the "run of the bass," and in water nearly twenty feet in depth. A few additional knots were laid on the grating, and the light penetrated to the bottom. Elizabeth then saw a fish of unusual size, floating above small pieces of logs and sticks. The animal was only distinguishable, at that distance, by a slight, but almost imperceptible motion of its fins and tail. The curiosity excited by this unusual exposure of the secrets of the lake, seemed to be mutual between the heiress of the land and the lord of these waters, for the "salmon-trout" soon announced his interest, by raising his head and body, for a few degrees above a horizontal line, and then dropping them again into a horizontal position.

"Whist, whist," said Natty, in a low voice, on hearing a slight sound made by Elizabeth, in bending over the side of the canoe, in curiosity; "'tis a sceary animal, and it's a far stroke for a spear. My handle is but fourteen foot, and the creater lies a good eighteen from the top of the water; but I'll try him, for he's a ten-pounder."

While speaking, the Leather-stocking was poising and directing his weapon. Elizabeth saw the bright, polished tines, as they slowly and silently entered the water, where the refraction pointed them many degrees from the true direction of the fish; and she thought that the intended victim saw them also, as he seemed to increase the play of his tail and fins, though without moving his station. At the next instant, the tall body of Natty bent to the water's edge, and the handle of his spear disappeared in the lake. The long, dark streak of the gliding weapon, and the little bubbling vortex, which followed its rapid flight, were easily to be seen; but it was not until the handle shot again into the air, by its own re-action, and its master, catching it in his hand, threw its tines uppermost, that Elizabeth was acquainted with the success of the blow. A fish of great size was transfixed by the barbed steel, and was very soon shaken from its impaled situation into the bottom of the canoe.

"That will do, John," said Natty, raising his prize by one of his fingers, and exhibiting it before the torch; "I shall not strike another blow to-night."

The Indian again waved his hand, and replied with the simple and energetic monosyllable of—

"Good."

Elizabeth was awakened from the trance, created by this scene, and by gazing in that unusual manner at the bottom of the lake, by the hoarse sounds of Benjamin's voice, and the dashing of oars, as the heavier boat of the seine-drawers approached the spot where the canoe lay, dragging after it the folds of the net.

"Haul off, haul off, Master Bumppo," cried Benjamin; "your top-light frightens the fish, who see the net, and sheer off soundings. A fish knows as much as a horse, or, for that matter, more, seeing that it's brought up on the water. Haul off, Master Bumppo, haul off, I say, and give a wide berth to the seine."

Mohegan guided their little canoe to a point where the movements of the fishermen could be observed, without interruption to the business, and then suffered it to lie quietly on the water, looking like an imaginary vessel floating in air. There appeared to be much ill-humour among the party in the batteau, for the directions of Benjamin were not only frequent, but issued in a voice that partook largely of dissatisfaction.

"Pull larboard oar, will ye, Master Kirby," cried the old seaman; "pull larboard, best. It would puzzle the oldest admiral in the British fleet to cast this here net fair, with a wake like a corkscrew. Pull starboard, boy, pull starboard oar, with a will."

"Harkee, Mister Pump," said Kirby, ceasing to row, and speaking with some spirit; "I'm a man that likes civil language and decent treatment; such as is right 'twixt man and man. If you want us to go hoy, say so, and hoy I'll go, for the benefit of the company; but I'm not used to being ordered about like dumb cattle."

"Who's dumb cattle!" echoed Benjamin, fiercely, turning his forbidding face to the glare of light from the canoe, and exhibiting every feature teeming with the expression of disgust. "If you want to come aft and cun the boat round, come and be damned, and pretty steerage you'll make of it. There's but another heave of the net in the stern-sheets, and we're clear of the thing. Give way, will ye? and shoot her ahead for a fathom or two, and if you catch me afloat again with such a horse-marine as yourself, why rate me a ship's jackass, that's all."

Probably encouraged by the prospect of a speedy termination to his labour, the wood-chopper resumed his oar, and, under strong excitement, gave a stroke, that not only cleared the boat of the net, but of the steward, at the same instant. Benjamin had stood on the little platform that held the seine, in the stern of the boat, and the violent whirl, occasioned by the vigour of the wood-chopper's arm, completely destroyed his balance. The position of the lights rendered objects in the batteau distinguishable, both from the canoe and the shore; and the heavy fall on the water drew all eyes to the steward, as he lay struggling, for a moment, in sight.

A loud burst of merriment, to which the lungs of Kirby contributed no small part, broke out like a chorus of laughter, and rung along the eastern mountain, in echoes, until it died away in distant, mocking mirth, among the rocks and woods. The body of the steward was seen slowly to disappear, as was expected; but when the light waves, which had been raised by his fall, begun to sink in calmness, and the water finally closed over his head, unbroken and still, a very different feeling pervaded the spectators.

"How fare you, Benjamin?" shouted Richard from the shore.

"The dumb devil can't swim a stroke!" exclaimed Kirby, rising, and beginning to throw aside his clothes.

"Paddle up, Mohegan," cried young Edwards, "the light will show us where he lies, and I will dive for the body."

"Oh! save him! for God's sake, save him!" exclaimed Elizabeth, bowing her head on the side of the canoe in horror.

A powerful and dexterous sweep of Mohegan's paddle sent the canoe directly over the spot, where the steward had fallen, and a loud shout from the Leather-stocking announced that he saw the body.

"Steady the boat while I dive," again cried Edwards.

"Gently, lad, gently," said Natty; "I'll spear the creater up in half the time, and no risk to any body."

The form of Benjamin was lying, about half way to the bottom, grasping with both hands some broken rushes. The blood of Elizabeth curdled to her heart, as she saw the figure of a fellow-creature thus extended under an immense sheet of water, apparently in motion, by the undulations of the dying waves, with its face and hands, viewed by that light, and through the medium of the fluid, already coloured with hues like death.

At the same instant, she saw the shining tines of Natty's spear approaching the head of the sufferer, and entwining themselves, rapidly and dexterously, in the hairs of his queue and the cape of his coat. The body was now raised slowly, looking ghastly and grim, as its features turned upward to the light, and approached the surface. The arrival of the nostrils of Benjamin into their own atmosphere, was announced by a breathing, that would have done credit to a porpoise. For a moment, Natty held the steward suspended, with his head just above the water, while his eyes slowly opened, and stared about him, as if he thought that he had reached a new and unexplored country.

As all the parties acted and spoke together, much less time was consumed in the occurrence of these events, than in their narration. To bring the batteau to the end of the spear, and to raise the form of Benjamin into the boat, and for the whole party to gain the shore, required but a minute. Kirby, aided by Richard, whose anxiety induced him to run into the water to meet his favourite assistant, carried the motionless steward up the bank, and seated him before the fire, while the Sheriff proceeded to order the most approved measures then in use, for the resuscitation of the drowned.

"Run, Billy," he cried, "to the village, and bring up the rum-hogshead that lies before the door, in which I am making vinegar, and be quick, boy, don't stay to empty the vinegar; and stop at Mr. Le Quoi's, and buy a paper of tobacco and half-a-dozen pipes; and ask Remarkable for some salt, and one of her flannel petticoats; and ask Dr. Todd to send his lancet, and to come himself; and——ha! 'duke, what are you about? would you strangle a man, who is full of water, by giving him rum! Help me to open his hand, that I may pat it."

All this time Benjamin sat, with his muscles fixed, his mouth shut, and his hands clenching the rushes, which he had seized in the confusion of the moment, and which, as he held fast, like a true seaman, had been the means of preventing his body from rising again to the surface. His eyes, however, were open, and stared wildly on the group about the fire, while his lungs were playing like a blacksmith's bellows, as if to compensate themselves for the minute of inaction to which they had been subjected. As he kept his lips compressed, with a most inveterate determination, the air was compelled to pass through his nostrils, and he rather snorted than breathed, and in such a manner, that nothing, but the excessive agitation of the Sheriff, could at all justify his precipitous orders.

The bottle, applied to the steward's lips by Marmaduke, acted like a charm. His mouth opened instinctively; his hands dropped the rushes, and seized the glass; his eyes raised from their horizontal stare, to the heavens; and the whole man was lost, for a moment, in a new sensation. Unhappily for the propensity of the steward, breath was as necessary after one of these draughts, as after his submersion, and the time at length arrived when he was compelled to let go the bottle.

"Why, Benjamin!" roared the Sheriff; "you amaze me! for a man of your experience in drownings to act so foolishly! just now, you were half full of water, and now you are"—

"Full of grog," interrupted the steward, his features settling down, with amazing flexibility, into their natural economy. "But, d'ye see, Squire, I kept my hatches close, and it is but little water that ever gets into my scuttle-butt.——Harkee, Master Kirby! I've follow'd the salt water for the better part of a man's life, and have seen some navigation on the fresh; but this here matter I will say in your favour, and that is, that you're the awk'ardest green'un that ever straddled a boat's thwart. Them that likes you for a shipmate, may sail with you, and no thanks; but dam'me if I even walk on the lake shore in your company. For why? you'd as lief drown a man as one of them there fish; not to throw a christian creature so much as a rope's end, when he was adrift, and no life-buoy in sight!—Natty Bumppo, give us your fist. There's them that says you're an Indian, and a scalper, but you've sarved me a good turn, and you may set me down for a friend; thof it would have been more ship-shape to lower the bight of a rope, or running bow-line, below me, than to seize an old seaman by his head-lanyard; but I suppose you are used to taking men by the hair, and seeing you did me good instead of harm thereby, why, it's the same thing, d'ye see."

Marmaduke prevented any reply, and assuming the direction of matters, with a dignity and discretion that at once silenced all opposition from his cousin, Benjamin was despatched to the village by land, and the net was hauled to shore, in such a manner that the fish, for once, escaped its meshes with impunity.

The division of the spoils was made in the ordinary manner, by placing one of the party with his back to the game, who named the owner of each pile. Billy Kirby stretched his large frame on the grass, by the side of the fire, as sentinel until morning, over net and fish; and the remainder of the party embarked in the batteau, to return to the village.

The wood-chopper was seen broiling his supper on the coals, as they lost sight of the fire; and when the boat approached the shore, the torch of Mohegan's canoe was shining again under the gloom of the eastern mountain. Its motion ceased suddenly; a scattering of brands was in the air, and then all remained dark as the conjunction of night, forest, and mountain, could render the scene.

The thoughts of Elizabeth wandered from the youth, who

was holding a canopy of shawls over herself and Louisa, to the hunter and the Indian warrior; and she felt an awakening curiosity to visit a hut, where men of such different habits and temperament were drawn together, as by common impulse.

Chapter XXV

"Cease all this parlance about hills and dales:
None listen to thy scenes of boyish frolic,
Fond dotard! with such tickled ears as thou dost;
Come! to thy tale."

Duo.

MR. JONES arose, on the following morning, with the sun, and, ordering his own and Marmaduke's steeds to be saddled, he proceeded, with a countenance big with some business of unusual moment, to the apartment of the Judge. The door was unfastened, and Richard entered, with the freedom that characterized, not only the intercourse between the cousins, but the ordinary manners of the Sheriff.

"Well, 'duke, to horse," he cried, "and I will explain to you my meaning in the allusions I made last night. David says, in the Psalms—no, it was Solomon, but it was all in the family—Solomon said, there was a time for all things; and, in my humble opinion, a fishing party is not the moment for discussing important subjects—Ha! why what the devil ails you, Marmaduke? an't you well? let me feel your pulse; my grandfather, you know"—

"Quite well in the body, Richard," interrupted the Judge, repulsing his cousin, who was about to assume the functions that properly belonged to Dr. Todd; "but ill at heart. I received letters by the post of last night, after we returned from the point, and this among the number."

The Sheriff took the letter, but without turning his eyes on the writing, for he was examining the appearance of the other with astonishment. From the face of his cousin, the gaze of Richard wandered to the table, which was covered with letters, packets, and newspapers; then to the apartment, and all that it contained. On the bed there was the impression that had been made by a human form, but the coverings were unmoved, and every thing indicated that the occupant of the room had passed a sleepless night. The candles were burnt to the sockets, and had evidently extinguished themselves in their own fragments. Marmaduke had drawn his curtains, and opened both the shutters and the sashes, to admit the balmy air of a spring morning; but his pale cheek, his quivering lip, and his sunken eye, presented, altogether, so very different an appearance from the usual calm, manly, and cheerful aspect of the Judge, that the Sheriff grew each moment more and more bewildered with astonishment. At length Richard found time to cast his eyes on the direction of the letter, which he still held unopened, crumbling it in his hand.

"What! a ship letter!" he exclaimed; "and from England! ha! 'duke, there must be news of importance indeed!"

"Read it," said Marmaduke, pacing the floor in excessive agitation.

Richard, who commonly thought aloud, was unable to read a letter, without suffering part of its contents to escape him in audible sounds. So much of the epistle as was divulged in that manner, we shall lay before the reader, accompanied by the passing remarks of the Sheriff:—

" 'London, February 12th, 1793.' What a devil of a passage she had! but the wind has been northwest, for six weeks, until within the last fortnight. 'Sir, your favours, of August 10th, September 23d, and of December 1st, were received in due season, and the first answered by return of packet. Since the receipt of the last, I' "—Here a long passage was rendered indistinct, by a kind of humming noise, made by the Sheriff. " 'I grieve to say, that'—hum, hum, bad enough, to be sure—'but trust that a merciful Providence has seen fit'—hum, hum, hum; seems to be a good, pious sort of a man, 'duke; belongs to the established church, I dare say; hum, hum—'vessel sailed from Falmouth on or about the 1st September of last year, and'—hum, hum, hum. 'If any thing should transpire, on this afflicting subject, shall not fail'—hum, hum; really a good-hearted man, for a lawyer—'but can communicate nothing further at present.'—Hum, hum. 'The national convention'—hum, hum—'unfortunate Louis'—hum, hum—'example of your Washington'—a very sensible man, I declare, and none of your crazy democrats. Hum, hum—'our gallant navy'—hum, hum—'under our most excellent monarch'—ay, a good man enough, that King George, but bad advisers; hum, hum—'I beg to conclude with assurances of my perfect respect,'—hum, hum—'ANDREW HOLT.'—Andrew Holt—a very sensible, feeling man, this Mr. Andrew Holt, but the writer of evil tidings. What will you do next, cousin Marmaduke?"

"What can I do, Richard, but trust to time, and the will of Heaven? Here is another letter, from Connecticut, but it only repeats the substance of the last. There is but one consoling reflection to be gathered from the English news, which is, that my last letter was received by him, before the ship sailed."

"This is bad enough indeed! 'duke, bad enough indeed! and away go all my plans of putting the wings to the house, to the devil. I had made arrangements for a ride, to introduce you to something of a very important nature. You know how much you think of mines"—

"Talk not of mines," interrupted the Judge; "there is a sacred duty to be performed, and that without delay. I must devote this day to writing; and thou must be my assistant, Richard; it will not do to employ Oliver in a matter of such secrecy and interest."

"No, no, 'duke," cried the Sheriff, squeezing his hand, "I am your man, just now; we are sisters' children, and blood, after all, is the best cement to make friendship stick together. Well, well, there is no hurry about the silver mine, just now; another time will do as well. We shall want Dirky Van, I suppose?"

Marmaduke assented to this indirect question, and the Sheriff relinquished all his intentions, on the subject of the ride, and, repairing to the breakfast parlour, he despatched a messenger to require the immediate presence of Dirck Van der School.

The village of Templeton, at that time, supported but two lawyers, one of whom was introduced to our readers in the bar-room of the "Bold Dragoon," and the other was the gentleman of whom Richard spoke, by the friendly, but familiar appellation of Dirck or Dirky Van. Great good nature, a very tolerable share of skill in his profession, and, considering the circumstances, no contemptible degree of honesty, were the principal ingredients in the character of this man; who was known to the settlers as Squire Van der School, and sometimes by the flattering, though anomalous title of "the Dutch," or "honest lawyer." We would not wish to mislead our readers in their conceptions of any of our characters, and we therefore feel it necessary to add, that the adjective, in the preceding agnomen of Mr. Van der School, was used in direct reference to its substantive. Our orthodox friends need not be told that all merit in this world is comparative; and, once for all, we desire to say, that where any thing which involves qualities or character is asserted, we must be understood to mean, "under the circumstances."

During the remainder of the day, the Judge was closeted with his cousin and his lawyer; and no one else was admitted to his apartment, excepting his daughter. The deep distress, that so evidently afflicted Marmaduke, was, in some measure, communicated to Elizabeth also; for a look of dejection shaded her intelligent features, and the buoyancy of her animated spirits was sensibly softened. Once, on that day, young Edwards, who was a wondering and observant spectator of the sudden alteration produced in the heads of the family, detected a tear stealing over the cheek of Elizabeth, and suffusing her bright eyes, with a softness that did not always belong to their expression.

"Have any evil tidings been received, Miss Temple?" he inquired, with an interest and voice that caused Louisa Grant to raise her head from her needle-work, with a quickness, at which she instantly blushed herself. "I would offer my services to your father, if, as I suspect, he needs an agent in some distant place, and I thought it would give you relief."

"We have certainly heard bad news," returned Elizabeth, "and it may be necessary that my father should leave home, for a short period; unless I can persuade him to trust my cousin Richard with the business, whose absence from the county, just at this time, too, might be inexpedient."

The youth paused a moment, and the blood gathered slowly to his temples, as he continued—

"If it be of a nature that I could execute"—

"It is such as can only be confided to one we know—one of ourselves."

"Surely, you know me, Miss Temple!" he added, with a warmth that he seldom exhibited, but which did sometimes escape him, in the moments of their frank communications—"Have I lived five months under your roof to be a stranger!"

Elizabeth was engaged with her needle, also; and she bent her head to one side, affecting to arrange her muslin; but her hand shook, her colour heightened, and her eyes lost their moisture, in an expression of ungovernable interest, as she said—

"How much do we know of you, Mr. Edwards?"

"How much!" echoed the youth, gazing from the speaker to the mild countenance of Louisa, that was also illuminated with curiosity; "how much! have I been so long an inmate with you, and not known?"

The head of Elizabeth slowly turned from its affected position, and the look of confusion that had blended so strongly with an expression of interest, changed to a smile.

"We know you, sir, indeed: you are called Mr. Oliver Edwards. I understand that you have informed my friend, Miss Grant, that you are a native"—

"Elizabeth!" exclaimed Louisa, blushing to the eyes, and trembling like an aspen; "you misunderstood me, dear Miss Temple; I—I—it was only conjecture. Besides, if Mr. Edwards is related to the natives, why should we reproach him! in what are we better? at least I, who am the child of a poor and unsettled clergyman?"

Elizabeth shook her head, doubtingly, and even laughed, but made no reply, until, observing the melancholy which pervaded the countenance of her companion, who was thinking of the poverty and labours of her father, she continued—

"Nay, Louisa, humility carries you too far. The daughter of a minister of the church can have no superiors. Neither I nor Mr. Edwards is quite your equal, unless," she added, again smiling, "he is in secret a king."

"A faithful servant of the King of kings, Miss Temple, is inferior to none on earth," said Louisa; "but his honours are his own; I am only the child of a poor and friendless man, and can claim no other distinction. Why, then, should I feel myself elevated above Mr. Edwards, because—because—perhaps, he is only very, very distantly related to John Mohegan?"

Glances of a very comprehensive meaning were exchanged

between the heiress and the young man, as Louisa betrayed, while vindicating his lineage, the reluctance with which she admitted his alliance to the old warrior; but not even a smile at the simplicity of their companion was indulged by either.

"On reflection, I must acknowledge that my situation here is somewhat equivocal," said Edwards, "though I may be said to have purchased it with my blood."

"The blood, too, of one of the native lords of the soil!" cried Elizabeth, who evidently put little faith in his aboriginal descent.

"Do I bear the marks of my lineage so very plainly impressed on my appearance? I am dark, but not very red—not more so than common?"

"Rather more so, just now."

"I am sure, Miss Temple," cried Louisa, "you cannot have taken much notice of Mr. Edwards. His eyes are not so black as Mohegan's, or even your own, nor is his hair!"

"Very possibly, then, I can lay claim to the same descent. It would be a great relief to my mind to think so, for I own that I grieve when I see old Mohegan walking about these lands, like the ghost of one of their ancient possessors, and feel how small is my own right to possess them."

"Do you!" cried the youth, with a vehemence that startled the ladies.

"I do, indeed," returned Elizabeth, after suffering a moment to pass in surprise; "but what can I do? what can my father do? Should we offer the old man a home and a maintenance, his habits would compel him to refuse us. Neither, were we so silly as to wish such a thing, could we convert these clearings and farms, again, into hunting-grounds, as the Leather-stocking would wish to see them."

"You speak the truth, Miss Temple," said Edwards. "What can you do, indeed! But there is one thing that I am certain you can and will do, when you become the mistress of these beautiful valleys—use your wealth with indulgence to the poor and charity to the needy;—indeed, you can do no more."

"And that will be doing a good deal," said Louisa, smiling in her turn. "But there will, doubtless, be one to take the direction of such things from her hands."

"I am not about to disclaim matrimony, like a silly girl, who dreams of nothing else from morning till night; but I am a nun, here, without the vow of celibacy. Where shall I find a husband, in these forests?"

"There is none, Miss Temple," said Edwards, quickly, "there is none who has a right to aspire to you, and I know that you will wait to be sought by your equal; or die, as you live, loved, respected, and admired, by all who know you."

The young man seemed to think that he had said all that was required by gallantry, for he arose, and taking his hat, hurried from the apartment. Perhaps Louisa thought that he had said more than was necessary, for she sighed, with an aspiration so low that it was scarcely audible to herself, and bent her head over her work again. And it is possible that Miss Temple wished to hear more, for her eyes continued fixed, for a minute, on the door through which the young man had passed, then glanced quickly towards her companion, when the long silence that succeeded manifested how much zest may be given to the conversation of two maidens under eighteen, by the presence of a youth of three and twenty.

The first person encountered by Mr. Edwards, as he rather rushed than walked from the house, was the little, square-built lawyer, with a large bundle of papers under his arm, a pair of green spectacles on his nose, with glasses at the sides, as if to multiply his power of detecting frauds, by additional organs of vision.

Mr. Van der School was a well-educated man, but of slow comprehension, who had imbibed a wariness in his speeches and actions, from having suffered by his collisions with his more mercurial and apt brethren who had laid the foundations of their practice in the eastern courts, and who had sucked in shrewdness with their mothers' milk. The caution of this gentleman was exhibited in his actions, by the utmost method and punctuality, tinctured with a good deal of timidity; and in his speeches, by a parenthetical style, that frequently left to his auditors a long search after his meaning.

"A good morning to you, Mr. Van der School," said Edwards; "it seems to be a busy day with us, at the Mansion-house."

"Good morning, Mr. Edwards, (if that is your name, (for, being a stranger, we have no other evidence of the fact than your own testimony,) as I understand you have given it to Judge Temple,) good morning, sir. It is, apparently, a busy day, (but a man of your discretion need not be told, (having, doubtless, discovered it of your own accord,) that appearances are often deceitful,) up at the Mansion-house."

"Have you papers of consequence, that will require copying? can I be of assistance in any way?"

"There are papers (as, doubtless, you see (for your eyes are young) by the outsides) that require copying."

"Well, then I will accompany you to your office, and receive such as are most needed, and by night I shall have them done, if there be much haste."

"I shall be always glad to see you, sir, at my office, (as in duty bound, (not that it is obligatory to receive any man within your dwelling, (unless so inclined,) which is a castle,) according to the forms of politeness,) or at any other place; but the papers are most strictly confidential, (and, as such, cannot be read by any one, (unless so directed,) by Judge Temple's solemn injunctions,) and are invisible to all eyes; excepting those whose duties (I mean assumed duties) require it of them."

"Well, sir, as I perceive that I can be of no service, I wish you another good morning; but beg you will remember that I am quite idle, just now, and I wish you would intimate as much to Judge Temple, and make him a tender of my services, in any part of the world; unless—unless—it be far from Templeton."

"I will make the communication, sir, in your name, (with your own qualifications,) as your agent. Good morning, sir.—But stay proceedings, Mr. Edwards, (so called,) for a moment. Do you wish me to state the offer of travelling, as a final contract, (for which consideration has been received, at former dates, (by sums advanced,) which would be binding,) or as a tender of services, for which compensation is to be paid (according to future agreement between the parties) on performance of the conditions?"

"Any way—any way," said Edwards—"he seems in distress, and I would assist him."

"The motive is good, sir, (according to appearances, (which are often deceitful,) on first impressions,) and does you honour. I will mention your wish, young gentleman, (as you now seem,) and will not fail to communicate the answer, by five o'clock, P.M. of this present day, (God willing,) if you give me an opportunity so to do."

The ambiguous nature of the situation and character of Mr. Edwards, had rendered him an object of peculiar suspicion to the lawyer, and the youth was consequently too much accustomed to similar equivocal and guarded speeches, to feel any unusual disgust at the present dialogue. He saw, at once, that it was the intention of the practitioner to conceal the nature of his business, even from the private secretary of Judge Temple; and he knew too well the difficulty of comprehending the meaning of Mr. Van der School, when the gentleman most wished to be luminous in his discourse, not to abandon all thoughts of a discovery, when he perceived that the attorney was endeavouring to avoid any thing like an approach to a cross-examination. They parted at the gate, the lawyer walking, with an important and hurried air, towards his office, keeping his right hand firmly clenched on the bundle of papers.

It must have been obvious to all our readers, that the youth entertained an unusual and deeply-seated prejudice against the character of the Judge; but, owing to some counteracting cause, his sensations were now those of powerful interest in the state of his patron's present feelings, and in the causes of his secret uneasiness.

He remained gazing after the lawyer, until the door closed on both the bearer and the mysterious packet, when he returned slowly to the dwelling, and endeavoured to forget his curiosity, in the usual avocations of his office.

When the Judge made his re-appearance in the circle of his family, his cheerfulness was tempered by a shade of melancholy, that lingered for many days around his manly brow; but the magical progression of the season aroused him from his temporary apathy, and his smiles returned with the summer.

The heats of the days, and the frequent occurrence of balmy showers, had completed, in an incredibly short period, the growth of plants, which the lingering spring had so long retarded in the germ; and the woods presented every shade of green that the American forests know. The stumps in the cleared fields were already hid beneath the wheat, that was waving with every breath of the summer air, shining, and changing its hues, like velvet.

During the continuance of his cousin's dejection, Mr. Jones forbore, with much consideration, to press on his attention a business that each hour was drawing nearer to the heart of the Sheriff, and which, if any opinion could be formed by his frequent private conferences with the man, who was introduced in these pages, by the name of Jotham, at the bar-room of the Bold Dragoon, was becoming also of great importance.

At length the Sheriff ventured to allude again to the subject, and one evening, in the beginning of July, Marmaduke made him a promise of devoting the following day to the desired excursion.

Chapter XXVI

"Speak on, my dearest father!
Thy words are like the breezes of the west."
Milman, *Belshazzar*, III.73–74.

IT WAS A mild and soft morning, when Marmaduke and Richard mounted their horses, to proceed on the expedition that had so long been uppermost in the thoughts of the latter; and Elizabeth and Louisa appeared at the same instant in the hall, attired for an excursion on foot.

The head of Miss Grant was covered by a neat, little hat of green silk, and her modest eyes peered from under its shade, with the soft languor that characterized her whole appearance; but Miss Temple trod her father's wide apartments, with the step of their mistress, holding in her hand, dangling by one of its ribands, the gipsy that was to conceal the glossy locks that curled around her polished forehead, in rich profusion.

"What, are you for a walk, Bess!" cried the Judge, suspending his movements for a moment, to smile, with a father's fondness, at the display of womanly grace and beauty that his child presented. "Remember the heats of July, my daughter; nor venture further than thou canst retrace before the meridian. Where is thy parasol, girl? thou wilt lose the polish of that brow, under this sun and southern breeze, unless thou guard it with unusual care."

"I shall then do more honour to my connexions," returned the smiling daughter. "Cousin Richard has a bloom that any lady might envy. At present, the resemblance between us is so trifling, that no stranger would know us to be 'sisters' children.' "

"Grand-children, you mean, cousin Bess," said the Sheriff. "But on, Judge Temple; time and tide wait for no man; and if you take my counsel, sir, in twelve months from this day, you may make an umbrella for your daughter of her camel's-hair shawl, and have its frame of solid silver. I ask nothing for myself, 'duke; you have been a good friend to me already; besides, all that I have will go to Bess, there, one of these melancholy days, so it's as long as it's short, whether I or you leave it. But we have a day's ride before us, sir; so move forward, or dismount, and say you won't go, at once."

"Patience, patience, Dickon," returned the Judge, checking his horse, and turning again to his daughter. "If thou art for the mountains, love, stray not too deep into the forest, I entreat thee; for, though it is done often with impunity, there is sometimes danger."

"Not at this season, I believe, sir," said Elizabeth; "for, I will confess, it is the intention of Louisa and myself to stroll among the hills."

"Less at this season than in the winter, dear; but still there may be danger in venturing too far. But though thou art resolute, Elizabeth, thou art too much like thy mother not to be prudent."

The eyes of the parent turned reluctantly from his child, and the Judge and Sheriff rode slowly through the gateway, and disappeared among the buildings of the village.

During this short dialogue, young Edwards stood, an attentive listener, holding in his hand a fishing-rod, the day and the season having tempted him also to desert the house, for the pleasure of exercise in the air. As the equestrians turned through the gate, he approached the young females, who were already moving towards the street, and was about to address them, as Louisa paused, and said quickly—

"Mr. Edwards would speak to us, Elizabeth."

The other stopped also, and turned to the youth, politely, but with a slight coldness in her air, that sensibly checked the freedom with which he had approached them.

"Your father is not pleased that you should walk unattended in the hills, Miss Temple. If I might offer myself as a protector"—

"Does my father select Mr. Oliver Edwards as the organ of his displeasure?" interrupted the lady.

"Good Heaven! you misunderstand my meaning; I should have said uneasy, for not pleased. I am his servant, madam, and in consequence yours. I repeat that, with your consent, I will change my rod for a fowling-piece, and keep nigh you on the mountain."

"I thank you, Mr. Edwards; but where there is no danger,

no protection is required. We are not yet reduced to wandering among these free hills accompanied by a body-guard. If such a one is necessary, there he is, however.—Here, Brave,—Brave—my noble Brave!"

The huge mastiff that has been already mentioned, appeared from his kennel, gaping and stretching himself, with pampered laziness; but as his mistress again called—"Come, dear Brave; once have you served your master well; let us see how you can do your duty by his daughter"—the dog wagged his tail, as if he understood her language, walked with a stately gait to her side, where he seated himself, and looked up at her face, with an intelligence but little inferior to that which beamed in her own lovely countenance.

She resumed her walk, but again paused, after a few steps, and added, in tones of conciliation—

"You can be serving us, equally, and, I presume, more agreeably to yourself, Mr. Edwards, by bringing us a string of your favourite perch, for the dinner-table."

When they again begun to walk, Miss Temple did not look back, to see how the youth bore this repulse; but the head of Louisa was turned several times, before they reached the gate, on that considerate errand.

"I am afraid, Elizabeth," she said, "that we have mortified Oliver. He is still standing where we left him, leaning on his rod. Perhaps he thinks us proud."

"He thinks justly," exclaimed Miss Temple, as if awaking from a deep musing; "he thinks justly, then. We are too proud to admit of such particular attentions from a young man whose situation is so equivocal. What! make him the companion of our most private walks! It is pride, Louisa, but it is the pride of our sex."

It was several minutes before Oliver aroused himself from the contemplative posture in which he was standing when Louisa last saw him; but when he did, he muttered something, rapidly and incoherently, and throwing his rod over his shoulder, he strode down the walk, through the gate, and along one of the streets of the village, until he reached the lake-shore, with the air of an emperor. At this spot boats were kept, for the use of Judge Temple and his family. The young man threw himself into a light skiff, and seizing the oars, he sent it across the lake, towards the hut of Leather-stocking, with a pair of vigorous arms. By the time he had rowed a quarter of a mile, his reflections were less bitter; and when he saw the bushes that lined the shore in front of Natty's habitation gliding by him, as if they possessed the motion which proceeded from his own efforts, he was quite cooled in mind, though somewhat heated in body. It is quite possible, that the very same reason which guided the conduct of Miss Temple, suggested itself to a man of the breeding and education of the youth; and it is very certain, that if such were the case, Elizabeth rose instead of falling in the estimation of Mr. Edwards.

The oars were now raised from the water, and the boat shot close into the land, where it lay gently agitated by waves of its own creating, while the young man, first casting a cautious and searching glance around him in every direction, put a small whistle to his mouth, and blew a long, shrill note, that rung among the echoing rocks behind the hut. At this alarm, the hounds of Natty rushed out of their bark kennel, and commenced their long, piteous howls, leaping about as if half frantic, though restrained by the leashes of buck-skin, by which they were fastened.

"Quiet, Hector, quiet," said Oliver, again applying his whistle to his mouth, and drawing out notes still more shrill than before. No reply was made, the dogs having returned to their kennel at the sounds of his voice.

Edwards pulled the bows of the boat on the shore, and landing, ascended the beach and approached the door of the cabin. The fastenings were soon undone, and he entered, closing the door after him, when all was as silent, in that retired spot, as if the foot of man had never trod the wilderness. The sounds of the hammers, that were in incessant motion in the village, were faintly heard across the water; but the dogs had crouched into their lairs, satisfied that none but the privileged had approached the forbidden ground.

A quarter of an hour elapsed before the youth re-appeared, when he fastened the door again and spoke kindly to the hounds. The dogs came out at the well-known tones, and the slut jumped upon his person, whining and barking, as if entreating Oliver to release her from prison. But Old Hector raised his nose to the light current of air, and opened a long howl, that might have been heard for a mile.

"Ha! what do you scent, old veteran of the woods?" cried Edwards. "If a beast, it is a bold one; and if a man, an impudent."

He sprung through the top of a pine, that had fallen near the side of the hut, and ascended a small hillock, that sheltered the cabin to the south, where he caught a glimpse of the formal figure of Hiram Doolittle, as it vanished, with unusual rapidity for the architect, amid the bushes.

"What can that fellow be wanting here?" muttered Oliver. "He has no business in this quarter, unless it be curiosity, which is an endemic in these woods. But against that I will effectually guard, though the dogs should take a liking to his ugly visage, and let him pass." The youth returned to the door, while giving vent to this soliloquy, and completed the fastenings, by placing a small chain through a staple, and securing it there by a padlock. "He is a pettifogger, and surely must know that there is such a thing as feloniously breaking into a man's house."

Apparently well satisfied with this arrangement, the youth again spoke to the hounds; and, descending to the shore, he launched his boat, and taking up his oars, pulled off into the lake.

There were several places in the Otsego that were celebrated fishing-ground for perch. One was nearly opposite to the cabin, and another, still more famous, was near a point, at the distance of a mile and a half above it, under the brow of the mountain, and on the same side of the lake with the hut. Oliver Edwards pulled his little skiff to the first, and sat, for a minute, undecided whether to continue there, with his eyes on the door of the cabin, or to change his ground, with a view to get superior game. While gazing about him, he saw the light-coloured bark canoe of his old companions, riding on the water, at the point we have mentioned, and containing two figures, that he at once knew to be Mohegan and the Leather-stocking. This decided the matter, and the youth pulled, in a very few minutes, to the place where his friends were fishing, and fastened his boat to the light vessel of the Indian.

The old men received Oliver with welcoming nods, but neither drew his line from the water, nor, in the least, varied his occupation. When Edwards had secured his own boat, he baited his hook and threw it into the lake, without speaking.

"Did you stop at the wigwam, lad, as you rowed past?" asked Natty.

"Yes, and I found all safe; but that carpenter and justice of the peace, Mr., or, as they call him, Squire Doolittle, was prowling through the woods. I made sure of the door, before I left the hut, and I think he is too great a coward to approach the hounds."

"There's little to be said in favour of that man," said Natty, while he drew in a perch and baited his hook. "He craves dreadfully to come into the cabin, and has as good as asked me as much to my face; but I put him off with unsartain answers, so that he is no wiser than Solomon. This comes of having so many laws that such a man may be called on to intarpret them."

"I fear he is more knave than fool," cried Edwards: "he makes a tool of that simple man, the Sheriff, and I dread that his impertinent curiosity may yet give us much trouble."

"If he harbours too much about the cabin, lad, I'll shoot the creater," said the Leather-stocking, quite simply.

"No, no, Natty, you must remember the law," said Edwards, "or we shall have you in trouble; and that, old man, would be an evil day, and sore tidings to us all."

"Would it, boy!" exclaimed the hunter, raising his eyes with a look of friendly interest towards the youth. "You have the true blood in your veins, Mr. Oliver, and I'll support it, to the face of Judge Temple, or in any court in the country. How is it, John? do I speak the true word? is the lad stanch, and of the right blood?"

"He is a Delaware," said Mohegan, "and my brother. The Young Eagle is brave, and he will be a chief. No harm can come."

"Well, well," cried the youth, impatiently; "say no more about it, my good friends; if I am not all that your partiality would make me, I am yours through life—in prosperity as in poverty. We will talk of other matters."

The old hunters yielded to his wish, which seemed to be their law. For a short time a profound silence prevailed, during which each man was very busy with his hook and line; but Edwards, probably feeling that it remained with him to renew the discourse, soon observed, with the air of one who knew not what he said—

"How beautifully tranquil and glassy the lake is. Saw you it ever more calm and even than at this moment, Natty?"

"I have known the Otsego water for five-and-forty year," said Leather-stocking, "and I will say that for it, which is, that a cleaner spring or better fishing is not to be found in the land. Yes, yes—I had the place to myself once; and a cheerful time I had of it. The game was plenty as heart could wish, and there was none to meddle with the ground, unless there might have been a hunting party of the Delawares crossing the hills, or, maybe, a rifling scout of them thieves, the Iroquois. There was one or two Frenchmen that squatted in the flats, further west, and married squaws; and some of the Scotch-Irishers, from the Cherry Valley, would come on to the lake, and borrow my canoe, to take a mess of parch, or drop a line for salmon-trout; but, in the main, it was a cheerful place, and I had but little to disturb me in it. John would come, and John knows."

Mohegan turned his dark face, at this appeal, and, moving his hand forward with a graceful motion of assent, he spoke, using the Delaware language—

"The land was owned by my people: we gave it to my brother, in council—to the Fire-Eater; and what the Delawares give, lasts as long as the waters run. Hawk-eye smoked at that council, for we loved him."

"No, no, John," said Natty, "I was no chief, seeing that I know'd nothing of scholarship, and had a white skin. But it was a comfortable hunting-ground then, lad, and would have been so to this day, but for the money of Marmaduke Temple, and the twisty ways of the law."

"It must have been a sight of melancholy pleasure, indeed," said Edwards, while his eye roved along the shores and over the hills, where the clearings, groaning with the golden corn, were cheering the forests with the signs of life, "to have roamed over these mountains, and along this sheet of beautiful water, without a living soul to speak to, or to thwart your humour."

"Haven't I said it was cheerful!" said Leather-stocking. "Yes, yes——when the trees begun to be kivered with leaves, and the ice was out of the lake, it was a second paradise. I have travelled the woods for fifty-three year, and have made them my home for more than forty, and I can say that I have met but one place that was more to my liking; and that was only to eyesight, and not for hunting or fishing."

"And where was that?" asked Edwards.

"Where! why up on the Cattskills. I used often to go up into the mountains after wolves' skins, and bears; once they paid me to get them a stuffed painter; and so I often went. There's a place in them hills that I used to climb to, when I wanted to see the carryings on of the world, that would well pay any man for a barked shin or a torn moccasin. You know the Cattskills, lad, for you must have seen them on your left, as you followed the river up from York, looking as blue as a piece of clear sky, and holding the clouds on their tops, as the smoke curls over the head of an Indian chief at the council fire. Well, there's the High-peak and the Round-top, which lay back, like a father and mother among their children, seeing they are far above all the other hills. But the place I mean is next to the river, where one of the ridges juts out a little from the rest, and where the rocks fall for the best part of a thousand feet, so much up and down, that a man standing on their edges is fool enough to think he can jump from top to bottom."

"What see you when you get there?" asked Edwards.

"Creation!" said Natty, dropping the end of his rod into the water, and sweeping one hand around him in a circle——"all creation, lad. I was on that hill when Vaughan burnt 'Sopus, in the last war, and I seen the vessels come out of the highlands as plain as I can see that lime-scow rowing into the Susquehanna, though one was twenty times further from me than the other. The river was in sight for seventy miles, looking like a curled shaving, under my feet, though it was eight long miles to its banks. I saw the hills in the Hampshire grants, the high lands of the river, and all that God had done or man could do, far as eye could reach—you know that the

Indians named me for my sight, lad——and from the flat on the top of that mountain, I have often found the place where Albany stands; and as for 'Sopus! the day the royal troops burnt the town, the smoke seemed so nigh, that I thought I could hear the screeches of the women."

"It must have been worth the toil, to meet with such a glorious view!"

"If being the best part of a mile in the air, and having men's farms and housen at your feet, with rivers looking like ribands, and mountains bigger than the 'Vision,' seeming to be haystacks of green grass under you, gives any satisfaction to a man, I can recommend the spot. When I first come into the woods to live, I used to have weak spells, when I felt lonesome; and then I would go into the Cattskills and spend a few days on that hill, to look at the ways of man; but it's now many a year since I felt any such longings, and I'm getting too old for rugged rocks. But there's a place, a short two miles back of that very hill, that in late times I relished better than the mountains; for it was kivered with the trees, and nateral."

"And where was that?" inquired Edwards, whose curiosity was strongly excited by the simple description of the hunter.

"Why, there's a fall in the hills, where the water of two little ponds that lie near each other breaks out of their bounds, and runs over the rocks into the valley. The stream is, maybe, such a one as would turn a mill, if so useless a thing was wanted in the wilderness. But the hand that made that 'Leap' never made a mill! There the water comes crooking and winding among the rocks, first so slow that a trout could swim in it, and then starting and running like a creater that wanted to make a far spring, till it gets to where the mountain divides, like the cleft hoof of a deer, leaving a deep hollow for the brook to tumble into. The first pitch is nigh two hundred feet, and the water looks like flakes of driven snow, afore it touches the bottom; and there the stream gathers together again for a new start, and maybe flutters over fifty feet of flat-rock, before it falls for another hundred, when it jumps about from shelf to shelf, first turning this-away and then turning that-away, striving to get out of the hollow, till it finally comes to the plain."

"I have never heard of this spot before: it is not mentioned in the books."

"I have never read a book in my life," said Leather-stocking; "and how should a man who has lived in towns and schools know any thing about the wonders of the woods! No, no, lad; there has that little stream of water been playing among them hills, since He made the world, and not a dozen white men have ever laid eyes on it. The rock sweeps like mason-work, in a half-round, on both sides of the fall, and shelves over the bottom for fifty feet; so that when I've been sitting at the foot of the first pitch, and my hounds have run into the caverns behind the sheet of water, they've looked no bigger than so many rabbits. To my judgment, lad, it's the best piece of work that I've met with in the woods; and none know how often the hand of God is seen in the wilderness, but them that rove it for a man's life."

"What becomes of the water? in which direction does it run? is it a tributary of the Delaware?"

"Anan!" said Natty.

"Does the water run into the Delaware?"

"No, no, it's a drop for the old Hudson; and a merry time it has till it gets down off the mountain. I've sat on the shelving rock many a long hour, boy, and watched the bubbles as they shot by me, and thought how long it would be before that very water, which seemed made for the wilderness, would be under the bottom of a vessel, and tossing in the salt sea. It is a spot to make a man solemnize. You can see right down into the valley that lies to the east of the High-Peak, where, in the fall of the year, thousands of acres of woods are afore your eyes, in the deep hollow, and along the side of the mountain, painted like ten thousand rainbows, by no hand of man, though not without the ordering of God's providence."

"You are eloquent, Leather-stocking!" exclaimed the youth.

"Anan!" repeated Natty.

"The recollection of the sight has warmed your blood, old man. How many years is it since you saw the place?"

The hunter made no reply; but, bending his ear near the water, he sat holding his breath, and listening attentively, as if to some distant sound. At length he raised his head, and said—

"If I hadn't fastened the hounds with my own hands, with a fresh leash of green buck-skin, I'd take a bible oath that I heard old Hector ringing his cry on the mountain."

"It is impossible," said Edwards; "it is not an hour since I saw him in his kennel."

By this time the attention of Mohegan was attracted to the sounds; but, notwithstanding the youth was both silent and attentive, he could hear nothing but the lowing of some cattle from the western hills. He looked at the old men, Natty sitting with his hand to his ear, like a trumpet, and Mohegan bending forward, with an arm raised to a level with his face, holding the fore finger elevated as a signal for attention, and laughed aloud at what he deemed to be their imaginary sounds.

"Laugh if you will, boy," said Leather-stocking; "the hounds be out, and be hunting a deer. No man can deceive me in such a matter. I wouldn't have had the thing happen for a beaver's skin. Not that I care for the law! but the venison is lean now, and the dumb things run the flesh off their own bones for no good. Now do you hear the hounds?"

Edwards started, as a full cry broke on his ear, changing from the distant sounds that were caused by some intervening hill, to confused echoes that rung among the rocks that the dogs were passing, and then directly to a deep and hollow baying that pealed under the forest on the lake shore. These variations in the tones of the hounds passed with amazing rapidity, and while his eyes were glancing along the margin of the water, a tearing of the branches of the alder and dogwood caught his attention, at a spot near them, and, at the next moment, a noble buck sprung on the shore, and buried himself in the lake. A full-mouthed cry followed, when Hector and the slut shot through the opening in the bushes, and darted into the lake also, bearing their breasts gallantly against the water.

Chapter XXVII

"Oft in the full-descending flood he tries
To lose the scent, and lave his burning sides."
Thomson, *The Seasons*, "Autumn," 445–46.

I KNOW'D IT—I know'd it!" cried Natty, when both deer and hounds were in full view;—"the buck has gone by them with the wind, and it has been too much for the poor rogues; but I must break them of these tricks, or they'll give me a deal of trouble. He-ere, he-ere—shore with you, rascals—shore with you—will ye?—Oh! off with you, old Hector, or I'll hatchel your hide with my ramrod when I get ye."

The dogs knew their master's voice, and, after swimming in a circle, as if reluctant to give over the chase, and yet afraid to persevere, they finally obeyed, and returned to the land, where they filled the air with their cries.

In the mean time, the deer, urged by his fears, had swam over half the distance between the shore and the boats, before his terror permitted him to see the new danger. But at the sounds of Natty's voice he turned short in his course, and, for a few moments, seemed about to rush back again, and brave the dogs. His retreat in this direction was, however, effectually cut off, and, turning a second time, he urged his course obliquely for the centre of the lake, with an intention of landing on the western shore. As the buck swam by the fishermen, raising his nose high into the air, curling the water before his slim neck like the beak of a galley, the Leather-stocking began to sit very uneasy in his canoe.

"'Tis a noble creater!" he exclaimed; "what a pair of horns! a man might hang up all his garments on the branches. Lets me see—July is the last month, and the flesh must be getting good." While he was talking, Natty had instinctively employed himself in fastening the inner end of the bark rope, that served him for a cable, to a paddle, and, rising suddenly on his legs, he cast this buoy away, and cried—"Strike out, John! let her go. The creater's a fool, to tempt a man in this way."

Mohegan threw the fastening of the youth's boat from the

canoe, and with one stroke of his paddle, sent the light bark over the water like a meteor.

"Hold!" exclaimed Edwards. "Remember the law, my old friends. You are in plain sight of the village, and I know that Judge Temple is determined to prosecute all, indiscriminately, who kill deer out of season."

The remonstrance came too late; the canoe was already far from the skiff, and the two hunters were too much engaged in the pursuit to listen to his voice.

The buck was now within fifty yards of his pursuers, cutting the water gallantly, and snorting at each breath with terror and his exertions, while the canoe seemed to dance over the waves, as it rose and fell with the undulations made by its own motion. Leather-stocking raised his rifle and freshened the priming, but stood in suspense whether to slay his victim or not.

"Shall I, John, or no?" he said. "It seems but a poor advantage to take of the dumb thing, too. I won't; it has taken to the water on its own nater, which is the reason that God has given to a deer, and I'll give it the lake play; so, John, lay out your arm, and mind the turn of the buck; it's easy to catch them, but they'll turn like a snake."

The Indian laughed at the conceit of his friend, but continued to send the canoe forward, with a velocity that proceeded much more from his skill than his strength. Both of the old men now used the language of the Delawares when they spoke.

"Hooh!" exclaimed Mohegan; "the deer turns his head. Hawk-eye, lift your spear."

Natty never moved abroad without taking with him every implement that might, by possibility, be of service in his pursuits. From his rifle he never parted; and, although intending to fish with the line, the canoe was invariably furnished with all its utensils, even to its grate. This precaution grew out of the habits of the hunter, who was often led, by his necessities or his sports, far beyond the limits of his original destination. A few years earlier than the date of our tale, the Leather-stocking had left his hut on the shores of the Otsego, with his rifle and his hounds, for a few days' hunting in the hills; but before he returned, he had seen the waters of Ontario.

One, two, or even three hundred miles, had once been nothing to his sinews, which were now a little stiffened by age. The hunter did as Mohegan advised, and prepared to strike a blow with the barbed weapon into the neck of the buck.

"Lay her more to the left, John," he cried, "lay her more to the left; another stroke of the paddle, and I have him."

While speaking, he raised the spear, and darted it from him like an arrow. At that instant the buck turned. The long pole glanced by him, the iron striking against his horn, and buried itself, harmlessly, in the lake.

"Back water," cried Natty, as the canoe glided over the place where the spear had fallen, "hold water, John."

The pole soon re-appeared, shooting upward from the lake, and as the hunter seized it in his hand, the Indian whirled the light canoe round, and renewed the chase. But this evolution gave the buck a great advantage; and it also allowed time for Edwards to approach the scene of action.

"Hold your hand, Natty," cried the youth, "hold your hand; remember it is out of season."

This remonstrance was made as the batteau arrived close to the place where the deer was struggling with the water, his back now rising to the surface, now sinking beneath it, as the waves curled from his neck, the animal still sustaining itself nobly against the odds.

"Hurrah!" shouted Edwards, inflamed beyond prudence at the sight; "mind him as he doubles—mind him as he doubles; sheer more to the right, Mohegan, more to the right, and I'll have him by the horns; I'll throw the rope over his antlers."

The dark eye of the old warrior was dancing in his head, with a wild animation, and the sluggish repose in which his aged frame had been resting in the canoe, was now changed to all the rapid inflections of practised agility. The canoe whirled, with each cunning evolution of the chase, like a bubble floating in a whirlpool; and when the direction of the pursuit admitted of a straight course, the little bark skimmed the lake with a velocity, that urged the deer to seek its safety in some new turn. The frequency of these circuitous movements, by confining the action to so small a compass, enabled the youth to keep near his companions. More than twenty times both the pursued and the pursuers glided by him, just without the reach of his oars, until he thought the best way to view the sport was to remain stationary, and, by watching a favourable opportunity, assist as much as he could in taking the victim.

He was not required to wait long, for no sooner had he adopted this resolution, and risen in the boat, than he saw the deer coming bravely towards him, with an apparent intention of pushing for a point of land at some distance from the hounds, which were still barking and howling on the shore. Edwards caught the painter of his skiff, and, making a noose, cast it from him with all his force, and luckily succeeded in drawing its knot close around one of the antlers of the buck.

For one instant, the skiff was drawn through the water, but in the next, the canoe glided before it, and Natty, bending low, passed his knife across the throat of the animal, whose blood followed the wound, dying the waters. The short time that was passed in the last struggles of the animal, was spent by the hunters in bringing their boats together, and securing them in that position; when Leather-stocking drew the deer from the water, and laid its lifeless form in the bottom of the canoe. He placed his hands on the ribs, and on different parts of the body of his prize, and then, raising his head, he laughed in his peculiar manner—

"So much for Marmaduke Temple's law!" he said. "This warms a body's blood, old John; I haven't killed a buck in the lake afore this, sin' many a year. I call that good venison, lad; and I know them that will relish the creater's steaks, for all the betterments in the land."

The Indian had long been drooping with his years, and perhaps under the calamities of his race, but this invigorating and exciting sport caused a gleam of sunshine to cross his swarthy face, that had long been absent from his features. It was evident the old man enjoyed the chase more as a memorial of his youthful sports and deeds, than with any expectation of profiting by the success. He felt the deer, however, lightly, his hand already trembling with the re-action of his unusual exertions, and smiled with a nod of approbation, as he said, in the emphatic and sententious manner of his people—

"Good."

"I am afraid, Natty," said Edwards, when the heat of the moment had passed, and his blood began to cool, "that we have all been equally transgressors of the law. But keep your own counsel, and there are none here to betray us. Yet, how came those dogs at large? I left them securely fastened, I know, for I felt the thongs, and examined the knots, when I was at the hut."

"It has been too much for the poor things," said Natty, "to have such a buck take the wind of them. See, lad, the pieces of the buck-skin are hanging from their necks yet. Let us paddle up, John, and I will call them in, and look a little into the matter."

When the old hunter landed, and examined the thongs that were yet fast to the hounds, his countenance sensibly changed, and he shook his head doubtingly.

"Here has been a knife at work," he said—"this skin was never torn, nor is this the mark of a hound's tooth. No, no—Hector is not in fault, as I feared."

"Has the leather been cut?" cried Edwards.

"No, no—I didn't say it had been cut, lad; but this is a mark that was never made by a jump or a bite."

"Could that rascally carpenter have dared!"

"Ay! he durst to do any thing when there is no danger," said Natty; "he is a curous body, and loves to be helping other people on with their concarns. But he had best not harbour so much near the wigwam."

In the mean time, Mohegan had been examining, with an Indian's sagacity, the place where the leather thong had been separated. After scrutinizing it closely, he said, in Delaware—

"It was cut with a knife—a sharp blade and a long handle—the man was afraid of the dogs."

"How is this, Mohegan!" exclaimed Edwards; "You saw it not! how can you know these facts?"

"Listen, son," said the warrior. "The knife was sharp, for the cut is smooth;—the handle was long, for a man's arm would not reach from this gash to the cut that did not go through the skin;—he was a coward, or he would have cut the thongs around the necks of the hounds."

"On my life," cried Natty, "John is on the scent! It was the carpenter; and he has got on the rock back of the kennel, and let the dogs loose by fastening his knife to a stick. It would be an easy matter to do it, where a man is so minded."

"And why should he do so?" asked Edwards; "who has done him wrong, that he should trouble two old men like you?"

"It's a hard matter, lad, to know men's ways, I find, since the settlers have brought in their new fashions. But is there nothing to be found out in the place? and maybe he is troubled with his longings after other people's business, as he often is."

"Your suspicions are just. Give me the canoe: I am young and strong, and will get down there yet, perhaps, in time to interrupt his plans. Heaven forbid, that we should be at the mercy of such a man!"

His proposal was accepted, the deer being placed in the skiff in order to lighten the canoe, and in less than five minutes the little vessel of bark was gliding over the glassy lake, and was soon hid by the points of land, as it shot close along the shore.

Mohegan followed slowly with the skiff, while Natty called his hounds to him, bade them keep close, and, shouldering his rifle, he ascended the mountain, with an intention of going to the hut by land.

Chapter XXVIII

"Ask me not what the maiden feels,
Left in that dreadful hour alone;
Perchance, her reason stoops, or reels;
Perchance, a courage not her own,
Braces her mind to desperate tone."
Scott, *Marmion*, VI.xxix.1–5.

WHILE THE CHASE was occurring on the lake, Miss Temple and her companion pursued their walk on the mountain. Male attendants, on such excursions, were thought to be altogether unnecessary, for none were ever known to offer an insult to a female who respected herself. After the embarrassment, created by the parting discourse with Edwards, had dissipated, the girls maintained a conversation that was as innocent and cheerful as themselves.

The path they took led them but a short distance above the hut of Leather-stocking, and there was a point in the road which commanded a bird's-eye view of the sequestered spot.

From a feeling, that might have been natural, and must have been powerful, neither of the friends, in their frequent and confidential dialogues, had ever trusted herself to utter one syllable concerning the equivocal situation in which the young man, who was now so intimately associated with them, had been found. If Judge Temple had deemed it prudent to make any inquiries on the subject, he had also thought it proper to keep the answers to himself; though it was so common an occurrence to find the well-educated youth of the eastern states, in every stage of their career to wealth, that the simple circumstance of his intelligence, connected with his poverty, would not, at that day, and in that country, have excited any very powerful curiosity. With his breeding it might have been different; but the youth himself had so effectually guarded against surprise on this subject, by his cold, and even, in some cases, rude deportment, that when his manners seemed to soften by time, the Judge, if he thought about it at all, would have been most likely to imagine that the improvement was the result of his late association. But women are always more alive to such subjects than men; and what the abstraction of the father had overlooked, the observation of the daughter had easily detected. In the thousand little courtesies of polished life, she had early discovered that Edwards was not wanting, though his gentleness was so often crossed by marks of what she conceived to be fierce and uncontrollable passions. It may, perhaps, be unnecessary to tell the reader that Louisa Grant never reasoned so much after the fashions of the world. The gentle girl, however, had her own thoughts on the subject, and, like others, she drew her own conclusions.

"I would give all my other secrets, Louisa," exclaimed Miss Temple, laughing, and shaking back her dark locks, with a look of childish simplicity that her intelligent face seldom expressed, "to be mistress of all that those rude logs have heard and witnessed."

They were both looking at the secluded hut, at the instant, and Miss Grant raised her mild eyes, as she answered—

"I am sure they would tell nothing to the disadvantage of Mr. Edwards."

"Perhaps not; but they might, at least, tell who he is."

"Why, dear Miss Temple, we know all that already. I have heard it all very rationally explained by your cousin"—

"The executive chief! he can explain any thing. His ingenuity will one day discover the philosopher's stone. But what did he say?"

"Say!" echoed Louisa, with a look of surprise; "why every thing that seemed to me to be satisfactory; and I have believed it to be true. He said that Natty Bumppo had lived most of his life in the woods, and among the Indians, by which means he had formed an acquaintance with old John, the Delaware chief."

"Indeed! that was quite a matter of fact tale for cousin Dickon. What came next?"

"I believe he accounted for their close intimacy, by some story about the Leather-stocking saving the life of John in a battle."

"Nothing more likely," said Elizabeth, a little impatiently; "but what is all this to the purpose?"

"Nay, Elizabeth, you must bear with my ignorance, and I will repeat all that I remember to have overheard; for the dialogue was between my father and the Sheriff, so lately as the last time they met. He then added, that the kings of England used to keep gentlemen as agents among the different tribes of Indians, and sometimes officers in the army, who frequently passed half their lives on the edge of the wilderness."

"Told with wonderful historical accuracy! And did he end there?"

"Oh! no—then he said that these agents seldom married; and—and—they must have been wicked men, Elizabeth! but I assure you he said so."

"Never mind," said Miss Temple, blushing and smiling, though so slightly that both were unheeded by her companion—"skip all that."

"Well, then he said that they often took great pride in the education of their children, whom they frequently sent to England, and even to the colleges; and this is the way that he accounts for the liberal manner in which Mr. Edwards has been taught; for he acknowledges that he knows almost as much as your father—or mine—or even himself!"

"Quite a climax in learning! And so he made Mohegan the grand-uncle or grandfather of Oliver Edwards."

"You have heard him yourself, then?" said Louisa.

"Often; but not on this subject. Mr. Richard Jones, you know, dear, has a theory for every thing; but has he one which will explain the reason why that hut is the only habitation within fifty miles of us, whose door is not open to every person who may choose to lift its latch?"

"I have never heard him say any thing on this subject," returned the clergyman's daughter; "but I suppose that, as they are poor, they very naturally are anxious to keep the little that they honestly own. It is sometimes dangerous to be rich, Miss Temple; but you cannot know how hard it is to be very, very poor."

"Nor you, I trust, Louisa; at least I should hope, that in this land of abundance, no minister of the church could be left to absolute suffering."

"There cannot be actual misery," returned the other, in a low and humble tone, "where there is a dependence on our

Maker; but there may be such suffering as will cause the heart to ache."

"But not you—not you," said the impetuous Elizabeth—"not you, dear girl; you have never known the misery that is connected with poverty."

"Ah! Miss Temple, you little understand the troubles of this life, I believe. My father has spent many years as a missionary, in the new countries, where his people were poor, and frequently we have been without bread; unable to buy, and ashamed to beg, because we would not disgrace his sacred calling. But how often have I seen him leave his home, where the sick and the hungry felt, when he left them, that they had lost their only earthly friend, to ride on a duty which could not be neglected for domestic evils. Oh! how hard it must be, to preach consolation to others, when your own heart is bursting with anguish!"

"But it is all over now! your father's income must now be equal to his wants—it must be—it shall be"—

"It is," replied Louisa, dropping her head on her bosom to conceal the tears which flowed in spite of her gentle Christianity, "for there are none left to be supplied but me."

The turn the conversation had taken drove from the minds of the young maidens all other thoughts but those of holy charity, and Elizabeth folded her friend in her arms, when the latter gave vent to her momentary grief in audible sobs. When this burst of emotion had subsided, Louisa raised her mild countenance, and they continued their walk in silence.

By this time they had gained the summit of the mountain, where they left the highway, and pursued their course, under the shade of the stately trees that crowned the eminence. The day was becoming warm, and the girls plunged more deeply into the forest, as they found its invigorating coolness agreeably contrasted to the excessive heat they had experienced in the ascent. The conversation, as if by mutual consent, was entirely changed to the little incidents and scenes of their walk, and every tall pine, and every shrub or flower, called forth some simple expression of admiration.

In this manner they proceeded along the margin of the precipice, catching occasional glimpses of the placid Otsego, or pausing to listen to the rattling of wheels and the sounds of hammers, that rose from the valley, to mingle the signs of men with the scenes of nature, when Elizabeth suddenly started, and exclaimed—

"Listen! there are the cries of a child on this mountain! is there a clearing near us? or can some little one have strayed from its parents?"

"Such things frequently happen," returned Louisa. "Let us follow the sounds; it may be a wanderer, starving on the hill."

Urged by this consideration, the females pursued the low, mournful sounds, that proceeded from the forest, with quick and impatient steps. More than once, the ardent Elizabeth was on the point of announcing that she saw the sufferer, when Louisa caught her by the arm, and pointing behind them, cried—

"Look at the dog!"

Brave had been their companion, from the time the voice of his young mistress lured him from his kennel, to the present moment. His advanced age had long before deprived him of his activity; and when his companions stopped to view the scenery, or to add to their bouquets, the mastiff would lay his huge frame on the ground, and await their movements, with his eyes closed, and a listlessness in his air that ill accorded with the character of a protector. But when, aroused by this cry from Louisa, Miss Temple turned, she saw the dog with his eyes keenly set on some distant object, his head bent near the ground, and his hair actually rising on his body, through fright or anger. It was most probably the latter, for he was growling in a low key, and occasionally showing his teeth, in a manner that would have terrified his mistress, had she not so well known his good qualities.

"Brave!" she said, "be quiet, Brave! what do you see, fellow?"

At the sounds of her voice, the rage of the mastiff, instead of being at all diminished, was very sensibly increased. He stalked in front of the ladies, and seated himself at the feet of his mistress, growling louder than before, and occasionally giving vent to his ire by a short, surly barking.

"What does he see?" said Elizabeth; "there must be some animal in sight."

Hearing no answer from her companion, Miss Temple turned her head, and beheld Louisa, standing with her face whitened to the colour of death, and her finger pointing upward, with a sort of flickering, convulsed motion. The quick eye of Elizabeth glanced in the direction indicated by her friend, where she saw the fierce front and glaring eyes of a female panther, fixed on them in horrid malignity, and threatening to leap.

"Let us fly!" exclaimed Elizabeth, grasping the arm of Louisa, whose form yielded like melting snow.

There was not a single feeling in the temperament of Elizabeth Temple, that could prompt her to desert a companion in such an extremity. She fell on her knees, by the side of the inanimate Louisa, tearing from the person of her friend, with instinctive readiness, such parts of her dress as might obstruct her respiration, and encouraging their only safeguard, the dog, at the same time, by the sounds of her voice.

"Courage, Brave," she cried, her own tones beginning to tremble, "courage, courage, good Brave."

A quarter-grown cub, that had hitherto been unseen, now appeared, dropping from the branches of a sapling, that grew under the shade of the beech which held its dam. This ignorant, but vitious creature, approached the dog, imitating the actions and sounds of its parent, but exhibiting a strange mixture of the playfulness of a kitten with the ferocity of its race.—Standing on its hind legs, it would rend the bark of a tree with its fore paws, and play the antics of a cat; and then, by lashing itself with its tail, growling, and scratching the earth, it would attempt the manifestations of anger that rendered its parent so terrific.

All this time Brave stood firm and undaunted, his short tail erect, his body drawn backward on its haunches, and his eyes following the movements of both dam and cub. At every gambol played by the latter, it approached nigher to the dog, the growling of the three becoming more horrid at each moment, until the younger beast overleaping its intended bound, fell directly before the mastiff. There was a moment of fearful cries and struggles, but they ended almost as soon as commenced, by the cub appearing in the air, hurled from the jaws of Brave, with a violence that sent it against a tree so forcibly, as to render it completely senseless.

Elizabeth witnessed the short struggle, and her blood was warming with the triumph of the dog, when she saw the form of the old panther in the air, springing twenty feet from the branch of the beech to the back of the mastiff. No words of ours can describe the fury of the conflict that followed. It was a confused struggle on the dried leaves, accompanied by loud and terrific cries. Miss Temple continued on her knees, bending over the form of Louisa, her eyes fixed on the animals, with an interest so horrid, and yet so intense, that she almost forgot her own stake in the result. So rapid and vigorous were the bounds of the inhabitant of the forest, that its active frame seemed constantly in the air, while the dog nobly faced his foe, at each successive leap. When the panther lighted on the shoulders of the mastiff, which was its constant aim, old Brave, though torn with her talons, and stained with his own blood, that already flowed from a dozen wounds, would shake off his furious foe, like a feather, and rearing on his hind legs, rush to the fray again, with jaws distended, and a dauntless eye. But age, and his pampered life, greatly disqualified the noble mastiff for such a struggle. In every thing but courage, he was only the vestige of what he had once been. A higher bound than ever, raised the wary and furious beast far beyond the reach of the dog, who was making a desperate, but fruitless dash at her, from which she alighted in a favourable position, on the back of her aged foe. For a single moment, only, could the panther remain there, the great strength of the dog returning with a convulsive effort. But Elizabeth saw, as Brave fastened his teeth in the side of his enemy, that the collar of brass around his neck, which had been glittering throughout the fray, was of the colour of blood, and directly, that his frame was sinking to the earth, where it soon lay prostrate and helpless. Several mighty efforts of the wild-cat to extricate herself from the jaws of the dog, followed, but they were fruitless, until the mastiff turned on his back, his lips collapsed, and his teeth loosened; when the short convulsions and stillness that succeeded, announced the death of poor Brave.

Elizabeth now lay wholly at the mercy of the beast. There

is said to be something in the front of the image of the Maker, that daunts the hearts of the inferior beings of his creation; and it would seem that some such power, in the present instance, suspended the threatened blow. The eyes of the monster and the kneeling maiden met, for an instant, when the former stooped to examine her fallen foe; next to scent her luckless cub. From the latter examination it turned, however, with its eyes apparently emitting flashes of fire, its tail lashing its sides furiously, and its claws projecting inches from its broad feet.

Miss Temple did not, or could not move. Her hands were clasped in the attitude of prayer, but her eyes were still drawn to her terrible enemy; her cheeks were blanched to the whiteness of marble, and her lips were slightly separated with horror. The moment seemed now to have arrived for the fatal termination, and the beautiful figure of Elizabeth was bowing meekly to the stroke, when a rustling of leaves behind seemed rather to mock the organs, than to meet her ears.

"Hist! hist!" said a low voice—"stoop lower, gall; your bunnet hides the creater's head."

It was rather the yielding of nature than a compliance with this unexpected order, that caused the head of our heroine to sink on her bosom; when she heard the report of the rifle, the whizzing of the bullet, and the enraged cries of the beast, who was rolling over on the earth, biting its own flesh, and tearing the twigs and branches within its reach. At the next instant the form of the Leather-stocking rushed by her, and he called aloud—

"Come in, Hector, come in, old fool; 'tis a hard-lived animal, and may jump ag'in."

Natty fearlessly maintained his position in front of the females, notwithstanding the violent bounds and threatening aspect of the wounded panther, which gave several indications of returning strength and ferocity, until his rifle was again loaded, when he stepped up to the enraged animal, and, placing the muzzle close to its head, every spark of life was extinguished by the discharge.

The death of her terrible enemy appeared to Elizabeth like a resurrection from her own grave. There was an elasticity in the mind of our heroine, that rose to meet the pressure of instant danger, and the more direct it had been, the more her nature had struggled to overcome it. But still she was a woman. Had she been left to herself, in her late extremity, she would probably have used her faculties to the utmost, and with discretion, in protecting her person, but encumbered with her inanimate friend, retreat was a thing not to be attempted.—Notwithstanding the fearful aspect of her foe, the eye of Elizabeth had never shrunk from its gaze, and long after the event, her thoughts would recur to her passing sensations, and the sweetness of her midnight sleep would be disturbed, as her active fancy conjured, in dreams, the most trifling movements of savage fury, that the beast had exhibited in its moment of power.

We shall leave the reader to imagine the restoration of Louisa's senses, and the expressions of gratitude which fell from the young women. The former was effected by a little water, that was brought from one of the thousand springs of those mountains, in the cap of the Leather-stocking; and the latter were uttered with the warmth that might be expected from the character of Elizabeth.—Natty received her vehement protestations of gratitude, with a simple expression of good will, and with indulgence for her present excitement, but with a carelessness that showed how little he thought of the service he had rendered.

"Well, well," he said, "be it so, gall; let it be so, if you wish it,—we'll talk the thing over another time. Come, come—let us get into the road, for you've had tirror enough to make you wish yourself in your father's house ag'in."

This was uttered as they were proceeding, at a pace that was adapted to the weakness of Louisa, towards the highway; on reaching which the ladies separated from their guide, declaring themselves equal to the remainder of the walk without his assistance, and feeling encouraged by the sight of the village, which lay beneath their feet, like a picture, with its limpid lake in front, the winding stream along its margin, and its hundred chimneys of whitened bricks.

The reader need not be told the nature of the emotions, which two youthful, ingenuous, and well-educated girls would experience, at their escape from a death so horrid as the one which had impended over them, while they pursued their way in silence along the track on the side of the mountain; nor how deep were their mental thanks to that Power which had given them their existence, and which had not deserted them in their extremity; neither how often they pressed each other's arms, as the assurance of their present safety came, like a healing balm, athwart their troubled spirits, when their thoughts were recurring to the recent moments of horror.

Leather-stocking remained on the hill, gazing after their retiring figures, until they were hid by a bend in the road, when he whistled in his dogs, and, shouldering his rifle, he returned into the forest.

"Well, it was a skeary thing to the young creaters," said Natty, while he retrod the path towards the slain. "It might frighten an older woman, to see a she-painter so near her, with a dead cub by its side. I wonder if I had aimed at the varmint's eye, if I shouldn't have touched the life sooner than in the forehead? but they are hard-lived animals, and it was a good shot, consid'ring that I could see nothing but the head and the peak of its tail. Ha! who goes there?"

"How goes it, Natty?" said Mr. Doolittle, stepping out of the bushes, with a motion that was a good deal accelerated by the sight of the rifle, that was already lowered in his direction. "What! shooting this warm day! mind old man, the law don't get hold on you."

"The law, Squire! I have shook hands with the law these forty year," returned Natty; "for what has a man who lives in the wilderness to do with the ways of the law?"

"Not much, maybe," said Hiram; "but you sometimes trade in ven'son. I s'pose you know, Leather-stocking, that there is an act passed to lay a fine of five pounds currency, or twelve dollars and fifty cents, by dicimals, on every man who kills a deer betwixt January and August. The Judge had a great hand in getting the law through."

"I can believe it," returned the old hunter; "I can believe that, or any thing, of a man who carries on as he does in the country."

"Yes, the law is quite positive, and the Judge is bent on putting it in force—five pounds penalty. I thought I heerd your hounds out on the scent of so'thing this morning: I didn't know but they might get you in difficulty."

"They know their manners too well," said Natty, carelessly. "And how much goes to the state's evidence, Squire?"

"How much!" repeated Hiram, quailing under the honest, but sharp look of the hunter—"the informer gets half, I—I b'lieve;—yes, I guess it's half. But there's blood on your sleeve, man;—you haven't been shooting any thing this morning?"

"I have, though," said the hunter, nodding his head significantly to the other, "and a good shot I made of it."

"He-e-m!" ejaculated the magistrate; "and where is the game? I s'pose it's of a good nater, for your dogs won't hunt any thing that isn't choish."

"They'll hunt any thing I tell them to, Squire," cried Natty, favouring the other with his laugh. "They'll hunt you, if I say so. He-e-e-re, he-e-e-re, Hector—he-e-e-re, slut—come this a-way, pups—come this a-way—come hither."

"Oh! I've always heern a good character of the dogs," returned Mr. Doolittle, quickening his pace by raising each leg in rapid succession, as the hounds scented around his person. "And where is the game, Leather-stocking?"

During this dialogue, the speakers had been walking at a very fast gait, and Natty swung the end of his rifle round, pointing through the bushes, and replied—

"There lays one. How do you like such meat?"

"This!" exclaimed Hiram, " why this is Judge Temple's dog Brave. Take kear, Leather-stocking, and don't make an inimy of the Judge. I hope you haven't harmed the animal?"

"Look for yourself, Mr. Doolittle," said Natty, drawing his knife from his girdle, and wiping it, in a knowing manner, once or twice across his garment of buck-skin; "does his throat look as if I had cut it with this knife?"

"It is dreadfully tore! it's an awful wownd!—no knife never did this deed. Who could have done it?"

"The painters behind you, Squire."

"Painters!" echoed Hiram, whirling on his heel, with an agility that would have done credit to a dancing master.

"Be easy, man," said Natty; "there's two of the vinimous things; but the dog finished one, and I have fastened the other's jaws for her; so don't be frightened, Squire; they won't hurt you."

"And where's the deer?" cried Hiram, staring about him with a bewildered air.

"Anan! deer!" repeated Natty.

"Sartain; an't there ven'son here, or didn't you kill a buck?"

"What! when the law forbids the thing, Squire!" said the old hunter. "I hope there's no law ag'in killing the painters."

"No; there's a bounty on the scalps—but—will your dogs hunt painters, Natty?"

"Any thing; didn't I tell you they'd hunt a man? He-e-re, he-e-re, pups"——

"Yes, yes, I remember. Well, they are strange dogs, I must say—I am quite in a wonderment."

Natty had seated himself on the ground, and having laid the grim head of his late ferocious enemy in his lap, was drawing his knife, with a practised hand, around the ears, which he tore from the head of the beast in such a manner as to preserve their connexion, when he answered—

"What at, Squire? did you never see a painter's scalp afore? Come, you be a magistrate. I wish you'd make me out an order for the bounty."

"The bounty!" repeated Hiram, holding the ears on the end of his finger, for a moment, as if uncertain how to proceed. "Well, let us go down to your hut, where you can take the oath, and I will write out the order. I s'pose you have a bible? all the law wants is the four evangelists and the Lord's prayer."

"I keep no books," said Natty, a little coldly; "not such a bible as the law needs."

"Oh! there's but one sort of bible that's good in law," returned the magistrate; "and yourn will do as well as another's. Come, the carcasses are worth nothing, man; let us go down and take the oath."

"Softly, softly, Squire," said the hunter, lifting his trophies very deliberately from the ground, and shouldering his rifle; "why do you want an oath at all, for a thing that your own eyes has seen? won't you believe yourself, that another man must swear to a fact that you know to be true? You have seen me scalp the creaters, and if I must swear to it, it shall be before Judge Temple, who needs an oath."

"But we have no pen or paper here, Leather-stocking; we must go to the hut for them, or how can I write the order?"

Natty turned his simple features on the cunning magistrate with another of his laughs, as he said—

"And what should I be doing with scholar's tools? I want no pens or paper, not knowing the use of 'ither; and I keep none. No, no, I'll bring the scalps into the village, Squire, and you can make out the order on one of your law-books, and it will be all the better for it. The deuce take this leather on the neck of the dog, it will strangle the old fool. Can you lend me a knife, Squire?"

Hiram, who seemed particularly anxious to be on good terms with his companion, unhesitatingly complied. Natty cut the thong from the neck of the hound, and, as he returned the knife to its owner, carelessly remarked—

"'Tis a good bit of steel, and has cut such leather as this very same before now, I dare to say."

"Do you mean to charge me with letting your hounds loose!" exclaimed Hiram, with a consciousness that disarmed his caution.

"Loose!" repeated the hunter—"I let them loose myself. I always let them loose before I leave the hut."

The ungovernable amazement with which Mr. Doolittle listened to this falsehood, would have betrayed his agency in the liberation of the dogs, had Natty wanted any further confirmation; and the coolness and management of the old man now disappeared in open indignation.

"Look you here, Mr. Doolittle," he said, striking the breech of his rifle violently on the ground: "what there is in the wigwam of a poor man like me, that one like you can crave, I don't know; but this I tell you to your face, that you never shall put foot under the roof of my cabin with my consent, and that if you harbour round the spot as you have done lately, you may meet with treatment that you will little relish."

"And let me tell you, Mr. Bumppo," said Hiram, retreating, however, with a quick step, "that I know you've broke the law, and that I'm a magistrate, and will make you feel it too, before you are a day older."

"That for you and your law too," cried Natty, snapping his

fingers at the justice of the peace—"away with you, you varmint, before the divil tempts me to give you your desarts. Take kear, if I ever catch your prowling face in the woods ag'in, that I don't shoot it for an owl."

There is something at all times commanding in honest indignation, and Hiram did not stay to provoke the wrath of the old hunter to extremities. When the intruder was out of sight, Natty proceeded to the hut, where he found all quiet as the grave. He fastened his dogs, and tapping at the door, which was opened by Edwards, asked—

"Is all safe, lad?"

"Every thing," returned the youth. "Some one attempted the lock, but it was too strong for him."

"I know the creater," said Natty; "but he'll not trust himself within reach of my rifle very soon—" What more was uttered by the Leather-stocking, in his vexation, was rendered inaudible by the closing of the door of the cabin.

Chapter XXIX

"It is noised, he hath a mass of treasure."
Timon of Athens, IV.iii.402.

WHEN MARMADUKE TEMPLE and his cousin rode through the gate of the former, the heart of the father had been too recently touched with the best feelings of our nature, to leave inclination for immediate discourse. There was an importance in the air of Richard, which would not have admitted of the ordinary informal conversation of the Sheriff, without violating all the rules of consistency; and the equestrians pursued their way with great diligence, for more than a mile, in profound silence. At length the soft expression of parental affection was slowly chased from the handsome features of the Judge, and was gradually supplanted by the cast of humour and benevolence that was usually seated on his brow.

"Well, Dickon," he said, "since I have yielded myself, so far, implicitly to your guidance, I think the moment has arrived, when I am entitled to further confidence. Why and wherefore are we journeying together in this solemn gait?"

The Sheriff gave a loud hem, that rung far in the forest, and keeping his eyes fixed on objects before him, like a man who is looking deep into futurity—

"There has always been one point of difference between us, Judge Temple, I may say, since our nativity," he replied; "not that I would insinuate that you are at all answerable for the acts of nature; for a man is no more to be condemned for the misfortunes of his birth, than he is to be commended for the natural advantages he may possess; but on one point we may be said to have differed from our births, and they, you know, occurred within two days of each other."

"I really marvel, Richard, what this one point can be; for, to my eyes, we seem to differ so materially, and so often"——

"Mere consequences, sir," interrupted the Sheriff; "all our minor differences proceed from one cause, and that is, our opinions of the universal attainments of genius."

"In what, Dickon?"

"I speak plain English, I believe, Judge Temple; at least I ought; for my father, who taught me, could speak"——

"Greek and Latin," interrupted Marmaduke—"I well know the qualifications of your family in tongues, Dickon. But proceed to the point; why are we travelling over this mountain to-day?"

"To do justice to any subject, sir, the narrator must be suffered to proceed in his own way," continued the Sheriff. "You are of opinion, Judge Temple, that a man is to be qualified by nature and education to do only one thing well, whereas I know that genius will supply the place of learning, and that a certain sort of man can do any thing and every thing."

"Like yourself, I suppose," said Marmaduke, smiling.

"I scorn personalities, sir, I say nothing of myself; but there are three men on your Patent, of the kind that I should term talented by nature, for her general purposes, though acting under the influence of different situations."

"We are better off, then, than I had supposed. Who are these triumviri?"

"Why, sir, one is Hiram Doolittle; a carpenter by trade, as you know, and I need only to point to the village to exhibit his merits. Then he is a magistrate, and might shame many a man, in his distribution of justice, who has had better opportunities."

"Well, he is one," said Marmaduke, with the air of a man that was determined not to dispute the point.

"Jotham Riddel is another."

"Who?"

"Jotham Riddel."

"What, that dissatisfied, shiftless, lazy, speculating fellow! he who changes his county every three years, his farm every six months, and his occupation every season! an agriculturist yesterday, a shoemaker to-day, and a schoolmaster to-morrow! that epitome of all the unsteady and profitless propensities of the settlers, without one of their good qualities to counterbalance the evil! Nay, Richard, this is too bad for even—but the third?"

"As the third is not used to hearing such comments on his character, Judge Temple, I shall not name him."

"The amount of all this, then, Dickon, is, that the trio, of which you are one, and the principal, have made some important discovery."

"I have not said that I am one, Judge Temple. As I told you before, I say nothing egotistical. But a discovery has been made, and you are deeply interested in it."

"Proceed—I am all ears."

"No, no, 'duke, you are bad enough, I own, but not so bad as that either; your ears are not quite full grown."

The Sheriff laughed heartily at his own wit, and put himself in good humour thereby, when he gratified his patient cousin with the following explanation:—

"You know, 'duke, there is a man living on your estate, that goes by the name of Natty Bumppo. Here has this man lived, by what I can learn, for more than forty years—by himself, until lately; and now with strange companions."

"Part very true, and all very probable," said the Judge.

"All true, sir; all true. Well, within these last few months have appeared as his companions, an old Indian chief, the last, or one of the last of his tribe, that is to be found in this part of the country, and a young man, who is said to be the son of some Indian agent, by a squaw."

"Who says that!" cried Marmaduke, with an interest that he had not manifested before.

"Who! why common sense—common report—the hue and cry. But listen, till you know all. This youth has very pretty talents—yes, what I call very pretty talents—and has been well educated, has seen very tolerable company, and knows how to behave himself, when he has a mind to. Now, Judge Temple, can you tell me what has brought three such men as Indian John, Natty Bumppo, and Oliver Edwards, together?"

Marmaduke turned his countenance, in evident surprise, to his cousin, and replied quickly—

"Thou hast unexpectedly hit on a subject, Richard, that has often occupied my mind. But knowest thou any thing of this mystery, or are they only the crude conjectures of"—

"Crude nothing, 'duke, crude nothing; but facts, stubborn facts. You know there are mines in these mountains; I have often heard you say that you believed in their existence"——

"Reasoning from analogy, Richard, but not with any certainty of the fact."

"You have heard them mentioned, and have seen specimens of the ore, sir; you will not deny that! and, reasoning from analogy, as you say, if there be mines in South America, ought there not to be mines in North America too?"

"Nay, nay, I deny nothing, my cousin. I certainly have heard many rumours of the existence of mines, in these hills; and I do believe that I have seen specimens of the precious metals that have been found here. It would occasion me no surprise to learn that tin and silver, or, what I consider of more consequence, good coal,"——

"Damn your coal," cried the Sheriff; " who wants to find coal, in these forests? No, no, silver, 'duke; silver is the one thing needful, and silver is to be found. But listen: you are not to be told that the natives have long known the use of gold and silver; now who so likely to be acquainted where they are to be found, as the ancient inhabitants of a country? I have the best reasons for believing that both Mohegan and the Leather-stocking have been privy to the existence of a mine, in this very mountain, for many years."

The Sheriff had now touched his cousin in a sensitive spot, and Marmaduke lent a more attentive ear to the speaker, who, after waiting a moment, to see the effect of this extraordinary development, proceeded—

"Yes, sir, I have my reasons, and at a proper time you shall know them."

"No time is so good as the present."

"Well, well, be attentive," continued Richard, looking cautiously about him, to make certain that no eavesdropper was hid in the forest, though they were in constant motion. "I have seen Mohegan and the Leather-stocking, with my own eyes—and my eyes are as good as any body's eyes—I have seen them, I say, both going up the mountain and coming down it, with spades and picks; and others have seen them carrying things into their hut, in a secret and mysterious manner, after dark. Do you call this a fact of importance?"

The Judge did not reply, but his brow had contracted, with a thoughtfulness that he always wore when much interested, and his eyes rested on his cousin in expectation of hearing more. Richard continued—

"It was ore. Now, sir, I ask if you can tell me who this Mr.

Oliver Edwards is, that has made a part of your household since Christmas?"

Marmaduke again raised his eyes, but continued silent, shaking his head in the negative.

"That he is a half-breed we know, for Mohegan does not scruple to call him, openly, his kinsman; that he is well educated we know. But as to his business here—do you remember that about a month before this young man made his appearance among us, Natty was absent from home several days? You do; for you inquired for him, as you wanted some venison to take to your friends, when you went for Bess. Well, he was not to be found. Old John was left in the hut alone; and when Natty did appear, although he came on in the night, he was seen drawing one of those jumpers that they carry their grain to mill in, and to take out something, with great care, that he had covered up under his bear-skins. Now let me ask you, Judge Temple, what motive could induce a man like the Leather-stocking to make a sled, and toil with a load over these mountains, if he had nothing but his rifle or his ammunition to carry?"

"They frequently make these jumpers to convey their game home, and you say he had been absent many days."

"How did he kill it? His rifle was in the village to be mended. No, no—that he was gone to some unusual place is certain; that he brought back some secret utensils is more certain; and that he has not allowed a soul to approach his hut since, is most certain of all."

"He was never fond of intruders"——

"I know it," interrupted Richard; "but did he drive them from his cabin morosely? Within a fortnight of his return, this Mr. Edwards appears. They spend whole days in the mountains, pretending to be shooting, but in reality exploring; the frosts prevent their digging at that time, and he avails himself of a lucky accident to get into good quarters. But even now, he is quite half of his time in that hut—many hours every night. They are smelting, 'duke, they are smelting, and as they grow rich you grow poor."

"How much of this is thine own, Richard, and how much comes from others? I would sift the wheat from the chaff."

"Part is my own, for I saw the jumper, though it was broken up and burnt in a day or two. I have told you that I saw the old man with his spades and picks. Hiram met Natty, as he was crossing the mountain, the night of his arrival with the sled, and very good-naturedly offered—Hiram *is* good natured—to carry up part of his load, for the old man had a heavy pull up the back of the mountain, but he wouldn't listen to the thing, and repulsed the offer in such a manner that the Squire said he had half a mind to swear the peace against him. Since the snow has been off, more especially after the frosts got out of the ground, we have kept a watchful eye on the gentleman, in which we have found Jotham useful."

Marmaduke did not much like the associates of Richard in this business; still he knew them to be cunning and ready in expedients; and as there was certainly something mysterious, not only in the connexion between the old hunters and Edwards, but in what his cousin had just related, he begun to revolve the subject in his own mind with more care. On reflection, he remembered various circumstances that tended to corroborate these suspicions, and, as the whole business favoured one of his infirmities, he yielded the more readily to their impression. The mind of Judge Temple, at all times comprehensive, had received, from his peculiar occupations, a bias to look far into futurity, in his speculations on the improvements that posterity were to make in his lands. To his eye, where others saw nothing but a wilderness, towns, manufactories, bridges, canals, mines, and all the other resources of an old country, were constantly presenting themselves, though his good sense suppressed, in some degree, the exhibition of these expectations.

As the Sheriff allowed his cousin full time to reflect on what he had heard, the probability of some pecuniary adventure being the connecting link in the chain that brought Oliver Edwards into the cabin of Leather-stocking, appeared to him each moment to be stronger. But Marmaduke was too much in the habit of examining both sides of a subject, not to perceive the objections, and he reasoned with himself aloud:—

"It cannot be so, or the youth would not be driven so near the verge of poverty."

"What so likely to make a man dig for money, as being poor?" cried the Sheriff.

"Besides, there is an elevation of character about Oliver, that proceeds from education, which would forbid so clandestine a proceeding."

"Could an ignorant fellow smelt?" continued Richard.

"Bess hints that he was reduced even to his last shilling, when we took him into our dwelling."

"He had been buying tools. And would he spend his last sixpence for a shot at a turkey, had he not known where to get more?"

"Can I have possibly been so long a dupe! His manner has been rude to me, at times; but I attributed it to his conceiving himself injured, and to his mistaking the forms of the world."

"Haven't you been a dupe all your life, 'duke? and an't what you call ignorance of forms deep cunning, to conceal his real character?"

"If he were bent on deception, he would have concealed his knowledge, and passed with us for an inferior man."

"He cannot. I could no more pass for a fool, myself, than I could fly. Knowledge is not to be concealed, like a candle under a bushel."

"Richard," said the Judge, turning to his cousin, "there are many reasons against the truth of thy conjectures; but thou hast awakened suspicions which must be satisfied. But why are we travelling here?"

"Jotham, who has been much in the mountain latterly, being kept there by me and Hiram, has made a discovery, which he will not explain, he says, for he is bound by an oath; but the amount is, that he knows where the ore lies, and he has this day begun to dig. I would not consent to the thing, 'duke, without your knowledge, for the land is yours;— and now you know the reason of our ride. I call this a countermine, ha!"

"And where is the desirable spot?" asked the Judge, with an air half comical, half serious.

"At hand; and when we have visited that, I will show you one of the places that we have found within a week, where our hunters have been amusing themselves for six months past."

The gentlemen continued to discuss the matter, while their horses picked their way under the branches of trees, and over the uneven ground of the mountain. They soon arrived at the end of their journey, where, in truth, they found Jotham already buried to his neck in a hole that he had been digging.

Marmaduke questioned the miner very closely, as to his reasons for believing in the existence of the precious metals near that particular spot; but the fellow maintained an obstinate mystery in his answers. He asserted that he had the best of reasons for what he did, and inquired of the Judge what portion of the profits would fall to his own share, in the event of success, with an earnestness that proved his faith. After spending an hour near the place, examining the stones, and searching for the usual indications of the proximity of ore, the Judge remounted, and suffered his cousin to lead the way to the place where the mysterious trio had been making their excavation.

The spot chosen by Jotham was on the back of the mountain that overhung the hut of Leather-stocking, and the place selected by Natty and his companions was on the other side of the same hill, but above the road, and, of course, in an opposite direction to the route taken by the ladies in their walk.

"We shall be safe in approaching the place now," said Richard, while they dismounted and fastened their horses; "for I took a look with the glass, and saw John and Leather-stocking in their canoe fishing, before we left home, and Oliver is in the same pursuit; but these may be nothing but shams, to blind our eyes, so we will be expeditious, for it would not be pleasant to be caught here by them."

"Not on my own land!" said Marmaduke, sternly. "If it be as you suspect, I will know their reasons for making this excavation."

"Mum," said Richard, laying a finger on his lip, and leading the way down a very difficult descent to a sort of a natural cavern, which was formed in the face of the rock, and was not unlike a fire-place in shape. In front of this place lay a pile of earth, which had evidently been taken from the recess, and part of which was yet fresh. An examination of the exterior of the cavern, left the Judge in doubt whether it was one of nature's frolics that had thrown it into that shape, or whether it had been wrought by the hands of man, at some earlier period. But there could be no doubt that the whole of the interior was of recent formation, and the marks of the pick were still visible, where the soft, lead-coloured rock had opposed itself to the progress of the miners. The whole formed an excavation of about twenty feet in width, and nearly twice that distance in depth. The height was much greater than was required for the ordinary purposes of experiment; but this was evidently the effect of chance, as the roof of the cavern was a natural stratum of rock, that projected many feet beyond the base of the pile. Immediately in front of the recess, or cave, was a little terrace, partly formed by nature, and partly by the earth that had been carelessly thrown aside by the labourers. The mountain fell off precipitously in front of the terrace, and the approach by its sides, under the ridge of the rocks, was difficult, and a little dangerous. The whole was wild, rude, and apparently incomplete; for, while looking among the bushes, the Sheriff found the very implements that had been used in the work.

When the Sheriff thought that his cousin had examined the spot sufficiently, he asked solemnly—

"Judge Temple, are you satisfied?"

"Perfectly—that there is something mysterious, and perplexing, in this business. It is a secret spot, and cunningly devised, Richard; yet I see no symptoms of ore."

"Do you expect, sir, to find gold and silver lying like pebbles on the surface of the earth?—dollars and dimes ready coined to your hands! No, no—the treasure must be sought after to be won. But let them mine; I shall countermine."

The Judge took an accurate survey of the place, and noted in his memorandum-book such marks as were necessary to find it again, in the event of Richard's absence; when the cousins returned to their horses.

On reaching the highway they separated, the Sheriff to summon twenty-four "good men and true," to attend as the inquest of the county, on the succeeding Monday, when Marmaduke held his stated court of "common pleas and general sessions of the peace," and the Judge to return, musing deeply on what he had seen and heard in the course of the morning.

When the horse of the latter reached the spot where the highway fell towards the valley, the eye of Marmaduke rested, it is true, on the same scene that had, ten minutes before, been so soothing to the feelings of his daughter and her friend, as they emerged from the forest; but it rested in vacancy. He threw the reins to his sure-footed beast, and suffered the animal to travel at its own gait, while he soliloquized as follows:—

"There may be more in this than I at first supposed. I have suffered my feeling to blind my reason, in admitting an unknown youth in this manner to my dwelling;—yet this is not the land of suspicion. I will have the Leather-stocking before me, and, by a few direct questions, extract the truth from the simple old man."——

At that instant the Judge caught a glimpse of the figures of Elizabeth and Louisa, who were slowly descending the mountain, a short distance before him. He put spurs to his horse, and riding up to them, dismounted, and drove his steed along the narrow path. While the agitated parent was listening to the vivid description that his daughter gave of her recent danger, and her unexpected escape, all thoughts of mines, vested rights, and examinations, were absorbed in emotion; and when the image of Natty again crossed his recollection, it was not as a lawless and depredating squatter, but as the preserver of his child.

Chapter XXX

"The court awards it, and the law doth give it."
The Merchant of Venice, IV.i.300.

REMARKABLE PETTIBONE, who had forgotten the wound received by her pride, in contemplation of the ease and comforts of her situation, and who still retained her station in the family of Judge Temple, was despatched to the humble dwelling which Richard already styled "the Rectory," in attendance on Louisa, who was soon consigned to the arms of her father.

In the mean time, Marmaduke and his daughter were closeted for more than an hour, nor shall we invade the sanctuary of parental love, by relating the conversation.—When the curtain rises on the reader, the Judge is seen walking up and down the apartment, with a tender melancholy in his air, and his child reclining on a settee, with a flushed cheek, and her dark eyes seeming to float in crystals.

"It was a timely rescue! it was, indeed, a timely rescue, my child!" cried the Judge. "Then thou didst not desert thy friend, my noble Bess?"

"I believe I may as well take the credit of fortitude," said Elizabeth, "though I much doubt if flight would have availed me any thing, had I even courage to execute such an intention. But I thought not of the expedient."

"Of what didst thou think, love? where did thy thoughts dwell most, at that fearful moment?"

"The beast! the beast!" cried Elizabeth, veiling her face with her hand; "Oh! I saw nothing, I thought of nothing, but the beast. I tried to think of better things, but the horror was too glaring, the danger too much before my eyes."

"Well, well, thou art safe, and we will converse no more on the unpleasant subject. I did not think such an animal yet remained in our forest; but they will stray far from their haunts when pressed by hunger, and"——

A loud knocking at the door of the apartment interrupted what he was about to utter, and he bid the applicant enter. The door was opened by Benjamin, who came in with a discontented air, as if he felt that he had a communication to make that would be out of season.

"Here is Squire Doolittle below, sir," commenced the Major-domo. "He has been standing off and on in the door-yard, for the matter of a glass; and he has sum'mat on his mind that he wants to heave up, d'ye see; but I tells him, says I, man, would you be coming aboard with your complaints, said I, when the Judge has gotten his own child, as it were, out of the jaws of a lion? But damn the bit of manners has the fellow any more than if he was one of them Guineas, down in the kitchen there; and so as he was sheering nearer, every stretch he made towards the house, I could do no better than to let your honour know that the chap was in the offing."

"He must have business of importance," said Marmaduke; "something in relation to his office, most probably, as the court sits so shortly."

"Ay, ay, you have it, sir," cried Benjamin, "it's sum'mat about a complaint that he has to make of the old Leather-stocking, who, to my judgment, is the better man of the two. It's a very good sort of a man is this Master Bumppo, and he has a way with a spear, all the same as if he was brought up at the bow oar of the captain's barge, or was born with a boat-hook in his hand."

"Against the Leather-stocking!" cried Elizabeth, rising from her reclining posture.

"Rest easy, my child; some trifle, I pledge you; I believe I am already acquainted with its import. Trust me, Bess, your champion shall be safe in my care.—Show Mr. Doolittle in, Benjamin."

Miss Temple appeared satisfied with this assurance, but fastened her dark eyes on the person of the architect, who profited by the permission, and instantly made his appearance.

All the impatience of Hiram seemed to vanish the instant he entered the apartment. After saluting the Judge and his daughter, he took the chair to which Marmaduke pointed, and sat for a minute, composing his straight black hair, with a gravity of demeanour, that was intended to do honour to his official station. At length he said—

"It's likely, from what I hear, that Miss Temple had a pretty narrow chance with the painters, on the mountain."

Marmaduke made a gentle inclination of his head, by way of assent, but continued silent.

"I s'pose the law gives a bounty on the scalps," continued Hiram, "in which case the Leather-stocking will make a good job on't."

"It shall be my care to see that he is rewarded," returned the Judge.

"Yes, yes, I rather guess that nobody hereabouts doubts the Judge's ginerosity. Doos he know whether the Sheriff has fairly made up his mind to have a reading-desk or a deacon's pew under the pulpit?"

"I have not heard my cousin speak on that subject lately," replied Marmaduke.

"I think it's likely that we will have a pretty dull court on't, from what I can gather. I hear that Jotham Riddel and the man who bought his betterments have agreen to leave their difference to men, and I don't think there'll be more than two civil cases in the calendar."

"I am glad of it," said the Judge; "nothing gives me more pain, than to see my settlers wasting their time and substance in the unprofitable struggles of the law. I hope it may prove true, sir."

"I rather guess 'twill be left out to men," added Hiram, with an air equally balanced between doubt and assurance, but which Judge Temple understood to mean certainty; "I some think that I am appointed a referee in the case myself. Jotham as much as told me that he should take me. The defendant, I guess, means to take Captain Hollister, and we two have partly agreen on Squire Jones for the third man."

"Are there any criminals to be tried?" asked Marmaduke.

"There's the counterfeiters," returned the magistrate; "as they were caught in the fact, I think it likely that they'll be indicted, in which case, it's probable they will be tried."

"Certainly, sir; I had forgotten those men. There are no more, I hope."

"Why, there is a threaten to come forrard with an assault, that happened at the last independence day; but I'm not sartain that the law'll take hold on't. There was plaguey hard words passed, but whether they struck or not I haven't heern. There's some folks talk of a deer or two being killed out of season, over on the west side of the Patent, by some of the squatters on the 'Fractions.' "

"Let a complaint be made, by all means," cried the Judge; "I am determined to see the law executed, to the letter, on all such depredators."

"Why, yes, I thought the Judge was of that mind; I come, partly, on such a business myself."

"You!" exclaimed Marmaduke, comprehending, in an instant, how completely he had been caught by the other's cunning; "and what have you to say, sir?"

"I some think that Natty Bumppo has the carcass of a deer in his hut at this moment, and a considerable part of my business was to get a sarch-warrant to examine."

"You think, sir! do you know that the law exacts an oath, before I can issue such a precept. The habitation of a citizen is not to be idly invaded on light suspicion."

"I rather think I can swear to it myself," returned the immoveable Hiram; "and Jotham is in the street, and as good as ready to come in and make oath to the same thing."

"Then issue the warrant thyself; thou art a magistrate, Mr. Doolittle; why trouble me with the matter?"

"Why, seeing it's the first complaint under the law, and knowing the Judge set his heart on the thing, I thought it best that the authority to sarch should come from himself. Besides, as I'm much in the woods, among the timber, I don't altogether like making an enemy of the Leather-stocking. Now the Judge has a weight in the county that puts him above fear."

Miss Temple turned her face to the callous architect, as she said—

"And what has any honest person to dread from so kind a man as Bumppo?"

"Why, it's as easy, Miss, to pull a rifle-trigger on a magistrate as on a painter. But if the Judge don't conclude to issoo the warrant, I must go home and make it out myself."

"I have not refused your application, sir," said Marmaduke, perceiving, at once, that his reputation for impartiality was at stake; "go into my office, Mr. Doolittle, where I will join you, and sign the warrant."

Judge Temple stopped the remonstrances which Elizabeth

was about to utter, after Hiram had withdrawn, by laying his hand on her mouth, and saying—

"It is more terrific in sound than frightful in reality, my child. I suppose that the Leather-stocking has shot a deer, for the season is nearly over, and you say that he was hunting with his dogs, when he came so timely to your assistance. But it will be only to examine his cabin, and find the animal, when you can pay the penalty out of your own pocket, Bess. Nothing short of the twelve dollars and a half will satisfy this harpy, I perceive; and surely my reputation as a Judge is worth that trifle."

Elizabeth was a good deal pacified with this assurance, and suffered her father to leave her, to fulfil his promise to Hiram.

When Marmaduke left his office, after executing his disagreeable duty, he met Oliver Edwards, walking up the gravelled walk in front of the Mansion-house, with great strides, and with a face agitated by feeling. On seeing Judge Temple, the youth turned aside, and with a warmth in his manner that was not often exhibited to Marmaduke, he cried—

"I congratulate you, sir; from the bottom of my soul I congratulate you, Judge Temple. Oh! it would have been too horrid to have recollected for a moment! I have just left the hut, where, after showing me his scalps, old Natty told me of the escape of the ladies, as a thing to be mentioned last. Indeed, indeed, sir, no words of mine can express half of what I have felt"—the youth paused a moment, as if suddenly recollecting that he was overstepping prescribed limits, and concluded with a good deal of embarrassment—"what I have felt, at this danger to Miss—Grant, and—and your daughter, sir."

But the heart of Marmaduke was too much softened, to admit of his cavilling at trifles, and, without regarding the confusion of the other, he replied—

"I thank thee, thank thee, Oliver; as thou sayest, it is almost too horrid to be remembered. But come, let us hasten to Bess, for Louisa has already gone to the Rectory."

The young man sprung forward, and, throwing open a door, barely permitted the Judge to precede him, when he was in the presence of Elizabeth in a moment.

The cold distance that often crossed the demeanour of the

heiress, in her intercourse with Edwards, was now entirely banished, and two hours were passed by the party, in the free, unembarrassed, and confiding manner of old and esteemed friends. Judge Temple had forgotten the suspicions engendered during his morning's ride, and the youth and maiden conversed, laughed, and were sad, by turns, as impulse directed. At length Edwards, after repeating his intention to do so for the third time, left the Mansion-house, to go to the Rectory on a similar errand of friendship.

During this short period, a scene was passing at the hut, that completely frustrated the benevolent intentions of Judge Temple in favour of the Leather-stocking, and at once destroyed the short-lived harmony between the youth and Marmaduke.

When Hiram Doolittle had obtained his search-warrant, his first business was to procure a proper officer to see it executed. The Sheriff was absent, summoning, in person, the grand inquest for the county; the deputy, who resided in the village, was riding on the same errand, in a different part of the settlement; and the regular constable of the township had been selected for his station from motives of charity, being lame of a leg. Hiram intended to accompany the officer as a spectator, but he felt no very strong desire to bear the brunt of the battle. It was, however, Saturday, and the sun was already turning the shadows of the pines towards the east; on the morrow the conscientious magistrate could not engage in such an expedition at the peril of his soul; and long before Monday, the venison, and all vestiges of the death of the deer, might be secreted or destroyed. Happily, the lounging form of Billy Kirby met his eye, and Hiram, at all times fruitful in similar expedients, saw his way clear at once. Jotham, who was associated in the whole business, and who had left the mountain in consequence of a summons from his coadjutor, but who failed, equally with Hiram, in the unfortunate particular of nerve, was directed to summon the wood-chopper to the dwelling of the magistrate.

When Billy appeared, he was very kindly invited to take the chair in which he had already seated himself, and was treated, in all respects, as if he were an equal.

"Judge Temple has set his heart on putting the deer law in force," said Hiram, after the preliminary civilities were over, "and a complaint has been laid before him that a deer has been killed. He has issooed a sarch-warrant, and sent for me to get somebody to execute it."

Kirby, who had no idea of being excluded from the deliberative part of any affair in which he was engaged, drew up his bushy head in a reflecting attitude, and, after musing a moment, replied by asking a few questions.

"The Sheriff is gone out of the way?"

"Not to be found."

"And his deputy too?"

"Both gone on the skirts of the Patent."

"But I seen the constable hobbling about town an hour ago."

"Yes, yes," said Hiram, with a coaxing smile and knowing nod, "but this business wants a man—not a cripple."

"Why," said Billy, laughing, " will the chap make fight?"

"He's a little quarrelsome at times, and thinks he's the best man in the county at rough-and-tumble."

"I heerd him brag once," said Jotham, "that there wasn't a man 'twixt the Mohawk Flats and the Pennsylvany line, that was his match at a close hug."

"Did you!" exclaimed Kirby, raising his huge frame in his seat, like a lion stretching in his lair; "I rather guess he never felt a Varmounter's knuckles on his back-bone. But who is the chap?"

"Why," said Jotham, "it's"——

"It's ag'in law to tell," interrupted Hiram, "unless you'll qualify to sarve. You'd be the very man to take him, Bill; and I'll make out a spicial deputation in a minute, when you will get the fees."

"What's the fees?" said Kirby, laying his large hand on the leaves of a statute-book, that Hiram had opened in order to give dignity to his office, which he turned over, in his rough manner, as if he were reflecting on a subject, about which he had, in truth, already decided; " will they pay a man for a broken head?"

"They'll be something handsome," said Hiram.

"Damn the fees," said Billy, again laughing—"doos the fellow think he's the best wrestler in the county, though? what's his inches?"

"He's taller than you be," said Jotham, "and one of the biggest"——

Talkers, he was about to add, but the impatience of Kirby interrupted him. The wood-chopper had nothing fierce, or even brutal in his appearance: the character of his expression was that of good-natured vanity. It was evident he prided himself on the powers of the physical man, like all who have nothing better to boast of; and, stretching out his broad hand, with the palm downward, he said, keeping his eyes fastened on his own bones and sinews—

"Come, give us a touch of the book. I'll swear, and you'll see that I'm a man to keep my oath."

Hiram did not give the wood-chopper time to change his mind, but the oath was administered without unnecessary delay. So soon as this preliminary was completed, the three worthies left the house, and proceeded by the nearest road towards the hut. They had reached the bank of the lake, and were diverging from the route of the highway, before Kirby recollected that he was now entitled to the privileges of the initiated, and repeated his question, as to the name of the offender.

"Which way, which way, Squire?" exclaimed the hardy wood-chopper; "I thought it was to sarch a house that you wanted me, not the woods. There is nobody lives on this side of the lake, for six miles, unless you count the Leather-stocking and old John for settlers. Come, tell me the chap's name, and I warrant me that I lead you to his clearing by a straighter path than this, for I know every sapling that grows within two miles of Templetown."

"This is the way," said Hiram, pointing forward, and quickening his step, as if apprehensive that Kirby would desert, "and Bumppo is the man."

Kirby stopped short, and looked from one of his companions to the other in astonishment. He then burst into a loud laugh, and cried—

"Who! Leather-stocking! he may brag of his aim and his rifle, for he has the best of both, as I will own myself, for sin he shot the pigeon I knock under to him; but for a wrestle! why, I would take the creatur between my finger and thumb, and tie him in a bow-knot around my neck for a Barcelony. The man is seventy, and was never any thing particular for strength."

"He's a deceiving man," said Hiram, "like all the hunters; he is stronger than he seems;—besides, he has his rifle."

"That for his rifle!" cried Billy; "he'd no more hurt me with his rifle than he'd fly. He is a harmless creater, and I must say that I think he has as good a right to kill deer as any man on the Patent. It's his main support, and this is a free country, where a man is privileged to follow any calling he likes."

"According to that doctrine," said Jotham, "any body may shoot a deer."

"This is the man's calling, I tell you," returned Kirby, "and the law was never made for such as he."

"The law was made for all," observed Hiram, who began to think that the danger was likely to fall to his own share, notwithstanding his management; "and the law is particular in noticing parjury."

"See here, Squire Doolittle," said the reckless wood-chopper, "I don't kear the valie of a beetle-ring for you and your parjury too. But as I have come so far, I'll go down and have a talk with the old man, and maybe we'll fry a steak of the deer together."

"Well, if you can get in peaceably, so much the better," said the magistrate. "To my notion, strife is very unpopular; I prefar, at all times, clever conduct to an ugly temper."

As the whole party moved at a great pace, they soon reached the hut, where Hiram thought it prudent to halt on the outside of the top of the fallen pine, which formed a chevaux-de-frize, to defend the approach to the fortress, on the side next the village. The delay was little relished by Kirby, who clapped his hands to his mouth, and gave a loud halloo, that brought the dogs out of their kennel, and, almost at the same instant, the scantily-covered head of Natty from the door.

"Lie down, old fool," cried the hunter; "do you think there's more painters about you?"

"Ha! Leather-stocking, I've an arrand with you," cried Kirby; "here's the good people of the state have been writing you a small letter, and they've hired me to ride post."

"What would you have with me, Billy Kirby?" said Natty, stepping across his threshold, and raising his hand over his eyes to screen them from the rays of the setting sun, while he took a survey of his visiter. "I've no land to clear; and Heaven knows I would set out six trees afore I would cut down one. Down, Hector, I say, into your kennel with ye."

"Would you, old boy!" roared Billy; "then so much the better for me. But I must do my arrand. Here's a letter for you, Leather-stocking. If you can read it it's all well, and if you can't, here's Squire Doolittle at hand to let you know what it means. It seems, you mistook the twentieth of July for the first of August, that's all."

By this time Natty had discovered the lank person of Hiram, drawn up under the cover of a high stump; and all that was complacent in his manner instantly gave way to marked distrust and dissatisfaction. He placed his head within the door of his hut, and said a few words in an under tone, when he again appeared, and continued—

"I've nothing for ye; so away, afore the evil one tempts me to do you harm. I owe you no spite, Billy Kirby, and what for should you trouble an old man, who has done you no harm?"

Kirby advanced through the top of the pine, to within a few feet of the hunter, where he seated himself on the end of a log with great composure, and begun to examine the nose of Hector, with whom he was familiar, from their frequently meeting in the woods, where he sometimes fed the dog from his own basket of provisions.

"You've outshot me, and I'm not ashamed to say it," said the wood-chopper; "but I don't owe you a grudge for that, Natty; though it seems, that you've shot once too often, for the story goes, that you've killed a buck."

"I've fired but twice to-day, and both times at the painters," returned the Leather-stocking; "see! here's the scalps! I was just going in with them to the Judge's to ask the bounty."

While Natty was speaking, he tossed the ears to Kirby, who continued playing with them, with a careless air, holding them to the dogs, and laughing at their movements when they scented the unusual game.

But Hiram, emboldened by the advance of the deputed constable, now ventured to approach also, and took up the discourse with the air of authority that became his commission. His first measure was to read the warrant aloud, taking care to give due emphasis to the most material parts, and concluding with the name of the Judge in very audible and distinct tones.

"Did Marmaduke Temple put his name to that bit of paper!" said Natty, shaking his head;—"well, well, that man loves the new ways, and his betterments, and his lands, afore his own flesh and blood. But I won't mistrust the gall: she has an eye like a full-grown buck! poor thing, she didn't choose her father, and can't help it.—I know but little of the law, Mr. Doolittle; what is to be done, now you've read your commission?"

"Oh! it's nothing but form, Natty," said Hiram, endeavouring to assume a friendly aspect. "Let's go in and talk the thing over in reason. I dare to say that the money can be easily found, and I partly conclude, from what passed, that Judge Temple will pay it himself."

The old hunter had kept a keen eye on the movements of his three visiters, from the beginning, and had maintained his position, just without the threshold of his cabin, with a determined manner, that showed he was not to be easily driven from his post. When Hiram drew nigher, as if expecting his proposition would be accepted, Natty lifted his hand and motioned for him to retreat.

"Haven't I told you, more than once, not to tempt me," he said. "I trouble no man; why can't the law leave me to myself? Go back—go back, and tell your Judge that he may keep his bounty; but I won't have his wasty ways brought into my hut."

This offer, however, instead of appeasing the curiosity of Hiram, seemed to inflame it the more; while Kirby cried—

"Well, that's fair, Squire; he forgives the county his demand, and the county should forgive him the fine; it's what I call an even trade, and should be concluded on the spot. I like quick dealings, and what's fair 'twixt man and man."

"I demand entrance into this house," said Hiram, summoning all the dignity he could muster to his assistance, "in the name of the people, and by vartoo of this warrant, and of my office, and with this peace-officer."

"Stand back, stand back, Squire, and don't tempt me," said the Leather-stocking, motioning for him to retire, with great earnestness.

"Stop us at your peril," continued Hiram—"Billy! Jotham! close up—I want testimony."

Hiram had mistaken the mild but determined air of Natty for submission, and had already put his foot on the threshold to enter, when he was seized unexpectedly by his shoulders, and hurled over the little bank towards the lake, to the distance of twenty feet. The suddenness of the movement, and the unexpected display of strength on the part of Natty, created a momentary astonishment in his invaders, that silenced all noises; but at the next instant Billy Kirby gave vent to his mirth in peals of laughter, that he seemed to heave up from his very soul.

"Well done, old stub!" he shouted; "the Squire know'd you better than I did. Come, come, here's a green spot; take it out like men, while Jotham and I see fair play."

"William Kirby, I order you to do your duty," cried Hiram, from under the bank; "seize that man; I order you to seize him in the name of the people."

But the Leather-stocking now assumed a more threatening attitude; his rifle was in his hand, and its muzzle was directed towards the wood-chopper.

"Stand off, I bid ye," said Natty; "you know my aim, Billy Kirby; I don't crave your blood, but mine and yourn both shall turn this green grass red, afore you put foot into the hut."

While the affair appeared trifling, the wood-chopper seemed disposed to take sides with the weaker party; but when the fire-arms were introduced, his manner very sensibly changed. He raised his large frame from the log, and, facing the hunter with an open front, he replied—

"I didn't come here as your enemy, Leather-stocking; but I don't valie the hollow piece of iron in your hand so much as a broken axe-helve;—so, Squire, say the word, and keep within the law, and we'll soon see who's the best man of the two."

But no magistrate was to be seen! The instant the rifle was produced Hiram and Jotham vanished; and when the wood-chopper bent his eyes about him in surprise at receiving no answer, he discovered their retreating figures, moving towards the village, at a rate that sufficiently indicated that they had not only calculated the velocity of a rifle-bullet, but also its probable range.

"You've skeared the creaters off," said Kirby, with great contempt expressed on his broad features; "but you are not a-going to skear me; so, Mr. Bumppo, down with your gun, or there'll be trouble 'twixt us."

Natty dropped his rifle, and replied—

"I wish you no harm, Billy Kirby; but I leave it to yourself, whether an old man's hut is to be run down by such varmint. I won't deny the buck to you, Billy, and you may take the skin in, if you please, and show it as tistimony. The bounty will pay the fine, and that ought to satisfy any man."

"'Twill, old boy, 'twill," cried Kirby, every shade of displeasure vanishing from his open brow at the peace-offering; "throw out the hide, and that shall satisfy the law."

Natty entered his hut, and soon re-appeared, bringing with him the desired testimonial, and the wood-chopper departed, as thoroughly reconciled to the hunter as if nothing had happened. As he paced along the margin of the lake, he would burst into frequent fits of laughter, while he recollected the summerset of Hiram; and, on the whole, he thought the affair a very capital joke.

Long before Billy reached the village, however, the news of his danger, and of Natty's disrespect of the law, and of Hiram's discomfiture, were in circulation. A good deal was said about sending for the Sheriff; some hints were given about calling out the posse comitatus to avenge the insulted laws; and many of the citizens were collected, deliberating how to proceed. The arrival of Billy with the skin, by removing all grounds for a search, changed the complexion of things materially. Nothing now remained but to collect the fine, and assert the dignity of the people; all of which, it was unanimously agreed, could be done as well on the succeeding Monday as on a Saturday night, a time kept sacred by a large portion of the settlers. Accordingly, all further proceedings were suspended for six-and-thirty hours.

Chapter XXXI

"And dar'st thou, then,
To beard the lion in his den,
The Douglass in his hall?"
Scott, *Marmion*, VI.xiv.23–25.

THE COMMOTION was just subsiding, and the inhabitants of the village had begun to disperse from the little groups they had formed, each retiring to his own home, and closing his door after him, with the grave air of a man who consulted public feeling in his exterior deportment, when Oliver Edwards, on his return from the dwelling of Mr. Grant, encountered the young lawyer, who is known to the reader as Mr. Lippet. There was very little similarity in the manners or opinions of the two; but as they both belonged to the more intelligent class of a very small community, they were, of course, known to each other; and, as their meeting was at a point where silence would have been rudeness, the following conversation was the result of their interview:—

"A fine evening, Mr. Edwards," commenced the lawyer, whose disinclination to the dialogue was, to say the least, very doubtful; "we want rain sadly;—that's the worst of this climate of ours, it's either a drought or a deluge. It's likely you've been used to a more equal temperatoore?"

"I am a native of this state," returned Edwards, coldly.

"Well, I've often heerd that point disputed; but it's so easy to get a man naturalized, that it's of little consequence where he was born. I wonder what course the Judge means to take in this business of Natty Bumppo?"

"Of Natty Bumppo!" echoed Edwards; "to what do you allude, sir?"

"Haven't you heerd!" exclaimed the other, with a look of surprise, so naturally assumed as completely to deceive his auditor; "it may turn out an ugly business. It seems that the old man has been out in the hills, and has shot a buck, this morning, and that, you know, is a criminal matter in the eyes of Judge Temple."

"Oh! he has, has he!" said Edwards, averting his face to conceal the colour that collected in his sun-burnt cheek. "Well, if that be all, he must even pay the fine."

"It's five pounds, currency," said the lawyer; "could Natty muster so much money at once?"

"Could he!" cried the youth. "I am not rich, Mr. Lippet; far from it—I am poor; and I have been hoarding my salary for a purpose that lies near my heart; but before that old man should lie one hour in a gaol, I would spend the last cent to prevent it. Besides, he has killed two panthers, and the bounty will discharge the fine many times over."

"Yes, yes," said the lawyer, rubbing his hands together with an expression of pleasure that had no artifice about it; "we shall make it out; I see plainly, we shall make it out."

"Make what out, sir? I must beg an explanation."

"Why, killing the buck is but a small matter, compared to what took place this afternoon," continued Mr. Lippet, with a confidential and friendly air, that insensibly won upon the youth, little as he liked the man. "It seems, that a complaint was made of the fact, and a suspicion that there was venison in the hut was sworn to, all which is provided for in the statoote, when Judge Temple granted a search-warrant"——

"A search-warrant!" echoed Edwards, in a voice of horror, and with a face that should have been again averted, to conceal its paleness; "and how much did they discover? What did they see?"

"They saw old Bumppo's rifle; and that is a sight which will quiet most men's curiosity in the woods."

"Did they! did they!" shouted Edwards, bursting into a convulsive laugh; "so the old hero beat them back—he beat them back! did he!"

The lawyer fastened his eyes in astonishment on the youth; but, as his wonder gave way to the thoughts that were commonly uppermost in his mind, he replied—

"It's no laughing matter, let me tell you, sir; the forty dollars of bounty, and your six months of salary, will be much redooced, before you get the matter fairly settled. Assaulting a magistrate in the execootion of his duty, and menacing a constable with fire-arms, at the same time, is a pretty serious affair, and punishable with both fine and imprisonment."

"Imprisonment!" repeated Oliver; "imprison the Leather-stocking! no, no, sir; it would bring the old man to his grave. They shall never imprison the Leather-stocking."

"Well, Mr. Edwards," said Lippet, dropping all reserve from his manner, "you are called a curious man; but if you can tell me how a jury is to be prevented from finding a verdict of guilty, if this case comes fairly before them, and the proof is clear, I shall acknowledge that you know more law than I do, who have had a license in my pocket for three years."

By this time the reason of Edwards was getting the ascendency of his feelings; and, as he begun to see the real difficulties of the case, he listened more readily to the conversation of the lawyer. The ungovernable emotion that escaped the youth, in the first moments of his surprise, entirely passed away, and, although it was still evident that he continued to be much agitated by what he had heard, he succeeded in yielding forced attention to the advice which the other uttered.

Notwithstanding the confused state of his mind, Oliver soon discovered that most of the expedients of the lawyer were grounded in cunning, and plans that required a time to execute them, that neither suited his disposition nor his necessities. After, however, giving Mr. Lippet to understand that he retained him, in the event of a trial, an assurance that at once satisfied the lawyer, they parted, one taking his course, with a deliberate tread, in the direction of the little building that had a wooden sign over its door, with "Chester Lippet, Attorney at Law," painted on it; and the other, pacing over the ground, with enormous strides, towards the Mansion-house. We shall take leave of the attorney for the present, and direct the attention of the reader to his client.

When Edwards entered the hall, whose enormous doors were opened to the passage of the air of a mild evening, he found Benjamin engaged in some of his domestic avocations, and, in a hurried voice, inquired where Judge Temple was to be found.

"Why, the Judge has stept into his office, with that master-carpenter, Mister Doolittle; but Miss Lizzy is in that there parlour. I say, Master Oliver, we'd like to have had a bad job of that panther, or painter's work—some calls it one, and some calls it t'other—but I know little of the beast, seeing that it's not of British growth. I said as much as that it was in the hills, the last winter; for I heard it moaning on the lake-shore, one evening in the fall, when I was pulling down from the fishing-point, in the skiff. Had the animal come into open water, where a man could see how and where to work his vessel, I would have engaged the thing myself; but looking aloft among the trees, is all the same to me as standing on the deck of one ship and looking at another vessel's tops. I never can tell one rope from another"——

"Well, well," interrupted Edwards; "I must see Miss Temple."

"And you shall see her, sir," said the steward; "she's in this here room. Lord, Master Edwards, what a loss she'd have been to the Judge! Dam'me if I know where he would have gotten such another daughter; that is, full-grown, d'ye see. I say, sir, this Master Bumppo is a worthy man, and seems to have a handy way with him, with fire-arms and boat-hooks. I'm his friend, Master Oliver, and he and you may both set me down as the same."

"We may want your friendship, my worthy fellow," cried Edwards, squeezing his hand convulsively—"we may want your friendship, in which case, you shall know it."

Without waiting to hear the earnest reply that Benjamin meditated, the youth extricated himself from the vigorous grasp of the steward, and entered the parlour.

Elizabeth was alone, and still reclining on the sofa, where we last left her. A hand, which exceeded all that the ingenuity of art could model, in shape and colour, veiled her eyes; and the maiden was sitting as if in deep communion with herself. Struck by the attitude and loveliness of the form that met his eye, the young man checked his impatience, and approached her with respect and caution.

"Miss Temple—Miss Temple," he said, "I hope I do not intrude; but I am anxious for an interview, if it be only for a moment."

Elizabeth raised her face, and exhibited her dark eyes swimming in moisture.

"Is it you, Edwards?" she said, with a sweetness in her

voice, and a softness in her air, that she often used to her father, but which, from its novelty to himself, thrilled on every nerve of the youth; "how left you our poor Louisa?"

"She is with her father, happy and grateful," said Oliver. "I never witnessed more feeling than she manifested, when I ventured to express my pleasure at her escape. Miss Temple, when I first heard of your horrid situation, my feelings were too powerful for utterance; and I did not properly find my tongue, until the walk to Mr. Grant's had given me time to collect myself. I believe—I do believe, I acquitted myself better there, for Miss Grant even wept at my silly speeches."

For a moment Elizabeth did not reply, but again veiled her eyes with her hand. The feeling that caused the action, however, soon passed away, and, raising her face again to his gaze, she continued, with a smile—

"Your friend, the Leather-stocking, has now become my friend, Edwards; I have been thinking how I can best serve him; perhaps you, who know his habits and his wants so well, can tell me"——

"I can," cried the youth, with an impetuosity that startled his companion—"I can, and may Heaven reward you for the wish. Natty has been so imprudent as to forget the law, and has this day killed a deer. Nay, I believe I must share in the crime and the penalty, for I was an accomplice throughout. A complaint has been made to your father, and he has granted a search"——

"I know it all," interrupted Elizabeth; "I know it all. The forms of the law must be complied with, however; the search must be made, the deer found, and the penalty paid. But I must retort your own question. Have you lived so long in our family, not to know us? Look at me, Oliver Edwards. Do I appear like one who would permit the man that has just saved her life to linger in a gaol, for so small a sum as this fine? No, no, sir; my father is a Judge, but he is a man, and a Christian. It is all understood, and no harm shall follow."

"What a load of apprehension do your declarations remove!" exclaimed Edwards. "He shall not be disturbed again! your father will protect him! I have your assurance, Miss Temple, that he will, and I must believe it."

"You may have his own, Mr. Edwards," returned Elizabeth, "for here he comes to make it."

But the appearance of Marmaduke, who entered the apartment, contradicted the flattering anticipations of his daughter. His brow was contracted, and his manner disturbed. Neither Elizabeth nor the youth spoke; but the Judge was allowed to pace once or twice across the room without interruption, when he cried—

"Our plans are defeated, girl; the obstinacy of the Leather-stocking has brought down the indignation of the law on his head, and it is now out of my power to avert it."

"How? in what manner?" cried Elizabeth; "the fine is nothing; surely"——

"I did not—I could not anticipate that an old, a friendless man, like him, would dare to oppose the officers of justice," interrupted the Judge; "I supposed that he would submit to the search, when the fine could have been paid, and the law would have been appeased; but now he will have to meet its rigour."

"And what must the punishment be, sir?" asked Edwards, struggling to speak with firmness.

Marmaduke turned quickly to the spot where the youth had withdrawn, and exclaimed—

"You here! I did not observe you. I know not what it will be, sir; it is not usual for a Judge to decide, until he has heard the testimony, and the jury have convicted. Of one thing, however, you may be assured, Mr. Edwards; it shall be whatever the law demands, notwithstanding any momentary weakness I may have exhibited, because the luckless man has been of such eminent service to my daughter."

"No one, I believe, doubts the sense of justice which Judge Temple entertains!" returned Edwards, bitterly. "But let us converse calmly, sir. Will not the years, the habits, nay, the ignorance of my old friend, avail him any thing against this charge?"

"Ought they? They may extenuate, but can they acquit? Would any society be tolerable, young man, where the ministers of justice are to be opposed by men armed with rifles? Is it for this that I have tamed the wilderness?"

"Had you tamed the beasts that so lately threatened the life of Miss Temple, sir, your arguments would apply better."

"Edwards!" exclaimed Elizabeth——

"Peace, my child," interrupted the father;—"the youth is unjust; but I have not given him cause. I overlook thy remark, Oliver, for I know thee to be the friend of Natty, and zeal in his behalf has overcome thy discretion."

"Yes, he is my friend," cried Edwards, "and I glory in the title. He is simple, unlettered, even ignorant; prejudiced, perhaps, though I feel that his opinion of the world is too true; but he has a heart, Judge Temple, that would atone for a thousand faults; he knows his friends, and never deserts them, even if it be his dog."

"This is a good character, Mr. Edwards," returned Marmaduke, mildly; "but I have never been so fortunate as to secure his esteem, for to me he has been uniformly repulsive; yet I have endured it, as an old man's whim. However, when he appears before me, as his judge, he shall find that his former conduct shall not aggravate, any more than his recent services shall extenuate his crime."

"Crime!" echoed Edwards; "is it a crime to drive a prying miscreant from his door? Crime! Oh! no, sir; if there be a criminal involved in this affair, it is not he."

"And who may it be, sir?" asked Judge Temple, facing the agitated youth, his features settled to their usual composure.

This appeal was more than the young man could bear. Hitherto he had been deeply agitated by his emotions; but now the volcano burst its boundaries.

"Who! and this to me!" he cried; "ask your own conscience, Judge Temple. Walk to that door, sir, and look out upon the valley, that placid lake, and those dusky mountains, and say to your own heart, if heart you have, whence came these riches, this vale, and those hills, and why am I their owner? I should think, sir, that the appearance of Mohegan and the Leather-stocking, stalking through the country, impoverished and forlorn, would wither your sight."

Marmaduke heard this burst of passion, at first, with deep amazement; but when the youth had ended, he beckoned to his impatient daughter for silence, and replied—

"Oliver Edwards, thou forgettest in whose presence thou standest. I have heard, young man, that thou claimest descent from the native owners of the soil; but surely thy education has been given thee to no effect, if it has not taught thee the validity of the claims that have transferred the title to the whites. These lands are mine by the very grants of thy ancestry, if thou art so descended; and I appeal to Heaven, for a testimony of the uses I have put them to. After this language, we must separate. I have too long sheltered thee in my dwelling; but the time has arrived when thou must quit it. Come to my office, and I will discharge the debt I owe thee. Neither shall thy present intemperate language mar thy future fortunes, if thou wilt hearken to the advice of one who is by many years thy senior."

The ungovernable feeling that caused the violence of the youth had passed away, and he stood gazing after the retiring figure of Marmaduke, with a vacancy in his eye, that denoted the absence of his mind. At length he recollected himself, and, turning his head slowly around the apartment, he beheld Elizabeth, still seated on the sofa, but with her head dropped on her bosom, and her face again concealed by her hands.

"Miss Temple," he said—all violence had left his manner—"Miss Temple—I have forgotten myself—forgotten you. You have heard what your father has decreed, and this night I leave here. With you, at least, I would part in amity."

Elizabeth slowly raised her face, across which a momentary expression of sadness stole; but as she left her seat, her dark eyes lighted with their usual fire, her cheek flushed to burning, and her whole air seemed to belong to another nature.

"I forgive you, Edwards, and my father will forgive you," she said, when she reached the door. "You do not know us, but the time may come, when your opinions shall change"——

"Of you! never!" interrupted the youth; "I"——

"I would speak, sir, and not listen. There is something in this affair that I do not comprehend; but tell the Leather-stocking he has friends as well as judges in us. Do not let the old man experience unnecessary uneasiness, at this rupture. It is impossible that you could increase his claims here; neither shall they be diminished by any thing you have said. Mr. Edwards, I wish you happiness, and warmer friends."

The youth would have spoken, but she vanished from the

door so rapidly, that when he reached the hall her form was nowhere to be seen. He paused a moment, in a stupor, and then, rushing from the house, instead of following Marmaduke to his "office," he took his way directly for the cabin of the hunters.

Chapter XXXII

"Who measured earth, described the starry spheres,
And traced the long records of lunar years."
Pope, "The Temple of Fame," ll. 111–12.

RICHARD DID NOT return from the exercise of his official duties, until late in the evening of the following day. It had been one portion of his business to superintend the arrest of part of a gang of counterfeiters, that had, even at that early period, buried themselves in the woods, to manufacture their base coin, which they afterwards circulated from one end of the Union to the other. The expedition had been completely successful, and about midnight the Sheriff entered the village, at the head of a posse of deputies and constables, in the centre of whom rode, pinioned, four of the malefactors. At the gate of the Mansion-house they separated, Mr. Jones directing his assistants to proceed with their charge to the county gaol, while he pursued his own way up the gravelled walk, with the kind of self-satisfaction that a man of his organization would feel, who had, really, for once, done a very clever thing.

"Holla! Aggy!" shouted the Sheriff, when he reached the door; " where are you, you black dog? will you keep me here in the dark all night?—Holla! Aggy! Brave! Brave! hoy, hoy—where have you got to, Brave? Off his watch! Every body is asleep but myself! poor I must keep my eyes open, that others may sleep in safety. Brave! Brave! Well, I will say this for the dog, lazy as he's grown, that it is the first time I ever knew him let any one come to the door after dark, without having a smell to know whether it was an honest man or not. He could tell by his nose, almost as well as I could myself by looking at them. Holla! you Agamemnon! where are you? Oh! here comes the dog at last."

By this time the Sheriff had dismounted, and observed a form, which he supposed to be that of Brave, slowly creeping out of the kennel; when, to his astonishment, it reared itself on two legs, instead of four, and he was able to distinguish, by the star-light, the curly head and dark visage of the negro.

"Ha! what the devil are you doing there, you black rascal?" he cried; "is it not hot enough for your Guinea blood in the house, this warm night, but you must drive out the poor dog and sleep in his straw!"

By this time the boy was quite awake, and, with a blubbering whine, he attempted to reply to his master.

"Oh! masser Richard! masser Richard! such a ting! such a ting! I nebber tink a could 'appen! nebber tink he die! Oh, Lor-a-gor! a'nt bury—keep 'em till masser Richard get back—got a grabe dug"——

Here the feelings of the negro completely got the mastery, and instead of making any intelligible explanation of the causes of his grief, he blubbered aloud.

"Eh! what! buried! grave! dead!" exclaimed Richard, with a tremour in his voice; "nothing serious? Nothing has happened to Benjamin, I hope? I know he has been bilious; but I gave him"——

"Oh! worser 'an dat! worser 'an dat!" sobbed the negro. "Oh! de Lor! Miss 'Lizzy an Miss Grant—walk—mountain—poor Bravy!—kill a lady—painter—Oh! Lor, Lor!—Natty Bumppo—tare he troat open—come a see, masser Richard—here he be—here he be."

As all this was perfectly inexplicable to the Sheriff, he was very glad to wait patiently until the black brought a lantern from the kitchen, when he followed Aggy to the kennel, where he beheld poor Brave, indeed, lying in his blood, stiff and cold, but decently covered with the great-coat of the negro. He was on the point of demanding an explanation; but the grief of the black, who had fallen asleep on his voluntary watch, having burst out afresh on his waking, utterly disqualified the lad from giving one. Luckily, at this moment the principal door of the house opened, and the coarse features of Benjamin were thrust over the threshold, with a candle elevated above them, shedding its dim rays around in such a manner as to exhibit the lights and shadows of his countenance. Richard threw his bridle to the black, and bidding him look to the horse, he entered the hall.

"What is the meaning of the dead dog?" he cried. "Where is Miss Temple?"

Benjamin made one of his square gestures, with the thumb

of his left hand pointing over his right shoulder, as he answered—

"Turned in."

"Judge Temple—where is he?"

"In his berth."

"But explain; why is Brave dead? and what is the cause of Aggy's grief?"

"Why, it's all down, Squire," said Benjamin, pointing to a slate that lay on the table, by the side of a mug of toddy, a short pipe, in which the tobacco was yet burning, and a prayer-book.

Among the other pursuits of Richard, he had a passion to keep a register of all passing events; and his diary, which was written in the manner of a journal, or log-book, embraced not only such circumstances as affected himself, but observations on the weather, and all the occurrences of the family, and frequently of the village. Since his appointment to the office of Sheriff, and his consequent absences from home, he had employed Benjamin to make memoranda, on a slate, of whatever might be thought worth remembering, which, on his return, were regularly transferred to the journal, with proper notations of the time, manner, and other little particulars. There was, to be sure, one material objection to the clerkship of Benjamin, which the ingenuity of no one but Richard could have overcome. The steward read nothing but his Prayer-book, and that only in particular parts, and by the aid of a good deal of spelling, and some misnomers; but he could not form a single letter with a pen. This would have been an insuperable bar to journalizing, with most men; but Richard invented a kind of hieroglyphical character, which was intended to note all the ordinary occurrences of a day, such as how the wind blew, whether the sun shone, or whether it rained, the hours, &c.; and for the extraordinary, after giving certain elementary lectures on the subject, the Sheriff was obliged to trust to the ingenuity of the Major-domo. The reader will at once perceive, that it was to this chronicle that Benjamin pointed, instead of directly answering the Sheriff's interrogatory.

When Mr. Jones had drunk a glass of toddy, he brought

forth, from its secret place, his proper journal, and, seating himself by the table, he prepared to transfer the contents of the slate to the paper, at the same time that he appeased his curiosity. Benjamin laid one hand on the back of the Sheriff's chair, in a familiar manner, while he kept the other at liberty, to make use of a fore-finger, that was bent like some of his own characters, as an index to point out his meaning.

The first thing referred to by the Sheriff was the diagram of a compass, cut in one corner of the slate for permanent use. The cardinal points were plainly marked on it, and all the usual divisions were indicated in such a manner, that no man who had ever steered a ship could mistake them.

"Oh!" said the Sheriff, settling himself down comfortably in his chair—"you'd the wind south-east, I see, all last night; I thought it would have blown up rain."

"Devil the drop, sir," said Benjamin; "I believe that the scuttle-butt up aloft is emptied, for there hasn't so much water fell in the country, for the last three weeks, as would float Indian John's canoe, and that draws just one inch nothing, light."

"Well, but didn't the wind change here this morning? there was a change where I was."

"To be sure it did, Squire; and haven't I logged it as a shift of wind?"

"I don't see where, Benjamin"——

"Don't see!" interrupted the steward, a little crustily; "an't there a mark ag'in east-and-by-nothe-half-nothe, with sum'mat like a rising sun at the end of it, to show 'twas in the morning watch?"

"Yes, yes, that is very legible; but where is the change noted?"

"Where! why doesn't it see this here tea-kettle, with a mark run from the spout straight, or mayhap a little crooked or so, into west-and-by-southe-half-southe? now I calls this a shift of wind, Squire. Well, do you see this here boar's head that you made for me, alongside of the compass"——

"Ay, ay—Boreas—I see. Why you've drawn lines from its mouth, extending from one of your marks to the other."

"It's no fault of mine, Squire Dickens; 'tis your d—d climate. The wind has been at all them there marks this very day; and that's all round the compass, except a little matter of an Irishman's hurricane at meridium, which you'll find marked right up and down. Now I've known a sow-wester blow for three weeks, in the Channel, with a clean drizzle in which you might wash your face and hands, without the trouble of hauling in water from alongside."

"Very well, Benjamin," said the Sheriff, writing in his journal; "I believe I have caught the idea. Oh! here's a cloud over the rising sun;—so you had it hazy in the morning?"

"Ay, ay, sir," said Benjamin.

"Ah! it's Sunday, and here are the marks for the length of the sermon—one, two, three, four—What! did Mr. Grant preach forty minutes!"

"Ay, sum'mat like it; it was a good half-hour by my own glass, and then there was the time lost in turning it, and some little allowance for lee-way in not being over smart about it."

"Benjamin, this is as long as a Presbyterian; you never could have been ten minutes in turning the glass!"

"Why, d'ye see, Squire, the parson was very solemn, and I just closed my eyes in order to think the better with myself, just the same as you'd put in the dead-lights to make all snug, and when I opened them ag'in I found the congregation were getting under way for home, so I calculated the ten minutes would cover the lee-way after the glass was out. It was only some such matter as a cat's nap."

"Oh, ho! Master Benjamin, you were asleep, were you! but I'll set down no such slander against an orthodox divine." Richard wrote twenty-nine minutes in his journal, and continued—"Why, what's this you've got opposite ten o'clock, A.M.? a full moon! had you a moon visible by day! I have heard of such portents before now, but—eh! what's this alongside of it? an hour-glass?"

"That!" said Benjamin, looking coolly over the Sheriff's shoulder, and rolling the tobacco about in his mouth with a jocular air; "why that's a small matter of my own. It's no moon, Squire, but only Betty Hollister's face; for, d'ye see, sir, hearing all the same as if she had got up a new cargo of Jamaiky from the river, I called in as I was going to the church this morning—ten, A.M. was it? just the time—and tried a glass; and so I logged it, to put me in mind of calling to pay her like an honest man."

"That was it, was it?" said the Sheriff, with some displeasure at this innovation on his memoranda; "and could you not make a better glass than this? it looks like a death's head and an hour-glass."

"Why, as I liked the stuff, Squire," returned the steward, "I turned in, homeward bound, and took t'other glass, which I set down at the bottom of the first, and that gives the thing the shape it has. But as I was there ag'in to-night, and paid for the three at once, your honour may as well run the sponge over the whole business."

"I will buy you a slate for your own affairs, Benjamin," said the Sheriff; "I don't like to have the journal marked over in this manner."

"You needn't—you needn't, Squire; for, seeing that I was likely to trade often with the woman while this barrel lasted, I've opened a fair account with Betty, and she keeps the marks on the back of her bar door, and I keeps the tally on this here bit of a stick."

As Benjamin concluded he produced a piece of wood, on which five very large, honest notches were apparent. The Sheriff cast his eyes on this new leger, for a moment, and continued—

"What have we here! Saturday, two, P.M.—why here's a whole family piece! two wine-glasses up-side-down!"

"That's two women; the one this a-way is Miss 'Lizzy, and t'other is the parson's young'un."

"Cousin Bess and Miss Grant!" exclaimed the Sheriff, in amazement; " what have they to do with my journal?"

"They'd enough to do to get out of the jaws of that there painter, or panther," said the immoveable steward. "This here thingum'y, Squire, that maybe looks sum'mat like a rat, is the beast, d'ye see; and this here t'other thing, keel uppermost, is poor old Brave, who died nobly, all the same as an admiral fighting for his king and country; and that there"——

"Scarecrow," interrupted Richard.

"Ay, mayhap it do look a little wild or so," continued the steward; "but, to my judgment, Squire, it's the best imager I've made, seeing it's most like the man himself;—well, that's

Natty Bumppo, who shot this here painter, that killed that there dog, who would have eaten or done worse to them here young ladies."

"And what the devil does all this mean?" cried Richard, impatiently.

"Mean!" echoed Benjamin; "it's as true as the Boadishey's log-book"——

He was interrupted by the Sheriff, who put a few direct questions to him, that obtained more intelligible answers, by which means he became possessed of a tolerably correct idea of the truth. When the wonder, and, we must do Richard the justice to say, the feelings also, that were created by this narrative, had in some degree subsided, the Sheriff turned his eyes again on his journal, where more inexplicable hieroglyphics met his view.

"What have we here!" he cried; "two men boxing! has there been a breach of the peace? ah! that's the way, the moment my back is turned"——

"That's the Judge and young Master Edwards," interrupted the steward, very cavalierly.

"How! 'duke fighting with Oliver! what the devil has got into you all? more things have happened within the last thirty-six hours, than in the preceding six months."

"Yes, it's so indeed, Squire," returned the steward; "I've known a smart chase, and a fight at the tail of it, where less has been logged than I've got on that there slate. Howsomnever, they didn't come to facers, only passed a little jaw fore and aft."

"Explain! explain!" cried Richard—"it was about the mines, ha!—ay, ay, I see it, I see it; here is a man with a pick on his shoulder. So you heard it all, Benjamin?"

"Why yes, it was about their minds, I believe, Squire," returned the steward; "and, by what I can learn, they spoke them pretty plainly to one another. Indeed, I may say that I overheard a small matter of it myself, seeing that the windows was open, and I hard by. But this here is no pick, but an anchor on a man's shoulder; and here's the other fluke down his back, maybe a little too close, which signifies that the lad has got under way and left his moorings."

"Has Edwards left the house?"

"He has."

Richard pursued this advantage, and, after a long and close examination, he succeeded in getting out of Benjamin all that he knew, not only concerning the misunderstanding, but of the attempt to search the hut, and Hiram's discomfiture. The Sheriff was no sooner possessed of these facts, which Benjamin related with all possible tenderness to the Leather-stocking, than, snatching up his hat, and bidding the astonished steward secure the doors and go to his bed, he left the house.

For at least five minutes after Richard disappeared, Benjamin stood with his arms a-kimbo, and his eyes fastened on the door; when, having collected his astonished faculties, he prepared to execute the orders he had received.

It has been already said, that the "court of common pleas and general sessions of the peace," or, as it is commonly called, the "county court," over which Judge Temple presided, held one of its stated sessions on the following morning. The attendants of Richard were officers who had come to the village as much to discharge their usual duties at this court, as to escort the prisoners; and the Sheriff knew their habits too well, not to feel confident he should find most, if not all of them, in the public room of the gaol, discussing the qualities of the keeper's liquors. Accordingly he held his way, through the silent streets of the village, directly to the small and insecure building, that contained all the unfortunate debtors, and some of the criminals of the county, and where justice was administered to such unwary applicants as were so silly as to throw away two dollars, in order to obtain one from their neighbours. The arrival of four malefactors in the custody of a dozen officers, was an event, at that day, in Templeton; and when the Sheriff reached the gaol, he found every indication that his subordinates intended to make a night of it.

The nod of the Sheriff brought two of his deputies to the door, who in their turn drew off six or seven of the constables. With this force Richard led the way through the village, towards the bank of the lake, undisturbed by any noise, except the barking of one or two curs, who were alarmed by the measured tread of the party, and by the low murmurs that run through their own numbers, as a few cautious questions and answers were exchanged, relative to the object of their expedition. When they had crossed the little bridge of hewn logs that was thrown over the Susquehanna, they left the highway, and struck into that field which had been the scene of the victory over the pigeons. From this they followed their leader into the low bushes of pines and chestnuts which had sprung up along the shores of the lake, where the plough had not succeeded the fall of the trees, and soon entered the forest itself. Here Richard paused, and collected his troop around him.

"I have required your assistance, my friends," he said, in a low voice, "in order to arrest Nathaniel Bumppo, commonly called the Leather-stocking. He has assaulted a magistrate, and resisted the execution of a search-warrant, by threatening the life of a constable with his rifle. In short, my friends, he has set an example of rebellion to the laws, and has become a kind of out-law. He is suspected of other misdemeanours and offences against private rights; and I have this night taken on myself, by the virtue of my office of sheriff, to arrest the said Bumppo, and bring him to the county gaol, that he may be present and forthcoming to answer to these heavy charges before the court to-morrow morning. In executing this duty, friends and fellow citizens, you are to use courage and discretion. Courage, that you may not be daunted by any lawless attempts that this man may make, with his rifle and his dogs, to oppose you; and discretion, which here means caution and prudence, that he may not escape from this sudden attack—and—for other good reasons that I need not mention. You will form yourselves in a complete circle around his hut, and at the word 'advance,' called aloud by me, you will rush forward, and, without giving the criminal time for deliberation, enter his dwelling by force and make him your prisoner. Spread yourselves for this purpose, while I shall descend to the shore with a deputy, to take charge of that point; and all communications must be made directly to me, under the bank in front of the hut, where I shall station myself, and remain in order to receive them."

This speech, which Richard had been studying during his walk, had the effect that all similar performances produce, of bringing the dangers of the expedition immediately before the eyes of his forces. The men divided, some plunging deeper into the forest, in order to gain their stations without giving an alarm, and others continuing to advance, at a gait that would allow the whole party to get in order; but all devising the best plan to repulse the attack of a dog, or to escape a rifle-bullet. It was a moment of dread expectation and interest.

When the Sheriff thought time enough had elapsed for the different divisions of his force to arrive at their stations, he raised his voice in the silence of the forest, and shouted the watchword. The sounds played among the arched branches of the trees in hollow cadences; but when the last sinking tone was lost on the ear, in place of the expected howls of the dogs, no other noises were returned but the crackling of torn branches and dried sticks, as they yielded before the advancing steps of the officers. Even this soon ceased, as if by a common consent, when, the curiosity and impatience of the Sheriff getting the complete ascendency over discretion, he rushed up the bank, and in a moment stood on the little piece of cleared ground in front of the spot where Natty had so long lived. To his amazement, in place of the hut, he saw only its smouldering ruins.

The party gradually drew together about the heap of ashes and the ends of smoking logs, while a dim flame in the centre of the ruin, which still found fuel to feed its lingering life, threw its pale light, flickering with the passing currents of the air, around the circle, now showing a face with eyes fixed in astonishment, and then glancing to another countenance, leaving the former shaded in the obscurity of night. Not a voice was raised in inquiry, nor an exclamation made in astonishment. This transition from excitement to disappointment was too powerful for speech, and even Richard lost the use of an organ that was seldom known to fail him.

The whole group were yet in the fulness of their surprise, when a tall form stalked from the gloom into the circle, treading down the hot ashes and dying embers with callous feet, and, standing over the light, lifted his cap, and exposed the bare head and weather-beaten features of the Leather-stocking. For a moment he gazed at the dusky figures who surrounded him, more in sorrow than in anger, before he spoke.

"What would ye have with an old and helpless man?" he

said. "You've driven God's creaters from the wilderness, where his providence had put them for his own pleasure, and you've brought in the troubles and diviltics of the law, where no man was ever known to disturb another. You have driven me, that have lived forty long years of my appointed time in this very spot, from my home and the shelter of my head, lest you should put your wicked feet and wasty ways in my cabin. You've driven me to burn these logs, under which I've eaten and drunk, the first of Heaven's gifts, and the other of the pure springs, for the half of a hundred years, and to mourn the ashes under my feet, as a man would weep and mourn for the children of his body. You've rankled the heart of an old man, that has never harmed you or yourn, with bitter feelings towards his kind, at a time when his thoughts should be on a better world; and you've driven him to wish that the beasts of the forest, who never feast on the blood of their own families, was his kindred and race; and now, when he has come to see the last brand of his hut, before it is melted into ashes, you follow him up, at midnight, like hungry hounds on the track of a worn-out and dying deer! What more would ye have? for I am here—one to many. I come to mourn, not to fight; and, if it is God's pleasure, work your will on me."

When the old man ended, he stood, with the light glimmering around his thinly-covered head, looking earnestly at the group, which receded from the pile, with an involuntary movement, without the reach of the quivering rays, leaving a free passage for his retreat into the bushes, where pursuit, in the dark, would have been fruitless. Natty seemed not to regard this advantage, but stood facing each individual in the circle, in succession, as if to see who would be the first to arrest him. After a pause of a few moments, Richard begun to rally his confused faculties, and advancing, apologized for his duty, and made him his prisoner. The party now collected, and, preceded by the Sheriff, with Natty in their centre, they took their way towards the village.

During the walk, divers questions were put to the prisoner concerning his reasons for burning the hut, and whither Mohegan had retreated, but to all of them he observed a profound silence, until, fatigued with their previous duties, and the lateness of the hour, the Sheriff and his followers reached the village, and dispersed to their several places of rest, after turning the key of a gaol on the aged and apparently friendless Leather-stocking.

Chapter XXXIII

"Fetch here the stocks, ho!
You stubborn ancient knave, you reverend braggart,
We'll teach you."

King Lear, II.ii.125–27.

THE LONG DAYS and early sun of July allowed time for a gathering of the interested, before the little bell of the academy announced that the appointed hour had arrived for administering right to the wronged, and punishment to the guilty. Ever since the dawn of day, the highways and wood-paths that, issuing from the forests, and winding along the sides of the mountains, centered in Templeton, had been thronged with equestrians and footmen, bound to the haven of justice. There was to be seen a well-clad yeoman, mounted on a sleek, switch-tailed steed, ambling along the highway, with his red face elevated in a manner that said, "I have paid for my land, and fear no man," while his bosom was swelling with the pride of being one of the grand inquest for the county. At his side rode a companion, his equal in independence of feeling, perhaps, but his inferior in thrift, as in property and consideration. This was a professed dealer in lawsuits,—a man whose name appeared in every calendar; whose substance, gained in the multifarious expedients of a settler's changeable habits, was wasted in feeding the harpies of the courts. He was endeavouring to impress the mind of the grand juror with the merits of a cause now at issue. Along with these was a pedestrian, who, having thrown a rifle frock over his shirt, and placed his best wool hat above his sun-burnt visage, had issued from his retreat in the woods by a footpath, and was striving to keep company with the others, on his way to hear and to decide the disputes of his neighbours as a petit juror. Fifty similar little knots of countrymen might have been seen, on that morning, journeying towards the shire-town on the same errand.

By ten o'clock the streets of the village were filled with busy faces, some talking of their private concerns, some listening to a popular expounder of political creeds, and others gaping in at the open stores, admiring the finery, or examining sithes, axes, and such other manufactures as attracted their curiosity or excited their admiration. A few women were in the crowd, most carrying infants, and followed, at a lounging, listless gait, by their rustic lords and masters. There was one young couple, in whom connubial love was yet fresh, walking at a respectful distance from each other, while the swain directed the timid steps of his bride, by a gallant offering of a thumb!

At the first stroke of the bell, Richard issued from the door of the "Bold Dragoon," flourishing a sheathed sword, that he was fond of saying his ancestors had carried in one of Cromwell's victories, and crying, in an authoritative tone, to "clear the way for the court." The order was obeyed promptly, though not servilely; the members of the crowd nodding familiarly to the members of the procession, as it passed. A party of constables with their staves followed the Sheriff, preceding Marmaduke and four plain, grave-looking yeomen, who were his associates on the bench. There was nothing to distinguish these subordinate judges from the better part of the spectators, except gravity, which they affected a little more than common, and that one of their number was attired in an old-fashioned military coat, with skirts that reached no lower than the middle of his thighs, and bearing two little silver epaulettes, not half so big as a modern pair of shoulder-knots. This gentleman was a colonel of the militia, in attendance on a court-martial, who found leisure to steal a moment from his military, to attend to his civil jurisdiction. But this incongruity excited neither notice nor comment. Three or four clean-shaved lawyers followed, as meekly as if they were lambs going to the slaughter. One or two of their number had contrived to obtain an air of scholastic gravity, by wearing spectacles. The rear was brought up by another posse of constables, and the mob followed the whole into the room where the court held its sittings.

The edifice was composed of a basement of squared logs, perforated here and there with small grated windows, through which a few wistful faces were gazing at the crowd without. Among the captives were the guilty, downcast countenances of the counterfeiters, and the simple but honest features of the Leather-stocking. The dungeons were to be distinguished, externally, from the debtors' apartments, only by the size of the apertures, the thickness of the grates, and by the heads of the spikes that were driven into the logs as a protection against the illegal use of edge-tools. The upper story was of frame-work, regularly covered with boards, and contained one room decently fitted up for the purposes of justice. A bench, raised on a narrow platform to the height of a man above the floor, and protected in front by a light railing, ran along one of its sides. In the centre was a seat, furnished with rude arms, that was always filled by the presiding judge. In front, on a level with the floor of the room, was a large table, covered with green baize, and surrounded by benches; and at either of its ends were rows of seats, rising one over the other, for jury-boxes. Each of these divisions was surrounded by a railing. The remainder of the room was an open square, appropriated to the spectators.

When the judges were seated, the lawyers had taken possession of the table, and the noise of moving feet had ceased in the area, the proclamations were made in the usual form, the jurors were sworn, the charge was given, and the court proceeded to hear the business before them.

We shall not detain the reader with a description of the captious discussions that occupied the court for the first two hours. Judge Temple had impressed on the jury, in his charge, the necessity for despatch on their part, recommending to their notice, from motives of humanity, the prisoners in the gaol, as the first objects of their attention. Accordingly, after the period we have mentioned had elapsed, the cry of the officer to "clear the way for the grand jury," announced the entrance of that body. The usual forms were observed, when the foreman handed up to the bench two bills, on both of which the Judge observed, at the first glance of his eye, the name of Nathaniel Bumppo. It was a leisure moment with the court; some low whispering passed between the bench and the Sheriff, who gave a signal to his officers, and in a very few minutes the silence that prevailed was interrupted by a general movement in the outer crowd; when presently the Leather-stocking made his appearance, ushered into the criminal's bar under the custody of two constables. The hum ceased, the people closed into the open space again, and the silence soon became so deep that the hard breathing of the prisoner was audible.

Natty was dressed in his buck-skin garments, without his coat, in place of which he wore only a shirt of coarse linen-check, fastened at his throat by the sinew of a deer, leaving his red neck and weather-beaten face exposed and bare. It was the first time that he had ever crossed the threshold of a court of justice, and curiosity seemed to be strongly blended with his personal feelings. He raised his eyes to the bench, thence to the jury-boxes, the bar, and the crowd without, meeting every where looks fastened on himself. After surveying his own person, as if searching for the cause of this unusual attraction, he once more turned his face around the assemblage, and opened his mouth in one of his silent and remarkable laughs.

"Prisoner, remove your cap," said Judge Temple.

The order was either unheard or unheeded.

"Nathaniel Bumppo, be uncovered," repeated the Judge.

Natty started at the sound of his name, and, raising his face earnestly towards the bench, he said—

"Anan!"

Mr. Lippet arose from his seat at the table, and whispered in the ear of the prisoner, when Natty gave him a nod of assent, and took the deer-skin covering from his head.

"Mr. District Attorney," said the Judge, "the prisoner is ready; we wait for the indictment."

The duties of public prosecutor were discharged by Dirck Van der School, who adjusted his spectacles, cast a cautious look around him at his brethren of the bar, which he ended by throwing his head aside so as to catch one glance over the glasses, when he proceeded to read the bill aloud. It was the usual charge for an assault and battery, on the person of Hiram Doolittle, and was couched in the ancient language of such instruments, especial care having been taken by the scribe, not to omit the name of a single offensive weapon known to the law. When he had done, Mr. Van der School removed his spectacles, which he closed and placed in his pocket, seemingly for the pleasure of again opening and replacing them on his nose. After this evolution was repeated once or twice, he handed the bill over to Mr. Lippet, with a cavalier air, that said as much as "pick a hole in that if you can."

Natty listened to the charge with great attention, leaning forward towards the reader with an earnestness that denoted his interest; and when it was ended he raised his tall body to the utmost, and drew a long sigh. All eyes were turned to the prisoner, whose voice was vainly expected to break the stillness of the room.

"You have heard the presentment that the grand jury have made, Nathaniel Bumppo," said the Judge; "what do you plead to the charge?"

The old man dropped his head for a moment in a reflecting attitude, and then raising it, he laughed before he answered—

"That I handled the man a little rough or so, is not to be denied; but that there was occasion to make use of all them things that the gentleman has spoken of, is downright untrue. I am not much of a wrestler, seeing that I'm getting old; but I was out among the Scotch-Irishers—lets me see—it must have been as long ago as the first year of the old war"——

"Mr. Lippet, if you are retained for the prisoner," interrupted Judge Temple, "instruct your client how to plead; if not, the court will assign him counsel."

Aroused from studying the indictment by this appeal, the attorney got up, and, after a short dialogue with the hunter in a low voice, he informed the court that they were ready to proceed.

"Do you plead guilty or not guilty?" said the Judge.

"I may say not guilty with a clean conscience," returned Natty; "for there's no guilt in doing what's right; and I'd rather died on the spot, than had him put foot in the hut at that moment."

Richard started at this declaration, and bent his eyes significantly on Hiram, who returned the look with a slight movement of his eye-brows.

"Proceed to open the cause, Mr. District Attorney," continued the Judge. "Mr. Clerk, enter the plea of not guilty."

After a short opening address from Mr. Van der School, Hiram was summoned to the bar to give his testimony. It was delivered to the letter, perhaps, but with all that moral colouring which can be conveyed under such expressions as, "thinking no harm," "feeling it my bounden duty as a magistrate," and "seeing that the constable was back'ard in the business." When he had done, and the District Attorney declined putting any further interrogatories, Mr. Lippet arose, with an air of keen investigation, and asked the following questions:—

"Are you a constable of this county, sir?"

"No, sir," said Hiram, "I'm only a justice-peace."

"I ask you, Mr. Doolittle, in the face of this court, putting it to your conscience and your knowledge of the law, whether you had any right to enter that man's dwelling?"

"Hem!" said Hiram, undergoing a violent struggle between his desire for vengeance and his love of legal fame; "I do suppose—that in—that is—strict law—that supposing—maybe I hadn't a real—lawful right;—but as the case was—and Billy was so back'ard—I thought I might come for'ard in the business."

"I ask you, again, sir," continued the lawyer, following up his success, "whether this old, this friendless old man, did or did not repeatedly forbid your entrance?"

"Why, I must say," said Hiram, "that he was considerable cross-grained; not what I call clever, seeing that it was only one neighbour wanting to go into the house of another."

"Oh! then you own it was only meant for a neighbourly visit on your part, and without the sanction of law. Remember, gentlemen, the words of the witness, 'one neighbour wanting to enter the house of another.' Now, sir, I ask you if Nathaniel Bumppo did not again and again order you not to enter?"

"There was some words passed between us," said Hiram, "but I read the warrant to him aloud."

"I repeat my question; did he tell you not to enter his habitation?"

"There was a good deal passed betwixt us—but I've the warrant in my pocket; maybe the court would wish to see it?"

"Witness," said Judge Temple, "answer the question directly; did or did not the prisoner forbid your entering his hut?"

"Why, I some think"——

"Answer without equivocation," continued the Judge, sternly.

"He did."

"And did you attempt to enter, after this order?"

"I did; but the warrant was in my hand."

"Proceed, Mr. Lippet, with your examination."

But the attorney saw that the impression was in favour of his client, and, waving his hand with a supercilious manner, as if unwilling to insult the understanding of the jury with any further defence, he replied—

"No, sir; I leave it for your honour to charge; I rest my case here."

"Mr. District Attorney," said the Judge, "have you any thing to say?"

Mr. Van der School removed his spectacles, folded them, and replacing them once more on his nose, eyed the other bill which he held in his hand, and then said, looking at the bar over the top of his glasses—

"I shall rest the prosecution here, if the court please."

Judge Temple arose and began the charge.

"Gentlemen of the jury," he said, "you have heard the testimony, and I shall detain you but a moment. If an officer meet with resistance in the execution of a process, he has an undoubted right to call any citizen to his assistance; and the acts of such assistant come within the protection of the law. I shall leave you to judge, gentlemen, from the testimony, how far the witness in this prosecution can be so considered, feeling less reluctance to submit the case thus informally to your decision, because there is yet another indictment to be tried, which involves heavier charges against the unfortunate prisoner."

The tone of Marmaduke was mild and insinuating, and as his sentiments were given with such apparent impartiality, they did not fail of carrying due weight with the jury. The grave-looking yeomen, who composed this tribunal, laid their heads together for a few minutes, without leaving the box, when the foreman arose, and, after the forms of the court were duly observed, he pronounced the prisoner to be—

"Not guilty."

"You are acquitted of this charge, Nathaniel Bumppo," said the Judge.

"Anan!" said Natty.

"You are found not guilty of striking and assaulting Mr. Doolittle."

"No, no, I'll not deny but that I took him a little roughly by the shoulders," said Natty, looking about him with great simplicity, "and that I"——

"You are acquitted," interrupted the Judge; "and there is nothing further to be done or said in the matter."

A look of joy lighted up the features of the old man, who now comprehended the case, and, placing his cap eagerly on his head again, he threw up the bar of his little prison, and said feelingly—

"I must say this for you, Judge Temple, that the law has not been as hard on me as I dreaded. I hope God will bless you for the kind things you've done to me this day."

But the staff of the constable was opposed to his egress, and Mr. Lippet whispered a few words in his ear, when the aged hunter sunk back into his place, and removing his cap, stroked down the remnants of his gray and sandy locks, with an air of mortification mingled with submission.

"Mr. District Attorney," said Judge Temple, affecting to busy himself with his minutes, "proceed with the second indictment."

Mr. Van der School took great care that no part of the presentment, which he now read, should be lost on his auditors. It accused the prisoner of resisting the execution of a search-warrant by force of arms, and particularized, in the vague language of the law, among a variety of other weapons, the use of the rifle. This was indeed a more serious charge than an ordinary assault and battery, and a corresponding degree of interest was manifested by the spectators in its result. The prisoner was duly arraigned, and his plea again demanded. Mr. Lippet had anticipated the answers of Natty, and in a whisper advised him how to plead. But the feelings of the old hunter were awakened by some of the expressions of the indictment, and, forgetful of his caution, he exclaimed—

" 'Tis a wicked untruth; I crave no man's blood. Them thieves, the Iroquois, won't say it to my face, that I ever thirsted after man's blood. I have fout as a soldier that feared his Maker and his officer, but I never pulled trigger on any but a warrior that was up and awake. No man can say that I ever struck even a Mingo in his blanket. I b'lieve there's some who thinks there's no God in a wilderness!"

"Attend to your plea, Bumppo," said the Judge; "you hear that you are accused of using your rifle against an officer of justice; are you guilty or not guilty?"

By this time the irritated feelings of Natty had found vent; and he rested on the bar for a moment, in a musing posture, when he lifted his face, with his silent laugh, and pointing to where the wood-chopper stood, he said—

"Would Billy Kirby be standing there, d'ye think, if I had used the rifle?"

"Then you deny it," said Mr. Lippet; "you plead not guilty?"

"Sartain," said Natty; "Billy knows that I never fired at all. Billy, do you remember the turkey last winter? ah! me! that was better than common firing; but I can't shoot as I used to could."

"Enter the plea of not guilty," said Judge Temple, strongly affected by the simplicity of the prisoner.

Hiram was again sworn, and his testimony given on the second charge. He had discovered his former error, and proceeded more cautiously than before. He related very distinctly, and, for the man, with amazing terseness, the suspicion against the hunter, the complaint, the issuing of the warrant, and the swearing in of Kirby; all of which, he affirmed, were done in due form of law. He then added the manner in which the constable had been received; and stated distinctly that Natty had pointed the rifle at Kirby, and threatened his life, if he attempted to execute his duty. All this was confirmed by Jotham, who was observed to adhere closely to the story of the magistrate. Mr. Lippet conducted an artful cross-examination of these two witnesses, but, after consuming much time, was compelled to relinquish the attempt to obtain any advantage, in despair.

At length the District Attorney called the wood-chopper to the bar. Billy gave an extremely confused account of the whole affair, although he evidently aimed at the truth, until Mr. Van der School aided him, by asking some direct questions:—

"It appears, from examining the papers, that you demanded admission into the hut legally; so you were put in bodily fear by his rifle and threats?"

"I didn't mind them that, man," said Billy, snapping his fingers; "I should be a poor stick, to mind old Leather-stocking."

"But I understood you to say, (referring to your previous words, (as delivered here in court,) in the commencement of your testimony,) that you thought he meant to shoot you?"

"To be sure I did; and so would you too, Squire, if you had seen the chap dropping a muzzle that never misses, and cocking an eye that has a nateral squint by long practice. I thought there would be a dust on't, and my back was up at once; but Leather-stocking gi'n up the skin, and so the matter ended."

"Ah! Billy," said Natty, shaking his head, " 'twas a lucky thought in me to throw out the hide, or there might have been blood spilt; and I'm sure, if it had been your'n, I should have mourned it sorely the little while I have to stay."

"Well, Leather-stocking," returned Billy, facing the prisoner, with a freedom and familiarity that utterly disregarded the presence of the court, "as you are on the subject, it may be that you've no"——

"Go on with your examination, Mr. District Attorney."

That gentleman eyed the familiarity between his witness and the prisoner with manifest disgust, and indicated to the court that he was done.

"Then you didn't feel frightened, Mr. Kirby?" said the counsel for the prisoner.

"Me! no," said Billy, casting his eyes over his own huge frame with evident self-satisfaction; "I'm not to be skeared so easy."

"You look like a hardy man; where were you born, sir?"

"Varmount state; 'tis a mountaynious place, but there's a stiff soil, and it's pretty much wooded with beech and maple."

"I have always heerd so," said Mr. Lippet, soothingly. "You have been used to the rifle yourself, in that country?"

"I pull the second best trigger in this county. I knock under to Natty Bumppo there, sin' he shot the pigeon."

Leather-stocking raised his head, and laughed again, when he abruptly thrust out a wrinkled hand, and said—

"You're young yet, Billy, and haven't seen the matches that I have; but here's my hand; I bear no malice to you, I don't."

Mr. Lippet allowed this conciliatory offering to be accepted, and judiciously paused, while the spirit of peace was exercising its influence over the two; but the Judge interposed his authority.

"This is an improper place for such dialogues," he said. "Proceed with your examination of this witness, Mr. Lippet, or I shall order the next."

The attorney started, as if unconscious of any impropriety, and continued—

"So you settled the matter with Natty amicably on the spot, did you?"

"He gi'n me the skin, and I didn't want to quarrel with an old man; for my part, I see no such mighty matter in shooting a buck!"

"And you parted friends? and you would never have thought of bringing the business up before a court, hadn't you been subpœnaed?"

"I don't think I should; he gi'n the skin, and I didn't feel a hard thought, though Squire Doolittle got some affronted."

"I have done, sir," said Mr. Lippet, probably relying on the charge of the Judge, as he again seated himself, with the air of a man who felt that his success was certain.

When Mr. Van der School arose to address the jury, he commenced by saying—

"Gentlemen of the jury, I should have interrupted the leading questions put by the prisoner's counsel, (by leading questions I mean telling him what to say,) did I not feel confident that the law of the land was superior to any advantages (I mean legal advantages) which he might obtain by his art. The counsel for the prisoner, gentlemen, has endeavoured to persuade you, in opposition to your own good sense, to believe that pointing a rifle at a constable (elected or deputed) is a very innocent affair; and that society (I mean the commonwealth, gentlemen,) shall not be endangered thereby. But let me claim your attention, while we look over the particulars of this heinous offence." Here Mr. Van der School favoured the jury with an abridgment of the testimony, recounted in such a manner as utterly to confuse the faculties of his worthy listeners. After this exhibition he closed as follows:—"And now, gentlemen, having thus made plain to your senses the crime of which this unfortunate man has been guilty, (unfortunate both on account of his ignorance and his guilt,) I shall leave you to your own consciences; not in the least doubting that you will see the importance (notwithstanding the prisoner's counsel (doubtless relying on your former verdict) wishes to appear so confident of success) of punishing the offender, and asserting the dignity of the laws."

It was now the duty of the Judge to deliver his charge. It consisted of a short, comprehensive summary of the testimony, laying bare the artifice of the prisoner's counsel, and placing the facts in so obvious a light that they could not well be misunderstood. "Living, as we do, gentlemen," he concluded, "on the skirts of society, it becomes doubly necessary to protect the ministers of the law. If you believe the witnesses, in their construction of the acts of the prisoner, it is your duty to convict him; but if you believe that the old man, who this day appears before you, meant not to harm the constable, but was acting more under the influence of habit than by the instigations of malice, it will be your duty to judge him, but to do it with lenity."

As before, the jury did not leave their box, but, after a consultation of some little time, their foreman arose, and pronounced the prisoner—

"Guilty."

There was but little surprise manifested in the court-room at this verdict, as the testimony, the greater part of which we have omitted, was too clear and direct to be passed over. The judges seemed to have anticipated this sentiment, for a consultation was passing among them also, during the deliberation of the jury, and the preparatory movements of the "bench" announced the coming sentence.

"Nathaniel Bumppo," commenced the Judge, making the customary pause.

The old hunter, who had been musing again, with his head on the bar, raised himself, and cried, with a prompt, military tone—

"Here."

The Judge waved his hand for silence, and proceeded—

"In forming their sentence, the court have been governed as much by the consideration of your ignorance of the laws, as by a strict sense of the importance of punishing such outrages as this of which you have been found guilty. They have, therefore, passed over the obvious punishment of whipping on the bare back, in mercy to your years; but as the dignity of the law requires an open exhibition of the consequences of your crime, it is ordered, that you be conveyed from this room to the public stocks, where you are to be confined for one hour; that you pay a fine to the state of one hundred dollars; and that you be imprisoned in the gaol of this county for one calendar month; and furthermore, that your imprisonment do not cease until the said fine shall be paid. I feel it my duty, Nathaniel Bumppo,"——

"And where should I get the money!" interrupted the Leather-stocking, eagerly; "where should I get the money! you'll take away the bounty on the painters, because I cut the throat of a deer; and how is an old man to find so much gold or silver in the woods? No, no, Judge; think better of it, and don't talk of shutting me up in a gaol for the little time I have to stay."

"If you have any thing to urge against the passing of the sentence, the court will yet hear you," said the Judge, mildly.

"I have enough to say ag'in it," cried Natty, grasping the bar, on which his fingers were working with a convulsed motion. "Where am I to get the money? Let me out into the woods and hills, where I've been used to breathe the clear air, and though I'm three score and ten, if you've left game enough in the country, I'll travel night and day but I'll make you up the sum afore the season is over. Yes, yes—you see the reason of the thing, and the wickedness of shutting up an old man, that has spent his days, as one may say, where he could always look into the windows of heaven."

"I must be governed by the law"——

"Talk not to me of law, Marmaduke Temple," interrupted the hunter. "Did the beast of the forest mind your laws, when it was thirsty and hungering for the blood of your own child! She was kneeling to her God for a greater favour than I ask, and he heard her; and if you now say no to my prayers, do you think he will be deaf?"

"My private feelings must not enter into"——

"Hear me, Marmaduke Temple," interrupted the old man, with melancholy earnestness, "and hear reason. I've travelled these mountains when you was no judge, but an infant in your mother's arms; and I feel as if I had a right and a privilege to travel them ag'in afore I die. Have you forgot the time that you come on to the lake-shore, when there wasn't even a gaol to lodge in; and didn't I give you my own bear-skin to sleep on, and the fat of a noble buck to satisfy the cravings of your hunger? Yes, yes—you thought it no sin then to kill a deer! And this I did, though I had no reason to love you, for you had never done any thing but harm to them that loved and sheltered me. And now will you shut me up in your dungeons to pay me for my kindness? A hundred dollars! where should I get the money? No, no—there's them that says hard things of you, Marmaduke Temple, but you an't so bad as to wish to see an old man die in a prison, because he stood up for the right. Come, friend, let me pass; it's long sin' I've been used to such crowds, and I crave to be in the woods ag'in. Don't fear me, Judge—I bid you not to fear me; for if there's beaver enough left on the streams, or the buckskins will sell for a shilling a-piece, you shall have the last penny of the fine. Where are ye, pups! come away, dogs! come away! we have a grievous toil to do for our years, but it shall be done—yes, yes, I've promised it, and it shall be done!"

It is unnecessary to say that the movement of the Leather-stocking was again intercepted by the constable; but before he had time to speak, a bustling in the crowd, and a loud hem, drew all eyes to another part of the room.

Benjamin had succeeded in edging his way through the people, and was now seen balancing his short body, with one foot in a window and the other on the railing of the jury-box. To the amazement of the whole court, the steward was evidently preparing to speak. After a good deal of difficulty, he succeeded in drawing from his pocket a small bag, and then found utterance.

"If-so-be," he said, "that your honour is agreeable to trust the poor fellow out on another cruise among the beasts, here's a small matter that will help to bring down the risk, seeing that there's just thirty-five of your Spaniards in it; and I wish, from the bottom of my heart, that they was raal British guineas, for the sake of the old boy. But 'tis as it is; and if Squire Dickens will just be so good as to overhaul this small bit of an account, and take enough from the bag to settle the same, he's welcome to hold on upon the rest, till such time as the Leather-stocking can grapple with them said beaver, or, for that matter, for ever, and no thanks asked."

As Benjamin concluded, he thrust out the wooden register of his arrears to the "Bold Dragoon" with one hand, while he offered his bag of dollars with the other. Astonishment at this singular interruption produced a profound stillness in the room, which was only interrupted by the Sheriff, who struck his sword on the table, and cried—

"Silence!"

"There must be an end to this," said the Judge, struggling to overcome his feelings. "Constable, lead the prisoner to the stocks. Mr. Clerk, what stands next on the calendar?"

Natty seemed to yield to his destiny, for he sunk his head on his chest, and followed the officer from the court-room in silence. The crowd moved back for the passage of the prisoner, and when his tall form was seen descending from the outer door, a rush of the people to the scene of his disgrace followed.

Chapter XXXIV

"Ha! ha! look! he wears cruel garters!"
King Lear, II.iv.8.

THE PUNISHMENTS of the common law were still known, at the time of our tale, to the people of New-York; and the whipping-post, and its companion the stocks, were not yet supplanted by the more merciful expedients of the public prisons. Immediately in front of the gaol, those relics of the elder times were situated, as a lesson of precautionary justice to the evil-doers of the settlement.

Natty followed the constables to this spot, bowing his head with submission to a power that he was unable to oppose, and surrounded by the crowd, that formed a circle about his person, exhibiting in their countenances strong curiosity. A constable raised the upper part of the stocks, and pointed with his finger to the holes where the old man was to place his feet. Without making the least objection to the punishment, the Leather-stocking quietly seated himself on the ground, and suffered his limbs to be laid in the openings, without even a murmur; though he cast one glance about him, in quest of that sympathy that human nature always seems to require under suffering. If he met no direct manifestations of pity, neither did he see any unfeeling exultation, or hear a single reproachful epithet. The character of the mob, if it could be called by such a name, was that of attentive subordination.

The constable was in the act of lowering the upper plank, when Benjamin, who had pressed close to the side of the prisoner, said, in his hoarse tones, as if seeking for some cause to create a quarrel—

"Where away, master constable, is the use of clapping a man in them here bilboes? it neither stops his grog nor hurts his back; what for is it that you do the thing?"

"'Tis the sentence of the court, Mr. Penguillum, and there's law for it, I s'pose."

"Ay, ay, I know that there's law for the thing; but where away do you find the use, I say? it does no harm, and it only keeps a man by the heels for the small matter of two glasses."

"Is it no harm, Benny Pump," said Natty, raising his eyes with a piteous look to the face of the steward—"is it no harm to show off a man in his seventy-first year, like a tamed bear, for the settlers to look on! Is it no harm to put an old soldier, that has sarved through the war of 'fifty-six, and seen the inimy in the 'seventy-six business, into a place like this, where the boys can point at him and say, I have known the time when he was a spictacle for the county! Is it no harm to bring down the pride of an honest man to be the equal of the beasts of the forest!"

Benjamin stared about him fiercely, and, could he have found a single face that expressed contumely, he would have been prompt to quarrel with its owner; but meeting every where with looks of sobriety, and occasionally of commiseration, he very deliberately seated himself by the side of the hunter, and placing his legs in the two vacant holes of the stocks, he said—

"Now lower away, master constable, lower away, I tell ye! If-so-be there's such a thing hereabouts as a man that wants to see a bear, let him look and be d—d, and he shall find two of them, and mayhap one of the same that can bite as well as growl."

"But I've no orders to put you in the stocks, Mr. Pump," cried the constable; "you must get up and let me do my duty."

"You've my orders, and what do you need better, to meddle with my own feet? so lower away, will ye, and let me see the man that chooses to open his mouth with a grin on it."

"There can't be any harm in locking up a creater that will enter the pound," said the constable, laughing, and closing the stocks on them both.

It was fortunate that this act was executed with decision, for the whole of the spectators, when they saw Benjamin assume the position he took, felt an inclination for merriment, which few thought it worth while to suppress. The steward struggled violently for his liberty again, with an evident intention of making battle on those who stood nearest to him; but the key was already turned, and all his efforts were vain.

"Hark ye, master constable," he cried, "just clear away your bilboes for the small matter of a log-glass, will ye, and let me show some of them there chaps who it is they are so merry about."

"No, no, you would go in, and you can't come out," returned the officer, "until the time has expired that the Judge directed for the keeping of the prisoner."

Benjamin, finding that his threats and his struggles were useless, had good sense enough to learn patience from the resigned manner of his companion, and soon settled himself down by the side of Natty, with a contemptuousness expressed in his hard features, that showed he had substituted disgust for rage. When the violence of the steward's feelings had in some measure subsided, he turned to his fellow sufferer, and, with a motive that might have vindicated a worse effusion, he attempted the charitable office of consolation.

"Taking it by and large, Master Bump-ho, 'tis but a small matter, after all," he said. "Now I've known very good sort of men, aboard of the Boadishey, laid by the heels, for nothing, mayhap, but forgetting that they'd drunk their allowance already, when a glass of grog has come in their way. This is nothing more than riding with two anchors ahead, waiting for a turn in the tide, or a shift of wind, d'ye see, with a soft bottom and plenty of room for the sweep of your hawse. Now I've seen many a man, for overshooting his reckoning, as I told ye, moored head and starn, where he couldn't so much as heave his broadside round, and mayhap a stopper clapt on his tongue too, in the shape of a plump-bolt lashed athwart-ship his jaws, all the same as an out-rigger alongside of a taffrel-rail."

The hunter appeared to appreciate the kind intentions of the other, though he could not understand his eloquence; and raising his humbled countenance, he attempted a smile, as he said—

"Anan!"

" 'Tis nothing, I say, but a small matter of a squall, that will soon blow over," continued Benjamin. "To you that has such a length of keel it must be all the same as nothing; thof, seeing that I'm a little short in my lower timbers, they've triced my heels up in such a way as to give me a bit of a cant.

But what cares I, Master Bump-ho, if the ship strains a little at her anchor; it's only for a dog-watch, and dam'me but she'll sail with you then on that cruise after them said beaver. I'm not much used to small arms, seeing that I was stationed at the ammunition-boxes, being sum'mat too low-rigged to see over the hammock-cloths; but I can carry the game, d'ye see, and mayhap make out to lend a hand with the traps; and if-so-be you're any way so handy with them as ye be with your boat-hook, 'twill be but a short cruise after all. I've squared the yards with Squire Dickens this morning, and I shall send him word that he needn't bear my name on the books again till such time as the cruise is over."

"You're used to dwell with men, Benny," said Leather-stocking, mournfully, "and the ways of the woods would be hard on you, if"——

"Not a bit—not a bit," cried the steward; "I'm none of your fair-weather chaps, Master Bump-ho, as sails only in smooth water. When I find a friend I sticks by him, d'ye see. Now, there's no better man a-going than Squire Dickens, and I love him about the same as I loves Mistress Hollister's new keg of Jamaiky." The steward paused, and turning his uncouth visage on the hunter, he survey'd him with a roguish leer of his eye, and gradually suffered the muscles of his hard features to relax, until his face was illuminated by the display of his white teeth, when he dropped his voice, and added—"I say, Master Leather-stocking, 'tis fresher and livelier than any Hollands you'll get in Garnsey. But we'll send a hand over and ask the woman for a taste, for I'm so jammed in these here bilboes, that I begin to want sum'mat to lighten my upper-works."

Natty sighed, and gazed about him on the crowd, that already begun to disperse, and which had now diminished greatly, as its members scattered in their various pursuits. He looked wistfully at Benjamin, but did not reply; a deeply-seated anxiety seeming to absorb every other sensation, and to throw a melancholy gloom over his wrinkled features, which were working with the movements of his mind.

The steward was about to act on the old principle, that silence gives consent, when Hiram Doolittle, attended by Jotham, stalked out of the crowd, across the open space, and approached the stocks. The magistrate passed by the end where Benjamin was seated, and posted himself, at a safe distance from the steward, in front of the Leather-stocking. Hiram stood, for a moment, cowering before the keen looks that Natty fastened on him, and suffering under an embarrassment that was quite new; when, having in some degree recovered himself, he looked at the heavens, and then at the smoky atmosphere, as if it were only an ordinary meeting with a friend, and said, in his formal, hesitating way—

"Quite a scurcity of rain lately; I some think we shall have a long drought on't."

Benjamin was occupied in untying his bag of dollars, and did not observe the approach of the magistrate, while Natty turned his face, in which every muscle was working, away from him in disgust, without answering. Rather encouraged than daunted by this exhibition of dislike, Hiram, after a short pause, continued—

"The clouds look as if they'd no water in them, and the earth is dreadfully parched. To my judgment, there'll be short crops this season, if the rain doosn't fall quite speedily."

The air with which Mr. Doolittle delivered this prophetical opinion was peculiar to his species. It was a jesuitical, cold, unfeeling, and selfish manner, that seemed to say, "I have kept within the law," to the man he had so cruelly injured. It quite overcame the restraint that the old hunter had been labouring to impose on himself, and he burst out in a warm glow of indignation.

"Why should the rain fall from the clouds," he cried, "when you force the tears from the eyes of the old, the sick, and the poor! Away with ye—away with ye! you may be formed in the image of the Maker, but Satan dwells in your heart. Away with ye, I say! I am mournful, and the sight of ye brings bitter thoughts."

Benjamin ceased thumbing his money, and raised his head, at the instant that Hiram, who was thrown off his guard by the invectives of the hunter, unluckily trusted his person within reach of the steward, who grasped one of his legs, with a hand that had the grip of a vice, and whirled the magistrate from his feet, before he had either time to collect his senses, or to exercise the strength he did really possess. Benjamin wanted neither proportions nor manhood in his head, shoulders and arms, though all the rest of his frame appeared to be originally intended for a very different sort of a man. He exerted his physical powers, on the present occasion, with much discretion, and as he had taken his antagonist at a great disadvantage, the struggle resulted, very soon, in Benjamin getting the magistrate fixed in a posture somewhat similar to his own, and manfully placed face to face.

"You're a ship's cousin, I tell ye, Master Doo-but-little," roared the steward—"some such matter as a ship's cousin, sir. I know you, I do, with your fair-weather speeches to Squire Dickens, to his face, and then you go and sarve out your grumbling to all the old women in the town, do ye. An't it enough for any christian, let him harbour never so much malice, to get an honest old fellow laid by the heels in this fashion, without carrying sail so hard on the poor dog, as if you would run him down as he lay at his anchors? But I've logged many a hard thing against your name, master, and now the time's come to foot up the day's work, d'ye see; so square yourself, you lubber, square yourself, and we'll soon know who's the better man."

"Jotham!" cried the frightened magistrate—"Jotham! call in the constables. Mr. Penguillum, I command the peace—I order you to keep the peace."

"There's been more peace than love atwixt us, master," cried the steward, making some very unequivocal demonstrations towards hostility; "so mind yourself! square yourself, I say! do you smell this here bit of a sledge-hammer?"

"Lay hands on me if you dare!" exclaimed Hiram, as well as he could under the grasp which the steward held on his throttle—"lay hands on me if you dare!"

"If ye call this laying, master, you are welcome to the eggs," roared the steward.

It becomes our disagreeable duty to record here, that the acts of Benjamin now became violent; for he darted his sledge-hammer violently on the anvil of Mr. Doolittle's countenance, and the place became, in an instant, a scene of tumult and confusion. The crowd rushed in a dense circle around the spot, while some run to the court-room to give the alarm, and one or two of the more juvenile part of the multitude had a desperate trial of speed, to see who should be the happy man to communicate the critical situation of the magistrate to his wife.

Benjamin worked away with great industry and a good deal of skill, at his occupation, using one hand to raise up his antagonist, while he knocked him over with the other; for he would have been disgraced in his own estimation, had he struck a blow on a fallen adversary. By this considerate arrangement he had found means to hammer the visage of Hiram out of all shape, by the time Richard succeeded in forcing his way through the throng to the point of combat. The Sheriff afterwards declared that, independently of his mortification, as preserver of the peace of the county at this interruption to its harmony, he was never so grieved in his life, as when he saw this breach of unity between his favourites. Hiram had in some degree become necessary to his vanity, and Benjamin, strange as it may appear, he really loved. This attachment was exhibited in the first words that he uttered.

"Squire Doolittle! Squire Doolittle! I am ashamed to see a man of your character and office forget himself so much as to disturb the peace, insult the court, and beat poor Benjamin in this manner!"

At the sound of Mr. Jones's voice the steward ceased his employment, and Hiram had an opportunity of raising his discomfited visage towards the mediator. Emboldened by the sight of the Sheriff, Mr. Doolittle again had recourse to his lungs.

"I'll have the law on you for this," he cried, desperately; "I'll have the law on you for this. I call on you, Mr. Sheriff, to seize this man, and I demand that you take his body into custody."

By this time Richard was master of the true state of the case, and, turning to the steward, he said, reproachfully—

"Benjamin, how came you in the stocks! I always thought you were mild and docile as a lamb. It was for your docility that I most esteemed you. Benjamin! Benjamin! you have not only disgraced yourself, but your friends, by this shameless conduct. Bless me! bless me! Mr. Doolittle, he seems to have knocked your face all of one side."

Hiram by this time had got on his feet again, and without the reach of the steward, when he broke forth in violent appeals for vengeance. The offence was too apparent to be passed over, and the Sheriff, mindful of the impartiality exhibited by his cousin in the recent trial of the Leather-stocking, came to the painful conclusion that it was necessary to commit his Major-domo to prison. As the time of Natty's punishment was expired, and Benjamin found that they were to be confined, for that night at least, in the same apartment, he made no very strong objections to the measure, nor spoke of bail, though, as the Sheriff preceded the party of constables that conducted them to the gaol, he uttered the following remonstrance:—

"As to being berthed with Master Bump-ho for a night or so, it's but little I think of it, Squire Dickens, seeing that I calls him an honest man, and one as has a handy way with boat-hooks and rifles; but as for owning that a man desarves any thing worse than a double allowance, for knocking that carpenter's face a-one-side, as you call it, I'll maintain it's ag'in reason and christianity. If there's a blood-sucker in this 'ere county, it's that very chap. Ay! I know him! and if he hasn't got all the same as dead-wood in his head-works, he knows sum'mat of me. Where's the mighty harm, Squire, that you take it so much to heart! It's all the same as any other battle, d'ye see, sir, being broadside to broadside, only that it was fout at anchor, which was what we did in Port Praya roads, when Suff'ring came in among us; and a suff'ring time he had of it, before he got out again."

Richard thought it unworthy of him to make any reply to this speech, but when his prisoners were safely lodged in an outer dungeon, ordering the bolts to be drawn and the key turned, he withdrew.

Benjamin held frequent and friendly dialogues with different people, through the iron gratings, during the afternoon; but his companion paced their narrow limits, in his moccasins, with quick, impatient treads, his face hanging on his breast in dejection, or when lifted, at moments, to the idlers at the window, lighted, perhaps, for an instant with the childish aspect of aged forgetfulness, which would vanish directly in an expression of deep and obvious anxiety.

At the close of the day Edwards was seen at the window, in earnest dialogue with his friend; and after he departed it was thought that he had communicated words of comfort to the hunter, who threw himself on his pallet, and was soon in a deep sleep. The curious spectators had exhausted the conversation of the steward, who had drank good fellowship with half of his acquaintance, and as Natty was no longer in motion, by eight o'clock, Billy Kirby, who was the last lounger at the window retired into the "Templetown Coffee-House," when Natty rose and hung a blanket before the opening, and the prisoners apparently retired for the night.

Chapter XXXV

"And to avoid the foe's pursuit,
With spurring put their cattle to't;
And till all four were out of wind,
And danger too, ne'er look'd behind."
Butler, *Hudibras*, II.ii.841–44.

AS THE SHADES of evening approached, the jurors, witnesses, and other attendants on the court, begun to disperse, and before nine o'clock the village was quiet, and its streets nearly deserted. At that hour, Judge Temple and his daughter, followed at a short distance by Louisa Grant, walked slowly down the avenue, under the slight shadows of the young poplars, holding the following discourse:—

"You can best soothe his wounded spirit, my child," said Marmaduke; "but it will be dangerous to touch on the nature of his offence; the sanctity of the laws must be respected."

"Surely, sir," cried the impatient Elizabeth, "those laws, that condemn a man like the Leather-stocking to so severe a punishment, for an offence that even I must think very venial, cannot be perfect in themselves."

"Thou talkest of what thou dost not understand, Elizabeth," returned her father. "Society cannot exist without wholesome restraints. Those restraints cannot be inflicted, without security and respect to the persons of those who administer them; and it would sound ill indeed, to report that a judge had extended favour to a convicted criminal, because he had saved the life of his child."

"I see—I see the difficulty of your situation, dear sir," cried the daughter; "but in appreciating the offence of poor Natty, I cannot separate the minister of the law from the man."

"There thou talkest as a woman, child; it is not for an assault on Hiram Doolittle, but for threatening the life of a constable, who was in the performance of"——

"It is immaterial whether it be one or the other," interrupted Miss Temple, with a logic that contained more feeling than reason; "I know Natty to be innocent, and thinking so, I must think all wrong who oppress him."

"His judge among the number! thy father, Elizabeth?"

"Nay, nay—nay, do not put such questions to me; give me my commission, father, and let me proceed to execute it."

The Judge paused a moment, smiling fondly on his child, and then dropped his hand affectionately on her shoulder, as he answered—

"Thou hast reason, Bess, and much of it too, but thy heart lies too near thy head. But listen: in this pocket-book are two hundred dollars. Go to the prison—there are none in this place to harm thee—give this note to the gaoler, and when thou seest Bumppo, say what thou wilt to the poor old man; give scope to the feelings of thy warm heart; but try to remember, Elizabeth, that the laws alone remove us from the condition of the savages; that he has been criminal, and that his judge was thy father."

Miss Temple made no reply, but she pressed the hand that held the pocket-book to her bosom, and taking her friend by the arm, they issued together from the enclosure into the principal street of the village.

As they pursued their walk in silence, under the row of houses, where the deeper gloom of the evening effectually concealed their persons, no sound reached them, excepting the slow tread of a yoke of oxen, with the rattling of a cart, that were moving along the street in the same direction with themselves. The figure of the teamster was just discernible by the dim light, lounging by the side of his cattle with a listless air, as if fatigued by the toil of the day. At the corner, where the gaol stood, the progress of the ladies was impeded, for a moment, by the oxen, who were turned up to the side of the building, and given a lock of hay, which they had carried on their necks, as a reward for their patient labour. The whole of this was so natural, and so common, that Elizabeth saw nothing to induce a second glance at the team, until she heard the teamster speaking to his cattle in a low voice—

"Mind yourself, Brindle; will you, sir! will you!"

The language itself was unusual to oxen, with which all who dwell in a new country are familiar; but there was something in the voice also, that startled Miss Temple. On turning the corner, she necessarily approached the man, and her look was enabled to detect the person of Oliver Edwards, concealed under the coarse garb of a teamster. Their eyes met at the same instant, and, notwithstanding the gloom, and the enveloping cloak of Elizabeth, the recognition was mutual.

"Miss Temple!" "Mr. Edwards!" were exclaimed simultaneously, though a feeling that seemed common to both rendered the words nearly inaudible.

"Is it possible!" exclaimed Edwards, after the moment of doubt had passed; "do I see you so nigh the gaol! but you are going to the Rectory. I beg pardon—Miss Grant, I believe; I did not recognise you at first."

The sigh which Louisa uttered, was so faint that it was only heard by Elizabeth, who replied, quickly—

"We are going not only to the gaol, Mr. Edwards, but into it. We wish to show the Leather-stocking that we do not forget his services, and that, at the same time we must be just, we are also grateful. I suppose you are on a similar errand; but let me beg that you will give us leave to precede you ten minutes. Good night, sir; I—I—am quite sorry, Mr. Edwards, to see you reduced to such labour; I am sure my father would"——

"I shall wait your pleasure, madam," interrupted the youth, coldly. "May I beg that you will not mention my being here?"

"Certainly," said Elizabeth, returning his bow by a slight inclination of her head, and urging the tardy Louisa forward. As they entered the gaoler's house, however, Miss Grant found leisure to whisper—

"Would it not be well to offer part of your money to Oliver? half of it will pay the fine of Bumppo; and he is so unused to hardships! I am sure my father will subscribe much of his little pittance, to place him in a station that is more worthy of him."

The involuntary smile that passed over the features of Elizabeth was blended with an expression of deep and heartfelt pity. She did not reply, however, and the appearance of the gaoler soon recalled the thoughts of both to the object of their visit.

The rescue of the ladies, and their consequent interest in his prisoner, together with the informal manners that prevailed in the country, all united to prevent any surprise, on the part of the gaoler, at their request for admission to

Bumppo. The note of Judge Temple, however, would have silenced all objections, if he had felt them, and he led the way without hesitation to the apartment that held the prisoners. The instant the key was put into the lock, the hoarse voice of Benjamin was heard, demanding—

"Yo! hoy! who comes there?"

"Some visiters that you'll be glad to see," returned the gaoler. "What have you done to the lock, that it won't turn?"

"Handsomely, handsomely, master," cried the steward; "I've just drove a nail into a berth alongside of this here bolt, as a stopper, d'ye see, so that master Doo-but-little can't be running in and breezing up another fight atwixt us, for, to my account, there'll be but a ban-yan with me soon, seeing that they'll mulct me of my Spaniards, all the same as if I'd overflogged the lubber. Throw your ship into the wind and lay by for a small matter, will ye? and I'll soon clear a passage."

The sounds of hammering gave an assurance that the steward was in earnest, and in a short time the lock yielded, when the door was opened.

Benjamin had evidently been anticipating the seizure of his money, for he had made frequent demands on the favourite cask at the "Bold Dragoon," during the afternoon and evening, and was now in that state which by marine imagery is called "half-seas-over." It was no easy thing to destroy the balance of the old tar by the effects of liquor, for, as he expressed it himself, "he was too low-rigged not to carry sail in all weathers;" but he was precisely in that condition which is so expressively termed "muddy." When he perceived who the visiters were, he retreated to the side of the room where his pallet lay, and, regardless of the presence of his young mistress, seated himself on it with an air of great sobriety, placing his back firmly against the wall.

"If you undertake to spoil my locks in this manner, Mr. Pump," said the gaoler, "I shall put a stopper, as you call it, on your legs, and tie you down to your bed."

"What for should ye, Master?" grumbled Benjamin; "I've rode out one squall to-day, anchored by the heels, and I wants no more of them. Where's the harm of doing all the same as yourself? Leave that there door free outboard, and you'll find no locking inboard, I'll promise ye."

"I must shut up for the night at nine," said the gaoler, "and it's now forty-two minutes past eight." He placed the little candle on a rough pine table, and withdrew.

"Leather-stocking!" said Elizabeth, when the key of the door was turned on them again, "my good friend Leather-stocking! I have come on a message of gratitude. Had you submitted to the search, worthy old man, the death of the deer would have been a trifle, and all would have been well"——

"Submit to the sarch!" interrupted Natty, raising his face from resting on his knees, without rising from the corner where he had seated himself; "d'ye think, gall, I would let such a varmint into my hut? No, no—I wouldn't have opened the door to your own sweet countenance then. But they are wilcome to sarch among the coals and ashes now; they'll find only some such heap as is to be seen at every pot-ashery in the mountains."

The old man dropped his face again on one hand, and seemed to be lost in melancholy.

"The hut can be rebuilt, and made better than before," returned Miss Temple; "and it shall be my office to see it done, when your imprisonment is ended."

"Can ye raise the dead, child!" said Natty, in a sorrowful voice; "can ye go into the place where you've laid your fathers, and mothers, and children, and gather together their ashes, and make the same men and women of them as afore! You do not know what 'tis to lay your head for more than forty year under the cover of the same logs, and to look on the same things for the better part of a man's life. You are young yet, child, but you are one of the most precious of God's creaters. I had a hope for ye that it might come to pass, but it's all over now; this put to that, will drive the thing quite out of his mind for ever."

Miss Temple must have understood the meaning of the old man better than the other listeners; for, while Louisa stood innocently by her side, commiserating the griefs of the hunter, she bent her head aside, so as to conceal her features. The action and the feeling that caused it lasted but a moment.

"Other logs, and better, though, can be had, and shall be found for you, my old defender," she continued. "Your confinement will soon be over, and before that time arrives I shall have a house prepared for you, where you may spend the close of your harmless life in ease and plenty."

"Ease and plenty! house!" repeated Natty, slowly. "You mean well, you mean well, and I quite mourn that it cannot be; but he has seen me a sight and a laughing-stock for"——

"Damn your stocks," said Benjamin, flourishing his bottle with one hand, from which he had been taking hasty and repeated draughts, while he made gestures of disdain with the other; "who cares for his bilboes? there's a leg that's been stuck up an end like a gib-boom for an hour, d'ye see, and what's it the worse for't, ha! canst tell me, what's it the worser, ha?"

"I believe you forget, Mr. Pump, in whose presence you are," said Elizabeth.

"Forget you, Miss 'Lizzy," returned the steward; "if I do dam'me; you're not to be forgot, like Goody Pretty-bones, up at the big house there. I say, old sharp-shooter, she may have pretty bones, but I can't say so much for her flesh, d'ye see, for she looks sum'mat like an otomy with another man's jacket on. Now, for the skin of her face, it's all the same as a new topsail with a taut bolt-rope, being snug at the leaches, but all in a bight about the inner cloths."

"Peace—I command you to be silent, sir," said Elizabeth.

"Ay, ay, ma'am," returned the steward. "You didn't say I shouldn't drink, though."

"We will not speak of what is to become of others," said Miss Temple, turning again to the hunter—"but of your own fortunes, Natty. It shall be my care to see that you pass the rest of your days in ease and plenty."

"Ease and plenty!" again repeated the Leather-stocking; "what ease can there be to an old man, who must walk a mile across the open fields, before he can find a shade to hide him from a scorching sun! or what plenty is there, where you may hunt a day and not start a buck, or see any thing bigger than a mink, or maybe a stray fox! Ah! I shall have a hard time after them very beavers, for this fine. I must go low toward the Pennsylvany line in sarch of the creaters, maybe a hundred mile, for they are not to be got here-away. No, no—your betterments and clearings have druv the knowing things out of the country; and instead of beaver-dams, which is the nater of the animal, and according to Providence, you turn back the waters over the low grounds with your mill-dams, as if 'twas in man to stay the drops from going where He wills them to go. Benny, unless you stop your hand from going so often to your mouth, you won't be ready to start when the time comes."

"Hark'ee, Master Bump-ho," said the steward; "don't you fear for Ben. When the watch is called, set me on my legs, and give me the bearings and distance of where you want to steer, and I'll carry sail with the best of you, I will."

"The time has come now," said the hunter, listening; "I hear the horns of the oxen rubbing ag'in the side of the gaol."

"Well, say the word, and then heave ahead, shipmate," said Benjamin.

"You won't betray us, gall?" said Natty, looking simply into the face of Elizabeth—"you won't betray an old man, who craves to breathe the clear air of heaven? I mean no harm, and if the law says that I must pay the hundred dollars, I'll take the season through, but it shall be forthcoming; and this good man will help me."

"You catch them," said Benjamin, with a sweeping gesture of his arm, "and if they get away again, call me a slink, that's all."

"What mean you!" cried the wondering Elizabeth. "Here you must stay for thirty days; but I have the money for your fine in this purse. Take it; pay it in the morning, and summon patience for your month. I will come often to see you, with my friend; we will make up your clothes with our own hands; indeed, indeed, you shall be comfortable."

"Would ye, children?" said Natty, advancing across the floor with an air of kindness, and taking the hand of Elizabeth; "would ye be so kearful of an old man, and just for shooting the beast, which cost him nothing? Such things doesn't run in the blood, I believe, for you seem not to forget a favour. Your little fingers couldn't do much on a buck-skin, nor be you used to such a thread as sinews. But if he hasn't got past hearing, he shall hear it and know it, that he may see, like me, there is some who know how to remember a kindness."

"Tell him nothing," cried Elizabeth, earnestly; "if you love me, if you regard my feelings, tell him nothing. It is of yourself only I would talk, and for yourself only I act. I grieve, Leather-stocking, that the law requires that you should be detained here so long; but, after all, it will be only a short month, and"——

"A month!" exclaimed Natty, opening his mouth with his usual laugh; "not a day, nor a night, nor an hour, gall. Judge Temple may sintence, but he can't keep, without a better dungeon than this. I was taken once by the French, and they put sixty-two of us in a block-house, nigh hand to old Frontinac; but 'twas easy to cut through a pine log to them that was used to timber." The hunter paused, and looked cautiously around the room, when, laughing again, he shoved the steward gently from his post, and removing the bed-clothes, discovered a hole recently cut in the logs with a mallet and chisel. "It's only a kick, and the outside piece is off, and then"——

"Off! ay, off!" cried Benjamin, rousing from his stupor; "well, here's off. Ay! ay! you catch 'em, and I'll hold on to them said beaver-hats."

"I fear this lad will trouble me much," said Natty; "'twill be a hard pull for the mountain, should they take the scent soon, and he is not in a state of mind to run."

"Run!" echoed the steward; "no, sheer alongside, and let's have a fight of it."

"Peace!" ordered Elizabeth.

"Ay, ay, ma'am."

"You will not leave us, surely, Leather-stocking," continued Miss Temple; "I beseech you, reflect that you will be driven to the woods entirely, and that you are fast getting old. Be patient for a little time, when you can go abroad openly, and with honour."

"Is there beaver to be catched here, gall?"

"If not, here is money to discharge the fine, and in a month you are free. See, here it is in gold."

"Gold!" said Natty, with a kind of childish curiosity; "it's long sin' I've seen a gold piece. We used to get the broad joes, in the old war, as plenty as the bears be now. I remember there was a man in Dieskau's army, that was killed, who had a dozen of the shining things sewed up in his shirt. I didn't handle them myself, but I seen them cut out, with my own eyes; they was bigger and brighter than them be."

"These are English guineas, and are yours," said Elizabeth; "an earnest of what shall be done for you."

"Me! why should you give me this treasure?" said Natty, looking earnestly at the maiden.

"Why! have you not saved my life? did you not rescue me from the jaws of the beast?" exclaimed Elizabeth, veiling her eyes, as if to hide some hideous object from her view.

The hunter took the money, and continued turning it in his hand for some time, piece by piece, talking aloud during the operation.

"There's a rifle, they say, out on the Cherry Valley, that will carry a hundred rods and kill. I've seen good guns in my day, but none quite equal to that. A hundred rods with any sartainty is great shooting! Well, well—I'm old, and the gun I have will answer my time. Here, child, take back your gold. But the hour has come; I hear him talking to the cattle, and I must be going. You won't tell of us, gall—you won't tell of us, will ye?"

"Tell of you!" echoed Elizabeth.—"But take the money, old man; take the money, even if you go into the mountains."

"No, no," said Natty, shaking his head kindly; "I wouldn't rob you so for twenty rifles. But there's one thing you can do for me, if ye will, that no other is at hand to do."

"Name it—name it."

"Why, it's only to buy a canister of powder;—'twill cost two silver dollars. Benny Pump has the money ready, but we daren't come into the town to get it. Nobody has it but the Frenchman. 'Tis of the best, and just suits a rifle. Will you get it for me, gall?—say, will you get it for me?"

"Will I! I will bring it to you, Leather-stocking, though I toil a day in quest of you through the woods. But where shall I find you, and how?"

"Where!" said Natty, musing a moment—"to-morrow, on the Vision; on the very top of the Vision I'll meet you, child, just as the sun gets over our heads. See that it's the fine grain; you'll know it by the gloss, and the price."

"I will do it," said Elizabeth, firmly.

Natty now seated himself, and placing his feet in the hole, with a slight effort he opened a passage through into the street. The ladies heard the rustling of hay, and well understood the reason why Edwards was in the capacity of a teamster.

"Come, Benny," said the hunter; " 'twill be no darker to-night, for the moon will rise in an hour."

"Stay!" exclaimed Elizabeth; "it should not be said that you escaped in the presence of the daughter of Judge Temple. Return, Leather-stocking, and let us retire, before you execute your plan."

Natty was about to reply, when the approaching footsteps of the gaoler announced the necessity of his immediate return. He had barely time to regain his feet, and to conceal the hole with the bed-clothes, across which Benjamin very opportunely fell, before the key was turned, and the door of the apartment opened.

"Isn't Miss Temple ready to go?" said the civil gaoler—"it's the usooal hour for locking up."

"I follow you, sir," returned Elizabeth. "Good night, Leather-stocking."

"It's a fine grain, gall, and I think 'twill carry lead further than common. I am getting old, and can't follow up the game with the step that I used to could."

Miss Temple waved her hand for silence, and preceded Louisa and the keeper from the apartment. The man turned the key once, and observed that he would return and secure his prisoners, when he had lighted the ladies to the street. Accordingly, they parted at the door of the building, when the gaoler retired to his dungeons, and the ladies walked, with throbbing hearts, towards the corner.

"Now the Leather-stocking refuses the money," whispered Louisa, "it can all be given to Mr. Edwards, and that added to"——

"Listen!" said Elizabeth; "I hear the rustling of the hay; they are escaping at this moment. Oh! they will be detected instantly!"

By this time they were at the corner, where Edwards and Natty were in the act of drawing the almost helpless body of Benjamin through the aperture. The oxen had started back from their hay, and were standing with their heads down the street, leaving room for the party to act in.

"Throw the hay into the cart," said Edwards, "or they will suspect how it has been done. Quick, that they may not see it."

Natty had just returned from executing this order, when the light of the keeper's candle shone through the hole, and instantly his voice was heard in the gaol, exclaiming for his prisoners.

"What is to be done now?" said Edwards—"this drunken fellow will cause our detection, and we have not a moment to spare."

"Who's drunk, ye lubber?" muttered the steward.

"A break-gaol! a break-gaol!" shouted five or six voices from within.

"We must leave him," said Edwards.

"Twouldn't be kind, lad," returned Natty; "he took half the disgrace of the stocks on himself to-day, and the creater has feeling."

At this moment two or three men were heard issuing from the door of the "Bold Dragoon," and among them the voice of Billy Kirby.

"There's no moon yet," cried the wood-chopper; "but it's a clear night. Come, who's for home? Hark! what a rumpus they're kicking up in the gaol—here's go and see what it's about."

"We shall be lost," said Edwards, "if we don't drop this man."

At that instant Elizabeth moved close to him, and said rapidly, in a low voice—

"Lay him in the cart, and start the oxen; no one will look there."

"There's a woman's quickness in the thought," said the youth.

The proposition was no sooner made than executed. The steward was seated on the hay, and enjoined to hold his peace, and apply the goad that was placed in his hand, while the oxen were urged on. So soon as this arrangement was completed, Edwards and the hunter stole along the houses for a short distance, when they disappeared through an opening that led into the rear of the buildings. The oxen were in brisk motion, and presently the cries of pursuit were heard in the street. The ladies quickened their pace, with a wish to escape the crowd of constables and idlers that were approaching, some execrating, and some laughing at the exploit of the prisoners. In the confusion, the voice of Kirby was plainly distinguishable above all the others, shouting and swearing that he would have the fugitives, threatening to bring back Natty in one pocket and Benjamin in the other.

"Spread yourselves, men," he cried, as he passed the ladies, his heavy feet sounding along the street like the tread of a dozen; "spread yourselves; to the mountains; they'll be in the mountain in a quarter of an hour, and then look out for a long rifle."

His cries were echoed from twenty mouths, for not only the gaol but the taverns had sent forth their numbers, some earnest in the pursuit, and others joining it as in sport.

As Elizabeth turned in at her father's gate, she saw the wood-chopper stop at the cart, when she gave Benjamin up for lost. While they were hurrying up the walk, two figures, stealing cautiously but quickly under the shades of the trees, met the eyes of the ladies, and in a moment Edwards and the hunter crossed their path.

"Miss Temple, I may never see you again," exclaimed the youth; "let me thank you for all your kindness; you do not, cannot know my motives."

"Fly! fly!" cried Elizabeth—"the village is alarmed. Do not be found conversing with me at such a moment, and in these grounds."

"Nay, I must speak, though detection were certain."

"Your retreat to the bridge is already cut off; before you can gain the wood your pursuers will be there.—If"—

"If what?" cried the youth. "Your advice has saved me once already; I will follow it to death."

"The street is now silent and vacant," said Elizabeth, after a pause; "cross it, and you will find my father's boat in the lake. It would be easy to land from it where you please in the hills."

"But Judge Temple might complain of the trespass."

"His daughter shall be accountable, sir."

The youth uttered something in a low voice, that was heard only by Elizabeth, and turned to execute what she had suggested. As they were separating, Natty approached the females, and said—

"You'll remember the canister of powder, children. Them beavers must be had, and I and the pups be getting old; we want the best of ammunition."

"Come, Natty," said Edwards, impatiently.

"Coming, lad, coming. God bless you, young ones, both of ye, for ye mean well and kindly to the old man."

The ladies paused until they had lost sight of the retreating figures, when they immediately entered the Mansion-house.

While this scene was passing in the walk, Kirby had overtaken the cart, which was his own, and had been driven by Edwards without asking the owner, from the place where the patient oxen usually stood at evening, waiting the pleasure of their master.

"Woa—come hither, Golden," he cried; "why, how come you off the end of the bridge, where I left you, dummies?"

"Heave ahead," muttered Benjamin, giving a random blow with his lash, that alighted on the shoulder of the other.

"Who the devil be you?" cried Billy, turning round in surprise, but unable to distinguish, in the dark, the hard visage that was just peering over the cart-rails.

"Who be I! why I'm helmsman aboard of this here craft, d'ye see, and a straight wake I'm making of it. Ay! ay! I've got the bridge right ahead, and the bilboes dead-aft; I calls that good steerage, boy. Heave ahead."

"Lay your lash in the right spot, Mr. Benny Pump," said the wood-chopper, "or I'll put you in the palm of my hand and box your ears.—Where be you going with my team?"

"Team!"

"Ay, my cart and oxen."

"Why, you must know, Master Kirby, that the Leather-stocking and I—that's Benny Pump—you knows Ben?—well, Benny and I—no, me and Benny—dam'me if I know how 'tis; but some of us are bound after a cargo of beaver-skins, d'ye see, and so we've pressed the cart to ship them

’ome in. I say, Master Kirby, what a lubberly oar you pull—you handle an oar, boy, pretty much as a cow would a musket, or a lady would a marling-spike.”

Billy had discovered the state of the steward’s mind, and he walked for some time alongside of the cart, musing within himself, when he took the goad from Benjamin, who fell back on the hay, and was soon asleep, and drove his cattle down the street, over the bridge, and up the mountain, towards a clearing in which he was to work the next day, without any other interruption than a few hasty questions from parties of the constables.

Elizabeth stood for an hour at the window of her room, and saw the torches of the pursuers gliding along the side of the mountain, and heard their shouts and alarms; but, at the end of that time, the last party returned, wearied and disappointed, and the village became as still as when she issued from the gate, on her mission to the gaol.

Chapter XXXVI

> " 'And I could weep'—th' Oneida chief
> His descant wildly thus begun—
> 'But that I may not stain with grief
> The death-song of my father's son.' "
> Campbell, *Gertrude of Wyoming*, III.xxxv.1–4.

It was yet early on the following morning, when Elizabeth and Louisa met by appointment, and proceeded to the store of Monsieur Le Quoi, in order to redeem the pledge the former had given to the Leather-stocking. The people were again assembling for the business of the day, but the hour was too soon for a crowd, and the ladies found the place in possession of its polite owner, Billy Kirby, one female customer, and the boy who did the duty of helper or clerk.

Monsieur Le Quoi was perusing a packet of letters, with manifest delight, while the wood-chopper, with one hand thrust in his bosom, and the other in the folds of his jacket, holding an axe under his right arm, stood sympathizing in the Frenchman's pleasure with good-natured interest. The freedom of manners that prevailed in the new settlements, commonly levelled all difference in rank, and with it, frequently, all considerations of education and intelligence. At the time the ladies entered the store they were unseen by the owner, who was saying to Kirby—

"Ah! ha! Monsieur Beel, dis lettair mak-a me de most happi of mans. Ah! ma chère France! I vill see you aga'n."

"I rejoice, Monsieur, at any thing that contributes to your happiness," said Elizabeth, "but hope we are not going to lose you entirely."

The complaisant shopkeeper changed the language to French, and recounted rapidly to Elizabeth his hopes of being permitted to return to his own country. Habit had, however, so far altered the manners of this pliable personage, that he continued to serve the wood-chopper, who was in quest of some tobacco, while he related to his more gentle visiter, the happy change that had taken place in the dispositions of his own countrymen.

The amount of it all was, that Mr. Le Quoi, who had fled from his own country more through terror than because he was offensive to the ruling powers in France, had succeeded at length in getting an assurance that his return to the West Indies would be unnoticed; and the Frenchman, who had sunk into the character of a country shopkeeper with so much grace, was about to emerge again from his obscurity into his proper level in society.

We need not repeat the civil things that passed between the parties on this occasion, nor recount the endless repetitions of sorrow that the delighted Frenchman expressed, at being compelled to quit the society of Miss Temple. Elizabeth took an opportunity, during this expenditure of polite expressions, to purchase the powder privately of the boy, who bore the generic appellation of Jonathan. Before they parted, however, Mr. Le Quoi, who seemed to think that he had not said enough, solicited the honour of a private interview with the heiress, with a gravity in his air that announced the importance of the subject. After conceding the favour, and appointing a more favourable time for the meeting, Elizabeth succeeded in getting out of the store, into which the countrymen now began to enter, as usual, where they met with the same attention and bienséance as formerly.

Elizabeth and Louisa pursued their walk as far as the bridge in profound silence, but when they reached that place, the latter stopped, and appeared anxious to utter something that her diffidence suppressed.

"Are you ill, Louisa?" exclaimed Miss Temple; "had we not better return, and seek another opportunity to meet the old man?"

"Not ill, but terrified. Oh! I never, never can go on that hill again with you only. I am not equal to it, indeed I am not."

This was an unexpected declaration to Elizabeth, who, although she experienced no idle apprehension of a danger that no longer existed, felt most sensitively all the delicacy of maiden modesty. She stood for some time, deeply reflecting within herself; but, sensible it was a time for action instead of reflection, she struggled to shake off her hesitation, and replied firmly—

"Well, then it must be done by me alone. There is no other than yourself to be trusted, or poor old Leather-stocking will be discovered. Wait for me in the edge of these woods, that at least I may not be seen strolling in the hills by myself just now. One would not wish to create remarks, Louisa—if—if—. You will wait for me, dear girl?"

"A year, in sight of the village, Miss Temple," returned the agitated Louisa, "but do not, do not ask me to go on that hill."

Elizabeth found that her companion was really unable to proceed, and they completed their arrangement by posting Louisa out of the observation of the people who occasionally passed, but nigh the road, and in plain view of the whole valley. Miss Temple then proceeded alone. She ascended the road which has been so often mentioned in our narrative, with an elastic and firm step, fearful that the delay in the store of Mr. Le Quoi, and the time necessary for reaching the summit, would prevent her being punctual to the appointment. Whenever she passed an opening in the bushes, she would pause for breath, or perhaps, drawn from her pursuits by the picture at her feet, would linger a moment to gaze at the beauties of the valley. The long drought had, however, changed its coat of verdure to a hue of brown, and, though the same localities were there, the view wanted the lively and cheering aspect of early summer. Even the heavens seemed to share in the dried appearance of the earth, for the sun was concealed by a haziness in the atmosphere, which looked like a thin smoke without a particle of moisture, if such a thing were possible. The blue sky was scarcely to be seen, though now and then there was a faint lighting up in spots, through which masses of rolling vapour could be discerned gathering around the horizon, as if nature were struggling to collect her floods for the relief of man. The very atmosphere that Elizabeth inhaled was hot and dry, and by the time she reached the point where the course led her from the highway, she experienced a sensation like suffocation. But, disregarding her feelings, she hastened to execute her mission, dwelling on nothing but the disappointment, and even the helplessness, the hunter would experience, without her aid.

On the summit of the mountain which Judge Temple had

named the "Vision," a little spot had been cleared, in order that a better view might be obtained of the village and the valley. At this point Elizabeth understood the hunter she was to meet him; and thither she urged her way, as expeditiously as the difficulty of the ascent and the impediments of a forest in a state of nature would admit. Numberless were the fragments of rocks, trunks of fallen trees, and branches, with which she had to contend; but every difficulty vanished before her resolution, and, by her own watch, she stood on the desired spot several minutes before the appointed hour.

After resting a moment on the end of a log, Miss Temple cast a glance about her in quest of her old friend, but he was evidently not in the clearing; she arose and walked around its skirts, examining every place where she thought it probable Natty might deem it prudent to conceal himself. Her search was fruitless; and, after exhausting not only herself, but her conjectures, in efforts to discover or imagine his situation, she ventured to trust her voice in that solitary place.

"Natty! Leather-stocking! old man!" she called aloud, in every direction; but no answer was given, excepting the reverberations of her own clear tones, as they were echoed in the parched forest.

Elizabeth approached the brow of the mountain, where a faint cry, like the noise produced by striking the hand against the mouth at the same time that the breath is strongly exhaled, was heard, answering to her own voice. Not doubting in the least that it was the Leather-stocking lying in wait for her, and who gave that signal to indicate the place where he was to be found, Elizabeth descended for near a hundred feet, until she gained a little natural terrace, thinly scattered with trees, that grew in the fissures of the rocks, which were covered by a scanty soil. She had advanced to the edge of this platform, and was gazing over the perpendicular precipice that formed its face, when a rustling among the dry leaves near her drew her eyes in another direction. Our heroine certainly was startled by the object that she then saw, but a moment restored her self-possession, and she advanced firmly, and with some interest in her manner, to the spot.

Mohegan was seated on the trunk of a fallen oak, with his tawny visage turned towards her, and his eyes fixed on her face with an expression of wildness and fire that would have terrified a less resolute female. His blanket had fallen from his shoulders, and was lying in folds around him, leaving his breast, arms, and most of his body bare. The medallion of Washington reposed on his chest, a badge of distinction that Elizabeth well knew he only produced on great and solemn occasions. But the whole appearance of the aged chief was more studied than common, and in some particulars it was terrific. The long black hair was plaited on his head, falling away, so as to expose his high forehead and piercing eyes. In the enormous incisions of his ears were entwined ornaments of silver, beads, and porcupine's quills, mingled in a rude taste, and after the Indian fashions. A large drop, composed of similar materials, was suspended from the cartilage of his nose, and, falling below his lips, rested on his chin. Streaks of red paint crossed his wrinkled brow, and were traced down his cheeks, with such variations in the lines as caprice or custom suggested. His body was also coloured in the same manner; the whole exhibiting an Indian warrior prepared for some event of more than usual moment.

"John! how fare you, worthy John?" said Elizabeth, as she approached him; "you have long been a stranger in the village. You promised me a willow basket, and I have long had a shirt of calico in readiness for you."

The Indian looked steadily at her for some time without answering, and then shaking his head, he replied, in his low, guttural tones—

"John's hand can make baskets no more—he wants no shirt."

"But if he should, he will know where to come for it," returned Miss Temple. "Indeed, old John, I feel as if you had a natural right to order what you will from us."

"Daughter," said the Indian, "listen:—Six times ten hot summers have passed, since John was young; tall like a pine; straight like the bullet of Hawk-eye; strong as the buffalo; spry as the cat of the mountain. He was strong, and a warrior like the Young Eagle. If his tribe wanted to track the Maquas for many suns, the eye of Chingachgook found the print of their moccasins. If the people feasted and were glad as they counted the scalps of their enemies, it was on his pole they hung. If the squaws cried because there was no meat for their children, he was the first in the chase. His bullet was swifter than the deer.—Daughter, then Chingachgook struck his tomahawk into the trees; it was to tell the lazy ones where to find him and the Mingos—but he made no baskets."

"Those times have gone by, old warrior," returned Elizabeth; "since then, your people have disappeared, and in place of chasing your enemies, you have learned to fear God and to live at peace."

"Stand here, daughter, where you can see the great spring, the wigwams of your father, and the land on the crooked-river. John was young, when his tribe gave away the country, in council, from where the blue mountain stands above the water, to where the Susquehannah is hid by the trees. All this, and all that grew in it, and all that walked over it, and all that fed there, they gave to the Fire-eater—for they loved him. He was strong, and they were women, and he helped them. No Delaware would kill a deer that run in his woods, nor stop a bird that flew over his land; for it was his. Has John lived in peace! Daughter, since John was young, he has seen the white man from Frontinac come down on his white brothers at Albany, and fight. Did they fear God! He has seen his English and his American Fathers burying their tomahawks in each other's brains, for this very land. Did they fear God, and live in peace! He has seen the land pass away from the Fire-eater, and his children, and the child of his child, and a new chief set over the country. Did they live in peace who did this! did they fear God!"

"Such is the custom of the whites, John. Do not the Delawares fight, and exchange their lands for powder, and blankets, and merchandise?"

The Indian turned his dark eyes on his companion, and kept them there, with a scrutiny that alarmed her a little.

"Where are the blankets and merchandise that bought the right of the Fire-eater?" he replied, in a more animated voice; "are they with him in his wigwam? Did they say to him, brother, sell us your land, and take this gold, this silver, these blankets, these rifles, or even this rum? No, they tore it from him, as a scalp is torn from an enemy; and they that did it looked not behind them, to see whether he lived or died. Do such men live in peace, and fear the Great Spirit?"

"But you hardly understand the circumstances," said Elizabeth, more embarrassed than she would own, even to herself. "If you knew our laws and customs better, you would judge differently of our acts. Do not believe evil of my father, old Mohegan, for he is just and good."

"The brother of Miquon is good, and he will do right. I have said it to Hawk-eye—I have said it to the Young Eagle, that the brother of Miquon would do justice."

"Whom call you the Young Eagle?" said Elizabeth, averting her face from the gaze of the Indian as she asked the question; " whence comes he, and what are his rights?"

"Has my daughter lived so long with him, to ask this question?" returned the Indian, warily. "Old age freezes up the blood, as the frosts cover the great spring in winter; but youth keeps the streams of the blood open, like a sun in the time of blossoms. The Young Eagle has eyes; had he no tongue?"

The loveliness to which the old warrior alluded was in no degree diminished by his allegorical speech; for the blushes of the maiden who listened, covered her burning cheeks, till her dark eyes seemed to glow with their reflection; but, after struggling a moment with shame, she laughed, as if unwilling to understand him seriously, and replied in pleasantry—

"Not to make me the mistress of his secret. He is too much of a Delaware, to tell his secret thoughts to a woman."

"Daughter, the Great Spirit made your father with a white skin, and he made mine with a red; but he coloured both their hearts with blood. When young, it is swift and warm; but when old, it is still and cold. Is there difference below the skin? No. Once John had a woman. She was the mother of so many sons"—he raised his hand with three fingers elevated—"and she had daughters that would have made the young Delawares happy. She was kind, daughter, and what I said she did. You have different fashions; but do you think John did not love the wife of his youth—the mother of his children!"

"And what has become of your family, John, your wife and

your children?" asked Elizabeth, touched by the Indian's manner.

"Where is the ice that covered the great spring? It is melted, and gone with the waters. John has lived till all his people have left him for the land of spirits; his time has come, and he is ready."

Mohegan dropped his head in his blanket, and sat in silence. Miss Temple knew not what to say. She wished to draw the thoughts of the old warrior from his gloomy recollections, but there was a dignity in his sorrow, and in his fortitude, that repressed her efforts to speak. After a long pause, however, she renewed the discourse, by asking—

"Where is the Leather-stocking, John? I have brought this canister of powder at his request; but he is nowhere to be seen. Will you take charge of it, and see it delivered?"

The Indian raised his head slowly, and looked earnestly at the gift, which she put into his hand.

"This is the great enemy of my nation. Without this, when could the white men drive the Delawares! Daughter, the Great Spirit gave your fathers to know how to make guns and powder, that they might sweep the Indians from the land. There will soon be no red-skin in the country. When John has gone, the last will leave these hills, and his family will be dead." The aged warrior stretched his body forward, leaning an elbow on his knee, and appeared to be taking a parting look at the objects of the vale, which were still visible through the misty atmosphere; though the air seemed to thicken at each moment around Miss Temple, who became conscious of an increased difficulty of respiration. The eye of Mohegan changed gradually, from its sorrowful expression to a look of wildness, that might be supposed to border on the inspiration of a prophet, as he continued—"But he will go to the country where his fathers have met. The game shall be plenty as the fish in the lakes. No woman shall cry for meat. No Mingo can ever come. The chase shall be for children, and all just red-men shall live together as brothers."

"John! this is not the heaven of a Christian!" cried Miss Temple; "you deal now in the superstition of your forefathers."

"Fathers! sons!" said Mohegan with firmness—"all gone—

all gone! I have no son but the Young Eagle, and he has the blood of a white man."

"Tell me, John," said Elizabeth, willing to draw his thoughts to other subjects, and at the same time yielding to her own powerful interest in the youth; "who is this Mr. Edwards? why are you so fond of him, and whence does he come?"

The Indian started at the question, which evidently recalled his recollection to earth. Taking her hand, he drew Miss Temple to a seat beside him, and pointed to the country beneath them—

"See, daughter," he said, directing her looks towards the north; "as far as your young eyes can see, it was the land of his"——

But immense volumes of smoke at that moment rolled over their heads, and whirling in the eddies formed by the mountains, interposed a barrier to their sight, while he was speaking. Startled by the circumstance, Miss Temple sprung on her feet, and turning her eyes toward the summit of the mountain, she beheld it covered by a similar canopy, while a roaring sound was heard in the forest above her, like the rushing of winds.

"What means it, John!" she exclaimed; "we are enveloped in smoke, and I feel a heat like the glow of a furnace."

Before the Indian could reply, a voice was heard, crying in the woods—

"John! where are you, old Mohegan! the woods are on fire, and you have but a minute for escape."

The chief put his hand before his mouth, and making it play on his lips, produced the kind of noise that had attracted Elizabeth to the place, when a quick and hurried step was heard dashing through the dried underbrush and bushes, and presently Edwards rushed to his side, with horror in every feature.

Chapter XXXVII

"Love rules the court, the camp, the grove."
Scott, *The Lay of the Last Minstrel*, III.ii.5.

IT WOULD HAVE been sad indeed, to lose you in such a manner, my old friend," said Oliver, catching his breath for utterance. "Up and away! even now we may be too late; the flames are circling round the point of the rock below, and unless we can pass there, our only chance must be over the precipice. Away! away! shake off your apathy, John; now is the time of need."

Mohegan pointed towards Elizabeth, who, forgetting her danger, had shrunk back to a projection of the rock as soon as she recognised the sounds of Edwards' voice, and said, with something like awakened animation—

"Save her—leave John to die."

"Her! whom mean you?" cried the youth, turning quickly to the place the other indicated;—but when he saw the figure of Elizabeth, bending towards him in an attitude that powerfully spoke terror, blended with reluctance to meet him in such a place, the shock deprived him of speech.

"Miss Temple!" he cried, when he found words; "you here! is such a death reserved for you!"

"No, no, no—no death, I hope, for any of us, Mr. Edwards," she replied, endeavouring to speak calmly: "there is smoke but no fire to harm us. Let us endeavour to retire."

"Take my arm," said Edwards; "there must be an opening in some direction for your retreat. Are you equal to the effort?"

"Certainly. You surely magnify the danger, Mr. Edwards. Lead me out the way you came."

"I will—I will," cried the youth, with a kind of hysterical utterance. "No, no—there is no danger—I have alarmed you unnecessarily."

"But shall we leave the Indian—can we leave him, as he says, to die?"

An expression of painful emotion crossed the face of the young man; he stopped, and cast a longing look at Mohegan;

but, dragging his companion after him, even against her will, he pursued his way, with enormous strides, towards the pass by which he had just entered the circle of flame.

"Do not regard him," he said, in those tones that denote a desperate calmness; "he is used to the woods, and such scenes; and he will escape up the mountain—over the rock—or he can remain where he is in safety."

"You thought not so this moment, Edwards! Do not leave him there to meet with such a death," cried Elizabeth, fixing a look on the countenance of her conductor, that seemed to distrust his sanity.

"An Indian burn! who ever heard of an Indian dying by fire! an Indian cannot burn; the idea is ridiculous. Hasten, hasten, Miss Temple, or the smoke may incommode you."

"Edwards! your look, your eye, terrifies me! tell me the danger; is it greater than it seems? I am equal to any trial."

"If we reach the point of yon rock before that sheet of fire, we are safe, Miss Temple!" exclaimed the young man, in a voice that burst without the bounds of his forced composure. "Fly! the struggle is for life!"

The place of the interview between Miss Temple and the Indian has already been described as one of those platforms of rock which form a sort of terrace in the mountains of that country, and the face of it, we have said, was both high and perpendicular. Its shape was nearly a natural arc, the ends of which blended with the mountain, at points where its sides were less abrupt in their descent. It was round one of these terminations of the sweep of the rock that Edwards had ascended, and it was towards the same place that he urged Elizabeth to a desperate exertion of speed.

Immense clouds of white smoke had been pouring over the summit of the mountain, and had concealed the approach and ravages of the element; but a crackling sound drew the eyes of Miss Temple, as she flew over the ground, supported by the young man, towards the outline of smoke, where she already perceived the waving flames shooting forward from the vapour, now flaring high in the air, and then bending to the earth, seeming to light into combustion every stick and shrub on which they breathed. The sight aroused them to redoubled efforts; but, unfortunately, a collection of the tops of trees, old and dried, lay directly across their course; and, at the very moment when both had thought their safety insured, the warm currents of the air swept a forked tongue of flame across the pile, which lighted at the touch; and when they reached the spot, the flying pair were opposed by the surly roaring of a body of fire, as if a furnace were glowing in their path. They recoiled from the heat, and stood on a point of the rock, gazing in a stupor at the flames, which were spreading rapidly down the mountain, whose side soon became a sheet of living fire. It was dangerous for one clad in the light and airy dress of Elizabeth to approach even the vicinity of the raging element; and those flowing robes, that gave such softness and grace to her form, seemed now to be formed for the instruments of her destruction.

The villagers were accustomed to resort to that hill in quest of timber and fuel; in procuring which, it was their usage to take only the bodies of the trees, leaving the tops and branches to decay under the operations of the weather. Much of the hill was, consequently, covered with such light fuel, which, having been scorched under the sun for the last two months, was ignited with a touch. Indeed, in some cases, there did not appear to be any contact between the fire and these piles, but the flames seemed to dart from heap to heap, as the fabulous fire of the temple is represented to relumine its neglected lamp.

There was beauty as well as terror in the sight, and Edwards and Elizabeth stood viewing the progress of the desolation, with a strange mixture of horror and interest. The former, however, shortly roused himself to new exertions, and, drawing his companion after him, they skirted the edge of the smoke, the young man penetrating frequently into its dense volumes in search of a passage, but in every instance without success. In this manner they proceeded in a semicircle around the upper part of the terrace, until, arriving at the verge of the precipice, opposite to the point where Edwards had ascended, the horrid conviction burst on both at the same instant, that they were completely encircled by the fire. So long as a single pass up or down the mountain was unexplored, there was hope; but when retreat seemed to be absolutely impracticable, the horror of their situation broke upon

Elizabeth as powerfully as if she had hitherto considered the danger light.

"This mountain is doomed to be fatal to me!" she whispered;—" we shall find our graves on it!"

"Say not so, Miss Temple; there is yet hope," returned the youth, in the same tone, while the vacant expression of his eye, contradicted his words; "let us return to the point of the rock; there is, there must be, some place about it where we can descend."

"Lead me there," exclaimed Elizabeth; "let us leave no effort untried." She did not wait for his compliance, but turning, retraced her steps to the brow of the precipice, murmuring to herself, in suppressed hysterical sobs, "My father—my poor, my distracted father!"

Edwards was by her side in an instant, and with aching eyes he examined every fissure in the crags, in quest of some opening that might offer the facilities for flight. But the smooth, even surface of the rocks afforded hardly a resting place for a foot, much less those continued projections which would have been necessary for a descent of nearly a hundred feet. Edwards was not slow in feeling the conviction that this hope was also futile, and, with a kind of feverish despair, that still urged him to action, he turned to some new expedient.

"There is nothing left, Miss Temple," he said, "but to endeavour to lower you from this place to the rock beneath. If Natty were here, or even that Indian could be roused, their ingenuity and long practice would easily devise methods to do it; but I am a child, at this moment, in every thing but daring. Where shall I find means? This dress of mine is so light, and there is so little of it—then the blanket of Mohegan. We must try—we must try—any thing is better than to see you a victim to such a death!"

"And what will become of you!" said Elizabeth. "Indeed, indeed, neither you nor John must be sacrificed to my safety."

He heard her not, for he was already by the side of Mohegan, who yielded his blanket without a question, retaining his seat with Indian dignity and composure, though his own situation was even more critical than that of the others. The blanket was cut into shreds, and the fragments fastened together; the loose linen jacket of the youth, and the light muslin shawl of Elizabeth, were attached to them, and the whole thrown over the rocks, with the rapidity of lightning; but the united pieces did not reach half way to the bottom.

"It will not do—it will not do!" cried Elizabeth; "for me there is no hope! The fire comes slowly, but certainly. See! it destroys the very earth before it!"

Had the flames spread on that rock with half the quickness with which they leaped from bush to tree, in other parts of the mountain, our painful task would have soon ended; for they would have consumed already the captives they enclosed. But the peculiarity of their situation afforded Elizabeth and her companion the respite, of which they had availed themselves to make the efforts we have recorded.

The thin covering of earth on the rock supported but a scanty and faded herbage, and most of the trees that had found root in the fissures had already died, during the intense heats of preceding summers. Those which still retained the appearance of life, bore a few dry and withered leaves, while the others were merely the wrecks of pines, oaks, and maples. No better materials to feed the fire could be found, had there been a communication with the flames; but the ground was destitute of the brush that led the destructive element like a torrent over the remainder of the hill. As auxiliary to this scarcity of fuel, one of the large springs which abound in that country gushed out of the side of the ascent above, and, after creeping sluggishly along the level land, saturating the mossy covering of the rock with moisture, it swept round the base of the little cone that formed the pinnacle of the mountain, and, entering the canopy of smoke near one of the terminations of the terrace, found its way to the lake, not by dashing from rock to rock, but by the secret channels of the earth. It would rise to the surface, here and there, in the wet seasons, but in the droughts of summer, it was to be traced only by the bogs and moss that announced the proximity of water. When the fire reached this barrier, it was compelled to pause, until a concentration of its heat could overcome the moisture, like an army waiting the operations of a battering train, to open its way to desolation.

That fatal moment seemed now to have arrived; for the hissing steams of the spring appeared to be nearly exhausted, and the moss of the rocks was already curling under the intense heat, while fragments of bark that yet clung to the dead trees, began to separate from their trunks, and fall to the ground in crumbling masses. The air seemed quivering with rays of heat, which might be seen playing along the parched stems of the trees. There were moments when dark clouds of smoke would sweep along the little terrace, and as the eye lost its power, the other senses contributed to give effect to the fearful horror of the scene. At such moments, the roaring of the flames, the crackling of the furious element, with the tearing of falling branches, and, occasionally, the thundering echoes of some falling tree, united to alarm the victims. Of the three, however, the youth appeared much the most agitated. Elizabeth, having relinquished entirely the idea of escape, was fast obtaining that resigned composure, with which the most delicate of her sex are sometimes known to meet unavoidable evils; while Mohegan, who was much nearer to the danger, maintained his seat with the invincible resignation of an Indian warrior. Once or twice the eye of the aged chief, which was ordinarily fixed in the direction of the distant hills, turned towards the young pair, who seemed doomed to so early a death, with a slight indication of pity crossing his composed features, but it would immediately revert again to its former gaze, as if already looking into the womb of futurity. Much of the time he was chanting a kind of low dirge, in the Delaware tongue, using the deep and remarkably guttural tones of his people.

"At such a moment, Mr. Edwards, all earthly distinctions end," whispered Elizabeth; "persuade John to move nearer to us—let us die together."

"I cannot—he will not stir," returned the youth, in the same horridly still tones. "He considers this as the happiest moment of his life. He is past seventy; and has been decaying rapidly for some time; he received some injury in chasing that unlucky deer, too, on the lake. Oh! Miss Temple, that was an unlucky chase indeed! it has led, I fear, to this awful scene."

The smile of Elizabeth was celestial: "Why name such a trifle now—at this moment the heart is dead to all earthly emotions!"

"If any thing could reconcile a man to this death," cried the youth, "it would be to meet it in such company!"

"Talk not so, Edwards, talk not so," interrupted Miss Temple, "I am unworthy of it; and it is unjust to yourself. We must die; yes—yes—we must die—it is the will of God, and let us endeavour to submit like his own children."

"Die!" the youth rather shrieked than exclaimed, "No—no—there must yet be hope—you at least must not, shall not die."

"In what way can we escape?" asked Elizabeth, pointing, with a look of heavenly composure, towards the fire. "Observe! the flame is crossing the barrier of wet ground—it comes slowly, Edwards, but surely.—Ah! see! the tree! the tree is already lighted!"

Her words were too true. The heat of the conflagration had, at length, overcome the resistance of the spring, and the fire was slowly stealing along the half-dried moss; while a dead pine kindled with the touch of a forked flame, that, for a moment, wreathed around the stem of the tree, as it whirled, in one of its evolutions, under the influence of the air. The effect was instantaneous. The flames danced along the parched trunk of the pine, like lightning quivering on a chain, and immediately a column of living fire was raging on the terrace. It soon spread from tree to tree, and the scene was evidently drawing to a close. The log on which Mohegan was seated lighted at its farther end, and the Indian appeared to be surrounded by fire. Still he was unmoved. As his body was unprotected, his sufferings must have been great, but his fortitude was superior to all. His voice could yet be heard, even in the midst of these horrors. Elizabeth turned her head from the sight, and faced the valley. Furious eddies of wind were created by the heat, and just at the moment, the canopy of fiery smoke that overhung the valley, was cleared away, leaving a distinct view of the peaceful village beneath them.

"My father!—My father!" shrieked Elizabeth. "Oh! this—this surely might have been spared me—but I submit."

The distance was not so great but the figure of Judge Temple could be seen, standing in his own grounds, and, apparently, contemplating, in perfect unconsciousness of the danger of his child, the mountain in flames. This sight was still more painful than the approaching danger; and Elizabeth again faced the hill.

"My intemperate warmth has done this!" cried Edwards, in the accents of despair. "If I had possessed but a moiety of your heavenly resignation, Miss Temple, all might yet have been well."

"Name it not—name it not," she said. "It is now of no avail. We must die, Edwards, we must die—let us do so as Christians. But—no—you may yet escape, perhaps. Your dress is not so fatal as mine. Fly! leave me. An opening may yet be found for you, possibly—certainly it is worth the effort. Fly! leave me—but stay! You will see my father; my poor, my bereaved father! Say to him, then, Edwards, say to him, all that can appease his anguish. Tell him that I died happy and collected; that I have gone to my beloved mother; that the hours of this life are as nothing when balanced in the scales of eternity. Say how we shall meet again. And say," she continued, dropping her voice, that had risen with her feelings, as if conscious of her worldly weaknesses, "how dear, how very dear, was my love for him. That it was near, too near, to my love for God."

The youth listened to her touching accents, but moved not. In a moment he found utterance and replied:

"And is it me that you command to leave you! to leave you on the edge of the grave! Oh! Miss Temple, how little have you known me," he cried, dropping on his knees at her feet, and gathering her flowing robe in his arms, as if to shield her from the flames. "I have been driven to the woods in despair; but your society has tamed the lion within me. If I have wasted my time in degradation, 'twas you that charmed me to it. If I have forgotten my name and family, your form supplied the place of memory. If I have forgotten my wrongs, 'twas you that taught me charity. No—no—dearest Elizabeth, I may die with you, but I can never leave you!"

Elizabeth moved not, nor answered. It was plain that her thoughts had been raised from the earth. The recollection of her father, and her regrets at their separation, had been mellowed by a holy sentiment, that lifted her above the level of earthly things, and she was fast losing the weakness of her sex, in the near view of eternity. But as she listened to these words, she became once more woman. She struggled against these feelings, and smiled, as she thought she was shaking off the last lingering feeling of nature, when the world, and all its seductions, rushed again to her heart, with the sounds of a human voice, crying in piercing tones—

"Gall! where be ye, gall! gladden the heart of an old man, if ye yet belong to 'arth!"

"List!" said Elizabeth, "'tis the Leather-stocking; he seeks me!"

"'Tis Natty!" shouted Edwards, "and we may yet be saved!"

A wide and circling flame glared on their eyes for a moment, even above the fire of the woods, and a loud report followed.

"'Tis the canister! 'tis the powder," cried the same voice, evidently approaching them. "'Tis the canister, and the precious child is lost!"

At the next instant Natty rushed through the steams of the spring, and appeared on the terrace, without his deer skin cap, his hair burnt to his head, his shirt of country check, black, and filled with holes, and his red features of a deeper colour than ever, by the heat he had encountered.

Chapter XXXVIII

"Even from the land of shadows, now,
My father's awful ghost appears."
Campbell, *Gertrude of Wyoming*, III.xxxix.3–4.

FOR AN HOUR after Louisa Grant was left by Miss Temple, in the situation already mentioned, she continued in feverish anxiety, awaiting the return of her friend. But, as the time passed by without the re-appearance of Elizabeth, the terror of Louisa gradually increased, until her alarmed fancy had conjured every species of danger that appertained to the woods, excepting the one that really existed. The heavens had become obscured, by degrees, and vast volumes of smoke were pouring over the valley; but the thoughts of Louisa were still recurring to beasts, without dreaming of the real cause for apprehension. She was stationed in the edge of the low pines and chestnuts that succeeded the first or large growth of the forest, and directly above the angle where the highway turned from the straight course to the village and ascended the mountain, laterally. Consequently she commanded a view not only of the valley, but of the road beneath her. The few travellers that passed, she observed, were engaged in earnest conversation, and frequently raised their eyes to the hill, and at length she saw the people leaving the court-house, and gazing upward also. While under the influence of the alarm excited by such unusual movements, reluctant to go, and yet fearful to remain, Louisa was startled by the low, cracking, but cautious treads, of some one approaching through the bushes. She was on the eve of flight, when Natty emerged from the cover and stood at her side. The old man laughed as he shook her kindly by a hand that was passive with fear.

"I am glad to meet you here, child," he said; "for the back of the mountain is a-fire, and it would be dangerous to go up it now, till it has been burnt over once, and the dead wood is gone. There's a foolish man, the comrad of that varmint, who has given me all this trouble, digging for ore, on the east side. I told him that the kearless fellows who thought to catch a practys'd hunter in the woods after dark, had thrown the lighted pine knots in the brush, and that 'twould kindle like tow, and warned him to leave the hill. But he was set upon his business, and nothing short of Providence could move him. If he isn't burnt and buried in a grave of his own digging, he's made of salamanders. Why, what ails the child! you look as skeary as if you see'd more painters! I wish there was more to be found, they'd count up faster than the beaver. But, where's the good child of a bad father? did she forget her promise to the old man?"

"The hill! the hill!" shrieked Louisa; "she seeks you on the hill, with the powder!"

Natty recoiled several feet, at this unexpected intelligence.

"The Lord of Heaven have mercy on her! She's on the Vision, and that's a sheet of fire ag'in this. Child, if ye love the dear one, and hope to find a friend when ye need it most, to the village, and give the alarm. The men be us'd to fighting fire, and there may be a chance left. Fly! I bid ye fly! nor stop even for breath."

The Leather-stocking had no sooner uttered this injunction, than he disappeared in the bushes, and when last seen by Louisa, was rushing up the mountain, with a speed that none but those who were accustomed to the toil, could attain.

"Have I found ye!" the old man exclaimed, when he burst out of the smoke; "God be praised, that I've found ye; but follow, there is no time for talking."

"My dress!" said Elizabeth; "it would be fatal to trust myself nearer to the flames in it."

"I bethought me of your flimsy things," cried Natty, throwing loose the folds of a covering of buckskin that he carried on his arm, and wrapping her form in it, in such a manner as to envelope her whole person; "now follow, for it's a matter of life and death to us all."

"But John! what will become of John," cried Edwards; "Can we leave the old warrior here to perish?"

The eyes of Natty followed the direction of Edwards' finger, when he beheld the Indian, still seated as before, with the very earth under his feet consuming with fire. Without delay, the hunter approached the spot, and spoke in Delaware—

"Up and away, Chingachgook! will ye stay here to burn, like a Mingo at the stake! The Moravians have teached ye better, I hope. The Lord preserve me if the powder has'nt flashed a-tween his legs, and the skin of his back is roasting. Will ye come, I say? will ye follow?"

"Why should Mohegan go?" returned the Indian, gloomily. "He has seen the days of an eagle, and his eye grows dim. He looks on the valley; he looks on the water; he looks in the hunting-grounds—but he sees no Delawares. Every one has a white skin. My fathers say, from the far-off land, come. My women, my young warriors, my tribe, say, come. The Great Spirit says, come. Let Mohegan die."

"But you forget your friend," cried Edwards.

" 'Tis useless to talk to an Indian with the death-fit on him, lad," interrupted Natty, who seized the strips of the blanket, and with wonderful dexterity strapped the passive chieftain to his own back; when he turned, and with a strength that seemed to bid defiance, not only to his years, but to his load, he led the way to the point whence he had issued. As they crossed the little terrace of rock, one of the dead trees, that had been tottering for several minutes, fell on the spot where they had stood, and filled the air with its cinders.

Such an event quickened the steps of the party, who followed the Leather-stocking with the urgency required by the occasion.

"Tread on the soft ground," he cried, when they were in a gloom where sight availed them but little, "and keep in the white smoke; keep the skin close on her, lad, she's a precious one, another will be hard to be found."

Obedient to the hunter's directions, they followed his steps and advice implicitly, and although the narrow passage along the winding of the spring led amid burning logs and falling branches, they happily achieved it in safety. No one but a man long accustomed to the woods could have traced his route through a smoke, in which respiration was difficult, and sight nearly useless; but the experience of Natty conducted them to an opening through the rocks, where, with a little difficulty, they soon descended to another terrace, and emerged at once into a tolerably clear atmosphere.

The feelings of Edwards and Elizabeth, at reaching this

spot, may be imagined, though not easily described. No one seemed to exult more than their guide, who turned, with Mohegan still lashed to his back, and laughing in his own manner, said, "I know'd 'twas the Frenchman's powder, gall; it went so altogether; your coarse grain will squib for a minute. The Iroquois had none of the best powder when I went ag'in the Canada tribes, under Sir William. Did I ever tell you the story, lad, concarning the skrimmage with"—

"For God's sake, tell me nothing now, Natty, until we are entirely safe——where shall we go next?"

"Why, on the platform of rock over the cave, to be sure, —you will be safe enough there, or we'll go into it if you be so minded."

The young man started, and appeared agitated; but looking around him with an anxious eye, said quickly—

"Shall we be safe on the rock? cannot the fire reach us there, too?"

"Can't the boy see?" said Natty, with the coolness of one accustomed to the kind of danger he had just encountered. "Had ye staid in the place above ten minutes longer, you would both have been in ashes, but here you may stay for ever, and no fire can touch you, until they burn the rocks as well as the woods."

With this assurance, which was obviously true, they proceeded to the spot, and Natty deposited his load, placing the Indian on the ground with his back against a fragment of the rocks. Elizabeth sunk on the ground, and buried her face in her hands, while her heart was swelling with a variety of conflicting emotions.

"Let me urge you to take a restorative, Miss Temple," said Edwards respectfully; "your frame will sink else."

"Leave me, leave me," she said, raising her beaming eyes for a moment to his; "I feel too much for words; I am grateful, Oliver, for this miraculous escape; and next to my God, to you."

Edwards withdrew to the edge of the rock, and shouted— "Benjamin! where are you, Benjamin?"

A hoarse voice replied, as if from the bowels of the earth, "Hereaway, master; stow'd in this here bit of a hole, which is all the same as hot as the cook's coppers. I'm tired of my berth, d'ye see, and if-so-be that Leather-stocking has got much overhauling to do before he sails after them said beaver, I'll go into dock again, and ride out my quarantine 'till I can get prottick from the law, and so hold on upon the rest of my 'spaniolas."

"Bring up a glass of water from the spring," continued Edwards, "and throw a little wine in it; hasten, I entreat you."

"I knows but little of your small drink, master Oliver," returned the steward, his voice issuing out of the cave into the open air, "and the Jamaiky held out no longer than to take a parting kiss with Billy Kirby, when he anchored me alongside the highway last night, where you run me down in the chase. But here's sum'mat of a red colour that may suit a weak stomach, mayhap. That master Kirby is no first rate in a boat, but he'll tack a cart among the stumps, all the same as a Lon'on pilot will back and fill through the colliers in the Pool."

As the steward ascended while talking, by the time he had ended his speech, he appeared on the rock, with the desired restoratives, exhibiting the worn out and bloated features of a man who had run deep in a debauch, and that lately.

Elizabeth took from the hand of Edwards the liquor which he offered, and then motioned to be left again to herself.

The youth turned at her bidding, and observed Natty kindly assiduous around the person of Mohegan. When their eyes met, the hunter said sorrowfully—

"His time has come, lad; I see it in his eyes;—when an Indian fixes his eye, he means to go but to one place; and what the wilful creaters put their minds on, they're sure to do."

A quick tread prevented the reply, and in a few moments, to the amazement of the whole party, Mr. Grant was seen clinging to the side of the mountain, and striving to reach the place where they stood. Oliver sprang to his assistance, and by their united efforts, the worthy divine was soon placed safely among them.

"How came you added to our number?" cried Edwards; "Is the hill alive with people, at a time like this?"

The hasty, but pious thanksgivings of the clergyman were soon ejaculated; and when he succeeded in collecting his bewildered senses, he replied—

"I heard that my child was seen coming to the mountain; and when the fire broke over its summit, my uneasiness drew me up the road, where I found Louisa, in terror for Miss Temple. It was to seek her that I came into this dangerous place; and I think but for God's mercy, through the dogs of Natty, I should have perished in the flames myself."

"Ay! follow the hounds, and if there's an opening they'll scent it out," said Natty; "their noses be given to them the same as man's reason."

"I did so, and they led me to this place; but, praise be to God, that I see you all safe and well."

"No, no," returned the hunter; "safe we be, but as for well, John can't be called in a good way, unless you'll say that for a man that's taking his last look at 'arth."

"He speaks the truth!" said the divine, with the holy awe with which he ever approached the dying;—"I have been by too many death-beds, not to see that the hand of the tyrant is laid on this old warrior. Oh! how consoling it is, to know that he has not rejected the offered mercy, in the hour of his strength and of worldly temptations! The offspring of a race of heathens, he has in truth been 'as a brand plucked from the burning.' "

"No, no," returned Natty, who alone stood with him by the side of the dying warrior, "it's no burning that ails him, though his Indian feelings made him scorn to move, unless it be the burning of man's wicked thoughts for near fourscore years; but it's nater giving out in a chase that's run too long.—Down with ye, Hector! down, I say!—Flesh isn't iron, that a man can live for ever, and see his kith and kin driven to a far country, and he left to mourn, with none to keep him company."

"John," said the divine, tenderly, "do you hear me? do you wish the prayers appointed by the church, at this trying moment?"

The Indian turned his ghastly face towards the speaker, and fastened his dark eyes on him, steadily, but vacantly. No sign of recognition was made; and in a moment he moved his head again slowly towards the vale, and begun to sing, using his own language, in those low, guttural tones that have been so often mentioned, his notes rising with his theme, till they swelled so loud as to be distinct.

"I will come! I will come! to the land of the just I will come! The Maquas I have slain!—I have slain the Maquas! and the Great Spirit calls to his son. I will come! I will come! to the land of the just I will come!"

"What says he, Leather-stocking?" inquired the priest, with tender interest; "sings he the Redeemer's praise?"

"No, no,—'tis his own praise that he speaks now," said Natty, turning in a melancholy manner from the sight of his dying friend; "and a good right he has to say it all, for I know every word to be true."

"May Heaven avert such self-righteousness from his heart! Humility and penitence are the seals of christianity; and without feeling them deeply seated in the soul, all hope is delusive, and leads to vain expectations. Praise himself! when his whole soul and body should unite to praise his Maker! John! you have enjoyed the blessings of a gospel ministry, and have been called from out a multitude of sinners and pagans, and, I trust, for a wise and gracious purpose. Do you now feel what it is to be justified by your Saviour's death, and reject all weak and idle dependence on good works, that spring from man's pride and vain-glory?"

The Indian did not regard his interrogator, but he raised his head again, and said, in a low, distinct voice—

"Who can say that the Maquas know the back of Mohegan! What enemy that trusted in him did not see the morning? What Mingo that he chased ever sung the song of triumph? Did Mohegan ever lie? No; the truth lived in him, and none else could come out of him. In his youth, he was a warrior, and his moccasins left the stain of blood. In his age, he was wise; his words at the council fire did not blow away with the winds."

"Ah! he has abandoned that vain relic of paganism, his songs," cried the divine;—"what says he now? is he sensible of his lost state?"

"Lord! man," said Natty, "he knows his ind is at hand as well as you or I, but, so far from thinking it a loss, he believes it to be a great gain. He is old and stiff, and you've made the game so scurce and shy, that better shots than him find it hard to get a livelihood. Now he thinks he shall travel where it will always be good hunting; where no wicked or unjust Indians can go; and where he shall meet all his tribe together ag'in. There's not much loss in that, to a man whose hands be hardly fit for basket-making. Loss! if there be any loss, 'twill be to me. I'm sure, after he's gone, there will be but little left for me but to follow."

"His example and end, which, I humbly trust, shall yet be made glorious," returned Mr. Grant, "should lead your mind to dwell on the things of another life. But I feel it to be my duty to smooth the way for the parting spirit. This is the moment, John, when the reflection that you did not reject the mediation of the Redeemer, will bring balm to your soul. Trust not to any act of former days, but lay the burthen of your sins at his feet, and you have his own blessed assurance that he will not desert you."

"Though all you say be true, and you have scripter gospels for it, too," said Natty, "you will make nothing of the Indian. He has'nt seen a Moravian priest sin' the war; and it's hard to keep them from going back to their native ways. I should think 'twould be as well to let the old man pass in peace. He's happy now; I know it by his eye; and that's more than I would say for the chief, sin' the time the Delawares broke up from the head-waters of their river, and went west. Ahs! me! 'tis a grievous long time that, and many dark days have we seen together, sin' it."

"Hawk-eye!" said Mohegan, rousing with the last glimmering of life. "Hawk-eye! listen to the words of your brother."

"Yes, John," said the hunter, in English, strongly affected by the appeal, and drawing to his side; " we have been brothers; and more so than it means in the Indian tongue. What would ye have with me, Chingachgook?"

"Hawk-eye! my fathers call me to the happy hunting-grounds. The path is clear, and the eyes of Mohegan grow young. I look—but I see no white-skins; there are none to be seen but just and brave Indians. Farewell, Hawk-eye—you shall go with the Fire-eater and the Young-eagle, to the white man's heaven; but I go after my fathers. Let the bow, and tomahawk, and pipe, and the wampum, of Mohegan, be laid in his grave; for when he starts 'twill be in the night, like a warrior on a war-party, and he cannot stop to seek them."

"What says he, Nathaniel?" cried Mr. Grant, earnestly, and with obvious anxiety; "does he recall the promises of the mediation? and trust his salvation to the Rock of ages?"

Although the faith of the hunter was by no means clear, yet the fruits of early instruction had not entirely fallen in the wilderness. He believed in one God, and in one heaven; and when the strong feeling excited by the leave-taking of his old companion, which was exhibited by the powerful working of every muscle in his weather beaten face, suffered him to speak, he replied—

"No—no—he trusts only to the Great Spirit of the savages, and to his own good deeds. He thinks, like all his people, that he is to be young ag'in, and to hunt, and be happy to the ind of etarnity. It's pretty much the same with all colours, parson. I could never bring myself to think that I shall meet with these hounds, or my piece, in another world; though the thoughts of leaving them for ever, sometimes brings hard feelings over me, and makes me cling to life with a greater craving than beseems three-score-and-ten."

"The Lord, in his mercy, avert such a death from one who has been sealed with the sign of the cross!" cried the minister, in holy fervour. "John—"

He paused for the elements. During the period occupied by the events which we have related, the dark clouds in the horizon had continued to increase in numbers and magnitude; and the awful stillness that now pervaded the air, announced a crisis in the state of the atmosphere. The flames, which yet continued to rage along the sides of the mountain, no longer whirled in the uncertain currents of their own eddies, but blazed high and steadily towards the heavens. There was even a quietude in the ravages of the destructive element, as if it foresaw that a hand, greater than even its own desolating power, was about to stay its progress. The piles of smoke which lay above the valley began to rise, and were dispelling rapidly; and streaks of vivid lightning were dancing through the masses of clouds that impended over the western hills. While Mr. Grant was speaking, a flash, which sent its quivering light through the gloom, laying bare the whole opposite horizon, was followed by a loud crash of thunder, that rolled away among the hills, seeming to shake the foundations of the earth to their centre. Mohegan raised himself, as if in obedience to a signal for his departure, and stretched his wasted arm towards the west. His dark face lighted with a look of joy; which, with all other expression, gradually disappeared; the muscles stiffening as they retreated to a state of rest; a slight convulsion played, for a single instant, about his lips; and his arm slowly dropped by his side; leaving the frame of the dead warrior reposing against the rock, with its glassy eyes open, and fixed on the distant hills, as if the deserted shell were tracing the flight of the spirit to its new abode.

All this Mr. Grant witnessed, in silent awe; but when the last echoes of the thunder died away, he clasped his hands together, with pious energy, and repeated, in the full rich tones of assured faith—

"O Lord! how unsearchable are thy judgments: And thy ways past finding out! 'I know that my Redeemer liveth, and that he shall stand at the latter day upon the earth: And though after my skin, worms destroy this body, yet in my flesh shall I see God; whom I shall see for myself, and mine eyes shall behold, and not another.' "

As the divine closed this burst of devotion, he bowed his head meekly to his bosom, and looked all the dependence and humility that the inspired language expressed.

When Mr. Grant retired from the body, the hunter approached, and taking the rigid hand of his friend, looked him wistfully in the face for some time without speaking; when he gave vent to his feelings by saying, in the mournful voice of one who felt deeply—

"Red skin, or white, it's all over now! He's to be judged by a righteous Judge, and by no laws that's made to suit times, and new ways. Well, there's only one more death, and the world be left to me and the hounds. Ahs! me! a man must wait the time of God's pleasure, but I begin to weary of life. There is scurcely a tree standing that I know, and it's hard to find a face that I was acquainted with in my younger days."

Large drops of rain began now to fall, and diffuse themselves over the dry rock, while the approach of the thunder shower was rapid and certain. The body of the Indian was hastily removed into the cave beneath, followed by the whining hounds, who missed, and moaned for, the look of intelligence that had always met their salutations to the chief.

Edwards made some hasty and confused excuse for not taking Elizabeth into the same place, which was now completely closed in front with logs and bark, saying something that she hardly understood about its darkness, and the unpleasantness of being with the dead body. Miss Temple, however, found a sufficient shelter against the torrent of rain that fell, under the projection of a rock which overhung them. But long before the shower was over, the sounds of voices were heard below them, crying aloud for Elizabeth, and men soon appeared, beating the dying embers of the bushes, as they worked their way cautiously among the unextinguished brands.

At the first short cessation in the rain, Oliver conducted Elizabeth to the road, where he left her. Before parting, however, he found time to say, in a fervent manner, that his companion was now at no loss to interpret—

"The moment of concealment is over, Miss Temple. By this time to-morrow, I shall remove a veil that perhaps it has been weakness to keep around me and my affairs so long. But I have had romantic and foolish wishes and weaknesses; and who has not, that is young and torn by conflicting passions! God bless you! I hear your father's voice; he is coming up the road, and I would not, just now, subject myself to detention. Thank Heaven, you are safe again; that alone removes the weight of a world from my spirit!"

He waited for no answer, but sprung into the woods. Elizabeth, notwithstanding she heard the cries of her father as he called upon her name, paused until he was concealed among the smoking trees, when she turned, and in a moment rushed into the arms of her half-distracted parent.

A carriage had been provided, into which Miss Temple hastily entered; when the cry was passed along the hill, that the lost one was found, and the people returned to the village, wet and dirty, but elated with the thought that the daughter of their landlord had escaped from so horrid and untimely an end.*

*The probability of a fire in the woods, similar to that here described, has been questioned. The writer can only say that he once witnessed a fire in another part of New York that compelled a man to desert his wagon and horses in the highway, and in which the latter were destroyed. In order to estimate the probability of such an event, it is necessary to remember the effects of a long drought in that climate, and the abundance of dead wood which is found in a forest like that described. The fires in the American forests frequently rage to such an extent as to produce a sensible effect on the atmosphere at the distance of fifty miles. Houses, barns, and fences are quite commonly swept away in their course.

Chapter XXXIX

"Selictar! unsheath then our chief's scimetar;
Tambourgi! thy 'larum gives promise of war;
Ye mountains! that see us descend to the shore,
Shall view us victors, or view us no more."
Byron, *Childe Harold's Pilgrimage*, II.lxxi.50–53.

THE HEAVY SHOWERS that prevailed during the remainder of the day, completely stopped the progress of the flames; though glimmering fires were observed during the night, on different parts of the hill, wherever there was a collection of fuel to feed the element. The next day the woods, for many miles, were black and smoking, and were stript of every vestige of brush and dead wood; but the pines and hemlocks still reared their heads proudly, among the hills, and even the smaller trees of the forest retained a feeble appearance of life and vegetation.

The many tongues of rumour were busy in exaggerating the miraculous escape of Elizabeth, and a report was generally credited, that Mohegan had actually perished in the flames. This belief became confirmed, and was indeed rendered probable, when the direful intelligence reached the village, that Jotham Riddel, the miner, was found in his hole, nearly dead with suffocation, and burnt to such a degree that no hopes were entertained of his life.

The public attention became much alive to the events of the last few days, and just at this crisis, the convicted counterfeiters took the hint from Natty, and, on the night succeeding the fire, found means to cut through their log prison also, and to escape unpunished. When this news begun to circulate through the village, blended with the fate of Jotham, and the exaggerated and tortured reports of the events on the hill, the popular opinion was freely expressed, as to the propriety of seizing such of the fugitives as remained within reach. Men talked of the cave, as a secret receptacle of guilt; and, as the rumour of ores and metals found its way into the confused medley of conjectures, counterfeiting, and every thing else that was wicked and dangerous to the peace of society, suggested themselves to the busy fancies of the populace.

While the public mind was in this feverish state, it was hinted that the wood had been set on fire by Edwards and the Leather-stocking, and that, consequently, they alone were responsible for the damages. This opinion soon gained ground, being most circulated by those who, by their own heedlessness, had caused the evil; and there was one irresistible burst of the common sentiment, that an attempt should be made to punish the offenders. Richard was by no means deaf to this appeal, and by noon he set about in earnest, to see the laws executed.

Several stout young men were selected, and taken apart, with an appearance of secrecy, where they received some important charge from the Sheriff, immediately under the eyes, but far removed from the ears, of all in the village. Possessed of a knowledge of their duty, these youths hurried into the hills, with a bustling manner, as if the fate of the world depended on their diligence, and, at the same time, with an air of mystery, as great as if they were engaged on secret matters of the state.

At twelve precisely, a drum beat the "long roll" before the "Bold Dragoon," and Richard appeared, accompanied by Captain Hollister, who was clad in his vestments as commander of the "Templeton Light-Infantry," when the former demanded of the latter the aid of the posse comitatus, in enforcing the laws of the country. We have not room to record the speeches of the two gentlemen on this occasion, but they are preserved in the columns of the little blue newspaper, which is yet to be found on file, and are said to be highly creditable to the legal formula of one of the parties, and to the military precision of the other. Every thing had been previously arranged, and as the red-coated drummer continued to roll out his clattering notes, some five-and-twenty privates appeared in the ranks, and arranged themselves in order of battle.

As this corps was composed of volunteers, and was commanded by a man who had passed the first five-and-thirty years of his life in camps and garrisons, it was the nonpareil of military science in that country, and was confidently pronounced, by the judicious part of the Templeton community, to be equal in skill and appearance to any troops in the known world; in physical endowments they were, certainly, much superior! To this assertion there were but three dissenting voices, and one dissenting opinion. The opinion belonged to Marmaduke, who, however, saw no necessity for its promulgation. Of the voices, one, and that a pretty loud one, came from the spouse of the commander himself, who frequently reproached her husband for condescending to lead such an irregular band of warriors, after he had filled the honourable station of sergeant-major to a dashing corps of Virginian cavalry through much of the recent war.

Another of these sceptical sentiments was invariably expressed by Mr. Pump, whenever the company paraded, generally in some such terms as these, which were uttered with that sort of meekness that a native of the island of our forefathers is apt to assume, when he condescends to praise the customs or character of her truant progeny—

"It's mayhap that they knows sum'mat about loading and firing, d'ye see; but as for working ship! why a corporal's guard of the Boadishey's marines would back and fill on their quarters in such a manner as to surround and captivate them all in half a glass." As there was no one to deny this assertion, the marines of the Boadicea were held in a corresponding degree of estimation.

The third unbeliever was Monsieur Le Quoi, who merely whispered to the Sheriff, that the corps was one of the finest he had ever seen, second only to the Mousquetaires of Le Bon Louis! However, as Mrs. Hollister thought there was something like actual service in the present appearances, and was, in consequence, too busily engaged with certain preparations of her own, to make her comments; as Benjamin was absent, and Monsieur Le Quoi too happy to find fault with any thing, the corps escaped criticism and comparison altogether on this momentous day, when they certainly had greater need of self-confidence, than on any other previous occasion. Marmaduke was said to be again closeted with Mr. Van der School, and no interruption was offered to the movements of the troops. At two o'clock precisely the corps shouldered arms, beginning on the right wing, next to the veteran, and carrying the motion through to the left with great regularity. When each musket was quietly fixed in its proper situation, the order was given to wheel to the left, and march. As this was bringing raw troops, at once, to face their enemy, it is not to be supposed that the manœuvre was executed with their usual accuracy, but as the music struck up the inspiring air of Yankee-doodle, and Richard, accompanied by Mr. Doolittle, preceded the troops boldly down the street, Captain Hollister led on, with his head elevated to forty-five degrees, with a little, low cocked hat, perched on his crown, carrying a tremendous dragoon sabre at a poise, and trailing at his heels a huge steel scabbard, that had war in its very clattering. There was a good deal of difficulty in getting all the platoons (there were six) to look the same way; but, by the time they reached the defile of the bridge, the troops were in sufficiently compact order. In this manner they marched up the hill to the summit of the mountain, no other alteration taking place in the disposition of the forces, excepting that a mutual complaint was made by the Sheriff and the magistrate, of a failure in wind, which gradually brought these gentlemen to the rear. It will be unnecessary to detail the minute movements that succeeded. We shall briefly say, that the scouts came in and reported, that, so far from retreating, as had been anticipated, the fugitives had evidently gained a knowledge of the attack, and were fortifying for a desperate resistance. This intelligence certainly made a material change, not only in the plans of the leaders, but in the countenances of the soldiery also. The men looked at one another with serious faces, and Hiram and Richard begun to consult together, apart.

At this conjuncture, they were joined by Billy Kirby, who came along the highway, with his axe under his arm, as much in advance of his team as Captain Hollister had been of his troops in the ascent. The wood-chopper was amazed at the military array, but the Sheriff eagerly availed himself of this powerful reinforcement, and commanded his assistance in putting the laws in force. Billy held Mr. Jones in too much deference to object; and it was finally arranged that he should be the bearer of a summons to the garrison to surrender, before they proceeded to extremities. The troops now divided, one party being led by the captain, over the Vision, and were brought in on the left of the cave, while the remainder advanced upon its right, under the orders of the lieutenant. Mr.

Jones and Dr. Todd, for the surgeon was in attendance also, appeared on the platform of rock, immediately over the heads of the garrison, though out of their sight. Hiram thought this approaching too near, and he therefore accompanied Kirby along the side of the hill, to within a safe distance of the fortifications, where he took shelter behind a tree. Most of the men discovered great accuracy of eye in bringing some object in range between them and their enemy, and the only two of the besiegers, who were left in plain sight of the besieged, were Captain Hollister on one side, and the woodchopper on the other. The veteran stood up boldly to the front, supporting his heavy sword, in one undeviating position, with his eye fixed firmly on his enemy, while the huge form of Billy was placed in that kind of quiet repose, with either hand thrust into his bosom, bearing his axe under his right arm, which permitted him, like his own oxen, to rest standing. So far, not a word had been exchanged between the belligerents. The besieged had drawn together a pile of black logs and branches of trees, which they had formed into a chevaux-de-frize, making a little circular abbatis, in front of the entrance to the cave. As the ground was steep and slippery in every direction around the place, and Benjamin appeared behind the works on one side, and Natty on the other, the arrangement was by no means contemptible, especially as the front was sufficiently guarded by the difficulty of the approach. By this time, Kirby had received his orders, and he advanced coolly along the mountain, picking his way with the same indifference as if he were pursuing his ordinary business. When he was within a hundred feet of the works, the long and much dreaded rifle of the Leather-stocking was seen issuing from the parapet, and his voice cried aloud—

"Keep off! Billy Kirby, keep off! I wish ye no harm; but if a man of ye all comes a step nigher, there'll be blood spilt atwixt us. God forgive the one that draws it first; but so it must be."

"Come, old chap," said Billy, good-naturedly, "don't be crabbed, but hear what a man has got to say. I've no concarn in the business, only to see right 'twixt man and man; and I don't kear the valie of a beetle-ring which gets the better; but there's Squire Doolittle, yonder behind the beech sapling, he has invited me to come in and ask you to give up to the law—that's all."

"I see the varmint! I see his clothes!" cried the indignant Natty; "and if he'll only show so much flesh as will bury a rifle bullet, thirty to the pound, I'll make him feel me. Go away, Billy, I bid ye; you know my aim, and I bear you no malice."

"You over calkilate your aim, Natty," said the other, as he stepped behind a pine that stood near him, "if you think to shoot a man through a tree with a three foot butt. I can lay this tree-top right across you, in ten minutes, by any man's watch, and in less time, too; so be civil—I want no more than what's right."

There was a simple seriousness in the countenance of Natty, that showed he was much in earnest; but it was, also, evident that he was reluctant to shed human blood. He answered the vaunt of the wood-chopper, by saying—

"I know you drop a tree where you will, Billy Kirby; but if you show a hand, or an arm, in doing it, there'll be bones to be set, and blood to stanch. If it's only to get into the cave that ye want, wait till a two hours' sun, and you may enter it in welcome; but come in now you shall not. There's one dead body, already, lying on the cold rocks, and there's another in which the life can hardly be said to stay. If you will come in, there'll be dead without as well as within."

The wood-chopper stept out fearlessly from his cover, and cried—

"That's fair; and what's fair, is right. He wants you to stop till it's two hours to sun-down; and I see reason in the thing. A man can give up when he's wrong, if you don't crowd him too hard; but you crowd a man, and he gets to be like a stubborn ox—the more you beat, the worse he kicks."

The sturdy notions of independence maintained by Billy, neither suited the emergency, nor the impatience of Mr. Jones, who was burning with a desire to examine the hidden mysteries of the cave. He, therefore, interrupted this amicable dialogue with his own voice.

"I command you, Nathaniel Bumppo, by my authority, to surrender your person to the law," he cried. "And I command you, gentlemen, to aid me in performing my duty. Benjamin Penguillan, I arrest you, and order you to follow me to the gaol of the county, by virtue of this warrant."

"I'd follow ye, Squire Dickens," said Benjamin, removing the pipe from his mouth, (for during the whole scene the ex-major domo had been very composedly smoking,) "Ay! I'd sail in your wake, to the end of the world, if-so-be that there was such a place, which there isn't, seeing that it's round. Now, mayhap, Master Hollister, having lived all your life on shore, you is'nt acquainted that the world, d'ye-see—"

"Surrender!" interrupted the veteran, in a voice that startled his hearers, and which actually caused his own forces to recoil several paces; "Surrender, Benjamin Penguillum, or expect no quarter."

"Damn your quarter," said Benjamin, rising from the log on which he was seated, and taking a squint along the barrel of the swivel, which had been brought on the hill, during the night, and now formed the means of defence on his side of the works. "Look you, Master, or Captain, thoff I questions if ye know the name of a rope, except the one that's to hang ye, there's no need of singing out, as if ye was hailing a deaf man on a top-gallant-yard. Mayhap you think you've got my true name in your sheep-skin; but what British sailor finds it worth while to sail in these seas, without a sham on his stern, in case of need, d'ye-see. If you call me Penguillan, you calls me by the name of the man on whose land, d'ye-see, I hove into daylight; and he was a gentleman; and that's more than my worst enimy will say of any of the family of Benjamin Stubbs."

"Send the warrant round to me, and I'll put in an alias," cried Hiram, from behind his cover.

"Put in a jackass, and you'll put in yourself, Mister Doo-but-little," shouted Benjamin, who kept squinting along his little iron tube, with great steadiness.

"I give you but one moment to yield," cried Richard. "Benjamin! Benjamin! This is not the gratitude I expected from you."

"I tell you, Richard Jones," said Natty, who dreaded the Sheriff's influence over his comrade; "though the canister the gall brought, be lost, there's powder enough in the cave to lift the rock you stand on. I'll take off my roof, if you don't hold your peace."

"I think it beneath the dignity of my office to parley further with the prisoners," the Sheriff observed to his companion, while they both retired with a precipitancy that Captain Hollister mistook for the signal to advance.

"Charge baggonet!" shouted the veteran; "march!"

Although this signal was certainly expected, it took the assailed a little by surprise, and the veteran approached the works, crying, "courage, my brave lads! give them no quarter unless they surrender," and struck a furious blow upwards with his sabre that would have divided the steward in moieties, by subjecting him to the process of decapitation, but for the fortunate interference of the muzzle of the swivel. As it was, the gun was dismounted at the critical moment that Benjamin was applying his pipe to the priming, and in consequence, some five or six dozen of rifle bullets were projected into the air, in, nearly, a perpendicular line. Philosophy teaches us that the atmosphere will not retain lead; and two pounds of the metal moulded into bullets, of thirty to the pound, after describing an ellipsis in their journey, returned to the earth, rattling among the branches of the trees directly over the heads of the troops stationed in the rear of their captain. Much of the success of an attack made by irregular soldiers, depends on the direction in which they are first got in motion. In the present instance, it was retrograde, and in less than a minute after the bellowing report of the swivel among the rocks and caverns, the whole weight of the attack, from the left, rested on the prowess of the single arm of the veteran. Benjamin received a severe contusion from the recoil of his gun, which produced a short stupor, during which period the ex-steward was prostrate on the ground. Capt. Hollister availed himself of this circumstance to scramble over the breast-work and obtain a footing in the bastion—for such was the nature of the fortress, as connected with the cave. The moment the veteran found himself within the works of his enemy, he rushed to the edge of the fortification, and waving his sabre over his head, shouted—

"Victory! come on, my brave boys, the work's our own!"

All this was perfectly military, and was such an example as

a gallant officer was in some measure bound to exhibit to his men; but the outcry was the unlucky cause of turning the tide of success. Natty, who had been keeping a vigilant eye on the wood-chopper, and the enemy immediately before him, wheeled at this alarm, and was appalled at beholding his comrade on the ground, and the veteran standing on his own bulwark, giving forth the cry of victory! The muzzle of the long rifle was turned instantly towards the captain. There was a moment when the life of the old soldier was in great jeopardy; but the object to shoot at was both too large and too near for the Leather-stocking, who, instead of pulling his trigger, applied the gun to the rear of his enemy, and by a powerful shove, sent him outside of the works with much greater rapidity than he had entered them. The spot on which Capt. Hollister alighted was directly in front, where, as his feet touched the ground, so steep and slippery was the side of the mountain, it seemed to recede from under them. His motion was swift, and so irregular, as utterly to confuse the faculties of the old soldier. During its continuance, he supposed himself to be mounted and charging through the ranks of his enemy. At every tree he made a blow, of course, as at a foot-soldier; and just as he was making the cut "St. George" at a half-burnt sapling, he landed in the highway, and, to his utter amazement, at the feet of his own spouse. When Mrs. Hollister, who was toiling up the hill, followed by at least twenty curious boys, leaning with one hand on the staff with which she ordinarily walked, and bearing in the other an empty bag, witnessed this exploit of her husband, indignation immediately got the better not only of her religion, but of her philosophy.

"Why, Sargeant! is it flying ye are?" she cried—"That I should live to see a husband of mine turn his back to the inimy! and sich a one! Here have I been telling the b'ys as we come along, all about the saige of Yorrektown, and how ye was hurted; and how ye'd be acting the same ag'in the day; and I mate ye retrating jist as the first gun is fired. Och! I may trow away the bag! for if there's plunder 'twill not be the wife of sich as yeerself that will be privileged to be getting the same. They do say too, there's a power of goold and silver in the place—the Lord forgive me for setting my heart on worreldly things; but what falls in the battle, there's Scripter for believing, is the just property of the victor."

"Retreating!" exclaimed the amazed veteran; "where's my horse? he has been shot under me—I—"

"Is the man mad!" interrupted his wife—"divil the horse do ye own, sargeant, and yee're nothing but a shabby captain of malaishy. Och! if the ra'al captain was here, 'tis the other way ye'd be riding, dear, or you would not follow your lader!"

While this worthy couple were thus discussing events, the battle began to rage more violently than ever, above them. When the Leather-stocking saw his enemy fairly under headway, as Benjamin would express it, he gave his attention again to the right wing of the assailants. It would have been easy for Kirby, with his powerful frame, to have seized the moment to scale the bastion, and with his great strength, to have sent both its defenders in pursuit of the veteran; but hostility appeared to be the passion that the wood-chopper indulged the least in, at that moment, for, in a voice that was heard by the retreating left wing, he shouted.

"Hurrah! well done, captain! keep it up! how he handles his bush hook! he makes nothing of a sapling!" and such other encouraging exclamations to the flying veteran, until, overcome by mirth, the good-natured fellow seated himself on the ground, kicking the earth with delight, and giving vent to peal after peal of laughter.

Natty stood all this time in a menacing attitude, with his rifle pointed over the breast-work, watching with a quick and cautious eye the least movement of the assailants. The outcry unfortunately tempted the ungovernable curiosity of Hiram to take a peep from behind his cover, at the state of the battle. Though this evolution was performed with great caution, in protecting his front, he left, like many a better commander, his rear exposed to the attacks of his enemy. Mr. Doolittle belonged physically to a class of his countrymen, to whom nature has denied, in their formation, the use of curved lines. Every thing about him was either straight or angular. But his tailor was a woman who worked like a regimental contractor, by a set of rules that gave the same configuration to the whole human species. Consequently, when Mr. Doolittle leaned forward in the manner described, a loose drapery appeared behind the tree, at which the rifle of Natty was pointed with the quickness of lightning. A less experienced man would have aimed at the flowing robe, which hung like a festoon half way to the earth; but the Leather-stocking knew both the man and his female tailor better, and when the smart report of the rifle was heard, Kirby, who watched the whole manœuvre in breathless expectation, saw the bark fly from the beech, and the cloth, at some distance above the loose folds, wave at the same instant. No battery was ever unmasked with more promptitude than Hiram advanced, from behind the tree, at this summons.

He made two or three steps, with great precision, to the front, and, placing one hand on the afflicted part, stretched forth the other, with a menacing air, towards Natty, and cried aloud—

"Gawl darn ye! this shan't be settled so easy; I'll follow it up from the 'common pleas' to the 'court of errors.' "

Such a shocking imprecation, from the mouth of so orderly a man as Squire Doolittle, with the fearless manner in which he exposed himself, together with, perhaps, the knowledge that Natty's rifle was unloaded, encouraged the troops in the rear, who gave a loud shout, and fired a volley into the tree-tops, after the contents of the swivel. Animated by their own noise, the men now rushed on in earnest, and Billy Kirby, who thought the joke, good as it was, had gone far enough, was in the act of scaling the works, when Judge Temple appeared on the opposite side, exclaiming—

"Silence and peace! why do I see murder and bloodshed attempted! is not the law sufficient to protect itself, that armed bands must be gathered, as in rebellion and war, to see justice performed!"

" 'Tis the posse comitatus," shouted the Sheriff, from a distant rock, "who"——

"Say rather a posse of demons. I command the peace."——

"Hold! shed not blood!" cried a voice from the top of the Vision—"Hold! for the sake of Heaven, fire no more! all shall be yielded! you shall enter the cave!"

Amazement produced the desired effect. Natty, who had reloaded his piece, quietly seated himself on the logs, and rested his head on his hand, while the "Light Infantry" ceased their military movements, and waited the issue in suspense.

In less than a minute Edwards came rushing down the hill, followed by Major Hartmann with a velocity that was surprising for his years. They reached the terrace in an instant, from which the youth led the way, by the hollow in the rock, to the mouth of the cave, into which they both entered; leaving all without silent and gazing after them with astonishment.

Chapter XL

"I am dumb.
Were you the Doctor, and I knew you not!"
The Merchant of Venice, V.i.279–80.

DURING THE FIVE or six minutes that elapsed before the youth and Major re-appeared, Judge Temple and the Sheriff, together with most of the volunteers, ascended to the terrace, where the latter begun to express their conjectures of the result, and to recount their individual services in the conflict. But the sight of the peace-makers, ascending the ravine, shut every mouth.

On a rude chair, covered with undressed deer-skins, they supported a human being, whom they seated carefully and respectfully in the midst of the assembly. His head was covered by long, smooth locks, of the colour of snow. His dress, which was studiously neat and clean, was composed of such fabrics as none but the wealthiest classes wear, but was threadbare and patched; and on his feet were placed a pair of moccasins, ornamented in the best manner of Indian ingenuity. The outlines of his face were grave and dignified, though his vacant eye, which opened and turned slowly to the faces of those around him in unmeaning looks, too surely announced that the period had arrived, when age brings the mental imbecility of childhood.

Natty had followed the supporters of this unexpected object to the top of the cave, and took his station at a little distance behind him, leaning on his rifle, in the midst of his pursuers, with a fearlessness that showed that heavier interests than those which affected himself were to be decided. Major Hartmann placed himself beside the aged man, uncovered, with his whole soul beaming through those eyes which so commonly danced with frolic and humour. Edwards rested with one hand familiarly, but affectionately, on the chair, though his heart was swelling with emotions that denied him utterance.

All eyes were gazing intently; but each tongue continued mute. At length the decrepit stranger, turning his vacant looks from face to face, made a feeble attempt to rise, while a faint smile crossed his wasted face, like an habitual effort at courtesy, as he said, in a hollow, tremulous voice—

"Be pleased to be seated, gentlemen. The council will open immediately. Each one who loves a good and virtuous king, will wish to see these colonies continue loyal. Be seated—I pray you, be seated, gentlemen. The troops shall halt for the night."

"This is the wandering of insanity!" said Marmaduke; "who will explain this scene?"

"No, sir," said Edwards, firmly, "'tis only the decay of nature; who is answerable for its pitiful condition, remains to be shown."

"Will the gentlemen dine with us, my son?" said the old stranger, turning to a voice that he both knew and loved. "Order a repast suitable for his Majesty's officers. You know we have the best of game always at command."

"Who is this man?" asked Marmaduke, in a hurried voice, in which the dawnings of conjecture united with interest to put the question.

"This man!" returned Edwards, calmly, his voice, however, gradually rising as he proceeded; "this man, sir, whom you behold hid in caverns, and deprived of every thing that can make life desirable, was once the companion and counsellor of those who ruled your country. This man, whom you see, helpless and feeble, was once a warrior, so brave and fearless, that even the intrepid natives gave him the name of the Fire-eater. This man, whom you now see destitute of even the ordinary comfort of a cabin in which to shelter his head, was once the owner of great riches; and, Judge Temple, he was the rightful proprietor of this very soil on which we stand. This man was the father of"——

"This, then," cried Marmaduke, with a powerful emotion, "this, then, is the lost Major Effingham!"

"Lost indeed," said the youth, fixing a piercing eye on the other.

"And you! and you!" continued the Judge, articulating with difficulty.

"I am his grandson."

A minute passed in profound silence. All eyes were fixed on

the speakers, and even the old German appeared to wait the issue in deep anxiety. But the moment of agitation soon passed. Marmaduke raised his head from his bosom, where it had sunk, not in shame, but in devout mental thanksgivings, and, as large tears fell over his fine, manly face, he grasped the hand of the youth warmly, and said—

"Oliver, I forgive all thy harshness—all thy suspicions. I now see it all. I forgive thee every thing, but suffering this aged man to dwell in such a place, when not only my habitation, but my fortune, were at his and thy command."

"He's true as ter steel!" shouted Major Hartmann; "titn't I tell't you, lat, dat Marmatuke Temple vast a frient dat woult never fail in ter dime as of neet!"

"It is true, Judge Temple, that my opinions of your conduct have been staggered by what this worthy gentleman has told me. When I found it impossible to convey my grandfather back whence the enduring love of this old man brought him, without detection and exposure, I went to the Mohawk in quest of one of his former comrades, in whose justice I had dependence. He is your friend, Judge Temple, but if what he says be true, both my father and myself may have judged you harshly."

"You name your father!" said Marmaduke, tenderly—"Was he, indeed, lost in the packet?"

"He was. He had left me, after several years of fruitless application and comparative poverty, in Nova-Scotia, to obtain the compensation for his losses, which the British commissioners had at length awarded. After spending a year in England, he was returning to Halifax, on his way to a government, to which he had been appointed, in the West-Indies, intending to go to the place where my grandfather had sojourned during and since the war, and take him with us."

"But, thou!" said Marmaduke, with powerful interest; "I had thought that thou hadst perished with him."

A flush passed over the cheeks of the young man, who gazed about him at the wondering faces of the volunteers, and continued silent. Marmaduke turned to the veteran captain, who just then rejoined his command, and said—

"March thy soldiers back again, and dismiss them; the zeal of the Sheriff has much mistaken his duty. Dr. Todd, I will thank you to attend to the injury which Hiram Doolittle has received in this untoward affair. Richard, you will oblige me by sending up the carriage to the top of the hill. Benjamin, return to your duty in my family."

Unwelcome as these orders were to most of the auditors, the suspicion that they had somewhat exceeded the wholesome restraints of the law, and the habitual respect with which all the commands of the Judge were received, induced a prompt compliance.

When they were gone, and the rock was left to the parties most interested in an explanation, Marmaduke, pointing to the aged Major Effingham, said to his grandson—

"Had we not better remove thy parent from this open place, until my carriage can arrive?"

"Pardon me, sir, the air does him good, and he has taken it whenever there was no dread of a discovery. I know not how to act, Judge Temple; ought I, can I, suffer Major Effingham to become an inmate of your family?"

"Thou shalt be thyself the judge," said Marmaduke. "Thy father was my early friend. He intrusted his fortune to my care. When we separated, he had such confidence in me, that he wished no security, no evidence of the trust, even had there been time or convenience for exacting it.—This thou hast heard?"

"Most truly, sir," said Edwards, or rather Effingham, as we must now call him.

"We differed in politics. If the cause of this country was successful, the trust was sacred with me, for none knew of thy father's interest. If the crown still held its sway, it would be easy to restore the property of so loyal a subject as Col. Effingham.—Is not this plain?"

"The premises are good, sir," continued the youth, with the same incredulous look as before.

"Listen—listen, poy," said the German. "Dere is not a hair as of ter rogue in ter het of ter Tchooge."

"We all know the issue of the struggle," continued Marmaduke, disregarding both; "Thy grandfather was left in Connecticut, regularly supplied by thy father with the means of such a subsistence as suited his wants. This I well knew, though I never had intercourse with him, even in our happiest days. Thy father retired with the troops to prosecute his claims on England. At all events, his losses must be great, for his real estates were sold, and I became the lawful purchaser. It was not unnatural to wish that he might have no bar to its just recovery?"

"There was none, but the difficulty of providing for so many claimants."

"But there would have been one, and an insuperable one, had I announced to the world that I held these estates, multiplied, by the times and my industry, a hundred fold in value, only as his trustee. Thou knowest that I supplied him with considerable sums, immediately after the war."

"You did, until"—

"My letters were returned unopened. Thy father had much of thy own spirit, Oliver; he was sometimes hasty and rash." The Judge continued, in a self-condemning manner—"Perhaps my fault lies the other way; I may possibly look too far ahead, and calculate too deeply. It certainly was a severe trial to allow the man, whom I most loved, to think ill of me for seven years, in order that he might honestly apply for his just remunerations. But had he opened my last letters, thou wouldst have learnt the whole truth. Those I sent him to England, by what my agent writes me, he did read. He died, Oliver, knowing all. He died my friend, and I thought thou hadst died with him."

"Our poverty would not permit us to pay for two passages," said the youth, with the extraordinary emotion with which he ever alluded to the degraded state of his family; "I was left in the Province to wait for his return, and when the sad news of his loss reached me, I was nearly pennyless."

"And what didst thou, boy?" asked Marmaduke, in a faltering voice.

"I took my passage here in search of my grandfather; for I well knew that his resources were gone, with the half-pay of my father. On reaching his abode, I learnt that he had left it in secret; though the reluctant hireling, who had deserted him in his poverty, owned to my urgent entreaties, that he believed he had been carried away by an old man, who had formerly been his servant. I knew at once it was Natty, for my father often"——

"Was Natty a servant of thy grandfather?" exclaimed the Judge.

"Of that too were you ignorant!" said the youth, in evident surprise.

"How should I know it? I never met the Major, nor was the name of Bumppo ever mentioned to me. I knew him only as a man of the woods, and one who lived by hunting. Such men are too common to excite surprise."

"He was reared in the family of my grandfather; served him for many years during their campaigns at the west, where he became attached to the woods; and he was left here as a kind of locum tenens on the lands that old Mohegan (whose life my grandfather once saved) induced the Delawares to grant to him, when they admitted him as an honorary member of their tribe."

"This, then, is thy Indian blood?"

"I have no other," said Edwards, smiling;—"Major Effingham was adopted as the son of Mohegan, who at that time was the greatest man in his nation; and my father, who visited those people when a boy, received the name of the Eagle from them, on account of the shape of his face, as I understand. They have extended his title to me. I have no other Indian blood or breeding; though I have seen the hour, Judge Temple, when I could wish that such had been my lineage and education."

"Proceed with thy tale," said Marmaduke.

"I have but little more to say, sir. I followed to the lake where I had so often been told that Natty dwelt, and found him maintaining his old master in secret; for even he could not bear to exhibit to the world, in his poverty and dotage, a man whom a whole people once looked up to with respect."

"And what did you?"

"What did I! I spent my last money in purchasing a rifle, clad myself in a coarse garb, and learned to be a hunter by the side of Leather-stocking. You know the rest, Judge Temple."

"Ant vere vast olt Fritz Hartmann!" said the German, reproachfully; "didst never hear a name as of olt Fritz Hartmann from ter mout of ter fader, lat?"

"I may have been mistaken, gentlemen," returned the

youth; "but I had pride, and could not submit to such an exposure as this day even has reluctantly brought to light. I had plans that might have been visionary; but, should my parent survive till autumn, I purposed taking him with me to the city, where we have distant relatives, who must have learnt to forget the Tory by this time. He decays rapidly," he continued, mournfully, "and must soon lie by the side of old Mohegan."

The air being pure, and the day fine, the party continued conversing on the rock, until the wheels of Judge Temple's carriage were heard clattering up the side of the mountain, during which time the conversation was maintained with deep interest, each moment clearing up some doubtful action, and lessening the antipathy of the youth to Marmaduke. He no longer objected to the removal of his grandfather, who displayed a childish pleasure when he found himself seated once more in a carriage. When placed in the ample hall of the Mansion-house, the eyes of the aged veteran turned slowly to the objects in the apartment, and a look like the dawn of intellect would, for moments, flit across his features, when he invariably offered some useless courtesies to those near him, wandering, painfully, in his subjects. The exercise and the change soon produced an exhaustion, that caused them to remove him to his bed, where he lay for hours, evidently sensible of the change in his comforts, and exhibiting that mortifying picture of human nature, which too plainly shows that the propensities of the animal continue, even after the nobler part of the creature appears to have vanished.

Until his parent was placed comfortably in bed, with Natty seated at his side, Effingham did not quit him. He then obeyed a summons to the library of the Judge, where he found the latter, with Major Hartmann, waiting for him.

"Read this paper, Oliver," said Marmaduke to him, as he entered, "and thou wilt find that, so far from intending thy family wrong during life, it has been my care to see that justice should be done at even a later day."

The youth took the paper, which his first glance told him was the will of the Judge. Hurried and agitated as he was, he discovered that the date corresponded with the time of the unusual depression of Marmaduke. As he proceeded, his eyes began to moisten, and the hand which held the instrument shook violently.

The will commenced with the usual forms, spun out by the ingenuity of Mr. Van der School; but after this subject was fairly exhausted, the pen of Marmaduke became plainly visible. In clear, distinct, manly, and even eloquent language, he recounted his obligations to Colonel Effingham, the nature of their connexion, and the circumstances in which they separated. He then proceeded to relate the motives of his long silence, mentioning, however, large sums that he had forwarded to his friend, which had been returned, with the letters unopened. After this, he spoke of his search for the grandfather, who had unaccountably disappeared, and his fears that the direct heir of the trust was buried in the ocean with his father.

After, in short, recounting in a clear narrative, the events which our readers must now be able to connect, he proceeded to make a fair and exact statement of the sums left in his care by Col. Effingham. A devise of his whole estate to certain responsible trustees followed; to hold the same for the benefit, in equal moieties, of his daughter, on one part, and of Oliver Effingham, formerly a major in the army of Great Britain, and of his son Edward Effingham, and of his son Edward Oliver Effingham, or to the survivor of them, and the descendants of such survivor, for ever, on the other part. The trust was to endure until 1810, when, if no person appeared, or could be found, after sufficient notice, to claim the moiety so devised, then a certain sum, calculating the principal and interest of his debt to Col. Effingham, was to be paid to the heirs at law of the Effingham family, and the bulk of his estate was to be conveyed in fee to his daughter, or her heirs.

The tears fell from the eyes of the young man, as he read this undeniable testimony of the good faith of Marmaduke, and his bewildered gaze was still fastened on the paper, when a voice, that thrilled on every nerve, spoke, near him, saying,

"Do you yet doubt us, Oliver?"

"I have never doubted *you*!" cried the youth, recovering his recollection and his voice, as he sprung to seize the hand of Elizabeth; "no, not one moment has my faith in you wavered."

"And my father—"

"God bless him!"

"I thank thee, my son," said the Judge, exchanging a warm pressure of the hand with the youth; "but we have both erred; thou hast been too hasty, and I have been too slow. One half of my estates shall be thine as soon as they can be conveyed to thee; and if what my suspicions tell me, be true, I suppose the other must follow speedily." He took the hand which he held, and united it with that of his daughter, and motioned towards the door to the Major.

"I telt you vat, gal!" said the old German, good humouredly; "if I vast, ast I vast, ven I servit mit his grantfader on ter lakes, ter lazy tog shouln't vin ter prize as for nottin."

"Come, come, old Fritz," said the Judge; "you are seventy, not seventeen; Richard waits for you with a bowl of egg-nog, in the hall."

"Richart! ter duyvel!" exclaimed the other, hastening out of the room; "he makes ter nog ast for ter horse. I vilt show ter Sheriff mit my own hants! Ter duyvel! I pelieve he sweetens mit ter yankee melasses!"

Marmaduke smiled and nodded affectionately at the young couple, and closed the door after them. If any of our readers expect that we are going to open it again, for their gratification, they are mistaken.

The tête-à-tête continued for a very unreasonable time; how long we shall not say; but it was ended by six o'clock in the evening, for at that hour Monsieur Le Quoi made his appearance, agreeably to the appointment of the preceding day, and claimed the ear of Miss Temple. He was admitted; when he made an offer of his hand, with much suavity, together with his "amis beeg and leet', his père, his mère, and his sucre-boosh." Elizabeth might, possibly, have previously entered into some embarrassing and binding engagements with Oliver, for she declined the tender of all, in terms as polite, though perhaps a little more decided, than those in which they were made.

The Frenchman soon joined the German and the Sheriff in the hall, who compelled him to take a seat with them at the table, where, by the aid of punch, wine, and egg-nog, they soon extracted from the complaisant Monsieur Le Quoi the nature of his visit. It was evident that he had made the offer, as a duty which a well-bred man owed to a lady in such a retired place, before he left the country, and that his feelings were but very little, if at all, interested in the matter. After a few potations, the waggish pair persuaded the exhilarated Frenchman that there was an inexcusable partiality in offering to one lady, and not extending a similar courtesy to another. Consequently, about nine, Monsieur Le Quoi sallied forth to the Rectory, on a similar mission to Miss Grant, which proved as successful as his first effort in love.

When he returned to the Mansion-house, at ten, Richard and the Major were still seated at the table. They attempted to persuade the Gaul, as the Sheriff called him, that he should next try Remarkable Pettibone. But, though stimulated by mental excitement and wine, two hours of abstruse logic were thrown away on this subject; for he declined their advice, with a pertinacity truly astonishing in so polite a man.

When Benjamin lighted Monsieur Le Quoi from the door, he said, at parting—

"If-so-be, Mounsheer, you'd run alongside Mistress Pretty-bones, as the Squire Dickens was bidding ye, 'tis my notion you'd have been grappled; in which case, d'ye see, you mought have been troubled in swinging clear again in a handsome manner; for thof Miss 'Lizzy and the parson's young 'un be tidy little vessels, that shoot by a body on a wind, Mistress Remarkable is sum'mat of a galliot fashion; when you once takes 'em in tow, they doesn't like to be cast off again."

Chapter XLI

"Yes, sweep ye on!—We will not leave,
For them who triumph, those who grieve.
With that armada gay
Be laughter loud, and jocund shout—
—But with that skiff
Abides the minstrel tale."
Scott, *The Lord of the Isles*, I.xvii.1–4, 11–12.

THE EVENTS of our tale carry us through the summer; and, after making nearly the circle of the year, we must conclude our labours in the delightful month of October. Many important incidents had, however, occurred in the intervening period; a few of which it may be necessary to recount.

The two principal were, the marriage of Oliver and Elizabeth, and the death of Major Effingham. They both took place early in September; and the former preceded the latter only by a few days. The old man passed away like the last glimmering of a taper; and though his death cast a melancholy over the family, grief could not follow such an end.

One of the chief concerns of Marmaduke was to reconcile the even conduct of a magistrate, with the course that his feelings dictated to the criminals. The day succeeding the discovery at the cave, however, Natty and Benjamin re-entered the gaol peaceably, where they continued, well fed and comfortable, until the return of an express to Albany, who brought the Governor's pardon to the Leather-stocking. In the mean time, proper means were employed to satisfy Hiram for the assaults on his person; and on the same day, the two comrades issued together into society again, with their characters not at all affected by the imprisonment.

Mr. Doolittle began to discover that neither his architecture, nor his law, was quite suitable to the growing wealth and intelligence of the settlement; and, after exacting the last cent that was attainable in his compromises, to use the language of the country, he "pulled up stakes," and proceeded further west, scattering his professional science and legal learning through the land; vestiges of both of which are to be discovered there even to the present hour.

Poor Jotham, whose life paid the forfeiture of his folly, acknowledged before he died, that his reasons for believing in a mine, were extracted from the lips of a sybil, who, by looking in a magic glass, was enabled to discover the hidden treasures of the earth. Such superstition was frequent in the new settlements; and after the first surprise was over, the better part of the community forgot the subject. But at the same time that it removed from the breast of Richard a lingering suspicion of the acts of the three hunters, it conveyed a mortifying lesson to him, which brought many quiet hours, in future, to his cousin Marmaduke. It may be remembered that the Sheriff confidently pronounced this to be no "visionary" scheme, and that word was enough to shut his lips, at any time within the next ten years.

Monsieur Le Quoi, who has been introduced to our readers, because no picture of that country would be faithful without some such character, found the island of Martinique, and his "sucre-boosh," in possession of the English; but Marmaduke, and his family, were much gratified in soon hearing that he had returned to his bureau, in Paris; where he afterwards issued yearly bulletins of his happiness, and of his gratitude to his friends in America.

With this brief explanation we must return to our narrative. Let the American reader imagine one of our mildest October mornings, when the sun seems a ball of silvery fire, and the elasticity of the air is felt while it is inhaled; imparting vigour and life to the whole system;—the weather, neither too warm, nor too cold, but of that happy temperature which stirs the blood, without bringing the lassitude of spring.

It was on such a morning, about the middle of the month, that Oliver entered the hall, where Elizabeth was issuing her usual orders for the day, and requested her to join him in a short excursion to the lake-side. The tender melancholy in the manner of her husband, caught the attention of Elizabeth, who instantly abandoned her concerns, threw a light shawl across her shoulders, and concealing her raven hair under a gypsey, she took his arm, and submitted herself, without a question, to his guidance. They crossed the bridge, and had turned from the highway, along the margin of the lake, before a word was exchanged. Elizabeth well knew, by the direction, the object of the walk, and respected the feelings of her companion too much to indulge in untimely conversation. But when they gained the open fields, and her eye roamed over the placid lake, covered with wild fowl, already journeying from the great northern waters, to seek a warmer sun, but lingering to play in the limpid sheet of the Otsego, and to the sides of the mountain, which were gay with the thousand dies of autumn, as if to grace their bridal, the swelling heart of the young wife burst out in speech.

"This is not a time for silence, Oliver!" she said, clinging more fondly to his arm; "every thing in nature seems to speak the praises of the Creator; why should we, who have so much to be grateful for, be silent."

"Speak on," said her husband, smiling; "I love the sounds of your voice. You must anticipate our errand hither; I have told you my plans, how do you like them?"

"I must first see them," returned his wife. "But I have had my plans, too; it is time I should begin to divulge them."

"You! It is something for the comfort of my old friend Natty, I know."

"Certainly of Natty; but we have other friends besides the Leather-stocking, to serve. Do you forget Louisa, and her father?"

"No, surely; have I not given one of the best farms in the county to the good divine. As for Louisa, I should wish you to keep her always near us."

"You do," said Elizabeth, slightly compressing her lips; "but poor Louisa may have other views for herself; she may wish to follow my example, and marry."

"I don't think it," said Effingham, musing a moment; "I really don't know any one hereabouts good enough for her."

"Perhaps not here; but there are other places besides Templeton, and other churches besides 'New St. Paul's.' "

"Churches, Elizabeth! you would not wish to lose Mr. Grant, surely! though simple, he is an excellent man. I shall never find another who has half the veneration for my orthodoxy. You would humble me from a saint to a very common sinner."

"It must be done, sir," returned the lady, with a half-concealed smile, "though it degrades you from an angel to a man."

"But you forget the farm."

"He can lease it, as others do. Besides, would you have a clergyman toil in the fields!"

"Where can he go? you forget Louisa."

"No, I do not forget Louisa," said Elizabeth, again compressing her beautiful lips. "You know, Effingham, that my father has told you that I ruled him, and that I should rule you. I am now about to exert my power."

"Any thing, any thing, dear Elizabeth, but not at the expense of us all; not at the expense of your friend."

"How do you know, sir, that it will be so much at the expense of my friend?" said the lady, fixing her eyes with a searching look on his countenance, where they met only the unsuspecting expression of manly regret.

"How do I know it! why, it is natural that she should regret us."

"It is our duty to struggle with our natural feelings," returned the lady; "and there is but little cause to fear that such a spirit as Louisa's will not effect it."

"But what is your plan?"

"Listen, and you shall know. My father has procured a call for Mr. Grant to one of the towns on the Hudson, where he can live more at his ease than in journeying through these woods; where he can spend the evening of his life in comfort and quiet; and where his daughter may meet with such society, and form such a connexion, as may be proper for one of her years and character."

"Bess! you amaze me! I did not think you had been such a manager!"

"Oh! I manage more deeply than you imagine, sir," said the wife, archly smiling, again; "but it is my will, and it is your duty to submit,—for a time at least."

Effingham laughed; but as they approached the end of their walk, the subject was changed by common consent.

The place at which they arrived was the little spot of level ground where the cabin of the Leather-stocking had so long stood. Elizabeth found it entirely cleared of rubbish, and beautifully laid down in turf, by the removal of sods, which, in common with the surrounding country, had grown gay, under the influence of profuse showers, as if a second spring had passed over the land. This little place was surrounded by a circle of mason-work, and they entered by a small gate, near which, to the surprise of both, the rifle of Natty was leaning against the wall. Hector and the slut reposed on the grass by its side, as if conscious that, however altered, they were lying on ground, and were surrounded by objects, with which they were familiar. The hunter himself was stretched on the earth, before a head-stone of white marble, pushing aside with his fingers the long grass that had already sprung up from the luxuriant soil around its base, apparently to lay bare the inscription. By the side of this stone, which was a simple slab at the head of a grave, stood a rich monument, decorated with an urn, and ornamented with the chisel.

Oliver and Elizabeth approached the graves, with a light tread, unheard by the old hunter, whose sunburnt face was working, and whose eyes twinkled as if something impeded their vision. After some little time, Natty raised himself slowly from the ground, and said aloud—

"Well, well—I'm bold to say it's all right! There's something that I suppose is reading; but I can't make any thing of it; though the pipe, and the tomahawk, and the moccasins, be pretty well—pretty well, for a man that, I dares to say, never seed 'ither of the things. Ah's me! there they lie, side by side, happy enough! Who will there be to put me in the 'arth, when my times comes!"

"When that unfortunate hour arrives, Natty, friends shall not be wanting to perform the last offices for you," said Oliver, a little touched at the hunter's soliloquy.

The old man turned, without manifesting surprise, for he had got the Indian habits in this particular, and running his hand under the bottom of his nose, seemed to wipe away his sorrow with the action.

"You've come out to see the graves, children, have ye?" he said; "well, well, they're wholesome sights to young as well as old."

"I hope they are fitted to your liking," said Effingham; "no one has a better right than yourself to be consulted in the matter."

"Why, seeing that I an't used to fine graves," returned the old man, "it is but little matter consarning my taste. Ye laid the Major's head to the west, and Mohegan's to the east, did ye, lad?"

"At your request it was done."

"It's so best," said the hunter; "they thought they had to journey different ways, children; though there is One greater than all, who'll bring the just together, at his own time, and who'll whiten the skin of a black-moor, and place him on a footing with princes."

"There is but little reason to doubt that," said Elizabeth, whose decided tones were changed to a soft, melancholy voice; "I trust we shall all meet again, and be happy together."

"Shall we, child! shall we!" exclaimed the hunter, with unusual fervour; "there's comfort in that thought too. But before I go, I should like to know what 'tis you tell these people, that be flocking into the country like pigeons in the spring, of the old Delaware, and of the bravest white man that ever trod the hills."

Effingham and Elizabeth were surprised at the manner of the Leather-stocking, which was unusually impressive and solemn; but attributing it to the scene, the young man turned to the monument, and read aloud—

"Sacred to the memory of Oliver Effingham, Esquire, formerly a Major in his B. Majesty's 60th Foot; a soldier of tried valour; a subject of chivalrous loyalty; and a man of honesty. To these virtues, he added the graces of a christian. The morning of his life was spent in honour, wealth, and power; but its evening was obscured by poverty, neglect, and disease, which were alleviated only by the tender care of his old, faithful, and upright friend and attendant, Nathaniel Bumppo. His descendants rear this stone to the virtues of the master, and to the enduring gratitude of the servant."

The Leather-stocking started at the sound of his own name, and a smile of joy illumined his wrinkled features, as he said—

"And did ye say it, lad? have ye got then the old man's name cut in the stone, by the side of his master's? God bless ye, children! 'twas a kind thought, and kindness goes to the heart as life shortens."

Elizabeth turned her back to the speakers. Effingham made a fruitless effort before he succeeded in saying—

"It is there cut in plain marble; but it should have been written in letters of gold!"

"Show me the name, boy," said Natty, with simple eagerness; "let me see my own name placed in such honour. 'Tis a gin'rous gift to a man who leaves none of his name and family behind him in a country, where he has tarried so long."

Effingham guided his finger to the spot, and Natty followed the windings of the letters to the end, with deep interest, when he raised himself from the tomb, and said—

"I suppose it's all right, and it's kindly thought, and kindly done! But what have ye put over the Red-skin?"

"You shall hear"—

"This stone is raised to the memory of an Indian Chief, of the Delaware tribe, who was known by the several names of John Mohegan; Mohican"—

"Mo-hee-can, lad; they call theirselves! 'hee-can."

"Mohican; and Chingagook"—

" 'Gach, boy;—'gach-gook; Chingachgook; which, intarpreted, means Big-sarpent. The name should be set down right, for an Indian's name has always some meaning in it."

"I will see it altered. 'He was the last of his people who continued to inhabit this country; and it may be said of him, that his faults were those of an Indian, and his virtues those of a man.' "

"You never said truer word, Mr. Oliver; ah's me! if you had know'd him as I did, in his prime, in that very battle, where, the old gentleman who sleeps by his side, sav'd his life, when them thieves, the Iroquois, had him at the stake, you'd have said all that, and more too. I cut the thongs with this very hand, and gave him my own tomahawk and knife, seeing that the rifle was always my fav'rite weepon. He did lay about him like a man! I met him as I was coming home from the trail, with eleven Mingo scalps on his pole. You needn't shudder, Madam Effingham, for they was all from shav'd heads and warriors. When I look about me, at these hills, where I used-to could count, sometimes twenty smokes, curling over the tree-tops, from the Delaware camps, it raises mournful thoughts, to think, that not a Red-skin is left of them all; unless it may be a drunken vagabond from the Oneidas, or them Yankee Indians, who, they say, be moving up from the sea-shore; and who belong to none of God's creaters, to my seeming; being, as it were, neither fish nor flesh; neither white-man, nor savage.—Well! well! the time has come at last, and I must go"—

"Go!" echoed Edwards, " whither do you go?"

The Leather-stocking, who had imbibed, unconsciously, many of the Indian qualities, though he always thought of himself, as of a civilized being, compared with even the Delawares, averted his face to conceal the workings of his muscles, as he stooped to lift a large pack from behind the tomb, which he placed deliberately on his shoulders.

"Go!" exclaimed Elizabeth, approaching him, with a hurried step; "you should not venture so far in the woods alone, at your time of life, Natty; indeed, it is imprudent. He is bent, Effingham, on some distant hunting."

"What Mrs. Effingham tells you, is true, Leather-stocking," said Edwards; "there can be no necessity for your submitting to such hardships now! So throw aside your pack, and confine your hunt to the mountains near us, if you will go."

"Hardship! 'tis a pleasure, children, and the greatest that is left me on this side the grave."

"No, no; you shall not go to such a distance," cried Elizabeth, laying her white hand on his deer-skin pack; "I am right! I feel his camp-kettle and a canister of powder! he must not be suffered to wander so far from us, Oliver; remember how suddenly Mohegan dropp'd away."

"I know'd the parting would come hard, children; I know'd it would!" said Natty, "and so I got aside to look at the graves by myself, and thought if I left ye the keep-sake which the Major gave me, when we first parted in the woods, ye wouldn't take it unkind, but would know, that let the old man's body go where it might, his feelings staid behind him."

"This means something more than common!" exclaimed the youth; " where is it, Natty, that you purpose going?"

The hunter drew nigh him with a confident reasoning air, as if what he had to say would silence all objections, and replied—

"Why, lad, they tell me, that on the Big-lakes, there's the best of hunting, and a great range, without a white man on it, unless it may be one like myself. I'm weary of living in clearings, and where the hammer is sounding in my ears from sun-rise to sun-down. And though I'm much bound to ye both, children; I wouldn't say it if it wasn't true; I crave to go into the woods ag'in, I do."

"Woods!" echoed Elizabeth, trembling with her feelings; "do you not call these endless forests woods?"

"Ah! child, these be nothing to a man that's used to the wilderness. I have took but little comfort sin' your father come on with his settlers; but I wouldn't go far, while the life was in the body that lies under the sod there. But now he's gone, and Chingachgook is gone; and you be both young and happy. Yes! the big-house has rung with merriment this month past! And now, I thought, was the time, to try to get a little comfort, in the close of my days. Woods! indeed! I doesn't call these woods, Madam Effingham, where I lose myself, every day of my life, in the clearings."

"If there be any thing wanting to your comfort, name it, Leather-stocking; if it be attainable, it is yours."

"You mean all for the best, lad; I know it; and so does Madam, too; but your ways isn't my ways. 'Tis like the dead there, who thought, when the breath was in them, that one went east and one went west, to find their heavens; but they'll meet at last; and so shall we, children.—Yes, ind as you've begun, and we shall meet in the land of the just, at last."

"This is so new! so unexpected!" said Elizabeth, in almost breathless excitement; "I had thought you meant to live with us, and die with us, Natty."

"Words are of no avail!" exclaimed her husband; "the habits of forty years are not to be dispossessed by the ties of a day. I know you too well to urge you further, Natty; unless you will let me build you a hut, on one of the distant hills, where we can sometimes see you, and know that you are comfortable."

"Don't fear for the Leather-stocking, children; God will see that his days be provided for, and his ind happy. I know you mean all for the best, but our ways doesn't agree. I love the woods, and ye relish the face of man; I eat when hungry and drink when a-dry, and ye keep stated hours and rules; nay, nay, you even over-feed the dogs, lad, from pure kindness; and hounds should be gaunty to run well. The meanest of God's creaters be made for some use, and I'm form'd for the wilderness; if ye love me, let me go where my soul craves to be ag'in!"

The appeal was decisive; and not another word of entreaty, for him to remain, was then uttered; but Elizabeth bent her head to her bosom and wept, while her husband dashed away the tears from his eyes, and, with hands that almost refused to perform their office, he produced his pocket-book, and extended a parcel of bank-notes to the hunter.

"Take these," he said, "at least, take these; secure them about your person, and, in the hour of need, they will do you good service."

The old man took the notes, and examined them with a curious eye.

"This, then, is some of the new-fashioned money that they've been making at Albany, out of paper! It can't be worth much to they that hasn't larning! No, no, lad—take back the stuff; it will do me no sarvice. I took kear to get all the Frenchman's powder, afore he broke up, and they say lead grows where I'm going. It isn't even fit for wads, seeing that I use none but leather!—Madam Effingham, let an old man kiss your hand, and wish God's choicest blessings on you and your'n."

"Once more let me beseech you, stay!" cried Elizabeth. "Do not, Leather-stocking, leave me to grieve for the man who has twice rescued me from death, and who has served those I love so faithfully. For my sake, if not for your own, stay. I shall see you, in those frightful dreams that still haunt my nights, dying in poverty and age, by the side of those terrific beasts you slew. There will be no evil that sickness, want, and solitude can inflict, that my fancy will not conjure as your fate. Stay with us, old man; if not for your own sake, at least for ours."

"Such thoughts and bitter dreams, Madam Effingham,"

returned the hunter, solemnly, "will never haunt an innocent parson long. They'll pass away with God's pleasure. And if the cat-a-mounts be yet brought to your eyes in sleep, 'tis not for my sake, but to show you the power of him that led me there to save you. Trust in God, Madam, and your honourable husband, and the thoughts for an old man like me can never be long nor bitter. I pray that the Lord will keep you in mind—the Lord that lives in clearings as well as in the wilderness—and bless you, and all that belong to you, from this time, till the great day when the whites shall meet the red-skins in judgment, and justice shall be the law, and not power."

Elizabeth raised her head, and offered her colourless cheek to his salute; when he lifted his cap, and touched it respectfully. His hand was grasped with convulsive fervour by the youth, who continued silent. The hunter prepared himself for his journey, drawing his belt tighter, and wasting his moments in the little reluctant movements of a sorrowful departure. Once or twice he essayed to speak, but a rising in his throat prevented it. At length he shouldered his rifle, and cried, with a clear huntsman's call, that echoed through the woods—

"He-e-e-re, he-e-e-re, pups—away, dogs, away;—ye'll be foot-sore afore ye see the ind of the journey!"

The hounds leaped from the earth at this cry, and, scenting around the graves and the silent pair, as if conscious of their own destination, they followed humbly at the heels of their master. A short pause succeeded, during which even the youth concealed his face on his grandfather's tomb. When the pride of manhood, however, had suppressed the feelings of nature, he turned to renew his entreaties, but saw that the cemetery was occupied only by himself and his wife.

"He is gone!" cried Effingham.

Elizabeth raised her face, and saw the old hunter standing, looking back for a moment, on the verge of the wood. As he caught their glances, he drew his hard hand hastily across his eyes again, waved it on high for an adieu, and, uttering a forced cry to his dogs, who were crouching at his feet, he entered the forest.

This was the last that they ever saw of the Leather-stocking, whose rapid movements preceded the pursuit which Judge Temple both ordered and conducted. He had gone far towards the setting sun,—the foremost in that band of Pioneers, who are opening the way for the march of the nation across the continent.

Finis.

THE LAST OF THE MOHICANS

A Narrative of 1757

"Mislike me not, for my complexion,
The shadowed livery of the burnished sun."
The Merchant of Venice, II.i.1–2.

Preface

THE READER, who takes up these volumes, in expectation of finding an imaginary and romantic picture of things which never had an existence, will probably lay them aside, disappointed. The work is exactly what it professes to be in its title-page—a narrative. As it relates, however, to matters which may not be universally understood, especially by the more imaginative sex, some of whom, under the impression that it is a fiction, may be induced to read the book, it becomes the interest of the author to explain a few of the obscurities of the historical allusions. He is admonished to discharge this duty, by the bitter cup of experience, which has often proved to him, that however ignorant the public may be of any thing before it is presented to their eyes, the instant it has been subjected to that terrible ordeal, they, individually and collectively, and he may add, intuitively, know more of it than the agent of the discovery; and yet, that, in direct opposition to this incontrovertible fact, it is a very unsafe experiment either for a writer or a projector to trust to the inventive powers of any one but himself. Therefore, nothing which can well be explained, should be left a mystery. Such an expedient would only impart a peculiar pleasure to readers of that description, who find a strange gratification in spending more of their time in making books, than of their money in buying them. With this preliminary explanation of his reasons for introducing so many unintelligible words, in the very threshold of his undertaking, the author will commence his task. Of course, nothing will, or need be told, with which any one, in the smallest degree acquainted with Indian antiquities, is not already familiar.

The greatest difficulty with which the student of Indian history has to contend, is the utter confusion that pervades the names. When, however, it is recollected, that the Dutch, the English, and the French, each took a conqueror's liberty in this particular; that the natives themselves not only speak different languages, and even dialects of those languages, but that they are also fond of multiplying their appellations, the difficulty is more a matter of regret than of surprise. It is hoped, that whatever other faults may exist in the following pages, their obscurity will be thought to arise from this fact.

The Europeans found that immense region which lies between the Penobscot and the Potomac, the Atlantic and the Mississippi, in the possession of a people who sprang from the same stock. In one or two points of this immense boundary, their limits may have been a little extended or curtailed, by the surrounding nations; but such, in general terms, was the extent of their territory. The generic name of this people was the Wapanachki. They were fond, however, of calling themselves the "Lenni Lenape," which of itself signifies, an "unmixed people." It would far exceed the information of the author, to enumerate a moiety of the communities, or tribes, into which this race of beings was subdivided. Each tribe had its name, its chiefs, its hunting grounds, and, frequently, its dialect. Like the feudal princes of the old world, they fought among themselves, and exercised most of the other privileges of sovereignty. Still, they admitted the claims of a common origin, a similar language, and of that moral interest, which was so faithfully and so wonderfully transmitted through their traditions. One branch of this numerous people was seated on a beautiful river, known as the "Lenapewihittuck," where the "long house," or Great Council Fire, of the nation was universally admitted to be established.

The tribe that possessed the country which now composes the south-western parts of New-England, and that portion of New-York that lies east of the Hudson, and the country even much farther to the south, was a mighty people, called the "Mahicanni," or, more commonly, the "Mohicans." The latter word has since been corrupted by the English, into "Mohegan."

The Mohicans were again subdivided. In their collective capacity, they even disputed the point of antiquity with their neighbours, who possessed the "long house;" but their claim to be the "eldest son" of their "grandfather," was freely allowed. Of course, this portion of the original proprietors of the soil was the first dispossessed by the whites. The few of them that now remain, are chiefly scattered among other tribes, and retain no other memorials of their power and greatness, than their melancholy recollections.

The tribe that guarded the sacred precincts of the council house, was distinguished for ages by its flattering title of the "Lenape;" but after the English changed the appellation of their river to "Delaware," they came gradually to be known by the same name. In the use of these terms, however, great delicacy of perception was observed among themselves. These shades of expression pervade their language, tempering all their communications, and frequently imparting its pathos or energy to their eloquence.

For many hundreds of miles along the northern boundaries of the Lenape, was seated another people, similarly situated as to subdivisions, descent, and language. They were called by their neighbours the "Mengwe." These northern savages were, for a time, however, less powerful, and less united, than the Lenape. In order to obviate this disadvantage, five of the most powerful and warlike of their tribes, who lay nearest to the council house of their enemies, confederated for the purposes of mutual defence; being, in truth, the oldest United Republics of which the history of North America furnishes any evidence. These tribes were the Mohawks, the Oneidas, the Senecas, the Cayugas, and the Onondagas. At a later day, a straggling band of their race, which had "gone nigher to the sun," was reclaimed, and admitted into a full communion of all their political privileges. This tribe (the Tuscarora) increased their number so far, that the English changed the appellation they had given the confederation, from the "Five" to the "Six Nations." It will be seen, in the course of the narrative, that the word nation is sometimes applied to a community, and sometimes to the people, in their most extended sense. The Mengwe were often called by their Indian neighbours, the "Maquas," and frequently, by way of contempt, "Mingoes." The French gave them the name of "Iroquois," which was probably a corruption of one of their own terms.

There is a well authenticated and disgraceful history of the means by which the Dutch on one side, and the Mengwe on the other, succeeded in persuading the Lenape to lay aside their arms, trusting their defence entirely to the latter, and becoming, in short, in the figurative language of the natives, "women." The policy on the part of the Dutch was a safe one, however generous it may have been. From that moment may be dated the downfall of the greatest and most civilized of the Indian nations, that existed within the limits of the present United States. Robbed by the whites, and murdered and oppressed by the savages, they lingered for a time around their council-fire, but finally broke off in bands, and sought refuge in the western wilds. Like the lustre of the dying lamp, their glory shone the brightest as they were about to become extinct.

Much more might be said concerning this interesting people, especially of their later history, but it is believed not to be essential to the plan of the present work. Since the death of the pious, the venerable, and the experienced Heckewelder, a fund of information of this nature has been extinguished, which, it is feared, can never again be collected in one individual. He laboured long and ardently in their behalf, and not less to vindicate their fame, than to improve their moral condition.

With this brief introduction to his subject, then, the author commits his book to the reader. As, however, candour, if not justice, requires such a declaration at his hands, he will advise all young ladies, whose ideas are usually limited by the four walls of a comfortable drawing room; all single gentlemen, of a certain age, who are under the influence of the winds; and all clergymen, if they have the volumes in hand, with intent to read them, to abandon the design. He gives this advice to such young ladies, because, after they have read the book, they will surely pronounce it shocking; to the bachelors, as it might disturb their sleep; and to the reverend clergy, because they might be better employed.

Introduction

IT IS BELIEVED that the scene of this tale, and most of the information necessary to understand its allusions, are rendered sufficiently obvious to the reader, in the text itself, or in the accompanying notes. Still there is so much obscurity in the Indian traditions, and so much confusion in the Indian names, as to render some explanation useful.

Few men exhibit greater diversity, or, if we may so express it, greater antithesis of character, than the native warrior of North America. In war, he is daring, boastful, cunning, ruthless, self-denying, and self-devoted; in peace, just, generous, hospitable, revengeful, superstitious, modest, and commonly chaste. These are qualities, it is true, which do not distinguish all alike; but they are so far the predominating traits of these remarkable people, as to be characteristic.

It is generally believed that the Aborigines of the American continent have an Asiatic origin. There are many physical as well as moral facts which corroborate this opinion, and some few that would seem to weigh against it.

The colour of the Indian, the writer believes, is peculiar to himself; and while his cheek-bones have a very striking indication of a Tartar origin, his eyes have not. Climate may have had great influence on the former, but it is difficult to see how it can have produced the substantial difference which exists in the latter. The imagery of the Indian, both in his poetry and his oratory, is Oriental,—chastened, and perhaps improved, by the limited range of his practical knowledge. He draws his metaphors from the clouds, the seasons, the birds, the beasts, and the vegetable world. In this, perhaps, he does no more than any other energetic and imaginative race would do, being compelled to set bounds to fancy by experience; but the North American Indian clothes his ideas in a dress that is so different from that of the African, and is Oriental in itself. His language has the richness and sententious fulness of the Chinese. He will express a phrase in a word, and he will qualify the meaning of an entire sentence by a syllable; he will even convey different significations by the simplest inflexions of the voice.

Philologists have said that there are but two or three languages, properly speaking, among all the numerous tribes which formerly occupied the country that now composes the United States. They ascribe the known difficulty one people have in understanding another to corruptions and dialects. The writer remembers to have been present at an interview between two chiefs of the Great Prairies west of the Mississippi, and when an interpreter was in attendance who spoke both their languages. The warriors appeared to be on the most friendly terms, and seemingly conversed much together; yet, according to the account of the interpreter, each was absolutely ignorant of what the other said. They were of hostile tribes, brought together by the influence of the American government; and it is worthy of remark, that a common policy led them both to adopt the same subject. They mutually exhorted each other to be of use in the event of the chances of war throwing either of the parties into the hands of his enemies. Whatever may be the truth, as respects the root and the genius of the Indian tongues, it is quite certain they are now so distinct in their words as to possess most of the disadvantages of strange languages: hence much of the embarrassment that has arisen in learning their histories, and most of the uncertainty which exists in their traditions.

Like nations of higher pretensions, the American Indian gives a very different account of his own tribe or race from that which is given by other people. He is much addicted to over-estimating his own perfections, and to undervaluing those of his rival or his enemy; a trait which may possibly be thought corroborative of the Mosaic account of the creation.

The Whites have assisted greatly in rendering the traditions of the Aborigines more obscure by their own manner of corrupting names. Thus, the term used in the title of this book has undergone the changes of Mahicanni, Mohicans, and Mohegans; the latter being the word commonly used by the Whites. When it is remembered that the Dutch (who first settled New York), the English, and the French, all gave appellations to the tribes that dwelt within the country which is the scene of this story, and that the Indians not only gave different names to their enemies, but frequently to themselves, the cause of the confusion will be understood.

In these pages, Lenni-Lenape, Lenope, Delawares, Wapanachki, and Mohicans, all mean the same people, or tribes of the same stock. The Mengwe, the Maquas, the Mingoes, and the Iroquois, though not all strictly the same, are identified frequently by the speakers, being politically confederated and opposed to those just named. Mingo was a term of peculiar reproach, as were Mengwe and Maqua in a less degree.

The Mohicans were the possessors of the country first occupied by the Europeans in this portion of the continent. They were, consequently, the first dispossessed; and the seemingly inevitable fate of all these people, who disappear before the advances, or it might be termed the inroads of civilisation, as the verdure of their native forests falls before the nipping frost, is represented as having already befallen them. There is sufficient historical truth in the picture to justify the use that has been made of it.

Before closing this introduction, it will not be improper to say a word of an important character of this legend, who is also a conspicuous actor in two other tales of the same writer. To portray an individual as a scout in the wars in which England and France contended for the possession of the American continent, a hunter in that season of activity which so immediately succeeded the peace of 1783, and a lone trapper in the Prairies after the policy of the republic threw open those interminable wastes to the enterprise of the half wild beings who hang between society and the wilderness, is poetically to furnish a witness to the truth of those wonderful alterations which distinguish the progress of the American nation, to a degree that has been hitherto unknown, and to which hundreds of living men might equally speak. In this particular the fiction has no merit as an invention.

Of the character in question, the writer has no more to say, than that he represents a man of native goodness, removed from the temptations of civilised life, though not entirely forgetful of its prejudices and lessons, exposed to the customs of barbarity, and yet perhaps more improved than injured by the association, and betraying the weaknesses as well as the virtues both of his situation and of his birth. It would, perhaps, have been more observant of reality to have drawn him of less moral elevation, but it would have also been less attractive;

and the business of a writer of fiction is to approach, as near as his powers will allow, to poetry. After this avowal, it is scarcely necessary to add, that individual character had little to do with either the conception or the filling up of this fanciful personage. It was believed that enough had been sacrificed to truth in preserving the language and the dramatic keeping necessary to the part.

In point of fact, the country which is the scene of the following tale has undergone as little change, since the historical events alluded to had place, as almost any other district of equal extent within the whole limits of the United States. There are fashionable and well-attended watering-places at and near the spring where Hawk-eye halted to drink, and roads traverse the forests where he and his friends were compelled to journey without even a path. Glenn's has a large village; and while William Henry, and even a fortress of later date, are only to be traced as ruins, there is another village on the shores of the Horican. But, beyond this, the enterprise and energy of a people who have done so much in other places have done little here. The whole of that wilderness, in which the latter incidents of the legend occurred is nearly a wilderness still, though the red man has entirely deserted this part of the state. Of all the tribes named in these pages, there exist only a few half-civilised beings of the Oneidas, on the reservations of their people in New York. The rest have disappeared, either from the regions in which their fathers dwelt, or altogether from the earth.

There is one point on which we would wish to say a word before closing this preface. Hawk-eye calls the *Lac du Saint Sacrement*, the "Horican." As we believe this to be an appropriation of the name that has its origin with ourselves, the time has arrived, perhaps, when the fact should be frankly admitted. While writing this book, fully a quarter of a century since, it occurred to us that the French name of this lake was too complicated, the American too commonplace, and the Indian too unpronounceable, for either to be used familiarly in a work of fiction. Looking over an ancient map, it was ascertained that a tribe of Indians, called "Les Horicans" by the

French, existed in the neighborhood of this beautiful sheet of water. As every word uttered by Natty Bumppo was not to be received as rigid truth, we took the liberty of putting the "Horican" into his mouth, as the substitute for "Lake George." The name has appeared to find favor, and all things considered, it may possibly be quite as well to let it stand, instead of going back to the House of Hanover for the appellation of our finest sheet of water. We relieve our conscience by the confession, at all events, leaving it to exercise its authority as it may see fit.

Chapter I

"Mine ear is open, and my heart prepared;
The worst is worldly loss thou canst unfold:—
Say, is my kingdom lost?"

Richard II, III.ii.93–95.

IT WAS A FEATURE peculiar to the colonial wars of North America, that the toils and dangers of the wilderness were to be encountered, before the adverse hosts could meet. A wide, and, apparently, an impervious boundary of forests, severed the possessions of the hostile provinces of France and England. The hardy colonist, and the trained European who fought at his side, frequently expended months in struggling against the rapids of the streams, or in effecting the rugged passes of the mountains, in quest of an opportunity to exhibit their courage in a more martial conflict. But, emulating the patience and self-denial of the practised native warriors, they learned to overcome every difficulty; and it would seem, that in time, there was no recess of the woods so dark, nor any secret place so lovely, that it might claim exemption from the inroads of those who had pledged their blood to satiate their vengeance, or to uphold the cold and selfish policy of the distant monarchs of Europe.

Perhaps no district, throughout the wide extent of the intermediate frontiers, can furnish a livelier picture of the cruelty and fierceness of the savage warfare of those periods, than the country which lies between the head waters of the Hudson and the adjacent lakes.

The facilities which nature had there offered to the march of the combatants, were too obvious to be neglected. The lengthened sheet of the Champlain stretched from the frontiers of Canada, deep within the borders of the neighbouring province of New-York, forming a natural passage across half the distance that the French were compelled to master in order to strike their enemies. Near its southern termination, it received the contributions of another lake, whose waters were so limpid, as to have been exclusively selected by the Jesuit missionaries, to perform the typical purification of baptism, and to obtain for it the title of the lake "du Saint Sacrement." The less zealous English thought they conferred a sufficient honour on its unsullied fountains, when they bestowed the name of their reigning prince, the second of the House of Hanover. The two united to rob the untutored possessors of its wooded scenery of their native right to perpetuate its original appellation of "Horican."*

Winding its way among countless islands, and imbedded in mountains, the "holy lake" extended a dozen leagues still farther to the south. With the high plain that there interposed itself to the further passage of the water, commenced a portage of as many miles, which conducted the adventurer to the banks of the Hudson, at a point, where, with the usual obstructions of the rapids, or rifts, as they were then termed in the language of the country, the river became navigable to the tide.

While, in the pursuit of their daring plans of annoyance, the restless enterprise of the French even attempted the distant and difficult gorges of the Alleghany, it may easily be imagined that their proverbial acuteness would not overlook the natural advantages of the district we have just described. It became, emphatically, the bloody arena, in which most of the battles for the mastery of the colonies were contested. Forts were erected at the different points that commanded the facilities of the route, and were taken and retaken, rased and rebuilt, as victory alighted on the hostile banners. While the husbandmen shrunk back from the dangerous passes, within the safer boundaries of the more ancient settlements, armies larger than those that had often disposed of the sceptres of the mother countries, were seen to bury themselves in these forests, whence they rarely returned but in skeleton bands, that were haggard with care, or dejected by defeat. Though the arts of peace were unknown to this fatal region, its forests

*As each nation of the Indians had either its language or its dialect, they usually gave different names to the same places, though nearly all of their appellations were descriptive of the object. Thus, a literal translation of the name of this beautiful sheet of water, used by the tribe that dwelt on its banks, would be "The tail of the Lake." Lake George, as it is vulgarly, and now indeed legally, called, forms a sort of tail to Lake Champlain, when viewed on the map. Hence the name.

were alive with men; its glades and glens rang with the sounds of martial music, and the echoes of its mountains threw back the laugh, or repeated the wanton cry, of many a gallant and reckless youth, as he hurried by them, in the noontide of his spirits, to slumber in a long night of forgetfulness.

It was in this scene of strife and bloodshed, that the incidents we shall attempt to relate occurred, during the third year of the war which England and France last waged, for the possession of a country, that neither was destined to retain.

The imbecility of her military leaders abroad, and the fatal want of energy in her councils at home, had lowered the character of Great Britain from the proud elevation on which it had been placed by the talents and enterprise of her former warriors and statesmen. No longer dreaded by her enemies, her servants were fast losing the confidence of self respect. In this mortifying abasement, the colonists, though innocent of her imbecility, and too humble to be the agents of her blunders, were but the natural participators. They had recently seen a chosen army, from that country, which, reverencing as a mother, they had blindly believed invincible—an army led by a chief who had been selected from a crowd of trained warriors for his rare military endowments, disgracefully routed by a handful of French and Indians, and only saved from annihilation by the coolness and spirit of a Virginian boy, whose riper fame has since diffused itself, with the steady influence of moral truth, to the uttermost confines of Christendom.* A wide frontier had been laid naked by this unexpected disaster, and more substantial evils were preceded by a thousand fanciful and imaginary dangers. The alarmed colonists believed that the yells of the savages mingled with every fitful gust of wind that issued from the interminable forests

*Washington: who, after uselessly admonishing the European general of the danger into which he was heedlessly running, saved the remnants of the British army, on this occasion, by his decision and courage. The reputation earned by Washington in this battle was the principal cause of his being selected to command the American armies at a later day. It is a circumstance worthy of observation, that, while all America rang with his well merited reputation, his name does not occur in any European account of the battle; at least, the author has searched for it without success. In this manner does the mother country absorb even the fame, under that system of rule.

of the west. The terrific character of their merciless enemies, increased, immeasurably, the natural horrors of warfare. Numberless recent massacres were still vivid in their recollections; nor was there any ear, in the provinces, so deaf as not to have drunk in with avidity the narrative of some fearful tale of midnight murder, in which the natives of the forests were the principal and barbarous actors. As the credulous and excited traveller related the hazardous chances of the wilderness, the blood of the timid curdled with terror, and mothers cast anxious glances even at those children which slumbered within the security of the largest towns. In short, the magnifying influence of fear began to set at nought the calculations of reason, and to render those who should have remembered their manhood, the slaves of the basest of passions. Even the most confident and the stoutest hearts, began to think the issue of the contest was becoming doubtful; and that abject class was hourly increasing in numbers, who thought they foresaw all the possessions of the English crown in America, subdued by their Christian foes, or laid waste by the inroads of their relentless allies.

When, therefore, intelligence was received at the fort which covered the southern termination of the portage between the Hudson and the lakes, that Montcalm had been seen moving up the Champlain with an army "numerous as the leaves on the trees," its truth was admitted with more of the craven reluctance of fear than with the stern joy that a warrior should feel, in finding an enemy within reach of his blow. The news had been brought towards the decline of a day in midsummer, by an Indian runner, who also bore an urgent request from Munro, the commander of a work on the shore of the "holy lake," for a speedy and powerful reinforcement. It has already been mentioned, that the distance between these two posts was less than five leagues. The rude path which originally formed their line of communication, had been widened for the passage of wagons, so that the distance which had been travelled by the son of the forest in two hours, might easily be effected by a detachment of troops, with their necessary baggage, between the rising and setting of a summer sun. The loyal servants of the British crown had given to one of these forest fastnesses the name of William Henry, and to the other that of Fort Edward; calling each after a favourite prince of the reigning family. The veteran Scotchman, just named, held the first, with a regiment of regulars and a few provincials, a force, really, by far too small to make head against the formidable power that Montcalm was leading to the foot of his earthen mounds. At the latter, however, lay General Webb, who commanded the armies of the king in the northern provinces, with a body of more than five thousand men. By uniting the several detachments of his command, this officer might have arrayed nearly double that number of combatants against the enterprising Frenchman, who had ventured so far from his reinforcements, with an army but little superior in numbers.

But, under the influence of their degraded fortunes, both officers and men appeared better disposed to await the approach of their formidable antagonists within their works, than to resist the progress of their march, by emulating the successful example of the French at Fort du Quesne, and striking a blow on their advance.

After the first surprise of the intelligence had a little abated, a rumour was spread through the intrenched camp, which stretched along the margin of the Hudson, forming a chain of outworks to the body of the fort itself, that a chosen detachment of fifteen hundred men was to depart with the dawn for William Henry, the post at the northern extremity of the portage. That which at first was only rumour, soon became certainty, as orders passed from the quarters of the commander-in-chief to the several corps he had selected for this service, to prepare for their speedy departure. All doubt as to the intention of Webb now vanished, and an hour or two of hurried footsteps and anxious faces succeeded. The novice in the military art flew from point to point, retarding his own preparations by the excess of his violent and somewhat distempered zeal; while the more practised veteran made his arrangements with a deliberation that scorned every appearance of haste; though his sober lineaments, and anxious eye, sufficiently betrayed that he had no very strong professional relish for the, as yet, untried and dreaded warfare of the wilderness. At length the sun set in a flood of glory behind the distant western hills, and as darkness drew its veil around the secluded spot, the sounds of preparation diminished; the last light finally disappeared from the log cabin of some officer; the trees cast their deeper shadows over the mounds, and the rippling stream, and a silence soon pervaded the camp, as deep as that which reigned in the vast forest by which it was environed.

According to the orders of the preceding night, the heavy sleep of the army was broken by the rolling of the warning drums, whose rattling echoes were heard issuing, on the damp morning air, out of every vista of the woods, just as day began to draw the shaggy outlines of some tall pines of the vicinity, on the opening brightness of a soft and cloudless eastern sky. In an instant, the whole camp was in motion; the meanest soldier arousing from his lair to witness the departure of his comrades, and to share in the excitement and incidents of the hour. The simple array of the chosen band was soon completed. While the regular and trained hirelings of the king marched with haughtiness to the right of the line, the less pretending colonists took their humbler position on its left, with a docility that long practice had rendered easy. The scouts departed; strong guards preceded and followed the lumbering vehicles that bore the baggage; and before the gray light of the morning was mellowed by the rays of the sun, the main body of the combatants wheeled into column, and left the encampment with a show of high military bearing, that served to drown the slumbering apprehensions of many a novice, who was now about to make his first essay in arms. While in view of their admiring comrades, the same proud front and ordered array was observed, until the notes of their fifes growing fainter in distance, the forest at length appeared to swallow up the living mass which had slowly entered its bosom.

The deepest sounds of the retiring and invisible column had ceased to be borne on the breeze to the listeners, and the latest straggler had already disappeared in pursuit, but there still remained the signs of another departure, before a log cabin of unusual size and accommodations, in front of which those sentinels paced their rounds, who were known to guard the person of the English general. At this spot were gathered some half dozen horses, caparisoned in a manner which showed that two, at least, were destined to bear the persons of females, of a rank that it was not usual to meet so far in the wilds of the country. A third wore the trappings and arms of an officer of the staff; while the rest, from the plainness of the housings, and the travelling mails with which they were encumbered, were evidently fitted for the reception of as many menials, who were, seemingly, already awaiting the pleasure of those they served. At a respectful distance from this unusual show, were gathered divers groupes of curious idlers; some admiring the blood and bone of the high-mettled military charger, and others gazing at the preparations with the dull wonder of vulgar curiosity. There was one man, however, who, by his countenance and actions, formed a marked exception to those who composed the latter class of spectators, being neither idle, nor seemingly very ignorant.

The person of this individual was to the last degree ungainly, without being in any particular manner deformed. He had all the bones and joints of other men, without any of their proportions. Erect, his stature surpassed that of his fellows; though, seated, he appeared reduced within the ordinary limits of the race. The same contrariety in his members, seemed to exist throughout the whole man. His head was large; his shoulders narrow; his arms long and dangling; while his hands were small, if not delicate. His legs and thighs were thin nearly to emaciation, but of extraordinary length; and his knees would have been considered tremendous, had they not been outdone by the broader foundations on which this false superstructure of blended human orders, was so profanely reared. The ill-assorted and injudicious attire of the individual only served to render his awkwardness more conspicuous. A sky-blue coat, with short and broad skirts and low cape, exposed a long thin neck, and longer and thinner legs, to the worst animadversions of the evil disposed. His nether garment was of yellow nankeen, closely fitted to the shape, and tied at his bunches of knees by large knots of white ribbon, a good deal sullied by use. Clouded cotton stockings, and shoes, on one of the latter of which was a plated spur, completed the costume of the lower extremity of this figure, no curve or angle of which was concealed, but, on the other hand, studiously exhibited, through the vanity or simplicity of its owner. From beneath the flap of an enormous pocket of a soiled vest of embossed silk, heavily ornamented with tarnished silver lace, projected an instrument, which, from being seen in such martial company, might have been easily mistaken for some mischievous and unknown implement of war. Small as it was, this uncommon engine had excited the curiosity of most of the Europeans in the camp, though several of the provincials were seen to handle it, not only without fear, but with the utmost familiarity. A large civil cocked hat, like those worn by clergymen within the last thirty years, surmounted the whole, furnishing dignity to a good natured, and somewhat vacant countenance, that apparently needed such artificial aid to support the gravity of some high and extraordinary trust.

While the common herd stood aloof, in deference to the quarters of Webb, the figure we have described stalked into the centre of the domestics, freely expressing his censures or commendations on the merits of the horses, as by chance they displeased or satisfied his judgment.

"This beast, I rather conclude, friend, is not of home raising, but is from foreign lands, or perhaps from the little island itself, over the blue water?" he said, in a voice as remarkable for the softness and sweetness of its tones, as was his person for its rare proportions: "I may speak of these things and be no braggart, for I have been down at both havens; that which is situate at the mouth of Thames, and is named after the capital of Old England, and that which is called 'Haven,' with the addition of the word 'New;' and have seen the snows and brigantines collecting their droves, like the gathering to the ark, being outward bound to the island of Jamaica, for the purpose of barter and traffic in four-footed animals; but never before have I beheld a beast which verified the true scripture war-horse like this; 'He paweth in the valley, and rejoiceth in his strength; he goeth on to meet the armed men.' 'He saith among the trumpets, ha ha! and he smelleth the battle afar off; the thunder of the captains and the shouting.'—It would seem that the stock of the horse of Israel has descended to our own time; would it not, friend?"

Receiving no reply to this extraordinary appeal, which, in truth, as it was delivered with the vigour of full and sonorous tones, merited some sort of notice, he who had thus sung forth the language of the holy book, turned to the silent figure to whom he had unwittingly addressed himself, and found a new and more powerful subject of admiration in the object that encountered his gaze. His eyes fell on the still, upright, and rigid form of the "Indian runner," who had borne to the camp the unwelcome tidings of the preceding evening. Although in a state of perfect repose, and apparently disregarding, with characteristic stoicism, the excitement and bustle around him, there was a sullen fierceness mingled with the quiet of the savage, that was likely to arrest the attention of much more experienced eyes, than those which now scanned him, in unconcealed amazement. The native bore both the tomahawk and knife of his tribe; and yet his appearance was not altogether that of a warrior. On the contrary, there was an air of neglect about his person, like that which might have proceeded from great and recent exertion, which he had not yet found leisure to repair. The colours of the war-paint had blended in dark confusion about his fierce countenance, and rendered his swarthy lineaments still more savage and repulsive, than if art had attempted an effect, which had been thus produced by chance. His eye, alone, which glistened like a fiery star amid lowering clouds, was to be seen in its state of native wildness. For a single instant, his searching, and yet wary glance, met the wondering look of the other, and then changing its direction, partly in cunning, and partly in disdain, it remained fixed, as if penetrating the distant air.

It is impossible to say what unlooked for remark this short and silent communication, between two such singular men, might have elicited from the white man, had not his active curiosity been again drawn to other objects. A general movement amongst the domestics, and a low sound of gentle voices, announced the approach of those whose presence alone was wanted to enable the cavalcade to move. The simple admirer of the war-horse instantly fell back to a low, gaunt, switch-tailed mare, that was unconsciously gleaning the faded herbage of the camp, nigh by, where, leaning with one elbow on the blanket that concealed an apology for a saddle, he became a spectator of the departure, while a foal was quietly making its morning repast, on the opposite side of the same animal.

A young man, in the dress of an officer, conducted to their steeds two females, who, it was apparent by their dresses, were prepared to encounter the fatigues of a journey in the woods. One, and she was the most juvenile in her appearance, though both were young, permitted glimpses of her dazzling complexion, fair golden hair, and bright blue eyes, to be caught, as she artlessly suffered the morning air to blow aside the green veil, which descended low from her beaver. The flush which still lingered above the pines in the western sky, was not more bright nor delicate than the bloom on her cheek; nor was the opening day more cheering than the animated smile which she bestowed on the youth, as he assisted her into the saddle. The other, who appeared to share equally in the attentions of the young officer, concealed her charms from the gaze of the soldiery with a care that seemed better fitted to the experience of four or five additional years. It could be seen, however, that her person, though moulded with the same exquisite proportions, of which none of the graces were lost by the travelling dress she wore, was rather fuller and more mature than that of her companion.

No sooner were these females seated, than their attendant sprang lightly into the saddle of the war-horse, when the whole three bowed to Webb, who, in courtesy, awaited their parting on the threshold of his cabin, and turning their horses' heads, they proceeded at a slow amble, followed by their train, towards the northern entrance of the encampment. As they traversed that short distance, not a voice was heard amongst them; but a slight exclamation proceeded from the younger of the females, as the Indian runner glided by her, unexpectedly, and led the way along the military road in her front. Though this sudden and startling movement of the Indian, produced no sound from the other, in the surprise, her veil also was allowed to open its folds, and betrayed an indescribable look of pity, admiration and horror, as her dark eye followed the easy motions of the savage. The tresses of this lady were shining and black, like the plumage of the raven. Her complexion was not brown, but it rather appeared charged with the colour of the rich blood, that seemed ready to burst its bounds. And yet there was neither coarseness, nor want of shadowing, in a countenance that was exquisitely regular and dignified, and surpassingly beautiful. She smiled, as if in pity at her own momentary forgetfulness, discovering by the act a row of teeth that would have shamed the purest ivory; when, replacing the veil, she bowed her face, and rode in silence, like one whose thoughts were abstracted from the scene around her.

Chapter II

"Sola, sola, wo ha, ho, sola!"
The Merchant of Venice, V.i.39.

WHILE ONE of the lovely beings we have so cursorily presented to the reader, was thus lost in thought, the other quickly recovered from the alarm which induced the exclamation, and, laughing at her own weakness, she inquired of the youth who rode by her side—

"Are such spectres frequent in the woods, Heyward; or is this sight an especial entertainment, ordered on our behalf. If the latter, gratitude must close our mouths; but if the former, both Cora and I shall have need to draw largely on that stock of hereditary courage of which we boast, even before we are made to encounter the redoubtable Montcalm."

"Yon Indian is a 'runner' of the army, and, after the fashion of his people, he may be accounted a hero," returned the officer. "He has volunteered to guide us to the lake, by a path but little known, sooner than if we followed the tardy movements of the column; and, by consequence, more agreeably."

"I like him not," said the lady, shuddering, partly in assumed, yet more in real terror. "You know him, Duncan, or you would not trust yourself so freely to his keeping?"

"Say, rather, Alice, that I would not trust you. I do know him, or he would not have my confidence, and least of all, at this moment. He is said to be a Canadian, too; and yet he served with our friends the Mohawks, who, as you know, are one of the six allied nations.* He was brought amongst us, as I have

*There existed for a long time a confederation among the Indian tribes which occupied the north-western part of the colony of New York, which was at first known as the "Five Nations." At a later day it admitted another tribe, when the appellation was changed to that of the "Six Nations." The original confederation consisted of the Mohawks, the Oneidas, the Senecas, the Cayugas, and the Onondagoes. The sixth tribe was the Tuscaroras. There are remnants of all these people still living on lands secured to them by the state; but they are daily disappearing, either by deaths or by removals to scenes more congenial to their habits. In a short time there will be no remains of these extraordinary people, in those regions in which they dwelt for centuries, but their names. The state of New York has counties named after all of them but the Mohawks and the Tuscaroras. The second river of that state is called the Mohawk.

heard, by some strange accident, in which your father was interested, and in which the savage was rigidly dealt by—but I forget the idle tale; it is enough, that he is now our friend."

"If he has been my father's enemy, I like him still less!" exclaimed the now really anxious girl. "Will you not speak to him, Major Heyward, that I may hear his tones? Foolish though it may be, you have often heard me avow my faith in the tones of the human voice!"

"It would be in vain; and answered, most probably, by an ejaculation. Though he may understand it, he affects, like most of his people, to be ignorant of the English; and least of all, will he condescend to speak it, now that war demands the utmost exercise of his dignity. But he stops; the private path by which we are to journey is, doubtless, at hand."

The conjecture of Major Heyward was true. When they reached the spot where the Indian stood, pointing into the thicket that fringed the military road, a narrow and blind path, which might, with some little inconvenience, receive one person at a time, became visible.

"Here, then, lies our way," said the young man, in a low voice. "Manifest no distrust, or you may invite the danger you appear to apprehend."

"Cora, what think you?" asked the reluctant fair one. "If we journey with the troops, though we may find their presence irksome, shall we not feel better assurance of our safety?"

"Being little accustomed to the practices of the savages, Alice, you mistake the place of real danger," said Heyward. "If enemies have reached the portage at all, a thing by no means probable, as our scouts are abroad, they will surely be found skirting the column, where scalps abound the most. The route of the detachment is known, while ours, having been determined within the hour, must still be secret."

"Should we distrust the man, because his manners are not our manners, and that his skin is dark!" coldly asked Cora.

Alice hesitated no longer; but giving her Narraganset* a

*In the state of Rhode Island, there is a bay called Narraganset, so named after a powerful tribe of Indians, which formerly dwelt on its banks. Accident, or one of those unaccountable freaks which nature sometimes plays in the animal world, gave rise to a breed of horses which were once well known in America by the name of the Narragansets. They were small, commonly of

smart cut of the whip, she was the first to dash aside the slight branches of the bushes, and to follow the runner along the dark and tangled path-way. The young man regarded the last speaker in open admiration, and even permitted her fairer, though certainly not more beautiful companion, to proceed unattended, while he sedulously opened a way himself, for the passage of her who has been called Cora. It would seem that the domestics had been previously instructed; for, instead of penetrating the thicket, they followed the route of the column; a measure, which Heyward stated, had been dictated by the sagacity of their guide, in order to diminish the marks of their trail, if, haply, the Canadian savages should be lurking so far in advance of their army. For many minutes, the intricacy of the route admitted of no further dialogue; after which they emerged from the broad border of underbrush, which grew along the line of the highway, and entered under the high, but dark arches of the forest. Here, their progress was less interrupted; and the instant the guide perceived that the females could command their steeds, he moved on, at a pace between a trot and a walk; and at a rate which kept the sure-footed and peculiar animals they rode, at a fast, and yet easy amble. The youth had turned, to speak to the dark-eyed Cora, when the distant sounds of horses' hoofs, clattering over the roots of the broken way in his rear, caused him to check his charger; and as his companions drew their reins at the same instant, the whole party came to a halt, in order to obtain an explanation of the unlooked for interruption.

In a few moments, a colt was seen gliding, like a fallow deer, amongst the straight trunks of the pines; and in another instant, the person of the ungainly man, described in the preceding chapter, came into view, with as much rapidity as he could excite his meager beast to endure, without coming to an open rupture. Until now this personage had escaped the observation of the travellers. If he possessed the power to

---

the colour called sorrel in America, and distinguished by their habit of pacing. Horses of this race were, and are still, in much request as saddle horses, on account of their hardiness and the ease of their movements. As they were also sure of foot, the Narragansets were greatly sought for by females who were obliged to travel over the roots and holes in the "new countries."

arrest any wandering eye, when exhibiting the glories of his altitude on foot, his equestrian graces were still more likely to attract attention. Notwithstanding a constant application of his one armed heel to the flanks of the mare, the most confirmed gait that he could establish, was a Canterbury gallop with the hind legs, in which those more forward assisted for doubtful moments, though generally content to maintain a lopeing trot. Perhaps the rapidity of the changes from one of these paces to the other, created an optical illusion, which might thus magnify the powers of the beast; for it is certain that Heyward, who possessed a true eye for the merits of a horse, was unable, with his utmost ingenuity, to decide, by what sort of movement his pursuer worked his sinuous way on his foot-steps, with such persevering hardihood.

The industry and movements of the rider were not less remarkable than those of the ridden. At each change in the evolutions of the latter, the former raised his tall person in the stirrups; producing, in this manner, by the undue elongation of his legs, such sudden growths and diminishings of the stature, as baffled every conjecture that might be made as to his dimensions. If to this be added the fact, that in consequence of the ex parte application of the spur, one side of the mare appeared to journey faster than the other; and that the aggrieved flank was resolutely indicated, by unremitted flourishes of a bushy tail, we finish the picture of both horse and man.

The frown which had gathered around the handsome, open, and manly brow of Heyward, gradually relaxed, and his lips curled into a slight smile, as he regarded the stranger. Alice made no very powerful effort to control her merriment; and even the dark, thoughtful eye of Cora, lighted with a humour that, it would seem, the habit, rather than the nature of its mistress, repressed.

"Seek you any here?" demanded Heyward, when the other had arrived sufficiently nigh to abate his speed; "I trust you are no messenger of evil tidings."

"Even so," replied the stranger, making diligent use of his triangular castor, to produce a circulation in the close air of the woods, and leaving his hearers in doubt, to which of the young man's questions he responded; when, however, he had cooled his face, and recovered his breath, he continued, "I hear you are riding to William Henry; as I am journeying thitherward myself, I concluded good company would seem consistent to the wishes of both parties."

"You appear to possess the privilege of a casting vote," returned Heyward: "we are three, whilst you have consulted no one but yourself."

"Even so. The first point to be obtained is to know one's own mind. Once sure of that, and where women are concerned it is not easy, the next is, to act up to the decision. I have endeavoured to do both, and here I am."

"If you journey to the lake, you have mistaken your route," said Heyward, haughtily; "the highway thither is at least half-a-mile behind you."

"Even so," returned the stranger, nothing daunted by this cold reception; "I have tarried at 'Edward' a week, and I should be dumb, not to have inquired the road I was to journey; and if dumb, there would be an end to my calling." After simpering in a small way, like one whose modesty prohibited a more open expression of his admiration of a witticism, that was perfectly unintelligible to his hearers, he continued, "It is not prudent for one of my profession to be too familiar with those he has to instruct; for which reason, I follow not the line of the army: besides which, I conclude that a gentleman of your character, has the best judgment in matters of wayfaring; I have therefore decided to join company, in order that the ride may be made agreeable, and partake of social communion."

"A most arbitrary, if not a hasty decision!" exclaimed Heyward, undecided whether to give vent to his growing anger, or to laugh in the other's face. "But you speak of instruction, and of a profession; are you an adjunct to the provincial corps, as a master of the noble science of defence and offence? or, perhaps, you are one who draws lines and angles, under the pretence of expounding the mathematics?"

The stranger regarded his interrogator a moment, in wonder; and then, losing every mark of self-satisfaction in an expression of solemn humility, he answered:

"Of offence, I hope there is none, to either party: of defence, I make none—by God's good mercy, having committed no palpable sin, since last entreating his pardoning grace. I understand not your allusions about lines and angles; and I leave expounding, to those who have been called and set apart for that holy office. I lay claim to no higher gift, than a small insight into the glorious art of petition and thanksgiving, as practised in psalmody."

"The man is, most manifestly, a disciple of Apollo," cried the amused Alice, "and I take him under my own especial protection. Nay, throw aside that frown, Heyward, and, in pity to my longing ears, suffer him to journey in our train. Besides," she added, in a low and hurried voice, casting a glance at the distant Cora, who slowly followed the footsteps of their silent but sullen guide, "it may be a friend added to our strength in time of need."

"Think you, Alice, that I would trust those I love by this secret path, did I imagine such need could happen?"

"Nay, nay, I think not of it now; but this strange man amuses me; and if he 'hath music in his soul,' let us not churlishly reject his company." She pointed persuasively along the path, with her riding whip, while their eyes met in a look, which the young man lingered a moment to prolong, then, yielding to her gentle influence, he clapt his spurs into his charger, and in a few bounds, was again at the side of Cora.

"I am glad to encounter thee, friend," continued the maiden, waving her hand to the stranger to proceed, as she urged her Narraganset to renew its amble. "Partial relatives have almost persuaded me, that I am not entirely worthless in a duette myself; and we may enliven our way-faring, by indulging in our favourite pursuit. It might be of signal advantage to one, ignorant as I, to hear the opinions and experience of a master in the art."

"It is refreshing both to the spirits and to the body, to indulge in psalmody, in befitting seasons," returned the master of song, unhesitatingly complying with her intimation to follow; "and nothing would relieve the mind more, than such a consoling communion. But four parts are altogether necessary to the perfection of melody. You have all the manifestations of a soft and rich treble; I can, by especial aid, carry a full tenor to the highest letter; but we lack counter and bass!

Yon officer of the king, who hesitated to admit me to his company, might fill the latter, if one may judge from the intonations of his voice in common dialogue."

"Judge not too rashly, from hasty and deceptive appearances," said the lady, smiling; "though Major Heyward can assume such deep notes, on occasion, believe me, his natural tones are better fitted for a mellow tenor, than the bass you heard."

"Is he, then, much practised in the art of psalmody?" demanded her simple companion.

Alice felt disposed to laugh, though she succeeded in suppressing her merriment, ere she answered,—

"I apprehend that he is rather addicted to profane song. The chances of a soldier's life, are but little fitted for the encouragement of more sober inclinations."

"Man's voice is given to him, like his other talents, to be used, and not to be abused. None can say they have ever known me neglect my gifts! I am thankful that, though my boyhood may be said to have been set apart, like the youth of the royal David, for the purposes of music, no syllable of rude verse has ever profaned my lips."

"You have, then, limited your efforts to sacred song?"

"Even so. As the psalms of David exceed all other language, so does the psalmody that has been fitted to them by the divines and sages of the land, surpass all vain poetry. Happily, I may say, that I utter nothing but the thoughts and the wishes of the King of Israel himself; for though the times may call for some slight changes, yet does this version, which we use in the colonies of New-England, so much exceed all other versions, that, by its richness, its exactness, and its spiritual simplicity, it approacheth, as near as may be, to the great work of the inspired writer. I never abide in any place, sleeping or waking, without an example of this gifted work. 'Tis the six-and-twentieth edition, promulgated at Boston, Anno Domini, 1744; and is entitled, 'The Psalms, Hymns, and Spiritual Songs of the Old and New Testaments; faithfully translated into English Metre, for the Use, Edification, and Comfort of the Saints in Public and Private, especially in New-England.' "

During this eulogium on the rare production of his native

poets, the stranger had drawn the book from his pocket, and fitting a pair of iron-rimmed spectacles to his nose, had opened the volume with a care and veneration suited to its sacred purposes. Then, without circumlocution or apology, first pronouncing the word, "Standish," and placing the unknown engine, already described, to his mouth, from which he drew a high, shrill sound, that was followed by an octave below, from his own voice, he commenced singing the following words, in full, sweet, and melodious tones, that set the music, the poetry, and even the uneasy motion of his ill-trained beast, at defiance:

"How good it is, O see,
   And how it pleaseth well,
 Together, e'en in unity,
   For brethren so to dwell.
 It's like the choice ointment,
   From head to th' beard did go:
 Down Aaron's beard, that downward went,
   His garment's skirts unto."

The delivery of these skilful rhymes was accompanied, on the part of the stranger, by a regular rise and fall of his right hand, which terminated at the descent, by suffering the fingers to dwell a moment on the leaves of the little volume; and on the ascent, by such a flourish of the member, as none but the initiated may ever hope to imitate. It would seem, that long practice had rendered this manual accompaniment necessary; for it did not cease, until the preposition which the poet had selected for the close of his verse, had been duly delivered like a word of two syllables.

Such an innovation on the silence and retirement of the forest, could not fail to enlist the ears of those who journeyed at so short a distance in advance. The Indian muttered a few words in broken English, to Heyward, who, in his turn, spoke to the stranger; at once interrupting, and, for the time, closing his musical efforts.

"Though we are not in danger, common prudence would teach us to journey through this wilderness in as quiet a manner as possible. You will, then, pardon me, Alice, should I diminish your enjoyments, by requesting this gentleman to postpone his chant until a safer opportunity."

"You will diminish them, indeed," returned the arch girl, "for never did I hear a more unworthy conjunction of execution and language, than that to which I have been listening; and I was far gone in a learned inquiry into the causes of such an unfitness between sound and sense, when you broke the charm of my musings by that bass of yours, Duncan!"

"I know not what you call my bass," said Heyward, piqued at her remark, "but I know that your safety, and that of Cora, is far dearer to me than could be any orchestra of Handel's music." He paused, and turned his head quickly towards a thicket, and then bent his eyes suspiciously on their guide, who continued his steady pace in undisturbed gravity. The young man smiled to himself, for he believed he had mistaken some shining berry of the woods, for the glistening eye-balls of a prowling savage, and he rode forward, continuing the conversation which had been interrupted by the passing thought.

Major Heyward was mistaken only in suffering his youthful and generous pride to suppress his active watchfulness. The cavalcade had not long passed, before the branches of the bushes that formed the thicket, were cautiously moved asunder, and a human visage, as fiercely wild as savage art and unbridled passions could make it, peered out on the retiring footsteps of the travellers. A gleam of exultation shot across the darkly painted lineaments of the inhabitant of the forest, as he traced the route of his intended victims, who rode unconsciously onward; the light and graceful forms of the females waving among the trees, in the curvatures of their path, followed at each bend by the manly figure of Heyward, until, finally, the shapeless person of the singing master was concealed behind the numberless trunks of trees, that rose in dark lines in the intermediate space.

Chapter III

"Before these fields were shorn and tilled,
Full to the brim our rivers flowed;
The melody of waters filled
The fresh and boundless wood;
And torrents dashed, and rivulets played,
And fountains spouted in the shade."
Bryant, "An Indian at the Burial-Place
of His Fathers," ll. 67–72.

LEAVING THE UNSUSPECTING Heyward, and his confiding companions, to penetrate still deeper into a forest that contained such treacherous inmates, we must use an author's privilege, and shift the scene a few miles to the westward of the place where we have last seen them.

On that day, two men were lingering on the banks of a small but rapid stream, within an hour's journey of the encampment of Webb, like those who awaited the appearance of an absent person, or the approach of some expected event. The vast canopy of woods spread itself to the margin of the river, overhanging the water, and shadowing its dark current with a deeper hue. The rays of the sun were beginning to grow less fierce, and the intense heat of the day was lessened, as the cooler vapours of the springs and fountains rose above their leafy beds, and rested in the atmosphere. Still that breathing silence, which marks the drowsy sultriness of an American landscape in July, pervaded the secluded spot, interrupted, only, by the low voices of the men, the occasional and lazy tap of a wood-pecker, the discordant cry of some gaudy jay, or a swelling on the ear, from the dull roar of a distant water-fall.

These feeble and broken sounds were, however, too familiar to the foresters, to draw their attention from the more interesting matter of their dialogue. While one of these loiterers showed the red skin and wild accoutrements of a native of the woods, the other exhibited, through the mask of his rude and nearly savage equipments, the brighter, though sunburnt and long-faded complexion of one who might claim descent from a European parentage. The former was seated on the end of a mossy log, in a posture that permitted him to heighten the effect of his earnest language, by the calm but expressive gestures of an Indian, engaged in debate. His body, which was nearly naked, presented a terrific emblem of death, drawn in intermingled colours of white and black. His closely shaved head, on which no other hair than the well known and chivalrous scalping tuft* was preserved, was without ornament of any kind, with the exception of a solitary eagle's plume, that crossed his crown, and depended over the left shoulder. A tomahawk and scalping-knife, of English manufacture, were in his girdle; while a short military rifle, of that sort with which the policy of the whites armed their savage allies, lay carelessly across his bare and sinewy knee. The expanded chest, full-formed limbs, and grave countenance of this warrior, would denote that he had reached the vigour of his days, though no symptoms of decay appeared to have yet weakened his manhood.

The frame of the white man, judging by such parts as were not concealed by his clothes, was like that of one who had known hardships and exertion from his earliest youth. His person, though muscular, was rather attenuated than full; but every nerve and muscle appeared strung and indurated, by unremitted exposure and toil. He wore a hunting-shirt of forest-green, fringed with faded yellow,† and a summer cap, of skins which had been shorn of their fur. He also bore a knife in a girdle of wampum, like that which confined the scanty garments of the Indian, but no tomahawk. His moccasins were ornamented after the gay fashion of the natives, while the only part of his under dress which appeared below the

*The North American warrior caused the hair to be plucked from his whole body; a small tuft, only, was left on the crown of his head, in order that his enemy might avail himself of it, in wrenching off the scalp in the event of his fall. The scalp was the only admissible trophy of victory. Thus, it was deemed more important to obtain the scalp than to kill the man. Some tribes lay great stress on the honour of striking a dead body. These practices have nearly disappeared among the Indians of the Atlantic states.

†The hunting-shirt is a picturesque smock-frock, being shorter, and ornamented with fringes and tassels. The colours are intended to imitate the hues of the wood, with a view to concealment. Many corps of American riflemen have been thus attired; and the dress is one of the most striking of modern times. The hunting shirt is frequently white.

hunting-frock, was a pair of buckskin leggings, that laced at the sides, and which were gartered above the knees, with the sinews of a deer. A pouch and horn completed his personal accoutrements, though a rifle of great length,* which the theory of the more ingenious whites had taught them, was the most dangerous of all fire-arms, leaned against a neighbouring sapling. The eye of the hunter, or scout, whichever he might be, was small, quick, keen, and restless, roving while he spoke, on every side of him, as if in quest of game, or distrusting the sudden approach of some lurking enemy. Notwithstanding these symptoms of habitual suspicion, his countenance was not only without guile, but at the moment at which he is introduced, it was charged with an expression of sturdy honesty.

"Even your traditions make the case in my favour, Chingachgook," he said, speaking in the tongue which was known to all the natives who formerly inhabited the country between the Hudson and the Potomack, and of which we shall give a free translation for the benefit of the reader; endeavouring, at the same time, to preserve some of the peculiarities, both of the individual and of the language. "Your fathers came from the setting sun, crossed the big river,† fought the people of the country, and took the land; and mine came from the red sky of the morning, over the salt lake, and did their work much after the fashion that had been set them by yours; then let God judge the matter between us, and friends spare their words!"

"My fathers fought with the naked red-man!" returned the Indian, sternly, in the same language. "Is there no difference, Hawk-eye, between the stone-headed arrow of the warrior, and the leaden bullet with which you kill?"

"There is reason in an Indian, though nature has made him with a red skin!" said the white man, shaking his head, like one on whom such an appeal to his justice was not thrown away. For a moment he appeared to be conscious of having

*The rifle of the army is short; that of the hunter is always long.

†The Mississippi. The scout alludes to a tradition which is very popular among the tribes of the Atlantic states. Evidence of their Asiatic origin is deduced from the circumstance, though great uncertainty hangs over the whole history of the Indians.

the worst of the argument, then rallying again, he answered the objection of his antagonist in the best manner his limited information would allow: "I am no scholar, and I care not who knows it; but judging from what I have seen at deer chaces, and squirrel hunts, of the sparks below, I should think a rifle in the hands of their grandfathers, was not so dangerous as a hickory bow, and a good flint-head might be, if drawn with Indian judgment, and sent by an Indian eye."

"You have the story told by your fathers," returned the other, coldly waving his hand. "What say your old men? do they tell the young warriors, that the pale-faces met the red-men, painted for war and armed with the stone hatchet or wooden gun?"

"I am not a prejudiced man, nor one who vaunts himself on his natural privileges, though the worst enemy I have on earth, and he is an Iroquois, daren't deny that I am genuine white," the scout replied, surveying, with secret satisfaction, the faded colour of his bony and sinewy hand; "and I am willing to own that my people have many ways, of which, as an honest man, I can't approve. It is one of their customs to write in books what they have done and seen, instead of telling them in their villages, where the lie can be given to the face of a cowardly boaster, and the brave soldier can call on his comrades to witness for the truth of his words. In consequence of this bad fashion, a man who is too conscientious to misspend his days among the women, in learning the names of black marks, may never hear of the deeds of his fathers, nor feel a pride in striving to outdo them. For myself, I conclude all the Bumppos could shoot; for I have a natural turn with a rifle, which must have been handed down from generation to generation, as our holy commandments tell us, all good and evil gifts are bestowed; though I should be loth to answer for other people in such a matter. But every story has its two sides; so I ask you, Chingachgook, what passed, according to the traditions of the red men, when our fathers first met?"

A silence of a minute succeeded, during which the Indian sat mute; then, full of the dignity of his office, he commenced his brief tale, with a solemnity that served to heighten its appearance of truth.

"Listen, Hawk-eye, and your ear shall drink no lie. 'Tis what my fathers have said, and what the Mohicans have done." He hesitated a single instant, and bending a cautious glance towards his companion, he continued in a manner that was divided between interrogation and assertion—"does not this stream at our feet, run towards the summer, until its waters grow salt, and the current flows upward!"

"It can't be denied, that your traditions tell you true in both these matters," said the white man; "for I have been there, and have seen them; though, why water, which is so sweet in the shade, should become bitter in the sun, is an alteration for which I have never been able to account."

"And the current!" demanded the Indian, who expected his reply with that sort of interest that a man feels in the confirmation of testimony, at which he marvels even while he respects it; "the fathers of Chingachgook have not lied!"

"The Holy Bible is not more true, and that is the truest thing in nature. They call this up-stream current the tide, which is a thing soon explained, and clear enough. Six hours the waters run in, and six hours they run out, and the reason is this; when there is higher water in the sea than in the river, they run in, until the river gets to be highest, and then it runs out again."

"The waters in the woods, and on the great lakes, run downward until they lie like my hand," said the Indian, stretching the limb horizontally before him, "and then they run no more."

"No honest man will deny it," said the scout, a little nettled at the implied distrust of his explanation of the mystery of the tides; "and I grant that it is true on the small scale, and where the land is level. But every thing depends on what scale you look at things. Now, on the small scale, the 'arth is level; but on the large scale it is round. In this manner, pools and ponds, and even the great fresh water lakes, may be stagnant, as you and I both know they are, having seen them; but when you come to spread water over a great tract, like the sea, where the earth is round, how in reason can the water be quiet? You might as well expect the river to lie still on the brink of those black rocks a mile above us, though your own ears tell you that it is tumbling over them at this very moment!"

If unsatisfied by the philosophy of his companion, the Indian was far too dignified to betray his unbelief. He listened like one who was convinced, and resumed his narrative in his former solemn manner.

"We came from the place where the sun is hid at night, over great plains where the buffaloes live, until we reached the big river. There we fought the Alligewi, till the ground was red with their blood. From the banks of the big river to the shores of the salt lake, there was none to meet us. The Maquas followed at a distance. We said the country should be ours from the place where the water runs up no longer, on this stream, to a river, twenty suns' journey toward the summer. The land we had taken like warriors, we kept like men. We drove the Maquas into the woods with the bears. They only tasted salt at the licks; they drew no fish from the great lake: we threw them the bones."

"All this I have heard and believe," said the white man, observing that the Indian paused; "but it was long before the English came into the country."

"A pine grew then, where this chestnut now stands. The first pale faces who came among us spoke no English. They came in a large canoe, when my fathers had buried the tomahawk with the red men around them. Then, Hawk-eye," he continued, betraying his deep emotion, only by permitting his voice to fall to those low, guttural tones, which render his language, as spoken at times, so very musical; "then, Hawk-eye, we were one people, and we were happy. The salt lake gave us its fish, the wood its deer, and the air its birds. We took wives who bore us children; we worshipped the Great Spirit; and we kept the Maquas beyond the sound of our songs of triumph!"

"Know you any thing of your own family, at that time?" demanded the white. "But you are a just man for an Indian! and as I suppose you hold their gifts, your fathers must have been brave warriors, and wise men at the council fire."

"My tribe is the grandfather of nations, but I am an unmixed man. The blood of chiefs is in my veins, where it must stay for ever. The Dutch landed, and gave my people the fire-water; they drank until the heavens and the earth seemed to meet, and they foolishly thought they had found the Great Spirit. Then they parted with their land. Foot by foot, they were driven back from the shores, until I, that am a chief and a Sagamore, have never seen the sun shine but through the trees, and have never visited the graves of my fathers."

"Graves bring solemn feelings over the mind," returned the scout, a good deal touched at the calm suffering of his companion; "and they often aid a man in his good intentions, though, for myself, I expect to leave my own bones unburied, to bleach in the woods, or to be torn asunder by the wolves. But where are to be found those of your race who came to their kin in the Delaware country, so many summers since?"

"Where are the blossoms of those summers!—fallen, one by one: so all of my family departed, each in his turn, to the land of spirits. I am on the hill-top, and must go down into the valley; and when Uncas follows in my footsteps, there will no longer be any of the blood of the Sagamores, for my boy is the last of the Mohicans."

"Uncas is here!" said another voice, in the same soft, guttural tones, near his elbow; " who speaks to Uncas?"

The white man loosened his knife in its leathern sheath, and made an involuntary movement of the hand towards his rifle, at this sudden interruption, but the Indian sat composed, and without turning his head at the unexpected sounds.

At the next instant, a youthful warrior passed between them, with a noiseless step, and seated himself on the bank of the rapid stream. No exclamation of surprise escaped the father, nor was any question asked or reply given for several minutes, each appearing to await the moment, when he might speak, without betraying womanish curiosity or childish impatience. The white man seemed to take counsel from their customs, and relinquishing his grasp of the rifle, he also remained silent and reserved. At length Chingachgook turned his eyes slowly towards his son, and demanded—

"Do the Maquas dare to leave the print of their moccasins in these woods?"

"I have been on their trail," replied the young Indian, "and know that they number as many as the fingers of my two hands; but they lie hid like cowards."

"The thieves are outlying for scalps and plunder!" said the white man, whom we shall call Hawk-eye, after the manner of his companions. "That busy Frenchman, Montcalm, will send his spies into our very camp, but he will know what road we travel!"

" 'Tis enough!" returned the father, glancing his eyes towards the setting sun; "they shall be driven like deer from their bushes. Hawk-eye, let us eat to-night, and show the Maquas that we are men to-morrow."

"I am as ready to do the one as the other; but to fight the Iroquois, 'tis necessary to find the skulkers; and to eat, 'tis necessary to get the game—talk of the devil and he will come; there is a pair of the biggest antlers I have seen this season, moving the bushes below the hill! Now, Uncas," he continued in a half whisper, and laughing with a kind of inward sound, like one who had learnt to be watchful, "I will bet my charger three times full of powder, against a foot of wampum, that I take him atwixt the eyes, and nearer to the right than to the left."

"It cannot be!" said the young Indian, springing to his feet with youthful eagerness; "all but the tips of his horns are hid!"

"He's a boy!" said the white man, shaking his head while he spoke, and addressing the father. "Does he think when a hunter sees a part of the creatur, he can't tell where the rest of him should be!"

Adjusting his rifle, he was about to make an exhibition of that skill, on which he so much valued himself, when the warrior struck up the piece with his hand, saying,

"Hawk-eye! will you fight the Maquas?"

"These Indians know the nature of the woods, as it might be by instinct!" returned the scout, dropping his rifle, and turning away like a man who was convinced of his error. "I must leave the buck to your arrow, Uncas, or we may kill a deer for them thieves, the Iroquois, to eat."

The instant the father seconded this intimation by an expressive gesture of the hand, Uncas threw himself on the ground, and approached the animal with wary movements. When, within a few yards of the cover, he fitted an arrow to his bow with the utmost care, while the antlers moved, as if their owner snuffed an enemy in the tainted air. In another moment the twang of the cord was heard, a white streak was seen glancing into the bushes, and the wounded buck plunged from the cover, to the very feet of his hidden enemy. Avoiding the horns of the infuriated animal, Uncas darted to his side, and passed his knife across the throat, when bounding to the edge of the river, it fell, dying the waters with its blood.

"'Twas done with Indian skill," said the scout, laughing inwardly, but with vast satisfaction; "and 'twas a pretty sight to behold! Though an arrow is a near shot, and needs a knife to finish the work."

"Hugh!" ejaculated his companion, turning quickly, like a hound who scented his game.

"By the Lord, there is a drove of them!" exclaimed the scout, whose eyes began to glisten with the ardour of his usual occupation; "if they come within range of a bullet, I will drop one, though the whole Six Nations should be lurking within sound! What do you hear, Chingachgook? for to my ears the woods are dumb."

"There is but one deer, and he is dead," said the Indian, bending his body, till his ear nearly touched the earth. "I hear the sounds of feet!"

"Perhaps the wolves have driven the buck to shelter, and are following on his trail."

"No. The horses of white men are coming!" returned the other, raising himself with dignity, and resuming his seat on the log with his former composure. "Hawk-eye, they are your brothers; speak to them."

"That will I, and in English that the king needn't be ashamed to answer," returned the hunter, speaking in the language of which he boasted; "but I see nothing, nor do I hear the sounds of man or beast; 'tis strange that an Indian should understand white sounds better than a man, who, his very enemies will own, has no cross in his blood, although he may have lived with the red skins long enough to be suspected! Ha! there goes something like the cracking of a dry stick, too—now I hear the bushes move—yes, yes, there is a trampling that I mistook for the falls—and—but here they come themselves; God keep them from the Iroquois!"

Chapter IV

"Well, go thy way; thou shalt not from this grove,
Till I torment thee for this injury."
A Midsummer Night's Dream, II.i.146–147.

THE WORDS were still in the mouth of the scout, when the leader of the party, whose approaching footsteps had caught the vigilant ear of the Indian, came openly into view. A beaten path, such as those made by the periodical passage of the deer, wound through a little glen at no great distance, and struck the river at the point where the white man and his red companions had posted themselves. Along this track the travellers, who had produced a surprise so unusual in the depths of the forest, advanced slowly towards the hunter, who was in front of his associates, in readiness to receive them.

"Who comes?" demanded the scout, throwing his rifle carelessly across his left arm, and keeping the fore finger of his right hand on the trigger, though he avoided all appearance of menace in the act—"Who comes hither, among the beasts and dangers of the wilderness?"

"Believers in religion, and friends to the law and to the king," returned he who rode foremost. "Men who have journeyed since the rising sun, in the shades of this forest, without nourishment, and are sadly tired of their wayfaring."

"You are, then, lost," interrupted the hunter, "and have found how helpless 'tis not to know whether to take the right hand or the left?"

"Even so; sucking babes are not more dependent on those who guide them, than we who are of larger growth, and who may now be said to possess the stature without the knowledge of men. Know you the distance to a post of the crown called William Henry?"

"Hoot!" shouted the scout, who did not spare his open laughter, though, instantly checking the dangerous sounds, he indulged his merriment at less risk of being overheard by any lurking enemies. "You are as much off the scent as a hound would be, with Horican atwixt him and the deer! William

Henry, man! if you are friends to the king, and have business with the army, your better way would be to follow the river down to Edward, and lay the matter before Webb; who tarries there, instead of pushing into the defiles, and driving this saucy Frenchman back across Champlain, into his den again."

Before the stranger could make any reply to this unexpected proposition, another horseman dashed the bushes aside, and leaped his charger into the pathway in front of his companion.

"What, then, may be our distance from Fort Edward?" demanded a new speaker; "the place you advise us to seek we left this morning, and our destination is the head of the lake."

"Then you must have lost your eyesight afore losing your way, for the road across the portage is cut to a good two rods, and is as grand a path, I calculate, as any that runs into London, or even before the palace of the king himself."

"We will not dispute concerning the excellence of the passage," returned Heyward, smiling, for, as the reader has anticipated, it was he. "It is enough, for the present, that we trusted to an Indian guide to take us by a nearer, though blinder path, and that we are deceived in his knowledge. In plain words, we know not where we are."

"An Indian lost in the woods!" said the scout, shaking his head doubtingly; "when the sun is scorching the tree tops, and the water courses are full; when the moss on every beech he sees, will tell him in which quarter the north star will shine at night! The woods are full of deer paths which run to the streams and licks, places well known to every body; nor have the geese done their flight to the Canada waters, altogether! 'Tis strange that an Indian should be lost atwixt Horican and the bend in the river! Is he a Mohawk?"

"Not by birth, though adopted in that tribe; I think his birth place was farther north, and he is one of those you call a Huron."

"Hugh!" exclaimed the two companions of the scout, who had continued until this part of the dialogue, seated, immoveable, and apparently indifferent to what passed, but who now sprang to their feet with an activity and interest that had evidently gotten the better of their reserve, by surprise.

"A Huron!" repeated the sturdy scout, once more shaking his head in open distrust; "they are a thievish race, nor do I care by whom they are adopted; you can never make any thing of them but skulks and vagabonds. Since you trusted yourself to the care of one of that nation, I only wonder that you have not fallen in with more."

"Of that there is little danger, since William Henry is so many miles in our front. You forget that I have told you our guide is now a Mohawk, and that he serves with our forces as a friend."

"And I tell you that he who is born a Mingo will die a Mingo," returned the other, positively. "A Mohawk! No, give me a Delaware or a Mohican for honesty; and when they will fight, which they won't all do, having suffered their cunning enemies, the Maquas, to make them women—but when they will fight at all, look to a Delaware or a Mohican for a warrior!"

"Enough of this," said Heyward, impatiently; "I wish not to inquire into the character of a man that I know, and to whom you must be a stranger. You have not yet answered my question; what is our distance from the main army at Edward?"

"It seems that may depend on who is your guide. One would think such a horse as that might get over a good deal of ground atwixt sun-up and sun-down."

"I wish no contention of idle words with you, friend," said Heyward, curbing his dissatisfied manner, and speaking in a more gentle voice; "if you will tell me the distance to Fort Edward, and conduct me thither, your labour shall not go without its reward."

"And in so doing, how know I that I don't guide an enemy, and a spy of Montcalm, to the works of the army? It is not every man who can speak the English tongue that is an honest subject."

"If you serve with the troops of whom I judge you to be a scout, you should know of such a regiment of the king as the 60th."

"The 60th! you can tell me little of the Royal Americans that I don't know, though I do wear a hunting shirt, instead of a scarlet jacket."

"Well, then, among other things, you may know the name of its major?"

"Its major!" interrupted the hunter, elevating his body like one who was proud of his trust. "If there is a man in the country who knows Major Effingham, he stands before you."

"It is a corps which has many majors; the gentleman you name is the senior, but I speak of the junior of them all; he who commands the companies in garrison at William Henry."

"Yes, yes, I have heard that a young gentleman of vast riches, from one of the provinces far south, has got the place. He is over young, too, to hold such rank, and to be put above men whose heads are beginning to bleach; and yet they say he is a soldier in his knowledge, and a gallant gentleman!"

"Whatever he may be, or however he may be qualified for his rank, he now speaks to you, and of course can be no enemy to dread."

The scout regarded Heyward in surprise, and then lifting his cap, he answered, in a tone less confident than before—though still expressing doubt—

"I have heard a party was to leave the encampment, this morning, for the lake shore?"

"You have heard the truth; but I preferred a nearer route, trusting to the knowledge of the Indian I mentioned."

"And he deceived you, and then deserted?"

"Neither, as I believe; certainly not the latter, for he is to be found in the rear."

"I should like to look at the creatur; if it is a true Iroquois I can tell him by his knavish look, and by his paint," said the scout, stepping past the charger of Heyward, and entering the path behind the mare of the singing master, whose foal had taken advantage of the halt to exact the maternal contribution. After shoving aside the bushes, and proceeding a few paces, he encountered the females, who awaited the result of the conference with anxiety, and not entirely without apprehension. Behind these, the runner leaned against a tree, where he stood the close examination of the scout with an air unmoved, though with a look so dark and savage, that it might in itself excite fear. Satisfied with his scrutiny, the hunter soon left him. As he repassed the females, he paused a moment to gaze upon their beauty, answering to the smile and nod of

Alice with a look of open pleasure. Thence he went to the side of the motherly animal, and spending a minute in a fruitless inquiry into the character of her rider, he shook his head and returned to Heyward.

"A Mingo is a Mingo, and God having made him so, neither the Mohawks nor any other tribe can alter him," he said, when he had regained his former position. "If we were alone, and you would leave that noble horse at the mercy of the wolves to night, I could show you the way to Edward myself within an hour, for it lies only about an hour's journey hence; but with such ladies in your company, 'tis impossible!"

"And why? they are fatigued, but they are quite equal to a ride of a few more miles."

" 'Tis a natural impossibility!" repeated the scout; "I wouldn't walk a mile in these woods after night gets into them, in company with that runner, for the best rifle in the colonies. They are full of outlying Iroquois, and your mongrel Mohawk knows where to find them too well, to be my companion."

"Think you so," said Heyward, leaning forward in the saddle, and dropping his voice nearly to a whisper; "I confess I have not been without my own suspicions, though I have endeavoured to conceal them, and affected a confidence I have not always felt, on account of my companions. It was because I suspected him, that I would follow no longer; making him, as you see, follow me."

"I knew he was one of the cheats as soon as I laid eyes on him!" returned the scout, placing a finger on his nose in sign of caution. "The thief is leaning against the foot of the sugar sapling that you can see over them bushes; his right leg is in a line with the bark of the tree, and," tapping his rifle, "I can take him, from where I stand, between the ankle and the knee, with a single shot, putting an end to his tramping through the woods for at least a month to come. If I should go back to him, the cunning varmint would suspect something, and be dodging through the trees like any frightened deer."

"It will not do. He may be innocent, and I dislike the act. Though, if I felt confident of his treachery"—

" 'Tis a safe thing to calculate on the knavery of an Iroquois," said the scout, throwing his rifle forward, by a sort of instinctive movement.

"Hold!" interrupted Heyward; "it will not do—we must think of some other scheme;—and yet, I have much reason to believe the rascal has deceived me."

The hunter, who had already abandoned his intention of maiming the runner, mused a moment, and then made a gesture, which instantly brought his two red companions to his side. They spoke together earnestly in the Delaware language, though in an under tone, and by the gestures of the white man, which were frequently directed towards the top of the sapling, it was evident he pointed out the situation of their hidden enemy. His companions were not long in comprehending his wishes, and laying aside their fire-arms, they parted, taking opposite sides of the path, and burying themselves in the thicket, with such cautious movements, that their steps were inaudible.

"Now go you back," said the hunter, speaking again to Heyward, "and hold the imp in talk; these Mohicans here, will take him, without breaking his paint."

"Nay," said Heyward, proudly, "I will seize him myself."

"Hist! what could you do, mounted, against an Indian, in the bushes?"

"I will dismount."

"And, think you, when he saw one of your feet out of the stirrup, he would wait for the other to be free! Whoever comes into the woods to deal with the natives, must use Indian fashions, if he would wish to prosper in his undertakings. Go, then; talk openly to the miscreant, and seem to believe him the truest friend you have on 'arth."

Heyward prepared to comply, though with strong disgust at the nature of the office he was compelled to execute. Each moment, however, pressed upon him a conviction of the critical situation in which he had suffered his invaluable trust to be involved, through his own confidence. The sun had already disappeared, and the woods, suddenly deprived of his light,* were assuming a dusky hue, which keenly reminded him, that the hour the savage usually chose for his most

*The scene of this tale was in the 42d degree of latitude, where the twilight is never of long continuance.

barbarous and remorseless acts of vengeance or hostility, was speedily drawing near. Stimulated by apprehension, he left the scout, who immediately entered into a loud conversation with the stranger that had so unceremoniously enlisted himself in the party of travellers that morning. In passing his gentler companions, Heyward uttered a few words of encouragement, and was pleased to find that, though fatigued with the exercise of the day, they appeared to entertain no suspicion that their present embarrassment was other than the result of accident. Giving them reason to believe he was merely employed in a consultation concerning the future route, he spurred his charger, and drew the reins again when the animal had carried him within a few yards of the place, where the sullen runner still stood leaning against the tree.

"You may see, Magua," he said, endeavouring to assume an air of freedom and confidence, "that the night is closing around us, and yet we are no nearer to William Henry than when we left the encampment of Webb, with the rising sun. You have missed the way, nor have I been more fortunate. But, happily, we have fallen in with a hunter, he whom you hear talking to the singer, that is acquainted with the deer-paths and by-ways of the woods, and who promises to lead us to a place where we may rest securely till the morning."

The Indian riveted his glowing eyes on Heyward as he asked, in his imperfect English, "Is he alone?"

"Alone!" hesitatingly answered Heyward, to whom deception was too new to be assumed without embarrassment. "Oh! not alone, surely, Magua, for you know that we are with him."

"Then le Renard Subtil will go," returned the runner, coolly raising his little wallet from the place where it had lain at his feet; "and the pale faces will see none but their own colour."

"Go! Whom call you le Renard?"

" 'Tis the name his Canada fathers have given to Magua," returned the runner, with an air that manifested his pride at the distinction. "Night is the same as day to le Subtil, when Munro waits for him."

"And what account will le Renard give the chief of William Henry concerning his daughters? will he dare to tell the hot-blooded Scotsman that his children are left without a guide, though Magua promised to be one?"

"Though the gray head has a loud voice, and a long arm, le Renard will not hear him or feel him in the woods."

"But what will the Mohawks say! They will make him petticoats, and bid him stay in the wigwam with the women, for he is no longer to be trusted with the business of a man."

"Le Subtil knows the path to the great lakes, and he can find the bones of his fathers," was the answer of the unmoved runner.

"Enough, Magua," said Heyward; "are we not friends! why should there be bitter words between us? Munro has promised you a gift for your services when performed, and I shall be your debtor for another. Rest your weary limbs, then, and open your wallet to eat. We have a few moments to spare; let us not waste them in talk like wrangling women. When the ladies are refreshed we will proceed."

"The pale faces make themselves dogs to their women," muttered the Indian, in his native language, "and when they want to eat, their warriors must lay aside the tomahawk to feed their laziness."

"What say you, Renard?"

"Le Subtil says it is good."

The Indian then fastened his eyes keenly on the open countenance of Heyward, but meeting his glance, he turned them quickly away, and seating himself deliberately on the ground, he drew forth the remnant of some former repast, and began to eat, though not without first bending his looks slowly and cautiously around him.

"This is well," continued Heyward; "and le Renard will have strength and sight to find the path in the morning;"—he paused, for sounds like the snapping of a dried stick, and the rustling of leaves, rose from the adjacent bushes, but recollecting himself instantly he continued—" we must be moving before the sun is seen, or Montcalm may lie in our path, and shut us out from the fortress."

The hand of Magua dropped from his mouth to his side, and though his eyes were fastened on the ground, his head was turned aside, his nostrils expanded, and his ears seemed even to stand more erect than usual, giving to him the appearance of a statue that was made to represent intense attention.

Heyward, who watched his movements with a vigilant eye, carelessly extricated one of his feet from the stirrup, while he passed a hand towards the bear-skin covering of his holsters. Every effort to detect the point most regarded by the runner, was completely frustrated by the tremulous glances of his organs, which seemed not to rest a single instant on any particular object, and which, at the same time, could be hardly said to move. While he hesitated how to proceed, le Subtil cautiously raised himself to his feet, though with a motion so slow and guarded, that not the slightest noise was produced by the change. Heyward felt it had now become incumbent on him to act. Throwing his leg over the saddle, he dismounted, with a determination to advance and seize his treacherous companion, trusting the result to his own manhood. In order, however, to prevent unnecessary alarm, he still preserved an air of calmness and friendship.

"Le Renard Subtil does not eat," he said, using the appellation he had found most flattering to the vanity of the Indian. "His corn is not well parched, and it seems dry. Let me examine; perhaps something may be found among my own provisions that will help his appetite."

Magua held out the wallet to the proffer of the other. He even suffered their hands to meet, without betraying the least emotion, or varying his riveted attitude of attention. But when he felt the fingers of Heyward moving gently along his own naked arm, he struck up the limb of the young man, and uttering a piercing cry, as he darted beneath it, plunged, at a single bound, into the opposite thicket. At the next instant, the form of Chingachgook appeared from the bushes, looking like a spectre in its paint, and glided across the path in swift pursuit. Next followed the shout of Uncas, when the woods were lighted by a sudden flash, that was accompanied by the sharp report of the hunter's rifle.

Chapter V

—"In such a night,
Did Thisbe fearfully o'ertrip the dew;
And saw the lion's shadow ere himself."—
The Merchant of Venice, V.i.7–8.

THE SUDDENNESS of the flight of his guide, and the wild cries of the pursuers, caused Heyward to remain fixed, for a few moments, in inactive surprise. Then recollecting the importance of securing the fugitive, he dashed aside the surrounding bushes, and pressed eagerly forward to lend his aid in the chase. Before he had, however, proceeded a hundred yards, he met the three foresters already returning from their unsuccessful pursuit.

"Why so soon disheartened!" he exclaimed; "the scoundrel must be concealed behind some of these trees, and may yet be secured. We are not safe while he goes at large."

"Would you set a cloud to chase the wind?" returned the disappointed scout; "I heard the imp, brushing over the dry leaves, like a black snake, and blinking a glimpse of him, just over ag'in yon big pine, I pulled as it might be on the scent; but 'twouldn't do! and yet for a reasoning aim, if any body but myself had touched the trigger, I should call it a quick sight; and I may be accounted to have experience in these matters, and one who ought to know. Look at this sumach; its leaves are red, though every body knows the fruit is in the yellow blossom, in the month of July!"

" 'Tis the blood of le Subtil! he is hurt, and may yet fall!"

"No, no," returned the scout, in decided disapprobation of this opinion, "I rubbed the bark off a limb, perhaps, but the creatur leaped the longer for it. A rifle bullet acts on a running animal, when it barks him, much the same as one of your spurs on a horse; that is, it quickens motion, and puts life into the flesh, instead of taking it away. But when it cuts the ragged hole, after a bound or two, there is, commonly, a stagnation of further leaping, be it Indian or be it deer!"

"We are four able bodies, to one wounded man!"

"Is life grievous to you?" interrupted the scout. "Yonder

red devil would draw you within swing of the tomahawks of his comrades, before you were heated in the chase. It was an unthoughtful act, in a man who has so often slept with the war-whoop ringing in the air, to let off his piece, within sound of an ambushment! But, then it was a natural temptation! 'twas very natural! Come, friends, let us move our station, and in such a fashion, too, as will throw the cunning of a Mingo on a wrong scent, or our scalps will be drying in the wind in front of Montcalm's marquee, ag'in this hour to-morrow."

This appalling declaration, which the scout uttered with the cool assurance of a man who fully comprehended, while he did not fear to face the danger, served to remind Heyward of the importance of the charge with which he himself had been intrusted. Glancing his eyes around, with a vain effort to pierce the gloom that was thickening beneath the leafy arches of the forest, he felt as if, cut off from human aid, his unresisting companions would soon lie at the entire mercy of those barbarous enemies, who, like beasts of prey, only waited till the gathering darkness might render their blows more fatally certain. His awakened imagination, deluded by the deceptive light, converted each waving bush, or the fragment of some fallen tree, into human forms, and twenty times he fancied he could distinguish the horrid visages of his lurking foes, peering from their hiding places, in never-ceasing watchfulness of the movements of his party. Looking upward, he found that the thin fleecy clouds, which evening had painted on the blue sky, were already losing their faintest tints of rose-colour, while the embedded stream which glided past the spot where he stood, was to be traced only by the dark boundary of its wooded banks.

"What is to be done?" he said, feeling the utter helplessness of doubt in such a pressing strait; "desert me not, for God's sake! remain to defend those I escort, and freely name your own reward!"

His companions, who conversed apart in the language of their tribe, heeded not this sudden and earnest appeal. Though their dialogue was maintained in low and cautious sounds, but little above a whisper, Heyward, who now approached, could easily distinguish the earnest tones of the younger warrior, from the more deliberate speeches of his seniors. It was evident, that they debated on the propriety of some measure, that nearly concerned the welfare of the travellers. Yielding to his powerful interest in the subject, and impatient of a delay that seemed fraught with so much additional danger, Heyward drew still nigher to the dusky groupe, with an intention of making his offers of compensation more definite, when the white man, motioning with his hand as if he conceded the disputed point, turned away, saying in a sort of soliloquy, and in the English tongue:—

"Uncas is right! it would not be the act of men, to leave such harmless things to their fate, even though it breaks up the harbouring place for ever. If you would save these tender blossoms from the fangs of the worst of sarpents, gentleman, you have neither time to lose nor resolution to throw away!"

"How can such a wish be doubted! have I not already offered"—

"Offer your prayers to Him, who can give us wisdom to carcumvent the cunning of the devils who fill these woods," calmly interrupted the scout, "but spare your offers of money, which neither you may live to realize, nor I to profit by. These Mohicans and I, will do what man's thoughts can invent, to keep such flowers, which, though so sweet, were never made for the wilderness, from harm, and that without hope of any other recompense but such as God always gives to upright dealings. First, you must promise two things, both in your own name, and for your friends, or without serving you, we shall only injure ourselves!"

"Name them."

"The one is to be still as these sleeping woods, let what will happen; and the other, is to keep the place where we shall take you forever a secret from all mortal men."

"I will do my utmost to see both these conditions fulfilled."

"Then follow, for we are losing moments that are as precious as the heart's blood to a stricken deer!"

Heyward could distinguish the impatient gesture of the scout, through the increasing shadows of the evening, and he moved in his footsteps, swiftly, towards the place where he had left the remainder of his party. When they rejoined the expecting and anxious females, he briefly acquainted them with the conditions of their new guide, and with the necessity that existed for their hushing every apprehension, in instant and serious exertions. Although his alarming communication was not received without much secret terror by the listeners, his earnest and impressive manner, aided perhaps by the nature of the danger, succeeded in bracing their nerves to undergo some unlooked for and unusual trial. Silently, and without a moment's delay, they permitted him to assist them from their saddles, when they descended, quickly, to the water's edge, where the scout had collected the rest of the party, more by the agency of his expressive gestures than by any use of words.

"What to do with these dumb creaturs!" muttered the white man, on whom the sole control of their future movements appeared to devolve; "it would be time lost to cut their throats, and cast them into the river; and to leave them here, would be to tell the Mingoes that they have not far to seek to find their owners!"

"Then give them their bridles, and let them range the woods!" Heyward ventured to suggest.

"No; it would be better to mislead the imps, and make them believe they must equal a horse's speed to run down their chase. Ay, ay, that will blind their fire-balls of eyes! Chingach—Hist! what stirs the bush?"

"The colt."

"That colt, at least, must die," muttered the scout, grasping at the mane of the nimble beast, which easily eluded his hand; "Uncas, your arrows!"

"Hold!" exclaimed the proprietor of the condemned animal, aloud, without regard to the whispering tones used by the others; "spare the foal of Miriam! it is the comely offspring of a faithful dam, and would, willingly, injure naught."

"When men struggle for the single life God has given them," said the scout, sternly, "even their own kind seem no more than the beasts of the wood. If you speak again, I shall leave you to the mercy of the Maquas! Draw to your arrow's head, Uncas; we have no time for second blows!"

The low, muttering sounds of his threatening voice, were still audible, when the wounded foal, first rearing on its hinder legs, plunged forward to its knees. It was met by Chingachgook, whose knife passed across its throat quicker than thought, and then precipitating the motion of the struggling victim, he dashed it into the river, down whose stream it glided away, gasping audibly for breath with its ebbing life. This deed of apparent cruelty, but of real necessity, fell upon the spirits of the travellers, like a terrific warning of the peril in which they stood, heightened, as it was, by the calm though steady resolution of the actors in the scene. The sisters shuddered, and clung closer to each other, while Heyward, instinctively, laid his hand on one of the pistols he had just drawn from their holsters, as he placed himself between his charge and those dense shadows, that seemed to draw an impenetrable veil before the bosom of the forest.

The Indians, however, hesitated not a moment, but taking the bridles, they led the frightened and reluctant horses into the bed of the river.

At a short distance from the shore, they turned, and were soon concealed by the projection of the bank, under the brow of which they moved, in a direction opposite to the course of the waters. In the mean time, the scout drew a canoe of bark from its place of concealment beneath some low bushes, whose branches were waving with the eddies of the current, into which he silently motioned for the females to enter. They complied without hesitation, though many a fearful and anxious glance was thrown behind them, towards the thickening gloom, which now lay like a dark barrier along the margin of the stream.

So soon as Cora and Alice were seated, the scout, without regarding the element, directed Heyward to support one side of the frail vessel, and posting himself at the other, they bore it up against the stream, followed by the dejected owner of the dead foal. In this manner they proceeded, for many rods, in a silence that was only interrupted by the rippling of the water, as its eddies played around them, or the low dash made by their own cautious footsteps. Heyward yielded the guidance of the canoe, implicitly, to the scout, who approached or receded from the shore, to avoid the fragments of rocks, or deeper parts of the river, with a readiness that showed his knowledge of the route they held. Occasionally he would stop; and in the midst of a breathing stillness, that the dull but increasing roar of the waterfall only served to render more impressive, he would listen with painful intenseness to catch any sounds that might arise from the slumbering forest. When assured that all was still, and unable to detect, even by the aid of his practised senses, any sign of his approaching foes, he would deliberately resume his slow and guarded progress. At length they reached a point in the river, where the roving eye of Heyward became riveted on a cluster of black objects, collected at a spot where the high bank threw a deeper shadow than usual on the dark waters. Hesitating to advance, he pointed out the place to the attention of his companion.

"Ay," returned the composed scout, "the Indians have hid the beasts with the judgment of natives! Water leaves no trail, and an owl's eyes would be blinded by the darkness of such a hole."

The whole party was soon reunited, and another consultation was held between the scout and his new comrades, during which, they, whose fates depended on the faith and ingenuity of these unknown foresters, had a little leisure to observe their situation more minutely.

The river was confined between high and cragged rocks, one of which impended above the spot where the canoe rested. As these, again, were surmounted by tall trees, which appeared to totter on the brows of the precipice, it gave the stream the appearance of running through a deep and narrow dell. All beneath the fantastic limbs and ragged tree-tops, which were, here and there, dimly painted against the starry zenith, lay alike in shadowed obscurity. Behind them, the curvature of the banks soon bounded the view, by the same dark and wooded outline; but in front, and apparently at no great distance, the water seemed piled against the heavens, whence it tumbled into caverns, out of which issued those sullen sounds, that had loaded the evening atmosphere. It seemed, in truth, to be a spot devoted to seclusion, and the sisters imbibed a soothing impression of security, as they gazed upon its romantic, though not unappalling beauties. A general movement among their conductors, however, soon recalled them from a contemplation of the wild charms that night had assisted to lend the place, to a painful sense of their real peril.

The horses had been secured to some scattering shrubs that grew in the fissures of the rocks, where, standing in the water, they were left to pass the night. The scout directed Heyward and his disconsolate fellow travellers to seat themselves in the forward end of the canoe, and took possession of the other himself, as erect and steady as if he floated in a vessel of much firmer materials. The Indians warily retraced their steps towards the place they had left, when the scout, placing his pole against a rock, by a powerful shove, sent his frail bark directly into the centre of the turbulent stream. For many minutes the struggle between the light bubble in which they floated, and the swift current, was severe and doubtful. Forbidden to stir even a hand, and almost afraid to breathe, lest they should expose the frail fabric to the fury of the stream, the passengers watched the glancing waters in feverish suspense. Twenty times they thought the whirling eddies were sweeping them to destruction, when the master-hand of their pilot would bring the bows of the canoe to stem the rapid. A long, a vigorous, and, as it appeared to the females, a desperate effort, closed the struggle. Just as Alice veiled her eyes in horror, under the impression that they were about to be swept within the vortex at the foot of the cataract, the canoe floated, stationary, at the side of a flat rock, that lay on a level with the water.

"Where are we? and what is next to be done?" demanded Heyward, perceiving that the exertions of the scout had ceased.

"You are at the foot of Glenn's," returned the other, speaking aloud, without fear of consequences, within the roar of the cataract; "and the next thing is to make a steady landing, lest the canoe upset, and you should go down again the hard road we have travelled, faster than you came up; 'tis a hard rift to stem, when the river is a little swelled; and five is an unnatural number to keep dry in the hurry-skurry, with a little birchen bark, and gum. There, go you all on the rock, and I will bring up the Mohicans with the venison. A man had better sleep without his scalp, than famish in the midst of plenty."

His passengers gladly complied with these directions. As the last foot touched the rock, the canoe whirled from its station, when the tall form of the scout was seen, for an instant, gliding above the waters, before it disappeared in the impenetrable darkness that rested on the bed of the river. Left by their guide, the travellers remained a few minutes in helpless ignorance, afraid even to move along the broken rocks, lest a false step should precipitate them down some one of the many deep and roaring caverns, into which the water seemed to tumble, on every side of them. Their suspense, however, was soon relieved; for, aided by the skill of the natives, the canoe shot back into the eddy, and floated again at the side of the low rock, before they thought the scout had even time to rejoin his companions.

"We are now fortified, garrisoned, and provisioned," cried Heyward, cheerfully, "and may set Montcalm and his allies at defiance. How, now, my vigilant sentinel, can you see any thing of those you call the Iroquois on the main land?"

"I call them Iroquois, because to me every native, who speaks a foreign tongue, is accounted an enemy, though he may pretend to serve the king! If Webb wants faith and honesty in an Indian, let him bring out the tribes of the Delawares, and send these greedy and lying Mohawks and Oneidas, with their six nations of varlets, where in nature they belong, among the French!"

"We should then exchange a warlike for a useless friend! I have heard that the Delawares have laid aside the hatchet, and are content to be called women!"

"Ay, shame on the Hollanders* and Iroquois, who carcumvented them by their deviltries into such a treaty! But I have known them for twenty years, and I call him liar, that says cowardly blood runs in the veins of a Delaware. You have driven their tribes from the sea-shore, and would now believe what their enemies say, that you may sleep at night upon an easy pillow. No, no; to me, every Indian who speaks a foreign tongue is an Iroquois, whether the castle† of his tribe be in Canada or be in York."

*The reader will remember that New York was originally a colony of the Dutch.

†The principal villages of the Indian are still called "castles" by the whites

Heyward perceiving that the stubborn adherence of the scout to the cause of his friends the Delawares or Mohicans, for they were branches of the same numerous people, was likely to prolong a useless discussion, changed the subject.

"Treaty or no treaty, I know full well, that your two companions are brave and cautious warriors! have they heard or seen any thing of our enemies?"

"An Indian is a mortal to be felt afore he is seen," returned the scout, ascending the rock, and throwing the deer carelessly down. "I trust to other signs than such as come in at the eye, when I am outlying on the trail of the Mingoes."

"Do your ears tell you that they have traced our retreat?"

"I should be sorry to think they had, though this is a spot that stout courage might hold for a smart skrimmage. I will not deny, however, but the horses cowered when I passed them, as though they scented the wolves; and a wolf is a beast that is apt to hover about an Indian ambushment, craving the offals of the deer the savages kill."

"You forget the buck at your feet! or, may we not owe their visit to the dead colt? Ha! what noise is that!"

"Poor Miriam," murmured the stranger; "thy foal was foreordained to become a prey to ravenous beasts!" Then suddenly lifting up his voice amid the eternal din of the waters, he sang aloud—

"First born of Egypt, smite did he,
Of mankind, and of beast also;
O Egypt! wonders sent 'midst thee,
On Pharaoh and his servants too!"

"The death of the colt sits heavy on the heart of its owner," said the scout; "but it's a good sign to see a man account upon his dumb friends. He has the religion of the matter, in believing what is to happen will happen; and with such a consolation, it wont be long afore he submits to the rationality of killing a four-footed beast, to save the lives of human men. It may be as you say," he continued, reverting to the purport of Heyward's last remark; "and the greater the reason

---

of New York. "Oneida castle" is no more than a scattered hamlet; but the name is in general use.

why we should cut our steaks, and let the carcass drive down the stream, or we shall have the pack howling along the cliffs, begrudging every mouthful we swallow. Besides, though the Delaware tongue is the same as a book to the Iroquois, the cunning varlets are quick enough at understanding the reason of a wolf's howl."

The scout, whilst making his remarks, was busied in collecting certain necessary implements; as he concluded, he moved silently by the groupe of travellers, accompanied by the Mohicans, who seemed to comprehend his intentions with instinctive readiness, when the whole three disappeared in succession, seeming to vanish against the dark face of a perpendicular rock, that rose to the height of a few yards, within as many feet of the water's edge.

Chapter VI

> "Those strains that once did sweet in Zion glide;
> He wales a portion with judicious care;
> And let us worship God, he says, with solemn air."
> Burns, "The Cotter's Saturday Night," ll. 106–108.

HEYWARD, and his female companions, witnessed this mysterious movement with secret uneasiness; for, though the conduct of the white man had hitherto been above reproach, his rude equipments, blunt address, and strong antipathies, together with the character of his silent associates, were all causes for exciting distrust in minds that had been so recently alarmed by Indian treachery. The stranger alone disregarded the passing incidents. He seated himself on a projection of the rocks, whence he gave no other signs of consciousness, than by the struggles of his spirit, as manifested in frequent and heavy sighs. Smothered voices were next heard, as though men called to each other in the bowels of the earth, when a sudden light flashed upon those without, and laid bare the much prized secret of the place.

At the farther extremity of a narrow, deep, cavern in the rock, whose length appeared much extended by the perspective and the nature of the light by which it was seen, was seated the scout, holding a blazing knot of pine. The strong glare of the fire fell full upon his sturdy, weather-beaten countenance and forest attire, lending an air of romantic wildness to the aspect of an individual, who, seen by the sober light of day, would have exhibited the peculiarities of a man remarkable for the strangeness of his dress, the iron-like inflexibility of his frame, and the singular compound of quick, vigilant sagacity, and of exquisite simplicity, that by turns usurped the possession of his muscular features. At a little distance in advance stood Uncas, his whole person thrown powerfully into view. The travellers anxiously regarded the upright, flexible figure of the young Mohican, graceful and unrestrained in the attitudes and movements of nature. Though his person was more than usually skreened by a green and fringed hunting shirt, like that of the white man, there was no concealment to his dark, glancing, fearless eye, alike terrible and calm; the bold outline of his high, haughty features, pure in their native red; or to the dignified elevation of his receding forehead, together with all the finest proportions of a noble head, bared to the generous scalping tuft. It was the first opportunity possessed by Duncan and his companions, to view the marked lineaments of either of their Indian attendants, and each individual of the party felt relieved from a burthen of doubt, as the proud and determined, though wild, expression of the features of the young warrior forced itself on their notice. They felt it might be a being partially benighted in the vale of ignorance, but it could not be one who would willingly devote his rich natural gifts to the purposes of wanton treachery. The ingenuous Alice gazed at his free air and proud carriage, as she would have looked upon some precious relic of the Grecian chisel, to which life had been imparted, by the intervention of a miracle; while Heyward, though accustomed to see the perfection of form which abounds among the uncorrupted natives, openly expressed his admiration at such an unblemished specimen of the noblest proportions of man.

"I could sleep in peace," whispered Alice, in reply, " with such a fearless and generous looking youth for my sentinel. Surely, Duncan, those cruel murders, those terrific scenes of torture, of which we read and hear so much, are never acted in the presence of such as he!"

"This, certainly, is a rare and brilliant instance of those natural qualities, in which these peculiar people are said to excel," he answered. "I agree with you, Alice, in thinking that such a front and eye were formed rather to intimidate than to deceive; but let us not practise a deception on ourselves, by expecting any other exhibition of what we esteem virtue, than according to the fashion of a savage. As bright examples of great qualities are but too uncommon among christians, so are they singular and solitary with the Indians; though, for the honour of our common nature, neither are incapable of producing them. Let us then hope, that this Mohican may not disappoint our wishes, but prove, what his looks assert him to be, a brave and constant friend."

"Now Major Heyward speaks, as Major Heyward should,"

said Cora; " who, that looks at this creature of nature, remembers the shades of his skin!"

A short, and apparently an embarrassed, silence succeeded this remark, which was interrupted by the scout calling to them aloud, to enter.

"This fire begins to show too bright a flame," he continued, as they complied, "and might light the Mingoes to our undoing. Uncas, drop the blanket, and show the knaves its dark side. This is not such a supper as a major of the Royal Americans has a right to expect, but I've known stout detachments of the corps glad to eat their venison raw, and without a relish too.* Here, you see, we have plenty of salt, and can make a quick broil. There's fresh saxafrax boughs for the ladies to sit on, which may not be as proud as their my-hog-guinea chairs, but which sends up a sweeter flavour than the skin of any hog can do, be it of Guinea, or be it of any other land. Come, friend, dont be mournful for the colt; 'twas an innocent thing, and had not seen much hardship. Its death will save the creatur many a sore back and weary foot!"

Uncas did as the other had directed, and when the voice of Hawk-eye ceased, the roar of the cataract sounded like the rumbling of distant thunder.

"Are we quite safe in this cavern?" demanded Heyward. "Is there no danger of surprise? A single armed man, at its entrance, would hold us at his mercy."

A spectral looking figure stalked from out the darkness behind the scout, and seizing a blazing brand, held it towards the further extremity of their place of retreat. Alice uttered a faint shriek, and even Cora rose to her feet, as this appalling object moved into the light; but a single word from Heyward calmed them, with the assurance it was only their attendant, Chingachgook, who, lifting another blanket, discovered that the cavern had two outlets. Then, holding the brand, he

*In vulgar parlance the condiments of a repast are called by the American "a relish," substituting the thing for its effect. These provincial terms are frequently put in the mouths of the speakers, according to their several conditions in life. Most of them are of local use, and others quite peculiar to the particular class of men to which the character belongs. In the present instance, the scout uses the word with immediate reference to the "salt," with which his own party was so fortunate as to be provided.

crossed a deep, narrow chasm in the rocks, which ran at right angles with the passage they were in, but which, unlike that, was open to the heavens, and entered another cave, answering to the description of the first, in every essential particular.

"Such old foxes as Chingachgook and myself, are not often caught in a burrow with one hole," said Hawk-eye, laughing; "you can easily see the cunning of the place—the rock is black limestone, which every body knows is soft; it makes no uncomfortable pillow, where brush and pine wood is scarce; well, the fall was once a few yards below us, and I dare to say was, in its time, as regular and as handsome a sheet of water as any along the Hudson. But old age is a great injury to good looks, as these sweet young ladies have yet to l'arn! The place is sadly changed! These rocks are full of cracks, and in some places, they are softer than at othersome, and the water has worked out deep hollows for itself, until it has fallen back, ay, some hundred feet, breaking here, and wearing there, until the falls have neither shape nor consistency."

"In what part of them are we?" asked Heyward.

"Why, we are nigh by the spot that Providence first placed them at, but where, it seems, they were too rebellious to stay. The rock proved softer on either side of us, and so they left the centre of the river bare and dry, first working out these two little holes for us to hide in."

"We are then on an island?"

"Ay! there are the falls on two sides of us, and the river above and below. If you had daylight, it would be worth the trouble to step up on the height of this rock, and look at the perversity of the water! It falls by no rule at all; sometimes it leaps, sometimes it tumbles; there, it skips; here, it shoots; in one place 'tis white as snow, and in another 'tis green as grass; hereabouts, it pitches into deep hollows, that rumble and quake the 'arth; and thereaway, it ripples and sings like a brook, fashioning whirlpools and gullies in the old stone, as if 'twas no harder than trodden clay. The whole design of the river seems disconcerted. First it runs smoothly, as if meaning to go down the descent as things were ordered; then it angles about and faces the shores; nor are there places wanting, where it looks backward, as if unwilling to leave the wilderness, to mingle with the salt! Ay, lady, the fine cobweb-looking cloth you wear at your throat, is coarse, and like a fish net, to little spots I can show you, where the river fabricates all sorts of images, as if, having broke loose from order, it would try its hand at every thing. And yet what does it amount to! After the water has been suffered to have its will for a time, like a headstrong man, it is gathered together by the hand that made it, and a few rods below you may see it all, flowing on steadily towards the sea, as was foreordained from the first foundation of the 'arth!"

While his auditors received a cheering assurance of the security of their place of concealment, from this untutored description of Glenn's,* they were much inclined to judge differently from Hawk-eye, of its wild beauties. But they were not in a situation to suffer their thoughts to dwell on the charms of natural objects; and, as the scout had not found it necessary to cease his culinary labours while he spoke, unless to point out, with a broken fork, the direction of some particularly obnoxious point in the rebellious stream, they now suffered their attention to be drawn to the necessary though more vulgar consideration of their supper.

The repast, which was greatly aided by the addition of a few delicacies, that Heyward had the precaution to bring with him, when they left their horses, was exceedingly refreshing to the wearied party. Uncas acted as attendant to the females, performing all the little offices within his power, with a mixture of dignity and anxious grace, that served to amuse Heyward, who well knew that it was an utter innovation on the Indian customs, which forbid their warriors to descend to any menial employment, especially in favour of their women. As

*Glenn's Falls are on the Hudson, some forty or fifty miles above the head of tide, or the place where that river becomes navigable for sloops. The description of this picturesque and remarkable little cataract, as given by the scout, is sufficiently correct, though the application of the water to the uses of civilised life has materially injured its beauties. The rocky island and the two caverns are well known to every traveller, since the former sustains a pier of a bridge, which is now thrown across the river, immediately above the fall. In explanation of the taste of Hawk-eye, it should be remembered that men always prize that most which is least enjoyed. Thus, in a new country, the woods and other objects, which in an old country would be maintained at great cost, are gotten rid of, simply with a view of "improving" as it is called.

the rites of hospitality were, however, considered sacred among them, this little departure from the dignity of manhood excited no audible comment. Had there been one there sufficiently disengaged to become a close observer, he might have fancied that the services of the young chief were not entirely impartial. That, while he tendered to Alice the gourd of sweet water, and the venison in a trencher, neatly carved from the knot of the pepperage, with sufficient courtesy, in performing the same offices to her sister, his dark eye lingered on her rich, speaking, countenance. Once or twice he was compelled to speak, to command the attention of those he served. In such cases, he made use of English, broken and imperfect, but sufficiently intelligible, and which he rendered so mild and musical, by his* deep, guttural voice, that it never failed to cause both ladies to look up in admiration and astonishment. In the course of these civilities, a few sentences were exchanged, that served to establish the appearance of an amicable intercourse between the parties.

In the meanwhile, the gravity of Chingachgook remained immovable. He had seated himself more within the circle of light, where the frequent, uneasy glances of his guests were better enabled to separate the natural expression of his face, from the artificial terrors of the war-paint. They found a strong resemblance between father and son, with the difference that might be expected from age and hardship. The fierceness of his countenance now seemed to slumber, and in its place was to be seen the quiet, vacant composure, which distinguishes an Indian warrior, when his faculties are not required for any of the greater purposes of his existence. It was, however, easy to be seen, by the occasional gleams that shot across his swarthy visage, that it was only necessary to arouse his passions in order to give full effect to the terrific device which he had adopted to intimidate his enemies. On the other hand, the quick, roving eye of the scout seldom rested. He ate and drank with an appetite that no sense of danger could disturb, but his vigilance seemed never to desert him. Twenty times the gourd or the venison was suspended before his lips, while his head was turned aside, as though he

*The meaning of Indian words is much governed by the emphasis and tones.

listened to some distant and distrusted sounds—a movement that never failed to recall his guests from regarding the novelties of their situation, to a recollection of the alarming reasons that had driven them to seek it. As these frequent pauses were never followed by any remark, the momentary uneasiness they created quickly passed away, and for a time was forgotten.

"Come, friend," said Hawk-eye, drawing out a keg from beneath a cover of leaves, towards the close of the repast, and addressing the stranger who sat at his elbow, doing great justice to his culinary skill, "try a little spruce; 'twill wash away all thoughts of the colt, and quicken the life in your bosom. I drink to our better friendship, hoping that a little horseflesh may leave no heart-burnings atween us. How do you name yourself?"

"Gamut—David Gamut," returned the singing-master, preparing to wash down his sorrows, in a powerful draught of the woodsman's high-flavoured and well-laced compound.

"A very good name, and, I dare say, handed down from honest forefathers. I'm an admirator of names, though the Christian fashions fall far below savage customs in this particular. The biggest coward I ever knew was called Lyon; and his wife, Patience, would scold you out of hearing in less time than a hunted deer would run a rod. With an Indian 'tis a matter of conscience; what he calls himself, he generally is—not that Chingachgook, which signifies a big sarpent, is really a snake, big or little; but that he understands the windings and turnings of human natur, and is silent, and strikes his enemies when they least expect him. What may be your calling?"

"I am an unworthy instructor in the art of psalmody."

"Anan!"

"I teach singing to the youths of the Connecticut levy."

"You might be better employed. The young hounds go laughing and singing too much already through the woods, when they ought not to breathe louder than a fox in his cover. Can you use the smooth bore, or handle the rifle?"

"Praised be God, I have never had occasion to meddle with murderous implements!"

"Perhaps you understand the compass, and lay down the

water courses and mountains of the wilderness on paper, in order that they who follow may find places by their given names?"

"I practise no such employment."

"You have a pair of legs that might make a long path seem short! you journey sometimes, I fancy, with tidings for the general."

"Never; I follow no other than my own high vocation, which is instruction in sacred music!"

" 'Tis a strange calling!" muttered Hawk-eye, with an inward laugh, "to go through life, like a cat-bird, mocking all the ups and downs that may happen to come out of other men's throats. Well, friend, I suppose it is your gift, and mustn't be denied any more than if 'twas shooting, or some other better inclination. Let us hear what you can do in that way; 'twill be a friendly manner of saying good night, for 'tis time these ladies should be getting strength for a hard and a long push, in the pride of the morning, afore the Maquas are stirring."

"With joyful pleasure do I consent," said David, adjusting his iron-rimmed spectacles, and producing his beloved little volume, which he immediately tendered to Alice. "What can be more fitting and consolatory, than to offer up evening praise after a day of such exceeding jeopardy!"

Alice smiled; but regarding Heyward, she blushed and hesitated.

"Indulge yourself," he whispered; "ought not the suggestion of the worthy namesake of the Psalmist to have its weight at such a moment?"

Encouraged by his opinion, Alice did what her pious inclinations and her keen relish for gentle sounds, had before so strongly urged. The book was open at a hymn not ill adapted to their situation, and in which the poet, no longer goaded by his desire to excel the inspired King of Israel, had discovered some chastened and respectable powers. Cora betrayed a disposition to support her sister, and the sacred song proceeded, after the indispensable preliminaries of the pitch-pipe and the tune had been duly attended to by the methodical David.

The air was solemn and slow. At times it rose to the fullest compass of the rich voices of the females, who hung over their little book in holy excitement, and again it sunk so low, that the rushing of the waters ran through their melody like a hollow accompaniment. The natural taste and true ear of David, governed and modified the sounds to suit their confined cavern, every crevice and cranny of which was filled with the thrilling notes of their flexible voices. The Indians riveted their eyes on the rocks, and listened with an attention that seemed to turn them into stone. But the scout, who had placed his chin in his hand, with an expression of cold indifference, gradually suffered his rigid features to relax, until, as verse succeeded verse, he felt his iron nature subdued, while his recollection was carried back to boyhood, when his ears had been accustomed to listen to similar sounds of praise, in the settlements of the colony. His roving eyes began to moisten, and before the hymn was ended, scalding tears rolled out of fountains that had long seemed dry, and followed each other down those cheeks that had oftener felt the storms of heaven, than any testimonials of weakness. The singers were dwelling on one of those low, dying chords, which the ear devours with such greedy rapture, as if conscious that it is about to lose them, when a cry, that seemed neither human, nor earthly, rose in the outward air, penetrating not only the recesses of the cavern, but to the inmost hearts of all who heard it. It was followed by a stillness apparently as deep as if the waters had been checked in their furious progress at such a horrid and unusual interruption.

"What is it?" murmured Alice, after a few moments of terrible suspense.

"What is it?" repeated Heyward, aloud.

Neither Hawk-eye, nor the Indians, made any reply. They listened, as if expecting the sound would be repeated, with a manner that expressed their own astonishment. At length, they spoke together, earnestly, in the Delaware language, when Uncas, passing by the inner and most concealed aperture, cautiously left the cavern. When he had gone, the scout first spoke in English.

"What it is, or what it is not, none here can tell; though two of us have ranged the woods for more than thirty years! I did believe there was no cry that Indian or beast could make, that my ears had not heard; but this has proved that I was only a vain and conceited mortal."

"Was it not, then, the shout the warriors make when they wish to intimidate their enemies?" asked Cora, who stood drawing her veil about her person, with a calmness to which her agitated sister was a stranger.

"No, no; this was bad, and shocking, and had a sort of unhuman sound; but when you once hear the war-whoop, you will never mistake it for any thing else! Well, Uncas!" speaking in the Delaware to the young chief as he re-entered, "what see you? do our lights shine through the blankets?"

The answer was short, and apparently decided, being given in the same tongue.

"There is nothing to be seen without," continued Hawk-eye, shaking his head in discontent; "and our hiding-place is still in darkness! Pass into the other cave, you that need it, and seek for sleep; we must be afoot long before the sun, and make the most of our time to get to Edward, while the Mingoes are taking their morning nap."

Cora set the example of compliance, with a steadiness that taught the more timid Alice the necessity of obedience. Before leaving the place, however, she whispered a request to Duncan that he would follow. Uncas raised the blanket for their passage, and as the sisters turned to thank him for this act of attention, they saw the scout seated again before the dying embers, with his face resting on his hands, in a manner which showed how deeply he brooded on the unaccountable interruption, which had broken up their evening devotions.

Heyward took with him a blazing knot, which threw a dim light through the narrow vista of their new apartment. Placing it in a favourable position, he joined the females, who now found themselves alone with him, for the first time since they had left the friendly ramparts of fort Edward.

"Leave us not, Duncan," said Alice; "we cannot sleep in such a place as this, with that horrid cry still ringing in our ears!"

"First let us examine into the security of your fortress," he answered, "and then we will speak of rest."

He approached the farther end of the cavern, to an outlet,

which, like the others, was concealed by blankets, and removing the thick skreen, breathed the fresh and reviving air from the cataract. One arm of the river flowed through a deep, narrow ravine, which its current had worn in the soft rock, directly beneath his feet, forming an effectual defence, as he believed, against any danger from that quarter; the water, a few rods above them, plunging, glancing, and sweeping along, in its most violent and broken manner.

"Nature has made an impenetrable barrier on this side," he continued, pointing down the perpendicular declivity into the dark current, before he dropped the blanket; "and as you know that good men and true, are on guard in front, I see no reason why the advice of our honest host should be disregarded. I am certain Cora will join me in saying, that sleep is necessary to you both!"

"Cora may submit to the justice of your opinion, though she cannot put it in practice," returned the elder sister, who had placed herself by the side of Alice, on a couch of sassafras; "there would be other causes to chase away sleep, though we had been spared the shock of this mysterious noise. Ask yourself, Heyward, can daughters forget the anxiety a father must endure, whose children lodge, he knows not where or how, in such a wilderness, and in the midst of so many perils!"

"He is a soldier, and knows how to estimate the chances of the woods."

"He is a father, and cannot deny his nature."

"How kind has he ever been to all my follies! how tender and indulgent to all my wishes!" sobbed Alice. "We have been selfish, sister, in urging our visit at such hazard!"

"I may have been a rash in pressing his consent in a moment of so much embarrassment, but I would have proved to him, that however others might neglect him, in his strait, his children at least were faithful!"

"When he heard of your arrival at Edward," said Heyward, kindly, "there was a powerful struggle in his bosom between fear and love; though the latter, heightened, if possible, by so long a separation, quickly prevailed. 'It is the spirit of my noble minded Cora that leads them, Duncan,' he said, 'and I will not balk it. Would to God, that he who holds the honor of our royal master in his guardianship, would show but half her firmness.' "

"And did he not speak of me, Heyward?" demanded Alice, with jealous affection. "Surely, he forgot not altogether his little Elsie!"

"That were impossible," returned the young man; "he called you by a thousand endearing epithets, that I may not presume to use, but to the justice of which I can warmly testify. Once, indeed, he said—"

Duncan ceased speaking; for while his eyes were rivetted on those of Alice, who had turned towards him with the eagerness of filial affection, to catch his words, the same strong, horrid cry, as before, filled the air, and rendered him mute. A long, breathless silence succeeded, during which, each looked at the others in fearful expectation of hearing the sound repeated. At length, the blanket was slowly raised, and the scout stood in the aperture with a countenance whose firmness evidently began to give way, before a mystery that seemed to threaten some danger, against which all his cunning and experience might prove of no avail.

Chapter VII

"They do not sleep.
On yonder cliffs, a grisly band,
I see them sit."
Gray, "The Bard," I.3 [Epode I.] ll. 43–45.

'TWOULD BE NEGLECTING a warning that is given for our good, to lie hid any longer," said Hawk-eye, "when such sounds are raised in the forest! These gentle ones may keep close, but the Mohicans and I will watch upon the rock, where I suppose a major of the 60th would wish to keep us company."

"Is then our danger so pressing?" asked Cora.

"He who makes strange sounds, and gives them out for man's information, alone knows our danger. I should think myself wicked unto rebellion against his will, was I to burrow with such warnings in the air! Even the weak soul, who passes his days in singing, is stirred by the cry, and, as he says, is 'ready to go forth to the battle.' If 'twere only a battle, it would be a thing understood by us all, and easily managed; but I have heard that when such shrieks are atween heaven and 'arth, it betokens another sort of warfare!"

"If all our reasons for fear, my friend, are confined to such as proceed from supernatural causes, we have but little occasion to be alarmed," continued the undisturbed Cora; "are you certain that our enemies have not invented some new and ingenious method to strike us with terror, that their conquest may become more easy?"

"Lady," returned the scout, solemnly, "I have listened to all the sounds of the woods for thirty years, as a man will listen, whose life and death depend on the quickness of his ears. There is no whine of the panther; no whistle of the cat-bird; nor any invention of the devilish Mingoes, that can cheat me! I have heard the forest moan like mortal men, in their affliction; often, and again, have I listened to the wind playing its music in the branches of the girdled trees; and I have heard the lightning cracking in the air, like the snapping of blazing brush, as it spitted forth sparks and forked flames; but never have I thought that I heard more than the pleasure of him, who sported with the things of his hand. But neither the Mohicans, nor I, who am a white man without a cross, can explain the cry just heard. We, therefore, believe it a sign given for our good."

"It is extraordinary!" said Heyward, taking his pistols from the place where he had laid them, on entering; "be it a sign of peace, or a signal of war, it must be looked to. Lead the way, my friend; I follow."

On issuing from their place of confinement, the whole party instantly experienced a grateful renovation of spirits, by exchanging the pent air of the hiding place, for the cool and invigorating atmosphere, which played around the whirlpools and pitches of the cataract. A heavy evening breeze swept along the surface of the river, and seemed to drive the roar of the falls into the recesses of their own caverns, whence it issued heavily and constant, like thunder rumbling beyond the distant hills. The moon had risen, and its light was already glancing here and there on the waters above them; but the extremity of the rock where they stood still lay in shadow. With the exception of the sounds produced by the rushing waters, and an occasional breathing of the air, as it murmured past them, in fitful currents, the scene was as still as night and solitude could make it. In vain were the eyes of each individual bent along the opposite shores, in quest of some signs of life, that might explain the nature of the interruption they had heard. Their anxious and eager looks were baffled by the deceptive light, or rested only on naked rocks, and straight and immovable trees.

"Here is nothing to be seen but the gloom and quiet of a lovely evening," whispered Duncan; "how much should we prize such a scene, and all this breathing solitude, at any other moment, Cora! Fancy yourselves in security, and what now, perhaps, increases your terror, may be made conducive to enjoyment—"

"Listen!" interrupted Alice.

The caution was unnecessary. Once more the same sound arose, as if from the bed of the river, and having broken out of the narrow bounds of the cliffs, was heard undulating through the forest, in distant and dying cadences.

"Can any here give a name to such a cry?" demanded Hawk-eye, when the last echo was lost in the woods; "if so, let him speak; for myself, I judge it not to belong to 'arth!"

"Here, then, is one who can undeceive you," said Duncan; "I know the sound full well, for often have I heard it on the field of battle, and in situations which are frequent in a soldier's life. 'Tis the horrid shriek that a horse will give in his agony; oftener drawn from him in pain, though sometimes in terror. My charger is either a prey to the beasts of the forest, or he sees his danger without the power to avoid it. The sound might deceive me in the cavern, but in the open air I know it too well to be wrong."

The scout and his companions listened to this simple explanation with the interest of men, who imbibe new ideas, at the same time that they get rid of old ones, which had proved disagreeable inmates. The two latter uttered their usual and expressive exclamation, "hugh!" as the truth first glanced upon their minds, while the former, after a short musing pause, took on himself to reply.

"I cannot deny your words," he said; "for I am little skilled in horses, though born where they abound. The wolves must be hovering above their heads on the bank, and the timorsome creatures are calling on man for help, in the best manner they are able. Uncas"—he spoke in Delaware—"Uncas, drop down in the canoe, and whirl a brand among the pack; or fear may do what the wolves can't get at to perform, and leave us without horses in the morning, when we shall have so much need to journey swiftly!"

The young native had already descended to the water, to comply, when a long howl was raised on the edge of the river, and was borne swiftly off into the depths of the forest, as though the beasts, of their own accord, were abandoning their prey, in sudden terror. Uncas, with instinctive quickness, receded, and the three foresters held another of their low, earnest conferences.

"We have been like hunters who have lost the points of the heavens, and from whom the sun has been hid for days," said Hawk-eye, turning away from his companions; "now we begin again to know the signs of our course, and the paths are cleared from briars! Seat yourselves in the shade, which the moon throws from yonder beech—'tis thicker than that of the pines—and let us wait for that which the Lord may choose to send next. Let all your conversation be in whispers; though it would be better, and perhaps, in the end, wiser, if each one held discourse with his own thoughts for a time."

The manner of the scout was seriously impressive, though no longer distinguished by any signs of unmanly apprehension. It was evident, that his momentary weakness had vanished with the explanation of a mystery, which his own experience had not served to fathom; and though he now felt all the realities of their actual condition, that he was prepared to meet them with the energy of his hardy nature. This feeling seemed also common to the natives, who placed themselves in positions which commanded a full view of both shores, while their own persons were effectually concealed from observation. In such circumstances, common prudence dictated that Heyward, and his companions, should imitate a caution that proceeded from so intelligent a source. The young man drew a pile of the sassafras from the cave, and placing it in the chasm which separated the two caverns, it was occupied by the sisters; who were thus protected by the rocks from any missiles, while their anxiety was relieved by the assurance that no danger could approach without a warning. Heyward himself was posted at hand, so near that he might communicate with his companions without raising his voice to a dangerous elevation; while David, in imitation of the woodsmen, bestowed his person in such a manner among the fissures of the rocks, that his ungainly limbs were no longer offensive to the eye.

In this manner, hours passed by without further interruption. The moon reached the zenith, and shed its mild light, perpendicularly, on the lovely sight of the sisters, slumbering peacefully in each other's arms. Duncan cast the wide shawl of Cora before a spectacle he so much loved to contemplate, and then suffered his own head to seek a pillow on the rock. David began to utter sounds that would have shocked his delicate organs in more wakeful moments; in short, all but Hawk-eye and the Mohicans lost every idea of consciousness, in uncontrollable drowsiness. But the watchfulness of these vigilant protectors, neither tired nor slumbered. Immovable as that rock, of which each appeared to form a part, they lay, with their eyes roving, without intermission, along the dark margin of trees that bounded the adjacent shores of the narrow stream. Not a sound escaped them; the most subtle examination could not have told they breathed. It was evident, that this excess of caution proceeded, from an experience, that no subtlety on the part of their enemies could deceive. It was, however, continued without any apparent consequences, until the moon had set, and a pale streak above the tree tops, at the bend of the river, a little below, announced the approach of day.

Then, for the first time, Hawk-eye was seen to stir. He crawled along the rock, and shook Duncan from his heavy slumbers.

"Now is the time to journey," he whispered; "awake the gentle ones, and be ready to get into the canoe when I bring it to the landing place."

"Have you had a quiet night?" said Heyward; "for myself, I believe sleep has gotten the better of my vigilance."

"All is yet still as midnight. Be silent, but be quick."

By this time Duncan was thoroughly awake, and he immediately lifted the shawl from the sleeping females. The motion caused Cora to raise her hand as if to repulse him, while Alice murmured, in her soft, gentle voice, "No, no, dear father, we were not deserted; Duncan was with us."

"Yes, sweet innocence," whispered the youth; "Duncan is here, and while life continue, or danger remain, he will never quit thee. Cora! Alice! awake! The hour has come to move!"

A loud shriek from the younger of the sisters, and the form of the other standing upright before him, in bewildered horror, was the unexpected answer he received. While the words were still on the lips of Heyward, there had arisen such a tumult of yells and cries, as served to drive the swift currents of his own blood, back from its bounding course into the fountains of his heart. It seemed, for near a minute, as if the demons of hell had possessed themselves of the air about them, and were venting their savage humours in barbarous sounds. The cries came from no particular direction, though it was evident they filled the woods, and, as the appalled listeners easily imagined, the caverns of the falls, the rocks, the bed of the river, and the upper air. David raised his tall person in the midst of the infernal din, with a hand on either ear, exclaiming—

"Whence comes this discord! Has hell broke loose, that man should utter sounds like these!"

The bright flashes, and the quick reports of a dozen rifles, from the opposite banks of the stream, followed this incautious exposure of his person, and left the unfortunate singing master, senseless, on that rock where he had been so long slumbering. The Mohicans boldly sent back the intimidating yell of their enemies, who raised a shout of savage triumph at the fall of Gamut. The flash of rifles was then quick and close between them, but either party was too well skilled to leave even a limb exposed to the hostile aim. Duncan listened with intense anxiety for the strokes of the paddle, believing that flight was now their only refuge. The river glanced by with its ordinary velocity, but the canoe was no where to be seen on its dark waters. He had just fancied they were cruelly deserted by the scout, as a stream of flame issued from the rock beneath him, and a fierce yell, blended with a shriek of agony, announced that the messenger of death, hurled from the fatal weapon of Hawk-eye, had found a victim. At this slight repulse the assailants instantly withdrew and, gradually, the place became as still as before the sudden tumult.

Duncan seized the favourable moment to spring to the body of Gamut, which he bore within the shelter of the narrow chasm that protected the sisters. In another minute the whole party was collected in this spot of comparative safety.

"The poor fellow has saved his scalp," said Hawk-eye, coolly passing his hand over the head of David; "but he is a proof that a man may be born with too long a tongue! 'Twas downright madness to show six feet of flesh and blood, on a naked rock, to the raging savages. I only wonder he has escaped with life."

"Is he not dead!" demanded Cora, in a voice whose husky tones showed how powerfully, natural horror struggled with her assumed firmness. "Can we do aught to assist the wretched man?"

"No, no! the life is in his heart yet, and after he has slept awhile he will come to himself, and be a wiser man for it, till the hour of his real time shall come," returned Hawk-eye, casting another oblique glance at the insensible body, while he filled his charger with admirable nicety. "Carry him in, Uncas, and lay him on the saxafrax. The longer his nap lasts the better it will be for him; as I doubt whether he can find a proper cover for such a shape on these rocks; and singing won't do any good with the Iroquois."

"You believe, then, the attack will be renewed?" asked Heyward.

"Do I expect a hungry wolf will satisfy his craving with a mouthful! They have lost a man, and 'tis their fashion, when they meet a loss, and fail in the surprise, to fall back; but we shall have them on again, with new expedients to circumvent us, and master our scalps. Our main hope," he continued, raising his rugged countenance, across which a shade of anxiety just then passed like a darkening cloud, " will be to keep the rock until Munro can send a party to our help! God send it may be soon, and under a leader that knows the Indian customs!"

"You hear our probable fortunes, Cora," said Duncan; "and you know we have every thing to hope from the anxiety and experience of your father. Come, then, with Alice, into this cavern, where you, at least, will be safe from the murderous rifles of our enemies, and where you may bestow a care suited to your gentle natures, on our unfortunate comrade."

The sisters followed him into the outer cave, where David was beginning, by his sighs, to give symptoms of returning consciousness, and, then, commending the wounded man to their attention, he immediately prepared to leave them.

"Duncan!" said the tremulous voice of Cora, when he had reached the mouth of the cavern. He turned, and beheld the speaker, whose colour had changed to a deadly paleness, and whose lip quivered, gazing after him, with an expression of interest which immediately recalled him to her side. "Remember, Duncan, how necessary your safety is to our own—how you bear a father's sacred trust—how much depends on your discretion and care—in short," she added, while the tell-tale blood stole over her features, crimsoning her very temples, "how very deservedly dear you are to all of the name of Munro."

"If any thing could add to my own base love of life," said Heyward, suffering his unconscious eyes to wander to the youthful form of the silent Alice; "it would be so kind an assurance. As major of the 60th, our honest host will tell you I must take my share of the fray; but our task will be easy; it is merely to keep these blood-hounds at bay for a few hours."

Without waiting for reply, he tore himself from the presence of the sisters, and joined the scout and his companions, who still lay within the protection of the little chasm, between the two caves.

"I tell you, Uncas," said the former, as Heyward joined them, "you are wasteful of your powder, and the kick of the rifle disconcerts your aim! Little powder, light lead, and a long arm, seldom fail of bringing the death screech from a Mingo! At least, such has been my experience with the creaturs. Come, friends; let us to our covers, for no man can tell when or where a Maqua* will strike his blow!"

The Indians silently repaired to their appointed stations, which were fissures in the rocks, whence they could command the approaches to the foot of the falls. In the centre of the little island, a few short and stunted pines had found root, forming a thicket, into which Hawk-eye darted, with the swiftness of a deer, followed by the active Duncan. Here they secured themselves, as well as circumstances would permit, among the shrubs and fragments of stone that were scattered about the place. Above them was a bare, rounded rock, on each side of which the water played its gambols, and plunged into the abysses beneath, in the manner already described. As the day had now dawned, the opposite shores no longer presented a confused outline, but they were able to look into the woods, and distinguish objects, beneath the canopy of gloomy pines.

A long and anxious watch succeeded, but without any further evidences of a renewed attack, and Duncan began to hope that their fire had proved more fatal than was supposed, and that their enemies had been effectually repulsed. When he

*It will be observed that Hawk-eye applies different names to his enemies. Mingo and Maqua are terms of contempt, and Iroquois is a name given by the French. The Indians rarely use the same name when different tribes speak of each other.

ventured to utter this impression to his companion, it was met by Hawk-eye with an incredulous shake of the head.

"You know not the nature of a Maqua, if you think he is so easily beaten back, without a scalp!" he answered. "If there was one of the imps yelling this morning, there were forty! and they know our number and quality too well to give up the chase so soon. Hist! look into the water above, just where it breaks over the rocks. I am no mortal, if the risky devils haven't swam down upon the very pitch, and as bad luck would have it, they have hit the head of the island! Hist! man, keep close! or the hair will be off your crown in the turning of a knife!"

Heyward lifted his head from the cover, and beheld what he justly considered a prodigy of rashness and skill. The river had worn away the edge of the soft rock in such a manner, as to render its first pitch less abrupt and perpendicular, than is usual at waterfalls. With no other guide than the ripple of the stream where it met the head of the island, a party of their insatiable foes had ventured into the current, and swam down upon this point, knowing the ready access it would give, if successful, to their intended victims. As Hawk-eye ceased speaking, four human heads could be seen peering above a few logs of drift wood, that had lodged on these naked rocks, and which had probably suggested the idea of the practicability of the hazardous undertaking. At the next moment, a fifth form was seen floating over the green edge of the fall, a little from the line of the island. The savage struggled powerfully to gain the point of safety, and favoured by the glancing water, he was already stretching forth an arm to meet the grasp of his companions, when he shot away again with the whirling current, appeared to rise into the air, with uplifted arms, and starting eye-balls, and fell, with a sullen plunge, into that deep and yawning abyss over which he hovered. A single, wild, despairing shriek, rose from the cavern, and all was hushed again as the grave.

The first generous impulse of Duncan, was to rush to the rescue of the hapless wretch, but he felt himself bound to the spot, by the iron grasp of the immoveable scout.

"Would ye bring certain death upon us, by telling the Mingoes where we lie?" demanded Hawk-eye, sternly; " 'tis a charge of powder saved, and ammunition is as precious now as breath to a worried deer! Freshen the priming of your pistols—the mist of the falls is apt to dampen the brimstone—and stand firm for a close struggle, while I fire on their rush."

He placed a finger in his mouth, and drew a long, shrill whistle, which was answered from the rocks, that were guarded by the Mohicans. Duncan caught glimpses of heads above the scattered drift wood, as this signal rose on the air, but they disappeared again as suddenly as they had glanced upon his sight. A low, rustling sound, next drew his attention behind him, and turning his head, he beheld Uncas within a few feet, creeping to his side. Hawk-eye spoke to him in Delaware, when the young chief took his position with singular caution, and undisturbed coolness. To Heyward this was a moment of feverish and impatient suspense; though the scout saw fit to select it as a fit occasion to read a lecture to his more youthful associates, on the art of using fire-arms with discretion.

"Of all we'pons," he commenced, "the long barrelled, true grooved, soft metalled rifle, is the most dangerous in skillful hands, though it wants a strong arm, a quick eye, and great judgment in charging, to put forth all its beauties. The gunsmiths can have but little insight into their trade, when they make their fowling-pieces and short horsemens'—"

He was interrupted by the low, but expressive "hugh" of Uncas.

"I see them, boy, I see them!" continued Hawk-eye; "they are gathering for the rush, or they would keep their dingy backs below the logs. Well, let them," he added, examining his flint; "the leading man certainly comes on to his death, though it should be Montcalm himself!"

At that moment the woods were filled with another burst of cries, and, at the signal, four savages sprang from the cover of the drift wood. Heyward felt a burning desire to rush forward to meet them, so intense was the delirious anxiety of the moment, but he was restrained by the deliberate examples of the scout and Uncas. When their foes, who leaped over the black rocks that divided them, with long bounds, uttering the wildest yells, were within a few rods, the rifle of Hawk-eye slowly rose among the shrubs, and poured out its fatal contents. The foremost Indian bounded like a stricken deer, and fell headlong among the clefts of the island.

"Now, Uncas!" cried the scout, drawing his long knife, while his quick eyes began to flash with ardour, "take the last of the screeching imps; of the other two we are sartain!"

He was obeyed; and but two enemies remained to be overcome. Heyward had given one of his pistols to Hawk-eye, and together they rushed down a little declivity towards their foes; they discharged their weapons at the same instant, and equally without success.

"I know'd it! and I said it!" muttered the scout, whirling the despised little implement over the falls, with bitter disdain. "Come on, ye bloody minded hell-hounds! ye meet a man without a cross!"

The words were barely uttered, when he encountered a savage of gigantic stature, and of the fiercest mien. At the same moment, Duncan found himself engaged with the other, in a similar contest of hand to hand. With ready skill, Hawk-eye and his antagonist each grasped that uplifted arm of the other, which held the dangerous knife. For near a minute, they stood looking one another in the eye, and gradually exerting the power of their muscles for the mastery. At length, the toughened sinews of the white man prevailed over the less practised limbs of the native. The arm of the latter slowly gave way before the increasing force of the scout, who suddenly wresting his armed hand from the grasp of his foe, drove the sharp weapon through his naked bosom to the heart. In the meantime, Heyward had been pressed in a more deadly struggle. His slight sword was snapped in the first encounter. As he was destitute of any other means of defence, his safety now depended entirely on bodily strength and resolution. Though deficient in neither of these qualities, he had met an enemy every way his equal. Happily, he soon succeeded in disarming his adversary, whose knife fell on the rock at their feet, and from this moment it became a fierce struggle, who should cast the other over the dizzy height, into a neighbouring cavern of the falls. Every successive struggle brought them nearer to the verge, where Duncan perceived the final and conquering effort must be made. Each of the combatants threw all his energies into that effort, and the result was, that both tottered on the brink of the precipice. Heyward felt the grasp of the other at his throat, and saw the grim smile the savage gave, under the revengeful hope that he hurried his enemy to a fate similar to his own, as he felt his body slowly yielding to a resistless power, and the young man experienced the passing agony of such a moment in all its horrors. At that instant of extreme danger, a dark hand, and glancing knife appeared before him; the Indian released his hold, as the blood flowed freely from around the severed tendons of his wrist; and while Duncan was drawn backward by the saving arm of Uncas, his charmed eyes were still riveted on the fierce and disappointed countenance of his foe, who fell sullenly and disappointed down the irrecoverable precipice.

"To cover! to cover!" cried Hawk-eye, who just then had despatched his enemy; "to cover, for your lives! the work is but half ended!"

The young Mohican gave a shout of triumph, and followed by Duncan, he glided up the acclivity they had descended to the combat, and sought the friendly shelter of the rocks and shrubs.

Chapter VIII

"They linger yet,
Avengers of their native land."
Gray, "The Bard," I.3. [Epode I.] ll. 45–46.

THE WARNING CALL of the scout was not uttered without occasion. During the occurrence of the deadly encounter just related, the roar of the falls was unbroken by any human sound whatever. It would seem, that interest in the result had kept the natives, on the opposite shores, in breathless suspense, while the quick evolutions and swift changes in the positions of the combatants, effectually prevented a fire, that might prove dangerous alike to friend and enemy. But the moment the struggle was decided, a yell arose, as fierce and savage as wild and revengeful passions could throw into the air. It was followed by the swift flashes of the rifles, which sent their leaden messengers across the rock in vollies, as though the assailants would pour out their impotent fury on the insensible scene of the fatal contest.

A steady, though deliberate, return was made from the rifle of Chingachgook, who had maintained his post throughout the fray with unmoved resolution. When the triumphant shout of Uncas was borne to his ears, the gratified father had raised his voice in a single responsive cry, after which his busy piece alone proved that he still guarded his pass with unwearied diligence. In this manner many minutes flew by with the swiftness of thought; the rifles of the assailants speaking, at times, in rattling vollies, and at others, in occasional, scattering shots. Though the rock, the trees, and the shrubs, were cut and torn in a hundred places around the besieged, their cover was so close, and so rigidly maintained, that, as yet, David had been the only sufferer in their little band.

"Let them burn their powder," said the deliberate scout, while bullet after bullet whizzed by the place where he securely lay; "there will be a fine gathering of lead when it is over, and I fancy the imps will tire of the sport, afore these old stones cry out for mercy! Uncas, boy, you waste the kernels by overcharging; and a kicking rifle never carries a true bullet. I told you to take that loping miscreant under the line of white paint; now, if your bullet went a hair's breadth, it went two inches above it. The life lies low in a Mingo, and humanity teaches us to make a quick end of the sarpents."

A quiet smile lighted the haughty features of the young Mohican, betraying his knowledge of the English language, as well as of the other's meaning, but he suffered it to pass away without vindication or reply.

"I cannot permit you to accuse Uncas of want of judgment or of skill," said Duncan; "he saved my life in the coolest and readiest manner, and he has made a friend who never will require to be reminded of the debt he owes."

Uncas partly raised his body, and offered his hand to the grasp of Heyward. During this act of friendship, the two young men exchanged looks of intelligence, which caused Duncan to forget the character and condition of his wild associate. In the meanwhile, Hawk-eye, who looked on this burst of youthful feeling with a cool but kind regard, made the following reply:

"Life is an obligation which friends often owe to each other in the wilderness. I dare say I may have served Uncas some such turn myself before now; and I very well remember, that he has stood between me and death five different times: three times from the Mingoes, once in crossing Horican, and—"

"That bullet was better aimed than common!" exclaimed Duncan, involuntarily shrinking from a shot which struck the rock at his side with a smart rebound.

Hawk-eye laid his hand on the shapeless metal, and shook his head, as he examined it, saying, "Falling lead is never flattened! had it come from the clouds this might have happened!"

But the rifle of Uncas was deliberately raised toward the heavens, directing the eyes of his companions to a point, where the mystery was immediately explained. A ragged oak grew on the right bank of the river, nearly opposite to their position, which, seeking the freedom of the open space, had inclined so far forward, that its upper branches overhung that arm of the stream which flowed nearest to its own shore. Among the topmost leaves, which scantily concealed the gnarled and stunted limbs, a savage was nestled, partly concealed by the trunk of the tree, and partly exposed, as though looking down upon them, to ascertain the effect produced by his treacherous aim.

"These devils will scale heaven to circumvent us to our ruin," said Hawk-eye; "keep him in play, boy, until I can bring 'kill-deer' to bear, when we will try his metal on each side of the tree at once."

Uncas delayed his fire until the scout uttered the word. The rifles flashed, the leaves and bark of the oak flew into the air, and were scattered by the wind, but the Indian answered their assault by a taunting laugh, sending down upon them another bullet in return, that struck the cap of Hawk-eye from his head. Once more the savage yells burst out of the woods, and the leaden hail whistled above the heads of the besieged, as if to confine them to a place where they might become easy victims to the enterprise of the warrior who had mounted the tree.

"This must be looked to!" said the scout, glancing about him with an anxious eye. "Uncas, call up your father; we have need of all our we'pons to bring the cunning varment from his roost."

The signal was instantly given; and, before Hawk-eye had reloaded his rifle, they were joined by Chingachgook. When his son pointed out to the experienced warrior the situation of their dangerous enemy, the usual exclamatory "hugh," burst from his lips; after which, no further expression of surprise or alarm was suffered to escape him. Hawk-eye and the Mohicans conversed earnestly together in Delaware for a few moments, when each quietly took his post, in order to execute the plan they had speedily devised.

The warrior in the oak had maintained a quick, though ineffectual, fire, from the moment of his discovery. But his aim was interrupted by the vigilance of his enemies, whose rifles instantaneously bore on any part of his person that was left exposed. Still his bullets fell in the centre of the crouching party. The clothes of Heyward, which rendered him peculiarly conspicuous, were repeatedly cut, and once blood was drawn from a slight wound in his arm.

At length, emboldened by the long and patient watchfulness of his enemies, the Huron attempted a better and more fatal aim. The quick eyes of the Mohicans caught the dark line of his lower limbs incautiously exposed through the thin foliage, a few inches from the trunk of the tree. Their rifles made a common report, when, sinking on his wounded limb, part of the body of the savage came into view. Swift as thought, Hawk-eye seized the advantage, and discharged his fatal weapon into the top of the oak. The leaves were unusually agitated; the dangerous rifle fell from its commanding elevation, and after a few moments of vain struggling, the form of the savage was seen swinging in the wind, while he still grasped a ragged and naked branch of the tree with hands clenched in desperation.

"Give him, in pity, give him, the contents of another rifle!" cried Duncan, turning away his eyes in horror from the spectacle of a fellow creature in such awful jeopardy.

"Not a karnel!" exclaimed the obdurate Hawk-eye; "his death is certain, and we have no powder to spare, for Indian fights, sometimes, last for days; 'tis their scalps, or ours!—and God, who made us, has put into our natures the craving to keep the skin on the head!"

Against this stern and unyielding morality, supported, as it was, by such visible policy, there was no appeal. From that moment the yells in the forest once more ceased, the fire was suffered to decline, and all eyes, those of friends, as well as enemies, became fixed on the hopeless condition of the wretch, who was dangling between heaven and earth. The body yielded to the currents of air, and though no murmur or groan escaped the victim, there were instants when he grimly faced his foes, and the anguish of cold despair might be traced, through the intervening distance, in possession of his swarthy lineaments. Three several times the scout raised his piece in mercy, and as often prudence getting the better of his intention, it was again silently lowered. At length, one hand of the Huron lost its hold, and dropped exhausted to his side. A desperate and fruitless struggle to recover the branch succeeded, and then the savage was seen for a fleeting instant, grasping wildly at the empty air. The lightning is not quicker than was the flame from the rifle of Hawk-eye; the limbs of the victim trembled and contracted, the head fell to the bosom, and the body parted the foaming waters, like lead, when the element closed above it, in its ceaseless velocity, and every vestige of the unhappy Huron was lost for ever.

No shout of triumph succeeded this important advantage, but even the Mohicans gazed at each other in silent horror. A single yell burst from the woods, and all was again still. Hawk-eye, who alone appeared to reason on the occasion, shook his head, at his own momentary weakness, even uttering his self-disapprobation aloud.

" 'Twas the last charge in my horn, and the last bullet in my pouch, and 'twas the act of a boy!" he said; "what mattered it whether he struck the rock living or dead! feeling would soon be over. Uncas, lad, go down to the canoe, and bring up the big horn; it is all the powder we have left, and we shall need it to the last grain, or I am ignorant of the Mingo nature."

The young Mohican complied, leaving the scout turning over the useless contents of his pouch, and shaking the empty horn with renewed discontent. From this unsatisfactory examination, however, he was soon called by a loud and piercing exclamation from Uncas, that sounded even to the unpractised ears of Duncan, as the signal of some new and unexpected calamity. Every thought filled with apprehension for the precious treasure he had concealed in the cavern, the young man started to his feet, totally regardless of the hazard he incurred by such an exposure. As if actuated by a common impulse, his movement was imitated by his companions, and, together, they rushed down the pass to the friendly chasm, with a rapidity that rendered the scattering fire of their enemies perfectly harmless. The unwonted cry had brought the sisters, together with the wounded David, from their place of refuge, and the whole party, at a single glance, was made acquainted with the nature of the disaster, that had disturbed even the practised stoicism of their youthful Indian protector.

At a short distance from the rock, their little bark was to be seen floating across the eddy, towards the swift current of the river, in a manner which proved that its course was directed by some hidden agent. The instant this unwelcome sight caught the eye of the scout, his rifle was levelled, as by instinct, but the barrel gave no answer to the bright sparks of the flint.

" 'Tis too late, 'tis too late!" Hawk-eye exclaimed, dropping the useless piece, in bitter disappointment; "the miscreant has struck the rapid, and had we powder, it could hardly send the lead swifter than he now goes!"

The adventurous Huron raised his head above the shelter of the canoe, and while it glided swiftly down the stream, he waved his hand, and gave forth the shout, which was the known signal of success. His cry was answered by a yell, and a laugh from the woods, as tauntingly exulting as if fifty demons were uttering their blasphemies at the fall of some Christian soul.

"Well may you laugh, ye children of the devil!" said the scout, seating himself on a projection of the rock, and suffering his gun to fall neglected at his feet, "for the three quickest and truest rifles in these woods, are no better than so many stalks of mullen, or the last year's horns of a buck!"

"What is to be done?" demanded Duncan, losing the first feeling of disappointment, in a more manly desire for exertion; " what will become of us?"

Hawk-eye made no other reply than by passing his finger around the crown of his head, in a manner so significant, that none who witnessed the action could mistake its meaning.

"Surely, surely, our case is not so desperate!" exclaimed the youth; "the Hurons are not here; we may make good the caverns; we may oppose their landing."

"With what?" coolly demanded the scout. "The arrows of Uncas, or such tears as women shed! No, no; you are young, and rich, and have friends, and at such an age I know it is hard to die! but," glancing his eyes at the Mohicans, "let us remember, we are men without a cross, and let us teach these natives of the forest, that white blood can run as freely as red, when the appointed hour is come."

Duncan turned quickly in the direction indicated by the other's eyes, and read a confirmation of his worst apprehensions in the conduct of the Indians. Chingachgook, placing himself in a dignified posture on another fragment of the rock, had already laid aside his knife and tomahawk, and was in the act of taking the eagle's plume from his head, and smoothing the solitary tuft of hair, in readiness to perform its last and revolting office. His countenance was composed, though thoughtful, while his dark, gleaming eyes, were gradually losing the fierceness of the combat in an expression better suited to the change he expected, momentarily, to undergo.

"Our case is not, cannot, be so hopeless!" said Duncan; "even at this very moment succour may be at hand. I see no enemies! they have sickened of a struggle, in which they risk so much with so little prospect of gain!"

"It may be a minute, or it may be an hour, afore the wily sarpents steal upon us, and it's quite in natur for them to be lying within hearing at this very moment," said Hawk-eye; "but come they will, and in such a fashion as will leave us nothing to hope! Chingachgook"—he spoke in Delaware—"my brother, we have fought our last battle together, and the Maquas will triumph in the death of the sage man of the Mohicans, and of the pale face, whose eyes can make night as day, and level the clouds to the mists of the springs!"

"Let the Mingo women go weep over their slain!" returned the Indian, with characteristic pride, and unmoved firmness; "the great snake of the Mohicans has coiled himself in their wigwams, and has poisoned their triumph with the wailings of children, whose fathers have not returned! Eleven warriors lie hid from the graves of their tribe, since the snows have melted, and none will tell where to find them, when the tongue of Chingachgook shall be silent! Let them draw the sharpest knife, and whirl the swiftest tomahawk, for their bitterest enemy is in their hands. Uncas, topmost branch of a noble trunk, call on the cowards to hasten, or their hearts will soften, and they will change to women!"

"They look among the fishes for their dead!" returned the low, soft voice of the youthful chieftain; "the Hurons float with the slimy eels! They drop from the oaks like fruit that is ready to be eaten! and the Delawares laugh!"

"Ay, ay," muttered the scout, who had listened to this peculiar burst of the natives with deep attention; "they have warmed their Indian feelings, and they'll soon provoke the Maquas to give them a speedy end. As for me, who am of the whole blood of the whites, it is befitting that I should die as becomes my colour, with no words of scoffing in my mouth, and without bitterness at the heart!"

"Why die at all!" said Cora, advancing from the place where natural horror had, until this moment, held her riveted to the rock; "the path is open on every side; fly, then, to the woods, and call on God for succour! Go, brave men, we owe you too much already; let us no longer involve you in our hapless fortunes!"

"You but little know the craft of the Iroquois, lady, if you judge they have left the path open to the woods!" returned Hawk-eye, who, however, immediately added in his simplicity; "the down stream current, it is certain, might soon sweep us beyond the reach of their rifles, or the sounds of their voices."

"Then try the river. Why linger, to add to the number of the victims of our merciless enemies?"

"Why!" repeated the scout, looking about him proudly, "because it is better for a man to die at peace with himself, than to live haunted by an evil conscience! What answer could we give to Munro, when he asked us, where and how we left his children?"

"Go to him, and say, that you left them with a message to hasten to their aid," returned Cora, advancing nigher to the scout, in her generous ardour; "that the Hurons bear them into the northern wilds, but that by vigilance and speed they may yet be rescued; and if, after all, it should please heaven, that his assistance come too late, bear to him," she continued, her voice gradually lowering, until it seemed nearly choked, "the love, the blessings, the final prayers of his daughters, and bid him not mourn their early fate, but to look forward with humble confidence to the Christian's goal to meet his children."

The hard, weather-beaten features of the scout began to work, and when she had ended, he dropped his chin to his hand, like a man musing profoundly on the nature of the proposal.

"There is reason in her words!" at length broke from his compressed and trembling lips; "ay, and they bear the spirit of christianity; what might be right and proper in a red skin, may be sinful in a man who has not even a cross in blood to plead for his ignorance. Chingachgook! Uncas! hear you the talk of the dark-eyed woman!"

He now spoke in Delaware to his companions, and his address, though calm and deliberate, seemed very decided. The elder Mohican heard him with deep gravity, and appeared to ponder on his words, as though he felt the importance of their import. After a moment of hesitation, he waved his hand in assent, and uttered the English word "good," with the peculiar emphasis of his people. Then, replacing his knife and tomahawk in his girdle, the warrior moved silently to the edge of the rock most concealed from the banks of the river. Here he paused a moment, pointed significantly to the woods below, and saying a few words in his own language, as if indicating his intended route, he dropped into the water, and sunk from before the eyes of the witnesses of his movements.

The scout delayed his departure to speak to the generous girl, whose breathing became lighter as she saw the success of her remonstrance.

"Wisdom is sometimes given to the young, as well as to the old," he said; "and what you have spoken is wise, not to call it by a better word. If you are led into the woods, that is, such of you as may be spared for a while, break the twigs on the bushes as you pass, and make the marks of your trail, as broad as you can, when, if mortal eyes can see them, depend on having a friend who will follow to the ends of the 'arth afore he desarts you."

He gave Cora an affectionate shake of the hand, lifted his rifle, and after regarding it a moment with melancholy solicitude, laid it carefully aside, and descended to the place where Chingachgook had just disappeared. For an instant he hung suspended by the rock; and looking about him, with a countenance of peculiar care, he added, bitterly, "Had the powder held out, this disgrace could never have befallen!" then, loosening his hold, the water closed above his head, and he also became lost to view.

All eyes were now turned on Uncas, who stood leaning against the ragged rock, in immoveable composure. After waiting a short time, Cora pointed down the river, and said—

"Your friends have not been seen, and are now, most probably, in safety; is it not time for you to follow?"

"Uncas will stay," the young Mohican calmly answered, in English.

"To increase the horror of our capture, and to diminish the chances of our release! Go, generous young man," Cora continued, lowering her eyes under the gaze of the Mohican, and, perhaps, with an intuitive consciousness of her power; "go to my father, as I have said, and be the most confidential of my messengers. Tell him to trust you with the means to buy the freedom of his daughters. Go; 'tis my wish, 'tis my prayer, that you will go!"

The settled, calm, look of the young chief, changed to an expression of gloom, but he no longer hesitated. With a noiseless step he crossed the rock, and dropped into the troubled stream. Hardly a breath was drawn by those he left behind, until they caught a glimpse of his head emerging for air, far down the current, when he again sunk, and was seen no more.

These sudden and apparently successful experiments had all taken place in a few minutes of that time, which had now become so precious. After the last look at Uncas, Cora turned, and, with a quivering lip, addressed herself to Heyward:

"I have heard of your boasted skill in the water, too, Duncan," she said; "follow, then, the wise example set you by these simple and faithful beings."

"Is such the faith that Cora Munro would exact from her protector," said the young man, smiling, mournfully, but with bitterness.

"This is not a time for idle subtleties and false opinions," she answered; "but a moment when every duty should be equally considered. To us you can be of no further service here, but your precious life may be saved for other and nearer friends."

He made no reply, though his eyes fell wistfully on the beautiful form of Alice, who was clinging to his arm with the dependency of an infant.

"Consider," continued Cora, after a pause, during which she seemed to struggle with a pang, even more acute than any that her fears had excited, "that the worst to us can be but death; a tribute that all must pay at the good time of God's appointment."

"There are evils worse than death," said Duncan, speaking hoarsely, and as if fretful at her importunity, "but which the presence of one who would die in your behalf may avert."

Cora ceased her entreaties, and veiling her face in her shawl, drew the nearly insensible Alice after her into the deepest recess of the inner cavern.

Chapter IX

"Be gay securely;
Dispel, my fair, with smiles, the tim'rous cloud,
That hangs on thy clear brow."
Gray, *Agrippina, A Tragedy*, Sc. II. 196–197.

THE SUDDEN and almost magical change, from the stirring incidents of the combat, to the stillness that now reigned around him, acted on the heated imagination of Heyward like some exciting dream. While all the images and events he had witnessed remained deeply impressed on his memory, he felt a difficulty in persuading himself of their truth. Still ignorant of the fate of those who had trusted to the aid of the swift current, he at first listened intently to any signal, or sounds of alarm, which might announce the good or evil fortune of their hazardous undertaking. His attention was, however, bestowed in vain; for with the disappearance of Uncas, every sign of the adventurers had been lost, leaving him in total uncertainty of their fate.

In a moment of such painful doubt, Duncan did not hesitate to look about him, without consulting that protection from the rocks which just before had been so necessary to his safety. Every effort, however, to detect the least evidence of the approach of their hidden enemies, was as fruitless as the inquiry after his late companions. The wooded banks of the river seemed again deserted by every thing possessing animal life. The uproar which had so lately echoed through the vaults of the forest was gone, leaving the rush of the waters to swell and sink on the currents of the air, in the unmingled sweetness of nature. A fish-hawk, which, secure on the topmost branches of a dead pine, had been a distant spectator of the fray, now stooped from his high and ragged perch, and soared, in wide sweeps, above his prey; while a jay, whose noisy voice had been stilled by the hoarser cries of the savages, ventured again to open his discordant throat, as though once more in undisturbed possession of his wild domains. Duncan caught from these natural accompaniments of the solitary scene a glimmering of hope, and he began to rally his faculties to renewed exertions, with something like a reviving confidence of success.

"The Hurons are not to be seen," he said, addressing David, who had by no means recovered from the effects of the stunning blow he had received; "let us conceal ourselves in the cavern, and trust the rest to Providence."

"I remember to have united with two comely maidens, in lifting up our voices in praise and thanksgiving," returned the bewildered singing-master; "since which time I have been visited by a heavy judgment for my sins. I have been mocked with the likeness of sleep, while sounds of discord have rent my ears; such as might manifest the fullness of time, and that nature had forgotten her harmony."

"Poor fellow! thine own period was, in truth, near its accomplishment! But arouse, and come with me; I will lead you where all other sounds, but those of your own psalmody, shall be excluded."

"There is melody in the fall of the cataract, and the rushing of many waters is sweet to the senses!" said David, pressing his hand confusedly on his brow. "Is not the air yet filled with shrieks and cries, as though the departed spirits of the damned—"

"Not now, not now," interrupted the impatient Heyward, "they have ceased; and they who raised them, I trust in God, they are gone too! every thing but the water is still and at peace; in, then, where you may create those sounds you love so well to hear."

David smiled sadly, though not without a momentary gleam of pleasure, at this allusion to his beloved vocation. He no longer hesitated to be led to a spot, which promised such unalloyed gratification to his wearied senses; and, leaning on the arm of his companion, he entered the narrow mouth of the cave. Duncan seized a pile of the sassafras, which he drew before the passage, studiously concealing every appearance of an aperture. Within this fragile barrier he arranged the blankets abandoned by the foresters, darkening the inner extremity of the cavern, while its outer received a chastened light from the narrow ravine, through which one arm of the river rushed, to form the junction with its sister branch, a few rods below.

"I like not that principle of the natives, which teaches them to submit without a struggle, in emergencies that appear desperate," he said, while busied in this employment; "our own maxim, which says, 'while life remains there is hope,' is more consoling, and better suited to a soldier's temperament. To you, Cora, I will urge no words of idle encouragement; your own fortitude and undisturbed reason, will teach you all that may become your sex; but cannot we dry the tears of that trembling weeper on your bosom?"

"I am calmer, Duncan," said Alice, raising herself from the arms of her sister, and forcing an appearance of composure through her tears; "much calmer, now. Surely, in this hidden spot, we are safe, we are secret, free from injury; we will hope every thing from those generous men, who have risked so much already in our behalf."

"Now does our gentle Alice speak like a daughter of Munro!" said Heyward, pausing to press her hand as he passed towards the outer entrance of the cavern. "With two such examples of courage before him, a man would be ashamed to prove other than a hero." He then seated himself in the centre of the cavern, grasping his remaining pistol with a hand convulsively clenched, while his contracted and frowning eye announced the sullen desperation of his purpose. "The Hurons, if they come, may not gain our position so easily as they think," he lowly muttered; and dropping his head back against the rock, he seemed to await the result in patience, though his gaze was unceasingly bent on the open avenue to their place of retreat.

With the last sound of his voice, a deep, a long, and almost breathless silence succeeded. The fresh air of the morning had penetrated the recess, and its influence was gradually felt on the spirits of its inmates. As minute after minute passed by, leaving them in undisturbed security, the insinuating feeling of hope was gradually gaining possession of every bosom, though each one felt reluctant to give utterance to expectations that the next moment might so fearfully destroy.

David alone formed an exception to these varying emotions. A gleam of light from the opening crossed his wan countenance, and fell upon the pages of the little volume, whose leaves he was again occupied in turning, as if searching for some song more fitted to their condition than any that had yet met his eye. He was most probably acting all this time under a confused recollection of the promised consolation of Duncan. At length, it would seem, his patient industry found its reward; for, without explanation or apology, he pronounced aloud the words "Isle of Wight," drew a long, sweet sound from his pitch-pipe, and then ran through the preliminary modulations of the air, whose name he had just mentioned, with the sweeter tones of his own musical voice.

"May not this prove dangerous?" asked Cora, glancing her dark eye at Major Heyward.

"Poor fellow! his voice is too feeble to be heard amid the din of the falls," was the answer; "besides, the cavern will prove his friend. Let him indulge his passion, since it may be done without hazard."

"Isle of Wight!" repeated David, looking about him with that dignity with which he had long been wont to silence the whispering echoes of his school; " 'tis a brave tune, and set to solemn words; let it be sung with meet respect!"

After allowing a moment of stillness to enforce his discipline, the voice of the singer was heard, in low, murmuring syllables, gradually stealing on the ear, until it filled the narrow vault, with sounds, rendered trebly thrilling by the feeble and tremulous utterance produced by his debility. The melody which no weakness could destroy, gradually wrought its sweet influence on the senses of those who heard it. It even prevailed over the miserable travesty of the song of David, which the singer had selected from a volume of similar effusions, and caused the sense to be forgotten, in the insinuating harmony of the sounds. Alice unconsciously dried her tears, and bent her melting eyes on the pallid features of Gamut, with an expression of chastened delight, that she neither affected, nor wished to conceal. Cora bestowed an approving smile on the pious efforts of the namesake of the Jewish prince, and Heyward soon turned his steady, stern, look from the outlet of the cavern, to fasten it, with a milder character, on the face of David, or to meet the wandering beams which at moments strayed from the humid eyes of Alice. The open sympathy of the listeners stirred the spirit of the votary of music, whose voice regained its richness and volume, without losing that touching softness which proved its secret charm. Exerting his renovated powers to their utmost, he was yet filling the arches of the cave with long and full tones, when a yell burst into the air without, that instantly stilled his pious strains, choking his voice suddenly, as though his heart had literally bounded into the passage of his throat.

"We are lost!" exclaimed Alice, throwing herself into the arms of Cora.

"Not yet, not yet," returned the agitated but undaunted Heyward; "the sound came from the centre of the island, and it has been produced by the sight of their dead companions. We are not yet discovered, and there is still hope."

Faint and almost despairing as was the prospect of escape, the words of Duncan were not thrown away, for it awakened the powers of the sisters in such a manner, that they awaited the result in silence. A second yell soon followed the first, when a rush of voices was heard pouring down the island, from its upper to its lower extremity, until they reached the naked rock above the caverns, where, after a shout of savage triumph, the air continued full of horrible cries and screams, such as man alone can utter, and he only when in a state of the fiercest barbarity.

The sounds quickly spread around them in every direction. Some called to their fellows from the water's edge, and were answered from the heights above. Cries were heard in the startling vicinity of the chasm between the two caves, which mingled with hoarser yells that arose out of the abyss of the deep ravine. In short, so rapidly had the savage sounds diffused themselves over the barren rock, that it was not difficult for the anxious listeners to imagine that they could be heard beneath, as, in truth, they were above, and on every side of them.

In the midst of this tumult, a triumphant yell was raised within a few yards of the hidden entrance to the cave. Heyward abandoned every hope, with the belief it was the signal that they were discovered. Again the impression passed away, as he heard the voices collect near the spot where the white man had so reluctantly abandoned his rifle. Amid the jargon of the Indian dialects that he now plainly heard, it was easy to distinguish not only words, but sentences in the patois of the Canadas. A burst of voices had shouted, simultaneously, "la Longue Carabine!" causing the opposite woods to re-echo with a name which, Heyward well remembered, had been given by his enemies to a celebrated hunter and scout of the English camp, and who he now learnt, for the first time, had been his late companion.

"La Longue Carabine! la Longue Carabine!" passed from mouth to mouth, until the whole band appeared to be collected around a trophy, which would seem to announce the death of its formidable owner. After a vociferous consultation, which was, at times, deafened by bursts of savage joy, they again separated, filling the air with the name of a foe, whose body, Heyward could collect from their expressions, they hoped to find concealed in some crevice of the island.

"Now," he whispered to the trembling sisters, "now is the moment of uncertainty! if our place of retreat escape this scrutiny, we are still safe! In every event, we are assured, by what has fallen from our enemies, that our friends have escaped, and in two short hours we may look for succour from Webb."

There were now a few minutes of fearful stillness, during which Heyward well knew that the savages conducted their search with greater vigilance and method. More than once he could distinguish their footsteps, as they brushed the sassafras, causing the faded leaves to rustle, and the branches to snap. At length, the pile yielded a little, a corner of a blanket fell, and a faint ray of light gleamed into the inner part of the cave. Cora folded Alice to her bosom in agony, and Duncan sprang to his feet. A shout was at that moment heard, as if issuing from the centre of the rock, announcing that the neighbouring cavern had at length been entered. In a minute, the number and loudness of the voices indicated that the whole party was collected in and around that secret place.

As the inner passages to the two caves were so close to each other, Duncan, believing that escape was no longer possible, passed David and the sisters, to place himself between the latter and the first onset of the terrible meeting. Grown desperate by his situation, he drew nigh the slight barrier which separated him only by a few feet from his relentless pursuers, and placing his face to the casual opening, he even looked out, with a sort of desperate indifference, on their movements.

Within reach of his arm was the brawny shoulder of a gigantic Indian, whose deep and authoritative voice appeared to give directions to the proceedings of his fellows. Beyond him again, Duncan could look into the vault opposite, which was filled with savages, upturning and rifling the humble furniture of the scout. The wound of David had died the leaves of sassafras with a colour, that the natives well knew was anticipating the season. Over this sign of their success, they set up a howl, like an opening from so many hounds, who had recovered a lost trail. After this yell of victory, they tore up the fragrant bed of the cavern, and bore the branches into the chasm, scattering the boughs, as if they suspected them of concealing the person of the man they had so long hated and feared. One fierce and wild looking warrior, approached the chief, bearing a load of the brush, and pointing, exultingly, to the deep red stains with which it was sprinkled, uttered his joy in Indian yells, whose meaning Heyward was only enabled to comprehend, by the frequent repetition of the name of "la Longue Carabine!" When his triumph had ceased, he cast the brush on the slight heap that Duncan had made before the entrance of the second cavern, and closed the view. His example was followed by others; who, as they drew the branches from the cave of the scout, threw them into one pile, adding unconsciously to the security of those they sought. The very slightness of the defence was its chief merit, for no one thought of disturbing a mass of brush, which all of them believed, in that moment of hurry and confusion, had been accidentally raised by the hands of their own party.

As the blankets yielded before the outward pressure, and the branches settled into the fissure of the rock by their own weight, forming a compact body, Duncan once more breathed freely. With a light step, and lighter heart, he returned to the centre of the cave, and took the place he had left, where he could command a view of the opening next the river. While he was in the act of making this movement, the Indians, as if changing their purpose by a common impulse, broke away from the chasm in a body, and were heard rushing up the island again, towards the point, whence they had originally descended. Here another wailing cry betrayed that they were again collected around the bodies of their dead comrades.

Duncan now ventured to look at his companions; for, during the most critical moments of their danger, he had been apprehensive that the anxiety of his countenance might communicate some additional alarm, to those who were so little able to sustain it.

"They are gone, Cora!" he whispered; "Alice, they are returned whence they came, and we are saved! To heaven, that has alone delivered us from the grasp of so merciless an enemy, be all the praise!"

"Then to heaven will I return my thanks!" exclaimed the younger sister, rising from the encircling arms of Cora, and casting herself, with enthusiastic gratitude, on the naked rock; "to that heaven who has spared the tears of a gray-headed father; has saved the lives of those I so much love—"

Both Heyward, and the more tempered Cora, witnessed the act of involuntary emotion with powerful sympathy, the former secretly believing that piety had never worn a form so lovely, as it had now assumed in the youthful person of Alice. Her eyes were radiant with the glow of grateful feelings; the flush of her beauty was again seated on her cheeks, and her whole soul seemed ready and anxious to pour out its thanksgivings, through the medium of her eloquent features. But when her lips moved, the words they should have uttered appeared frozen by some new and sudden chill. Her bloom gave place to the paleness of death; her soft and melting eyes grew hard, and seemed contracting with horror; while those hands, which she had raised, clasped in each other, towards heaven, dropped in horizontal lines before her, the fingers pointing forward in convulsed motion. Heyward turned the instant she gave a direction to his suspicions, and, peering just above the ledge which formed the threshold of the open outlet of the cavern, he beheld the malignant, fierce, and savage features of le Renard Subtil.

In that moment of surprise, the self-possession of Heyward did not desert him. He observed by the vacant expression of the Indian's countenance, that his eye, accustomed to the open air, had not yet been able to penetrate the dusky light which pervaded the depth of the cavern. He had even thought of retreating beyond the curvature in the natural wall, which might still conceal him and his companions, when, by the sudden gleam of intelligence that shot across the features of the savage, he saw it was too late, and that they were betrayed.

The look of exultation and brutal triumph which announced this terrible truth, was irresistibly irritating. Forgetful of every thing but the impulses of his hot blood, Duncan levelled his pistol and fired. The report of the weapon made the cavern bellow like an eruption from a volcano, and when the smoke, it vomited, had been driven away before the current of air which issued from the ravine, the place so lately occupied by the features of his treacherous guide was vacant. Rushing to the outlet, Heyward caught a glimpse of his dark figure, stealing around a low and narrow ledge, which soon hid him entirely from sight.

Among the savages, a frightful stillness succeeded the explosion, which had just been heard bursting from the bowels of the rock. But when le Renard raised his voice in a long and intelligible whoop, it was answered by a spontaneous yell from the mouth of every Indian within hearing of the sound. The clamorous noises again rushed down the island, and before Duncan had time to recover from the shock, his feeble barrier of brush was scattered to the winds, the cavern was entered at both its extremities, and he and his companions were dragged from their shelter, and borne into the day, where they stood surrounded by the whole band of the triumphant Hurons.

Chapter X

"I fear we shall outsleep the coming morn,
As much as we this night have overwatched!"
A Midsummer Night's Dream, V.i.365–366.

THE INSTANT the shock of this sudden misfortune had abated, Duncan began to make his observations on the appearance and proceedings of their captors. Contrary to the usages of the natives in the wantonness of their success, they had respected, not only the persons of the trembling sisters, but his own. The rich ornaments of his military attire, had indeed been repeatedly handled by different individuals of the tribe, with eyes expressing a savage longing to possess the baubles, but before the customary violence could be resorted to, a mandate, in the authoritative voice of the large warrior already mentioned, stayed the uplifted hand, and convinced Heyward that they were to be reserved for some object of particular moment.

While, however, these manifestations of weakness were exhibited by the young and vain of the party, the more experienced warriors continued their search throughout both caverns, with an activity that denoted they were far from being satisfied with those fruits of their conquest, which had already been brought to light. Unable to discover any new victim, these diligent workers of vengeance soon approached their male prisoners, pronouncing the name of "la Longue Carabine," with a fierceness that could not easily be mistaken. Duncan affected not to comprehend the meaning of their repeated and violent interrogatories, while his companion was spared the effort of a similar deception, by his ignorance of French. Wearied, at length, by their importunities, and apprehensive of irritating his captors by too stubborn a silence, the former looked about him in quest of Magua, who might interpret his answers to questions which were, at each moment, becoming more earnest and threatening.

The conduct of this savage had formed a solitary exception to that of all his fellows. While the others were busily occupied in seeking to gratify their childish passion for finery, by plundering even the miserable effects of the scout, or had been searching, with such blood-thirsty vengeance in their looks, for their absent owner, le Renard had stood at a little distance from the prisoners, with a demeanour so quiet and satisfied, as to betray, that he had already effected the grand purpose of his treachery. When the eyes of Heyward first met those of his recent guide, he turned them away, in horror, at the sinister though calm look he encountered. Conquering his disgust, however, he was able, with an averted face, to address his successful enemy:

"Le Renard Subtil is too much of a warrior," said the reluctant Heyward, "to refuse telling an unarmed man what his conquerors say."

"They ask for the hunter who knows the paths through the woods," returned Magua, in his broken English, laying his hand, at the same time, with a ferocious smile, on the bundle of leaves, with which a wound on his own shoulder was bandaged; "la Longue Carabine! his rifle is good, and his eye never shut; but, like the short gun of the white chief, it is nothing against the life of le Subtil!"

"Le Renard is too brave to remember the hurts received in war, or the hands that gave them!"

"Was it war, when the tired Indian rested at the sugar tree, to taste his corn! who filled the bushes with creeping enemies! who drew the knife! whose tongue was peace, while his heart was coloured with blood! Did Magua say that the hatchet was out of the ground, and that his hand had dug it up?"

As Duncan dared not retort upon his accuser, by reminding him of his own premeditated treachery, and disdained to deprecate his resentment by any words of apology, he remained silent. Magua seemed also content to rest the controversy, as well as all further communication, there, for he resumed the leaning attitude against the rock, from which, in momentary energy, he had arisen. But the cry of "la Longue Carabine," was renewed, the instant the impatient savages perceived that the short dialogue was ended.

"You hear," said Magua, with stubborn indifference; "the red Hurons call for the life of the 'long rifle,' or they will have the blood of them that keep him hid!"

"He is gone—escaped; he is far beyond their reach."

Renard smiled with cold contempt, as he answered:

"When the white man dies, he thinks he is at peace; but the red men know how to torture even the ghosts of their enemies. Where is his body? Let the Hurons see his scalp!"

"He is not dead, but escaped."

Magua shook his head incredulously.

"Is he a bird, to spread his wings; or is he a fish, to swim without air! The white chief reads in his books, and he believes the Hurons are fools!"

"Though no fish, the 'long rifle' can swim. He floated down the stream when the powder was all burnt, and when the eyes of the Hurons were behind a cloud."

"And why did the white chief stay?" demanded the still incredulous Indian. "Is he a stone, that goes to the bottom, or does the scalp burn his head?"

"That I am not a stone, your dead comrade, who fell into the falls, might answer, were the life still in him," said the provoked young man, using, in his anger, that boastful language which was most likely to excite the admiration of an Indian. "The white man thinks none but cowards desert their women."

Magua muttered a few words, inaudibly, between his teeth, before he continued, aloud—

"Can the Delawares swim, too, as well as crawl in the bushes? Where is 'le Gros Serpent'? "

Duncan, who perceived by the use of these Canadian appellations, that his late companions were much better known to his enemies than to himself, answered, reluctantly: "He also is gone down with the water."

" 'Le Cerf Agile' is not here?"

"I know not whom you call the 'nimble deer,' " said Duncan, gladly profiting by any excuse to create delay.

"Uncas," returned Magua, pronouncing the Delaware name with even greater difficulty than he spoke his English words. " 'Bounding elk' is what the white man says when he calls to the young Mohican."

"Here is some confusion in names between us, le Renard," said Duncan, hoping to provoke a discussion. "Daim is the French for deer, and cerf for stag; élan is the true term, when one would speak of an elk."

"Yes," muttered the Indian, in his native tongue; "the pale faces are prattling women! they have two words for each thing, while a red skin will make the sound of his voice speak for him." Then changing his language, he continued, adhering to the imperfect nomenclature of his provincial instructers, "The deer is swift, but weak; the elk is swift, but strong; and the son of 'le serpent' is 'le cerf agile.' Has he leaped the river to the woods?"

"If you mean the younger Delaware, he too is gone down with the water."

As there was nothing improbable to an Indian, in the manner of the escape, Magua admitted the truth of what he had heard, with a readiness that afforded additional evidence how little he would prize such worthless captives. With his companions, however, the feeling was manifestly different.

The Hurons had awaited the result of this short dialogue with characteristic patience, and with a silence, that increased, until there was a general stillness in the band. When Heyward ceased to speak, they turned their eyes, as one man, on Magua, demanding, in this expressive manner, an explanation of what had been said. Their interpreter pointed to the river, and made them acquainted with the result, as much by the action as by the few words he uttered. When the fact was generally understood, the savages raised a frightful yell, which declared the extent of their disappointment. Some ran furiously to the water's edge, beating the air with frantic gestures, while others spat upon the element, to resent the supposed treason it had committed against their acknowledged rights as conquerors. A few, and they not the least powerful and terrific of the band, threw lowering looks, in which the fiercest passion was only tempered by habitual self-command, at those captives who still remained in their power; while one or two even gave vent to their malignant feelings by the most menacing gestures, against which neither the sex, nor the beauty of the sisters, was any protection. The young soldier made a desperate, but fruitless, effort to spring to the side of Alice, when he saw the dark hand of a savage twisted in the rich tresses, which were flowing in volumes over her shoulders, while a knife was passed around the head from which they fell, as if to denote the horrid manner in which it was about to be robbed of its beautiful ornament. But his hands were bound, and at the first movement he made, he felt the grasp of the powerful Indian, who directed the band, pressing his shoulder like a vice. Immediately conscious how unavailing any struggle against such an overwhelming force must prove, he submitted to his fate, encouraging his gentle companions, by a few low and tender assurances, that the natives seldom failed to threaten more than they performed.

But, while Duncan resorted to these words of consolation, to quiet the apprehensions of the sisters, he was not so weak as to deceive himself. He well knew that the authority of an Indian chief was so little conventional, that it was oftener maintained by physical superiority, than by any moral supremacy he might possess. The danger was, therefore, magnified exactly in proportion to the number of the savage spirits by which they were surrounded. The most positive mandate from him, who seemed the acknowledged leader, was liable to be violated, at each moment, by any rash hand that might choose to sacrifice a victim to the manes of some dead friend or relative. While, therefore, he sustained an outward appearance of calmness and fortitude, his heart leaped into his throat, whenever any of their fierce captors drew nigher than common to the helpless sisters, or fastened one of their sullen wandering looks on those fragile forms, which were so little able to resist the slightest assault.

His apprehensions were however greatly relieved, when he saw that the leader had summoned his warriors to himself in council. Their deliberations were short, and it would seem, by the silence of most of the party, the decision unanimous. By the frequency with which the few speakers pointed in the direction of the encampment of Webb, it was apparent they dreaded the approach of danger from that quarter. This consideration probably hastened their determination, and quickened the subsequent movements.

During this short conference, Heyward finding a respite from his greatest fears, had leisure to admire the cautious manner in which the Hurons had made their approaches, even after hostilities had ceased.

It has already been stated, that the upper half of the island was a naked rock, and destitute of any other defences than a few scattering logs of drift wood. They had selected this point to make their descent, having borne the canoe through the wood, around the cataract, for that purpose. Placing their arms in the little vessel, a dozen men, clinging to its sides, had trusted themselves to the direction of the canoe, which was controlled by two of the most skilful warriors, in attitudes, that enabled them to command a view of the dangerous passage. Favoured by this arrangement, they touched the head of the island, at that point which had proved so fatal to their first adventurers, but with the advantages of superior numbers, and the possession of fire arms. That such had been the manner of their descent, was rendered quite apparent to Duncan, for they now bore the light bark from the upper end of the rock, and placed it in the water, near the mouth of the outer cavern. As soon as this change was made, the leader made signs to the prisoners to descend and enter.

As resistance was impossible, and remonstrance useless, Heyward set the example of submission, by leading the way into the canoe, where he was soon seated with the sisters, and the still wondering David. Notwithstanding the Hurons were necessarily ignorant of the little channels among the eddies and rapids of the stream, they knew the common signs of such a navigation too well, to commit any material blunder. When the pilot chosen for the task of guiding the canoe had taken his station, the whole band plunged again into the river, the vessel glided down the current, and in a few moments the captives found themselves on the south bank of the stream, nearly opposite to the point where they had struck it, the preceding evening.

Here was held another short but earnest consultation, during which, the horses, to whose panic their owners ascribed their heaviest misfortune, were led from the cover of the woods, and brought to the sheltered spot. The band now divided. The great chief, so often mentioned, mounting the charger of Heyward, led the way directly across the river, followed by most of his people, and disappeared in the woods, leaving the prisoners in charge of six savages, at whose head was le Renard Subtil. Duncan witnessed all their movements with renewed uneasiness.

He had been fond of believing, from the uncommon forbearance of the savages, that he was reserved as a prisoner, to be delivered to Montcalm. As the thoughts of those who are in misery seldom slumber, and the invention is never more lively, than when it is stimulated by hope, however feeble and remote, he had even imagined that the parental feelings of Munro were to be made instrumental in seducing him from his duty to the king. For though the French commander bore a high character for courage and enterprise, he was also thought to be expert in those political practices, which do not always respect the nicer obligations of morality, and which so generally disgraced the European diplomacy of that period.

All those busy and ingenious speculations were now annihilated by the conduct of his captors. That portion of the band who had followed the huge warrior, took the route towards the foot of the Horican, and no other expectation was left for himself and companions, than that they were to be retained as hopeless captives by their savage conquerors. Anxious to know the worst, and willing, in such an emergency, to try the potency of gold, he overcame his reluctance to speak to Magua. Addressing himself to his former guide, who had now assumed the authority and manner of one who was to direct the future movements of the party, he said, in tones as friendly and confiding as he could assume—

"I would speak to Magua, what is fit only for so great a chief to hear."

The Indian turned his eyes on the young soldier, scornfully, as he answered—

"Speak; trees have no ears!"

"But the red Hurons are not deaf; and counsel that is fit for the great men of a nation, would make the young warriors drunk. If Magua will not listen, the officer of the king knows how to be silent."

The savage spoke carelessly to his comrades, who were busied, after their awkward manner, in preparing the horses for the reception of the sisters, and moved a little to one side, whither, by a cautious gesture, he induced Heyward to follow.

"Now speak," he said; "if the words are such as Magua should hear."

"Le Renard Subtil has proved himself worthy of the honourable name given to him by his Canada fathers," commenced Heyward; "I see his wisdom, and all that he has done for us, and shall remember it, when the hour to reward him arrives. Yes! Renard has proved that he is not only a great chief in council, but one who knows how to deceive his enemies!"

"What has Renard done?" coldly demanded the Indian.

"What! has he not seen that the woods were filled with outlying parties of the enemies, and that the serpent could not steal through them without being seen? Then, did he not lose his path, to blind the eyes of the Hurons? Did he not pretend to go back to his tribe, who had treated him ill, and driven him from their wigwams, like a dog? And, when we saw what he wished to do, did we not aid him, by making a false face, that the Hurons might think the white man believed that his friend was his enemy? Is not all this true? And when le Subtil had shut the eyes and stopped the ears of his nation by his wisdom, did they not forget that they had once done him wrong, and forced him to flee to the Mohawks? And did they not leave him on the south side of the river, with their prisoners, while they have gone foolishly on the north? Does not Renard mean to turn like a fox on his footsteps, and carry to the rich and gray headed Scotchman, his daughters? Yes, Magua, I see it all, and I have already been thinking how so much wisdom and honesty should be repaid. First, the chief of William Henry will give as a great chief should, for such a service. The medal* of Magua will no longer be of tin, but of beaten gold; his horn will run over with powder; dollars will be as plenty in his pouch, as pebbles on the shore of Horican; and the deer will lick his hand, for they will know it to be vain to fly from the rifle he will carry! As for myself, I know not how

*It has long been a practice with the whites to conciliate the important men, of the Indians, by presenting medals, which are worn in the place of their own rude ornaments. Those given by the English generally bear the impression of the reigning king, and those given by the Americans that of the president.

to exceed the gratitude of the Scotchman, but I—yes, I will—"

"What will the young chief, who comes from towards the sun, give?" demanded the Huron, observing that Heyward hesitated in his desire to end the enumeration of benefits with that which might form the climax of an Indian's wishes.

"He will make the fire-water from the islands in the salt lake, flow before the wigwam of Magua, until the heart of the Indian shall be lighter than the feathers of the humming-bird, and his breath sweeter than the wild honeysuckle."

Le Renard had listened gravely as Heyward slowly proceeded in this subtle speech. When the young man mentioned the artifice he supposed the Indian to have practised on his own nation, the countenance of the listener was veiled in an expression of cautious gravity. At the allusion to the injury which Duncan affected to believe had driven the Huron from his native tribe, a gleam of such ungovernable ferocity flashed from the other's eyes, as induced the adventurous speaker to believe he had struck the proper chord. And by the time he reached the part where he so artfully blended the thirst of vengeance with the desire of gain, he had, at least, obtained a command of the deepest attention of the savage. The question put by le Renard had been calm, and with all the dignity of an Indian; but it was quite apparent, by the thoughtful expression of the listener's countenance, that the answer was most cunningly devised. The Huron mused a few moments, and then laying his hand on the rude bandages of his wounded shoulder, he said, with some energy—

"Do friends make such marks?"

"Would 'la Longue Carabine' cut one so light on an enemy?"

"Do the Delawares crawl upon those they love like snakes, twisting themselves to strike?"

"Would 'le Gros Serpent' have been heard by the ears of one he wished to be deaf?"

"Does the white chief burn his powder in the faces of his brothers?"

"Does he ever miss his aim, when seriously bent to kill?" returned Duncan, smiling with well acted sincerity.

Another long and deliberative pause succeeded these sententious questions and ready replies. Duncan saw that the Indian hesitated. In order to complete his victory, he was in the act of recommencing the enumeration of the rewards, when Magua made an expressive gesture, and said—

"Enough; le Renard is a wise chief, and what he does will be seen. Go, and keep the mouth shut. When Magua speaks, it will be the time to answer."

Heyward, perceiving that the eyes of his companion were warily fastened on the rest of the band, fell back immediately, in order to avoid the appearance of any suspicious confederacy with their leader. Magua approached the horses, and affected to be well pleased with the diligence and ingenuity of his comrades. He then signed to Heyward to assist the sisters into the saddles, for he seldom deigned to use the English tongue, unless urged by some motive of more than usual moment.

There was no longer any plausible pretext for delay, and Duncan was obliged, however reluctantly, to comply. As he performed this office, he whispered his reviving hopes in the ears of the trembling females, who, through dread of encountering the savage countenances of their captors, seldom raised their eyes from the ground. The mare of David had been taken with the followers of the large chief; in consequence, its owners, as well as Duncan, were compelled to journey on foot. The latter did not, however, so much regret this circumstance, as it might enable him to retard the speed of the party—for he still turned his longing looks in the direction of fort Edward, in the vain expectation of catching some sound from that quarter of the forest, which might denote the approach of succour.

When all were prepared, Magua made the signal to proceed, advancing in front, to lead the party in person. Next followed David, who was gradually coming to a true sense of his condition, as the effects of the wound became less and less apparent. The sisters rode in his rear, with Heyward at their side, while the Indians flanked the party, and brought up the close of the march, with a caution that seemed never to tire.

In this manner they proceeded in uninterrupted silence, except when Heyward addressed some solitary word of comfort to the females, or David gave vent to the moanings of his spirit, in piteous exclamations, which he intended should express the humility of resignation. Their direction lay towards the south, and in a course nearly opposite to the road to William Henry. Notwithstanding this apparent adherence in Magua to the original determination of his conquerors, Heyward could not believe his tempting bait was so soon forgotten; and he knew the windings of an Indian path too well, to suppose that its apparent course led directly to its object, when artifice was at all necessary. Mile after mile was, however, passed through the boundless woods in this painful manner, without any prospect of a termination to their journey. Heyward watched the sun, as he darted his meridian rays through the branches of the trees, and pined for the moment when the policy of Magua should change their route to one more favourable to his hopes. Sometimes he fancied that the wary savage, despairing of passing the army of Montcalm, in safety, was holding his way towards a well known border settlement, where a distinguished officer of the crown, and a favoured friend of the Six Nations, held his large possessions, as well as his usual residence. To be delivered into the hands of Sir William Johnson, was far preferable to being led into the wilds of Canada; but in order to effect even the former, it would be necessary to traverse the forest for many weary leagues, each step of which was carrying him further from the scene of the war, and, consequently, from the post, not only of honour, but of duty.

Cora alone remembered the parting injunctions of the scout, and whenever an opportunity offered, she stretched forth her arm to bend aside the twigs that met her hands. But the vigilance of the Indians rendered this act of precaution both difficult and dangerous. She was often defeated in her purpose, by encountering their watchful eyes, when it became necessary to feign an alarm she did not feel, and occupy the limb, by some gesture of feminine apprehension. Once, and once only, was she completely successful; when she broke down the bough of a large sumach, and, by a sudden thought, let her glove fall at the same instant. This sign intended for those that might follow, was observed by one of her conductors, who restored the glove, broke the remaining branches of the bush in such a manner, that it appeared to proceed from the struggling of some beast in its branches, and then laid his hand on his tomahawk, with a look so significant, that it put an effectual end to these stolen memorials of their passage.

As there were horses, to leave the prints of their footsteps, in both bands of the Indians, this interruption cut off any probable hopes of assistance being conveyed through the means of their trail.

Heyward would have ventured a remonstrance, had there been any thing encouraging in the gloomy reserve of Magua. But the savage, during all this time, seldom turned to look at his followers, and never spoke. With the sun for his only guide, or aided by such blind marks as are only known to the sagacity of a native, he held his way along the barrens of pine, through occasional little fertile vales, across brooks and rivulets, and over undulating hills, with the accuracy of instinct, and nearly with the directness of a bird. He never seemed to hesitate. Whether the path was hardly distinguishable, whether it disappeared, or whether it lay beaten and plain before him, made no sensible difference in his speed or certainty. It seemed as if fatigue could not affect him. Whenever the eyes of the wearied travellers rose from the decayed leaves over which they trode, his dark form was to be seen glancing among the stems of the trees in front, his head immoveably fastened in a forward position, with the light plume on its crest, fluttering in a current of air, made solely by the swiftness of his own motion.

But all this diligence and speed was not without an object. After crossing a low vale, through which a gushing brook meandered, he suddenly ascended a hill, so steep and difficult of ascent, that the sisters were compelled to alight, in order to follow. When the summit was gained, they found themselves on a level spot, but thinly covered with trees, under one of which Magua had thrown his dark form, as if willing and ready to seek that rest, which was so much needed by the whole party.

Chapter XI

—"Cursed be my tribe,
If I forgive him."
The Merchant of Venice, I.iii.51–52.

THE INDIAN had selected for this desirable purpose, one of those steep, pyramidal hills, which bear a strong resemblance to artificial mounds, and which so frequently occur in the valleys of America. The one in question was high, and precipitous; its top flattened, as usual; but with one of its sides more than ordinarily irregular. It possessed no other apparent advantages for a resting place, than in its elevation and form, which might render defence easy, and surprise nearly impossible. As Heyward, however, no longer expected that rescue, which time and distance now rendered so improbable, he regarded these little peculiarities with an eye devoid of interest, devoting himself entirely to the comfort and condolence of his feebler companions. The Narragansets were suffered to browse on the branches of the trees and shrubs, that were thinly scattered over the summit of the hill, while the remains of their provisions were spread under the shade of a beech, that stretched its horizontal limbs like a canopy above them.

Notwithstanding the swiftness of their flight, one of the Indians had found an opportunity to strike a straggling fawn with an arrow, and had borne the more preferable fragments of the victim, patiently on his shoulders, to the stopping place. Without any aid from the science of cookery, he was immediately employed, in common with his fellows, in gorging himself with this digestable sustenance. Magua alone sat apart, without participating in the revolting meal, and apparently buried in the deepest thought.

This abstinence, so remarkable in an Indian, when he possessed the means of satisfying hunger, at length attracted the notice of Heyward. The young man willingly believed that the Huron deliberated on the most eligible manner of eluding the vigilance of his associates. With a view to assist his plans by any suggestion of his own, and to strengthen the temptation, he left the beech, and straggled, as if without an object, to the spot where le Renard was seated.

"Has not Magua kept the sun in his face long enough to escape all danger from the Canadians?" he asked, as though no longer doubtful of the good intelligence established between them; "and will not the chief of William Henry be better pleased to see his daughters before another night may have hardened his heart to their loss, to make him less liberal in his reward?"

"Do the pale faces love their children less in the morning than at night?" asked the Indian, coldly.

"By no means," returned Heyward, anxious to recall his error, if he had made one; "the white man may, and does often, forget the burial place of his fathers; he sometimes ceases to remember those he should love, and has promised to cherish; but the affection of a parent for his child is never permitted to die."

"And is the heart of the white-headed chief soft, and will he think of the babes that his squaws have given him? He is hard to his warriors, and his eyes are made of stone!"

"He is severe to the idle and wicked, but to the sober and deserving he is a leader, both just and humane. I have known many fond and tender parents, but never have I seen a man whose heart was softer towards his child. You have seen the gray-head in front of his warriors, Magua, but I have seen his eyes swimming in water, when he spoke of those children who are now in your power!"

Heyward paused, for he knew not how to construe the remarkable expression that gleamed across the swarthy features of the attentive Indian. At first it seemed as if the remembrance of the promised reward grew vivid in his mind, while he listened to the sources of parental feeling which were to assure its possession; but as Duncan proceeded, the expression of joy became so fiercely malignant, that it was impossible not to apprehend it proceeded from some passion more sinister than avarice.

"Go," said the Huron, suppressing the alarming exhibition in an instant, in a death-like calmness of countenance; "go to the dark-haired daughter, and say, Magua waits to speak. The father will remember what the child promises."

Duncan, who interpreted this speech to express a wish for some additional pledge that the promised gifts should not be withheld, slowly and reluctantly repaired to the place where the sisters were now resting from their fatigue, to communicate its purport to Cora.

"You understand the nature of an Indian's wishes," he concluded, as he led her towards the place where she was expected, "and must be prodigal of your offers of powder and blankets. Ardent spirits are, however, the most prized by such as he; nor would it be amiss to add some boon from your own hand, with that grace you so well know how to practise. Remember, Cora, that on your presence of mind and ingenuity, even your life, as well as that of Alice, may in some measure depend."

"Heyward, and yours!"

"Mine is of little moment; it is already sold to my king, and is a prize to be seized by any enemy who may possess the power. I have no father to expect me, and but few friends to lament a fate, which I have courted with the unsatiable longings of youth after distinction. But, hush; we approach the Indian. Magua, the lady, with whom you wish to speak, is here."

The Indian rose slowly from his seat, and stood for near a minute silent and motionless. He then signed with his hand for Heyward to retire, saying, coldly—

"When the Huron talks to the women, his tribe shut their ears."

Duncan still lingering, as if refusing to comply, Cora said, with a calm smile—

"You hear, Heyward, and delicacy at least should urge you to retire. Go to Alice, and comfort her with our reviving prospects."

She waited until he had departed, and then turning to the native, with the dignity of her sex, in her voice and manner, she added: "What would le Renard say to the daughter of Munro?"

"Listen," said the Indian, laying his hand firmly upon her arm, as if willing to draw her utmost attention to his words; a movement that Cora as firmly, but quietly repulsed, by extricating the limb from his grasp—"Magua was born a chief and a warrior among the red Hurons of the lakes; he saw the suns of twenty summers make the snows of twenty winters run off in the streams, before he saw a pale-face; and he was happy! Then his Canada fathers came into the woods, and taught him to drink the fire-water, and he became a rascal. The Hurons drove him from the graves of his fathers, as they would chase the hunted buffalo. He ran down the shores of the lakes, and followed their outlet to the 'city of cannon.' There he hunted and fished, till the people chased him again through the woods into the arms of his enemies. The chief, who was born a Huron, was at last a warrior among the Mohawks!"

"Something like this I had heard before," said Cora, observing that he paused to suppress those passions which began to burn with too bright a flame, as he recalled the recollection of his supposed injuries.

"Was it the fault of le Renard that his head was not made of rock? Who gave him the fire-water? who made him a villain? 'Twas the pale-faces, the people of your own colour."

"And am I answerable that thoughtless and unprincipled men exist, whose shades of countenance may resemble mine?" Cora calmly demanded of the excited savage.

"No; Magua is a man, and not a fool; such as you never open their lips to the burning stream; the Great Spirit has given you wisdom!"

"What then have I to do, or say, in the matter of your misfortunes, not to say of your errors?"

"Listen," repeated the Indian, resuming his earnest attitude; "when his English and French fathers dug up the hatchet, le Renard struck the war-post of the Mohawks, and went out against his own nation. The pale-faces have driven the red-skins from their hunting grounds, and now, when they fight, a white man leads the way. The old chief at Horican, your father, was the great captain of our war party. He said to the Mohawks do this, and do that, and he was minded. He made a law, that if an Indian swallowed the fire-water, and came into the cloth wigwams of his warriors, it should not be forgotten. Magua foolishly opened his mouth, and the hot liquor led him into the cabin of Munro. What did the gray-head? let his daughter say."

"He forgot not his words, and did justice, by punishing the offender," said the undaunted daughter.

"Justice!" repeated the Indian, casting an oblique glance of the most ferocious expression at her unyielding countenance; "is it justice to make evil, and then punish for it! Magua was not himself; it was the fire-water that spoke and acted for him! but Munro did not believe it. The Huron chief was tied up before all the pale-faced warriors, and whipped like a dog."

Cora remained silent, for she knew not how to palliate this imprudent severity on the part of her father, in a manner to suit the comprehension of an Indian.

"See!" continued Magua, tearing aside the slight calico that very imperfectly concealed his painted breast; "here are scars given by knives and bullets—of these a warrior may boast before his nation; but the gray-head has left marks on the back of the Huron chief, that he must hide, like a squaw, under this painted cloth of the whites."

"I had thought," resumed Cora, "that an Indian warrior was patient, and that his spirit felt not, and knew not, the pain his body suffered?"

"When the Chippewas tied Magua to the stake, and cut this gash," said the other, laying his finger on a deep scar, "the Huron laughed in their faces, and told them, women struck so light! His spirit was then in the clouds! But when he felt the blows of Munro, his spirit lay under the birch. The spirit of a Huron is never drunk; it remembers for ever!"

"But it may be appeased. If my father has done you this injustice, show him how an Indian can forgive an injury, and take back his daughters. You have heard from Major Heyward—"

Magua shook his head, forbidding the repetition of offers he so much despised.

"What would you have," continued Cora, after a most painful pause, while the conviction forced itself on her mind, that the too sanguine and generous Duncan had been cruelly deceived by the cunning of the savage.

"What a Huron loves—good for good; bad for bad!"

"You would then revenge the injury inflicted by Munro, on

his helpless daughters. Would it not be more like a man to go before his face, and take the satisfaction of a warrior?"

"The arms of the pale-faces are long, and their knives sharp!" returned the savage, with a malignant laugh; "why should le Renard go among the muskets of his warriors, when he holds the spirit of the gray-head in his hand?"

"Name your intention, Magua," said Cora, struggling with herself to speak with steady calmness. "Is it to lead us prisoners to the woods, or do you contemplate even some greater evil? Is there no reward, no means of palliating the injury, and of softening your heart? At least, release my gentle sister, and pour out all your malice on me. Purchase wealth by her safety, and satisfy your revenge with a single victim. The loss of both his daughters might bring the aged man to his grave, and where would then be the satisfaction of le Renard?"

"Listen," said the Indian again. "The light eyes can go back to the Horican, and tell the old chief what has been done, if the dark-haired woman will swear, by the Great Spirit of her fathers, to tell no lie."

"What must I promise?" demanded Cora, still maintaining a secret ascendancy over the fierce native, by the collected and feminine dignity of her presence.

"When Magua left his people, his wife was given to another chief; he has now made friends with the Hurons, and will go back to the graves of his tribe, on the shores of the great lake. Let the daughter of the English chief follow, and live in his wigwam for ever."

However revolting a proposal of such a character might prove to Cora, she retained, notwithstanding her powerful disgust, sufficient self-command to reply, without betraying the weakness.

"And what pleasure would Magua find in sharing his cabin with a wife he did not love; one who would be of a nation and colour different from his own? It would be better to take the gold of Munro, and buy the heart of some Huron maid with his gifts."

The Indian made no reply for near a minute, but bent his fierce looks on the countenance of Cora, in such wavering glances, that her eyes sunk with shame, under an impression, that, for the first time, they had encountered an expression that no chaste female might endure. While she was shrinking within herself, in dread of having her ears wounded by some proposal still more shocking than the last, the voice of Magua answered, in its tones of deepest malignancy—

"When the blows scorched the back of the Huron, he would know where to find a woman to feel the smart. The daughter of Munro would draw his water, hoe his corn, and cook his venison. The body of the gray-head would sleep among his cannon, but his heart would lie within reach of the knife of le Subtil."

"Monster! well dost thou deserve thy treacherous name!" cried Cora, in an ungovernable burst of filial indignation. "None but a fiend could meditate such a vengeance! But thou overratest thy power! You shall find it is, in truth, the heart of Munro you hold, and that it will defy your utmost malice!"

The Indian answered this bold defiance by a ghastly smile, that showed an unaltered purpose, while he motioned her away, as if to close the conference, for ever. Cora, already regretting her precipitation, was obliged to comply; for Magua instantly left the spot, and approached his gluttonous comrades. Heyward flew to the side of the agitated female, and demanded the result of a dialogue, that he had watched at a distance with so much interest. But unwilling to alarm the fears of Alice, she evaded a direct reply, betraying only by her countenance her utter want of success, and keeping her anxious looks fastened on the slightest movements of their captors. To the reiterated and earnest questions of her sister, concerning their probable destination, she made no other answer, than by pointing towards the dark groupe, with an agitation she could not control, and murmuring, as she folded Alice to her bosom—

"There, there; read our fortunes in their faces; we shall see! we shall see!"

The action, and the choked utterance of Cora, spoke more impressively than any words, and quickly drew the attention of her companions on that spot, where her own was riveted with an intenseness, that nothing but the importance of the stake could create.

When Magua reached the cluster of lolling savages, who, gorged with their disgusting meal, lay stretched on the earth, in brutal indulgence, he commenced speaking with the dignity of an Indian chief. The first syllables he uttered, had the effect to cause his listeners to raise themselves in attitudes of respectful attention. As the Huron used his native language, the prisoners, notwithstanding the caution of the natives had kept them within the swing of their tomahawks, could only conjecture the substance of his harangue, from the nature of those significant gestures with which an Indian always illustrates his eloquence.

At first, the language, as well as the action of Magua, appeared calm and deliberative. When he had succeeded in sufficiently awakening the attention of his comrades, Heyward fancied, by his pointing so frequently toward the direction of the great lakes, that he spoke of the land of their fathers, and of their distant tribe. Frequent indications of applause escaped the listeners, who, as they uttered the expressive "hugh!" looked at each other in commendation of the speaker. Le Renard was too skilful to neglect his advantage. He now spoke of the long and painful route by which they had left those spacious hunting grounds and happy villages, to come and battle against the enemies of their Canadian fathers. He enumerated the warriors of the party; their several merits; their frequent services to the nation; their wounds, and the numbers of the scalps they had taken. Whenever he alluded to any present, (and the subtle Indian neglected none,) the dark countenance of the flattered individual gleamed with exultation, nor did he even hesitate to assert the truth of the words, by gestures of applause and confirmation. Then the voice of the speaker fell, and lost the loud, animated tones of triumph with which he had enumerated their deeds of success and victory. He described the cataract of Glenn's; the impregnable position of its rocky island, with its caverns, and its numerous rapids and whirlpools; he named the name of 'la Longue Carabine,' and paused until the forest beneath them had sent up the last echo of a loud and long yell, with which the hated appellation was received. He pointed toward the youthful military captive, and described the death of a favourite warrior, who had been precipitated into the deep ravine by his hand. He not only mentioned the fate of him who, hanging between heaven and earth, had presented such a spectacle of horror to the whole band, but he acted anew the terrors of his situation, his resolution and his death, on the branches of a sapling; and, finally, he rapidly recounted the manner in which each of their friends had fallen, never failing to touch upon their courage, and their most acknowledged virtues. When this recital of events was ended, his voice once more changed, and became plaintive, and even musical, in its low, guttural sounds. He now spoke of the wives and children of the slain; their destitution; their misery, both physical and moral; their distance; and, at last, of their unavenged wrongs. Then suddenly lifting his voice to a pitch of terrific energy, he concluded, by demanding—

"Are the Hurons dogs, to bear this? Who shall say to the wife of Menowgua, that the fishes have his scalp, and that his nation have not taken revenge! Who will dare meet the mother of Wassawattimie, that scornful woman, with his hands clean! What shall be said to the old men, when they ask us for scalps, and we have not a hair from a white head to give them! The women will point their fingers at us. There is a dark spot on the names of the Hurons, and it must be hid in blood!—"

His voice was no longer audible in the burst of rage, which now broke into the air, as if the wood, instead of containing so small a band, was filled with their nation. During the foregoing address, the progress of the speaker was too plainly read by those most interested in his success, through the medium of the countenances of the men he addressed. They had answered his melancholy and mourning, by sympathy and sorrow; his assertions, by gestures of confirmation; and his boastings, with the exultation of savages. When he spoke of courage, their looks were firm and responsive; when he alluded to their injuries, their eyes kindled with fury; when he mentioned the taunts of the women, they dropped their heads in shame; but when he pointed out their means of vengeance, he struck a chord which never failed to thrill in the breast of an Indian. With the first intimation that it was within their reach, the whole band sprang upon their feet, as one man, and giving utterance to their rage in the most frantic cries, they rushed upon their prisoners in a body, with drawn knives and uplifted tomahawks. Heyward threw himself between the sisters and the foremost, whom he grappled with a desperate strength that for a moment checked his violence. This unexpected resistance gave Magua time to interpose, and with rapid enunciation and animated gestures, he drew the attention of the band again to himself. In that language he knew so well how to assume, he diverted his comrades from their instant purpose, and invited them to prolong the misery of their victims. His proposal was received with acclamations, and executed with the swiftness of thought.

Two powerful warriors cast themselves on Heyward, while another was occupied in securing the less active singing-master. Neither of the captives, however, submitted without a desperate though fruitless struggle. Even David hurled his assailant to the earth; nor was Heyward secured, until the victory over his companion enabled the Indians to direct their united force to that object. He was then bound and fastened to the body of the sapling, on whose branches Magua had acted the pantomime of the falling Huron. When the young soldier regained his recollection, he had the painful certainty before his eyes, that a common fate was intended for the whole party. On his right was Cora, in a durance similar to his own, pale and agitated, but with an eye, whose steady look still read the proceedings of their enemies. On his left, the withes which bound her to a pine, performed that office for Alice which her trembling limbs refused, and alone kept her fragile form from sinking. Her hands were clasped before her in prayer, but instead of looking upward to that power which alone could rescue them, her unconscious looks wandered to the countenance of Duncan, with infantile dependency. David had contended; and the novelty of the circumstance held him silent, in deliberation, on the propriety of the unusual occurrence.

The vengeance of the Hurons had now taken a new direction, and they prepared to execute it, with that barbarous ingenuity, with which they were familiarized by the practice of centuries. Some sought knots, to raise the blazing pile; one was riving the splinters of pine, in order to pierce the flesh of their captives with the burning fragments; and others bent the tops of two saplings to the earth, in order to suspend Heyward by the arms between the recoiling branches. But the vengeance of Magua sought a deeper and a more malignant enjoyment.

While the less refined monsters of the band prepared, before the eyes of those who were to suffer, these well known and vulgar means of torture, he approached Cora, and pointed out, with the most malign expression of countenance, the speedy fate that awaited her—

"Ha!" he added, " what says the daughter of Munro? Her head is too good to find a pillow in the wigwam of le Renard; will she like it better when it rolls about this hill, a plaything for the wolves? Her bosom cannot nurse the children of a Huron; she will see it spit upon by Indians!"

"What means the monster!" demanded the astonished Heyward.

"Nothing!" was the firm reply. "He is a savage, a barbarous and ignorant savage, and knows not what he does. Let us find leisure, with our dying breath, to ask for him penitence and pardon."

"Pardon!" echoed the fierce Huron, mistaking, in his anger, the meaning of her words; "the memory of an Indian is longer than the arm of the pale-faces; his mercy shorter than their justice! Say; shall I send the yellow-hair to her father, and will you follow Magua to the great lakes, to carry his water, and feed him with corn?"

Cora beckoned him away, with an emotion of disgust she could not control.

"Leave me," she said, with a solemnity that for a moment checked the barbarity of the Indian; "you mingle bitterness in my prayers; you stand between me and my God!"

The slight impression produced on the savage was, however, soon forgotten, and he continued pointing, with taunting irony, towards Alice.

"Look! the child weeps! She is young to die! Send her to Munro, to comb his gray hairs, and keep life in the heart of the old man."

Cora could not resist the desire to look upon her youthful sister, in whose eyes she met an imploring glance, that betrayed the longings of nature.

"What says he, dearest Cora?" asked the trembling voice of Alice. "Did he speak of sending me to our father?"

For many moments the elder sister looked upon the younger, with a countenance that wavered with powerful and contending emotions. At length she spoke, though her tones had lost their rich and calm fulness, in an expression of tenderness, that seemed maternal.

"Alice," she said, "the Huron offers us both life—nay, more than both; he offers to restore Duncan—our invaluable Duncan, as well as you, to our friends—to our father—to our heart-stricken, childless father, if I will bow down this rebellious, stubborn pride of mine, and consent—"

Her voice became choked, and clasping her hands, she looked upward, as if seeking, in her agony, intelligence from a wisdom that was infinite.

"Say on," cried Alice; "to what, dearest Cora? Oh! that the proffer were made to me! to save you, to cheer our aged father! to restore Duncan, how cheerfully could I die!"

"Die!" repeated Cora, with a calmer and firmer voice, "that were easy! Perhaps the alternative may not be less so. He would have me," she continued, her accents sinking under a deep consciousness of the degradation of the proposal, "follow him to the wilderness; to go to the habitations of the Hurons; to remain there: in short, to become his wife! Speak then, Alice; child of my affections! sister of my love! And you too, Major Heyward, aid my weak reason with your counsel. Is life to be purchased by such a sacrifice? Will you, Alice, receive it at my hands, at such a price? And *you*, Duncan; guide me; control me between you; for I am wholly yours."

"Would I!" echoed the indignant and astonished youth. "Cora! Cora! you jest with our misery! Name not the horrid alternative again; the thought itself is worse than a thousand deaths."

"That such would be *your* answer, I well knew!" exclaimed Cora, her cheeks flushing, and her dark eyes once more sparkling with the lingering emotions of a woman. "What says my Alice? for her will I submit without another murmur."

Although both Heyward and Cora listened with painful suspense and the deepest attention, no sounds were heard in reply. It appeared as if the delicate and sensitive form of Alice had shrunk into itself, as she listened to this proposal. Her arms had fallen lengthwise before her, the fingers moving in slight convulsions; her head dropped upon her bosom, and her whole person seemed suspended against the tree, looking like some beautiful emblem of the wounded delicacy of her sex, devoid of animation, and yet keenly conscious. In a few moments, however, her head began to move slowly, in a sign of deep, unconquerable disapprobation.

"No, no, no; better that we die, as we have lived, together!"

"Then die!" shouted Magua, hurling his tomahawk with violence at the unresisting speaker, and gnashing his teeth with a rage that could no longer be bridled, at this sudden exhibition of firmness in the one he believed the weakest of the party. The axe cleaved the air in front of Heyward, and cutting some of the flowing ringlets of Alice, quivered in the tree above her head. The sight maddened Duncan to desperation. Collecting all his energies in one effort, he snapped the twigs which bound him, and rushed upon another savage, who was preparing, with loud yells, and a more deliberate aim, to repeat the blow. They encountered, grappled, and fell to the earth together. The naked body of his antagonist, afforded Heyward no means of holding his adversary, who glided from his grasp, and rose again with one knee on his chest, pressing him down with the weight of a giant. Duncan already saw the knife gleaming in the air, when a whistling sound swept past him, and was rather accompanied, than followed, by the sharp crack of a rifle. He felt his breast relieved from the load it had endured; he saw the savage expression of his adversary's countenance change to a look of vacant wildness, when the Indian fell dead on the faded leaves by his side.

Chapter XII

> "*Clo.*—I am gone, sir,
> And anon, sir,
> I'll be with you again."
> *Twelfth Night*, IV.ii.120–122.

THE HURONS stood aghast at this sudden visitation of death on one of their band. But, as they regarded the fatal accuracy of an aim, which had dared to immolate an enemy, at so much hazard to a friend, the name of "la Longue Carabine" burst simultaneously from every lip, and was succeeded by a wild and a sort of plaintive howl. The cry was answered by a loud shout from a little thicket, where the incautious party had piled their arms; and, at the next moment, Hawk-eye, too eager to load the rifle he had regained, was seen advancing upon them, brandishing the clubbed weapon, and cutting the air with wide and powerful sweeps. Bold and rapid as was the progress of the scout, it was exceeded by that of a light and vigorous form, which bounding past him, leaped, with incredible activity and daring, into the very centre of the Hurons, where it stood, whirling a tomahawk, and flourishing a glittering knife, with fearful menaces, in front of Cora. Quicker than the thoughts could follow these unexpected and audacious movements, an image, armed in the emblematic panoply of death, glided before their eyes, and assumed a threatening attitude at the other's side. The savage tormentors recoiled before these warlike intruders, and uttered, as they appeared, in such quick succession, the often repeated and peculiar exclamation of surprise, followed by the well known and dreaded appellations of—

"Le Cerf Agile! le Gros Serpent!"

But the wary and vigilant leader of the Hurons, was not so easily disconcerted. Casting his keen eyes around the little plain, he comprehended the nature of the assault, at a glance, and encouraging his followers by his voice, as well as by his example, he unsheathed his long and dangerous knife, and rushed, with a loud whoop, upon the expecting Chingachgook. It was the signal for a general combat. Neither party had fire-arms, and the contest was to be decided in the deadliest manner; hand to hand, with weapons of offence, and none of defence.

Uncas answered the whoop, and leaping on an enemy, with a single, well-directed blow of his tomahawk, cleft him to the brain. Heyward tore the weapon of Magua from the sapling, and rushed eagerly towards the fray. As the combatants were now equal in number, each singled an opponent from the adverse band. The rush and blows passed with the fury of a whirlwind, and the swiftness of lightning. Hawk-eye soon got another enemy within reach of his arm, and with one sweep of his formidable weapon, he beat down the slight and inartificial defences of his antagonist, crushing him to the earth with the blow. Heyward ventured to hurl the tomahawk he had seized, too ardent to await the moment of closing. It struck the Indian he had selected on the forehead, and checked for an instant his onward rush. Encouraged by this slight advantage, the impetuous young man continued his onset, and sprang upon his enemy with naked hands. A single instant was sufficient to assure him of the rashness of the measure, for he immediately found himself fully engaged, with all his activity and courage, in endeavouring to ward the desperate thrusts made with the knife of the Huron. Unable longer to foil an enemy so alert and vigilant, he threw his arms about him, and succeeded in pinning the limbs of the other to his side, with an iron grasp, but one that was far too exhausting to himself to continue long. In this extremity he heard a voice near him, shouting—

"Extarminate the varlets! no quarter to an accursed Mingo!"

At the next moment, the breech of Hawk-eye's rifle fell on the naked head of his adversary, whose muscles appeared to wither under the shock, as he sunk from the arms of Duncan, flexible and motionless.

When Uncas had brained his first antagonist, he turned, like a hungry lion, to seek another. The fifth and only Huron disengaged at the first onset, had paused a moment, and then seeing that all around him were employed in the deadly strife, he had sought, with hellish vengeance, to complete the baffled work of revenge. Raising a shout of triumph, he had sprung towards the defenceless Cora, sending his keen axe, as the dreadful precursor of his approach. The tomahawk grazed her shoulder, and cutting the withes which bound her to the tree, left the maiden at liberty to fly. She eluded the grasp of the savage, and reckless of her own safety, threw herself on the bosom of Alice, striving, with convulsed and ill-directed fingers, to tear asunder the twigs which confined the person of her sister. Any other than a monster would have relented at such an act of generous devotion to the best and purest affection; but the breast of the Huron was a stranger to any sympathy. Seizing Cora by the rich tresses which fell in confusion about her form, he tore her from her frantic hold, and bowed her down with brutal violence to her knees. The savage drew the flowing curls through his hand, and raising them on high with an outstretched arm, he passed the knife around the exquisitely moulded head of his victim, with a taunting and exulting laugh. But he purchased this moment of fierce gratification, with the loss of the fatal opportunity. It was just then the sight caught the eye of Uncas. Bounding from his footsteps, he appeared for an instant darting through the air, and descending in a ball he fell on the chest of his enemy, driving him many yards from the spot, headlong and prostrate. The violence of the exertion cast the young Mohican at his side. They arose together, fought, and bled, each in his turn. But the conflict was soon decided; the tomahawk of Heyward, and the rifle of Hawk-eye, descended on the skull of the Huron, at the same moment that the knife of Uncas reached his heart.

The battle was now entirely terminated, with the exception of the protracted struggle between "le Renard Subtil" and "le Gros Serpent." Well did these barbarous warriors prove that they deserved those significant names, which had been bestowed for deeds in former wars. When they engaged, some little time was lost in eluding the quick and vigorous thrusts which had been aimed at their lives. Suddenly darting on each other, they closed, and came to the earth, twisted together, like twining serpents, in pliant and subtle folds. At the moment when the victors found themselves unoccupied, the spot where these experienced and desperate combatants lay, could only be distinguished by a cloud of dust and leaves, which moved from the centre of the little plain towards its boundary, as if raised by the passage of a whirlwind. Urged by the different motives of filial affection, friendship, and gratitude, Heyward and his companions rushed with one accord to the place, encircling the little canopy of dust which hung above the warriors. In vain did Uncas dart around the cloud, with a wish to strike his knife into the heart of his father's foe; the threatening rifle of Hawk-eye was raised and suspended in vain; while Duncan endeavoured to seize the limbs of the Huron, with hands that appeared to have lost their power. Covered, as they were, with dust and blood, the swift evolutions of the combatants seemed to incorporate their bodies into one. The death-like looking figure of the Mohican, and the dark form of the Huron, gleamed before their eyes in such quick and confused succession, that the friends of the former knew not where nor when to plant the succouring blow. It is true, there were short and fleeting moments, when the fiery eyes of Magua were seen glittering, like the fabled organs of the basilisk, through the dusty wreath by which he was enveloped, and he read by those short and deadly glances, the fate of the combat in the presence of his enemies; ere, however, any hostile hand could descend on his devoted head, its place was filled by the scowling visage of Chingachgook. In this manner, the scene of the combat was removed from the centre of the little plain to its verge. The Mohican now found an opportunity to make a powerful thrust with his knife; Magua suddenly relinquished his grasp, and fell backward, without motion, and, seemingly, without life. His adversary leaped on his feet, making the arches of the forest ring with the sounds of triumph.

"Well done for the Delawares! victory to the Mohican!" cried Hawk-eye, once more elevating the butt of the long and fatal rifle; "a finishing blow from a man without a cross, will never tell against his honour, nor rob him of his right to the scalp!"

But, at the very moment when the dangerous weapon was in the act of descending, the subtle Huron rolled swiftly from beneath the danger, over the edge of the precipice, and falling on his feet, was seen leaping, with a single bound, into the centre of a thicket of low bushes, which clung along its sides.

The Delawares, who had believed their enemy dead, uttered their exclamation of surprise, and were following with speed and clamour, like hounds in open view of the deer, when a shrill and peculiar cry from the scout, instantly changed their purpose, and recalled them to the summit of the hill.

"'Twas like himself!" cried the inveterate forester, whose prejudices contributed so largely to veil his natural sense of justice in all matters which concerned the Mingoes; "a lying and deceitful varlet as he is! An honest Delaware now, being fairly vanquished, would have laid still, and been knocked on the head, but these knavish Maquas cling to life like so many cats-o'-the-mountain. Let him go—let him go; 'tis but one man, and he without rifle or bow, many a long mile from his French commerades; and, like a rattler that has lost his fangs, he can do no farther mischief, until such time as he, and we too, may leave the prints of our moccasins over a long reach of sandy plain. See, Uncas," he added, in Delaware, "your father is flaying the scalps already! It may be well to go round and feel the vagabonds that are left, or we may have another of them loping through the woods, and screeching like any jay that has been winged!"

So saying, the honest, but implacable scout, made the circuit of the dead, into whose senseless bosoms he thrust his long knife, with as much coolness, as though they had been so many brute carcasses. He had, however, been anticipated by the elder Mohican, who had already torn the emblems of victory from the unresisting heads of the slain.

But Uncas, denying his habits, we had almost said his nature, flew with instinctive delicacy, accompanied by Heyward to the assistance of the females, and quickly releasing Alice, placed her in the arms of Cora. We shall not attempt to describe the gratitude to the Almighty Disposer of events which glowed in the bosoms of the sisters, who were thus unexpectedly restored to life, and to each other. Their thanskgivings were deep and silent; the offerings of their gentle spirits, burning brightest and purest on the secret altars of their hearts; and their renovated and more earthly feelings exhibiting themselves in long and fervent, though speechless caresses. As Alice rose from her knees, where she had sunk, by the side of Cora, she threw herself on the bosom of the latter, and sobbed aloud the name of their aged father, while her soft, dove-like eyes, sparkled with the rays of hope.

"We are saved! we are saved!" she murmured; "to return to the arms of our dear, dear father, and his heart will not be broken with grief! And you too, Cora, my sister; my more than sister, my mother; you too are spared! and Duncan," she added, looking round upon the youth, with a smile of ineffable innocence, "even our own brave and noble Duncan has escaped without a hurt!"

To these ardent and nearly incoherent words, Cora made no other answer than by straining the youthful speaker to her heart, as she bent over her, in melting tenderness. The manhood of Heyward felt no shame, in dropping tears over this spectacle of affectionate rapture; and Uncas stood, fresh and blood-stained from the combat, a calm, and, apparently, an unmoved looker-on, it is true, but with eyes that had already lost their fierceness, and were beaming with a sympathy, that elevated him far above the intelligence, and advanced him probably centuries before the practices of his nation.

During this display of emotions so natural in their situation, Hawk-eye, whose vigilant distrust had satisfied itself that the Hurons, who disfigured the heavenly scene, no longer possessed the power to interrupt its harmony, approached David, and liberated him from the bonds he had, until that moment, endured with the most exemplary patience.

"There," exclaimed the scout, casting the last withe behind him, "you are once more master of your own limbs, though you seem not to use them with much greater judgment than that, in which they were first fashioned. If advice from one who is not older than yourself, but who, having lived most of his time in the wilderness, may be said to have experience beyond his years, will give no offence, you are welcome to my thoughts; and these are, to part with the little tooting instrument in your jacket to the first fool you meet with, and buy some useful we'pon with the money, if it be only the barrel of a horseman's pistol. By industry and care, you might thus come to some prefarment; for by this time, I should think, your eyes would plainly tell you, that a carrion crow is a better bird than a mocking thresher. The one will, at least, remove foul sights from before the face of man, while the other is only good to brew disturbances in the woods, by cheating the ears of all that hear them."

"Arms and the clarion for the battle, but the song of thanksgiving to the victory!" answered the liberated David. "Friend," he added, thrusting forth his lean, delicate hand, toward Hawk-eye, in kindness, while his eyes twinkled and grew moist, "I thank thee that the hairs of my head still grow where they were first rooted by Providence; for, though those of other men may be more glossy and curling, I have ever found mine own well suited to the brain they shelter. That I did not join myself to the battle, was less owing to disinclination, than to the bonds of the heathen. Valiant and skilful hast thou proved thyself in the conflict, and I hereby thank thee, before proceeding to discharge other and more important duties, because thou hast proved thyself well worthy of a Christian's praise!"

"The thing is but a trifle, and what you may often see, if you tarry long among us," returned the scout, a good deal softened toward the man of song, by this unequivocal expression of gratitude. "I have got back my old companion, 'killdeer,' " he added, striking his hand on the breech of his rifle, "and that in itself is a victory. These Iroquois are cunning, but they outwitted themselves when they placed their firearms out of reach; and had Uncas, or his father, been gifted with only their common Indian patience, we should have come in upon the knaves with three bullets instead of one, and that would have made a finish of the whole pack; yon lopeing varlet, as well as his commerades. But 'twas all foreordered, and for the best!"

"Thou sayest well," returned David, "and has caught the true spirit of christianity. He that is to be saved will be saved, and he that is predestined to be damned will be damned! This is the doctrine of truth, and most consoling and refreshing it is to the true believer."

The scout, who by this time was seated, examining into the state of his rifle with a species of parental assiduity, now looked up at the other in a displeasure that he did not affect to conceal, roughly interrupting further speech.

"Doctrine, or no doctrine," said the sturdy woodsman, " 'tis the belief of knaves, and the curse of an honest man! I can credit that yonder Huron was to fall by my hand, for with my own eyes have I seen it; but nothing short of being a witness, will cause me to think he has met with any reward, or that Chingachgook, there, will be condemned at the final day."

"You have no warranty for such an audacious doctrine, nor any covenant to support it," cried David, who was deeply tinctured with the subtle distinctions, which, in his time, and more especially in his province, had been drawn around the beautiful simplicity of revelation, by endeavouring to penetrate the awful mystery of the divine nature, supplying faith by self-sufficiency, and by consequence, involving those who reasoned from such human dogmas in absurdities and doubt; "your temple is reared on the sands, and the first tempest will wash away its foundation. I demand your authorities for such an uncharitable assertion; (like other advocates of a system, David was not always accurate in his use of terms.) Name chapter and verse; in which of the holy books do you find language to support you?"

"Book!" repeated Hawk-eye, with singular and ill-concealed disdain; "do you take me for a whimpering boy, at the apron string of one of your old gals; and this good rifle on my knee for the feather of a goose's wing, my ox's horn for a bottle of ink, and my leathern pouch for a cross-barred handkercher to carry my dinner! Book! what have such as I, who am a warrior of the wilderness, though a man without a cross, to do with books! I never read but in one, and the words that are written there are too simple and too plain to need much schooling; though I may boast that of forty long and hard working years."

"What call you the volume?" said David, misconceiving the other's meaning.

" 'Tis open before your eyes," returned the scout; "and he who owns it is not a niggard of its use. I have heard it said, that there are men who read in books, to convince themselves there is a God! I know not but man may so deform his works in the settlements, as to leave that which is so clear in the wilderness, a matter of doubt among traders and priests. If any such there be, and he will follow me from sun to sun, through the windings of the forest, he shall see enough to teach him that he is a fool, and that the greatest of his folly lies in striving to rise to the level of one he can never equal, be it in goodness, or be it in power."

The instant David discovered that he battled with a disputant who imbibed his faith from the lights of nature, eschewing all subtleties of doctrine, he willingly abandoned a controversy, from which he believed neither profit nor credit was to be derived. While the scout was speaking, he had also seated himself, and producing the ready little volume, and the iron-rimmed spectacles, he prepared to discharge a duty, which nothing but the unexpected assault he had received in his orthodoxy, could have so long suspended. He was, in truth, a minstrel of the western continent, of a much later day, certainly, than those gifted bards, who formerly sung the profane renown of baron and prince, but after the spirit of his own age and country; and he was now prepared to exercise the cunning of his craft, in celebration of, or rather in thanksgiving for, the recent victory. He waited patiently for Hawk-eye to cease, then lifting his eyes, together with his voice, he said, aloud—

"I invite you, friends, to join in praise for this signal deliverance from the hands of barbarians and infidels, to the comfortable and solemn tones of the tune, called 'Northampton.' "

He next named the page and verse where the rhymes selected were to be found, and applied the pitch-pipe to his lips, with the decent gravity, that he had been wont to use in the temple. This time he was, however, without any accompaniment, for the sisters were just then pouring out those tender effusions of affection, which have been already alluded to. Nothing deterred by the smallness of his audience, which, in truth, consisted only of the discontented scout, he raised his voice, commencing and ending the sacred song, without accident or interruption of any kind.

Hawk-eye listened, while he coolly adjusted his flint and reloaded his rifle, but the sounds wanting the extraneous assistance of scene and sympathy, failed to awaken his slumbering emotions. Never minstrel, or by whatever more suitable name David should be known, drew upon his talents in the presence of more insensible auditors; though considering the singleness and sincerity of his motive, it is probable that no bard of profane song ever uttered notes that ascended so near to that throne, where all homage and praise is due. The scout shook his head, and muttering some unintelligible words, among which "Throat" and "Iroquois," were alone audible, he walked away, to collect and to examine into the state of the captured arsenal of the Hurons. In this office he was now joined by Chingachgook, who found his own, as well as the rifle of his son, among the arms. Even Heyward and David were furnished with weapons, nor was ammunition wanting to render them all effectual.

When the foresters had made their selection, and distributed their prizes, the scout announced, that the hour had arrived when it was necessary to move. By this time the song of Gamut had ceased, and the sisters had learned to still the exhibition of their emotions. Aided by Duncan and the younger Mohican, the two latter descended the precipitous sides of that hill which they had so lately ascended, under so very different auspices, and whose summit had so nearly proved the scene of their massacre. At the foot, they found the Narragansets browsing the herbage of the bushes, and having mounted, they followed the movements of a guide, who, in the most deadly straits, had so often proved himself their friend. The journey was, however, short. Hawk-eye, leaving the blind path that the Hurons had followed, turned short to his right, and entering the thicket, he crossed a babbling brook, and halted in a narrow dell, under the shade of a few water elms. Their distance from the base of the fatal hill was but a few rods, and the steeds had been serviceable only in crossing the shallow stream.

The scout and the Indians appeared to be familiar with the sequestered place where they now were; for, leaning their rifles against the trees, they commenced throwing aside the dried leaves, and opening the blue clay, out of which a clear and sparkling spring of bright, glancing water, quickly bubbled. The white man then looked about him, as though seeking for some object, which was not to be found as readily as he expected—

"Them careless imps, the Mohawks, with their Tuscarora and Onondaga brethren, have been here slaking their thirst," he muttered, "and the vagabonds have thrown away the gourd! This is the way with benefits, when they are bestowed on such disremembering hounds! Here has the Lord laid his hand, in the midst of the howling wilderness, for their good, and raised a fountain of water from the bowels of the 'arth, that might laugh at the richest shop of apothecary's ware in all the colonies; and see! the knaves have trodden in the clay, and deformed the cleanliness of the place, as though they were brute beasts, instead of human men!"

Uncas silently extended towards him the desired gourd, which the spleen of Hawk-eye had hitherto prevented him from observing, on a branch of an elm. Filling it with water, he retired a short distance, to a place where the ground was more firm and dry; here he coolly seated himself, and after taking a long, and, apparently, a grateful draught, he commenced a very strict examination of the fragments of food left by the Hurons, which had hung in a wallet on his arm.

"Thank you, lad," he continued, returning the empty gourd to Uncas; "now we will see how these rampaging Hurons lived, when outlying in ambushments. Look at this! The varlets know the better pieces of the deer, and one would think they might carve and roast a saddle, equal to the best cook in the land! But every thing is raw, for them Iroquois are thorough savages. Uncas, take my steel, and kindle a fire; a mouthful of a tender broil will give natur a helping hand, after so long a trail."

Heyward, perceiving that their guides now set about their repast in sober earnest, assisted the ladies to alight, and placed himself at their side, not unwilling to enjoy a few moments of grateful rest, after the bloody scene he had just gone through. While the culinary process was in hand, curiosity induced him to inquire into the circumstances which had led to their timely and unexpected rescue—

"How is it that we see you so soon, my generous friend," he asked, "and without aid from the garrison of Edward?"

"Had we gone to the bend in the river, we might have been in time to rake the leaves over your bodies, but too late to have saved your scalps," coolly answered the scout. "No, no; instead of throwing away strength and opportunity by crossing to the fort, we lay by, under the bank of the Hudson, waiting to watch the movements of the Hurons."

"You were, then, witnesses of all that passed!"

"Not of all; for Indian sight is too keen to be easily cheated, and we kept close. A difficult matter it was, too, to keep this Mohican boy snug in the ambushment! Ah! Uncas, Uncas, your behaviour was more like that of a curious woman, than of a warrior on his scent!"

Uncas permitted his eyes to turn for an instant on the sturdy countenance of the speaker, but he neither spoke, nor gave any indication of repentance. On the contrary, Heyward thought the manner of the young Mohican was disdainful, if not a little fierce, and that he suppressed passions that were ready to explode, as much in compliment to the listeners, as from the deference he usually paid to his white associate.

"You saw our capture?" Heyward next demanded.

"We heard it," was the significant answer. "An Indian yell is plain language to men who have passed their days in the woods. But when you landed, we were driven to crawl, like sarpents, beneath the leaves; and then we lost sight of you entirely, until we placed eyes on you again trussed to the trees, and ready bound for an Indian massacre."

"Our rescue was the deed of Providence! It was nearly a miracle that you did not mistake the path, for the Hurons divided, and each band had its horses!"

"Ay! there we were thrown off the scent, and might, indeed, have lost the trail, had it not been for Uncas; we took the path, however, that led into the wilderness; for we judged, and judged rightly, that the savages would hold that course with their prisoners. But when we had followed it for many miles, without finding a single twig broken, as I had advised, my mind misgave me; especially as all the footsteps had the prints of moccasins."

"Our captors had the precaution to see us shod like themselves," said Duncan, raising a foot, and exhibiting the buskin he wore.

"Ay! 'twas judgmatical, and like themselves; though we were too expart to be thrown from a trail by so common an invention."

"To what then are we indebted for our safety?"

"To what, as a white man who has no taint of Indian blood, I should be ashamed to own; to the judgment of the young Mohican, in matters which I should know better than he, but which I can now hardly believe to be true, though my own eyes tell me it is so."

" 'Tis extraordinary! will you not name the reason?"

"Uncas was bold enough to say, that the beasts ridden by the gentle ones," continued Hawk-eye, glancing his eyes, not without curious interest on the fillies of the ladies, "planted the legs of one side on the ground at the same time, which is contrary to the movements of all trotting four-footed animals of my knowledge, except the bear! And yet here are horses that always journey in this manner, as my own eyes have seen, and as their trail has shown for twenty long miles!"

" 'Tis the merit of the animal! They come from the shores of Narraganset Bay, in the small province of Providence Plantations, and are celebrated for their hardihood, and the ease of this peculiar movement; though other horses are not unfrequently trained to the same."

"It may be—it may be," said Hawk-eye, who had listened with singular attention to this explanation; "though I am a man who has the full blood of the whites, my judgment in deer and beaver is greater than in beasts of burthen. Major Effingham has many noble chargers, but I have never seen one travel after such a sideling gait!"

"True, for he would value the animals for very different properties. Still, is this a breed highly esteemed, and as you witness, much honoured with the burthens it is often destined to bear."

The Mohicans had suspended their operations about the glimmering fire, to listen, and when Duncan had done, they looked at each other significantly, the father uttering the never-failing exclamation of surprise. The scout ruminated, like a man digesting his newly acquired knowledge, and once more stole a curious glance at the horses.

"I dare to say there are even stranger sights to be seen in the settlements!" he said, at length; "natur is sadly abused by man, when he once gets the mastery. But, go sideling, or go straight, Uncas had seen the movement, and their trail led us on to the broken bush. The outer branch, near the prints of one of the horses, was bent upward, as a lady breaks a flower from its stem, but all the rest were ragged and broken down, as if the strong hand of a man had been tearing them! So I concluded, that the cunning varments had seen the twig bent, and had torn the rest, to make us believe a buck had been feeling the boughs with his antlers."

"I do believe your sagacity did not deceive you; for some such thing occurred!"

"That was easy to see," added the scout, in no degree conscious of having exhibited any extraordinary sagacity; "and a very different matter it was from a waddling horse! It then struck me the Mingoes would push for this spring, for the knaves well know the vartue of its waters!"

"Is it, then, so famous?" demanded Heyward, examining, with a more curious eye, the secluded dell, with its bubbling fountain, surrounded, as it was, by earth of a deep dingy brown.

"Few red-skins, who travel south and east of the great lakes, but have heard of its qualities. Will you taste for yourself?"

Heyward took the gourd, and after swallowing a little of the water, threw it aside with grimaces of discontent. The scout laughed in his silent, but heartfelt manner, and shook his head with vast satisfaction.

"Ah! you want the flavour that one gets by habit; the time was when I liked it as little as yourself; but I have come to my taste, and I now crave it, as a deer does the licks.* Your high spiced wines are not better liked than a red-skin relishes this water; especially when his natur is ailing. But Uncas has made his fire, and it is time we think of eating, for our journey is long, and all before us."

Interrupting the dialogue by this abrupt transition, the scout had instant recourse to the fragments of food, which had escaped the voracity of the Hurons. A very summary pro-

*Many of the animals of the American forests resort to those spots where salt springs are found. These are called "licks" or "salt licks," in the language of the country, from the circumstance that the quadruped is often obliged to lick the earth, in order to obtain the saline particles. These licks are great places of resort with the hunters, who way-lay their game near the paths that lead to them.

cess completed the simple cookery, when he and the Mohicans commenced their humble meal, with the silence and characteristic diligence of men, who ate in order to enable themselves to endure great and unremitting toil.

When this necessary, and, happily, grateful duty had been performed, each of the foresters stooped and took a long and parting draught, at that solitary and silent spring,* around which and its sister fountains, within fifty years, the wealth, beauty, and talents, of a hemisphere, were to assemble in throngs, in pursuit of health and pleasure. Then Hawk-eye announced his determination to proceed. The sisters resumed their saddles; Duncan and David grasped their rifles, and followed on their footsteps; the scout leading the advance, and the Mohicans bringing up the rear. The whole party moved swiftly through the narrow path, towards the north, leaving the healing waters to mingle unheeded with the adjacent brook, and the bodies of the dead to fester on the neighbouring mount, without the rites of sepulture; a fate but too common to the warriors of the woods, to excite either commiseration or comment.

*The scene of the foregoing incidents is on the spot where the village of Ballston now stands; one of the two principal watering places of America.

Chapter XIII

"I'll seek a readier path."
Parnell, "A Night-Piece on Death," l. 7.

THE ROUTE taken by Hawk-eye lay across those sandy plains, relieved by occasional valleys and swells of land, which had been traversed by their party on the morning of the same day, with the baffled Magua for their guide. The sun had now fallen low towards the distant mountains, and as their journey lay through the interminable forest, the heat was no longer oppressive. Their progress, in consequence, was proportionate, and long before the twilight gathered about them, they had made good many toilsome miles, on their return.

The hunter, like the savage whose place he filled, seemed to select among the blind signs of their wild route with a species of instinct, seldom abating his speed, and never pausing to deliberate. A rapid and oblique glance at the moss on the trees, with an occasional upward gaze towards the setting sun, or a steady but passing look at the direction of the numerous water courses, through which he waded, were sufficient to determine his path, and remove his greatest difficulties. In the mean time, the forest began to change its hues, losing that lively green which had embellished its arches, in the graver light, which is the usual precursor of the close of day.

While the eyes of the sisters were endeavouring to catch glimpses, through the trees, of the flood of golden glory, which formed a glittering halo around the sun, tinging here and there, with ruby streaks, or bordering with narrow edgings of shining yellow, a mass of clouds that lay piled at no great distance above the western hills, Hawk-eye turned suddenly, and pointing upward towards the gorgeous heavens, he spoke.

"Yonder is the signal given to man to seek his food and natural rest," he said; "better and wiser would it be, if he could understand the signs of nature, and take a lesson from the fowls of the air, and the beasts of the fields! Our night, however, will soon be over, for, with the moon, we must be up and moving again. I remember to have fout the Maquas hereaways, in the first war in which I ever drew blood from man; and we threw up a work of blocks, to keep the ravenous varments from handling our scalps. If my marks do not fail me, we shall find the place a few rods further to our left."

Without waiting for an assent, or, indeed, for any reply, the sturdy hunter moved boldly into a dense thicket of young chestnuts, shoving aside the branches of the exuberant shoots which nearly covered the ground, like a man who expected, at each step, to discover some object he had formerly known. The recollection of the scout did not deceive him. After penetrating through the brush, matted as it was with briars, for a few hundred feet, he entered an open space, that surrounded a low, green hillock, which was crowned by the decayed block-house in question. This rude and neglected building was one of those deserted works, which, having been thrown up on an emergency, had been abandoned with the disappearance of danger, and was now quietly crumbling in the solitude of the forest, neglected, and nearly forgotten, like the circumstances which had caused it to be reared. Such memorials of the passage and struggles of man are yet frequent throughout the broad barrier of wilderness, which once separated the hostile provinces, and form a species of ruins, that are intimately associated with the recollections of colonial history, and which are in appropriate keeping with the gloomy character of the surrounding scenery.* The roof of bark had

*Some years since, the writer was shooting in the vicinity of the ruins of Fort Oswego, which stands on the shores of Lake Ontario. His game was deer, and his chase a forest that stretched, with little interruption, fifty miles inland. Unexpectedly he came upon six or eight ladders lying in the woods within a short distance of each other. They were rudely made and much decayed. Wondering what could have assembled so many of these instruments in such a place, he sought an old man who resided near for the explanation.

During the war of 1776 Fort Oswego was held by the British. An expedition had been sent two hundred miles through the wilderness to surprise the fort. It appears that the Americans, on reaching the spot named, which was within a mile or two of the fort, first learned that they were expected, and in great danger of being cut off. They threw away their scaling ladders, and made a rapid retreat. These ladders had lain unmolested thirty years, in the spot where they had thus been cast.

long since fallen and mingled with the soil, but the huge logs of pine, which had been hastily thrown together, still preserved their relative positions, though one angle of the work had given way under the pressure, and threatened a speedy downfall to the remainder of the rustic edifice. While Heyward and his companions hesitated to approach a building so decayed, Hawk-eye and the Indians entered within the low walls, not only without fear, but with obvious interest. While the former surveyed the ruins, both internally and externally, with the curiosity of one whose recollections were reviving at each moment, Chingachgook related to his son, in the language of the Delawares, and with the pride of a conqueror, the brief history of the skirmish which had been fought in his youth, in that secluded spot. A strain of melancholy, however, blended with his triumph, rendering his voice, as usual, soft and musical.

In the mean time, the sisters gladly dismounted, and prepared to enjoy their halt in the coolness of the evening, and in a security which they believed nothing but the beasts of the forest could invade.

"Would not our resting-place have been more retired, my worthy friend," demanded the more vigilant Duncan, perceiving that the scout had already finished his short survey, "had we chosen a spot less known, and one more rarely visited than this?"

"Few live who know the block-house was ever raised," was the slow and musing answer; " 'tis not often that books are made, and narratives written, of such a skrimmage as was here fout atween the Mohicans and the Mohawks, in a war of their own waging. I was then a younker, and went out with the Delawares, because I know'd they were a scandalized and wronged race. Forty days and forty nights did the imps crave our blood around this pile of logs, which I designed and partly reared, being, as you'll remember, no Indian myself, but a man without a cross. The Delawares lent themselves to the work, and we made it good, ten to twenty, until our numbers were nearly equal, and then we sallied out upon the hounds, and not a man of them ever got back to tell the fate of his party. Yes, yes; I was then young, and new to the sight of blood, and not relishing the thought that creatures who had spirits like myself, should lay on the naked ground, to be torn asunder by beasts, or to bleach in the rains, I buried the dead with my own hands, under that very little hillock, where you have placed yourselves; and no bad seat does it make neither, though it be raised by the bones of mortal men."

Heyward and the sisters arose on the instant from the grassy sepulchre; nor could the two latter, notwithstanding the terrific scenes they had so recently passed through, entirely suppress an emotion of natural horror, when they found themselves in such familiar contact with the grave of the dead Mohawks. The gray light, the gloomy little area of dark grass, surrounded by its border of brush, beyond which the pines rose, in breathing silence, apparently, into the very clouds, and the death-like stillness of the vast forest, were all in unison to deepen such a sensation.

"They are gone, and they are harmless," continued Hawkeye, waving his hand, with a melancholy smile, at their manifest alarm; "they'll never shout the warwhoop, nor strike a blow with the tomahawk, again! And of all those who aided in placing them where they lie, Chingachgook and I only are living! The brothers and family of the Mohican formed our war party, and you see before you, all that are now left of his race."

The eyes of the listeners involuntarily sought the forms of the Indians, with a compassionate interest in their desolate fortune. Their dark persons were still to be seen within the shadows of the block-house, the son listening to the relation of his father, with that sort of intenseness, which would be created by a narrative, that redounded so much to the honour of those, whose names he had long revered for their courage and savage virtues.

"I had thought the Delawares a pacific people," said Duncan, "and that they never waged war in person; trusting the defence of their lands to those very Mohawks that you slew!"

" 'Tis true in part," returned the scout, "and yet, at the bottom, 'tis a wicked lie. Such a treaty was made in ages gone by, through the deviltries of the Dutchers, who wished to disarm the natives that had the best right to the country, where they had settled themselves. The Mohicans, though a part of the same nation, having to deal with the English, never entered into the silly bargain, but kept to their manhood; as in truth did the Delawares, when their eyes were opened to their folly. You see before you, a chief of the great Mohican Sagamores! Once his family could chase their deer over tracts of country wider than that which belongs to the Albany Patteroon, without crossing brook or hill, that was not their own; but what is left to their descendant! He may find his six feet of earth, when God chooses; and keep it in peace, perhaps, if he has a friend who will take the pains to sink his head so low, that the ploughshares cannot reach it!"

"Enough!" said Heyward, apprehensive that the subject might lead to a discussion that would interrupt the harmony, so necessary to the preservation of his fair companions; "we have journeyed far, and few among us are blest with forms like that of yours, which seems to know neither fatigue nor weakness."

"The sinews and bones of a man carry me through it all," said the hunter, surveying his muscular limbs with a simplicity that betrayed the honest pleasure the compliment afforded him; "there are larger and heavier men to be found in the settlements, but you might travel many days in a city, before you could meet one able to walk fifty miles without stopping to take breath, or who has kept the hounds within hearing during a chase of hours. However, as flesh and blood are not always the same, it is quite reasonable to suppose, that the gentle ones are willing to rest, after all they have seen and done this day. Uncas, clear out the spring, while your father and I make a cover for their tender heads of these chestnut shoots, and a bed of grass and leaves."

The dialogue ceased, while the hunter and his companions busied themselves in preparations for the comfort and protection of those they guided. A spring, which many long years before had induced the natives to select the place for their temporary fortification, was soon cleared of leaves, and a fountain of crystal gushed from the bed, diffusing its waters over the verdant hillock. A corner of the building was then roofed in such a manner, as to exclude the heavy dew of the climate, and piles of sweet shrubs and dried leaves were laid beneath it, for the sisters to repose on.

While the diligent woodsmen were employed in this manner, Cora and Alice partook of that refreshment, which duty required, much more than inclination prompted, them to accept. They then retired within the walls, and first offering up their thanksgivings for past mercies, and petitioning for a continuance of the Divine favour throughout the coming night, they laid their tender forms on the fragrant couch, and in spite of recollections and forebodings, soon sunk into those slumbers which nature so imperiously demanded, and which were sweetened by hopes for the morrow. Duncan had prepared himself to pass the night in watchfulness, near them, just without the ruin; but the scout, perceiving his intention, pointed towards Chingachgook, as he coolly disposed his own person on the grass, and said—

"The eyes of a white man are too heavy, and too blind, for such a watch as this! The Mohican will be our sentinel; therefore, let us sleep."

"I proved myself a sluggard on my post during the past night," said Heyward, "and have less need of repose than you, who did more credit to the character of a soldier. Let all the party seek their rest, then, while I hold the guard."

"If we lay among the white tents of the 60th, and in front of an enemy like the French, I could not ask for a better watchman," returned the scout; "but in the darkness, and among the signs of the wilderness, your judgment would be like the folly of a child, and your vigilance thrown away. Do, then, like Uncas and myself; sleep, and sleep in safety."

Heyward perceived, in truth, that the younger Indian had thrown his form on the side of the hillock, while they were talking, like one who sought to make the most of the time allotted to rest, and that his example had been followed by David, whose voice literally 'clove to his jaws' with the fever of his wound, heightened, as it was, by their toilsome march. Unwilling to prolong a useless discussion, the young man affected to comply, by posting his back against the logs of the block-house, in a half-recumbent posture, though resolutely determined, in his own mind, not to close an eye until he had delivered his precious charge into the arms of Munro himself. Hawk-eye, believing he had prevailed, soon fell asleep, and a silence as deep as the solitude in which they had found it, pervaded the retired spot.

For many minutes Duncan succeeded in keeping his senses on the alert, and alive to every moaning sound that arose from the forest. His vision became more acute, as the shades of evening settled on the place, and even after the stars were glimmering above his head, he was able to distinguish the recumbent forms of his companions, as they lay stretched on the grass, and to note the person of Chingachgook, who sat upright, and motionless as one of the trees, which formed the dark barrier on every side of them. He still heard the gentle breathings of the sisters, who lay within a few feet of him, and not a leaf was ruffled by the passing air, of which his ear did not detect the whispering sound. At length, however, the mournful notes of a whip-poor-will, became blended with the moanings of an owl; his heavy eyes occasionally sought the bright rays of the stars, and then he fancied he saw them through the fallen lids. At instants of momentary wakefulness, he mistook a bush for his associate sentinel; his head next sunk upon his shoulder, which, in its turn, sought the support of the ground; and, finally, his whole person became relaxed and pliant, and the young man sunk into a deep sleep, dreaming that he was a knight of ancient chivalry, holding his midnight vigils before the tent of a re-captured princess, whose favour he did not despair of gaining, by such a proof of devotion and watchfulness.

How long the tired Duncan lay in this insensible state he never knew himself, but his slumbering visions had been long lost in total forgetfulness, when he was awakened by a light tap on the shoulder. Aroused by this signal, slight as it was, he sprang upon his feet, with a confused recollection of the self-imposed duty he had assumed with the commencement of the night—

"Who comes?" he demanded, feeling for his sword, at the place where it was usually suspended. "Speak! friend or enemy?"

"Friend," replied the low voice of Chingachgook; who, pointing upward at the luminary which was shedding its mild light through the opening in the trees, directly on their bivouac, immediately added, in his rude English, "moon comes, and white man's fort far—far off; time to move, when sleep shuts both eyes of the Frenchman!"

"You say true! call up your friends, and bridle the horses, while I prepare my own companions for the march."

"We are awake, Duncan," said the soft, silvery tones of Alice within the building, "and ready to travel very fast, after so refreshing a sleep; but you have watched through the tedious night, in our behalf, after having endured so much fatigue the livelong day!"

"Say, rather, I would have watched, but my treacherous eyes betrayed me; twice have I proved myself unfit for the trust I bear."

"Nay, Duncan, deny it not," interrupted the smiling Alice, issuing from the shadows of the building into the light of the moon, in all the loveliness of her freshened beauty; "I know you to be a heedless one, when self is the object of your care, and but too vigilant in favour of others. Can we not tarry here a little longer, while you find the rest you need. Cheerfully, most cheerfully, will Cora and I keep the vigils, while you, and all these brave men, endeavour to snatch a little sleep!"

"If shame could cure me of my drowsiness, I should never close an eye again," said the uneasy youth, gazing at the ingenuous countenance of Alice, where, however, in its sweet solicitude, he read nothing to confirm his half awakened suspicion. "It is but too true, that after leading you into danger by my heedlessness, I have not even the merit of guarding your pillows, as should become a soldier."

"No one but Duncan himself, should accuse Duncan of such a weakness. Go, then, and sleep; believe me, neither of us, weak girls as we are, will betray our watch."

The young man was relieved from the awkwardness of making any further protestations of his own demerits, by an exclamation from Chingachgook, and the attitude of riveted attention assumed by his son.

"The Mohicans hear an enemy!" whispered Hawk-eye, who, by this time, in common with the whole party, was awake and stirring. "They scent danger in the wind!"

"God forbid!" exclaimed Heyward. "Surely, we have had enough of bloodshed!"

While he spoke, however, the young soldier seized his rifle, and advancing towards the front, prepared to atone for his venial remissness, by freely exposing his life in defence of those he attended.

" 'Tis some creature of the forest prowling around us in quest of food!" he said, in a whisper, as soon as the low, and, apparently, distant sounds, which had startled the Mohicans, reached his own ears.

"Hist!" returned the attentive scout; " 'tis man; even I can now tell his tread, poor as my senses are, when compared to an Indian's! That scampering Huron has fallen in with one of Montcalm's outlying parties, and they have struck upon our trail. I shouldn't like myself to spill more human blood in this spot," he added, looking around with anxiety in his features, at the dim objects by which he was surrounded; "but what must be, must! Lead the horses into the block-house, Uncas; and, friends, do you follow to the same shelter. Poor and old as it is, it offers a cover, and has rung with the crack of a rifle afore to night!"

He was instantly obeyed, the Mohicans leading the Narragansets within the ruin, whither the whole party repaired, with the most guarded silence.

The sounds of approaching footsteps were now too distinctly audible, to leave any doubts as to the nature of the interruption. They were soon mingled with voices, calling to each other, in an Indian dialect, which the hunter, in a whisper, affirmed to Heyward, was the language of the Hurons. When the party reached the point where the horses had entered the thicket which surrounded the block-house, they were evidently at fault, having lost those marks which, until that moment, had directed their pursuit.

It would seem by the voices that twenty men were soon collected at that one spot, mingling their different opinions and advice, in noisy clamour.

"The knaves know our weakness," whispered Hawk-eye, who stood by the side of Heyward, in deep shade, looking through an opening in the logs, "or they wouldn't indulge their idleness in such a squaw's march. Listen to the reptiles! each man among them seems to have two tongues, and but a single leg!"

Duncan, brave as he was in the combat, could not, in such a moment of painful suspense, make any reply to the cool and characteristic remark of the scout. He only grasped his rifle more firmly, and fastened his eyes upon the narrow opening, through which he gazed upon the moonlight view with increasing anxiety. The deeper tones of one who spoke as having authority, were next heard, amid a silence that denoted the respect with which his orders, or rather advice, was received. After which, by the rustling of leaves, and cracking of dried twigs, it was apparent the savages were separating in pursuit of the lost trail. Fortunately for the pursued, the light of the moon, while it shed a flood of mild lustre, upon the little area around the ruin, was not sufficiently strong to penetrate the deep arches of the forest, where the objects still lay in deceptive shadow. The search proved fruitless; for so short and sudden had been the passage from the faint path the travellers had journeyed into the thicket, that every trace of their footsteps was lost in the obscurity of the woods.

It was not long, however, before the restless savages were heard beating the brush, and gradually approaching the inner edge of that dense border of young chestnuts, which encircled the little area.

"They are coming!" muttered Heyward, endeavouring to thrust his rifle through the chink in the logs; "let us fire on their approach!"

"Keep every thing in the shade," returned the scout; "the snapping of a flint, or even the smell of a single karnel of the brimstone, would bring the hungry varlets upon us in a body. Should it please God, that we must give battle for the scalps, trust to the experience of men who know the ways of the savages, and who are not often backward when the war-whoop is howled."

Duncan cast his eyes behind him, and saw that the trembling sisters were cowering in the far corner of the building, while the Mohicans stood in the shadow, like two upright posts, ready, and apparently willing, to strike, when the blow should be needed. Curbing his impatience, he again looked out upon the area, and awaited the result in silence. At that instant the thicket opened, and a tall and armed Huron advanced a few paces into the open space. As he gazed upon the silent block-house, the moon fell full upon his swarthy countenance, and betrayed its surprise and curiosity. He made the exclamation, which usually accompanies the former emotion in an Indian, and calling in a low voice, soon drew a companion to his side.

These children of the woods stood together for several moments, pointing at the crumbling edifice, and conversing in the unintelligible language of their tribe. They then approached, though with slow and cautious steps, pausing every instant to look at the building, like startled deer, whose curiosity struggled powerfully with their awakened apprehensions for the mastery. The foot of one of them suddenly rested on the mound, and he stooped to examine its nature. At this moment, Heyward observed that the scout loosened his knife in its sheath, and lowered the muzzle of his rifle. Imitating these movements, the young man prepared himself for the struggle, which now seemed inevitable.

The savages were so near, that the least motion in one of the horses, or even a breath louder than common, would have betrayed the fugitives. But, in discovering the character of the mound, the attention of the Hurons appeared directed to a different object. They spoke together, and the sounds of their voices were low and solemn, as if influenced by a reverence that was deeply blended with awe. Then they drew warily back, keeping their eyes riveted on the ruin, as if they expected to see the apparitions of the dead issue from its silent walls, until having reached the boundary of the area, they moved slowly into the thicket, and disappeared.

Hawk-eye dropped the breech of his rifle to the earth, and drawing a long, free breath, exclaimed, in an audible whisper—

"Ay! they respect the dead, and it has this time saved their own lives, and it may be, the lives of better men too!"

Heyward lent his attention, for a single moment, to his companion, but without replying, he again turned towards those who just then interested him more. He heard the two Hurons leave the bushes, and it was soon plain that all the pursuers were gathered about them, in deep attention to their report. After a few minutes of earnest and solemn dialogue, altogether different from the noisy clamour with which they had first collected about the spot, the sounds grew fainter, and more distant, and finally were lost in the depths of the forest.

Hawk-eye waited until a signal from the listening Chingachgook assured him, that every sound from the retiring party was completely swallowed by the distance, when he motioned to Heyward to lead forth the horses, and to assist the sisters into their saddles. The instant this was done, they issued through the broken gate-way, and stealing out by a direction opposite to the one by which they had entered, they quitted the spot, the sisters casting furtive glances at the silent grave and crumbling ruin, as they left the soft light of the moon, to bury themselves in the gloom of the woods.

Chapter XIV

"*Guard.*——Qui est là?
Puc.——Paisans, pauvres gens de France."
1 Henry VI, III.ii.13–14.

DURING THE RAPID movement from the block-house, and until the party was deeply buried in the forest, each individual was too much interested in the escape, to hazard a word even in whispers. The scout resumed his post in the advance, though his steps, after he had thrown a safe distance between himself and his enemies, were more deliberate than in their previous march, in consequence of his utter ignorance of the localities of the surrounding woods. More than once he halted to consult with his confederates, the Mohicans, pointing upwards at the moon, and examining the barks of the trees with care. In these brief pauses, Heyward and the sisters listened, with senses rendered doubly acute by the danger, to detect any symptoms which might announce the proximity of their foes. At such moments, it seemed as if a vast range of country lay buried in eternal sleep; not the least sound arising from the forest, unless it was the distant and scarcely audible rippling of a water-course. Birds, beasts, and man, appeared to slumber alike, if, indeed, any of the latter were to be found in that wide tract of wilderness. But the sounds of the rivulet, feeble and murmuring as they were, relieved the guides at once from no trifling embarrassment, and towards it they immediately held their way.

When the banks of the little stream were gained, Hawk-eye made another halt; and, taking the moccasins from his feet, he invited Heyward and Gamut to follow his example. He then entered the water, and for near an hour they travelled in the bed of the brook, leaving no trail. The moon had already sunk into an immense pile of black clouds, which lay impending above the western horizon, when they issued from the low and devious water-course to rise, again, to the light and level of the sandy but wooded plain. Here the scout seemed to be once more at home, for he held on his way, with the certainty and diligence of a man, who moved in the security of his own knowledge. The path soon became more uneven, and the travellers could plainly perceive, that the mountains drew nigher to them on each hand, and that they were, in truth, about entering one of their gorges. Suddenly, Hawk-eye made a pause, and waiting until he was joined by the whole party, he spoke; though in tones so low and cautious, that they added to the solemnity of his words, in the quiet and darkness of the place.

"It is easy to know the path-ways, and to find the licks and water-courses of the wilderness," he said; "but who that saw this spot, could venture to say, that a mighty army was at rest among yonder silent trees and barren mountains!"

"We are then at no great distance from William Henry?" said Heyward, advancing nigher to the scout.

"It is yet a long and weary path, and when and where to strike it, is now our greatest difficulty. See," he said, pointing through the trees towards a spot where a little basin of water reflected the stars from its placid bosom, "here is the 'bloody pond;' and I am on ground that I have not only often travelled, but over which I have fou't the enemy, from the rising to the setting sun!"

"Ha! that sheet of dull and dreary water, then, is the sepulchre of the brave men who fell in the contest! I have heard it named, but never have I stood on its banks before!"

"Three battles did we make with the Dutch Frenchman* in a day!" continued Hawk-eye, pursuing the train of his own thoughts, rather than replying to the remark of Duncan. "He met us hard by, in our outward march to ambush his advance, and scattered us, like driven deer, through the defile, to the shores of Horican. Then we rallied behind our fallen trees, and made head against him, under Sir William—who was made Sir William for that very deed; and well did we pay him for the disgrace of the morning! Hundreds of Frenchmen saw the sun that day for the last time; and even their leader, Dieskau himself, fell into our hands, so cut and torn with the lead, that he has gone back to his own country, unfit for further acts in war."

*Baron Dieskau, a German, in the service of France. A few years previously to the period of the tale, this officer was defeated by Sir William Johnson of Johnstown, New York, on the shores of Lake George.

" 'Twas a noble repulse!" exclaimed Heyward in the heat of his youthful ardour; "the fame of it reached us early in our southern army."

"Ay! but it did not end there. I was sent by Major Effingham, at Sir William's own bidding, to out-flank the French, and carry the tidings of their disaster across the portage, to the fort on the Hudson. Just hereaway, where you see the trees rise into a mountain swell, I met a party coming down to our aid, and I led them where the enemy were taking their meal, little dreaming that they had not finished the bloody work of the day."

"And you surprised them!"

"If death can be a surprise to men who are thinking only of the cravings of their appetites! we gave them but little breathing time, for they had borne hard upon us in the fight of the morning, and there were few in our party who had not lost friend or relative by their hands. When all was over, the dead, and some say the dying, were cast into that little pond. These eyes have seen its waters coloured with blood, as natural water never yet flowed from the bowels of the 'arth."

"It was a convenient, and, I trust, will prove a peaceful grave for a soldier! You have, then, seen much service on this frontier?"

"I!" said the scout, erecting his tall person with an air of military pride; "there are not many echoes among these hills that haven't rung with the crack of my rifle, nor is there the space of a square mile atwixt Horican and the river, that 'kill-deer' hasn't dropped a living body on, be it an enemy, or be it a brute beast. As for the grave there, being as quiet as you mention, it is another matter. There are them in the camp, who say and think, man to lie still, should not be buried while the breath is in the body; and certain it is, that in the hurry of that evening, the doctors had but little time to say who was living, and who was dead. Hist! see you nothing walking on the shore of the pond?"

" 'Tis not probable that any are as houseless as ourselves, in this dreary forest."

"Such as he may care but little for house or shelter, and night dew can never wet a body that passes its days in the water!" returned the scout, grasping the shoulder of Heyward, with such convulsive strength, as to make the young soldier painfully sensible how much superstitious terror had gotten the mastery of a man usually so dauntless.

"By heaven! there is a human form, and it approaches! stand to your arms, my friends, for we know not whom we encounter."

"Qui vive?" demanded a stern, quick voice, which sounded like a challenge from another world, issuing out of that solitary and solemn place.

"What says it?" whispered the scout; "it speaks neither Indian nor English!"

"Qui vive?" repeated the same voice, which was quickly followed by the rattling of arms, and a menacing attitude.

"France," cried Heyward, advancing from the shadow of the trees, to the shore of the pond, within a few yards of the sentinel.

"D'où venez-vous—où allez-vous d'aussi bonne heure?" demanded the grenadier, in the language, and with the accent of a man from old France.

"Je viens de la découverte, et je vais me coucher."

"Etes-vous officier du roi?"

"Sans doute, mon camarade; me prends-tu pour un provincial! Je suis capitaine de chasseurs (Heyward well knew that the other was of a regiment in the line)—j'ai ici, avec moi, les filles du commandant de la fortification. Aha! tu en as entendu parler! je les ai fait prisonnières près de l'autre fort, et je les conduis au général."

"Ma foi! mesdames; j'en suis fâché pour vous," exclaimed the young soldier, touching his cap with grace; "mais—fortune de guerre! vous trouverez notre général un brave homme, et bien poli avec les dames."

"C'est le caractère des gens de guerre," said Cora, with admirable self-possession; "Adieu, mon ami; je vous souhaiterais un devoir plus agréable, à remplir."

The soldier made a low and humble acknowledgment for her civility; and Heyward adding a "bonne nuit, mon camarade," they moved deliberately forward; leaving the sentinel pacing the banks of the silent pond, little suspecting an enemy of so much effrontery, and humming to himself those words which were recalled to his mind by the sight of women, and, perhaps, by recollections of his own distant and beautiful France—

"Vive le vin, vive l'amour," &c. &c.

" 'Tis well you understood the knave!" whispered the scout, when they had gained a little distance from the place, and letting his rifle fall into the hollow of his arm again; "I soon saw that he was one of them uneasy Frenchers, and well for him it was, that his speech was friendly, and his wishes kind; or a place might have been found for his bones amongst those of his countrymen."

He was interrupted by a long and heavy groan, which arose from the little basin, as though, in truth, the spirits of the departed lingered about their watery sepulchre.

"Surely, it was of flesh!" continued the scout; "no spirit could handle its arms so steadily!"

"It *was* of flesh, but whether the poor fellow still belongs to this world, may well be doubted," said Heyward, glancing his eyes around him, and missing Chingachgook from their little band. Another groan, more faint than the former, was succeeded by a heavy and sullen plunge into the water, and all was as still again, as if the borders of the dreary pool had never been awakened from the silence of creation. While they yet hesitated in uncertainty, the form of the Indian was seen gliding out of the thicket. As the chief rejoined them, with one hand he attached the reeking scalp of the unfortunate young Frenchman to his girdle, and with the other he replaced the knife and tomahawk that had drunk his blood. He then took his wonted station, with the air of a man who believed he had done a deed of merit.

The scout dropped one end of his rifle to the earth, and leaning his hands on the other, he stood musing in profound silence. Then shaking his head in a mournful manner, he muttered—

" 'Twould have been a cruel and an unhuman act for a white-skin; but 'tis the gift and natur of an Indian, and I suppose it should not be denied! I could wish, though, it had befallen an accursed Mingo, rather than that gay, young boy, from the old countries!"

"Enough!" said Heyward, apprehensive the unconscious

sisters might comprehend the nature of the detention, and conquering his disgust by a train of reflections very much like that of the hunter; " 'tis done, and though better it were left undone, cannot be amended. You see we are, too obviously, within the sentinels of the enemy; what course do you propose to follow?"

"Yes," said Hawk-eye, rousing himself again, " 'tis, as you say, too late to harbour further thoughts about it! Ay, the French have gathered around the fort in good earnest, and we have a delicate needle to thread in passing them."

"And but little time to do it in," added Heyward; glancing his eyes upward, towards the bank of vapour that concealed the setting moon.

"And little time to do it in!" repeated the scout. "The thing may be done in two fashions, by the help of Providence, without which it may not be done at all!"

"Name them quickly, for time presses."

"One would be, to dismount the gentle ones, and let their beasts range the plain; by sending the Mohicans in front, we might then cut a lane through their sentries, and enter the fort over the dead bodies."

"It will not do—it will not do!" interrupted the generous Heyward; "a soldier might force his way in this manner, but never with such a convoy."

" 'Twould be, indeed, a bloody path for such tender feet to wade in!" returned the equally reluctant scout, "but I thought it befitting my manhood to name it. We must then turn on our trail, and get without the line of their look-outs, when we will bend short to the west, and enter the mountains; where I can hide you, so that all the devil's hounds in Montcalm's pay would be thrown off the scent, for months to come."

"Let it be done, and that instantly."

Further words were unnecessary; for Hawk-eye, merely uttering the mandate to "follow," moved along the route, by which they had just entered their present, critical, and even dangerous situation. Their progress, like their late dialogue, was guarded, and without noise; for none knew at what moment a passing patrol, or a crouching picquet, of the enemy, might rise upon their path. As they held their silent way along the margin of the pond, again, Heyward and the scout stole furtive glances at its appalling dreariness. They looked in vain for the form they had so recently seen stalking along its silent shores, while a low and regular wash of the little waves, by announcing that the waters were not yet subsided, furnished a frightful memorial of the deed of blood they had just witnessed. Like all that passing and gloomy scene, the low basin, however, quickly melted in the darkness, and became blended with the mass of black objects in the rear of the travellers.

Hawk-eye soon deviated from the line of their retreat, and striking off towards the mountains which form the western boundary of the narrow plain, he led his followers, with swift steps, deep within the shadows, that were cast from their high and broken summits. The route was now painful; lying over ground ragged with rocks, and intersected with ravines, and their progress proportionately slow. Bleak and black hills lay on every side of them, compensating, in some degree, for the additional toil of the march, by the sense of security they imparted. At length the party began slowly to rise a steep and rugged ascent, by a path that curiously wound among rocks and trees, avoiding the one, and supported by the other, in a manner that showed it had been devised by men long practised in the arts of the wilderness. As they gradually rose from the level of the valleys, the thick darkness which usually precedes the approach of day, began to disperse, and objects were seen in the plain and palpable colours with which they had been gifted by nature. When they issued from the stunted woods which clung to the barren sides of the mountain, upon a flat and mossy rock, that formed its summit, they met the morning, as it came blushing above the green pines of a hill, that lay on the opposite side of the valley of the Horican.

The scout now told the sisters to dismount, and taking the bridles from the mouths and the saddles off the backs of the jaded beasts, he turned them loose, to glean a scanty subsistence, among the shrubs and meager herbage of that elevated region.

"Go," he said, "and seek your food where natur gives it you; and beware that you become not food to ravenous wolves yourselves, among these hills."

"Have we no further need of them?" demanded Heyward.

"See, and judge with your own eyes," said the scout, advancing towards the eastern brow of the mountain, whither he beckoned for the whole party to follow; "if it was as easy to look into the heart of man, as it is to spy out the nakedness of Montcalm's camp from this spot, hypocrites would grow scarce, and the cunning of a Mingo might prove a losing game, compared to the honesty of a Delaware."

When the travellers had reached the verge of the precipice, they saw, at a glance, the truth of the scout's declaration, and the admirable foresight with which he had led them to their commanding station.

The mountain on which they stood, elevated perhaps a thousand feet in the air, was a high cone, that rose a little in advance of that range which stretches for miles along the western shores of the lake, until meeting its sister piles, beyond the water, it ran off towards the Canadas, in confused and broken masses of rock, thinly sprinkled with evergreens. Immediately at the feet of the party the southern shore of the Horican swept in a broad semi-circle, from mountain to mountain, marking a wide strand, that soon rose into an uneven and somewhat elevated plain. To the north, stretched the limpid, and, as it appeared from that dizzy height, the narrow sheet of the "holy lake," indented with numberless bays, embellished by fantastic head-lands, and dotted with countless islands. At the distance of a few leagues, the bed of the waters became lost among mountains, or was wrapped in the masses of vapour, that came slowly rolling along their bosom, before a light morning air. But a narrow opening between the crests of the hills, pointed out the passage by which they found their way still farther north, to spread their pure and ample sheets again, before pouring out their tribute into the distant Champlain. To the south stretched the defile, or, rather, broken plain, so often mentioned. For several miles, in this direction, the mountains appeared reluctant to yield their dominion, but within reach of the eye they diverged, and finally melted into the level and sandy lands, across which we have accompanied our adventurers in their double journey. Along both ranges of hills, which bounded the opposite sides of the lake and valley, clouds of light vapour were rising in spiral wreaths from the uninhabited woods, looking like the smokes of hidden cottages, or rolled lazily down the declivities, to mingle with the fogs of the lower land. A single, solitary, snow-white cloud, floated above the valley, and marked the spot, beneath which lay the silent pool of the 'bloody pond.'

Directly on the shore of the lake, and nearer to its western than to its eastern margin, lay the extensive earthen ramparts and low buildings of William Henry. Two of the sweeping bastions appeared to rest on the water, which washed their bases, while a deep ditch and extensive morasses guarded its other sides and angles. The land had been cleared of wood for a reasonable distance around the work, but every other part of the scene lay in the green livery of nature, except where the limpid water mellowed the view, or the bold rocks thrust their black and naked heads above the undulating outlines of the mountain ranges. In its front, might be seen the scattered sentinels, who held a weary watch against their numerous foes; and within the walls themselves, the travellers looked down upon men still drowsy with a night of vigilance. Towards the south-east, but in immediate contact with the fort, was an entrenched camp, posted on a rocky eminence, that would have been far more eligible for the work itself, in which Hawk-eye pointed out the presence of those auxiliary regiments that had so recently left the Hudson, in their company. From the woods, a little farther to the south, rose numerous dark and lurid smokes, that were easily to be distinguished from the purer exhalations of the springs, and which the scout also showed to Heyward, as evidences that the enemy lay in force in that direction.

But the spectacle which most concerned the young soldier, was on the western bank of the lake, though quite near to its southern termination. On a stripe of land, which appeared, from his stand, too narrow to contain such an army, but which, in truth, extended many hundreds of yards from the shores of the Horican to the base of the mountain, were to be seen the white tents and military engines of an encampment of ten thousand men. Batteries were already thrown up in their front, and even while the spectators above them were looking down, with such different emotions, on a scene, which lay like a map beneath their feet, the roar of artillery rose from the valley, and passed off, in thundering echoes, along the eastern hills.

"Morning is just touching them below," said the deliberate and musing scout, "and the watchers have a mind to wake up the sleepers by the sound of cannon. We are a few hours too late! Montcalm has already filled the woods with his accursed Iroquois."

"The place is, indeed, invested," returned Duncan; "but is there no expedient by which we may enter? capture in the works would be far preferable to falling, again, into the hands of roving Indians."

"See!" exclaimed the scout, unconsciously directing the attention of Cora to the quarters of her own father, "how that shot has made the stones fly from the side of the commandant's house! Ay! these Frenchers will pull it to pieces faster than it was put together, solid and thick though it be!"

"Heyward, I sicken at the sight of danger, that I cannot share," said the undaunted but anxious daughter. "Let us go to Montcalm, and demand admission; he dare not deny a child the boon!"

"You would scarce find the tent of the Frenchman with the hair on your head!" said the blunt scout. "If I had but one of the thousand boats which lie empty along that shore, it might be done. Ha! here will soon be an end of the firing, for yonder comes a fog that will turn day to night, and make an Indian arrow more dangerous than a moulded cannon. Now, if you are equal to the work, and will follow, I will make a push; for I long to get down into that camp, if it be only to scatter some Mingo dogs, that I see lurking in the skirts of yonder thicket of birch."

"We are equal!" said Cora, firmly; "on such an errand we will follow to any danger!"

The scout turned to her with a smile of honest and cordial approbation, as he answered—

"I would I had a thousand men, of brawny limbs and quick eyes, that feared death as little as you! I'd send them jabbering Frenchers back into their den again, afore the week was ended, howling like so many fettered hounds, or hungry wolves. But stir," he added, turning from her to the rest of the party, "the fog comes rolling down so fast, we shall have but just the time to meet it on the plain, and use it as a cover. Remember, if any accident should befall me, to keep the air blowing on your left cheeks—or, rather, follow the Mohicans; they'd scent their way, be it in day, or be it at night."

He then waved his hand for them to follow, and threw himself down the steep declivity, with free but careful footsteps. Heyward assisted the sisters to descend, and in a few minutes they were all far down a mountain, whose sides they had climbed with so much toil and pain.

The direction taken by Hawk-eye soon brought the travellers to the level of the plain, nearly opposite to a sally-port, in the western curtain of the fort, which lay, itself, at the distance of about half a mile from the point where he halted, to allow Duncan to come up with his charge. In their eagerness, and favoured by the nature of the ground, they had anticipated the fog, which was rolling heavily down the lake, and it became necessary to pause, until the mists had wrapped the camp of the enemy in their fleecy mantle. The Mohicans profited by the delay, to steal out of the woods, and to make a survey of surrounding objects. They were followed, at a little distance, by the scout, with a view to profit early by their report, and to obtain some faint knowledge for himself of the more immediate localities.

In a very few moments he returned, his face reddened with vexation, while he muttered his disappointment in words of no very gentle import.

"Here, has the cunning Frenchman been posting a picquet directly in our path," he said; "red-skins and whites; and we shall be as likely to fall into their midst, as to pass them in the fog!"

"Cannot we make a circuit to avoid the danger," asked Heyward, "and come into our path again when it is past?"

"Who that once bends from the line of his march, in a fog, can tell when or how to turn to find it again! The mists of Horican are not like the curls from a peace-pipe, or the smoke which settles above a mosquetoe fire!"

He was yet speaking, when a crashing sound was heard, and a cannon ball entered the thicket, striking the body of a sapling, and rebounding to the earth, its force being much expended by previous resistance. The Indians followed instantly like busy attendants on the terrible messenger, and Uncas commenced speaking earnestly, and with much action, in the Delaware tongue.

"It may be so, lad," muttered the scout, when he had ended; "for desperate fevers are not to be treated like a toothache. Come, then, the fog is shutting in."

"Stop!" cried Heyward; "first explain your expectations."

" 'Tis soon done, and a small hope it is; but it is better than nothing. This shot that you see," added the scout, kicking the harmless iron with his foot, "has ploughed the 'arth in its road from the fort, and we shall hunt for the furrow it has made, when all other signs may fail. No more words, but follow; or the fog may leave us in the middle of our path, a mark for both armies to shoot at."

Heyward perceiving that, in fact, a crisis had arrived, when acts were more required than words, placed himself between the sisters, and drew them swiftly forward, keeping the dim figure of their leader in his eye. It was soon apparent that Hawk-eye had not magnified the power of the fog, for before they had proceeded twenty yards, it was difficult for the different individuals of the party to distinguish each other, in the vapour.

They had made their little circuit to the left, and were already inclining again towards the right, having, as Heyward thought, got over nearly half the distance to the friendly works, when his ears were saluted with the fierce summons, apparently within twenty feet of them, of—

"Qui va là?"

"Push on!" whispered the scout, once more bending to the left.

"Push on!" repeated Heyward; when the summons was renewed by a dozen voices, each of which seemed charged with menace.

"C'est moi," cried Duncan, dragging, rather than leading, those he supported, swiftly, onward.

"Bête! qui? moi!"

"Ami de la France."

"Tu m'as plus l'air d'un *ennemi* de la France; arrete! ou pardieu je te ferai ami du diable. Non! feu; camarades; feu!"

The order was instantly obeyed, and the fog was stirred by the explosion of fifty muskets. Happily, the aim was bad, and the bullets cut the air in a direction a little different from that taken by the fugitives; though still so nigh them, that to the unpractised ears of David and the two females, it appeared as if they whistled within a few inches of the organs. The outcry was renewed, and the order, not only to fire again, but to pursue, was too plainly audible. When Heyward briefly explained the meaning of the words they heard, Hawk-eye halted, and spoke with quick decision and great firmness.

"Let us deliver our fire," he said; "they will believe it a sortie, and give way; or they will wait for reinforcements."

The scheme was well conceived, but failed in its effect. The instant the French heard the pieces, it seemed as if the plain was alive with men, muskets rattling along its whole extent, from the shores of the lake to the farthest boundary of the woods.

"We shall draw their entire army upon us, and bring on a general assault," said Duncan. "Lead on my friend, for your own life, and ours!"

The scout seemed willing to comply; but, in the hurry of the moment, and in the change of position, he had lost the direction. In vain he turned either cheek towards the light air; they felt equally cool. In this dilemma, Uncas lighted on the furrow of the cannon ball, where it had cut the ground in three adjacent ant-hills.

"Give me the range!" said Hawk-eye, bending to catch a glimpse of the direction, and then instantly moving onward.

Cries, oaths, voices calling to each other, and the reports of muskets, were now quick and incessant, and, apparently, on every side of them. Suddenly, a strong glare of light flashed across the scene, the fog rolled upward in thick wreaths, and several cannon belched across the plain, and the roar was thrown heavily back from the bellowing echoes of the mountain.

" 'Tis from the fort!" exclaimed Hawk-eye, turning short on his tracks; "and we, like stricken fools, were rushing to the woods, under the very knives of the Maquas."

The instant their mistake was rectified, the whole party retraced the error with the utmost diligence. Duncan willingly relinquished the support of Cora to the arm of Uncas, and Cora as readily accepted the welcome assistance. Men, hot and angry in pursuit, were evidently on their footsteps, and each instant threatened their capture, if not their destruction.

"Point de quartier, aux coquins!" cried an eager pursuer, who seemed to direct the operations of the enemy.

"Stand firm, and be ready, my gallant 60ths!" suddenly exclaimed a voice above them; " wait to see the enemy; fire low, and sweep the glacis."

"Father! father!" exclaimed a piercing cry from out the mist; "it is I! Alice! thy own Elsie! spare, oh! save, your daughters!"

"Hold!" shouted the former speaker, in the awful tones of parental agony, the sound reaching even to the woods, and rolling back in solemn echo. " 'Tis she! God has restored me my children! Throw open the sally-port; to the field, 60ths, to the field; pull not a trigger, lest ye kill my lambs! Drive off these dogs of France with your steel."

Duncan heard the grating of the rusty hinges, and darting to the spot, directed by the sound, he met a long line of dark-red warriors, passing swiftly towards the glacis. He knew them for his own battalion of the Royal Americans, and flying to their head, soon swept every trace of his pursuers from before the works.

For an instant, Cora and Alice had stood trembling and bewildered by this unexpected desertion; but, before either had leisure for speech, or even thought, an officer of gigantic frame, whose locks were bleached with years and service, but whose air of military grandeur had been rather softened than destroyed by time, rushed out of the body of the mist, and folded them to his bosom, while large, scalding tears rolled down his pale and wrinkled cheeks, and he exclaimed, in the peculiar accent of Scotland—

"For this I thank thee, Lord! Let danger come as it will, thy servant is now prepared!"

Chapter XV

"Then go we in, to know his embassy;
Which I could, with a ready guess, declare,
Before the Frenchman speak a word of it."
Henry V, I.i.95–97.

A FEW SUCCEEDING DAYS were passed amid the privations, the uproar, and the dangers of the siege, which was vigorously pressed by a power, against whose approaches Munro possessed no competent means of resistance. It appeared as if Webb, with his army, which lay slumbering on the banks of the Hudson, had utterly forgotten the strait to which his countrymen were reduced. Montcalm had filled the woods of the portage with his savages, every yell and whoop from whom rang through the British encampment, chilling the hearts of men, who were already but too much disposed to magnify the danger.

Not so, however, with the besieged. Animated by the words, and stimulated by the examples of their leaders, they had found their courage, and maintained their ancient reputation, with a zeal that did justice to the stern character of their commander. As if satisfied with the toil of marching through the wilderness to encounter his enemy, the French general, though of approved skill, had neglected to seize the adjacent mountains; whence the besieged might have been exterminated with impunity, and which, in the more modern warfare of the country, would not have been neglected for a single hour. This sort of contempt for eminences, or rather dread of the labour of ascending them, might have been termed the besetting weakness of the warfare of the period. It originated in the simplicity of the Indian contests, in which, from the nature of the combats, and the density of the forests, fortresses were rare, and artillery next to useless. The carelessness engendered by these usages, descended even to the war of the revolution, and lost the states the important fortress of Ticonderoga, opening a way for the army of Burgoyne, into what was then the bosom of the country. We look back at this ignorance, or infatuation, which ever it may be called, with wonder, knowing that the neglect of an eminence, whose difficulties, like those of Mount Defiance, had been so greatly exaggerated, would, at the present time, prove fatal to the reputation of the engineer who had planned the works at their base, or to that of the general, whose lot it was to defend them.

The tourist, the valetudinarian, or the amateur of the beauties of nature, who, in the train of his four-in-hand, now rolls through the scenes we have attempted to describe, in quest of information, health, or pleasure, or floats steadily towards his object on those artificial waters, which have sprung up under the administration of a statesman,* who has dared to stake his political character on the hazardous issue, is not to suppose that his ancestors traversed those hills, or struggled with the same currents with equal facility. The transportation of a single heavy gun, was often considered equal to a victory gained; if happily the difficulties of the passage had not so far separated it from its necessary concomitants, the ammunition, as to render it no more than an useless tube of unwieldy iron.

The evils of this state of things pressed heavily on the fortunes of the resolute Scotsman, who now defended William Henry. Though his adversary neglected the hills, he had planted his batteries with judgment on the plain, and caused them to be served with vigour and skill. Against this assault, the besieged could only oppose the imperfect and hasty preparations of a fortress in the wilderness.

It was in the afternoon of the fifth day of the siege, and the fourth of his own service in it, that Major Heyward profited by a parley that had just been beaten, by repairing to the ramparts of one of the water bastions, to breathe the cool air from the lake, and to take a survey of the progress of the siege. He was alone, if the solitary sentinel who paced the mound be excepted; for the artillerists had hastened also to profit by the temporary suspension of their arduous duties. The evening was delightfully calm, and the light air from the limpid water fresh and soothing. It seemed as if, with the termination to the roar of artillery, and the plunging of shot, nature had also seized the moment to assume her mildest and

*Evidently the late De Witt Clinton, who died governor of New York, in 1828.

most captivating form. The sun poured down his parting glory on the scene, without the oppression of those fierce rays that belong to the climate and the season. The mountains looked green, and fresh, and lovely; tempered with the milder light, or softened in shadow, as thin vapours floated between them and the sun. The numerous islands rested on the bosom of the Horican, some low and sunken, as if imbedded in the waters, and others appearing to hover above the element, in little hillocks of green velvet; among which the fishermen of the beleaguering army peacefully rowed their skiffs, or floated at rest on the glassy mirror, in quiet pursuit of their employment.

The scene was at once animated and still. All that pertained to nature was sweet, or simply grand; while those parts which depended on the temper and movements of man, were lively and playful.

Two little spotless flags were abroad, the one on a salient angle of the fort, and the other on the advanced battery of the besiegers; emblems of the truce which existed, not only to the acts, but it would seem, also, to the enmity of the combatants. Behind these, again, swung, heavily opening and closing in silken folds, the rival standards of England and France.

A hundred gay and thoughtless young Frenchmen were drawing a net to the pebbly beach, within dangerous proximity to the sullen but silent cannon of the fort, while the eastern mountain was sending back the loud shouts and gay merriment that attended their sport. Some were rushing eagerly to enjoy the aquatic games of the lake, and others were already toiling their way up the neighbouring hills, with the restless curiosity of their nation. To all these sports and pursuits, those of the enemy who watched the besieged, and the besieged themselves, were, however, merely the idle, though sympathizing spectators. Here and there a picquet had, indeed, raised a song, or mingled in a dance, which had drawn the dusky savages around them, from their lairs in the forest. In short, every thing wore rather the appearance of a day of pleasure, than of an hour stolen from the dangers and toil of a bloody and vindictive warfare.

Duncan had stood in a musing attitude, contemplating this

scene a few minutes, when his eyes were directed to the glacis in front of the sally-port, already mentioned, by the sounds of approaching footsteps. He walked to an angle of the bastion, and beheld the scout advancing, under the custody of a French officer, to the body of the fort. The countenance of Hawk-eye was haggard and care-worn, and his air dejected, as though he felt the deepest degradation at having fallen into the power of his enemies. He was without his favourite weapon, and his arms were even bound behind him with thongs, made of the skin of a deer. The arrival of flags, to cover the messengers of summons, had occurred so often of late, that when Heyward first threw his careless glance on this groupe, he expected to see another of the officers of the enemy, charged with a similar office; but the instant he recognised the tall person, and still sturdy, though downcast, features of his friend, the woodsman, he started with surprise, and turned to descend from the bastion into the bosom of the work.

The sounds of other voices, however, caught his attention, and for a moment caused him to forget his purpose. At the inner angle of the mound, he met the sisters, walking along the parapet, in search, like himself, of air and relief from confinement. They had not met since that painful moment when he deserted them, on the plain, only to assure their safety. He had parted from them, worn with care, and jaded with fatigue; he now saw them refreshed and blooming, though timid and anxious. Under such an inducement, it will cause no surprise, that the young man lost sight, for a time, of other objects, in order to address them. He was, however, anticipated by the voice of the ingenuous and youthful Alice.

"Ah! thou truant! thou recreant knight! he who abandons his damsels in the very lists!" she cried; "here have we been days, nay, ages, expecting you at our feet, imploring mercy and forgetfulness of your craven backsliding, or, I should rather say, back-running—for verily you fled in a manner that no stricken deer, as our worthy friend the scout would say, could equal!"

"You know that Alice means our thanks and our blessings," added the graver and more thoughtful Cora. "In truth, we have a little wondered why you should so rigidly absent yourself from a place, where the gratitude of the daughters might receive the support of a parent's thanks."

"Your father himself could tell you, that though absent from your presence, I have not been altogether forgetful of your safety," returned the young man; "the mastery of yonder village of huts," pointing to the neighbouring entrenched camp, "has been keenly disputed; and he who holds it, is sure to be possessed of this fort, and that which it contains. My days and my nights have all been passed there, since we separated, because I thought that duty called me thither. But," he added, with an air of chagrin, which he endeavoured, though unsuccessfully, to conceal, "had I been aware, that what I then believed a soldier's conduct, could be so construed, shame would have been added to the list of reasons."

"Heyward!—Duncan!" exclaimed Alice, bending forward to read his half-averted countenance, until a lock of her golden hair rested on her flushed cheek, and nearly concealed the tear that had started to her eye; "did I think this idle tongue of mine had pained you, I would silence it for ever! Cora can say, if Cora would, how justly we have prized your services, and how deep—I had almost said, how fervent—is our gratitude!"

"And will Cora attest the truth of this?" cried Duncan, suffering the cloud to be chased from his countenance by a smile of open pleasure. "What says our graver sister? Will she find an excuse for the neglect of the knight, in the duty of a soldier?"

Cora made no immediate answer, but turned her face toward the water, as if looking on the sheet of the Horican. When she did bend her dark eyes on the young man, they were yet filled with an expression of anguish that at once drove every thought but that of kind solicitude from his mind.

"You are not well, dearest Miss Munro!" he exclaimed; "we have trifled, while you are in suffering!"

"'Tis nothing," she answered, refusing his offered support, with feminine reserve. "That I cannot see the sunny side of the picture of life, like this artless but ardent enthusiast," she added, laying her hand lightly, but affectionately, on the arm of her sister, "is the penalty of experience, and, perhaps, the misfortune of my nature. See," she continued, as if determined to shake off infirmity, in a sense of duty; "look around you, Major Heyward, and tell me what a prospect is this, for the daughter of a soldier, whose greatest happiness is his honour and his military renown!"

"Neither ought nor shall be tarnished by circumstances, over which he has had no control," Duncan warmly replied. "But your words recall me to my own duty. I go now to your gallant father, to hear his determination in matters of the last moment to the defence. God bless you in every fortune, noble—Cora—I may, and must call you." She frankly gave him her hand, though her lip quivered, and her cheeks gradually became of an ashy paleness. "In every fortune, I know you will be an ornament and honour to your sex. Alice, adieu"—his tone changed from admiration to tenderness—"adieu, Alice; we shall soon meet again; as conquerors, I trust, and amid rejoicings!"

Without waiting for an answer from either, the young man threw himself down the grassy steps of the bastion, and moving rapidly across the parade, he was quickly in the presence of their father. Munro was pacing his narrow apartment with a disturbed air, and gigantic strides, as Duncan entered.

"You have anticipated my wishes, Major Heyward," he said; "I was about to request this favour."

"I am sorry to see, sir, that the messenger I so warmly recommended, has returned in custody of the French! I hope there is no reason to distrust his fidelity?"

"The fidelity of the 'Long Rifle' is well known to me," returned Munro, "and is above suspicion; though his usual good fortune seems, at last, to have failed. Montcalm has got him, and with the accursed politeness of his nation, he has sent him in with a doleful tale, of 'knowing how I valued the fellow, he could not think of retaining him.' A jesuitical way, that, Major Duncan Heyward, of telling a man of his misfortunes!"

"But the general and his succour?—"

"Did ye look to the south as ye entered, and could ye not see them!" said the old soldier, laughing bitterly. "Hoot! hoot! you're an impatient boy, sir, and cannot give the gentlemen leisure for their march!"

"They are coming then? The scout has said as much?"

"When? and by what path? for the dunce has omitted to tell me this! There is a letter, it would seem, too; and that is the only agreeable part of the matter. For the customary attentions of your Marquis of Montcalm—I warrant me, Duncan, that he of Lothian would buy a dozen such marquessates—but, if the news of the letter were bad, the gentility of this French monsieur would certainly compel him to let us know it!"

"He keeps the letter, then, while he releases the messenger?"

"Ay, that does he, and all for the sake of what you call your 'bonhommie.' I would venture, if the truth was known, the fellow's grandfather taught the noble science of dancing!"

"But what says the scout? he has eyes and ears, and a tongue! what verbal report does he make?"

"Oh! sir, he is not wanting in natural organs, and he is free to tell all that he has seen and heard. The whole amount is this: there is a fort of his majesty's on the banks of the Hudson, called Edward, in honour of his gracious highness of York, you'll know, and it is well filled with armed men, as such a work should be!"

"But was there no movement, no signs, of any intention to advance to our relief?"

"There were the morning and evening parades, and when one of the provincial loons—you'll know, Duncan, your're half a Scotsman yourself—when one of them dropped his powder over his porretch, if it touched the coals, it just burnt!" Then suddenly changing his bitter, ironical manner, to one more grave and thoughtful, he continued; "and yet there might, and must be, something in that letter, which it would be well to know!"

"Our decision should be speedy," said Duncan, gladly availing himself of this change of humour, to press the more important objects of their interview; "I cannot conceal from you, sir, that the camp will not be much longer tenable; and I am sorry to add, that things appear no better in the fort;—more than half the guns are bursted."

"And how should it be otherwise! some were fished from the bottom of the lake; some have been rusting in the woods since the discovery of the country; and some were never guns at all—mere privateersmen's playthings! Do you think, sir, you can have Woolwich Warren in the midst of a wilderness; three thousand miles from Great Britain!"

"The walls are crumbling about our ears, and provisions begin to fail us," continued Heyward, without regarding this new burst of indignation; "even the men show signs of discontent and alarm."

"Major Heyward," said Munro, turning to his youthful associate with the dignity of his years and superior rank; "I should have served his majesty for half a century, and earned these gray hairs, in vain, were I ignorant of all you say, and of the pressing nature of our circumstances; still, there is every thing due to the honour of the king's arms, and something to ourselves. While there is hope of succour, this fortress will I defend, though it be to be done with pebbles gathered on the lake shore. It is a sight of the letter, therefore, that we want, that we may know the intentions of the man, the Earl of Loudon has left among us as his substitute."

"And can I be of service in the matter."

"Sir, you can; the Marquis of Montcalm has, in addition to his other civilities, invited me to a personal interview between the works and his own camp; in order, as he says, to impart some additional information. Now, I think it would not be wise to show any undue solicitude to meet him, and I would employ you, an officer of rank, as my substitute; for it would but ill comport with the honour of Scotland, to let it be said, one of her gentlemen was outdone in civility, by a native of any other country on earth!"

Without assuming the supererogatory task of entering into a discussion of the comparative merits of national courtesy, Duncan cheerfully assented to supply the place of the veteran, in the approaching interview. A long and confidential communication now succeeded, during which the young man received some additional insight into his duty, from the experience and native acuteness of his commander, and then the former took his leave.

As Duncan could only act as the representative of the commandant of the fort, the ceremonies which should have accompanied a meeting between the heads of the adverse forces, were of course dispensed with. The truce still existed, and with a roll and beat of the drum, and covered by a little white flag, Duncan left the sally-port, within ten minutes after his instructions were ended. He was received by the French officer in advance, with the usual formalities, and immediately accompanied to the distant marquee of the renowned soldier, who led the forces of France.

The general of the enemy received the youthful messenger, surrounded by his principal officers, and by a swarthy band of the native chiefs, who had followed him to the field, with the warriors of their several tribes. Heyward paused short, when, in glancing his eyes rapidly over the dark groupe of the latter, he beheld the malignant countenance of Magua, regarding him with the calm but sullen attention which marked the expression of that subtle savage. A slight exclamation of surprise even burst from the lips of the young man; but, instantly recollecting his errand, and the presence in which he stood, he suppressed every appearance of emotion, and turned to the hostile leader, who had already advanced a step to receive him.

The Marquis of Montcalm was, at the period of which we write, in the flower of his age, and it may be added, in the zenith of his fortunes. But even in that enviable situation, he was affable, and distinguished as much for his attention to the forms of courtesy, as for that chivalrous courage, which, only two short years afterwards, induced him to throw away his life, on the plains of Abraham. Duncan, in turning his eyes from the malign expression of Magua, suffered them to rest with pleasure on the smiling and polished features, and the noble, military air of the French general.

"Monsieur," said the latter, "J'ai beaucoup de plaisir à—bah! où est cet interprête?"

"Je crois, monsieur, qu'il ne sera pas nécessaire," Heyward modestly replied; "je parle un peu Français."

"Ah! j'en suis bien aise," said Montcalm, taking Duncan familiarly by the arm, and leading him deep into the marquee, a little out of earshot; "je déteste ces fripons-là; on ne sait jamais sur quel piè, on est avec eux. Eh, bien! monsieur," he continued, still speaking in French; "though I should have been proud of receiving your commandant, I am very happy that he has seen proper to employ an officer so distinguished, and who, I am sure, is so amiable, as yourself."

Duncan bowed low, pleased with the compliment, in spite of a most heroic determination to suffer no artifice to lure him into forgetfulness of the interests of his prince; and Montcalm, after a pause of a moment, as if to collect his thoughts, proceeded—

"Your commandant is a brave man, and well qualified to repel my assaults. Mais, monsieur, is it not time to begin to take more counsel of humanity, and less of your own courage? The one as strongly characterizes the hero, as the other!"

"We consider the qualities as inseparable," returned Duncan, smiling; "but, while we find in the vigour of your excellency, every motive to stimulate the one, we can, as yet, see no particular call for the exercise of the other."

Montcalm, in his turn, slightly bowed, but it was with the air of a man too practised to remember the language of flattery. After musing a moment, he added—

"It is possible my glasses have deceived me, and that your works resist our cannon better than I had supposed. You know our force?"

"Our accounts vary," said Duncan, carelessly; "the highest, however, has not exceeded twenty thousand men."

The Frenchman bit his lip, and fastened his eyes keenly on the other, as if to read his thoughts; then, with a readiness peculiar to himself, he continued, as if assenting to the truth of an enumeration, which quite doubled his army—

"It is a poor compliment to the vigilance of us soldiers, monsieur, that, do what we will, we never can conceal our numbers. If it were to be done at all, one would believe it might succeed in these woods. Though you think it too soon to listen to the calls of humanity," he added, smiling, archly, "I may be permitted to believe that gallantry is not forgotten by one so young as yourself. The daughters of the commandant, I learn, have passed into the fort, since it was invested?"

"It is true, monsieur; but so far from weakening our efforts, they set us an example of courage in their own fortitude. Were nothing but resolution necessary to repel so accomplished a soldier, as M. de Montcalm, I would gladly trust the defence of William Henry to the elder of those ladies."

"We have a wise ordinance in our Salique laws, which says, 'the crown of France shall never degrade the lance to the distaff,' " said Montcalm, dryly, and with a little hauteur; but, instantly adding, with his former frank and easy air, "as all the nobler qualities are hereditary, I can easily credit you; though, as I said before, courage has its limits, and humanity must not be forgotten. I trust, monsieur, you come authorized to treat for the surrender of the place?"

"Has your excellency found our defence so feeble, as to believe the measure necessary!"

"I should be sorry to have the defence protracted in such a manner, as to irritate my red friends there," continued Montcalm, glancing his eyes at the groupe of grave and attentive Indians, without attending to the other's question; "I find it difficult, even now, to limit them to the usages of war."

Heyward was silent; for a painful recollection of the dangers he had so recently escaped came over his mind, and recalled the images of those defenceless beings, who had shared in all his sufferings.

"Ces messieurs-là," said Montcalm, following up the advantage which he conceived he had gained, "are most formidable when baffled; and it is unnecessary to tell you, with what difficulty they are restrained in their anger. Eh bien, monsieur! shall we speak of the terms?"

"I fear your excellency has been deceived as to the strength of William Henry, and the resources of its garrison!"

"I have not set down before Quebec, but an earthen work, that is defended by twenty-three hundred gallant men," was the laconic reply.

"Our mounds are earthen, certainly—nor are they seated on the rocks of Cape Diamond;—but they stand on that shore which proved so destructive to Dieskau, and his army. There is also a powerful force within a few hours' march of us, which we account upon as part of our means."

"Some six or eight thousand men," returned Montcalm, with much apparent indifference, " whom their leader, wisely, judges to be safer in their works, than in the field."

It was now Heyward's turn to bite his lip with vexation, as

the other so coolly alluded to a force which the young man knew to be overrated. Both mused a little while in silence, when Montcalm renewed the conversation, in a way that showed he believed the visit of his guest was, solely, to propose terms of capitulation. On the other hand, Heyward began to throw sundry inducements in the way of the French general, to betray the discoveries he had made through the intercepted letter. The artifice of neither, however, succeeded; and, after a protracted and fruitless interview, Duncan took his leave, favourably impressed with an opinion of the courtesy and talents of the enemy's captain, but as ignorant of what he came to learn, as when he arrived. Montcalm followed him as far as the entrance of the marquee, renewing his invitations to the commandant of the fort, to give him an immediate meeting in the open ground, between the two armies.

There they separated, and Duncan returned to the advanced post of the French, accompanied as before; whence he instantly proceeded to the fort, and to the quarters of his own commander.

Chapter XVI

"*Edg.*—Before you fight the battle, ope this letter."
King Lear, V.i.40.

MAJOR HEYWARD found Munro attended only by his daughters. Alice sate upon his knee, parting the gray hairs on the forehead of the old man, with her delicate fingers; and whenever he affected to frown on her trifling, appeasing his assumed anger, by pressing her ruby lips fondly on his wrinkled brow. Cora was seated nigh them, a calm and amused looker-on; regarding the wayward movements of her more youthful sister, with that species of maternal fondness, which characterised her love for Alice. Not only the dangers through which they had passed, but those which still impended above them, appeared to be momentarily forgotten, in the soothing indulgence of such a family meeting. It seemed as if they had profited by the short truce, to devote an instant to the purest and best affections: the daughters forgetting their fears, and the veteran his cares, in the security of the moment. Of this scene, Duncan, who, in his eagerness to report his arrival, had entered unannounced, stood many moments an unobserved and a delighted spectator. But the quick and dancing eyes of Alice soon caught a glimpse of his figure, reflected from a glass, and she sprang blushing from her father's knee, exclaiming aloud—

"Major Heyward!"

"What of the lad?" demanded her father; "I have sent him to crack a little with the Frenchman. Ha! sir, you are young, and your're nimble! Away with you, ye baggage; as if there were not troubles enough for a soldier, without having his camp filled with such prattling hussies as yourself!"

Alice laughingly followed her sister, who instantly led the way from an apartment, where she perceived their presence was no longer desirable. Munro, instead of demanding the result of the young man's mission, paced the room for a few moments, with his hands behind his back, and his head inclined towards the floor, like a man lost in thought. At length, he raised his eyes, glistening with a father's fondness, and exclaimed—

"They are a pair of excellent girls, Heyward, and such as any one may boast of!"

"You are not now to learn my opinion of your daughters, Colonel Munro."

"True, lad, true," interrupted the impatient old man; "you were about opening your mind more fully on that matter the day you got in; but I did not think it becoming an old soldier to be talking of nuptial blessings, and wedding jokes, when the enemies of his king were likely to be unbidden guests at the feast! But I was wrong, Duncan, boy, I was wrong there; and I am now ready to hear what you have to say."

"Notwithstanding the pleasure your assurance gives me, dear sir, I have, just now, a message from Montcalm—"

"Let the Frenchman, and all his host, go to the devil, sir!" exclaimed the hasty veteran. "He is not yet master of William Henry, nor shall he ever be, provided Webb proves himself the man he should. No, sir! thank heaven, we are not yet in such a strait, that it can be said, Munro is too much pressed to discharge the little domestic duties of his own family! Your mother was the only child of my bosom friend, Duncan; and I'll just give you a hearing, though all the knights of St. Louis were in a body at the sally-port, with the French saint at their head, craving to speak a word, under favour. A pretty degree of knighthood, sir, is that which can be bought with sugar-hogsheads! and then your two-penny marquessates! The Thistle is the order for dignity and antiquity; the veritable 'nemo me impune lacessit' of chivalry! Ye had ancestors in that degree, Duncan, and they were an ornament to the nobles of Scotland."

Heyward, who perceived that his superior took a malicious pleasure in exhibiting his contempt for the message of the French general, was fain to humour a spleen that he knew would be short lived; he, therefore, replied with as much indifference as he could assume on such a subject—

"My request, as you know, sir, went so far as to presume to the honour of being your son."

"Ay, boy, you found words to make yourself very plainly

comprehended! But, let me ask ye, sir; have you been as intelligible to the girl?"

"On my honour, no," exclaimed Duncan, warmly; "there would have been an abuse of a confided trust, had I taken advantage of my situation, for such a purpose!"

"Your notions are those of a gentleman, Major Heyward, and well enough in their place. But Cora Munro is a maiden too discreet, and of a mind too elevated and improved, to need the guardianship, even of a father."

"Cora!"

"Ay—Cora! we are talking of your pretensions to Miss Munro, are we not, sir?"

"I—I—I, was not conscious of having mentioned her name," said Duncan, stammering.

"And, to marry whom, then, did you wish my consent, Major Heyward," demanded the old soldier, erecting himself in the dignity of offended feeling.

"You have another, and not less lovely child."

"Alice!" exclaimed the father, in an astonishment equal to that with which Duncan had just repeated the name of her sister.

"Such was the direction of my wishes, sir."

The young man awaited in silence, the result of the extraordinary effect produced by a communication which, as it now appeared, was so unexpected. For several minutes, Munro paced the chamber with long and rapid strides, his rigid features working convulsively, and every faculty seemingly absorbed in the musings of his own mind. At length, he paused directly in front of Heyward, and riveting his eyes upon those of the other, he said, with a lip that quivered violently—

"Duncan Heyward, I have loved you for the sake of him whose blood is in your veins; I have loved you for your own good qualities; and I have loved you, because I thought you would contribute to the happiness of my child. But all this love would turn to hatred, were I assured, that what I so much apprehend is true!"

"God forbid that any act or thought of mine should lead to such a change!" exclaimed the young man, whose eye never quailed under the penetrating look it encountered. Without adverting to the impossibility of the other's comprehending those feelings which were hid in his own bosom, Munro suffered himself to be appeased by the unaltered countenance he met, and with a voice sensibly softened, he continued—

"You would be my son, Duncan, and you're ignorant of the history of the man you wish to call your father. Sit ye down, young man, and I will open to you the wounds of a seared heart, in as few words as may be suitable."

By this time, the message of Montcalm was as much forgotten by him who bore it, as by the man for whose ears it was intended. Each drew a chair, and while the veteran communed a few moments with his own thoughts, apparently in sadness, the youth suppressed his impatience in a look and attitude of respectful attention. At length, the former spoke—

"You'll know, already, Major Heyward, that my family was both ancient and honourable," commenced the Scotsman, "though it might not altogether be endowed with that amount of wealth, that should correspond with its degree. I was, may be, such an one as yourself, when I plighted my faith to Alice Graham; the only child of a neighbouring laird of some estate. But the connexion was disagreeable to her father, on more accounts than my poverty. I did, therefore, what an honest man should; restored the maiden her troth, and departed the country, in the service of my king. I had seen many regions, and had shed much blood in different lands, before duty called me to the islands of the West Indies. There it was my lot to form a connexion with one who in time became my wife, and the mother of Cora. She was the daughter of a gentleman of those isles, by a lady, whose misfortune it was, if you will," said the old man, proudly, "to be descended, remotely, from that unfortunate class, who are so basely enslaved to administer to the wants of a luxurious people! Ay, sir, that is a curse entailed on Scotland, by her unnatural union with a foreign and trading people. But could I find a man among them, who would dare to reflect on my child, he should feel the weight of a father's anger! Ha! Major Heyward, you are yourself born at the south, where these unfortunate beings are considered of a race inferior to your own!"

" 'Tis most unfortunately true, sir," said Duncan, unable any longer to prevent his eyes from sinking to the floor in embarrassment.

"And you cast it on my child as a reproach! You scorn to mingle the blood of the Heywards, with one so degraded—lovely and virtuous though she be?" fiercely demanded the jealous parent.

"Heaven protect me from a prejudice so unworthy of my reason!" returned Duncan, at the same time conscious of such a feeling, and that as deeply rooted as if it had been engrafted in his nature. "The sweetness, the beauty, the witchery of your younger daughter, Colonel Munro, might explain my motives, without imputing to me this injustice."

"Ye are right, sir," returned the old man, again changing his tones to those of gentleness, or rather softness; "the girl is the image of what her mother was at her years, and before she had become acquainted with grief. When death deprived me of my wife, I returned to Scotland, enriched by the marriage; and would you think it, Duncan! the suffering angel had remained in the heartless state of celibacy twenty long years, and that for the sake of a man who could forget her! She did more, sir; she overlooked my want of faith, and all difficulties being now removed, she took me for her husband."

"And became the mother of Alice!" exclaimed Duncan, with an eagerness, that might have proved dangerous, at a moment when the thoughts of Munro were less occupied than at present.

"She did, indeed," said the old man, "and dearly did she pay for the blessing she bestowed. But she is a saint in heaven, sir; and it ill becomes one whose foot rests on the grave, to mourn a lot so blessed. I had her but a single year, though; a short term of happiness, for one who had seen her youth fade in hopeless pining!"

There was something so commanding in the distress of the old man, that Heyward did not dare to venture a syllable of consolation. Munro sat utterly unconscious of the other's presence, his features exposed and working with the anguish of his regrets, while heavy tears fell from his eyes, and rolled unheeded from his cheeks to the floor. At length he moved, as if suddenly recovering his recollection; when he arose, and taking a single turn across the room, he approached his companion with an air of military grandeur, and demanded—

"Have you not, Major Heyward, some communication, that I should hear, from the Marquis de Montcalm?"

Duncan started, in his turn, and immediately commenced, in an embarrassed voice, the half-forgotten message. It is unnecessary to dwell upon the evasive, though polite manner, with which the French general had eluded every attempt of Heyward to worm from him the purport of the communication he had proposed making, or on the decided, though still polished message, by which he now gave his enemy to understand, that unless he chose to receive it in person, he should not receive it at all. As Munro listened to the detail of Duncan, the excited feelings of the father gradually gave way before the obligations of his station, and when the other was done, he saw before him nothing but the veteran, swelling with the wounded feelings of a soldier.

"You have said enough, Major Heyward!" exclaimed the angry old man; "enough to make a volume of commentary on French civility! Here has this gentleman invited me to a conference, and when I send him a capable substitute, for ye're all that Duncan, though your years are but few, he answers me with a riddle!"

"He may have thought less favourably of the substitute, my dear sir; and you will remember that the invitation, which he now repeats, was to the commandant of the works, and not to his second."

"Well, sir, is not a substitute clothed with all the power and dignity of him who grants the commission! He wishes to confer with Munro! Faith, sir, I have much inclination to indulge the man, if it should only be to let him behold the firm countenance we maintain, in spite of his numbers and his summons! There might be no bad policy in such a stroke, young man."

Duncan, who believed it of the last importance, that they should speedily come at the contents of the letter borne by the scout, gladly encouraged this idea.

"Without doubt, he could gather no confidence by witnessing our indifference," he said.

"You never said truer word. I could wish, sir, that he would visit the works in open day, and in the form of a storming party: that is the least failing method of proving the countenance of an enemy, and would be far preferable to the battering system he has chosen. The beauty and manliness of warfare has been much deformed, Major Heyward, by the arts of your Monsieur Vauban. Our ancestors were far above such scientific cowardice!"

"It may be very true, sir; but we are, now, obliged to repel art by art. What is your pleasure in the matter of the interview?"

"I will meet the Frenchman, and that without fear or delay; promptly, sir, as becomes a servant of my royal master. Go, Major Heyward, and give them a flourish of the music, and send out a messenger to let them know who is coming. We will follow with a small guard, for such respect is due to one who holds the honour of his king in keeping; and, hark'ee, Duncan," he added, in a half whisper, though they were alone, "it may be prudent to have some aid at hand, in case there should be treachery at the bottom of it all."

The young man availed himself of this order, to quit the apartment; and, as the day was fast coming to a close, he hastened, without delay, to make the necessary arrangements. A very few minutes only were necessary to parade a few files, and to despatch an orderly with a flag, to announce the approach of the commandant of the fort. When Duncan had done both these, he led the guard to the sally-port, near which he found his superior ready, waiting his appearance. As soon as the usual ceremonials of a military departure were observed, the veteran, and his more youthful companion, left the fortress, attended by the escort.

They had proceeded only a hundred yards from the works, when the little array which attended the French general to the conference, was seen issuing from the hollow way, which formed the bed of a brook, that ran between the batteries of the besiegers and the fort. From the moment that Munro left his own works, to appear in front of his enemies, his air had been grand, and his step and countenance highly military. The instant he caught a glimpse of the white plume that waved in the hat of Montcalm, his eye lighted, and age no longer appeared to possess any influence over his vast and still muscular person.

"Speak to the boys to be watchful, sir," he said, in an under tone, to Duncan; "and to look well to their flints and steel, for one is never safe with a servant of these Louis; at the same time, we will show them the front of men in deep security. Ye'll understand me, Major Heyward!"

He was interrupted by the clamour of a drum from the approaching Frenchmen, which was immediately answered, when each party pushed an orderly in advance, bearing a white flag, and the wary Scotsman halted, with his guard close at his back. As soon as this slight salutation had passed, Montcalm moved towards them with a quick but graceful step, baring his head to the veteran, and dropping his spotless plume nearly to the earth, in courtesy. If the air of Munro was more commanding and manly, it wanted both the ease and insinuating polish of that of the Frenchman. Neither spoke for a few moments, each regarding the other with curious and interested eyes. Then, as became his superior rank, and the nature of the interview, Montcalm broke the silence. After uttering the usual words of greeting, he turned to Duncan, and continued, with a smile of recognition, speaking always in French—

"I am rejoiced, monsieur, that you have given us the pleasure of your company on this occasion. There will be no necessity to employ an ordinary interpreter, for in your hands I feel the same security, as if I spoke your language myself."

Duncan acknowledged the compliment, when Montcalm, turning to his guard, which, in imitation of that of their enemies, pressed close upon him, continued—

"En arrière, mes enfans—il fait chaud; retirez-vous un peu."

Before Major Heyward would imitate this proof of confidence, he glanced his eyes around the plain, and beheld, with uneasiness, the numerous dusky groupes of savages, who looked out from the margin of the surrounding woods, curious spectators of the interview.

"Monsieur de Montcalm will readily acknowledge the difference in our situation," he said, with some embarrassment, pointing, at the same time, towards those dangerous foes, who were to be seen in almost every direction. "Were we to dismiss our guard, we should stand here at the mercy of our enemies."

"Monsieur, you have the plighted faith of 'un gentilhomme Français,' for your safety," returned Montcalm, laying his hand impressively on his heart; "it should suffice."

"It shall. Fall back," Duncan added to the officer who led the escort; "fall back, sir, beyond hearing, and wait for orders."

Munro witnessed this movement with manifest uneasiness; nor did he fail to demand an instant explanation.

"Is it not our interest, sir, to betray no distrust?" retorted Duncan. "Monsieur de Montcalm pledges his word for our safety, and I have ordered the men to withdraw a little, in order to prove how much we depend on his assurance."

"It may be all right, sir, but I have no overweening reliance on the faith of these marquesses, or marquis, as they call themselves. Their patents of nobility are too common, to be certain that they bear the seal of true honour."

"You forget, dear sir, that we confer with an officer, distinguished alike in Europe and America, for his deeds. From a soldier of his reputation we can have nothing to apprehend."

The old man made a gesture of resignation, though his rigid features still betrayed his obstinate adherence to a distrust, which he derived from a sort of hereditary contempt of his enemy, rather than from any present signs, which might warrant so uncharitable a feeling. Montcalm waited, patiently, until this little dialogue in demi-voice was ended, when he drew nigher, and opened the subject of their conference.

"I have solicited this interview from your superior, monsieur," he said, "because I believe he will allow himself to be persuaded, that he has already done every thing which is necessary for the honour of his prince, and will now listen to the admonitions of humanity. I will forever bear testimony that his resistance has been gallant, and was continued, as long as there was hope."

When this opening was translated to Munro, he answered with dignity, but with sufficient courtesy,

"However I may prize such testimony from Monsieur Montcalm, it will be more valuable when it shall be better merited."

The French general smiled, as Duncan gave him the purport of this reply, and observed—

"What is now so freely accorded to approved courage, may be refused to useless obstinacy. Monsieur would wish to see my camp, and witness, for himself, our numbers, and the impossibility of his resisting them with success?"

"I know that the king of France is well served," returned the unmoved Scotsman, as soon as Duncan ended his translation; "but my own royal master has as many and as faithful troops."

"Though not at hand, fortunately for us," said Montcalm, without waiting, in his ardour, for the interpreter. "There is a destiny in war, to which a brave man knows how to submit, with the same courage that he faces his foes."

"Had I been conscious that Monsieur Montcalm was master of the English, I should have spared myself the trouble of so awkward a translation," said the vexed Duncan, dryly; remembering instantly his recent by-play with Munro.

"Your pardon, monsieur," rejoined the Frenchman, suffering a slight colour to appear on his dark cheek. "There is a vast difference between understanding and speaking a foreign tongue; you will, therefore, please to assist me still." Then after a short pause, he added, "These hills afford us every opportunity of reconnoitring your works, messieurs, and I am possibly as well acquainted with their weak condition as you can be yourselves."

"Ask the French general if his glasses can reach to the Hudson," said Munro, proudly; "and if he knows when and where to expect the army of Webb."

"Let général Webb be his own interpreter," returned the politic Montcalm, suddenly extending an open letter towards Munro, as he spoke; "you will there learn, monsieur, that his movements are not likely to prove embarrassing to my army."

The veteran seized the offered paper without waiting for Duncan to translate the speech, and with an eagerness that betrayed how important he deemed its contents. As his eye passed hastily over the words, his countenance changed from its look of military pride, to one of deep chagrin; his lip began to quiver; and, suffering the paper to fall from his hand, his head dropped upon his chest, like that of a man whose hopes were withered at a single blow. Duncan caught the letter from the ground, and without apology for the liberty he took, he read, at a glance, its cruel purport. Their common superior, so far from encouraging them to resist, advised a speedy surrender, urging, in the plainest language, as a reason, the utter impossibility of his sending a single man to their rescue.

"Here is no deception!" exclaimed Duncan, examining the billet both inside and out; "this is the signature of Webb, and must be the captured letter!"

"The man has betrayed me!" Munro at length bitterly exclaimed; "he has brought dishonour to the door of one, where disgrace was never before known to dwell, and shame has he heaped heavily on my gray hairs!"

"Say not so!" cried Duncan; "we are yet masters of the fort, and of our honour! Let us then sell our lives at such a rate, as shall make our enemies believe the purchase too dear!"

"Boy, I thank thee!" exclaimed the old man, rousing himself from his stupor; "you have, for once, reminded Munro of his duty. We will go back, and dig our graves behind those ramparts!"

"Messieurs," said Montcalm, advancing towards them a step, in generous interest; "you little know Louis de St. Véran, if you believe him capable of profiting by this letter, to humble brave men, or to build up a dishonest reputation for himself. Listen to my terms before you leave me."

"What says the Frenchman," demanded the veteran, sternly; "does he make a merit of having captured a scout, with a note from head-quarters? Sir, he had better raise this siege, to go and sit down before Edward, if he wishes to frighten his enemy with words!"

Duncan explained the other's meaning.

"Monsieur de Montcalm, we will hear you," the veteran added, more calmly, as Duncan ended.

"To retain the fort is now impossible," said his liberal enemy; "it is necessary to the interests of my master, that it should be destroyed; but, as for yourselves, and your brave comrades, there is no privilege dear to a soldier that shall be denied."

"Our colours?" demanded Heyward.

"Carry them to England, and show them to your king."

"Our arms!"

"Keep them; none can use them better!"

"Our march; the surrender of the place?"

"Shall all be done in a way most honourable to yourselves."

Duncan now turned to explain these proposals to his commander, who heard him with amazement, and a sensibility that was deeply touched by so unusual and unexpected generosity.

"Go you, Duncan," he said; "go with this marquess, as indeed marquess he should be; go to his marquee, and arrange it all. I have lived to see two things in my old age, that never did I expect to behold. An Englishman afraid to support a friend, and a Frenchman too honest to profit by his advantage!"

So saying, the veteran again dropped his head to his chest, and returned slowly towards the fort, exhibiting, by the dejection of his air, to the anxious garrison, a harbinger of evil tidings.

From the shock of this unexpected blow the haughty feelings of Munro never recovered; but from that moment there commenced a change in his determined character, which accompanied him to a speedy grave. Duncan remained to settle the terms of the capitulation. He was seen to re-enter the works during the first watches of the night, and immediately after a private conference with the commandant, to leave them again. It was then openly announced, that hostilities must cease—Munro having signed a treaty, by which the place was to be yielded to the enemy, with the morning; the garrison to retain their arms, their colours, and their baggage, and consequently, according to military opinion, their honour.

Chapter XVII

"Weave we the woof. The thread is spun.
The web is wove. The work is done."
Gray, "The Bard," III.i [Strophe 3.], ll. 98, 100.

THE HOSTILE ARMIES, which lay in the wilds of the Horican, passed the night of the ninth of August, 1757, much in the manner they would, had they encountered on the fairest field of Europe. While the conquered were still, sullen and dejected, the victors triumphed. But, there are limits, alike, to grief and joy; and long before the watches of the morning came, the stillness of those boundless woods was only broken, by a gay call from some exulting young Frenchman of the advanced piquets, or a menacing challenge from the fort, which sternly forbade the approach of any hostile footsteps before the stipulated moment. Even these occasional threatening sounds ceased to be heard in that dull hour which precedes the day, at which period a listener might have sought, in vain, any evidence of the presence of those armed powers, that then slumbered on the shores of the 'holy lake.'

It was during these moments of deep silence, that the canvass which concealed the entrance to a spacious marquee, in the French encampment, was shoved aside, and a man issued from beneath the drapery into the open air. He was enveloped in a cloak that might have been intended as a protection from the chilling damps of the woods, but which served equally well, as a mantle, to conceal his person. He was permitted to pass the grenadier, who watched over the slumbers of the French commander, without interruption, the man making the usual salute, which betokens military deference, as the other passed swiftly through the little city of tents, in the direction of William Henry. Whenever this unknown individual encountered one of the numberless sentinels, who crossed his path, his answer was prompt, and as it appeared satisfactory; for he was uniformly allowed to proceed, without further interrogation.

With the exception of such repeated, but brief interruptions, he had moved, silently, from the centre of the camp, to its most advanced outposts, when he drew nigh the soldier, who held his watch nearest to the works of the enemy. As he approached, he was received with the usual challenge.

"Qui vive?"

"France"—was the reply.

"Le mot d'ordre?"

"La victoire," said the other, drawing so nigh, as to be heard in a loud whisper.

"C'est bien," returned the sentinel, throwing his musket from the charge to his shoulder; "vous vous promenez bien matin, monsieur!"

"Il est necessaire d'être vigilant, mon enfant," the other observed, dropping a fold of his cloak, and looking the soldier close in the face, as he passed him, still continuing his way towards the British fortification. The man started; his arms rattled heavily, as he threw them forward, in the lowest and most respectful salute; and when he had again recovered his piece, he turned to walk his post, muttering between his teeth,

"Il faut être vigilant, en vérité! je crois que nous avons là, un caporal qui ne dort jamais!"

The officer proceeded, without affecting to hear the words which escaped the sentinel in his surprise; nor did he, again, pause, until he had reached the low strand, and in a somewhat dangerous vicinity to the western water bastion of the fort. The light of an obscured moon, was just sufficient to render objects, though dim, perceptible in their outlines. He, therefore, took the precaution to place himself against the trunk of a tree, where he leaned, for many minutes, and seemed to contemplate the dark and silent mounds of the English works, in profound attention. His gaze at the ramparts was not that of a curious or idle spectator; but his looks wandered from point to point, denoting his knowledge of military usages, and betraying that his search was not unaccompanied by distrust. At length he appeared satisfied; and having cast his eyes, impatiently, upward, towards the summit of the eastern mountain, as if anticipating the approach of the morning, he was in the act of turning on his footsteps, when a light sound on the nearest angle of the bastion, caught his ear, and induced him to remain.

Just then a figure was seen to approach the edge of the rampart, where it stood, apparently, contemplating in its turn the distant tents of the French encampment. Its head was then turned towards the east, as though equally anxious for the appearance of light, when the form leaned against the mound, and seemed to gaze upon the glassy expanse of the waters, which, like a submarine firmament, glittered with its thousand mimic stars. The melancholy air, the hour, together with the vast frame of the man who thus leaned, in musing, against the English ramparts, left no doubt as to his person, in the mind of the observant spectator. Delicacy, no less than prudence, now urged him to retire; and he had mov'd cautiously round the body of the tree, for that purpose, when another sound drew his attention, and once more arrested his footsteps. It was a low, and almost inaudible movement of the water, and was succeeded by a grating of pebbles, one against the other. In a moment, he saw a dark form rise, as it were, out of the lake, and steal, without farther noise, to the land, within a few feet of the place where he himself stood. A rifle next slowly rose between his eyes and the watery mirror; but before it could be discharged, his own hand was on the lock.

"Hugh!" exclaimed the savage, whose treacherous aim was so singularly and so unexpectedly interrupted.

Without making any reply, the French officer laid his hand on the shoulder of the Indian, and led him, in profound silence, to a distance from the spot, where their subsequent dialogue might have proved dangerous, and where, it seemed, that one of them, at least, sought a victim. Then, throwing open his cloak, so as to expose his uniform, and the cross of St. Louis, which was suspended at his breast, Montcalm sternly demanded—

"What means this! does not my son know, that the hatchet is buried between the English and his Canadian father?"

"What can the Hurons do?" returned the savage, speaking, also, though imperfectly, in the French language. "Not a warrior has a scalp, and the pale faces make friends!"

"Ha! le Renard Subtil! Methinks this is an excess of zeal for a friend, who was so late an enemy! How many suns have set, since le Renard struck the war post of the English?"

"Where is that sun!" demanded the sullen savage. "Behind the hill; and it is dark and cold. But when he comes again, it will be bright and warm. Le Subtil is the sun of his tribe. There have been clouds, and many mountains between him and his nation; but now he shines, and it is a clear sky!"

"That le Renard has power with his people, I well know," said Montcalm; "for yesterday he hunted for their scalps, and to-day, they hear him at the council fire!"

"Magua is a great chief!"

"Let him prove it, by teaching his nation how to conduct towards our new friends!"

"Why did the chief of the Canadas bring his young men into the woods, and fire his cannon at the earthen house?" demanded the subtle Indian.

"To subdue it. My master owns the land, and your father was ordered to drive off these English squatters. They have consented to go, and now he calls them enemies no longer."

" 'Tis well. Magua took the hatchet to colour it with blood. It is now bright; when it is red, it shall be buried."

"But Magua is pledged not to sully the lilies of France. The enemies of the great king across the salt lake, are his enemies; his friends, the friends of the Hurons."

"Friends!" repeated the Indian, in scorn. "Let his father give Magua a hand."

Montcalm, who felt that his influence over the warlike tribes he had gathered, was to be maintained by concession, rather than by power, complied, reluctantly, with the other's request. The savage placed the finger of the French commander on a deep scar in his bosom, and then exultingly demanded—

"Does my father know that?"

"What warrior does not! 'tis where a leaden bullet has cut."

"And this!" continued the Indian, who had turned his naked back to the other, his body being without its usual calico mantle.

"This!—my son, has been sadly injured, here! who has done this?"

"Magua slept hard in the English wigwams, and the sticks have left their mark," returned the savage, with a hollow laugh, which did not conceal the fierce temper that nearly choked him. Then, recollecting himself, with sudden and native dignity, he added—"Go; teach your young men, it is peace! le Renard Subtil knows how to speak to a Huron warrior!"

Without deigning to bestow farther words, or to wait for any answer, the savage cast his rifle into the hollow of his arm, and moved, silently, through the encampment towards the woods, where his own tribe was known to lie. Every few yards, as he proceeded, he was challenged by the sentinels; but he stalked, sullenly, onward, utterly disregarding the summons of the soldiers, who only spared his life, because they knew the air and tread, no less than the obstinate daring, of an Indian.

Montcalm lingered long and melancholy on the strand, where he had been left by his companion, brooding deeply on the temper which his ungovernable ally had just discovered. Already had his fair fame been tarnished by one horrid scene, and in circumstances fearfully resembling those, under which he now found himself. As he mused, he became keenly sensible of the deep responsibility they assume, who disregard the means to attain their end, and of all the danger of setting in motion an engine, which it exceeds human power to control. Then shaking off a train of reflections, that he accounted a weakness in such a moment of triumph, he retraced his steps towards his tent, giving the order, as he passed, to make the signal that should arouse the army from its slumbers.

The first tap of the French drums was echoed from the bosom of the fort; and, presently, the valley was filled with the strains of martial music, rising long, thrilling, and lively, above the rattling accompaniment. The horns of the victors sounded merry and cheerful flourishes, until the last laggard of the camp was at his post; but the instant the British fifes had blown their shrill signal, they became mute. In the mean time the day had dawned, and when the line of the French army was ready to receive its general, the rays of a brilliant sun were glancing along the glittering array. Then, that success which was already so well known, was officially announced; the favoured band, who were selected to guard the gates of the fort, were detailed, and defiled before their chief; the signal of their approach was given, and all the usual preparations for a change of masters, were ordered and executed directly under the guns of the contested works.

A very different scene presented itself within the lines of the Anglo-American army. As soon as the warning signal was given, it exhibited all the signs of a hurried and forced departure. The sullen soldiers shouldered their empty tubes, and fell into their places, like men whose blood had been heated by the past contest, and who only desired the opportunity to revenge an indignity, which was still wounding to their pride, concealed, as it was, under all the observances of military etiquette. Women and children ran from place to place, some bearing the scanty remnants of their baggage, and others searching, in the ranks, for those countenances they looked up to for protection.

Munro appeared among his silent troops, firm, but dejected. It was evident that the unexpected blow had struck deep into his heart, though he struggled to sustain his misfortune with the port of a man.

Duncan was touched at the quiet and impressive exhibition of his grief. He had discharged his own duty, and he now pressed to the side of the old man, to know in what particular he might serve him.

"My daughters," was the brief, but expressive reply.

"Good heavens! Are not arrangements already made for their convenience?"

"To-day I am only a soldier, Major Heyward," said the veteran. "All that you see here, claim alike to be my children."

Duncan had heard enough. Without losing one of those moments which had now become so precious, he flew towards the quarters of Munro, in quest of the sisters. He found them on the threshold of the low edifice, already prepared to depart, and surrounded by a clamorous and weeping assemblage of their own sex, that had gathered about the place, with a sort of instinctive consciousness, that it was the point most likely to be protected. Though the cheeks of Cora were pale, and her countenance anxious, she had lost none of her firmness; but the eyes of Alice were inflamed, and betrayed how long and bitterly she had wept. They both, however, received the young man with undisguised pleasure; the former, for a novelty, being the first to speak.

"The fort is lost," she said, with a melancholy smile; "though our good name, I trust, remains!"

" 'Tis brighter than ever! But, dearest Miss Munro, it is time to think less of others, and to make some provision for yourself. Military usage—pride—that pride on which you so much value yourself, demands that your father and I should, for a little while, continue with the troops. Then where to seek a proper protecter for you, against the confusion and chances of such a scene!"—

"None is necessary," returned Cora; " who will dare to injure or insult the daughter of such a father, at a time like this!"

"I would not leave you alone," continued the youth, looking about him in a hurried manner, "for the command of the best regiment in the pay of the king! Remember, our Alice is not gifted with all your firmness, and God only knows the terror she might endure."

"You may be right," Cora replied, smiling again, but far more sadly than before. "Listen; chance has already sent us a friend when he is most needed."

Duncan did listen, and on the instant comprehended her meaning. The low, and serious sounds of the sacred music, so well known to the eastern provinces, caught his ear, and instantly drew him to an apartment in an adjacent building, which had, already, been deserted by its customary tenants. There he found David, pouring out his pious feelings, through the only medium in which he ever indulged. Duncan waited, until by the cessation of the movement of the hand, he believed the strain was ended, when, by touching his shoulder, he drew the attention of the other to himself, and in a few words explained his wishes.

"Even so," replied the single minded disciple of the King of Israel, when the young man had ended; "I have found much that is comely and melodious in the maidens, and it is fitting that we, who have consorted in so much peril, should abide together in peace. I will attend them, when I have completed my morning praise, to which nothing is now wanting, but the doxology. Wilt thou bear a part, friend? The metre is common, and the tune 'Southwell.' "

Then, extending the little volume, and giving the pitch of

the air, anew, with considerate attention, David re-commenced and finished his strains, with a fixedness of manner that it was not easy to interrupt. Heyward was fain to wait until the verse was ended; when seeing David relieving himself from the spectacles, and replacing the book, he continued—

"It will be your duty, to see that none dare to approach the ladies, with any rude intention, or to offer insult or taunt at the misfortune of their brave father. In this task, you will be seconded by the domestics of their household."

"Even so."

"It is possible, that the Indians and stragglers of the enemy may intrude; in which case, you will remind them of the terms of the capitulation, and threaten to report their conduct to Montcalm. A word will suffice."

"If not, I have that here which shall," returned David, exhibiting his book, with an air, in which meekness and confidence were singularly blended. "Here are words, which uttered, or rather thundered, with proper emphasis, and in measured time, shall quiet the most unruly temper.

"Why rage the heathen furiously!"—

"Enough," said Heyward, interrupting the burst of his musical invocation; "we understand each other; it is time that we should, now, assume our respective duties."

Gamut cheerfully assented, and together they sought the females. Cora received her new, and somewhat extraordinary, protector, courteously at least; and even the pallid features of Alice lighted, again, with some of their native archness, as she thanked Heyward for his care. Duncan took occasion to assure them he had done the best that circumstances permitted, and, as he believed, quite enough for the security of their feelings; of danger there was none. He then spoke gladly of his intention to rejoin them, the moment he had led the advance a few miles towards the Hudson, and immediately took his leave.

By this time the signal of departure had been given, and the head of the English column was in motion. The sisters started at the sound, and glancing their eyes around, they saw the white uniforms of the French grenadiers, who had, already, taken possession of the gates of the fort. At that moment, an enormous cloud seemed to pass suddenly above their heads, and looking upward, they discovered that they stood beneath the wide folds of the standard of France.

"Let us go," said Cora; "this is no longer a fit place for the children of an English officer!"

Alice clung to the arm of her sister, and together they left the parade, accompanied by the moving throng, that surrounded them.

As they passed the gates, the French officers, who had learned their rank, bowed often and low, forbearing, however, to intrude those attentions, which they saw, with peculiar tact, might not be agreeable. As every vehicle, and each beast of burthen, was occupied by the sick and wounded, Cora had decided to endure the fatigues of a foot march, rather than interfere with their comforts. Indeed, many a maimed and feeble soldier was compelled to drag his exhausted limbs, in the rear of the columns, for the want of the necessary means of conveyance, in that wilderness. The whole, however, was in motion; the weak and wounded, groaning, and in suffering; their comrades, silent, and sullen; and the women and children in terror, they knew not of what.

As the confused and timid throng, left the protecting mounds of the fort, and issued on the open plain, the whole scene was, at once, presented to their eyes. At a little distance on the right, and somewhat in the rear, the French army stood to their arms, Montcalm having collected his parties, so soon as his guards had possession of the works. They were attentive, but silent observers of the proceedings of the vanquished, failing in none of the stipulated military honours, and offering no taunt or insult, in their success, to their less fortunate foes. Living masses of the English, to the amount, in the whole, of near three thousand, were moving slowly across the plain, towards the common center, and gradually approached each other, as they converged to the point of their march, a vista cut through the lofty trees, where the road to the Hudson entered the forest. Along the sweeping borders of the woods, hung a dark cloud of savages, eyeing the passage of their enemies, and hovering, at a distance, like vultures, who were only kept from stooping on their prey, by the presence and restraint of a superior army. A few had straggled among the conquered columns, where they stalked, in sullen discontent; attentive, though, as yet, passive observers of the moving multitude.

The advance, with Heyward at its head, had already reached the defile, and was slowly disappearing, when the attention of Cora was drawn to a collection of stragglers, by the sounds of contention. A truant provincial was paying the forfeit of his disobedience, by being plundered of those very effects, which had caused him to desert his place in the ranks. The man was of powerful frame, and too avaricious to part with his goods, without a struggle. Individuals from either party interfered; the one side to prevent, and the other to aid in the robbery. Voices grew loud and angry, and a hundred savages appeared, as it were, by magic, where a dozen only had been seen, a minute before. It was, then, that Cora saw the form of Magua, gliding among his countrymen, and speaking, with his fatal and artful eloquence. The mass of women and children stopped, and hovered together, like alarmed and fluttering birds. But the cupidity of the Indian was soon gratified, and the different bodies, again, moved slowly onward.

The savages now fell back, and seemed content to let their enemies advance, without further molestation. But as the female crowd approached them, the gaudy colours of a shawl attracted the eyes of a wild and untutored Huron. He advanced to seize it, without the least hesitation. The woman, more in terror, than through love of the ornament, wrapped her child in the coveted article, and folded both more closely to her bosom. Cora was in the act of speaking, with an intent to advise the woman to abandon the trifle, when the savage relinquished his hold of the shawl, and tore the screaming infant from her arms. Abandoning every thing to the greedy grasp of those around her, the mother darted, with distraction in her mien, to reclaim her child. The Indian smiled grimly, and extended one hand, in sign of a willingness to exchange, while, with the other, he flourished the babe above his head, holding it by the feet, as if to enhance the value of the ransom.

"Here—here—there—all—any—every thing!" exclaimed the breathless woman; tearing the lighter articles of dress from her person, with ill-directed and trembling fingers—"Take all, but give me my babe!"

The savage spurned the worthless rags, and perceiving that the shawl had already become a prize to another, his bantering, but sullen smile, changing to a gleam of ferocity, he dashed the head of the infant against a rock, and cast its quivering remains to her very feet. For an instant, the mother stood, like a statue of despair, looking wildly down at the unseemly object, which had so lately nestled in her bosom and smiled in her face; and then she raised her eyes and countenance towards heaven, as if calling on God to curse the perpetrator of the foul deed. She was spared the sin of such a prayer; for, maddened at his disappointment, and excited by the sight of blood, the Huron mercifully drove his tomahawk into her own brain. The mother sunk under the blow, and fell, grasping at her child, in death, with the same engrossing love, that had caused her to cherish it when living.

At that dangerous moment Magua placed his hands to his mouth, and raised the fatal and appalling whoop. The scattered Indians started at the well known cry, as coursers bound at the signal to quit the goal; and, directly, there arose such a yell along the plain, and through the arches of the wood, as seldom bursted from human lips before. They who heard it, listened with a curdling horror at the heart, little inferior to that dread which may be expected to attend the blasts of the final summons.

More than two thousand raging savages broke from the forest at the signal, and threw themselves across the fatal plain with instinctive alacrity. We shall not dwell on the revolting horrors that succeeded.—Death was every where, and in his most terrific and disgusting aspects. Resistance only served to inflame the murderers, who inflicted their furious blows long after their victims were beyond the power of their resentment. The flow of blood might be likened to the outbreaking of a torrent; and as the natives became heated and maddened by the sight, many among them even kneeled to the earth, and drank freely, exultingly, hellishly, of the crimson tide.

The trained bodies of the troops threw themselves, quickly, into solid masses, endeavouring to awe their assailants by the imposing appearance of a military front. The experiment in some measure succeeded, though far too many suffered their unloaded muskets to be torn from their hands, in the vain hope of appeasing the savages.

In such a scene, none had leisure to note the fleeting moments. It might have been ten minutes, (it seemed an age,) that the sisters had stood, rivetted to one spot, horror-stricken, and nearly helpless. When the first blow was struck, their screaming companions had pressed upon them in a body, rendering flight impossible; and now that fear or death had scattered most, if not all, from around them, they saw no avenue open, but such as conducted to the tomahawks of their foes. On every side arose shrieks, groans, exhortations, and curses. At this moment, Alice caught a glimpse of the vast form of her father, moving rapidly across the plain, in the direction of the French army. He was, in truth, proceeding to Montcalm, fearless of every danger, to claim the tardy escort, for which he had before conditioned. Fifty glittering axes, and barbed spears, were offered unheeded at his life, but the savages respected his rank and calmness, even in their fury. The dangerous weapons were brushed aside by the still nervous arm of the veteran, or fell of themselves, after menacing an act, that it would seem no one had courage to perform. Fortunately, the vindictive Magua was searching for his victim in the very band the veteran had just quitted.

"Father—father—we are here!" shrieked Alice, as he passed, at no great distance, without appearing to heed them. "Come to us, father, or we die!"

The cry was repeated, and in terms and tones, that might have melted a heart of stone, but it was unanswered. Once, indeed, the old man appeared to catch the sounds, for he paused, and listened; but Alice had dropped senseless on the earth, and Cora had sunk at her side, hovering, in untiring tenderness, over her lifeless form. Munro shook his head, in disappointment, and proceeded, bent on the high duty of his station.

"Lady," said Gamut, who, helpless and useless as he was, had not yet dreamed of deserting his trust, "it is the jubilee of the devils, and this is not a meet place for christians to tarry in. Let us up and fly!"

"Go," said Cora, still gazing at her unconscious sister; "save thyself. To me thou canst not be of further use."

David comprehended the unyielding character of her resolution, by the simple, but expressive, gesture, that accompanied her words. He gazed, for a moment, at the dusky forms that were acting their hellish rites on every side of him, and his tall person grew more erect, while his chest heaved, and every feature swelled, and seemed to speak with the power of the feelings by which he was governed.

"If the Jewish boy might tame the evil spirit of Saul, by the sound of his harp, and the words of sacred song, it may not be amiss," he said, "to try the potency of music here."

Then raising his voice to its highest tones, he poured out a strain so powerful as to be heard, even amid the din of that bloody field. More than one savage rushed towards them, thinking to rifle the unprotected sisters of their attire, and bear away their scalps; but when they found this strange and unmoved figure, rivetted to his post, they paused to listen. Astonishment soon changed to admiration, and they passed on to other, and less courageous victims, openly expressing their satisfaction at the firmness with which the white warrior sung his death song. Encouraged and deluded by his success, David exerted all his powers to extend what he believed so holy an influence. The unwonted sounds caught the ears of a distant savage, who flew, raging from groupe to groupe, like one who, scorning to touch the vulgar herd, hunted for some victim more worthy of his renown. It was Magua, who uttered a yell of pleasure when he beheld his ancient prisoners again at his mercy.

"Come," he said, laying his soiled hand on the dress of Cora, "the wigwam of the Huron is still open. Is it not better than this place?"

"Away!" cried Cora, veiling her eyes from his revolting aspect.

The Indian laughed tauntingly as he held up his reeking hand, and answered—"It is red, but it comes from white veins!"

"Monster! there is blood, oceans of blood, upon thy soul; thy spirit has moved this scene."

"Magua is a great chief!" returned the exulting savage— "will the dark-hair go to his tribe!"

"Never! strike, if thou wilt, and complete thy revenge."

He hesitated a moment; and then catching the light and senseless form of Alice in his arms, the subtle Indian moved swiftly across the plain toward the woods.

"Hold!" shrieked Cora, following wildly on his footsteps, "release the child! wretch! what is't you do!"

But Magua was deaf to her voice; or rather he knew his power, and was determined to maintain it.

"Stay—lady—stay," called Gamut, after the unconscious Cora. "The holy charm is beginning to be felt, and soon shalt thou see this horrid tumult stilled."

Perceiving that, in his turn, he was unheeded, the faithful David followed the distracted sister, raising his voice again in sacred song, and sweeping the air to the measure, with his long arm, in diligent accompaniment. In this manner they traversed the plain, through the flying, the wounded, and the dead. The fierce Huron was, at any time, sufficient for himself and the victim that he bore; though Cora would have fallen, more than once, under the blows of her savage enemies, but for the extraordinary being who stalked in her rear, and who now appeared to the astonished natives gifted with the protecting spirit of madness.

Magua, who knew how to avoid the more pressing dangers, and, also, to elude pursuit, entered the woods through a low ravine, where he quickly found the Narragansetts, which the travellers had abandoned so shortly before, awaiting his appearance, in custody of a savage as fierce and as malign in his expression as himself. Laying Alice on one of the horses, he made a sign for Cora to mount the other.

Notwithstanding the horror excited by the presence of her captor, there was a present relief in escaping from the bloody scene enacting on the plain, to which Cora could not be altogether insensible. She took her seat, and held forth her arms for her sister, with an air of entreaty and love, that even the Huron could not deny. Placing Alice, then, on the same animal with Cora, he seized the bridle, and commenced his route by plunging deeper into the forest. David, perceiving that he was left alone, utterly disregarded, as a subject too worthless even to destroy, threw his long limb across the saddle of the beast they had deserted, and made such progress in the pursuit, as the difficulties of the path permitted.

They soon began to ascend; but as the motion had a tendency to revive the dormant faculties of her sister, the attention of Cora was too much divided between the tenderest solicitude in her behalf, and in listening to the cries, which were still too audible on the plain, to note the direction in which they journeyed. When, however, they gained the flattened surface of the mountain top, and approached the eastern precipice, she recognised the spot to which she had, once before, been led, under the more friendly auspices of the scout. Here Magua suffered them to dismount, and, notwithstanding their own captivity, the curiosity which seems inseparable from horror, induced them to gaze at the sickening sight below.

The cruel work was still unchecked. On every side the captured were flying before their relentless persecutors, while the armed columns of the Christian King stood fast, in an apathy which has never been explained, and which has left an immoveable blot on the, otherwise, fair escutcheon of their leader. Nor was the sword of death stayed, until cupidity got the mastery of revenge. Then, indeed, the shrieks of the wounded, and the yells of their murderers, grew less frequent, until finally the cries of horror were lost to their ear, or were drowned in the loud, long and piercing whoops of the triumphant savages.*

*The accounts of the number who fell in this unhappy affair, vary between five and fifteen hundred.

Chapter XVIII

"Why, any thing:
An honourable murderer, if you will;
For nought I did in hate, but all in honour."
Othello, V.ii.294–295.

THE BLOODY and inhuman scene rather incidentally mentioned than described, in the preceding chapter, is conspicuous in the pages of colonial history, by the merited title of "The massacre of William Henry." It so far deepened the stain which a previous and very similar event had left upon the reputation of the French commander, that it was not entirely erased by his early and glorious death. It is now becoming obscured by time; and thousands, who know that Montcalm died like a hero on the plains of Abraham, have yet to learn how much he was deficient in that moral courage, without which no man can be truly great. Pages might be written to prove, from this illustrious example, the defects of human excellence; to show how easy it is for generous sentiments, high courtesy, and chivalrous courage, to lose their influence beneath the chilling blight of selfishness, and to exhibit to the world a man who was great in all the minor attributes of character, but who was found wanting, when it became necessary to prove how much principle is superior to policy. But the task would exceed our prerogatives; and, as history, like love, is so apt to surround her heroes with an atmosphere of imaginary brightness, it is probable that Louis de Saint Véran will be viewed by posterity only as the gallant defender of his country, while his cruel apathy on the shores of the Oswego and of the Horican, will be forgotten. Deeply regretting this weakness on the part of a sister muse, we shall at once retire from her sacred precincts, within the proper limits of our own humbler vocation.

The third day from the capture of the fort was drawing to a close, but the business of the narrative must still detain the reader on the shores of the "holy lake." When last seen, the environs of the works were filled with violence and uproar.

They were now possessed by stillness and death. The blood-stained conquerors had departed; and their camp, which had so lately rung with the merry rejoicings of a victorious army, lay a silent and deserted city of huts. The fortress was a smouldering ruin; charred rafters, fragments of exploded artillery, and rent mason-work, covering its earthen mounds, in confused disorder.

A frightful change had also occurred in the season. The sun had hid its warmth behind an impenetrable mass of vapour, and hundreds of human forms, which had blackened beneath the fierce heats of August, were stiffening in their deformity, before the blasts of a premature November. The curling and spotless mists, which had been seen sailing above the hills, towards the north, were now returning in an interminable dusky sheet, that was urged along by the fury of a tempest. The crowded mirror of the Horican was gone; and, in its place, the green and angry waters lashed the shores, as if indignantly casting back its impurities to the polluted strand. Still, the clear fountain retained a portion of its charmed influence; but it reflected only the sombre gloom that fell from the impending heavens. That humid and congenial atmosphere which commonly adorned the view, veiling its harshness, and softening its asperities, had disappeared, and the northern air poured across the waste of water so harsh and unmingled, that nothing was left to be conjectured by the eye, or fashioned by the fancy.

The fiercer element had cropped the verdure of the plain, which looked as though it were scathed by the consuming lightning. But, here and there, a dark green tuft rose in the midst of the desolation; the earliest fruits of a soil that had been fattened with human blood. The whole landscape, which, seen by a favouring light, and in a genial temperature, had been found so lovely, appeared now like some pictured allegory of life, in which objects were arrayed in their harshest but truest colours, and without the relief of any shadowing.

The solitary and arid blades of grass arose from the passing gusts fearfully perceptible; the bold and rocky mountains were too distinct in their barrenness, and the eye even sought relief, in vain, by attempting to pierce the illimitable void of heaven, which was shut to its gaze, by the dusky sheet of ragged and driving vapour.

The wind blew unequally; sometimes sweeping heavily along the ground, seeming to whisper its moanings in the cold ears of the dead, then rising in a shrill and mournful whistling, it entered the forest with a rush that filled the air with the leaves and branches it scattered in its path. Amid the unnatural shower, a few hungry ravens struggled with the gale; but no sooner was the green ocean of woods, which stretched beneath them, passed, than they gladly stooped, at random, to their hideous banquet.

In short, it was a scene of wildness and desolation; and it appeared as if all who had profanely entered it, had been stricken, at a blow, by the relentless arm of death. But the prohibition had ceased; and, for the first time since the perpetrators of those foul deeds, which had assisted to disfigure the scene, were gone, living human beings had now presumed to approach the place.

About an hour before the setting of the sun, on the day already mentioned, the forms of five men might have been seen issuing from the narrow vista of trees, where the path to the Hudson entered the forest, and advancing in the direction of the ruined works. At first their progress was slow and guarded, as though they entered with reluctance amid the horrors of the spot, or dreaded the renewal of its frightful incidents. A light figure preceded the rest of the party, with the caution and activity of a native; ascending every hillock to reconnoitre, and indicating, by gestures, to his companions, the route he deemed it most prudent to pursue. Nor were those in the rear wanting in every caution and foresight known to forest warfare. One among them, and he also was an Indian, moved a little on one flank, and watched the margin of the woods, with eyes long accustomed to read the smallest sign of danger. The remaining three were white, though clad in vestments adapted, both in quality and colour, to their present hazardous pursuit; that of hanging on the skirts of a retiring army, in the wilderness.

The effects produced by the appalling sights, that constantly arose, in their path to the lake shore, were as different as the characters of the respective individuals who composed the party. The youth in front threw serious but furtive glances at the mangled victims, as he stepped lightly across the plain, afraid to exhibit his feelings, and yet too inexperienced to quell entirely their sudden and powerful influence. His red associate, however, was superior to such a weakness. He passed the groupes of dead with a steadiness of purpose, and an eye so calm, that nothing but long and inveterate practice could enable him to maintain. The sensations produced in the minds of even the white men, were different, though uniformly sorrowful. One, whose gray locks and furrowed lineaments, blending with a martial air and tread, betrayed, in spite of the disguise of a woodsman's dress, a man long experienced in scenes of war, was not ashamed to groan aloud, whenever a spectacle of more than usual horror came under his view. The young man at his elbow shuddered, but seemed to suppress his feelings in tenderness to his companion. Of them all, the straggler who brought up the rear, appeared alone to betray his real thoughts, without fear of observation or dread of consequences. He gazed at the most appalling sight with eyes and muscles that knew not how to waver, but with execrations so bitter and deep, as to denote how much he denounced the crime of his enemies.

The reader will perceive, at once, in these respective characters, the Mohicans, and their white friend, the scout; together with Munro and Heyward. It was, in truth, the father in quest of his children, attended by the youth who felt so deep a stake in their happiness, and those brave and trusty foresters, who had already proved their skill and fidelity, through the trying scenes related.

When Uncas, who moved in front, had reached the centre of the plain, he raised a cry that drew his companions, in a body, to the spot. The young warrior had halted over a groupe of females, who lay in a cluster, a confused mass of dead. Notwithstanding the revolting horror of the exhibition, Munro and Heyward flew towards the festering heap, endeavouring, with a love that no unseemliness could extinguish, to discover whether any vestiges of those they sought, were to be seen among the tattered and many-coloured garments. The father and the lover found instant relief in the search;

though each was condemned again to experience the misery of an uncertainty, that was hardly less insupportable than the most revolting truth. They were standing, silent and thoughtful, around the melancholy pile, when the scout approached. Eyeing the sad spectacle with an angry countenance, the sturdy woodsman, for the first time since entering the plain, spoke intelligibly and aloud.

"I have been on many a shocking field, and have followed a trail of blood for weary miles," he said, "but never have I found the hand of the devil so plain as it is here to be seen! Revenge is an Indian feeling, and all who know me, know that there is no cross in my veins; but this much will I say—here, in the face of heaven, and with the power of the Lord so manifest in this howling wilderness, that should these Frenchers ever trust themselves again within the range of a ragged bullet, there is one rifle shall play its part, so long as flint will fire, or powder burn!—I leave the tomahawk and knife to such as have a natural gift to use them. What say you, Chingachgook," he added, in Delaware; "shall the Hurons boast of this to their women when the deep snows come?"

A gleam of resentment flashed across the dark lineaments of the Mohican chief; he loosened his knife in his sheath; and then turning calmly from the sight, his countenance settled into a repose as deep as if he never knew the instigation of passion.

"Montcalm! Montcalm!" continued the deeply resentful and less self-restrained scout; "they say a time must come, when all the deeds done in the flesh will be seen at a single look; and that by eyes cleared from mortal infirmities. Wo betide the wretch who is born to behold this plain, with the judgment hanging above his soul! Ha—as I am a man of white blood, yonder lies a red-skin, without the hair of his head where nature rooted it! Look to him, Delaware; it may be one of your missing people; and he should have burial like a stout warrior. I see it in your eye, Sagamore; a Huron pays for this, afore the fall winds have blown away the scent of the blood!"

Chingachgook approached the mutilated form, and turning it over, he found the distinguishing marks of one of those six allied tribes, or nations, as they were called, who, while they fought in the English ranks, were so deadly hostile to his own people. Spurning the loathsome object with his foot, he turned from it with the same indifference he would have quitted a brute carcass. The scout comprehended the action, and very deliberately pursued his own way, continuing, however, his denunciations against the French commander in the same resentful strain.

"Nothing but vast wisdom and onlimited power should dare to sweep off men in multitudes," he added; "for it is only the one that can know the necessity of the judgment; and what is there short of the other, that can replace the creatures of the Lord? I hold it a sin to kill the second buck afore the first is eaten; unless a march in the front, or an ambushment, be contemplated. It is a different matter with a few warriors in open and rugged fight, for 'tis their gift to die with the rifle or the tomahawk in hand; according as their natures may happen to be, white or red. Uncas, come this way, lad, and let the raven settle upon the Mingo. I know, from often seeing it, that they have a craving for the flesh of an Oneida; and it is as well to let the bird follow the gift of its natural appetite."

"Hugh!" exclaimed the young Mohican, rising on the extremities of his feet, and gazing intently in his front, frightening the raven to some other prey, by the sound and the action.

"What is it, boy?" whispered the scout, lowering his tall form into a crouching attitude, like a panther about to take his leap; "God send it be a tardy Frencher, skulking for plunder. I do believe 'kill-deer' would take an oncommon range to-day!"

Uncas, without making any reply, bounded away from the spot, and in the next instant he was seen tearing from a bush, and waving, in triumph, a fragment of the green riding veil of Cora. The movement, the exhibition, and the cry, which again burst from the lips of the young Mohican, instantly drew the whole party about him.

"My child!" said Munro, speaking quick and wildly; "give me my child!"

"Uncas will try," was the short and touching answer.

The simple, but meaning assurance was lost on the father, who seized the piece of gauze, and crushed it in his hand, while his eyes roamed fearfully among the bushes, as if he equally dreaded and hoped for the secrets they might reveal.

"Here are no dead!" said Heyward; "the storm seems not to have passed this way."

"That's manifest; and clearer than the heavens above our heads," returned the undisturbed scout; "but either she, or they that have robbed her, have passed the bush; for I remember the rag she wore to hide a face that all did love to look upon. Uncas, you are right; the dark-hair has been here, and she has fled, like a frighted fawn, to the wood; none who could fly would remain to be murdered! Let us search for the marks she left; for to Indian eyes, I sometimes think even a humming-bird leaves his trail in the air!"

The young Mohican darted away at the suggestion, and the scout had hardly done speaking, before the former raised a cry of success from the margin of the forest. On reaching the spot, the anxious party perceived another portion of the veil fluttering on the lower branch of a beech.

"Softly, softly," said the scout, extending his long rifle in front of the eager Heyward; " we now know our work, but the beauty of the trail must not be deformed. A step too soon may give us hours of trouble. We have them though; that much is beyond denial!"

"Bless ye, bless ye! worthy man!" exclaimed Munro; " whither then have they fled, and where are my babes?"

"The path they have taken depends on many chances. If they have gone alone, they are quite as likely to move in a circle as straight, and they may be within a dozen miles of us; but if the Hurons, or any of the French Indians, have laid hands on them, 'tis probable they are now near the borders of the Canadas. But what matters that!" continued the deliberate scout, observing the powerful anxiety and disappointment the listeners exhibited; "here are the Mohicans and I on one end of the trail, and, rely on it, we'll find the other, though they should be a hundred leagues asunder! Gently, gently, Uncas, you are as impatient as a man in the settlements; you forget that light feet leave but faint marks!"

"Hugh!" exclaimed Chingachgook, who had been occupied in examining an opening that had been evidently made through the low underbrush, which skirted the forest; and who now stood erect, as he pointed downwards, in the attitude and with the air of a man, who beheld a disgusting serpent.

"Here is the palpable impression of the footstep of a man!" cried Heyward, bending over the indicated spot; "he has trod in the margin of this pool, and the mark cannot be mistaken. They are captives!"

"Better so than left to starve in the wilderness," returned the scout; "and they will leave a wider trail. I would wager fifty beaver skins against as many flints, that the Mohicans and I enter their wigwams within the month! Stoop to it, Uncas, and try what you can make of that moccasin; for moccasin it plainly is, and no shoe."

The young Mohican bent over the track, and removing the scattered leaves from around the place, he examined it with much of that sort of scrutiny, that a money-dealer, in these days of pecuniary doubts, would bestow on a suspected due-bill. At length, he arose from his knees, satisfied with the result of the examination.

"Well, boy," demanded the attentive scout, "what does it say? can you make any thing of the tell-tale?"

"Le Renard Subtil!"

"Ha! that rampaging devil again! there never will be an end of his loping, till 'kill-deer' has said a friendly word to him."

Heyward reluctantly admitted the truth of this intelligence, and now expressed rather his hopes, than his doubts, by saying—

"One moccasin is so much like another, it is probable there is some mistake."

"One moccasin like another! you may as well say that one foot is like another; though we all know, that some are long, and others short; some broad, and others narrow; some with high, and some with low, insteps; some in-toed, and some out! One moccasin is no more like another, than one book is like another; though they who can read in one, are seldom able to tell the marks of the other. Which is all ordered for the best, giving to every man his natural advantages. Let me get down to it, Uncas; neither book nor moccasin is the worse for having two opinions, instead of one." The scout stooped to the task, and instantly added, "you are right, boy; here is the patch we saw so often in the other chase. And the fellow will drink when he can get an opportunity; your drinking Indian always learns to walk with a wider toe than the natural savage, it being the gift of a drunkard to straddle, whether of white or red skin. 'Tis just the length and breadth too! look at it, Sagamore; you measured the prints more than once, when we hunted the varments from Glenn's to the health-springs."

Chingachgook complied, and after finishing his short examination, he arose, and with a quite demeanour, he merely pronounced the word—

"Magua."

"Ay, 'tis a settled thing; here then have passed the dark hair and Magua."

"And not Alice?" demanded Heyward.

"Of her we have not yet seen the signs," returned the scout, looking closely around at the trees, the bushes, and the ground. "What have we there! Uncas, bring hither the thing you see dangling from yonder thorn-bush."

When the Indian had complied, the scout received the prize, and holding it on high, he laughed in his silent but heartfelt manner.

" 'Tis the tooting we'pon of the singer! now we shall have a trail a priest might travel," he said. "Uncas, look for the marks of a shoe that is long enough to uphold six feet two of tottering human flesh. I begin to have some hopes of the fellow, since he has given up squalling, to follow some better trade."

"At least, he has been faithful to his trust," said Heyward; "and Cora and Alice are not without a friend."

"Yes," said Hawk-eye, dropping his rifle, and leaning on it with an air of visible contempt, "he will do their singing! Can he slay a buck for their dinner; journey by the moss on the beeches, or cut the throat of a Huron? If not, the first cat-bird* he meets is the cleverest fellow of the two. Well, boy, any signs of such a foundation?"

"Here is something like the footstep of one who has worn a shoe; can it be that of our friend?"

"Touch the leaves lightly, or you'll disconsart the formation. That! that, is the print of a foot, but 'tis the dark hair's; and small it is, too, for one of such a noble heighth and grand appearance! The singer would cover it with his heel!"

"Where! let me look on the footsteps of my child!" said Munro, shoving the bushes aside, and bending fondly over the nearly obliterated impression. Though the tread, which had left the mark, had been light and rapid, it was still plainly visible. The aged soldier examined it with eyes that grew dim as he gazed; nor did he rise from his stooping posture, until Heyward saw that he had watered the trace of his daughter's passage, with a scalding tear. Willing to divert a distress which threatened, each moment, to break through the restraint of appearances, by giving the veteran something to do, the young man said to the scout—

"As we now possess these infallible signs, let us commence our march. A moment, at such a time, will appear an age to the captives."

"It is not the swiftest leaping deer that gives the longest chase," returned Hawk-eye, without moving his eyes from the different marks that had come under his view; "we know that the rampaging Huron has passed—and the dark hair—and the singer—but where is she of the yellow locks and blue eyes? Though little, and far from being as bold as her sister, she is fair to the view, and pleasant in discourse. Has she no friend, that none care for her?"

"God forbid she should ever want hundreds! Are we not now in her pursuit? for one, I will never cease the search till she be found!"

"In that case we may have to journey by different paths;

*The powers of the American mocking-bird are generally known. But the true mocking-bird is not found so far north, as the state of New-York, where it has, however, two substitutes of inferior excellence; the cat-bird, so often named by the scout, and the bird vulgarly called ground-thresher. Either of these two last birds is superior to the nightingale or the lark, though, in general, the American birds are less musical than those of Europe.

for here she has not passed, light and little as her footstep would be."

Heyward drew back, all his ardour to proceed seeming to vanish on the instant. Without attending to this sudden change in the other's humour, the scout, after musing a moment, continued—

"There is no woman in this wilderness could leave such a print as that, but the dark-hair, or her sister! We know that the first has been here, but where are the signs of the other? Let us push deeper on the trail, and if nothing offers, we must go back to the plain, and strike another scent. Move on, Uncas, and keep your eyes on the dried leaves. I will watch the bushes, while your father shall run with a low nose to the ground. Move on, friends; the sun is getting behind the hills."

"Is there nothing that I can do?" demanded the anxious Heyward.

"You!" repeated the scout, who, with his red friends, was already advancing in the order he had prescribed; "yes, you can keep in our rear, and be careful not to cross the trail."

Before they had proceeded many rods, the Indians stopped, and appeared to gaze at some signs on the earth, with more than their usual keenness. Both father and son spoke quick and loud, now looking at the object of their mutual admiration, and now regarding each other with the most unequivocal pleasure.

"They have found the little foot!" exclaimed the scout, moving forward, without attending further to his own portion of the duty. "What have we here! An ambushment has been planted in the spot! No, by the truest rifle on the frontiers, here have been them one-sided horses again! Now the whole secret is out, and all is plain as the north star at midnight. Yes, here they have mounted. There the beasts have been bound to a sapling, in waiting; and yonder runs the broad path away to the north, in full sweep for the Canadas."

"But still there are no signs of Alice—of the younger Miss Munro," said Duncan.

"Unless the shining bauble Uncas has just lifted from the ground, should prove one. Pass it this way, lad, that we may look at it."

Heyward instantly knew it for a trinket, that Alice was fond of wearing, and which he recollected, with the tenacious memory of a lover, to have seen on the fatal morning of the massacre, dangling from the fair neck of his mistress. He seized the highly prized jewel, and as he proclaimed the fact, it vanished from the eyes of the wondering scout, who in vain looked for it on the ground, long after it was warmly pressed against the beating heart of Duncan.

"Pshaw!" said the disappointed Hawk-eye, ceasing to rake the leaves with the breech of his rifle; " 'tis a certain sign of age, when the sight begins to weaken. Such a glittering gewgaw, and not to be seen! Well, well, I can squint along a clouded barrel yet, and that is enough to settle all disputes between me and the Mingoes. I should like to find the thing too, if it were only to carry it to the right owner, and that would be bringing the two ends of what I call a long trail together—for by this time the broad St. Lawrence, or perhaps, the Great Lakes, themselves, are atwixt us."

"So much the more reason why we should not delay our march," returned Heyward; "let us proceed."

"Young blood and hot blood, they say, are much the same thing. We are not about to start on a squirrel hunt, or to drive a deer into the Horican, but to outlie for days and nights, and to stretch across a wilderness where the feet of men seldom go, and where no bookish knowledge would carry you through, harmless. An Indian never starts on such an expedition without smoking over his council fire; and though a man of white blood, I honour their customs in this particular, seeing that they are deliberate and wise. We will, therefore, go back, and light our fire to night in the ruins of the old fort, and in the morning we shall be fresh, and ready to undertake our work like men, and not like babbling women, or eager boys."

Heyward saw, by the manner of the scout, that altercation would be useless. Munro had again sunk into that sort of apathy which had beset him since his late overwhelming misfortunes, and from which he was, apparently, to be roused only by some new and powerful excitement. Making a merit of necessity, the young man took the veteran by the arm, and followed in the footsteps of the Indians and the scout, who had already begun to retrace the path which conducted them to the plain.

Chapter XIX

Salar. "Why, I am sure, if he forfeit, thou wilt not take his flesh; what's that good for?"

Shy. "To bait fish withal: if it will feed nothing else, it will feed my revenge."

The Merchant of Venice, III.i.51–54.

THE SHADES OF EVENING had come to increase the dreariness of the place, when the party entered the ruins of William Henry. The scout and his companions immediately made their preparations to pass the night there; but with an earnestness and sobriety of demeanour, that betrayed how much the unusual horrors they had just witnessed, worked on even their practised feelings. A few fragments of rafters were reared against a blackened wall; and when Uncas had covered them slightly with brush, the temporary accommodations were deemed sufficient. The young Indian pointed toward his rude hut, when his labour was ended; and Heyward, who understood the meaning of the silent gesture, gently urged Munro to enter. Leaving the bereaved old man alone with his sorrows, Duncan immediately returned into the open air, too much excited himself to seek the repose he had recommended to his veteran friend.

While Hawk-eye and the Indians lighted their fire, and took their evening's repast, a frugal meal of dried bear's meat, the young man paid a visit to that curtain of the dilapidated fort, which looked out on the sheet of the Horican. The wind had fallen, and the waves were already rolling on the sandy beach beneath him, in a more regular and tempered succession. The clouds, as if tired of their furious chase, were breaking asunder; the heavier volumes, gathering in black masses about the horizon, while the lighter scud still hurried above the water, or eddied among the tops of the mountains, like broken flights of birds, hovering around their roosts. Here and there, a red and fiery star struggled through the drifting vapour, furnishing a lurid gleam of brightness to the dull aspect of the heavens. Within the bosom of the encircling hills, an impenetrable darkness had already settled, and the plain lay like a vast and deserted charnel-house, without omen or whisper, to disturb the slumbers of its numerous and hapless tenants.

Of this scene, so chillingly in accordance with the past, Duncan stood, for many minutes, a rapt observer. His eyes wandered from the bosom of the mound, where the foresters were seated around their glimmering fire, to the fainter light, which still lingered in the skies, and then rested long and anxiously on the embodied gloom, which lay like a dreary void on that side of him where the dead reposed. He soon fancied that inexplicable sounds arose from the place, though so indistinct and stolen, as to render not only their nature, but even their existence, uncertain. Ashamed of his apprehensions, the young man turned towards the water, and strove to divert his attention to the mimic stars, that dimly glimmered on its moving surface. Still, his too conscious ears performed their ungrateful duty, as if to warn him of some lurking danger. At length, a swift trampling seemed, quite audibly, to rush athwart the darkness. Unable any longer to quiet his uneasiness, Duncan spoke in a low voice to the scout, requesting him to ascend the mound, to the place where he stood. Hawk-eye threw his rifle across an arm, and complied, but with an air so unmoved and calm, as to prove how much he accounted on the security of their position.

"Listen," said Duncan, when the other had placed himself deliberately at his elbow; "there are suppressed noises on the plain, which may show that Montcalm has not yet entirely deserted his conquest."

"Then ears are better than eyes," said the undisturbed scout, who having just deposited a portion of a bear between his grinders, spoke thick and slow, like one whose mouth was doubly occupied; "I, myself, saw him caged in Ty, with all his host; for your Frenchers, when they have done a clever thing, like to get back, and have a dance, or a merry-making, with the women, over their success."

"I know not. An Indian seldom sleeps in war, and plunder may keep a Huron here, after his tribe has departed. It would be well to extinguish the fire, and have a watch—Listen! you hear the noise I mean!"

"An Indian more rarely lurks about the graves. Though

ready to slay, and not over regardful of the means, he is commonly content with the scalp, unless when blood is hot, and temper up; but after the spirit is once fairly gone, he forgets his enmity, and is willing to let the dead find their natural rest. Speaking of spirits, major, are you of opinion that the heaven of a red-skin, and of us whites, will be one and the same?"

"No doubt—no doubt. I thought I heard it again! or was it the rustling of the leaves in the top of the beech?"

"For my own part," continued Hawk-eye, turning his face, for a moment, in the direction indicated by Heyward, but with a vacant and careless manner, "I believe that paradise is ordained for happiness; and that men will be indulged in it according to their dispositions and gifts. I therefore judge, that a red-skin is not far from the truth, when he believes he is to find them glorious hunting grounds of which his traditions tell; nor, for that matter, do I think it would be any disparagement to a man without a cross, to pass his time—"

"You hear it again!" interrupted Duncan.

"Ay, ay; when food is scarce, and when food is plenty, a wolf grows bold," said the unmoved scout. "There would be picking, too, among the skins of the devils, if there was light and time for the sport! But, concerning the life that is to come, major. I have heard preachers say, in the settlements, that heaven was a place of rest. Now men's minds differ as to their ideas of enjoyment. For myself, and I say it with reverence to the ordering of Providence, it would be no great indulgence to be kept shut up in those mansions of which they preach, having a natural longing for motion and the chase."

Duncan, who was now made to understand the nature of the noises he had heard, answered, with more attention to the subject which the humour of the scout had chosen for discussion, by saying—

"It is difficult to account for the feelings that may attend the last great change."

"It would be a change indeed, for a man who has passed his days in the open air," returned the single-minded scout; "and who has so often broken his fast on the head waters of the Hudson, to sleep within sound of the roaring Mohawk! But it is a comfort to know we serve a merciful Master, though we do it each after his fashion, and with great tracts of wilderness atween us—What goes there?"

"Is it not the rushing of the wolves you have mentioned?"

Hawk-eye slowly shook his head, and beckoned for Duncan to follow him to a spot, to which the glare from the fire did not extend. When he had taken this precaution, the scout placed himself in an attitude of intense attention, and listened, long and keenly, for a repetition of the low sound that had so unexpectedly startled him. His vigilance, however, seemed exercised in vain; for, after a fruitless pause, he whispered to Duncan—

"We must give a call to Uncas. The boy has Indian senses, and may hear what is hid from us; for, being a white-skin, I will not deny my nature."

The young Mohican, who was conversing in a low voice with his father, started as he heard the moaning of an owl, and springing on his feet, he looked toward the black mounds, as if seeking the place whence the sounds proceeded. The scout repeated the call, and in a few moments, Duncan saw the figure of Uncas stealing cautiously along the rampart, to the spot where they stood.

Hawk-eye explained his wishes in a very few words, which were spoken in the Delaware tongue. So soon as Uncas was in possession of the reason why he was summoned, he threw himself flat on the turf; where, to the eyes of Duncan, he appeared to lie quiet and motionless. Surprised at the immovable attitude of the young warrior, and curious to observe the manner in which he employed his faculties to obtain the desired information, Heyward advanced a few steps, and bent over the dark object, on which he had kept his eyes riveted. Then it was he discovered that the form of Uncas had vanished, and that he beheld only the dark outline of an inequality in the embankment.

"What has become of the Mohican?" he demanded of the scout, stepping back in amazement; "it was here that I saw him fall, and I could have sworn that here he yet remained!"

"Hist! speak lower; for we know not what ears are open, and the Mingoes are a quick-witted breed. As for Uncas, he is out on the plain, and the Maquas, if any such are about us, will find their equal."

"You think that Montcalm has not called off all his Indians! Let us give the alarm to our companions, that we may stand to our arms. Here are five of us, who are not unused to meet an enemy."

"Not a word to either, as you value life! Look at the Sagamore, how like a grand Indian chief he sits by the fire! If there are any skulkers out in the darkness, they will never discover, by his countenance, that we suspect danger at hand!"

"But they may discover him, and it will prove his death. His person can be too plainly seen by the light of that fire, and he will become the first and most certain victim!"

"It is undeniable, that now you speak the truth," returned the scout, betraying more anxiety in his manner than was usual; "yet what can be done! A single suspicious look might bring on an attack before we are ready to receive it. He knows, by the call I gave to Uncas, that we have struck a scent; I will tell him that we are on the trail of the Mingoes; his Indian nature will teach him how to act."

The scout applied his fingers to his mouth, and raised a low hissing sound, that caused Duncan, at first, to start aside, believing that he heard a serpent. The head of Chingachgook was resting on a hand, as he sat musing by himself; but the moment he heard the warning of the animal whose name he bore, it arose to an upright position, and his dark eyes glanced swiftly and keenly on every side of him. With this sudden and perhaps involuntary movement, every appearance of surprise or alarm ended. His rifle lay untouched, and apparently unnoticed, within reach of his hand. The tomahawk that he had loosened in his belt, for the sake of ease, was even suffered to fall from its usual situation to the ground, and his form seemed to sink, like that of a man whose nerves and sinews were suffered to relax for the purpose of rest. Cunningly resuming his former position, though with a change of hands, as if the movement had been made merely to relieve the limb, the native awaited the result with a calmness and fortitude, that none but an Indian warrior would have known how to exercise.

But Heyward saw, that while to a less instructed eye the Mohican chief appeared to slumber, his nostrils were expanded, his head was turned a little to one side, as if to assist the organs of hearing, and that his quick and rapid glances ran incessantly over every object within the power of his vision.

"See the noble fellow!" whispered Hawk-eye, pressing the arm of Heyward; "he knows that a look, or a motion, might disconsart our schemes, and put us at the mercy of them imps—"

He was interrupted by the flash and report of a rifle. The air was filled with sparks of fire, around that spot where the eyes of Heyward were still fastened, with admiration and wonder. A second look told him, that Chingachgook had disappeared in the confusion. In the mean time, the scout had thrown forward his rifle, like one prepared for service, and awaited, impatiently, the moment, when an enemy might rise to view. But with the solitary and fruitless attempt made on the life of Chingachgook, the attack appeared to have terminated. Once or twice the listeners thought they could distinguish the distant rustling of bushes, as bodies of some unknown description rushed through them; nor was it long before Hawk-eye pointed out the "scampering of the wolves," as they fled precipitately before the passage of some intruder on their proper domains. After an impatient and breathless pause, a plunge was heard in the water, and it was immediately followed by the report of another rifle.

"There goes Uncas!" said the scout; "the boy bears a smart piece! I know its crack, as well as a father knows the language of his child, for I carried the gun myself until a better offered."

"What can this mean!" demanded Duncan; "we are watched, and, as it would seem, marked for destruction."

"Yonder scattered brand can witness that no good was intended, and this Indian will testify that no harm has been done," returned the scout, dropping his rifle across his arm again, and following Chingachgook, who just then re-appeared within the circle of light, into the bosom of the works. "How is it, Sagamore! Are the Mingoes upon us in earnest, or is it only one of those reptyles who hang upon the skirts of a war party, to scalp the dead, go in, and make their boast among the squaws of the valiant deeds done on the pale-faces!"

Chingachgook very quietly resumed his seat, nor did he make any reply, until after he had examined the firebrand which had been struck by the bullet, that had nearly proved fatal to himself. After which, he was content to reply, holding a single finger up to view, with the English monosyllable—

"One."

"I thought as much," returned Hawk-eye, seating himself; "and as he had got the cover of the lake afore Uncas pulled upon him, it is more than probable the knave will sing his lies about some great ambushment, in which he was outlying on the trail of two Mohicans and a white hunter—for the officers can be considered as little better than idlers in such a skrimmage. Well, let him—let him. There are always some honest men in every nation, though heaven knows, too, that they are scarce among the Maquas, to look down an upstart when he brags ag'in the face of reason! The varlet sent his lead within whistle of your ears, Sagamore."

Chingachgook turned a calm and incurious eye towards the place where the ball had struck, and then resumed his former attitude, with a composure that could not be disturbed by so trifling an incident. Just then Uncas glided into the circle, and seated himself at the fire, with the same appearance of indifference as was maintained by his father.

Of these several movements, Heyward was a deeply interested and wondering observer. It appeared to him as though the foresters had some secret means of intelligence, which had escaped the vigilance of his own faculties. In place of that eager and garrulous narration, with which a white youth would have endeavoured to communicate, and perhaps exaggerate, that which had passed out in the darkness of the plain, the young warrior was seemingly content to let his deeds speak for themselves. It was, in fact, neither the moment nor the occasion for an Indian to boast of his exploits; and it is probable, that had Heyward neglected to inquire, not another syllable would, just then, have been uttered on the subject.

"What has become of our enemy, Uncas?" demanded Duncan; "we heard your rifle, and hoped you had not fired in vain."

The young chief removed a fold of his hunting shirt, and quietly exposed the fatal tuft of hair, which he bore as the symbol of victory. Chingachgook laid his hand on the scalp, and considered it for a moment with deep attention. Then dropping it, with disgust depicted in his strong features, he ejaculated—

"Oneida!"

"Oneida!" repeated the scout, who was fast losing his interest in the scene, in an apathy nearly assimilated to that of his red associates, but who now advanced with uncommon earnestness to regard the bloody badge. "By the Lord, if the Oneidas are outlying upon our trail, we shall be flanked by devils on every side of us! Now, to white eyes there is no difference between this bit of skin and that of any other Indian, and yet the Sagamore declares it came from the poll of a Mingo; nay, he even names the tribe of the poor devil, with as much ease as if the scalp was the leaf of a book, and each hair a letter. What right have christian whites to boast of their learning, when a savage can read a language, that would prove too much for the wisest of them all! What say *you*, lad; of what people was the knave?"

Uncas raised his eyes to the face of the scout, and answered, in his soft voice—

"Oneida."

"Oneida again! when one Indian makes a declaration it is commonly true; but when he is supported by his people, set it down as gospel!"

"The poor fellow has mistaken us for French!" said Heyward, "or he would not have attempted the life of a friend."

"He mistake a Mohican, in his paint, for a Huron! You would be as likely to mistake them white coated grenadiers of Montcalm, for the scarlet jackets of the 'Royal Americans,' " returned the scout. "No, no, the sarpent knew his errand; nor was there any great mistake in the matter, for there is but little love atween a Delaware and a Mingo, let their tribes go out to fight for whom they may, in a white quarrel. For that matter, though the Oneidas do serve his sacred majesty, who is my own sovereign lord and master, I should not have deliberated long about letting off 'killdeer' at the imp myself, had luck thrown him in my way."

"That would have been an abuse of our treaties, and unworthy of your character."

"When a man consorts much with a people," continued Hawk-eye, "if they are honest, and he no knave, love will grow up atwixt them. It is true, that white cunning has managed to throw the tribes into great confusion, as respects friends and enemies; so that the Hurons and the Oneidas, who speak the same tongue, or what may be called the same, take each other's scalps, and the Delawares are divided among themselves; a few hanging about their great council fire, on their own river, and fighting on the same side with the Mingoes, while the greater part are in the Canadas, out of natural enmity to the Maquas—thus throwing every thing into disorder, and destroying all the harmony of warfare. Yet a red natur is not likely to alter with every shift of policy! so that the love atwixt a Mohican and a Mingo is much like the regard between a white man and a sarpent."

"I regret to hear it; for I had believed, those natives who dwelt within our boundaries had found us too just and liberal, not to identify themselves, fully, with our quarrels."

"Why, I believe it is natur to give a preference to one's own quarrels before those of strangers. Now, for myself, I do love justice; and therefore—I will not say I hate a Mingo, for that may be unsuitable to my colour and my religion—though I will just repeat, it may have been owing to the night that 'killdeer' had no hand in the death of this skulking Oneida."

Then, as if satisfied with the force of his own reasons, whatever might be their effect on the opinions of the other disputant, the honest but implacable woodsman turned from the fire, content to let the controversy slumber. Heyward withdrew to the rampart, too uneasy and too little accustomed to the warfare of the woods, to remain at ease under the possibility of such insidious attacks. Not so, however, with the scout and the Mohicans. Those acute and long practised senses, whose powers so often exceed the limits of all ordinary credulity, after having detected the danger, had enabled them to ascertain its magnitude and duration. Not one of the three appeared in the least to doubt their perfect security, as was indicated by the preparations that were soon made, to sit in council over their future proceedings.

The confusion of nations, and even of tribes, to which Hawk-eye alluded, existed at that period in the fullest force.

The great tie of language, and, of course, of a common origin, was severed in many places; and it was one of its consequences that the Delaware and the Mingo, (as the people of the Six Nations were called,) were found fighting in the same ranks, while the latter sought the scalp of the Huron, though believed to be the root of his own stock. The Delawares were even divided among themselves. Though love for the soil which had belonged to his ancestors, kept the Sagamore of the Mohicans, with a small band of followers who were serving at Edward, under the banners of the English king, by far the largest portion of his nation were known to be in the field as allies of Montcalm. The reader probably knows, if enough has not already been gleaned from this narrative, that the Delaware, or Lenape, claimed to be the progenitors of that numerous people, who once were masters of most of the eastern and northern states of America, of whom the community of the Mohicans was an ancient and highly honoured member.

It was, of course, with a perfect understanding of the minute and intricate interests, which had armed friend against friend, and brought natural enemies to combat by each other's side, that the scout and his companions now disposed themselves to deliberate on the measures that were to govern their future movements, amid so many jarring and savage races of men. Duncan knew enough of Indian customs, to understand the reason that the fire was replenished, and why the warriors, not excepting Hawk-eye, took their seats within the curl of its smoke, with so much gravity and decorum. Placing himself at an angle of the works, where he might be a spectator of the scene within, while he kept a watchful eye against any danger from without, he awaited the result, with as much patience as he could summon.

After a short and impressive pause, Chingachgook lighted a pipe, whose bowl was curiously carved in one of the soft stones of the country, and whose stem was a tube of wood, and commenced smoking. When he had inhaled enough of the fragrance of the soothing weed, he passed the instrument into the hands of the scout. In this manner the pipe had made its rounds three several times, amid the most profound silence, before either of the party opened his lips. Then the Sagamore, as the oldest and highest in rank, in a few calm and dignified words, proposed the subject for deliberation. He was answered by the scout; and Chingachgook rejoined, when the other objected to his opinions. But the youthful Uncas continued a silent and respectful listener, until Hawk-eye, in complaisance, demanded his opinion. Heyward gathered from the manners of the different speakers, that the father and son espoused one side of a disputed question, while the white man maintained the other. The contest gradually grew warmer, until it was quite evident the feelings of the speakers began to be somewhat enlisted in the debate.

Notwithstanding the increasing warmth of the amicable contest, the most decorous christian assembly, not even excepting those in which its reverend ministers are collected, might have learned a wholesome lesson of moderation from the forbearance and courtesy of the disputants. The words of Uncas were received with the same deep attention as those which fell from the maturer wisdom of his father; and so far from manifesting any impatience, neither spoke, in reply, until a few moments of silent meditation were, seemingly, bestowed in deliberating on what had already been said.

The language of the Mohicans was accompanied by gestures so direct and natural, that Heyward had but little difficulty in following the thread of their argument. On the other hand, the scout was obscure; because, from the lingering pride of colour, he rather affected the cold and inartificial manner, which characterizes all classes of Anglo-Americans, when unexcited. By the frequency with which the Indians described the marks of a forest trail, it was evident they urged a pursuit by land, while the repeated sweep of Hawk-eye's arm toward the Horican, denoted that he was for a passage across its waters.

The latter was, to every appearance, fast losing ground, and the point was about to be decided against him, when he arose to his feet, and shaking off his apathy, he suddenly assumed the manner of an Indian, and adopted all the arts of native eloquence. Elevating an arm, he pointed out the track of the sun, repeating the gesture for every day that was necessary to accomplish their object. Then he delineated a long and painful path, amid rocks and water courses. The age and weakness of the slumbering and unconscious Munro, were indicated by signs too palpable to be mistaken. Duncan perceived that even his own powers were spoken lightly of, as the scout extended his palm, and mentioned him by the appellation of the "open hand;" a name his liberality had purchased of all the friendly tribes. Then came the representation of the light and graceful movements of a canoe, set in forcible contrast to the tottering steps of one enfeebled and tired. He concluded by pointing to the scalp of the Oneida, and apparently urging the necessity of their departing speedily, and in a manner that should leave no trail.

The Mohicans listened gravely, and with countenances that reflected the sentiments of the speaker. Conviction gradually wrought its influence, and towards the close of Hawk-eye's speech, his sentences were accompanied by the customary exclamation of commendation. In short, Uncas and his father became converts to his way of thinking, abandoning their own previously expressed opinions, with a liberality and candour, that, had they been the representatives of some great and civilized people, would have infallibly worked their political ruin, by destroying, for ever, their reputation for consistency.

The instant the matter in discussion was decided, the debate, and every thing connected with it, except the result, appeared to be forgotten. Hawk-eye, without looking round to read his triumph in applauding eyes, very composedly stretched his tall frame before the dying embers, and closed his own organs in sleep.

Left now in a measure to themselves, the Mohicans, whose time had been so much devoted to the interests of others, seized the moment to devote some attention to themselves. Casting off, at once, the grave and austere demeanour of an Indian chief, Chingachgook commenced speaking to his son in the soft and playful tones of affection. Uncas gladly met the familiar air of his father, and before the hard breathing of the scout announced that he slept, a complete change was effected in the manner of his two associates.

It is impossible to describe the music of their language, while thus engaged in laughter and endearments, in such a way as to render it intelligible to those whose ears have never listened to its melody. The compass of their voices, particularly that of the youth, was wonderful; extending from the deepest bass, to tones that were even feminine in softness. The eyes of the father followed the plastic and ingenious movements of the son with open delight, and he never failed to smile in reply to the other's contagious, but low laughter. While under the influence of these gentle and natural feelings, no trace of ferocity was to be seen in the softened features of the Sagamore. His figured panoply of death looked more like a disguise assumed in mockery, than a fierce annunciation of a desire to carry destruction and desolation in his footsteps.

After an hour passed in the indulgence of their better feelings, Chingachgook abruptly announced his desire to sleep, by wrapping his head in his blanket, and stretching his form on the naked earth. The merriment of Uncas instantly ceased; and carefully raking the coals, in such a manner that they should impart their warmth to his father's feet, the youth sought his own pillow among the ruins of the place.

Imbibing renewed confidence from the security of these experienced foresters, Heyward soon imitated their example; and long before the night had turned, they who lay in the bosom of the ruined work, seemed to slumber as heavily as the unconscious multitude, whose bones were already beginning to bleach, on the surrounding plain.

Chapter XX

> "Land of Albania! let me bend mine eyes
> On thee, thou rugged nurse of savage men!"
> Byron, *Childe Harold's Pilgrimage*,
> Canto II, Stanza xxxii. 5–6.

THE HEAVENS were still studded with stars, when Hawk-eye came to arouse the sleepers. Casting aside their cloaks, Munro and Heyward were on their feet, while the woodsman was still making his low calls, at the entrance of the rude shelter where they had passed the night. When they issued from beneath its concealment, they found the scout awaiting their appearance nigh by, and the only salutation between them was the significant gesture for silence, made by their sagacious leader.

"Think over your prayers," he whispered, as they approached him; "for he, to whom you make them, knows all tongues; that of the heart, as well as those of the mouth. But speak not a syllable; it is rare for a white voice to pitch itself properly in the woods, as we have seen by the example of that miserable devil, the singer. Come," he continued, turning towards a curtain of the works; "let us get into the ditch on this side, and be regardful to step on the stones and fragments of wood as you go."

His companions complied, though to two of them the reasons of this extraordinary precaution were yet a mystery. When they were in the low cavity, that surrounded the earthen fort on three of its sides, they found the passage nearly choked by the ruins. With care and patience, however, they succeeded in clambering after the scout, until they reached the sandy shore of the Horican.

"That's a trail that nothing but a nose can follow," said the satisfied scout, looking back along their difficult way; "grass is a treacherous carpet for a flying party to tread on, but wood and stone take no print from a moccasin. Had you worn your armed boots, there might, indeed, have been something to fear! but with the deer-skin suitably prepared, a man may trust himself, generally, on rocks with safety. Shove in the canoe nigher to the land, Uncas; this sand will take a stamp as easily as the butter of the Jarmans on the Mohawk. Softly, lad, softly; it must not touch the beach, or the knaves will know by what road we have left the place."

The young man observed the precaution; and the scout, laying a board from the ruins to the canoe, made a sign for the two officers to enter. When this was done, every thing was studiously restored to its former disorder; and then Hawk-eye succeeded in reaching his little birchen vessel, without leaving behind him any of those marks which he appeared so much to dread. Heyward was silent, until the Indians had cautiously paddled the canoe some distance from the fort, and within the broad and dark shadow that fell from the eastern mountain, on the glassy surface of the lake; then he demanded—

"What need have we for this stolen and hurried departure?"

"If the blood of an Oneida could stain such a sheet of pure water as this we float on," returned the scout, "your two eyes would answer your own question. Have you forgotten the skulking reptyle that Uncas slew?"

"By no means. But he was said to be alone, and dead men give no cause for fear!"

"Ay, he was alone in his deviltry! but an Indian, whose tribe counts so many warriors, need seldom fear his blood will run, without the death-shriek coming speedily from some of his enemies."

"But our presence—the authority of Colonel Munro, would prove a sufficient protection against the anger of our allies, especially in a case where the wretch so well merited his fate. I trust, in Heaven, you have not deviated a single foot from the direct line of our course, with so slight a reason."

"Do you think the bullet of that varlet's rifle would have turned aside, though his sacred majesty the king had stood in its path!" returned the stubborn scout. "Why did not the grand Frencher, he who is captain general of the Canadas, bury the tomahawks of the Hurons, if a word from a white can work so strongly on the natur of an Indian?"

The reply of Heyward was interrupted by a groan from Munro; but after he had paused a moment, in deference to the sorrow of his aged friend, he resumed the subject.

"The Marquis of Montcalm can only settle that error with his God," said the young man, solemnly.

"Ay, ay, now there is reason in your words, for they are bottomed on religion and honesty. There is a vast difference between throwing a regiment of white coats atwixt the tribes and the prisoners, and coaxing an angry savage to forget he carries a knife and a rifle, with words that must begin with calling him 'your son.' No, no," continued the scout, looking back at the dim shore of William Henry, which was now fast receding, and laughing in his own silent but heartfelt manner; "I have put a trail of water atween us; and unless the imps can make friends with the fishes, and hear who has paddled across their basin, this fine morning, we shall throw the length of the Horican behind us, before they have made up their minds which path to take."

"With foes in front, and foes in our rear, our journey is like to be one of danger!"

"Danger!" repeated Hawk-eye, calmly; "no, not absolutely of danger; for, with vigilant ears and quick eyes, we can manage to keep a few hours ahead of the knaves; or, if we must try the rifle, there are three of us who understand its gifts as well as any you can name on the borders. No, not of danger; but that we shall have what you may call a brisk push of it, is probable; and it may happen, a brush, a skrimmage, or some such divarsion, but always where covers are good, and ammunition abundant."

It is possible that Heyward's estimate of danger differed in some degree from that of the scout, for, instead of replying, he now sat in silence, while the canoe glided over several miles of water. Just as the day dawned, they entered the narrows of the lake,* and stole swiftly and cautiously among their numberless little islands. It was by this road that Mont-

*The beauties of Lake George are well known to every American tourist. In the height of the mountains which surround it, and in artificial accessories, it is inferior to the finest of the Swiss and Italian lakes, while in outline and purity of water it is fully their equal; and in the number and disposition of its isles and islets much superior to them all together. There are said to be some hundreds of islands in a sheet of water, less than thirty miles long. The narrows which connect what may be called, in truth, two lakes, are crowded with islands to such a degree as to leave passages between them, frequently

calm had retired with his army, and the adventurers knew not but he had left some of his Indians in ambush, to protect the rear of his forces, and collect the stragglers. They, therefore, approached the passage with the customary silence of their guarded habits.

Chingachgook laid aside his paddle; while Uncas and the scout urged the light vessel through crooked and intricate channels, where every foot that they advanced exposed them to the danger of some sudden rising on their progress. The eyes of the Sagamore moved warily from islet to islet, and copse to copse, as the canoe proceeded; and when a clearer sheet of water permitted, his keen vision was bent along the bald rocks and impending forests, that frowned upon the narrow strait.

Heyward, who was a doubly interested spectator, as well from the beauties of the place as from the apprehension natural to his situation, was just believing that he had permitted the latter to be excited without sufficient reason, when the paddles ceased moving, in obedience to a signal from Chingachgook.

"Hugh!" exclaimed Uncas, nearly at the moment that the light tap his father had made on the side of the canoe, notified them of the vicinity of danger.

"What now?" asked the scout; "the lake is as smooth as if the winds had never blown, and I can see along its sheet for miles; there is not so much as the black head of a loon dotting the water!"

The Indian gravely raised his paddle, and pointed in the direction in which his own steady look was riveted. Duncan's eyes followed the motion. A few rods in their front lay another of the low wooded islets, but it appeared as calm and peaceful, as if its solitude had never been disturbed by the foot of man.

---

of only a few feet in width. The lake, itself, varies in breadth from one to three miles.

The state of New-York is remarkable for the number and beauty of its lakes. One of its frontiers lies on the vast sheet of Ontario, while Champlain stretches nearly a hundred miles along another. Oneida, Cayuga, Canandaigua, Seneca, and George, are all lakes of thirty miles in length, while those of a size smaller are without number. On most of these lakes, there are now beautiful villages, and on many of them steam-boats.

"I see nothing," he said, "but land and water; and a lovely scene it is!"

"Hist!" interrupted the scout. "Ay, Sagamore, there is always a reason for what you do! 'Tis but a shade, and yet it is not natural. You see the mist, major, that is rising above the island; you can't call it a fog, for it is more like a streak of thin cloud"—

"It is vapour from the water!"

"That a child could tell. But what is the edging of blacker smoke, that hangs along its lower side, and which you may trace down into the thicket of hazle? 'Tis from a fire; but one that, in my judgment, has been suffered to burn low."

"Let us then push for the place, and relieve our doubts," said the impatient Duncan; "the party must be small that can lie on such a bit of land."

"If you judge of Indian cunning by the rules you find in books, or by white sagacity, they will lead you astray, if not to your death," returned Hawk-eye, examining the signs of the place with that acuteness which distinguished him. "If I may be permitted to speak in this matter, it will be to say, that we have but two things to choose between: the one is, to return, and give up all thoughts of following the Hurons—"

"Never!" exclaimed Heyward, in a voice far too loud for their circumstances.

"Well, well," continued Hawk-eye, making a hasty sign to repress his impatience; "I am much of your mind myself; though I thought it becoming my experience to tell the whole. We must then make a push, and if the Indians or Frenchers are in the narrows, run the gauntlet through these topping mountains. Is there reason in my words, Sagamore?"

The Indian made no other answer than by dropping his paddle into the water, and urging forward the canoe. As he held the office of directing its course, his resolution was sufficiently indicated by the movement. The whole party now plied their paddles vigorously, and in a very few moments they had reached a point whence they might command an entire view of the northern shore of the island, the side that had hitherto been concealed.

"There they are, by all the truth of signs!" whispered the

scout; "two canoes and a smoke! The knaves have'nt yet got their eyes out of the mist, or, we should hear the accursed whoop. Together, friends—we are leaving them, and are already nearly out of whistle of a bullet."

The well known crack of a rifle, whose ball came skipping along the placid surface of the strait, and a shrill yell from the island, interrupted his speech, and announced that their passage was discovered. In another instant several savages were seen rushing into the canoes, which were soon dancing over the water, in pursuit. These fearful precursors of a coming struggle, produced no change in the countenances and movements of his three guides, so far as Duncan could discover, except that the strokes of their paddles were longer and more in unison, and caused the little bark to spring forward like a creature possessing life and volition.

"Hold them there, Sagamore," said Hawk-eye, looking coolly backward over his left shoulder, while he still plied his paddle; "keep them just there. Them Hurons have never a piece in their nation that will execute at this distance; but 'kill-deer' has a barrel on which a man may calculate."

The scout having ascertained that the Mohicans were sufficient of themselves to maintain the requisite distance, deliberately laid aside his paddle, and raised the fatal rifle. Three several times he brought the piece to his shoulder, and when his companions were expecting its report, he as often lowered it, to request the Indians would permit their enemies to approach a little nigher. At length, his accurate and fastidious eye seemed satisfied, and throwing out his left arm on the barrel, he was slowly elevating the muzzle, when an exclamation from Uncas, who sat in the bow, once more caused him to suspend the shot.

"What now, lad?" demanded Hawk-eye; "you saved a Huron from the death-shriek by that word; have you reason for what you do?"

Uncas pointed towards the rocky shore, a little in their front, whence another war canoe was darting directly across their course. It was too obvious, now, that their situation was imminently perilous, to need the aid of language to confirm it. The scout laid aside his rifle, and resumed the paddle, while Chingachgook inclined the bows of the canoe a little towards the western shore, in order to increase the distance between them and this new enemy. In the mean time, they were reminded of the presence of those who pressed upon their rear, by wild and exulting shouts. The stirring scene awakened even Munro from his apathy.

"Let us make for the rocks on the main," he said, with the mien of a tried soldier, "and give battle to the savages. God forbid that I, or those attached to me and mine, should ever trust again to the faith of any servant of the Louises!"

"He who wishes to prosper in Indian warfare," returned the scout, "must not be too proud to learn from the wit of a native. Lay her more along the land, Sagamore; we are doubling on the varlets, and perhaps they may try to strike our trail on the long calculation."

Hawk-eye was not mistaken; for, when the Hurons found their course was likely to throw them behind their chase, they rendered it less direct, until by gradually bearing more and more obliquely, the two canoes were, ere long, gliding on parallel lines, within two hundred yards of each other. It now became entirely a trial of speed. So rapid was the progress of the light vessels, that the lake curled in their front, in miniature waves, and their motion became undulating by its own velocity. It was, perhaps, owing to this circumstance, in addition to the necessity of keeping every hand employed at the paddles, that the Hurons had not immediate recourse to their fire-arms. The exertions of the fugitives were too severe to continue long, and the pursuers had the advantage of numbers. Duncan observed, with uneasiness, that the scout began to look anxiously about him, as if searching for some further means of assisting their flight.

"Edge her a little more from the sun, Sagamore," said the stubborn woodsman; "I see the knaves are sparing a man to the rifle. A single broken bone might lose us our scalps. Edge more from the sun, and we will put the island between us."

The expedient was not without its use. A long, low island lay at a little distance before them, and as they closed with it, the chasing canoe was compelled to take a side opposite to that on which the pursued passed. The scout and his companions did not neglect this advantage, but the instant they were hid from observation by the bushes, they redoubled efforts that before had seemed prodigious. The two canoes came round the last low point, like two coursers at the top of their speed, the fugitives taking the lead. This change had brought them nigher to each other, however, while it altered their relative positions.

"You showed knowledge in the shaping of birchen bark, Uncas, when you chose this from among the Huron canoes," said the scout, smiling, apparently, more in satisfaction at their superiority in the race, than from that prospect of final escape, which now began to open a little upon them. "The imps have put all their strength again at the paddles, and we are to struggle for our scalps with bits of flattened wood, instead of clouded barrels and true eyes! A long stroke, and together, friends."

"They are preparing for a shot," said Heyward; "and as we are in a line with them, it can scarcely fail."

"Get you then into the bottom of the canoe," returned the scout; "you and the colonel; it will be so much taken from the size of the mark."

Heyward smiled, as he answered—

"It would be but an ill example for the highest in rank to dodge, while the warriors were under fire!"

"Lord! Lord! that is now a white man's courage!" exclaimed the scout; "and like too many of his notions, not to be maintained by reason. Do you think the Sagamore, or Uncas, or even I, who am a man without a cross, would deliberate about finding a cover in a skrimmage, when an open body would do no good! For what have the Frenchers reared up their Quebec, if fighting is always to be done in the clearings?"

"All that you say is very true, my friend," replied Heyward; "still, our customs must prevent us from doing as you wish."

A volley from the Hurons interrupted the discourse, and as the bullets whistled about them, Duncan saw the head of Uncas turned, looking back at himself and Munro. Notwithstanding the nearness of the enemy, and his own great personal danger, the countenance of the young warrior expressed no other emotion, as the former was compelled to think, than amazement at finding men willing to encounter so useless an exposure. Chingachgook was probably better acquainted with the notions of white men, for he did not even cast a glance aside from the riveted look his eye maintained on the object, by which he governed their course. A ball soon struck the light and polished paddle from the hands of the chief, and drove it through the air far in the advance. A shout arose from the Hurons, who seized the opportunity to fire another volley. Uncas described an arc in the water with his own blade, and as the canoe passed swiftly on, Chingachgook recovered his paddle, and flourishing it on high, he gave the war-whoop of the Mohicans, and then lent his strength and skill, again, to the important task.

The clamorous sounds of "le Gros Serpent," "la Longue Carabine," "le Cerf Agile," burst at once from the canoes behind, and seemed to give new zeal to the pursuers. The scout seized "kill-deer" in his left hand, and elevating it above his head, he shook it in triumph at his enemies. The savages answered the insult with a yell, and immediately another volley succeeded. The bullets pattered along the lake, and one even pierced the bark of their little vessel. No perceptible emotion could be discovered in the Mohicans during this critical moment, their rigid features expressing neither hope nor alarm; but the scout again turned his head, and laughing in his own silent manner, he said to Heyward—

"The knaves love to hear the sounds of their pieces; but the eye is not to be found among the Mingoes that can calculate a true range in a dancing canoe! You see the dumb devils have taken off a man to charge, and by the smallest measurement that can be allowed, we move three feet to their two!"

Duncan, who was not altogether as easy under this nice estimate of distances as his companions, was glad to find, however, that owing to their superior dexterity, and the diversion among their enemies, they were very sensibly obtaining the advantage. The Hurons soon fired again, and a bullet struck the blade of Hawk-eye's paddle without injury.

"That will do," said the scout, examining the slight indentation with a curious eye; "it would not have cut the skin of an infant, much less of men, who, like us, have been blown upon by the Heavens in their anger. Now, major, if you will try to use this piece of flattened wood, I'll let 'kill-deer' take a part in the conversation."

Heyward seized the paddle, and applied himself to the work with an eagerness that supplied the place of skill, while Hawk-eye was engaged in inspecting the priming of his rifle. The latter then took a swift aim, and fired. The Huron in the bows of the leading canoe had risen with a similar object, and he now fell backward, suffering his gun to escape from his hands into the water. In an instant, however, he recovered his feet, though his gestures were wild and bewildered. At the same moment his companions suspended their efforts, and the chasing canoes clustered together, and became stationary. Chingachgook and Uncas profited by the interval to regain their wind, though Duncan continued to work with the most persevering industry. The father and son now cast calm but inquiring glances at each other, to learn if either had sustained any injury by the fire; for both well knew that no cry or exclamation would, in such a moment of necessity, have been permitted to betray the accident. A few large drops of blood were trickling down the shoulder of the Sagamore, who, when he perceived that the eyes of Uncas dwelt too long on the sight, raised some water in the hollow of his hand, and washing off the stain, was content to manifest, in this simple manner, the slightness of the injury.

"Softly, softly, major," said the scout, who by this time had reloaded his rifle; " we are a little too far already for a rifle to put forth its beauties, and you see yonder imps are holding a council. Let them come up within striking distance—my eye may well be trusted in such a matter—and I will trail the varlets the length of the Horican, guaranteeing that not a shot of theirs shall, at the worst, more than break the skin, while 'kill-deer' shall touch the life twice in three times."

"We forget our errand," returned the diligent Duncan. "For God's sake, let us profit by this advantage, and increase our distance from the enemy."

"Give me my children," said Munro, hoarsely; "trifle no longer with a father's agony, but restore me my babes!"

Long and habitual deference to the mandates of his superiors, had taught the scout the virtue of obedience. Throwing a last and lingering glance at the distant canoes, he laid aside his rifle, and relieving the wearied Duncan, resumed the paddle, which he wielded with sinews that never tired. His efforts were seconded by those of the Mohicans, and a very few minutes served to place such a sheet of water between them and their enemies, that Heyward once more breathed freely.

The lake now began to expand, and their route lay along a wide reach, that was lined, as before, by high and ragged mountains. But the islands were few, and easily avoided. The strokes of the paddles grew more measured and regular, while they who plied them continued their labour, after the close and deadly chase from which they had just relieved themselves, with as much coolness as though their speed had been tried in sport, rather than under such pressing, nay, almost desperate, circumstances.

Instead of following the western shore, whither their errand led them, the wary Mohican inclined his course more towards those hills, behind which, Montcalm was known to have led his army into the formidable fortress of Ticonderoga. As the Hurons, to every appearance, had abandoned the pursuit, there was no apparent reason for this excess of caution. It was, however, maintained for hours, until they had reached a bay, nigh the northern termination of the lake. Here the canoe was driven upon the beach, and the whole party landed. Hawk-eye and Heyward ascended an adjacent bluff, where the former, after considering the expanse of water beneath him, pointed out to the latter a small black object, hovering under a head-land, at the distance of several miles.

"Do you see it?" demanded the scout. "Now, what would you account that spot, were you left alone to white experience to find your way through this wilderness?"

"But for its distance and its magnitude, I should suppose it a bird. Can it be a living object?"

" 'Tis a canoe of good birchen bark, and paddled by fierce and crafty Mingoes! Though Providence has lent to those who inhabit the woods eyes that would be needless to men in the settlements, where there are inventions to assist the sight, yet no human organs can see all the dangers which at this moment circumvent us. These varlets pretend to be bent chiefly on their sun-down meal, but the moment it is dark, they will be on our trail, as true as hounds on the scent. We must throw them off, or our pursuit of le Renard Subtil may be given up. These lakes are useful at times, especially when the game takes the water," continued the scout, gazing about him with a countenance of concern, "but they give no cover, except it be to the fishes. God knows what the country would be, if the settlements should ever spread far from the two rivers. Both hunting and war would lose their beauty."

"Let us not delay a moment, without some good and obvious cause."

"I little like that smoke, which you may see worming up along the rock above the canoe," interrupted the abstracted scout. "My life on it, other eyes than ours see it, and know its meaning! Well, words will not mend the matter, and it is time that we were doing."

Hawk-eye moved away from the look out, and descended, musing profoundly, to the shore. He communicated the result of his observations to his companions, in Delaware, and a short and earnest consultation succeeded. When it terminated, the three instantly set about executing their new resolutions.

The canoe was lifted from the water, and borne on the shoulders of the party. They proceeded into the wood, making as broad and obvious a trail as possible. They soon reached a water-course, which they crossed, and continued onward, until they came to an extensive and naked rock. At this point, where their footsteps might be expected to be no longer visible, they retraced their route to the brook, walking backwards, with the utmost care. They now followed the bed of the little stream to the lake, into which they immediately launched their canoe again. A low point concealed them from the head land, and the margin of the lake was fringed for some distance with dense and overhanging bushes. Under the cover of these natural advantages, they toiled their way, with patient industry, until the scout pronounced that he believed it would be safe once more to land.

The halt continued until evening rendered objects indistinct and uncertain to the eye. Then they resumed their route, and, favoured by the darkness, pushed silently and vigorously toward the western shore. Although the rugged outline of mountain, to which they were steering, presented no distinctive marks to the eyes of Duncan, the Mohican entered the little haven he had selected with the confidence and accuracy of an experienced pilot.

The boat was again lifted, and borne into the woods, where it was carefully concealed under a pile of brush. The adventurers assumed their arms and packs, and the scout announced to Munro and Heyward, that he and the Indians were at last in readiness to proceed.

Chapter XXI

"If you find a man there, he shall die a flea's death."
The Merry Wives of Windsor, IV.ii.150–151.

THE PARTY had landed on the border of a region that is, even to this day, less known to the inhabitants of the states, than the deserts of Arabia, or the steppes of Tartary. It was the sterile and rugged district, which separates the tributaries of Champlain from those of the Hudson, the Mohawk, and of the St. Lawrence. Since the period of our tale, the active spirit of the country has surrounded it with a belt of rich and thriving settlements, though none but the hunter or the savage is ever known, even now, to penetrate its wild recesses.

As Hawk-eye and the Mohicans had, however, often traversed the mountains and valleys of this vast wilderness, they did not hesitate to plunge into its depths, with the freedom of men accustomed to its privations and difficulties. For many hours the travellers toiled on their laborious way, guided by a star, or following the direction of some water-course, until the scout called a halt, and holding a short consultation with the Indians, they lighted their fire, and made the usual preparations to pass the remainder of the night where they then were.

Imitating the example, and emulating the confidence of their more experienced associates, Munro and Duncan slept without fear, if not without uneasiness. The dews were suffered to exhale, and the sun had dispersed the mists, and was shedding a strong and clear light in the forest, when the travellers resumed their journey.

After proceeding a few miles, the progress of Hawk-eye, who led the advance, became more deliberate and watchful. He often stopped to examine the trees; nor did he cross a rivulet, without attentively considering the quantity, the velocity, and the colour of its waters. Distrusting his own judgment, his appeals to the opinion of Chingachgook were frequent and earnest. During one of these conferences, Heyward observed that Uncas stood a patient and silent, though, as he imagined, an interested listener. He was strongly tempted to address the young chief, and demand his opinion of their progress; but the calm and dignified demeanour of the native, induced him to believe, that, like himself, the other was wholly dependent on the sagacity and intelligence of the seniors of the party. At last, the scout spoke in English, and at once explained the embarrassment of their situation.

"When I found that the home path of the Hurons run north," he said, "it did not need the judgment of many long years to tell that they would follow the valleys, and keep atween the waters of the Hudson and the Horican, until they might strike the springs of the Canada streams, which would lead them into the heart of the country of the Frenchers. Yet here are we, within a short range of the Scaroon, and not a sign of a trail have we crossed! Human natur is weak, and it is possible we may not have taken the proper scent."

"Heaven protect us from such an error!" exclaimed Duncan. "Let us retrace our steps, and examine as we go, with keener eyes. Has Uncas no counsel to offer in such a strait?"

The young Mohican cast a glance at his father, but maintaining his quiet and reserved mien, he continued silent. Chingachgook had caught the look, and motioning with his hand, he bade him speak. The moment this permission was accorded, the countenance of Uncas changed from its grave composure to a gleam of intelligence and joy. Bounding forward like a deer, he sprang up the side of a little acclivity, a few rods in advance, and stood, exultingly, over a spot of fresh earth, that looked as though it had been recently upturned by the passage of some heavy animal. The eyes of the whole party followed the unexpected movement, and read their success in the air of triumph that the youth assumed.

" 'Tis the trail!" exclaimed the scout, advancing to the spot; "the lad is quick of sight and keen of wit, for his years."

" 'Tis extraordinary, that he should have withheld his knowledge so long," muttered Duncan, at his elbow.

"It would have been more wonderful had he spoken, without a bidding! No, no; your young white, who gathers his learning from books, and can measure what he knows by the page, may conceit that his knowledge, like his legs, outruns that of his father; but where experience is the master, the scholar is made to know the value of years, and respects them accordingly."

"See!" said Uncas, pointing north and south, at the evident marks of the broad trail on either side of him; "the dark-hair has gone towards the frost."

"Hound never ran on a more beautiful scent," responded the scout, dashing forward, at once, on the indicated route; "we are favoured, greatly favoured, and can follow with high noses. Ay, here are both your waddling beasts; this Huron travels like a white general! The fellow is stricken with a judgment, and is mad! Look sharp for wheels, Sagamore," he continued, looking back and laughing, in his newly awakened satisfaction; "we shall soon have the fool journeying in a coach, and that with three of the best pair of eyes on the borders in his rear."

The spirits of the scout, and the astonishing success of the chase, in which a circuitous distance of more than forty miles had been passed, did not fail to impart a portion of hope to the whole party. Their advance was rapid; and made with as much confidence as a traveller would proceed along a wide highway. If a rock, or a rivulet, or a bit of earth harder than common, severed the links of the clue they followed, the true eye of the scout recovered them at a distance, and seldom rendered the delay of a single moment necessary. Their progress was much facilitated by the certainty that Magua had found it necessary to journey through the valleys; a circumstance which rendered the general direction of the route sure. Nor had the Huron entirely neglected the arts uniformly practised by the natives, when retiring in front of an enemy. False trails, and sudden turnings, were frequent, wherever a brook, or the formation of the ground, rendered them feasible; but his pursuers were rarely deceived, and never failed to detect their error, before they had lost either time or distance on the deceptive track.

By the middle of the afternoon they had passed the Scaroon, and were following the route of the declining sun. After descending an eminence to a low bottom, through which a swift stream glided, they suddenly came to a place where the party of le Renard had made a halt. Extinguished brands were lying around a spring, the offals of a deer were scattered about the place, and the trees bore evident marks of having been browsed by the horses. At a little distance, Heyward discovered, and contemplated with tender emotion, the small bower under which, he was fain to believe, that Cora and Alice had reposed. But while the earth was trodden, and the footsteps of both men and beasts were so plainly visible around the place, the trail appeared to have suddenly ended.

It was easy to follow the tracks of the Narragansetts, but they seemed only to have wandered without guides, or any other object than the pursuit of food. At length Uncas, who, with his father, had endeavoured to trace the route of the horses, came upon a sign of their presence, that was quite recent. Before following the clue, he communicated his success to his companions, and while the latter were consulting on the circumstance, the youth re-appeared, leading the two fillies, with their saddles broken, and the housings soiled, as though they had been permitted to run, at will, for several days.

"What should this prove?" said Duncan, turning pale, and glancing his eyes around him, as if he feared the brush and leaves were about to give up some horrid secret.

"That our march is come to a quick end, and that we are in an enemy's country," returned the scout. "Had the knave been pressed, and the gentle ones wanted horses to keep up with the party, he might have taken their scalps; but without an enemy at his heels, and with such rugged beasts as these, he would not hurt a hair of their heads. I know your thoughts, and shame be it to our colour, that you have reason for them; but he who thinks that even a Mingo would ill treat a woman, unless it be to tomahawk her, knows nothing of Indian natur, or the laws of the woods. No, no; I have heard that the French Indians had come into these hills, to hunt the moose, and we are getting within scent of their camp. Why should they not? the morning and evening guns of Ty, may be heard any day among these mountains; for the Frenchers are running a new line atween the provinces of the king and the Canadas. It is true, that the horses are here, but the Hurons are gone; let us then hunt for the path by which they departed."

Hawk-eye and the Mohicans now applied themselves to

their task in good earnest. A circle of a few hundred feet in circumference was drawn, and each of the party took a segment for his portion. The examination, however, resulted in no discovery. The impressions of footsteps were numerous, but they all appeared like those of men who had wandered about the spot, without any design to quit it. Again the scout and his companions made the circuit of the halting-place, each slowly following the other, until they assembled in the centre, once more, no wiser than when they started.

"Such cunning is not without its deviltry!" exclaimed Hawk-eye, when he met the disappointed looks of his assistants. "We must get down to it, Sagamore, beginning at the spring, and going over the ground by inches. The Huron shall never brag in his tribe that he has a foot which leaves no print!"

Setting the example himself, the scout engaged in the scrutiny with renewed zeal. Not a leaf was left unturned. The sticks were removed, and the stones lifted—for Indian cunning was known frequently to adopt these objects as covers, labouring with the utmost patience and industry, to conceal each footstep as they proceeded. Still, no discovery was made. At length Uncas, whose activity had enabled him to achieve his portion of the task the soonest, raked the earth across the turbid little rill which ran from the spring, and diverted its course into another channel. So soon as its narrow bed below the dam was dry, he stooped over it with keen and curious eyes. A cry of exultation immediately announced the success of the young warrior. The whole party crowded to the spot, where Uncas pointed out the impression of a moccasin in the moist alluvion.

"The lad will be an honour to his people!" said Hawk-eye, regarding the trail with as much admiration as a naturalist would expend on the tusk of a mammoth, or the rib of a mastodon; "ay, and a thorn in the sides of the Hurons. Yet that is not the footstep of an Indian! the weight is too much on the heel, and the toes are squared, as though one of the French dancers had been in, pigeon-winging his tribe! Run back, Uncas, and bring me the size of the singer's foot. You will find a beautiful print of it just opposite yon rock, ag'in the hill side."

While the youth was engaged in this commission, the scout and Chingachgook were attentively considering the impressions. The measurements agreed, and the former unhesitatingly pronounced that the footstep was that of David, who had, once more, been made to exchange his shoes for moccasins.

"I can now read the whole of it, as plainly as if I had seen the arts of le Subtil," he added; "the singer, being a man whose gifts lay chiefly in his throat and feet, was made to go first, and the others have trod in his steps, imitating their formation."

"But," cried Duncan, "I see no signs of—"

"The gentle ones," interrupted the scout; "the varlet has found a way to carry them, until he supposed he had thrown any followers off the scent. My life on it, we see their pretty little feet again, before many rods go by."

The whole party now proceeded, following the course of the rill, keeping anxious eyes on the regular impressions. The water soon flowed into its bed again, but watching the ground on either side, the foresters pursued their way, content with knowing that the trail lay beneath. More than half a mile was passed, before the rill rippled close around the base of an extensive and dry rock. Here they paused to make sure that the Hurons had not quitted the water.

It was fortunate they did so. For the quick and active Uncas soon found the impression of a foot on a bunch of moss, where it would seem an Indian had inadvertently trodden. Pursuing the direction given by this discovery, he entered the neighbouring thicket, and struck the trail, as fresh and obvious as it had been before they reached the spring. Another shout announced the good fortune of the youth to his companions, and at once terminated the search.

"Ay, it has been planned with Indian judgment," said the scout, when the party was assembled around the place; "and would have blinded white eyes."

"Shall we proceed?" demanded Heyward.

"Softly, softly; we know our path, but it is good to examine the formation of things. This is my schooling, major; and if one neglects the book, there is little chance of learning from the open hand of Providence. All is plain but one thing, which is, the manner that the knave contrived to get the gentle ones along the blind trail. Even a Huron would be too proud to let their tender feet touch the water."

"Will this assist in explaining the difficulty?" said Heyward, pointing towards the fragments of a sort of hand-barrow, that had been rudely constructed of boughs, and bound together with withes, and which now seemed carelessly cast aside as useless.

" 'Tis explained!" cried the delighted Hawk-eye. "If them varlets have passed a minute, they have spent hours in striving to fabricate a lying end to their trail! Well, I've known them waste a day in the same manner, to as little purpose. Here we have three pair of moccasins, and two of little feet. It is amazing that any mortal beings can journey on limbs so small! Pass me the thong of buckskin, Uncas, and let me take the length of this foot. By the Lord, it is no longer than a child's, and yet the maidens are tall and comely. That Providence is partial in its gifts, for its own wise reasons, the best and most contented of us must allow!"

"The tender limbs of my daughters are unequal to these hardships!" said Munro, looking at the light footsteps of his children with a parent's love; "we shall find their fainting forms in this desert."

"Of that there is little cause of fear," returned the scout, slowly shaking his head; "this is a firm and straight, though a light step, and not over long. See, the heel has hardly touched the ground; and there the dark-hair has made a little jump, from root to root. No, no; my knowledge for it, neither of them was nigh fainting, hereaway. Now, the singer was beginning to be foot-sore and leg-weary, as is plain by his trail. There you see he slipped; here he has travelled wide, and tottered; and there, again, it looks as though he journeyed on snow-shoes. Ay, ay, a man who uses his throat altogether, can hardly give his legs a proper training!"

From such undeniable testimony, did the practised woodsman arrive at the truth, with nearly as much certainty and precision, as if he had been a witness of all those events, which his ingenuity so easily elucidated. Cheered by these assurances, and satisfied by a reasoning that was so obvious, while it was so simple, the party resumed its course, after making a short halt, to take a hurried repast.

When the meal was ended, the scout cast a glance upward at the setting sun, and pushed forward with a rapidity, which compelled Heyward and the still vigorous Munro to exert all their muscles to equal. Their route, now, lay along the bottom which has already been mentioned. As the Hurons had made no further efforts to conceal their footsteps, the progress of the pursuers was no longer delayed by uncertainty. Before an hour had elapsed, however, the speed of Hawk-eye sensibly abated, and his head, instead of maintaining its former direct and forward look, began to turn suspiciously from side to side, as if he were conscious of approaching danger. He soon stopped again, and awaited for the whole party to come up.

"I scent the Hurons," he said, speaking to the Mohicans; "yonder is open sky, through the tree-tops, and we are getting too nigh their encampment. Sagamore, you will take the hill side, to the right; Uncas will bend along the brook to the left, while I will try the trail. If any thing should happen, the call will be three croaks of a crow. I saw one of the birds fanning himself in the air, just beyond the dead oak—another sign that we are touching an encampment."

The Indians departed their several ways, without reply, while Hawk-eye cautiously proceeded with the two gentlemen. Heyward soon pressed to the side of their guide, eager to catch an early glimpse of those enemies he had pursued with so much toil and anxiety. His companion told him to steal to the edge of the wood, which, as usual, was fringed with a thicket, and wait his coming, for he wished to examine certain suspicious signs a little on one side. Duncan obeyed, and soon found himself in a situation to command a view which he found as extraordinary as it was novel.

The trees of many acres had been felled, and the glow of a mild summer's evening had fallen on the clearing, in beautiful contrast to the gray light of the forest. A short distance from the place where Duncan stood, the stream had seemingly expanded into a little lake, covering most of the low land, from mountain to mountain. The water fell out of this wide basin, in a cataract so regular and gentle, that it appeared rather to be the work of human hands, than fashioned by nature. A hundred earthen dwellings stood on the margin of the lake, and even in its water, as though the latter had overflowed its usual banks. Their rounded roofs, admirably moulded for defence against the weather, denoted more of industry and foresight, than the natives were wont to bestow on their regular habitations, much less on those they occupied for the temporary purposes of hunting and war. In short, the whole village, or town, which ever it might be termed, possessed more of method and neatness of execution, than the white men had been accustomed to believe belonged, ordinarily, to the Indian habits. It appeared, however, to be deserted. At least, so thought Duncan for many minutes; but, at length, he fancied he discovered several human forms, advancing towards him on all fours, and apparently dragging in their train some heavy, and, as he was quick to apprehend, some formidable engine. Just then a few dark looking heads gleamed out of the dwellings, and the place seemed suddenly alive with beings, which, however, glided from cover to cover so swiftly, as to allow no opportunity of examining their humours or pursuits. Alarmed at these suspicious and inexplicable movements, he was about to attempt the signal of the crows, when the rustling of leaves at hand, drew his eyes in another direction.

The young man started, and recoiled a few paces instinctively, when he found himself within a hundred yards of a stranger Indian. Recovering his recollection on the instant, instead of sounding an alarm, which might prove fatal to himself, he remained stationary, an attentive observer of the other's motions.

An instant of calm observation, served to assure Duncan that he was undiscovered. The native, like himself, seemed occupied in considering the low dwellings of the village, and the stolen movements of its inhabitants. It was impossible to discover the expression of his features, through the grotesque masque of paint, under which they were concealed; though Duncan fancied it was rather melancholy than savage. His head was shaved, as usual, with the exception of the crown, from whose tuft three or four faded feathers, from a hawk's wing, were loosely dangling. A ragged calico mantle half encircled his body, while his nether garment was composed of an ordinary shirt, the sleeves of which were made to perform the office that is usually executed by a much more commodious arrangement. His legs were bare, and sadly cut and torn by briars. The feet were, however, covered with a pair of good deer-skin moccasins. Altogether, the appearance of the individual was forlorn and miserable.

Duncan was still curiously observing the person of his neighbour, when the scout stole silently and cautiously to his side.

"You see we have reached their settlement, or encampment," whispered the young man; "and here is one of the savages himself in a very embarrassing position for our further movements."

Hawk-eye started, and dropped his rifle, when, directed by the finger of his companion, the stranger came under his view. Then lowering the dangerous muzzle, he stretched forward his long neck, as if to assist a scrutiny that was already intensely keen.

"The imp is not a Huron," he said, "nor of any of the Canada tribes! and yet you see by his clothes, the knave has been plundering a white. Ay, Montcalm, has raked the woods for his inroad, and a whooping, murdering set of varlets has he gathered together! Can you see where he has put his rifle, or his bow?"

"He appears to have no arms; nor does he seem to be viciously inclined. Unless he communicate the alarm to his fellows, who, as you see, are dodging about the water, we have but little to fear from him."

The scout turned to Heyward, and regarded him a moment with unconcealed amazement. Then opening wide his mouth, he indulged in unrestrained and heartfelt laughter, though in that silent and peculiar manner, which danger had so long taught him to practise.

Repeating the words, "fellows who are dodging about the water!" he added, "so much for schooling and passing a boyhood in the settlements! The knave has long legs though, and shall not be trusted. Do you keep him under your rifle, while I creep in behind, through the bush, and take him alive. Fire on no account."

Heyward had already permitted his companion to bury part of his person in the thicket, when stretching forth an arm, he arrested him, in order to ask—

"If I see you in danger, may I not risk a shot?"

Hawk-eye regarded him a moment, like one who knew not how to take the question; then nodding his head, he answered, still laughing, though inaudibly—

"Fire a whole platoon, major."

In the next moment he was concealed by the leaves. Duncan waited several minutes in feverish impatience, before he caught another glimpse of the scout. Then he re-appeared, creeping along the earth, from which his dress was hardly distinguishable, directly in the rear of his intended captive. Having reached within a few yards of the latter, he arose to his feet, silently and slowly. At that instant, several loud blows were struck on the water, and Duncan turned his eyes just in time to perceive that a hundred dark forms were plunging, in a body, into the troubled little sheet. Grasping his rifle, his looks were again bent on the Indian near him. Instead of taking the alarm, the unconscious savage stretched forward his neck, as if he also watched the movements about the gloomy lake, with a sort of silly curiosity. In the mean time, the uplifted hand of Hawk-eye was above him. But, without any apparent reason, it was withdrawn, and its owner indulged in another long, though still silent, fit of merriment. When the peculiar and hearty laughter of Hawk-eye was ended, instead of grasping his victim, by the throat, he tapped him lightly on the shoulder, and exclaimed aloud—

"How now, friend! have you a mind to teach the beavers to sing?"

"Even so," was the ready answer. "It would seem that the Being that gave them power to improve his gifts so well, would not deny them voices to proclaim his praise."

Chapter XXII

Bot. "Are we all met?"
Qui. "Pat-pat; and here's a marvellous
Convenient place for our rehearsal."
A Midsummer Night's Dream, III.i.1–3.

THE READER may better imagine, than we describe, the surprise of Heyward. His lurking Indians were suddenly converted into four-footed beasts; his lake into a beaver pond; his cataract into a dam, constructed by those industrious and ingenious quadrupeds; and a suspected enemy into his tried friend, David Gamut, the master of psalmody. The presence of the latter created so many unexpected hopes relative to the sisters, that, without a moment's hesitation, the young man broke out of his ambush, and sprang forward to join the two principal actors in the scene.

The merriment of Hawk-eye was not easily appeased. Without ceremony, and with a rough hand, he twirled the supple Gamut around on his heel, and more than once affirmed that the Hurons had done themselves great credit in the fashion of his costume. Then seizing the hand of the other, he squeezed it with a gripe that brought the tears into the eyes of the placid David, and wished him joy of his new condition.

"You were about opening your throat-practysings among the beavers, were ye!" he said. "The cunning devils know half the trade already, for they beat the time with their tails, as you heard just now; and in good time it was too, or 'kill-deer' might have sounded the first note among them. I have known greater fools, who could read and write, than an experienced old beaver; but as for squalling, the animals are born dumb!—What think you of such a song as this?"

David shut his sensitive ears, and even Heyward, apprised as he was of the nature of the cry, looked upward in quest of the bird, as the cawing of a crow rang in the air about them.

"See," continued the laughing scout, as he pointed towards the remainder of the party, who, in obedience to the signal, were already approaching; "this is music, which has its natural virtues; it brings two good rifles to my elbow, to say nothing of the knives and tomahawks. But we see that you are safe; now tell us what has become of the maidens."

"They are captives to the heathen," said David; "and though greatly troubled in spirit, enjoying comfort and safety in the body."

"Both?" demanded the breathless Heyward.

"Even so. Though our wayfaring has been sore, and our sustenance scanty, we have had little other cause for complaint, except the violence done our feelings, by being thus led in captivity into a far land."

"Bless ye for these very words!" exclaimed the trembling Munro; "I shall then receive my babes spotless, and angel like, as I lost them!"

"I know not that their delivery is at hand," returned the doubting David; "the leader of these savages is possessed of an evil spirit, that no power, short of Omnipotence, can tame. I have tried him, sleeping and waking, but neither sounds nor language seem to touch his soul."

"Where is the knave?" bluntly interrupted the scout.

"He hunts the moose to day, with his young men; and to-morrow, as I hear, they pass further into these forests, and nigher to the borders of Canada. The elder maiden is conveyed to a neighbouring people, whose lodges are situate beyond yonder black pinnacle of rock; while the younger is detained among the women of the Hurons, whose dwellings are but two short miles hence, on a table land, where the fire has done the office of the ax, and prepared the place for their reception."

"Alice, my gentle Alice!" murmured Heyward; "she has lost the consolation of her sister's presence!"

"Even so. But so far as praise and thanksgiving in psalmody can temper the spirit in affliction, she has not suffered."

"Has she then a heart for music?"

"Of the graver and more solemn character; though it must be acknowledged, that in spite of all my endeavours, the maiden weeps oftener than she smiles. At such moments I forbear to press the holy songs; but there are many sweet and comfortable periods of satisfactory communication, when the ears of the savages are astounded with the upliftings of our voices."

"And why are you permitted to go at large, unwatched?"

David composed his features into what he intended should express an air of modest humility, before he meekly replied—

"Little be the praise to such a worm as I. But, though the power of psalmody was suspended in the terrible business of that field of blood, through which we passed, it has recovered its influence, even over the souls of the heathen, and I am suffered to go and come at will."

The scout laughed, and tapping his own forehead significantly, he perhaps explained the singular indulgence more satisfactorily, when he said—

"The Indians never harm a non-composser. But why, when the path lay open before your eyes, did you not strike back on your own trail, (it is not so blind as that which a squirrel would make,) and bring in the tidings to Edward?"

The scout, remembering only his own sturdy and iron nature, had probably exacted a task, that David, under no circumstances, could have performed. But, without entirely losing the meekness of his air, the latter was content to answer—

"Though my soul would rejoice to visit the habitations of christendom once more, my feet would rather follow the tender spirits intrusted to my keeping, even into the idolatrous province of the Jesuits, than take one step backward, while they pined in captivity and sorrow."

Though the figurative language of David was not very intelligible, the sincere and steady expression of his eye, and the glow on his honest countenance, were not easily mistaken. Uncas pressed closer to his side, and regarded the speaker with a look of commendation, while his father expressed his satisfaction by the ordinary pithy exclamation of approbation. The scout shook his head, as he rejoined—

"The Lord never intended that the man should place all his endeavours in his throat, to the neglect of other and better gifts! But he has fallen into the hands of some silly woman, when he should have been gathering his education under a blue sky, and among the beauties of the forest. Here, friend;

I did intend to kindle a fire with this tooting whistle of thine, but as you value the thing, take it, and blow your best on it!"

Gamut received his pitch-pipe with as strong an expression of pleasure, as he believed compatible with the grave functions he exercised. After essaying its virtues, repeatedly, in contrast with his own voice, and satisfying himself that none of its melody was lost, he made a very serious demonstration towards achieving a few stanzas of one of the longest effusions in the little volume, so often mentioned.

Heyward, however, hastily interrupted his pious purpose, by continuing questions concerning the past and present condition of his fellow captives, and in a manner more methodical than had been permitted by his feelings in the opening of their interview. David, though he regarded his treasure with longing eyes, was constrained to answer; especially, as the venerable father took a part in the interrogatories, with an interest too imposing to be denied. Nor did the scout fail to throw in a pertinent inquiry, whenever a fitting occasion presented. In this manner, though with frequent interruptions, which were filled with certain threatening sounds from the recovered instrument, the pursuers were put in possession of such leading circumstances, as were likely to prove useful in accomplishing their great and engrossing object—the recovery of the sisters. The narrative of David was simple, and the facts but few.

Magua had waited on the mountain until a safe moment to retire presented itself, when he had descended, and taken the route along the western side of the Horican, in the direction of the Canadas. As the subtle Huron was familiar with the paths, and well knew there was no immediate danger of pursuit, their progress had been moderate, and far from fatiguing. It appeared, from the unembellished statement of David, that his own presence had been rather endured than desired; though even Magua had not been entirely exempt from that veneration with which the Indians regard those whom the Great Spirit has visited in their intellects. At night, the utmost care had been taken of the captives, both to prevent injury from the damps of the woods, and to guard against an escape. At the spring, the horses were turned loose, as has been seen;

and notwithstanding the remoteness and length of their trail, the artifices already named were resorted to, in order to cut off every clue to their place of retreat. On their arrival at the encampment of his people, Magua, in obedience to a policy seldom departed from, separated his prisoners. Cora had been sent to a tribe that temporarily occupied an adjacent valley, though David was far too ignorant of the customs and history of the natives, to be able to declare any thing satisfactory concerning their name or character. He only knew that they had not engaged in the late expedition against William Henry; that, like the Hurons themselves, they were allies of Montcalm; and that they maintained an amicable, though a watchful, intercourse with the warlike and savage people, whom chance had, for a time, brought in such close and disagreeable contact with themselves.

The Mohicans and the scout listened to his interrupted and imperfect narrative, with an interest that obviously increased as he proceeded, and it was while attempting to explain the pursuits of the community, in which Cora was detained, that the latter abruptly demanded—

"Did you see the fashion of their knives? were they of English or French formation?"

"My thoughts were bent on no such vanities, but rather mingled in consolation with those of the maidens."

"The time may come when you will not consider the knife of a savage such a despisable vanity," returned the scout, with a strong expression of contempt for the other's dulness. "Had they held their corn-feast—or can you say any thing of the totems of their tribe?"

"Of corn, we had many and plentiful feasts; for the grain, being in the milk, is both sweet to the mouth and comfortable to the stomach. Of totem, I know not the meaning; but if it appertaineth in any wise to the art of Indian music, it need not be inquired after at their hands. They never join their voices in praise, and it would seem that they are among the profanest of the idolatrous."

"Therein you belie the nature of an Indian. Even the Mingo adores but the true and living God! 'Tis a wicked fabrication of the whites, and I say it to the shame of my colour, that would make the warrior bow down before images of his own creation. It is true, they endeavour to make truces with the wicked one—as who would not with an enemy he cannot conquer—but they look up for favour and assistance to the Great and Good Spirit only."

"It may be so," said David; "but I have seen strange and fantastic images drawn in their paint, of which their admiration and care, savoured of spiritual pride; especially one, and that too a foul and loathsome object."

"Was it a sarpent?" quickly demanded the scout.

"Much the same. It was in the likeness of an abject and creeping tortoise!"

"Hugh!" exclaimed both the attentive Mohicans in a breath; while the scout shook his head with the air of one who had made an important, but by no means a pleasing discovery. Then the father spoke, in the language of the Delawares, and with a calmness and dignity that instantly arrested the attention even of those, to whom his words were unintelligible. His gestures were impressive, and, at times, energetic. Once he lifted his arm on high, and as it descended, the action threw aside the folds of his light mantle, a finger resting on his breast, as if he would enforce his meaning by the attitude. Duncan's eyes followed the movement, and he perceived that the animal just mentioned was beautifully, though faintly, worked in a blue tint, on the swarthy breast of the chief. All that he had ever heard of the violent separation of the vast tribes of the Delawares, rushed across his mind, and he awaited the proper moment to speak, with a suspense that was rendered nearly intolerable, by his interest in the stake. His wish, however, was anticipated by the scout, who turned from his red friend, saying—

"We have found that which may be good or evil to us, as Heaven disposes. The Sagamore is of the high blood of the Delawares, and is the great chief of their Tortoises! That some of this stock are among the people of whom the singer tells us, is plain, by his words; and had he but spent half the breath in prudent questions, that he has blown away in making a trumpet of his throat, we might have known how many warriors they numbered. It is, altogether, a dangerous path we move in; for a friend whose face is turned from you, often bears a bloodier mind, than the enemy who seeks your scalp!"

"Explain," said Duncan.

" 'Tis is a long and melancholy tradition, and one I little like to think of; for it is not to be denied, that the evil has been mainly done by men with white skins. But it has ended in turning the tomahawk of brother against brother, and brought the Mingo and the Delaware to travel in the same path."

"You then suspect it is a portion of that people among whom Cora resides?"

The scout nodded his head in assent, though he seemed anxious to waive the further discussion of a subject that appeared painful. The impatient Duncan now made several hasty and desperate propositions to attempt the release of the sisters. Munro seemed to shake off his apathy, and listened to the wild schemes of the young man, with a deference that his gray hairs and reverend years should have denied. But the scout, after suffering the ardour of the lover to expend itself a little, found means to convince him of the folly of precipitation, in a matter that would require their coolest judgment and utmost fortitude.

"It would be well," he added, "to let this man go in again, as usual, and for him to tarry in the lodges, giving notice to the gentle ones of our approach, until we call him out, by signal, to consult. You know the cry of a crow, friend, from the whistle of the whip-poor-will?"

" 'Tis a pleasing bird," returned David, "and has a soft and melancholy note! though the time is rather quick and ill-measured."

"He speaks of the wish-ton-wish," said the scout; " well, since you like his whistle, it shall be your signal. Remember, then, when you hear the whip-poor-will's call three times repeated, you are to come into the bushes, where the bird might be supposed—"

"Stop," interrupted Heyward; "I will accompany him."

"You!" exclaimed the astonished Hawk-eye; "are you tired of seeing the sun rise and set?"

"David is a living proof that the Hurons can be merciful."

"Ay, but David can use his throat, as no man, in his senses, would pervart the gift."

"I too can play the madman, the fool, the hero; in short,

any or every thing, to rescue her I love. Name your objections no longer; I am resolved."

Hawk-eye regarded the young man a moment in speechless amazement. But Duncan, who, in deference to the other's skill and services, had hitherto submitted somewhat implicitly to his dictation, now assumed the superior, with a manner that was not easily resisted. He waved his hand, in sign of his dislike to all remonstrance, and then, in more tempered language, he continued—

"You have the means of disguise; change me; paint me too, if you will; in short, alter me to any thing—a fool."

"It is not for one like me to say that he who is already formed by so powerful a hand as Providence, stands in need of a change," muttered the discontented scout. "When you send your parties abroad in war, you find it prudent, at least, to arrange the marks and places of encampment, in order that they who fight on your side, may know when and where to expect a friend?"

"Listen," interrupted Duncan; "you have heard from this faithful follower of the captives, that the Indians are of two tribes, if not of different nations. With one, whom you think to be a branch of the Delawares, is she you call the 'dark-hair;' the other, and younger of the ladies, is undeniably with our declared enemies, the Hurons. It becomes my youth and rank to attempt the latter adventure. While you, therefore, are negotiating with your friends for the release of one of the sisters, I will effect that of the other, or die."

The awakened spirit of the young soldier gleamed in his eyes, and his form became imposing under its influence. Hawk-eye, though too much accustomed to Indian artifices not to foresee the danger of the experiment, knew not well how to combat this sudden resolution. Perhaps there was something in the proposal that suited his own hardy nature, and that secret love of desperate adventure, which had increased with his experience, until hazard and danger had become, in some measure, necessary to the enjoyment of his existence. Instead of continuing to oppose the scheme of Duncan, his humour suddenly altered, and he lent himself to its execution.

"Come," he said, with a good humoured smile; "the buck

that will take to the water must be headed, and not followed! Chingachgook has as many different paints, as the engineer officer's wife, who takes down natur on scraps of paper, making the mountains look like cocks of rusty hay, and placing the blue sky in reach of your hand—the Sagamore can use them too! Seat yourself on the log, and my life on it, he can soon make a natural fool of you, and that, well, to your liking."

Duncan complied, and the Mohican, who had been an attentive listener to the discourse, readily undertook the office. Long practised in all the subtle arts of his race, he drew, with great dexterity and quickness, the fantastic shadow that the natives were accustomed to consider as the evidence of a friendly and jocular disposition. Every line that could possibly be interpreted into a secret inclination for war, was carefully avoided; while, on the other hand, he studied those conceits that might be construed into amity. In short, he entirely sacrificed every appearance of the warrior, to the masquerade of a buffoon. Such exhibitions were not uncommon among the Indians; and as Duncan was already sufficiently disguised in his dress, there certainly did exist some reason for believing, that with his knowledge of French, he might pass for a juggler from Ticonderoga, straggling among the allied and friendly tribes.

When he was thought to be sufficiently painted, the scout gave him much friendly advice; concerted signals, and appointed the place where they should meet, in the event of mutual success. The parting between Munro and his young friend was more melancholy; still, the former submitted to the separation with an indifference, that his warm and honest nature would never have permitted in a more healthful state of mind. The scout led Heyward aside, and acquainted him with his intention to leave the veteran in some safe encampment, in charge of Chingachgook, while he and Uncas pursued their inquiries among the people they had reason to believe were Delawares. Then renewing his cautions and advice, he concluded, by saying, with a solemnity and warmth of feeling, with which Duncan was deeply touched—

"And now God bless you! You have shown a spirit that I like; for it is the gift of youth, more especially one of warm blood and a stout heart. But believe the warning of a man, who has reason to know all he says to be true. You will have occasion for your best manhood, and for a sharper wit than what is to be gathered in books, afore you outdo the cunning, or get the better of the courage of a Mingo! God bless you! if the Hurons master your scalp, rely on the promise of one, who has two stout warriors to back him—They shall pay for their victory, with a life for every hair it holds! I say, young gentleman, may Providence bless your undertaking, which is altogether for good; and remember, that to outwit the knaves it is lawful to practise things, that may not be naturally the gift of a white skin."

Duncan shook his worthy and reluctant associate warmly by the hand, once more recommended his aged friend to his care, and returning his good wishes, he motioned to David to proceed. Hawk-eye gazed after the high-spirited and adventurous young man for several moments, in open admiration; then shaking his head, doubtingly, he turned, and led his own division of the party into the concealment of the forest.

The route taken by Duncan and David, lay directly across the clearing of the beavers, and along the margin of their pond. When the former found himself alone with one so simple, and so little qualified to render any assistance in desperate emergencies, he first began to be sensible of the difficulties of the task he had undertaken. The fading light increased the gloominess of the bleak and savage wilderness, that stretched so far on every side of him, and there was even a fearful character in the stillness of those little huts, that he knew were so abundantly peopled. It struck him, as he gazed at the admirable structures, and the wonderful precautions of their sagacious inmates, that even the brutes of these vast wilds were possessed of an instinct nearly commensurate with his own reason; and he could not reflect, without anxiety, on the unequal contest that he had so rashly courted. Then came the glowing image of Alice; her distress; her actual danger; and all the peril of his situation was forgotten. Cheering David, he moved on, with the light and vigorous step of youth and enterprise.

After making nearly a semi-circle around the pond, they

diverged from the water-course, and began to ascend to the level of a slight elevation in that bottom land, over which they journeyed. Within half an hour they gained the margin of another opening, that bore all the signs of having been also made by the beavers, and which those sagacious animals had probably been induced, by some accident, to abandon, for the more eligible position they now occupied. A very natural sensation caused Duncan to hesitate a moment, unwilling to leave the cover of their bushy path, as a man pauses to collect his energies, before he essays any hazardous experiment, in which he is secretly conscious they will all be needed. He profited by the halt, to gather such information as might be obtained from his short and hasty glances.

On the opposite side of the clearing, and near the point where the brook tumbled over some rocks, from a still higher level, some fifty or sixty lodges, rudely fabricated of logs, brush, and earth, intermingled, were to be discovered. They were arranged without any order, and seemed to be constructed with very little attention to neatness or beauty. Indeed, so very inferior were they, in the two latter particulars, to the village Duncan had just seen, that he began to expect a second surprise, no less astonishing than the former. This expectation was in no degree diminished, when, by the doubtful twilight, he beheld twenty or thirty forms, rising alternately, from the cover of the tall, coarse grass, in front of the lodges, and then sinking again from the sight, as it were to burrow in the earth. By the sudden and hasty glimpses that he caught of these figures, they seemed more like dark glancing spectres, or some other unearthly beings, than creatures fashioned with the ordinary and vulgar materials of flesh and blood. A gaunt, naked form, was seen, for a single instant, tossing its arms wildly in the air, and then the spot it had filled was vacant; the figure appearing, suddenly, in some other and distant place, or being succeeded by another, possessing the same mysterious character. David, observing that his companion lingered, pursued the direction of his gaze, and in some measure recalled the recollection of Heyward, by speaking—

"There is much fruitful soil uncultivated here," he said; "and I may add, without the sinful leaven of self-commendation, that, since my short sojourn in these heathenish abodes, much good seed has been scattered by the way-side."

"The tribes are fonder of the chase, than of the arts of men of labour," returned the unconscious Duncan, still gazing at the objects of his wonder.

"It is rather joy than labour to the spirit, to lift up the voice in praise; but sadly do these boys abuse their gifts! Rarely have I found any of their age, on whom nature has so freely bestowed the elements of psalmody; and surely, surely, there are none who neglect them more. Three nights have I now tarried here, and three several times have I assembled the urchins to join in sacred song, and as often have they responded to my efforts with whoopings and howlings that have chilled my soul!"

"Of whom speak you?"

"Of those children of the devil, who waste the precious moments in yonder idle antics. Ah! the wholesome restraint of discipline is but little known among this self-abandoned people! In a country of birches, a rod is never seen; and it ought not to appear a marvel in my eyes, that the choicest blessings of Providence are wasted in such cries as these."

David closed his ears against the juvenile pack, whose yells just then rang shrilly through the forest; and Duncan, suffering his lip to curl, as in mockery of his own superstition, said firmly—

"We will proceed."

Without removing the safeguards from his ears, the master of song complied, and together they pursued their way towards what David was sometimes wont to call "the tents of the Philistines."

Chapter XXIII

—"But though the beast of game
The privilege of chase may claim;
Though space and law the stag we lend,
Ere hound we slip, or bow we bend;
Whoever recked, where, how, or when,
The prowling fox was trapped or slain."
Scott, *The Lady of the Lake*, Canto IV, xxx.14–19.

IT IS UNUSUAL to find an encampment of the natives, like those of the more instructed whites, guarded by the presence of armed men. Well informed of the approach of every danger, while it is yet at a distance, the Indian generally rests secure under his knowledge of the signs of the forest, and the long and difficult paths that separate him from those he has most reason to dread. But the enemy who, by any lucky concurrence of accidents, has found means to elude the vigilance of the scouts, will seldom meet with sentinels nearer home to sound the alarm. In addition to this general usage, the tribes friendly to the French knew too well the weight of the blow that had just been struck, to apprehend any immediate danger from the hostile nations that were tributary to the crown of Britain.

When Duncan and David, therefore, found themselves in the centre of the children, who played the antics already mentioned, it was without the least previous intimation of their approach. But so soon as they were observed, the whole of the juvenile pack raised, by common consent, a shrill and warning whoop; and then sunk, as it were, by magic, from before the sight of their visiters. The naked, tawny bodies of the crouching urchins, blended so nicely, at that hour, with the withered herbage, that at first it seemed as if the earth had, in truth, swallowed up their forms; though when surprise had permitted Duncan to bend his look more curiously about the spot, he found it every where met by dark, quick, and rolling eye-balls.

Gathering no encouragement from this startling presage, of the nature of the scrutiny he was likely to undergo from the more mature judgments of the men, there was an instant when the young soldier would have retreated. It was, however, too late to appear to hesitate. The cry of the children had drawn a dozen warriors to the door of the nearest lodge, where they stood, clustered in a dark and savage groupe, gravely awaiting the nearer approach of those who had unexpectedly come among them.

David, in some measure familiarized to the scene, led the way, with a steadiness that no slight obstacle was likely to disconcert, into this very building. It was the principal edifice of the village, though roughly constructed of the bark and branches of trees; being the lodge in which the tribe held its councils and public meetings, during their temporary residence on the borders of the English province. Duncan found it difficult to assume the necessary appearance of unconcern, as he brushed the dark and powerful frames of the savages who thronged its threshold; but, conscious that his existence depended on his presence of mind, he trusted to the discretion of his companion, whose footsteps he closely followed, endeavouring, as he proceeded, to rally his thoughts for the occasion. His blood curdled when he found himself in absolute contact with such fierce and implacable enemies; but he so far mastered his feelings, as to pursue his way into the centre of the lodge, with an exterior that did not betray the weakness. Imitating the example of the deliberate Gamut, he drew a bundle of fragrant brush from beneath a pile, that filled a corner of the hut, and seated himself, in silence.

So soon as their visiter had passed, the observant warriors fell back from the entrance, and arranging themselves about him, they seemed patiently to await the moment when it might comport with the dignity of the stranger to speak. By far the greater number stood leaning, in lazy, lounging attitudes, against the upright posts that supported the crazy building, while three or four of the oldest and most distinguished of the chiefs placed themselves on the earth, a little more in advance.

A flaring torch was burning in the place, and sent its red glare from face to face, and figure to figure, as it waved in the currents of air. Duncan profited by its light, to read the probable character of his reception, in the countenances of his hosts. But his ingenuity availed him little, against the cold artifices of the people he had encountered. The chiefs in front scarce cast a glance at his person, keeping their eyes on the ground, with an air that might have been intended for respect, but which it was quite easy to construe into distrust. The men, in shadow, were less reserved. Duncan soon detected their searching, but stolen looks, which, in truth, scanned his person and attire inch by inch; leaving no emotion of the countenance, no gesture, no line of the paint, nor even the fashion of a garment, unheeded, and without comment.

At length, one whose hair was beginning to be sprinkled with gray, but whose sinewy limbs and firm tread announced that he was still equal to the duties of manhood, advanced out of the gloom of a corner, whither he had probably posted himself to make his observations unseen, and spoke. He used the language of the Wyandots, or Hurons: his words were, consequently, unintelligible to Heyward, though they seemed, by the gestures that accompanied them, to be uttered more in courtesy than anger. The latter shook his head, and made a gesture indicative of his inability to reply.

"Do none of my brothers speak the French or the English?" he said, in the former language, looking about him, from countenance to countenance, in hopes of finding a nod of assent.

Though more than one head turned, as if to catch the meaning of his words, they remained unanswered.

"I should be grieved to think," continued Duncan, speaking slowly, and using the simplest French of which he was the master, "to believe that none of this wise and brave nation understand the language that the 'Grand Monarque' uses, when he talks to his children. His heart would be heavy, did he believe his red warriors paid him so little respect!"

A long and grave pause succeeded, during which no movement of a limb, nor any expression of an eye, betrayed the impression produced by his remark. Duncan, who knew that silence was a virtue amongst his hosts, gladly had recourse to the custom, in order to arrange his ideas. At length, the same warrior, who had before addressed him, replied, by dryly demanding, in the language of the Canadas—

"When our Great Father speaks to his people, is it with the tongue of a Huron?"

"He knows no difference in his children, whether the colour of the skin be red, or black, or white," returned Duncan, evasively; "though chiefly is he satisfied with the brave Hurons."

"In what manner will he speak," demanded the wary chief, "when the runners count, to him, the scalps which five nights ago grew on the heads of the Yengeese?"

"They were his enemies," said Duncan, shuddering involuntarily; "and, doubtless, he will say it is good—my Hurons are very gallant."

"Our Canada father does not think it. Instead of looking forward to reward his Indians, his eyes are turned backward. He sees the dead Yengeese, but no Huron. What can this mean?"

"A great chief, like him, has more thoughts than tongues. He looks to see that no enemies are on his trail."

"The canoe of a dead warrior will not float on the Horican," returned the savage, gloomily. "His ears are open to the Delawares, who are not our friends, and they fill them with lies."

"It cannot be. See; he has bid me, who am a man that knows the art of healing, to go to his children, the red Hurons of the Great Lakes, and ask if any are sick!"

Another silence succeeded this annunciation of the character Duncan had assumed. Every eye was simultaneously bent on his person, as if to inquire into the truth or falsehood of the declaration, with an intelligence and keenness, that caused the subject of their scrutiny to tremble for the result. He was, however, relieved again, by the former speaker.

"Do the cunning men of the Canadas paint their skins," the Huron, coldly, continued; "we have heard them boast that their faces were pale."

"When an Indian chief comes among his white fathers," returned Duncan, with great steadiness, "he lays aside his buffalo robe, to carry the shirt that is offered him. My brothers have given me paint, and I wear it."

A low murmur of applause announced that the compliment to the tribe was favourably received. The elderly chief made a gesture of commendation, which was answered by most of his companions, who each threw forth a hand, and uttered a brief exclamation of pleasure. Duncan began to breathe more freely, believing that the weight of his examination was past; and as he had already prepared a simple and probable tale to support his pretended occupation, his hopes of ultimate success grew brighter.

After a silence of a few moments, as if adjusting his thoughts, in order to make a suitable answer to the declaration their guest had just given, another warrior arose, and placed himself in an attitude to speak. While his lips were yet in the act of parting, a low, but fearful sound, arose from the forest, and was immediately succeeded by a high, shrill yell, that was drawn out, until it equalled the longest and most plaintive howl of the wolf. The sudden and terrible interruption caused Duncan to start from his seat, unconscious of every thing, but the effect produced by so frightful a cry. At the same moment, the warriors glided in a body from the lodge, and the outer air was filled with loud shouts, that nearly drowned those awful sounds, which were still ringing beneath the arches of the woods. Unable to command himself any longer, the youth broke from the place, and presently stood in the centre of a disorderly throng, that included nearly every thing having life, within the limits of the encampment. Men, women, and children; the aged, the infirm, the active, and the strong, were alike abroad; some exclaiming aloud, others clapping their hands with a joy that seemed frantic, and all expressing their savage pleasure in some unexpected event. Though astounded, at first, by the uproar, Heyward was soon enabled to find its solution by the scene that followed.

There yet lingered sufficient light in the heavens, to exhibit those bright openings among the tree-tops, where different paths left the clearing to enter the depths of the wilderness. Beneath one of them, a line of warriors issued from the woods, and advanced slowly towards the dwellings. One in front bore a short pole, on which, as it afterwards appeared, were suspended several human scalps. The startling sounds that Duncan had heard, were what the whites have, not inappropriately, called the "death-halloo;" and each repetition of the cry was intended to announce to the tribe, the fate of an enemy. Thus far the knowledge of Heyward assisted him in the explanation; and as he now knew that the interruption was caused by the unlooked-for return of a successful war-party, every disagreeable sensation was quieted, in inward congratulations, for the opportune relief and insignificance it conferred on himself.

When at the distance of a few hundred feet from the lodges, the newly arrived warriors halted. Their plaintive and terrific cry, which was intended to represent, equally, the wailings of the dead and the triumph of the victors, had entirely ceased. One of their number now called aloud, in words that were far from appalling, though not more intelligible to those for whose ears they were intended, than their expressive yells. It would be difficult to convey a suitable idea of the savage ecstacy with which the news, thus imparted, was received. The whole encampment, in a moment, became a scene of the most violent bustle and commotion. The warriors drew their knives, and flourishing them, they arranged themselves in two lines, forming a lane, that extended from the war-party to the lodges. The squaws seized clubs, axes, or whatever weapon of offence first offered itself to their hands, and rushed eagerly to act their part in the cruel game that was at hand. Even the children would not be excluded; but boys, little able to wield the instruments, tore the tomahawks from the belts of their fathers, and stole into the ranks, apt imitators of the savage traits exhibited by their parents.

Large piles of brush lay scattered about the clearing, and a wary and aged squaw was occupied in firing as many as might serve to light the coming exhibition. As the flame arose, its power exceeded that of the parting day, and assisted to render objects, at the same time, more distinct and more hideous. The whole scene formed a striking picture, whose frame was composed of the dark and tall border of pines. The warriors just arrived were the most distant figures. A little in advance, stood two men, who were apparently selected from the rest, as the principal actors in what was to follow. The light was not strong enough to render their features distinct, though it was quite evident, that they were governed by very different emotions. While one stood erect and firm, prepared to meet his fate like a hero, the other bowed his head, as if palsied by terror, or stricken with shame. The high spirited Duncan felt a powerful impulse of admiration and pity towards the former, though no opportunity could offer to exhibit his generous emotions. He watched his slightest movement, however, with eager eyes; and as he traced the fine outline of his admirably proportioned and active frame, he endeavoured to persuade himself, that if the powers of man, seconded by such noble resolution, could bear one harmless through so severe a trial, the youthful captive before him, might hope for success in the hazardous race he was about to run. Insensibly, the young man drew nigher to the swarthy lines of the Hurons, and scarcely breathed, so intense became his interest in the spectacle. Just then the signal yell was given, and the momentary quiet, which had preceded it, was broken by a burst of cries, that far exceeded any before heard. The most abject of the two victims continued motionless; but the other bounded from the place, at the cry, with the activity and swiftness of a deer. Instead of rushing through the hostile lines, as had been expected, he just entered the dangerous defile, and before time was given for a single blow, turned short, and leaping the heads of a row of children, he gained at once the exterior and safer side of the formidable array. The artifice was answered by a hundred voices raised in imprecations, and the whole of the excited multitude broke from their order, and spread themselves about the place in wild confusion.

A dozen blazing piles now shed their lurid brightness on the place, which resembled some unhallowed and supernatural arena, in which malicious demons had assembled to act their bloody and lawless rites. The forms in the back ground, looked like unearthly beings, gliding before the eye, and cleaving the air with frantic and unmeaning gestures; while the savage passions of such as passed the flames, were rendered fearfully distinct, by the gleams that shot athwart their inflamed visages.

It will easily be understood, that amid such a concourse of vindictive enemies, no breathing time was allowed the fugitive. There was a single moment, when it seemed as if he would have reached the forest, but the whole body of his captors threw themselves before him, and drove him back into the centre of his relentless persecutors. Turning like a headed deer, he shot, with the swiftness of an arrow, through a pillar of forked flame, and passing the whole multitude harmless, he appeared on the opposite side of the clearing. Here, too, he was met and turned by a few of the older and more subtle of the Hurons. Once more he tried the throng, as if seeking safety in its blindness, and then several moments succeeded, during which Duncan believed the active and courageous young stranger was lost.

Nothing could be distinguished but a dark mass of human forms, tossed and involved in inexplicable confusion. Arms, gleaming knives, and formidable clubs, appeared above them, but the blows were evidently given at random. The awful effect was heightened by the piercing shrieks of the women, and the fierce yells of the warriors. Now and then, Duncan caught a glimpse of a light form cleaving the air in some desperate bound, and he rather hoped than believed, that the captive yet retained the command of his astonishing powers of activity. Suddenly, the multitude rolled backward, and approached the spot where he himself stood. The heavy body in the rear pressed upon the women and children in front, and bore them to the earth. The stranger re-appeared in the confusion. Human power could not, however, much longer endure so severe a trial. Of this the captive seemed conscious. Profiting by the momentary opening, he darted from among the warriors, and made a desperate, and what seemed to Duncan, a final effort to gain the wood. As if aware that no danger was to be apprehended from the young soldier, the fugitive nearly brushed his person in his flight. A tall and powerful Huron, who had husbanded his forces, pressed close upon his heels, and with an uplifted arm, menaced a fatal blow. Duncan thrust forth a foot, and the shock precipitated the eager savage, headlong, many feet in advance of his intended victim. Thought itself is not quicker than was the motion with which the latter profited by the advantage; he turned, gleamed like a meteor again before the eyes of Duncan, and at the next moment, when the latter recovered his recollection, and gazed around in quest of the captive, he saw him quietly leaning against a small painted post, which stood before the door of the principal lodge.

Apprehensive that the part he had taken in the escape

might prove fatal to himself, Duncan left the place without delay. He followed the crowd, which drew nigh the lodges, gloomy and sullen, like any other multitude that had been disappointed in an execution. Curiosity, or, perhaps, a better feeling, induced him to approach the stranger. He found him, standing, with one arm cast about the protecting post, and breathing thick and hard, after his exertions, but disdaining to permit a single sign of suffering to escape. His person was now protected, by immemorial and sacred usage, until the tribe in council had deliberated and determined on his fate. It was not difficult, however, to foretell the result, if any presage could be drawn from the feelings of those who crowded the place.

There was no term of abuse known to the Huron vocabulary, that the disappointed women did not lavishly expend on the successful stranger. They flouted at his efforts, and told him, with bitter scoffs, that his feet were better than his hands, and that he merited wings, while he knew not the use of an arrow, or a knife. To all this, the captive made no reply; but was content to preserve an attitude, in which dignity was singularly blended with disdain. Exasperated as much by his composure as by his good fortune, their words became unintelligible, and were succeeded by shrill, piercing yells. Just then, the crafty squaw, who had taken the necessary precaution to fire the piles, made her way through the throng, and cleared a place for herself in front of the captive. The squalid and withered person of this hag, might well have obtained for her the character of possessing more than human cunning. Throwing back her light vestment, she stretched forth her long, skinny, arm in derision, and using the language of the Lenape, as more intelligible to the subject of her gibes, she commenced aloud.

"Look you, Delaware!" she said, snapping her fingers in his face; "your nation is a race of women, and the hoe is better fitted to your hands than the gun! Your squaws are the mothers of deer; but if a bear, or a wild cat, or a serpent, were born among you, ye would flee! The Huron girls shall make you petticoats, and we will find you a husband."

A burst of savage laughter succeeded this attack, during which the soft and musical merriment of the younger females, strangely chimed with the cracked voice of their older and more malignant companion. But the stranger was superior to all their efforts. His head was immovable; nor did he betray the slightest consciousness that any were present, except when his haughty eye rolled towards the dusky forms of the warriors, who stalked in the back ground, silent and sullen observers of the scene.

Infuriated at the self-command of the captive, the woman placed her arms akimbo, and throwing herself into a posture of defiance, she broke out anew, in a torrent of words, that no art of ours could commit, successfully, to paper. Her breath was, however, expended in vain; for, although distinguished in her nation as a proficient in the art of abuse, she was permitted to work herself into such a fury, as actually to foam at the mouth, without causing a muscle to vibrate in the motionless figure of the stranger. The effect of his indifference began to extend itself to the other spectators; and a youngster, who was just quitting the condition of a boy, to enter the state of manhood, attempted to assist the termagant, by flourishing his tomahawk before their victim, and adding his empty boasts to the taunts of the woman. Then, indeed, the captive turned his face towards the light, and looked down on the stripling with an expression that was superior to contempt. At the next moment, he resumed his quiet and reclining attitude against the post. But the change of posture had permitted Duncan to exchange glances with the firm and piercing eyes of Uncas.

Breathless with amazement, and heavily oppressed with the critical situation of his friend, Heyward recoiled before the look, trembling lest its meaning might, in some unknown manner, hasten the prisoner's fate. There was not, however, any instant cause for such an apprehension. Just then a warrior forced his way into the exasperated crowd. Motioning the women and children aside with a stern gesture, he took Uncas by the arm, and led him towards the door of the council lodge. Thither all the chiefs, and most of the distinguished warriors, followed, among whom the anxious Heyward found means to enter, without attracting any dangerous attention to himself.

A few minutes were consumed in disposing of those present in a manner suitable to their rank and influence in the tribe. An order very similar to that adopted in the preceding interview was observed; the aged and superior chiefs occupying the area of the spacious apartment, within the powerful light of a glaring torch, while their juniors and inferiors were arranged in the back ground, presenting a dark outline of swarthy and marked visages. In the very centre of the lodge, immediately under an opening that admitted the twinkling light of one or two stars, stood Uncas, calm, elevated, and collected. His high and haughty carriage was not lost on his captors, who often bent their looks on his person, with eyes, which, while they lost none of their inflexibility of purpose, plainly betrayed their admiration of the stranger's daring.

The case was different with the individual, whom Duncan had observed to stand forth with his friend, previously to the desperate trial of speed; and who, instead of joining in the chase, had remained, throughout its turbulent uproar, like a cringing statue, expressive of shame and disgrace. Though not a hand had been extended to greet him, nor yet an eye had condescended to watch his movements, he had also entered the lodge, as though impelled by a fate, to whose decrees he submitted, seemingly, without a struggle. Heyward profited by the first opportunity to gaze in his face, secretly apprehensive he might find the features of another acquaintance, but they proved to be those of a stranger, and what was still more inexplicable, of one who bore all the distinctive marks of a Huron warrior. Instead of mingling with his tribe, however, he sat apart, a solitary being in a multitude, his form shrinking into a crouching and abject attitude, as if anxious to fill as little space as possible. When each individual had taken his proper station, and silence reigned in the place, the gray-haired chief, already introduced to the reader, spoke aloud, in the language of the Lenni Lenape.

"Delaware," he said, "though one of a nation of women, you have proved yourself a man. I would give you food, but he who eats with a Huron, should become his friend. Rest in peace till the morning sun, when our last words shall be spoken."

"Seven nights, and as many summer days, have I fasted on the trail of the Hurons," Uncas coldly replied; "the children of the Lenape know how to travel the path of the just, without lingering to eat."

"Two of my young men are in pursuit of your companion," resumed the other, without appearing to regard the boast of his captive; " when they get back, then will our wise men say to you—live or die."

"Has a Huron no ears?" scornfully exclaimed Uncas; "twice since he has been your prisoner, has the Delaware heard a gun that he knows! Your young men will never come back."

A short and sullen pause succeeded this bold assertion. Duncan, who understood the Mohican to allude to the fatal rifle of the scout, bent forward in earnest observation of the effect it might produce on the conquerors; but the chief was content with simply retorting—

"If the Lenape are so skilful, why is one of their bravest warriors here?"

"He followed in the steps of a flying coward, and fell into a snare. The cunning beaver may be caught!"

As Uncas thus replied, he pointed with his finger towards the solitary Huron, but without deigning to bestow any other notice on so unworthy an object. The words of the answer, and the air of the speaker, produced a strong sensation among his auditors. Every eye rolled sullenly toward the individual indicated by the simple gesture, and a low, threatening murmur, passed through the crowd. The ominous sounds reached the outer door, and the women and children pressing into the throng, no gap had been left, between shoulder and shoulder, that was not, now, filled with the dark lineaments of some eager and curious human countenance.

In the mean time, the more aged chiefs, in the centre, communed with each other, in short and broken sentences. Not a word was uttered, that did not convey the meaning of the speaker, in the simplest and most energetic form. Again, a long and deeply solemn pause took place. It was known, by all present, to be the grave precursor of a weighty and important judgment. They who composed the outer circle of faces, were on tiptoe to gaze; and even the culprit, for an instant, forgot his shame, in a deeper emotion, and exposed his abject features, in order to cast an anxious and troubled glance at the dark assemblage of chiefs. The silence was finally broken by the aged warrior, so often named. He arose from the earth, and moving past the immovable form of Uncas, placed himself in a dignified attitude before the offender. At that moment, the withered squaw, already mentioned, moved into the circle, in a slow, sideling sort of a dance, holding the torch, and muttering the indistinct words of what might have been a species of incantation. Though her presence was altogether an intrusion, it was unheeded.

Approaching Uncas, she held the blazing brand in such a manner, as to cast its red glare on his person, and to expose the slightest emotion of his countenance. The Mohican maintained his firm and haughty attitude; and his eye, so far from deigning to meet her inquisitive look, dwelt steadily on the distance, as though it penetrated the obstacles which impeded the view, and looked into futurity. Satisfied with her examination, she left him, with a slight expression of pleasure, and proceeded to practise the same trying experiment on her delinquent countryman.

The young Huron was in his war paint, and very little of a finely moulded form was concealed by his attire. The light rendered every limb and joint discernible, and Duncan turned away in horror, when he saw they were writhing in irrepressible agony. The woman was commencing a low and plaintive howl, at the sad and shameful spectacle, when the chief put forth his hand, and gently pushed her aside.

"Reed-that-bends," he said, addressing the young culprit by name, and in his proper language, "though the Great Spirit has made you pleasant to the eyes, it would have been better that you had not been born. Your tongue is loud in the village, but in battle it is still. None of my young men strike the tomahawk deeper into the war-post—none of them so lightly on the Yengeese. The enemy know the shape of your back, but they have never seen the colour of your eyes. Three times have they called on you to come, and as often did you forget to answer. Your name will never be mentioned, again, in your tribe—it is already forgotten."

As the chief slowly uttered these words, pausing impressively between each sentence, the culprit raised his face, in deference to the other's rank and years. Shame, horror, and pride, struggled in its lineaments. His eye, which was contracted with inward anguish, gleamed around on the persons of those whose breath was his fame, and the latter emotion, for an instant predominated. He arose to his feet, and baring his bosom, looked steadily on the keen, glittering knife, that was already upheld by his inexorable judge. As the weapon passed slowly into his heart, he even smiled, as if in joy, at having found death less dreadful than he had anticipated, and fell heavily on his face, at the feet of the rigid and unyielding form of Uncas.

The squaw gave a loud and plaintive yell, dashed the torch to the earth, and buried every thing in darkness. The whole shuddering groupe of spectators glided from the lodge, like troubled sprites; and Duncan thought that he and the yet throbbing body of the victim of an Indian judgment, had now become its only tenants.

Chapter XXIV

"Thus spoke the sage: the kings without delay
Dissolve the council, and their chief obey."
Pope, *The Iliad*, Book II, ll. 107–108.

A SINGLE MOMENT served to convince the youth that he was mistaken. A hand was laid, with a powerful pressure, on his arm, and the low voice of Uncas muttered in his ears—

"The Hurons are dogs! The sight of a coward's blood can never make a warrior tremble. The 'gray head' and the Sagamore are safe, and the rifle of Hawk-eye is not asleep. Go—Uncas and the 'open hand' are now strangers. It is enough."

Heyward would gladly have heard more, but a gentle push from his friend, urged him toward the door, and admonished him of the danger that might attend the discovery of their intercourse. Slowly and reluctantly yielding to the necessity, he quitted the place, and mingled with the throng that hovered nigh. The dying fires in the clearing, cast a dim and uncertain light on the dusky figures, that were silently stalking to and fro; and, occasionally, a brighter gleam than common glanced into the lodge, and exhibited the figure of Uncas, still maintaining its upright attitude near the dead body of the Huron.

A knot of warriors soon entered the place again, and reissuing, they bore the senseless remains into the adjacent woods. After this termination of the scene, Duncan wandered among the lodges, unquestioned and unnoticed, endeavouring to find some trace of her, in whose behalf he incurred the risk he ran. In the present temper of the tribe, it would have been easy to have fled and rejoined his companions, had such a wish crossed his mind. But, in addition, to the never-ceasing anxiety on account of Alice, a fresher, though feebler, interest in the fate of Uncas, assisted to chain him to the spot. He continued, therefore, to stray from hut to hut, looking into each only to encounter additional disappointment, until he had made the entire circuit of the village. Abandoning a species of inquiry that proved so fruitless, he retraced his steps to the council lodge, resolved to seek and question David, in order to put an end to his doubts.

On reaching the building, which had proved alike the seat of judgment and the place of execution, the young man found that the excitement had already subsided. The warriors had re-assembled, and were now calmly smoking, while they conversed gravely on the chief incidents of their recent expedition to the head of the Horican. Though the return of Duncan was likely to remind them of his character, and the suspicious circumstances of his visit, it produced no visible sensation. So far, the terrible scene that had just occurred, proved favourable to his views, and he required no other prompter than his own feelings to convince him of the expediency of profiting by so unexpected an advantage.

Without seeming to hesitate, he walked into the lodge, and took his seat with a gravity that accorded, admirably, with the deportment of his hosts. A hasty, but searching glance, sufficed to tell him, that though Uncas still remained where he had left him, David had not re-appeared. No other restraint was imposed on the former, than the watchful looks of a young Huron, who had placed himself at hand; though an armed warrior leaned against the post that formed one side of the narrow door-way. In every other respect, the captive seemed at liberty; still, he was excluded from all participation in the discourse, and possessed much more of the air of some finely moulded statue, than of a man having life and volition.

Heyward had, too recently, witnessed a frightful instance of the prompt punishments of the people, into whose hands he had fallen, to hazard an exposure by any officious boldness. He would greatly have preferred silence and meditation to speech, when a discovery of his real condition might prove so instantly fatal. Unfortunately for this prudent resolution, his entertainers appeared otherwise disposed. He had not long occupied the seat wisely taken, a little in the shade, when another of the elder warriors, who spoke the French language, addressed him—

"My Canada father does not forget his children!" said the chief; "I thank him. An evil spirit lives in the wife of one of my young men. Can the cunning stranger frighten him away?"

Heyward possessed some knowledge of the mummery practised among the Indians, in the cases of such supposed vistations. He saw, at a glance, that the circumstance might possibly be improved to further his own ends. It would, therefore, have been difficult, just then, to have uttered a proposal, that would have given him more satisfaction. Aware of the necessity of preserving the dignity of his imaginary character, however, he repressed his feelings, and answered with suitable mystery—

"Spirits differ; some yield to the power of wisdom, while others are too strong."

"My brother is a great medicine!" said the cunning savage; "he will try?"

A gesture of assent was the answer. The Huron was content with the assurance, and resuming his pipe, he awaited the proper moment to move. The impatient Heyward, inwardly execrating the cold customs of the savages, which required such a sacrifice to appearances, was fain to assume an air of indifference, equal to that maintained by the chief, who was, in truth, a near relative of the afflicted woman. The minutes lingered, and the delay had seemed an hour to the adventurer in empiricism, when the Huron laid aside his pipe, and drew his robe across his breast, as if about to lead the way to the lodge of the invalid. Just then, a warrior of powerful frame darkened the door, and stalking silently among the attentive groupe, he seated himself on one end of the low pile of brush, which sustained Duncan. The latter cast an impatient look at his neighbour, and felt his flesh creep with uncontrollable horror, when he found himself in actual contact with Magua.

The sudden return of this artful and dreaded chief, caused a delay in the departure of the Huron. Several pipes, that had been extinguished, were lighted again; while the new comer, without speaking a word, drew his tomahawk from his girdle, and filling the bowl on its head, began to inhale the vapours of the weed through the hollow handle, with as much indifference, as if he had not been absent two weary days, on a long and toilsome hunt. Ten minutes, which appeared so many ages to Duncan, might have passed in this manner; and the warriors were fairly enveloped in a cloud of white smoke, before any of them spoke.

"Welcome!" one at length uttered; "has my friend found the moose?"

"The young men staggered under their burthens," returned Magua. "Let 'Reed-that-bends' go on the hunting path; he will meet them."

A deep and awful silence succeeded the utterance of the forbidden name. Each pipe dropped from the lips of its owner, as though all had inhaled an impurity at the same instant. The smoke wreathed above their heads in little eddies, and curling in a spiral form, it ascended swiftly through the opening in the roof of the lodge, leaving the place beneath clear of its fumes, and each dark visage distinctly visible. The looks of most of the warriors were riveted on the earth; though a few of the younger and less gifted of the party, suffered their wild and glaring eye-balls to roll in the direction of a white headed savage, who sate between two of the most venerated chiefs of the tribe. There was nothing in the air or attire of this Indian, that would seem to entitle him to such a distinction. The former was rather depressed, than remarkable for the bearing of the natives; and the latter was such as was commonly worn by the ordinary men of the nation. Like most around him, for more than a minute, his look, too, was on the ground; but trusting his eyes, at length, to steal a glance aside, he perceived that he was becoming an object of general attention. Then he arose, and lifted his voice in the general silence.

"It was a lie," he said; "I had no son! He who was called by that name is forgotten; his blood was pale, and it came not from the veins of a Huron; the wicked Chippewas cheated my squaw! The Great Spirit has said, that the family of Wiss-en-tush should end—he is happy who knows that the evil of his race dies with himself! I have done."

The speaker, who was the father of the recreant young Indian, looked round and about him, as if seeking commendation of his stoicism, in the eyes of his auditors. But the stern customs of his people had made too severe an exaction of the feeble old man. The expression of his eye contradicted his figurative and boastful language, while every muscle in his wrinkled visage was working with anguish. Standing a single minute to enjoy his bitter triumph, he turned away, as if sickening at the gaze of men, and veiling his face in his blanket, he walked from the lodge, with the noiseless step of an Indian, and sought, in the privacy of his own abode, the sympathy of one like himself, aged, forlorn, and childless.

The Indians, who believe in the hereditary transmission of virtues and defects in character, suffered him to depart in silence. Then, with an elevation of breeding that many in a more cultivated state of society might profitably emulate, one of the chiefs drew the attention of the young men from the weakness they had just witnessed, by saying, in a cheerful voice, addressing himself in courtesy to Magua, as the newest comer—

"The Delawares have been like bears after the honey-pots, prowling around my village. But who has ever found a Huron asleep!"

The darkness of the impending cloud which precedes a burst of thunder, was not blacker than the brow of Magua, as he exclaimed—

"The Delawares of the Lakes!"

"Not so. They who wear the petticoats of squaws on their own river. One of them has been passing the tribe."

"Did my young men take his scalp?"

"His legs were good, though his arm is better for the hoe than the tomahawk," returned the other, pointing to the immovable form of Uncas.

Instead of manifesting any womanish curiosity to feast his eyes with the sight of a captive from a people he was known to have so much reason to hate, Magua continued to smoke, with the meditative air that he usually maintained, when there was no immediate call on his cunning or his eloquence. Although secretly amazed at the facts communicated by the speech of the aged father, he permitted himself to ask no questions, reserving his inquiries for a more suitable moment. It was only after a sufficient interval, that he shook the ashes from his pipe, replaced the tomahawk, tightened his girdle, and arose, casting, for the first time, a glance in the direction of the prisoner, who stood a little behind him. The wary, though seemingly abstracted, Uncas, caught a glimpse of the movement, and turning suddenly to the light, their looks met. Near a minute these two bold and untamed spirits stood regarding one another steadily in the eye, neither quailing in the least before the fierce gaze he encountered. The form of Uncas dilated, and his nostrils opened, like those of a tiger at bay; but so rigid and unyielding was his posture, that he might easily have been converted, by the imagination, into an exquisite and faultless representation of the warlike deity of his tribe. The lineaments of the quivering features of Magua proved more ductile; his countenance gradually lost its character of defiance in an expression of ferocious joy, and heaving a breath from the very bottom of his chest, he pronounced aloud the formidable name of—

"Le Cerf Agile!"

Each warrior sprang upon his feet at the utterance of the well-known appellation, and there was a short period, during which the stoical constancy of the natives was completely conquered by surprise. The hated and yet respected name was repeated, as by one voice, carrying the sound even beyond the limits of the lodge. The women and children, who lingered around the entrance, took up the words in an echo, which was succeeded by another shrill and plaintive howl. The latter was not yet ended, when the sensation among the men had entirely abated. Each one in presence seated himself, as though ashamed of his precipitation, but it was many minutes before their meaning eyes ceased to roll towards their captive, in curious examination of a warrior, who had so often proved his prowess on the best and proudest of their nation.

Uncas enjoyed his victory, but was content with merely exhibiting his triumph, by a quiet smile—an emblem of scorn which belongs to all time and every nation. Magua caught the expression, and raising his arm, he shook it at the captive—the light silver ornaments attached to his bracelet rattling with the trembling agitation of the limb, as, in a tone of vengeance, he exclaimed, in English—

"Mohican, you die!"

"The healing waters will never bring the dead Hurons to life!" returned Uncas, in the music of the Delawares; "the tumbling river washes their bones! their men are squaws; their women owls. Go—call together the Huron dogs, that they may look upon a warrior. My nostrils are offended; they scent the blood of a coward!"

The latter allusion struck deep, and the injury rankled. Many of the Hurons understood the strange tongue in which the captive spoke, among which number was Magua. This cunning savage beheld, and instantly profited by, his advantage. Dropping the light robe of skin from his shoulder, he stretched forth his arm, and commenced a burst of his dangerous and artful eloquence. However much his influence among his people had been impaired by his occasional and besetting weakness, as well as by his desertion of the tribe, his courage, and his fame as an orator, were undeniable. He never spoke without auditors, and rarely without making converts to his opinions. On the present occasion, his native powers were stimulated by the thirst of revenge.

He again recounted the events of the attack on the island at Glenn's; the death of his associates; and the escape of their most formidable enemies. Then he described the nature and position of the mount whither he had led such captives as had fallen into their hands. Of his own bloody intentions towards the maidens, and of his baffled malice, he made no mention, but passed rapidly on to the surprise by the party of "la Longue Carabine," and its fatal termination. Here he paused, and looked about him, in affected veneration for the departed—but, in truth, to note the effect of his opening narrative. As usual, every eye was riveted on his face. Each dusky figure seemed a breathing statue, so motionless was the posture, so intense the attention of the individual.

Then Magua dropped his voice, which had hitherto been clear, strong, and elevated, and touched upon the merits of the dead. No quality that was likely to command the sympathy of an Indian, escaped his notice. One had never been known to follow the chase in vain; another had been indefatigable on the trail of their enemies. This was brave; that, generous. In short, he so managed his allusions, that in a nation which was composed of so few families, he contrived to strike every chord that might find, in its turn, some breast in which to vibrate.

"Are the bones of my young men," he concluded, "in the burial place of the Hurons! You know they are not. Their spirits are gone towards the setting sun, and are already crossing the great waters, to the happy hunting grounds. But they departed without food, without guns or knives, without moccasins, naked and poor, as they were born. Shall this be? Are their souls to enter the land of the just, like hungry Iroquois, or unmanly Delawares; or shall they meet their friends with arms in their hands, and robes on their backs? What will our fathers think the tribes of the Wyandots have become? They will look on their children with a dark eye, and say, go; a Chippewa has come hither with the name of a Huron. Brothers, we must not forget the dead; a red skin never ceases to remember. We will load the back of this Mohican, until he staggers under our bounty, and despatch him after my young men. They call to us for aid, though our ears are not open; they say, forget us not. When they see the spirit of this Mohican toiling after them, with his burthen, they will know we are of that mind. Then will they go on happy; and our children will say, 'so did our fathers to their friends, so must we do to them.' What is a Yengee! we have slain many, but the earth is still pale. A stain on the name of a Huron can, only, be hid by blood that comes from the veins of an Indian. Let this Delaware die."

The effect of such an harangue, delivered in the nervous language, and with the emphatic manner of a Huron orator, could scarcely be mistaken. Magua had so artfully blended the natural sympathies with the religious superstition of his auditors, that their minds, already prepared by custom to sacrifice a victim to the manes of their countrymen, lost every vestige of humanity in a wish for revenge. One warrior in particular, a man of wild and ferocious mien, had been conspicuous for the attention he had given to the words of the speaker. His countenance had changed with each passing emotion, until it settled into a look of deadly malice. As Magua ended, he arose, and uttering the yell of a demon, his polished little axe was seen glancing in the torch light, as he whirled it above his head. The motion and the cry were too sudden for words to interrupt his bloody intention. It appeared as if a bright gleam shot from his hand, which was crossed at the same moment by a dark and powerful line. The former was the tomahawk in its passage; the latter the arm that Magua darted forward to divert its aim. The quick and ready motion of the chief was not entirely too late. The keen weapon cut the war-plume from the scalping tuft of Uncas, and passed through the frail wall of the lodge, as though it were hurled from some formidable engine.

Duncan had seen the threatening action, and sprang upon his feet, with a heart which, while it leaped into his throat, swelled with the most generous resolution in behalf of his friend. A glance told him that the blow had failed, and terror changed to admiration. Uncas stood, still looking his enemy in the eye, with features that seemed superior to emotion. Marble could not be colder, calmer, or steadier, than the countenance he put upon this sudden and vindictive attack. Then, as if pitying a want of skill, which had proved so fortunate to himself, he smiled, and muttered a few words of contempt, in his own tongue.

"No!" said Magua, after satisfying himself of the safety of the captive; "the sun must shine on his shame; the squaws must see his flesh tremble, or our revenge will be like the play of boys. Go—take him where there is silence; let us see if a Delaware can sleep at night, and, in the morning, die!"

The young men whose duty it was to guard the prisoner, instantly passed their ligaments of bark across his arms, and led him from the lodge, amid a profound and ominous silence. It was only as the figure of Uncas stood in the opening of the door, that his firm step hesitated. There he turned, and in the sweeping and haughty glance that he threw around the circle of his enemies, Duncan caught a look, which he was glad to construe into an expression that he was not entirely deserted by hope.

Magua was content with his success, or too much occupied with his secret purposes, to push his inquiries any further. Shaking his mantle, and folding it on his bosom, he also quitted the place, without pursuing a subject that might have proved so fatal to the individual at his elbow. Notwithstanding his rising resentment, his natural firmness, and his anxiety in behalf of Uncas, Heyward felt sensibly relieved by the absence of so dangerous and so subtle a foe. The excitement produced by the speech gradually subsided. The warriors resumed their seats, and clouds of smoke once more filled the lodge. For near half an hour, not a syllable was uttered, or scarcely a look cast aside—a grave and meditative silence being in the ordinary succession to every scene of violence and commotion, amongst those beings, who were alike so impetuous, and yet so self-restrained.

When the chief who had solicited the aid of Duncan had finished his pipe, he made a final and successful movement towards departing. A motion of a finger was the intimation he gave the supposed physician to follow; and passing through the clouds of smoke, Duncan was glad, on more accounts than one, to be able, at last, to breathe the pure air of a cool and refreshing summer evening.

Instead of pursuing his way among those lodges, where Heyward had already made his unsuccessful search, his companion turned aside, and proceeded directly toward the base of an adjacent mountain, which overhung the temporary village. A thicket of brush skirted its foot, and it became necessary to proceed through a crooked and narrow path. The boys had resumed their sports in the clearing, and were enacting a mimic chase to the post, among themselves. In order to render their games as like the reality as possible, one of the boldest of their number had conveyed a few brands into some piles of tree-tops, that had hitherto escaped the burning. The blaze of one of these fires lighted the way of the chief and Duncan, and gave a character of additional wildness to the rude scenery. At a little distance from a bald rock, and directly in its front, they entered a grassy opening, which they prepared to cross. Just then, fresh fuel was added to the fire, and a powerful light penetrated even to that distant spot. It fell upon the white surface of the mountain, and was reflected downward upon a dark and mysterious looking being, that arose, unexpectedly, in their path.

The Indian paused, as if doubtful whether to proceed, and permitted his companion to approach his side. A large black ball, which at first seemed stationary, now began to move in a manner, that to the latter was inexplicable. Again the fire brightened, and its glare fell more distinctly on the object. Then even Duncan knew it, by its restless and sideling attitudes, which kept the upper part of its form in constant motion, while the animal itself appeared seated, to be a bear. Though it growled loudly and fiercely, and there were instants when its glistening eye-balls might be seen, it gave no other indication of hostility. The Huron, at least, seemed assured that the intentions of this singular intruder were peaceable, for after giving it an attentive examination, he quietly pursued his course.

Duncan, who knew that the animal was often domesticated among the Indians, followed the example of his companion, believing that some favourite of the tribe had found its way into the thicket, in search of food. They passed it unmolested. Though obliged to come nearly in contact with the monster, the Huron, who had at first so warily determined the character of his strange visiter, was now content with proceeding without wasting a moment in further examination; but Heyward was unable to prevent his eyes from looking backward, in salutary watchfulness against attacks in the rear. His uneasiness was in no degree diminished, when he perceived the beast rolling along their path, and following their footsteps. He would have spoken, but the Indian at that moment shoved aside a door of bark, and entered a cavern in the bosom of the mountain.

Profiting by so easy a method of retreat, Duncan stepped after him, and was gladly closing the slight cover to the opening, when he felt it drawn from his hand by the beast, whose shaggy form immediately darkened the passage. They were now in a straight and long gallery, in a chasm of the rocks, where retreat, without encountering the animal, was impossible. Making the best of the circumstances, the young man pressed forward, keeping as close as possible to his conductor. The bear growled frequently at his heels, and once or twice its enormous paws were laid on his person, as if disposed to prevent his further passage into the den.

How long the nerves of Heyward would have sustained him in this extraordinary situation, it might be difficult to decide, for, happily, he soon found relief. A glimmer of light had constantly been in their front, and they now arrived at the place whence it proceeded.

A large cavity in the rock had been rudely fitted to answer

the purposes of many apartments. The subdivisions were simple, but ingenious; being composed of stone, sticks, and bark, intermingled. Openings above admitted the light by day, and at night fires and torches supplied the place of the sun. Hither the Hurons had brought most of their valuables, especially those which more particularly pertained to the nation; and hither, as it now appeared, the sick woman, who was believed to be the victim of supernatural power, had been transported also, under an impression, that her tormentor would find more difficulty in making his assaults through walls of stone, than through the leafy coverings of the lodges. The apartment into which Duncan and his guide first entered, had been exclusively devoted to her accommodation. The latter approached her bed-side, which was surrounded by females, in the centre of whom, Heyward was surprised to find his missing friend David.

A single look was sufficient to apprise the pretended leech, that the invalid was far beyond his powers of healing. She lay in a sort of paralysis, indifferent to the objects which crowded before her sight, and happily unconscious of suffering. Heyward was far from regretting that his mummeries were to be performed on one who was much too ill to take an interest in their failure or success. The slight qualm of conscience which had been excited by the intended deception, was instantly appeased, and he began to collect his thoughts, in order to enact his part with suitable spirit, when he found he was about to be anticipated in his skill, by an attempt to prove the power of music.

Gamut, who had stood prepared to pour forth his spirit in song when the visiters entered, after delaying a moment, drew a strain from his pipe, and commenced a hymn, that might have worked a miracle, had faith in its efficacy been of much avail. He was allowed to proceed to the close, the Indians respecting his imaginary infirmity, and Duncan too glad of the delay to hazard the slightest interruption. As the dying cadence of his strains was falling on the ears of the latter, he started aside at hearing them repeated behind him, in a voice half human and half sepulchral. Looking around, he beheld the shaggy monster seated on end, in a shadow of the cavern, where, while his restless body swung in the uneasy manner of the animal, it repeated, in a sort of low growl, sounds, if not words, which bore some slight resemblance to the melody of the singer.

The effect of so strange an echo, on David, may better be imagined than described. His eyes opened, as if he doubted their truth; and his voice became instantly mute, in excess of wonder. A deep laid scheme of communicating some important intelligence to Heyward, was driven from his recollection by an emotion which very nearly resembled fear, but which he was fain to believe was admiration. Under its influence, he exclaimed aloud—"She expects you, and is at hand"—and precipitately left the cavern.

Chapter XXV

Snug. "Have you the lion's part written? Pray you, if it be,
give it me, for I am slow of study.
Quince. You may do it extempore, for it is nothing but
roaring."

A Midsummer Night's Dream, I.ii.66–69.

THERE WAS A strange blending of the ridiculous, with that which was solemn, in this scene. The beast still continued its rolling, and apparently untiring, movements, though its ludicrous attempt to imitate the melody of David ceased the instant the latter abandoned the field. The words of Gamut were, as has been seen, in his native tongue; and to Duncan they seemed pregnant with some hidden meaning, though nothing present assisted him in discovering the object of their allusion. A speedy end was, however, put to every conjecture on the subject, by the manner of the chief, who advanced to the bed-side of the invalid, and beckoned away the whole groupe of female attendants, that had clustered there to witness the skill of the stranger. He was implicitly, though reluctantly, obeyed; and when the low echo which rang along the hollow, natural gallery, from the distant closing door, had ceased, pointing towards his insensible daughter, he said—

"Now let my brother show his power."

Thus unequivocally called on to exercise the functions of his assumed character, Heyward was apprehensive that the smallest delay might prove dangerous. Endeavouring then to collect his ideas he prepared to commence that species of incantation, and those uncouth rites, under which the Indian conjurers are accustomed to conceal their ignorance and impotency. It is more than probable, that in the disordered state of his thoughts, he would soon have fallen into some suspicious, if not fatal error, had not his incipient attempts been interrupted by a fierce growl from the quadruped. Three several times did he renew his efforts to proceed, and as often was he met by the same unaccountable opposition, each interruption seeming more savage and threatening than the preceding.

"The cunning ones are jealous," said the Huron; "I go. Brother, the woman is the wife of one of my bravest young men; deal justly by her. Peace," he added, beckoning to the discontented beast to be quiet; "I go."

The chief was as good as his word, and Duncan now found himself alone in that wild and desolate abode, with the helpless invalid, and the fierce and dangerous brute. The latter listened to the movements of the Indian, with that air of sagacity that a bear is known to possess, until another echo announced that he had also left the cavern, when it turned and came waddling up to Duncan, before whom it seated itself, in its natural attitude, erect like a man. The youth looked anxiously about him for some weapon, with which he might make a resistance against the attack he now seriously expected.

It seemed, however, as if the humour of the animal had suddenly changed. Instead of continuing its discontented growls, or manifesting any further signs of anger, the whole of its shaggy body shook violently, as if agitated by some strange, internal, convulsion. The huge and unwieldy talons pawed stupidly about the grinning muzzle, and while Heyward kept his eyes riveted on its movements, with jealous watchfulness, the grim head fell on one side, and in its place appeared the honest, sturdy countenance of the scout, who was indulging, from the bottom of his soul, in his own peculiar expression of merriment.

"Hist!" said the wary woodsman, interrupting Heyward's exclamation of surprise; "the varlets are about the place, and any sounds that are not natural to witchcraft, would bring them back upon us in a body!"

"Tell me the meaning of this masquerade; and why you have attempted so desperate an adventure!"

"Ah! reason and calculation are often outdone by accident," returned the scout. "But as a story should always commence at the beginning, I will tell you the whole in order. After we parted, I placed the Commandant and the Sagamore in an old beaver lodge, where they are safer from the Hurons, than they would be in the garrison of Edward; for your high norwest Indians, not having as yet got the traders much among them, continue to venerate the beaver. After which, Uncas and I pushed for the other encampment, as was agreed; have you seen the lad?"

"To my great grief!—he is captive, and condemned to die at the rising of the sun."

"I had misgivings that such would be his fate," resumed the scout, in a less confident and joyous tone. But soon regaining his naturally firm voice, he continued—"His bad fortune is the true reason of my being here, for it would never do to abandon such a boy to the Hurons! A rare time the knaves would have of it, could they tie the 'bounding elk' and the 'longue carabine,' as they call me, to the same stake! Though why they have given me such a name, I never knew, there being as little likeness between the gifts of 'killdeer' and the performance of one of your real Canada carabynes, as there is between the natur of a pipe-stone and a flint!"

"Keep to your tale," said the impatient Heyward; "we know not at what moment the Hurons may return."

"No fear of them. A conjuror must have his time, like a straggling priest in the settlements. We are as safe from interruption, as a missionary would be at the beginning of a two hours' discourse. Well, Uncas and I fell in with a return party of the varlets; the lad was much too forward for a scout; nay, for that matter, being of hot blood, he was not so much to blame; and, after all, one of the Hurons proved a coward, and in fleeing, led him into an ambushment!"

"And dearly has he paid for the weakness!"

The scout significantly passed his hand across his own throat, and nodded, as if he said, "I comprehend your meaning." After which, he continued, in a more audible, though scarcely more intelligible language—

"After the loss of the boy, I turned upon the Hurons, as you may judge. There have been skrimmages atween one or two of their outlyers and myself; but that is neither here nor there. So, after I had shot the imps, I got in pretty nigh to the lodges, without further commotion. Then, what should luck do in my favour, but lead me to the very spot where one of the most famous conjurors of the tribe was dressing himself, as I well knew, for some great battle with Satan—though why should I call that luck, which it now seems was an especial ordering of Providence! So, a judgematical rap, over the head, stiffened the lying impostor for a time, and leaving him a bit of walnut for his supper, to prevent any uproar, and stringing him up atween two saplings, I made free with his finery, and took the part of a bear on myself, in order that the operations might proceed."

"And admirably did you enact the character! the animal itself might have been shamed by the representation."

"Lord, major," returned the flattered woodsman, "I should be but a poor scholar, for one who has studied so long in the wilderness, did I not know how to set forth the movements and natur of such a beast! Had it been now a catamount, or even a full sized painter, I would have embellished a performance, for you, worth regarding! But it is no such marvellous feat to exhibit the feats of so dull a beast; though, for that matter too, a bear may be over acted! Yes, yes; it is not every imitator that knows natur may be outdone easier than she is equalled. But all our work is yet before us! where is the gentle one?"

"Heaven knows; I have examined every lodge in the village, without discovering the slightest trace of her presence in the tribe."

"You heard what the singer said, as he left us—'she is at hand, and expects you.' "

"I have been compelled to believe he alluded to this unhappy woman."

"The simpleton was frightened, and blundered through his message, but he had a deeper meaning. Here are walls enough to separate the whole settlement. A bear ought to climb; therefore will I take a look above them. There may be honey-pots hid in these rocks, and I am a beast, you know, that has a hankering for the sweets."

The scout looked behind him, laughing at his own conceit, while he clambered up the partition, imitating, as he went, the clumsy motions of the beast he represented; but the instant the summit was gained, he made a gesture for silence, and slid down with the utmost precipitation.

"She is here," he whispered, "and by that door you will find her. I would have spoken a word of comfort to the afflicted soul, but the sight of such a monster might upset her reason.

Though, for that matter, major, you are none of the most inviting yourself, in your paint."

Duncan, who had already sprung eagerly forward, drew instantly back, on hearing these discouraging words.

"Am I then so very revolting?" he demanded, with an air of chagrin.

"You might not startle a wolf, or turn the Royal Americans from a charge; but I have seen the time when you had a better favoured look; your streaked countenances are not ill judged of by the squaws, but young women of white blood give the preference to their own colour. See," he added, pointing to a place where the water trickled from a rock, forming a little crystal spring, before it found an issue through the adjacent crevices; "you may easily get rid of the Sagamore's daub, and when you come back, I will try my hand at a new embellishment. It's as common for a conjuror to alter his paint, as for a buck in the settlements to change his finery."

The deliberate woodsman had little occasion to hunt for arguments to enforce his advice. He was yet speaking, when Duncan availed himself of the water. In a moment, every frightful or offensive mark was obliterated, and the youth appeared again in the lineaments with which he had been gifted by nature. Thus prepared for an interview with his mistress, he took a hasty leave of his companion, and disappeared through the indicated passage. The scout witnessed his departure with complacency, nodding his head after him, and muttering his good wishes; after which, he very coolly set about an examination of the state of the larder among the Hurons—the cavern, among other purposes, being used as a receptacle for the fruits of their hunts.

Duncan had no other guide than a distant glimmering light, which served, however, the office of a polar star to the lover. By its aid, he was enabled to enter the haven of his hopes, which was merely another apartment of the cavern, that had been solely appropriated to the safe keeping of so important a prisoner, as a daughter of the commandant of William Henry. It was profusely strewed with the plunder of that unlucky fortress. In the midst of this confusion he found her he sought, pale, anxious, and terrified, but lovely. David had prepared her for such a visit.

"Duncan!" she exclaimed, in a voice that seemed to tremble at the sounds created by itself.

"Alice!" he answered, leaping carelessly among trunks, boxes, arms, and furniture, until he stood at her side.

"I knew that you would never desert me," she said, looking up with a momentary glow on her otherwise dejected countenance. "But you are alone! grateful as it is to be thus remembered, I could wish to think you are not entirely alone!"

Duncan, observing that she trembled in a manner which betrayed her inability to stand, gently induced her to be seated, while he recounted those leading incidents which it has been our task to record. Alice listened with breathless interest; and though the young man touched lightly on the sorrows of the stricken father, taking care, however, not to wound the self-love of his auditor, the tears ran as freely down the cheeks of the daughter, as though she had never wept before. The soothing tenderness of Duncan, however, soon quieted the first burst of her emotions, and she then heard him to the close with undivided attention, if not with composure.

"And now, Alice," he added, "you will see how much is still expected of you. By the assistance of our experienced and invaluable friend, the scout, we may find our way from this savage people, but you will have to exert your utmost fortitude. Remember, that you fly to the arms of your venerable parent, and how much his happiness, as well as your own, depends on those exertions."

"Can I do otherwise for a father who has done so much for me!"

"And for me too!" continued the youth, gently pressing the hand he held in both his own.

The look of innocence and surprise which he received, in return, convinced Duncan of the necessity of being more explicit.

"This is neither the place nor the occasion to detain you with selfish wishes," he added; "but what heart loaded like mine would not wish to cast its burthen! They say misery is the closest of all ties; our common suffering in your behalf, left but little to be explained between your father and myself."

"And dearest Cora, Duncan; surely Cora was not forgotten!"

"Not forgotten! no; regretted as woman was seldom mourned, before. Your venerable father knew no difference between his children; but I—Alice, you will not be offended, when I say, that to me her worth was in a degree obscured—"

"Then you knew not the merit of my sister," said Alice, withdrawing her hand; "of you she ever speaks, as of one who is her dearest friend!"

"I would gladly believe her such," returned Duncan, hastily; "I could wish her to be even more; but with you, Alice, I have the permission of your father to aspire to a still nearer and dearer tie."

Alice trembled violently, and there was an instant, during which she bent her face aside, yielding to the emotions common to her sex; but they quickly passed away, leaving her mistress of her deportment, if not of her affections.

"Heyward," she said, looking him full in the face, with a touching expression of innocence and dependency, "give me the sacred presence and the holy sanction of that parent, before you urge me farther."

"Though more I should not, less I could not say," the youth was about to answer, when he was interrupted by a light tap on his shoulder. Starting to his feet, he turned, and confronting the intruder, his looks fell on the dark form and malignant visage of Magua. The deep, guttural laugh of the savage, sounded, at such a moment, to Duncan, like the hellish taunt of a demon. Had he pursued the sudden and fierce impulse of the instant, he would have cast himself on the Huron, and committed their fortunes to the issue of a deadly struggle. But, without arms of any description, ignorant of what succours his subtle enemy could command, and charged with the safety of one who was just then dearer than ever to his heart, he no sooner entertained, than he abandoned the desperate intention.

"What is your purpose?" said Alice, meekly folding her arms on her bosom, and struggling to conceal an agony of apprehension in behalf of Heyward, in the usual cold and distant manner with which she received the visits of her captor.

The exulting Indian had resumed his austere countenance, though he drew warily back before the menacing glance of the young man's fiery eye. He regarded both his captives for a moment with a steady look, and then stepping aside, he dropped a log of wood across a door different from that by which Duncan had entered. The latter now comprehended the manner of his surprise, and believing himself irretrievably lost, he drew Alice to his bosom, and stood prepared to meet a fate which he hardly regretted, since it was to be suffered in such company. But Magua meditated no immediate violence. His first measures were very evidently taken to secure his new captive; nor did he even bestow a second glance at the motionless forms in the centre of the cavern, until he had completely cut off every hope of retreat through the private outlet he had himself used. He was watched in all his movements by Heyward, who however remained firm, still folding the fragile form of Alice to his heart, at once too proud and too hopeless to ask favour of an enemy so often foiled. When Magua had effected his object, he approached his prisoners, and said, in English—

"The pale-faces trap the cunning beavers; but the red-skins known how to take the Yengeese!"

"Huron, do your worst!" exclaimed the excited Heyward, forgetful that a double stake was involved in his life; "you and your vengeance are alike despised."

"Will the white man speak these words at the stake?" asked Magua; manifesting, at the same time, how little faith he had in the other's resolution, by the sneer that accompanied his words.

"Here; singly to your face, or in the presence of your nation!"

"Le Renard Subtil is a great chief!" returned the Indian; "he will go and bring his young men, to see how bravely a pale-face can laugh at the tortures."

He turned away while speaking, and was about to leave the place through the avenue by which Duncan had approached, when a growl caught his ear, and caused him to hesitate. The figure of the bear appeared in the door, where it sate rolling from side to side, in its customary restlessness. Magua, like the father of the sick woman, eyed it keenly for a moment, as if to ascertain its character. He was far above the more vulgar superstitions of his tribe, and so soon as he recognised the well known attire of the conjuror, he prepared to pass it in cool contempt. But a louder and more threatening growl caused him again to pause. Then he seemed as if suddenly resolved to trifle no longer, and moved resolutely forward. The mimic animal, which had advanced a little, retired slowly in his front, until it arrived again at the pass, when rearing on its hinder legs, it beat the air with its paws, in the manner practised by its brutal prototype.

"Fool!" exclaimed the chief, in Huron, "go play with the children and squaws; leave men to their wisdom."

He once more endeavoured to pass the supposed empyric, scorning even the parade of threatening to use the knife, or tomahawk, that was pendant from his belt. Suddenly, the beast extended its arms, or rather legs, and enclosed him in a grasp, that might have vied with the far-famed power of the "bear's hug" itself. Heyward had watched the whole procedure, on the part of Hawk-eye, with breathless interest. At first he relinquished his hold of Alice; then he caught up a thong of buckskin, which had been used around some bundle, and when he beheld his enemy with his two arms pinned to his side, by the iron muscles of the scout, he rushed upon him, and effectually secured them there. Arms, legs, and feet, were encircled in twenty folds of the thong, in less time than we have taken to record the circumstance. When the formidable Huron was completely pinioned, the scout released his hold, and Duncan laid his enemy on his back, utterly helpless.

Throughout the whole of this sudden and extraordinary operation, Magua, though he had struggled violently, until assured he was in the hands of one whose nerves were far better strung than his own, had not uttered the slightest exclamation. But when Hawk-eye, by way of making a summary explanation of his conduct, removed the shaggy jaws of the beast, and exposed his own rugged and earnest countenance to the gaze of the Huron, the philosophy of the latter was so far mastered, as to permit him to utter the never-failing—

"Hugh!"

"Ay! you've found your tongue!" said his undisturbed conqueror; "now, in order that you shall not use it to our ruin, I must make free to stop your mouth."

As there was no time to be lost, the scout immediately set about effecting so necessary a precaution; and when he had gagged the Indian, his enemy might safely have been considered as "hors de combat."

"By what place did the imp enter?" asked the industrious scout, when his work was ended. "Not a soul has passed my way since you left me."

Duncan pointed out the door by which Magua had come, and which now presented too many obstacles to a quick retreat.

"Bring on the gentle one then," continued his friend; "we must make a push for the woods by the other outlet."

"'Tis impossible!" said Duncan; "fear has overcome her, and she is helpless. Alice! my sweet, my own Alice, arouse yourself; now is the moment to fly. 'Tis in vain! she hears, but is unable to follow. Go, noble and worthy friend; save yourself, and leave me to my fate!"

"Every trail has its end, and every calamity brings its lesson!" returned the scout. "There, wrap her in them Indian cloths. Conceal all of her little form. Nay, that foot has no fellow in the wilderness; it will betray her. All, every part. Now take her in your arms, and follow. Leave the rest to me."

Duncan, as may be gathered from the words of his companion, was eagerly obeying; and as the other finished speaking, he took the light person of Alice in his arms, and followed on the footsteps of the scout. They found the sick woman as they had left her, still alone, and passed swiftly on, by the natural gallery, to the place of entrance. As they approached the little door of bark, a murmur of voices without announced that the friends and relatives of the invalid were gathered about the place, patiently awaiting a summons to re-enter.

"If I open my lips to speak," Hawk-eye whispered, "my

English, which is the genuine tongue of a white-skin, will tell the varlets that an enemy is among them. You must give 'em your jargon, major; and say, that we have shut the evil spirit in the cave, and are taking the woman to the woods, in order to find strengthening roots. Practyse all your cunning, for it is a lawful undertaking."

The door opened a little, as if one without was listening to the proceedings within, and compelled the scout to cease his directions. A fierce growl repelled the eaves-dropper, and then the scout boldly threw open the covering of bark, and left the place, enacting the character of the bear as he proceeded. Duncan kept close at his heels, and soon found himself in the centre of a cluster of twenty anxious relatives and friends.

The crowd fell back a little, and permitted the father, and one who appeared to be the husband of the woman, to approach.

"Has my brother driven away the evil spirit?" demanded the former. "What has he in his arms?"

"Thy child," returned Duncan, gravely; "the disease has gone out of her; it is shut up in the rocks. I take the woman to a distance, where I will strengthen her against any further attacks. She shall be in the wigwam of the young man when the sun comes again."

When the father had translated the meaning of the stranger's words into the Huron language, a suppressed murmur announced the satisfaction with which this intelligence was received. The chief himself waved his hand for Duncan to proceed, saying aloud, in a firm voice, and with a lofty manner—

"Go—I am a man, and I will enter the rock and fight the wicked one!"

Heyward had gladly obeyed, and was already past the little groupe, when these startling words arrested him.

"Is my brother mad!" he exclaimed; "is he cruel! He will meet the disease, and it will enter him; or he will drive out the disease, and it will chase his daughter into the woods. No—let my children wait without, and if the spirit appears, beat him down with clubs. He is cunning, and will bury himself in the mountain, when he sees how many are ready to fight him."

This singular warning had the desired effect. Instead of entering the cavern, the father and husband drew their tomahawks, and posted themselves in readiness to deal their vengeance on the imaginary tormentor of their sick relative, while the women and children broke branches from the bushes, or seized fragments of the rock, with a similar intention. At this favourable moment the counterfeit conjurors disappeared.

Hawk-eye, at the same time that he had presumed so far on the nature of the Indian superstitions, was not ignorant that they were rather tolerated than relied on by the wisest of the chiefs. He well knew the value of time in the present emergency. Whatever might be the extent of the self-delusion of his enemies, and however it had tended to assist his schemes, the slightest cause of suspicion, acting on the subtle nature of an Indian, would be likely to prove fatal. Taking the path, therefore, that was most likely to avoid observation, he rather skirted than entered the village. The warriors were still to be seen in the distance, by the fading light of the fires, stalking from lodge to lodge. But the children had abandoned their sports for their beds of skins, and the quiet of night was already beginning to prevail over the turbulence and excitement of so busy and important an evening.

Alice revived under the renovating influence of the open air, and as her physical rather than her mental powers had been the subject of weakness, she stood in no need of any explanation of that which had occurred.

"Now let me make an effort to walk," she said, when they had entered the forest, blushing, though unseen, that she had not been sooner able to quit the arms of Duncan; "I am, indeed, restored."

"Nay, Alice, you are yet too weak."

The maiden struggled gently to release herself, and Heyward was compelled to part with his precious burthen. The representative of the bear had certainly been an entire stranger to the delicious emotions of the lover, while his arms encircled his mistress, and he was, perhaps, a stranger also to the nature of that feeling of ingenuous shame, that oppressed the trembling Alice. But when he found himself at a suitable distance from the lodges, he made a halt, and spoke on a subject of which he was thoroughly the master.

"This path will lead you to the brook," he said; "follow its northern bank until you come to a fall; mount the hill on your right, and you will see the fires of the other people. There you must go, and demand protection; if they are true Delawares, you will be safe. A distant flight with that gentle one, just now, is impossible. The Hurons would follow up our trail, and master our scalps, before we had got a dozen miles. Go, and Providence be with you."

"And you!" demanded Heyward, in surprise; "surely we part not here!"

"The Hurons hold the pride of the Delawares; the last of the high blood of the Mohicans, is in their power!" returned the scout; "I go to see what can be done in his favour. Had they mastered your scalp, major, a knave should have fallen for every hair it held, as I promised; but if the young Sagamore is to be led to the stake, the Indians shall see also how a man without a cross can die!"

Not in the least offended with the decided preference that the sturdy woodsman gave to one who might, in some degree, be called the child of his adoption, Duncan still continued to urge such reasons against so desperate an effort, as presented themselves. He was aided by Alice, who mingled her entreaties with those of Heyward, that he would abandon a resolution that promised so much danger, with such little hopes of success. Their eloquence and ingenuity were expended in vain. The scout heard them attentively, but impatiently, and finally closed the discussion, by answering, in a tone that instantly silenced Alice, while it told Heyward how fruitless any further remonstrances would be.

"I have heard," he said, "that there is a feeling in youth, which binds man to woman, closer than the father is tied to the son. It may be so. I have seldom been where women of my colour dwell; but such may be the gifts of natur in the settlements! You have risked life, and all that is dear to you, to bring off this gentle one, and I suppose that some such disposition is at the bottom of it all. As for me, I taught the lad the real character of a rifle; and well has he paid me for it! I have fou't at his side in many a bloody skrimmage; and so long as I could hear the crack of his piece in one ear, and that of the Sagamore in the other, I knew no enemy was on my back. Winters and summers, nights and days, have we roved the wilderness in company, eating of the same dish, one sleeping while the other watched; and afore it shall be said that Uncas was taken to the torment, and I at hand—— There is but a single Ruler of us all, whatever may be the colour of the skin; and him I call to witness—that before the Mohican boy shall perish for the want of a friend, good faith shall depart the 'arth, and 'kill-deer' become as harmless as the tooting we'pon of the singer!"

Duncan released his hold on the arm of the scout, who turned, and steadily retraced his steps towards the lodges. After pausing a moment to gaze at his retiring form, the successful and yet sorrowful Heyward, and Alice, took their way together towards the distant village of the Delawares.

Chapter XXVI

Bot. "Let me play the lion too."
A Midsummer Night's Dream, I.ii.70.

NOTWITHSTANDING the high resolution of Hawk-eye, he fully comprehended all the difficulties and dangers he was about to incur. In his return to the camp, his acute and practised intellects were intently engaged in devising means to counteract a watchfulness and suspicion on the part of his enemies, that he knew were, in no degree, inferior to his own. Nothing but the colour of his skin had saved the lives of Magua and the conjuror, who would have been the first victims sacrificed to his own security, had not the scout believed such an act, however congenial it might be to the nature of an Indian, utterly unworthy of one who boasted a descent from men that knew no cross of blood. Accordingly, he trusted to the withes and ligaments with which he had bound his captives, and pursued his way directly towards the centre of the lodges.

As he approached the buildings, his steps became more deliberate, and his vigilant eye suffered no sign, whether friendly or hostile, to escape him. A neglected hut was a little in advance of the others, and appeared as if it had been deserted when half completed—most probably on account of failing in some of the more important requisites; such as wood or water. A faint light glimmered through its cracks, however, and announced, that notwithstanding its imperfect structure, it was not without a tenant. Thither, then, the scout proceeded, like a prudent general, who was about to feel the advanced positions of his enemy, before he hazarded the main attack.

Throwing himself into a suitable posture for the beast he represented, Hawk-eye crawled to a little opening, where he might command a view of the interior. It proved to be the abiding-place of David Gamut. Hither the faithful singing-master had now brought himself, together with all his sorrows, his apprehensions, and his meek dependence on the protection of Providence. At the precise moment when his ungainly person came under the observation of the scout, in the manner just mentioned, the woodsman himself, though in his assumed character, was the subject of the solitary being's profoundest reflections.

However implicit the faith of David was in the performance of ancient miracles, he eschewed the belief of any direct supernatural agency in the management of modern morality. In other words, while he had implicit faith in the ability of Balaam's ass to speak, he was somewhat sceptical on the subject of a bear's singing; and yet he had been assured of the latter, on the testimony of his own exquisite organs! There was something in his air and manner, that betrayed to the scout the utter confusion of the state of his mind. He was seated on a pile of brush, a few twigs from which occasionally fed his low fire, with his head leaning on his arm, in a posture of melancholy musing. The costume of the votary of music had undergone no other alteration from that so lately described, except that he had covered his bald head with the triangular beaver, which had not proved sufficiently alluring to excite the cupidity of any of his captors.

The ingenious Hawk-eye, who recalled the hasty manner in which the other had abandoned his post at the bed-side of the sick woman, was not without his suspicions concerning the subject of so much solemn deliberation. First making the circuit of the hut, and ascertaining that it stood quite alone, and that the character of its inmate was likely to protect it from visiters, he ventured through its low door, into the very presence of Gamut. The position of the latter brought the fire between them; and when Hawk-eye had seated himself on end, near a minute elapsed, during which the two remained regarding each other without speaking. The suddenness and the nature of the surprise, had nearly proved too much for—we will not say the philosophy—but for the faith and resolution of David. He fumbled for his pitch-pipe, and arose with a confused intention of attempting a musical exorcism.

"Dark and mysterious monster!" he exclaimed, while with trembling hands he disposed of his auxiliary eyes, and sought his never-failing resource in trouble, the gifted version of the Psalms; "I know not your nature nor intents; but if aught you meditate against the person and rights of one of the humblest servants of the temple, listen to the inspired language of the youth of Israel, and repent."

The bear shook his shaggy sides, and then a well-known voice replied—

"Put up the tooting we'pon, and teach your throat modesty. Five words of plain and comprehendible English, are worth, just now, an hour of squalling."

"What art thou?" demanded David, utterly disqualified to pursue his original intention, and nearly gasping for breath.

"A man like yourself; and one whose blood is as little tainted by the cross of a bear, or an Indian, as your own. Have you so soon forgotten from whom you received the foolish instrument you hold in your hand?"

"Can these things be?" returned David, breathing more freely, as the truth began to dawn upon him. "I have found many marvels during my sojourn with the heathen, but, surely, nothing to excel this!"

"Come, come," returned Hawk-eye, uncasing his honest countenance, the better to assure the wavering confidence of his companion; "you may see a skin, which, if it be not as white as one of the gentle ones, has no tinge of red to it, that the winds of the heaven and the sun have not bestowed. Now let us to business."

"First tell me of the maiden, and of the youth who so bravely sought her," interrupted David.

"Ay, they are happily freed from the tomahawks of these varlets! But can you put me on the scent of Uncas?"

"The young man is in bondage, and much I fear his death is decreed. I greatly mourn, that one so well disposed should die in his ignorance, and I have sought a goodly hymn—"

"Can you lead me to him?"

"The task will not be difficult," returned David, hesitating; "though I greatly fear your presence would rather increase than mitigate his unhappy fortunes."

"No more words, but lead on," returned Hawk-eye, concealing his face again, and setting the example in his own person, by instantly quitting the lodge.

As they proceeded, the scout ascertained that his companion found access to Uncas, under privilege of his imaginary infirmity, aided by the favour he had acquired with one of the guards, who, in consequence of speaking a little English, had been selected by David as the subject of a religious conversion. How far the Huron comprehended the intentions of his new friend, may well be doubted; but as exclusive attention is as flattering to a savage as to a more civilized individual, it had produced the effect we have mentioned. It is unnecessary to repeat the shrewd manner with which the scout extracted these particulars from the simple David, neither shall we dwell, in this place, on the nature of the instructions he delivered, when completely master of all the necessary facts, as the whole will be sufficiently explained to the reader in the course of the narrative.

The lodge in which Uncas was confined, was in the very centre of the village, and in a situation, perhaps, more difficult than any other to approach or leave without observation. But it was not the policy of Hawk-eye to affect the least concealment. Presuming on his disguise, and his ability to sustain the character he had assumed, he took the most plain and direct route to the place. The hour, however, afforded him some little of that protection, which he appeared so much to despise. The boys were already buried in sleep, and all the women, and most of the warriors, had retired to their lodges for the night. Four or five of the latter, only, lingered about the door of the prison of Uncas, wary, but close observers of the manner of their captive.

At the sight of Gamut, accompanied by one in the well known masquerade of their most distinguished conjuror, they readily made way for them both. Still, they betrayed no intention to depart. On the other hand, they were evidently disposed to remain bound to the place by an additional interest in the mysterious mummeries that they, of course, expected from such a visit. From the total inability of the scout to address the Hurons, in their own language, he was compelled to trust the conversation entirely to David. Notwithstanding the simplicity of the latter, he did ample justice to the instructions he had received, more than fulfilling the strongest hopes of his teacher.

"The Delawares are women!" he exclaimed, addressing himself to the savage who had a slight understanding of the language, in which he spoke; "the Yengeese, my foolish countrymen, have told them to take up the tomahawk, and strike their fathers in the Canadas, and they have forgotten their sex. Does my brother wish to hear 'le Cerf Agile' ask for his petticoats, and see him weep before the Hurons, at the stake?"

The exclamation, "hugh," delivered in a strong tone of assent, announced the gratification the savage would receive, in witnessing such an exhibition of weakness in an enemy so long hated and so much feared.

"Then let him step aside, and the cunning man will blow upon the dog! Tell it to my brothers."

The Huron explained the meaning of David to his fellows, who, in their turn, listened to the project with that sort of satisfaction, that their untamed spirits might be expected to find, in such a refinement in cruelty. They drew back a little from the entrance, and motioned to the supposed conjuror to enter. But the bear, instead of obeying, maintained the seat it had taken, and growled.

"The cunning man is afraid that his breath will blow upon his brothers, and take away their courage too," continued David, improving the hint he received; "they must stand further off."

The Hurons, who would have deemed such a misfortune the heaviest calamity that could befall them, fell back in a body, taking a position where they were out of ear-shot, though, at the same time, they could command a view of the entrance to the lodge. Then, as if satisfied of their safety, the scout left his position, and slowly entered the place. It was silent and gloomy, being tenanted solely by the captive, and lighted by the dying embers of a fire, which had been used for the purposes of cookery.

Uncas occupied a distant corner, in a reclining attitude, being rigidly bound, both hands and feet, by strong and painful withes. When the frightful object first presented itself to the young Mohican, he did not deign to bestow a single glance on the animal. The scout, who had left David at the door, to ascertain they were not observed, thought it prudent to preserve his disguise until assured of their privacy. Instead of speaking, therefore, he exerted himself to enact one of the antics of the animal he represented. The young Mohican, who, at first, believed his enemies had sent in a real beast to torment him, and try his nerves, detected, in those performances that to Heyward had appeared so accurate, certain blemishes, that at once betrayed the counterfeit. Had Hawk-eye been aware of the low estimation in which the more skilful Uncas held his representations, he would, probably, have prolonged the entertainment a little in pique. But the scornful expression of the young man's eye, admitted of so many constructions, that the worthy scout was spared the mortification of such a discovery. As soon, therefore, as David gave the preconcerted signal, a low, hissing sound, was heard in the lodge, in place of the fierce growlings of the bear.

Uncas had cast his body back against the wall of the hut, and closed his eyes, as if willing to exclude so contemptible and disagreeable an object from his sight. But the moment the noise of the serpent was heard, he arose, and cast his looks on each side of him, bending his head low, and turning it inquiringly in every direction, until his keen eye rested on the shaggy monster, where it remained riveted, as though fixed by the power of a charm. Again the same sounds were repeated, evidently proceeding from the mouth of the beast. Once more the eyes of the youth roamed over the interior of the lodge, and returning to their former resting-place, he uttered, in a deep, suppressed voice—

"Hawk-eye!"

"Cut his bands," said Hawk-eye to David, who just then approached them.

The singer did as he was ordered, and Uncas found his limbs released. At the same moment, the dried skin of the animal rattled, and presently the scout arose to his feet, in proper person. The Mohican appeared to comprehend the nature of the attempt his friend had made, intuitively; neither tongue nor feature betraying another symptom of surprise. When Hawk-eye had cast his shaggy vestment, which was done by simply loosing certain thongs of skin, he drew a long glittering knife, and put it in the hands of Uncas.

"The red Hurons are without," he said; "let us be ready."

At the same time, he laid his finger significantly on another similar weapon; both being the fruits of his prowess among their enemies during the evening.

"We will go!" said Uncas.

"Whither?"

"To the Tortoises—they are the children of my grandfathers!"

"Ay, lad," said the scout in English, a language he was apt to use when a little abstracted in mind; "the same blood runs in your veins, I believe; but time and distance has a little changed its colour! What shall we do with the Mingoes at the door! They count six, and this singer is as good as nothing."

"The Hurons are boasters!" said Uncas, scornfully; "their 'totem' is a moose; and they run like snails. The Delawares are children of the tortoise; and they outstrip the deer!"

"Ay, lad, there is truth in what you say; and I doubt not, on a rush, you would pass the whole nation; and in a straight race of two miles, would be in, and get your breath again, afore a knave of them all was within hearing of the other village! But the gift of a white man lies more in his arms than in his legs. As for myself, I can brain a Huron, as well as a better man, but when it comes to a race, the knaves would prove too much for me."

Uncas, who had already approached the door, in readiness to lead the way, now recoiled, and placed himself, once more, in the bottom of the lodge. But Hawk-eye, who was too much occupied with his own thoughts to note the movement, continued speaking more to himself than to his companion.

"After all," he said, "it is unreasonable to keep one man in bondage to the gifts of another. So, Uncas, you had better take the leap, while I will put on the skin again, and trust to cunning for want of speed."

The young Mohican made no reply, but quietly folded his arms, and leaned his body against one of the upright posts that supported the wall of the hut.

"Well," said the scout, looking up at him, "why do you tarry; there will be time enough for me, as the knaves will give chase to you at first."

"Uncas will stay," was the calm reply.

"For what?"

"To fight with his father's brother, and die with the friend of the Delawares."

"Ay, lad," returned Hawk-eye, squeezing the hand of

Uncas between his own iron fingers; " 'twould have been more like a Mingo than a Mohican, had you left me. But I thought I would make the offer, seeing that youth commonly loves life. Well, what can't be done by main courage, in war, must be done by circumvention. Put on the skin—I doubt not you can play the bear nearly as well as myself."

Whatever might have been the private opinion of Uncas of their respective abilities, in this particular, his grave countenance manifested no opinion of his own superiority. He silently and expeditiously encased himself in the covering of the beast, and then awaited such other movements as his more aged companion saw fit to dictate.

"Now, friend," said Hawk-eye, addressing David, "an exchange of garments will be a great convenience to you, inasmuch as you are but little accustomed to the make-shifts of the wilderness. Here, take my hunting shirt and cap, and give me your blanket and hat. You must trust me with the book and spectacles, as well as the tooter, too; if we ever meet again, in better times, you shall have all back again, with many thanks in the bargain."

David parted with the several articles named with a readiness that would have done great credit to his liberality, had he not certainly profited, in many particulars, by the exchange. Hawk-eye was not long in assuming his borrowed garments; and when his restless eyes were hid behind the glasses, and his head was surmounted by the triangular beaver, as their statures were not dissimilar, he might readily have passed for the singer, by star-light. As soon as these dispositions were made, the scout turned to David, and gave him his parting instructions.

"Are you much given to cowardice?" he bluntly asked, by way of obtaining a suitable understanding of the whole case, before he ventured a prescription.

"My pursuits are peaceful, and my temper, I humbly trust, is greatly given to mercy and love," returned David, a little nettled at so direct an attack on his manhood; "but there are none who can say, that I have ever forgotten my faith in the Lord, even in the greatest straits."

"Your chiefest danger will be at the moment when the savages find out that they have been deceived. If you are not then knocked in the head, your being a non-compossur will protect you, and you'll then have good reason to expect to die in your bed. If you stay, it must be to sit down here in the shadow, and take the part of Uncas, until such time as the cunning of the Indians discover the cheat, when, as I have already said, your time of trial will come. So choose for yourself, to make a rush, or tarry here."

"Even so," said David, firmly; "I will abide in the place of the Delaware; bravely and generously has he battled in my behalf, and this, and more, will I dare in his service."

"You have spoken as a man, and like one who, under wiser schooling, would have been brought to better things. Hold your head down, and draw in your legs; their formation might tell the truth too early. Keep silent as long as may be; and it would be wise when you do speak, to break out suddenly in one of your shoutings, which will serve to remind the Indians that you are not altogether as responsible as men should be. If, however, they take your scalp, as I trust and believe they will not, depend on it, Uncas and I will not forget the deed, but revenge it, as becomes true warriors and trusty friends."

"Hold!" said David, perceiving that with this assurance they were about to leave him; "I am an unworthy and humble follower of one, who taught not the damnable principle of revenge. Should I fall, therefore, seek no victims to my manes, but rather forgive my destroyers; and if you remember them at all, let it be in prayers for the enlightening of their minds, and for their eternal welfare!"

The scout hesitated, and appeared to muse.

"There is a principle in that," he said, "different from the law of the woods! and yet it is fair and noble to reflect upon!" Then, heaving a heavy sigh, probably among the last he ever drew in pining for the condition he had so long abandoned, he added—"It is what I would wish to practyse myself, as one without a cross of blood, though it is not always easy to deal with an Indian, as you would with a fellow christian. God bless you, friend; I do believe your scent is not greatly wrong, when the matter is duly considered, and keeping eternity before the eyes, though much depends on the natural gifts, and the force of temptation."

So saying, the scout returned, and shook David cordially by the hand; after which act of friendship, he immediately left the lodge, attended by the new representative of the beast.

The instant Hawk-eye found himself under the observation of the Hurons, he drew up his tall form in the rigid manner of David, threw out his arm in the act of keeping time, and commenced, what he intended for an imitation of his psalmody. Happily, for the success of this delicate adventure, he had to deal with ears but little practised in the concord of sweet sounds, or the miserable effort would infallibly have been detected. It was necessary to pass within a dangerous proximity of the dark groupe of savages, and the voice of the scout grew louder as they drew nigher. When at the nearest point, the Huron who spoke the English, thrust out an arm, and stopped the supposed singing-master.

"The Delaware dog!" he said, leaning forward, and peering through the dim light to catch the expression of the other's features; "is he afraid? will the Hurons hear his groans?"

A growl, so exceedingly fierce and natural, proceeded from the beast, that the young Indian released his hold, and started aside, as if to assure himself that it was not a veritable bear, and no counterfeit, that was rolling before him. Hawk-eye, who feared his voice would betray him to his subtle enemies, gladly profited by the interruption, to break out anew, in such a burst of musical expression, as would, probably, in a more refined state of society, have been termed a "grand crash." Among his actual auditors, however, it merely gave him an additional claim to that respect, which they never withhold from such as are believed to be the subjects of mental alienation. The little knot of Indians drew back, in a body, and suffered, as they thought, the conjuror and his inspired assistant to proceed.

It required no common exercise of fortitude in Uncas and the scout, to continue the dignified and deliberate pace they had assumed in passing the lodges; especially, as they immediately perceived, that curiosity had so far mastered fear, as to induce the watchers to approach the hut, in order to witness the effect of the incantations. The least injudicious or impatient movement on the part of David, might betray them, and time was absolutely necessary to insure the safety of the scout.

The loud noise the latter conceived it politic to continue, drew many curious gazers to the doors of the different huts, as they passed; and once or twice a dark looking warrior stepped across their path, led to the act by superstition or watchfulness. They were not, however, interrupted; the darkness of the hour, and the boldness of the attempt, proving their principal friends.

The adventurers had got clear of the village, and were now swiftly approaching the shelter of the woods, when a loud and long cry arose from the lodge where Uncas had been confined. The Mohican started on his feet, and shook his shaggy covering, as though the animal he counterfeited was about to make some desperate effort.

"Hold!" said the scout, grasping his friend by the shoulder, "let them yell again! 'Twas nothing but wonderment."

He had no occasion to delay, for at the next instant a burst of cries filled the outer air, and ran along the whole extent of the village. Uncas cast his skin, and stepped forth in his own beautiful proportions. Hawk-eye tapped him lightly on the shoulder, and glided ahead.

"Now let the devils strike our scent!" said the scout, tearing two rifles, with all their attendant accoutrements from beneath a bush, and flourishing 'kill-deer' as he handed Uncas a weapon; "two, at least, will find it to their deaths."

Then throwing their pieces to a low trail, like sportsmen in readiness for their game, they dashed forward, and were soon buried in the sombre darkness of the forest.

Chapter XXVII

Ant. "I shall remember:
When Cæsar says, *do this*, it is performed."
Julius Cæsar, I.ii.9–10.

THE IMPATIENCE of the savages who lingered about the prison of Uncas, as has been seen, had overcome their dread of the conjuror's breath. They stole cautiously, and with beating hearts, to a crevice, through which the faint light of the fire was glimmering. For several minutes, they mistook the form of David for that of their prisoner; but the very accident which Hawk-eye had foreseen, occurred. Tired of keeping the extremities of his long person so near together, the singer gradually suffered the lower limbs to extend themselves, until one of his misshapen feet actually came in contact with, and shoved aside, the embers of the fire. At first, the Hurons believed the Delaware had been thus deformed by witchcraft. But when David, unconscious of being observed, turned his head, and exposed his simple, mild countenance, in place of the haughty lineaments of their prisoner, it would have exceeded the credulity of even a native to have doubted any longer. They rushed together into the lodge, and laying their hands, with but little ceremony, on their captive, immediately detected the imposition. Then arose the cry first heard by the fugitives. It was succeeded by the most frantic and angry demonstrations of vengeance. David, however firm in his determination to cover the retreat of his friends, was compelled to believe that his own final hour had come. Deprived of his book and his pipe, he was fain to trust to a memory that rarely failed him on such subjects, and breaking forth in a loud and impassioned strain, he endeavoured to smooth his passage into the other world, by singing the opening verse of a funeral anthem. The Indians were seasonably reminded of his infirmity, and rushing into the open air, they aroused the village in the manner described.

A native warrior fights as he sleeps, without the protection of any thing defensive. The sounds of the alarm were, therefore, hardly uttered, before two hundred men were afoot, and ready for the battle, or the chase, as either might be required. The escape was soon known, and the whole tribe crowded, in a body, around the council lodge, impatiently awaiting the instruction of their chiefs. In such a sudden demand on their wisdom, the presence of the cunning Magua could scarcely fail of being needed. His name was mentioned, and all looked round in wonder, that he did not appear. Messengers were then despatched to his lodge, requiring his presence.

In the mean time, some of the swiftest and most discreet of the young men were ordered to make the circuit of the clearing, under cover of the woods, in order to ascertain that their suspected neighbours, the Delawares, designed no mischief. Women and children ran to and fro; and, in short, the whole encampment exhibited another scene of wild and savage confusion. Gradually, however, these symptoms of disorder diminished, and in a few minutes the oldest and most distinguished chiefs were assembled in the lodge, in grave consultation.

The clamour of many voices soon announced that a party approached, who might be expected to communicate some intelligence that would explain the mystery of the novel surprise. The crowd without gave way, and several warriors entered the place, bringing with them the hapless conjuror, who had been left so long by the scout in duresse.

Notwithstanding this man was held in very unequal estimation among the Hurons, some believing implicitly in his power, and others deeming him an impostor, he was now listened to by all, with the deepest attention. When his brief story was ended, the father of the sick woman stepped forth, and in a few pithy expressions, related, in his turn, what he knew. These two narratives gave a proper direction to the subsequent inquiries, which were now made with the characteristic cunning of savages.

Instead of rushing in a confused and disorderly throng to the cavern, ten of the wisest and firmest among the chiefs were selected to prosecute the investigation. As no time was to be lost, the instant the choice was made, the individuals appointed rose, in a body, and left the place without speaking. On reaching the entrance, the younger men in advance made way for their seniors, and the whole proceeded along the low, dark gallery, with the firmness of warriors ready to devote themselves to the public good, though, at the same time, secretly doubting the nature of the power with which they were about to contend.

The outer apartment of the cavern was silent and gloomy. The woman lay in her usual place and posture, though there were those present who affirmed they had seen her borne to the woods, by the supposed "medicine of the white men." Such a direct and palpable contradiction of the tale related by the father, caused all eyes to be turned on him. Chafed by the silent imputation, and inwardly troubled by so unaccountable a circumstance, the chief advanced to the side of the bed, and stooping, cast an incredulous look at the features, as if distrusting their reality. His daughter was dead.

The unerring feeling of nature for a moment prevailed, and the old warrior hid his eyes in sorrow. Then recovering his self-possession, he faced his companions, and pointing towards the corpse, he said, in the language of his people—

"The wife of my young man has left us! the Great Spirit is angry with his children."

The mournful intelligence was received in solemn silence. After a short pause, one of the elder Indians was about to speak, when a dark looking object was seen rolling out of an adjoining apartment, into the very centre of the room where they stood. Ignorant of the nature of the beings they had to deal with, the whole party drew back a little, and gazed in admiration, until the object fronted the light, and rising on end, exhibited the distorted, but still fierce and sullen, features of Magua. The discovery was succeeded by a general exclamation of amazement.

As soon, however, as the true situation of the chief was understood, several ready knives appeared, and his limbs and tongue were quickly released. The Huron arose, and shook himself like a lion quitting his lair. Not a word escaped him, though his hand played convulsively with the handle of his knife, while his lowering eyes scanned the whole party, as if they sought an object suited to the first burst of his vengeance.

It was happy for Uncas and the scout, and even David, that they were all beyond the reach of his arm at such a moment, for assuredly, no refinement in cruelty would then have deferred their deaths, in opposition to the promptings of the fierce temper that nearly choked him. Meeting every where faces that he knew as friends, the savage grated his teeth together, like rasps of iron, and swallowed his passion, for want of a victim on whom to vent it. This exhibition of anger was noted by all present, and from an apprehension of exasperating a temper that was already chafed nearly to madness, several minutes were suffered to pass before another word was uttered. When, however, suitable time had elapsed, the oldest of the party spoke.

"My friend has found an enemy!" he said. "Is he nigh, that the Hurons may take revenge!"

"Let the Delaware die!" exclaimed Magua, in a voice of thunder.

Another long and expressive silence was observed, and was broken, as before, with due precaution, by the same individual.

"The Mohican is swift of foot, and leaps far," he said; "but my young men are on his trail."

"Is he gone?" demanded Magua, in tones so deep and guttural, that they seemed to proceed from his inmost chest.

"An evil spirit has been among us, and the Delaware has blinded our eyes."

"An evil spirit!" repeated the other, mockingly; " 'tis the spirit that has taken the lives of so many Hurons. The spirit that slew my young men at 'the tumbling river;' that took their scalps at the 'healing spring;' and who has, now, bound the arms of le Renard Subtil!"

"Of whom does my friend speak?"

"Of the dog who carries the heart and cunning of a Huron under a pale skin—la Longue Carabine."

The pronunciation of so terrible a name, produced the usual effect among his auditors. But when time was given for reflection, and the warriors remembered that their formidable and daring enemy had even been in the bosom of their encampment, working injury, fearful rage took the place of wonder, and all those fierce passions with which the bosom of Magua had just been struggling, were suddenly transferred to his companions. Some among them gnashed their teeth in anger, others vented their feelings in yells, and some, again, beat the air as frantically, as if the object of their resentment was suffering under their blows. But this sudden outbreaking of temper, as quickly subsided in the still and sullen restraint they most affected in their moments of inaction.

Magua, who had, in his turn, found leisure for reflection, now changed his manner, and assumed the air of one who knew how to think and act with a dignity worthy of so grave a subject.

"Let us go to my people," he said; "they wait for us."

His companions consented, in silence, and the whole of the savage party left the cavern, and returned to the council lodge. When they were seated, all eyes turned on Magua, who understood, from such an indication, that, by common consent, they had devolved the duty of relating what had passed, on him. He arose, and told his tale, without duplicity or reservation. The whole deception practised by both Duncan and Hawk-eye, was, of course, laid naked; and no room was found, even for the most superstitious of the tribe, any longer to affix a doubt on the character of the occurrences. It was but too apparent, that they had been insultingly, shamefully, disgracefully, deceived. When he had ended, and resumed his seat, the collected tribe—for his auditors, in substance, included all the fighting men of the party—sate regarding each other like men astonished equally at the audacity and the success of their enemies. The next consideration, however, was the means and opportunities for revenge.

Additional pursuers were sent on the trail of the fugitives; and then the chiefs applied themselves in earnest to the business of consultation. Many different expedients were proposed by the elder warriors, in succession, to all of which Magua was a silent and respectful listener. That subtle savage had recovered his artifice and self-command, and now proceeded towards his object with his customary caution and skill. It was only when each one disposed to speak had uttered his sentiments, that he prepared to advance his own opinions. They were given with additional weight, from the circumstance, that some of the runners had already returned, and reported, that their enemies had been traced so far, as to leave no doubt of their having sought safety in the neighbouring camp of their suspected allies, the Delawares. With the advantage of possessing this important intelligence, the chief warily laid his plans before his fellows, and, as might have been anticipated from his eloquence and cunning, they were adopted without a dissenting voice. They were, briefly, as follows, both in opinions and in motives.

It has been already stated, that in obedience to a policy rarely departed from, the sisters were separated so soon as they reached the Huron village. Magua had early discovered, that in retaining the person of Alice, he possessed the most effectual check on Cora. When they parted, therefore, he kept the former within reach of his hand, consigning the one he most valued to the keeping of their allies. The arrangement was understood to be merely temporary, and was made as much with a view to flatter his neighbours, as in obedience to the invariable rule of Indian policy.

While goaded, incessantly, by those revengeful impulses that in a savage seldom slumber, the chief was still attentive to his more permanent, personal interests. The follies and disloyalty committed in his youth, were to be expiated by a long and painful penance, ere he could be restored to the full enjoyment of the confidence of his ancient people; and without confidence, there could be no authority in an Indian tribe. In this delicate and arduous situation, the crafty native had neglected no means of increasing his influence; and one of the happiest of his expedients, had been the success with which he had cultivated the favour of their powerful and dangerous neighbours. The result of his experiment had answered all the expectations of his policy—for the Hurons were in no degree exempt from that governing principle of nature, which induces man to value his gifts precisely in the degree that they are appreciated by others.

But while he was making this ostensible sacrifice to general considerations, Magua never lost sight of his individual motives. The latter had been frustrated by the unlooked-for events, which had placed all his prisoners beyond his control, and he now found himself reduced to the necessity of suing for favours to those whom it had so lately been his policy to oblige.

Several of the chiefs had proposed deep and treacherous

schemes to surprise the Delawares, and by gaining possession of their camp, to recover their prisoners by the same blow; for all agreed that their honour, their interests, and the peace and happiness of their dead countrymen, imperiously required them speedily to immolate some victims to their revenge. But plans so dangerous to attempt, and of such doubtful issue, Magua found little difficulty in defeating. He exposed their risque and fallacy with his usual skill; and it was only after he had removed every impediment, in the shape of opposing advice, that he ventured to propose his own projects.

He commenced by flattering the self-love of his auditors; a never-failing method of commanding attention. When he had enumerated the many different occasions on which the Hurons had exhibited their courage and prowess, in the punishment of insults, he digressed in a high encomium on the virtue of wisdom. He painted the quality, as forming the great point of difference between the beaver and other brutes; between brutes and men; and, finally, between the Hurons, in particular, and the rest of the human race. After he had sufficiently extolled the property of discretion, he undertook to exhibit in what manner its use was applicable to the present situation of their tribe. On the one hand, he said, was their great pale father, the governor of the Canadas, who had looked upon his children with a hard eye, since their tomahawks had been so red; on the other, a people as numerous as themselves, who spoke a different language, possessed different interests, and loved them not, and who would be glad of any pretence to bring them in disgrace with the great white chief. Then he spoke of their necessities; of the gifts they had a right to expect for their past services; of their distance from their proper hunting grounds and native villages; and of the necessity of consulting prudence more, and inclination less, in so critical circumstances. When he perceived, that, while the old men applauded his moderation, many of the fiercest and most distinguished of the warriors listened to these politic plans with lowering looks, he cunningly led them back to the subject which they most loved. He spoke openly of the fruits of their wisdom, which he boldly pronounced would be a complete and final triumph over their enemies. He even darkly hinted that their success might be extended, with proper caution, in such a manner, as to include the destruction of all whom they had reason to hate. In short, he so blended the warlike with the artful, the obvious with the obscure, as to flatter the propensities of both parties, and to leave to each subject of hope, while neither could say, it clearly comprehended his intentions.

The orator, or the politician, who can produce such a state of things, is commonly popular with his contemporaries, however he may be treated by posterity. All perceived that more was meant than was uttered, and each one believed that the hidden meaning was precisely such as his own faculties enabled him to understand, or his own wishes led him to anticipate.

In this happy state of things, it is not surprising that the management of Magua prevailed. The tribe consented to act with deliberation, and with one voice they committed the direction of the whole affair to the government of the chief, who had suggested such wise and intelligible expedients.

Magua had now attained one great object of all his cunning and enterprise. The ground he had lost in the favour of his people was completely regained, and he found himself even placed at the head of affairs. He was, in truth, their ruler; and so long as he could maintain his popularity, no monarch could be more despotic, especially while the tribe continued in a hostile country. Throwing off, therefore, the appearance of consultation, he assumed the grave air of authority, necessary to support the dignity of his office.

Runners were despatched for intelligence, in different directions; spies were ordered to approach and feel the encampment of the Delawares; the warriors were dismissed to their lodges, with an intimation that their services would soon be needed; and the women and children were ordered to retire, with a warning, that it was their province to be silent. When these several arrangements were made, Magua passed through the village, stopping here and there, to pay a visit where he thought his presence might be flattering to the individual. He confirmed his friends in their confidence; fixed the wavering; and gratified all. Then he sought his own lodge. The wife the Huron chief had abandoned, when he was chased from among his people, was dead. Children he had none; and he now occupied a hut, without companion of any sort. It was, in fact, the dilapidated and solitary structure in which David had been discovered, and whom he had tolerated in his presence, on those few occasions when they met, with the contemptuous indifference of a haughty superiority.

Hither, then, Magua retired, when his labours of policy were ended. While others slept, however, he neither knew nor sought repose. Had there been one sufficiently curious to have watched the movements of the newly elected chief, he would have seen him seated in a corner of his lodge, musing on the subject of his future plans, from the hour of his retirement, to the time he had appointed for the warriors to assemble again. Occasionally, the air breathed through the crevices of the hut, and the low flames that fluttered about the embers of the fire, threw their wavering light on the person of the sullen recluse. At such moments, it would not have been difficult to have fancied the dusky savage the Prince of Darkness, brooding on his own fancied wrongs, and plotting evil.

Long before the day dawned, however, warrior after warrior entered the solitary hut of Magua, until they had collected to the number of twenty. Each bore his rifle, and all the other accoutrements of war; though the paint was uniformly peaceful. The entrance of these fierce looking beings was unnoticed; some seating themselves in the shadows of the place, and others standing like motionless statues, until the whole of the designated band was collected.

Then Magua arose, and gave the signal to proceed, marching himself in advance. They followed their leader singly, and in that well known order, which has obtained the distinguishing appellation of "Indian file." Unlike other men engaged in the spirit-stirring business of war, they stole from their camp, unostentatiously and unobserved, resembling a band of gliding spectres, more than warriors seeking the bubble reputation by deeds of desperate daring.

Instead of taking the path which led directly towards the camp of the Delawares, Magua led his party for some distance down the windings of the stream, and along the little artificial lake of the beavers. The day began to dawn as they entered the clearing, which had been formed by those sagacious and industrious animals. Though Magua, who had resumed his ancient garb, bore the outline of a fox, on the dressed skin which formed his robe, there was one chief of his party, who carried the beaver as his peculiar symbol, or "totem." There would have been a species of profanity in the omission, had this man passed so powerful a community of his fancied kindred, without bestowing some evidence of his regard. Accordingly, he paused, and spoke in words as kind and friendly, as if he were addressing more intelligent beings. He called the animals his cousins, and reminded them that his protecting influence was the reason they remained unharmed, while so many avaricious traders were prompting the Indians to take their lives. He promised a continuance of his favours, and admonished them to be grateful. After which, he spoke of the expedition in which he was himself engaged, and intimated, though with sufficient delicacy and circumlocution, the expediency of bestowing on their relative a portion of that wisdom for which they were so renowned.*

During the utterance of this extraordinary address, the companions of the speaker were as grave and as attentive to his language, as though they were all equally impressed with its propriety. Once or twice black objects were seen rising to the surface of the water, and the Huron expressed pleasure, conceiving that his words were not bestowed in vain. Just as he had ended his address, the head of a large beaver was thrust from the door of a lodge, whose earthen walls had been much injured, and which the party had believed, from its situation, to be uninhabited. Such an extraordinary sign of confidence was received by the orator as a highly favourable omen; and, though the animal retreated a little precipitately, he was lavish of his thanks and commendations.

When Magua thought sufficient time had been lost, in gratifying the family affection of the warrior, he again made the signal to proceed. As the Indians moved away in a body, and with a step that would have been inaudible to the ears of any common man, the same venerable looking beaver once more

*These harangues of the beasts are frequent among the Indians. They often address their victims in this way, reproaching them for cowardice, or commending their resolution, as they may happen to exhibit fortitude, or the reverse, in suffering.

ventured his head from its cover. Had any of the Hurons turned to look behind them, they would have seen the animal watching their movements with an interest and sagacity that might easily have been mistaken for reason. Indeed, so very distinct and intelligible were the devices of the quadruped, that even the most experienced observer would have been at a loss to account for its actions, until the moment when the party entered the forest, when the whole would have been explained, by seeing the entire animal issue from the lodge, uncasing, by the act, the grave features of Chingachgook from his mask of fur.

Chapter XXVIII

"Brief, I pray you; for you see, 'tis a busy time with me."
Much Ado about Nothing, III.v.4–5.

THE TRIBE, or rather half-tribe, of Delawares, which has been so often mentioned, and whose present place of encampment was so nigh the temporary village of the Hurons, could assemble about an equal number of warriors with the latter people. Like their neighbours, they had followed Montcalm into the territories of the English crown, and were making heavy and serious inroads on the hunting grounds of the Mohawks, though they had seen fit, with the mysterious reserve so common among the natives, to withhold their assistance at the moment when it was most required. The French had accounted for this unexpected defection on the part of their ally in various ways. It was the prevalent opinion, however, that they had been influenced by veneration for the ancient treaty, that had once made them dependent on the Six Nations for military protection, and now rendered them reluctant to encounter their former masters. As for the tribe itself, it had been content to announce to Montcalm, through his emissaries, with Indian brevity, that their hatchets were dull, and time was necessary to sharpen them. The politic captain of the Canadas had deemed it wiser to submit to entertain a passive friend, than, by any acts of ill-judged severity, to convert him into an open enemy.

On that morning when Magua led his silent party from the settlement of the beavers into the forest, in the manner described, the sun rose upon the Delaware encampment, as if it had suddenly burst upon a busy people, actively employed in all the customary avocations of high noon. The women ran from lodge to lodge, some engaged in preparing their morning's meal, a few earnestly bent on seeking the comforts necessary to their habits, but more pausing to exchange hasty and whispered sentences with their friends. The warriors were lounging in groupes, musing more than they conversed; and when a few words were uttered, speaking like men who

deeply weighed their opinions. The instruments of th
were to be seen in abundance among the lodges; but
departed. Here and there, a warrior was examining his ar
with an attention that is rarely bestowed on the implemen
when no other enemy than the beasts of the forest is expected
to be encountered. And, occasionally, the eyes of a whole groupe were turned simultaneously towards a large and silent lodge in the centre of the village, as if it contained the subject of their common thoughts.

During the existence of this scene, a man suddenly appeared at the farthest extremity of a platform of rock which formed the level of the village. He was without arms, and his paint tended rather to soften than increase the natural sternness of his austere countenance. When in full view of the Delawares, he stopped, and made a gesture of amity, by throwing his arm upward towards heaven, and then letting it fall impressively on his breast. The inhabitants of the village answered his salute by a low murmur of welcome, and encouraged him to advance by similar indications of friendship. Fortified by these assurances, the dark figure left the brow of the natural rocky terrace, where it had stood a moment, drawn in a strong outline against the blushing morning sky, and moved, with dignity, into the very centre of the huts. As he approached, nothing was audible but the rattling of the light silver ornaments that loaded his arms and neck, and the tinkling of the little bells that fringed his deer-skin moccasins. He made, as he advanced, many courteous signs of greeting to the men he passed, neglecting to notice the women, however, like one who deemed their favour, in the present enterprise, of no importance. When he had reached the groupe, in which it was evident, by the haughtiness of their common mien, that the principal chiefs were collected, the stranger paused, and then the Delawares saw that the active and erect form that stood before them, was that of the well known Huron chief, le Renard Subtil.

His reception was grave, silent, and wary. The warriors in front stepped aside, opening the way to their most approved orator by the action; one who spoke all those languages, that were cultivated among the northern aborigines.

"The wise Huron is welcome," said the Delaware, in the language of the Maquas; "he is come to eat his 'suc-ca-tush'* with his brothers of the lakes!"

"He is come;" repeated Magua, bending his head with the dignity of an eastern prince.

The chief extended his arm, and taking the other by the wrist, they once more exchanged friendly salutations. Then the Delaware invited his guest to enter his own lodge, and share his morning meal. The invitation was accepted, and the two warriors, attended by three or four of the old men, walked calmly away, leaving the rest of the tribe devoured by a desire to understand the reasons of so unusual a visit, and yet not betraying the least impatience, by sign or word.

During the short and frugal repast that followed, the conversation was extremely circumspect, and related entirely to the events of the hunt, in which Magua had so lately been engaged. It would have been impossible for the most finished breeding to wear more of the appearance of considering the visit as a thing of course, than did his hosts, notwithstanding every individual present was perfectly aware, that it must be connected with some secret object, and that, probably, of importance to themselves. When the appetites of the whole were appeased, the squaws removed the trenchers and gourds, and the two parties began to prepare themselves for a subtle trial of their wits.

"Is the face of my great Canada father turned again towards his Huron children?" demanded the orator of the Delawares.

"When was it ever otherwise!" returned Magua. "He calls my people 'most beloved.' "

The Delaware gravely bowed his acquiescence to what he knew to be false, and continued—

"The tomahawks of your young men have been very red!"

"It is so; but they are now bright and dull—for the Yengeese are dead, and the Delawares are our neighbours!"

The other acknowledged the pacific compliment by a gesture of the hand, and remained silent. Then Magua, as if recalled to such a recollection, by the allusion to the massacre, demanded—

*A dish composed of cracked corn and beans. It is much used also by the whites. By corn is meant maize.

"Does my prisoner give trouble to my brothers?"

"She is welcome."

"The path between the Hurons and the Delawares is short, and it is open; let her be sent to my squaws, if she gives trouble to my brother."

"She is welcome," returned the chief of the latter nation, still more emphatically.

The baffled Magua continued silent several minutes, apparently indifferent, however, to the repulse he had received in this, his opening, effort to regain possession of Cora.

"Do my young men leave the Delawares room on the mountains for their hunts?" he, at length, continued.

"The Lenape are rulers of their own hills," returned the other, a little haughtily.

"It is well. Justice is the master of a red-skin! Why should they brighten their tomahawks, and sharpen their knives against each other! Are not the pale-faces thicker than the swallows in the season of flowers?"

"Good!" exclaimed two or three of his auditors at the same time.

Magua waited a little, to permit his words to soften the feelings of the Delawares, before he added—

"Have there not been strange moccasins in the woods? Have not my brothers scented the feet of white men?"

"Let my Canada father come!" returned the other, evasively; "his children are ready to see him."

"When the Great Chief comes, it is to smoke with the Indians, in their wigwams. The Hurons say, too, he is welcome. But the Yengeese have long arms, and legs that never tire! My young men dreamed they had seen the trail of the Yengeese nigh the village of the Delawares!"

"They will not find the Lenape asleep."

"It is well. The warrior whose eye is open, can see his enemy," said Magua, once more shifting his ground, when he found himself unable to penetrate the caution of his companion. "I have brought gifts to my brother. His nation would not go on the war-path, because they did not think it well; but their friends have remembered where they lived."

When he had thus announced his liberal intention, the crafty chief arose, and gravely spread his presents before the dazzled eyes of his hosts. They consisted principally of trinkets of little value, plundered from the slaughtered females of William Henry. In the division of the baubles, the cunning Huron discovered no less art than in their selection. While he bestowed those of greater value on the two most distinguished warriors, one of whom was his host, he seasoned his offerings to their inferiors with such well-timed and apposite compliments, as left them no grounds of complaint. In short, the whole ceremony contained such a happy blending of the profitable with the flattering, that it was not difficult for the donor immediately to read the effect of a generosity so aptly mingled with praise, in the eyes of those he addressed.

This well judged and politic stroke on the part of Magua, was not without instantaneous results. The Delawares lost their gravity, in a much more cordial expression; and the host, in particular, after contemplating his own liberal share of the spoil, for some moments, with peculiar gratification, repeated, with strong emphasis, the words—

"My brother is a wise chief. He is welcome!"

"The Hurons love their friends the Delawares," returned Magua. "Why should they not! they are coloured by the same sun, and their just men will hunt in the same grounds after death. The red-skins should be friends, and look with open eyes on the white men. Has not my brother scented spies in the woods?"

The Delaware, whose name, in English, signified "Hard-heart," an appellation that the French had translated into "Le-cœur-dur," forgot that obduracy of purpose, which had probably obtained him so significant a title. His countenance grew very sensibly less stern, and he now deigned to answer more directly.

"There have been strange moccasins about my camp. They have been tracked into my lodges."

"Did my brother beat out the dogs?" asked Magua, without adverting in any manner to the former equivocation of the chief.

"It would not do. The stranger is always welcome to the children of the Lenape."

"The stranger, but not the spy!"

"Would the Yengeese send their women as spies? Did not the Huron chief say he took women in the battle?"

"He told no lie. The Yengeese have sent out their scouts. They have been in my wigwams, but they found there no one to say welcome. Then they fled to the Delawares—for say they, the Delawares are our friends; their minds are turned from their Canada father!"

This insinuation was a home thrust, and one that, in a more advanced state of society, would have entitled Magua to the reputation of a skilful diplomatist. The recent defection of the tribe had, as they well knew themselves, subjected the Delawares to much reproach among their French allies, and they were now made to feel that their future actions were to be regarded with jealousy and distrust. There was no deep insight, into causes and effects, necessary to foresee that such a situation of things was likely to prove highly prejudicial to their future movements. Their distant villages, their hunting grounds, and hundreds of their women and children, together with a material part of their physical force, were actually within the limits of the French territory. Accordingly, this alarming annunciation was received, as Magua intended, with manifest disapprobation, if not with alarm.

"Let my father look in my face," said Le-cœur-dur; "he will see no change. It is true, my young men did not go out on the war-path; they had dreams for not doing so. But they love and venerate the great white chief."

"Will he think so, when he hears that his greatest enemy is fed in the camp of his children! When he is told, a bloody Yengee smokes at your fire! That the pale-face, who has slain so many of his friends, goes in and out among the Delawares! Go—my great Canada Father is not a fool!"

"Where is the Yengee that the Delawares fear!" returned the other; " who has slain my young men! who is the mortal enemy of my Great Father!"

"La Longue Carabine."

The Delaware warriors started at the well known name, betraying, by their amazement, that they now learnt, for the first time, one so famous among the Indian allies of France, was within their power.

"What does my brother mean?" demanded Le-cœur-dur, in

a tone that, by its wonder, far exceeded the usual apathy of his race.

"A Huron never lies," returned Magua, coldly, leaning his head against the side of the lodge, and drawing his slight robe across his tawny breast. "Let the Delawares count their prisoners; they will find one whose skin is neither red nor pale."

A long and musing pause succeeded. The chief consulted, apart, with his companions, and messengers were despatched to collect certain others of the most distinguished men of the tribe.

As warrior after warrior dropped in, they were each made acquainted, in turn, with the important intelligence that Magua had just communicated. The air of surprise, and the usual, low, deep, guttural exclamation, were common to them all. The news spread from mouth to mouth, until the whole encampment became powerfully agitated. The women suspended their labours, to catch such syllables as unguardedly fell from the lips of the consulting warriors. The boys deserted their sports, and walking fearlessly among their fathers, looked up in curious admiration, as they heard the brief exclamations of wonder they so freely expressed, at the temerity of their hated foe. In short, every occupation was abandoned, for the time; and all other pursuits seemed discarded, in order that the tribe might freely indulge, after their own peculiar manner, in an open expression of feeling.

When the excitement had a little abated, the old men disposed themselves seriously to consider that which it became the honour and safety of their tribe to perform, under circumstances of so much delicacy and embarrassment. During all these movements, and in the midst of the general commotion, Magua had not only maintained his seat, but the very attitude he had originally taken, against the side of the lodge, where he continued as immovable, and, apparently, as unconcerned, as if he had no interest in the result. Not a single indication of the future intentions of his hosts, however, escaped his vigilant eyes. With his consummate knowledge of the nature of the people with whom he had to deal, he anticipated every measure on which they decided; and it might almost be said, that in many instances, he knew their intentions even before they became known to themselves.

The council of the Delawares was short. When it was ended, a general bustle announced that it was to be immediately succeeded by a solemn and formal assemblage of the nation. As such meetings were rare, and only called on occasions of the last importance, the subtle Huron, who still sate apart, a wily and dark observer of the proceedings, now knew that all his projects must be brought to their final issue. He, therefore, left the lodge, and walked silently forth to the place, in front of the encampment, whither the warriors were already beginning to collect.

It might have been half an hour before each individual, including even the women and children, was in his place. The delay had been created by the grave preparations that were deemed necessary to so solemn and unusual a conference. But, when the sun was seen climbing above the tops of that mountain, against whose bosom the Delawares had constructed their encampment, most were seated; and as his bright rays darted from behind the outline of trees that fringed the eminence, they fell upon as grave, as attentive, and as deeply interested a multitude, as was probably ever before lighted by his morning beams. Its number somewhat exceeded a thousand souls.

In a collection of so serious savages, there is never to be found any impatient aspirant after premature distinction, standing ready to move his auditors to some hasty, and, perhaps, injudicious discussion, in order that his own reputation may be the gainer. An act of so much precipitancy and presumption, would seal the downfall of precocious intellect for ever. It rested solely with the oldest and most experienced of the men to lay the subject of the conference before the people. Until such a one chose to make some movement, no deeds in arms, no natural gifts, nor any renown as an orator, would have justified the slightest interruption. On the present occasion, the aged warrior whose privilege it was to speak, was silent, seemingly oppressed with the magnitude of his subject. The delay had already continued long beyond the usual, deliberative pause, that always precedes a conference; but no sign of impatience, or surprise, escaped even the youngest boy. Occasionally, an eye was raised from the earth, where the looks of most were riveted, and strayed towards a particular lodge, that was, however, in no manner distinguished from those around it, except in the peculiar care that had been taken to protect it against the assaults of the weather.

At length, one of those low murmurs that are so apt to disturb a multitude, was heard, and the whole nation arose to their feet by a common impulse. At that instant, the door of the lodge in question opened, and three men issuing from it, slowly approached the place of consultation. They were all aged, even beyond that period to which the oldest present had reached; but one in the centre, who leaned on his companions for support, had numbered an amount of years, to which the human race is seldom permitted to attain. His frame, which had once been tall and erect, like the cedar, was now bending under the pressure of more than a century. The elastic, light step of an Indian was gone, and in its place, he was compelled to toil his tardy way over the ground, inch by inch. His dark, wrinkled countenance, was in singular and wild contrast with the long white locks, which floated on his shoulders, in such thickness, as to announce that generations had probably passed away, since they had last been shorn.

The dress of this patriarch, for such, considering his vast age, in conjunction with his affinity and influence with his people, he might very properly be termed, was rich and imposing, though strictly after the simple fashions of the tribe. His robe was of the finest skins, which had been deprived of their fur, in order to admit of a hieroglyphical representation of various deeds in arms, done in former ages. His bosom was loaded with medals, some in massive silver, and one or two even in gold, the gifts of various christian potentates, during the long period of his life. He also wore armlets, and cinctures above the ancles, of the latter precious metal. His head, on the whole of which the hair had been permitted to grow, the pursuits of war having so long been abandoned, was encircled by a sort of plated diadem, which, in its turn, bore lesser and more glittering ornaments, that sparkled amid the glossy hues of three drooping ostrich feathers, dyed a deep black, in touching contrast to the colour of his snow-white locks. His tomahawk was nearly hid in silver, and the handle of his knife shone like a horn of solid gold.

So soon as the first hum of emotion and pleasure, which the sudden appearance of this venerated individual created, had a little subsided, the name of "Tamenund" was whispered from mouth to mouth. Magua had often heard the fame of this wise and just Delaware; a reputation that even proceeded so far as to bestow on him the rare gift of holding secret communion with the Great Spirit, and which has since transmitted his name, with some slight alteration, to the white usurpers of his ancient territory, as the imaginary, tutelar saint* of a vast empire. The Huron chief, therefore, stepped eagerly out a little from the throng, to a spot whence he might catch a nearer glimpse of the features of the man, whose decision was likely to produce so deep an influence on his own fortunes.

The eyes of the old man were closed, as though the organs were wearied with having so long witnessed the selfish workings of human passions. The colour of his skin differed from that of most around him, being richer and darker; the latter hue having been produced by certain delicate and mazy lines of complicated and yet beautiful figures, which had been traced over most of his person by the operation of tattooing. Notwithstanding the position of the Huron, he passed the observant and silent Magua without notice, and leaning on his two venerable supporters, proceeded to the high place of the multitude, where he seated himself in the centre of his nation, with the dignity of a monarch, and the air of a father.

Nothing could surpass the reverence and affection with which this unexpected visit, from one who belonged rather to another world than to this, was received by his people. After a suitable and decent pause, the principal chiefs arose, and approaching the patriarch, they placed his hands reverently on their heads, seeming to intreat a blessing. The younger men were content with touching his robe, or even with drawing nigh his person, in order to breathe in the atmosphere of one so aged, so just, and so valiant. None but the most distinguished among the youthful warriors even presumed so far as to perform the latter ceremony; the great mass of the multi-

*The Americans sometimes called their tutelar saint Tamenay, a corruption of the name of the renowned chief here introduced. There are many traditions which speak of the character and power of Tamenund.

tude deeming it a sufficient happiness to look upon a form so deeply venerated, and so well beloved. When these acts of affection and respect were performed, the chiefs drew back again to their several places, and silence reigned in the whole encampment.

After a short delay, a few of the young men, to whom instructions had been whispered by one of the aged attendants of Tamenund, arose, left the crowd, and entered the lodge which has already been noted as the object of so much attention, throughout that morning. In a few minutes they reappeared, escorting the individuals who had caused all these solemn preparations, towards the seat of judgment. The crowd opened in a lane, and when the party had re-entered, it closed in again, forming a large and dense belt of human bodies, arranged in an open circle.

Chapter XXIX

"The assembly seated, rising o'er the rest,
Achilles thus the king of men address'd."
Pope, *The Iliad*, Book II, ll. 77–78.

CORA STOOD FOREMOST among the prisoners, entwining her arms in those of Alice, in the tenderness of sisterly love. Notwithstanding the fearful and menacing array of savages on every side of her, no apprehension on her own account could prevent the noble-minded maiden from keeping her eyes fastened on the pale and anxious features of the trembling Alice. Close at their side stood Heyward, with an interest in both, that, at such a moment of intense uncertainty, scarcely knew a preponderance in favour of her whom he most loved. Hawk-eye had placed himself a little in the rear, with a deference to the superior rank of his companions, that no similarity in the state of their present fortunes could induce him to forget. Uncas was not there.

When perfect silence was again restored, and after the usual, long, impressive pause, one of the two aged chiefs, who sate at the side of the patriarch, arose, and demanded aloud, in very intelligible English—

"Which of my prisoners is la Longue Carabine?"

Neither Duncan nor the scout answered. The former, however, glanced his eyes around the dark and silent assembly, and recoiled a pace, when they fell on the malignant visage of Magua. He saw, at once, that this wily savage had some secret agency in their present arraignment before the nation, and determined to throw every possible impediment in the way of the execution of his sinister plans. He had witnessed one instance of the summary punishments of the Indians, and now dreaded that his companion was to be selected for a second. In this dilemma, with little or no time for reflection, he suddenly determined to cloak his invaluable friend, at any or every hazard to himself. Before he had time, however, to speak, the question was repeated in a louder voice, and with a clearer utterance.

"Give us arms," the young man haughtily replied, "and place us in yonder woods. Our deeds shall speak for us!"

"This is the warrior whose name has filled our ears!" returned the chief, regarding Heyward with that sort of curious interest, which seems inseparable from man, when first beholding one of his fellows, to whom merit or accident, virtue or crime, has given notoriety. "What has brought the white man into the camp of the Delawares?"

"My necessities. I come for food, shelter, and friends."

"It cannot be. The woods are full of game. The head of a warrior needs no other shelter than a sky without clouds, and the Delawares are the enemies, and not the friends, of the Yengeese. Go—the mouth has spoken, while the heart said nothing."

Duncan, a little at a loss in what manner to proceed, remained silent; but the scout, who had listened attentively to all that passed, now advanced steadily to the front.

"That I did not answer to the call for la Longue Carabine, was not owing either to shame or fear," he said; "for neither one nor the other is the gift of an honest man. But I do not admit the right of the Mingoes to bestow a name on one, whose friends have been mindful of his gifts, in this particular; especially, as their title is a lie, 'kill-deer' being a grooved barrel, and no carabyne. I am the man, however, that got the name of Nathaniel from my kin; the compliment of Hawkeye from the Delawares, who live on their own river; and whom the Iroquois have presumed to style the 'long rifle,' without any warranty from him who is most concerned in the matter."

The eyes of all present, which had hitherto been gravely scanning the person of Duncan, were now turned, on the instant, towards the upright, iron frame of this new pretender to the distinguished appellation. It was in no degree remarkable, that there should be found two who were willing to claim so great an honour, for impostors, though rare, were not unknown amongst the natives; but it was altogether material to the just and severe intentions of the Delawares, that there should be no mistake in the matter. Some of their old men consulted together, in private, and then, as it would seem, they determined to interrogate their visiter on the subject.

"My brother has said that a snake crept into my camp," said the chief to Magua; "which is he?"

The Huron pointed to the scout.

"Will a wise Delaware believe the barking of a wolf!" exclaimed Duncan, still more confirmed in the evil intentions of his ancient enemy; "a dog never lies, but when was a wolf known to speak the truth!"

The eyes of Magua flashed fire; but suddenly recollecting the necessity of maintaining his presence of mind, he turned away in silent disdain, well assured that the sagacity of the Indians would not fail to extract the real merits of the point in controversy. He was not deceived; for, after another short consultation, the wary Delaware turned to him again, and expressed the determination of the chiefs, though in the most considerate language.

"My brother has been called a liar," he said; "and his friends are angry. They will show that he has spoken the truth. Give my prisoners guns, and let them prove which is the man."

Magua affected to consider the expedient, which he well knew proceeded from distrust of himself, as a compliment, and made a gesture of acquiescence, well content that his veracity should be supported by so skilful a marksman as the scout. The weapons were instantly placed in the hands of the friendly opponents, and they were bid to fire, over the heads of the seated multitude, at an earthen vessel, which lay, by accident, on a stump, some fifty yards from the place where they stood.

Heyward smiled to himself, at the idea of a competition with the scout, though he determined to persevere in the deception, until apprised of the real designs of Magua. Raising his rifle with the utmost care, and renewing his aim three several times, he fired. The bullet cut the wood within a few inches of the vessel, and a general exclamation of satisfaction announced that the shot was considered a proof of great skill in the use of the weapon. Even Hawk-eye nodded his head, as if he would say, it was better than he had expected. But, instead of manifesting an intention to contend with the successful marksman, he stood leaning on his rifle for more than a minute, like a man who was completely buried in thought. From this reverie he was, however, awakened by one of the young Indians who had furnished the arms, and who now touched his shoulder, saying, in exceedingly broken English—

"Can the pale-face beat it?"

"Yes, Huron!" exclaimed the scout, raising the short rifle in his right hand, and shaking it at Magua, with as much apparent ease as if it were a reed; "yes, Huron, I could strike you now, and no power of 'arth could prevent the deed! The soaring hawk is not more certain of the dove, than I am this moment of you, did I choose to send a bullet to your heart! Why should I not! Why!—because the gifts of my colour forbid it, and I might draw down evil on tender and innocent heads! If you know such a being as God, thank him, therefore, in your inward soul—for you have reason!"

The flushed countenance, angry eye, and swelling figure of the scout, produced a sensation of secret awe in all that heard him. The Delawares held their breath in expectation; but Magua himself, even while he distrusted the forbearance of his enemy, remained immovable and calm, where he stood, wedged in by the crowd, as one who grew to the spot.

"Beat it," repeated the young Delaware at the elbow of the scout.

"Beat what; fool!—what!"—exclaimed Hawk-eye, still flourishing the weapon angrily above his head, though his eye no longer sought the person of Magua.

"If the white man is the warrior he pretends," said the aged chief, "let him strike nigher to the mark."

The scout laughed aloud—a noise that produced the startling effect of an unnatural sound on Heyward—then dropping the piece, heavily, into his extended left hand, it was discharged, apparently by the shock, driving the fragments of the vessel into the air, and scattering them on every side. Almost at the same instant, the rattling sound of the rifle was heard, as he suffered it to fall, contemptuously, to the earth.

The first impression of so strange a scene was engrossing admiration. Then a low, but increasing murmur, ran through the multitude, and finally swelled into sounds, that denoted lively opposition in the sentiments of the spectators. While some openly testified their satisfaction at so unexampled dexterity, by far the larger portion of the tribe were inclined to believe the success of the shot was the result of accident. Heyward was not slow to confirm an opinion that was so favourable to his own pretensions.

"It was chance!" he exclaimed; "none can shoot without an aim!"

"Chance!" echoed the excited woodsman, who was now stubbornly bent on maintaining his identity, at every hazard, and on whom the secret hints of Heyward to acquiesce in the deception were entirely lost. "Does yonder lying Huron, too, think it chance? Give him another gun, and place us face to face, without cover or dodge, and let Providence, and our own eyes, decide the matter atween us! I do not make the offer to you, major; for our blood is of a colour, and we serve the same master."

"That the Huron is a liar, is very evident," returned Heyward, coolly; "you have, yourself, heard him assert you to be la Longue Carabine."

It were impossible to say what violent assertion the stubborn Hawk-eye would have next made, in his headlong wish to vindicate his identity, had not the aged Delaware once more interposed.

"The hawk which comes from the clouds, can return when he will," he said; "give them the guns."

This time the scout seized the rifle with avidity; nor had Magua, though he watched the movement of the marksman with jealous eyes, any further cause for apprehension.

"Now let it be proved, in the face of this tribe of Delawares, who is the better man," cried the scout, tapping the butt of his piece with that finger which had pulled so many fatal triggers. "You see the gourd hanging against yonder tree, major; if you are a marksman, fit for the borders, let me see you break its shell!"

Duncan noted the object, and prepared himself to renew the trial. The gourd was one of the usual little vessels used by the Indians, and it was suspended from a dead branch of a small pine, by a thong of deer-skin, at the full distance of a hundred yards. So strangely compounded is the feeling of self-love, that the young soldier, while he knew the utter worthlessness of the suffrages of his savage umpires, forgot the sudden motives of the contest, in a wish to excel. It has been seen, already, that his skill was far from being contemptible, and he now resolved to put forth its nicest qualities. Had his life depended on the issue, the aim of Duncan could not have been more deliberate or guarded. He fired; and three or four young Indians, who sprang forward at the report, announced with a shout, that the ball was in the tree, a very little on one side of the proper object. The warriors uttered a common ejaculation of pleasure, and then turned their eyes, inquiringly, on the movements of his rival.

"It may do for the Royal Americans!" said Hawk-eye, laughing once more in his own silent, heartfelt, manner; "but had my gun often turned so much from the true line, many a martin, whose skin is now in a lady's muff, would still be in the woods; ay, and many a bloody Mingo, who has departed to his final account, would be acting his deviltries at this very day, atween the provinces. I hope the squaw who owns the gourd, has more of them in her wigwam, for this will never hold water again!"

The scout had shook his priming, and cocked his piece, while speaking; and, as he ended, he threw back a foot, and slowly raised the muzzle from the earth. The motion was steady, uniform, and in one direction. When on a perfect level, it remained for a single moment without tremor or variation, as though both man and rifle were carved in stone. During that stationary instant, it poured forth its contents, in a bright, glancing, sheet of flame. Again the young Indians bounded forward, but their hurried search and disappointed looks announced, that no traces of the bullet were to be seen.

"Go," said the old chief to the scout, in a tone of strong disgust; "thou art a wolf in the skin of a dog. I will talk to the 'long rifle' of the Yengeese."

"Ah! had I that piece which furnished the name you use, I would obligate myself to cut the thong, and drop the gourd, without breaking it!" returned Hawk-eye, perfectly undisturbed by the other's manner. "Fools, if you would find the bullet of a sharp-shooter of these woods, you must look *in* the object, and not around it!"

The Indian youths instantly comprehended his meaning—for this time he spoke in the Delaware tongue—and tearing the gourd from the tree, they held it on high, with an exulting shout, displaying a hole in its bottom, which had been cut by the bullet, after passing through the usual orifice in the centre of its upper side. At this unexpected exhibition, a loud and vehement expression of pleasure burst from the mouth of every warrior present. It decided the question, and effectually established Hawk-eye in the possession of his dangerous reputation. Those curious and admiring eyes which had been turned again on Heyward, were finally directed to the weather-beaten form of the scout, who immediately became the principal object of attention, to the simple and unsophisticated beings, by whom he was surrounded. When the sudden and noisy commotion had a little subsided, the aged chief resumed his examination.

"Why did you wish to stop my ears?" he said, addressing Duncan; "are the Delawares fools, that they could not know the young panther from the cat?"

"They will yet find the Huron a singing-bird," said Duncan, endeavouring to adopt the figurative language of the natives.

"It is good. We will know who can shut the ears of men. Brother," added the chief, turning his eyes on Magua, "the Delawares listen."

Thus singled, and directly called on, to declare his object, the Huron arose, and advancing with great deliberation and dignity, into the very centre of the circle, where he stood confronted to the prisoners, he placed himself in an attitude to speak. Before opening his mouth, however, he bent his eyes slowly along the whole living boundary of earnest faces, as if to temper his expressions to the capacities of his audience. On Hawk-eye he cast a glance of respectful enmity; on Duncan, a look of inextinguishable hatred; the shrinking figure of Alice, he scarcely deigned to notice; but when his glance met the firm, commanding, and yet lovely form of Cora, his eye lingered a moment, with an expression, that it might have been difficult to define. Then, filled with his own dark intentions, he spoke in the language of the Canadas, a tongue that he well knew was comprehended by most of his auditors.

"The Spirit that made men, coloured them differently," commenced the subtle Huron. "Some are blacker than the sluggish bear. These he said should be slaves; and he ordered them to work for ever, like the beaver. You may hear them groan, when the south wind blows, louder than the lowing buffaloes, along the shores of the great salt lake, where the big canoes come and go with them in droves. Some he made with faces paler than the ermine of the forests: and these he ordered to be traders; dogs to their women, and wolves to their slaves. He gave this people the nature of the pigeon; wings that never tire; young, more plentiful than the leaves on the trees, and appetites to devour the earth. He gave them tongues like the false call of the wild-cat; hearts like rabbits; the cunning of the hog, (but none of the fox,) and arms longer than the legs of the moose. With his tongue, he stops the ears of the Indians; his heart teaches him to pay warriors to fight his battles; his cunning tells him how to get together the goods of the earth; and his arms enclose the land from the shores of the salt water, to the islands of the great lake. His gluttony makes him sick. God gave him enough, and yet he wants all. Such are the pale-faces.

"Some the Great Spirit made with skins brighter and redder than yonder sun," continued Magua, pointing impressively upward to the lurid luminary, which was struggling through the misty atmosphere of the horizon; "and these did he fashion to his own mind. He gave them this island as he had made it, covered with trees, and filled with game. The wind made their clearings; the sun and rains ripened their fruits; and the snows came to tell them to be thankful. What need had they of roads to journey by! They saw through the hills! When the beavers worked, they lay in the shade, and looked on. The winds cooled them in summer; in winter, skins kept them warm. If they fought among themselves, it was to prove that they were men. They were brave; they were just; they were happy."

Here the speaker paused, and again looked around him, to discover if his legend had touched the sympathies of his listeners. He met every where with eyes riveted on his own, heads erect, and nostrils expanded, as if each individual present felt himself able and willing, singly, to redress the wrongs of his race.

"If the Great Spirit gave different tongues to his red children," he continued, in a low, still, melancholy voice, "it was, that all animals might understand them. Some he placed among the snows, with their cousin the bear. Some he placed near the setting sun, on the road to the happy hunting grounds. Some on the lands around the great fresh waters; but to his greatest, and most beloved, he gave the sands of the salt lake. Do my brothers know the name of this favoured people?"

"It was the Lenape!" exclaimed twenty eager voices, in a breath.

"It was the Lenni Lenape," returned Magua, affecting to bend his head in reverence to their former greatness. "It was the tribes of the Lenape! The sun rose from water that was salt, and set in water that was sweet, and never hid himself from their eyes. But why should I, a Huron of the woods, tell a wise people their own traditions? Why remind them of their injuries; their ancient greatness; their deeds; their glory; their happiness—their losses; their defeats; their misery? Is there not one among them who has seen it all, and who knows it to be true? I have done. My tongue is still, for my heart is of lead. I listen."

As the voice of the speaker suddenly ceased, every face and all eyes turned, by a common movement, towards the venerable Tamenund. From the moment that he took his seat, until the present instant, the lips of the patriarch had not severed, and scarcely a sign of life had escaped him. He had sate, bent in feebleness, and apparently unconscious of the presence he was in, during the whole of that opening scene, in which the skill of the scout had been so clearly established. At the nicely graduated sounds of Magua's voice, however, he had betrayed some evidence of consciousness, and once or twice he had even raised his head, as if to listen. But when the crafty Huron spoke of his nation by name, the eyelids of the old man raised themselves, and he looked out upon the multitude, with that sort of dull, unmeaning expression, which might be supposed to belong to the countenance of a spectre. Then he made an effort to rise, and being upheld by his supporters, he gained his feet, in a posture commanding by its dignity, while he tottered with weakness.

"Who calls upon the children of the Lenape!" he said, in a

deep, guttural voice, that was rendered awfully audible by the breathless silence of the multitude; " who speaks of things gone! Does not the egg become a worm—the worm a fly—and perish! Why tell the Delawares of good that is past? Better thank the Manitto for that which remains."

"It is a Wyandot," said Magua, stepping nigher to the rude platform on which the other stood; "a friend of Tamenund."

"A friend!" repeated the sage, on whose brow a dark frown settled, imparting a portion of that severity, which had rendered his eye so terrible in middle age—"Are the Mingoes rulers of the earth! What brings a Huron here?"

"Justice. His prisoners are with his brothers, and he comes for his own."

Tamenund turned his head towards one of his supporters, and listened to the short explanation the man gave. Then facing the applicant, he regarded him a moment with deep attention; after which, he said, in a low and reluctant voice—

"Justice is the law of the Great Manitto. My children, give the stranger food. Then, Huron, take thine own, and depart."

On the delivery of this solemn judgment, the patriarch seated himself, and closed his eyes again, as if better pleased with the images of his own ripened experience, than with the visible objects of the world. Against such a decree, there was no Delaware sufficiently hardy to murmur, much less oppose himself. The words were barely uttered, when four or five of the younger warriors stepping behind Heyward and the scout, passed thongs so dexterously and rapidly around their arms, as to hold them both in instant bondage. The former was too much engrossed with his precious and nearly insensible burthen, to be aware of their intentions before they were executed; and the latter, who considered even the hostile tribes of the Delawares a superior race of beings, submitted without resistance. Perhaps, however, the manner of the scout would not have been so passive, had he fully comprehended the language in which the preceding dialogue had been conducted.

Magua cast a look of triumph around the whole assembly, before he proceeded to the execution of his purpose. Perceiving that the men were unable to offer any resistance, he turned his looks on her he valued most. Cora met his gaze with an eye so calm and firm, that his resolution wavered. Then recollecting his former artifice, he raised Alice from the arms of the warrior, against whom she leaned, and beckoning Heyward to follow, he motioned for the encircling crowd to open. But Cora, instead of obeying the impulse he had expected, rushed to the feet of the patriarch, and raising her voice, exclaimed aloud—

"Just and venerable Delaware, on thy wisdom and power we lean for mercy! Be deaf to yonder artful and remorseless monster, who poisons thy ears with falsehoods, to feed his thirst for blood. Thou, that hast lived long, and that hast seen the evil of the world, should know how to temper its calamities to the miserable."

The eyes of the old man opened heavily, and he once more looked upward at the multitude. As the piercing tones of the supplicant swelled on his ears, they moved slowly in the direction of her person, and finally settled there, in a steady gaze. Cora had cast herself to her knees, and with hands clenched in each other, and pressed upon her bosom, she remained like a beauteous and breathing model of her sex, looking up in his faded, but majestic countenance, with a species of holy reverence. Gradually, the expression of Tamenund's features changed, and losing their vacancy in admiration, they lighted with a portion of that intelligence, which, a century before, had been wont to communicate his youthful fire to the extensive bands of the Delawares. Rising, without assistance, and, seemingly, without an effort, he demanded, in a voice that startled its auditors by its firmness—

"What art thou?"

"A woman. One of a hated race, if thou wilt—a Yengee. But one who has never harmed thee, and who cannot harm thy people, if she would; who asks for succour."

"Tell me, my children," continued the patriarch, hoarsely, motioning to those around him, though his eyes still dwelt upon the kneeling form of Cora, "where have the Delawares 'camped?"

"In the mountains of the Iroquois; beyond the clear springs of the Horican."

"Many parching summers are come and gone," continued the sage, "since I drank of the waters of my own river. The children of Miquon* are the justest white men; but they were thirsty, and they took it to themselves. Do they follow us so far?"

"We follow none; we covet nothing;" answered Cora. "Captives, against our wills, have we been brought amongst you; and we ask but permission to depart to our own, in peace. Art thou not Tamenund—the father—the judge—I had almost said, the prophet—of this people?"

"I am Tamenund, of many days."

" 'Tis now some seven years that one of thy people was at the mercy of a white chief, on the borders of this province. He claimed to be of the blood of the good and just Tamenund. 'Go,' said the white man, 'for thy parent's sake, thou art free.' Dost thou remember the name of that English warrior?"

"I remember, that when a laughing boy," returned the patriarch, with the peculiar recollection of vast age, "I stood upon the sands of the sea-shore, and saw a big canoe, with wings whiter than the swan's, and wider than many eagles, come from the rising sun—"

"Nay, nay; I speak not of a time so very distant; but of favour shown to thy kindred by one of mine, within the memory of thy youngest warrior."

"Was it when the Yengeese and the Dutchemanne fought for the hunting grounds of the Delawares? Then Tamenund was a chief, and first laid aside the bow for the lightning of the pale-faces—"

"Nor yet then," interrupted Cora, "by many ages; I speak of a thing of yesterday. Surely, surely, you forget it not!"

"It was but yesterday," rejoined the aged man, with touching pathos, "that the children of the Lenape were masters of the world! The fishes of the salt-lake, the birds, the beasts, and the Mengwe of the woods, owned them for Sagamores."

*William Penn was termed Miquon by the Delawares, and, as he never used violence or injustice in his dealings with them, his reputation for probity passed into a proverb. The American is justly proud of the origin of his nation, which is perhaps unequalled in the history of the world, but the Pennsylvanian and Jerseyman have more reason to value themselves in their ancestors than the natives of any other state, since no wrong was done the original owners of the soil.

Cora bowed her head in disappointment, and, for a bitter moment, struggled with her chagrin. Then elevating her rich features and beaming eyes, she continued, in tones scarcely less penetrating than the unearthly voice of the patriarch himself,

"Tell me, is Tamenund a father?"

The old man looked down upon her, from his elevated stand, with a benignant smile on his wasted countenance, and then casting his eyes slowly over the whole assemblage, he answered—

"Of a nation."

"For myself I ask nothing. Like thee and thine, venerable chief," she continued, pressing her hands convulsively on her heart, and suffering her head to droop, until her burning cheeks were nearly concealed in the maze of dark, glossy tresses, that fell in disorder upon her shoulders, "the curse of my ancestors has fallen heavily on their child! But yonder is one, who has never known the weight of Heaven's displeasure until now. She is the daughter of an old and failing man, whose days are near their close. She has many, very many, to love her, and delight in her; and she is too good, much too precious, to become the victim of that villain."

"I know that the pale-faces are a proud and hungry race. I know that they claim, not only to have the earth, but that the meanest of their colour is better than the Sachems of the red man. The dogs and crows of their tribes," continued the earnest old chieftain, without heeding the wounded spirit of his listener, whose head was nearly crushed to the earth, in shame, as he proceeded, "would bark and caw, before they would take a woman to their wigwams, whose blood was not of the colour of snow. But let them not boast before the face of the Manitto too loud. They entered the land at the rising, and may yet go off at the setting sun! I have often seen the locust strip the leaves from the trees, but the season of blossoms has always come again!"

"It is so," said Cora, drawing a long breath, as if reviving from a trance, raising her face, and shaking back her shining veil, with a kindling eye, that contradicted the death-like paleness of her countenance; "but why—it is not permitted us to inquire! There is yet one of thine own people, who has not been brought before thee; before thou lettest the Huron depart in triumph, hear him speak."

Observing Tamenund to look about him doubtingly, one of his companions said—

"It is a snake—a red-skin in the pay of the Yengeese. We keep him for the torture."

"Let him come," returned the sage.

Then Tamenund once more sunk into his seat, and a silence so deep prevailed, while the young men prepared to obey his simple mandate, that the leaves, which fluttered in the draught of the light morning air, were distinctly heard rustling in the surrounding forest.

Chapter XXX

> "If you deny me, fie upon your law!
> There is no force in the decrees of Venice:
> I stand for judgment: answer; shall I have it?"
> *The Merchant of Venice*, IV.i.101–103.

THE SILENCE continued unbroken by human sounds for many anxious minutes. Then the waving multitude opened, and shut again, and Uncas stood in the living circle. All those eyes, which had been curiously studying the lineaments of the sage, as the source of their own intelligence, turned, on the instant, and were now bent in secret admiration on the erect, agile, and faultless person of the captive. But neither the presence in which he found himself, nor the exclusive attention that he attracted, in any manner disturbed the self-possession of the young Mohican. He cast a deliberate and observing look on every side of him, meeting the settled expression of hostility, that lowered in the visages of the chiefs, with the same calmness as the curious gaze of the attentive children. But when, last in his haughty scrutiny, the person of Tamenund came under his glance, his eye became fixed, as though all other objects were already forgotten. Then advancing with a slow and noiseless step, up the area, he placed himself immediately before the footstool of the sage. Here he stood unnoted, though keenly observant himself, until one of the chiefs apprised the latter of his presence.

"With what tongue does the prisoner speak to the Manitto?" demanded the patriarch, without unclosing his eyes.

"Like his fathers," Uncas replied; "with the tongue of a Delaware."

At this sudden and unexpected annunciation, a low, fierce yell, ran through the multitude, that might not inaptly be compared to the growl of the lion, as his choler is first awakened—a fearful omen of the weight of his future anger. The effect was equally strong on the sage, though differently exhibited. He passed a hand before his eyes, as if to exclude the least evidence of so shameful a spectacle, while he repeated, in his low guttural tones, the words he had just heard.

"A Delaware! I have lived to see the tribes of the Lenape driven from their council fires, and scattered, like broken herds of deer, among the hills of the Iroquois! I have seen the hatchets of a strange people sweep woods from the valleys, that the winds of Heaven had spared! The beasts that run on the mountains, and the birds that fly above the trees, have I seen living in the wigwams of men; but never before have I found a Delaware so base, as to creep, like a poisonous serpent, into the camps of his nation."

"The singing-birds have opened their bills," returned Uncas, in the softest notes of his own musical voice; "and Tamenund has heard their song."

The sage started, and bent his head aside, as if to catch the fleeting sounds of some passing melody.

"Does Tamenund dream!" he exclaimed. "What voice is at his ear! Have the winters gone backward! Will summer come again to the children of the Lenape!"

A solemn and respectful silence succeeded this incoherent burst from the lips of the Delaware prophet. His people readily construed his unintelligible language into one of those mysterious conferences, he was believed to hold so frequently, with a superior intelligence, and they awaited the issue of the revelation in awe. After a patient pause, however, one of the aged men perceiving that the sage had lost the recollection of the subject before them, ventured to remind him again of the presence of the prisoner.

"The false Delaware trembles lest he should hear the words of Tamenund," he said. " 'Tis a hound that howls, when the Yengeese show him a trail."

"And ye," returned Uncas, looking sternly around him, "are dogs that whine when the Frenchman casts ye the offals of his deer!"

Twenty knives gleamed in the air, and as many warriors sprang to their feet, at this biting, and perhaps merited, retort; but a motion from one of the chiefs suppressed the outbreaking of their tempers, and restored the appearance of quiet. The task might probably have been more difficult, had not a movement, made by Tamenund, indicated that he was again about to speak.

"Delaware," resumed the sage, "little art thou worthy of

thy name. My people have not seen a bright sun in many winters; and the warrior who deserts his tribe, when hid in clouds, is doubly a traitor. The law of the Manitto is just. It is so; while the rivers run and the mountains stand, while the blossoms come and go on the trees, it must be so. He is thine, my children; deal justly by him."

Not a limb was moved, nor was a breath drawn louder and longer than common, until the closing syllable of this final decree had passed the lips of Tamenund. Then a cry of vengeance burst at once, as it might be, from the united lips of the nation; a frightful augury of their ruthless intentions. In the midst of these prolonged and savage yells, a chief proclaimed, in a high voice, that the captive was condemned to endure the dreadful trial of torture by fire. The circle broke its order, and screams of delight mingled with the bustle and tumult of preparation. Heyward struggled madly with his captors; the anxious eyes of Hawk-eye began to look around him, with an expression of peculiar earnestness; and Cora again threw herself at the feet of the patriarch, once more a supplicant for mercy.

Throughout the whole of these trying moments, Uncas had alone preserved his serenity. He looked on the preparations with a steady eye, and when the tormentors came to seize him, he met them with a firm and upright attitude. One among them, if possible, more fierce and savage than his fellows, seized the hunting shirt of the young warrior, and at a single effort, tore it from his body. Then, with a yell of frantic pleasure, he leaped toward his unresisting victim, and prepared to lead him to the stake. But, at that moment, when he appeared most a stranger to the feelings of humanity, the purpose of the savage was arrested as suddenly, as if a supernatural agency had interposed in the behalf of Uncas. The eye-balls of the Delaware seemed to start from their sockets; his mouth opened, and his whole form became frozen in an attitude of amazement. Raising his hand with a slow and regulated motion, he pointed with a finger to the bosom of the captive. His companions crowded about him, in wonder, and every eye was, like his own, fastened intently on the figure of a small tortoise, beautifully tattooed on the breast of the prisoner, in a bright blue tint.

For a single instant, Uncas enjoyed his triumph, smiling calmly on the scene. Then motioning the crowd away, with a high and haughty sweep of his arm, he advanced in front of the nation with the air of a king, and spoke in a voice louder than the murmur of admiration that ran through the multitude.

"Men of the Lenni Lenape!" he said, "my race upholds the earth! Your feeble tribe stands on my shell! What fire, that a Delaware can light, would burn the child of my fathers," he added, pointing proudly to the simple blazonry on his skin; "the blood that came from such a stock, would smother your flames! My race is the grandfather of nations!"

"Who art thou!" demanded Tamenund, rising, at the startling tones he heard, more than at any meaning conveyed by the language of the prisoner.

"Uncas, the son of Chingachgook," answered the captive, modestly, turning from the nation, and bending his head in reverence to the other's character and years; "a son of the Great Unâmis."*

"The hour of Tamenund is nigh!" exclaimed the sage; "the day is come, at last, to the night! I thank the Manitto, that one is here to fill my place at the council-fire. Uncas, the child of Uncas, is found! Let the eyes of a dying eagle gaze on the rising sun."

The youth stepped lightly, but proudly, on the platform, where he became visible to the whole agitated and wondering multitude. Tamenund held him long at the length of his arm, and read every turn in the fine lineaments of his countenance, with the untiring gaze of one who recalled the days of happiness.

"Is Tamenund a boy!" at length the bewildered prophet exclaimed. "Have I dreamt of so many snows—that my people were scattered like floating sands—of Yengeese, more plenty than the leaves on the trees! The arrow of Tamenund would not frighten the fawn; his arm is withered like the branch of a dead oak; the snail would be swifter in the race; yet is Uncas before him, as they went to battle, against the pale-faces! Uncas, the panther of his tribe, the eldest son of the Lenape, the

*Turtle.

wisest Sagamore of the Mohicans! Tell me, ye Delawares, has Tamenund been a sleeper for a hundred winters?"

The calm and deep silence which succeeded these words, sufficiently announced the awful reverence with which his people received the communication of the patriarch. None dared to answer, though all listened in breathless expectation of what might follow. Uncas, however, looking in his face, with the fondness and veneration of a favoured child, presumed on his own high and acknowledged rank, to reply.

"Four warriors of his race have lived and died," he said, "since the friend of Tamenund led his people in battle. The blood of the Turtle has been in many chiefs, but all have gone back into the earth, from whence they came, except Chingachgook and his son."

"It is true—it is true," returned the sage—a flash of recollection destroying all his pleasing fancies, and restoring him, at once, to a consciousness of the true history of his nation. "Our wise men have often said that two warriors of the 'unchanged' race were in the hills of the Yengeese; why have their seats at the council fires of the Delawares been so long empty?"

At these words, the young man raised his head, which he had still kept bowed a little, in reverence, and lifting his voice, so as to be heard by the multitude, as if to explain, at once, and for ever, the policy of his family, he said, aloud—

"Once we slept where we could hear the salt lake speak in its anger. Then we were rulers and Sagamores over the land. But when a pale-face was seen on every brook, we followed the deer back to the river of our nation. The Delawares were gone! Few warriors of them all stayed to drink of the stream they loved. Then said my fathers—'here will we hunt. The waters of the river go into the salt lake. If we go towards the setting sun, we shall find streams that run into the great lakes of sweet water; there would a Mohican die, like fishes of the sea, in the clear springs. When the Manitto is ready, and shall say, "come," we will follow the river to the sea, and take our own again.' Such, Delawares, is the belief of the children of the Turtle! Our eyes are on the rising, and not towards the setting sun! We know whence he comes, but we know not whither he goes. It is enough."

The men of the Lenape listened to his words with all the respect that superstition could lend, finding a secret charm even in the figurative language with which the young Sagamore imparted his ideas. Uncas himself watched the effect of his brief explanation with intelligent eyes, and gradually dropped the air of authority he had assumed, as he perceived that his auditors were content. Then permitting his looks to wander over the silent throng that crowded around the elevated seat of Tamenund, he first perceived Hawk-eye, in his bonds. Stepping eagerly from his stand, he made a way for himself to the side of his friend, and cutting his thongs with a quick and angry stroke of his own knife, he motioned to the crowd to divide. The Indians silently obeyed, and once more they stood ranged in their circle, as before his appearance among them. Uncas took the scout by the hand, and led him to the feet of the patriarch.

"Father," he said, "look at this pale-face; a just man, and the friend of the Delawares."

"Is he a son of Miquon?"

"Not so; a warrior known to the Yengeese, and feared by the Maquas."

"What name has he gained by his deeds?"

"We call him Hawk-eye," Uncas replied, using the Delaware phrase; "for his sight never fails. The Mingoes know him better by the death he gives their warriors; with them he is the 'long rifle.' "

"La Longue Carabine!" exclaimed Tamenund, opening his eyes, and regarding the scout, sternly. "My son has not done well to call him friend!"

"I call him so who proves himself such," returned the young chief, with great calmness, but with a steady mien. "If Uncas is welcome among the Delawares, then is Hawk-eye with his friends."

"The pale-face has slain my young men; his name is great for the blows he has struck the Lenape."

"If a Mingo has whispered that much in the ear of the Delaware, he has only shown that he is a singing-bird," said the scout, who now believed it was time to vindicate himself from such offensive charges, and who spoke in the tongue of the man he addressed, modifying his Indian figures, however, with his own peculiar notions. "That I have slain the Maquas, I am not the man to deny, even at their own council fires; but that, knowingly, my hand has ever harmed a Delaware, is opposed to the reason of my gifts, which is friendly to them, and all that belongs to their nation."

A low exclamation of applause passed among the warriors, who exchanged looks with each other, like men that first began to perceive their error.

"Where is the Huron?" demanded Tamenund. "Has he stopped my ears!"

Magua, whose feelings, during that scene in which Uncas had triumphed, may be much better imagined than described, answered to the call, by stepping boldly in front of the patriarch.

"The just Tamenund," he said, " will not keep what a Huron has lent."

"Tell me, son of my brother," returned the sage, avoiding the dark countenance of le Subtil, and turning gladly to the more ingenuous features of Uncas; "has the stranger a conqueror's right over you?"

"He has none. The panther may get into snares set by the women, but he is strong, and knows how to leap through them."

"La Longue Carabine?"

"Laughs at the Mingoes. Go, Huron; ask your squaws the colour of a bear!"

"The stranger and the white maiden that came into my camp together?"

"Should journey on an open path."

"And the woman that the Huron left with my warriors?"

Uncas made no reply.

"And the woman that the Mingo has brought into my camp?" repeated Tamenund, gravely.

"She is mine!" cried Magua, shaking his hand in triumph at Uncas. "Mohican, you know that she is mine."

"My son is silent," said Tamenund, endeavouring to read the expression of the face that the youth turned from him, in sorrow.

"It is so," was the low answer.

A short and impressive pause succeeded, during which it

was very apparent with what reluctance the multitude admitted the justice of the Mingo's claim. At length the sage, on whom alone the decision depended, said, in a firm voice—

"Huron, depart."

"As he came, just Tamenund," demanded the wily Magua; "or with hands filled with the faith of the Delawares? The wigwam of le Renard Subtil is empty. Make him strong with his own."

The aged man mused with himself for a time, and then bending his head towards one of his venerable companions, he asked—

"Are my ears open?"

"It is true."

"Is this Mingo a chief?"

"The first in his nation."

"Girl, what wouldst thou! A great warrior takes thee to wife. Go—thy race will not end."

"Better, a thousand times, it should," exclaimed the horror-struck Cora, "than meet with such a degradation!"

"Huron, her mind is in the tents of her fathers. An unwilling maiden makes an unhappy wigwam."

"She speaks with the tongue of her people," returned Magua, regarding his victim with a look of bitter irony. "She is of a race of traders, and will bargain for a bright look. Let Tamenund speak the words."

"Take you the wampum, and our love."

"Nothing hence, but what Magua brought hither."

"Then depart with thine own. The Great Manitto forbids that a Delaware should be unjust."

Magua advanced, and seized his captive strongly by the arm; the Delawares fell back, in silence; and Cora, as if conscious that remonstrance would be useless, prepared to submit to her fate without resistance.

"Hold, hold!" cried Duncan, springing forward; "Huron, have mercy! Her ransom shall make thee richer than any of thy people were ever yet known to be."

"Magua is a red-skin; he wants not the beads of the pale-faces."

"Gold, silver, powder, lead—all that a warrior needs, shall be in thy wigwam; all that becomes the greatest chief."

"Le Subtil is very strong," cried Magua, violently shaking the hand which grasped the unresisting arm of Cora; "he has his revenge!"

"Mighty Ruler of Providence!" exclaimed Heyward, clasping his hands together in agony, "can this be suffered! To you, just Tamenund, I appeal for mercy."

"The words of the Delaware are said," returned the sage, closing his eyes, and dropping back into his seat, alike wearied with his mental and his bodily exertion. "Men speak not twice."

"That a chief should not misspend his time in unsaying what has once been spoken, is wise and reasonable," said Hawk-eye, motioning to Duncan to be silent; "but it is also prudent in every warrior to consider well before he strikes his tomahawk into the head of his prisoner. Huron, I love you not; nor can I say that any Mingo has ever received much favour at my hands. It is fair to conclude, that if this war does not soon end, many more of your warriors will meet me in the woods. Put it to your judgment, then, whether you would prefer taking such a prisoner as that lady into your encampment, or one like myself, who am a man that it would greatly rejoice your nation to see with naked hands."

"Will the 'long rifle' give his life for the woman?" demanded Magua, hesitatingly; for he had already made a motion towards quitting the place with his victim.

"No, no; I have not said so much as that," returned Hawk-eye, drawing back, with suitable discretion, when he noted the eagerness with which Magua listened to his proposal. "It would be an unequal exchange, to give a warrior, in the prime of his age and usefulness, for the best woman on the frontiers. I might consent to go into winter quarters, now—at least six weeks afore the leaves will turn—on condition you will release the maiden."

Magua shook his head, and made an impatient sign for the crowd to open.

"Well, then," added the scout, with the musing air of a man who had not half made up his mind, "I will throw 'kill-deer' into the bargain. Take the word of an experienced hunter, the piece has not its equal atween the provinces."

Magua still disdained to reply, continuing his efforts to disperse the crowd.

"Perhaps," added the scout, losing his dissembled coolness, exactly in proportion as the other manifested an indifference to the exchange, "if I should condition to teach your young men the real virtue of the we'pon, it would smooth the little differences in our judgments."

Le Renard fiercely ordered the Delawares, who still lingered in an impenetrable belt around him, in hopes he would listen to the amicable proposal, to open his path, threatening, by the glance of his eye, another appeal to the infallible justice of their "prophet."

"What is ordered, must sooner or later arrive," continued Hawk-eye, turning with a sad and humbled look to Uncas. "The varlet knows his advantage, and will keep it! God bless you, boy; you have found friends among your natural kin, and I hope they will prove as true as some you have met, who had no Indian cross. As for me, sooner or later, I must die; it is therefore fortunate there are but few to make my death-howl! After all, it is likely the imps would have managed to master my scalp, so a day or two will make no great difference in the everlasting reckoning of time. God bless you," added the rugged woodsman, bending his head aside, and then instantly changing its direction again, with a wistful look towards the youth; "I loved both you and your father, Uncas, though our skins are not altogether of a colour, and our gifts are somewhat different. Tell the Sagamore I never lost sight of him in my greatest trouble; and, as for you, think of me sometimes, when on a lucky trail; and depend on it, boy, whether there be one heaven or two, there is a path in the other world, by which honest men may come together, again. You'll find the rifle in the place we hid it; take it, and keep it for my sake; and harkee, lad, as your natural gifts dont deny you the use of vengeance, use it a little freely on the Mingoes; it may unburthen your grief at my loss, and ease your mind. Huron, I accept your offer; release the woman. I am your prisoner."

A suppressed, but still distinct murmur of approbation, ran through the crowd at this generous proposition; even the fiercest among the Delaware warriors manifesting pleasure at the manliness of the intended sacrifice. Magua paused, and for an anxious moment, it might be said, he doubted; then casting his eyes on Cora, with an expression in which ferocity and admiration were strangely mingled, his purpose became fixed for ever.

He intimated his contempt of the offer, with a backward motion of his head, and said, in a steady and settled voice—

"Le Renard Subtil is a great chief; he has but one mind. Come," he added, laying his hand too familiarly on the shoulder of his captive, to urge her onward; "a Huron is no tattler; we will go."

The maiden drew back in lofty, womanly reserve, and her dark eye kindled, while the rich blood shot, like the passing brightness of the sun, into her very temples, at the indignity.

"I am your prisoner, and at a fitting time shall be ready to follow, even to my death. But violence is unnecessary," she coldly said; and immediately turning to Hawk-eye, added, "generous hunter! from my soul I thank you. Your offer is vain, neither could it be accepted; but still you may serve me, even more than in your own noble intention. Look at that drooping, humbled child! Abandon her not until you leave her in the habitations of civilized men. I will not say," wringing the hard hand of the scout, "that her father will reward you—for such as you are above the rewards of men—but he will thank you, and bless you. And, believe me, the blessing of a just and aged man, has virtue in the sight of Heaven. Would to God, I could hear one from his lips at this awful moment!" Her voice became choked, and for an instant she was silent; then advancing a step nigher to Duncan, who was supporting her unconscious sister, she continued, in more subdued tones, but in which feeling and the habits of her sex, maintained a fearful struggle—"I need not tell you to cherish the treasure you will possess. You love her, Heyward; that would conceal a thousand faults, though she had them. She is kind, gentle, sweet, good, as mortal may be. There is not a blemish in mind or person, at which the proudest of you all would sicken. She is fair—Oh! how surpassingly fair!" laying her own beautiful, but less brilliant hand, in melancholy affection, on the alabaster forehead of Alice, and parting the golden hair which clustered about her brows; "and yet her soul is pure and spotless as her skin! I could say much—more, perhaps, than cooler reason would approve; but I will spare you and myself—" Her voice became inaudible, and her face was bent over the form of her sister. After a long and burning kiss, she arose, and with features of the hue of death, but without even a tear in her feverish eye, she turned away, and added, to the savage, with all her former elevation of manner—"Now, sir, if it be your pleasure, I will follow."

"Ay, go," cried Duncan, placing Alice in the arms of an Indian girl; "go, Magua, go. These Delawares have their laws, which forbid them to detain you; but I—I have no such obligation. Go, malignant monster—why do you delay!"

It would be difficult to describe the expression with which Magua listened to this threat to follow. There was at first a fierce and manifest display of joy, and then it was instantly subdued in a look of cunning coldness.

"The woods are open," he was content with answering; "the 'open hand' can come."

"Hold," cried Hawk-eye, seizing Duncan by the arm, and detaining him by violence; "you know not the craft of the imp. He would lead you to an ambushment, and your death—"

"Huron," interrupted Uncas, who, submissive to the stern customs of his people, had been an attentive and grave listener to all that passed; "Huron, the justice of the Delawares comes from the Manitto. Look at the sun. He is now in the upper branches of the hemlock. Your path is short and open. When he is seen above the trees, there will be men on your trail."

"I hear a crow!" exclaimed Magua, with a taunting laugh. "Go," he added, shaking his hand at the crowd, which had slowly opened to admit his passage—"Where are the petticoats of the Delawares! Let them send their arrows and their guns to the Wyandots; they shall have venison to eat, and corn to hoe. Dogs, rabbits, thieves—I spit on you!"

His parting gibes were listened to in a dead, boding, silence; and, with these biting words in his mouth, the triumphant Magua passed unmolested into the forest, followed by his passive captive, and protected by the inviolable laws of Indian hospitality.

Chapter XXXI

Flue. "Kill the poys and the luggage! 'tis expressly against the law of arms: 'tis as arrant a piece of knavery, mark you now, as can be offered in the 'orld."

Henry V, IV.vii.1–4.

So long as their enemy and his victim continued in sight, the multitude remained, motionless as beings charmed to the place by some power that was friendly to the Huron; but the instant he disappeared, it became tossed and agitated by fierce and powerful passion. Uncas maintained his elevated stand, keeping his eyes on the form of Cora, until the colours of her dress were blended with the foliage of the forest; when he descended, and moving silently through the throng, he disappeared in that lodge, from which he had so recently issued. A few of the graver and more attentive warriors, who caught the gleams of anger that shot from the eyes of the young chief, in passing, followed him to the place he had selected for his meditations. After which, Tamenund and Alice were removed, and the women and children were ordered to disperse. During the momentous hour that succeeded, the encampment resembled a hive of troubled bees, who only awaited the appearance and example of their leader, to take some distant and momentous flight.

A young warrior, at length, issued from the lodge of Uncas, and moving deliberately, with a sort of grave march, towards a dwarf pine, that grew in the crevices of the rocky terrace, he tore the bark from its body, and then returned whence he came, without speaking. He was soon followed by another, who stripped the sapling of its branches, leaving it a naked and blazed* trunk. A third coloured the post with stripes of a dark red paint; all which indications of a hostile design in the leaders of the nation, were received by the men without, in a gloomy and ominous silence. Finally, the Mohican himself reappeared, devested of all his attire, except his

*A tree which has been partially or entirely stripped of its bark is said, in the language of the country, to be "blazed." The term is strictly English; for a horse is said to be blazed when it has a white mark.

girdle and leggings, and with one half of his fine features hid under a cloud of threatening black.

Uncas moved with a slow and dignified tread towards the post, which he immediately commenced encircling with a measured step, not unlike an ancient dance, raising his voice, at the same time, in the wild and irregular chant of his war-song. The notes were in the extremes of human sounds; being sometimes melancholy and exquisitely plaintive, even rivalling the melody of birds—and then, by sudden and startling transitions, causing the auditors to tremble by their depth and energy. The words were few, and often repeated, proceeding gradually from a sort of invocation, or hymn, to the deity, to an intimation of the warrior's object, and terminating as they commenced, with an acknowledgment of his own dependence on the Great Spirit. If it were possible to translate the comprehensive and melodious language in which he spoke, the ode might read something like the following—

Manitto! Manitto! Manitto!
Thou art great—thou art good—thou art wise—
Manitto! Manitto!
Thou art just!

In the heavens, in the clouds, Oh! I see!
Many spots—many dark—many red—
In the heavens, Oh! I see!
Many clouds.

In the woods, in the air, Oh! I hear!
The whoop, the long yell, and the cry—
In the woods, Oh! I hear!
The loud whoop!

Manitto! Manitto! Manitto!
I am weak—thou art strong—I am slow—
Manitto! Manitto!
Give me aid.

At the end of what might be called each verse, he made a pause, by raising a note louder and longer than common, that was peculiarly suited to the sentiment just expressed. The first close was solemn, and intended to convey the idea of veneration; the second descriptive, bordering on the alarming; and the third was the well-known and terrific war-whoop, which burst from the lips of the young warrior, like a combination of all the frightful sounds of battle. The last was like the first, humble and imploring. Three times did he repeat this song, and as often did he encircle the post, in his dance.

At the close of the first turn, a grave and highly esteemed chief of the Lenape, followed his example, singing words of his own, however, to music of a similar character. Warrior after warrior enlisted in the dance, until all of any renown and authority were numbered in its mazes. The spectacle now became wildly terrific; the fierce looking and menacing visages of the chiefs receiving additional power, from the appalling strains in which they mingled their guttural tones. Just then, Uncas struck his tomahawk deep into the post, and raised his voice in a shout, which might be termed his own battle cry. The act announced that he had assumed the chief authority in the intended expedition.

It was a signal that awakened all the slumbering passions of the nation. A hundred youths, who had hitherto been restrained by the diffidence of their years, rushed in a frantic body on the fancied emblem of their enemy, and severed it asunder, splinter by splinter, until nothing remained of the trunk but its roots in the earth. During this moment of tumult, the most ruthless deeds of war were performed on the fragments of the tree, with as much apparent ferocity, as if they were the living victims of their cruelty. Some were scalped; some received the keen and trembling axe; and others suffered by thrusts from the fatal knife. In short, the manifestations of zeal and fierce delight were so great and unequivocal, that the expedition was declared to be a war of the nation.

The instant Uncas had struck the blow, he moved out of the circle, and cast his eyes up at the sun, which was just gaining the point, when the truce with Magua was to end. The fact was soon announced by a significant gesture, accompanied by a corresponding cry, and the whole of the excited multitude abandoned their mimic warfare, with shrill yells of pleasure, to prepare for the more hazardous experiment of the reality.

The whole face of the encampment was instantly changed. The warriors, who were already armed and painted, became as still, as if they were incapable of any uncommon burst of emotion. On the other hand, the women broke out of the lodges, with the songs of joy and those of lamentation, so strangely mingled, that it might have been difficult to have said which passion preponderated. None, however, were idle. Some bore their choicest articles, others their young, and some their aged and infirm, into the forest, which spread itself like a verdant carpet of bright green, against the side of the mountain. Thither Tamenund also retired, with calm composure, after a short and touching interview with Uncas; from whom the sage separated with the reluctance that a parent would quit a long lost, and just recovered, child. In the mean time, Duncan saw Alice to a place of safety, and then sought the scout, with a countenance that denoted how eagerly he, also, panted for the approaching contest.

But Hawk-eye was too much accustomed to the war-song and the enlistments of the natives, to betray any interest in the passing scene. He merely cast an occasional look at the number and quality of the warriors, who, from time to time, signified their readiness to accompany Uncas to the field. In this particular he was soon satisfied; for, as has been already seen, the power of the young chief quickly embraced every fighting man in the nation. After this material point was so satisfactorily decided, he despatched an Indian boy, in quest of "kill-deer" and the rifle of Uncas, to the place where they had deposited the weapons, on approaching the camp of the Delawares—a measure of double policy, inasmuch as it protected the arms from their own fate, if detained as prisoners, and gave them the advantage of appearing among the strangers rather as sufferers, than as men provided with the means of defence and subsistence. In selecting another to perform the office of reclaiming his highly prized rifle, the scout had lost sight of none of his habitual caution. He knew that Magua had not come unattended, and he also knew that Huron spies watched the movements of their new enemies, along the whole boundary of the woods. It would, therefore, have been fatal to himself to have attempted the experiment; a warrior would have fared no better; but the danger of a boy would not be likely to commence until after his object was discovered. When Heyward joined him, the scout was coolly awaiting the result of this experiment.

The boy, who had been well instructed, and was sufficiently crafty, proceeded, with a bosom that was swelling with the pride of such a confidence, and all the hopes of young ambition, carelessly across the clearing to the wood, which he entered at a point at some little distance from the place where the guns were secreted. The instant, however, he was concealed by the foliage of the bushes, his dusky form was to be seen gliding, like that of a serpent, towards the desired treasure. He was successful; and in another moment he appeared, flying across the narrow opening that skirted the base of the terrace on which the village stood, with the velocity of an arrow, and bearing a prize in each hand. He had actually gained the crags, and was leaping up their sides with incredible activity, when a shot from the woods showed how accurate had been the judgment of the scout. The boy answered it with a feeble, but contemptuous shout, and immediately a second bullet was sent after him, from another part of the cover. At the next instant he appeared on the level above, elevating his guns in triumph, while he moved, with the air of a conqueror, towards the renowned hunter, who had honoured him by so glorious a commission.

Notwithstanding the lively interest Hawk-eye had taken in the fate of his messenger, he received "kill-deer" with a satisfaction that, momentarily, drove all other recollections from his mind. After examining the piece with an intelligent eye, and opening and shutting the pan some ten or fifteen times, and trying sundry other equally important experiments on the lock, he turned to the boy, and demanded, with great manifestations of kindness, if he was hurt. The urchin looked proudly up in his face, but made no reply.

"Ay! I see, lad, the knaves have barked your arm!" added the scout, taking up the limb of the patient sufferer, across which a deep flesh wound had been made by one of the bullets; "but a little bruised alder will act like a charm. In the mean time, I will wrap it in a badge of wampum! You have commenced the business of a warrior early, my brave boy, and are likely to bear a plenty of honourable scars to your grave. I know many young men that have taken scalps, who cannot show such a mark as this! Go;" having bound up the arm; "you will be a chief!"

The lad departed, prouder of his flowing blood than the vainest courtier could be of his blushing riband; and stalked among the fellows of his age, an object of general admiration and envy.

But in a moment of so many serious and important duties, this single act of juvenile fortitude, did not attract the general notice and commendation it would have received under milder auspices. It had, however, served to apprise the Delawares of the position and the intentions of their enemies. Accordingly, a party of adventurers, better suited to the task than the weak, though spirited boy, was ordered to dislodge the skulkers. The duty was soon performed, for most of the Hurons retired of themselves, when they found they had been discovered. The Delawares followed to a sufficient distance from their own emcampment, and then halted for orders, apprehensive of being led into an ambush. As both parties secreted themselves, the woods were again as still and quiet, as a mild summer morning and deep solitude could render them.

The calm, but still impatient Uncas, now collected his chiefs, and divided his power. He presented Hawk-eye as a warrior, often tried, and always found deserving of confidence. When he found his friend met with a favourable reception, he bestowed on him the command of twenty men, like himself, active, skilful, and resolute. He gave the Delawares to understand the rank of Heyward among the troops of the Yengeese, and then tendered to him a trust of equal authority. But Duncan declined the charge, professing his readiness to serve as a volunteer by the side of the scout. After this disposition, the young Mohican appointed various native chiefs to fill the different situations of responsibility, and the time pressing, he gave forth the word to march. He was cheerfully, but silently, obeyed, by more than two hundred men.

Their entrance into the forest was perfectly unmolested; nor did they encounter any living objects, that could either give the alarm, or furnish the intelligence they needed, until they came upon the lairs of their own scouts. Here a halt was ordered, and the chiefs were assembled to hold a "whispering council." At this meeting, divers plans of operation were suggested, though none of a character to meet the wishes of their ardent leader. Had Uncas followed the promptings of his own inclinations, he would have led his followers to the charge without a moment's delay, and put the conflict to the hazard of an instant issue; but such a course would have been in opposition to all the received practices and opinions of his countrymen. He was, therefore, fain to adopt a caution, that in the present temper of his mind, he execrated, and to listen to advice at which his fiery spirit chafed, under the vivid recollection of Cora's danger, and Magua's insolence.

After an unsatisfactory conference of many minutes, a solitary individual was seen advancing from the side of the enemy, with such apparent haste, as to induce the belief, he might be a messenger charged with pacific overtures. When within a hundred yards, however, of the cover, behind which the Delaware council had assembled, the stranger hesitated, appeared uncertain what course to take, and finally halted. All eyes were now turned on Uncas, as if seeking directions how to proceed.

"Hawk-eye," said the young chief, in a low voice, "he must never speak to the Hurons again."

"His time has come," said the laconic scout, thrusting the long barrel of his rifle through the leaves, and taking his deliberate and fatal aim. But, instead of pulling the trigger, he lowered the muzzle again, and indulged himself in a fit of his peculiar mirth. "I took the imp for a Mingo, as I'm a miserable sinner!" he said; "but when my eye ranged along his ribs, for a place to get the bullet in—would you think it, Uncas—I saw the musicianer's blower! and so, after all, it is the man they call Gamut, whose death can profit no one, and whose life, if his tongue can do any thing but sing, may be made serviceable to our own ends. If sounds have not lost their virtue, I'll soon have a discourse with the honest fellow, and that in a voice he'll find more agreeable than the speech of 'kill-deer.' "

So saying, Hawk-eye laid aside his rifle, and crawling through the bushes, until within hearing of David, he attempted to repeat the musical effort, which had conducted himself, with so much safety and eclat, through the Huron encampment. The exquisite organs of Gamut could not readily be deceived, (and, to say the truth, it would have been difficult for any other than Hawk-eye to produce a similar noise,) and, consequently, having once before heard the sounds, he now knew whence they proceeded. The poor fellow appeared relieved from a state of great embarrassment; for pursuing the direction of the voice—a task that to him was not much less arduous, than it would have been to have gone up in face of a battery—he soon discovered the hidden songster.

"I wonder what the Hurons will think of that!" said the scout, laughing, as he took his companion by the arm, and urged him towards the rear. "If the knaves lie within ear-shot, they will say there are two non-compossurs, instead of one! But here we are safe," he added, pointing to Uncas and his associates. "Now give us the history of the Mingo inventions, in natural English, and without any ups-and-downs of voice."

David gazed about him, at the fierce and wild looking chiefs, in mute wonder; but assured by the presence of faces that he knew, he soon rallied his faculties so far, as to make an intelligent reply.

"The heathen are abroad in goodly numbers," said David; "and, I fear, with evil intent. There has been much howling and ungodly revelry, together with such sounds as it is profanity to utter, in their habitations within the past hour; so much so, in truth, that I have fled to the Delawares in search of peace."

"Your ears might not have profited much by the exchange, had you been quicker of foot," returned the scout, a little drily. "But let that be as it may; where are the Hurons?"

"They lie hid in the forest, between this spot and their village, in such force, that prudence would teach you instantly to return."

Uncas cast a glance along the range of trees which concealed his own band, and mentioned the name of—

"Magua?"—

"Is among them. He brought in the maiden that had sojourned with the Delawares, and leaving her in the cave, has put himself, like a raging wolf, at the head of his savages. I know not what has troubled his spirit so greatly!"

"He has left her, you say, in the cave!" interrupted Heyward; " 'tis well that we know its situation! May not something be done for her instant relief?"

Uncas looked earnestly at the scout, before he asked—

"What says Hawk-eye?"

"Give me my twenty rifles, and I will turn to the right, along the stream, and passing by the huts of the beaver, will join the Sagamore and the Colonel. You shall then hear the whoop from that quarter; with this wind one may easily send it a mile. Then, Uncas, do you drive in their front; when they come within range of our pieces, we will give them a blow, that I pledge the good name of an old frontiersman, shall make their line bend, like an ashen bow. After which, we will carry their village, and take the woman from the cave; when the affair may be finished with the tribe, according to a white man's battle, by a blow and a victory; or, in the Indian fashion, with dodge and cover. There may be no great learning, major, in this plan, but with courage and patience it can all be done."

"I like it much," cried Duncan, who saw that the release of Cora was the primary object in the mind of the scout; "I like it much. Let it be instantly attempted."

After a short conference, the plan was matured, and rendered more intelligible to the several parties; the different signals were appointed, and the chiefs separated, each to his allotted station.

Chapter XXXII

"But plagues shall spread, and funeral fires increase,
Till the great King, without a ransom paid,
To her own Chrysa, send the black-eyed maid."
Pope, *The Iliad*, Book I, ll. 122–124.

During the time Uncas was making this disposition of his forces, the woods were as still, and, with the exception of those who had met in council, apparently, as much untenanted, as when they came fresh from the hands of their Almighty Creator. The eye could range, in every direction, through the long and shadowed vistas of the trees; but no where was any object to be seen, that did not properly belong to the peaceful and slumbering scenery. Here and there a bird was heard fluttering among the branches of the beeches, and occasionally a squirrel dropped a nut, drawing the startled looks of the party, for a moment, to the place; but the instant the casual interruption ceased, the passing air was heard murmuring above their heads, along that verdant and undulating surface of forest, which spread itself unbroken, unless by stream or lake, over such a vast region of country. Across the tract of wilderness, which lay between the Delawares and the village of their enemies, it seemed as if the foot of man had never trodden, so breathing and deep was the silence in which it lay. But Hawk-eye, whose duty led him foremost in the adventure, knew the character of those with whom he was about to contend, too well, to trust the treacherous quiet.

When he saw his little band collected, the scout threw "kill-deer" into the hollow of his arm, and making a silent signal that he would be followed, he led them many rods towards the rear, into the bed of a little brook, which they had crossed in advancing. Here he halted, and after waiting for the whole of his grave and attentive warriors to close about him, he spoke in Delaware, demanding—

"Do any of my young men know whither this run will lead us?"

A Delaware stretched forth a hand, with the two fingers separated, and indicating the manner in which they were joined at the root, he answered—

"Before the sun could go his own length, the little water will be in the big." Then he added, pointing in the direction of the place he mentioned, "the two make enough for the beavers."

"I thought as much," returned the scout, glancing his eye upward at the opening in the tree-tops, "from the course it takes, and the bearings of the mountains. Men, we will keep within the cover of its banks till we scent the Hurons."

His companions gave the usual brief exclamation of assent, but perceiving that their leader was about to lead the way, in person, one or two made signs that all was not as it should be. Hawk-eye, who comprehended their meaning glances, turned, and perceived that his party had been followed thus far by the singing-master.

"Do you know, friend," asked the scout, gravely, and perhaps with a little of the pride of conscious deserving in his manner, "that this is a band of rangers, chosen for the most desperate service, and put under the command of one, who, though another might say it with a better face, will not be apt to leave them idle. It may not be five, it cannot be thirty, minutes before we tread on the body of a Huron, living or dead."

"Though not admonished of your intentions in words," returned David, whose face was a little flushed, and whose ordinarily quiet and unmeaning eyes glimmered with an expression of unusual fire, "your men have reminded me of the children of Jacob going out to battle against the Shechemites, for wickedly aspiring to wedlock with a woman of a race that was favoured of the Lord. Now, I have journeyed far, and sojourned much, in good and evil, with the maiden ye seek; and, though not a man of war, with my loins girded and my sword sharpened, yet would I gladly strike a blow in her behalf."

The scout hesitated, as if weighing the chances of such a strange enlistment in his mind, before he answered—

"You know not the use of any we'pon. You carry no rifle; and believe me, what the Mingoes take, they will freely give again."

"Though not a vaunting and bloodily disposed Goliah," returned David, drawing a sling from beneath his particoloured and uncouth attire, "I have not forgotten the example of the Jewish boy. With this ancient instrument of war have I practised much in my youth, and peradventure the skill has not entirely departed from me."

"Ay!" said Hawk-eye, considering the deer-skin thong and apron, with a cold and discouraging eye; "the thing might do its work among arrows, or even knives; but these Mengwe have been furnished by the Frenchers with a good grooved barrel a man. However, it seems to be your gift to go unharmed amid fire; and as you have hitherto been favoured ——Major, you have left your rifle at a cock; a single shot before the time, would be just twenty scalps lost to no purpose—Singer, you can follow; we may find use for you in the shoutings."

"I thank you, friend," returned David, supplying himself, like his royal namesake, from among the pebbles of the brook, "though not given to the desire to kill, had you sent me away, my spirit would have been troubled."

"Remember," added the scout, tapping his own head significantly on that spot where Gamut was yet sore, "we come to fight, and not to musickate. Until the general whoop is given, nothing speaks but the rifle."

David nodded, as much as to signify his acquiescence with the terms, and then Hawk-eye, casting another observant glance over his followers, made the signal to proceed.

Their route lay, for the distance of a mile, along the bed of the water course. Though protected from any great danger of observation by the precipitous banks, and the thick shrubbery which skirted the stream, no precaution, known to an Indian attack, was neglected. A warrior rather crawled than walked on each flank, so as to catch occasional glimpses into the forest; and every few minutes the band came to a halt, and listened for hostile sounds, with an acuteness of organs, that would be scarcely conceivable to a man in a less natural state. Their march was, however, unmolested, and they reached the point where the lesser stream was lost in the greater, without the smallest evidence that their progress had been noted. Here the scout again halted, to consult the signs of the forest.

"We are likely to have a good day for a fight," he said, in English, addressing Heyward, and glancing his eye upwards at the clouds, which began to move in broad sheets across the firmament; "a bright sun and a glittering barrel are no friends to true sight. Every thing is favourable; they have the wind, which will bring down their noises and their smoke too, no little matter in itself; whereas, with us, it will be first a shot and then a clear view. But here is an end of our cover; the beaver have had the range of this stream for hundreds of years, and what atween their food and their dams, there is, as you see, many a girdled stub, but few living trees."

Hawk-eye had, in truth, in these few words, given no bad description of the prospect that now lay in their front. The brook was irregular in its width, sometimes shooting through narrow fissures in the rocks, and at others, spreading over acres of bottom land, forming little areas, that might be termed ponds. Every where along its banks were the mouldering relics of dead trees, in all the stages of decay, from those that groaned on their tottering trunks, to such as had recently been robbed of those rugged coats, that so mysteriously contain their principle of life. A few long, low, and moss covered piles, were scattered among them, like the memorials of a former and long departed generation.

All these minute particulars were noted by the scout, with a gravity and interest, that they probably had never before attracted. He knew that the Huron encampment lay a short half mile up the brook, and, with the characteristic anxiety of one who dreaded a hidden danger, he was greatly troubled at not finding the smallest trace of the presence of his enemy. Once or twice he felt induced to give the order for a rush, and to attempt the village by surprise; but his experience quickly admonished him of the danger of so useless an experiment. Then he listened intently, and with painful uncertainty, for the sounds of hostility in the quarter where Uncas was left; but nothing was audible except the sighing of the wind, that began to sweep over the bosom of the forest in gusts, which threatened a tempest. At length, yielding rather to his unusual impatience, than taking counsel from his knowledge, he determined to bring matters to an issue, by unmasking his force, and proceeding cautiously, but steadily, up the stream.

The scout had stood, while making his observations, sheltered by a brake, and his companions still lay in the bed of the ravine, through which the smaller stream debouched; but on hearing his low, though intelligible signal, the whole party stole up the bank, like so many dark spectres, and silently arranged themselves around him. Pointing in the direction he wished to proceed, Hawk-eye advanced, the band breaking off in single files, and following so accurately in his footsteps, as to leave, if we except Heyward and David, the trail of but a single man.

The party was, however, scarcely uncovered, before a volley from a dozen rifles was heard in their rear, and a Delaware leaping high into the air, like a wounded deer, fell at his whole length, perfectly dead.

"Ah! I feared some deviltry like this!" exclaimed the scout, in English; adding, with the quickness of thought, in his adopted tongue, "to cover men, and charge!"

The band dispersed at the word, and before Heyward had well recovered from his surprise, he found himself standing alone with David. Luckily, the Hurons had already fallen back, and he was safe from their fire. But this state of things was evidently to be of short continuance, for the scout set the example of pressing on their retreat, by discharging his rifle, and darting from tree to tree, as his enemy slowly yielded ground.

It would seem that the assault had been made by a very small party of the Hurons, which, however, continued to increase in numbers, as it retired on its friends, until the return fire was very nearly, if not quite equal, to that maintained by the advancing Delawares. Heyward threw himself among the combatants, and imitating the necessary caution of his companions, he made quick discharges with his own rifle. The contest now grew warm and stationary. Few were injured, as both parties kept their bodies as much protected as possible by the trees; never, indeed, exposing any part of their persons, except in the act of taking aim. But the chances were gradually growing unfavourable to Hawk-eye and his band. The quick sighted scout perceived his danger, without knowing how to remedy it. He saw it was more dangerous to retreat than to maintain his ground; while he found his enemy throwing out men on his flank, which rendered the task of keeping themselves covered so very difficult to the Delawares, as nearly to silence their fire. At this embarrassing moment, when they began to think the whole of the hostile tribe was gradually encircling them, they heard the yell of combatants, and the rattling of arms, echoing under the arches of the wood, at the place where Uncas was posted; a bottom which, in a manner, lay beneath the ground on which Hawk-eye and his party were contending.

The effects of this attack were instantaneous, and to the scout and his friends greatly relieving. It would seem, that while his own surprise had been anticipated, and had consequently failed, the enemy, in their turn, having been deceived in its object and in his numbers, had left too small a force to resist the impetuous onset of the young Mohican. This fact was doubly apparent, by the rapid manner in which the battle in the forest rolled upward towards the village, and by an instant falling off in the number of their assailants, who rushed to assist in maintaining the front, and, as it now proved to be, the principal point of defence.

Animating his followers by his voice, and his own example, Hawk-eye then gave the word to bear down upon their foes. The charge, in that rude species of warfare, consisted merely in pushing from cover to cover, nigher to the enemy; and in this manœuvre he was instantly and successfully obeyed. The Hurons were compelled to withdraw, and the scene of the contest rapidly changed from the more open ground on which it had commenced, to a spot where the assailed found a thicket to rest upon. Here the struggle was protracted, arduous, and, seemingly, of doubtful issue. The Delawares, though none of them fell, beginning to bleed freely, in consequence of the disadvantage at which they were held.

In this crisis, Hawk-eye found means to get behind the same tree, as that which served for a cover to Heyward; most of his own combatants being within call, a little on his right, where they maintained rapid, though fruitless, discharges on their sheltered enemies.

"You are a young man, major," said the scout, dropping the butt of 'kill-deer' to the earth, and leaning on the barrel, a little fatigued with his previous industry; "and it may be your gift to lead armies, at some future day, ag'in these imps, the Mingoes. You may here see the philosophy of an Indian fight. It consists, mainly, in a ready hand, a quick eye, and a good cover. Now, if you had a company of the Royal Americans here, in what manner would you set them to work in this business?"

"Thy bayonet would make a road."

"Ay, there is white reason in what you say; but a man must ask himself, in this wilderness, how many lives he can spare. No—horse,"* continued the scout, shaking his head, like one who mused; "horse, I am ashamed to say, must, sooner or later, decide these skrimmages. The brutes are better than men, and to horse must we come at last! Put a shodden hoof on the moccasin of a red-skin, and if his rifle be once emptied, he will never stop to load it again."

"This is a subject that might better be discussed another time," returned Heyward; "shall we charge?"

"I see no contradiction to the gifts of any man, in passing his breathing spells in useful reflections," the scout replied. "As to a rush, I little relish such a measure, for a scalp or two must be thrown away in the attempt. And yet," he added, bending his head aside, to catch the sounds of the distant combat, "if we are to be of use to Uncas, these knaves in our front must be gotten rid of!"

Then turning, with a prompt and decided air, he called aloud to his Indians, in their own language. His words were answered by a shout, and at a given signal, each warrior made a swift movement around his particular tree. The sight of so many dark bodies, glancing before their eyes at the same instant, drew a hasty, and, consequently, an ineffectual fire from the Hurons. Without stopping to breathe, the Delawares leaped, in long bounds, towards the wood, like so many

*The American forest admits of the passage of horse, there being little underbrush, and few tangled brakes. The plan of Hawk-eye is the one which has always proved the most successful in the battles between the whites and the Indians. Wayne, in his celebrated campaign on the Miami, received the fire of his enemies in line; and then causing his dragoons to wheel round his flanks, the Indians were driven from their covers before they had time to load. One of the most conspicuous of the chiefs who fought in the battle of Miami assured the writer, that the red-men could not fight the warriors with "long knives and leather-stockings;" meaning the dragoons, with their sabres and boots.

panthers springing upon their prey. Hawk-eye was in front, brandishing his terrible rifle, and animating his followers by his example. A few of the older and more cunning Hurons, who had not been deceived by the artifice which had been practised to draw their fire, now made a close and deadly discharge of their pieces, and justified the apprehensions of the scout, by felling three of his foremost warriors. But the shock was insufficient to repel the impetus of the charge. The Delawares broke into the cover, with the ferocity of their natures, and swept away every trace of resistance by the fury of the onset.

The combat endured only for an instant, hand to hand, and then the assailed yielded ground rapidly, until they reached the opposite margin of the thicket, where they clung to the cover, with the sort of obstinacy that is so often witnessed in hunted brutes. At this critical moment, when the success of the struggle was again becoming doubtful, the crack of a rifle was heard behind the Hurons, and a bullet came whizzing from among some beaver lodges, which were situated in the clearing, in their rear, and was followed by the fierce and appalling yell of the war-whoop.

"There speaks the Sagamore!" shouted Hawk-eye, answering the cry with his own stentorian voice; "we have them now in face and back!"

The effect on the Hurons was instantaneous. Discouraged by an assault from a quarter that left them no opportunity for cover, their warriors uttered a common yell of disappointment, and breaking off in a body, they spread themselves across the opening, heedless of every consideration but flight. Many fell, in making the experiment, under the bullets and the blows of the pursuing Delawares.

We shall not pause to detail the meeting between the scout and Chingachgook, or the more touching interview that Duncan held with Munro. A few brief and hurried words served to explain the state of things to both parties; and then Hawk-eye, pointing out the Sagamore to his band, resigned the chief authority into the hands of the Mohican chief. Chingachgook assumed the station to which his birth and experience gave him so distinguished a claim, with the grave dignity that always gives force to the mandates of a native warrior.

Following the footsteps of the scout, he led the party back through the thicket, his men scalping the fallen Hurons, and secreting the bodies of their own dead as they proceeded, until they gained a point where the former was content to make a halt.

The warriors who had breathed themselves freely in the preceding struggle, were now posted on a bit of level ground, sprinkled with trees, in sufficient numbers to conceal them. The land fell away rather precipitously in front, and beneath their eyes stretched, for several miles, a narrow, dark, and wooded vale. It was through this dense and dark forest, that Uncas was still contending with the main body of the Hurons.

The Mohican and his friends advanced to the brow of the hill, and listened, with practised ears, to the sounds of the combat. A few birds hovered over the leafy bosom of the valley, frightened from their secluded nests, and here and there a light vapoury cloud, which seemed already blending with the atmosphere, arose above the trees, and indicated some spot where the struggle had been fierce and stationary.

"The fight is coming up the ascent," said Duncan, pointing in the direction of a new explosion of fire-arms; "we are too much in the centre of their line to be effective."

"They will incline into the hollow, where the cover is thicker," said the scout, "and that will leave us well on their flank. Go, Sagamore; you will hardly be in time to give the whoop, and lead on the young men. I will fight this skrimmage with warriors of my own colour! You know me, Mohican; not a Huron of them all shall cross the swell, into your rear, without the notice of 'kill-deer.' "

The Indian chief paused another moment to consider the signs of the contest, which was now rolling rapidly up the ascent, a certain evidence that the Delawares triumphed; nor did he actually quit the place, until admonished of the proximity of his friends, as well as enemies, by the bullets of the former, which began to patter among the dried leaves on the ground, like the bits of falling hail which precede the bursting of the tempest. Hawk-eye and his three companions withdrew a few paces to a shelter, and awaited the issue with calmness that nothing but great practice could impart, in such a scene.

It was not long before the reports of the rifles began to lose the echoes of the woods, and to sound like weapons discharged in the open air. Then a warrior appeared, here and there, driven to the skirts of the forest, and rallying as he entered the clearing, as at the place where the final stand was to be made. These were soon joined by others, until a long line of swarthy figures was to be seen clinging to the cover, with the obstinacy of desperation. Heyward began to grow impatient, and turned his eyes anxiously in the direction of Chingachgook. The chief was seated on a rock, with nothing visible but his calm visage, considering the spectacle with an eye as deliberate, as if he were posted there merely to view the struggle.

"The time is come for the Delaware to strike!" said Duncan.

"Not so, not so," returned the scout; "when he scents his friends, he will let them know that he is here. See, see; the knaves are getting in that clump of pines, like bees settling after their flight. By the Lord, a squaw might put a bullet into the centre of such a knot of dark-skins!"

At that instant the whoop was given, and a dozen Hurons fell by a discharge from Chingachgook and his band. The shout that followed, was answered by a single war-cry from the forest, and a yell passed through the air, that sounded as if a thousand throats were united in a common effort. The Hurons staggered, deserting the centre of their line, and Uncas issued from the forest through the opening they left, at the head of a hundred warriors.

Waving his hands right and left, the young chief pointed out the enemy to his followers, who separated in pursuit. The war now divided, both wings of the broken Hurons seeking protection in the woods again, hotly pressed by the victorious warriors of the Lenape. A minute might have passed, but the sounds were already receding in different directions, and gradually losing their distinctness beneath the echoing arches of the woods. One little knot of Hurons, however, had disdained to seek a cover, and were retiring, like lions at bay, slowly and sullenly up the acclivity, which Chingachgook and his band had just deserted to mingle, more closely, in the fray. Magua was conspicuous in this party, both by his fierce and savage mien, and by the air of haughty authority he yet maintained.

In his eagerness to expedite the pursuit, Uncas had left himself nearly alone; but the moment his eye caught the figure of le Subtil, every other consideration was forgotten. Raising his cry of battle, which recalled some six or seven warriors, and reckless of the disparity in their numbers, he rushed upon his enemy. Le Renard, who watched the movement, paused to receive him with secret joy. But at the moment when he thought the rashness of his impetuous young assailant had left him at his mercy, another shout was given, and la Longue Carabine was seen rushing to the rescue, attended by all his white associates. The Huron instantly turned, and commenced a rapid retreat up the ascent.

There was no time for greetings or congratulations; for Uncas, though unconscious of the presence of his friends, continued the pursuit with the velocity of the wind. In vain Hawk-eye called to him to respect the covers; the young Mohican braved the dangerous fire of his enemies, and soon compelled them to a flight as swift as his own headlong speed. It was fortunate that the race was of short continuance, and that the white men were much favoured by their position, or the Delaware would soon have outstripped all his companions, and fallen a victim to his own temerity. But ere such a calamity could happen, the pursuers and pursued entered the Wyandot village, within striking distance of each other.

Excited by the presence of their dwellings, and tired of the chase, the Hurons now made a stand, and fought around their council lodge with the fury of despair. The onset and the issue were like the passage and destruction of a whirlwind. The tomahawk of Uncas, the blows of Hawk-eye, and, even, the still nervous arm of Munro, were all busy for that passing moment, and the ground was quickly strewed with their enemies. Still Magua, though daring and much exposed, escaped from every effort against his life, with that sort of fabled protection, that was made to overlook the fortunes of favoured heroes in the legends of ancient poetry. Raising a yell that spoke volumes of anger and disappointment, the subtle chief, when he saw his comrades fallen, darted away from the place, attended by his two only surviving friends, leaving the Delawares engaged in stripping the dead of the bloody trophies of their victory.

But Uncas, who had vainly sought him in the mêlée, bounded forward in pursuit; Hawk-eye, Heyward, and David, still pressing on his footsteps. The utmost that the scout could effect, was to keep the muzzle of his rifle a little in advance of his friend, to whom, however, it answered every purpose of a charmed shield. Once Magua appeared disposed to make another and a final effort to revenge his losses; but abandoning his intentions as soon as demonstrated, he leaped into a thicket of bushes, through which he was followed by his enemies, and suddenly entered the mouth of the cave already known to the reader. Hawk-eye, who had only forborne to fire in tenderness to Uncas, raised a shout of success, and proclaimed aloud, that now they were certain of their game. The pursuers dashed into the long and narrow entrance, in time to catch a glimpse of the retreating forms of the Hurons. Their passage through the natural galleries and subterraneous apartments of the cavern was preceded by the shrieks and cries of hundreds of women and children. The place, seen by its dim and uncertain light, appeared like the shades of the infernal regions, across which unhappy ghosts and savage demons were flitting in multitudes.

Still Uncas kept his eye on Magua, as if life to him possessed but a single object. Heyward and the scout still pressed on his rear, actuated, though, possibly, in a less degree, by a common feeling. But their way was becoming intricate, in those dark and gloomy passages, and the glimpses of the retiring warriors less distinct and frequent; and for a moment the trace was believed to be lost, when a white robe was seen fluttering in the farther extremity of a passage that seemed to lead up the mountain.

" 'Tis Cora!" exclaimed Heyward, in a voice in which horror and delight were wildly mingled.

"Cora! Cora!" echoed Uncas, bounding forward like a deer.

" 'Tis the maiden!" shouted the scout. "Courage, lady; we come—we come."

The chase was renewed with a diligence rendered tenfold encouraging, by this glimpse of the captive. But the way was rugged, broken, and, in spots, nearly impassable. Uncas abandoned his rifle, and leaped forward with headlong precipitation. Heyward rashly imitated his example, though both were, a moment afterwards, admonished of its madness, by hearing the bellowing of a piece, that the Hurons found time to discharge down the passage in the rocks, the bullet from which even gave the young Mohican a slight wound.

"We must close!" said the scout, passing his friends by a desperate leap; "the knaves will pick us all off at this distance; and see; they hold the maiden so as to shield themselves!"

Though his words were unheeded, or rather unheard, his example was followed by his companions, who, by incredible exertions, got near enough to the fugitives to perceive that Cora was borne along between the two warriors, while Magua prescribed the direction and manner of their flight. At this moment, the forms of all four were strongly drawn against an opening in the sky, and they disappeared. Nearly frantic with disappointment, Uncas and Heyward increased efforts that already seemed superhuman, and they issued from the cavern on the side of the mountain, in time to note the route of the pursued. The course lay up the ascent, and still continued hazardous and laborious.

Encumbered by his rifle, and, perhaps, not sustained by so deep an interest in the captive as his companions, the scout suffered the latter to precede him a little; Uncas, in his turn, taking the lead of Heyward. In this manner, rocks, precipices, and difficulties, were surmounted, in an incredibly short space, that at another time, and under other circumstances, would have been deemed almost insuperable. But the impetuous young men were rewarded, by finding, that, encumbered with Cora, the Hurons were losing ground in the race.

"Stay; dog of the Wyandots!" exclaimed Uncas, shaking his bright tomahawk at Magua; "a Delaware girl calls stay!"

"I will go no farther," cried Cora, stopping unexpectedly on a ledge of rocks, that overhung a deep precipice, at no great distance from the summit of the mountain. "Kill me if thou wilt, detestable Huron, I will go no farther!"

The supporters of the maiden raised their ready tomahawks

with the impious joy that fiends are thought to take in mischief, but Magua suddenly stayed the uplifted arms. The Huron chief, after casting the weapons he had wrested from his companions over the rock, drew his knife, and turned to his captive, with a look in which conflicting passions fiercely contended.

"Woman," he said, "choose; the wigwam or the knife of le Subtil!"

Cora regarded him not; but dropping on her knees, she raised her eyes and stretched her arms towards Heaven, saying, in a meek and yet confiding voice—

"I am thine! do with me as thou seest best!"

"Woman," repeated Magua, hoarsely, and endeavouring in vain to catch a glance from her serene and beaming eye, "choose."

But Cora neither heard nor heeded his demand. The form of the Huron trembled in every fibre, and he raised his arm on high, but dropped it again, with a bewildered air, like one who doubted. Once more he struggled with himself, and lifted the keen weapon again—but just then a piercing cry was heard above them, and Uncas appeared, leaping frantically, from a fearful height, upon the ledge. Magua recoiled a step, and one of his assistants, profiting by the chance, sheathed his own knife in the bosom of Cora.

The Huron sprang like a tiger on his offending and already retreating countryman, but the falling form of Uncas separated the unnatural combatants. Diverted from his object by this interruption, and maddened by the murder he had just witnessed, Magua buried his weapon in the back of the prostrate Delaware, uttering an unearthly shout, as he committed the dastardly deed. But Uncas arose from the blow, as the wounded panther turns upon his foe, and struck the murderer of Cora to his feet, by an effort, in which the last of his failing strength was expended. Then, with a stern and steady look, he turned to le Subtil, and indicated, by the expression of his eye, all that he would do, had not the power deserted him. The latter seized the nerveless arm of the unresisting Delaware, and passed his knife into his bosom three several times, before his victim, still keeping his gaze riveted on his enemy with a look of inextinguishable scorn, fell dead at his feet.

"Mercy! mercy! Huron," cried Heyward, from above, in tones nearly choked by horror; "give mercy, and thou shalt receive it!"

Whirling the bloody knife up at the imploring youth, the victorious Magua uttered a cry, so fierce, so wild, and yet so joyous, that it conveyed the sounds of savage triumph to the ears of those who fought in the valley, a thousand feet below. He was answered by a burst from the lips of the scout, whose tall person was just then seen moving swiftly towards him, along those dangerous crags, with steps as bold and reckless, as if he possessed the power to move in air. But when the hunter reached the scene of the ruthless massacre, the ledge was tenanted only by the dead.

His keen eye took a single look at the victims, and then shot its glances over the difficulties of the ascent in his front. A form stood at the brow of the mountain, on the very edge of the giddy height, with uplifted arms, in an awful attitude of menace. Without stopping to consider his person, the rifle of Hawk-eye was raised, but a rock, which fell on the head of one of the fugitives below, exposed the indignant and glowing countenance of the honest Gamut. Then Magua issued from a crevice, and stepping with calm indifference over the body of the last of his associates, he leaped a wide fissure, and ascended the rocks at a point where the arm of David could not reach him. A single bound would carry him to the brow of the precipice, and assure his safety. Before taking the leap, however, the Huron paused, and shaking his hand at the scout, he shouted—

"The pale-faces are dogs! the Delawares women! Magua leaves them on the rocks, for the crows!"

Laughing hoarsely, he made a desperate leap, and fell short of his mark; though his hands grasped a shrub on the verge of the height. The form of Hawk-eye had crouched like a beast about to take its spring, and his frame trembled so violently with eagerness, that the muzzle of the half raised rifle played like a leaf fluttering in the wind. Without exhausting himself with fruitless efforts, the cunning Magua suffered his body to drop to the length of his arms, and found a fragment for his feet to rest upon. Then summoning all his powers, he renewed the attempt, and so far succeeded, as to draw his knees on the edge of the mountain. It was now, when the body of his enemy was most collected together, that the agitated weapon of the scout was drawn to his shoulder. The surrounding rocks, themselves, were not steadier than the piece became for the single instant that it poured out its contents. The arms of the Huron relaxed, and his body fell back a little, while his knees still kept their position. Turning a relentless look on his enemy, he shook his hand in grim defiance. But his hold loosened, and his dark person was seen cutting the air with its head downwards, for a fleeting instant, until it glided past the fringe of shrubbery which clung to the mountain, in its rapid flight to destruction.

Chapter XXXIII

"They fought—like brave men, long and well,
They piled that ground with Moslem slain,
They conquered—but Bozzaris fell,
Bleeding at every vein.
His few surviving comrades saw
His smile when rang their proud hurrah,
And the red field was won;
Then saw in death his eyelids close
Calmly, as to a night's repose,
Like flowers at set of sun."
Halleck, "Marco Bozzaris," ll. 37–46.

THE SUN found the Lenape, on the succeeding day, a nation of mourners. The sounds of the battle were over, and they had fed fat their ancient grudge, and had avenged their recent quarrel with the Mengwe, by the destruction of a whole community. The black and murky atmosphere that floated around the spot where the Hurons had encamped, sufficiently announced, of itself, the fate of that wandering tribe; while hundreds of ravens, that struggled above the bleak summits of the mountains, or swept, in noisy flocks, across the wide ranges of the woods, furnished a frightful direction to the scene of the combat. In short, any eye, at all practised in the signs of a frontier warfare, might easily have traced all those unerring evidences of the ruthless results which attend an Indian vengeance.

Still, the sun rose on the Lenape, a nation of mourners. No shouts of success, no songs of triumph, were heard, in rejoicings for their victory. The latest straggler had returned from his fell employment, only to strip himself of the terrific emblems of his bloody calling, and to join in the lamentations of his countrymen, as a stricken people. Pride and exultation were supplanted by humility, and the fiercest of human passions was already succeeded by the most profound and unequivocal demonstrations of grief.

The lodges were deserted; but a broad belt of earnest faces encircled a spot in their vicinity, whither every thing possessing life had repaired, and where all were now collected, in deep and awful silence. Though beings of every rank and age, of both sexes, and of all pursuits, had united to form this breathing wall of bodies, they were influenced by a single emotion. Each eye was riveted on the centre of that ring, which contained the objects of so much, and of so common, an interest.

Six Delaware girls, with their long, dark, flowing, tresses, falling loosely across their bosoms, stood apart, and only gave proofs of their existence, as they occasionally strewed sweet scented herbs and forest flowers on a litter of fragrant plants, that, under a pall of Indian robes, supported all that now remained of the ardent, high souled, and generous Cora. Her form was concealed in many wrappers of the same simple manufacture, and her face was shut for ever from the gaze of men. At her feet was seated the desolate Munro. His aged head was bowed nearly to the earth, in compelled submission to the stroke of Providence; but a hidden anguish struggled about his furrowed brow, that was only partially concealed by the careless locks of gray that had fallen, neglected, on his temples. Gamut stood at his side, his meek head bared to the rays of the sun, while his eyes, wandering and concerned, seemed to be equally divided between that little volume, which contained so many quaint but holy maxims, and the being, in whose behalf his soul yearned to administer consolation. Heyward was also nigh, supporting himself against a tree, and endeavouring to keep down those sudden risings of sorrow, that it required his utmost manhood to subdue.

But sad and melancholy as this groupe may easily be imagined, it was far less touching than another, that occupied the opposite space of the same area. Seated, as in life, with his form and limbs arranged in grave and decent composure, Uncas appeared, arrayed in the most gorgeous ornaments that the wealth of the tribe could furnish. Rich plumes nodded above his head; wampum, gorgets, bracelets, and medals, adorned his person in profusion; though his dull eye, and vacant lineaments, too strongly contradicted the idle tale of pride they would convey.

Directly in front of the corpse, Chingachgook was placed, without arms, paint, or adornment of any sort, except the bright blue blazonry of his race, that was indelibly impressed on his naked bosom. During the long period that the tribe had been thus collected, the Mohican warrior had kept a steady, anxious, look on the cold and senseless countenance of his son. So riveted and intense had been that gaze, and so changeless his attitude, that a stranger might not have told the living from the dead, but for the occasional gleamings of a troubled spirit, that shot athwart the dark visage of one, and the deathlike calm that had for ever settled on the lineaments of the other.

The scout was hard by, leaning, in a pensive posture, on his own fatal and avenging weapon; while Tamenund, supported by the elders of his nation, occupied a high place at hand, whence he might look down on the mute and sorrowful assemblage of his people.

Just within the inner edge of the circle, stood a soldier, in the military attire of a strange nation; and without it, was his war-horse, in the centre of a collection of mounted domestics, seemingly in readiness to undertake some distant journey. The vestments of the stranger announced him to be one who held a responsible situation near the person of the Captain of the Canadas; and who, as it would now seem, finding his errand of peace frustrated by the fierce impetuosity of his allies, was content to become a silent and sad spectator of the fruits of a contest, that he had arrived too late to anticipate.

The day was drawing to the close of its first quarter, and yet had the multitude maintained its breathing stillness, since its dawn. No sound louder than a stifled sob had been heard among them, nor had even a limb been moved throughout that long and painful period, except to perform the simple and touching offerings that were made, from time to time, in commemoration of the dead. The patience and forbearance of Indian fortitude, could alone support such an appearance of abstraction, as seemed now to have turned each dark and motionless figure into stone.

At length, the sage of the Delawares stretched forth an arm, and leaning on the shoulders of his attendants, he arose with an air as feeble, as if another age had already intervened between the man who had met his nation the preceding day, and him who now tottered on his elevated stand.

"Men of the Lenape!" he said, in hollow tones, that

sounded like a voice charged with some prophetic mission; "the face of the Manitto is behind a cloud! his eye is turned from you; his ears are shut; his tongue gives no answer. You see him not; yet his judgments are before you. Let your hearts be open, and your spirits tell no lie. Men of the Lenape, the face of the Manitto is behind a cloud!"

As this simple and yet terrible annunciation stole on the ears of the multitude, a stillness as deep and awful succeeded, as if the venerated spirit they worshipped had uttered the words, without the aid of human organs; and even the inanimate Uncas appeared a being of life, compared with the humbled and submissive throng by whom he was surrounded. As the immediate effect, however, gradually passed away, a low murmur of voices commenced a sort of chant in honour of the dead. The sounds were those of females, and were thrillingly soft and wailing. The words were connected by no regular continuation, but as one ceased, another took up the eulogy, or lamentation, which ever it might be called, and gave vent to her emotions, in such language as was suggested by her feelings and the occasion. At intervals, the speaker was interrupted by general and loud bursts of sorrow, during which the girls around the bier of Cora plucked the plants and flowers, blindly, from her body, as if bewildered with grief. But, in the milder moments of their plaint, these emblems of purity and sweetness were cast back to their places, with every sign of tenderness and regret. Though rendered less connected by many and general interruptions and outbreakings, a translation of their language would have contained a regular descant, which, in substance, might have proved to possess a train of consecutive ideas.

A girl, selected for the task by her rank and qualifications, commenced by modest allusions to the qualities of the deceased warrior, embellishing her expressions with those oriental images, that the Indians have probably brought with them from the extremes of the other continent, and which form, of themselves, a link to connect the ancient histories of the two worlds. She called him the "panther of his tribe;" and described him as one whose moccasin left no trail on the dews; whose bound was like the leap of the young fawn; whose eye was brighter than a star in the dark night; and whose voice, in battle, was loud as the thunder of the Manitto. She reminded him of the mother who bore him, and dwelt forcibly on the happiness she must feel in possessing such a son. She bade him tell her, when they met in the world of spirits, that the Delaware girls had shed tears above the grave of her child, and had called her blessed.

Then, they who succeeded, changing their tones to a milder and still more tender strain, alluded, with the delicacy and sensitiveness of women, to the stranger maiden, who had left the upper earth at a time so near his own departure, as to render the will of the Great Spirit too manifest to be disregarded. They admonished him to be kind to her, and to have consideration for her ignorance of those arts, which were so necessary to the comfort of a warrior like himself. They dwelt upon her matchless beauty, and on her noble resolution, without the taint of envy, and as angels may be thought to delight in a superior excellence; adding, that these endowments should prove more than equivalent for any little imperfections in her education.

After which, others again, in due succession, spoke to the maiden herself, in the low, soft language of tenderness and love. They exhorted her to be of cheerful mind, and to fear nothing for her future welfare. A hunter would be her companion, who knew how to provide for her smallest wants; and a warrior was at her side, who was able to protect her against every danger. They promised that her path should be pleasant, and her burthen light. They cautioned her against unavailing regrets for the friends of her youth, and the scenes where her fathers had dwelt; assuring her that the "blessed hunting grounds of the Lenape" contained vales as pleasant, streams as pure, and flowers as sweet, as the "Heaven of the pale-faces." They advised her to be attentive to the wants of her companion, and never to forget the distinction which the Manitto had so wisely established between them. Then, in a wild burst of their chant, they sung, with united voices, the temper of the Mohican's mind. They pronounced him noble, manly, and generous; all that became a warrior, and all that a maid might love. Clothing their ideas in the most remote and subtle images, they betrayed, that, in the short period of their intercourse, they had discovered, with the intuitive perception of their sex, the truant disposition of his inclinations. The Delaware girls had found no favour in his eyes! He was of a race that had once been lords on the shores of the salt lake, and his wishes had led him back to a people who dwelt about the graves of his fathers. Why should not such a predilection be encouraged! That she was of a blood purer and richer than the rest of her nation, any eye might have seen. That she was equal to the dangers and daring of a life in the woods, her conduct had proved; and, now, they added, the " wise one of the earth" had transplanted her to a place where she would find congenial spirits, and might be for ever happy.

Then, with another transition in voice and subject, allusions were made to the virgin who wept in the adjacent lodge. They compared her to flakes of snow; as pure, as white, as brilliant, and as liable to melt in the fierce heats of summer, or congeal in the frosts of winter. They doubted not that she was lovely in the eyes of the young chief, whose skin and whose sorrow seemed so like her own; but, though far from expressing such a preference, it was evident, they deemed her less excellent than the maid they mourned. Still they denied her no meed, her rare charms might properly claim. Her ringlets were compared to the exuberant tendrils of the vine, her eye to the blue vault of the heavens, and the most spotless cloud, with its glowing flush of the sun, was admitted to be less attractive than her bloom.

During these and similar songs, nothing was audible but the murmurs of the music; relieved, as it was, or rather rendered terrible, by those occasional bursts of grief, which might be called its choruses. The Delawares themselves listened like charmed men; and it was very apparent, by the variations of their speaking countenances, how deep and true was their sympathy. Even David was not reluctant to lend his ears to the tones of voices so sweet; and long ere the chant was ended, his gaze announced that his soul was enthralled.

The scout, to whom alone, of all the white men, the words were intelligible, suffered himself to be a little aroused from his meditative posture, and bent his face aside, to catch their meaning, as the girls proceeded. But when they spoke of the future prospects of Cora and Uncas, he shook his head, like one who knew the error of their simple creed, and resuming his reclining attitude, he maintained it until the ceremony—if that might be called a ceremony, in which feeling was so deeply imbued—was finished. Happily for the self-command of both Heyward and Munro, they knew not the meaning of the wild sounds they heard.

Chingachgook was a solitary exception to the interest manifested by the native part of the audience. His look never changed throughout the whole of the scene, nor did a muscle move in his rigid countenance, even at the wildest, or the most pathetic parts of the lamentation. The cold and senseless remains of his son was all to him, and every other sense but that of sight seemed frozen, in order that his eyes might take their final gaze at those lineaments he had so long loved, and which were now about to be closed for ever from his view.

In this stage of the funeral obsequies, a warrior, much renowned for deeds in arms, and more especially for services in the recent combat, a man of stern and grave demeanour, advanced slowly from the crowd, and placed himself nigh the person of the dead.

"Why hast thou left us, pride of the Wapanachki!" he said, addressing himself to the dull ears of Uncas, as if the empty clay retained the faculties of the animated man; "thy time has been like that of the sun when in the trees; thy glory brighter than his light at noon-day. Thou art gone, youthful warrior, but a hundred Wyandots are clearing the briars from thy path to the world of spirits. Who that saw thee in battle, would believe that thou couldst die! Who before thee hast ever shown Uttawa the way into the fight. Thy feet were like the wings of eagles; thine arm heavier than falling branches from the pine; and thy voice like the Manitto, when he speaks in the clouds. The tongue of Uttawa is weak," he added, looking about him with a melancholy gaze, "and his heart exceeding heavy. Pride of the Wapanachki, why hast thou left us!"

He was succeeded by others, in due order, until most of the high and gifted men of the nation had sung or spoken their tribute of praise over the manes of the deceased chief. When each had ended, another deep and breathing silence reigned in all the place.

Then a low, deep sound was heard, like the suppressed accompaniment of distant music, rising just high enough on the air to be audible, and yet so indistinctly, as to leave its character, and the place whence it proceeded, alike matters of conjecture. It was, however, succeeded by another and another strain, each in a higher key, until they grew on the ear, first in long drawn and often repeated interjections, and finally in words. The lips of Chingachgook had so far parted, as to announce that it was the monody of the father. Though not an eye was turned towards him, nor the smallest sign of impatience exhibited, it was apparent, by the manner in which the multitude elevated their heads to listen, that they drunk in the sounds with an intenseness of attention, that none but Tamenund himself had ever before commanded. But they listened in vain. The strains rose just so loud, as to become intelligible, and then grew fainter and more trembling, until they finally sunk on the ear, as if borne away by a passing breath of wind. The lips of the Sagamore closed, and he remained silent in his seat, looking, with his riveted eye and motionless form, like some creature that had been turned from the Almighty hand with the form, but without the spirit of a man. The Delawares, who knew, by these symptoms, that the mind of their friend was not prepared for so mighty an effort of fortitude, relaxed in their attention, and, with innate delicacy, seemed to bestow all their thoughts on the obsequies of the stranger maiden.

A signal was given, by one of the elder chiefs, to the women, who crowded that part of the circle near which the body of Cora lay. Obedient to the sign, the girls raised the bier to the elevation of their heads, and advanced with slow and regulated steps, chanting, as they proceeded, another wailing song in praise of the deceased. Gamut, who had been a close observer of rites he deemed so heathenish, now bent his head over the shoulder of the unconscious father, whispering—

"They move with the remains of thy child; shall we not follow, and see them interred with Christian burial?"

Munro started, as if the last trumpet had sounded in his ear, and bestowing one anxious and hurried glance around him, he arose and followed in the simple train, with the mien of a soldier, but bearing the full burthen of a parent's suffering. His friends pressed around him with a sorrow that was too strong to be termed sympathy—even the young Frenchman joining in the procession, with the air of a man who was sensibly touched at the early and melancholy fate of one so lovely. But when the last and humblest female of the tribe had joined in the wild, and yet ordered, array, the men of the Lenape contracted their circle, and formed, again, around the person of Uncas, as silent, as grave, and as motionless, as before.

The place which had been chosen for the grave of Cora, was a little knoll, where a cluster of young and healthful pines had taken root, forming, of themselves, a melancholy and appropriate shade over the spot. On reaching it, the girls deposited their burthen, and continued, for many minutes, waiting, with characteristic patience, and native timidity, for some evidence, that they whose feelings were most concerned, were content with the arrangement. At length, the scout, who alone understood their habits, said, in their own language—

"My daughters have done well; the white men thank them."

Satisfied with this testimony in their favour, the girls proceeded to deposit the body in a shell, ingeniously, and not inelegantly, fabricated of the bark of the birch; after which, they lowered it into its dark and final abode. The ceremony of covering the remains, and concealing the marks of the fresh earth, by leaves and other natural and customary objects, was conducted with the same simple and silent forms. But when the labours of the kind beings, who had performed these sad and friendly offices, were so far completed, they hesitated, in a way to show, that they knew not how much farther they might proceed. It was in this stage of the rites, that the scout again addressed them—

"My young women have done enough," he said; "the spirit of a pale-face has no need of food or raiment—their gifts being according to the heaven of their colour. I see," he added, glancing an eye at David, who was preparing his book in a manner that indicated an intention to lead the way in sacred song, "that one who better knows the Christian fashions is about to speak."

The females stood modestly aside, and, from having been the principal actors in the scene, they now became the meek and attentive observers of that which followed. During the time David was occupied in pouring out the pious feelings of his spirit in this manner, not a sign of surprise, nor a look of impatience, escaped them. They listened like those who knew the meaning of the strange words, and appeared as if they felt the mingled emotions of sorrow, hope, and resignation, they were intended to convey.

Excited by the scene he had just witnessed, and perhaps influenced by his own secret emotions, the master of song exceeded his usual efforts. His full, rich, voice, was not found to suffer by a comparison with the soft tones of the girls; and his more modulated strains possessed, at least for the ears of those to whom they were peculiarly addressed, the additional power of intelligence. He ended the anthem, as he had commenced it, in the midst of a grave and solemn stillness.

When, however, the closing cadence had fallen on the ears of his auditors, the secret, timorous glances of the eyes, and the general, and yet subdued movement of the assemblage, betrayed, that something was expected from the father of the deceased. Munro seemed sensible that the time was come for him to exert what is, perhaps, the greatest effort of which human nature is capable. He bared his gray locks, and looked around the timid and quiet throng, by which he was encircled, with a firm and collected countenance. Then motioning with his hand for the scout to listen, he said—

"Say to these kind and gentle females, that a heart-broken and failing man, returns them his thanks. Tell them, that the Being we all worship, under different names, will be mindful of their charity; and that the time shall not be distant, when we may assemble around his throne, without distinction of sex, or rank, or colour!"

The scout listened to the tremulous voice in which the veteran delivered these words, and shook his head, slowly, when they were ended, as one who doubted their efficacy.

"To tell them this," he said, "would be to tell them that the snows come not in the winter, or that the sun shines fiercest when the trees are stripped of their leaves!"

Then turning to the women, he made such a communication of the other's gratitude, as he deemed most suited to the capacities of his listeners. The head of Munro had already sunken upon his chest, and he was again fast relapsing into melancholy, when the young Frenchman before named, ventured to touch him lightly on the elbow. As soon as he had gained the attention of the mourning old man, he pointed towards a groupe of young Indians, who approached with a light, but closely covered litter, and then pointed upward towards the sun.

"I understand you, sir," returned Munro, with a voice of forced firmness; "I understand you. It is the will of Heaven, and I submit. Cora, my child! if the prayers of a heart-broken father could avail thee now, how blessed shouldst thou be! Come, gentlemen," he added, looking about him with an air of lofty composure, though the anguish that quivered in his faded countenance was far too powerful to be concealed, "our duty here is ended; let us depart."

Heyward gladly obeyed a summons that took them from a spot, where, each instant, he felt his self-control was about to desert him. While his companions were mounting, however, he found time to press the hand of the scout, and to repeat the terms of an engagement they had made, to meet again within the posts of the British army. Then gladly throwing himself into the saddle, he spurred his charger to the side of the litter, whence low and stifled sobs, alone announced the presence of Alice. In this manner, the head of Munro again dropping on his bosom, with Heyward and David following in sorrowing silence, and attended by the Aide of Montcalm with his guard, all the white men, with the exception of Hawk-eye, passed from before the eyes of the Delawares, and were soon buried in the vast forests of that region.

But the tie which, through their common calamity, had united the feelings of these simple dwellers in the woods with the strangers who had thus transiently visited them, was not so easily broken. Years passed away before the traditionary tale of the white maiden, and of the young warrior of the Mohicans, ceased to beguile the long nights and tedious marches, or to animate their youthful and brave with a desire for vengeance. Neither were the secondary actors in these momentous incidents forgotten. Through the medium of the scout, who served for years afterwards, as a link between them and civilized life, they learned, in answer to their inquiries, that the "gray-head" was speedily gathered to his fathers—borne down, as was erroneously believed, by his military misfortunes; and that the "open hand" had conveyed his surviving daughter far into the settlements of the "pale-faces," where her tears had, at last, ceased to flow, and had been succeeded by the bright smiles which were better suited to her joyous nature.

But these were events of a time later than that which concerns our tale. Deserted by all of his colour, Hawk-eye returned to the spot where his own sympathies led him, with a force that no ideal bond of union could bestow. He was just in time to catch a parting look of the features of Uncas, whom the Delawares were already enclosing in his last vestments of skins. They paused to permit the longing and lingering gaze of the sturdy woodsman, and when it was ended, the body was enveloped, never to be unclosed again. Then came a procession like the other, and the whole nation was collected about the temporary grave of the chief—temporary, because it was proper, that at some future day, his bones should rest among those of his own people.

The movement, like the feeling, had been simultaneous and general. The same grave expression of grief, the same rigid silence, and the same deference to the principal mourner, were observed, around the place of interment, as have been already described. The body was deposited, in an attitude of repose, facing the rising sun, with the implements of war and of the chase at hand, in readiness for the final journey. An opening was left in the shell, by which it was protected from the soil, for the spirit to communicate with its earthly tenement, when necessary; and the whole was concealed from the instinct, and protected from the ravages of the beasts of prey, with an ingenuity peculiar to the natives. The manual rites then ceased, and all present reverted to the more spiritual part of the ceremonies.

Chingachgook became, once more, the object of the common attention. He had not yet spoken, and something consolatory and instructive was expected from so renowned a chief, on an occasion of such interest. Conscious of the wishes of the people, the stern and self-restrained warrior raised his face, which had latterly been buried in his robe, and looked about him, with a steady eye. His firmly compressed and expressive lips then severed, and for the first time during the long ceremonies, his voice was distinctly audible.

"Why do my brothers mourn!" he said, regarding the dark race of dejected warriors, by whom he was environed; "why do my daughters weep! that a young man has gone to the happy hunting grounds! that a chief has filled his time with honour! He was good. He was dutiful. He was brave. Who can deny it? The Manitto had need of such a warrior, and he has called him away. As for me, the son and the father of Uncas, I am a 'blazed pine, in a clearing of the pale-faces.' My race has gone from the shores of the salt lake, and the hills of the Delawares. But who can say that the serpent of his tribe has forgotten his wisdom! I am alone—"

"No, no," cried Hawk-eye, who had been gazing with a yearning look at the rigid features of his friend, with something like his own self-command, but whose philosophy could endure no longer; "no, Sagamore, not alone. The gifts of our colours may be different, but God has so placed us as to journey in the same path. I have no kin, and I may also say, like you, no people. He was your son, and a red-skin by nature; and it may be, that your blood was nearer;—but if ever I forget the lad, who has so often fou't at my side in war, and slept at my side in peace, may He who made us all, whatever may be our colour or our gifts, forget me. The boy has left us for a time, but, Sagamore, you are not alone!"

Chingachgook grasped the hand that, in the warmth of feeling, the scout had stretched across the fresh earth, and in that attitude of friendship, these two sturdy and intrepid woodsmen bowed their heads together, while scalding tears fell to their feet, watering the grave of Uncas, like drops of falling rain.

In the midst of the awful stillness with which such a burst of feeling, coming, as it did, from the two most renowned warriors of that region, was received, Tamenund lifted his voice, to disperse the multitude.

"It is enough!" he said. "Go, children of the Lenape; the anger of the Manitto is not done. Why should Tamenund stay? The pale-faces are masters of the earth, and the time of the red-men has not yet come again. My day has been too long. In the morning I saw the sons of Unâmis happy and strong; and yet, before the night has come, have I lived to see the last warrior of the wise race of the Mohicans!"

THE END

THE PRAIRIE

A Tale

Preface

THE MANNER in which the writer of this book, came into possession of most of its materials is mentioned in the work itself. Any well bred reader will readily conceive that there may exist a thousand reasons, why he should not reveal any more of his private sources of information. He will only say, on his own responsibility, that the portions of the tale for which no authorities are given are quite as true as those which are not destitute of this peculiar advantage, and that all may be believed alike.

There is however to be found in the following pages an occasional departure from strict historical veracity which it may be well to mention. In the endless confusion of names, customs, opinions and languages which exists among the tribes of the West, the author, has paid much more attention to sound and convenience than to literal truth. He has uniformly called the Great Spirit, for instance, the Wahcondah, though he is not ignorant that there are different names for that being in the two nations he has introduced. So in other matters he has rather adhered to simplicity than sought to make his narrative strictly correct at the expense of all order and clearness. It was enough for his purpose that the picture should possess the general features of the original. In the shading, attitude, and disposition of the figure a little liberty has been taken. Even this brief explanation would have been spared, did not the author know that there was a certain class of 'learned Thebans,' who are just as fit to read any thing which depends for its success on the imagination, as they are to write it.

It may be necessary to meet much graver and less easily explained objections in the minds of a far higher class of readers. The introduction of one and the same character, as a principal actor, in no less than three books, and the selection of a comparative desert, which is aided by no historical recollections and embellished by so few or no poetical associations for the scene of a legend, in these times of perilous adventure in works of this description, may need more vindication. If the first objection can be removed, the latter must fall of course, as it clearly became the duty of a faithful chronicler, to follow his hero wherever he might choose to go.

It is quite probable that the narrator of these simple events has deceived himself as to the importance they may have in the eyes of other people. But he has seen or thought he has seen, something sufficiently instructive and touching in the life of a veteran of the forest, who, having commenced his career near the Atlantic had been driven, by the increasing and unparalleled advance of population, to seek a final refuge from society in the broad and tenantless plains of the West, to induce him to hazard the experiment of publication. That the changes, which might have driven a man so constituted to such an expedient, have actually occurred within a single life, is a matter of undeniable history;—that they did produce such an effect on the Scout of the Mohicans, the Leather-stocking of the Pioneers and the Trapper of the Prairie, rests on an authority no less imposing than these veritable pages, from which the reader shall no longer be detained, if he be disposed to peruse them, after this frank arrival of the poverty of their contents.

Introduction

THE GEOLOGICAL FORMATION of that portion of the American Union, which lies between the Alleghanies and the Rocky Mountains, has given rise to many ingenious theories. Virtually, the whole of this immense region is a plain. For a distance extending nearly 1500 miles east and west, and 600 north and south, there is scarcely an elevation worthy to be called a mountain. Even hills are not common; though a good deal of the face of the country has more or less of the "rolling" character, which is described in the opening pages of this work.

There is much reason to believe that the territory which now composes Ohio, Illinois, Indiana, Michigan, and a large portion of the country west of the Mississippi, lay formerly under water. The soil of all the former states has the appearance of an alluvial deposit; and isolated rocks have been found, of a nature and in situations which render it difficult to refute the opinion that they have been transferred to their present beds by floating ice. This theory assumes that the Great Lakes were the deep pools of one immense body of fresh water, which lay too low to be drained by the irruption that laid bare the land.

It will be remembered that the French, when masters of the Canadas and Louisiana, claimed the whole of the territory in question. Their hunters and advanced troops held the first communications with the savage occupants, and the earliest written accounts we possess of these vast regions, are from the pens of their missionaries. Many French words have, consequently, become of local use in this quarter of America, and not a few names given in that language have been perpetuated. When the adventurers, who first penetrated these wilds, met, in the centre of the forests, immense plains, covered with rich verdure or rank grasses, they naturally gave them the appellation of meadows. As the English succeeded the French, and found a peculiarity of nature, differing from all they had yet seen on the continent, already distinguished by a word that did not express any thing in their own language, they left these natural meadows in possession of their title of convention. In this manner has the word "Prairie" been adopted into the English tongue.

The American prairies are of two kinds. Those which lie east of the Mississippi are comparatively small, and exceedingly fertile, and are always surrounded by forests. They are susceptible of high cultivation, and are fast becoming settled. They abound in Ohio, Michigan, Illinois, and Indiana. They labour under the disadvantages of a scarcity of wood and water,—evils of a serious character, until art has had time to supply the deficiencies of nature. As coal is said to abound in all that region, and wells are generally successful, the enterprise of the emigrants is gradually prevailing against these difficulties.

The second description of these natural meadows lies west of the Mississippi, at a distance of a few hundred miles from that river, and is called the Great Prairies. They resemble the steppes of Tartary more than any other known portion of the world; being, in fact, a vast country, incapable of sustaining a dense population, in the absence of the two great necessaries already named. Rivers abound, it is true; but this region is nearly destitute of brooks and the smaller water courses, which tend so much to comfort and fertility.

The origin and date of the Great American Prairies form one of nature's most majestic mysteries. The general character of the United States, of the Canadas, and of Mexico, is that of luxuriant fertility. It would be difficult to find another portion of the world, of the same extent, which has so little useless land as the inhabited parts of the American Union. Most of the mountains are arable, and even the prairies, in this section of the republic, are of deep alluvion. The same is true between the Rocky Mountains and the Pacific. Between the two lies the broad belt, of comparative desert, which is the scene of this tale, appearing to interpose a barrier to the progress of the American people westward.

The Great Prairies appear to be the final gathering place of the red men. The remnants of the Mohicans, and the Delawares, of the Creeks, Choctaws, and Cherokees, are destined to fulfil their time on these vast plains. The entire number of the Indians, within the Union, is differently computed, at between one and five hundred thousand souls. Most of them inhabit the country west of the Mississippi. At the period of the tale, they dwelt in open hostility; national feuds passing from generation to generation. The power of the republic has done much to restore peace to these wild scenes, and it is now possible to travel in security, where civilized man did not dare to pass unprotected five-and-twenty years ago.

The reader, who has perused the two former works, of which this is the natural successor, will recognise an old acquaintance in the principal character of the story. We have here brought him to his end, and we trust he will be permitted to slumber in the peace of the just.

—*Paris, June, 1832*

Chapter I

"I pray thee, shepherd, if that love or gold
Can in this desert place buy entertainment,
Bring us where we may rest ourselves and feed."
As You Like It, II.iv.71–73.

MUCH WAS SAID and written, at the time, concerning the policy of adding the vast regions of Louisiana, to the already immense, and but half-tenanted territories of the United-States. As the warmth of the controversy however subsided, and party considerations gave place to more liberal views, the wisdom of the measure began to be generally conceded. It soon became apparent, to the meanest capacity, that, while nature had placed a barrier of desert to the extension of our population in the west, the measure had made us the masters of a belt of fertile country, which, in the revolutions of the day, might have become the property of a rival nation. It gave us the sole command of the great thoroughfare of the interior, and placed the countless tribes of savages, who lay along our borders, entirely within our controul; it reconciled conflicting rights, and quieted national distrusts; it opened a thousand avenues to the inland trade, and to the waters of the Pacific; and, if ever time or necessity shall require a peaceful division of this vast empire, it assures us a neighbour that will possess our language, our religion, our institutions, and it is also to be hoped, our sense of political justice.

Although the purchase was made in 1803, the spring of the succeeding year was permitted to open, before the official prudence of the Spaniard, who held the province for his European master, admitted the authority, or even of the entrance, of its new proprietors. But the forms of the transfer were no sooner completed, and the new government acknowledged, than swarms of that restless people, which is ever found hovering on the skirts of American society, plunged into the thickets that fringed the right bank of the Mississippi, with the same careless hardihood, as had already sustained so many of them in their toilsome progress from the Atlantic states, to the eastern shores of the "Father of rivers."*

Time was necessary to blend the numerous and affluent colonists of the lower province with their new compatriots; but the thinner and more humble population, above, was almost immediately swallowed in the vortex which attended the tide of instant emigration. The inroad from the east was a new and sudden out-breaking of a people, who had endured a momentary restraint, after having been rendered nearly resistless by success. The toils and hazards of former undertakings were forgotten, as these endless and unexplored regions, with all their fancied as well as real advantages, were laid open to their enterprise. The consequences were such as might easily have been anticipated, from so tempting an offering, placed as it was before the eyes of a race long trained in adventure and nurtured in difficulties.

Thousands of the elders, of what were then called the *New*-States,† broke up from the enjoyment of their hard-earned indulgencies, and were to be seen leading long files of descendants, born and reared in the forests of Ohio and Kentucky, deeper into the land, in quest of that which might be termed, without the aid of poetry, their natural and more congenial atmosphere. The distinguished and resolute forester, who first penetrated the wilds of the latter state, was of the number. This adventurous and venerable patriarch was now seen making his last remove; placing the "endless river" between him and the multitude his own success had drawn around him, and seeking for the renewal of enjoyments which were rendered worthless in his eyes, when trammelled by the forms of human institutions.‡

*The Mississippi is thus termed in several of the Indian languages. The reader will gain a more just idea of the importance of this stream, if he recall to mind the fact, that the Missouri and the Mississippi are properly the same river. Their united lengths cannot be greatly short of four thousand miles.

†All the states admitted to the American Union, since the revolution are called *New*-States, with the exception of Vermont that had claims before the war which were not, however, admitted until a later day.

‡Col. Boon, the patriarch of Kentucky. This venerable and hardy pioneer of civilization emigrated to an estate three hundred miles west of the Mississippi, in his ninety second year, because he found a population of ten to the square mile, inconveniently crowded!

In the pursuit of adventures, such as these, men are ordinarily governed by their habits or deluded by their wishes. A few, led by the phantoms of hope, and ambitious of sudden affluence, sought the mines of the virgin territory; but by far the greater portion of the emigrants were satisfied to establish themselves along the margins of the larger water-courses, content with the rich returns that the generous alluvial bottoms of the rivers never fail to bestow on the most desultory industry. In this manner were communities formed with magical rapidity; and most of those who witnessed the purchase of the empty empire, have lived to see already a populous and sovereign state, parcelled from its inhabitants, and received into the bosom of the national Union, on terms of political equality.

The incidents and scenes which are connected with this legend, occurred in the earliest periods of the enterprises which have led to so great and so speedy a result.

The harvest of the first year of our possession had long been passed, and the fading foliage of a few scattered trees was, already, beginning to exhibit the hues and tints of autumn, when a train of wagons issued from the bed of a dry rivulet, to pursue its course across the undulating surface of what, in the language of the country of which we write, is called a "rolling Prairie." The vehicles, loaded with household goods and implements of husbandry, the few straggling sheep and cattle that were herded in the rear, and the rugged appearance and careless mien of the sturdy men who loitered at the sides of the lingering teams, united to announce a band of emigrants seeking for the Eldorado of the West. Contrary to the usual practice of the men of their caste, this party had left the fertile bottoms of the low country, and had found its way, by means only known to such adventurers, across glen and torrent, over deep morasses and arid wastes, to a point far beyond the usual limits of civilized habitations. In their front were stretched those broad plains, which extend, with so little diversity of character, to the bases of the Rocky Mountains; and many long and dreary miles in their rear, foamed the swift and turbid waters of La Platte.

The appearance of such a train, in that bleak and solitary place, was rendered the more remarkable by the fact, that the surrounding country offered so little, that was tempting to the cupidity of speculation and, if possible, still less that was flattering to the hopes of an ordinary settler of new lands.

The meagre herbage of the Prairie promised nothing, in favor of a hard and unyielding soil, over which the wheels of the vehicles rattled as lightly as if they travelled on a beaten road; neither wagons nor beasts making any deeper impression, than to mark that bruised and withered grass, which the cattle plucked, from time to time, and as often rejected, as food too sour, for even hunger to render palatable.

Whatever might be the final destination of these adventurers, or the secret causes of their apparent security in so remote and unprotected a situation, there was no visible sign of uneasiness, uncertainty, or alarm among them. Including both sexes, and every age, the number of the party exceeded twenty.

At some little distance in front of the whole, marched the individual who, by his position and air, appeared to be the leader of the band. He was a tall, sun-burnt man, past the middle age, of a dull countenance and listless manner. His frame appeared loose and flexible; but it was vast, and in reality of prodigious power. It was only at moments, however, as some slight impediment opposed itself to his loitering progress, that his person, which, in its ordinary gait seemed so lounging and nerveless, displayed any of those energies which lay latent in his system, like the slumbering and unwieldy, but terrible, strength of the elephant. The inferior lineaments of his countenance were coarse, extended and vacant; while the superior, or those nobler parts which are thought to affect the intellectual being, were low, receding and mean.

The dress of this individual was a mixture of the coarsest vestments of a husbandman, with the leathern garments, that fashion as well as use had in some degree rendered necessary to one engaged in his present pursuits. There was, however, a singular and wild display of prodigal and ill-judged ornaments blended with his motley attire. In place of the usual deer-skin belt, he wore around his body a tarnished silken sash of the most gaudy colours; the buck-horn haft of his knife was profusely decorated with plates of silver; the marten's fur of his cap was of a fineness and shadowing that a queen might covet; the buttons of his rude and soiled blanket-coat were of the glittering coinage of Mexico; the stock of his rifle was of beautiful mahogany, riveted and banded with the same precious metal, and the trinkets of no less than three worthless watches dangled from different parts of his person. In addition to the pack and the rifle which were slung at his back, together with the well-filled, and carefully guarded pouch and horn, he had carelessly cast a keen and bright wood-axe across his shoulder, sustaining the weight of the whole with as much as apparent ease as if he moved, unfettered in limb, and free from incumbrance.

A short distance in the rear of this man, came a groupe of youths very similarly attired, and bearing sufficient resemblance to each other, and to their leader, to distinguish them as the children of one family. Though the youngest of their number could not much have passed the period, that, in the nicer judgment of the law, is called the age of discretion, he had proved himself so far worthy of his progenitors as to have reared already his aspiring person to the standard height of his race. There were one or two others, of different mould, whose descriptions must however be referred to the regular course of the narrative.

Of the females, there were but two who had arrived at womanhood; though several white-headed, olive-skinn'd faces were peering out of the foremost wagon of the train, with eyes of lively curiosity and characteristic animation. The elder of the two adults was the sallow and wrinkled mother of most of the party, and the younger was a sprightly, active girl of eighteen, who in figure, dress and mien, seemed to belong to a station in society several gradations above that of any one of her visible associates. The second vehicle was covered with a top of cloth so tightly drawn, as to conceal its contents, with the nicest care. The remaining wagons were loaded with such rude furniture and other personal effects as might be supposed to belong to one ready, at any moment to change his abode, without reference to season or distance.

Perhaps there was little in this train, or in the appearance of its proprietors, that is not daily to be encountered on the highways of this changeable and moving country. But the solitary and peculiar scenery, in which it was so unexpectedly exhibited, gave to the party a marked character of wildness and adventure.

In the little vallies which, in the regular formation of the land, occurred at every mile of their progress, the view was bounded, on two of the sides, by the gradual and low elevations, which give name to the description of Prairie we have mentioned; while on the others, the meagre prospect ran off in long, narrow, barren perspectives, but slightly relieved by a pitiful show of coarse, though somewhat luxuriant vegetation. From the summits of the swells, the eye became fatigued with the sameness and chilling dreariness of the landscape. The earth was not unlike the ocean, when its restless waters are heaving heavily, after the agitation and fury of the tempest have begun to lessen. There was the same waving and regular surface, the same absence of foreign objects, and the same boundless extent to the view. Indeed so very striking was the resemblance between the water and the land, that, however much the geologist might sneer at so simple a theory, it would have been difficult for a poet not to have felt that the formation of the one had been produced by the subsiding dominion of the other. Here and there a tall tree rose out of the bottoms, stretching its naked branches abroad, like some solitary vessel; and, to strengthen the delusion, far in the distance, appeared two or three rounded thickets, looming in the misty horizon like islands resting on the waters. It is unnecessary to warn the practised reader, that the sameness of the surface, and the low stands of the spectators exaggerated the distances; but, as swell appeared after swell, and island succeeded island, there was a disheartening assurance that long, and seemingly interminable, tracts of territory must be passed, before the wishes of the humblest agriculturist could be realized.

Still the leader of the emigrants steadily pursued his way, with no other guide than the sun, turning his back resolutely on the abodes of civilization, and plunging, at each step, more deeply if not irretrievably, into the haunts of the barbarous and savage occupants of the country. As the day drew nigher to a close however, his mind, which was, perhaps, incapable of maturing any connected system of forethought, beyond that which related to the interests of the present moment, became, in some slight degree, troubled with the care of providing for the wants of the hours of darkness.

On reaching the crest of a swell that was a little higher than the usual elevations, he lingered a minute, and cast a half curious eye on either hand, in quest of those well-known signs, which might indicate a place, where the three grand requisites of water, fuel and fodder were to be obtained in conjunction.

It would seem that his search was fruitless; for after a few moments of indolent and listless examination, he suffered his huge frame to descend the gentle declivity, in the same sluggish manner that an over-fatted beast would have yielded to the downward pressure.

His example was silently followed by those who succeeded him, though not until the young men had manifested much more of interest, if not of concern, in the brief inquiry which each, in his turn, made on gaining the same look-out. It was now evident, by the tardy movements both of beasts and men, that the time of necessary rest was not far distant. The matted grass of the lower land presented obstacles which fatigue began to render formidable, and the whip was becoming necessary to urge the lingering teams to their labour. At this moment, when, with the exception of the principal individual, a general lassitude was getting the mastery of the travellers, and every eye was cast, by a sort of common impulse, wistfully forward, the whole party was brought to a halt, by a spectacle as sudden as it was unexpected.

The sun had fallen below the crest of the nearest wave of the Prairie, leaving the usual rich and glowing train on its track. In the centre of this flood of fiery light a human form appeared, drawn against the gilded background, as distinctly, and seemingly as palpable, as though it would come within the grasp of any extended hand. The figure was colossal; the attitude musing and melancholy, and the situation directly in the route of the travellers. But embedded, as it was, in its setting of garish light, it was impossible to distinguish its just proportions or true character.

The effect of such a spectacle was instantaneous and powerful. The man in front of the emigrants came to a stand, and remained gazing at the mysterious object, with a dull interest, that soon quickened into superstitious awe. His sons, so soon as the first emotions of surprise had a little abated, drew slowly around him, and, as they who governed the teams gradually followed their example, the whole party was soon collected in one silent and wondering groupe. Notwithstanding the impression of a supernatural agency was very general among the travellers, the ticking of gun-locks was heard, and one of two of the bolder youths cast their rifles forward, in readiness for service.

"Send the boys off to the right," exclaimed the resolute wife and mother, in a sharp, dissonant voice; "I warrant me Asa or Abner will give me some account of the creature!"

"It may be well enough to try the rifle," muttered a dull looking man, whose features, both in outline and expression, bore no small resemblance to the first speaker, and who loosened the stock of his piece and brought it dexterously to the front, while delivering this opinion; "the Pawnee Loups are said to be hunting by hundreds in the plains; if so, they'll never miss a single man from their tribe."

"Stay!" exclaimed a soft-toned but alarmed female voice, which was easily to be traced to the trembling lips of the younger of the two women; "we are not all together; it may be a friend!"

"Who is scouting, now?" demanded the father, scanning, at the same time, the cluster of his stout sons, with a displeased and sullen eye. "Put by the piece, put by the piece;" he continued diverting the other's aim with the finger of a giant, and with the air of one it might be dangerous to deny. "My job is not yet ended; let us finish the little that remains in peace."

The man, who had manifested so hostile an intention, appeared to understand the other's allusion, and suffered himself to be diverted from his object. The sons turned their inquiring looks on the girl, who had so eagerly spoken, to require an explanation; but, as if content with the respite she had obtained for the stranger, she sunk back in her seat, and chose to affect a maidenly silence.

In the mean time the hues of the heavens had often changed. In place of the brightness, which had dazzled the eye, a gray and more sober light had succeeded, and, as the setting lost its brilliancy, the proportions of the fanciful form became less exaggerated, and finally distinct. Ashamed to hesitate, now that the truth was no longer doubtful, the leader of the party resumed his journey, using the precaution, as he ascended the slight acclivity, to release his own rifle from the strap, and to cast it into a situation more convenient for sudden use.

There was little apparent necessity, however, for such watchfulness. From the moment when it had thus unaccountably appeared, as it were, between the heavens and the earth, the stranger's figure had neither moved nor given the smallest evidence of hostility. Had he harboured any such evil intention, the individual who now came plainly into view, seemed but little qualified to execute them.

A frame, that had endured the hardships of more than eighty seasons, was not qualified to awaken apprehension in the breast of one as powerful as the emigrant. Notwithstanding his years, and his look of emaciation, if not of suffering, there was that about this solitary being however, which said that time, and not disease, had laid his hand heavily on him. His form had withered, but it was not wasted. The sinews and muscles, which had once denoted great strength, though shrunken, were still visible; and his whole figure had attained an appearance of induration, which, if it were not for the well-known frailty of humanity, would have seemed to bid defiance to the further approaches of decay. His dress was chiefly of skins, worn with the hair to the weather; a pouch and horn were suspended from his shoulders; and he leaned on a rifle of uncommon length, but which, like its owner exhibited the wear of long and hard service.

As the party drew nigher to this solitary being, and came within a distance to be heard, a low growl issued from the grass at his feet, and then a tall, gaunt, toothless hound arose lazily from his lair, and shaking himself made some show of resisting the nearer approach of the travellers.

"Down! Hector, down!" said his master, in a voice that was a little tremulous and hollow with age. "What have ye to do, pup, with men who journey on their lawful callings?"

"Stranger, if you ar' much acquainted in this country," said the leader of the emigrants, "can you tell a traveller where he may find necessaries for the night."

"Is the land filled on the other side of the Big River!" demanded the old man, solemnly, and without appearing to hearken to the other's question; "or why do I see a sight I had never thought to behold again?"

"Why there is country left, it is true, for such as have money, and ar' not particular in the choice," returned the emigrant; "but to my taste it is getting crowdy. What may a man call the distance from this place to the nighest point on the main river?"

"A hunted deer could not cool his sides, in the Mississippi, without travelling a weary five hundred miles."

"And what may you name the district, hereaway?"

"By what name," returned the old man pointing significantly upward, " would you call the spot, where you see yonder cloud?"

The emigrant looked at the other, like one who did not comprehend his meaning and who half suspected he was trifled with, but he contented himself by saying—

"You ar' but a new inhabitant, like myself, I reckon, stranger, otherwise you wouldn't be backward in helping a traveller to some advice; words cost but little, and sometimes lead to friendships."

"Advice is not a gift, but a debt that the old owe to the young. What would you wish to know?"

"Where I may 'camp for the night. I'm no great difficulty maker, as to bed and board, but all old journeyers, like myself, know the virtue of sweet water, and a good browse for the cattle."

"Come then with me, and you shall be master of both; and little more is it that I can offer on this hungry Prairie."

As the old man was speaking, he raised his heavy rifle to his shoulder, with a facility a little remarkable for his years and appearance, and without further words led the way over the acclivity into the adjacent bottom.

Chapter II

"Up with my tent: here will I lie to night;
But where, to-morrow?—Well, all's one for that."
Richard III, V.iii.7, 8.

THE TRAVELLERS soon discovered the usual and unerring evidences, that the several articles necessary to their situation were not far distant. A clear and gurgling spring burst out of the side of the declivity, and joining its waters to those of other similar little fountains in its vicinity, their united contributions formed a run, which was easily to be traced, for miles along the Prairie, by the scattering foliage and verdure which occasionally grew within the influence of its moisture. Hither, then, the stranger held his way, eagerly followed by the willing teams, whose instinct gave them a prescience of refreshment and rest.

On reaching what he deemed a suitable spot, the old man halted, and with an enquiring look he seemed to demand if it possessed the needed conveniences. The leader of the emigrants cast his eyes understandingly about him, and examined the place with the keenness of one competent to judge of so nice a question, though in that dilatory and heavy manner which rarely permitted him to betray precipitation.

"Ay, this may do," he said, when satisfied with his scrutiny, "boys, you have seen the last of the sun; be stirring."

The young men manifested a characteristic obedience. The order, for such in tone and manner it was, in truth, was received with respect; but the utmost movement was the falling of an axe or two from the shoulder to the ground, while their owners continued to regard the place with listless and incurious eyes. In the mean time, the elder traveller, as if familiar with the nature of the impulses by which his children were governed, disencumbered himself of his pack and rifle, and, assisted by the man already mentioned as disposed to appeal so promptly to the rifle, he quietly proceeded to release the cattle from the gears.

At length the eldest of the sons stepped heavily forward, and, without any apparent effort, he buried his axe to the eye in the soft body of a cotton-wood tree. He stood, a moment, regarding the effect of the blow, with that sort of contempt with which a giant might be supposed to contemplate the puny resistance of a dwarf, and then flourishing the implement above his head, with the grace and dexterity with which a master of the art of offense would wield his nobler though less useful weapon, he quickly severed the trunk of the tree, bringing its tall top crashing to the earth, in submission to his prowess. His companions regarded the operation with indolent curiosity, until they saw the prostrate trunk stretch'd on the ground, when, as if a signal for a general attack had been given, they advanced in a body to the work, and in a space of time, and with a neatness of execution that would have astonished an ignorant spectator, they stripped a small but suitable spot of its burthen of forest, as effectually, and almost as promptly, as if a whirlwind had passed along the place.

The stranger had been a silent, but attentive observer of their progress. As tree after tree came whistling down, he cast his eyes upward, at the vacancies they left in the heavens, with a melancholy gaze, and finally turned away, muttering to himself with a bitter smile, like one who disdained giving a more audible utterance to his discontent. Pressing through the groupe of active and busy children, who had already lighted a cheerful fire, the attention of the old man became next fixed on the movements of the leader of the emigrants and of his savage looking assistant.

These two had already liberated the cattle, which were eagerly browsing the grateful and nutritious extremities of the fallen trees, and were now employed about the wagon, which has been described, as having its contents concealed with so much apparent care. Notwithstanding this particular conveyance appeared to be as silent, and as tenantless as the rest of the vehicles, the men applied their strength to its wheels, and rolled it apart from the others, to a dry and elevated spot, near the edge of the thicket. Here they brought certain poles, which had seemingly been long employed in such a service, and fastening their larger ends firmly in the ground, the smaller were attached to the hoops that supported the covering of the wagon. Large folds of cloth were next drawn out of the vehicle, and after being spread around the whole, were pegged to the earth in such a manner as to form a tolerably capacious and an exceedingly convenient tent. After surveying their work with inquisitive, and perhaps jealous eyes, arranging a fold here and driving a peg more firmly there, the men once more applied their strength to the wagon, pulling it, by its projecting tongue, from the centre of the canopy, until it appeared in the open air, deprived of its covering, and destitute of any other freight than a few light articles of furniture. The latter were immediately removed, by the traveller into the tent with his own hands, as though to enter it were a privilege to which even his bosom companion was not entitled.

Curiosity is a passion that is rather quickened than destroyed by seclusion, and the old inhabitant of the Prairies did not view these precautionary and mysterious movements, without experiencing some of its impulses. He approached the tent, and was about to sever two of its folds, with the very obvious intention of examining, more closely, into the nature of its contents, when the man, who had once already placed his life in jeopardy, seized him by the arm, and with a rude exercise of his strength threw him from the spot he had selected as the one most convenient for his object.

"It's an honest regulation, friend," the fellow drily observed, though with an eye that threatened volumes, "and sometimes it is a safe one, which says, mind your own business."

"Men seldom bring any thing to be concealed into these deserts," returned the old man, as if willing, and yet a little ignorant how to apologize for the liberty he had been about to take, "and I had hop'd no offence, in examining your comforts."

"They seldom bring themselves, I reckon though this has the look of an old country, to my eye it seems not to be overly peopled."

"The land is as aged as the rest of the works of the Lord, I believe; but you say true, concerning its inhabitants. Many months have passed since I have laid eyes on a face of my own colour, before your own. I say again, friend, I meant no harm; I did not know, but there was something behind the cloth, that might bring former days to my mind."

As the stranger ended his simple explanation, he walked meekly away, like one who felt the deepest sense of the right which every man has to the quiet enjoyment of his own, without any troublesome interference on the part of his neighbour; a wholesome and just principle, that he had, also, most probably imbibed from the habits of his secluded life. As he passed towards the little encampment of the emigrants, for such the place had now become, he heard the voice of the leader calling aloud, in its hoarse tones, the name of—

"Ellen Wade."

The girl, who has been already introduced to the reader, and who was occupied with the others of her sex, around the fires, sprang willingly forward at this summons, and passing the stranger with the activity of a young antelope, she was instantly lost behind the forbidden folds of the tent. Neither her sudden disappearance, nor any of the arrangements we have mentioned, seemed, however, to excite the smallest surprise among the remainder of the party. The young men, who had already completed their tasks with the axe, were all engaged after their lounging and listless manner; some in bestowing equitable portions of the fodder among the different animals; others in plying the heavy pestle of a moveable hommany-mortar,* and one or two, in wheeling the remainder of the wagons aside and arranging them in such a manner as to form a sort of outwork for their otherwise defenceless bivouac.

These several duties were soon performed, and, as darkness now began to conceal the objects on the surrounding Prairie, the shrill-toned termagant, whose voice since the halt had been diligently exercised among her idle and drowsy offspring, announced in tones that might have been heard at a dangerous distance, that the evening meal waited only for the approach of those who were to consume it. Whatever may be the other qualities of a border-man, he is seldom deficient in the virtue of hospitality. The emigrant no sooner heard the sharp call of his wife, than he cast his eyes about him in quest of the stranger, in order to offer him the place of distinction, in the rude entertainment to which they were so unceremoniously summoned.

*Hommany, is a dish composed chiefly of cracked corn, or maize.

"I thank you, friend," the old man replied to the rough invitation to take a seat nigh the smoking kettle; "you have my hearty thanks; but I have eaten for the day, and I am not one of them who dig their graves with their teeth. Well; as you wish it, I will take a place, for it is long sin' I have seen people of my colour eating their daily bread."

"You ar' an old settler, in these districts, then?" the emigrant rather remarked than inquired, with a mouth filled nearly to overflowing with the delicious hommany, prepared by his skillful, though repulsive spouse. "They told us below we should find settlers something thinnish, hereaway, and I must say, the report was mainly true; for, unless, we count the Canada traders on the big river, you ar' the first white face I have met, in a good five hundred miles; that is calculating according to your own reckoning."

"Though I have spent some years in this quarter, I can hardly be called a settler, seeing that I have no regular abode, and seldom pass more than a month, at a time, in the same range."

"A hunter, I reckon?" the other continued, glancing his eyes aside, as if to examine the equipments of his new acquaintance; "your fixen seem none of the best, for such a calling."

"They are old, and nearly ready to be laid aside, like their master," said the old man regarding his rifle, with a look in which affection and regret were singularly blended; "and I may say they are but little needed, too. You are mistaken, friend, in calling me a hunter; I am nothing better than a trapper."*

"If you ar' much of the one, I'm bold to say you ar' something of the other; for the two callings go mainly together, in these districts."

"To the shame of the man who is able to follow the first be it so said!" returned the trapper, whom in future we shall choose to designate by his pursuit; "for more than fifty years did I carry my rifle in the wilderness, without so much as

*It is scarcely necessary to say, that this American word means one who takes his game in a trap. It is of general use on the frontiers. The beaver, an animal too sagacious to be easily killed, is oftener taken in this way than in any other.

setting a snare for even a bird that flies the heavens;—much less a beast, that has nothing but legs, for its gifts."

"I see but little difference whether a man gets his peltry by the rifle or by the trap," said the ill-looking companion of the emigrant, in his rough manner. "The 'arth was made for our comfort; and, for that matter, so ar' its creatur's."

"You seem to have but little plunder,* stranger, for one who is far abroad," bluntly interrupted the emigrant, as if he had a reason for wishing to change the conversation. "I hope you ar' better off for skins."

"I make but little use of either," the trapper quietly replied. "At my time of life, food and clothing be all that is needed, and I have little occasion for what you call plunder, unless it may be, now and then, to barter for a horn of powder or a bar of lead."

"You ar' not, then, of these parts, by natur', friend?" the emigrant continued, having in his mind the exception which the other had taken to the very equivocal word, which he himself, according to the custom of the country, had used for "baggage" or "effects."

"I was born on the sea-shore, though most of my life has been passed in the woods."

The whole party now looked up at him, as men are apt to turn their eyes on some unexpected object of general interest. One or two of the young men, repeated the words "sea-shore," and the woman tendered him one of those civilities with which, uncouth as they were, she was little accustomed to grace her hospitality, as if in deference to the travelled dignity of her guest. After a long, and seemingly a meditating silence, the emigrant, who had, however, seen no apparent necessity to suspend the functions of his masticating powers, resumed the discourse.

"It is a long road, as I have heard, from the waters of the west to the shores of the main sea?"

*The cant word for luggage in the western States is "plunder." The term might easily mislead one as to the character of the people, who, notwithstanding their pleasant use of so expressive a word, are, like the inhabitants of all new settlements hospitable and honest. Knavery of the description conveyed by "plunder," is chiefly found in regions more civilized.

"It is a weary path, indeed, friend; and much have I seen, and something have I suffered in journeying over it."

"A man would see a good deal of hard travel in going its length?"

"Seventy and five years I have been upon the road, and there are not half that number of leagues in the whole distance, after you leave the Hudson, on which I have not tasted venison of my own killing. But this is vain boasting! of what use are former deeds, when time draws to an end!"

"I once met a man, that had boated on the river he names," observed the eldest son, speaking in a low tone of voice, like one who distrusted his knowledge, and deemed it prudent to assume a becoming diffidence in the presence of a man who had seen so much; "from his tell, it must be a considerable stream, and deep enough for a keelboat, from top to bottom."

"It is a wide and deep water-course, and many sightly towns are there growing on its banks," returned the trapper; "and yet it is but a brook, to the waters of the endless river!"

"I call nothing a stream, that a man can travel round," exclaimed the ill-looking associate of the emigrant; "a real river must be crossed; not headed, like a bear in a county hunt."*

"Have you been far towards the sun-down, friend?" interrupted the emigrant, as if he desired to keep his rough companion, as much as possible out of the discourse. "I find it is a wide tract of clearing, this, into which I have fallen."

"You may travel weeks, and you will see it the same. I often think the Lord has placed this barren belt of Prairie, behind the States, to warn men to what their folly may yet bring the land! Ay, weeks if not months, may you journey in these open fields, in which there is neither dwelling, nor habitation for man or beast. Even the savage animals travel miles on miles to seek their dens. And yet the wind seldom blows from the east, but I conceit the sounds of axes, and the crash of falling trees are in my ears."

*There is a practice, in the new countries, to assemble the men of a large district, sometimes of an entire county, to exterminate the beasts of prey. They form themselves into a circle of several miles in extent, and gradually draw nearer, killing all before them. The allusion is to this custom, in which the hunted beast is turned from one to another.

As the old man spoke with the seriousness and dignity that age seldom fails to communicate even to less striking sentiments, his auditors were deeply attentive, and as silent as the grave. Indeed the trapper was left to renew the dialogue, himself, which he soon did by asking a question, in the indirect manner so much in use by the border inhabitants.

"You found it no easy matter to ford the water-courses, and to make your way so deep into the Prairies, friend, with teams of horses, and herds of horned beasts?"

"I kept the left bank of the main river," the emigrant replied, "until I found the stream leading too much to the north, when we rafted ourselves across, without any great suffering. The woman lost a fleece or two from the next year's sheering, and the girls have one cow less to their dairy. Since then, we have done bravely, by bridging a creek every day or two."

"It is likely you will continue west, until you come to land more suitable for a settlement?"

"Until I see reason to stop, or to turn ag'in," the emigrant bluntly answered, rising at the same time, and cutting short the dialogue, by the suddenness of the movement. His example was followed by the trapper, as well as the rest of the party, and then, without much deference to the presence of their guest, the travellers proceeded to make their dispositions to pass the night. Several little bowers, or rather huts, had already been formed of the tops of trees, blankets of coarse country manufacture, and the skins of buffaloes, united without much reference to any other object than temporary comfort. Into these covers the children with their mother soon drew themselves, and where, it is more than possible, they were all speedily lost in the oblivion of sleep. Before the men, however, could seek their rest, they had sundry little duties to perform; such as completing their works of defence; carefully concealing the fires; replenishing the fodder of their cattle, and setting the watch that was to protect the party, in the approaching hours of night.

The former was effected by dragging the trunks of a few trees into the intervals left by the wagons, and along the open space, between the vehicles and the thicket, on which, in military language, the encampment would be said to have rested;

thus forming a sort of chevaux-de-frise on three sides of the position. Within these narrow limits (with the exception of what the tent contained), both man and beast were now collected; the latter being far too happy in resting their weary limbs, to give any undue annoyance to their scarcely more intelligent associates. Two of the young men took their rifles, and, first renewing the priming and examining the flints with the utmost care, they proceeded, the one to the extreme right and the other to the left of the encampment, where they posted themselves, within the shadows of the thicket, but in such positions, as enabled each to overlook a portion of the Prairie.

The trapper loitered about the place, declining to share the straw of the emigrant, until the whole arrangement was completed; and then, without the ceremony of an adieu, he slowly retired from the spot.

It was now in the first watch of the night, and the pale, quivering, and deceptive light, from a new moon, was playing over the endless waves of the Prairie, tipping the swells with gleams of brightness, and leaving the interval land in deep shadow. Accustomed to scenes of solitude like the present, the old man, as he left the encampment proceeded alone into the waste, like a bold vessel leaving its haven to enter on the trackless field of the ocean. He appeared to move for some time, without object, or indeed, without any apparent consciousness, whither his limbs were carrying him. At length, on reaching the rise of one of the undulations, he came to a stand, and for the first time, since leaving the band, who had caused such a flood of reflections and recollections to crowd upon his mind, the old man became aware of his present situation. Throwing one end of his rifle to the earth, he stood leaning on the other, again lost in deep contemplation for several minutes, during which time his hound came and crouched at his feet. A deep, menacing growl from the faithful animal, first aroused him from his musing.

"What now, dog?" he said, looking down at his companion, as if he addressed a being of an intelligence equal to his own, and speaking in a voice of great affection. "What is it, pup? ha! Hector; what is it noseing, now? It won't do, dog; it won't do; the very fa'ns play in open view of us, without minding so worn out curs, as you and I. Instinct is their gift, Hector; and they have found out how little we are to be fear'd, they have!"

The dog stretched his head upward, and responded to the words of his master by a long and plaintive whine, which he even continued after he had again buried his head in the grass, as if he held an intelligent communication with one who so well knew how to interpret his dumb discourse.

"This is a manifest warning, Hector!" The trapper continued, dropping his voice, to the tones of caution and looking warily about him. "What is it, pup; speak plainer, dog; what is it?"

The hound had, however, already laid his nose to the earth, and was silent; appearing to slumber. But the keen quick glances of his master, soon caught a glimpse of a distant figure, which seemed, through the deceptive light, floating along the very elevation on which he had placed himself. Presently its proportions became more distinct, and then an airy, female form appeared to hesitate, as if considering whether it would be prudent to advance. Though the eyes of the dog were now to be seen glancing in the rays of the moon, opening and shutting lazily, he gave no further signs of displeasure.

"Come nigher; we are friends," said the trapper, associating himself with his companion by long use, and, probably, through the strength of the secret tie that connected them together; " we are your friends; none will harm you."

Encouraged by the mild tones of his voice, and perhaps led on by the earnestness of her purpose, the female approached, until she stood at his side; when the old man perceived his visiter to be the young woman, with whom the reader, has already become acquainted by the name of Ellen Wade.

"I had thought you were gone," she said, looking timidly and anxiously around. "They said you were gone; and that we should never see you again. I did not think it was you!"

"Men are no common objects in these empty fields," returned the trapper, "and I humbly hope, though I have so long consorted with the beasts of the wilderness, that I have not yet lost the look of my kind."

"Oh! I knew you to be a man, and I thought I knew the

whine of the hound, too," she answered hastily, as if willing to explain she knew not what, and then checking herself, like one fearful of having already said too much.

"I saw no dogs among the teams of your father," the trapper remarked.

"Father!" exclaimed the girl, feelingly, "I have no father! I had nearly said no friend."

The old man, turned towards her, with a look of kindness and interest, that was even more conciliating than the ordinary, upright, and benevolent expression of his weather-beaten countenance.

"Why then do you venture in a place where none but the strong should come?" he demanded. "Did you not know that, when you crossed the big river, you left a friend behind you that is always bound to look to the young and feeble, like yourself."

"Of whom do you speak?"

"The law—'Tis bad to have it, but, I sometimes think, it is worse to be entirely without it. Age and weakness have brought me to feel such weakness, at times. Yes—yes, the law is needed, when such as have not the gifts of strength and wisdom are to be taken care of. I hope, young woman, if you have no father, you have at least a brother."

The maiden felt the tacit reproach conveyed in this covert question, and for a moment she remained in an embarrassed silence. But catching a glimpse of the mild and serious features of her companion, as he continued to gaze on her with a look of interest, she replied, firmly, and in a manner that left no doubt she comprehended his meaning:

"Heaven forbid that any such as you have seen, should be a brother of mine, or any thing else near or dear to me! But, tell me, do you then actually live alone, in this desert district, old man; is there really none here besides yourself?"

"There are hundreds, nay, thousands of the rightful owners of the country, roving about the plains; but few of our own colour."

"And have you then met none who are white, but us?" interrupted the girl, like one too impatient to await the tardy explanation of age and deliberation.

"Not in many days—Hush, Hector, hush," he added in

reply to a low, and nearly inaudible growl from his hound. "The dog scents mischief in the wind! The black bears from the mountains sometimes make their way, even lower than this. The pup is not apt to complain of the harmless game. I am not so ready and true with the piece as I used-to-could-be, yet I have struck even the fiercest animals of the Prairie, in my time; so, you have little reason for fear, young woman."

The girl raised her eyes, in that peculiar manner which is so often practised by her sex, when they commence their glances, by examining the earth at their feet, and terminate them by noting every thing within the power of human vision; but she rather manifested the quality of impatience, than any feeling of alarm.

A short bark from the dog, however, soon gave a new direction to the looks of both, then the real object of his second warning became dimly visible.

Chapter III

"Come, come, thou art as hot a Jack in thy mood, as any in Italy; and as soon mov'd to be moody, and as soon moody to be moved."
Romeo and Juliet, III.i.11–13.

THOUGH THE TRAPPER manifested some surprise when he perceived that another human figure was approaching him, and that, too, from a direction opposite to the place where the emigrant had made his encampment, it was with the steadiness of one long accustomed to scenes of danger.

"This is a man," he said; "and one who has white blood in his veins, or his step would be lighter. It will be well to be ready for the worst, as the half-and-halfs,* that one meets in these distant districts, are altogether more barbarous than the real savage."

He raised his rifle while he spoke, and assured himself of the state of its flint, as well as of the priming by manual examination. But his arm was arrested, while in the act of throwing forward the muzzle of the piece, by the eager and trembling hands of his companion.

"For God's sake, be not too hasty," she said; "it may be a friend—an acquaintance—a neighbour!"

"A friend!" the old man repeated, deliberately releasing himself, at the same time, from her grasp. "Friends are rare in any land, and less in this, perhaps, than in another; and the neighbourhood is too thinly settled to make it likely, that he who comes towards us is even an acquaintance."

"But though a stranger, you would not seek his blood!"

The trapper earnestly regarded her anxious and frightened features, and then he dropped the butt of his rifle on the ground, like one whose purpose had undergone a sudden change.

"No," he said, speaking rather to himself, than to his companion, "she is right; blood is not to be spilt, to save the life

*Half-breeds; men born of Indian women by white fathers. This race has much of the depravity of civilization without the virtues of the savage.

of one so useless, and so near his time. Let him come on; my skins, my traps, and even my rifle shall be his, if he sees fit to demand them."

"He will ask for neither—He wants neither," returned the girl; "if he be an honest man, he will surely be content with his own, and ask for nothing that is the property of another."

The trapper had not time to express the surprise he felt at this incoherent and contradictory language, for the man who was advancing, was, already, within fifty feet of the place where they stood.—In the mean time Hector had not been an indifferent witness of what was passing. At the sound of the distant footsteps, he had arisen, from his warm bed at the feet of his master; and now, as the stranger appeared in open view, he stalked slowly towards him, crouching to the earth like a panther about to take his leap.

"Call in your dog," said a firm, deep, manly voice, in tones of friendship, rather than of menace; "I love a hound, and should be sorry to do an injury to the animal."

"You hear what is said about you, pup?" the trapper answered; "come hither, fool. His growl and his bark are all that is left him now; you may come on, friend; the hound is toothless."

The stranger profited by the intelligence. He sprang eagerly forward, and at the next instant stood at the side of Ellen Wade. After assuring himself of the identity of the latter, by a hasty but keen glance, he turned his attention, with a quickness and impatience that proved the interest he took in the result, to a similar examination of her companion.

"From what cloud have you fallen, my good old man?" he said in a careless, off-hand, heedless manner that seemed too natural to be assumed: "Or do you actually live, hereaway, in the Prairies?"

"I have been long on earth, and never I hope nigher to Heaven than I am at this moment," returned the trapper; "my dwelling, if dwelling I may be said to have, is not far distant. Now may I take the liberty with you, that you are so willing to take with others? Whence do you come, and where is your home?"

"Softly, softly; when I have done with my catechism it will be time to begin with yours. What sport is this, you follow by moonlight? You are not dodging the buffaloes at such an hour!"

"I am, as you see, going from an encampment of travellers, which lies over yonder swell in the land, to my own wigwam; in doing so I wrong no man."

"All fair and true. And you got this young woman to show you the way, because she knows it so well and you know so little about it yourself."

"I met her, as I have met you, by accident. For ten tiresome years have I dwelt on these open fields, and never, before to-night, have I found human beings with white skins on them at this hour. If my presence here gives offence, I am sorry; and will go my way. It is more than likely that when your young friend has told her story, you will be better given to believe mine."

"Friend!" said the youth, lifting a cap of skins from his head, and running his fingers leisurely through a dense mass of black and shaggy locks, "if I ever laid eyes on the girl before to night, may I—"

"You've said enough, Paul," interrupted the female, laying her hand on his mouth with a familiarity that gave something very like the lie direct to his intended asseveration. "Our secret will be safe with this honest old man. I know it by his looks and kind words."

"Our secret! Ellen, have you forgot—"

"Nothing. I have not forgotten any thing I should remember. But still I say we are safe with this honest trapper."

"Trapper! is he then a trapper! Give me your hand, father; our trades should bring us acquainted."

"There is little call for handicrafts in this region," returned the other, examining the athletic and active form of the youth, as he leaned carelessly and not ungracefully on his rifle; "the art of taking the creatur's of God, in traps and nets is one that needs more cunning than manhood; and yet am I brought to practise it in my age! But it would be quite as seemly, in one like you, to follow a pursuit better becoming your years and courage."

"I! I never took even a slinking mink or a paddling musk-rat in a cage; though I admit having peppered a few of the dark-skin'd devils, when I had much better have kept my powder in the horn and the lead in its pouch. Not I, old man; nothing that crawls the earth is for my sport."

"What then may you do for a living, friend; for little profit is to be made in these districts, if a man denies himself his lawful right in the beasts of the fields."

"I deny myself nothing. If a bear crosses my path he is soon the mere ghost of Bruin. The deer begin to nose me; and as for the buffaloe, I have kill'd more beef, old stranger, than the largest butcher in all Kentucky."

"You can shoot, then!" demanded the trapper, with a glow of latent fire glimmering about his eyes; "is your hand true, and your look quick?"

"The first is like a steel-trap, and the last nimbler than a buck-shot. I wish it was hot noon, now, grand'ther; and that there was an acre or two of your white swans or of black feathered ducks going south, over our heads; you, or Ellen here, might set your heart on the finest in the flock, and my character against a horn of powder, that the bird would be hanging head downwards in five minutes, and that too with a single ball. I scorn a shotgun! No man can say he ever knew me carry one, a rod."

"The lad has good in him! I see it plainly by his manner;" said the trapper turning to Ellen with an encouraging air; "I will take it on myself to say that you are not unwise in meeting him as you do. Tell me, lad; did you ever strike a leaping buck atwixt the antlers? Hector; quiet, pup; quiet. The very name of venison quickens the blood of the cur;—did you ever take an animal in that fashion, on the long leap?"

"You might just as well ask me, did you ever eat? There is no fashion, old stranger, that a deer has not been touched by my hand, unless it was when asleep."

"Ay, ay; you have a long, and a happy—ay, and an honest life afore you! I am old, and I suppose I might also say, worn out and useless; but, if it was given me to choose my time and place, again,—as such things are not and ought not ever to be given to the will of man—though, if such a gift was to be given me, I would say, twenty and the wilderness! But, tell me; how do you part with the peltry?"

"With my pelts! I never took a skin from a buck, nor a quill from a goose, in my life! I knock them over, now and then, for a meal, and sometimes to keep my finger true to the touch; but when hunger is satisfied, the Prairie wolves get the remainder. No—no—I keep to my calling; which pays me better, than all the fur I could sell on the other side of the big river."

The old man appeared to ponder a little; but shaking his head, he soon continued—

"I know of but one business that can be followed here with profit—"

He was interrupted by the youth, who raised a small cup of tin, which dangled at his neck, before the other's eyes, and springing its lid, the delicious odour of the finest flavoured honey diffused itself over the organs of the trapper.

"A bee-hunter!" observed the latter, with a readiness that proved he understood the nature of the occupation, though not without some little surprise at discovering one of the other's spirited mien engaged in so humble a pursuit. "It pays well in the skirts of the settlements, but I should call it a doubtful trade in the more open districts."

"You think a tree is wanting for a swarm to settle in! But I know differently; and so I have stretched out a few hundred miles farther west, than common, to taste your honey. And now I have bated your curiosity, stranger, you will just move aside, while I tell the remainder of my story to this young woman."

"It is not necessary, I'm sure it is not necessary, that he should leave us," said Ellen, with a haste that implied some little consciousness of the singularity if not of the impropriety of the request. "You can have nothing to say that the whole world might not hear."

"No! well, may I be stung to death by drones if I understand the buzzings of a woman's mind! For my part, Ellen, I care for nothing nor any body; and am just as ready to go down to the place where your uncle, if uncle you can call one who I'll swear is no relation, has hoppled his teams, and tell the old man my mind now, as I shall be a year hence. You have only to say a single word, and the thing is done; let him like it or not."

"You are ever so hasty and so rash, Paul Hover, that I seldom know when I am safe with you. How can you, who know the danger of our being seen together, speak of going before my uncle and his sons?"

"Has he done that of which he has reason to be ashamed?" demanded the trapper, who had not moved an inch from the place he first occupied.

"Heaven forbid! But there are reasons why he should not be seen, just now, that could do him no harm if known, but which may not yet be told. And so if you will wait, father, near yonder willow bush, until I have heard what Paul can possibly have to say, I shall be sure to come and wish you a good-night, before I return to the camp."

The trapper drew slowly aside, as if satisfied with the somewhat incoherent reason Ellen had given why he should retire. When completely out of ear-shot of the earnest and hurried dialogue, that instantly commenced between the two he had left, the old man again paused, and patiently awaited the moment when he might renew his conversation with beings in whom he felt a growing interest, no less from the mysterious character of their intercourse, than from a natural sympathy in the welfare of a pair so young, and who, as in the simplicity of his heart he was also fain to believe, were also so deserving. He was accompanied by his indolent but attached dog, who once more made his bed at the feet of his master, and soon lay slumbering as usual, with his head nearly buried in the dense fog of the Prairie grass.

It was so unusual a spectacle to see the human form amid the solitude in which he dwelt, that the trapper bent his eyes on the dim figures of his new acquaintances, with sensations to which he had long been a stranger. Their presence awakened recollections and emotions, to which his sturdy but honest nature had latterly paid but little homage, and his thoughts began to wander over the varied scenes of a life of hardships, that had been strangely blended with scenes of wild and peculiar enjoyment. The train taken by his thoughts had already conducted him, in imagination, far into an ideal world, when he was once more suddenly recalled to the reality of his situation, by the movements of the faithful hound.

The dog who, in submission to his years and infirmities, had manifested such a decided propensity to sleep, now arose, and stalked from out the shadow cast by the tall person of his master, and looked abroad into the Prairie, as if his instinct apprised him of the presence of still another visiter. Then, seemingly content with his examination, he returned to his comfortable post, and disposed of his weary limbs with the deliberation and care of one who was no novice in the art of self-preservation.

"What; again, Hector!" said the trapper in a soothing voice, which he had the caution, however, to utter in an under tone; "what is it, dog? tell it all to his master, pup; what is it?"

Hector answered with another growl, but was content to continue in his lair. These were evidences of intelligence and distrust, to which one as practised as the trapper could not turn an inattentive ear. He again spoke to the dog, encouraging him to watchfulness by a low, guarded whistle. The animal, however, as if conscious of having already discharged his duty, obstinately refused to raise his head from the grass.

"A hint from such a friend is far better than man's advice!" muttered the trapper, as he slowly moved towards the couple, who were yet too earnestly and abstractedly engaged in their own discourse to notice his approach; "and none but a conceited settler would hear it and not respect it, as he ought. Children," he added, when near enough to address his companions, "we are not alone in these dreary fields; there are others stirring, and, therefore, to the shame of our kind be it said, danger is nigh."

"If one of the lazy sons of Skirting Ishmael is prowling out of his camp to night," said the young bee-hunter, with great vivacity, and in tones that might easily have been excited to a menace, "he may have an end put to his journey, sooner either than he or his father has calculated!"

"My life on it, they are all with the teams," hurriedly answered the girl. "I saw the whole of them asleep, myself, except the two on watch; and their natures have greatly changed, if they, too, are not both dreaming of a turkey-hunt, or a court-house fight, at this very moment."

"Some beast, with a strong scent, has passed between the wind and the hound, father, and it makes him uneasy; or perhaps he too is dreaming. I had a pup of my own in Kentucky, that would start upon a long chase from a deep sleep; and all upon the fancy of some dream. Go to him, and pinch his ear that the beast may feel the life within him."

"Not so—not so," returned the trapper, shaking his head as one who better understood the qualities of his dog.—"Youth sleeps, ay, and dreams too; but age is awake and watchful. The pup is never false with his nose, and long experience tells me to heed his warnings."

"Did you ever run him upon the trail of carrion?"

"Why I must say that the ravenous beasts have sometimes tempted me to let him loose, for they are as greedy as men after the venison, in its season; but then I knew the reason of the dog would tell him the object!—No—no, Hector is an animal known in the ways of man, and will never strike a false trail when a true one is to be followed!"

"Ay, ay, the secret is out! you have run the hound on the track of a wolf, and his nose has a better memory than his master!" said the bee-hunter, laughing.

"I have seen the creatur' sleep for hours, with pack after pack, in open view. A wolf might eat out of his tray without a snarl, unless there was a scarcity; then, indeed, Hector would be apt to claim his own."

"There are panthers down from the mountains; I saw one make a leap at a sick deer, as the sun was setting. Go; go you back to the dog, and tell him the truth, father; in a minute I—"

He was interrupted by a long, loud, and piteous howl from the hound, which rose on the air of the evening like the wailing of some spirit of the place, and passed off into the Prairie, in cadences that rose and fell like its own undulating surface. The trapper was impressively silent, listening intently. Even the reckless bee-hunter was struck with the wailing wildness of the sounds. After a short pause the former whistled the dog to his side, and turning to his companions, he said, with the seriousness which, in his opinion, the occasion demanded—

"They who think man enjoys all the knowledge of the creatur's of God, will live to be disappointed, if they reach, as I have done, the age of fourscore years. I will not take upon myself to say what mischief is brewing, nor will I vouch that even the hound himself knows so much; but that evil is nigh, and that wisdom invites us to avoid it, I have heard from the mouth of one who never lies. I did think the pup had become unused to the footsteps of man, and that your presence made him uneasy; but his nose has been on a long scent the whole evening, and what I mistook as a notice of your coming, has been intended for something more serious. If the advice of an old man is, then, worth hearkening to, children, you will quickly go different ways to your places of shelter and safety."

"If I quit Ellen, at such a moment," exclaimed the youth, "may I—"

"You've said enough!" the girl interrupted, by again interposing a hand that might, both by its delicacy and colour, have graced a far more elevated station in life; "my time is out; and we must part, at all events—So good-night, Paul—father—good-night."

"Hist!" said the youth seizing her arm, as she was in the very act of tripping from his side—"Hist! do you hear nothing? There are buffaloes playing their pranks at no great distance—That sound beats the earth like a herd of the mad scampering devils!"

His two companions listened, as people in their situation would be apt to lend their faculties to discover the meaning of any doubtful noises, especially when heard after so many and such startling warnings. The unusual sounds were unequivocally though still faintly audible. The youth and his female companion had made several hurried and vacillating conjectures concerning their nature, when a current of the night air brought the rush of trampling footsteps too sensibly to their ears, to render mistake any longer possible.

"I am right!" said the bee-hunter; "a panther is driving a herd before him; or, may-be, there is a battle among the beasts."

"Your ears are cheats;" returned the old man, who, from the moment his own organs had been able to catch the distant sounds, stood like a statue made to represent deep attention—"The leaps are too long for the buffaloe, and too regular for terror. Hist; now they are in a bottom where the grass is high, and the sound is deadened! Ay, there they go on the hard earth! And now they come up the swell, dead upon us; they will be here afore you can find a cover."

"Come, Ellen," cried the youth seizing his companion by the hand, "let us make a trial for the encampment."

"Too late! too late!" exclaimed the trapper, "for the creatur's are in open view; and a bloody band of accursed Siouxes they are, by their thieving look and the random fashion in which they ride!"

"Siouxes or devils, they shall find *us* men!" said the bee-hunter, with a mien as fierce as if he led a party of superior strength, and of a courage equal to his own—"You have a piece, old man, and will pull a trigger in behalf of a helpless, Christian girl!"

"Down, down into the grass—down with ye both," whispered the trapper, intimating to them to turn aside to the tall weeds, which grew in a denser body than common near the place where they stood. "You've not the time to fly nor the numbers to fight, foolish boy. Down into the grass, if you prize the young woman or value the gift of life!"

His remonstrance, seconded as it was by a prompt and energetic action, did not fail to produce the submission to his order, which the occasion seemed, indeed, imperiously to require. The moon had fallen behind a sheet of thin, fleecy clouds, which skirted the horizon, leaving just enough of its faint and fluctuating light to render objects visible, dimly revealing their forms and proportions. The trapper, by exercising that species of influence over his companions, which experience and decision usually assert, in cases of emergency, had effectually succeeded in concealing them in the grass, and, by the aid of the feeble rays of the luminary, he was enabled to scan the disorderly party, which was riding like so many madmen directly upon them.

A band of beings, who resembled demons rather than men sporting in their nightly revels across the bleak plain, was in truth approaching, at a fearful rate, and in a direction to leave little hope that some one among them, at least, would not pass over the spot where the trapper and his companions lay. At intervals, the clattering of hoofs was borne along by the night wind quite audibly in their front, and then, again, their progress through the fog of the autumnal grass was swift and silent; adding to the unearthly appearance of the spectacle. The trapper, who had called in his hound, and bidden him crouch at his side, now kneeled in the cover, also, and kept a keen and watchful eye on the route of the band, soothing the fears of the girl, and restraining the impatience of the youth, in the same breath.

"If there's one, there's thirty of the miscreants!" he said, in a sort of episode to his whispered comments. "Ay, ay; they are edging towards the river—Peace, pup—pup—peace—no, here they come this-a-way again—the thieves dont seem to know their own errand! If there were just six of us, lad, what a beautiful ambushment we might make upon them, from this very spot—it wont do, it wont do, boy; keep yourself closer, or your head will be seen—besides, I'm not altogether strong in the opinion it would be lawful, as they have done us no harm—There they bend again to the river—no; here they come up the swell—now is the moment to be as still as if the breath had done its duty and departed the body."

The old man sunk into the grass while he was speaking, as if the final separation to which he alluded had in his own case actually occurred, and, at the next instant, a band of wild horsemen whirled by them, with the noiseless rapidity in which it might be imagined a troop of spectres would pass. The dark and fleeting forms were already vanished, when the trapper ventured again to raise his head to a level with the tops of the bending herbage, motioning at the same time to his companions, to maintain their positions and their silence.

"They are going down the swell, towards the encampment," he continued, in his former guarded tones; "no, they halt in the bottom, and are clustering together like deer in council. By the Lord they are turning again, and we are not yet done with the reptiles!"

Once more he sought his friendly cover, and at the next instant the dark troop were to be seen riding, in a disorderly manner, on the very summit of the little elevation on which the trapper and his companions lay. It was now soon apparent that they had returned to avail themselves of the height of the ground, in order to examine the dim horizon.

Some dismounted, while others rode to and fro, like men engaged in a local inquiry of much interest. Happily for the hidden party, the grass in which they were concealed not only served to skreen them from the eyes of the savages, but opposed an obstacle to prevent their horses, which were no less rude and untrained than their riders, from trampling on them, in their irregular and wild paces.

At length an athletic and dark-looking Indian, who, by his air of authority, would seem to be the leader, summoned his chiefs about him to a consultation, which was held mounted. This body was collected on the very margin of that mass of herbage in which the trapper and his companions were hid. As the young man looked up and saw the fierce aspect of the groupe, which was increasing at each instant by the accession of some countenance and figure, apparently more forbidding than any which had preceded it, he drew his rifle, by a very natural impulse, from beneath him, and commenced putting it in a state for service. The female, at his side, buried her face in the grass, by a feeling that was, possibly, quite as natural to her sex and habits, leaving him to follow the impulses of his hot blood; but his aged and more prudent adviser whispered sternly in his ear.

"The tick of the lock is as well known to the knaves as the blast of a trumpet to a soldier! Lay down the piece—lay down the piece—should the moon touch the barrel, it could not fail to be seen by the devils, whose eyes are keener than the blackest snake's! The smallest motion, now, would be sure to bring an arrow among us."

The bee-hunter so far obeyed as to continue immoveable and silent. But there was still sufficient light to convince his companion, by the contracted brow and threatening eye of the young man, that a discovery would not bestow a bloodless victory on the savages. Finding his advice disregarded, the trapper took his measures accordingly, and awaited the result with a resignation and calmness that were characteristics of the individual.

In the mean time the Siouxes (for the sagacity of the old man was not deceived in the character of his dangerous neighbors) had terminated their council, and were again dispersed along the ridge of land as if they sought some hidden object.

"The imps have heard the hound!" whispered the trapper, "and their ears are too true to be cheated in the distance.

Keep close, lad, keep close; down with your head to the very earth, like a dog that sleeps."

"Let us rather take to our feet, and trust to manhood," returned his impatient companion.

He would have proceeded, but feeling a hand laid rudely on his shoulder he turned his eyes upward, and beheld the dark and savage countenance of an Indian glooming full upon him. Notwithstanding the surprise and the disadvantage of his attitude, the youth was not disposed to become a captive so easily. Quicker than the flash of his own gun, he sprang upon his feet, and was throttling his opponent with a power that would soon have terminated the contest, when he felt the arms of the trapper thrown around his body, confining his exertions by a strength very little inferior to his own. Before he had time to reproach his comrade for this apparent treachery, a dozen Siouxes, were around them, and the whole party were compelled to yield themselves as prisoners.

Chapter IV

——"With much more dismay
I view the fight, than those that make the fray."
The Merchant of Venice, III.ii.61–62.

THE UNFORTUNATE bee-hunter and his companions had become the captives of a people, who might, without exaggeration, be called the Ishmaelites of the American deserts. From time immemorial, the hands of the Siouxes had been turned against their neighbors of the Prairies, and even at this day, when the influence and authority of a civilized government are beginning to be felt around them, they are considered a treacherous and dangerous race. At the period of our tale, the case was far worse; few white men trusting themselves in the remote and unprotected regions where so false a tribe was known to dwell.

Notwithstanding the peaceable submission of the trapper, he was quite aware of the character of the band into whose hands he had fallen. It would have been difficult, however, for the nicest judge to have determined whether fear, policy or resignation formed the secret motive of the old man, in permitting himself to be plundered, as he did, without a murmur. So far from opposing any remonstrance to the rude and violent manner, in which his conquerors performed this customary office, he even anticipated their cupidity, by tendering to the chiefs, such articles as he thought might prove the most acceptable. On the other hand, Paul Hover, who had been literally a conquered man, manifested the strongest repugnance to submit to the violent liberties that were taken with his person and property. He, even, gave several exceedingly unequivocal demonstrations of his displeasure during the summary process, and would, more than once, have broken out into open and desperate resistance, but for the admonitions and intreaties of the trembling girl, who clung to his side, in a manner so dependant, as to show the youth, that her hopes were now placed, no less on his discretion, than on his disposition to serve her.

The Indians had, however, no sooner deprived the captives of their arms, and ammunition, and stript them of a few articles of dress of little use and perhaps of less value, than they appeared disposed to grant them a respite. Business of greater moment pressed on their hands, and required their attention. Another consultation of the chiefs was convened, and it was apparent, by the earnest and vehement manner of the few who spoke, that the warriors conceived their success, as yet, to be far from complete.

"It will be well," whispered the trapper, who knew enough of the language he heard, to comprehend perfectly the subject of the discussion, "if the travellers who lie near the willow brake, are not awoke out of their sleep by a visit from these miscreants. They are too cunning to believe that a woman of the pale faces is to be found so far from the settlements, without having a white man's inventions and comforts at hand."

"If they will carry the tribe of wandering Ishmael to the Rocky Mountains," said the young bee-hunter, laughing in his vexation with a sort of bitter merriment, "I may forgive the rascals!"

"Paul! Paul," exclaimed his companion in a tone of reproach, "you forget all! Think of the dreadful consequences!"

"Ay, it was thinking of what you call consequences, Ellen, that prevented me from putting the matter, at once, to yonder red-devil, and making it a real knock-down and drag out. Old trapper, the sin of this cowardly business lies on your shoulders! But it is no more than your daily calling, I reckon, to take men as well as beasts in snares!"

"I implore you, Paul, to be calm, to be patient."

"Well, since it is your wish, Ellen," returned the youth, endeavoring to swallow his spleen, "I will make the trial, though, as you ought to know, it is part of the religion of a Kentuckian, to fret himself, a little, at a mischance."

"I fear your friends, in the other bottom, will not escape the eyes of the imps," continued the trapper, as coolly as though he had not heard a syllable of the intervening discourse. "They scent plunder, and it would be as hard to drive a hound from his game, as to throw the varmints from its trail!"

"Is there nothing to be done?" asked Ellen, in an imploring manner which proved the sincerity of her concern.

"It would be an easy matter to call out, in so loud a voice, as to make old Ishmael dream that the wolves were among his flock," Paul replied, "I can make myself heard a mile in these open fields, and his camp is but a short quarter from us."

"And get knock'd on the head for your pains," returned the trapper—"No, no, cunning must match cunning, or the hounds, will murder the whole family."

"Murder! no—no murder. Ishmael loves travel, so well, there would be no harm in his having a look at the other sea, but the old fellow is in a bad condition to take the long journey. I would try a look myself, before he should be quite murdered!"

"His party is strong in number and well armed; do you think it will fight?"

"Look here, old trapper. Few men love Ishmael Bush and his seven sledge-hammer sons, less than one Paul Hover, but I scorn to slander even a Tennessee shot-gun. There is as much of the true stand-up courage among them, as there is in any family, that was ever raised in Kentuck, itself. They are a long-sided and double jointed breed, and let me tell you, that he, who takes the measure of one of them on the ground, must be a workman at a hug."

"Hist! The savages have done their talk, and are about to set their accursed devices in motion. Let us be patient, something may yet offer, in favor of your friends."

"Friends! call none of the race a friend of mine, trapper, if you have the smallest regard for my affection. What I say in their favor is less from love than honesty."

"I did not know but the young woman was of the kin," returned the other, a little drily. "But no offence should be taken where none was intended."

The mouth of Paul was again stopped by the hand of Ellen, who took on herself to reply, in her conciliating tones, "We should be all of a family, when it is in our power to serve each other. We depend entirely on your experience, honest old man, to discover the means to apprise our friends of their danger."

"There will be a real time of it," muttered the bee-hunter,

laughing, "if the boys get at work, in good earnest, with these red-skins."

He was interrupted by a general movement which took place among the band. The Indians dismounted to a man, giving their horses in charge of three or four of the party, who were, also, entrusted with the safe keeping of the prisoners. They then, formed themselves in a circle around a warrior, who appeared to possess the chief authority, and at a given signal the whole array mov'd slowly, and cautiously from the centre, in straight, and consequently, in diverging lines. Most of their dark forms were soon blended with the brown covering of the Prairie, though the captives, who watched the slightest movements, of their enemies with vigilant eyes, were, now and then, enabled to discern a human figure drawn against the horizon, as some one more eager than the rest rose to his greatest height in order to extend the limits of his view. But it was not long, before even these fugitive glimpses of the moving and constantly increasing circle, were lost, and uncertainty and conjecture were added to apprehension. In this manner passed many anxious and weary minutes, during the close of which the listeners expected at each moment, to hear the whoop, of the assailants and the shrieks of the assailed, rising together on the stillness of the night. But it would seem, that the search which was so evidently making was without a sufficient object, for at the expiration of half an hour the different individuals of the band began to return singly, gloomy and sullen, like men who were disappointed.

"Our time is at hand," observed the trapper, who noted the smallest incident, or the slightest indication of hostility among the savages; "we are now to be questioned; and if I know any thing of the policy of our case, I should say it would be wise to choose one among us, to hold the discourse, in order that our testimony may agree. And furthermore if an opinion from one as old and as worthless as a hunter of fourscore is to be regarded, I would just venture to say, that man should be the one most skill'd in the natur' of an Indian, and that he should also, know something of their language. Are you acquainted with the tongue of the Siouxes, friend?"

"Swarm your own hive," returned the discontented bee-hunter. "You are good at buzzing, old trapper, if you are good at nothing else."

"'Tis the gift of youth to be rash and heady," the trapper calmly, retorted. "The day has been, boy, when my blood was like your own, too swift and too hot to run quietly in my veins. But what will it profit to talk of silly risks and foolish acts at this time of life! A gray head should cover a brain of reason and not the tongue of a boaster."

"True, true," whispered Ellen, "and we have other things to attend to now! here comes the Indian to put his questions."

The girl, whose apprehensions had quickened her senses was not deceived. She was yet speaking when a tall, half naked savage approached the spot where they stood, and after examining the whole party as closely as the dim light permitted, for more than a minute in perfect stillness, he gave the usual salutation in the harsh and guttural tones of his own language. The trapper replied as well as he could, which it seems, was sufficiently well to be understood. In order to escape the imputation of pedantry we shall render the substance, and, so far as it is possible, the form of the dialogue that succeeded, into the English tongue.

"Have the pale faces eaten their own buffaloes, and taken the skins from all their own beavers," continued the savage, allowing the usual moment of decorum to elapse after the words of greeting, before he again spoke, "that they come to count how many are left among the Pawnees?"

"Some of us are here to buy and some to sell," returned the trapper, "but none will follow if they hear it is not safe to come nigh the lodge of a Sioux."

"The Siouxes are thieves, and they live in the snows, why do we talk of a people who are so far, when we are in the country of the Pawnees."

"If the Pawnees are the owners of this land, then white and red are here by equal right."

"Have not the Pale-faces stolen enough from the Red men, that you come so far to carry a lie! I have said that this is a hunting ground of my tribe."

"My right to be here is equal to your own," the trapper

rejoined with undisturbed coolness: "I do not speak as I might—It is better to be silent. The Pawnees and the white men are brothers, but a Sioux dare not show his face in the village of the Loups."

"The Dahcotahs are men!" exclaimed the savage fiercely, forgetting, in his anger, to maintain the character he had assumed, and using the appellation of which his nation was most proud, "The Dahcotahs have no fear. Speak; what brings you so far from the villages of the Pale-faces?"

"I have seen the sun rise and set on many Councils, and have heard the words of wise men. Let your Chiefs come, and my mouth shall not be shut."

"I am a great Chief," said the savage, affecting an air of offended dignity. "Do you take me for an Assiniboine! Weucha is a warrior often named, and much beloved!"

"Am I a fool not to know a 'burnt-wood Teton'!" demanded the trapper with a steadiness that did great credit to his nerves. "Go: it is dark, and you do not see that my head is gray."

The Indian, now, appeared convinced that he had adopted too shallow an artifice to deceive one so practised as the man he addressed, and he was deliberating what fiction he should next invent, in order to obtain his real object, when a slight commotion among the band, put an end at once, to all his schemes. Casting his eyes behind him, as if fearful of a speedy interruption, he said in tones much less pretending than those he had first resorted to—

"Give Weucha the milk of the Long-knives, and he will sing your name in the ears of the great men of his tribe."

"Go," repeated the trapper motioning him away, with strong disgust. "Your young men are speaking of Mahtoree. My words are for the ears of a chief."

The savage cast a look on the other which, notwithstanding the dim light, was sufficiently indicative of implacable hostility. He then stole away among his fellows, anxious to conceal the counterfeit he had attempted to practise, no less than the treachery he had contemplated against a fair division of the spoils, from the man named by the trapper, whom he now also knew to be approaching, by the manner in which his name passed from one to another in the band. He had hardly disappeared, before a warrior of powerful frame, advanced out of the dark circle, and placed himself before the captives with that high and proud bearing for which a distinguished Indian chief is ever so remarkable. He was followed by all the party, who arranged themselves around his person, in a deep and respectful silence.

"The earth is very large," the Chief commenced, after a pause of that true dignity, which his counterfeit had so miserably affected. "Why can the children of my Great White Father never find room on it?"

"Some among them have heard, that their friends in the Prairies are in want of many things," returned the trapper, "and they have come to see if it be true. Some want, in their turns, what the red men are willing to sell, and they come to make their friends rich, with powder and blankets."

"Do traders cross the big river, with empty hands!"

"Our hands are empty because your young men thought we were tired, and they have lightened us of our loads. They were mistaken. I am old, but I am still strong."

"It cannot be. Your load has fallen in the Prairies. Show my young men the place, that they may pick it up, before the Pawnees find it."

"The path to the spot is crooked, and it is night. The hour is come for sleep," said the trapper with perfect composure—"bid your warriors go over yonder hill. There is water and there is wood; let them light their fires and sleep with warm feet. When the sun comes again I will speak to you."

A low murmur, but one that was clearly indicative of dissatisfaction passed among the attentive listeners, and served to inform the old man, that he had not been sufficiently wary in proposing a measure, that he intended should notify the travellers in the brake, of the presence of their dangerous neighbors. Mahtoree, however, without betraying, in the slightest degree, the excitement which was so strongly exhibited by his companions, continued the discourse in the same lofty manner, as before.

"I know that my friend is rich," he said, "that he has many warriors not far off, and that horses are plentier with him than dogs among the red skins."

"You see my warriors and my horses."

"What! has the woman the feet of a Dahcotah, that she can walk for thirty nights in the Prairies, and not fall! I know that the red men of the woods make long marches on foot, but we who live where the eye cannot see from one lodge to another, love our horses."

The trapper now hesitated, in his turn. He was perfectly aware that deception, if detected, might prove dangerous, and for one of his pursuits and character, he was strongly troubled with an unaccommodating regard for the truth. But recollecting that he controlled the fate of others as well as of himself, he determined to let things take their course, and to permit the Dahcotah Chief to deceive himself if he would.

"The women of the Siouxes and of the white men are not of the same wigwam," he answered evasively. "Would a Teton warrior make his wife greater than himself. I know he would not; and yet, my ears have heard that there are lands, where the Councils are held by squaws."

Another slight movement in the dark circle, apprised the trapper, that his declaration was not received without surprise, if entirely without distrust. The Chief, alone, seem'd unmoved, nor was he disposed to relax from the loftiness and high dignity of his air.

"My white Fathers who live on the Great Lakes have declared," he said, "that their brothers towards the rising sun are not men; and, now, I know they did not lie! Go. What is a nation, whose chief is a squaw! are you the dog and not the husband of this woman?"

"I am neither. Never did I see her face before this day. She came into the Prairies, because they had told her a great and generous nation called the Dahcotahs liv'd there, and she wish'd to look on men. The women of the pale-faces, like the women of the Siouxes, open their eyes to see things that are new; but she is poor, like myself, and she will want corn and buffaloe, if you take away the little that she and her friend still have."

"My ears listen to many wicked lies!" exclaimed the Teton warrior, in a voice so stern, that it startled even his red auditors. "Am I a woman! Has not a Dacotah eyes! Tell me, white hunter, who are the men of your colour, that sleep near the fallen trees!"

As he spoke, the indignant Chief pointed in the direction of Ishmael's encampment, leaving the trapper no reason to doubt that the superior industry and sagacity of this man had effected a discovery which had eluded the search of the rest of his party. Notwithstanding his regret at an event that might prove fatal to the sleepers, and some little vexation at having been so completely outwitted in the dialogue, just related, the old man continued to maintain his air of inflexible composure.

"It may be true," he answered, "that white men are sleeping on the Prairie. If my brother says it, it is true; but what men thus trust to the generosity of the Tetons, I cannot tell. If there be strangers asleep, send your young men to wake them up and let them say why they are here; every pale-face has a tongue."

The Chief shook his head with a wild and fierce smile, answering abruptly, as he turned away to put an end to the conference.

"The Dacotahs are a wise race, and Mahtoree is their Chief. He will not call to the strangers, that they may rise and speak to him, with their carabines. He will whisper softly in their ears. When this is done let the men of their own colour come and awake them!"

As he uttered these words and turned on his heel, a low, and approving laugh passed around the dark circle, which instantly broke its order and followed him to a little distance, from the stand of the captives, where those who might presume to mingle opinions with so great a warrior, again, gathered about him, in consultation. Weucha profited by the occasion to renew his importunities, but the trapper, who had discovered how great a counterfeit he was, shook him off, in displeasure. An end was, however, more effectually put to the annoyance of this malignant savage by a mandate for the whole party, including men and beasts, to change their position. The movement was made in dead silence, and with an order that would have done credit to more enlightened beings. A halt, however, was soon made, and when the captives had time to look about them, they found they were in view of the low, dark outline of the copse, near which lay the slumbering party of Ishmael.

Here another short but grave and deliberative consultation was held.

The beasts, which seem'd trained to such covert and silent attacks, were once more plac'd under the care of keepers, who, as before were charged with the duty of watching the prisoners. The mind of the trapper was in no degree relieved from the uneasiness, which was, at each instant, getting a stronger possession of him, when he found that Weucha was plac'd nearest to his own person, and, as it appeared by the air of triumph and authority he assumed, at the head of the guard also. The savage, however, who doubtless had his secret instructions, was content, for the present, with making a significant gesture with his tomahawk, which menaced death to Ellen. After admonishing in this expressive manner his male captives of the fate that would instantly attend their female companion, on the slightest alarm proceeding from any of the party, he was content to maintain a rigid silence. This unexpected forbearance, on the part of Weucha, enabled the trapper and his two associates to give their undivided attention to the little that might be seen of the interesting movements which were passing in their front.

Mahtoree took the entire disposition of the arrangements on himself. He pointed out the precise situation he wished each individual to occupy, like one intimately acquainted with the qualifications of his respective followers, and he was obeyed with the deference and promptitude with which an Indian warrior is wont to submit to the instructions of his chief, in moments of trial. Some he despatched to the right, and others to the left. Each man departed with the noiseless and quick step peculiar to the race, until all had assumed their allotted stations, with the exception of two chosen warriors, who remained nigh the person of their leader. When the rest had disappeared, Mahtoree turned to these select companions, and intimated by a sign, that the critical moment had arrived, when the enterprise he contemplated was to be put in execution.

Each man laid aside the light fowling piece which, under the name of a carabyne, he carried in virtue of his rank, and divesting himself of every article of exterior or heavy clothing, he stood resembling a dark and fierce looking statue, in the attitude and nearly in the garb of nature. Mahtoree assured himself of the right position of his tomahawk, felt that his knife was secure in its sheath of skin, tightened his girdle of wampum, and saw that the lacing of his fringed and ornamented leggings was secure and likely to offer no impediment to his exertions. Thus prepared at all points, and ready for his desperate undertaking, the Teton gave the signal to proceed.

The three advanced in a line with the encampment of the travellers, until, in the dim light by which they were seen, their dusky forms were nearly lost to the eyes of the prisoners. Here they paused, looking around them like men who deliberate and ponder long on the consequences before they take a desperate leap. Then sinking together, they became lost in the grass of the Prairie.

It is not difficult to imagine the distress and anxiety of the different spectators of these threatening movements. Whatever might be the reasons of Ellen for entertaining no strong attachment to the family in which she has first been seen by the reader, the feelings of her sex, and, perhaps, some lingering seeds of kindness, predominated. More than once she felt tempted to brave the awful and instant danger that awaited such an offence, and to raise her feeble and in truth impotent voice in warning. So strong, indeed, and so very natural was the inclination, that she would most probably have put it in execution, but for the often-repeated though whispered remonstrances of Paul Hover. In the breast of the young bee-hunter himself, there was a singular union of emotions. His first and chiefest solicitude was certainly in behalf of his gentle and dependant companion; but the sense of her danger was mingled in the breast of the reckless woods-man with a consciousness of a high and wild, and by no means an unpleasant excitement. Though united to the emigrants by ties still less binding than those of Ellen, he longed to hear the crack of their rifles, and, had occasion offered, he would gladly have been among the first to rush to their rescue. There were in truth moments when he felt in his turn an impulse, that was nearly resistless, to spring forward and awake the unconscious sleepers; but a glance at Ellen would serve to recall his tottering prudence, and to admonish him of the consequences. The trapper, alone, remained calm and observant, as if nothing that involved his personal comfort or safety had occurred. His ever-moving, vigilant eyes, watched the smallest change, with the composure of one too long inured to scenes of danger to be easily moved, and with an expression of cool determination which denoted the intention he actually harboured, of profiting by the smallest oversight on the part of the captors.

In the mean time the Teton warriors had not been idle. Profiting by the high fog which grew in the bottoms, they had worm'd their way, through the matted grass, like so many treacherous serpents stealing on their prey, until the point was gained, where an extraordinary caution became necessary to their further advance. Mahtoree, alone, had occasionally elevated his dark, grim countenance above the herbage, straining his eye balls to penetrate the gloom which skirted the border of the brake. In these momentary glances he gained sufficient knowledge, added to that he had obtained in his former search, to be the perfect master of the position of his intended victims, though he was still profoundly ignorant of their numbers, and of their means of defence.

His efforts to possess himself of the requisite knowledge concerning these two latter and essential points were, however, completely baffled by the stillness of the camp, which lay in a quiet as deep as if it were literally a place of the dead. Too wary and distrustful to rely, in circumstances of so much doubt, on the discretion of any less firm and crafty than himself, the Dahcotah, bade his companions remain where they lay, and pursued the adventure alone.

The progress of Mahtoree was now slow, and to one less accustomed to such a species of exercise, it would have proved painfully laborious. But the advance of the wily snake itself is not more certain or noiseless, than was his approach. He drew his form, foot by foot, through the bending grass, pausing at each movement to catch the smallest sound that might betray any knowledge, on the part of the travellers, of his proximity. He succeeded, at length, in dragging himself, out of the sickly light of the moon, into the shadows of the brake, where not only his own dark person was much less liable to be seen, but where the surrounding objects became more distinctly visible to his keen and active glances.

Here the Teton paused long and warily to make his observations, before he ventured further. His position enabled him to bring the whole encampment, with its tent, wagons and lodges, into a dark but clearly marked profile, furnishing a clue by which the practised warrior was led to a tolerably accurate estimate of the force he was about to encounter. Still an unnatural silence pervaded the spot, as if men suppressed even the quiet breathings of sleep, in order to render the appearance of their confidence more evident. The chief bent his head to the earth, and listened intently. He was about to raise it again, in disappointment, when the long drawn and trembling respiration of one who slumbered imperfectly met his ear. The Indian was too well skilled in all the means of deception to become himself the victim of any common artifice. He knew the sound to be natural, by its peculiar quivering, and he hesitated no longer.

A man of nerves less tried than those of the fierce and conquering Mahtoree would have been keenly sensible of all the hazard he incurred. The reputation of those hardy and powerful white adventurers, who so often penetrated the wilds inhabited by his people, was well known to him; but while he drew nigher, with the respect and caution that a brave enemy never fails to inspire, it was with the vindictive animosity of a red man, jealous and resentful of the inroads of the stranger.

Turning from the line of his former route, the Teton dragged himself directly towards the margin of the thicket. When this material object was effected in safety, he arose to his seat, and took a better survey of his situation. A single moment served to apprise him of the place where the unsuspecting traveller lay. The reader will readily anticipate that the savage had succeeded in gaining a dangerous proximity to one of those slothful sons of Ishmael, who were deputed to watch over the isolated encampment of the travellers.

When certain that he was undiscovered, the Dahcotah raised his person again, and bending forward, he mov'd his dark visage above the face of the sleeper, in that sort of wanton and subtle manner with which the reptile is seen to play about its victim before it strikes. Satisfied at length, not only of the condition but of the character of the stranger,

Mahtoree was in the act of withdrawing his head, when a slight movement of the sleeper announced the symptoms of reviving consciousness. The savage seized the knife which hung at his girdle, and in an instant it was poised above the breast of the young emigrant. Then changing his purpose, with an action as rapid as his own flashing thoughts, he sunk back behind the trunk of the fallen tree against which the other reclined, and lay in its shadow, as dark, as motionless and apparently as insensible as the wood itself.

The slothful sentinel opened his heavy eyes, and gazing upward for a moment at the hazy heavens, he made an extraordinary exertion and raised his powerful frame from the support of the log. Then he looked about him, with an air of something like watchfulness, suffering his dull glances to run over the misty objects of the encampment until they finally settled on the distant and dim field of the open Prairie. Meeting with nothing more attractive than the same faint outlines of swell and interval, which everywhere rose before his drowsy eyes, he changed his position so as completely to turn his back on his dangerous neighbour, and suffered his person to sink sluggishly down into its former recumbent attitude. A long and, on the part of the Teton, an anxious and painful silence succeeded, before the deep breathing of the traveller again announced that he was indulging in his slumbers. The savage was however far too jealous of a counterfeit to trust to the first appearance of sleep. But the fatigues of a day of unusual toil lay too heavy on the sentinel to leave the other long in doubt. Still the motion with which Mahtoree again raised himself to his knees was so noiseless and guarded, that even a vigilant observer might have hesitated to believe he stirred. The change was, however, at length effected, and the Dacotah chief, then bent again over his enemy, without having produced a noise louder than that of the cotton-wood leaf which fluttered at his side in the currents of the passing air.

Mahtoree now felt himself master of the sleeper's fate. At the same time that he scanned the vast proportions and athletic limbs of the youth, in that sort of admiration which physical excellence seldom fails to excite in the breast of a savage, he coolly prepared to extinguish the principle of vitality which could alone render them formidable. After making himself sure of the seat of life, by gently removing the folds of the intervening cloth, he raised his keen weapon, and was about to unite his strength and skill in the impending blow, when the young man threw his brawny arm carelessly backward, exhibiting in the action the vast volume of its muscles.

The sagacious and wary Teton paused. It struck his acute faculties that sleep was less dangerous to him, at that moment, than even death itself might prove. The smallest noise, the agony of struggling, with which such a frame would probably relinquish its hold of life, suggested themselves to his rapid thoughts, and were all present to his experienced senses. He looked back into the encampment, turned his head into the thicket, and glanced his glowing eyes abroad into the wild and silent Prairies. Bending once more over the respited victim, he assured himself that he was sleeping heavily, and then abandoned his immediate purpose in obedience alone to the suggestions of a more crafty policy.

The retreat of Mahtoree was as still and guarded as had been his approach. He now took the direction of the encampment, stealing along the margin of the brake, as a cover into which he might easily plunge at the smallest alarm. The drapery of the solitary hut attracted his notice in passing. After examining the whole of its exterior, and listening with painful intensity, in order to gather counsel from his ears, the savage ventured to raise the cloth at the bottom, and to thrust his dark visage beneath. It might have been a minute before the Teton chief drew back, and seated himself with the whole of his form without the linen tenement. Here he sat, seemingly brooding over his discovery, for many moments, in rigid inaction. Then he resumed his crouching attitude, and once more projected his visage beyond the covering of the tent. His second visit to the interior was longer and, if possible, more ominous than the first. But it had, like every thing else, its termination, and the savage again withdrew his glaring eyes from the secrets of the place.

Mahtoree had drawn his person many yards from the spot, in his slow progress towards the cluster of objects which pointed out the centre of the position, before he again stopped. He made another pause, and looked back at the solitary little dwelling he had left, as if doubtful whether he should not return. But the chevaux-de-frise of branches now lay within reach of his arm, and the very appearance of precaution it presented, as it announced the value of the effects it encircled, tempted his cupidity, and induced him to proceed.

The passage of the savage, through the tender and brittle limbs of the cotton-wood, could be likened only to the sinuous and noiseless winding of the reptiles which he imitated. When he had effected his object, and had taken an instant to become acquainted with the nature of the localities within the enclosure, the Teton used the precaution to open a way through which he might make a swift retreat. Then raising himself on his feet, he stalked through the encampment, like the master of evil, seeking whom and what he should first devote to his fell purposes. He had already ascertained the contents of the lodge in which were collected the woman and her young children, and had passed several gigantic frames, stretched on different piles of brush, which happily for him lay in unconscious helplessness, when he reached the spot occupied by Ishmael in person. It could not escape the sagacity of one like Mahtoree that he had now within his power the principal man among the travellers. He stood long hovering above the recumbent and Herculean form of the emigrant, keenly debating in his own mind the chances of his enterprise, and the most effectual means of reaping its richest harvest.

He sheathed the knife which, under the hasty and burning impulse of his thoughts, he had been tempted to draw, and was passing on, when Ishmael turned in his lair, and demanded roughly who was moving before his half-opened eyes. Nothing short of the readiness and cunning of a savage could have evaded the crisis. Imitating the gruff tones and nearly unintelligible sounds he heard, Mahtoree threw his body heavily on the earth, and appeared to dispose himself to sleep. Though the whole movement was seen by Ishmael, in a sort of stupid observation, the artifice was too bold and too admirably executed to fail. The drowsy father closed his eyes, and slept heavily, with this treacherous inmate in the very bosom of his family.

It was necessary for the Teton to maintain the position he had taken, for many long weary minutes, in order to make sure that he was no longer watched. Though his body lay so motionless, his active mind was not idle. He profited by the delay to mature a plan which he intended should put the whole encampment, including both its effects and their proprietors, entirely at his mercy. The instant he could do so with safety, the indefatigable savage was again in motion. He took his way towards the slight pen which contained the domestic animals, worming himself along the ground in his former subtle and guarded manner.

The first animal he encountered among the beasts occasioned a long and hazardous delay. The weary creature, perhaps conscious, through its secret instinct, that in the endless wastes of the Prairies its surest protector was to be found in man, was so exceedingly docile as quietly to submit to the close examination it was doomed to undergo. The hand of the wandering Teton passed over the downy coat, the meek countenance, and the slender limbs of the gentle creature with untiring curiosity; but he finally abandoned the prize, as useless in his predatory expeditions, and offering too little temptation to the appetite. As soon however as he found himself among the beasts of burthen, his gratification was extreme, and it was with difficulty that he restrained the customary ejaculations of pleasure that were more than once on the point of bursting from his lips. Here he lost sight of the hazards by which he had gained access to his dangerous position, and the watchfulness of the wary and long practised warrior was momentarily forgotten in the exultation of the savage.

Chapter V

"Why, worthy father, what have we to lose?
—The law
Protects us not. Then why should we be tender
To let an arrogant piece of flesh threat us!
Play judge and executioner."

Cymbeline, IV.ii.124–28.

WHILE THE TETON thus enacted his subtle and characteristic part, not a sound broke the stillness of the surrounding Prairie. The whole band, lay at their several posts, waiting, with the well known patience of the Natives, for the signal which was to summon them to action. To the eyes of the anxious spectators, who occupied the little eminence, already described as the position of the captives, the scene presented the broad, solemn view, of a waste dimly lighted, by the glimmering rays of a clouded moon. The place of the encampment was marked by a gloom deeper than that which faintly shadowed out the courses of the bottoms, and here and there, a brighter streak tinged the rolling summits of the ridges. As for the rest, it was the deep, imposing quiet, of a desert.

But to those who so well knew, how much was brooding beneath this mantle of stillness and night, it was a scene of high and wild excitement. Their anxiety gradually increased, as minute after minute, passed away, and not the smallest sound of life arose out of the calm and darkness which enveloped the brake. The breathing of Paul grew louder and deeper, and more than once Ellen trembled at she knew not what, as she felt the quivering of his active frame, while she leaned dependantly on his arm, for support.

The shallow honesty, as well as the besetting infirmity of Weucha, have, already, been exhibited. The reader therefore will not be surprised to learn, that he was the first to forget the regulations he had himself imposed. It was at the precise moment, when we left, Mahtoree yielding to his nearly ungovernable delight, as he surveyed the number and quality of Ishmael's beasts of burthen, that the man he had selected to watch his captives, chose to indulge in the malignant pleasure of tormenting those it was his duty to protect. Bending his head nigh the ear of the trapper, the savage, rather muttered than whispered—

"If the Tetons lose their Great Chief, by the hands of the Long-knives,* old shall die, as well as young!"

"Life is the gift of the Wahcondah," was the unmov'd reply. "The burnt-wood warrior must submit to his laws, as well as his other children. Men only die when *he* chooses; and no Dahcotah can change the hour."

"Look!" returned the savage thrusting the blade of his knife before the face of his captive. "Weucha is the Wahcondah of a dog!"

The old man raised his eyes to the fierce visage of his keeper, and, for a moment, a gleam of honest and powerful disgust shot from their deep cells; but it instantly pass'd away, leaving in its place, an expression of commiseration, if not of sorrow.

"Why should one made in the real image of God, suffer his natur' to be provoked by a mere effigy of reason!" he said in English, and in tones much louder than those, in which Weucha had chosen to pitch the conversation. The latter profited by the unintentional offence of his captive, and seizing him, by the thin, gray locks that fell from beneath his cap, was on the point of passing the blade of his knife in malignant triumph around their roots, when a long, shrill yell rent the air, and was instantly echoed from the surrounding waste, as if a thousand demons opened their throats in common at the summons. Weucha relinquished his grasp, and uttered a cry of exultation.

"Now!" shouted Paul, unable to controul his impatience any longer, "now, old Ishmael, is the time to show the native blood of Kentucky! Fire, low, boys—Level into the swales, for the red-skins are settling to the very earth!"

His voice was however, lost, or rather unheeded, in the midst of the shrieks, shouts, and yells, that were, by this time, bursting from fifty mouths on every side of him. The guards still maintained their posts, at the side of the captives, but it was with that sort of difficulty with which steeds are re-

*The whites are so called by the Indians, from their swords.

strained at the starting-post, when expecting the signal to commence the trial of speed. They toss'd their arms wildly in the air, leaping up and down, more like exulting children than sober men, and continued to utter the most frantic cries.

In the midst of this tumultuous disorder, a rushing sound was heard, similar to that which might be expected to precede the passage of a flight of buffaloes, and then came the flocks and cattle of Ishmael, in one confused and frightened drove.

"They have robbed the squatter of his beasts!" said the attentive trapper. "The reptiles have left him as hoofless as a beaver!" He was yet speaking, when the whole body of the terrified animals rose the little acclivity and swept by the place where he stood, followed by a band of dusky, and demon-like looking figures, who pressed madly on their rear.

The impulse was communicated to the Teton horses, long accustomed to sympathise in the untutored passions of their owners, and it was with difficulty that their keepers were enabled to restrain their impatience. At this moment, when all eyes were directed to the passing whirlwind of men and beasts, the trapper caught the knife, from the hands of his inattentive keeper, with a power that his age would have seemed to contradict, and, at a single blow, severed the thong of hide which connected the whole of the drove. The wild animals snorted with joy and terror, and tearing the earth with their heels, they dash'd away into the broad Prairies in a dozen different directions.

Weucha turned upon his assailant with the ferocity and agility of a tiger. He felt for the weapon of which he had been so suddenly deprived, fumbled, with impotent haste for the handle of his tomahawk, and at the same moment, glanced his eyes after the flying cattle, with the longings of a Western Indian. The struggle between thirst for vengeance and cupidity was severe but short. The latter quickly predominated in the bosom of one whose passions were proverbially grovelling, and scarcely a moment intervened between the flight of the animals and the swift pursuit of the guards. The trapper had continued calmly facing his foe, during the instant of suspense that succeeded his hardy act, and now that Weucha was seen following his companions, he pointed after the dark train, saying, with his deep and nearly inaudible laugh—

"Red-natur' is red-natur', let it show itself on a Prairie, or in a Forest. A knock on the head, would be the smallest reward to him, who should take such a liberty with a Christian sentinel, but there goes the Teton after his horses as if he thought two legs as good as four in such a race! And yet the imps will have every hoof of them afore the day sets in, because it's reason ag'in instinct. Poor reason, I allow; but still there is a great deal of the man in an Indian. Ah's me! your Delawares were the red-skins of which America might boast; but few and scattered is that mighty people now! Well! the traveller may just make his pitch where he is; he has plenty of water, though natur' has cheated him of the pleasure of stripping the 'arth of its lawful trees. He has seen the last of his four-footed creaturs or I am but little skilled in Sioux cunning!"

"Had we not better join the party of Ishmael," said the Bee-hunter. "There will be a regular fight about this matter, or the old fellow has suddenly grown chicken hearted."

"No, no, no," hastily exclaimed Ellen—

She was stopped by the trapper, who laid his hand gently on her mouth, as he answered—

"Hist—hist—the sound of voices, might bring us into danger. Is your friend," he added, turning to Paul, "a man of spirit, enough . . . ."

"Dont call the squatter a friend of mine!" interrupted the youth. "I never, yet, harbored with one, who could not show hand and seal for the land which fed him."

"Well, well, let it then be acquaintance. Is he a man to maintain his own, stoutly, by dint of powder and lead?"

"His own! ay, and that which is not his own, too! Can you tell me, old trapper, who held the rifle that did the deed for the sheriff's deputy, that thought to rout the unlawful settlers who had gathered nigh the Buffaloe Lick, in old Kentuck. I had lin'd a beautiful swarm that very day into the hollow of a dead beech, and there lay the People's Officer at its roots with a hole directly through the 'Grace of God', which he carried in his jacket pocket, covering his heart, as if he thought a bit of sheepskin was a breast plate, against a squatter's bullet. Now, Ellen, you need'n't be troubled, for it never strictly was brought home to him; and there were fifty others who had pitch'd in that neighbourhood with just the same authority from the law."

The poor girl shuddered, struggling powerfully to suppress the sigh, which arose, in spite of her efforts, as if from the very bottom of her heart.

Thoroughly satisfied that he understood the character of the emigrants by the short but comprehensive description conveyed in Paul's reply, the old man, raised no further question concerning the readiness of Ishmael to revenge his wrongs, but rather, followed the train of thought which was suggested to his experience, by the occasion.

"Each one knows the ties which bind him to his fellow creatur's best," he answered. "Though it is greatly to be mourned, that colour, and property, and tongue, and l'arning, should make so wide a difference in those who, after all, are but the children of one Father! Howsomever," he continued, by a transition, not a little characteristic of the pursuits and feelings of the man, "as this is a business in which there is much more likelihood of a fight than need for a sermon, it is best to be prepared for what may follow. Hush. There is a movement below, it is an equal chance that we are seen."

"The family is stirring," cried Ellen with a tremor that announced nearly as much terror at the approach of her friends as she had before manifested at the presence of her enemies. "Go, Paul, leave me. *You*, at least must not be seen!"

"If I leave you, Ellen, in this desert before I see you safe, in the care of old Ishmael at least, may I never hear the hum of another bee, or what is worse fail in sight, to line him to his hive!"

"You forget, this good old man. He will not leave me. Though I am sure, Paul, we have parted before, where there has been more of a desert than this."

"Never. These Indians may come whooping back, and then where are you? Half way to the Rocky Mountains before a man can fairly strike the line of your flight. What think you, old trapper? How long may it be before these Tetons, as you call them, will be coming for the rest of old Ishmael's goods and chattels!"

"No fear of them," returned the old man laughing in his

own peculiar and silent manner, "I warrant me, the devils will be scampering after their beasts, these six hours yet! Listen, you may hear them in the willow bottoms, at this very moment, ay, your real Sioux cattle will run like so many long-legged Elks. Hist, crouch again into the grass, down with ye both; as I'm a miserable piece of clay, I heard the ticking of a gun-lock!"

The trapper did not allow his companions time to hesitate, but dragging them both after him, he nearly buried his own person in the fog of the Prairie, while he was speaking. It was fortunate that the senses of the aged hunter remained so acute, and that he had lost none of his readiness of action. The three were scarcely bowed to the ground, when their ears were saluted with the well known, sharp, short, reports of the western rifle, and instantly, the whizzing of the ragged lead was heard, buzzing within dangerous proximity of their heads.

"Well done young chips! well done old block!" whispered Paul, whose spirits no danger or situation could entirely depress. "As pretty a volley, as one would wish to hear on the wrong end of a rifle! What d'ye say, trapper! here is likely to be a three-cornered war, shall I give 'em as good as they send?"

"Give them nothing but fair words," returned the other, hastily, "or you are both lost."

"I'm not certain it would much mend the matter, if I were to speak with my tongue, instead of the piece," said Paul, in a tone half jocular, half bitter.

"For the sake of Heaven, do not let them hear you!" cried Ellen. "Go, Paul, go, you can easily quit us now!"

Several shots in quick succession, each sending its dangerous messenger, still nearer than the preceding discharge, cut short her speech, no less in prudence than in terror.

"This must end," said the trapper rising with the dignity of one bent only on the importance of his object. "I know not what need, ye may have, children, to fear those you should both love and honour; but something must be done to save your lives. A few hours more or less, can never be missed from the time of one, who has, already numbered so many days, therefore I will advance. Here is a clear space around you. Profit by it, as you need, and may God bless and prosper each of you as ye deserve."

Without waiting for any reply, the trapper walked boldly down the declivity in his front, taking the direction of the encampment, neither quickening his pace in trepidation nor suffering it to be retarded by fear. The light of the moon fell brighter for a moment, on his tall, gaunt, form, and served to warn the emigrants of his approach. Indifferent however, to this unfavorable circumstance, he held his way, silently and steadily towards the copse, until a threatening voice met him with the challenge of—

"Who comes. Friend or Foe?"

"Friend," was the reply, "one who has liv'd too long, to disturb the close of life with quarrels."

"But not so long as to forget the tricks of his youth," said Ishmael, rearing his huge frame from beneath the slight covering of a low bush, and meeting the trapper face to face. "Old man, you have brought this tribe of red devils upon us, and to-morrow you will be sharing the booty."

"What have you lost?" calmly demanded the trapper.

"Eight as good mares, as ever travelled in gears, besides a foal, that is worth thirty of the brightest Mexicans that bear the face of the King of Spain. Then the woman has not a cloven hoof for her dairy, or her loom, and I believe even the grunters, foot sore as they be, are ploughing the Prairie. And now, stranger," he added dropping the butt of his rifle on the hard earth with a violence and clatter that would have intimidated one less firm than the man he addressed, "how many of these creatures may fall to your lot?"

"Horses have I never craved, nor even used, though few have journeyed over more of the wide lands of America than myself, old and feeble as I seem. But little use is there for a horse among the hills and woods of York; that is as York was, but as I greatly fear York is no longer. As for woolen covering and cow's milk, I covet no such womanly fashions! The beasts of the field give me food and raiment. No, I crave no cloth better than the skin of a deer, nor any meat richer than his flesh."

The sincere manner of the trapper, as he uttered this simple vindication, was not entirely thrown away on the emigrant, whose dull nature was gradually quickening into a flame, that might speedily have burst forth, with dangerous violence. He listened like one who doubted, though not entirely convinced, and he muttered between his teeth, the denunciation, with which, a moment before, he intended to precede the summary vengeance he had certainly meditated.

"This is brave talking," he at length grumbled; "but to my judgement, too lawyer like for a straight forward, fair weather, and foul weather, hunter."

"I claim to be no better than a trapper," the other meekly answered.

"Hunter or trapper—There is little difference. I have come, old man, into these districts because I found the law sitting too tight upon me, and am not over fond of neighbors who cant settle a dispute without troubling a justice and twelve men; but I didn't come to be robbed of my plunder and then to say thank'ee to the man who did it!"

"He who ventures far into the Prairies, must abide by the ways of its owners."

"Owners!" echoed the squatter, "I am as rightful an owner of the land I stand on, as any governor in the States! Can you tell me, stranger, where the law or the reason, is to be found, which says that one man shall have a section, or a town, or perhaps a county, to his use, and another have to beg for 'arth to make his grave in. This is not natur and I deny that it is law. That is, your legal law."

"I cannot say that you are wrong," returned the trapper, whose opinions on this important topic, though drawn from very different premises were in singular accordance, with those of his companion, "and I have often thought and said as much, when and where I have believed my voice could be heard. But your beasts are stolen by them who claim to be masters of all they find in these deserts."

"They had better not dispute that matter with a man who knows better," said the other, in a portentous voice, though it seem'd deep and sluggish as he who spoke; "I call myself a fair trader, and one who gives to his chaps as good as he receives. You saw the Indians?"

"I did. They held me a prisoner, while they stole into your camp."

"It would have been more like a white-man and a christian to have let me known as much, in better season," retorted Ishmael, casting another ominous sidelong glance at the trapper, as if still meditating evil. "I am not much given to call every man, I fall in with, cousin, but colour should be something, when christians meet in such a place as this. But what is done, is done, and cannot be mended by words. Come out of your ambush, boys; here is no one but the old man: he has eaten of my bread, and should be our friend, though there is such good reason to suspect him of harboring with our enemies."

The trapper made no reply to the harsh suspicion which the other did not scruple to utter without the smallest delicacy, notwithstanding the explanations and denials to which he had just listened. The summons of the unnurtured squatter brought an immediate accession to their party. Four or five of his sons, made their appearance from beneath as many covers, where they had been posted under the impression that the figures they had seen on the swell of the Prairies, were a part of the Sioux band. As each man approached, and dropped his rifle into the hollow of his arm, he cast an indolent but inquiring glance at the stranger, though none of them expressed the least curiosity to know whence he had come or why he was there. This forebearance, however, proceeded only in part from the sluggishness of their common temper, for long and frequent experience in scenes of a similar character, had taught them the virtue of discretion. The trapper endured their sullen scrutiny with the steadiness of one as practised as themselves, and with the entire composure of innocence. Content with the momentary examination he had made, the eldest of the groupe, who was in truth the delinquent sentinel, by whose remissness the wily Mahtoree had so well profited, turned towards his father, and said bluntly—

"If this man is all that is left of the party I saw on the upland, yonder, we haven't altogether thrown away our ammunition."

"Asa, you are right," said the Father, turning suddenly on the trapper, a lost idea being recalled by the hint of his son. "How is it, stranger, there were three of you, just now, or there is no virtue in moonlight!"

"If you had seen the Tetons racing across the Prairies, like so many black-looking evil ones, on the heels of your cattle, my friend, it would have been an easy matter to have fancied them a thousand."

"Ay! for a town bred boy, or a skeary woman; though, for that matter, there is old Esther, she has no more fear of a red skin than of a crawling cub or of a wolf pup. I'll warrant ye, had your thievish devils made their push, by the light of the sun, the good woman would have been smartly at work among them, and the Siouxes would have found she was not given to part with her cheese and her butter without a price. But there'll come a time, stranger, right soon, when justice will have its dues, and that, too, without the help of what is called the law. We ar' of a slow breed, it may be said, and it is often said, of us, but slow is sure, and there ar' few men living who can say they ever struck a blow that they did not get one as hard in return from Ishmael Bush."

"Then has Ishmael Bush followed the instinct of the beasts, rather than the principle which ought to belong to his kind," returned the stubborn trapper. "I have struck many a blow, myself, but never have I felt the same ease of mind, that of right belongs to a man who follows his reason, after slaying, even, a fa'an when there was no call for his meat or hide, as I have felt at leaving a Mingo unburied in the woods, when following the trade of open and honest warfare."

"What, you have been a soldier, have you, trapper! I made a forage or two among the Cherokees when I was a lad myself; and I followed Mad Anthony* one season, through the beeches, but there was, altogether, too much tatooing and regulating among his troops for me, so I left him, without calling on the Paymaster to settle my arrearages. Though as Esther afterward boasted, she had made such use of the pay-ticket, that the States gained no great sum, by the oversight. You have heard of such a man as Mad Anthony, if you tarried long among the soldiers?"

*Anthony Wayne, a Pennsylvanian distinguished in the war of the revolution, and subsequently against the Indians of the west, for his daring as a general, by which he gained from his followers the title of Mad Anthony. General Wayne was the son of the person mentioned in the life of West as commanding the regiment which excited his military ardor.

"I fout my last battle, as I hope, under his orders," returned the trapper, a gleam of sunshine shooting from his dim eyes, as if the event was recollected with pleasure, and then a sudden shade of sorrow succeeding, as though he felt a secret admonition against dwelling on the violent scenes in which he had so often been an actor. "I was passing from the states on the sea shore, into these far regions, when I cross'd the trail of his army and I fell in, on his rear, just as a looker-on, but when they got to blows, the crack of my rifle was heard among the rest, though to my shame it may be said I never knew the right of the quarrel as well as a man of three score and ten, should know the reason of his acts afore he takes mortal life, which is a gift he never can return!"

"Come, stranger," said the Emigrant, his rugged nature a good deal softened when he found that they had fought on the same side in the wild warfare of the West. "It is of small account, what may be the ground-work of the disturbance, when it's a Christian ag'in a savage. We shall hear more of this horse-stealing to-morrow; to-night we can do no wiser or safer thing than to sleep."

So saying Ishmael deliberately led the way back towards his rifled encampment, and ushered the man, whose life a few minutes before had been in real jeopardy from his resentment, into the presence of his family. Here, with a very few words of explanation, mingled with scarce but ominous denunciations against the plunderers, he made his wife acquainted with the state of things on the Prairies, and announced his own determination to compensate himself for his broken rest, by devoting the remainder of the night to sleep.

The trapper gave his ready assent to the measure and adjusted his gaunt form on the pile of brush that was offered him, with as much composure as a Sovereign could resign himself to sleep, in the security of his Capital and surrounded by his armed protectors. The old man did not close his eyes, however, until he had assured himself, that Ellen Wade was among the females of the family, and that her relative, or lover, whichever he might be, had observed the caution of keeping himself out of view. After which he slept though with the peculiar watchfulness of one long accustomed to vigilance even in the hours of deepest night.

Chapter VI

"He is too picked, too spruce, too affected, too odd,
As it were too peregrinate, as I may call it."
Love's Labor's Lost, V.i.12–14.

THE ANGLO-AMERICAN is apt to boast, and not without reason, that his nation may claim a descent more truly honorable than that of any other people whose history is to be credited. Whatever might have been the weaknesses of the original colonists, their virtues have rarely been disputed. If they were superstitious, they were sincerely pious, and, consequently, honest. The descendants of these simple and single minded provincials have been content to reject the ordinary and artificial means by which honors have been perpetuated in families, and have substituted a standard which brings the individual himself to the ordeal of the public estimation, paying as little deference as may be to those who have gone before him. This forbearance, self denial, or common sense, or by whatever term it may be thought proper to distinguish the measure, has subjected the nation to the imputation of having an ignoble origin. Were it worth the inquiry, it would be found that more than a just proportion of the renowned names of the mother country are, at this hour, to be found in her ci-devant colonies, and it is a fact well known to the few who have wasted sufficient time to become the masters of so unimportant a subject, that the direct descendants of many a failing line, which the policy of England has seen fit to sustain by collateral supporters, are now discharging the simple duties of citizens in the bosom of this republic. The hive has remained stationary, and they who flutter around the venerable straw are wont to claim the empty distinction of antiquity, regardless alike of the frailty of their tenement and of the enjoyments of the numerous and vigorous swarms that are culling the fresher sweets of a virgin world. But as this is a subject which belongs rather to the politician and historian than to the humble narrator of the home-bred incidents we are about to reveal, we must confine our reflexions to such matters as have an immediate relation to the subject of the tale.

Although the citizen of the United States may claim so just an ancestry, he is far from being exempt from the penalties of his fallen race. Like causes are well known to produce like effects. That tribute, which it would seem nations must ever pay, by way of a weary probation, around the shrine of Ceres before they can be indulged in her fullest favors, is in some measure exacted in America, from the descendant instead of the ancestor. The march of civilization with us, has a strong analogy to that of all coming events, which are known "to cast their shadows before." The gradations of society, from that state which is called refined to that which approaches as near barbarity as connexion with an intelligent people will readily allow, are to be traced from the bosom of the states, where wealth, luxury and the arts are beginning to seat themselves, to those distant, and ever-receding borders which mark the skirts, and announce the approach, of the nation, as moving mists precede the signs of day.

Here, and here only, is to be found that widely spread, though far from numerous class, which may be at all likened to those who have paved the way for the intellectual progress of nations, in the old world. The resemblance between the American borderer and his European prototype is singular, though not always uniform. Both might be called without restraint; the one being above, the other beyond the reach of the law—brave, because they were inured to dangers—proud, because they were independant, and vindictive, because each was the avenger of his own wrongs. It would be unjust to the borderer to pursue the parallel much farther. He is irreligious, because he has inherited the knowledge that religion does not exist in forms, and his reason rejects a mockery. He is not a knight, because he has not the power to bestow distinctions; and he has not the power, because he is the offspring and not the parent of a system. In what manner these several qualities are exhibited, in some of the most strongly marked of the latter class, will be seen in the course of the ensuing narrative.

Ishmael Bush had passed the whole of a life of more than fifty years on the skirts of society. He boasted that he had never dwelt where he might not safely fell every tree he could view from his own threshold; that the law had rarely been known to enter his clearing, and that his ears had never willingly admitted the sound of a church bell. His exertions seldom exceeded his wants, which were peculiar to his class, and rarely failed of being supplied. He had no respect for any learning except that of the leech; because he was ignorant of the application of any other intelligence, than such as met the senses. His deference to this particular branch of science had induced him to listen to the application of a medical man, whose thirst for natural history had led him to the desire of profiting by the migratory propensities of the squatter. This gentleman he had cordially received into his family, or rather under his protection, and they had journeyed together, thus far through the Prairies, in perfect harmony: Ishmael often felicitating his wife on the possession of a companion, who would be so serviceable in their new abode, wherever it might chance to be, until the family were thoroughly "acclimated." The pursuits of the naturalist frequently led him, however, for days at a time, from the direct line of the route of the squatter, who rarely seemed to have any other guide than the sun. Most men would have deem'd themselves fortunate to have been absent on the perilous occasion of the Sioux inroad, as was Obed Bat, (or as he was fond of hearing himself called, Battius) M.D. and fellow of several cis-atlantic learned societies—the adventurous gentleman in question.

Although the sluggish nature of Ishmael was not actually awakened, it was sorely pricked by the liberties which had just been taken with his property. He slept, however, for it was the hour he had allotted to that refreshment, and because he knew how impotent any exertions to recover his effects must prove in the darkness of mid-night. He also knew the danger of his present situation too well, to hazard what was left, in pursuit of that which was lost. Much as the inhabitants of the Prairies were known to love horses, their attachment to many other articles, still in the possession of the travellers, was equally well understood. It was a common artifice to scatter the herds, and to profit by the confusion. But, Mahtoree had, it would seem in this particular, undervalued the acuteness of the man he had assailed. The phlegm with which the squatter learned his loss, has already been seen, and it now remains to exhibit the results of his more matured determinations.

Though the encampment contained many an eye that was long unclosed, and many an ear that listened greedily to catch the faintest evidence of any new alarm, it lay in deep quiet, during the remainder of the night. Silence and fatigue finally performed their accustomed offices, and before the morning, all but the sentinels were again buried in sleep. How well these indolent watchers discharged their duties after the assault, has never been known, inasmuch as nothing occurred to confirm or to disprove their subsequent vigilance.

Just as day, however, began to dawn, and a gray light was falling from the heavens on the dusky objects of the plain, the half-startled, anxious, and yet blooming countenance of Ellen Wade was reared above the confused mass of children, among whom she had clustered, on her stolen return to the camp. Arising warily, she stepp'd lightly across the recumbent bodies, and proceeded, with the same caution to the utmost limits of the defences of Ishmael. Here, she listened, as if doubting the propriety of venturing further. The pause was only momentary, however, and long before the drowsy eyes of the sentinel, who overlooked the spot where she stood, had time to catch a glimpse of her active form, it had glided along the bottom, and stood on the summit of the nearest eminence.

Ellen now listened, intently anxious to catch some other sound, than the breathing of the morning air, which faintly rustled the herbage at her feet. She was about to turn, in disappointment, from the inquiry, when the tread of human feet, making their way, through the matted grass, met her ear. Springing eagerly forward, she soon beheld the outlines of a figure advancing up the eminence, on the side opposite to the camp. She had already uttered the name of Paul, and was beginning to speak in the hurried and eager voice with which female affection is apt to greet a friend, when drawing back, the disappointed girl, clos'd her salutations, by coldly adding—

"I did not expect, Doctor, to meet you, at this unusual hour."

"All hours, and all seasons are alike, my good Ellen, to the genuine lover of nature," returned a small, slightly made, but exceedingly active man dressed in an odd mixture of cloth and skins, a little past the middle age, and who advanced directly

to her side, with the familiarity of an old acquaintance, "and he who does not know how to find things to admire by this gray light, is ignorant of a large portion of the blessings he enjoys."

"Very true," said Ellen, suddenly recollecting the necessity of accounting for her own appearance abroad, at that unseasonable hour, "I know many who think the earth has a pleasanter look, in the night, than when seen by the brightest sunshine."

"Ah! Their organs of sight must be too convex! But the man who wishes to study the active habits of the feline race or the variety, Albinos, must indeed be stirring at this hour. I dare say there are men, who prefer even looking at objects by twilight, for the simple reason, that they see better at that time of the day."

"And is this the cause why you are so much abroad, in the night?"

"I am abroad at night, my good girl, because the earth in its diurnal revolutions, leaves the light of the sun, but half the time on any given meridian, and because what I have to do, cannot be performed in twelve or fifteen consecutive hours. Now have I been off, two days from the family, in search of a plant, that is known to exist on the tributaries of La Platte, without seeing even a blade of grass that is not already enumerated and classed."

"You have been unfortunate, Doctor, but—"

"Unfortunate!" echoed the little man sideling nigher to his companion and producing his tabletts with an air, in which exultation struggled strangely with an affectation of self abasement. "No, no, Ellen, I am any thing but unfortunate. Unless indeed, a man may be so called, whose fortune is made—whose fame may be said to be established forever—whose name will go down to posterity with that of Buffon—Buffon! a mere compiler! one who flourishes on the foundation of other men's labours—no, pari passu, with Solander who bought his knowledge, with pain and privations!"

"Have you discovered a mine, Doctor Bat?"

"More than a mine; a treasure, coined, and fit for instant use, girl. Listen! I was making the angle, necessary to intersect the line of your uncle's march, after my fruitless search, when I heard sounds like the explosion produced by fire arms."

"Yes," exclaimed Ellen eagerly. "We had an alarm—"

"And thought I was lost," continued the man of science too much bent on his own ideas, to understand her interruption. "Little danger of that! I made my own base, knew the length of the perpendicular by calculation, and to draw the hypothenuse had nothing to do, but to work my angle. I supposed the guns were fired for my benefit, and changed my course for the sounds; not that I think the senses more accurate, or even as accurate as a mathematical calculation, but I feared, that some of the children might need my services."

"They are all happily—"

"Listen;" interrupted the other, already forgetting his affected anxiety for his patients, in the greater importance of the present subject. "I had crossed a large tract of Prairie, for sound is conveyed far, where there is little obstruction, when I heard the trampling of feet, as if Bisons, were beating the earth. Then I caught a distant view of a herd of quadrupeds, rushing up and down the swells, animals, which would have still remained unknown and undescribed, had it not been for a most felicitous accident. One, and he a noble specimen of the whole! was running a little apart from the rest. The herd made an inclination in my direction, in which the solitary animal coincided and this brought him, within fifty yards of the spot where I stood. I profited by the opportunity, and by the aid of steel and taper, I wrote his description on the spot. I would have given a thousand dollars, Ellen, for a single shot from the rifle of one of the boys."

"You carry a pistol, Doctor, why didn't you use it?" said the half inattentive girl, anxiously examining the Prairie, but still lingering where she stood, quite willing to be detained.

"Ay, but it carries nothing but the most minute particles of lead, adapted to the destruction of the larger insects and reptiles. No. I did better than to attempt waging a war, in which I could not be the victor. I recorded the event, noting each particular, with the precision necessary to science. You shall hear, Ellen, for you are a good and improving girl, and by retaining what you learn in this way, may yet be of great service to learning, should any accident occur to me. Indeed, my worthy Ellen, mine is a pursuit, which has its dangers as well as that of the warrior. This very night," he continued, glancing his eye behind him, "this awful night has the principle of life, itself, been in great danger of extinction!"

"By what?"

"By the monster I have discovered. It approached me, often, and ever as I receded it continued to advance. I believe nothing but the little lamp I carried was my protector. I kept it between us whilst I wrote, making it serve the double purpose of luminary and shield. But you shall hear the character of the beast, and you may then, judge of the risks we promoters of science run in behalf of mankind."

The naturalist raised his tabletts to the heavens and disposed himself to read as well as he could, by the dim light, they yet shed upon the plain, premising with saying—

"Listen, girl, and you shall hear, with what a treasure it has been my happy lot to enrich the pages of Natural History."

"Is it then a creature of your forming," said Ellen, turning away from her fruitless examination, with a sudden lighting of her sprightly blue eyes, that shewed she knew how to play with the foible of her learned companion.

"Is the power to give life to inanimate matter the gift of man; I would it were! You should speedily see a Historia Naturalis, Americana, that would put the sneering imitators of the Frenchman de Buffon to shame! A great improvement might be made in the formation of all quadrupeds; especially those in which velocity is a virtue. Two of the inferior limbs should be on the principle of the lever—wheels, perhaps as they are now formed, though I have not yet determined whether the improvement might be better applied to the anterior or posterior members, inasmuch as I am yet to learn whether dragging or shoving requires the greatest muscular exertion. A natural exudation of the animal, might assist in overcoming the friction, and a powerful momentum be obtained. But all this is hopeless; at least for the present," he added, raising his tabletts, again to the light and reading aloud. "Oct. 6, 1805, that's merely the date which I dare say you know better than I, mem. *Quadruped*; seen by star-light, and by the aid of a pocket lamp, in the Prairies of North America, see journal for Latitude and Meridian. *Genus*, unknown, therefore named after the Discoverer, and from the happy coincidence of having been seen in the evening—*Vespertilio*; *Horribilis*, *Americanus*. *Dimensions* (by estimation). *Greatest length* eleven feet, *height*, six feet. *Head*, erect, *nostrils*, expansive, *eyes*, expressive and fierce, *teeth*, serrated and abundant. *Tail*, horizontal, waving, and slightly feline. *Feet*, large and hairy. *Talons*, long, arquated, dangerous. *Ears*, inconspicuous. *Horns*, elongated, diverging and formidable, *colour*, plumbeous-ashy, with fiery spots. *Voice*, sonorous, martial and appalling. *Habits*, gregarious, carnivorous, fierce, and fearless. There," exclaimed Obed, when he had ended this sententious but comprehensive description, "there is an animal, which will be likely to dispute with the Lion, his title to be called the King of the Beasts!"

"I know not the meaning of all you have said, Doctor Battius," returned the quick witted girl, who understood the weakness of the Philosopher, and often indulged him with a title he loved so well to hear, "but I shall think it dangerous to venture far from the camp, if such monsters are prowling over the Prairies."

"You may well call it prowling," returned the Naturalist nestling still closer to her side, and dropping his voice to such low, and undignified tones, of confidence, as conveyed a meaning, still more pointed than he had intended. "I have never before experienced such a trial of the nervous system; there was a moment I acknowledge when the *fortiter in re* faltered before so terrible an enemy; but the love of Natural Science, bore me up, and brought me off in triumph!"

"You speak a language so different from that we use in Tennessee," said Ellen, struggling to conceal her laughter, "that I hardly know, whether I understand your meaning. If I am right, you wish to say you were chicken-hearted."

"An absurd simile, drawn from an ignorance of the formation of the biped. The heart of a chicken, bears a just proportion to its other organs, and the domestic fowl is, in a state of nature, a gallant bird. Ellen," he added with a countenance so solemn as to produce an impression on the attentive girl, "I was pursued—hunted—and in a danger that I scorn to dwell on—what's that."

Ellen started, for the earnestness and simple sincerity of her companion's manner had produced a certain degree of credulity, even on her buoyant mind. Looking in the direction indicated by the Doctor, she beheld, in fact, a beast coursing over the Prairie, and making a straight and rapid approach to the spot they occupied. The day was not yet sufficiently advanced, to enable her to distinguish its form and character, though enough was discernible to induce her to imagine it a fierce and savage animal.

"It comes! it comes!" exclaimed the Doctor, fumbling, by a sort of instinct for his tablets, while he fairly tottered on his feet, under the powerful efforts he made to maintain his ground. "Now Ellen, has fortune given me an opportunity to correct the errors made by star-light, hold, ashey plumbeous, no ears. Horns, excessive—"

His voice, and hand, were both arrested, by a roar, or rather a shriek from the beast, that was sufficiently terrific to appal even a stouter heart, than that of the Naturalist. The cries of the animal passed over the Prairie in strange cadences, and then succeeded a deep and solemn silence, that was only broken by an uncontrolled fit of merriment from the more musical voice of Ellen Wade. In the mean time, the Naturalist stood like a statue of amazement, permitting a well grown Ass, against whose approach he no longer offered his boasted shield of light, to smell about his person, without comment or hindrance.

"It is your own ass!" cried Ellen, the instant she found breath for words, "your own patient, hard-working hack!"

The Doctor roll'd his eyes from the beast to the speaker, and from the speaker to the beast, but gave no audible expression of his wonder.

"Do you refuse to know an animal that has laboured so long in your service!" continued the laughing girl. "A beast, that I have heard you say a thousand times, has served you well, and whom you loved like a brother!"

"Asinus Domesticus!" ejaculated the Doctor, drawing his breath like one who had been near suffocation. "There is no doubt of the genus; and I will always maintain that the animal is not of the species, equus. This is undeniably Asinus himself, Ellen Wade; but this is not the Vespertilio Horribilis of the Prairies! Very different animals, I can assure you, young woman, and differently characterised in every important particular. That, carnivorous," he continued glancing his eye at the open page of his tablets; "this, granivorous; *habits*, fierce, dangerous; *habits*, patient, abstemious; *ears*, inconspicuous; *ears*, elongated; *horns*, diverging, etc. *horns*, none!"

He was interrupted by another burst of merriment from Ellen, which served, in some measure, to recall him to his recollection.

"The image of the Vespertilio was on the retina," the astounded enquirer into the secrets of nature observed, in a manner that seemed a little apologetic, "and I was silly enough to mistake my own faithful beast for the monster? Though even now I greatly marvel to see this animal running at large!"

Ellen then proceeded to explain, the history of the attack and its results. She described, with an accuracy that might have raised suspicions of her own movements in the mind of one less simple than her auditor, the manner in which the beasts burst out of the encampment and the headlong speed with which they had dispersed themselves over the open plain. Although she forbore to say as much in terms, she so managed as to present before the eyes of her listener the strong probability of his having mistaken the frightened drove for savage beasts, and then terminated her account by a lamentation for their loss, and some very natural remarks on the helpless condition in which it had left the family. The naturalist listened in silent wonder, neither interrupting her narrative nor suffering a single exclamation of surprise to escape him. The keen-eyed girl, however, saw that as she proceeded the important leaf was torn from the tablets, in a manner which shewed that their owner had got rid of his delusion at the same instant. From that moment the world has heard no more of the Vespertilio Horribilis Americanus, and the natural sciences have irretrieveably lost an important link in that great animated chain which is said to connect earth and heaven, and in which man is thought to be so familiarly complicated with the monkey.

When Dr. Batt was put in full possession of all the circumstances of the inroad, his concern immediately took a different direction. He had left sundry folios, and certain boxes well stored with botanical specimens and defunct animals, under the good keeping of Ishmael, and it immediately struck his acute mind, that marauders as subtle as the Siouxes would never neglect the opportunity to despoil him of these treasures. Nothing that Ellen could say to the contrary served to appease his apprehensions, and, consequently, they separated; he to relieve his doubts and fears together, and she to glide, as swiftly and silently as she had just before passed it, into the still and solitary tent.

Chapter VII

"What, fifty of my followers, at a clap!"
King Lear, I.iv.294.

THE DAY had now fairly opened on the seemingly, interminable waste of the Prairie. The entrance of Obed, at such a moment into the camp, accompanied, as it was, by vociferous lamentations over his anticipated loss, did not fail to rouse the drowsy family of the squatter. Ishmael and his sons, together with the forbidding looking brother of his wife, were all, speedily afoot; and then, as the sun began to shed his light on the place, they became gradually apprised of the extent of their loss.

Ishmael look'd round upon the motionless and heavily loaded vehicles, with his teeth firmly compressed, cast a glance at the amazed and helpless groupe of children which clustered around their sullen but desponding, mother, and walked out upon the open land, as if he found the air of the encampment, too confined. He was followed by several of the men, who were attentive observers, watching the dark expression of his eye, as the index of their own future movements. The whole proceeded in profound and moody silence to the summit of the nearest swell, whence they could command an almost boundless view of the naked plains. Here, nothing was visible, but a solitary buffaloe, that gleaned a meagre subsistence from the decaying herbage, at no great distance, and the Ass of the Physician, who profited by his freedom to enjoy a meal richer than common.

"Yonder is one of the creaturs left by the villians to mock us!" said Ishmael, glancing his eye towards the latter, "and that the meanest of the stock. This is a hard country to make a crop in, boys; and yet food must be found to fill many hungry mouths!"

"The rifle, is better than the hoe in such a place as this," returned the eldest of his sons, kicking the hard and thirsty soil on which he stood, with an air of contempt. "It is good for such as they, who make their dinner better on beggar's beans, than on homminy. A crow would shed tears, if obliged by its errand to fly across this district!"

"What say you, trapper," resumed the Father, showing the slight impression his powerful heel, had made on the compact earth, and laughing with frightful ferocity. "Is this the quality of land a man would choose, who never troubles the County Clerk with Title deeds!"

"There is richer soil in the bottoms," returned the old man, calmly, "and you have passed millions of acres, to get to this dreary spot, where he who loves to till the 'arth might have received bushels in return for pints, and that too at the cost of no very grievous labour. If you have come in search of land, you have journeyed hundreds of miles too far, or as many leagues too little."

"There is, then, a better choice, towards the other Ocean?" demanded the squatter pointing in the direction of the Pacific.

"There is; and I have seen it all," was the answer of the other, who dropped his rifle to the earth, and stood leaning on its barrel like one who recalled the scenes he had witnessed, with melancholy pleasure. "I have seen the waters of the two seas. On one of them, was I born, and raised to be a lad, like yonder tumbling boy. America has grown, my man, since the days of my youth, to be a country larger than I once had thought the world itself to be. Near seventy years, I dwelt in York, Province and State, together. You've been in York, 'tis like?"

"Not I—not I, I never visited the towns; but often have heard the place you speak of named. 'Tis a wide clearing, there, I reckon!"

"Too wide! Too wide! They scourge the very 'arth with their axes. Such hills and hunting grounds as I have seen stripped of the gifts of the Lord; without remorse or shame! I tarried till the mouths of my hounds were deafened by the blows of the choppers, and then I came west, in search of quiet. It was a grievous journey, that I made; a grievous toil to pass through falling timber, and to breathe the thick air of smoky clearings week after week, as I did. 'Tis a far country too, that State of York, from this!"

"It lies ag'in the outer edge of old Kentuck I reckon; though what the distance may be, I never knew."

"A gull, would have to fan a thousand miles of air, to find

the Eastern Sea. And yet it is no mighty reach to hunt across, when shade and game are plenty! The time has been, when I followed the deer in the mountains of the Delaware and Hudson, and took the beaver on the streams of the Upper Lakes in the same season; but my eye was quick and certain at that day, and my limbs were like the legs of a moose. The dam of Hector," dropping his look kindly to the aged hound that crouch'd at his feet, "was then a pup, and apt to open on the game, the moment she struck the scent. She gave me a deal of trouble, that slut; she did!"

"Your hound is old, stranger, and a rap on the head would prove a mercy to the beast."

"The dog is like his master," returned the trapper without appearing to heed the brutal advice the other gave, "and will number his days when his work amongst the game is over, and not before. To my eye, things seem ordered to meet each other, in this creation. Tis not the swiftest running deer that always throws off the hounds, nor the biggest arm that holds the truest rifle. Look around you, men; what will the Yankee choppers say, when they have cut their path from the eastern to the western waters, and find that a hand, which can lay the 'arth bare at a blow, has been here, and swept the country, in very mockery of their wickedness. They will turn on their tracks, like a fox that doubles, and then the rank smell of their own footsteps, will show them the madness of their waste. Howsom'ever, these are thoughts that are more likely to rise in him who has seen the folly of Eighty seasons, than to teach wisdom to men, still bent on the pleasures of their kind! You have need yet of a stirring time, if you think to escape the craft and hatred of the burnt-wood Indians. They claim to be the lawful owners of this Country, and seldom leave a white, more than the skin he boasts of, when once they get the power, as they always have the will, to do him harm."

"Old man," said Ishmael, sternly, "to which people do you belong? You have the colour and speech of a Christian, while it seems that your heart is with the red-skins."

"To me there is little difference in Nations. The people I lov'd most, are scattered as the sands of the dry river-beds fly before the Fall hurricanes, and life is too short, to make use and custom, with strangers, as one can do with such as he has dwelt amongst for years. Still am I a man, without the cross of Indian blood; and what is due from a warrior to his Nation, is owing by me to the people of the States; though little need, have they, with their militia and their armed boats, of help from a single arm of fourscore."

"Since you own your kin, I may ask a simple question. Where are the Siouxes who have stolen my cattle?"

"Where is the herd of Buffaloe, which was chased by the Panther across this plain, no later, than the morning of yesterday. It is as hard—"

"Friend," said Dr. Battius, who had hitherto been an attentive listener, but who, now, felt a sudden impulse to mingle in the discourse, "I am grieved when I find a venator or hunter of your experience and observation, following the current of vulgar error. The animal you describe, is in truth a species of the bos ferus or bos sylvestris, as he has been happily called by the poets, but, though of close affinity it is altogether distinct, from the common Bubulus. Bison is the better word, and I would suggest the necessity of adopting it in future, when you shall have occasion to allude to the species."

"Bison or Buffaloe, it makes but little matter. The creatur' is the same, call it by what name you will, and—"

"Pardon me, venerable venator; as classification is the very soul of the Natural Sciences, the animal or vegetable, must, of necessity, be characterised by the peculiarities of its species, which is always indicated by the name."

"Friend," said the trapper, a little positively, "would the tail of a beaver make the worse dinner, for calling it a mink? or could you eat of the wolf, with relish, because some bookish man, had given it the name of venison?"

As these questions were put with no little earnestness and some spirit, there was every probability that a hot discussion would have succeeded between two men, of whom one was so purely practical and the other so much given to theory, had not Ishamel, seen fit to terminate the dispute by bringing into view a subject that was much more important to his own immediate interests.

"Beavers' tails, and minks-flesh may do to talk about, before a maple fire and a quiet hearth," interrupted the squatter, without the smallest deference to the interested feelings of the disputants, "but, something more than foreign words, or words of any sort, is now needed. Tell me, trapper; where are your Siouxes, skulking?"

"It would be as easy to tell you the colours of the hawk, that is floating beneath yonder white cloud! When a red-skin strikes his blow, he is not apt to wait, until he is paid for the evil deed, in lead."

"Will the beggarly savages believe they have enough, when they find themselves master of all the stock?"

"Natur is much the same, let it be covered by what skin it may. Do you ever find your longings after riches less when you have made a good crop than before you were master of a kernel of corn. If you do, you differ from what the experience of a long life, tells me is the common cravings of man."

"Speak plainly, old stranger," said the squatter, striking the butt of his rifle heavily on the earth, his dull capacity finding no pleasure in a discourse that was conducted in so obscure allusions, "I have asked a simple question, and one I know well that you can answer."

"You are right, you are right, I can answer; for I have too often seen the disposition of my kind, to mistake it, when evil is stirring. When the Siouxes have gathered in the beasts, and have made sure that you are not upon their heels, they will be back nibbling like hungry wolves to take the bait they have left. Or it may be they'll show the temper of the Great Bears that are found at the falls of the Long River, and strike at once with the paw, without stopping to nose their prey."

"You have then, seen, the animals you mention!" exclaimed Dr. Battius, who had now been thrown out of the conversation quite as long as his impatience could well brook, and who approached the subject, with his tabletts ready opened, as a book of reference. "Can you tell me if what you encountered was of the species, Ursus Horribilis, with the *ears* rounded, *front*, arquated, *eyes*, destitute of the remarkable supplemental lid, with six insicores—one false, and four perfect molares—"

"Trapper, go on, for we are engaged in reasonable discourse," interrupted Ishmael; "you believe we shall see more of these robbers."

"Nay, nay, I do not call them robbers, for it is the usage of their people, and what may be called the Prairie law."

"I have come five hundred miles to find a place, where no man can ding the words of the Law, in my ears," said Ishmael, fiercely, "and I am not in a humour to stand quietly at a bar, while a red-skin sits in judgement. I tell you, trapper, if another Sioux is seen prowling around my camp, wherever it may be, he shall feel the contents of old Kentuck," slapping his rifle in a manner that could not be easily misconstrued, "though he wore the medal of Washington* himself. I call the man a robber who takes that which is not his own."

"The Teton and the Pawnee and the Konza, and men of a dozen other tribes claim to own these naked fields."

"Natur gives them the lie, in their teeth. The air, the water and the ground are free gifts to man, and no one has the power to portion them out in parcels. Man must drink, and breathe and walk, and therefore each has a right to his share of 'arth. Why do not the Surveyors of the States, set their compasses and run their lines over our heads, as well as beneath our feet? Why do they not, cover their shining sheep skins with big words, giving to this land-holder, or perhaps he should be called air-holder, so many rods of heaven, with the use of such a star for a boundary mark and such a cloud to turn a mill!"

As the squatter uttered his wild conceit, he laughed from the very bottom of his chest, in scorn. The deriding but frightful merriment pass'd from the mouth of one of his ponderous sons to that of the other, until it had made the circuit of the whole family.

"Come, trapper," continued Ishmael in a tone of better humour, like a man who feels that he has triumphed, "neither of us, I reckon, has ever had much to do with title deeds or County Clerks, or blazed trees; therefore we will not waste words on fooleries. You ar' a man, that has tarried long in this clearing, and, now I ask your opinion, face to face, without fear or favor, if you had the lead in my business, what would you do."

*The American government creates chiefs among the western tribes, and decorates them with silver medals bearing the impression of the different Presidents. That of Washington is the most prized.

The old man hesitated, and seem'd to give the required advice with deep reluctance. As every eye, however, was fastened on him, and whichever way he turned his face, he encountered a look rivetted on the lineaments of his own working countenance, he answered in a low, melancholy, tone.

"I have seen too much mortal blood, poured out in empty quarrels, to wish ever to hear an angry rifle, again. Ten weary years have I sojourned alone, on these naked plains, waiting for my hour, and not a blow have I struck ag'in an enemy more humanized than the grizzly bear."

"Ursus horribilis!" muttered the Doctor.

The speaker paused at the sound of the other's voice, but perceiving it was no more than a sort of mental ejaculation, he continued in the same strain—

"More humanized than the grizzly bear, or the Panther of the Rocky Mountains; unless the Beaver, which is a wise and knowing animal may be so reckoned. What would I advise! Even the female Buffaloe will fight for her young!"

"It never then shall be said, that Ishmael Bush, has less kindness for his children, than the bear for her cubs."

"And yet this is but a naked spot, for a dozen men to make head in, ag'in five hundred."

"Ay, it is so," returned the squatter glancing his eye towards his humble camp, "but something might be done, with the wagons and the cotton wood."

The trapper shook his head, incredulously, and pointed across the rolling plain in the direction of the west, as he answered.

"A rifle would send a bullet from these hills into your very sleeping-cabins; nay, arrows from the thicket in your rear would keep you, all, burrowed like so many Prairie dogs: it wouldn't do—it wouldn't do. Three long miles from this spot, is a place where, as I have often thought, in passing across this desert, a stand might be made, for days and weeks together, if there were hearts and hands ready to engage in the bloody work."

Another low, deriding laugh, passed among the young men, announcing in a manner sufficiently intelligible their readiness to undertake a task, even more arduous. The squatter himself, eagerly seized the hint, which had been so reluctantly extorted from the trapper, who by some singular process of reasoning had, evidently, persuaded himself that it was his duty to be strictly neutral. A few direct and pertinent inquiries, served to obtain the little additional information that was necessary, in order to make the contemplated movement, and then Ishmael, who was, on emergencies, as terrifically energetic, as he was sluggish in common, set about effecting his object without delay.

Notwithstanding the industry and zeal of all engaged, the task was one of great labor and difficulty. The loaded vehicles were to be drawn by hand across a wide distance of plain, without track, or guide of any sort, except that which the trapper furnished, by communicating his knowledge of the cardinal points of the compass. In accomplishing this object, the gigantic strength of the men was taxed to the utmost, nor were the females or the children spared a heavy proportion of the toil. While the sons distributed themselves about the heavily loaded wagons and drew them, by main strength up the neighboring swell, their mother and Ellen, surrounded by the amazed groupe of little ones, followed slowly in the rear, bending under the weight of such different articles, as were suited to their several strengths.

Ishmael, himself, superintended and directed the whole, occasionally applying his colossal shoulder to some lagging vehicle until he saw that the chief difficulty, that of gaining the level of their intended route, was accomplished. Then he pointed out the required course, cautioning his sons to proceed, in such a manner, that they should not lose the advantage they had with so much labour obtained, and beckoning to the brother of his wife, they returned, together, to the empty camp.

Throughout the whole of this movement, which occupied an hour of time, the trapper had stood apart, leaning on his rifle with the aged hound slumbering at his feet, a silent but attentive observer of all that passed. Occasionally, a smile, lighted his hard, muscular, but wasted features, like a gleam of sunshine, flitting across a ragged ruin, and betrayed the momentary pleasure he found, in witnessing from time to time the vast power the youths discovered. Then, as the train drew slowly up the ascent, a cloud of thought and sorrow threw all into the shade again, leaving the expression of his countenance, in its usual state of quiet melancholy. As vehicle, after vehicle left the place of the encampment, he noted the change, with increasing attention, seldom failing to cast an enquiring look at the little, neglected tent, which with its proper wagon, still remained, as before, solitary and apparently forgotten. The summons of Ishmael to his gloomy associate, had, however, as it would now seem, this, hitherto, neglected portion of his effects, for its object.

First casting a cautious and suspicious glance on every side of him, the squatter and his companion advanced to the little wagon, and caused it to enter within the folds of the cloth, much in the manner, that it had been extricated the preceding evening. They both then disappeared behind the drapery, and many moments of suspense succeeded, during which, the old man, secretly urged by a burning desire to know the meaning of so much mystery, insensibly drew nigh to the place, until he stood within a few yards of the proscribed spot. The agitation of the cloth, betrayed the nature of the occupation of those whom it concealed, though their work was conducted in rigid silence. It would appear that long practice had made each of the two, acquainted with his particular duty, for neither sign nor direction of any sort was necessary from Ishmael, in order to apprise his surly associate of the manner in which he was to proceed. In less time, than has been consumed in relating it, the interior portion of the arrangement was complete, when the men re-appeared without the tent. Too busy with his occupation to heed the presence of the trapper, Ishmael, began to release the folds of the cloth from the ground, and to dispose of them, in such a manner, around the vehicle, as to form a sweeping train to the new form the little pavillion had now assumed. The arch'd roof trembled with the occasional movement of the light vehicle, which, it was now apparent, once more supported its secret burthen. Just as the work was ended, the scowling eye of Ishmael's assistant caught a glimpse of the figure of the attentive observer of their movements. Dropping the shaft, which he had already lifted from the ground, preparatory to occupying the place, that was usually filled by an animal less reasoning, and perhaps less dangerous than himself, he bluntly exclaimed—

"I am a fool, as you often say! But look for yourself: if that man is not an enemy, I will disgrace father and mother, call myself an Indian, and go hunt with the Siouxes."

The cloud, as it is about to discharge the subtle lightning, is not more dark nor threatening, than the look with which Ishmael greeted the intruder. He turned his head on every side of him, as if seeking some engine sufficiently terrible to annihilate the offending trapper at a blow, and, then, possibly recollecting the further occasion he might have for his counsel, he forced himself, to say with an appearance of moderation that nearly choked him—

"Stranger, I did believe this prying into the concerns of others, was the business of women in the towns and settlements, and not the manner in which men, who are used to live where each has room for himself, deal with the secrets of their neighbors. To what lawyer or sheriff do you calculate to sell your news?"

"I hold but little discourse except with one; and, then, chiefly of my own affairs," returned the old man, without the least observable apprehension, and pointing imposingly upward, "a judge; and judge of all. Little does he need knowledge from my hands, and but little will your wish to keep any thing secret from him, profit you, even, in this desert."

The mounting tempers of his unnurtured listeners were rebuked by the simple, solemn, manner of the trapper. Ishmael stood, sullen and thoughtful; while his companion stole a furtive and involuntary glance at the placid sky which spread, so wide and blue above his head, as if he expected, to see, the Almighty eye, itself, beaming from the heavenly vault. But impressions of a serious character are seldom lasting on minds long indulged in forgetfulness. The hesitation of the squatter was consequently of short duration. The language, however, as well as the firm and collected air of the speaker, were the means of preventing much subsequent abuse if not violence.

"It would be shewing more of the kindness of a friend and comrade," Ishmael returned in a tone sufficiently sullen to betray his humour, though it was no longer threatening, "had your shoulder been put to the wheel of one of yonder wagons, instead of edging itself in here, where none are wanted, but such as are invited."

"I can put the little strength that is left me," returned the trapper, "to this as well as to another of your loads."

"Do you take us for boys!" exclaimed Ishmael, laughing half in ferocity and half in derision, applying his powerful strength at the same time, to the little vehicle, which rolled over the grass, with as much seeming facility, as if it were drawn by its usual team.

The trapper paused, and followed the departing wagon with his eye, marvelling greatly as to the nature of its concealed contents, until it had, also, gained the summit of the eminence, and, in its turn, disappeared behind the swell of the land. Then, he turned to gaze at the desolation of the scene around him. The absence of human forms would have scarce created a sensation in the bosom of one so long accustomed to solitude, had not the site of the deserted camp, furnished such strong memorials of its recent visiters, and, as the old man was quick to detect, of their waste also. He cast his eye upwards with a shake of the head, at the vacant spot in the heavens, which had so lately been filled by the branches of those trees, that now lay, stripped of their verdure, worthless and deserted logs at his feet.

"Ay!" he muttered to himself, "I might have know'd it! I might have know'd it! Often have I seen the same before, and yet I brought them to the spot myself, and have now sent them to the only neighborhood of their kind, within many long leagues of the spot where I stand. This is man's wish, and pride, and waste, and sinfulness. He tames the beasts of the field, to feed his idle wants, and having robbed the brutes of their natural food, he teaches them to strip the 'arth of its trees, to quiet their hunger."

A rustling in the low bushes, which still grew, for some distance, along the swale that formed the thicket on which the camp of Ishmael had rested, caught his ear, at the moment, and cut short the soliloquy. The habits of so many years spent in the wilderness, caused the old man to bring his rifle to a poise with something like the activity and promptitude of his youth, but suddenly recovering his recollection, he dropped it into the hollow of his arm again, and resumed his air of melancholy resignation.

"Come forth, come forth," he said aloud, "be ye bird or be ye beast, ye are safe from these old hands. I have eaten and I have drunk, why should I take life, when my wants call for no sacrifice. It will not be long afore the birds will peck at eyes that shall not see them, and perhaps light on my very bones, for if things like these are only made to perish, why am I to expect to live forever. Come, forth. Come, forth! you are safe from harm at these weak hands."

"Thank you for the good word, old trapper," cried Paul Hover, springing actively forward from his place of concealment. "There was an air about you, when you threw forward the muzzle of the piece, that I did not like; for it seem'd to say that you were master of all the rest of the motions."

"You are right! you are right!" cried the trapper laughing, with inward self-complacency, at the recollection of his former skill. "The day has been, when few men knew the virtues of a long rifle, like this I carry, better than myself, old and useless as I now seem. You are right, young man, and the time was, when it was dangerous to move a leaf, within ear-shot of my stand, or," he added dropping his voice and looking serious, "for a red Mingo, to show an eye-ball from his ambushment. You have heard of the Red Mingos."

"I have heard of minks," said Paul, taking the old man by the arm, and gently urging him towards the thicket as he spoke, while at the same time, he cast quick and uneasy glances behind him, in order to make sure he was not observed. "Of your common black minks, but none of any other colour."

"Lord, Lord," continued the trapper, shaking his head and still laughing in his deep but quiet manner, "the boy mistakes a brute for a man. Though, a Mingo is little better than a beast, or, for that matter, he is worse, when rum and opportunity are placed before his eyes. There was that accursed Huron, from the Upper Lakes, that I knocked from his perch, among the rocks, in the hills back of the Hori—"

His voice was lost in the thicket, into which he had suffered himself to be led by Paul, while speaking, too much occupied by thoughts which dwelt on scenes and acts that had taken place, half a century earlier, in the History of the Country, to offer the smallest resistance.

Chapter VIII

"Now they are clapper-clawing one another; I'll go look on. That dissembling abominable varlet, Diomed, has got that same scurvy, doting, foolish young knave in his helm."

Troilus and Cressida, V.iv.1–4.

IT IS NECESSARY, in order that the thread of the narrative should not be spun to a length which might fatigue the reader, that he should imagine a week to have intervened between the scene, with which the preceding chapter closed, and the events, with which it is our intention to resume its relation in this. The season was on the point of changing its character, the verdure of summer giving place, more rapidly, to the brown and party coloured livery of the Fall.* The heavens were clothed in driving clouds, piled in vast masses one above the other, which whirled violently, in the gusts, opening, occasionally, to admit transient glimpses of the bright and glorious sight of the heavens, dwelling in a magnificence by far too grand and durable, to be disturbed by the fitful efforts of the lower world. Beneath, the wind swept across the wild and naked Prairies, with a violence that is seldom witnessed, in any section of the continent less open. It would have been easy to have imagined, in the ages of Fable, that the god of the winds had permitted his subordinate agents to escape from their den, and that they now rioted, in wantonness, across wastes, where neither tree, nor work of man, nor mountain, nor obstacle of any sort opposed itself to their gambols.

Though nakedness, might, as usual, be given as the pervading character of the spot, whither it is now necessary to transfer the scene of the tale, it was not, entirely without the signs of human life. Amid the monotonous rolling of the Prairies, a single, naked, and ragged rock arose, on the margin of a little water course, which found its way, after winding a vast distance through the plains, into one of the numerous tributaries of the Father of Rivers. A swale of low land, lay near the base of the eminence, and as it was still fringed with a

*The Americans call the autumn the "fall," from the fall of the leaf.

thicket of alders and sumack, it bore the signs of having once nurtured a feeble growth of wood. The trees themselves, had been transferred, however, to the summit and crags of the neighboring rocks. On this elevation the signs of man to which this allusion just made applies were to be found.

Seen from beneath, there were visible a breast-work of logs and stones, intermingled in such a manner as to save all unnecessary labour, a few low roofs made of bark and boughs of trees, an occasional barrier, constructed like the defences on the summit, and placed on such points of the acclivity as were easier of approach than the general face of the eminence, and a little dwelling of cloth, perched on the apex of a small pyramid that shot up, on one angle of the rock, the white covering of which glimmered from a distance like a spot of snow, or to make the simile more suitable to the rest of the subject, like a spotless and carefully guarded standard, which was to be protected by the dearest blood of those who defended the citadel beneath. It is hardly necessary to add that this rude and characteristic fortress was the place, where Ishmael Bush had taken refuge, after the robbery of his flocks and herds.

On the day to which the narrative is advanced, the squatter was standing near the base of the rocks, leaning on his rifle, and regarding the sterile soil that supported him, with a look, in which contempt and disappointment were strongly blended.

"'Tis time to change our naturs," he observed to the brother of his wife, who was rarely far from his elbow, "and to become ruminaters instead of people used to the fare of Christians and free men. I reckon, Abiram, you could glean a living among the grasshoppers; you ar' an active man, and might outrun the nimblest skipper of them all."

"The country will never do," returned the other, who relished but little the forced humour of his kinsman; "and it is well, to remember that a lazy traveller, makes a long journey!"

"Would you have me draw a cart at my heels, across this desert, for weeks; ay, months!" retorted Ishmael, who like all of his class could labor with incredible efforts on emergencies, but who too seldom exerted continued industry on any occasion to brook a proposal that offered so little repose. "It may do for your people who live in settlements, to hasten on, to their houses. But thank Heaven, my farm is too big, for its owner ever to want a resting place."

"Since you like the Plantation, then, you have only to make your crop!"

"That is easier said than done, on this corner of the estate. I tell you, Abiram, there is need of moving for more reasons than one. You know I'm a man, that very seldom enters into a bargain, but who always fulfils his agreements better than your dealers in wordy contracts written on rags of paper. If there's one mile, there ar' a hundred still needed to make up the distance for which you have my honour."

As he spoke, the squatter glanced his eye upward at the little tenement of cloth, which crowned the summit of his ragged fortress. The look was understood and answered by the other, and by some secret influence, which operated either through their interests or feelings, it served to re-establish that harmony between them which had just been threatened with something like a momentary breach.

"I know it, and feel it, in every bone of my body. But I remember the reason why I have set myself on this accursed journey, too well, to forget the distance between me and the end. Neither you nor I, will ever be the better for what we have done, unless we thoroughly finish what is so well begun. Ay, that is the doctrine of the whole world, I judge: I heard a travelling Preacher, who was skirting it down the Ohio, a time since, say that if a man should live up to the faith, for a hundred years, and then fall from his work a single day, he would find the settlement was to be made for the finishing blow that he had put to his job, and that all the bad and none of the good would come into the final account."

"And you believed the hungry hypocrite?"

"Who said that I believed it!" retorted Abiram with a bullying look, that betrayed how much, his fears had dwelt on the subject he affected to despise. "Is it believing to tell what a roguish—and yet Ishmael, the man might have been honest after all. He told us that the world was, in truth, no better than a desert, and that there was but one hand that could lead the most learned man through all its crooked windings. Now, if this be true of the whole, it may be true of a part."

"Abiram, out with your grievances like a man," interrupted the squatter with a hoarse laugh. "You want to pray! But of what use will it be, according to your own doctrine, to serve God, five minutes and the Devil an hour. Harkee, friend, I'm not much of a husbandman, but this I know to my cost; that to make a right good crop even on the richest bottom, there must be hard labor, and your snufflers liken the 'arth to a field of corn, and the men who live on it, to its yield. Now I tell you, Abiram; that you are no better than a thistle or a mullen; yea, ye ar' wood, of too open a pore to be good even to burn."

The malign glance, which shot from the scowling eye of Abiram, announced the angry character of his feelings, but as the furtive look quailed, immediately before the unmoved, steady, countenance of the squatter, it also betrayed how much the bolder spirit of the latter had obtained the mastery over his craven nature.

Content with his ascendancy, which was too apparent, and had been too often exerted on similar occasions, to leave him in any doubt of its extent, Ishmael coolly continued the discourse, by adverting more directly to his future plans.

"You will own the justice of paying every one, in kind," he said. "I have been robbed of my stock; and I have a scheme to make myself as good as before, by taking hoof for hoof, or, for that matter, when a man is put to the trouble of bargaining for both sides, he is a fool if he dont pay himself, something in the way of commission."

As the squatter made this declaration in a tone, which was a little excited by the humour of the moment, four or five of his lounging sons, who had been leaning against the foot of the rock, came forward, with the indolent step, so common to the family.

"I have been calling Ellen Wade, who is on the rock keeping the look out, to know if there is any thing to be seen," observed the eldest of the young men; "and she shakes her head, for an answer. Ellen is sparing of her words for a woman; and might be taught manners, at least, without spoiling her good looks."

Ishmael cast his eye upward, to the place where the offending, but unconscious girl was holding her anxious watch. She was seated at the edge of the uppermost crag, by the side of the little tent, and, at least, two hundred feet, above the level of the plain. Little else was to be distinguished at that distance, but the outline of her form, her fair hair streaming, in the gusts beyond her shoulders, and the steady, and seemingly unchangeable look that she had rivetted on some remote point of the Prairie.

"What is it, Nell?" cried Ishmael, lifting his powerful voice a little above the rushing of the element. "Have you got a glimpse of any thing, bigger than a burrowing barker?"

The lips of the attentive Ellen parted, she rose to the utmost height her small stature admitted, seeming still to regard the unknown object, but her voice, if she spoke at all, was not sufficiently loud to be heard amid the wind.

"It ar' a fact, that the child sees something more uncommon than a buffaloe or a Prairie dog!" continued Ishmael. "Why, Nell; girl, ar' ye deaf? Nell, I say: I hope it is an army of red-skins she has in her eye; for I should relish the chance to pay them, for their kindness, under the favor of these logs and rocks!"

As the squatter accompanied his vaunt with corresponding gestures, and directed his eyes to the circle of his equally confident sons while speaking, he drew their gaze from Ellen to himself; but, now, when they turned together to note the succeeding movements of their female sentinel, the place which had, so lately, been occupied by her form, was vacant.

"As I am a sinner," exclaimed Asa, usually one of the most phlegmatic of the youths, "the girl is blown away by the wind!"

Something like a sensation was exhibited among them, which might have denoted that the influence of the laughing blue eyes, flaxen hair, and glowing cheeks of Ellen had not been lost on the dull natures of the young men, and looks of amazement mingled slightly with concern, passed from one to the other, as they gazed in dull wonder at the point of the naked rock.

"It might well be!" added another. "She sat on a slivered stone, and, I have been thinking, of telling her she was in danger, for more than an hour."

"Is that a ribband of the child, dangling from the corner of the hill below!" cried Ishmael, "Ha! who is moving about the tent! Have I not told you, all—"

"Ellen! tis Ellen!" interrupted the whole body of his sons in a breath; and at that instant she re-appeared to put an end to their different surmises, and, to relieve more than one sluggish nature from its unwonted excitement. As Ellen issued from beneath the folds of the tent, she advanced with a light and fearless step to her former giddy stand, and pointed, toward the Prairie, appearing to speak in an eager and rapid voice to some invisible auditor.

"Nell is mad!" said Asa, half in contempt, and yet not a little in concern. "The girl is dreaming with her eyes open; and thinks she sees some of them fierce creaturs with hard names, with which the Doctor fills her ears."

"Can it be the child has found a scout of the Siouxes!" said Ishmael, bending his look towards the plain; but, a low, significant whisper from Abiram, drew his eyes quickly upward, again, where they were turned just in time, to perceive that the cloth of the tent, was agitated by a motion very evidently different from the quivering occasioned by the wind. "Let her, if she dare!" the squatter muttered, in his teeth. "Abiram; they know my temper too well, to play the prank with me."

"Look for yourself! if the curtain is not lifted, I can see no better than the owl, by day light."

Ishmael struck the breech of his rifle violently on the earth, and shouted, in a voice that might easily have been heard by Ellen, had not her attention still continued rapt on the object, which, so unaccountably attracted her eyes in the distance.

"Nell!" continued the squatter, "Away with you, fool! Will you bring down punishment on your own head. Why, Nell! She has forgotten her native speech; let us see, if she can understand another language."

Ishmael threw his rifle to his shoulder, and at the next moment it was pointed upward at the summit of the rock. Before time was given for a word of remonstrance, it had sent forth its contents, in its usual streak of bright flame. Ellen started like the frightened chamois, and uttering a piercing scream, she darted into the tent, with a swiftness, that left it uncertain, whether terror or actual injury, had been the penalty of her offence.

The action of the squatter was too sudden and unexpected to admit of prevention, but the instant it was done, his sons manifested, in an unequivocal manner the temper with which they witnessed the desperate measure. Angry and fierce glances were interchanged, and a murmur of disapprobation was uttered by the whole, in common.

"What has Ellen done, Father," said Asa, with a degree of spirit, which was the more striking from being unusual, "that she should be shot at, like a straggling deer or a hungry wolf!"

"Mischief," deliberately returned the squatter, but with a cool expression of defiance in his eye, that show'd, how little he was mov'd by the ill concealed humour of his children. "Mischief, boy; mischief. Take you heed, that the disorder dont spread."

"It would need a different treatment in a man, than in yon screaming girl."

"Asa, you ar' a man, as you have often boasted; but, remember I am your Father, and your better."

"I know it well—and what sort of a Father!"

"Harkee, boy: I more than half believe, that your drowsy head, let in the Siouxes. Be modest in speech, my watchful son, or you may have to answer yet for the mischief, your own bad conduct has brought upon us."

"I'll stay no longer to be hectored like a child in petticoats. You talk of law, as if you knew of none; and yet you keep me, down, as though I had not life and wants of my own. I'll stay no longer to be treated like one of your meanest cattle!"

"The world is wide, my gallant boy, and there's many a noble plantation, on it, without a tenant. Go, you have title deeds, sign'd and seal'd to your hand. Few Fathers portion their children better than Ishmael Bush, you will say that for me, at least when you get to be a wealthy land holder."

"Look, Father, look!" exclaimed several voices at once, seizing with avidity, an opportunity to interrupt a dialogue, which threatened to become more violent.

"Look!" repeated Abiram, in a voice, which sounded hollow and warning. "If you have time for any thing but quarrels, Ishmael, look!"

The squatter turned slowly from his offending son, and cast

an eye that still lowered with deep resentment upward, but, which, the instant it caught a view of the object that now attracted the attention of all around him, chang'd its expression to one of astonishment and dismay.

A female stood on the spot, from which Ellen had been so fearfully expelled. Her person, was of the smallest size that is believed to comport with beauty, and which poets and artists have chosen as the beau idéal of female loveliness. Her dress was of a dark and glossy silk, and fluttered like gossamer, around her form. Long, flowing, and curling tresses of hair, still blacker and more shining than her robe, fell at times about her shoulders, completely enveloping the whole of her delicate bust in their ringlets, or at others, streamed long and waving in the wind. The elevation at which she stood prevented a close examination of the lineaments of a countenance, which, however, it might be seen was youthful, and, at the moment of her unlooked for appearance eloquent with feeling. So young indeed, did this fair and fragile being appear, that it might be doubted whether the age of childhood was entirely passed. One small and exquisitely moulded hand was pressed on her heart, while with the other she made an impressive gesture, which seem'd to invite Ishmael, if further violence was meditated, to direct it against her bosom.

The silent wonder with which the groupe of borderers gazed upward at so extraordinary a spectacle, was only interrupted, as the person of Ellen was seen, emerging with timidity from the tent, as if equally urged by apprehensions in behalf of herself, and the fears which she felt on account of her companion to remain concealed and to advance. She spoke; but her words were unheard by those below, and unheeded by her, to whom they were addressed. The latter, however, as if content with the offer she had made of herself as a victim to the resentment of Ishmael, now, calmly retired, and the spot she had so lately occupied became vacant, leaving a sort of stupid impression on the spectators beneath, not unlike that which it might be supposed would have been created, had they just been gazing at some supernatural vision.

More than a minute of profound silence succeeded, during which the sons of Ishmael, still continued gazing at the naked rock, in stupid wonder. Then as eye met eye, an expression of novel intelligence passed from one to the other, indicating that to them at least the appearance of this extraordinary tenant of the pavilion was as unexpected as it was incomprehensible. At length, Asa, in right of his years, and moved by the rankling impulse of the recent quarrel, took on himself the office of interrogator. Instead, however, of braving the resentment of his father, of whose fierce nature, when roused, he had had too frequent evidence, to excite it wantonly, he turned upon the cowering person of Abiram, observing with a sneer—

"This then is the beast, you were bringing into the Prairies for a decoy! I know you to be a man who seldom troubles truth, when any thing worse may answer, but I never knew you to outdo yourself, so thoroughly, before. The newspapers of Kentuck have called you a dealer in black flesh, a hundred times, but little did they reckon that you drove the trade into white families."

"Who is a kidnapper!" demanded Abiram, with a blustering show of resentment. "Am I to be called to account for every lie, they put in print, throughout the States! Look to your own family, boy; look to yourselves. The very stumps, of Kentucky and Tennessee, cry out ag'in ye! Ay, my tonguey gentleman, I have seen, Father and Mother, and three children, yourself for one, published on the logs and stubs of the settlements with dollars enough for reward to have made an honest man rich, for—"

He was interrupted by a back handed, but violent blow on the mouth, that caused him to totter, and which left the impression of its weight in the starting blood, and swelling lips.

"Asa!" said the Father, advancing with a portion of that dignity with which the hand of Nature seems to have invested the parental character. "You have struck the brother of your Mother!"

"I have struck the abuser of the whole family," returned the angry youth, "and unless he teach his tongue a wiser language, he had better part with it, altogether, as the unruly member. I'm no great performer with the knife, but, on an occasion, could make out, myself, to cut off a slande—"

"Boy; twice have you forgotten yourself to-day. Be careful

that it does not happen the third time. Where the law of the land is weak, it is right that the law of natur should be strong. You understand me, Asa, and you know me. As for you, Abiram, the child has done you wrong, and it is my place to see you righted. Remember; I tell you, justice shall be done; it is enough. But you have said hard things ag'in me and my family. If the hounds of the law have put their bills on the trees and stumps of the clearings, it was for no act of dishonesty, as you know, but because we maintain the rule that 'arth is common property. No, Abiram; could I wash my hands, of things done by your advice, as easily as I can of the things done by the whisperings of the devil, my sleep would be quieter at night, and none, who bear my name, need blush to hear it mentioned. Peace, Asa, and you too, man; enough has been said. Let us all think well, before any thing is added, that may make what is already so bad still more bitter."

Ishmael wav'd his hand, with authority, as he ended, and turned away with the air of one, who felt assured, that those he addressed would not have the temerity to dispute his commands. Asa, evidently struggled with himself to compel the required obedience, but his heavy nature quietly sunk into its ordinary repose, and he soon appeared, again, the being he really was; dangerous, only, at moments, and one whose passions were too sluggish to be long maintained at the point of ferocity. Not so with Abiram. While there was an appearance of a personal conflict between him and his colossal nephew, his mien had expressed the infallible evidences of engrossing apprehension, but, now, that the authority, as well as gigantic strength of the Father were interposed, between him and his assailant, his countenance changed from paleness to a livid hue, that bespoke how deeply, the injury he had received, rankled in his breast. Like Asa, however, he acquiesced in the decision of the squatter, and the appearance, at least, of harmony was restored again among a set of beings who were restrained, by no obligations more powerful, than the frail web, of authority, with which Ishmael had been able to envelope his children.

One effect of the quarrel, had been to divert the thoughts of the young men, from their recent visiter. With the dispute, that succeeded the disappearance of the fair stranger, all recollection of her existence appeared to have vanished. A few ominous and secret conferences, it is true were held apart, during which the direction of the eyes of the different speakers betrayed their subject; but these threatening symptoms soon disappeared, and the whole party, was again seen broken into its usual, listless, silent, and lounging groupes.

"I will go upon the rock, boys, and look abroad for the savages," said Ishmael, shortly after advancing towards them, with a mien which he intended should be conciliating, at the same time that it was authoritative. "If there is nothing to fear, we will go out on the plain; the day is too good to be lost in words, like women in the towns wrangling over their tea and sugared cakes."

Without waiting for approbation or dissent, the squatter advanced to the base of the rock, which formed a sort of perpendicular wall, nearly twenty feet high, around the whole acclivity. Ishmael, however, directed his footsteps to a point, where an ascent might be made, through a narrow cleft, which he had taken the precaution to fortify, with a breastwork of cotton wood logs, and which in its turn was defended by a chevaux de frieze of the branches of the same tree. Here, an armed man was usually kept, as at the key of the whole position, and here one of the young men, now stood, indolently leaning against the rock, ready to protect the pass, if it should prove necessary until the whole party, could be mustered at the several points of defence.

From this place the squatter found the ascent still difficult, partly by nature, and partly by artificial impediments, until he reach'd a sort of terrace, or to speak more properly the plain of the elevation, where he had established the huts, in which the whole family dwelt. These tenements were, as already mentioned, of that class, which are so often seen on the borders, and such as belong'd to the infancy of architecture, being simply formed of logs, bark, and poles. The area on which they stood contained several hundred square feet, and was sufficiently elevated above the plain, greatly to lessen if not to remove all danger from Indian missiles. Here Ishmael, believed he might leave his infants in comparative security, under the protection of their spirited mother, and here he, now, found Esther, engaged, at her ordinary domestic employments, surrounded by her daughters, and lifting her voice in declamatory censure, as one or another of the idle fry incurred her displeasure, and far too much engrossed with the tempest of her own conversation to know any thing of the violent scene which had been passing below.

"A fine windy place, you have chosen for the camp, Ishmael!" she commenced, or rather continued, by merely, diverting the attack from a sobbing girl of ten at her elbow, to her husband. "My word, if I haven't to count the young ones, every ten minutes, to see, they are not flying away among the buzzards, or the ducks. Why do ye all keep hovering round the rock, like lolloping reptiles in the spring, when the heavens are beginning to be alive with birds, man? D'ye think mouths can be fill'd, and hunger satisfied, by laziness and sleep!"

"You'll have your say, Eester," said the husband, using the provincial pronunciation of America for the name, and regarding his noisy companions with a look of habitual tolerance rather than of affection. "But the birds you shall have, if your own tongue dont frighten them, to take too high a flight. Ay, woman," he continued, standing on the very spot whence he had so rudely banished Ellen, which he had, by this time, gained, "and buffaloe too, if my eye can tell the animal, at the distance of a Spanish league."

"Come down; come down and be doing instead of talking. A talking man is no better than a barking dog. Nell shall hang out the cloth, if any of the red-skins show themselves, in time to give you notice. But, Ishmael, what have you been killing, my man, for it was your rifle, I heard a few minutes agone, unless I have lost my skill in sounds."

"Poh! 'twas to frighten the hawk you see, sailing above the rock."

"Hawk, indeed! at your time of day, to be shooting at hawks and buzzards, with eighteen open mouths to feed! Look at the bee, and at the beaver, my good man, and learn to be a provider. Why, Ishmael! I believe my soul," she continued, dropping the tow she was twisting on a distaff, "the man is in that tent ag'in! More than half his time is spent about that worthless, good-for-nothing—"

The sudden re-appearance of her husband closed the mouth

of the wife, and as the former descended to the place where Esther had resumed her employment, she was content to grumble forth her dissatisfaction, instead of expressing it, in more audible terms.

The dialogue that now took place between the affectionate pair was sufficiently succinct and expressive. The woman was at first a little brief and sullen in her answers, but care for her family soon rendered her more complaisant. As the purport of the conversation was merely an engagement to hunt during the remainder of the day, in order to provide the chief necessary of life, we shall not stop to record it.

With this resolution, then, the squatter descended to the plains, and divided his forces, into two parts; one of which was to remain as a guard with the fortress, and the other to accompany him to the field. He warily included, Asa and Abiram in his own party, well knowing that no authority short of his own was competent to repress the fierce disposition of his head-strong son, if fairly awakened. When these arrangements were completed, the hunters sallied forth, separating, at no great distance from the rock in order to form a circle about the distant herd of Buffaloes.

Chapter IX

"Priscian a little scratch'd;
'Twill serve."
Love's Labor's Lost, V.i.28–29.

Having made the reader acquainted with the manner in which Ishmael Bush had disposed of his family, under circumstances that might have proved so embarrassing to most other men, we shall again shift the scene a few short miles from the place last described, preserving, however, the due and natural succession of time. At the very moment that the squatter and his sons departed in the manner mentioned in the preceding chapter, two men were intently occupied in a swale that lay along the borders of a little run, just out of cannon-shot from the encampment, discussing the merits of a savoury bison's hump, that had been prepared for their palates with the utmost attention to the particular merits of that description of food. The choice morsel had been judiciously separated from the adjoining and less worthy parts of the beast, and, enveloped in the hairy coating provided by nature, it had duly undergone the heat of the customary subterraneous oven, and was now laid before its proprietors in all the culinary glory of the Prairies. So far as richness, delicacy, and wildness of flavour, and substantial nourishment were concerned, the viand might well have claimed a decided superiority over the meretricious cookery and laboured compounds of the most renowned artist; though the service of the dainty was certainly achieved in a manner far from artificial. It would appear that the two fortunate mortals, to whose happy lot it fell to enjoy a meal in which health and appetite lent so keen a relish to the exquisite food of the American deserts, were far from being insensible of the advantage they possessed.

The one, to whose knowledge in the culinary art the other was indebted for his banquet, seemed the least disposed of the two to profit by his own skill. He ate, it is true, and with a relish; but it was always with the moderation with which age is apt to temper the appetite. No such restraint, however, was imposed on the inclination of his companion. In the very flower of his days and in the vigour of manhood, the homage that he paid to the work of his more aged friend's hands was of the most profound and engrossing character. As one delicious morsel succeeded another he rolled his eyes towards his companion, and seemed to express that gratitude which he had not speech to utter, in looks of the most benignant nature.

"Cut more into the heart of it, lad," said the trapper, for it was the venerable inhabitant of those vast wastes, who had served the bee-hunter with the banquet in question; "cut more into the centre of the piece; there you will find the genuine riches of natur'; and that without need from spices, or any of your biting mustard to give it a foreign relish."

"If I had but a cup of metheglin," said Paul, stopping to perform the necessary operation of breathing, "I should swear this was the strongest meal that was ever placed before the mouth of man!"

"Ay, ay, well you may call it strong!" returned the other, laughing after his peculiar manner, in pure satisfaction at witnessing the infinite contentment of his companion; "strong it is, and strong it makes him who eats it! Here, Hector," tossing the patient hound, who was watching his eye with a wistful look, a portion of the meat, "you have need of strength, my friend, in your old days as well as your master. Now, lad, there is a dog that has eaten and slept wiser and better, ay, and that of richer food, than any king of them all! and why? because he has used and not abused the gifts of his Maker. He was made a hound, and like a hound has he feasted. Them did He create men; but they have eaten like famished wolves! A good and prudent dog has Hector proved, and never have I found one of his breed false in nose or friendship. Do you know the difference between the cookery of the wilderness and that which is found in the settlements? No; I see plainly you don't, by your appetite; then I will tell you. The one follows man, the other natur'. One thinks he can add to the gifts of the Creator, while the other is humble enough to enjoy them; therein lies the secret."

"I tell you, trapper," said Paul, who was very little edified by the morality with which his associate saw fit to season their repast, "that, every day while we are in this place, and they are likely to be many, I will shoot a buffaloe and you shall cook his hump!"

"I cannot say that, I cannot say that. The beast is good, take him in what part you will, and it was to be food for man that he was fashioned; but I cannot say that I will be a witness and a helper to the waste of killing one daily."

"The devil a bit of waste shall there be, old man. If they all turn out as good as this, I will engage to eat them clean myself, even to the hoofs—how now, who comes here! some one with a long nose I will answer; and one that has led him on a true scent, if he is following the trail of a dinner."

The individual who interrupted the conversation, and who had elicited the foregoing remark of Paul, was seen advancing along the margin of the run, with a deliberate pace, in a direct line for the two revellers. As there was nothing formidable nor hostile in his appearance, the bee-hunter, instead of suspending his operations, rather increased his efforts, in a manner which would seem to imply that he doubted whether the hump would suffice for the proper entertainment of all who were now likely to partake of the delicious morsel. With the trapper, however, the case was different. His more tempered appetite was already satisfied, and he faced the new comer with a look of cordiality, that plainly evinced how very opportune he considered his arrival.

"Come on, friend," he said waving his hand, as he observed the stranger to pause a moment, apparently in doubt. "Come on, I say: if hunger be your guide it has led you to a fitting place. Here is meat, and this youth can give you corn, parch'd till it be whiter than the upland snow; come on, without fear. We are not ravenous beasts, eating of each other, but Christian men, receiving thankfully that which the Lord hath seen fit to give."

"Venerable hunter," returned the Doctor, for it was no other than the naturalist on one of his daily exploring expeditions, "I rejoice greatly at this happy meeting; we are lovers of the same pursuits, and should be friends."

"Lord, lord!" said the old man laughing, without much deference to the rules of decorum, in the philosopher's very face, "it is the man who wanted to make me believe that a name could change the natur' of a beast! Come, friend; you are welcome, though your notions are a little blinded with reading too many books. Sit ye down, and after eating of this morsel, tell me, if you can, the name of the creatur' that has bestowed on you its flesh for a meal?"

The eyes of Dr. Battius (for we deem it decorous to give the good man the appellation he most preferred), the eyes of Dr. Battius sufficiently denoted the satisfaction with which he listened to this proposal. The exercise he had taken, and the sharpness of the wind, proved excellent stimulants, and Paul himself had hardly been in better plight to do credit to the trapper's cookery, than was the lover of nature, when the grateful invitation met his ears. Indulging in a small laugh, which his exertions to repress reduced nearly to a simper, he took the indicated seat by the old man's side, and made the customary dispositions to commence his meal without further ceremony.

"I should be ashamed of my profession," he said, swallowing a morsel of the hump with evident delight, slily endeavouring at the same time to distinguish the peculiarities of the singed and defaced skin, "I ought to be ashamed of my profession were there beast, or bird, on the continent of America that I could not tell by some one of the many evidences which science has enlisted in her cause. This—then—the food is nutritious and savoury—a mouthful of your corn, friend, if you please?"

Paul, who continued eating with increasing industry, looking askaunt not unlike a dog when engaged in the same agreeable pursuit, threw him his pouch, without deeming it at all necessary to suspend his own labours.

"You were saying, friend, that you have many ways of telling the creatur'?"—observed the attentive trapper.

"Many; many and infallible. Now, the animals that are carnivorous are known by their incisores."

"Their what!" demanded the trapper.

"The teeth with which nature has furnished them for defence, and in order to tear their food. Again—"

"Look you then for the teeth of this creatur'," interrupted the trapper, who was bent on convicting a man who had presumed to enter into competition with himself, in matters pertaining to the wilds, of gross ignorance; "turn the piece round and find your inside-overs."

The doctor complied, and of course without success; though he profited by the occasion to take another fruitless glance at the wrinkled hide.

"Well, friend, do you find the things you need, before you can pronounce the creatur' a duck or a salmon?"

"I apprehend the entire animal is not here?"

"You may well say as much," cried Paul, who was now compelled to pause from pure repletion; "I will answer for some pounds of the fellow, weighed by the truest steel-yards west of the Alleghanies. Still you may make out to keep soul and body together, with what is left," reluctantly eyeing a piece large enough to feed twenty men, but which he felt compelled to abandon from satiety; "cut in nigher to the heart, as the old man says, and you will find the riches of the piece."

"The heart!" exclaimed the doctor, inwardly delighted to learn there was a distinct organ to be submitted to his inspection. "Ay, let me see the heart—it will at once determine the character of the animal—certes this is not the cor—ay, sure enough it is—the animal must be of the order belluae, from its obese habits!"

He was interrupted by a long and hearty, but still a noiseless fit of merriment, from the trapper, which was considered so ill-timed by the offended naturalist, as to produce an instant cessation of speech, if not a stagnation of ideas.

"Listen to his beasts' habits and belly orders," said the old man delighted with the evident embarrassment of his rival; "and then he says it is not the core! Why, man, you are farther from the truth than you are from the settlements, with all your bookish l'arning and hard words; which I have once for all, said cannot be understood by any tribe or nation east of the Rocky Mountains. Beastly habits or no beastly habits, the creatur's are to be seen cropping the Prairies, by tens of thousands, and the piece in your hand is the core of as juicy a buffaloe-hump as stomach need crave!"

"My aged companion," said Obed, struggling to keep down a rising irascibility, that he conceived would ill comport with the dignity of his character, "your system is erroneous from the premises to the conclusion, and your classification so faulty, as utterly to confound the distinctions of science. The buffaloe is not gifted with a hump at all. Nor is his flesh savoury and wholesome, as I must acknowledge it would seem the subject before us may well be characterized—"

"There I'm dead against you, and clearly with the trapper," interrupted Paul Hover. "The man who denies that buffaloe beef is good, should scorn to eat it!"*

The Doctor, whose observation of the bee-hunter had hitherto been exceedingly cursory, stared at the new speaker with a look which denoted something like recognition.

"The principal characteristics of your countenance, friend," he said, "are familiar; either you, or some other specimen of your class, is known to me."

"I am the man you met in the woods east of the big river, and whom you tried to persuade to line a yellow hornet to his nest: as if my eye was not too true to mistake any other animal for a honey-bee, in a clear day! we tarried together a week, as you may remember; you at your toads and lizards, and I at my high holes and hollow trees. And a good job we made of it, between us! I filled my tubs with the sweetest honey I ever sent to the settlements, besides housing a dozen hives; and your bag was near bursting with a crawling museum. I never was bold enough to put the question to your face, stranger, but I reckon you are a keeper of curiosities?"†

"Ay! that is another of their wanton wickednesses!" exclaimed the trapper. "They slay the buck, and the moose, and the wild cat, and all the beasts that range the woods, and stuffing them with worthless rags, and placing eyes of glass

*It is scarcely necessary to tell the reader, that the animal so often alluded to in this book, and which is vulgarily called the buffaloe, is in truth the bison; hence so many contre tems between the man of the Prairies and the man of science.

†The pursuit of a bee-hunter is not uncommon on the skirts of American society, though it is a little embellished here. When the bees are seen sucking the flowers, their pursuer contrives to capture one or two. He then chooses a proper spot, and suffering one to escape, the insect invariably takes its flight towards the hive. Changing his ground to a greater or less distance, according to circumstances the bee-hunter then permits another to escape. Having watched the courses of the bees, which is technically called "lining," he is enabled to calculate the intersecting angle of the two lines, which is the hive.

into their heads, they set them up to be stared at, and call them the creatur's of the Lord; as if any mortal effigy could equal the works of his hand!"

"I know you well," returned the Doctor, on whom the plaint of the old man produced no visible impression. "I know you," offering his hand cordially to Paul; "it was a prolific week, as my herbal and catalogues shall one day prove. Ay, I remember you well, young man. You are of the *class*, mammalia; *order*, primates; *genus*, homo; *species*, Kentucky." Pausing to smile at his own humour, the naturalist proceeded. "Since our separation, I have journeyed far, having entered into a compactum or agreement with a certain man, named Ishmael—"

"Bush!" interrupted the impatient and reckless Paul. "By the Lord, trapper, this is the very blood-letter that Ellen told me of!"

"Then Nelly has not done me credit for what I trust I deserve;" returned the single-minded Doctor, "for I am not of the phlebotomizing school at all; greatly preferring the practice which purifies the blood instead of abstracting it."

"It was a blunder of mine, good stranger; the girl called you a skilful man."

"Therein she may have exceeded my merits," Dr. Battius continued, bowing with sufficient meekness. "But Ellen is a good, and a kind, and a spirited girl, too. A kind and a sweet girl I have ever found Nelly Wade to be!"

"The devil you have!" cried Paul, dropping the morsel he was sucking, from sheer reluctance to abandon the hump, and casting a fierce and direct look into the very teeth of the unconscious physician. "I reckon, stranger, you have a mind to bag Ellen, too!"

"The riches of the whole vegetable and animal world united, would not tempt me to harm a hair of her head! I love the child, with what may be called amor naturalis—or rather paternus.—The affection of a father."

"Ay—that indeed is more befitting the difference in your years," Paul coolly rejoined, stretching forth his hand to regain the rejected morsel. "You would be no better than a drone at your time of day, with a young hive to feed and swarm."

"Yes, there is reason, because there is natur', in what he says," observed the trapper: "But friend, you have said you were a dweller in the camp of one Ishmael Bush?"

"True; it is, in virtue of compactum—"

"I know but little of the virtue of packing, though I follow trapping, in my old age, for a livelihood. They tell me that skins are well kept, in the new fashion, but it is long since I have left off killing more than I need for food and garments. I was an eye-witness, myself, of the manner in which the Siouxes broke into your encampment, and drove off the cattle; stripping the poor man you call Ishmael of his smallest hoofs, counting even the cloven feet."

"Asinus excepted;" muttered the Doctor, who by this time was discussing his portion of the hump, in utter forgetfulness of all its scientific attributes. "Asinus domesticus Americanus excepted."

"I am glad to hear that so many of them are saved, though I know not the value of the animals you name; which is nothing uncommon, seeing how long it is that I have been out the settlements. But can you tell me, friend, what the traveller carries under the white cloth, he guards with teeth as sharp as a wolf that quarrels for the carcass the hunter has left?"

"You've heard of it!" exclaimed the other, dropping the morsel he was conveying to his mouth, in manifest surprise.

"Nay, I have heard nothing; but I have seen the cloth, and had like to have been bitten for no greater crime than wishing to know what it covered."

"Bitten! then after all the animal must be carnivorous! It is too tranquil for the ursus horridus; if it were the canis latrans, the voice would betray it. Nor would Nelly Wade be so familiar with any of the *genus*, feræ. Venerable hunter! the solitary animal confined in that wagon by day, and in the tent at night, has occasioned me more perplexity of mind than the whole catalogue of quadrupeds besides: and for this plain reason; I did not know how to class it."

"You think it a ravenous beast?"

"I know it to be a quadruped: your own danger proves it to be carnivorous."

During this broken explanation, Paul Hover sat silent and thoughtful, regarding each speaker with deep attention. But, suddenly moved by the manner of the Doctor, the latter had scarcely time to utter his positive assertion, before the young man bluntly demanded—

"And pray, friend, what may you call a quadruped?"

"A vagary of nature, wherein she has displayed less of her infinite wisdom than is usual. Could rotary levers be substituted for two of the limbs, agreeably to the improvement in my new order of phalangacrura, which might be rendered into the vernacular as lever-legged, there would be a delightful perfection and harmony in the construction. But, as the quadruped is now formed, I call it a mere vagary of nature; no other than a vagary."

"Harkee, stranger! in Kentucky we are but small dealers in dictionaries. Vagary is as hard a word to turn into English as quadruped."

"A quadruped is an animal with four legs—a beast."

"A beast! Do you then reckon that Ishmael Bush travels with a beast caged in that wagon?"

"I know it, and lend me your ear—not literally, friend," observing Paul to start and look surprised, "but figuratively, through its functions, and you shall hear. I have already made known that, in virtue of a compactum I journey with the aforesaid Ishmael Bush; but though I am bound to perform certain duties while the journey lasts, there is no condition which says that the said journey shall be sempiternum, or eternal. Now, though this region may scarcely be said to be wedded to science, being to all intents a virgin territory as respects the inquirer into natural history, still it is greatly destitute of the treasures of the vegetable kingdom. I should therefore have tarried some hundreds of miles more to the eastward, were it not for the inward propensity that I feel to have the beast in question inspected and suitably described and classed. For that matter," he continued, dropping his voice, like one who imparts an important secret, "I am not without hopes of persuading Ishmael to let me dissect it."

"You have seen the creature?"

"Not with the organs of sight; but with much more infallible instruments of vision: the conclusions of reason, and the deductions of scientific premises. I have watched the habits of the animal, young man; and can fearlessly pronounce, by evidence that would be thrown away on ordinary observers, that it is of vast dimensions, inactive, possibly torpid, of voracious appetite, and, as it now appears by the direct testimony of this venerable hunter, ferocious and carnivorous!"

"I should be better pleased, stranger," said Paul, on whom the Doctor's description was making a very sensible impression, "to be sure the creature was a beast at all."

"As to that, if I wanted evidence of a fact, which is abundantly apparent by the habits of the animal, I have the word of Ishmael, himself. A reason can be given for my smallest deductions. I am not troubled, young man, with a vulgar and idle curiosity, but all my aspirations after knowledge, as I humbly believe, are, first, for the advancement of learning, and secondly, for the benefit of my fellow-creatures. I pined greatly in secret to know the contents of the tent, which Ishmael guarded so carefully, and which he had covenanted that I should swear, (jurare per deos) not to approach nigher than a defined number of cubits, for a definite period of time. Your jusjurandum, or oath, is a serious matter, and not to be dealt in lightly; but, as my expedition depended on complying, I consented to the act, reserving to myself at all times the power of distant observation. It is now some ten days since Ishmael, pitying the state in which he saw me, a humble lover of science, imparted the fact that the vehicle contained a beast, which he was carrying into the Prairies as a decoy, by which he intends to entrap others of the same genus, or perhaps species. Since then my task, has been reduced simply to watch the habits of the animal, and to record the results. When we reach a certain distance where these beasts are said to abound, I am to have the liberal examination of the specimen."

Paul continued to listen, in the most profound silence, until the Doctor concluded his singular but characteristic explanation; then the incredulous bee-hunter shook his head, and saw fit to reply, by saying—

"Stranger, old Ishmael has burrowed you in the very bottom of a hollow tree, where your eyes will be of no more use than the sting of a drone. I, too, know something of that very wagon, and I may say that I have lined the squatter down into a flat lie. Harkee, friend; do you think a girl, like Ellen Wade, would become the companion of a wild beast?"

"Why not! why not!" repeated the naturalist; "Nelly has a taste, and often listens with pleasure to the treasures that I am sometimes compelled to scatter in this desert. Why should she not study the habits of any animal, even though it were a rhinoceros!"

"Softly, softly," returned the equally positive, and, though less scientific, certainly, on this subject, better instructed bee-hunter; "Ellen is a girl of spirit, and one too that knows her own mind, or I'm much mistaken; but with all her courage and brave looks, she is no better than a woman after all. Haven't I often had the girl, crying—"

"You are an acquaintance, then, of Nelly's?"

"The devil a bit. But I know woman is woman; and all the books in Kentucky couldn't make Ellen Wade go into a tent alone with a ravenous beast!"

"It seems to me," the trapper calmly observed, "that there is something dark and hidden in this matter. I am a witness that the traveller likes none to look into the tent, and I have a proof more sure than what either of you can lay claim to, that the wagon does not carry the cage of a beast. Here is Hector, come of a breed with noses as true and faithful as a hand that is all-powerful has made any of their kind, and had there been a beast in the place, the hound would long since have told it to his master."

"Do you pretend to oppose a dog to a man! brutality to learning! instinct to reason!" exclaimed the Doctor in some heat. "In what manner, pray, can a hound distinguish the habits, species, or even the genus of an animal, like reasoning, learned, scientific, triumphant man!"

"In what manner!" coolly repeated the veteran woodsman. "Listen; and if you believe that a schoolmaster can make a quicker wit than the Lord, you shall be made to see how much you're mistaken. Do you not hear something move in the brake? it has been cracking the twigs these five minutes. Now tell me what the creatur' is?"

"I hope nothing ferocious!" exclaimed the Doctor, who still retained a lively impression of his rencounter with the vespertilio horribilis. "You have rifles, friends; would it not be prudent to prime them; for this fowling-piece of mine is little to be depended on."

"There may be reason in what he says," returned the trapper, so far complying as to take his piece from the place where it had lain during the repast, and raising its muzzle in the air. "Now tell me the name of the creatur'?"

"It exceeds the limits of earthly knowledge! Buffon himself could not tell whether the animal was a quadruped, or of the *order*, serpens! a sheep, or a tiger!"

"Then was your buffoon a fool to my Hector! Here; pup!—What is it, dog!—Shall we run it down, pup—or shall we let it pass?"

The hound, which had already manifested to the experienced trapper, by the tremulous motion of his ears, his consciousness of the proximity of a strange animal, lifted his head from his fore paws and slightly parted his lips, as if about to shew the remnants of his teeth. But, suddenly abandoning his hostile purpose, he snuffed the air a moment, gaped heavily, shook himself, and peaceably resumed his recumbent attitude.

"Now, Doctor," cried the trapper, triumphantly, "I am well convinced there is neither game nor ravenous beast in the thicket; and that I call substantial knowledge to a man who is too old to be a spendthrift of his strength, and yet who would not wish to be a meal for a panther!"

The dog interrupted his master by a growl, but still kept his head crouched to the earth.

"It is a man!" exclaimed the trapper rising. "It is a man, if I am a judge of the creatur's ways. There is but little said atwixt the hound and me, but we seldom mistake each other's meaning!"

Paul Hover sprang to his feet like lightning, and, throwing forward his rifle, he cried in a voice of menace—

"Come forward, if a friend; if an enemy, stand ready for the worst!"

"A friend, a white man, and I hope a Christian," returned a voice from the thicket; which opened at the same instant, and at the next, the speaker made his appearance.

Chapter X

"Go apart, Adam, and thou shalt hear
How he will shake me up."
As You Like It, I.i.27–28.

IT IS WELL KNOWN, that even long before the immense regions of Louisiana changed their masters, for the second, and, as it is to be hoped for the last time, its unguarded territory was by no means, safe from the inroads of white adventurers. The semi-barbarous hunters from the Canadas, the same description of population, a little more enlightened from the States, and the metiffs or half breeds who claimed to be ranked in the class of white men, were scattered, among the different Indian tribes or gleaned a scanty livelihood, in solitude, amid the haunts of the beaver and the bison; or, to adopt the popular nomenclature of the country, of the buffaloe.*

It was, therefore, no unusual thing for strangers to encounter each other in the endless wastes of the West. By signs which an unpractised eye would pass unobserved, a borderer, knew when one of his fellows was in his vicinity, and he avoided or approached the intruder, as best comported with his feelings or his interests. Generally, these interviews were pacific, for the whites had a common enemy to dread in the ancient, and perhaps more lawful, occupants, of the country, but instances were not rare, in which jealousy and cupidity, had caused them to terminate in scenes of the most violent and ruthless treachery. The meeting of two hunters on the American desert, as we find it convenient, sometimes, to call this region, was, consequently, somewhat in the suspicious and wary manner in which two vessels draw together in a sea, that is known to be infested with pirates. While neither party is willing to betray its weakness by exhibiting distrust, neither is disposed to commit itself, by any acts of confidence from which it may be difficult to recede.

*In addition to the scientific distinctions which mark the two species, it may be added, with due deference to Dr. Battius, that a much more important particular is, the fact, that while the former of these animals is delicious and nourishing food, the latter is scarcely edible.

Such, was, in some degree, the character of the present interview. The stranger drew nigh, deliberately, keeping his eyes steadily fastened on the movements of the other party, while he purposely created little difficulties to impede an approach which might prove too hasty. On the other hand, Paul stood, playing with the lock of his rifle, too proud to let it appear that three men could manifest any apprehension of a solitary individual, and yet too prudent, to omit, entirely, the customary precautions. The principal reason of the marked difference which the two legitimate proprietors of the banquet, made in the receptions of their guests, was to be explained by the entire difference which existed in their respective appearances.

While the exterior of the Naturalist was decidedly pacific, not to say, abstracted, that of the new comer was distinguished by an air of vigour, and a front and step, which it would not have been difficult to have at once pronounced to be military. He wore a forage cap, of fine blue cloth, from which depended a soiled tassel in gold, and which was nearly buried, in a mass of exuberant, curling, jet-black hair. Around his throat, he had, negligently, fastened a stock of black silk. His body was enveloped in a hunting shirt, of dark green, trimmed with the yellow fringes and ornaments that were sometimes seen among the border-troops of the Confederacy. Beneath this, however, were visible the collar and lapels of a jacket, similar in colour and cloth to the cap. His lower limbs were protected by buckskin leggings, and his feet, by the ordinary Indian moccasins. A richly ornamented, and exceedingly dangerous, straight dirk was stuck in a sash of red-silk, net-work; another girdle, or rather belt, of uncolored leather, contained a pair of the smallest sized pistols, in holsters nicely made to fit, and across his shoulder was thrown a short, heavy, military rifle; its horn and pouch occupying the usual places, beneath his arms. At his back he bore, a knapsack, marked by the well known initials, that have since, gained for the Government of the United States, the good humoured and quaint appellation of Uncle Sam.

"I come in amity," the stranger said, like one too much accustomed to the sight of arms, to be startled at the ludicrously belligerent attitude which Doctor Battius had seen fit to assume. "I come as a friend; and am one, whose pursuits and wishes will not at all interfere with your own."

"Harkee, stranger," said Paul Hover, bluntly, "do you understand lining a bee, from this open place, into a wood, distant, perhaps a dozen miles."

"The bee is a bird, I have never been compelled to seek," returned the other, laughing, "though I have too, been something of a fowler, in my time."

"I thought as much," exclaimed Paul, thrusting forth his hand, frankly, and with the true freedom of manner, that marks an American borderer. "Let us cross fingers. You and I will never quarrel about the comb, since you set so little store, by the honey. And, now, if your stomach has an empty corner, and you know how to relish a genuine dew drop when it falls into your very mouth, there lies the exact morsel to put into it. Try it, stranger; and having tried it, if you dont call it as snug a fit, as you have made since—How long ar' you from the settlements, pray?"

"'Tis many weeks, and I fear, it may be as many more, before I can return. I will however gladly profit by your invitation; for I have fasted since the rising of yesterday's sun, and I know too well the merits of a bison's hump, to reject the food."

"Ah! you ar' acquainted with the dish! Well, therein, you have the advantage of me, in setting out, though I think, I may say we could now, start on equal grounds. I should be the happiest fellow, between Kentuck and the Rocky Mountains, if I had a snug cabin, near some old wood that was filled with hollow trees, just such a hump every day as that for dinner; a load of fresh straw for hives, and little El—"

"Little what?" demanded the stranger, evidently amused with the communicative and frank disposition of the bee-hunter.

"Something that I shall have one day, and which concerns no body so much as myself," returned Paul, pecking the flint of his rifle, and beginning very cavalierly to whistle an air well known on the waters of the Mississippi.

During this preliminary discourse the stranger had taken his seat by the side of the hump, and was already making a serious inroad on its relicks. Dr. Battius however watch'd his movements, with a jealousy, still more striking than the cordial reception which the open hearted Paul had just exhibited.

But the doubts, or rather apprehensions, of the naturalist, were of a character altogether different from the confidence of the bee-hunter. He had been struck with the stranger's using the legitimate instead of the perverted name of the animal off which he was making his repast, and as he had been among the foremost, himself, to profit by the removal of the impediments which the policy of Spain had plac'd in the way of all explorers of her Trans-Atlantic dominions; whether bent on the purposes of commerce, or like himself on the more laudable pursuits of science, he had a sufficiency of every day philosophy to feel, that the same motives which had so powerfully urged himself to his present undertaking, might produce a like result on the mind of some other student of Nature. Here, then, was the prospect of an alarming rivalry, which bade fair to strip him of, at least, a moiety of the just rewards of all his labors, privations and dangers. Under these views of his character, therefore, it is not at all surprising that the native meekness of the naturalist's disposition was a little disturbed, and that he watch'd the proceedings of the other, with such a degree of vigilance, as he believed best suited to detect his sinister designs.

"This is, truly, a delicious repast," observed the unconscious young stranger; for both young and handsome, he was fairly entitled to be considered, "either hunger has given a peculiar relish to the viand, or the bison may lay claim to be the finest of the ox family!"

"Naturalists, sir, are apt, when they speak familiarly, to give the cow the credit of the genus," said Doctor Battius, swelling with secret distrust, and clearing his throat before speaking, much in the manner that a duellist examines the point of the weapon he is about to put into the body of his foe. "The figure is more perfect, as the bos, meaning the ox, is unable to perpetuate his kind; and the bos, in its most extended meaning, or vacca, is altogether the nobler animal of the two."

The Doctor uttered this opinion with a certain air, that he intended should express his readiness to come, at once, to any of the numerous points of difference, which he doubted not existed between them, and he now awaited the blow of his antagonist, intending that his next thrust should be still more vigorous. But the young stranger appeared much better disposed to partake of the good cheer with which he had been so providently provided, than to take up the cudgels of argument on this or on any other of the knotty points, which are so apt to furnish the lovers of science, with the materials of a mental joust.

"I dare say, you are very right, sir," he replied, with a most provoking indifference to the importance of the points he conceded. "I dare say, you are quite right, and that vacca, would have been the better word."

"Pardon me, sir; you are giving a very wrong construction to my language, if you suppose I include, without many and particular qualifications, the bibulus Americanus, in the family of the vacca. For as you well know, sir—or, as I presume I should say, Doctor—you have the Medical Diploma, no doubt?"

"You give me credit for an honour I can not claim," interrupted the other.

"An under-graduate! or perhaps your degrees have been taken in some other of the liberal sciences?"

"Still wrong, I do assure you."

"Surely, young man, you have not entered on this important—I may say this awful service, without some evidence of your fitness for the task!—some commission by which you can assert an authority to proceed, or by which you may claim, an affinity and a communion with your fellow-workers, in the same beneficent pursuits!"

"I know not, by what means, or for what purposes, you have made yourself master of my objects!" exclaimed the youth, reddening, and rising with a quickness, which manifested how little he regarded the grosser appetites, when a subject nearer his heart was approached. "Still, sir, your language is incomprehensible. That pursuit which in another might perhaps be justly called beneficent, is, in me a dear and cherished duty; though why a commission should be demanded or needed, is, I confess, no less a subject of surprise."

"It is customary to be provided with such a document," returned the Doctor gravely, "and, on all suitable occasions to produce it, in order that congenial and friendly minds, may at once, reject unworthy suspicions, and stepping over, what may be called the elements of discourse, come at once, to those points which are desiderata, to both."

"It is a strange request!" the youth muttered, turning his frowning eye, from one to the other, as if examining the characters of his companions, with a view to weigh their physical powers. Then, putting his hand into his bosom he drew forth a small box and extending it, with an air of dignity towards the Doctor, he continued—"you will find by this, sir, that I have some right, to travel in a country, which is now the property of the American States."

"What have we here!" exclaimed the Naturalist, opening the folds of a large parchment. "Why, this is the sign manual of the Philosopher Jefferson! The seal of State! Countersigned, by the Minister of War! Why this is a commission, creating Duncan Uncas Middleton a Captain of Artillery."

"Of whom! of whom!" repeated the trapper, who had sat regarding the stranger, during the whole discourse, with eyes that seem'd greedily to devour each lineament. "How is the name! did you call him Uncas? Uncas! was it, Uncas?"

"Such is my name," returned the youth, a little haughtily. "It is the appellation of a native chief, that both my uncle and myself, bear with pride; for it is the memorial of an important service done my family, by a warrior, in the old wars of the Provinces!"

"Uncas! did ye call him, Uncas!" repeated the trapper, approaching the youth, and parting the dark curls which clustered over his brow, without the slightest resistance on the part, of their wondering owner. "Ah! my eyes are old, and not so keen as when I was a warrior, myself, but I can see the look of the father in the son! I saw it, when he first came nigh, but so many things have, since, passed before my failing sight, that I could not name, the place, where I had met his likeness! Tell me, lad, by what name is your father known?"

"He was an officer of the States in the war of the revolution, of my own name of course; my mother's brother was called Duncan Uncas Heyward."

"Still Uncas! still, Uncas!" echoed the other, trembling with eagerness. "And *his* father?"

"Was called the same, without the appellation of the native chief. It was to him and to my grandmother, that the service of which I have just spoken was rendered."

"I know'd it! I know'd it!" shouted the old man, in his tremulous voice, his rigid features working, powerfully, as if the names the other mentioned, awakened some long dormant emotions, connected with the events of an anterior age. "I know'd it! son or grandson, it is all the same, it is the blood, and 'tis the look! Tell me, is he they call'd Duncan, without the Uncas, is he living."

The young man shook his head sorrowfully as he replied in the negative.

"He died full of days, and of honours. Beloved, happy and bestowing happiness."

"Full of days!" repeated the trapper looking down at his own meagre, but still muscular hands. "Ah! he liv'd in the settlements, and was wise, only, after their fashions. But you have often seen him, and you have heard him discourse of Uncas, and of the wilderness?"

"Often! He was then an Officer of the King; but when the war took place between the Crown and her Colonies, my grandfather did not forget his birth-place, but threw off the empty allegiance of names, and was true to his proper country; he fought on the side of Liberty."

"There was reason in it; and what is better, there was Natur. Come, sit ye down, beside me lad; sit ye down and tell me of what your grand'ther used to speak, when his mind dwelt on the wonders of the wilderness."

The youth smiled, no less at the importunity than at the interest manifested by the old man, but, as he found that there was no longer, the least appearance of any violence being contemplated, he unhesitatingly complied.

"Give it all, to the trapper, by rule and by figures of speech," said Paul, very coolly taking his seat on the other side of the young soldier. "It is the fashion of old age to relish these ancient traditions, and, for that matter, I can say, that I dont dislike to listen to them, myself."

Middleton smiled, again, and perhaps with a slight air of derision; but good naturedly turning to the trapper, he continued—

"It is a long, and might prove a painful story. Blood-shed and all the horrors of Indian cruelty and of Indian warfare, are fearfully mingled in the narrative."

"Ay, give it all to us, stranger," continued Paul; "we are used to these matters in Kentuck; and I must say, I think a story none the worse, for having a few scalps in it!"

"But he told you of Uncas, did he!" resumed the trapper, without regarding the slight interruptions of the bee hunter, which amounted to no more than a sort of by-play. "And, what thought he, and said he, of the lad, in his parlour, with the comforts and ease of the settlements at his elbow?"

"I doubt not, he used a language similar to that he would have adopted in the woods, and had he stood face to face with his friend—"

"Did he call the savage his friend! the poor, naked, painted warrior; he was not too proud then, to call the Indian his friend?"

"He even boasted of the connexion; and as you have already heard, bestowed a name on his first-born, which is likely to be handed down, as an heir loom among the rest of his descendants."

"It was well done! Like a man, ay! and like a christian too! He used to say the Delaware was swift of foot—did he remember that?"

"As the antelope. Indeed he often spoke of him, by the appellation of Le Cerf Agile, a name he had obtained by his activity."

"And bold and fearless, lad!" continued the trapper looking up into the eyes of his companion, with a wistfulness that bespoke the delight he received in listening to the praises of one, whom it was so very evident, he had once, tenderly lov'd.

"Brave as a blooded hound! Without fear. He always quoted Uncas and his father, who from his wisdom, was called the Grand Serpent, as models of heroism and constancy."

"He did them justice! He did them justice! Truer men, were not to be found in tribe or nation, be their skins of what colour they might. I see your grand'ther was just; and did his duty, too, by his offspring. 'Twas a perilous time he had of it, among them hills, and nobly did he play his own part. Tell, me, lad, or, officer, I should say, since officer, you be, was this all?"

"Certainly not; it was as I have said a fearful tale, full of moving incidents, and the memories both of my grandfather and of my grandmother."

"Ah!" exclaimed the trapper tossing a hand into the air, as his whole countenance lighted with the recollections the name revived. "They called her Alice! Elsie or Alice, 'tis all the same. A laughing, playful, child she was, when happy, and tender and weeping in her misery. Her hair was shining and yellow as the coat of the young fawn, and her skin clearer than the purest water that drips from the rocks. Well do I remember her! I remember her right well!"

The lip of the youth slightly curled, and he regarded the old man, with an expression, which might easily have been construed into a declaration that such were not his own recollections of his venerable and revered ancestor, though it would seem he did not think it necessary to say as much in words. He was content to answer:—

"They both retained impressions of the dangers they had passed, by far too vivid easily to lose the recollection of any of their fellow actors."

The trapper look'd aside, and seem'd to struggle with some deeply innate feeling; then turning again, towards his companion, though his honest eyes no longer dwelt with the same open interest, as before, on the countenance of the other, he continued—

"Did he tell you of them *all*? were they *all* red-skins, but himself and the daughters of Munro?"

"No. There was a white man, associated with the Delawares. A scout of the English Army, but a native of the Provinces."

"A drunken, worthless, vagabond, like most of his colour who harbor with the savages, I warrant you!"

"Old man, your gray hairs, should caution you against slander. The man, I speak of, was of great simplicity of mind, but of sterling worth. Unlike most of those who live a border life, he united the better, instead of the worst qualities of the two people. He was a man, endowed with the choicest and perhaps rarest gift of nature, that of distinguishing, good from evil, his virtues were those of simplicity, because such were the fruits of his habits, as were, indeed, his very prejudices. In courage, he was the equal of his red associates, in warlike skill, being better instructed, their superior. In short, he was a noble shoot from the stock of human nature, which never could attain its proper elevation and importance, for no other reason, than because it grew in the forest: such, old hunter, were the very words of my grandfather, when speaking of the man, you imagine so worthless."

The eyes of the trapper had sunk to the earth as the stranger delivered this character in the ardent tones of generous youth. He play'd with the ears of his hound, fingered his own rustic garment, and open'd and shut the pan of his rifle, with hands that trembled in a manner, that would have implied their total unfitness to wield the weapon. When the other had concluded he hoarsely added—

"Your grand'ther didn't then entirely forget the white man!"

"So far from that, there are already three, among us, who have also names derived from that scout."

"A name, did you say!" exclaimed the old man, starting, "what, the name, of the solitary, unl'arned hunter! Do the great, and the rich, and the honored, and what is better, still, the just, do they bear his very actual name!"

"It is borne, by my brother, and by two of my cousins, whatever may be their titles to be described by the terms you have mentioned."

"Do you mean, the actual name itself: spelt with the very same letters; beginning with an N. and ending with an L."

"Exactly the same," the youth smilingly replied. "No, no, we have forgotten nothing that was his; I have at this moment a dog brushing a deer, not far from this, who is come of a hound, that very scout sent as a present after his friends, and which was of the stock he always used himself: a truer breed in nose and foot, is not to be found in the wide Union."

"Hector!" said the old man, struggling to conquer an emotion that nearly suffocated him, and speaking to his hound, in the sort of tones he would have used to a child, "do ye hear that, Pup. Your kin and blood, are on the Prairies! A name! it is wonderful! very wonderful!"

Nature could endure no more. Overcome by a flood of unusual and extraordinary sensations, and stimulated by tender and long dormant recollections strangely and unexpectedly revived, the old man had just self command enough to add, in a voice that was hollow and unnatural, through the efforts he made to command it—

"Boy, I am that scout; a warrior once, a miserable trapper now!" when the tears broke over his wasted cheeks out of fountains that had long been dried and, sinking his face between his knees, he covered it decently, with his buckskin garment, and sobb'd aloud.

The spectacle produced correspondent emotions in his companions. Paul Hover had actually swallowed each syllable of the discourse as they fell, alternately, from the different speakers, his feelings keeping equal pace with the increasing interest of the scene. Unused to such strange sensations, he was turning his face on every side of him, to avoid he knew not what, until he saw the tears and heard the sobs of the old man, when he sprang to his feet, and grappling his guest fiercely by the throat, he demanded, by what authority he had made his aged companion weep. A flash of recollection crossing his brain, at the same instant, he released his hold, and stretching forth an arm in the very wantonness of gratification, he seized the Doctor by the hair, which instantly revealed its artificial formation, by cleaving to his hand, leaving the white and shining poll of the Naturalist with a covering no warmer than the skin.

"What think you of that, Mr. Bug-gatherer!" he rather shouted, than cried, "is not this a strange bee to line into his hole!"

"Tis remarkable! wonderful! edifying!" returned the lover of nature, good humouredly recovering his wig, with twinkling eyes and a husky voice. "Tis rare and commendable! Though I doubt not in the exact order of causes and effects."

With this sudden outbreaking, however, the commotion instantly subsided, the three spectators clustering around the trapper with a species of awe, at beholding the tears of one so aged.

"It must be so, or how could he be so familiar with a history that is little known beyond my own family," at length the youth observed, not ashamed to acknowledge how much he had been affected by unequivocally drying his own eyes.

"True!" echoed Paul: "If you want any more evidence I will swear to it! I know every word of it, myself, to be true as the gospel!"

"And yet we had long supposed him dead!" continued the soldier. "My grandfather had filled his days, with honor, and we had believed him the junior of the two."

"It is not often that youth, has an opportunity of thus looking down on the weakness of age!" the trapper observed, raising his head, and looking around him with composure and dignity. "That I am still here, young man, is the pleasure of the Lord, who has spared me, until I have seen fourscore long and laborious years, for his own secret ends. That I am the man I say, you need not doubt, for why should I go to my grave with so cheap a lie in my mouth?"

"I do not hesitate to believe, I only marvel that it should be so. But why do I find you, venerable and excellent friend of my parents, in these wastes so far from the comforts and safety of the lower country?"

"I have come into these plains to escape the sound of the axe, for, here, surely the choppers can never follow. But, I may put the like question to yourself. Are you of the party which the States have sent into their new purchase to look after the natur of the bargain they have made?"

"I am not. Lewis is working his way up the river, some hundreds of miles from this. I come on a private adventure."

"Though it is no cause of wonder that a man whose strength and eyes have failed him as a hunter, should be seen nigh the haunts of the beaver, using a trap instead of a rifle, it is strange, that one so young and prosperous, and bearing the commission of the Great Father, should be moving among the Prairies, without even a camp-colour-man to do his biddings!"

"You would think my reasons sufficient did you know them, as know them you shall, if you are disposed to listen to my story. I think you all, honest, and men who would rather aid than betray one, bent on a worthy object."

"Come, then, and tell us at your leisure," said the trapper, seating himself, and beckoning to the youth to follow his example. The latter willingly complied, and after Paul and the Doctor, had disposed of themselves to their several likings, the new-comer, entered into a narrative of the singular reasons which had led him so far into the deserts.

Chapter XI

"So foul a sky clears not without a storm."
King John, IV.ii.108.

IN THE MEAN TIME the industrious and irreclaimable hours continued their labours. The sun, which had been struggling through such masses of vapor throughout the day, fell slowly into a streak of clear sky, and thence sunk, gloriously, into the gloomy wastes, as he is wont to settle into the waters of the ocean. The vast herds, which had been grazing among the wild pastures of the Prairies, gradually disappeared, and the endless flocks of aquatic birds, that were pursuing their customary annual journey from the virgin Lakes of the North towards the Gulf of Mexico, ceased to fan that air, which had now become loaded with dew and vapour. In short, the shadows of night, fell upon the rock, adding the mantle of darkness to the other dreary accompanyments of the place.

As the light began to fail, Esther collected her younger children at her side, and placing herself on a projecting point of her insulated fortress, she sat patiently awaiting the return of the hunters. Ellen Wade was at no great distance, seeming to keep a little aloof from the anxious circle, as if willing to mark the distinction which existed in their characters.

"Your uncle is, and always will be a dull calculator, Nell," observed the mother, after a long pause in a conversation that had turned on the labors of the day; "A lazy hand at figures, and foreknowledge is that said Ishmael Bush! Here he sat, lolloping about the rock from light till noon, doing nothing, but scheme—scheme—scheme, with seven as noble boys at his elbows, as woman ever gave to man, and what's the upshot! why, night is setting in, and his needful work not yet ended."

"It is not prudent, certainly, aunt," Ellen replied, with a vacancy in her air, that proved how little she knew what she was saying; "and it is setting a very bad example to his sons."

"Hoity toity, girl, who has reared you up as a judge over your elders, ay! and your betters, too! I should like to see the man on the whole frontier, who sets a more honest example to his children than this same Ishmael Bush! Show me if you can, Miss fault-finder, but not fault-mender, a set of boys who will, on occasion, sooner chop a piece of logging, and dress it for the crop, than my own children, though I say it, myself, who, perhaps should be silent; or a cradler that knows better how to lead a gang of hands through a field of wheat leaving a cleaner stubble, in his track, than my own good man! Then as a father, he is as generous as a Lord; for his sons have only to name the spot where they would like to pitch, and he gives 'em a deed of the Plantation, and no charge for papers, is ever made."

As the wife of the squatter concluded, she raised a hollow taunting laugh, that was echoed from the mouths of several juvenile imitators, whom she was training to a life as shiftless and lawless as her own, but which notwithstanding its uncertainty was not without its secret charms.

"Holla! old Eester;" shouted the well known voice of her husband from the plain beneath; "ar' you keeping your junketts, while we ar' finding you in venison and buffaloe beef. Come down, come down, old girl, with all your young and lend us a hand to carry up the meat! why what a frolick, you ar' in, woman! Come down, come down; for the boys are at hand, and we have work here for double your number."

Ishmael might have spared his lungs, more than a moiety of the effort they were compelled to make, in order that he should be heard. He had hardly uttered the name of his wife, before the whole of the crouching circle rose in a body, and tumbling over each other, they precipitated themselves down the dangerous passes of the rock, with ungovernable impatience. Esther followed the young fry, with a more measured gait, nor did Ellen deem it wise, or rather discreet, to remain behind. Consequently, the whole were soon assembled at the base of the citadel, on the open plain.

Here the squatter was found, staggering under the weight of a fine fat buck, attended by one or two of his younger sons. Abiram quickly appeared, and before many minutes had elapsed most of the hunters dropped in, singly and in pairs, each man bringing with him some fruits of his prowess in the field.

"The plain is free from red-skins to night, at least," said

Ishmael, after the bustle of reception had a little subsided: "for I have scoured the Prairie, for many long miles, on my own feet, and I call myself a judge of the print of an Indian moccasin. So, old woman, you can give us a few steaks of the venison, and then we will sleep on the day's work."

"I'll not swear there are no savages near us," said Abiram. "I, too, know something of the trail of a red-skin, and unless my eyes have lost some of their sight, I would swear, boldly, that there ar' Indians at hand. But wait till Asa, comes in. He pass'd the spot where I found the marks, and the boy knows something of such matters too."

"Ay, the boy, knows too much of many things," returned Ishmael, gloomily. "It will be better for him, when he thinks he knows less. But what matters it, Hetty, if all the Sioux tribes west of the big river, are within a mile of us; they will find it no easy matter to scale this rock in the teeth of ten bold men."

"Call 'em twelve, at once, Ishmael, call 'em twelve," cried his termigant assistant. "For if your moth gathering, bug hunting friend, can be counted a man, I beg you will set me down as two. I will not turn my back to him, with the rifle or the shot-gun, and for courage, the yearling heifer that them skulking devils the Tetons stole, was the biggest coward among us all, and after her comes your drivelling Doctor. Ah! Ishmael, you rarely attempt a regular trade, but you come out the loser; and this man, I reckon, is the hardest bargain among them all. Would you think it, the fellow ordered me a blister around my mouth, because I complained of a pain in the foot!"

"It is a pity, Eester," the husband, coolly answered, "that you did not take it, I reckon, it would have done considerable good. But, boys, if it should turn out as Abiram thinks, that there are Indians near us, we may have to scamper up the rock, and lose our suppers after all. Therefore we will make sure of the game, and talk over the performances of the Doctor, when we have nothing better to do."

The hint was taken, and in a few minutes, the exposed situation in which the family was collected, was exchanged for the more secure elevation of the rock. Here Esther busied herself, working and scolding with equal industry, until the repast was prepared, when she summoned her husband to his meal, in a voice as sonorous as that with which the Imaum reminds the Faithful of a more important duty.

When each had assumed his proper and customary place around the smoking viand, the squatter set the example, by beginning to partake of a delicious venison steak, prepared like the hump of the bison, with a skill, that rather increased than concealed its natural properties. A painter would gladly have seized the moment, to transfer the wild and characteristic scene to the canvass.

The reader will remember that the citadel of Ishmael, stood insulated, lofty, ragged, and nearly inaccessible. A bright, flashing fire, that was burning on the centre of its summit, and around which the busy groupe was clustered, lent it the appearance of some tall Pharos, placed in the centre of the deserts, to light such adventurers as wandered through their broad wastes. The flashing flame, gleamed from one sun burnt countenance to another, exhibiting every variety of expression, from the juvenile simplicity of the children, mingled as it was with a shade of the wildness peculiar to their semi-barbarous lives, to the dull and immovable apathy that dwelt on the features of the squatter, when unexcited. Occasionally a gust of wind, would fan the embers, and as a brighter light shot upward, the little solitary tent, was seen, as it were suspended in the gloom of the upper air. All beyond was enveloped as usual at that hour in an impenetrable body of darkness.

"It is unaccountable that Asa, should choose to be out of the way, at such a time as this," Esther pettishly observed. "When all is finished and to rights, we shall have the boy coming up grumbling for his meal, and hungry as a bear after his winter's nap. His stomach is as true as the best clock in Kentucky, and seldom wants winding up, to tell the time, whether of day, or night. A desperate eater, is Asa, when a-hungered by a little work!"

Ishmael look'd, sternly, around the circle of his silent sons, as if to see whether any among them would presume to say aught in favour of the absent delinquent. But, now, when no exciting cause existed to arouse their slumbering tempers, it seemed to be too great an effort to enter on the defence of their rebellious brother. Abiram, however, who since the pacification either felt or affected to feel a more generous interest in his late adversary, saw fit to express an anxiety, to which the others were strangers.

"It will be well if the boy has escaped the Tetons!" he muttered. "I should be sorry to have Asa, who is one of the stoutest of our party, both in heart and hand, fall into the power of the red devils."

"Look to yourself, Abiram; and spare your breath if you can use it only to frighten the woman and her huddling girls. You have whitened the face of Ellen Wade, already, who looks as pale, as if she was staring to-day at the very Indians you name, when I was forced to speak to her through the rifle, because I couldn't reach her ears with my tongue. How was it, Nell; you have never given the reason of your deafness?"

The colour of Ellen's cheek changed, as suddenly as the squatter's piece had flash'd, on the occasion to which he alluded, the burning glow, suffusing her features, until even her throat mantled with its fine healthful tinge. She hung her head abashed, but, did not seem to think it necessary to reply.

Ishmael, too sluggish to pursue the subject, or content with the pointed allusion he had just made, rose from his seat on the rock, and stretching his heavy frame, like a well fed and fattened ox, he announced his intention to sleep. Among a race who liv'd chiefly for the indulgence of the natural wants, such a declaration, could not fail of meeting with sympathetic dispositions. One after another disappeared each seeking his or her rude dormitory, and before many minutes, Esther, who by this time had scolded the younger fry to sleep, found, herself, if we except the usual watchman below, in solitary possession of the naked rock.

Whatever less valuable fruits had been produced, in this uneducated woman, by her migratory habits, the great principle of female nature was too deeply rooted ever to be entirely eradicated. Of a powerful, not to say fierce temperament, her passions, were violent and difficult to be smothered. But, however she might and did abuse the accidental prerogatives of her situation, love for her offspring, while it often, slumbered, could never be said to become extinct. She lik'd not the protracted absence of Asa. Too fearless herself to have hesitated, an instant, on her own account about crossing the dark abyss, into which she now sat looking with longing eyes, her busy imagination, in obedience to this inextinguishable sentiment, began to conjure nameless evils on account of her son. It might be true, as Abiram had hinted, that he had become a captive to some of the tribes who were hunting the buffaloe in that vicinity, or even a still more dreadful calamity might have befallen. So thought the mother, while silence and darkness lent their aid to the secret impulses of nature.

Agitated by these reflexions, which put sleep at defiance, Esther, continued at her post, listening with that sort of acuteness, which is termed instinct in the animals a few degrees below her in the scale of intelligence, for any of those noises which might indicate the approach of footsteps. At length, her wishes had an appearance of being realized, for the long desired sounds were distinctly audible, and presently she distinguished the dim form of a man, at the base of the rock.

"Now, Asa, richly do you deserve to be left with an earthen bed this blessed night!" the woman began to mutter, with a revolution in her feelings that will not be surprising to those who have made the contradictions that give variety to the human character a study. "And a hard one, I've mind it shall be. Why Abner; Abner; you Abner, do you sleep? Let me not see you dare to open the hole, till I get down. I will know who it is that wishes to disturb a peaceable, ay, and an honest family too, at such a time, in the night, as this!"

"Woman!" exclaimed a voice, that intended to bluster, while the speaker was manifestly, a little apprehensive of the consequences; "Woman, I forbid you, on pain of the Law to project any of your infernal missiles. I am a citizen, and a freeholder, and a graduate of two universities, and I stand upon my rights. Beware of malice prepense—of chance medley and of man-slaughter. It is I—your amicus, a Friend and inmate, I—Doctor Obed Battius!"

"Who!" demanded Esther in a voice that nearly refused to convey her words to the ears of the anxious listener beneath. "Did you say it was not Asa?"

"Nay, I am neither Asa nor Absolem, nor any of the Hebrew Princes; but Obed, the root and stock of them all. Have I not said, woman, that you keep one, in attendance, who is entitled, to a peaceable as well as an honorable admission. Do you take me for an animal of the class Amphibia, and that I can play with my lungs, as a blacksmith does with his bellows!"

The naturalist might have expended his breath much longer, without producing any desirable result, had Esther been his only auditor. Disappointed and alarmed, the woman had already sought her pallet, and was preparing with a sort of desperate indifference, to compose herself to sleep. Abner, the sentinel below, however, had been aroused from an exceedingly equivocal situation, by the outcry, and as he had now regained sufficient consciousness to recognize the voice of the Physician, the latter was admitted, with the least possible delay. Doctor Battius bustled through the narrow entrance, with an air of singular impatience, and was already beginning to mount the difficult ascent, when catching a view of the porter, he paused to observe with an air that he intended should be impressively admonitory—

"Abner, there are dangerous symptoms of somnolency about thee! It is sufficiently exhibited in the tendency to hiation, and may prove dangerous not only to yourself, but to all thy father's family!"

"You never made a greater mistake, Doctor," returned the youth, gaping like an indolent lion; "I haven't a symptom, as you call it, about any part of me, and as to father and the children, I reckon, the small-pox, and the measles, have been thoroughly through the breed these many months ago."

Content with his brief admonition, the Naturalist, had surmounted half the difficulties of the ascent, before the deliberate Abner ended his justification. On the summit, Obed fully expected to encounter Esther, of whose linguacious powers, he had too often been furnished with the most sinister proofs, and of which he stood in an awe too salutary to covet a repetition of the attacks. The reader can foresee that he was to be agreeably disappointed. Treading lightly, and looking timidly over his shoulder as if he apprehended a shower of something, even more formidable than words, the

Doctor, proceeded to the place, which had been allotted to himself, in the general disposition of the dormitories.

Instead of sleeping the worthy naturalist sat ruminating over what he had both seen and heard that day, until the tossing and mutterings which proceeded from the cabin of Esther, who was his nearest neighbor, advertised him of the wakeful situation of its inmate. Perceiving the necessity of doing something to disarm this female Cerberus, before his own purpose could be accomplished, the Doctor, reluctant as he was to encounter her tongue, found himself compelled, to invite a colloquial communication.

"You appear not to sleep, my very kind and worthy Mrs. Bush," he said, determined to commence his applications with a plaister that was usually found to adhere; "you appear to rest badly, my excellent hostess. Can I administer to your ailings?"

"What would you give me, man," grumbled Esther. "A blister to make me sleep!"

"Say, rather a cataplasm. But if you are in pain, here are some cordial drops, which, taken in a glass of my own Cogniac, will give you rest, if I know aught of the Materia Medica."

The Doctor, as he very well knew, had assailed Esther on her weak side; and as he doubted not of the acceptable quality of his prescription he set himself at work, without unnecessary delay, to prepare it. When he made his offering, it was received in a snappish and threatening manner, but swallowed with a facility that sufficiently proclaimed how much it was relished. The woman muttered her thanks, and her leech re-seated himself, in silence, to await the operation of the dose. In less than half an hour, the breathing of Esther became so profound, and as the Doctor himself, might have termed it, so very abstracted, that, had he not known how easy it was to ascribe this new instance of somnolency to the powerful dose of opium with which he had garnished the brandy, he might have seen reason to distrust his own prescription. With the sleep of the restless woman, the stillness became profound and general.

Then Dr. Battius saw fit, to arise, with the silence and caution, of the midnight robber, and to steal out of his own cabin, or rather kennel, for it deserved no better name, towards the adjoining dormitories. Here he took time to assure himself that all his neighbors were buried in deep sleep. Once advised of this important fact, he hesitated no longer, but commenced the difficult ascent which led to the upper pinnacle of the rock. His advance, though abundantly guarded, was not entirely noiseless, but while he was felicitating himself on having successfully effected his object, and he was in the very act of placing his foot on the highest ledge, a hand was laid upon the skirts of his coat, which as effectually put an end to his advance, as if the gigantic strength of Ishmael himself had pinned him to the earth.

"Is there sickness in the tent," whispered a soft voice in his very ear, "that Doctor Battius, is called to visit it at such an hour?"

So soon as the heart of the Naturalist had returned from its hasty expedition into his throat, as one less skilled than Dr. Battius in the formation of the animal, would have been apt to have accounted for the extraordinary sensation with which he received this unlook'd for interruption, he found resolution to reply, using, as much in terror as in prudence, the same precaution in the indulgence of his voice.

"My worthy Nelly, I am greatly rejoiced to find it is no other than thee! Hist! child, hist! Should Ishmael gain a knowledge of our plans, he would not hesitate to cast us both, from this rock, upon the plain beneath. Hist, Nelly, hist."

As the Doctor delivered his injunctions between the intervals of his ascent, by the time they were concluded, both he and his auditor had gained the upper level.

"And now, Doctor Battius," the girl gravely demanded, "may I know the reason why you have run so great a risk of flying from this place, without wings, and at the certain expense of your neck?"

"Nothing shall be concealed from thee, worthy and trusty Nelly—but are you certain, that Ishmael will not awake."

"No fear of him; he will sleep until the sun scorches his eye lids. The danger is from my aunt."

"Esther sleepeth," the Doctor sententiously replied. "Ellen, you have been watching, on this rock, to-day?"

"I was ordered to do so."

"And you have seen the bison, and the antelope, and the wolf, and the deer, as usual; animals of the *orders*, pecora, belluæ and feræ."

"I have seen the creatures you nam'd in English; but I know nothing of the Indian languages."

"There is still an *order* that I have not named, which you have also seen. The Primates—is it not true?"

"I cannot say. I know no animal by that name."

"Nay, Ellen, you confer with a friend. Of the *genus*, homo, child."

"Whatever else I may have had in view, I have not seen the vespertilio horribi—"

"Hush, Nelly, thy vivacity will betray us. Tell me, girl; have you not seen certain *bipeds* called, *men*, wandering about the Prairie."

"Surely. My uncle and his sons, have been hunting the buffaloe since the sun began to fall."

"I must speak in the vernacular to be comprehended! Ellen, I would say of the *species*, Kentucky."

Though Ellen reddened like the rose, her blushes were concealed by the darkness. She hesitated an instant, and then summoned sufficient spirit to say, decidedly—

"If you wish to speak in parables, Doctor Battius, you must find another listener. Put your questions plainly, in English, and I will answer them honestly in the same tongue."

"I have been journeying in this desert, as thou knowest, Nelly, in quest of animals, that have been hidden from the eyes of science, until now. Among others, I have discovered a Primates, of the *genus* homo; *species*, Kentucky; which I term Paul—"

"Hist, for the sake of mercy!" said Ellen, "speak lower, Doctor, or we shall be ruined."

"Hover, by profession a collector of the Apes, or Bee," continued the other. "Do I use the vernacular now—am I understood."

"Perfectly, perfectly," returned the girl, breathing with difficulty in her surprise. "But what of him—did he tell you to mount this rock—he knows nothing, himself, for the oath I gave my uncle, has shut my mouth."

"Ay, but there is one, that has taken no oath, who has revealed all. I would that the mantle which is wrapped around the mysteries of nature, were as effectually withdrawn from its hidden treasures! Ellen. Ellen, the man with whom I have unwittingly formed a compactum, or agreement, is sadly forgetful of the obligations of honesty! Thy uncle, child."

"You mean, Ishmael Bush, my father's brother's widow's husband," returned the offended girl, a little proudly—"Indeed, indeed, it is cruel to reproach me with a tie, that chance has formed, and which I would rejoice so much to break for ever!"

The humbled Ellen could utter no more, but sinking on a projection of the rock, she began to sob in a manner that rendered their situation doubly critical. The Doctor muttered a few words, which he intended as an apologetic explanation, but before he had time to complete his laboured vindication, she arose and said with decision—

"I did not come here to pass my time in foolish tears, nor you to try to stop them. What then has brought you hither?"

"I must see the inmate of that tent."

"You know what it contains?"

"I am taught to believe I do; and I bear a letter, which I must deliver with my own hands. If the animal prove a quadruped, Ishmael is a true man—if a biped, fledged or unfledged, I care not, he is false, and our compactum at an end!"

Ellen made a sign for the Doctor to remain where he was, and to be silent. She then glided into the tent, where she continued many minutes, that proved exceedingly weary and anxious to the expectant without, but the instant she returned, she took him by the arm and together they entered beneath the folds of the mysterious cloth.

Chapter XII

"Pray God the Duke of York excuse himself!"
2 Henry VI, I.iii.178.

THE MUSTERING of the borderers on the following morning, was silent, sullen and gloomy. The repast of that hour, was wanting in the inharmonious accompanyment, with which Esther ordinarily enlivened their meals, for the effects of the powerful opiate the Doctor had administered, still muddled her intellects. The young men brooded over the absence of their elder brother, and the brows of Ishmael, himself, were knit, as he cast his scowling eyes from one to the other, like a man preparing to meet and to repel an expected assault on his authority. In the midst of this family distrust, Ellen and her midnight confederate, the Naturalist, took their usual places, among the children, without awakening suspicion or exciting comment. The only apparent fruits of the adventure in which they had been engaged, were occasional upliftings of the eyes, on the part of the Doctor, which were mistaken by the observers for some of his scientific contemplations of the heavens, but which, in reality, were no other than furtive glances at the fluttering walls of the proscribed tent.

At length the squatter, who had waited, in vain for some more decided manifestation of the expected rising among his sons, resolved to make a demonstration of his own intentions.

"Asa shall account to me, for this undutiful conduct!" he observed. "Here has the live-long night gone by, and he outlying on the Prairie, when his hand and his rifle might both have been wanted in a brush with the Siouxes, for any right he had to know the contrary."

"Spare your breath, good man;" retorted his wife, "be saving of your breath; for you may have to call long enough for the boy before he will answer."

"It ar' a fact, that some men be so womanish, as to let the young master the old! But you, old Eester, should know better, than to think such will ever be the natur of things, in the family of Ishmael Bush."

"Ah! you ar' a hectorer with the boys, when need calls! I know it, well, Ishmael, and one of your sons, have you driven from you, by your temper; and that, too, at a time when he is most wanted."

"Father," said Abner, whose sluggish nature had, gradually, been stimulating itself to the exertion of taking so bold a stand, "the boys and I have pretty generally concluded, to go out on the search of Asa. We are disagreeable, about his camping on the Prairie, instead of coming in to his own bed, as we all know, he would like to do—"

"Pshaw!" muttered Abiram; "the boy, has killed a buck, or, perhaps a buffaloe, and he is sleeping by the carcass to keep off the wolves 'till day; we shall soon see him, or hear him, bawling for help to bring in his load."

"Tis little help, that a son of mine will call for, to shoulder a buck or to quarter your wild beef!" returned the Mother. "And you, Abiram, to say so uncertain a thing! you, who said yourself, that the red skins had been prowling around this place, no later than the yesterday."

"I!" exclaimed her brother, hastily, as if anxious to retract an error. "I said it then, and I say it now, and so you will find it to be. The Tetons are in our neighborhood, and happy will it prove for the boy, if he is well shut of them."

"It seems to me," said Doctor Battius, speaking with the sort of deliberation and dignity one is apt to use, after having thoroughly ripened his opinions by sufficient reflection, "it seems to me, a man but little skilled in the signs and tokens of Indian warfare, especially as practised in these remote plains, but one, who I may say without vanity has some insight into the mysteries of nature; it seems, then, to me thus humbly qualified, that when doubts exist, in a matter of moment, it would, always be the wisest course to appease them."

"No more of your doctoring for me," cried the grum Esther, "no more of your quiddities in a healthy family, say I. Here, was I doing well, only a little out of sorts with over instructing the young, and you dos'd me with a drug, that hangs about my tongue, like a pound weight on a humming bird's wing."

"Is the medicine out?" drily demanded Ishmael: "it must be

a rare dose that gives a heavy feel to the tongue of old Eester!"

"Friends," continued the Doctor, waving his hand for the angry wife to maintain the peace, "that it cannot perform all that is said of it, the very charge of good Mrs. Bush is a sufficient proof. But to speak of the absent, Asa. There is doubt, as to his fate, and there is a proposition to solve it. Now in the natural sciences, truth is always a desideratum, and I confess it would seem to be equally so, in the present case of domestick uncertainty, which may be called a vacuum, where, according to the laws of physick, there should exist some pretty palpable proofs of materiality."

"Don't mind him, don't mind him," cried Esther, observing that the rest of his auditors listened with an attention which might proceed, equally, from acquiescence in his proposal or ignorance of its meaning. "There is a drug in every word he utters."

"Doctor Battius wishes to say," Ellen modestly interposed, "that as some of us, think Asa is in danger, and some think otherwise, the whole family might pass an hour or two, in looking for him."

"Does he," interrupted the woman, "then Dr. Battius has more sense in him, than I believed. She is right, Ishmael; and what she says shall be done. I will shoulder a rifle myself, and woe betide, the red-skin, that crosses my path! I have pulled a trigger before to day, ay, and heard an Indian yell, too, to my sorrow."

The spirit of Esther diffused itself, like the stimulus which attends a war-cry, among her sons. They arose in a body and declared their determination to second so bold a resolution. Ishmael prudently yielded to an impulse that he could not resist, and in a few minutes, the woman appeared, shouldering her arms, prepared to lead forth in person, such of her descendants as chose to follow.

"Let them stay with the children that please," she said, "and them follow me who ar' not chicken-hearted."

"Abiram, it will not do to leave the huts without some guard," Ishmael whispered, glancing his eye upward.

The man whom he address'd started, and betrayed extraordinary eagerness in his reply.

"I will tarry and watch the camp."

A dozen voices were instantly raised in objections to this proposal. He was wanted to point out the places where the hostile tracks had been seen, and his termagant sister openly scouted at the idea, as unworthy of his manhood. The reluctant Abiram was compelled to yield, and Ishmael, made a new disposition for the defence of the place, which was admitted, by every one, to be all important to their security and comfort.

He offered the post of Commandant to Dr. Battius, who, however peremptorily and somewhat haughtily declined the doubtful honor, exchanging looks of intelligence with Ellen as he did so. In this dilemma the squatter was obliged to constitute the girl, herself, castellan; taking care, however, in deputing this important trust to omit no words of caution and instruction. When this preliminary point was settled, the young men, proceeded to arrange certain means of defence, and signals of alarm, that were adapted to the weakness and character of the garrison. Several masses of rock were drawn to the edge of the upper level, and, so placed, as to leave it at the discretion of the feeble Ellen and her associates to cast them or not, as they might choose, on the heads of any invaders, who would, of necessity, be obliged to mount the eminence, by the difficult and narrow passage already so often mentioned. In addition to this formidable obstruction, the barriers were strengthened, and rendered nearly impassable. Smaller missiles, that might be hurled even by the hands of the younger children, but which would prove, from the elevation of the place, exceedingly dangerous, were provided in profusion. A pile of dried leaves and splinters, was placed as a beacon on the upper rock, and then even in the jealous judgment of the squatter, the post was deemed competent to maintain a creditable siege.

The moment the rock was thought to be in a state of sufficient security, the party who composed what might be called the sortie, sallied forth, on their anxious expedition. The advance was led by Esther in person, who, attired in a dress half-masculine, and bearing a weapon like the rest, seem'd no unfit leader for the groupe of wildly clad frontier-men, that followed in her rear.

"Now, Abiram," cried the Amazon in a voice that was cracked and harsh, for the simple reason of being used too often on a strained and unnatural key, "now, Abiram, run with your nose low, show yourself a hound of the true breed, and do some credit to your training. You it was, that saw the prints of the Indian moccasin, and it behoves you, to let others be as wise as yourself. Come; come to the front, man, and give us a bold lead."

The brother, who appeared, at all times, to stand in awe of his sister's authority, complied, though it was with a reluctance so evident, as to excite sneers, even among the unobservant and indolent sons of the squatter. Ishmael, himself, mov'd among his tall children like one who expected nothing from the search, and who was indifferent, alike to its success or failure. In this manner the party proceeded until their distant fortress had sunk so low, as to present an object no larger nor more distinct than a hazy point, on the margin of the Prairie. Hitherto their progress, had been silent, and somewhat rapid, for as swell after swell, was mounted and passed, without varying, or discovering a living object to enliven the monotony of the view, even the tongue of Esther was hushed in increasing anxiety. Here, however, Ishmael chose to pause; and casting the butt of his rifle from his shoulder to the ground, he observed—

"This is enough. Buffaloe signs, and deer signs, ar' plenty; but where ar' thy Indian footsteps, Abiram?"

"Still farther West," returned the other pointing in the direction he named. "This was the spot where I struck the tracks of the buck; it was after I took the deer, that I fell upon the Teton trail."

"And a bloody piece of work you made of it, man," cried the squatter, pointing tauntingly to the soiled garments of his kinsman, and then directing the attention of the spectators to his own, by the way of a triumphant contrast. "Here have I cut the throat of two lively does, and a scampering fawn without spot or stain, while you, blundering dog as you ar', have made as much work for Eester and her girls, as though butchering was your regular calling. Come, boys: it is enough. I am too old, not to know the signs of the frontiers; no Indian has been here since the last fall of water. Follow me, and I will make a turn that shall give us at least the beef of a fallow cow, for our trouble."

"Follow *me*!" echoed Esther, stepping undauntedly forward. "I am leader to day, and I *will* be followed—who so proper, let me know, as a mother to head a search for her own lost child!"

Ishmael regarded his untractable mate with a smile of indulgent pity. Observing that she had already struck out a path for herself, different both from that of Abiram and the one he had seen fit to choose, and being unwilling to draw the cord of authority too tight, just at that moment, he submitted to her will. But Doctor Battius, who had hitherto, been a silent and thoughtful, attendant on the woman, now, saw fit to raise his feeble voice, in the way of remonstrance.

"I agree with thy partner in life, worthy and gentle Mrs. Bush," he said, "in believing that some ignuus fatuus of the imagination, has deceived Abiram, in the signs or symptoms of which he has spoken."

"Symptoms, yourself!" interrupted the termagant. "This is no time for bookish words, nor is this a place to stop, and swallow medicines. If you ar' a-leg weary say so, as a plain-speaking man should; then seat yourself on the Prairie, like a hound that is foot-sore, and take your natural rest."

"I accord in the opinion," the Naturalist calmly replied, complying literally with the opinion of the deriding Esther, by taking his seat, very coolly by the side of an indigenous shrub, the examination of which he commenced, on the instant, in order, that science might not lose any of its just and important dues. "I honor your excellent advice, Mistress Esther, as you may perceive. Go thou in quest of thy offspring, while I tarry here, in pursuit of that which is better; viz, an insight into the arcana of nature's volume."

The woman answered with a hollow, unnatural and scornful laugh, and even her heavy sons, as they slowly passed the seat of the already abstracted naturalist, did not disdain to manifest their contempt in smiles. In a few minutes, the train mounted the nearest eminence, and as it turned the rounded acclivity, the Doctor was left to pursue his profitable investigations in entire solitude.

Another half-hour passed during which Esther, continued

to advance on her, seemingly, fruitless search. Her pauses, however, were becoming frequent and her looks wandering and uncertain, when footsteps, were heard, clattering through the bottom, and at the next instant, a buck was seen to bound up the ascent, and to dart from before their eyes, in the direction of the naturalist. So sudden and unlooked-for had been the passage of the animal, and so much had he been favored by the shape of the ground, that, before any one of the foresters had time to bring his rifle to his shoulder, it was already beyond the range of a bullet.

"Look out for the wolf!" shouted Abner, shaking his head, in vexation at being a single moment too late. "A wolf's skin, will be no bad gift, in a winter's night. Ay, yonder the hungry devil comes."

"Hold!" cried Ishmael, knocking up the levelled weapon of his too eager son. " 'Tis not a wolf; but a hound of thorough blood and bottom! Ha! we have hunters nigh. There ar' two of them!"

He was still speaking when the animals in question, came leaping, on the track of the deer, striving with noble ardor to outdo each other. One was an aged dog, whose strength seem'd to be sustained purely by generous emulation, and the other a pup, that gamboled, even, while he press'd most warmly on the chace. They both ran, however, with clean and powerful leaps, carrying their noses high, like animals of the most keen and subtle scent. They had passed; and in another minute, they would have been, running open-mouthed with the deer in view, had not the younger dog, suddenly bounded from the course, and uttered a cry of surprise. His aged companion, stopped also, and returned panting and exhausted, to the place where the other was whirling around in swift, and apparently in mad evolutions, circling the spot in his own footsteps and continuing his outcry, in a short, snappish barking. But when the elder hound, had reach'd the spot, he seated himself, and lifting his nose high into the air, he raised a long, loud, and wailing howl.

"It must be a strong scent," said Abner, who had been, with the rest of the family, an admiring observer of the movements of the dogs, "that can break off two such creaturs so suddenly from their trail."

"Murder them!" cried Abiram; "I'll swear to the old hound, 'tis the dog of the trapper, whom we now know to be our mortal enemy."

Though the brother of Esther gave so hostile advice, he appeared in no way ready to put it in execution, himself. The surprise which had taken possession of the whole party exhibited itself, in his own vacant, wondering stare, as strongly as in any of the admiring visages, by whom he was surrounded. His denunciation, therefore, notwithstanding its dire import was disregarded, and the dogs were left to obey the impulses of their mysterious instinct, without let or hindrance.

It was long before any of the spectators broke the silence; but the squatter, at length, so far recollected his authority, as to take on himself the right to controul the movements of his children.

"Come away, boys; come, away and leave the hounds to sing their tunes for their own amusement," Ishmael said in his coldest manner. "I scorn to take the life of a beast because its master has pitch'd himself too nigh my clearing—come, away, boys; come away; we have enough of our own work before us, without turning aside to do that of the whole neighbourhood."

"Come *not*, away!" cried Esther, in tones that sounded like the admonitions of some Sybil. "I say, come, *not* away, my children. There is a meaning and a warning in this; and as I am a woman and a mother, will I know the truth of it all."

So saying, the awakened wife brandished her weapon with an air, that was not without its wild and secret influence, and led the way, towards the spot, where the dogs, still remained, filling the air with their long drawn and piteous complaints. The whole party, followed in her steps, some too indolent to oppose, others obedient to her will, and all more or less excited by the uncommon character of the scene.

"Tell me, you Abner—Abiram—Ishmael—" the woman cried, standing over a spot where the earth was trampled and beaten, and plainly sprinkled with blood; "tell me, you who ar' hunters, what sort of animal, has here met his death?—Speak!—ye ar' men, and used to the signs of the plains; is it the blood of wolf or panther?"

"A buffaloe, and a noble and powerful creatur has it been,"

returned the squatter, who look'd down calmly on these fatal signs, which so strangely affected his wife. "Here are the marks of the spot, where he has struck his hoofs into the earth in the death-struggle, and yonder he has plunged and torn the ground with his horns. Ay, a buffaloe bull, of wonderful strength and courage has he been!"

"And who has slain him!" continued Esther; "man! where—are the offals?—wolves!—they devour not the hide. Tell me, ye men and hunters, is this the blood of a beast?"

"The creatur, has plunged over the hillock," said Abner, who had proceeded a short distance beyond the rest of the party. "Ah! there you will find it, in yon swale of alders. Look! a thousand carrion birds, ar' hovering, above the carcass."

"The animal has still life in him," returned the squatter, "or the buzzards would settle upon their prey! By the action of the dogs, it must be something ravenous, I reckon it is the white bear from the upper falls. They are said to cling desperately to life."

"Let us go back," said Abiram; "there may be danger, and there can be no good, in attacking a ravenous beast. Remember, Ishmael, 'twill be a risky job, and one of small profit."

The young men smil'd at this new proof of the well known pusilanimity of their uncle. The oldest even proceeded, so far as to express his contempt, by bluntly saying—

"It will do, to cage with the other animal we carry. Then we may go back double-handed into the settlements, and set up for showmen around the court-houses and gaols of Kentuck."

The threatening frown which gathered on the brow of his father admonished the young man to forbear. Exchanging looks that were half-rebellious with his brethren, he saw fit to be silent. But instead of observing the caution recommended by Abiram, they proceeded in a body until, they, again, came to a halt within a few yards of the matted cover of the thicket.

The scene had, now, indeed, become wild and striking enough, to have produced a powerful effect on minds better prepared than those of the unnurtured family of the squatter, to resist the impressions of so exciting a spectacle. The heavens were as usual at the season covered with dark driving clouds, beneath which interminable flocks of aquatic birds, were again on the wing, holding their toilsome and heavy way, towards the distant waters of the south. The wind had risen, and was once more sweeping over the Prairie in gusts, which it was often vain to oppose, and then again the blasts would seem to mount into the upper air, as if to sport with the drifting vapour, whirling and rolling, vast masses of the dusky and ragged volumes over each other, in a terrific and yet grand disorder. Above the little brake, the flocks of birds, still held their flight, circling with heavy wings about the spot, struggling at times against the torrent of wind, and then, favored by their position and height, making bold swoops upon the thicket, away from which, however, they never fail'd to sail, screaming in terror, as if apprised, either by sight or instinct, that the hour of their voracious dominion had not yet fully arrived.

Ishmael stood for many minutes, with his wife and children clustered together, in an amazement with which awe was singularly mingled, gazing in death-like stillness on the sight. The voice of Esther, at length, broke the charm, and reminded the spectators of the necessity of resolving their doubts, in some manner more worthy of their manhood, than by dull and inactive observation.

"Call in the dogs!" she said, "call in the hounds, and put them into the thicket. There ar' men enough of ye, if ye have not lost the spirit, with which I know ye were born, to tame the tempers of all the bears, west of the big river. Call in the dogs, I say, you, Enoch—Abner, Gabriel, has wonder made ye deaf!"

One of the young men complied; and having succeeded in detaching the hounds from the place, around which, until then, they had not ceased to hover, he led them down to the margin of the thicket.

"Put them in, boy. Put them in," continued the woman; "and you, Ishmael and Abiram, if anything wicked or hurtful comes forth, show them the use of your rifles, like frontiermen. If ye ar' wanting in spirit, before the eyes of my children will I put ye both to shame!"

The youths who, until now, had detained the hounds, let slip the thongs of skin by which they had been held, and urged them to the attack, by their voices. But it would seem, that the elder dog, was restrained by some extraordinary sensation, or that he was much too experienced to attempt the rash adventure. After proceeding a few yards to the very verge of the brake, he made a sudden pause, and stood trembling in all his aged limbs, apparently as unable to recede as to advance. The encouraging calls of the young men were disregarded, or only answered by a low and plaintive whining. For a minute, the pup also was similarly affected; but less sage, or more easily excited, he was induced at length, to leap forward, and finally to dash into the cover. An alarmed and startling howl was heard, and at the next minute he broke out of the thicket, and commenced circling the spot in the same wild and unsteady manner as before.

"Have I a man among my children!" demanded Esther. "Give me, a truer piece than a childish shot-gun, and I will show ye, what the courage of a frontier woman can do!"

"Stay, mother," exclaimed Abner and Enoch; "if you *will* see the creatur, let *us* drive it into view."

This was quite as much, as the youths were accustomed to utter even on more important occasions, but having given a pledge of their intentions, they were far from being backward in redeeming it. Preparing their arms with the utmost care, they advanced with steadiness, to the brake. Nerves less often tried, than those of the young borderers might have shrunk before the dangers of so uncertain an undertaking. As they proceeded, the howls of the dogs, became more shrill and plaintive, the vultures and buzzards settled so low, as to flap the bushes with their heavy wings, and the wind came hoarsely sweeping along the naked Prairie, as if the spirits of the air, had, also descended, to witness the approaching developement.

There was a breathless moment, when the blood of the undaunted Esther, flowed backward to her heart, as she saw her sons push aside the matted branches of the thicket, and bury themselves in its labyrinth. A deep and solemn pause succeeded. Then arose two loud and piercing cries, in quick succession, which were followed by a quiet still more awful and appalling.

"Come back, come back, my children," cried the woman, the feelings of a mother getting the ascendancy.

But her voice, was hushed, and every faculty seem'd frozen with horror, as at that instant, the bushes once more parted, and the two adventurers reappeared, pale and nearly insensible themselves and laid at her feet, the stiff and motionless body of the lost Asa, with the marks of a violent death but too plainly stamp'd on every pallid lineament.

The dogs uttered a long and closing howl and then breaking off, together, they disappeared on the forsaken trail of the deer. The flight of birds, wheeled upward into the heavens, filling the air with their complaints at having been robbed of a victim, which, frightful and disgusting as it was, still bore too much of the impression of humanity to become the prey of their obscene appetites.

Chapter XIII

"A pickaxe, and a spade, a spade.
For,—and a shrouding sheet:
O, a pit of clay for to be made
For such a guest is meet."
Hamlet, V.i.94–97.

STAND BACK! stand off, the whole of ye!" said Esther, hoarsely, to the crowd which press'd too closely on the corpse, "I am his mother, and my right is better than that of ye all. Who has done this! Tell, me, Ishmael, Abiram, Abner, open your mouths and your hearts, and let God's truth and no other issue from them. Who has done this bloody deed?"

Her husband made no reply but stood, leaning on his rifle, looking sadly, but with an unaltered eye, at the mangled remains of his son. Not so the mother: She threw herself on the earth, and receiving the cold and ghastly head into her lap, she sat contemplating those muscular features, on which the death-agony was still horridly impressed, in a silence, far more expressive than any language of lamentation could have proved.

The voice of the woman was frozen in grief. In vain Ishmael attempted a few words of rude consolation; she neither listened nor answered. Her sons gathered about her in a circle, and expressed after their uncouth manner, their sympathy in her sorrows, as well as their sense of their own loss; but she motioned them away, impatiently, with her hand. At times, her fingers play'd in the matted hair of the dead, and at others, they lightly attempted to smooth the painfully expressive muscles of its ghastly visage, as the hand of the mother, is seen lingering fondly about the features of her sleeping child. Then starting from their revolting office, her hands would flutter around her, and seem to seek some fruitless remedy against the violent blow, which had thus suddenly destroyed the child, in whom she had not only plac'd her greatest hopes, but so much of her maternal pride. While engaged in the latter incomprehensible manner, the lethargic Abner, turned aside, and swallowing the unwonted emotions which were rising in his own throat, he observed—

"Mother means, that we should look for the signs, that we may know in what manner, Asa has come by his end."

"We owe it to the accursed Siouxes," answered Ishmael. "Twice have they put me deeply in their debt! The third time, the score shall be cleared!"

But, not content with this plausible explanation, and perhaps secretly glad to avert their eyes from a spectacle which awakened so extraordinary and unusual sensations in their sluggish bosoms, the sons of the squatter turned away, in a body, from their mother and the corpse, and proceeded to make the enquiries, which they fancied the former had so repeatedly demanded. Ishmael, made no objections; but, though he accompanied his children, while they proceeded in the investigation, it was more with the appearance of complying with their wishes, at a time when resistance might not be seemly, than with any visible interest in the result. As the borderers, notwithstanding their usual dullness, were well instructed in most things connected with their habits of life, an inquiry, the success of which depended so much on signs and evidences that bore so strong a resemblance to a forest trail, was likely to be conducted, with skill and acuteness. Accordingly, they proceeded to the melancholy task with great readiness and intelligence.

Abner and Enoch, agreed in their accounts as to the position in which they had found the body. It was seated nearly upright, the back supported by a mass of matted brush, and one hand still grasping a broken twig of the alders. It was, most probably, owing to the former circumstance, that the body had escaped the rapacity of the carrion birds, which had been seen hovering above the thicket, and the latter prov'd that life had not yet entirely abandoned the hapless victim when he entered the brake. The opinion now became general that the youth had received his death wound in the open Prairie, and had dragged his enfeebled form into the cover of the thicket for the purpose of concealment. A trail through the bushes confirmed this opinion. It also appeared, on examination, that a desperate struggle had taken place on the very margin of the thicket. This was sufficiently apparent by the trodden branches, the deep impressions on the moist ground, and the lavish flow of blood.

"He has been shot in the open ground and come here for a cover," said Abiram, "these marks would clearly prove it. The boy has been set upon by the savages, in a body, and has fout like a hero as he was, until they have mastered his strength, and then drawn him to the bushes."

To this probable opinion there was now but one dissenting voice; that of the slow-minded Ishmael who demanded that the corpse, itself, should be examined in order to obtain a more accurate knowledge of its injuries. On examination, it appeared, that a rifle bullet had passed directly through the body of the deceased, entering beneath one of his brawny shoulders and making its exit, by the breast. It required some knowledge in gun-shot wounds to decide this delicate point, but the experience of the borderers was quite equal to the scrutiny, and a smile of wild, and certainly of singular satisfaction passed among the sons of Ishmael, when Abner confidently announced that the enemies of Asa had assailed him in the rear.

"It must be so," said the gloomy but attentive squatter. "He was of too good a stock and too well trained, knowingly to turn the weak side to man or beast! Remember, boys, that while the front of manhood is to your enemy, let him be who or what he may, you ar' safe from cowardly surprise—Why Eester, woman! you ar' getting beside yourself, with picking at the hair and the garments of the child! Little good can you do him, now, old girl."

"See!" interrupted Enoch extricating from the fragments of cloth, the morsel of lead which had prostrated the strength of one so powerful. "Here is the very bullet!"

Ishmael took it in his hand, and eyed it long and closely.

"There's no mistake"—at length he muttered, through his compressed teeth. "It is from the pouch of that accursed trapper. Like many of the hunters, he has a mark in his mould in order to know the work his rifle performs, and here you see it plainly—six little holes laid crossways."

"I'll swear to it!" cried Abiram, triumphantly; "he show'd me his private mark, himself, and boasted of the number of deer he had laid upon the Prairies with these very bullets! Now, Ishmael, will you believe me, when I tell you the old knave is a spy of the red-skins."

The lead pass'd from the hand of one to that of another, and unfortunately for the reputation of the old man, several among them remembered also to have seen the aforesaid private bullet-mark, during the curious examination which all had made of his accoutrements. In addition to this wound, however, were many others of a less dangerous nature, all of which were deemed to confirm the supposed guilt of the trapper.

The traces of many different struggles were to be seen, between the spot, where the first blood was spilt and the thicket to which it was now generally believed Asa had retreated as a place of refuge. These were interpreted into so many proofs of the weakness of the murderer, who would have sooner dispatched his victim had not even the dying strength of the youth rendered him formidable to the infirmities of one so old. The danger of drawing some others of the hunters to the spot, by repeated firing, was deem'd a sufficient reason for not again resorting to the rifle after it had performed the important duty of disabling the victim. The weapon of the dead man, was not to be found, and had doubtless, together with many other less valuable and lighter articles, that he was accustomed to carry about his person, become a prize to his destroyer.

But what, in addition to the tell tale bullet, appeared to fix the ruthless deed with peculiar certainty on the trapper, was the accumulated evidence, furnished by the trail, which proved, notwithstanding his deadly hurt, that the wounded man had still been able to make a long and desperate resistance to the subsequent efforts of his murderer. Ishmael seemed to press this proof, with a singular mixture of sorrow and pride—sorrow at the loss of a son, whom in their moments of amity he highly valued; and pride at the courage and power he had manifested to his last and weakest breath.

"He died as a son of mine should die," said the squatter, gleaning a hollow consolation from so unnatural an exultation, "a dread to his enemy to the last, and without help from the law. Come, children; we have the grave to make, and then to hunt his murderer!"

The sons of the squatter set about their melancholy office in silence and in sadness. An excavation was made in the hard earth, at a great expense of toil and time, and the body was wrapped in such spare vestments as could be collected among the laborers. When these arrangements were completed, Ishmael approached the seemingly, unconscious Esther, and announced his intention to inter the dead. She heard him, and quietly relinquished her grasp of the corpse, rising in silence to follow it to its narrow resting place. Here she seated herself, again, at the head of the grave, watching each movement of the youths, with eager and jealous eyes. When a sufficiency of earth was laid upon the senseless clay of Asa, to protect it from injury, Enoch and Abner, entered the cavity, and trode it into a solid mass, by the weight of their huge frames, with an appearance of a strange, not to say savage mixture, of care and indifference. This well-known precaution was adopted to prevent the speedy exhumation of the body, by some of the carnivorous beasts of the Prairie, whose instinct was sure to guide them to the spot. Even the rapacious birds, appeared to comprehend the nature of the ceremony, for, mysteriously apprised that the miserable victim was now about to be abandoned by the human race, they once more began to make their airy circuits above the place, screaming, as if to frighten the kinsmen from their labour of caution and love.

Ishmael stood with folded arms, steadily watching the manner in which this necessary duty was performed, and when the whole was completed, he lifted his cap to his sons, to thank them for their services, with a dignity that would have become one much better nurtured. Throughout the whole of a ceremony, which is ever solemn and admonitory, the squatter had maintained a grave and serious deportment. His vast features were visibly stamp'd with an expression of deep concern, but at no time did they falter, until he turned his back, as he believed forever, on the grave of his first-born. Nature was then stirring powerfully within him, and the muscles of his stern visage began to work perceptibly. His children fastened their eyes on his, as if to seek a direction to the strange emotions which were moving their own heavy natures, when the struggle in the bosom of the squatter, suddenly ceased, and taking his wife by the arm he raised her to her feet as if she had been an infant, saying in a voice that was perfectly steady, though a nice observer would have discovered that it was kinder than usual—

"Eester, we have now done all that man and woman can do. We raised the boy, and made him such, as few others were like, on the frontiers of America; and, we have given him a grave. Let us go our way."

The woman turned her eyes slowly from the fresh earth, and laying her hands on the shoulders of her husband, stood looking him, anxiously in the eyes.

"Ishmael! Ishmael!" she said, "you parted from the boy, in your wrath!"

"May the Lord pardon his sins, as freely as I have forgiven his worst misdeeds," calmly returned the squatter; " woman, go you back to the rock, and read your bible, a chapter in that book always does you good. You *can* read, Eester; which is a privilege I never did enjoy."

"Yes, yes," muttered the woman yielding to his strength and suffering herself to be led, though with powerful reluctance, from the spot. "I *can* read; and how have I used the knowledge! But he, Ishmael, he has not the sin, of wasted l'arning to answer for. We have spared him *that*, at least, whether it be in mercy or in cruelty, I know not."

Her husband made no reply, but continued steadily to lead her in the direction of their temporary abode. When they reached the summit of the swell of land, which they knew, was the last spot, from which the situation of the grave of Asa could be seen, they all turned, as by common concurrence to take a farewell view of the place. The little mound itself, was not visible, but it was frightfully indicated by the flock of screaming birds, which hovered above. In the opposite direction, a low blue hillock, in the skirts of the horizon, pointed out the place where Esther had left, the rest of her young, and served as an attraction to draw her reluctant steps from the last abode of her eldest born. Nature quickened in the bosom of the mother at the sight, and she finally yielded the rights of the dead, to the more urgent claims of the living.

The foregoing occurrences had struck a spark from the stern tempers of a set of beings so singularly moulded in the habits of their uncultivated lives, which served to keep alive among them the dying embers of family affection. United to their parents by ties no stronger than those which use had created, there had been great danger, as Ishmael had foreseen, that the overloaded hive would swarm, and leave him, saddled with the difficulties of a young and helpless brood, unsupported by the exertions of those, whom he had, already, brought to a state of maturity. The spirit of insubordination, which emanated from the unfortunate Asa, had spread among his juniors, and the squatter had been made painfully to remember the time, when in the wantonness of his youth and vigor, he had, reversing the order of the brutes, cast off his own aged and failing parents, to enter into the world unshackled and free. But the danger had now abated, for a time at least, and if his authority was not restored with all its former influence, it was admitted to exist, and to maintain its ascendancy a little longer.

It is true, that his slow-minded sons, even while they submitted to the impressions of the recent event, had glimmerings of terrible distrusts, as to the manner in which their elder brother had met with his death. There were, faint and indistinct images in the minds of two or three of the oldest, which portrayed the father, himself, as ready to imitate the example of Abraham, without the justification of the sacred authority, which commanded the holy man to attempt the revolting office. But, then, these images were so transient and so much obscured in intellectual mists as to leave no very strong impressions, and the tendency of the whole transaction, as we have already said, was rather to strengthen, than to weaken the authority of Ishmael.

In this disposition of mind, the party continued their route towards the place, whence, they had that morning issued on a search which had been crowned with so melancholy a success. The long and fruitless march, which they had made under the direction of Abiram, the discovery of the body and its subsequent interment had so far consumed the day, that by the time, their steps were retraced across the broad tract of waste which lay between the grave of Asa and the rock, the sun had fallen, far below his meridian altitude. The hill had gradually risen, as they approached, like some tower, emerging from the bosom of the sea, and when within a mile the minuter objects that crowned its height came, dimly into view.

"It will be a sad meeting for the girls!" said Ishmael, who, from time to time, did not cease to utter something which he intended should be consolatory to the bruised spirit of his partner. "Asa was much regarded, by all the young, and seldom failed to bring in from his hunts something, that they lov'd."

"He did, he did," murmured Esther, "the boy was the pride of the family—My other children are as nothing to him!"

"Say not so, good woman," returned the Father glancing his eye, a little proudly at the athletic train which followed at no great distance in their rear. "Say not so, old Eester for few fathers and mothers, have greater reason to be boastful than ourselves."

"Thankful, thankful," muttered the humbled woman; "ye mean thankful, Ishmael!"

"Then thankful, let it be, if you like the word better, my good girl—but what has become of Nelly and the young! The child has forgotten the charge I gave her, and has not only suffered the children to sleep, but I warrant you, is dreaming of the fields of Tennessee at this very moment. The mind of your niece is mainly fix'd on the settlements, I reckon."

"Ay, she is not for us. I said it, and thought it, when I took her, because death had stripped her of all other friends. Death is a sad worker in the bosom of families, Ishmael. Asa had a kind feeling to the child, and they might have come, one day, into our places, had things been so ordered."

"Nay, she is not gifted for a frontier wife if this is the manner she is to keep house, while the husband, is on the hunt. Abner, let off your rifle, that they may know we ar' coming. I fear Nelly, and the young, ar' asleep."

The young man complied with an alacrity, that manifested how gladly he would see, the rounded, active figure of Ellen, enliven the ragged summit of the rock. But the report was succeeded by neither signal nor answer of any sort. For a moment, the whole party stood in suspense, awaiting the result, and then a simultaneous impulse caused the whole to let off their pieces at the same instant, producing a noise, which might not fail to reach the ears of all within so short a distance.

"Ah! there they come at last!" cried Abiram, who was usually among the first to seize on any circumstance which promised relief from disagreeable apprehensions.

"It is a petticoat fluttering on the line," said Esther; "I put it there myself."

"You ar' right—but now she comes. The jade has been taking her comfort in the tent!"

"It is not so," said Ishmael, whose usually inflexible features were beginning to manifest the uneasiness he felt. "It is the tent, itself, blowing about, loosely, in the wind. They have loosened the bottom, like silly children as they ar', and unless care is had, the whole will come down!"

The words were scarcely uttered, before a rushing blast of wind, swept by the spot where they stood, raising the dust in little eddies, in its progress, and then, as if guided by a master hand, it quitted the earth and mounted, to the precise spot, on which all eyes were just then rivetted. The loosened linen felt its influence and tottered, but regained its poise, and for a moment, it became tranquil. The cloud of leaves next play'd in circling revolutions around the place, and then descended with the velocity of a swooping hawk, and sailed away into the Prairie in long straight lines, like a flight of swallows resting on their expanded wings. They were followed, for some distance by the snow-white tent, which, however, soon fell behind the rock, leaving its highest peak as naked, as when it lay in the entire solitude of the desert.

"The murderers have been here!" moaned Esther. "My babes, my babes!"

For a moment even Ishmael faltered before the weight of so unexpected a blow. But shaking himself, like an awakened lion, he sprang forward and pushing aside the impediments of the barrier, as if they had been feathers, he rushed up the ascent with an impetuosity, which proved how formidable a sluggish nature may become when thoroughly aroused.

Chapter XIV

"Whose party do the townsmen yet admit?"
King John, II.i.361.

IN ORDER to preserve an even pace between the incidents of the tale, it becomes necessary to revert to such events as occurred during the ward of Ellen Wade.

For the few first hours, the cares of the honest and warm hearted girl were confined to the simpler offices of satisfying the often repeated demands which her younger associates made on her time and patience, under the pretences of hunger, thirst, and all the other, ceaseless wants of captious and inconsiderate childhood. She had seized a moment, from their importunities, to steal into the tent, where she was administering to the comforts of one far more deserving of her tenderness, when an outcry, among the children, recalled her to the duties she had momentarily forgotten.

"See, Nelly, see," exclaimed half a dozen eager voices, "yonder ar' men, and Phoebe says that they ar' Sioux Indians!"

Ellen turned her eyes in the direction in which so many arms were already extended, and to her consternation, beheld several men, advancing manifestly and swiftly in a straight line towards the rock. She counted four, but was unable to make out any thing concerning their characters except, that they were not any of those, who of right, were entitled to admission into the fortress. It was a fearful moment for Ellen. Looking around at the juvenile and frightened flock that press'd upon the skirts of her garments, she endeavored to recall to her confused faculties some one of the many tales of female heroism, with which the history of the western frontier abounded. In one a stockade had been successfully defended by a single man supported by three or four women, for days against the assaults of a hundred enemies. In another, the women alone had been able to protect the children and the less valuable effects of their absent husbands; and a third was not wanting, in which a solitary female, had destroyed her sleeping captors and given liberty not only to herself, but to a brood of helpless young. This was the case most nearly assimilated to the situation in which Ellen now found herself, and with flushing cheeks and kindling eyes, the girl began to consider, and to prepare her slender means of defence.

She posted the larger girls, at the little levers that were to cast the rocks on the assailants, the smaller were to be used more for show than any positive service they could perform, while, like any other leader, she reserved her own person, as a superintendant, and encourager of the whole. When these dispositions were made, she endeavored to await the issue, with an air of composure that she intended should inspire her assistants with the confidence necessary to insure success.

Although Ellen was vastly their superior in that spirit which emanates from moral qualities, she was by no means the equal of the two eldest daughters of Esther in the important military property, of insensibility to danger. Reared in the hardihood of a migrating life, on the skirts of society, where they had become familiarised to the sights and dangers of the wilderness, these girls, promised fairly, to become at some future day no less distinguished than their mother, for daring and for that singular mixture of good and evil, which in a wider sphere of action, would probably have enabled the wife of the squatter to enroll her name, among the remarkable females of her time. Esther had already, on one occasion, made good the log tenement of Ishmael, against an inroad of savages, and on another, she had been left for dead, by her enemies, after a defence that with a more civilized foe, would have entitled her to the honours of a liberal capitulation. These facts, and sundry others, of a similar nature, had often been recapitulated with suitable exaltation, in the presence of her daughters, and the bosoms of the young Amazons, were now strangely fluctuating between natural terror, and the ambitious wish to do something that might render them worthy of being the children of such a mother. It appeared that the opportunity for distinction of this wild character, was no longer to be denied them.

The party of strangers was, already within a hundred rods of the rock. Either consulting their usual wary method of advancing, or admonished by the threatening attitudes of two figures, who had thrust forth the barrels of as many old muskets, from behind the stone entrenchment, the new comers halted, under favor of an inequality in the ground, where a growth of grass thicker than common, offered the advantage of concealment. From this spot, they reconnoitred the fortress, for several anxious, and to Ellen, interminable minutes. Then, one advanced singly, and apparently more in the character of a herald than of an assailant.

"Phoebe, *do you* fire," and "no, Hetty, *you*," were beginning to be heard between the half frightened and yet eager daughters of the squatter, when Ellen probably saved the advancing stranger from some imminent alarm, if from no greater danger, by exclaiming—

"Lay down the muskets! 'tis Dr. Battius!"

Her subordinates so far complied, as to withdraw their hands from the locks, though the threatening barrels still maintained the portentous levels. The Naturalist who had advanced with sufficient deliberation to note the smallest hostile demonstration of the garrison, now raised a white handkerchief on the end of his fusee, and came within speaking distance of the fortress. Then, assuming what he intended should be an imposing and dignified semblance of authority, he blustered forth in a voice that might have been heard at a much greater distance—

"What, ho! I summon ye all, in the name of the Confederacy of the United, Sovereign States of North America, to submit yourselves to the laws."

"Doctor or no Doctor; he is an enemy, Nelly; hear him! hear him! he talks of the law!"

"Stop! stay, till I hear his answer!" said the nearly breathless Ellen, pushing aside the dangerous weapons which were again pointed in the direction of the shrinking person of the herald.

"I admonish and forewarn ye all," continued the startled Doctor, "that I am a peaceful Citizen of the before named Confederacy, or, to speak with greater accuracy, Union, a supporter of the Social Compact, and a lover of good order and amity." Then perceiving that the danger, was at least, temporarily, removed, he once more raised his voice to the hostile pitch. "I charge ye all, therefore, to submit to the laws."

"I thought you were a friend," Ellen replied, "and that you travelled with my uncle in virtue of an agreement—"

"It is void! I have been deceived in the very premises; and I, hereby, pronounce a certain compactum, entered into and concluded between Ishmael Bush, squatter, and Obed Battius M. D. to be incontinently null and of non-effect. Nay; children, to be null is merely a negative property, and is fraught with no evil to thy worthy parent, so lay aside the fire arms and listen to the admonitions of reason. I declare it vicious—null—abrogated. As for thee, Nelly, my feelings towards thee are not at all given to hostility; therefore listen to that which I have to utter, nor turn away thine ears in the wantonness of security. Thou knowest the character of the man with whom thou dwellest, young woman, and thou also knowest the danger of being found in evil company. Abandon then the trifling advantages of thy situation, and yield the rock peacably to the will of those who accompany me—a legion, young woman, I do assure you, an invincible and powerful legion. Render therefore the effects of this lawless, and wicked squatter—nay, children, such disregard of human life, is frightful in those who have so recently received the gift, in their own persons, point those dangerous weapons aside, I entreat of you, more for your own sakes than for mine. Hetty, hast thou forgotten who appeased thine anguish when thy auricular nerves were tortured by the colds and damps, of the naked earth! and thou, Phoebe, ungrateful, and forgetful Phoebe! but for this very arm, which you would prostrate with an endless paralysis, thine incisores would still be giving thee pain and sorrow! Lay, then, aside thy weapons, and hearken to the advice of one who has always been thy friend. And, now, young woman," still keeping a jealous eye on the muskets, which the girl had suffered to be diverted a little from their aim, "And now, young woman, for the last, and therefore the most solemn, asking, I demand of thee, the surrender of this rock, without delay or resistance, in the joint names of Power, of justice and of the—" Law, he would have added; but recollecting that this ominous word would again provoke the hostility of the squatter's children, he succeeded in swallowing it, in good season and concluded with the less dangerous and more convertible term of Reason.

This extraordinary summons, failed however, of producing the desired effect. It proved utterly unintelligible to his younger listeners, with the exception of the few offensive terms, already sufficiently distinguished, and though Ellen better comprehended the meaning of the herald, she appeared as little moved by his rhetoric as her companions. At those passages, which he intended should be tender and affecting, the intelligent girl, though tortured by painful feelings, had even manifested a disposition to laugh, while to the threats she turned an utterly insensible ear.

"I know not the meaning of all you wish to say, Dr. Battius," she quietly replied, when he had ended, "but I am sure if it would teach me to betray my trust, it is what I ought not to hear. I caution you to attempt no violence, for let my wishes be what they may, you see I am surrounded by a force that can easily put me down, and you know, or ought to know, too well the temper of this family, to trifle in such a matter, with any of its members, let them be of what sex or age they may."

"I am not entirely ignorant of human character," returned the Naturalist, prudently receding a little from the position, which he had, until now, stoutly maintained at the very base of the hill. "But here comes one, who may know its secret windings still better than I."

"Ellen! Ellen Wade," cried Paul Hover, who had advanced to his elbow, without betraying any of that sensitiveness which had so manifestly discomposed the Doctor, "I didn't expect to find an enemy in you!"

"Nor shall you, when you ask that, which I can grant, without treachery. You know that my uncle has trusted his family to my care, and shall I so far betray the trust, as to let in his bitterest enemies, to murder his children, perhaps, and to rob him of the little which the Indians have left!"

"Am I a murderer! is this old man, this Officer of the States," pointing to the trapper and his newly discovered friend, both of whom by this time, stood at his side, "is either of them likely to do the things you name."

"What is it then, you ask of me?" said Ellen, wringing her hands in excessive doubt.

"The beast—nothing more nor less than the squatter's hidden, ravenous, dangerous beast!"

"Excellent young woman," commenced the young stranger, who had so lately joined himself to the party on the Prairie—but his mouth was immediately stopped by a significant sign from the trapper, who whispered in his ear—

"Let the lad be our spokesman. Natur *will* work in the bosom of the child, and we shall gain our object, in good time."

"The whole truth is out, Ellen," Paul continued, "and we have lined the squatter into his most secret misdoings. We have come, to right the wronged, and to free the imprisoned, now if you are the girl of a true heart, as I have always believed, so far from throwing straws in our way, you will join in the general swarming, and leave old Ishmael and his hive to the bees of his own breed."

"I have sworn a solemn oath—"

"A compactum which is entered into, through ignorance or in duresse, is null in the sight of all good moralists," cried the Doctor.

"Hush, hush," again the trapper whispered; "leave it all to natur and the lad!"

"I have sworn, in the sight and by the name of him, who is the founder and ruler of all that is good, whether it be in morals or in religion," Ellen continued, "neither to reveal the contents of that tent, nor to help its prisoner to escape. We are both solemnly, terribly sworn; our lives perhaps have been the gift we received for the promises. It is true you are masters of the secret, but not through any means of ours; nor do I know that I can justify myself for even being neutral, while you attempt to invade the dwelling of my uncle, in this hostile manner."

"I can prove beyond the power of refutation," the Naturalist eagerly exclaimed, "by Payley, Berkeley, ay even by the immortal Binkerschoef, that a compactum concluded, while one of the parties, be it a state or be it an individual, is in durence—"

"You will ruffle the temper of the child with your abusive language," said the cautious trapper, " while the lad, if left to human feelings, will bring her down to the meekness of a fawn—Ah! you are, like myself, little knowing in the natur' of hidden kindnesses!"

"Is this the only vow you have taken, Ellen!" Paul continued, in a tone which for the gay light-hearted bee-hunter, sounded dolorous and reproachful. "Have you sworn only to this! are the words which the squatter says to be as honey in your mouth and all other promises like so much useless comb?"

The paleness which had taken possession of the usually cheerful countenance of Ellen was hid in a bright glow, that was plainly visible even, at the distance at which she stood. She hesitated a moment, as if struggling to repress something very like resentment, before she answered, with all her native spirit—

"I know not what right any one has to question me, about oaths and promises, which can only concern her who has made them, if, indeed any of the sort, you mention, have ever been made at all. I shall hold no further discourse with one, who thinks so much of himself and takes advice merely of his own feelings."

"Now, old trapper! do you hear that;" said the unsophisticated bee-hunter, turning abruptly to his aged friend. "The meanest insect that skims the heavens, when it has got its load, flies, straight and honestly to its nest or hive, according to its kind; but the ways of a woman's mind, are as knotty as a gnarled oak, and more crooked than the windings of the Mississippi!"

"Nay, nay, child," said the trapper good naturedly interfering in behalf of the offending Paul, "you are to consider that youth is hasty and not overgiven to thought. But then a promise is a promise, and not to be thrown aside and forgotten, like the hoofs and horns of a buffaloe."

"I thank you for reminding me of my oath," said the still resentful Ellen, biting her pretty nether lip with vexation; "I might else have proved forgetful!"

"Ah! female natur is awakened in her," said the old man, shaking his head in a manner to show how much he was disappointed in the result; "but it manifests itself against the true spirit!"

"Ellen!" cried the young stranger, who until now, had been an attentive listener to the parly—"since Ellen is the name by which you are known—"

"They often add to it another. I am sometimes called by the name of my father."

"Call her Nelly Wade, at once," muttered Paul. "It is her rightful name, and I care not if she keeps it forever!"

"Wade, I should have added," continued the youth, "you will acknowledge that, though bound by no oath myself, I at least, have known how to respect those of others. You are a witness, yourself, that I have foreborn to utter a single call, while I am certain it could reach those ears, it would gladden so much. Permit me then to ascend the rock, singly; I promise a perfect indemnity to your kinsman against any injury his effects may sustain."

Ellen seem'd to hesitate, but catching a glimpse of Paul, who stood, leaning proudly on his rifle, whistling with an appearance of the utmost indifference the air of a boating song, she recovered her recollection in time to answer—

"I have been left the Captain of the rock, while my uncle, and his sons hunt, and Captain will I remain, 'till he returns to receive back the charge."

"This is wasting moments that will not soon return, and neglecting an opportunity that may never occur again;" the young soldier, gravely, remarked. "The sun is beginning to fall, already, and many minutes cannot elapse, before the squatter and his savage brood, will be returning to their huts."

Doctor Battius, cast a glance behind him, and took up the discourse, by saying—

"Perfection is always found in maturity, whether it be in the Animal or in the Intellectual world. Reflection is the mother of wisdom, and wisdom the Parent of success. I propose that we retire to a discreet distance from this impregnable position, and there hold a convocation, or council, to deliberate in what manner we may sit down regularly before the place, or perhaps, by postponing the siege to another season, gain the aid of auxiliaries from the inhabited countries, and thus secure the dignity of the laws, from any danger of a repulse."

"A storm would be better," the soldier smilingly answered, measuring the height, and scanning all its difficulties with a deliberate eye—"twould be but a broken arm, or a bruised head at the worst."

"Then have at it!" shouted the impetuous bee-hunter, making a spring that at once put him out of danger from shot, by carrying him beneath the projecting ledge on which the garrison was posted. "Now do your worst, young devils of a wicked breed; you have but a moment to work your mischief in!"

"Paul! rash Paul!" shrieked Ellen; "another step, and these rocks will crush you! they hang but by a thread, and the girls are ready and willing to let them fall!"

"Then drive the accursed swarm from the hive; for scale the rock I will, though I find it covered with hornets!"

"Let her if she dare!" tauntingly cried the eldest of the girls, brandishing a musket with a mien and resolution, that would have done credit to her Amazonian dam. "I know you, Nelly Wade; you are with the lawyers in your heart, and if you come a foot nigher, you shall have frontier punishment. Put in another pry girls, in with it! I should like to see the man, of them all, that dare come up into the camp of Ishmael Bush, without asking leave of his children!"

"Stir not, Paul! for your life keep beneath the rock!—"

Ellen was interrupted by the same bright vision which on the preceding day, had stay'd another scarcely less portentous tumult, by exhibiting itself on the same giddy height, where it was now seen.

"In the name of him, who commandeth all, I implore you to pause—both you who so madly incur the risk and you, who so rashly offer to take that, which you never can return!" said a voice, in a slightly foreign accent, that instantly drew all eyes, upward.

"Inez!" cried the Officer. "Do I again see you! mine shall you, now, be, though a million devils, were posted on this rock. Push up, brave woodsman, and give room for another!"

The sudden appearance of the figure from the tent, had created a momentary stupor, among the defendants of the rock, which might, with suitable forbearance, have been happily improved; but startled by the voice of Middleton, the surprised Phoebe, discharged her musket at the female, scarcely knowing whether she aimed at the life of a mortal, or at some being which belonged to another world. Ellen uttered a cry of horror, and darted after her alarmed or wounded friend, she knew not which, into the tent.

During this moment of dangerous bye-play the sounds of a serious attack, were very distinctly audible, beneath. Paul had profited by the commotion over his head, to change his place so far, as to make room for Middleton. The latter was followed by the naturalist, who in a state of mental aberration produced by the report of the musket, had instinctively rushed towards the rocks, for cover. The trapper remained, where he was last seen, an unmoved but close observer of the several proceedings. Though averse to enter into actual hostilities, the old man was, however, far from being useless. Favored by his position, he was enabled to apprise his friends of the movements of those who plotted their destruction above, and to advise and control their advance, accordingly.

In the mean time the children of Esther were true to the spirit they had inherited from their redoubtable mother. The instant they found themselves relieved from the presence of Ellen and her unknown companion, they bestowed an undivided attention on their more masculine, and certainly more dangerous assailants, who by this time had made a complete lodgement among the crags of their citadel. The repeated summons to surrender, which Paul uttered in a voice that he intended should strike terror in their young bosoms, were as little heeded as were the calls of the trapper, to abandon a resistance which might prove fatal to some among them, without offering the smallest probability of eventual success. Encouraging each other to persevere, they poised the fragments of rocks, prepared the lighter missiles for immediate service, and thrust forward the barrels of the muskets, with a business like air, and a coolness, that would have done credit to men long practised in warfare.

"Keep under the ledge," said the trapper pointing out to Paul the manner in which he should proceed, "keep in your foot, more, lad—ah! you see the warning was not amiss! had the stone struck it, the bees would have had the Prairies to themselves. Now—namesake of my Friend! Uncas, in name and spirit! now if you have the activity of le Cerf Agile, you may make a far leap to the right, and gain a good twenty feet, without danger. Beware the bush. Beware the bush! 'twill prove a treacherous hold! Ah! he has done it, safely and bravely has he done it! Your turn comes next, friend that follows the fruits of natur. Push you to the left, and divide the attention of the children. Nay, girls, fire. My old ears are used to the whistling of lead, and little reason have I to prove a doe-heart, with fourscore years on my back." He shook his head with a melancholy smile, but without flinching in a muscle, as the bullet which the exasperated Hetty fired, passed innocently, at no great distance from the spot where he stood. "It is safer keeping in your track than dodging when a weak finger pulls the trigger," he continued, "but it is a solemn sight to witness how much human natur' is inclined to evil, in one so young! Well done, my man of beasts and plants! Another such leap, and you may laugh at all the squatter's bars and walls. The Doctor has got his temper up! I see it in his eye, and something good will come of him! keep closer, man, keep, closer."

The trapper though he was not deceived as to the state of Doctor Battius' mind, was, however, greatly in error as to the exciting cause. While imitating the movements of his companions, and toiling his way upward, with the utmost caution, and not without great inward tribulation, the eye of the Naturalist had caught a glimpse of an unknown plant, a few yards above his head, and in a situation more than commonly exposed to the missiles which the girls were unceasingly hurling in the direction of the assailants. Forgetting, in an instant, every thing but the glory of being the first to give this jewel to the catalogues of science, he sprang upward at the prize, with the avidity with which the sparrow darts upon the butterfly. The rock which instantly came thundering down, announced that he was seen, and for a moment, while his form was concealed, in the cloud of dust and fragments, which followed the furious descent, the trapper gave him up for lost. At the next instant, he was seen, safely seated in a cavity formed by some of the projecting stones, which had yielded to the shock, holding, triumphantly, in his hand, the captured stem, which he was already devouring with delighted and, certainly, not unskillful, eyes. Paul profited by the opportunity. Turning his course, with the quickness of thought, he sprang to the post, which Obed thus securely occupied, and unceremoniously making a footstool of his shoulder, as the latter stooped over his treasure he bounded through the breach left by the fallen rock, and gained the level. He was followed by Middleton who joined him in seizing and disarming the girls. In this manner a bloodless and complete victory, was obtained over that citadel which Ishmael had vainly flattered himself, might prove impregnable.

Chapter XV

"So smile the heavens upon this holy act,
That after-hours with sorrow chide us not!"
Romeo and Juliet, II.vi.1–2.

IT IS PROPER that the course of the narrative should be staied, while we revert to those causes, which have brought in their train of consequences, the singular contest, just related. The interruption must, necessarily, be as brief, as we hope it may prove satisfactory to that class of readers who require, that no gap should be left, by those who assume the office of historians, for their own fertile imaginations to fill.

Among the troops sent, by the Government of the United States, to take possession of its newly acquired territory in the west, was a detachment led by the young soldier, who has become so busy an actor in the scenes of our Legend. The mild and indolent descendants of the Ancient Colonists received their new compatriots without distrust, well knowing that the transfer, raised them from the condition of subjects, to the more enviable distinction of citizens in a Government of Laws. The new rulers exercised their functions with discretion, and wielded their delegated authority without offence. In such a novel intermixture, however, of men born and nurtured in freedom and the compliant minions of absolute power, the catholic and the protestant, the active and the indolent, some little time was necessary to blend the discrepant elements of society. In attaining so desirable an end, woman was made to perform her accustomed and grateful office. The barriers of Prejudice and religion were broken through by the irresistible power of the Master Passion, and family unions, ere long, began to cement the political tie which had made a forced conjunction, between people so opposite in their habits, their educations, and their opinions.

Middleton was among the first of the new possessors of the soil, who became captive to the charms of a Louisianian Lady. In the immediate vicinity of the post he had been directed to occupy, dwelt the chief of one of those ancient colonial families, which had been content to slumber for ages amid the ease, indolence, and wealth of the spanish provinces. He was an officer of the crown, and had been induced to remove from the Floridas, among the French of the adjoining province, by a rich succession of which he had become the inheritor. The name of Don Augustin de Certavallos was scarcely known beyond the limits of the little town in which he resided, though he found a secret pleasure, himself, in pointing it out, in large scrolls of musty documents, to an only child, as enrolled among the former heroes and grandees of old and of New Spain. This fact, so important to himself and of so little moment to any body else, was the principal reason, that while his more vivacious Gallic neighbors were not slow to open a frank communion with their visiters, he chose to keep aloof, seemingly content with the society of his daughter, who was a girl just emerging from the condition of childhood into that of a woman.

The curiosity of the youthful Inez, however, was not so inactive. She had not heard the martial music of the garrison, melting on the evening air, nor seen the strange banner which fluttered over the height, that rose at no great distance from her Father's extensive grounds, without experiencing some of those secret impulses which are thought to distinguish the sex. Natural timidity, and that retiring and perhaps peculiar lassitude which forms the very ground work of female fascination, in the tropical Provinces of Spain, held her, in their, seemingly, indissoluble bonds, and it is more than probable that had not an accident occurred, in which Middleton was of some personal service to her father, so long a time would have elapsed before they met, that another direction might have been given to the wishes of one, who was just of an age to be alive to all the power of youth and beauty.

Providence, or if that imposing word is too just to be classical, Fate had otherwise decreed. The haughty and reserved Don Augustin was by far, too cbservant of the forms of that station, on which he so much valued himself to forget the duties of a gentleman. Gratitude for the kindness of Middleton, induced him to open his doors to the Officers of the Garrison, and to admit of a guarded but polite intercourse. Reserve gradually gave way before the propriety and candor of their spirited young leader, and it was not long ere, the affluent Planter rejoiced as much as his daughter, whenever the well known signal, at the gate, announced one of these agreeable visits from the commander of the post.

It is unnecessary to dwell on the impression which the charms of Inez produced on the soldier, or to delay the tale in order to write a wire-drawn account of the progressive influence, that elegance of deportment, manly beauty, and undivided assiduity, and intelligence were likely to produce on the sensitive mind of a romantic, warm-hearted and secluded girl of sixteen. It is sufficient for our purpose to say, that they lov'd—that the youth was not backward to declare his feelings, that he prevailed with some facility over the scruples of the maiden, and with no little difficulty over the objections of her father, and that, before the Province of Louisiana had been six months in the possession of the States, the officer of the latter, was the affianced husband of the richest heiress on the banks of the Mississippi.

Although we have presumed the reader to be acquainted with the manner in which such results are, commonly, attained, it is not to be supposed that the triumph of Middleton, either over the prejudices of the father or over those of the daughter, was achieved without difficulty. Religion formed a stubborn and, nearly, irremovable obstacle with both. The devoted young man patiently submitted to a formidable essay, which Father Ignatius was deputed to make, in order to convert him to the true faith. The effort on the part of the worthy priest was systematic, vigorous, and long sustained. A dozen times (it was at those moments when glimpses of the light, sylph like form of Inez flitted, like some fairy being past the scene of their conferences) the good Father fancied he was on the eve of a glorious triumph over infidelity; but all his hopes were frustrated by some unlook'd for opposition, on the part of the subject of his pious labors. So long as the assault on his faith was distant and feeble, Middleton, who was no great proficient in Polemics, submitted to its effects with the patience and humility of a martyr; but the moment the good father who felt such concern in his future happiness, was tempted to improve his vantage ground, by calling in the aid of some of the peculiar subtilties of his own creed, the young man was too good a soldier not to make head against the hot attack. He came to the contest, it is true, with no weapons more formidable than common sense, and some little knowledge of the habits of his country as contrasted with that of his adversary; but with these home-bred implements he never failed to repulse the father with something of the power with which a nervous cudgel player would deal with a skilful master of the rapier, setting at naught his passados, by the direct and unanswerable arguments of a broken head and a shivered weapon.

Before the controversy was terminated, an inroad of Protestants had come to aid the soldier. The reckless freedom of such among them, as thought only of this life, and the consistent and tempered piety of others, caused the honest priest to look about him, in concern. The influence of example on one hand and the contamination of too free an intercourse on the other began to manifest themselves, even, in that portion of his own flock, which he had supposed to be too thoroughly folded in spiritual government ever to stray. It was time to turn his thoughts from the offensive, and to prepare his followers to resist the lawless deluge of opinion, which threatened to break down the barriers of their faith. Like a wise commander who finds he has occupied too much ground for the amount of his force, he began to curtail his out-works. The relics were concealed from profane eyes; his people were admonished not to speak of miracles before a race that not only denied their existence but who had even the desperate hardihood to challenge their proofs, and even the bible itself, was prohibited with terrible denunciations, for the triumphant reason that it was liable to be misinterpreted.

In the mean time, it became necessary to report to Don Augustin, the effects his arguments and prayers had produced on the heretical disposition of the young soldier. No man is prone to confess his weakness, at the very moment, when circumstances demand the utmost efforts of his strength. By a species of pious fraud, for which no doubt the worthy Priest found his absolution in the purity of his motives, he declared that, while no positive change was actually wrought in the mind of Middleton, there was every reason to hope, the entering wedge of argument had been driven to its head, and that in consequence an opening was left, through which, it might rationally be hoped, the blessed seeds of a religious fructification would find their way, especially if the subject was left uninterruptedly to enjoy the advantage of catholic communion.

Don Augustin, himself, was now seized with the desire of proselyting. Even, the soft and amiable Inez thought it would be a glorious consummation of her wishes, to be a humble instrument of bringing her lover into the bosom of the true church. The offers of Middleton were promptly accepted, and, while the father looked forward, impatiently, to the day assigned for the nuptials, as to the pledge of his own success, the daughter thought of it with feelings in which the holy emotions of her faith, were blended with the softer sensations of her years and situation.

The sun rose, the morning of her nuptials, on a day so bright and cloudless that Inez hailed it as a harbinger of future happiness. Father Ignatius performed the offices of the church, in a little chapel attached to the estate of Don Augustin, and long ere the sun had begun to fall, Middleton pressed the blushing and timid young creole to his bosom, his acknowledged and unalienable wife. It had pleased the parties to pass the day of the wedding in retirement dedicating it solely to the best and purest affections, aloof from the noisy and heartless rejoicings of a compelled festivity.

Middleton was returning through the grounds of Don Augustin, from a visit of duty, to his encampment, at that hour, in which the light of the sun begins to melt into the shadows of evening, when a glimpse of a robe similar to that, in which Inez had accompanied him to the altar, caught his eye, through the foliage of a retired arbour. He approached the spot, with a delicacy that was rather increased than diminished, by the claim she had perhaps given him to intrude on her private moments, but the sounds of her soft voice, which was offering up prayers, in which he heard himself named by the dearest of all appellations, overcame his scruples, and induced him to take a position where he might listen without the fear of detection. It was certainly grateful to the feelings of a husband to be able, in this manner, to lay bare the spotless soul of his wife, and to find that his own image lay enshrined amid its purest and holiest aspirations. His self esteem was too much flattered, not to induce him to overlook, the immediate object of the petitioner. While she prayed that she might become the humble instrument of bringing him into the flock of the faithful, she petitioned for forgiveness, on her own behalf, if presumption, or indifference to the counsel of the church, had caused her to set too high a value on her influence, and led her into the dangerous error of hazarding her own soul, by espousing a heretic. There was so much of fervent piety, mingled with so strong a burst of natural feeling, so much of the woman blended with the angel, in her prayers, that Middleton could have forgiven her, had she termed him a pagan, for the sweetness and interest with which she petitioned in his favor.

The young man waited until his bride arose from her knees, and then he joined her, as if entirely ignorant of what had occurred.

"It is getting late, my Inez," he said, "and Don Augustin would be apt to reproach you with inattention to your health, in being abroad at such an hour. What then am I to do, who am charged with all his authority and twice his love."

"Be like him, in *every* thing," she answered, looking up in his face, with tears in her eyes, and speaking with emphasis; "in *every* thing. Imitate my father, Middleton, and I can ask no more of you."

"Nor *for* me, Inez? I doubt not that I should be all you can wish, were I to become as good, as the worthy and respectable Don Augustin. But you are to make some allowances for the infirmities and habits of a soldier. Now, let us go, and join this excellent father."

"Not yet," said his bride, gently extricating herself from the arm that he had thrown around her slight form, while he urged her from the place; "I have still another duty to perform, before I can submit, so implicitly to your orders, soldier though you are. I promised the worthy Inesella, my faithful nurse, she who, as you heard, has so long been a mother to me, Middleton—I promised her a visit at this hour. It is the last, as she thinks, that she can receive from her own child, and I cannot disappoint her. Go you then to Don Augustin; in one short hour, I will rejoin you."

"Remember, it is but an hour!"

"One hour," repeated Inez, as she kissed her hand to him; and then blushing ashamed at her own boldness, she darted from the arbor, and was seen for an instant gliding toward the cottage of her nurse, in which, at the next moment, she disappeared.

Middleton returned, slowly and thoughtfully, to the house, often bending his eyes in the direction in which he had last seen his wife, as if he would fain trace her lovely form, in the gloom of the evening, still floating through the vacant space. Don Augustin received him with warmth and for many minutes his mind was amused by relating to his new kinsman, plans for the future. The exclusive old Spaniard, listened to his glowing but true account of the prosperity and happiness of those States, of which he had been an ignorant neighbor half his life, partly in wonder, and partly with that sort of incredulity, with which one attends to what he fancies are the exaggerated descriptions of a too partial friendship.

In this manner the hour for which Inez had conditioned pass'd away much sooner than her husband could have thought possible, in her absence. At length his looks began to wander to the clock, and then the minutes were counted, as one roll'd by after another, and Inez did not appear. The hand had already made half of another circuit, around the face of the dial, when Middleton arose, and announced his determination to go, and offer himself, as an escort to the absentee. He found the night dark, and the heavens charged with threatening vapor, which in that climate, was the infallible forerunner of a gust. Stimulated no less, by the unpropitious aspect of the skies, than by his secret uneasiness, he quickened his pace, making long and rapid strides in the direction of the cottage of Inesella. Twenty times he stopp'd, fancying that he caught glimpses of the fairy form of Inez, tripping across the grounds, on her return to the mansion-house, and as often he was obliged to resume his course, in disappointment. He reached the gate of the cottage, knocked, opened the door, entered, and even, stood in the presence of the aged nurse, without meeting the person of her he sought. She had, already, left the place, and had returned to her father's house! Believing that he must have passed her in the darkness, Middleton retraced his steps, to meet with another disappointment. Inez had not been seen. Without communicating his intention to any one, the bridegroom proceeded with a palpitating heart to the little sequestered arbor, where he had overheard his bride offering up those petitions for his happiness and conversion. Here too, he was disappointed, and then all was afloat, in the painful incertitude of doubt and conjecture.

For many hours, a secret distrust of the motives of his wife, caused Middleton to proceed in the search with delicacy and caution. But as day dawned, without restoring her to the arms of her father or her husband, reserve was thrown aside, and her unaccountable absence was loudly proclaimed. The inquiries after the lost Inez were now direct and open; but they prov'd equally fruitless. No one had seen her, or heard of her, from the moment that she left the cottage, of her nurse.

Day succeeded day, and still no tidings rewarded the search that was immediately instituted, until she was finally given over by most of her relatives and friends as irretrievably lost.

An event of so extraordinary a character was not likely to be soon forgotten. It excited speculation, gave rise to an infinity of rumours, and not a few inventions. The prevalent opinion, among such of those emigrants who were overrunning the country as had time, in the multitude of their employments, to think of any foreign concerns, was the simple and direct conclusion, that the absent bride, was no more nor less than a felo de se. Father Ignatius had many doubts and much secret compunction of conscience, but like a wise chief, he endeavored to turn the sad event to some account, in the impending warfare of faith. Changing his battery, he whispered in the ears of a few of his oldest parishioners, that he had been deceived in the state of Middleton's mind, which he was now compelled to believe was completely stranded on the quicksands of heresy. He began to show his relicks again, and was even heard to allude once more, to the delicate and nearly forgotten subject of modern miracles. In consequence of these demonstrations, on the part, of the venerable priest, it came to be whispered among the faithful, and finally it was adopted as part of the parish creed, that Inez had been translated to heaven.

Don Augustin had all the feelings of a Father, but they

were smothered in the lassitude of a Creole. Like his spiritual governor, he began to think that they had been wrong in consigning one so pure, so young, so lovely, and above all so pious to the arms of a heretic, and he was fain to believe that the calamity which had befallen his age, was a judgment on his presumption and want of adherence to established forms. It is true, that as the whispers of the congregation came to his ears, he found present consolation in their belief, but then nature was too powerful and had too strong a hold of the old man's heart, not to give rise to the rebellious thought, that the succession of his daughter to the heavenly inheritance was a little premature.

But Middleton, the lover, the husband, the bridegroom—Middleton was nearly crushed by the weight of the unexpected and terrible blow. Educated himself, under the dominion of a simple and rational faith, in which nothing is attempted to be concealed from the believers, he could have no other apprehensions for the fate of Inez, than such as grew out of his knowledge of the superstitious opinions, she entertained of his own church. It is needless to dwell on the mental tortures that he endured, or all the various surmises, hopes, and disappointments that he was fated to experience in the first few weeks of his misery. A jealous distrust of the motives of Inez, and a secret, lingering, hope that he should yet find her, had tempered his enquiries, without, however, causing him to abandon them entirely. But time was beginning to deprive him, even, of the mortifying reflection that he was intentionally, though perhaps temporarily, deserted, and he was gradually yielding to the more painful conviction that she was dead, when his hopes were suddenly revived, in a new and singular manner.

The young commander, was slowly and sorrowfully returning from an evening parade of his troops, to his own quarters, which stood at some little distance from the place of the encampment and on the same high bluff of land, when his vacant eyes fell on the figure of a man, who by the regulations of the place, was not entitled to be there, at that forbidden hour. The stranger was meanly dress'd, with every appearance, about his person and countenance, of squalid poverty and of the most dissolute habits. Sorrow had softened the military pride of Middleton, and as he passed the crouching form of the intruder, he said in tones of great mildness or rather of kindness—

"You will be given a night in the guard house, friend, should the patrole find you here. Here is a dollar—go: and get a better place to sleep in, and something to eat."

"I swallow all my food, Captain, without chewing;" returned the vagabond, with the low exultation of an accomplished villain, as he eagerly seized the silver. "Make this Mexican, twenty, and I will sell you a secret."

"Go, go," said the other, with a little of a soldier's severity, returning to his manner. "Go, before I order the guard to seize you."

"Well, go I will. But if I do go, captain, I shall take my knowledge with me, and then you may live a widower bewitched, 'till the tatoo of life is beat off."

"What mean, you, fellow!" exclaimed Middleton, turning quickly toward the wretch who was already dragging his diseased limbs from the place.

"I mean to have the value of this dollar in Spanish Brandy, and then come back and sell you my secret for enough to buy a barrel."

"If you have any thing to say, speak now," continued Middleton, restraining with difficulty the impatience that urged him to betray his feeling.

"I am a dry, and I can never talk with elegance, when my throat is husky, captain. How much will you give, to know what I can tell you, let it be something, handsome; such as one gentleman can offer to another."

"I believe it would be better justice, to order the drummer to pay you a visit, fellow. To what does your boasted secret relate?"

"Matrimony. A wife and no wife, a pretty face, and a rich bride; do I speak plain, now, captain?"

"If you know any thing relating to my wife, say it at once, you need not fear for your reward."

"Ay, Captain, I have drove many a bargain in my time, and sometimes I have been paid in money, and sometimes I have been paid in promises. Now, the last are what I call pinching food."

"Name your price."

"Twenty—no damnit, it's worth thirty dollars if it's worth a cent!"

"Here, then, is your money, but remember, if you tell me nothing worth knowing, I have a force that can easily deprive you of it, again, and punish your insolence, in the bargain."

The fellow examined the bank-bills he received, with a jealous eye, and then pocketted them, apparently well satisfied of their being genuine.

"I like a northern note," he said, very coolly, "they have a charcatur to lose, like myself. No fear of me, captain; I am a man of honour and I shall not tell you a word more, nor a word less, than I know of my own knowledge to be true."

"Proceed then, without further delay, or I may repent, and order you to be deprived of all your gains, the silver as well as the notes."

"Honor if you die for it!" returned the miscreant, holding up a hand in affected horror at so treacherous a threat. "Well, Captain, you must know, that gentlemen don't all live by the same calling, some keep what they've got, and some get what they can."

"You have been a thief."

"I scorn the word. I have been a humanity-hunter. Do you know what that means? ay, it has many interpretations! Some people think the woolly-heads are miserable, working on hot plantations under a broiling sun—and all such sorts of inconveniences. Well, captain, I have been, in my time, a man who has been willing to give them the pleasures of variety, at least, by changing the scene for them. You understand me?"

"You are, in plain language a kidnapper."

"Have been—my worthy Captain—have been; but just now a little reduced, like a merchant who leaves off selling tobacco by the hogshead to deal in it, by the yard. I have been a soldier, too, in my day. What is said to be the great secret of our trade; can you tell me that?"

"I know not," said Middleton beginning to tire of the fellow's trifling, "courage."

"No, legs—legs, to fight with and legs to run away with. And therein you see my two callings agreed. My legs are none of the best, just now, and without legs a kidnapper would carry on a losing trade. But then there are men enough left, better provided than I am."

"Stolen!" groaned the horror struck husband.

"On her travels, as sure as you are standing still!"

"Villain, what reason have you, for believing a thing so shocking!"

"Hands off—hands off—do you think my tongue can do its work the better, for a little squeezing of the throat! Have patience and you shall know it all; but if you treat me so ungenteelly again, I shall be obliged to call in the assistance of the Lawyers."

"Say on; but if you utter a single word more or less than the truth, expect instant vengeance."

"Are you fool enough to believe what such a scoundrel as I am, tells you, captain, unless it has probability to back it. I know you are not: therefore, I will give my facts and my opinions, and then leave you to chew on them, while I go and drink of your generosity. I know a man, who is called Abiram White. I believe the knave took that name to show his enmity to the race of blacks! But this gentleman is now, and has been, for years, to my certain knowledge a regular translator of the human body from one State to another. I have dealt with him, in my time, and a cheating dog he is! No more honor, in him, than meat in my stomach. I saw him, here, in this very town, the day of your wedding. He was in company with his wife's brother, and pretended to be a settler on the hunt for new land. A noble set they were, to carry on business—seven sons, each of them as tall as your sergeant with his cap on. Well, the moment I heard that your wife was lost, I saw at once that Abiram had laid his hands on her."

"Do you know this—can this be true! What reason have you to fancy a thing so wild!"

"Reason enough; I know Abiram White. Now, will you add a trifle just to keep my throat from parching?"

"Go, go, you are stupified with drink, already, miserable man, and know not what you say. Go, go, and beware the drummer."

"Experience is a good guide," the fellow call'd after the retiring Middleton, and then turning with a chuckling laugh, like one well satisfied with himself, he made the best of his way towards the shop of the suttler.

A hundred times in the course of that night did Middleton fancy that the communication of the miscreant was entitled to some attention, and as often did he reject the idea, as too wild and visionary for another thought. He was awakened early on the following morning, after passing a restless and, nearly, sleepless night, by his orderly who came, to report that a man was found dead on the parade, at no great distance from his quarters. Throwing on his clothes, he proceeded to the spot, and beheld the individual, with whom he had held the preceding conference in the precise situation in which he had first been found.

The miserable wretch had fallen a victim to his intemperance. This revolting fact was sufficiently proclaimed by his obtruding eye-balls, his bloated countenance, and the nearly insufferable odours that were even, then exhaling from his carcass. Disgusted with the odious spectacle, the youth was turning from the sight, after ordering the corpse to be removed, when the position of one of the dead man's hands struck him. On examination he found the fore finger extended, as if in the act of writing in the sand, with the following incomplete sentence, nearly illegible, but yet in a state to be deciphered. "Capt. it is true, as I am a gentle—" He had either died or fallen into a sleep, the forerunner of his death, before the latter word was finished.

Concealing this fact from the others, Middleton, repeated his orders and departed. The pertinacity of the deceased, and all the circumstances united, induced, him to set on foot some secret inquiries. He found that a family answering the description which had been given him, had, in fact passed the place the day of his nuptials. They were traced along the margin of the Mississippi, for some distance, until they took boat, and ascended the river to its confluence with the Missouri. Here they had disappeared, like hundreds of others, in pursuit of the hidden wealth of the interior.

Furnished with these facts, Middleton, detailed a small guard of his most trusty men, took leave of Don Augustin without declaring his hopes or his fears, and having arrived at the indicated point, he pushed into the wilderness, in pursuit. It was not difficult to trace a train like that of Ishmael, until he was well assured, its object lay far beyond the usual limits of the settlements. This circumstance, in itself, quickened his suspicions, and gave additional force to his hopes of final success.

After getting beyond the assistance of verbal directions, the anxious husband had recourse to the usual signs of a trail, in order to follow the fugitives. This he also found a task of no difficulty, until he reached the hard and unyielding soil of the rolling Prairies. Here, indeed, he was completely at fault. He found himself, at length, compelled to divide his followers, appointing a place of rendezvous at a distant day, and to endeavor to find the lost trail, by multiplying, as much as possible, the number of his eyes. He had been alone a week, when accident brought him in contact with the trapper and the bee-hunter. Part of their interview has been related, and the reader can readily imagine the explanations that succeeded the tale he recounted, and which led as has already been seen to the recovery of his bride.

Chapter XVI

"These likelihoods confirm her flight from hence.
Therefore, I pray you, stay not to discourse,
But mount you presently;—"
Two Gentlemen of Verona, V.ii.43–45.

An hour had slid by, in hasty and nearly incoherent questions and answers, before Middleton, hanging over his recovered treasure with that sort of jealous watchfullness, with which a miser would regard his hoards, closed the disjointed narrative of his own proceedings by demanding—

"And you, my Inez: in what manner were you treated?"

"In every thing, but the great injustice they did in separating me so forcibly from my friends, as well, perhaps, as the circumstances of my captors would allow. I think the man, who is certainly the master here, is but a new beginner in wickedness. He quarrelled, frightfully, in my presence, with the wretch who seized me, and then they made an impious bargain, to which I was compelled to acquiesce, and to which they bound me as well as themselves by oaths. Ah! Middleton, I fear the heretics are not so heedful of their vows as we who are nurtured in the bosom of the true church!"

"Believe it not. These villains are of no religion—did they foreswear themselves?"

"No; but perjured. But was it not awful to call upon the good God, to witness so sinful a compact!"

"And so we think, Inez, as truly as the most virtuous Cardinal of Rome. But how did they observe their oath, and what was its purport?"

"They conditioned to leave me unmolested and free from their odious presence, provided I would give a pledge to make no effort to escape, and that I would not, even, show myself, until a time that my masters saw fit to name."

"And that time!—" demanded the impatient Middleton, who so well knew the religious scruples of his wife—"That time—"

"It is already passed. I was sworn by my Patron Saint, and faithfully did I keep the vow, until the man they call Ishmael forgot the terms by offering violence. I then made one appearance on the rock; for the time, too, was passed—though I even, think that Father Ignatius would have absolved me from the vow, on account of the treachery of my keepers."

"If he had not," muttered the youth between his compressed teeth; "I would have absolved him forever from his spiritual care of your conscience."

"You, Middleton!" returned his wife looking up into his flush'd face while a bright blush suffused her own sweet countenance; "you may *receive* my vows; but, surely, you can have no power to *absolve* me from their observance!"

"No, no, no, Inez, you are right. I know but little of these conscientious subtilties, and I am any thing but a priest. Yet tell me, what has induced these monsters to play this desperate game—to trifle thus with my happiness?"

"You know my ignorance of the world, and how ill I am qualified to furnish reasons for the conduct of beings so different from any I have ever seen, before. But does not love of money drive men to acts, even, worse than this! I believe they thought that an aged and wealthy father could be tempted to pay them a rich ransom for his child; and perhaps," she added, stealing an enquiring glance through her tears, at the attentive Middleton, "they counted something on the fresh affections of a bridegroom."

"They might have extracted the blood from my heart, drop by drop!"

"Yes," resumed his young and timid wife, instantly withdrawing the stolen look she had hazarded, and, hurriedly, pursuing the train of the discourse as if glad to make him forget the liberty she had just taken, "I have been told there are men so base, as to perjure themselves at the altar, in order to command the gold of ignorant and confiding girls, and if love of money will lead to such baseness, we may surely expect it will hurry those who devote themselves to gain, into acts of lesser fraud!"

"It must be so, and, now Inez, though I am here to guard you, with my life, and we are in possession of this rock, our difficulties, perhaps our dangers, are not ended. You will summon all your courage to meet the trial, and prove yourself a soldier's wife, my Inez?"

"I am ready to depart this instant. The letter you sent by the physician, had prepared me to hope for the best, and I have every thing arranged for flight, at the shortest warning."

"Let us then leave this place, and join our friends."

"Friends!" interrupted Inez, glancing her eyes around the little tent in quest of the form of Ellen. "I too have a friend who must not be forgotten, but who is pledged to pass the remainder of her life with us. She is gone!"

Middleton gently led her from the spot, as he smilingly answered—

"She may have had like myself her own private communications for some favored ear."

The young man had not, however, done justice to the motives of Ellen Wade. The sensitive and intelligent girl, had readily perceived how little her presence was necessary in the interview, that has just been related, and had retired with that intuitive delicacy of feeling which seems to belong more properly to her sex. She was now to be seen seated on a point of the rock, with her person so entirely enveloped in her dress, as to conceal her features. Here she had remained for near an hour, no one approaching to address her, and as it appeared to her own quick and jealous eyes totally unobserved. In the latter particular, however, even, the vigilance of the quicksighted Ellen was deceived.

The first act of Paul Hover, on finding himself the master of Ishmael's citadel, had been to sound the note of victory, after the quaint and ludicrous manner, that is so often practised among the borderers of the west. Flapping his sides, with his hands, as the conquering game cock is wont to do with his wings, he raised a loud and laughable imitation of the exultation of this bird, a cry which might have proved a dangerous challenge, had any one of the athletic sons of the squatter been within hearing.

"This has been a regular knock-down and drag-out," he cried, "and no bones broke! How now, old trapper, you have been one of your training, platoon, rank-and-file soldiers in your day, and have seen forts taken and batteries stormed, before this: am I right?"

"Ay, ay, that have I," answered the old man, who still maintained his post at the foot of the rock, so little disturbed by what he had just witnessed, as to return the grin of Paul, with a hearty indulgence in his own silent and peculiar laughter. "You have gone through the exploit like men!"

"Now tell me, is it not in rule, to call over the names of the living and to bury the dead, after every bloody battle."

"Some did and other some didn't. When Sir William push'd the German, Dieskau, thro' the defiles at the foot of the Hori—"

"Your Sir William was a drone to Sir Paul, and knew nothing of regularity. So here begins the roll call—by-the-bye, old man, what between bee-hunting and buffaloe humps, and certain other matters, I have been too busy to ask your name; for I intend to begin with my rear guard, well knowing that my man in front is too busy to answer."

"Lord, lad, I've been called in my time, by as many names, as there are people among whom I've dwelt. Now, the Delawares nam'd me for my eyes, and I was called after the far-sighted hawk. Then ag'in the settlers in the Otsego hills christened me anew, from the fashion of my leggings, and various have been the names by which I have gone through life: But little will it matter when the time shall come that all are to be muster'd, face to face, by what titles a mortal has play'd his part; I humbly trust I shall be able to answer to any of mine, in a loud and manly voice."

Paul paid little or no attention to this reply, more than half of which was lost in the distance, but pursuing the humour of the moment, he called out, in a stentorian voice to the naturalist to answer to his name. Doctor Battius had not thought it necessary to push his success beyond the comfortable niche, which accident had so opportunely formed for his protection and in which he now reposed from his labors, with a pleasing consciousness of security, added to great exultation at the possession of the botanical treasure already mentioned.

"Mount. Mount, my worthy mole-catcher! come and behold the prospect of skirting Ishmael! Come and look nature boldly in the face, and not go sneaking, any longer, among the Prairie grass and mullen tops, like a gobbler nibbling for grass hoppers."

The mouth of the light-hearted and reckless bee hunter was

instantly closed, and he was rendered as mute, as he had just been boisterous and talkative, by the appearance of Ellen Wade. When the melancholy maiden took her seat on the point of the rock, as mentioned, Paul affected to employ himself in conducting a close inspection of the household effects of the squatter. He rummaged the drawers of Esther with no delicate hands, scattered the rustic finery of her girls on the ground without the least deference to its quality or elegance, and toss'd her pots and kettles here, and there, as though they had been vessels of wood instead of iron. All this industry, was, however, manifestly without an object. He reserved nothing for himself, not even, appearing conscious of the nature of the articles which suffered by his familiarity. When he had examined the inside of every cabin, taken a fresh survey of the spot where he had confined the children and where he had thoroughly secured them with cord, and kick'd one of the pails of the woman, like a foot-ball, fifty feet into the air, in sheer wantonness, he returned to the edge of the rock, and thrusting both his hands through his wampum belt, he began to whistle the Kentucky hunters, as diligently as if he had been hired to supply his auditors with music, by the hour. In this manner pass'd the remainder of the time, until Middleton, as has been related, led Inez forth from the tent, and gave a new direction to the thoughts of the whole party. He summoned Paul from his flourish of music, tore the Doctor from the study of his plant, and as acknowledged leader, gave the necessary orders for immediate departure.

In the bustle and confusion that were likely to succeed such a mandate, there was little opportunity to indulge in complaints or reflections. As the adventurers had not come unprepared for victory, each individual employed himself in such offices, as were best adapted to his strength and situation. The trapper had already made himself master of the patient Asinus, who was quietly feeding at no great distance from the rock, and he was now busy in fitting his back with the complicated machinery, that Doctor Battius, saw fit to term a saddle of his own invention. The naturalist himself, seized upon his port-folios, herbals, and collection of insects, which he quickly transferred from the encampment of the squatter to certain pockets in the aforesaid ingenious invention, and which the trapper as uniformly cast away, the moment his back was turned. Paul showed his dexterity in removing such light articles as Inez and Ellen had prepared for their flight to the foot of the citadel, while Middleton, after mingling threats and promises, in order to induce the children to remain quietly in their bondage, assisted the females to descend. As time began to press upon them, and there was great danger of Ishmael's returning, these several movements were made with singular industry and despatch.

The trapper bestowed such articles as he conceived, were necessary to the comfort of the weaker and more delicate members of the party in those pockets, from which he had so unceremoniously expelled the treasures of the unconscious naturalist, and then gave way for Middleton to place Inez in one of those seats, which he had prepared on the back of the animal for her and her companion.

"Go, child," the old man said, motioning to Ellen to follow the example of the lady, and turning his head a little anxiously to examine the waste behind him, "It cannot be long afore the owner of this place will be coming to look after his house hold, and he is not a man to give up his property, however obtained, without complaint."

"It is true," cried Middleton, " we have wasted moments that are precious, and have the utmost need of industry."

"Ay, ay, I thought it; and would have said it, Captain; but I remembered how your grand'ther used to love to look upon the face of her he led away for a wife, in the days of his youth and his happiness! 'Tis natur', 'tis natur, and 'tis wiser to give way a little before its feelings than to try to stop a current that will have its course."

Ellen advanced to the side of the beast, and seizing Inez by the hand, she said with heart-felt warmth, after struggling to suppress an emotion that nearly choked her—

"God bless you, sweet lady. I hope you will forget and forgive the wrongs you have received from my uncle—"

The humbled and sorrowful girl could say no more; her voice becoming entirely inaudible in an ungovernable burst of grief.

"How is this!" cried Middleton, "did you not say, Inez, that this excellent young woman was to accompany us, and to live with us, for the remainder of her life, or, at least, until she found some more agreeable residence for herself."

"I did; and I still hope it. She has always given me reason to believe, that, after having shown so much commiseration and friendship in my misery, she would not desert me, should happier times return."

"I cannot, I ought not," continued Ellen, getting the better of her momentary weakness. "It has pleased God to cast my lot among these people, and I ought not to quit them. It would be adding the appearance of treachery to what will already seem bad enough, with one of his opinions. He has been kind to me, an orphan, after his rough customs, and I cannot steal from him at such a moment!"

"She is just as much a relation of skirting Ishmael, as I am a Bishop!" said Paul, with a loud hem, as if his throat wanted clearing. "If the old fellow has done the honest thing by her, in giving her a morsel of venison, now and then, or a spoon around his homminy dish, hasn't she pay'd him, in teaching the young devils to read their bible, or in helping old Esther to put her finery in shape and fashion. Tell me that a drone has a sting, and I'll believe you, as easily as I will that this young woman is a debtor to any of the tribe of Bush!"

"It is but little matter, who owns me, or where I'm in debt. There are none to care for a girl, who is fatherless and motherless and whose nearest kin are the offcasts of all honest people—no, no, go, lady, and heaven forever bless you. I am better here, in this desert, where there are none to know my shame."

"Now old trapper," retorted Paul, "this is what I call knowing which way the wind blows! You ar' a man that has seen life and you know something of fashions; I put it to your judgement, plainly, isn't it in the nature of things for the hive to swarm when the young get their growth, and if children will quit their parents, ought one who is of no kith nor kin—"

"Hist!" interrupted the man he addressed. "Hector is discontented. Say it out, plainly, pup. What is it, dog, what is it!"

The venerable hound had risen, and was scenting the fresh breeze which continued to sweep heavily over the Prairies. At the words of his master, he growled, and contracted the muscles of his lips, as if half disposed to threaten with the remnants of his teeth. The younger dog, who was resting after the chace of the morning, also made some signs that his nose detected a taint in the air, and then the two resumed their slumbers as if they had done enough.

The trapper seized the bridle of the Ass, and cried urging the beast onward—

"There is no time for words. The squatter and his brood are within a mile or two of this blessed spot!"

Middleton lost all recollection of Ellen, in the danger which now so imminently beset his recovered bride, nor is it necessary to add that Doctor Battius did not wait for a second admonition to commence his retreat. Following the route indicated by the old man, they turned the rock in a body, and pursued their way, as fast as possible across the Prairie, under the favor of the cover it afforded.

Paul Hover, however, remained in his tracks sullenly leaning on his rifle. Near a minute had elapsed, before he was observed by Ellen, who had buried her face in her hands, to conceal her fancied desolation from herself.

"Why do you not fly!" the weeping girl, exclaimed the instant she perceived she was not alone.

"I'm not used to it."

"My uncle will soon be here! you have nothing to hope from his pity."

"Nor from that of his niece, I reckon. Let him come; he can only knock me on the head!"

"Paul, Paul, if you love me, fly—"

"Alone! if I do, may I be—"

"If you value, your life, fly!"

"I value it not, compared to you."

"Paul!"

"Ellen!"

She extended both her hands, and burst into another and a still more violent flood of tears. The bee-hunter put one of his sturdy arms around her waist, and in another moment he was urging her over the plain, in rapid pursuit of their flying friends.

Chapter XVII

"Approach the chamber, and destroy your sight
With a new Gorgon:—Do not bid me speak:
See, and then speak yourselves."
Macbeth, II.iii.71–73.

THE LITTLE RUN which supplied the family of the squatter with water, and nourished the trees and bushes that grew near the base of the rocky eminence, took its rise at no great distance from the latter, in a small thicket of cotton-wood, and vines. Hither, then the trapper directed the flight, as to the place affording the only available cover, in so pressing an emergency. It will be remembered that the sagacity of the old man, which from long practice in similar scenes amounted nearly to an instinct in all cases of sudden danger, had first induced him to take this course, as it plac'd the hill between them and the approaching party. Favored by this circumstance he succeeded in reaching the bushes in sufficient time, and Paul Hover had just hurried the breathless Ellen into the tangled brush as Ishmael gained the summit of the rock, in the manner already described, where he stood like a man momentarily bereft of senses, gazing at the confusion which had been created among his chattels, or at his gagged and bound children, who had been safely bestowed, by the forethought of the bee-hunter, under the cover of a bark roof in a sort of irregular pile. A long rifle would have thrown a bullet from the height on which the squatter now stood, into the very cover, where the fugitives who had wrought all this mischief were clustered.

The trapper, was the first to speak, as the man on whose intelligence and experience they all depended for counsel, after running his eye over the different individuals, who gathered about him, in order to see that none were missing.

"Ah! natur' is natur' and has done its work!" he said, nodding to the exulting Paul with a smile of approbation, "I thought it would be hard for them who had so often met in fair and foul, by star-light and under the clouded moon, to part at last, in anger! Now, is there little time to lose, in talk, and every thing to gain, by industry! It cannot be long afore some of yonder brood will be nosing along the 'arth for our trail, and, should they find it, as find it they surely will, and should they push us to stand on our courage, the dispute must be settled with the rifle; which may He in Heaven forbid! Captain, can you lead us to the place where any of your warriors lie?—for the stout sons of the squatter will make a manly brush of it, or I am but little of a judge in warlike dispositions!"

"The place of rendezvous is many leagues from this, on the banks of La Platte."

"It is bad! it is bad—If fighting is to be done, it is always wise to enter on it, on equal terms. But what has one so near his time, to do with ill-blood and hot-blood, at his heart! Listen to what a gray head and some experience have to offer, and then if any among you can point out a wiser fashion for a retreat, we can just follow his design and forget that I have spoken. This thicket stretches for near a mile, as it may be slanting from the rock, and leads towards the sun-set instead of the settlements."

"Enough. Enough," cried Middleton too impatient to wait until the deliberative and perhaps loquacious old man could end his minute explanation. "Time is too precious, for words: Let us fly."

The trapper made a gesture of compliance, and turning in his tracks he lead Asinus across the trembling earth of the swale, and quickly emerged on the hard ground, on the side opposite to the encampment of the squatter.

"If old Ishmael gets a squint at that highway through the brush," cried Paul casting, as he left the place, a hasty glance, at the broad trail the party had made through the thicket, "he'll need no finger board to tell him which way his road lies. But let him follow! I know the vagabond would gladly cross his breed with a little honest blood, but if any son of his ever gets to be the husband of—"

"Hush, Paul, hush," said the terrified young woman who leaned on his arm for support, "your voice might be heard."

The bee-hunter was silent, though he did not cease to cast ominous looks behind him, as they flew along the edge of the run, which sufficiently betrayed the belligerent condition of his mind. As each one was busy for himself, but a few minutes elapsed before the party rose a swell of the Prairie, and descending, without a moment's delay on the opposite side, they were at once removed from every danger of being seen, by the sons of Ishmael, unless the pursuers should happen to fall upon their trail. The old man, now profited by the formation of the land, to take another direction, with a view to elude pursuit, as a vessel changes her course in fogs and darkness, to escape from the vigilance of her enemies.

Two hours passed in the utmost diligence, enabled them to make a half-circuit around the rock, and to reach a point that was exactly opposite to the original direction of their flight. To most of the fugitives their situation was as entirely unknown, as is that of a ship in the middle of the ocean to the uninstructed voyager, but the old man proceeded at every turn, and through every bottom with a decision that inspired his followers with confidence, as it spoke favorably of his own knowledge of the localities. His hound, stopping now and then to catch the expression of his eye, had preceded the trapper, throughout the whole distance, with as much certainty as though a previous and intelligible communion between them had established the route by which they were to proceed. But, at the expiration of the time, just named, the dog suddenly came to a stand; and then seating himself on the Prairie, he snuffed the air, a moment, and began a low and piteous whining.

"Ay, pup—ay. I know the spot. I know the spot, and reason there is to remember it well!" said the old man, stopping by the side of his uneasy associate, until those who followed had time to come up. "Now yonder is a thicket before us," he continued pointing forward, "where we may lie till tall trees grow on these naked fields, afore any of the squatter's kin, will venture to molest us."

"This is the spot where the body of the dead man lay!" cried Middleton examining the place with an eye that revolted at the recollection.

"The very same. But whether his friends have put him in the bosom of the ground or not remains to be seen. The hound knows the scent, but seems to be a little at a loss, too. It is therefore necessary that you advance, friend bee-hunter to examine, while I tarry to keep the dogs from complaining in too loud a voice."

"I!" exclaimed Paul thrusting his hand into his shaggy locks, like one who thought it prudent to hesitate before he undertook so formidable an adventure: "now, heark'ee, old trapper; I've stood in my thinnest cottons, in the midst of many a swarm that has lost its queen bee, without winking, and let me tell you, the man who can do that is not likely to fear any living son of skirting Ishmael; but as to meddling with dead men's bones, why it is neither my calling nor my inclination, so after thanking you for the favor of your choice, as they say when they make a man a corporal in Kentucky, I decline serving."

The old man turned a disappointed look towards Middleton who was too much occupied in solacing Inez to observe his embarrassment, which was, however, suddenly relieved from a quarter, whence, from previous circumstances, there was little reason to expect such a demonstration of fortitude.

Doctor Battius, had rendered himself a little remarkable throughout the whole of the preceding retreat, for the exceeding diligence with which he had labored to effect that desirable object. So very conspicuous was his zeal, indeed, as to have entirely gotten the better of all his ordinary predilections. The worthy naturalist belong'd to that species of discoverers who make the worst possible travelling-companions to a man who has reason to be in a hurry. No stone, no bush, no plant is ever suffered to escape the examination of their vigilant eyes, and thunder may mutter and rain fall, without disturbing the abstraction of their reveries. Not so, however, with the disciple of Linnæus, during the momentous period, that it remained a mooted point at the tribunal of his better judgement, whether the stout descendants of the squatter were not likely to dispute his right to traverse the Prairie, in freedom. The highest blooded and best trained hound with his game in view, could not have run with an eye more rivetted than that with which the Doctor had pursued his curvilinear course. It was perhaps lucky for his fortitude that he was ignorant of the artifice of the trapper in leading them around the citadel of Ishmael, and that he had imbibed, the soothing impression, that every inch of Prairie he traversed was just so much added to the distance between his own person and the detested rock. Notwithstanding the momentary shock he certainly experienced when he discovered this error, he now boldly volunteered to enter the thicket in which there was some reason to believe the body of the murdered Asa still lay. Perhaps the naturalist was urged to show his spirit on this occasion, by some secret consciousness that his excessive industry in the retreat, might be liable to misconstruction, and it is certain, that whatever might be his peculiar notions of danger from the quick, his habits and his knowledge had plac'd him far above the apprehension of suffering harm from any communication with the dead.

"If there is any service to be performed, which requires the perfect command of the nervous system," said the man of science, with a look that was slightly blustering, "you have only to give a direction to his intellectual faculties, and here stands one, on whose physical powers you may depend."

"The man is given to speak in parables," muttered the single minded trapper, "but I conclude there is always some meaning hidden in his words, though it is as hard to find sense in his speeches, as to discover three eagles on the same tree. It will be wise, friend, to make a cover, lest the sons of the squatter should be out skirting on our trail, and as you well know, there is some reason to fear yonder thicket contains a sight that may horrify a woman's mind. Are you man enough to look death in the face, or shall I run the risk of the hounds raising an outcry and go in myself. You see the pup is willing to run with an open mouth, already."

"Am I man enough! venerable trapper, our communications have a recent origin, or thy interrogatory might have a tendency to embroil us in angry disputation. Am I man enough! I claim to be of the *class*, mammalia; *order*, Primates; *genus*, homo! Such are my physical attributes; of my moral properties, let posterity speak; it becomes me to be mute."

"Physick may do for such as relish it; to my taste and judgment, it is neither palatable nor healthy, but morals never did harm to any living mortal, be it that he was a sojourner in the forest, or a dweller in the midst of glazed windows, and smoking chimnies. It is only a few hard words that divide us, friend; for I'm of an opinion that, with use and freedom, we should come to understand one another, and mainly settle down into the same judgments of mankind and of the ways of the world. Quiet, Hector, quiet, what ruffles your temper, pup; is it not used to the scent of human blood!"

The Doctor bestowed a gracious but commiserating smile on the Philosopher of nature, as he retrograded a step or two from the place whither he had been impelled by his excess of spirit, in order to reply with less expenditure of breath and with a greater freedom of action and attitude. "A homo, is certainly a homo," he said, stretching forth an arm in an argumentative manner, "so far as the animal functions extend there are the connecting links of harmony, order, conformity, and design, between the whole genus; but there the resemblance ends. Man may be degraded to the very margin of the line which separates him from the brute, by ignorance; or he may be elevated to a communion with the Great Master Spirit of All by knowledge—nay, I know not, if time and opportunity were given him, but he might become the Master of all learning, and consequently equal to the great moving principle."

The old man, who stood leaning on his rifle, in a thoughtful attitude, shook his head, as he answered with a native steadiness that entirely eclipsed the imposing air which his antagonist had seen fit to assume—

"This is neither more nor less than mortal wickedness! Here have I been a dweller on the 'arth for fourscore and six changes of the seasons, and all that time have I look'd at the growing and the dying trees, and yet do I not know the reasons why the bud starts under the summer sun, or the leaf falls when it is pinch'd by the frosts. Your l'arning, though it is man's boast, is folly in the eyes of him, who sits in the clouds and looks down in sorrow at the pride and vanity of his creatur's. Many is the hour, that I've pass'd, lying in the shades of the woods, or stretch'd upon the hills of these open fields, looking up into the blue skies, where I could fancy, the Great One had taken his stand, and was solemnizing on the waywardness of man and brute, below, as I myself had often look'd at the ants tumbling over each other in their eagerness, though in a way and a fashion more suited to his mightiness and Power. Knowledge! it is his plaything—say, you who think it so easy to climb into the judgment seat above, can you tell me any thing of the beginning and the end? Nay, you're a dealer in ailings and cures—what is life, and what is death? Why does the eagle live, so long, and why is the time of the butterfly so short? Tell me a simpler thing: why is this hound so uneasy, while you, who have passed your days in looking into books can see no reason to be disturbed?"

The Doctor who had been a little astounded by the dignity and energy of the old man, drew a long breath, like a fallen wrestler who is just released from the throttling grasp of his antagonist, and seized on the opportunity of the pause, to reply—

"It is his instinct."

"And what is the gift of instinct?"

"An inferior gradation of reason—a sort of mysterious combination of thought and matter."

"And what is that which you call thought?"

"Venerable venator, this is a method of reasoning which sets at naught the uses of definitions, and such as I do assure you is not at all tolerated in the schools."

"Then is there more cunning in your schools than I had thought, for it is a certain method of showing them their vanity," returned the trapper, suddenly abandoning a discussion from which the naturalist was just beginning to anticipate great delight, by turning to his dog, whose restlessness he attempted to appease by playing with his ears. "This is foolish, Hector; more like an untrained pup, than a sensible hound—one who has got his education by hard experience, and not by nosing over the trails of other dogs, as a boy, in the settlements, follows on the track of his masters, be it right or be it wrong. Well, friend; you who can do so much, are you equal to looking into the thicket, or must I go in myself?"

The Doctor again assumed his air of resolution and without further parlance proceeded to do as desired. The dogs were so far restrained by the remonstrances of the old man, as to confine their complaints to low, but often repeated whinings. When they saw the naturalist advance, the pup, however, broke through all restraint and made a swift circuit around his person, scenting the earth as he proceeded, and then returning to his companion, he howled aloud.

"The squatter and his brood have left a strong taint upon the 'arth!" said the old man, watching as he spoke for some signal from his learned Pioneer, to follow; "I hope yonder school-bred man knows enough, to remember the errand on which I have sent him."

Doctor Battius had already disappeared in the bushes, and the trapper was beginning to betray additional evidences of impatience, when the person of the former was seen retiring from the thicket backwards with his face fastened on the place he had just left, as if his look was bound in the thraldom of some charm.

"Here is something skeary, by the wildness of the man's countenance!" exclaimed the old man, relinquishing his hold of Hector, and moving stoutly to the side of the totally unconscious naturalist. "How is it, friend, have you found a new leaf in your book of wisdom."

"It is a basilisk!" muttered the Doctor, whose altered visage betrayed the utter confusion which beset his faculties. "An animal of the *order* serpens. I had thought its attributes were fabulous, but mighty nature is equal to all that man can imagine!"

"What is't?—what is't? The snakes of the Prairies are harmless, unless it be, now and then, an angered rattler, and he always gives you notice with his tail, afore he works his mischief with his fangs. Lord, Lord, what a humbling thing is fear! Here is one who in common delivers words too big for a humble mouth to hold, so much beside himself that his voice is as fine as the whistle of the whip-poor-will!—Courage!—what is it, man?—what is't?"

"A Prodigy! a lusus naturæ! a monster that nature has delighted to form, in order to exhibit her power. Never before have I witnessed such an utter confusion in her Laws, or a specimen that so completely bids defiance to the distinctions of *Class* and *Genera*. Let me record its appearance," fumbling for his tabletts with hands that trembled too much to perform their office, "while time and opportunity are allowed—*eyes*, enthralling. *Colour*, various, complex, and profound—"

"One would think the man was craz'd, with his enthralling looks and pieball'd colours!" interrupted the discontented trapper, who began to grow a little uneasy that his party was, all this time, neglecting to seek the protection of some cover. "If there is a reptile in the brush, show me the creatur' and should it refuse to depart peaceably, why there must be a quarrel for the possession of the place."

"There!" said the Doctor pointing into a dense mass of the thicket, to a spot within fifty feet of that where they both stood. The trapper turned his look with perfect composure in the required direction, but the instant his practised glance met the object which had so utterly upset the philosophy of the naturalist, he gave a start, himself, threw his rifle rapidly forward and as instantly recovered it, as if a second flash of thought convinced him he was wrong. Neither the instinctive movement, nor the sudden recollection, was without a sufficient object. At the very margin of the thicket, and in absolute contact with the earth, lay an animate ball that might easily, by the singularity and fierceness of its aspect, have justified the disturbed condition of the naturalist's mind. It were difficult to describe the shape or colours of this extraordinary substance, except to say in general terms that it was nearly spherical and exhibited all the hues of the rainbow intermingled, without reference to harmony and without any very ostensible design. The predominant hues were a black and a bright vermillion. With these, however, the several tints of white, yellow, and crimson, were strangely and wildly blended. Had this been all, it would have been difficult to have pronounced that the object was possessed of life, for it lay motionless as any stone: but a pair of dark, glaring, and moving eye-balls, which watch'd with jealousy the smallest movement of the trapper and his companion, sufficiently established the important fact of its possessing vitality.

"Your reptile is a scouter, or I'm no judge of Indian paints and Indian deviltries," muttered the old man, dropping the butt of his weapon to the ground, and gazing with a steady eye at the frightful object, as he leaned on its barrel, in an attitude of great composure. "He wants to face us out of sight and reason, and make us think the head of a red-skin is a stone covered with the autumn leaf, or he has some other devilish artifice in his mind!"

"Is the animal human!" demanded the Doctor, "of the *genus* homo! I had fancied it a non-descript."

"It's as human, and as mortal too, as a warrior of these Prairies is ever known to be. I have seen the time when a red-skin would have shown a foolish daring to peep out of his ambushment in that fashion on a hunter I could name, but who is too old now, and too near his time, to be any thing better than a miserable trapper. It will be well to speak to the imp, and to let him know he deals with men whose beards are grown. Come, forth from your cover, friend," he continued in the language of the extensive tribes of the Dahcotahs; "there is room on the Prairie for another warrior."

The eyes appeared to glare more fiercely than before, but the mass which according to the trapper's opinion was neither more nor less than a human head, shorn, as usual among the warriors of the west, of its hair, still continued without motion, or any other sign of life.

"It is a mistake!" exclaimed the Doctor. "The animal is not even of the *class* Mammalia, much less a man."

"So much for your knowledge!" returned the trapper laughing with great exultation. "So much for the l'arning of one who has look'd into so many books that his eyes are not able to tell a moose from a wildcat! Now, my Hector, here, is a dog of education after his fashion, and though the meanest primmer in the settlements would puzzle his schooling, you could'nt cheat the hound in a matter like this. As you think the object no man, you shall see his whole formation, and then let an ignorant old trapper who never passed a day within reach of a spelling book in his life, know by what name to call it. Mind, I mean no violence, but just to brush the devil from his ambushment."

The trapper very deliberately examined the priming of his rifle, taking care to make as great a parade as possible of his hostile intentions, in going through the necessary evolutions with the weapon. When he thought the stranger began seriously to apprehend some danger, he very deliberately presented the piece, and called aloud—

"Now, friend, am I all for peace, or all for war, as you may say. No! well it *is* no man, as the wise one, here, says, and there can be no harm in just firing into a bunch of leaves."

The muzzle of the rifle fell as he concluded, and the weapon was gradually settling into a steady, and what would easily have proved a fatal aim, when a tall Indian sprang from beneath that bed of leaves, and brush, which he had collected about his person at the approach of the party, and stood upright uttering the exclamation,

"Wagh!"

Chapter XVIII

"My visor is Philemon's roof; within the house is Jove."

Much Ado about Nothing, II.i.96–97.

THE TRAPPER, who had meditated no violence, dropped his rifle again, and laughing at the success of his experiment, with great seeming self complacency, he drew the astounded gaze of the naturalist from the person of the savage to himself by saying—

"The imps will lie for hours like sleeping alligators, brooding their deviltries in dreams and other craftiness, till such time as they see some real danger is at hand and then they look to themselves the same as other mortals. But this is a scouter in his war-paint! There should be more of his tribe at no great distance. Let us draw the truth out of him, for an unlucky war-party may prove more dangerous to us, than a visit from the whole family of the squatter."

"It is truly a desperate and a dangerous species!" said the Doctor, relieving his amazement by a breath that seem'd to exhaust his lungs of air; "a violent race; and one that it is difficult to define or class within the usual boundaries of definitions. Speak to him, therefore, but let thy words be strong in amity."

The old man cast a keen eye, on every side of him, to ascertain the important particular whether the stranger was supported by any associates, and then making the usual signs of peace by exhibiting the palm of his naked hand he boldly advanced. In the mean time, the Indian betrayed no evidences, of uneasiness. He suffered the trapper to draw nigh, maintaining by his own mien and attitude a striking air of dignity and fearlessness. Perhaps the wary warrior also knew that owing to the difference in their weapons, he should be plac'd more on an equality, by being brought nearer to the stranger.

As a description of this individual may furnish some idea of the personal appearance of a whole race, it may be well to detain the narrative in order to present it to the reader in our hasty and imperfect manner. Would the truant eyes of Alston or Greenough turn, but for a time, from their gaze at the models of antiquity to contemplate this wronged and humbled people, little would be left for such inferior artists as ourselves to delineate.

The Indian in question was in every particular a warrior of fine stature and admirable proportions. As he cast aside his masque composed of such party-coloured leaves, as he had hurriedly collected, his countenance appeared in all the gravity, the dignity and it may be added in the terror, of his profession. The outlines of his lineaments were strikingly noble, and nearly approaching to Roman, though the secondary features of his face were slightly marked with the well known traces of his Asiatic origin. The peculiar tint of the skin, which in itself is so well designed to aid the effect of a martial expression, had received an additional aspect of wild ferocity from the colours of the war-paint. But as if he disdained the usual artifices of his people, he bore none of those strange and horrid devices with which the children of the forest are accustomed, like the more civilized heroes of the moustache, to back their reputation for courage, contenting himself with a broad and deep shadowing of black that served as a sufficient and an admirable foil to the brighter gleamings of his native swarthiness. His head was as usual shaved to the crown where a large and gallant scalplock seem'd to challenge the grasp of his enemies. The ornaments that in peace were pendant from the cartilages of his ear had been removed on account of his present pursuit. His body, notwithstanding the lateness of the season, was nearly naked, and the portion that was clad, bore a vestment no warmer than a light robe of the finest dress'd deer skin, beautifully stained with the rude design of some daring exploit, and which was carelessly worn, as if more in pride than from any unmanly regard to comfort. His leggins were of bright scarlet cloth, the only evidence about his person that he had held communion with the traders of Pale faces. But as if to furnish some offset to this solitary submission to a womanish vanity, they were fearfully fringed, from the gartered knee to the bottom of the mockasin, with the hair of human scalps. He leaned lightly with one hand on a short hickory bow, while the other rather touched than sought support, from the long, delicate handle of an ashen lance. A quiver, made of the cougar skin, from which the tail of the animal depended, as a characteristic ornament, was slung at his back, and a shield of hides, quaintly emblazoned with another of his warlike deeds, was suspended from his neck by a thong of sinews.

As the trapper approached, this warrior maintained his calm, upright attitude, discovering neither an eagerness to ascertain the character of those who advanced upon him, nor the smallest wish to avoid a scrutiny in his own person. An Eye, that was darker and more shining than that of the stag, was incessantly glancing, however, from one to another of the strange party, seemingly never knowing rest for an instant.

"Is my brother far from his village;" demanded the old man, in the Pawnee language, after examining the paint and those other little signs by which a practised eye, knows the tribe of the warrior he encounters in the American desert, with the same readiness and by the same sort of mysterious observation as that by which the seaman knows the distant sail.

"It is farther to the towns of the Big-knives," was the laconick reply.

"Why is a Pawnee-Loup so far from the Fork of his own river, without a horse to journey on, and in a spot empty as this?"

"Can the women and children of a Pale-face live without the meat of the bison! There was hunger in my lodge!"

"My brother is very young to be already the master of a lodge," returned the trapper looking steadily into the unmoved countenance of the youthful warrior; "but I dare say he is brave and that many a chief has offered him his daughters for wives. But he has been mistaken," pointing to the arrow which was dangling from the hand that held the bow, "in bringing a loose and barbed arrow head to kill the buffaloe. Do the Pawnees wish the wounds they give their game to rankle?"

"It is good to be ready for the Sioux; though he is not in sight, a bush may hide him."

"The man is a living proof of the truth of his words," muttered the trapper in English, "and a close-jointed and gallant looking lad he is, but far too young for a chief of any importance. It is wise, however to speak him fair, for a single arm thrown into either party if we come to blows with the squatter and his brood may turn the day. You see my children are weary," he continued in the dialect of the Prairie, pointing as he spoke to the rest of the party, who by this time were also approaching. "We wish to camp and eat. Does my brother own this spot?"

"The runners from the people on the Big-river tell us, that your nation have traded with the Tawney-faces who live beyond the salt lake, and that the Prairies are now the hunting grounds of the Big-knives."

"It is true as I hear, also from the hunters and trappers on La Platte. Though it is with the Frenchers and not with the men who claim to own the Mexicos, that my people have bargained."

"And warriors are wading up the Long River, to see that they have not been cheated, in what they have bought?"

"Ay, that is partly true, too, I fear; and it will not be long afore an accursed band of choppers and loggers will be following on their heels to humble the wilderness which lies so broad and rich on the western banks of the Mississippi, and then the land will be a peopled desert from the shores of the Maine sea to the foot of the Rocky Mountains, fill'd with all the abominations and craft of man and stript of the comfort and loveliness it received from the hand of the Lord!"

"And where were the chiefs of the Pawnee Loups, when this bargain was made!" suddenly demanded the youthful warrior, a look of startling fierceness gleaming at the same instant, athwart his dark visage. "Is a nation to be sold like the skin of a beaver!"

"Right enough, right enough; and where were truth and honesty also. But might is right according to the fashions of the 'arth and what the strong choose to do, the weak must call justice. If the Law of the Wahcondah was as much hearkened to, Pawnee, as the laws of the Long knives, your right to the Prairies would be as good as that of the greatest chief in the settlements, to the house which covers his head."

"The skin of the traveller is white," said the young native laying a finger impressively on the hard and wrinkled hand of the trapper, "does his heart say one thing and his tongue another?"

"The Wahcondah of a white-man has ears, and he shuts them to a lie. Look at my head; it is like a frosted pine, and must soon be laid in the ground. Why then should I wish to meet the Great Spirit, face to face, while his countenance is dark upon me."

The Pawnee gracefully threw his shield over one shoulder, and placing a hand on his chest he bent his head in deference to the gray locks exhibited by the trapper, after which his eye became more steady and his countenance less fierce. Still he maintained every appearance of a distrust and watchfulness that were rather tempered and subdued than forgotten. When this equivocal species of amity was established between the warrior of the Prairies and the experienced old trapper, the latter proceeded to give his directions to Paul, concerning the arrangements of the contemplated halt. While Inez and Ellen were dismounting and Middleton and the bee-hunter were attending to their comforts, the discourse was continued, sometimes in the language of the natives, but often as Paul and the Doctor mingled their opinions with the two principal speakers, in the English tongue. There was a keen and subtle trial of skill between the Pawnee and the trapper, in which each endeavored to discover the objects of the other, without betraying his own interest in the investigation. As might be expected when the struggle was between adversaries so equal, the result of the encounter answered the expectations of neither. The latter had put all the interrogatories his ingenuity and practice could suggest concerning the state of the tribe of the Loups, their crops, their store of provisions for the coming winter and their relations with their different warlike neighbors, without extorting any answer, that, in the slightest degree, elucidated the reason why he found a solitary warrior so far from his people. On the other hand, while the questions of the Indian were far more dignified and delicate, they were equally ingenious. He commented on the state of the trade in peltries; spoke of the good or ill success of many white hunters whom he had either encountered or heard named, and even alluded to the steady march, which the nation of his 'Great Father' as he courteously termed the government of the States, was making towards the hunting-grounds of his tribe. It was apparent, however, by this singular mixture of interest, contempt and indignation that were occasionally gleaming through the reserved manner of this warrior, that he knew the strange people, who were thus trespassing on his native rights, much more by report than by any actual intercourse. This personal ignorance of the whites, was as much betrayed by the manner in which he regarded the females, as by the brief, but energetick, expressions which, occasionally escaped him.

While speaking to the trapper he suffered his wandering glances, to stray towards the intellectual and nearly infantile beauty of Inez, as one might be supposed to gaze upon the loveliness of an ethereal being. It was very evident that he now saw, for the first time, one of those females, of whom the fathers of his tribe so often spoke, and who were considered of such rare excellence as to equal all that savage ingenuity could imagine in the way of loveliness. His observation of Ellen was less marked, but, notwithstanding the warlike and chastened expression of his eye, there was much of the homage which man is wont to pay to woman, even in the more cursory look he sometimes turned on her maturer and perhaps more animated beauty. This admiration, however, was so tempered by his habits and so smothered in the pride of a warrior, as completely to elude every eye but that of the trapper, who was too well skilled in Indian customs and was too well instructed in the importance of rightly conceiving the character of the stranger to let the smallest trait, or the most trifling of his movements escape him. In the mean time, the unconscious Ellen, herself, mov'd about the feeble, and less resolute Inez, with her accustomed assiduity and tenderness, exhibiting in her frank features those changing emotions of joy and regret, which occasionally beset her, as her active mind dwelt on the decided step she had just taken, with the contending doubts and hopes, and possibly with some of the mental vacillation, that was natural to her situation and sex.

Not so Paul; conceiving himself to have attained the two things dearest to his heart, the possession of Ellen and a triumph over the sons of Ishmael, he, now, enacted his part in the business of the moment, with as much coolness as though he were already leading his willing bride from solemnizing their nuptials before a border magistrate to the security of his own dwelling. He had hovered around the moving family during the tedious period of their weary march, concealing himself by day, and seeking interviews with his betrothed, as opportunities offered, in the manner already described, until fortune and his own intrepidity had united to render him successful, at the very moment when he was beginning to despair. He now cared neither for distance, nor violence, nor hardships. To his sanguine fancy and determined resolution, all the rest was easily to be achieved. Such were his feelings and such in truth they seem'd to be. With his cap cast on one side, and whistling a low air, he thrashed among the bushes, in order to make a place suitable for the females to repose on, while from time to time, he cast an approving glance at the agile form of Ellen as she tripp'd past him engaged in her own share of the duty.

"And so the wolf-tribe of the Pawnees have buried the hatchet with their neighbors, the Konzas," said the trapper pursuing a discourse which he had scarcely permitted to flag, though it had been, occasionally, interrupted by the different directions with which he saw fit to interlard it—the reader will remember that while he spoke to the native warrior in his own tongue, he necessarily addressed his white companions in English—"The Loups and the light-fac'd red-skins are again friends. Doctor, that is a tribe of which I'll engage you've often read, and of which many a round lie has been whispered in the ears of the ignorant people who live in the settlements. There was a story of a nation of Welshers, that liv'd, hereaway, in the Prairies, and how they came into the land, afore the uneasy-minded man who first let in the Christians to rob the heathens of their inheritance, had even dreamt that the sun set on a country as big as that it rose from. And how they knew the white ways and spoke with white tongues, and a thousand other follies and idle conceits."

"Have I not heard of them!" exclaimed the Naturalist, dropping a piece of jerked bison's meat which he was rather roughly discussing, at the moment. "I should be greatly ignorant not to have often dwelt with delight on so beautiful a theory, and one which so triumphantly establishes two positions which I have often maintained are unanswerable even without such living testimony in their favor, viz, that this continent can claim a more remote affinity with civilization than the time of Columbus, and that colour is the fruit of climate and condition and not a regulation of nature. Propound the latter question to this Indian gentleman, venerable hunter, he is of a reddish tint, himself, and his opinion may be said to make us masters of the two sides of the disputed point."

"Do you think a Pawnee is a reader of books, and a believer of printed lies, like the idlers in the towns!" contemptuously retorted the old man. "But it may be as well to humour the likings of the man, which after all, it is quite probable, are neither more nor less than his natural gifts, and therefore to be followed although they may be pitied. What does my brother think? all whom he sees here have white skins, but the Pawnee warriors are red, does he believe that man changes with the season, and that the son is not like his fathers?"

The young warrior regarded his interrogator for a moment with a steady and deliberating eye; then raising his finger upward he answered, with dignity—

"The Wahcondah pours the rain from his clouds; when he speaks he shakes the hills, and the fire which scorches the trees is the anger of his eye; but he fashioned his children with care and thought. What he has thus made never alters!"

"Ay, 'tis in the reason of natur' that it should be so, Doctor," continued the trapper when he had interpreted this answer to the disappointed naturalist. "The Pawnees are a wise and a great people, and I'll engage they abound in many a wholesome and honest tradition. The hunters and trappers I sometimes see speak of a great warrior of your race."

"My tribe are not women. A brave is no stranger in my village."

"Ay, but he they speak of most, is a chief far beyond the renown of common warriors, and one that might have done credit to that once mighty but now fallen people the Delawares of the Hills."

"Such a warrior should have a name."

"They call him Hard-Heart from the stoutness of his resolution; and well is he named if all I have heard of his deeds be true."

The stranger cast a glance which seem'd to read the guileless soul of the old man, as he demanded.—

"Has the pale face seen the Partizan of my tribe?"

"Never. It is not with me, now, as it used to be some forty years agone, when warfare and bloodshed were my calling and my gifts."

A loud shout from the reckless Paul interrupted his speech, and at the next moment the bee-hunter appeared leading an Indian war-horse from the side of the thicket opposite to the one occupied by the party.

"Here is a beast for a red-skin to straddle!" He cried, as he made the animal go through some of its wild paces. "There's not a brigadier in all Kentuck that can call himself master of so sleek and well jointed a nag! A Spanish saddle too, like a Grandee of the Mexico's, and look at the mane and tail! braided and platted down with little silver balls, as if it were Ellen, herself, getting her shining hair ready for a dance, or a husking frolick! Isn't this a real trotter, old trapper, to eat out of the manger of a savage!"

"Softly, lad, softly. The Loups are famous for their horses, and it's often that you see a warrior on the Prairies far better mounted, than a Congress-man in the settlements. But this, indeed, is a beast that none but a powerful chief should ride! The saddle, as you rightly think, has been sat upon in its day by a great Spanish Captain, who has lost it and his life together, in some of the battles, which this people often fight against the Southern Provinces. I warrant me, I warrant me, this youngster is the son of a great Chief, maybe of the mighty Hard-Heart himself."

During this rude interruption to the discourse the young Pawnee manifested neither impatience nor displeasure, but when he thought his beast had been the subject of sufficient comment, he very coolly, and with the air of one accustomed to have his will respected, relieved Paul of the bridle, and throwing the reins on the neck of the animal, he sprang upon his back with the activity of a professor of the equestrian art. Nothing could be finer or firmer than the seat of the savage. The highly wrought and cumbrous saddle was evidently more for show than use. Indeed it impeded rather than aided the action of limbs, which disdained to seek assistance, or admit of restraint from so womanish inventions as stirrups. The horse, which immediately began to prance, was like its rider, wild and untutored in all his motions, but while there was so little of art, there was all the freedom and grace of nature in the movements of both. The animal was probably indebted to the blood of Araby for its excellence, through a long Pedigree that embraced the steed of Mexico, the spanish barb, and the Moorish charger. The rider, in obtaining his steed from the Provinces of Central-America, had also obtained that spirit and grace in controlling him, which unite to form the most intrepid and perhaps the most skilful horsemen in the world.

Notwithstanding this sudden occupation of his animal the Pawnee discovered no hasty wish to depart. More at his ease, and possibly more independant now he found himself secure of the means of retreat, he rode back and forth, eyeing the different individuals of the party with far greater freedom than before. But, at each extremity of his ride, just as the sagacious trapper, expected to see him profit by his advantage and fly, he would turn his horse and pass over the same ground, sometimes with the rapidity of the flying antelope, and at others more slowly, and with greater dignity of mien and movement. Anxious to ascertain such facts as might have an influence on his future proceedings the old man, determined to invite him to a renewal of their conference. He therefore made a gesture expressive at the same time of his wish to resume the interrupted discourse and of his own pacific intentions. The quick eye of the stranger was not slow to note the action, but it was not until a sufficient time had passed to allow him to debate the prudence of the measure in his own mind, that he seem'd willing to trust himself, again, so near a party that was so much superior to himself in physical power, and consequently one that was able, at any instant, to command his life, or controul his personal liberty. When he did approach nigh enough to converse with facility it was with a singular mixture of haughtiness and of distrust.

"It is far to the village of the Loups," he said, stretching his arm in a direction contrary to that in which the trapper well knew that the tribe dwelt, "and the road is very crooked—what has the Big-Knife to say?"

"Ay crooked enough!" muttered the old man in English, "if you are to set out on your journey by that path, but not half so winding as the cunning of an Indian's mind. Say, my Brother; do the chiefs of the Pawnees love to see strange faces in their lodges?"

The young warrior bent his body gracefully, though but slightly, over the saddle bow, as he replied—

"When have my people forgotten to give food to the stranger!"

"If I lead my daughters to the doors of the Loups, will the women take them by the hand and will the warriors smoke with my young men?"

"The country of the Pale faces is behind them. Why do they journey so far towards the setting sun! Have they lost the path or are these the women of the white-warriors, that I hear are wading up the river of 'the troubled water'?"

"Neither. They who wade the Missouri are the warriors of my Great Father, who has sent them on his message. But we are peace-runners. The White-men and the Red are neighbors, and they wish to be friends. Do not the Omahaws visit the Loups, when the tomahawk is buried in the path between the two nations?"

"The Omahaws are welcome."

"And the Yanktons, and the Burnt-wood Tetons who live in the elbow of the river with muddy water, do they not come into the lodges of the Loups, and smoke?"

"The Tetons are liars!" exclaimed the other. "They dare not shut their eyes in the night. No; they sleep in the sun. See," he added pointing with fierce triumph to the frightful ornaments of his leggings, "their scalps are so plenty, that the Pawnees tread on them! Go: let a Sioux live in banks of snow; the plains and buffaloes are for men!"

"Ah! The secret is out," said the trapper to Middleton who was an attentive, because a deeply interested, observer of what was passing. "This good-looking young Indian is scouting on the track of the Siouxes. You may see it by his arrow-heads, and his paint, ay, by his eye, too: for a red-skin lets his natur' follow the business he is on, be it for peace, or be it for war.

Quiet, Hector, quiet. Have you never scented a Pawnee afore, pup; keep down, dog, keep down. My brother is right. The Siouxes are thieves. Men of all colours and nations say it of them, and say it truly. But the people from the rising-sun are not Siouxes, and they wish to visit the lodges of the Loups."

"The head of my brother is white," returned the Pawnee throwing one of those glances at the trapper which were so remarkably expressive of distrust, intelligence and pride, and then pointing as he continued, towards the eastern horizon, "and his eyes have look'd on many things. Can he tell me the name of what he sees yonder. Is it a buffaloe?"

"It looks more like a cloud, peeping above the skirt of the plain, with the sunshine lighting its edges. It is the smoke of the heavens!"

"It is a hill of the earth. And on its top, are the lodges of Pale-faces. Let the women of my brother wash their feet with the people of their own colour."

"The eyes of a Pawnee are good if he can see a white skin so far."

The Indian turned slowly towards the speaker, and after a pause of a moment, he sternly demanded—

"Can my brother hunt?"

"Alas! I claim to be no better than a miserable trapper!"

"When the plain is covered with the buffaloes, can he see them?"

"No doubt, no doubt, it is far easier to see than to take a scampering bull."

"And when the birds are flying from the cold, and the clouds are black with their feathers, can he see *them* too?"

"Ay—ay—it is not hard to find a duck, or a goose, when millions are darkening the heavens."

"When the snow falls, and covers the lodges of the Long-knives, can the stranger see flakes in the air?"

"My eyes are none of the best, now," returned the old man a little resentfully, "but the time has been, Pawnee, when I had a name for my sight."

"The Red-skins find the Big-knives as easily as the stranger sees the buffaloe, or the travelling birds, or the falling snow. Your warriors think the Master of Life has made the whole earth white; they are mistaken. They are pale, and it is their own faces that they see. Go, a Pawnee is not blind, that he need look long for your people!—"

The warrior suddenly paused, and bent his face aside like one who listened with all his faculties absorbed in the act. Then turning the head of his horse he rode to the nearest angle of the thicket and look'd intently across the bleak Prairie, in a direction opposite to the side on which the party stood. Returning slowly from this unaccountable, and to his observers startling, procedure, he rivetted his eyes on Inez, and pac'd back and forth several times, with the air of one who maintained a warm struggle on some difficult point, in the recesses of his own thought. He had drawn the reins of his impatient steed, and was seemingly about to speak, when his head again sunk on his chest, and he resumed his former attitude of attention. Galloping like a deer to the place of his former observations, he rode for a moment swiftly in short and rapid circles, as if still uncertain of his course, and then darted away like a bird that had been fluttering around its nest before it takes a distant flight. After scouring the plain for a minute, he was lost to the eye behind a swell of the land.

The hounds, who had also manifested great uneasiness for some time, followed him for a little distance and then terminated their chase, by seating themselves on the ground, and raising their usual, low, whining and warning howls.

Chapter XIX

"How if he will not stand?"
Much Ado about Nothing, III.iii.27.

THE SEVERAL movements, related in the close of the preceding chapter had passed in so short a space of time, that the old man, while he neglected not to note the smallest incident, had no opportunity of expressing his opinion concerning the stranger's motives. After the Pawnee had disappeared, however, he shook his head, and muttered while he walked slowly to the angle of the thicket that the Pawnee had just quitted.

"There are both scents and sounds in the air, though my miserable senses are not good enough to hear the one or to catch the taint of the other."

"There is nothing to be seen," cried Middleton who kept close at his side. "My eyes and my ears are good, and yet I can assure you that I neither hear nor see any thing."

"Your eyes are good! and you are not deaf!" returned the other with a slight air of contempt, "no, lad, no—they may be good to see across a church or to hear a town bell, but afore you had passed a year on these Prairies you would find yourself mistaking a turkey for a horse, or conceiting fifty times that the roar of a buffaloe bull was the thunder of the Lord. There is a deception of natur' in these naked plains, in which the air throws up the image like water, and then is it hard to tell the Prairies from a sea. But yonder is a sign that a hunter never fails to know!"

The trapper pointed to a flight of vultures that were sailing over the plain at no great distance, and apparently in the direction in which the Pawnee had rivetted his eye. At first Middleton could not distinguish the small dark objects that were dotting the dusky clouds, but as they came swiftly onward, first their forms and then their heavy waving wings became distinctly visible.

"Listen;" said the trapper, when he had succeeded in making Middleton see the moving column of birds; "now you hear the buffaloes, or bisons as your knowing Doctor sees fit to call them, though buffaloes is their name among all the hunters of these regions. Now, I conclude that a hunter is a better judge of a beast and of its name," he added winking to the young soldier, "than any man who has turn'd over the leaves of a book, instead of travelling over the face of the 'arth, in order to find out the natur's of its inhabitants."

"Of their habits, I will grant you," cried the Naturalist, who rarely miss'd an opportunity to agitate any point which touched his favorite studies, "that is provided, always, that deference is had to the proper use of definitions, and that they are contemplated with scientific eyes."

"Eyes of a mole! as if man's eyes were not as good for names as the eyes of any other creatur'! who named the works of His hand, can you tell me that, with your books and college wisdom? Was it not the first man in the Garden, and is it not a plain consequence that his children inherit his gifts!"

"That is certainly the Mosaic account of the event," said the Doctor, "though your reading is by far too literal."

"My reading—nay, if you suppose that I have wasted my time in schools you do such a wrong to my knowledge, as one mortal should never lay to the door of another without sufficient reason. If I have ever craved the art of reading, it has been that I might better know the sayings of the book you name for it is a book, which speaks in every line according to human feelings and therein according to reason."

"And do you then believe," said the Doctor a little provoked by the dogmatism of his stubborn adversary, and perhaps secretly triumphing in his own more liberal, though scarcely as profitable, attainments. "Do you then believe that all these beasts were literally collected in a garden to be enrolled in the nomenclature of the first man?"

"Why not. I understand your meaning, for it is not needful to live in towns to hear all the devilish devices that the conceit of man can invent to upset his own happiness. What does it prove, except, indeed that it may be said to prove that the garden He made was not after the miserable fashions of our times, thereby directly giving the lie to what the world calls its civilizing. No, no, the Garden of the Lord, was the forest then and is the forest now, where the fruits do grow and the birds do sing according to his own wise ordering—Now, lads, you may see through the mystery of the vultures. There come the buffaloes themselves, and a noble herd it is! I warrant me, that Pawnee has a troop of his people in some of the hollows nigh by, and as he has gone scampering after them, you are about to see a glorious chase. It will serve to keep the squatter and his brood under cover, and for ourselves there is little reason to fear. A Pawnee is not apt to be a malicious savage."

Every eye was now drawn to the striking spectacle that succeeded. Even the timid Inez hastened to the side of Middleton to gaze at the sight, and Paul summoned Ellen from her culinary labors, to become a witness of the lively scene.

Throughout the whole of those moving events which it has been our duty to record, the Prairies had lain in the majesty of perfect solitude. The heavens had been blackened with the passage of the migratory birds, it is true, but the dogs of the party, and the ass of the Doctor, were the only quadrupeds that had enlivened the broad surface of the waste beneath. There was now a sudden exhibition of animal life which changed the scene, as it were by magic, to the very opposite extreme.

A few enormous Bison bulls were first observed scouring along the most distant roll of the Prairie, and then succeeded long files of single beasts, which in their turns were followed by a dark mass of bodies, until the dun-coloured herbage of the plain was entirely lost, in the deeper hue of their shaggy coats. The herd, as the column spread and thickened, was like the endless flocks of the smaller birds, whose extended flanks are so often seen to heave up out the abyss of the heavens, until they appear as countless and as interminable, as the leaves in those forests over which they wing their endless flight. Clouds of dust shot up in little columns from the centre of the mass, as some animal more furious than the rest ploughed the plain with his horns, and from time to time a deep hollow bellowing was borne along on the wind, as if a thousand throats vented their plaints in a discordant murmuring.

A long and musing silence reigned in the party as they gazed on this spectacle of wild and peculiar grandeur. It was at length broken by the trapper, who having been long accustomed to similar sights felt less of its influence, or rather felt it in a less thrilling and absorbing manner, than those to whom the scene was more novel.

"There go ten thousand oxen in one drove without keeper or master, except him, who made them and gave them these open plains for their pasture! Ay it is here that man may see the proofs of his wantonness and folly! Can the proudest Governer in all the States go into his fields and slaughter a nobler bullock than is here offered to the meanest hand, and when he has gotten his surloin, or his steak can he eat it with as good a relish as he who has sweetened his food with wholesome toil, and earned it according to the law of natur' by honestly mastering that which the Lord hath put before him?"

"If the Prairie platter is smoking with a buffaloe's hump, I answer, no;" interrupted the luxurious bee-hunter.

"Ay, boy; you have tasted and you feel the genuine reasoning of the thing! But the herd is heading a little, this-a-way, and it behoves us to make ready for their visit. If we hide ourselves, altogether, the horned brutes will break through the place, and trample us beneath their feet like so many creeping worms; so we will just put the weak ones apart, and take post as becomes men and hunters in the van."

As there was but little time to make the necessary arrangements the whole party set about them in good earnest. Inez and Ellen were placed in the edge of the thicket on the side farthest from the approaching herd, Asinus was posted in the centre, in consideration of his nerves, and then the old man with his three male companions divided themselves in such a manner as they thought would enable them to turn the head of the rushing column, should it chance to approach too nigh their position. By the vacillating movements of some fifty or a hundred bulls that led the advance it remained questionable for many moments what course they intended to pursue. But a tremendous and painful roar which came from behind the cloud of dust that rose in the centre of the horde, and which was horridly answered by the screams of the carrion birds that were greedily sailing directly above the flying drove, appeared to give a new impulse to their flight, and at once, to remove every symptom of indecision. As if glad to seek the smallest signs of the forest the whole of the affrighted herd became steady in its direction rushing in a straight line toward the little cover of bushes which has already been so often named.

The appearance of danger was now, in reality, of a character to try the stoutest nerves. The flanks of the dark, moving mass were advanced in such a manner as to make a concave line of the front, and every fierce eye that was glaring from the shaggy wilderness of hair in which the entire heads of the males were enveloped, was rivetted with mad anxiety on the thicket. It seem'd as if each beast strove to outstrip his neighbor, in gaining this desired cover, and as thousands in the rear press'd blindly on those in front, there was the appearance of an imminent risk that the leaders of the herd would be precipitated on the crouching party, in which case the destruction of every one of them was certain. Each of our adventurers felt the danger of his situation in a manner peculiar to his individual character and circumstances.

Middleton wavered. At times, he felt inclined to rush through the bushes and seizing Inez attempt to fly, then recollecting the impossibility of outstripping the furious speed of an alarmed bison, he felt for his arms, determined to make head against the countless drove. The faculties of Doctor Battius were quickly wrought up to the very summit of mental delusion. The dark forms of the herd lost their distinctness and then the Naturalist began to fancy he beheld a wild collection of all the creatures of the world rushing upon him in a body as if to revenge the various injuries, which in the course of a life of indefatigable labour in behalf of the natural sciences, he had inflicted on their several genera. The paralysis it occasioned in his system was like the effect of the Incubus. Equally unable to fly or to advance he stood rivetted to the spot, until the infatuation became so complete, that the worthy naturalist was beginning, by a desperate effort of scientific resolution, even to class the different specimens. On the other hand, Paul shouted and call'd on Ellen to come and assist him in shouting, but his voice was lost in the bellowings and trampling of the herd. Furious, and yet strangely excited by the obstinacy of the brutes and the wildness of the sight, and nearly maddened by sympathy and a species of unconscious apprehension, in which the claims of nature were singularly mingled with concern for his mistress, he nearly split his throat in exhorting his aged friend to interfere.

"Come forth, old trapper," he shouted, " with your Prairie inventions or we shall be all smothered under a mountain of buffaloe humps."

The old man, who had stood all this while leaning on his rifle and regarding the movements of the herd with a steady eye, now deem'd it time to strike his blow. Levelling his piece at the foremost bull, with an agility that would have done credit to his youth, he fired. The animal received the bullet on the matted hair between his horns, and fell to his knees: but shaking his head he instantly arose, the very shock seeming to increase his exertions. There was now, no longer time to hesitate. Throwing down his rifle, the trapper stretched forth his arms and advanced from the cover with naked hands, directly towards the rushing column of the beasts.

The figure of a man, when sustained by the firmness and steadiness that intellect can only impart rarely fails of commanding respect from all the inferior animals of the creation. The leading bulls recoiled and for a single instant there was a sudden stop to their speed, a dense mass of bodies rolling up in front, until hundreds were seen floundering and tumbling on the plain. Then came another of those hollow bellowings from the rear, and set the herd again, in motion. The head of the column, however, divided, the immovable form of the trapper cutting it, as it were, into two gliding streams of life. Middleton and Paul instantly profited by his example, and extended the feeble barrier by a similar exhibition of their own persons.

For a few moments the new impulse given to the animals in front served to protect the thicket, but as the body of the herd press'd more and more upon the open line of its defenders, and the dust thickened, so as to obscure their persons, there was, at each instant, a renewed danger of the brutes breaking through. It became necessary for the trapper and his companions to become still more and more alert, and they were gradually yielding before the headlong multitude, when a furious bull darted by Middleton, so near as to brush his person, and at the next instant swept through the thicket with the velocity of the wind.

"Close, and die for the ground," shouted the old man, "or a thousand of the devils will be at his heels."

All their efforts would have prov'd fruitless however, against the living torrent, had not Asinus, whose domains had just been so rudely entered lifted his voice, in the midst of the uproar. The most sturdy and furious of the bulls trembled at the alarming and unknown cry, and then each individual brute was seen madly pressing from that very thicket, which, the moment before, he had endeavored to reach, with the eagerness with which the murderer seeks the sanctuary.

As the stream divided, the place became clear, the two dark columns moving obliquely from the copse, to unite, again, at the distance of a mile on its opposite side. The instant the old man saw the sudden effect which the voice of Asinus had produced, he coolly commenced reloading his rifle, indulging at the same time in a heartfelt fit of his silent and peculiar merriment.

"There they go like dogs with so many half-filled shot pouches dangling at their tails, and no fear of their breaking their order, for what the brutes in the rear didn't hear with their own ears they'll conceit they did: besides, if they change their minds it may be no hard matter to get the Jack to sing the rest of his tune."

"The ass has spoken, but Balaam is silent!" cried the Bee-hunter, catching his breath after a repeated burst of noisy mirth that might possibly have added to the panic of the buffaloes by its vociferation—"The man is as completely dumb-founded as if a swarm of young bees had settled on the end of his tongue, and he not willing to speak for fear of their answer."

"How now, friend;" continued the trapper, addressing the still motionless and entranced naturalist. "How now, friend; are you, who make your livelihood by booking the names and natur's of the beasts of the fields and the fowls of the air, frightened at a herd of scampering buffaloes. Though perhaps you are ready to dispute my right to call them by a word, that is in the mouth of every hunter and trader on the frontier!"

The old man was, however, mistaken in supposing he could excite the benumbed faculties of the Doctor, by provoking a discussion. From that time henceforth, he was never known except on one occasion to utter a word that indicated either the species, or the genus, of the animal. He obstinately refused the nutritious food of the whole ox family, and even to the present hour, now that he is established in all the scientific dignity and security of a *savan* in one of the maritime towns, he turns his back, with a shudder, on those delicious and unrivalled viands that are so often seen at the suppers of the craft, and which are unequalled by any thing that is served under the same name at the boasted chop-houses of London, or at the most renowned of the Parisian restaurans. In short the distaste of the worthy naturalist for beef was not unlike that which the shepherd sometimes produces by first muzzling and fettering his delinquent dog, and then leaving him as a stepping stone for the whole flock to use in its transit over a wall, or through the opening of a sheep-fold, a process which is said to produce in the culprit a species of surfeit on the subject of mutton, forever after. By the time Paul and the trapper saw fit to terminate the fresh bursts of merriment, which the continued abstraction of their learned companion did not fail to excite, he commenced breathing again as if the suspended action of his lungs had been renewed by the application of a pair of artificial bellows, and was heard to make use of the ever afterwards proscribed term on that solitary occasion to which we have just alluded.

"Boves Americani Horridi!" exclaimed the Doctor, laying great stress on the latter word after which he continued mute, like one who pondered on strange and unaccountable events.

"Ay, horrid eyes enough I will willingly allow," returned the trapper, "and altogether the creatur' has a frightful look, to one unused to the sights and bustle of a natural life. But then the courage of the beast is in no way equal to its countenance. Lord, man, if you should once get fairly beset by a brood of grizzly bears, as happened to Hector and I, at the great falls of the Miss—ah! here comes the tail of the herd, and yonder goes a pack of hungry wolves, ready to pick up the sick, or such as get a disjointed neck by a tumble—ha! there are mounted men on their trail, or I'm no sinner! here, lad; you may see them, hereaway, just where the dust is scattering afore the wind. They are hovering around a wounded buffaloe, making an end of the surly devil with their arrows!"

Middleton and Paul soon caught a glimpse of the dark groupe, that the quick eye of the old man had so readily detected. Some fifteen or twenty horsemen were, in truth, to be seen riding in quick circuits about a noble bull, which stood at bay, too grievously hurt to fly, and yet seeming to disdain to fall notwithstanding his hardy body had already been the target for a hundred arrows. A thrust from the lance of a powerful Indian, however, completed his conquest, and the brute gave up his obstinate hold of life with a roar, that past bellowing over the place where our adventurers stood, and reaching the ears of the affrighted herd, added a new impulse to their flight.

"How well that Pawnee knew the philosophy, of a buffaloe hunt!" said the old man, after he had stood regarding the animated scene for a few moments with evident satisfaction. "You saw how he went off like the wind before the drove. It was in order that he might not taint the air, and that he might turn the flank and join—Ha! how is this! yonder red-skins are not Pawnees. The feathers in their heads are from the wings and tails of owls. Ah, as I am but a miserable, half sighted, trapper it is a band of the accursed Siouxes! To cover, lads, to cover. A single cast of an eye this-a-way, would strip us of every rag of clothes as surely as the lightning scorches the bush, and it might be that our very lives would be far from safe."

Middleton had already turned from the spectacle to seek that which pleased him better; the sight of his young and beautiful bride. Paul seized the Doctor by the arm, and as the trapper followed with the smallest possible delay, the whole party was quickly collected within the cover of the thicket. After a few short explanations concerning the character of this new danger, the old man, on whom the whole duty of directing their movements was devolved in deference to his great experience, continued his discourse, as follows—

"This is a region, as you must all know, where a strong arm is far better than the right, and where the white law is as little known as heeded, therefore, does every thing, now, depend on judgment and power. If," he continued, laying his finger on his cheek, like one who considered deeply all sides of the embarrassing situation in which he found himself, "if, an invention could be framed which would set these Siouxes and the brood of the squatter by the ears, then might we come in like the buzzards after a fight atween the beasts and pick up the gleanings of the ground. There are Pawnees nigh us too! It is a certain matter; for yonder lad is not so far from his village without an errand. Here are therefore four parties within sound of a cannon, not one of whom can trust the other. All which makes movement a little difficult in a district where covers are far from plenty. But we are three well armed, and I think I may say three stout-hearted men—"

"Four;" interrupted Paul.

"Anan!" said the old man, looking up simply at his companion.

"Four," repeated the bee-hunter pointing to the Naturalist.

"Every army has its hangers-on and idlers," rejoined the blunt border man. "Friend, it will be necessary to slaughter this ass."

"To slay Asinus! such a deed would be an act of supererogatory cruelty!"

"I know nothing of your words, which hide their meaning in sound; but that is cruel which sacrifices a christian to a brute. This is what I call the reason of marcy. It would be just as safe to blow a trumpet as to let the animal raise his voice ag'in; inasmuch as it would prove a manifest challenge to the Siouxes."

"I will answer for the discretion of Asinus, who seldom speaks without a reason."

"They say a man can be known by the company he keeps," retorted the old man, "and why not a brute! I once made a forced march and went through a great deal of jeopardy with a companion who never opened his mouth but to sing; and trouble enough and great concern of mind did the fellow give me. It was in that very business with your grand'ther, Captain, but, then, he had a human throat, and well did he know how to use it, on occasion, though he didn't always stop to regard the time and seasons fit for such outcries. Ah's! me: if I was now, as I was then, it wouldn't be a band of thieving

Siouxes that should easily drive me from such a lodgment as this! But what signifies boasting, when sight and strength are both failing. The warrior that the Delawares once saw fit to call after the Hawk for the goodness of his eyes, would now be better termed the Mole! In my judgement, therefore, it will be well to slay the brute."

"There's argument and good logic in it," said Paul. "Music is music, and it's always noisy whether it comes from a fiddle or a Jack-Ass. Therefore I agree with the old man, and say, kill the beast."

"Friends," said the naturalist looking with a sorrowful eye from one to another of his bloodily disposed companions, "slay not Asinus. He is a specimen of his kind of whom much good and little evil can be said. Hardy and docile for his *genus*, abstemious and patient even for his humble *species*. We have journeyed much together and his death would grieve me. How would it trouble thy spirit, venerable venator, to separate in such an untimely manner from your faithful hound?"

"The animal shall not die," said the old man, suddenly clearing his throat, in a manner that proved he felt the force of the appeal, "but his voice must be smothered. Bind his jaws with the halter, and then I think we may trust the rest to providence."

With this double security for the discretion of Asinus, for Paul instantly bound the muzzle of the ass in the manner required, the trapper seem'd content. After which he proceeded to the margin of the thicket to reconnoitre.

The uproar which attended the passage of the herd was now gone, or rather it was heard rolling along the Prairie, at the distance of a mile. The clouds of dust were already blown away by the wind, and a clear range was left to the eye, in that place, where ten minutes before there existed a scene of so much wildness and confusion.

The Siouxes had completed their conquest, and, apparently satisfied with this addition to the numerous previous captives they had made, they now seemed content to let the remainder of the herd escape. A dozen remained around the carcass, over which a few buzzards were balancing themselves with steady wings and greedy eyes, while the rest were riding about in quest of such further booty as might come in their way, on the trail of so vast a drove. The trapper measured the proportions and scanned the equipments of such individuals as drew nearer to the side of the thicket, with careful eyes. At length he pointed out one among them to Middleton as Weucha.

"Now, know we not only who they are, but their errand;" the old man continued deliberately shaking his head. "They have lost the trail of the squatter, and are on its hunt. These buffaloes have cross'd their path, and in chasing the animals bad luck has led them, in open sight of the hill on which the brood of Ishmael have harbored. Do you see, yon birds watching for the offals of the beast they have killed? Therein is a moral which teaches the manner of a Prairie life. A band of Pawnees are outlying for these very Siouxes as you see the buzzards looking down for their food, and it behooves us as Christian men who have so much at stake to look down upon them both. Ha! what brings yonder two skirting reptiles to a stand! As you live, they have found the place where the miserable son of the squatter met his death!"

The old man was not mistaken. Weucha and a savage who accompanied him, had reached that spot which has already been mentioned as furnishing the frightful evidences of violence and bloodshed. There they sat on their horses, examining the well known signs, with the intelligence that distinguishes the habits of Indians. Their scrutiny was long, and apparently not without distrust. At length they raised a cry, that was scarcely less hideous and startling than that which the hounds had before made over the same fatal signs, and which did not fail to draw the whole band immediately around them, as the fell bark of the jackall is said to gather his comrades to the chase.

Chapter XX

"Welcome, ancient Pistol."
2 Henry IV, II.iv.III.

IT WAS NOT long, before the trapper pointed out the commanding person of Mahtoree as the leader of the Siouxes. This chief who had been among the last to obey the vociferous summons of Weucha, no sooner reach'd the spot where his whole party was now gathered than he threw himself from his horse and proceeded to examine the marks of the extraordinary trail, with that degree of dignity and attention which became his high and responsible station. The warriors, for it was but too evident that they were to a man of that fearless and ruthless class, awaited the result of his investigation with patient reserve; none, but a few of the principal braves, presuming even to speak while their leader was thus gravely occupied. It was several minutes before Mahtoree seem'd satisfied. He, then, directed his eyes along the ground to those several places where Ishmael had found the same revolting evidences of the passage of some bloody struggle, and motioned to his people to follow.

The whole band advanced in a body towards the thicket until they came to a halt, within a few yards of the precise spot, where Esther had stimulated her sluggish sons to break into the cover. The reader will readily imagine that the trapper and his companions were not indifferent observers of so threatening a movement. The old man summoned all who were capable of bearing arms to his side, and demanded in very unequivocal terms, though in a voice that was suitably lowered in order to escape the ears of their dangerous neighbors, whether they were disposed to make battle for their liberty or whether they should try the milder expedient of conciliation. As it was a subject in which all had an equal interest he put the question as to a Council of war, and not without some slight exhibition of the lingering vestiges of a nearly extinct military pride. Paul and the Doctor were diametrically opposed to each other in opinion; the former declaring for an immediate appeal to arms, and the latter as warmly espousing the policy of pacific measures. Middleton, who saw that there was great danger of a hot verbal dispute between two men who were governed by feelings so diametrically opposed, saw fit to assume the office of arbiter, or rather to decide the question, his situation making him a sort of umpire. He also leaned to the side of peace, for he evidently saw that in consequence of the vast superiority of their enemies violence would irretrievably lead to their destruction.

The trapper listened to the reasons of the young soldier with great attention, and as they were given with the steadiness of one who did not suffer apprehension to blind his judgement, they did not fail to produce a suitable impression.

"It is rational," rejoined the trapper, when the other had delivered his reasons; "It is very rational, for what man cannot move with his strength he must circumvent with his wits. It is reason that makes him stronger than the buffaloe, and swifter than the moose. Now stay you, here, and keep yourselves close. My life, and my traps are but of little value, when the welfare of so many human souls is concerned, and, moreover, I may say that I know the windings of Indian cunning. Therefore will I go alone upon the Prairie. It may so happen that I can yet draw the eyes of a Sioux from this spot, and give you time and room to fly."

As if resolved to listen to no remonstrance the old man quietly shouldered his rifle, and moving leisurely through the thicket, he issued on the plain at a point whence he might first appear before the eyes of the Siouxes without exciting their suspicions that he came from its cover.

The instant that the figure of a man, dressed in the garb of a hunter and bearing the well known and much dreaded rifle, appeared before the eyes of the Siouxes, there was a sensible, though a suppressed sensation in the band. The artifice of the trapper had so far succeeded, as to render it extremely doubtful whether he came from some point on the open Prairie, or from the thicket; though the Indians still continued to cast frequent and suspicious glances at the cover. They had made their halt at the distance of an arrow-flight from the bushes, but when the stranger came sufficiently nigh to show that the deep coating of red and brown, which time and exposure had given to his features, was laid upon the original colour of a

Pale Face, they slowly receded from the spot until they reached a distance that might defeat the aim of fire-arms.

In the mean time the old man continued to advance until he had got nigh enough to make himself heard without difficulty. Here, he stopped and dropping his rifle to the earth, he raised his hand with the palm outward, in token of peace. After uttering a few words of reproach to his hound, who watch'd the savage groupe with eyes that seem'd to recognize them he spoke in the Sioux tongue—

"My brothers are welcome;" he said, cunningly constituting himself the master of the region in which they had met, and assuming the offices of hospitality. "They are far from their villages, and are hungry. Will they follow to my lodge, to eat and sleep."

No sooner was his voice heard, than the yell of pleasure, which burst from a dozen mouths, convinced the sagacious trapper that he also was recognized. Feeling that it was too late to retreat, he profited by the confusion which prevailed among them, while Weucha was explaining his character, to advance, until he was again face to face with the redoubtable Mahtoree. The second interview between these two men, each of whom was extraordinary in his way, was marked by the usual caution of the frontiers. They stood for nearly a minute examining each other without speaking.

"Where are your young men?" sternly demanded the Teton chieftain, after he found that the immoveable features of the trapper refused to betray any of their master's secrets, under his intimidating look.

"The Long-knives do not come in bands to trap the beaver. I am alone."

"Your head is white, but you have a forked tongue. Mahtoree has been in your camp. He knows that you are not alone. Where is your young wife, and the warrior that I found upon the Prairie?"

"I have no wife. I have told my brother, that the woman and her friend were strangers. The words of a gray head, should be heard, and not forgotten. The Dahcotahs found travellers asleep and they thought they had no need of horses. The women and children of a Pale-face are not used to go far on foot. Let them be sought, where you left them."

The eyes of the Teton flash'd fire, as he answered—

"They are gone; but Mahtoree is a wise chief and his eyes can see a great distance."

"Does the Partizan of the Tetons see men on these naked fields?" retorted the trapper with great steadiness of mien, "I am very old and my eyes grow dim: where do they stand?"

The chief remained silent a moment as if he disdained to contest any further, the truth of a fact concerning which he was already satisfied, then pointing to the traces on the earth, he said, with a sudden transition to mildness in his eye and manner—

"My father has learnt wisdom in many winters; can he tell me whose moccasin has left this trail?"

"There have been wolves and buffaloes on the Prairies, and there may have been cougars too."

Mahtoree glanced his eye at the thicket as if he thought the latter suggestion not impossible. Pointing to the place he ordered his young men reconnoitre it more closely, cautioning them at the same time with a stern look at the trapper to beware of treachery from the Big-knives. Three or four half-naked, eager-looking youths lash'd their horses, at the word, and darted away to obey the mandate. The old man trembled a little for the discretion of Paul when he saw this demonstration. The Tetons encircled the place, two or three times, approaching nigher and nigher, at each circuit, and then galloped back to their leader to report that the copse seem'd empty. Notwithstanding the trapper watch'd the eye of Mahtoree, in order to detect the inward movements of his mind and, if possible to anticipate in order to direct his suspicions, the utmost sagacity of one so long accustomed to study the cold habits of the Indian race could however detect no symptom, or expression, that denoted how far he credited or distrusted this intelligence. Instead of replying to the information of his scouts, he spoke kindly to his horse, and motioning to a youth to receive the bridle, or rather halter, by which he governed the animal, he took the trapper by the arm and led him a little apart from the rest of the band.

"Has my father been a warrior?" said the wily Teton, in a tone that he intended should be conciliating.

"Do the leaves cover the trees, in the season of fruits! Go.

The Dahcotahs have not seen as many warriors living as I have look'd on in their blood! But what signifies idle remembrancing," he added in English, "when limbs grow stiff, and sight is failing!"

The chief regarded him a moment with a severe look as if he would lay bare the falsehood he had heard, but meeting in the calm eye and steady mien of the trapper a confirmation of the truth of what he said, he took the hand of the old man and laid it gently on his head, in token of the respect that was due to the other's years and experience.

"Why then do the Big-knives tell their red brethren to bury the tomahawk," he said, "when their own young men never forget that they are braves, and meet each other so often with bloody hands."

"My nation is more numerous than the buffaloes on the Prairies or the pigeons in the air. Their quarrels are frequent, yet their warriors are few. None go out on the war path, but they who are gifted with the qualities of a brave, and therefore such see many battles."

"It is not so—my Father is mistaken;" returned Mahtoree, indulging in a smile of exulting penetration, at the very instant he corrected the force of his denial, in deference to the years and services of one so aged. "The Big-knives are very wise; and they are men; all of them would be warriors. They would leave the red skins to dig roots and hoe the corn. But a Dahcotah is not born to live like a woman; he must strike the Pawnee and the Omawhaw, or he will lose the name of his Fathers."

"The Master of Life looks with an open eye on his children who die in a battle that is fought for the right; but he is blind, and his ears are shut to the cries of an Indian who is killed when plundering, or doing evil to his neighbor."

"My father is old," said Mahtoree looking at his aged companion, with an expression of irony that sufficiently denoted he was one of those who overstep the trammels of education, and who are perhaps a little given to abuse the mental liberty they thus obtain. "He is *very* old: Has he made a journey to the far country, and has he been at the trouble to come back to tell the young men what he has seen?"

"Teton," returned the trapper, throwing the breech of his

rifle to the earth with startling vehemence, and regarding his companion with steady severity. "I have heard that there are men among my people who study their great medecines until they believe themselves to be Gods, and who laugh at all faith except in their own vanities. It may be true. It *is* true; for I have seen them. When man is shut up in towns and schools with his own follies, it may be easy to believe himself greater than the Master of Life; but a warrior who lives in a house with the clouds for its roof, where he can at any moment look both at the heavens and at the earth, and who daily sees the power of the Great Spirit, should be more humble. A Dahcotah chieftain ought to be too wise to laugh at justice."

The crafty Mahtoree, who saw that his free-thinking was not likely to produce a favorable impression on the old man, instantly changed his ground, by alluding to the more immediate subject of their interview. Laying his hand gently on the shoulder of the trapper, he led him forward until they both stood within fifty feet of the margin of the thicket. Here he fastened his penetrating eyes on the other's honest countenance, and continued the discourse—

"If my father has hid his young men in the bush, let him tell them to come forth. You see that a Dahcotah is not afraid. Mahtoree is a great Chief! A warrior whose head is white and who is about to go to the Land of Spirits cannot have a tongue with two ends, like a serpent."

"Dahcotah, I have told no lie. Since the Great Spirit made me a man, I have liv'd in the wilderness, or on these naked plains, without lodge or family. I am a hunter, and go on my path alone."

"My father has a good carabyne. Let him point it in the bush and fire."

The old man hesitated a moment, and then slowly prepared himself to give this delicate assurance of the truth of what he said, without which he plainly perceived the suspicions of his crafty companion could not be lulled. As he lowered his rifle, his eye, although greatly dimmed and weakened by age, ran over the confused collection of objects that lay embedded amid the party coloured foliage of the thicket until it succeeded in catching a glimpse of the brown covering of the stem of a small tree. With this object in view he raised the piece to a level and fired. The bullet had no sooner glided from the barrel, than a tremor seized the hands of the trapper which, had it occurred a moment sooner would have utterly disqualified him for so hazardous an experiment. A frightful silence succeeded the report, during which he expected to hear the shrieks of the females, and then as the smoke whirled away in the wind, he caught a view of the fluttering bark, and felt assured that all his former skill was not entirely departed from him. Dropping the piece to the earth, he turned again to his companion with an air of the utmost composure and demanded—

"Is my brother satisfied?"

"Mahtoree is a chief of the Dahcotahs," returned the cunning Teton laying his hand on his chest, in acknowledgement of the other's sincerity. "He knows that a warrior who has smoked at so many Council fires, until his head has grown white, would not be found in wicked company. But did not my father once ride on a horse, like a rich chief of the Pale-faces, instead of travelling on foot like a hungry Konza?"

"Never. The Wahcondah has given me legs, and he has given me resolution to use them. For sixty summers and winters did I journey in the woods of America, and ten tiresome years have I dwelt on these open fields, without finding need to call often upon the gifts of the other cre'turs of the Lord, to carry me from place to place."

"If my Father has so long liv'd in the shade, why has he come upon the Prairies. The sun will scorch him?"

The old man look'd sorrowfully about for a moment, and then turning with a confidential air to the other he replied—

"I passed the spring, summer, and autumn of life among the trees. The winter of my days had come, and found me where I lov'd to be, in the quiet, ay and in the honesty of the woods! Teton; then I slept, happily, where my eyes could look up through the branches of the pines and the beeches, to the very dwelling of the Good Spirit of my people. If I had need to open my heart to him, while his fires were burning above my head, the door was open and before my eyes. But the axes of the choppers awoke me. For a long time my ears heard nothing but the uproar of clearings. I bore it, like a warrior and a man; there was a reason that I should bear it.

But when that reason was ended, I bethought me to get beyond the accursed sounds. It was trying to the courage and to the habits, but I had heard of these vast and naked fields, and I came hither to escape the wasteful temper of my people. Tell me, Dahcotah, have I not done well?"

The trapper laid his long, lean finger on the naked shoulder of the Indian as he ended, and seem'd to demand his felicitations on his ingenuity and success, with a ghastly smile in which triumph was singularly blended with regret. His companion listened intently, and replied to the question, by saying in the sententious manner of his race—

"The head of my Father is very gray; he has always liv'd with men, and he has seen every thing. What he does is good; what he speaks is wise. Now let him say, is he sure that he is a stranger to the Big-knives who are looking for their beasts on every side of the Prairies and cannot find them."

"Dahcotah, what I have said is true. I live alone, and never do I mingle with men whose skins are white, if—"

His mouth was suddenly closed by an interruption that was as mortifying as it was unexpected. The words were still on his tongue when the bushes on the side of the thicket where they stood opened, and the whole of the party whom he had just left, and in whose behalf he was endeavoring to reconcile his love of truth, to the necessity of prevaricating, came openly into view. A pause of mute astonishment succeeded this unlooked-for spectacle. Then, Mahtoree, who did not suffer a muscle or a joint to betray the wonder and surprise he actually experienced motioned towards the advancing friends of the trapper, with an air of assumed civility, and a smile, that lighted his fierce, dark, visage, as the glare of the setting sun reveals the volume and load of the cloud, that is surcharged to bursting with the electric fluid. He, however, disdained to speak, or to give any other evidence of his intentions, than by calling to his side the distant band, who sprang forward at his beck, with the alacrity of willing subordinates.

In the mean time, the friends of the old man continued to advance. Middleton himself was foremost, supporting the light and aerial looking figure of Inez, on whose anxious and shaking countenance, he cast such occasional glances of tender interest, as, in similar circumstances, a father would have given to his child. Paul led Ellen, close in their rear. But while the eye of the bee-hunter did not neglect his blooming companion, it scowled angrily, resembling more the aspect of the sullen and retreating bear, than the soft intelligence of a favored suitor. Obed and Asinus came last, the former leading his companion with a degree of fondness that could hardly be said to be exceeded by any other of the Party. The approach of the naturalist was far less rapid than that of those who preceded him. His feet seem'd equally reluctant to advance, or to remain stationary; his position bearing a great analogy to that of Mahomet's coffin, with the exception that the quality of repulsion rather than that of attraction held him in a state of rest. The repulsive power in his rear, however, appeared to predominate, and by a singular exception, as he would have said himself, to all philosophical principles, it rather increased than diminished by distance. As the eyes of the naturalist steadily maintained a position that was the opposite of his route they served to give a direction to those of the observers of all these movements, and at once, furnished a sufficient clue by which to unravel the mystery of so sudden a debouchement from the cover.

Another cluster of stout, and armed men, was seen at no great distance, just rounding a point of the thicket, and moving directly though cautiously towards the place where the band of the Siouxes was posted, as a squadron of cruisers is often seen to steer across the waste of waters towards the rich but well-protected convoy. In short, the family of the squatter, or at least such among them as were capable of bearing arms, appeared in view, on the broad Prairie, evidently bent on revenging their wrongs.

Mahtoree and his party slowly retired from the thicket, the moment they caught a view of the strangers, until they halted on a swell that commanded a wide and unobstructed view of the naked fields on which they stood. Here the Dahcotah appeared disposed to make his stand, and to bring matters to an issue. Notwithstanding this retreat, in which he compelled the trapper to accompany him, Middleton still advanced until he too, halted on the same elevation, and within speaking distance of the warlike Siouxes. The borderers in their turn took a favourable position, though at a much greater distance.

The three groupes now resembled so many fleets at sea, lying with their top-sails to the masts, with the commendable precaution of reconnoitring, before each could ascertain who among the strangers might be considered as friends, and who as foes.

During this moment of suspense the dark, threatening, eye of Mahtoree rolled from one of the strange parties to the other, in keen and hasty examination, and then it turned its withering look on the old man, as the chief said, in a tone of high and bitter scorn—

"The Big-knives are fools. It is easier to catch the Cougar asleep, than to find a blind Dahcotah. Did the 'white-head' think to ride on the horse of a Sioux?"

The trapper, who had found time to collect his perplexed faculties, saw at once that Middleton, having perceived Ishmael on the trail by which they had fled, preferred trusting to the hospitality of the savages than to the treatment he would be likely to receive from the hands of the squatter. He therefore disposed himself to clear the way for the favorable reception of his friends, since he found that the unnatural coalition became necessary to secure the liberty, if not, the lives of the party.

"Did my brother ever go on a war path to strike my people?" he calmly demanded of the indignant chief, who still awaited his reply.

The lowering aspect of the Teton warrior so far lost its severity, as to suffer a gleam of pleasure and triumph to lighten its ferocity as, sweeping his arm in an entire circle around his person, he answered.

"What tribe or nation has not felt the blows of the Dahcotahs? Mahtoree is their Partizan."

"And has he found the Big-knives women, or has he found them men?"

A multitude of fierce passions were struggling in the tawny countenance of the Indian. For a moment inextinguishable hatred seem'd to hold the mastery, and then a nobler expression, and one that better became the character of a brave got possession of his features and maintained itself, until, first throwing aside his light robe of pictured deer-skin, and pointing to the scar of a bayonet on his breast, he replied—

"It was given, as it was taken; face to face."

"It is enough. My brother is a brave chief, and he should be wise. Let him look; is that a warrior of the Pale-faces? Was it one such as that, who gave the Great Dahcotah his hurt?"

The eyes of Mahtoree followed the direction of the old man's extended arm, until they rested on the drooping form of Inez. The look of the Teton was long, rivetted, and admiring. Like that of the young Pawnee, it resembled more the gaze of a mortal on some heavenly image, than the admiration with which man is wont to contemplate even the loveliness of woman. Starting, as if suddenly self-convicted of forgetfulness, the chief next turned his eyes on Ellen, where they lingered an instant with a much more intelligible expression of admiration, and then pursued their course until they had taken another glance at each individual of the party.

"My brother sees that my tongue is not forked," continued the trapper watching the emotions the other betrayed, with a readiness of comprehension little inferior to that of the Teton himself. "The Big-knives do not send their women to war. I know that the Dahcotahs will smoke with the strangers."

"Mahtoree is a great chief! The Big-knives are welcome," said the Teton, laying his hand on his breast with an air of lofty politeness that would have done credit to any state of society. "The arrows of my young men are in their quivers."

The trapper motioned to Middleton to approach, and in a few moments the two parties were blended, in one, each of the males having exchanged friendly greetings, after the fashions of the Prairie warriors. But even while engaged in this hospitable manner, the Dahcotah did not fail to keep a strict watch on the more distant party of white men, as if he still distrusted an artifice, or sought further explanation. The old man, in his turn, perceived the necessity of being more explicit, and of securing the slight and equivocal advantage he had, already obtained. While affecting to examine the groupe, which still lingered at the spot where it had first halted, as if to discover the characters of those who composed it, he plainly saw that Ishmael contemplated immediate hostilities. The result of a conflict, on the open Prairies, between a dozen resolute border men, and the half armed natives, even though seconded by their white allies, was in his experienced judgment a point of great uncertainty, and, though far from reluctant to engage in the struggle on account of himself, the aged trapper thought it far more worthy of his years, and his character, to avoid than to court the contest. His feelings were, for obvious reasons, in accordance with those of Paul and Middleton, who had lives still more precious than their own to watch over and protect. In this dilemma, the three consulted on the means of escaping the frightful consequences which might immediately follow a single act of hostility on the part of the borderers, the old man taking care that their communication should, in the eyes of those who noted the expression of their countenances with jealous watchfulness, bear the appearance of explanations, as to the reason why such a party of travellers was met so far in the deserts.

"I know that the Dahcotahs are a wise and great people," at length the trapper commenced, again addressing himself to the chief—"but does not their partizan know a single brother who is base?"

The eye of Mahtoree wandered proudly around his band, but rested a moment reluctantly, on Weucha as he answered—

"The Master of Life has made chiefs, and warriors, and women," conceiving that he thus embraced all the gradations of human excellence from the highest to the lowest.

"And he has also made pale faces who are wicked. Such are they, whom my brother sees yonder."

"Do they go on foot, to do wrong," demanded the Teton, with a wild gleam from his eyes, that sufficiently betrayed how well he knew the reason why they were reduced to so humble an expedient.

"Their beasts are gone. But their powder and their lead and their blankets remain."

"Do they carry their riches in their hands, like miserable Konzas, or are they brave, and leave them with the women, as men should do, who know where to find what they lose?"

"My brother sees the spot of blue, across the Prairie, look, the sun has touch'd it for the last time, to-day."

"Mahtoree is not a mole."

"It is a rock, and on it are the goods of the Big-knives."

An expression of savage joy shot into the dark countenance

of the Teton as he listened. Turning to the old man, he seem'd to read his soul, as if to assure himself he was not deceived. Then he bent his look on the party of Ishmael, and counted its numbers.

"One warrior is wanting;" he said.

"Does my brother see the buzzards. There is his grave. Did he find blood, on the Prairie. It was his."

"Enough; Mahtoree is a wise chief. Put your women on the horses of the Dahcotahs—we shall see, for our eyes are open very wide."

The trapper wasted no unnecessary words in explanation. Familiar with the brevity and promptitude of the Natives he immediately communicated the result to his companions. Paul was mounted in an instant, with Ellen at his back. A few more moments were necessary to assure Middleton of the security and ease of Inez. While he was thus engaged, Mahtoree advanced to the side of the beast he had allotted to this service, which was his own, and manifested an intention to occupy his customary place on its back. The young soldier seized the reins of the animal, and glances of sudden anger and lofty pride were exchanged between them.

"No man takes this seat but myself!" said Middleton, sternly, in English.

"Mahtoree is a great chief!" retorted the savage, neither comprehending the meaning of the other's words.

"The Dahcotah will be too late," whispered the old man at his elbow; "see, the Big-knives are afraid, and they will soon run."

The Teton chief instantly abandoned his claim, and threw himself on another horse, directing one of his young men to furnish a similar accommodation for the trapper. The warriors who were dismounted, got up behind as many of their companions; Doctor Battius, bestrode Asinus, and, notwithstanding the brief interruption, in half the time we have taken to relate it, the whole party was prepared to move.

When he saw that all were ready, Mahtoree, gave the signal to advance. A few of the best mounted of the warriors, the chief himself included, moved a little in front, and made a threatening demonstration, as if they intended to attack the strangers. The squatter who was in truth slowly retiring, instantly halted his party, and showed a willing front. Instead, however, of coming within reach of the dangerous aim of the western rifle, the subtle savages, kept wheeling about the strangers, until they had made a half circuit, keeping the latter in constant expectation of an assault. Then perfectly secure of their object, the Tetons raised a loud shout, and darted across the Prairie in a line for the distant rock, as directly and nearly with the velocity of the arrow, that has just been shot from its bow.

Chapter XXI

"Dally not with the gods, but get thee gone."
The Taming of the Shrew, IV.iv.68.

MAHTOREE HAD scarcely given the first intimation of his real design, before a general discharge from the borderers proved how well they understood it. The distance and the rapidity of the flight, however, rendered the fire harmless. As a proof of how little he regarded the hostility of their Party, the Dahcotah chieftain answered the report with a yell, and flourishing his carabyne above his head, he made a circuit on the plain, followed by his chosen warriors, in scorn of the impotent attempt of his enemies. As the main body continued the direct course, this little band of the *elite*, in returning from its wild exhibition of savage contempt, took its place in the rear, with a dexterity, and a concert of action, that showed the manoeuvre had been contemplated.

Volley swiftly succeeded volley, until the enraged squatter was reluctantly compelled to abandon the idea of injuring his enemies, by means so feeble. Relinquishing his fruitless attempt, he commenced a rapid pursuit, occasionally discharging a rifle in order to give the alarm to the garrison, which he had prudently left, under the command of the redoubtable Esther, herself. In this manner the chase was continued for many minutes, the horsemen gradually gaining on their pursuers, who maintained the race, however, with an incredible power of foot.

As the little speck of blue rose against the heavens, like an island issuing from the deep, the savages occasionally raised a yell of triumph. But the mists of evening were already gathering along the whole of the eastern margin of the Prairie, and before the band had made half of the necessary distance, the dim outline of the rock had melted into the haze of the background. Indifferent to this circumstance, which rather favored than disconcerted his plans, Mahtoree, who had again ridden in front, held on his course, with the accuracy of a hound of the truest scent, merely slackening his speed a little, as the horses of his party were, by this time, thoroughly blown. It was at this stage of the enterprise, that the old man rode up to the side of Middleton, and addressed him, as follows, in English—

"Here is likely to be a thieving business, and one in which I must say, I have but little wish to be a partner."

"What would you do. It would be fatal to trust ourselves in the hands of the miscreants in our rear."

"Tut for miscreants, be they red or be they white. Look ahead, lad, as if ye were talking of our medecines, or perhaps, praising the Teton beasts. For the knaves love to hear their horses commended, the same as a foolish mother, in the settlements, is fond of hearing the praises of her wilful child. So pat the animal and lay your hand on the gew-gaws with which the red-skins have ornamented his mane, giving your eye, as it were, to one thing, and your mind to another. Listen, if matters are managed with judgement we may leave these Tetons as the night sets in."

"A blessed thought!" exclaimed Middleton, who retained a painful remembrance of the look of admiration with which Mahtoree had contemplated the loveliness of Inez, as well as of his subsequent presumption in daring to wish to take the office of her protecter on himself.

"Lord, Lord! what a weak creatur' is man, when the gifts of natur' are smothered in bookish knowledge, and womanly manners! Such another start would tell these imps at our elbows that we were plotting against them, just as plainly as if it were whispered in their ears by a Sioux tongue. Ay, Ay, I know the devils: they look as innocent as so many frisky fawns, but there is not one among them all that has not an eye on our smallest motions. Therefore what is to be done is to be done, in wisdom, in order to circumvent their cunning. That is right, pat his neck, and smile as if you praised the horse, and keep the ear on my side open to my words. Be careful not to worry your beast, for though but little skilled in horses, reason teaches that breath is needful in a hard push, and that a weary leg makes a dull race. Be ready to mind the signal when you hear a whine from old Hector. The first will be to make ready, the second to edge out of the crowd, and the third to go. Am I understood?"

"Perfectly, perfectly;" said Middleton, trembling in his excessive eagerness to put the plan in instant execution, and pressing the little arm which encircled his body, to his heart. "Perfectly. Hasten. Hasten."

"Ay, the beast is no sloth," continued the trapper in the Teton language, as if he continued the discourse, edging cautiously through the dusky throng at the same time, until he found himself riding at the side of Paul. He communicated his intentions in the same guarded manner as before. The high-spirited and fearless bee-hunter received the intelligence with delight declaring his readiness to engage the whole of the savage band should it become necessary to effect their object. When the old man drew off from the side of this pair also, he cast his eyes about him to discover the situation occupied by the naturalist.

The Doctor with infinite labor to himself and Asinus had maintained a position in the very centre of the Siouxes, so long as there existed the smallest reason for believing that any of the missiles of Ishmael might arrive in contact with his person. After this danger had diminished or rather disappeared, entirely, his own courage revived while that of his steed began to droop. To this mutual but very material change was owing the fact that the rider and the ass were now to be sought among that portion of the band who formed a sort of rear guard. Hither then the trapper contrived to turn his steed without exciting the suspicions of any of his subtle companions.

"Friend," commenced the old man when he found himself in a situation favorable to discourse, "should you like to pass a dozen years among the savages, with a shaved head, and a painted countenance, with perhaps a couple of wives and five or six children, of the half-breed to call you father?"

"Impossible!" exclaimed the startled naturalist, "I am indisposed to matrimony, in general, and more especially to all admixture of the varieties of *species*, which only tend to tarnish the beauty and to interrupt the harmony of nature. Moreover, it is a painful innovation on the order of all nomenclatures!"

"Ay, ay, you have reason, enough for your distaste to such a life, but should these Siouxes get you fairly into their village such would be your luck, as certain as that the sun rises and sets at the pleasure of the Lord."

"Marry me to a woman who is not adorned with the comeliness of the *species*!" responded the Doctor. "Of what crime have I been guilty that so grievous a punishment should await the offense. To marry a man against the movements of his will is to do a violence to human nature!"

"Now that you speak of natur' I have hopes that the gift of reason has not altogether deserted your brain," returned the old man, with a covert expression playing about the angles of his deep set eyes, which betrayed he was not entirely destitute of humour. "Nay, they may conceive you a remarkable subject for their kindness, and, for that matter, marry you to five or six. I have known, in my day, favored chiefs who had numberless wives."

"But why should they meditate this vengeance?" demanded the Doctor, whose hair began to rise as if each fibre was possessed of sensibility; " what evil have I done?"

"It is the fashion of their kindness. When they come to learn that you are a great medecine, they will adopt you in the tribe, and some mighty chief will give you his name, and perhaps his daughter, or it may be a wife or two of his own, who have dwelt long in his lodge and of whose value he is a judge, by experience."

"The Governor and Founder of Natural Harmony Protect me!" ejaculated the Doctor. "I have no affinity to a single consort, much less to duplicates and triplicates of the *class*! I shall certainly essay a flight from their abodes, before I mingle in so violent a conjunction."

"There is reason in your words: but why not attempt the race you speak of, now?"

The naturalist look'd fearfully around, as if he had an inclination to make an instant exhibition of his desperate intention, but the dusky figures who were riding on every side of him, seem'd suddenly tripled in number and the darkness that was already thickening on the Prairie appeared, in his eyes, to possess the glare of high noon.

"It would be premature, and reason forbids it;" he answered: "Leave me, venerable venator, to the council of my own thoughts, and when my plans are properly classed, I will advise you of my resolutions."

"Resolutions!" repeated the old man, shaking his head a

little contemptuously, as he gave the rein to his horse and allowed him to mingle with the steeds of the savages, "Resolution is a word that is talk'd of in the settlements, and felt on the borders! Does my brother know the beast on which the Pale face rides?" he continued, addressing a gloomy looking warrior, in his own tongue, and making a motion with his arm that at the same time directed his attention to the Naturalist and the meek Asinus.

The Teton turned his eyes for a minute, on the animal, but disdained to manifest the smallest portion of that wonder he had felt, in common with all his companions, on first viewing so rare a quadruped. The trapper was not ignorant that, while asses and mules were beginning to be known to those tribes who dwelt nearest the Mexicos they were not usually encountered so far north as the waters of La Platte. He, therefore, managed to read the mute astonishment, that lay so deeply concealed in the tawny visage of the savage, and took his measures accordingly.

"Does my brother think that the rider is a warrior of the Pale-faces?" he demanded, when he believed that sufficient time had elapsed, for a full examination of the pacific mien of the naturalist.

The flash of scorn, which shot across the features of the Teton, was visible, even by the dim light of the stars.

"Is a Dahcotah a fool," was the answer.

"They are a wise nation whose eyes are never shut; much do I wonder, that they have not seen the Great Medecine of the Big knives!"

"Wah!" exclaimed his companion, suffering the whole of his amazement to burst out of his dark rigid countenance, at the surprise, like a flash of lightning illuminating the gloom of midnight.

"The Dahcotah knows that my tongue is not forked. Let him open his eyes wider. Does he not see a very great Medicine!"

The light was not necessary to recall to the savage, each feature in the really remarkable costume and equipage of Doctor Battius. In common with the rest of the band, and in conformity with the universal practice of the Indians, this warrior, while he had suffered no gaze of idle curiosity to disgrace his manhood, had not permitted a single distinctive mark which might characterize any one of the strangers to escape his vigilance. He knew the air, the stature, the dress, and the features, even to the colour of the eyes and of the hair, of every one of the Big-knives whom he had thus strangely encountered, and deeply had he ruminated on the causes which could have led a party so singularly constituted into the haunts of the rude inhabitants of his native wastes. He had, already considered the several physical powers of the whole party; and had duly compared their abilities with what he supposed might have been their intentions. Warriors they were not, for the Big knives, like the Siouxes, left their women in their villages when they went out on the bloody path. The same objections applied to them as hunters, and even as traders, the two characters under which the white men, commonly appeared in their villages. He had heard of a Great Council, at which the Menahashah, or Long knives and the Washsheomantiqua, or Spaniards, had smoked together, when the latter had sold to the former their incomprehensible rights over those vast regions, through which his nation had roam'd, in freedom, for so many ages. His simple mind had not been able to embrace the reasons why one people should thus assume a superiority over the possessions of another, and it will readily be perceived, that, at the hint just received from the trapper, he was not indisposed to fancy that some of the hidden subtilty of that magical influence of which he was so firm a believer, was about to be practised by the unsuspecting subject of their conversation in furtherance of these mysterious claims. Abandoning, therefore, all the reserve and dignity of his manner, under the conscious helplessness of ignorance, he turned to the old man, and stretching forth his arms, as if to denote how much he lay at his mercy, he said:

"Let my father look at me. I am a wild man of the Prairies. My body is naked; my hands, empty; my skin, red. I have struck the Pawnees, the Konzas, the Omawhaws, the Osages, and even the Long knives. I am a man amid warriors, but a woman among the conjurors. Let my Father speak; the ears of the Teton are open. He listens like a deer to the step of the cougar."

"Such are the wise and uns'archable ways of one, who

alone knows, good from evil!" exclaimed the trapper in English. "To some he grants cunning and on others he bestows the gift of manhood! It is humbling, and it is afflicting to see so noble a creatur' as this, who has fou't in many a bloody fray, truckling before his superstition, like a beggar asking for the bones you would throw to the dogs. The Lord will forgive me, for playing with the ignorance of the savage, for he knows I do it, in no mockery of his state or in idle vaunting of my own, but in order to save mortal life, and to give justice to the wronged, while I defeat the deviltries of the wicked! Teton," speaking again in the language of the listener, "I ask you, is not that a wonderful medicine? If the Dahcotahs are wise they will not breathe the air he breathes, nor touch his robes. They know that the Wahconshecheh (bad spirit) loves his own children, and will not turn his back on him that does them harm."

The old man delivered this opinion in an ominous and sententious manner, and then rode apart, as if he had said enough. The result justified his expectations. The warrior to whom he had addressed himself was not slow to communicate his important knowledge to the rest of the rear guard, and in a very few moments the naturalist was the object of general observation and reverence. The trapper, who understood that the natives often worshipped, with a view to propitiate, the evil spirit, awaited the workings of his artifice, with the coolness of one who had not the smallest interest in its effects. It was not long before he saw one dark figure after another, lashing his horse and galloping ahead into the centre of the band, until Weucha, alone, remained nigh the persons of himself and Obed. The very dullness of this grovelling-minded savage, who continued gazing at the supposed conjuror with a sort of stupid admiration, opposed, now, the only obstacle to the complete success of his artifice.

Thoroughly understanding the character of this Indian, the old man lost no time in getting rid of him also. Riding to his side, he said in an affected whisper—

"Has Weucha drunk of the milk of the Big knives, to day?"

"Hugh!" exclaimed the savage, every dull thought instantly recalled from heaven to earth by the question.

"Because the Great Captain of my people, who rides in

front, has a cow that is never empty. I know it will not be long before he will say, 'are any of my red brethren dry?' "

The words were scarcely uttered, before Weucha in his turn, quickened the gait of his beast, and was soon blended with the rest of the dark groupe who were riding at a more moderate pace a few rods in advance. The trapper, who knew how fickle and sudden were the changes of a savage mind, did not lose a moment, in profiting by this advantage. He loosened the reins of his own impatient steed and in an instant, he was again at the side of Obed.

"Do you see the twinkling star, that is, maybe, the length of four rifles above the Prairie, hereaway to the North I mean."

"Ay, it is of the Constellation—"

"A tut for your Constellation man; do you see the star I mean?—tell me in the English of the Land, yes or no."

"Yes."

"The moment my back is turned, pull upon the rein of your ass, until you lose sight of the savages. Then take the Lord for your dependance and yonder star for your guide. Turn neither to the right hand, nor to the left, but make diligent use of your time, for your beast is not quick of foot, and every inch of Prairie you gain is a day added to your liberty, or to your life!" Without waiting to listen to the queries which the Naturalist was about to put, the old man, again loosened the reins of his horse and presently he too, was blended with the groupe in front.

Obed was now, alone. Asinus willingly obeyed the hint which his master soon, gave rather in desperation, than with any very collected understanding of the orders he had received, and checked his pace, accordingly. As the Tetons, however, rode at a hard gallop, but a moment of time was necessary, after the ass began to walk, to remove them effectually from before the vision of his rider. Without plan, expectation or hope of any sort, except that of escaping from his dangerous neighbors, the Doctor, first feeling to assure himself that the package which contained the miserable remnants of his specimens, and notes was safe at his crupper, turned the head of the beast in the required direction, and kicking him with a species of fury, he soon succeeded in exciting the speed of the patient animal into a smart run. He had barely time to descend into a hollow and ascend the adjoining swell of the prairie, before he heard, or fancied he heard, his name shouted, in good English, from the throats of twenty Tetons. The delusion gave a new impulse to his ardor, and no professor of the saltant art ever applied himself with greater industry, than the naturalist now used his heels on the ribs of Asinus. The conflict endured for several minutes without interruption, and to all appearances it might have continued to the present moment, had not the meek temper of the beast become unduly excited. Borrowing an idea from the manner in which his master exhibited his agitation, Asinus so far changed the application of his own heels as to raise them simultaneously with a certain indignant flourish into the air; a measure that instantly decided the controversy in his favor. Obed took leave of his seat, as of a position no longer tenable, continuing however the direction of his flight, while the Ass like a conqueror took possession of the field of battle, beginning to crop the dry herbage, as the fruits of victory.

When Doctor Battius had recovered his feet, and rallied his faculties, which were in a good deal of disorder from the hurried manner in which he had abandoned his former situation, he returned in quest of his specimens and of his Ass. Asinus displayed enough of magnanimity to render the interview amicable, and thenceforth the Naturalist continued the required route with very commendable industry but with a much more tempered discretion.

In the mean time, the old trapper had not lost sight of the important movements that he had undertaken to control. Obed had not been mistaken in supposing that he was already missed and sought, though his imagination had corrupted certain savage cries into the well known sounds that composed his own latinized name. The truth was simply this. The warriors of the rear guard had not failed to apprise those in front of the mysterious character, with which it had pleased the trapper, to invest the unsuspecting naturalist. The same untutored admiration which on the receipt of this intelligence had driven those in the rear to the front, now drove many of the front to the rear. The Doctor was of course absent, and the outcry was no more than the wild yells which were raised in the first burst of savage disappointment.

But the authority of Mahtoree was prompt to aid the ingenuity of the trapper, in suppressing these dangerous sounds. When order was restored, and the former was made acquainted with the reason why his young men had betrayed so strong a mark of indiscretion, the old man, who had taken a post at his elbow, saw, with alarm, the gleam of keen distrust that flashed in his swarthy visage.

"Where is your conjuror?" demanded the chief, turning suddenly to the trapper, as if he meant to make him responsible for the reappearance of Obed.

"Can I tell, my brother the number of the stars! the ways of a great medicine, are not like the ways of other men."

"Listen to me, gray-head; and count my words;" continued the other bending on his rude saddle bow, like some Chevalier of a more civilized race, and speaking in the haughty tones of absolute power; "the Dahcotahs have not chosen a woman for their Chief. When Mahtoree feels the power of a great medicine, he will tremble. Until then, he will look with his own eyes, without borrowing sight from a Pale face. If your conjuror is not with his friends, in the morning, my young men shall look for him. Your ears are open. Enough."

The trapper was not sorry to find that so long a respite was granted. He had before found reason to believe, that the Teton Partizan was one of those bold spirits, who overstep the limits, which use and education fix to the opinions of man, in every state of society, and he now saw, plainly, that he must adopt some artifice to deceive him, different from that which had succeeded so well with his followers. The sudden appearance of the rock, however, which hove up, a black and ragged mass, out of the darkness ahead, put an end, for the present, to their discourse, Mahtoree giving all his thoughts to the execution of his designs on the rest of the squatter's moveables. A murmur ran through the band, as each dark warrior caught a glimpse of the desired haven, after which the nicest ear might have listened in vain, to catch a sound louder than the rustling of feet among the tall grass of the Prairie.

But the vigilance of Esther was not easily deceived. She had long listened anxiously to the suspicious sounds which approached the rock across the naked waste, nor had the sudden outcry been unheard by the unwearied sentinels of the rock. The savages, who had dismounted at some little distance, had not time to draw around the base of the hill, in their customary silent and insidious manner, before the voice of the Amazon was raised, demanding—

"Who is beneath? answer: for your lives? Siouxes or devils I fear ye not!"

No answer was given to this challenge, every warrior halting where he stood, confident that his dusky form was blended with the shadows of the plain. It was at this moment that the trapper determined to escape. He had been left, with the rest of his friends, under the surveillance of those who were assigned to the duty of watching the horses, as they all continued mounted, the moment appeared favorable to his project. The attention of the guards was drawn to the rock, and a heavy cloud driving above them, at that instant, obscured even the feeble light which fell from the stars. Leaning on the neck of his horse the old man muttered—

"Where's my pup? where is it, Hector, where is it, dog?"

The hound caught the well known sounds and answered by a whine of friendship, which threatened to break out into one of his piercing howls. The trapper was in the act of raising himself, from this successful exploit, when he felt the hand of Weucha grasping his throat, as if determined to suppress his voice, by the very unequivocal process of strangulation. Profiting by the circumstance, he raised another low sound as if in the natural effort of breathing, which drew a second responsive cry from the faithful hound. Weucha, instantly abandoned his hold of the master in order to wreak his vengeance on the dog. But the voice of Esther was again heard, and every other design was abandoned in order to listen.

"Ay, whine, and deform your throats as you may, ye imps of darkness," she said, with a cracked but scornful laugh, "I know ye! Tarry and ye shall have light for your misdeeds. Put in the coals, Phoebe; put in the coal, your Father and the boys shall see that they are wanted at home, to welcome their guests!"

As she spoke, a strong light, like that of a brilliant star was seen on the very pinnacle of the rock; then followed a forked flame which curled for a moment, amid the windings of an enormous pile of brush, and flashing upward in an united sheet, it wavered to and fro, in the passing air, shedding a bright glare on every object within its influence. A taunting laugh, was heard from the height, in which the voices of all ages mingled, as though they triumphed in having so successfully exposed the treacherous intentions of the Tetons.

The trapper look'd about him to ascertain in what situations he might find his friends. True to the signals, Middleton and Paul had drawn a little apart, and now stood ready, by every appearance, to commence their flight at the third repetition of the cry. Hector had escaped his savage pursuer, and was again crouching at the heels of his master's horse. But the broad circle of light was gradually increasing in extent and power, and the old man, whose eye and judgment so rarely failed him, patiently awaited a more propitious moment for his enterprise.

"Now Ishmael, my man, if sight and hand ar' true as ever, now is the time, to work upon these red-skins, who claim to own all your property, even to wife and children! Now, my good man, prove both breed and character!"

A distant shout was heard, in the direction of the approaching party of the squatter, assuring the female garrison that succour was not far distant. Esther answered to the grateful sounds, by a crack'd cry of her own, lifting her form in the first burst of her exultation above the rock, in a manner to be visible to all below. Not content with this dangerous exposure of her person, she was in the act of tossing her arms in triumph, when the dark figure of Mahtoree, shot into the light, and pinioned them to her side. The forms of three other warriors glided across the top of the rock, looking like naked demons, flitting among the clouds. The air was filled with the brands of the beacon, and a heavy darkness succeeded, not unlike that of the appalling instant when the last rays of the sun are excluded by the intervening mass of the moon. A yell of triumph burst from the savages in their turn, and was rather accompanied than followed by a long, loud whine from Hector.

In an instant the old man was between the horses of Middleton and Paul, extending a hand to the bridle of each, in order to check the impatience of their riders.

"Softly. Softly," he whispered, "their eyes are as marvellously shut, for the minute, as if the Lord had stricken them blind: but their ears are open. Softly, softly, for fifty rods at least we must move no faster than a walk."

The five minutes of doubt that succeeded seemed like an age to all but the trapper. As their sight was gradually restored, it appeared to each that the momentary gloom which followed the extinction of the beacon, was to be replaced by as broad a light as that of noon day. Gradually the old man, however, suffered the animals to quicken their steps until they had gained the centre of one of the Prairie bottoms, then laughing in his quiet manner, he released the reins and said—

"Now, let them give play to their legs, but keep on the old fog, to deaden the sounds."

It is needless to say how cheerfully he was obeyed. In a few more minutes they ascended and cross'd a swell of the land, after which the flight was continued at the top of their horses' speed, keeping the indicated star in view, as the laboring bark steers for the light which points the way to a haven and security.

Chapter XXII

"The clouds and sunbeams o'er his eye,
That once their shades and glories threw,
Have left in yonder silent sky,
No vestige where they flew."
Montgomery, "The Common Lot," ll. 33–36.

A STILLNESS as deep as that which marked the gloomy waste in their front, was observed by the fugitives to distinguish the spot they had just abandoned. Even the trapper lent his practised faculties, in vain, to detect any of the well known signs which might establish the important fact, that hostilities had actually commenced between the parties of Mahtoree and Ishmael, but their horses carried them out of the reach of sounds, without the occurrence of the smallest evidence of that sort. The old man, from time to time, muttered his discontent, but manifested the uneasiness he actually entertained in no other manner, unless it might be in exhibiting a growing anxiety to urge the animals to increase their speed. He pointed out in passing, the deserted swale, where the family of the squatter had encamped the night they were introduced to the reader, and afterwards he maintained an ominous silence; ominous, because his companions had already seen enough of his character, to be convinced that the circumstances must be critical, indeed, which possessed the power to disturb the well regulated tranquility of the old man's mind.

"Have we not done, enough," Middleton demanded, in tenderness to the inability of Inez and Ellen to endure so much fatigue, at the end of some hours; "we have ridden hard, and have cross'd a wide tract of Plain. It is time to seek a place of rest."

"You must seek it then, in heaven, if you find yourselves unequal to a longer march;" murmured the old trapper. "Had the Tetons and the squatters come to blows, as any one might see in the natur' of things they were bound to do, there would be time to look about us, and to calculate, not only the chances but the comforts of the journey; but as the case actually is, I should consider it certain death, or endless captivity to trust our eyes with sleep until our heads are fairly hid in some uncommon cover."

"I know not;" returned the youth who reflected more on the sufferings of the fragile being he supported than on the experience of his companion. "I know not. We have ridden leagues, and I can see no extraordinary signs of danger. If you fear for yourself, my good friend, believe me, you are wrong, for—"

"Your grand'ther were he living and here," interrupted the old man, stretching forth a hand and laying a finger impressively on the arm of Middleton, "would have spared those words. He had some reason to think, that in the prime of my days, when my eye was quicker than the hawk's and my limbs were as active as the legs of the fallow deer, I never clung too eagerly and fondly to life: then, why should I, now, feel such childish affection for a thing that I know to be vain and the companion of pain and sorrow. Let the Tetons do their worst; they will not find a miserable and worn out trapper the loudest in his complaints, or his prayers!"

"Pardon me, my worthy, my inestimable friend," exclaimed the repentant young man, warmly grasping the hand which the other was in the act of withdrawing; "I knew not what I said—or rather I thought, only, of those whose tenderness we are most bound to consider."

"Enough. It is natur', and it is right. Therein your grand'ther would have done the very same. Ah's me! what a number of seasons, hot and cold, wet and dry, have rolled over my poor head since the time we worried it out together, among the red Hurons of the Lakes, back in those rugged mountains of old York! and many a noble buck, has since that day fallen by my hand; ay! and many a thieving Mingo, too! Tell me, lad, did the General, for General I know he got to be, did he ever tell you of the deer we took, that night the outlyers of the accursed tribe drove us to the caves, on the island, and how we feasted and drunk in security?"

"I have often heard him mention the smallest circumstance of the night you mean; but—"

"And the singer; and his open throat, and his shoutings in

the fights?" continued the old man, laughing joyously at the strength of his own recollections.

"All—All—he forgot nothing, even to the most trifling incident. Do you not—"

"What did he tell you of the imp behind the log—and of the miserable devil who went over the fall—or of the wretch in the tree?"

"Of each and all, with every thing that concerned them.* I should think—"

"Ay," continued the old man, in a voice which betrayed how powerfully his own faculties retained the impression of the spectacle. "I have been a dweller in forests, and in the wilderness for threescore and ten years, and if any man can pretend to know the world or to have seen scary sights, it is myself! But never before nor since have I seen human man in such a state of mortal despair as that very savage, and yet he scorned to speak or to cry out, or to own his forlorn condition! It is their gift, and nobly did he maintain it!"

"Harkee, old trapper," interrupted Paul, who, content with the knowledge that his waist was grasped by one of the arms of Ellen, had hitherto ridden in unusual silence, "my eyes are as true and as delicate as a humming bird's in the day, but they are nothing worth boasting of by star-light. Is that a sick buffaloe, crawling along, in the bottom, there, or is it one of the stray cattle of the savages?"

The whole party drew up, in order to examine the object which Paul had pointed out. During most of the time they had ridden in the little vales in order to seek the protection of the shadows, but just at that moment, they had ascended a roll of the Prairie, in order to cross into the very bottom where this unknown animal was now seen.

"Let us descend," said Middleton. "Be it beast or man, we are too strong to have any cause of fear."

"Now if the thing was not morally impossible," cried the trapper, who, the reader must have already discovered, was not always exact in the use of qualifying words, "if the thing was not morally impossible, I should say that was the man

*They who have read the preceding books, in which the trapper appears as a hunter and a scout, will readily understand the allusions.

who journeys in search of reptiles and insects: our fellow traveller the Doctor."

"Why, impossible? did you not direct him to pursue this course, in order to rejoin us."

"Ay, but I did not tell him to make an Ass outdo the speed of a horse—you are right, you are right," said the trapper, interrupting himself, as by gradually lessening the distance between them, his eyes assured him it was Obed and Asinus whom he saw, "you are right, as certainly as the thing is a miracle. Lord, what a thing is fear! How now, friend; you have been industrious to have got so far ahead in so short a time. I marvel at the speed of the ass!"

"Asinus, is overcome," returned the Naturalist, mournfully. "The animal has certainly not been idle since we separated, but he declines all my admonitions and invitations to proceed. I hope there is no instant fear from the savages?"

"I cannot say that; I cannot say that; matters are not as they should be, atween the squatter and the Tetons, nor will I answer, as yet, for the safety of any scalp among us. The beast is broken down! you have urged him beyond his natural gifts, and he is like a worried hound. There is pity and discretion in all things, even, though a man be a-riding for his life."

"You indicated the star," returned the Doctor, "and I deem'd it expedient to use great diligence in pursuing the direction."

"Did you expect to reach it, by such haste! Go, go; you talk boldly of the creatur's of the Lord, though I plainly see that you are but a child in matters that concern their gifts and instincts. What plight would you now be in, if there was need for a long and a quick push, with our heels!"

"The fault exists in the formation of the quadruped," said Obed, whose placid temper began to revolt under so many scandalous imputations. "Had there been rotary levers for two of the members, a moiety of the fatigue would have been saved, for one item—"

"That, for your moiety's and rotary's, and items, man; a jaded ass is a jaded ass, and he who denies it is but a brother of the beast itself! Now, Captain are we driven to choose one of two evils. We must either abandon this man, who has been too much with us, through good and bad to be easily cast away, or we must seek a cover to let the animal rest."

"Venerable venator!" exclaimed the alarmed Obed. "I conjure you by all the secret sympathies of our common nature, by all the hidden—"

"Ah, fear has brought him to talk a little rational sense! It is not natur' truly to abandon a brother in distress, and the Lord he knows, that I have never yet done the shameful deed. You are right, friend, you are right, we must all be hidden, and that speedily. But what to do with the Ass! Friend, Doctor, do you truly value the life of the creatur'?"

"He is an ancient and faithful servant," returned the disconsolate Obed, "and with pain should I see him come to any harm. Fetter his lower limbs, and leave him to repose in this bed of herbage. I will engage he shall be found where he is left, in the morning."

"And, the Siouxes? What would become of the beast, should any of the red imps catch a peep at his ears, growing up out of the grass, like two mullein tops!" cried the bee-hunter. "They would stick him as full of arrows, as a woman's cushion, is full of pins, and then believe that they had done the job for the Father of all rabbits! My word for it, but they would find out their blunder, at the first mouthful!"

Middleton who began to grow impatient under the protracted discussion, interposed, and as a good deal of deference was paid to his rank, he quickly prevailed in his efforts to effect a sort of compromise. The humble Asinus, too meek and too weary to make any resistance was soon tethered and deposited in his bed of dying grass, where he was left, with a perfect confidence on the part of his master, of finding him again at the expiration of a few hours. The old man strongly remonstrated against this arrangement and more than once hinted that the knife was much more certain than the tether, but the petitions of Obed, aided perhaps by the secret reluctance of the trapper to destroy the beast, were the means of saving its life. When Asinus was thus secured, and as his master believed secreted, the whole party proceeded to find some place, where they might rest, themselves, during the time required for the repose of the animal.

According to the calculations of the trapper, they had ridden twenty miles since the commencement of their flight. The delicate frame of Inez began to droop under the excessive fatigue, nor was the more robust, but still feminine person of Ellen insensible to the extraordinary effort she had made. Middleton himself, was not sorry to repose, nor did the vigorous and high spirited Paul hesitate to confess that he should be all the better for a little rest. The old man, alone, seem'd indifferent to the usual claims of nature. Although but little accustomed to the unusual description of exercise he had just been taking, he appeared to bid defiance to all the usual attacks of human infirmities. Though evidently so near its dissolution, his attenuated frame still stood like the shaft of seasoned oak, dry, naked, and tempest-riven, but unbending, and apparently indurated to the consistency of stone. On the present occasion he conducted the search for a resting place, which was immediately commenced, with all the energy of youth tempered by the discretion and experience of his great age.

The bed of grass in which the Doctor had been met, and in which his ass had just been left, was followed, a little distance, until it was found that the rolling swells of the Prairie were melting away into one vast, level plain, that was covered for miles on miles, with the same species of herbage.

"Ah! this may do, this may do," said the old man, when they arrived on the borders of this sea of withered grass: "I know the spot, and often have I lain in its secret holes, for days at a time, while the savages have been hunting the buffaloes on the open ground. We must enter it with great care, for a broad trail might be seen, and Indian curiosity is a dangerous neighbor."

Leading the way, himself, he selected a spot where the tall coarse herbage stood most erect, growing not unlike a bed of reeds, both in height and density. Here he entered, singly, directing the others to follow as nearly as possible in his own footsteps. When they had passed for some hundred or two feet into the wilderness of weeds, he gave his directions to Paul and Middleton, who continued a direct route deeper into the place, while he dismounted and returned on his tracks to the margin of the meadow. Here he passed many minutes in replacing the trodden grass, and in effacing, as far as possible every evidence of their passage.

In the mean time, the rest of the party continued their progress, not without toil and consequently at a very moderate gait, until they had penetrated a mile into the place. Here they found a spot suited to their circumstances, and dismounting they began to make their dispositions to pass the remainder of the night. By this time the trapper had rejoined the party, and again resumed the direction of their proceedings.

The weeds and grass were soon plucked and cut from an area of sufficient extent, and a bed for Inez and Ellen was speedily made, a little apart, which for sweetness and ease might have rivalled one of down. The exhausted females, after receiving some light refreshments from the provident stores of Paul and the old man soon sought their repose, leaving their more stout companions at liberty to provide for their own necessities. Middleton and Paul were not long in following the examples of their betrothed, leaving the trapper and the Naturalist still seated around a savory dish of bison's meat, which had been cooked at a previous halt, and which was, as usual, eaten cold.

A certain lingering sensation which had so long been uppermost in the mind of Obed temporarily banished sleep, and as for the old man, his wants were rendered by habit and necessity, as seemingly subject to his will, as if they altogether depended on the pleasures of the moment. Like his companion he chose, therefore, to watch instead of sleeping.

"If the children of ease and security knew the hardships and dangers, the students of nature encounter in their behalf," said Obed, after a moment of silence when Middleton took his leave for the night, "pillars of silver and statues of brass would be reared as the everlasting monuments of their glory!"

"I know not, I know not," returned his companion. "Silver is far from plenty, at least in the wilderness, and your brazen idols are forbidden in the Commandments of the Lord."

"Such indeed was the opinion of the Great Law Giver of the Jews, but the Egyptians, and the Chaldeans, the Greeks, and the Romans were wont to manifest their gratitude, in these types of the human form. Indeed, many of the illustrious masters of Antiquity have by the aid of science and skill, even outdone the works of nature, and exhibited a beauty and perfection in the human form, that are difficult to be found in the rarest living specimens of any of the species, *genus*, homo."

"Can your idols, walk, or speak, or have they the glorious gift of reason!" demanded the trapper, with some indignation in his voice; "though but little given to run into the noise and chatter of the settlements, yet have I been into the towns, in my day, to barter the Peltry for lead and powder, and often have I seen your waxen dolls, with their tawdry clothes and glass eyes—"

"Waxen dolls!" interrupted Obed, "it is profanation in the view of the arts to liken the miserable handy work of the dealers in wax to the pure models of antiquity."

"It is profanation in the eyes of the Lord," retorted the old man, "to liken the works of his creatur's, to the power of his own hand!"

"Venerable venator," resumed the naturalist clearing his throat, like one who was much in earnest, "let us discuss understandingly, and in amity. You speak of the dross of ignorance, whereas my memory dwells on those precious jewels which it was my happy fortune, formerly, to witness, among the treasured glories of the old world."

"*Old* World!" retorted the trapper, "that is the miserable cry of all the half-starved miscreants that have come into this blessed land, since the days of my boyhood! They tell you of the *old* world, as if the Lord had not the power and the will to create the universe in a day! or, as if he had not bestowed his gifts with an equal hand, though, not with an equal mind, or equal wisdom, have they been received and used! were they to say a *worn* out, and an *abused*, and a *sacrilegious* world, they might not be so far from the truth!"

Doctor Battius, who found it quite as arduous a task to maintain any of his favorite positions with so irregular an antagonist, as he would have found it difficult to keep his feet within the hug of a western wrestler, hemmed aloud, and profited, by the new opening the trapper had made, to shift the grounds of the discussion—

"By old and new world, my excellent associate," he said; "it is not to be understood, that the hills, and the vallies, the rocks and the rivers of our own moiety of the earth, do not, physically speaking, bear a date as ancient, as the spot on which the bricks of Babylon are found. It merely signifies that its moral existence is not co-equal with its physical, or geological formation."

"Anan!" said the old man looking up inquiringly into the face of the Philosopher.

"Merely, that it has not been so long known in morals, as the other countries of Christendom."

"So much the better, so much the better. I am no great admirator of your old morals, as you call them, for I have ever found, and I have liv'd long, as it were, in the very heart of natur', that your old morals are never of the best. Mankind twist and turn the rules of the Lord, to suit their own wickedness when their devilish cunning has had too much time to trifle with his commands."

"Nay, venerable hunter, still am I not comprehended. By morals, I do not mean the limited and literal signification of the term, such as is convey'd in its synonyme, morality, but the practices of men, as connected with their daily intercourse, their institutions, and their laws."

"And such I call, barefaced and downright wantonness and waste," interrupted his sturdy disputant.

"Well be it so," returned the Doctor, abandoning the explanation in despair. "Perhaps I have conceded too much," he, then, instantly added, fancying that he still saw the glimmerings of an argument through another chink in the discourse, "Perhaps I have conceded too much, in saying that this hemisphere is literally as old in its formation, as that which embraces the venerable quarters of Europe, Asia and Africa."

"It is easy to say that a pine is not so tall as an alder, but it would be hard to prove. Can you give a reason for such a belief?"

"The reasons are numerous and powerful," returned the Doctor delighted by this encouraging opening. "Look into the plains of Egypt and Araby, their sandy deserts teem with the monuments of their antiquity; and then we have also recorded documents of their glory, doubling the proofs of their former greatness, now that they lie stripped of their fertility, while we look in vain for similar evidences that man has ever reach'd the summit of civilization on this Continent, or search without our reward for the path, by which he has made the downward journey to his present condition of second childhood."

"And what see you in all this?" demanded the trapper, who, though a little confused by the terms of his companion, seized the thread of his ideas.

"A demonstration of my Problem, that nature did not make so vast a region to lie so many ages an uninhabited waste. This is merely the moral view of the subject; as to the more exact and geological—"

"Your morals are exact enough for me," returned the old man, "for I think I see in them the very *pride* of *folly*. I am but little gifted in the fables of what you call the *old* world, seeing that my time has been mainly passed looking natur' steadily in the face, and in reasoning on what I've seen rather than on what I've heard in traditions. But I have never shut my ears to the words of the good book, and many is the long winter evening that I have passed, in the wigwams of the Delawares, listening to the good Moravians as they dealt forth the history and doctrines of the elder times to the people of the Lenape. It was pleasant to hearken to such wisdom after a weary hunt! Right pleasant did I find it, and often have I talked the matter over with the Great Serpent of the Delawares, in the more peaceful hours of our outlyings, whether it might be on the trail of a war-party of the Mingoes, or on the watch for a York deer. I remember to have heard it, then and there said that the blessed Land was once fertile as the bottoms of the Mississippi, and groaning with its stores of grain and fruits; but that the judgement has since fallen upon it, and that it is now more remarkable for its barrenness than any qualities to boast of."

"It is true; but Egypt, nay much of Africa furnishes still more striking proofs of this exhaustion of nature."

"Tell me," interrupted the old man, "is it a certain truth that buildings are still standing in that land of Pharoah, which may be likened in their stature to the hills of the 'arth?"

"It is as true, as that nature never refuses to bestow her incisores on the *animals*, mamalia; *genus*, Homo;—"

"It is very marvellous! and it proves how great He must be, when his miserable creatur's can accomplish such wonders!

Many men, must have been needed to finish such an edifice; ay! and men gifted with strength and skill, too! Does the land abound with such a race, to this hour."

"Far from it. Most of the Country is a desert, and but for a mighty river all would be so."

"Yes; rivers are rare gifts to such as till the ground, as any one may see, who journeys far atween the Rocky Mountains and the Mississippi. But how do you account for these changes on the face of the 'arth itself, and for this downfall of nations; you men of the schools?"

"It is to be ascribed to moral cau—"

"You're right! it is their morals! their wickedness and their pride, and chiefly their waste that has done it all! now listen to what the experience of an old man teaches him. I have lived long, as these gray hairs and wrinkled hands will show, even though my tongue should fail in the wisdom of my years. And I have seen much of the folly of man; for his natur' is the same, be he born in the wilderness or be he born in the towns. To my weak judgement it hath ever seem'd that his gifts are not equal to his wishes. That he would mount into the Heavens with all his deformities about him, if he only knew the road, no one will gainsay that witnesses his bitter strivings upon 'arth. If his power is not equal to his will, it is because the wisdom of the Lord hath set bounds to his evil workings."

"It is much too certain that certain facts will warrant a theory which teaches the natural depravity of the *genus*; but if science could be fairly brought to bear on a whole species, at once, for instance, education might eradicate the evil principle."

"That, for your education! the time has been when I have thought it possible to make a companion of a beast. Many are the cubs, and many are the speckled fawns that I have reared with these old hands, until I have even fancied them rational and altered beings, but what did it amount to! the bear would bite, and the deer would run, notwithstanding my wicked conceit, in fancying I could change a temper that the Lord himself had seen fit to bestow! Now if man is so blinded in his folly, as to go on, ages on ages, doing harm chiefly to himself, there is the same reason to think that he has wrought his evil here, as in the Countries you call so old. Look about you, man; where are the multitudes that once peopled these Prairies; the Kings, and the Palaces; the riches and the riotousnesses, of this desert?"

"Where are the monuments, that would prove the truth of so vague a theory?"

"I know not what you call a monument."

"The works of man! the glories of Thebes and Balbec. Columns, catacombs and Pyramids, standing amid the sands of the East, like wrecks on a rocky shore, to testify to the storms of ages!"

"They are gone. Time has lasted too long for them; for why? time was made by the Lord, and they were made by man. This very spot of reeds and grass on which you now sit, may, once have been the garden of some mighty King. It is the fate of all things, to ripen, and then to decay. The tree blossoms, and bears its fruit, which falls, rots, withers, and even the seed is lost. Go count the rings of the oak and of the sycamore; they lie in circles, one about another, until the eye is blinded in striving to make out their numbers, and yet a full change of the seasons comes round while the stem is winding one of those little lines about itself, like the buffaloe changing his coat, or the buck his horns, and what does it all amount to! there does the noble tree fill its place in the forest, loftier, and grander, and richer, and more difficult to imitate, than any of your pitiful pillars, for a thousand years, until the time which the Lord hath given it, is full. Then come the winds, that you cannot see, to rive its bark, and the waters from the heavens to soften its pores, and the rot, which all can feel and none can understand, to humble its pride and bring it to the ground. From that moment its beauty begins to perish. It lies another hundred years, a mouldering log, and then a mound of moss and 'arth, a sad effigy of a human grave. This is one of your genuine monuments, though made by a very different power than such as belongs to your chiselling masons; and after all the cunningest scout of the whole Dahcotah nation might pass his life in searching for the spot where it fell, and be no wiser when his eyes grew dim, than when they were first opened. As if that was not enough to convince man of his ignorance, and as though it were put there in mockery of his conceit, a pine shoots up from the roots of the oak, just as barrenness comes after fertility, or as these wastes have been spread, where a garden may have been created. Tell me not of your worlds that are old, it is blasphemous to set bounds and seasons in this manner, to the works of the Almighty, like a woman counting the ages of her young."

"Friend hunter, or trapper," returned the naturalist clearing his throat in some intellectual confusion at the vigorous attack of his companion, "your deductions, if admitted by the world, would sadly circumscribe the efforts of reason, and much abridge the boundaries of knowledge."

"So much the better, so much the better; for I have always found that a conceited man never knows content. All things prove it. Why have we not the wings of the pigeon, the eyes of the eagle and the legs of the moose, if it had been intended that man should be equal to all his wishes?"

"These are mere physical defects, venerable trapper, in which I am always ready to admit great and happy alterations might be suggested. For example, in my own order of Phalangacru—"

"Cruel enough would be the order that should come from miserable hands like thine! A touch from such a finger would destroy the mocking deformity of a monkey! Go, go, human folly is not needed to fill up the great design of God. There is no stature, no beauty, no proportions nor any colours, in which man himself can well be fashioned that is not already done to his hand."

"That is touching another great and much disputed question!" exclaimed the Doctor, who seized upon every distinct idea that the ardent and somewhat dogmatic old man left exposed to his mental grasp, with the vain hope of inducing a logical discussion in which he might bring his battery of syllogisms to annihilate the unscientific defences of his antagonist.

It is however unnecessary to our narrative to relate the erratic discourse that ensued. The old man eluded the annihilating blows of his adversary, as the light armed soldier is wont to escape the efforts of the more regular warrior even while he annoys him most, and an hour passed away without bringing any of the numerous subjects on which they touch'd to a satisfactory conclusion. The arguments acted however, on the nervous system of the Doctor like so many soothing soporifics, and by the time his aged companion was disposed to lay his head on his pack, Obed, refreshed by his recent mental joust, was in a condition to seek his natural rest, without enduring the torments of the Incubus in the shapes of Teton warriors and bloody tomahawks.

Chapter XXIII

"—Save you, sir."
Coriolanus, IV.iv.6.

THE SLEEP of the fugitives lasted for several hours. The trapper was the first to shake off its influence as he had been the last to court its refreshment. Rising, just as the gray light of day began to brighten that portion of the studded vault which rested on the eastern margin of the plain, he summoned his companions from their warm lairs, and pointed out the necessity of their being, once more, on the alert. While Middleton attended to the arrangements necessary to the comforts of Inez and Ellen in the long and painful journey which lay before them, the old man and Paul prepared the meal, which the former had advised them to take before they proceeded to horse. These several dispositions were not long in making, and the little groupe was soon seated about a repast, which though it might want the elegancies to which the bride of Middleton had been accustomed, was not deficient in the more important requisites of savour and nutriment.

"When we get lower into the hunting grounds of the Pawnees," said the trapper, laying a morsel of delicate venison before Inez on a little trencher neatly made of horn, and expressly for his own use, "we shall find the buffaloe fatter and sweeter, the deer in more abundance, and all the gifts of the Lord abounding to satisfy our wants. Perhaps we may even strike a beaver, and get a morsel from his tail,* by way of a rare mouthful."

"What course do you mean to pursue when you have once thrown these blood-hounds from the chace?" demanded Middleton.

"If I might advise," said Paul, "it would be to strike a water-course, and get upon its downward current, as soon as may be. Give me a cotton-wood, and I will turn you out a canoe that shall carry us all, the jackass excepted, in perhaps

*The American hunters consider the tail of the beaver the most nourishing of all food.

the work of a day and a night. Ellen, here, is a lively girl enough, but then she is no great race-rider, and it would be far more comfortable to boat six or eight hundred miles, than to go loping along like so many elks measuring the Prairies: besides, water leaves no trail."

"I will not swear to that," returned the trapper; "I have often thought the eyes of a red skin would find a trail in the air."

"See, Middleton!" exclaimed Inez in a sudden burst of youthful pleasure, that caus'd her for a moment to forget her situation. "How lovely is that sky! surely it contains a promise of happier times!"

"It is glorious!" returned her husband. "Glorious and heavenly is that streak of vivid red—and here is a still brighter crimson—rarely have I seen a richer rising of the sun."

"Rising of the sun!" slowly repeated the old man, lifting his tall person from its seat, with a deliberate and abstracted air, while he kept his eye rivetted on the changing and certainly beautiful tints that were garnishing the vault of heaven. "Rising of the sun! I like not such risings of the sun! Ah's me; the imps have circumvented us with a vengeance. The Prairie is on fire!"

"God in Heaven protect us!" cried Middleton catching Inez to his bosom, under the instant impression of the imminence of their danger. "There is no time to lose, old man; each instant is a day; let us fly!"

"Whither?" demanded the trapper motioning him with calmness and dignity to arrest his steps. "In this wilderness of grass and reeds, you are like a vessel on the broad lakes without a compass. A single step on the wrong course might prove the destruction of us all. It is seldom that danger is so pressing, that there is not time enough for reason to do its work, young officer; therefore let us await its biddings."

"For my own part," said Paul Hover, looking about him with no equivocal expression of concern, "I acknowledge that should this dry bed of weeds get fairly in a flame a bee would have to make a flight higher than common to prevent his wings from scorching. Therefore, old trapper, I agree with the Captain, and say mount and run."

"Ye are wrong, ye are wrong, man is not a beast to follow

the gift of instinct, and to snuff up his knowledge by a taint in the air or a rumbling in the sound, but he must see, and reason, and then conclude. So follow me a little to the left, where there is a rise in the ground, whence we may make our reconnoitrings."

The old man waved his hand with authority, and led the way without further parlance to the spot he had indicated, followed by the whole of his alarmed companions. An eye less practised than that of the trapper might have failed in discovering the gentle elevation, to which he alluded, and which look'd on the surface of the meadow like a growth a little taller than common. When they reach'd the place, however, the stunted grass, itself, announced the absence of that moisture which had fed the rank weeds of most of the plain, and furnished a clue to the evidence by which he had judged of the formation of the ground hidden beneath. Here a few minutes were lost in breaking down the tops of the surrounding herbage, which, notwithstanding the advantage of their position, rose even above the heads of Middleton and Paul, and in obtaining a look-out, that might command a view of the surrounding sea of fire.

The frightful prospect added nothing to the hopes of those who had so fearful a stake in the result. Although the day was beginning to dawn, the vivid colours of the sky continued to deepen, as if the fierce element were bent on an impious rivalry of the light of the sun. Bright flashes of flame shot up, here and there, along the margin of the waste, like the nimble corruscations of the North, but far more angry and threatening in their colour and changes. The anxiety on the rigid features of the trapper sensibly deepened as he leisurely traced these evidences of a conflagration, which spread in a broad belt about their place of refuge, until he had encircled the whole horizon.

Shaking his head, as he again turned his face to the point where the danger seem'd nighest and most rapidly approaching, the old man said—

"Now have we been cheating ourselves with the belief, that we had thrown those Tetons from our trail, while here is proof enough that they not only know where we lie, but that they intend to smoke us out, like so many skulking beasts of prey. See; they have lighted the fire, around the whole bottom at the same moment, and we are as completely hemm'd in by the Devils, as an island by its waters."

"Let us mount and ride;" cried Middleton. "Is life not worth a struggle!"

"Whither would ye go! Is a Teton horse a salamander that can walk amid fiery flames, unhurt; or do ye think the Lord will show his might in your behalf as in the days of old, and carry you harmless through such a furnace as you may see glowing beneath yonder red sky! There are Siouxes too, hemming the fire with their arrows and knives on every side of us, or I am no judge of their murderous deviltries."

"We will ride into the centre of the whole tribe," retorted the youth, fiercely, "and put their manhood to the test."

"Ay, it's well in words, but what would it prove in deeds! Here is a dealer in bees, who can teach you wisdom in a matter like this."

"Now, for that matter, old trapper," said Paul, stretching his athletic form like a mastiff conscious of his strength, "I am on the side of the Captain, and am clearly for a race, against the fire, though it line me into a Teton wigwam. Here is Ellen, who will—"

"Of what use, of what use, are your stout hearts when the element of the Lord is to be conquered as well as human men. Look about you, friends; the wreath of smoke that is rising from the bottoms, plainly says that there is no outlet from the spot, without crossing a belt of fire. Look for yourselves, my men; look for yourselves; if you can find a single opening, I will engage to follow."

The examination which his companions so instantly and so intently made, rather served to assure them of their desperate situation, than to appease their fears. Huge columns of smoke were rolling up from the plain, and thickening in gloomy masses, around the horizon. The red glow which gleamed upon their enormous folds, now lighting their volumes with the glare of the conflagration and now flashing to another point, as the flame beneath glided ahead, leaving all behind enveloped in awful darkness, and proclaiming, louder than words, the character of the imminent and approaching danger.

"This is terrible!" exclaimed Middleton, folding the trembling Inez to his heart. "At such a time as this, and in such a manner!"

"The gates of Heaven are open to all who truly believe," murmured the pious devotee in his bosom.

"This resignation is maddening! But we are men and will make a struggle for our lives! How now, my brave and spirited friend; shall we yet mount and push across the flames, or shall we stand here, and see these we most love perish, in this frightful manner, without an effort!"

"I am for a swarming time and a flight, before the hive is too hot to hold us;" said the bee-hunter, to whom it will be at once seen that Middleton addressed himself. "Come, old trapper, you must acknowledge this is but a slow way of getting out of danger: if we tarry here much longer, it will be in the fashion that the bees lie around the straw after the hive has been smoked for its honey. You may hear the fire begin to roar, already, and I know by experience that when the flame once gets fairly into the Prairie grass, it is no sloth that can outrun it."

"Think you," returned the old man pointing scornfully at the mazes of the dry and matted grass which environed them, "that mortal feet can outstrip the speed of fire, on such a path. If I only knew now on which side them miscreants lay."

"What say you, friend, Doctor," cried the bewildered Paul, turning to the naturalist, with that sort of helplessness with which the strong are often apt to seek aid of the weak when human power is baffled by the hand of a mightier being. "What say you, have you no advice to give away in a case of life and death?"

The naturalist stood, tabletts in hand, looking at the awful spectacle with as much composure as if the conflagration had been lighted in order to solve the difficulties of some scientific problem. Aroused by the question of his companion, he turned to his equally calm, though differently occupied associate the trapper, demanding with the most provoking insensibility to the urgent nature of their situation—

"Venerable hunter, you have often witnessed similar prismatick experiments—"

He was rudely interrupted by Paul, who struck the tabletts

from his hands, with a violence that betrayed the utter intellectual confusion which had overset the equanimity of his mind. Before time was allowed for remonstrance, the old man, who had continued during the whole scene like one much at a loss how to proceed though also like one who was rather perplexed than alarmed, suddenly assumed a decided air, as if he no longer doubted on the course it was most adviseable to pursue.

"It is time to be doing," he said interrupting the controversy that was about to ensue between the Naturalist and the bee-hunter. "It is time to leave off books and moanings and to be doing."

"You have come to your recollections too late, miserable old man;" cried Middleton. "The flames are within a quarter of a mile of us, and the wind is bringing them down upon us, in this quarter, with dreadful rapidity."

"Anan! the flames! I care but little for the flames. If I only knew how to circumvent the cunning of the Tetons as I know how to cheat the fire of its prey, there would be nothing needed but thanks to the Lord for our deliverance. Do you call this a fire! If you had seen what I have witnessed in the Eastern hills, when mighty mountains were like the furnace of a smith, you would have known what it was to fear the flames and to be thankful that you were spared. Come, lads, come; 'tis time to be doing, now, and to cease talking; for yonder curling flame is truly coming on like a trotting moose. Put hands upon this short and withered grass where we stand and lay bare the 'arth."

"Would you think to deprive the fire of its victims in this childish manner!" exclaimed Middleton.

A faint but solemn smile passed over the features of the old man as he answered—

"Your gran'ther would have said, that when the enemy was nigh a soldier could do no better than to obey."

The Captain felt the reproof and instantly began to imitate the industry of Paul, who was tearing the decayed herbage from the ground in a sort of desperate compliance with the trapper's directions. Even Ellen lent her hands to the labor, nor was it long before Inez was seen similarly employed, though none amongst them, knew why or wherefore. When life is thought to be the reward of labor, men are wont to be industrious. A very few minutes sufficed to lay nearly bare a spot of some thirty feet in diameter. Into one edge of this little area the trapper brought the females, directing Middleton and Paul to cover their light and inflammable dresses with the blankets of the party. So soon as this precaution was observed the old man approached the opposite margin of the grass which still environed them in a tall and dangerous circle, and selecting a handful of the driest of the herbage he placed it over the pan of his rifle. The light combustible kindled at the flash. Then he placed the little flame in a bed of the standing fog, and withdrawing from the spot, to the centre of the ring, he patiently awaited the result.

The subtle element seized with avidity upon its new fuel, and, in a moment, forked flames were gliding among the grass, as the tongues of ruminating animals are seen rolling among their food, apparently in quest of its sweetest portions.

"Now," said the old man, holding up a finger and laughing in his peculiarly silent manner, "you shall see fire fight fire! Ah's me; many is the time I have burnt a smooty path from wanton laziness to pick my way across a tangled bottom!"

"But is this not fatal," cried the amazed Middleton; "are you not bringing the enemy nigher to us instead of avoiding it?"

"Do ye scorch so easily! Your Gran'ther had a tougher skin. But we shall live to see, we shall all live to see."

The experience of the trapper was in the right. As the fire gained strength and heat, it began to spread on three sides, dying of itself on the fourth for want of aliment. As it increased, and the sullen roaring announced its power, it cleared every thing before it, leaving the black and smoking soil far more naked than if the scythe had swept the place. The situation of the fugitives would have still been hazardous had not the area enlarged as the flame encircled them. But by advancing, to the spot where the trapper had kindled the grass, they avoided the heat, and in a very few moments the flames began to recede in every quarter, leaving them enveloped in a cloud of smoke, but perfectly safe from the torrent of fire that was still furiously rolling onward.

The spectators regarded the simple expedient of the trapper with that species of wonder, with which the courtiers of Ferdinand are said to have viewed the manner in which Columbus made his egg stand on its end, though with feelings that were filled with gratitude instead of envy.

"Most wonderful!" said Middleton, when he saw the complete success of the means by which they had been rescued from a danger that he had conceived to be unavoidable. "The thought was a gift from heaven, and the hand that executed it should be immortal!"

"Old trapper," cried Paul, thrusting his fingers through his shaggy locks, "I have lined many a loaded bee into his hole, and know something of the nature of the woods, but this is robbing a hornet of his sting without touching the insect!"

"It will do, it will do," returned the old man, who after the first moment of his success, seem'd to think no more of the exploit; "now get the horses in readiness. Let the flames do their work for a short half hour, and then we will mount. That time is needed to cool the meadow for these unshod Teton beasts are as tender on the hoof, as a bare-footed girl."

Middleton and Paul who considered their unlooked-for escape as a species of resurrection, patiently awaited the time the trapper mentioned with renewed confidence in the infallibility of his judgement. The Doctor regained his tabletts, a little the worse from having fallen among the grass which had been subject to the dominion of the flames, and was consoling himself for this slight misfortune, by recording, uninterruptedly, such different vacillations in light and shadow as he chose to consider phenomena.

In the mean time, the veteran, on whose experience they all so implicitly relied for protection, employed himself in reconnoitring objects in the distance, through the openings which the air occasionally made in the immense bodies of smoke that, by this time, lay in enormous piles on every part of the plain.

"Look you here, lads," the trapper said, after a long and anxious examination; "your eyes are young and may prove better than my worthless sight—though the time has been when a wise and brave people saw reason to think me quick on a look-out, but those times are gone, and many a true and tried friend has passed away with them. Ah's me! If I could choose a change in the orderings of providence—which I cannot, and which it would be blasphemy to attempt, seeing that all things are governed by a wiser mind than belongs to mortal weakness—but if I were to choose a change it would be to say, that such as they who have liv'd long together in friendship and kindness, and who have prov'd their fitness to go in company by many acts of suffering and daring in each other's behalf, should be permitted to give up life at such times, as when the death of one, leaves the other but little reason to wish to live."

"Is it an Indian that you see?" demanded the impatient Middleton.

"Red-skin or white-skin it is much the same. Friendship and use can tie men as strongly together in the woods as in the towns—ay, or for that matter, stronger. Here are the young warriors of the Prairies—Often do they sort themselves in pairs, and set apart their lives for deeds of friendship, and well and truly do they act up to their promises. The death blow to one is commonly mortal to the other! I have been a solitary man much of my time, if he can be called solitary who has lived for seventy years in the very bosom of natur' and where he could at any instant open his heart to God, without having to strip it of the cares and wickednesses of the settlements, but making that allowance, have I been a solitary man, and yet have I always found that intercourse with my kind was pleasant, and painful to break off, provided that the companion was brave and honest. Brave because a skeary comrade in the woods" suffering his eyes inadvertently to rest a moment on the person of the abstracted naturalist, "is apt to make a short path, long, and honest, inasmuch, as craftiness is rather an instinct of the brutes than a gift becoming the reason of a human man."

"But the object that you saw—was it a Sioux?"

"What this world of America is coming to, and where the machinations and inventions of its people are to have an end, the Lord, he only knows. I have seen in my day, the chief, who in his time, had beheld the first christian that plac'd his wicked foot in the regions of York! How much has the beauty of the wilderness been deformed in two short lives! My own eyes were first opened on the shores of the Eastern sea, and well do I remember that I tried the virtues of the first rifle I ever bore, after such a march, from the door of my father to the forest, as a stripling could make between sun and sun, and that without offence to the rights, or prejudices, of any man who set himself up to be the owner of the beasts of the fields. Natur' then lay in its glory along the whole coast, giving a narrow stripe between the woods and the ocean to the greediness of the settlers. And where am I now! Had I the wings of an eagle, they would tire before a tenth of the distance, which separates me from that sea, could be passed; and towns, and villages, farms and high ways, churches, and schools, in short all the inventions and deviltries of man are spread across the region! I have known the time when a few red-skins shouting along the borders, could set the Provinces in a fever, and men were to be armed, and troops were to be called to aid from a distant land, and prayers were said, and the women frighted, and few slept in quiet, because the Iroquois was on the war path, the accursed Mingo had the tomahawk in hand. How is it now. The country sends out her ships to foreign lands to wage their battles, cannon are plentier than the rifle used to be, and trained soldiers are never wanting in tens of thousands, when need calls for their services. Such is the difference atween a Province and a State, my men; and I, miserable and worn out as I seem, have liv'd to see it all!"

"That you must have seen many a chopper skimming the cream from the face of the earth, and many a settler gathering the very honey of nature, old trapper," said Paul, "no reasonable man can, or for that matter, shall doubt. But here is Ellen growing uneasy about the Siouxes, and now you have opened your mind, so freely, concerning these matters, if you will just put us on the line of our flight, the swarm will make another move."

"Anan!"

"I say that Ellen is getting uneasy, and as the smoke is lifting from the plain, it may be prudent to take another flight."

"The boy is reasonable. I had forgotten we were in the midst of a raging fire and that Siouxes were round about us, like hungry wolves watching a drove of buffaloes. But when memory is at work in my old brain, on times long past, it is apt to overlook the matters of the day. You say right, my children; it is time to be moving, and now comes the real nicety of our case. It is easy to outwit a furnace for it is nothing but a raging element, and it is not always difficult to throw a grizzly bear from his scent, for the creatur' is both enlightened and blinded by his instinct, but to shut the eyes of a waking Teton is a matter of greater judgement, inasmuch, as his deviltry is backed by reason."

Notwithstanding the old man appeared so conscious of the difficulty of the undertaking, he set about its achievement with great steadiness and alacrity. After completing the examination which had been interrupted by the melancholy wanderings of his mind, he gave the signal to his companions to mount. The horses, which had continued passive and trembling amid the raging of the fire, received their burthens with a satisfaction so very evident as to furnish a favorable augury of their future industry. The trapper invited the Doctor to take his own steed, declaring his intention to proceed on foot.

"I am but little used to journeying with the feet of others," he added as a reason for the measure, "and my legs are weary of doing nothing. Besides, should we light, suddenly, on an ambushment, which is a thing far from impossible, the horse will be in a better condition for a hard run, with one man on his back, than with two. As for me, what matters it whether my time is to be a day shorter, or longer! Let the Tetons take my scalp, if it be God's pleasure; they will find it covered with gray hairs, and it is beyond the craft of man to cheat me of the knowledge and experience by which they have been whitened."

As no one, among the impatient listeners seemed disposed to dispute the arrangement it was acceded to in silence. The Doctor though he muttered a few mourning exclamations on behalf of the lost Asinus, was by far too well pleased in finding that his speed was likely to be sustained by four legs instead of two, to be long in complying, and consequently, in a very few moments, the bee-hunter, who was never last to speak on such occasions, vociferously announced that they were ready to proceed.

"Now look off, yonder, to the east," said the old man, as

he began to lead the way across the murky and still smoking plain; "little fear of cold feet in journeying such a path as this—but look you off to the east, and if you see a sheet of shining white, glistening like a plate of beaten silver through the openings of the smoke, why that is water. A noble stream is running, thereaway, and I thought I got a glimpse of it a while since, but other thoughts came, and I lost it. It is a broad and swift river, such as the Lord has made many of its fellows in this desert. For here may natur' be seen in all its richness, trees alone excepted. Trees, which are to the 'arth as fruits are to a garden; without them nothing can be pleasant, or thoroughly useful. Now watch all of you, with open eyes, for that stripe of glittering water; we shall not be safe until it is flowing between our trail and these sharp sighted Tetons."

The latter declaration was enough to insure a vigilant look-out for the desired steam, on the part of all the trapper's followers. With this object in view the party proceeded, in profound silence, the old man having admonished them of the necessity of caution, as they entered the clouds of smoke which were rolling like masses of fog along the plain, more particularly over those spots where the fire had encountered occasional pools of stagnant water.

They travelled near a league, in this manner, without obtaining the desired glimpse of the river. The fire was still raging in the distance and as the air swept away the first vapor of the conflagration fresh volumes rolled along the place, limiting the view. At length the old man, who had begun to betray some little uneasiness which caused his followers to apprehend that even his acute faculties were beginning to be confused, in the mazes of the smoke, made a sudden pause, and dropping his rifle to the ground, he stood apparently musing over some object at his feet. Middleton and the rest, rode up to his side and demanded the reason of the halt.

"Look ye here," returned the trapper, pointing to the mutilated carcass of a horse that lay more than half consumed in a little hollow of the ground, "here may you see the power of a Prairie conflagration. The 'arth is moist, hereaway, and the grass has been taller than usual. This miserable beast has been caught in his bed. You see the bones—the crackling and scorched hide, and the grinning teeth. A thousand winters could not wither an animal so thoroughly, as the element has done it, in a minute."

"And this might have been our fate!" said Middleton, "had the flames come upon us, in our sleep!"

"Nay, I do not say that. I do not say that. Not but what man will burn as well as tinder, but that being more reasoning than a horse, he would better know how to avoid the danger."

"Perhaps this then has been but the carcass of an animal; or he too would have fled?"

"See you these marks in the damp soil? Here have been his hoofs, and there is a moccasin print, as I'm a sinner! The owner of the beast has tried hard to move him from the place, but it is in the instinct of the creatur' to be faint-hearted and obstinate in a fire!"

"It is a well known fact. But if the animal has had a rider, where is he?"

"Ay, therein lies the mystery;" returned the trapper stooping to examine the signs in the ground, with a closer eye. "Yes, yes, it is plain there has been a long struggle atween the two. The master has tried hard to save his beast, and the flames must have been very greedy, or he would have had better success."

"Harkee, old trapper," interrupted Paul, pointing to a little distance where the ground was drier, and the herbage had, in consequence, been less luxuriant, "just call them two horses. Yonder lies another."

"The boy is right! can it be that the Tetons have been caught in their own snares! Such things do happen; and here is an example to all evil-doers. Ay, look you, here; this is iron; there have been some white inventions about the trappings of this beast, it must be so, it must be so. A party of the knaves have been skirting in the grass after us, while their friends have fired the Prairie, and look you at the consequences; they have lost their beasts and happy have they been if their own souls are not now skirting along the path, which leads to the Indian heaven."

"They had the same expedient at command as yourself," rejoined Middleton as the party slowly proceeded, approaching the other carcass which lay directly on their route.

"I know not that. It is not every savage that carries his steel and flint, or a good rifle pan, like this old friend of mine. It is slow making a fire with two sticks, and a little time was given to consider, or invent, just at this spot, as you may see by yon streak of flame, which is flashing along afore the wind, as if it were on a trail of powder. It is not many minutes since the fire has passed, hereaway, and it may be well to look at our primings, not that I would willingly combat the Tetons, God forbid, but if a fight needs be, it is always wise to get the first shot."

"This has been a strange beast, old man," said Paul, who had pulled the bridle, or rather halter, of his steed, over the second carcass, which the rest of the party were already, passing, in their eagerness to proceed. "A strange horse do I call it: it has neither head nor hoofs!"

"The fire has not been idle," returned the trapper, keeping his eye vigilantly employed in profiting by those glimpses of the horizon which the whirling smoke offered to his examination. "It would soon bake you a buffaloe whole, or for that matter powder his hoofs and horns into white ashes. Shame, shame, old Hector; as for the captain's pup, it is to be expected that he would show his want of years and I may say I hope without offence, his want of education too; but for a hound like you, who have liv'd so long in the forest afore you came into these plains, it is very disgraceful, Hector, to be showing your teeth and growling at the carcass of a roasted horse, the same as if you were telling your master that you found the trail of a grizzly bear."

"I tell you, old trapper, this is no horse, neither in hoofs, head, nor hide."

"Anan. Not a horse! your eyes are good for the bees, and for the hollow trees, my lad, but—bless me, the boy is right! That I should mistake the hide of a buffaloe, scorched and crimpled as it is, for the carcass of a horse! Ah's, me! The time has been, my men, when I would tell you the name of a beast as far as eye could reach, and that too with most of the particulars of colour, age, and sex."

"An inestimable advantage have you, then, enjoyed in your day, venerable venator," observed the attentive naturalist. "The man who can make these distinctions in a desert is saved the pain of many a weary walk, and, often, of an inquiry that in its result proves useless. Pray tell now did your exceeding excellence of vision extend so far as to enable you to decide on their *Order*, or *Genus*?"

"I know not what you mean by your orders of genius."

"No!" interrupted the bee-hunter a little disdainfully for him when speaking to his aged friend. "Now, old trapper, that is admitting your ignorance of the English language, in a way I should not expect from a man of your experience and understanding. By order, our comrade, means, whether they go in promiscuous droves like a swarm that is following its Queen-bee, or, in single file, as you often see the Buffaloe trailing each other through a Prairie. And as for genius, I'm sure *that* is a word well understood, and in every body's mouth. There is the congress-man, in our district, and that tonguey little fellow who puts out the paper in our County, they are both so called, for their smartness, which is what the Doctor means, as I take it, seeing that he seldom speaks without a particular meaning."

When Paul finished this very clever explanation, he look'd behind him with an expression which rightly interpreted would have said, "You see, though I don't often trouble myself in these matters; I am no fool."

Ellen admired Paul for any thing but his learning. There was enough in his frank, fearless, and manly character, backed as it was by great personal attraction, to awaken her sympathies, without the necessity of prying into his mental attainments. The poor girl reddened like a rose, her pretty fingers played with the belt by which she sustained herself on the horse, and she hurriedly observed, as if anxious to divert the attentions of the other listeners from a weakness on which her own thoughts could not bear to dwell—

"And this is not a horse after all?"

"It is nothing more, nor less, than the hide of a buffaloe," continued the trapper, who had been no less puzzled by the explanation of Paul than by the language of the Doctor. "The hair is beneath, and the fire has run over it, as you see, for being fresh, the flames could take no hold. The beast has not been long killed, and it may be that some of the beef is, still, here away."

"Lift the corner of the skin, old trapper," said Paul, with the tone of one who felt, as if he had now proved his right to mingle his voice in any council. "If there is a morsel of the hump, left, it must be well cooked, and it shall be welcome."

The old man laughed, heartily, at the conceit of his companion. Thrusting his foot beneath the skin, it moved. Then it was suddenly cast aside, and an Indian warrior sprang from its cover, to his feet, with an agility that bespoke how urgent he deemed the occasion.

Chapter XXIV

"But tell me, Hal; art thou not horribly afeard?"—

1 Henry IV, II.iv.365–66.

A SECOND GLANCE sufficed to convince the whole of the startled party that the young Pawnee, whom they had already encountered, again stood before them. Surprise kept both sides mute, and more than a minute was passed in surveying each other, with eyes of astonishment, if not of distrust. The wonder of the young warrior was, however, much more tempered and dignified than that of his christian acquaintances. While Middleton and Paul felt the tremors which shook the persons of their dependant companions, thrilling through their own quickened blood, the glowing eye of the Indian rolled from one to another as if it could never quail, before the rudest assaults. His gaze after making the circuit of every wondering countenance finally settled in a steady look on the equally immoveable features of the trapper. The silence was first broken by Doctor Battius, in the ejaculation of,

"*Order*, primates; *genus*, homo; *species*, Prairie!"

"Ay, ay, the secret is out!" said the old trapper, shaking his head like one who congratulated himself on having mastered the mystery of some knotty difficulty. "The lad has been in the grass for a cover; the fire has come upon him, in his sleep, and having lost his horse, he has been driven to save himself under that fresh hide of buffaloe. No bad invention when powder and flint were wanting to kindle a ring! I warrant me, now, this is a clever youth, and one that it would be safe to journey with! I will speak to him kindly, for anger can at least serve no turn of ours. My brother is welcome, again," using the language which the other understood; "the Tetons have been smoking him, as they would a raccoon."

The young Pawnee roll'd his eye over the place, as if he were examining the terrific danger from which he had just escaped, but he disdained to betray the smallest emotion, at its imminency. His brow contracted as he answered to the remark of the trapper, by saying—

"A Teton is a dog. When the Pawnee war-whoop is in their ears, the whole nation howls."

"It is true. The imps are on our trail, and I am glad to meet a warrior with the tomahawk in his hand, who does not love them. Will my brother lead my children to his village? If the Siouxes follow on our path, my young men shall help him to strike them."

The young Pawnee turned his eyes from one to another of the strangers, in a keen scrutiny, before he saw fit to answer so important an interrogatory. His examination of the males was short and apparently satisfactory. But his gaze was fastened long and admiringly, as in their former interview, on the surpassing and unwonted beauty of a being so fair and so unknown as Inez. Though his glance wandered, for moments, from her countenance to the more intelligible and yet extraordinary charms of Ellen, it did not fail to return promptly, to the study of a creature, who, in the view of his unpractised eye and untutored imagination, was formed with all that perfection, with which the youthful poet is apt to endow the glowing images of his brain. Nothing so fair, so ideal, so every way worthy to reward the courage and self devotion of a warrior had ever before been encountered on the Prairies, and the young brave appeared to be deeply and intuitively sensible to the influence of so rare a model of the loveliness of the sex. Perceiving, however, that his gaze gave uneasiness to the subject of his admiration, he withdrew his eyes, and laying his hand, impressively, on his chest, he, modestly, answered—

"My father shall be welcome. The young men of my nation shall hunt with his sons; Chiefs shall smoke with the grey head. The Pawnee girls will sing in the ears of his daughters."

"And if we meet the Tetons?"—demanded the trapper, who wished to understand, thoroughly, the more important conditions of this new alliance.

"The enemy of the Big-knives shall feel the blow of the Pawnee."

"It is well. Now let my brother and I meet in Council, that we may not go on a crooked path, but that our road to his village may be like the flight of the pigeons."

The young Pawnee made a significant gesture of assent, and

followed the other a little apart, in order to be removed from all danger of interruption from the reckless Paul, or the abstracted naturalist. Their conference was short, but, as it was conducted in the sententious manner of the natives, it served to make each of the parties acquainted with all the necessary information of the other. When they rejoined their associates the old man saw fit to explain a portion of what had passed between them, as follows—

"Ay, I was not mistaken," he said, "this good looking young warrior, for good looking and noble looking he is, though a little horrified perhaps with paint,—this good looking youth, then, tells me he is out on the scout for these very Tetons. His party was not strong enough to strike the devils, who are down from their towns in great numbers to hunt the buffaloe, and runners have gone to the Pawnee villages for aid. It would seem that this lad is a fearless boy, for he has been hanging on their skirts alone, until like ourselves he was driven to the grass for a cover. But he tells me more, my men, and what I am mainly sorry to hear, which is, that the cunning Mahtoree, instead of going to blows with the squatter has become his friend, and that both broods, red and white, are on our heels, and outlying around this very burning plain to circumvent us to our destruction."

"How knows he all this to be true?" demanded Middleton.

"Anan!"

"In what manner does he know that these things are so?"

"In what manner! Do you think news-papers and town criers are needed to tell a scout what is doing on the Prairies, as they are in the bosom of the States. No gossipping woman, who hurries from house to house to spread evil of her neighbor, can carry tidings with her tongue, so fast as these people will spread their meaning, by signs and warnings that they alone understand. 'Tis their l'arning, and what is better, it is got in the open air, and not within the walls of a school. I tell you, Captain, that what he says is true."

"For that matter," said Paul, "I'm ready to swear to it. It is reasonable, and therefore it must be true."

"And well you might, lad; well you might. He furthermore declares that my old eyes, for once, were true to me, and that the river lies, hereaway, at about the distance of half a league.

You see the fire has done most of its work in that quarter, and our path is clouded in smoke. He also agrees that it is needful to wash our trail in water. Yes, we must put that river atween us and the Sioux eyes, and then by the favor of the Lord, not forgetting our own industry, we may gain the village of the Loups."

"Words will not forward us a foot," said Middleton; "let us move."

The old man assented, and the party once more prepared to renew its route. The Pawnee threw the skin of the buffaloe over his shoulder, and led the advance, casting many a stolen glance behind him, as he proceeded, in order to fix his gaze on the extraordinary, and, to him, unaccountable loveliness of the unconscious Inez.

An hour sufficed to bring the fugitives to the bank of the stream, which was one of the hundred rivers that serve to conduct, through the mighty arteries of the Missouri and Mississippi, the waters of that vast and still uninhabited region to the ocean. The river was not deep, but its current was troubled and rapid. The flames had scorched the earth to its very margin, and as the warm steams of the fluid mingled, in the cooler air of the morning, with the smoke of the raging conflagration, most of its surface was wrapped in a mantle of moving vapour. The trapper pointed out the circumstance with pleasure, saying as he assisted Inez to dismount on the margin of the water course—

"The knaves have outwitted themselves! I am far from certain that I should not have fired the Prairie to have got the benefit of this very smoke to hide our movements, had not the heartless imps saved us the trouble. I've known such things done in my day, and done with success. Come, lady; put your tender foot upon the ground, for a fearful time has it been to one of your breeding and skeary qualities. Ahs! me: what have I not known the young, and the delicate, and the virtuous and the modest to undergo, in my time, among the horrifications and circumventions of Indian warfare!—Come, it is a short quarter of a mile to the other bank, and then our trail, at least, will be broken."

Paul had by this time assisted Ellen to dismount, and he now stood looking with rueful eyes at the naked banks of the river. Neither tree nor shrub grew along its borders, with the exception, of here and there, a solitary thicket of low bushes, from among which it would not have been an easy matter to have found a dozen stems of a size sufficient to make an ordinary walking-stick.

"Harkee, old trapper," the moody looking bee-hunter exclaimed; "it is very well to talk of the other side of this ripple of a river or brook or whatever you may call it, but in my judgement it would be a smart rifle that would throw its lead across it, that is to any detriment to Indian, or deer."

"That it would, that it would; though I carry a piece here, that has done its work, in time of need, at as great a distance."

"And do you mean to shoot Ellen, and the Captain's lady, across or do you intend them to go trout fashion with their mouths under water?"

"Is this river too deep to be forded?" asked Middleton, who like Paul began to consider the impossibility of transporting her whose safety he valued more than his own to the opposite shore.

"When the mountains above, feed it with their torrents, it is as you see a swift and powerful stream. Yet have I crossed its sandy bed, in my time, without wetting a knee. But we have the Sioux horses, I warrant me, that the kicking imps will swim like so many deer."

"Old trapper," said Paul, thrusting his fingers into his mop of a head, as was usual with him, when any difficulty confounded his philosophy, "I have swam like a fish, in my day and I can do it again, when there is need; nor do I much regard the weather. But I question if you get Nelly to sit a horse, with this water whirling like a mill-race before her eyes—besides it is manifest the thing is not to be done dry shod."

"Ah! the lad is right! We must to our inventions, therefore, or the river cannot be crossed." Cutting the discourse short, he turned to the Pawnee, and explained to him the difficulty which existed in relation to the women. The young warrior listened gravely, and throwing the buffaloe skin from his shoulder he immediately commenced, assisted by the occasional aid of the understanding old man, the preparations necessary to effect this desirable object.

The hide was soon drawn into the shape of an umbrella top or an inverted parachute, by thongs of deer-skin, with which both the laborers were well provided. A few light sticks served to keep the parts from collapsing or falling in. When this simple and natural expedient was arranged, it was placed on the water, the Indian making a sign that it was ready to receive its freight. Both Inez and Ellen hesitated to trust themselves in a bark of so frail a construction, nor would Middleton or Paul consent that they should do so, until each had assured himself by actual experiment that the vessel was capable of sustaining a load much heavier than it was destined to receive. Then, indeed, their scruples were reluctantly overcome, and the skin was made to receive its precious burthen.

"Now, leave the Pawnee to be the pilot," said the trapper, "my hand is not so steady as it used to be, but he has limbs like toughened hickory. Leave all to the wisdom of the Pawnee."

The husband and lover could not well do otherwise, and they were fain to become, deeply interested it is true, but passive spectators of this primitive species of ferrying. The Pawnee selected the beast of Mahtoree, from among the three horses, with a readiness that proved he was far from being ignorant of the properties of that noble animal, and throwing himself upon its back, he rode into the margin of the river. Thrusting an end of his lance into the hide, he bore the light vessel up against the stream, and giving his steed the rein, they push'd boldly into the current. Middleton and Paul followed, pressing as nigh the bark, as prudence would at all warrant. In this manner, the young warrior bore his precious cargo to the opposite bank, in perfect safety, without the slightest inconvenience to the passengers, and with a steadiness and celerity which proved that both horse and rider were not unused to the operation. When the shore was gained, the young Indian undid his work, threw the skin over his shoulder, plac'd the sticks under his arm, and returned without speaking, to transfer the remainder of the party, in a similar manner, to what was very justly considered the safer side of the river.

"Now, friend Doctor," said the old man, when he saw the Indian plunging into the river a second time, "do I know there is faith in yonder red-skin. He is a good-looking, ay, and an honest looking youth, but the winds of heaven are not more deceitful than these savages when the devil has fairly beset them. Had the Pawnee been a Teton, or one of them heartless Mingos that used to be prowling through the woods of York, a time back, that is, some sixty years agone, we should have seen his back and not his face turned towards us. My heart had its misgivings when I saw the lad choose the better horse, for it would be as easy to leave us, with that beast, as it would for a nimble pigeon to part company from a flock of noisy and heavy winged crows. But you see, the truth is in the boy, and make a red-skin once your friend he is yours so long as you deal honestly by him."

"What may be the distance to the sources of this stream?" demanded Doctor Battius, whose eyes were rolling over the whirling eddies of the current, with a very portentous expression of doubt. "At what distance may its secret springs be found?"

"That may be as the weather proves. I warrant me your legs would be a-weary before you had followed its bed into the Rocky Mountains, but then there are seasons when it might be done without wetting a foot."

"And in what particular divisions of the year do these periodical seasons occur?"

"He that passes this spot a few months from this time, will find that foaming watercourse a desert of drifting sand."

The naturalist pondered deeply. Like most others who are not endowed with a superfluity of physical fortitude, the worthy man had found the danger of passing the river, in so simple a manner, magnifying itself, in his eyes, so rapidly as the moment of adventure approached, that he actually contemplated the desperate effort of going round the river in order to escape the hazard of crossing it. It may not be necessary to dwell on the incredible ingenuity with which terror will at any time, prop a tottering argument. The worthy Obed had gone over the whole subject with commendable diligence, and had just arrived at the consoling conclusion that there was nearly as much glory in discerning the hidden sources of so considerable a stream, as in adding a plant, or an insect, to the lists of the learned, when the Pawnee reach'd the shore for the second time. The old man took his seat with the utmost deliberation in the vessel of skin (so soon as it had been duly arranged for his reception) and having carefully disposed of Hector, between his legs he beckoned to his companion to occupy the third place.

The naturalist plac'd a foot in the frail vessel, as an elephant will try a bridge, or a horse is often seen to make a similar experiment before he will trust the whole of his corporeal treasure on the dreaded flat, and then withdrew, just as the old man believed he was about to seat himself.

"Venerable venator," he said, mournfully, "this is a most unscientific bark! there is an inward monitor which bids me distrust its security!"

"Anan!" said the old man, who was pinching the ears of the hound, as a father would play with the same members in a favorite child.

"I incline not to this irregular mode of experimenting on fluids. The vessel has neither form, nor proportions."

"It is not as handsomely turned as I have seen a canoe in birchen bark, but comfort may be taken in a wigwam as well as in a Palace."

"It is impossible that any vessel constructed on principles so repugnant to science can be safe. This tub, venerable hunter, will never reach the opposite shore in safety!"

"You are a witness of what it has done."

"Ay; but it was an anomaly in prosperity. If exceptions were to be taken as rules, in the government of things, the human race would speedily be plunged in the abysses of ignorance. Venerable trapper, this expedient in which you would repose your safety is, in the annals of regular inventions, what a lusus naturæ may be termed in the lists of Natural History—a monster."

How much longer Doctor Battius might have felt disposed to prolong the discourse it is difficult to say, for in addition to the powerful personal considerations which induced him to procrastinate an experiment which was certainly not without its dangers, the pride of reason was beginning to sustain him in the discussion. But fortunately for the credit of the old man's forbearance, when the naturalist reach'd the word with which he terminated his last speech, a sound arose on the air, that seem'd a sort of supernatural echo to the idea itself. The young Pawnee, who had awaited the termination of the incomprehensible discussion with grave and characteristic patience, raised his head, and listened to the unknown cry, like a stag whose mysterious faculties had detected the footsteps of the distant hounds in the gale. The trapper and the Doctor were not, however, entirely so uninstructed as to the nature of the extraordinary sounds. The latter recognized in them, the well known voice of his own beast, and he was about to rush up the little bank which confined the current, with all the longings of strong affection, when Asinus himself, galloped into view, at no great distance, urged to the unnatural gait, by the impatient and brutal Weucha, who bestrode him.

The eyes of the Teton and those of the fugitives met. The former raised a long, loud and piercing yell in which the notes of exultation were fearfully blended with those of warning. The signal served for a finishing blow to the discussion on the merits of the bark, the Doctor stepping as promptly to the side of the old man, as if a mental mist had been miraculously removed from his eyes. In another instant the steed of the young Pawnee was struggling with the torrent.

The utmost strength of the horse was needed to urge the fugitives, beyond the flight of arrows that came sailing through the air at the next moment. The cry of Weucha had brought fifty of his comrades to the shore, but fortunately among them all, there was not one of a rank sufficient to entitle him to the privilege of bearing a fusee. One half the stream, however, was not passed, before the form of Mahtoree, himself, was seen on its bank and an ineffectual discharge of fire arms announced the rage and disappointment of the chief. More than once, the trapper had raised his rifle, as if about to try its power, on his enemies, but he as often, lowered it, without firing. The eyes of the Pawnee warrior glared like those of the cougar, at the sight of so many of the hostile tribe, and he answered the impotent effort of their chief, by tossing a hand into the air in contempt, and raising the war-cry of his nation. The challenge was too taunting to be endured. The Tetons dashed into the stream, in a body, and the river became dotted with the dark forms of beasts and riders.

There was now a fearful struggle for the friendly bank. As the Dahcotahs advanced with beasts which had not, like that of the Pawnee, expended their strength in former efforts, and as they moved unincumbered by any thing but their riders, the speed of the pursuers greatly outstripped that of the fugitives. The trapper who clearly comprehended the whole danger of their situation, calmly turned his eyes from the Tetons to his young Indian associate, in order to examine whether the resolution of the latter began to falter as the former lessened the distance between them. Instead of betraying fear, however, or any of that concern which might so readily have been excited by the peculiarity of his risque, the brow of the young warrior contracted to a look which indicated high and deadly hostility.

"Do you greatly value life, friend Doctor?" demanded the old man, with a sort of philosophical calmness which made the question doubly appalling to his companion.

"Not for itself," returned the naturalist sipping some of the water of the river from the hollow of his hand, in order to clear his husky throat. "Not for itself. But exceedingly, inasmuch as Natural History has so deep a stake in my existence. Therefore—"

"Ay," resumed the other who mused too deeply to dissect the ideas of the Doctor with his usual sagacity, "tis in truth the history of natur', and a base and craven feeling it is! Now is life as precious to this young Pawnee as to any Governor in the States, and he might save it, or at least stand some chance of saving it, by letting us go down the stream, and yet you see he keeps his faith, manfully and like an Indian warrior. For myself, I am old, and willing to take the fortune that the Lord may see fit to give, nor do I conceit that you are of much benefit to mankind, and it is a crying shame if not a sin, that so fine a youth as this should lose his scalp for two beings so worthless as ourselves. I am therefore disposed, provided that it shall prove agreeable to you, to tell the lad to make the best of his way, and to leave us to the mercy of the Tetons."

"I repel the proposition, as repugnant to nature, and as treason to science!" exclaimed the alarmed naturalist. "Our progress is miraculous and as this admirable invention moves with so wonderful a facility a few more minutes will serve to bring us to land."

The old man regarded him, intently, for an instant and shaking his head, he said—

"Lord, what a thing is fear! it transforms the creatur's of the world and the craft of man, making that which is ugly, seemly in our eyes, and that which is beautiful, unsightly! Lord, Lord, what a thing is fear!"

A termination was, however, put to the discussion by the increasing interest of the chace. The horses of the Dahcotahs had, by this time, gained the middle of the current, and their riders, were already filling the air with yells of triumph. At this moment, Middleton and Paul, who had led the females to a little thicket, appeared again on the margin of the stream, menacing their enemies with the rifle.

"Mount, mount," shouted the trapper, the instant he beheld them. "Mount and fly, if you value those who lean on you for help. Mount, and leave us in the hands of the Lord."

"Stoop your head, old trapper," returned the voice of Paul. "Down with ye both into your nest. The Teton Devil is in your line—down with your heads, and make way for a Kentucky bullet."

The old man turned his head, and saw that the eager Mahtoree, who preceded his party some distance, had brought himself nearly in a line with the bark and the bee-hunter, who stood perfectly ready to execute his hostile threat. Bending his body low, the rifle was discharged and the swift lead whizzed harmlessly past him, on its more distant errand. But the eye of the Teton chief was not less quick and certain than that of his enemy. He threw himself from his horse, the moment preceding the report, and sunk into the water. The beast snorted with terror and anguish, throwing half his form out of the river in a desperate plunge. Then he was seen drifting away in the torrent, and dying the turbid waters with his blood.

The Teton chief soon reappeared on the surface, and understanding the nature of his loss, he swam with vigorous strokes to the nearest of the young men, who relinquished his steed, as a matter of course, to so renowned a warrior. The incident, however, created a confusion in the whole of the

Dahcotah band, who appeared to await the intention of their leader, before they renewed their efforts to reach the shore. In the mean time, the vessel of skin had reach'd the land, and the fugitives were once more united on the margin of the river.

The savages were now swimming about in indecision, as a flock of pigeons is often seen to hover, in confusion, after receiving a heavy discharge into its leading column, apparently hesitating on the risk of storming a bank so formidably defended. The well known precaution of Indian warfare prevailed, and Mahtoree, admonished by his recent adventure, led his warriors back to the shore from which they had come, in order to relieve their beasts, which were already becoming unruly.

"Now, mount you, with the tender ones, and ride for yonder hillock," said the trapper, "beyond it, you will find another stream, into which you must enter, and turning to the sun follow its bed for a mile, until you reach a high and sandy plain. There will I meet you. Go. Mount. This Pawnee youth and I, and my stout friend the Physicianer, who is a desperate warrior are men enough to keep the bank, seeing that show and not use is all that is needed."

Middleton and Paul saw no use in wasting their breath in remonstrances against this proposal. Glad to know that their rear was to be covered even in this imperfect manner, they hastily got their horses in motion and soon disappeared on the required route. Some twenty or thirty minutes succeeded this movement, before the Tetons on the opposite shore seem'd inclined to enter on any new enterprise. Mahtoree was distinctly visible in the midst of his warriors, issuing his mandates, and betraying his desire for vengeance, by occasionally shaking an arm in the direction of the fugitives, but no step was taken which appeared to threaten any further act of immediate hostility. At length a yell arose among the savages which announced the occurrence of some fresh event. Then Ishmael and his sluggish sons were seen in the distance, and soon the whole of the united force mov'd down to the very limits of the stream. The squatter proceeded to examine the position of his enemies, with his usual coolness, and, as if to try the power of his rifle, he sent a bullet among them with a force sufficient to do execution even at the distance at which he stood.

"Now let us depart!" exclaimed Obed, endeavoring to catch a furtive glimpse of the lead, which he fancied was whizzing at his very ear, " we have maintained the bank, in a gallant manner; for a sufficient length of time, quite as much military skill is to be displayed in a retreat as in an advance."

The old man cast a look behind him, and seeing that the equestrians had reached the cover of the hill, he made no objections to the proposal. The remaining horse was given to the Doctor with instructions to pursue the course just taken by Middleton and Paul. When the naturalist was mounted and in full retreat, the trapper and the young Pawnee stole from the spot, in such a manner as to leave their enemies some time in doubt as to their movements. Instead, however, of proceeding across the plain towards the hill, a route on which they must have been in open view, they took a shorter path, covered by the formation of the ground, and intersected the little water course at the point where Middleton had been directed to leave it, and just in season to join his party. The Doctor had used so much diligence in the retreat as to have already overtaken his friends, and of course all the fugitives were again assembled.

The trapper, now look'd about him for some convenient spot, where the whole party might halt, as he expressed it for some five or six hours.

"Halt!" exclaimed the Doctor, when the alarming proposal reached his ears, "venerable hunter, it would seem that on the contrary, many days should be passed in industrious flight!"

Middleton and Paul were both of his opinion, and each in his particular manner expressed as much.

The old man heard them with patience, but shook his head like one who was unconvinced, and then answered all their arguments, in one general and positive reply.

"Why should we fly?" he asked. "Can the legs of mortal men out strip the speed of horses! Do you think the Tetons will lie down and sleep, or will cross the water and nose for our trail. Thanks be to the Lord we have washed it well in this stream, and if we leave the place with discretion and wisdom we may yet throw them off its track. But a Prairie is not a wood. *There* a man may journey long, caring for nothing but the prints his moccasin leaves, whereas in these open plains, a runner, plac'd on yonder hill for instance, could see far on every side of him like a hovering hawk, looking down on his prey. No, no, night must come, and darkness be upon us afore we leave this spot. But listen to the words of the Pawnee, he is a lad of spirit, and I warrant me, many is the hard race that he has run with the Sioux bands! Does my brother think our trail is long enough?" he demanded in the Indian tongue.

"Is a Teton a fish, that he can see it in the river?"

"But my young men think we should stretch it, until it reaches across the Prairie."

"Mahtoree has eyes—he will see it."

"What does my brother counsel?"

The young warrior studied the heavens a moment and appeared to hesitate. He mused some time with himself, and then he replied like one whose opinion was fixed.

"The Dahcotahs are not asleep," he said, "we must lie in the grass."

"Ah! the lad is of my mind," said the old man, briefly explaining the opinion of his companion to his white friends. Middleton was obliged to acquiesce, and, as it was confessedly dangerous to remain upon their feet, each one set about assisting in the means to be adopted for their security. Inez and Ellen were quickly bestowed, beneath the warm and not uncomfortable shelter of the buffaloe skins, which formed a thick covering, and tall grass was drawn over the place, in such a manner as to evade any examination from a common eye. Paul and the Pawnee fettered the beasts and cast them to the earth, where after supplying them with food, they were also left concealed in the fog of the Prairie. No time was lost when these several arrangements were completed, before each of the others sought a place of rest and concealment, and then the plain appeared again deserted to its solitude.

The old man had advised his companions of the absolute necessity of their continuing for hours in this concealment. All their hopes of escape depended on the success of the artifice. If they might elude the cunning of their pursuers, by this simple and therefore less suspected expedient, they could renew their flight as the evening approached, and by changing their course, the chance of final success would be greatly increased. Influenced by these momentous considerations, the whole party lay, musing on their situation, until thoughts grew weary, and sleep finally settled on them all, one after another.

The deepest silence had prevailed for hours, when the quick ears of the trapper and the Pawnee were startled, by a faint cry of surprise from Inez. Springing to their feet like men who were about to struggle for their lives, they found the vast plain, the rolling swells, the little hillock, and the scattered thickets covered in one white dazzling sheet of snow.

"The Lord have mercy on ye all!" exclaimed the old man, regarding the prospect with a rueful eye, "now, Pawnee, do I know the reason why you studied the clouds so closely; but it is too late, it is too late. A squirrel would leave his trail on this light coating of the 'arth! Ha! there come the imps to a certainty. Down with ye all, down with ye, your chance is but small, and yet it must not be wilfully cast away."

The whole party was instantly concealed, again, though many an anxious and stolen glance was directed through the tops of the grass on the movements of their enemies. At the distance of half a mile, the Teton band was seen riding in a circuit which was gradually contracting itself, and evidently closing upon the very spot where the fugitives lay. There was but little difficulty in solving the mystery of this movement. The snow had fallen in time to assure them, that those they sought were in their rear, and they were now employed with the unwearied perseverance and patience of Indian warriors in circling the certain boundaries of their place of concealment.

Each minute added to the jeopardy of the fugitives. Paul and Middleton deliberately prepared their rifles, and as the occupied Mahtoree came, at length, within fifty feet of them, keeping his eyes riveted on the grass through which he rode, they levelled them together and pulled the triggers. The effort was answered by the mere snapping of the locks.

"Enough," said the old man, rising with dignity, "I have cast away the priming, for certain death would follow your rashness. Now, let us meet our fates like men. Cringing and complaining find no favor in Indian eyes."

His appearance was greeted by a yell, that spread far and wide over the plain, and in a moment a hundred savages were seen riding madly to the spot. Mahtoree received his prisoners with great self-restraint, though gleams of fierce joy broke through his clouded brow, and the heart of Middleton grew cold as he caught the expression of that eye, which the chief turned on the nearly insensible but still lovely Inez.

The exultation of receiving the white captives was so great, as, for a time to throw the dark and immovable form of their young Indian companion entirely out of view. He stood apart, disdaining to turn an eye on his enemies, as motionless, as if he were frozen in that attitude of dignity and composure. But when a little time had passed, even this secondary object attracted the attention of the Tetons. Then it was that the trapper first learned by the shout of triumph and the long drawn yell of delight, which burst at once from a hundred throats, as well as by the terrible name which fill'd the air, that his youthful friend was no other than that redoubtable and hitherto invincible warrior, Hard-Heart.

Chapter XXV

"What, are ancient pistol and
You friends, yet?"
Henry V, II.i.3–4.

THE CURTAIN of our imperfect drama must fall to rise upon another scene. The time is advanced several days; during which very material changes had occurred in the situation of the actors. The hour is noon, and the place an elevated plain, that rose, at no great distance from the water, somewhat abruptly from a fertile bottom which stretched along the margin of one of the numberless water-courses of that region. The river took its rise near the base of the Rocky Mountains, and after washing a vast extent of plain, it mingled its waters with a still larger stream, to become finally lost in the turbid current of the Missouri.

The landscape was changed materially for the better, though the hand which had impressed so much of the desert on the surrounding region, had laid a portion of its power on this spot. The appearance of vegetation was, however, less discouraging than in the more sterile wastes of the rolling Prairies. Clusters of trees were scattered in greater profusion, and a long outline of ragged forest marked the northern boundary of the view. Here and there on the bottom, were to be seen the evidences of a hasty and imperfect culture of such indigenous vegetables as were of a quick growth, and which were known to flourish, without the aid of art, in deep and alluvial soils. On the very edge of what might be called the table-land, were pitch'd the hundred lodges of a horde of wandering Siouxes. These light tenements were arranged without the least attention to order. Proximity to the water seemed to be the only consideration which had been consulted in their disposition, nor had even this important convenience been always regarded. While most of the lodges stood along the brow of the plain, many were to be seen at greater distances, occupying such places, as had first pleased the capricious eyes of their untutored owners. The encampment was not military or in the slightest degree protected from surprise by its position or defences. It was open on every side, and on every side as accessible as any other point in those wastes, if the imperfect and natural obstruction offered by the river, be excepted. In short, the place bore the appearance of having been tenanted longer than its occupants had originally intended, while it was not wanting in the signs of readiness for a hasty or even a compelled departure.

This was the temporary encampment of that portion of his people who had long been hunting under the direction of Mahtoree, on those grounds which separated the stationary abodes of his nation from those of the warlike tribes of the Pawnees. The lodges were tents of skin, high, conical and of the most simple and primitive construction. The shield, the quiver, the lance and the bow of its master were to be seen suspended from a light post before the opening, or door of each habitation; the different domestic implements of his one, two or three wives, as the brave was of greater or lesser renown, were carelessly thrown at its side, and, here and there, the round, full, patient countenance of an infant might be found, peeping from its comfortless wrappers of bark, as, suspended by a deer skin thong, from the same post, it rocked in the passing air. Children of a larger growth were tumbling over each other in piles, the males, even at that early age, making themselves distinguished for that species of domination, which, in after life, was to mark the vast distinction between the sexes. Youths were on the bottom, essaying their juvenile powers in curbing the wild steeds of their fathers, while here and there a truant girl was to be seen, stealing from her labors, to admire their fierce and impatient daring.

Thus far the picture was the daily exhibition of an encampment confident in its security. But immediately in front of the lodges was a gathering that seemed to forbode some movements of more than usual interest. A few of the withered and remorseless crones of the band were clustering together, in readiness to lend their fell voices if needed, to aid in exciting their descendants to an exhibition, which their depraved tastes covetted, as the luxurious Roman dame witnessed the struggles and the agony of the gladiator. The men were subdivided into groupes, assorted according to the deeds and reputations of the several individuals of whom they were composed.

They, who were of that equivocal age which admitted them to the hunts while their discretion was still too doubtful to permit them to be trusted on the war-path, hung around the skirts of the whole, catching, from the fierce models before them, that gravity of demeanour and restraint of manner, which in time, was to become so deeply engrafted in their own characters. A few of a still older class, and who had heard the whoop in anger, were a little more presuming, pressing nigher to the chiefs, though far from presuming to mingle in their Councils, sufficiently distinguished by being permitted to catch the wisdom which fell from lips so venerated. The ordinary warriors of the band were still less diffident, not hesitating to mingle among the chiefs of lesser note, though far from assuming the right to dispute the sentiments of any established brave, or to call in question the prudence of measures that were recommended by the more gifted counsellors of the nation.

Among the chiefs themselves there was a singular compound of exterior. They were divided into two classes; those who were mainly indebted for their influence to physical causes and to deeds in arms, and those who had become more distinguished rather for their wisdom than for their services in the field. The former was by far the most numerous and the most important class. These were men of stature and mien, whose stern countenances were often rendered doubly imposing by those evidences of their valour which had been roughly traced on their lineaments by the hands of their enemies. That class which had gained its influence by a moral ascendancy was extremely limited. They were uniformly to be distinguished by the quick and lively expression of their eyes, by the air of distrust that marked their movements, and occasionally by the vehemence of their utterance in those sudden outbreakings of the mind, by which their present consultations were from time to time, distinguished.

In the very centre of a ring formed by these chosen counsellors, was to be seen the person of the disquieted, but seemingly calm, Mahtoree. There was a conjunction of all the several qualities of the others in his person and character.

Mind as well as matter had contributed to establish his authority. His scars were as numerous and deep, as those of the whitest head in his nation; his limbs were in their greatest vigor; his courage at its fullest height. Endowed with this rare combination of moral and physical influence, the keenest eye in all that assembly was wont to lower before his threatening glance. Courage and cunning had established his ascendancy, and it had been rendered, in some degree sacred by time. He knew so well how to unite the powers of reason and force, that in a state of society which admitted of a greater display of his energies, the Teton would in all probability have been both a conqueror and a despot.

A little apart from the gathering of the band, was to be seen a set of beings of an entirely different origin. Taller and far more muscular in their persons, the lingering vestiges of their Saxon and Norman ancestry were yet to be found beneath the swarthy complexions, which had been bestowed by an American sun. It would have been a curious investigation, for one skilled in such an inquiry, to have traced those points of difference by which the offspring of the most western European was still to be distinguished from the descendant of the most remote Asiatic, now that the two, in the revolutions of the world, were approximating in their habits, their residence and not a little in their characters. The groupe of whom we write was composed of the family of the squatter. They stood, indolent, lounging and inert, as usual when no immediate demand was made on their dormant energies, clustered in front of some four or five habitations of skin, for which they were indebted to the hospitality of their Teton allies. The terms of their unexpected confederation were sufficiently explained, by the presence of the horses and domestic cattle, that were quietly grazing on the bottom beneath, under the jealous eyes of the spirited Hetty. The wagons were drawn about the lodges in a sort of irregular barrier, which at once manifested, that their confidence was not entirely restored, while, on the other hand, their policy or indolence prevented any very positive exhibition of distrust. There was a singular union of passive enjoyment and of dull curiosity slumbering in every dull countenance, as each of the party stood leaning on his rifle, regarding the movements of the Sioux conference. Still no sign of expectation or interest escaped from the youngest among them, the whole appearing to emulate the most phlegmatic of their savage allies, in an exhibition of patience. They rarely spoke; and when they did, it was in some short and contemptuous remark, which served to put the physical superiority of a white man, and that of an Indian, in a sufficiently striking point of view. In short, the family of Ishmael appeared now, to be in the plentitude of an enjoyment which depended on inactivity, but which was not entirely free from certain confused glimmerings of a perspective, in which their security stood in some little danger of a rude interruption from Teton treachery. Abiram alone, formed a solitary exception to this state of equivocal repose.

After a life passed in the commission of a thousand mean and insignificant villainies, the mind of the kidnapper had become hardy enough to attempt the desperate adventure which has been laid before the reader, in the course of the narrative. His influence over the bolder, but less active spirit of Ishmael was far from great, and had not the latter been suddenly expelled from a fertile bottom of which he had taken possession with intent to keep it, without much deference to the forms of law, he would never have succeeded in enlisting the husband of his sister, in an enterprise that required so much decision and forethought. Their original success and subsequent disappointment have been seen, and Abiram now sat apart, plotting the means by which he might secure to himself the advantages of his undertaking, which he perceived were each moment becoming more uncertain, through the open admiration of Mahtoree, for the innocent subject of his villainy. We shall leave him to his vacillating and confused expedients in order to pass to the description of certain other personages in the drama.

There was still another corner of the picture that was occupied. On a little bank, at the extreme right of the encampment, lay the forms of Middleton and Paul. Their limbs were painfully bound with thongs, cut from the skin of a bison, while by a sort of refinement in cruelty, they were so placed that each could see a reflection of his own misery in that of his neighbor. Within a dozen yards of them, a post was set firmly in the ground, and against it was bound the light and

Apollo-like person of Hard-Heart. Between the two stood the trapper, deprived of his rifle, his pouch and his horn, but otherwise left in a sort of contemptuous liberty. Some five or six young warriors however with quivers at their backs and long tough bows dangling from their shoulders, who stood with grave watchfullness at no great distance from the spot, sufficiently proclaimed how fruitless any attempt to escape on the part of one so aged and so feeble might prove. Unlike the other spectators of the important conference, these individuals were engaged in a discourse, that for them contained an interest of its own.

"Captain," said the bee-hunter, with an expression of comical concern that no misfortune could repress in one of his buoyant feelings, "do you really find that accursed strap of untanned leather cutting into your shoulder, or is it only the tickling in my own arm, that I feel?"

"When the spirit suffers so deeply, the body is insensible to pain," returned the more refined, though scarcely so spirited Middleton, "would to Heaven that some of my trusty artillerists might fall upon this accursed encampment!"

"You might as well wish that these Teton lodges were so many hives of hornets, and that the insects would come forth and battle with yonder tribe of half-naked savages." Then chuckling with his own conceit, the bee-hunter turned away from his companion, and sought a momentary relief from his misery, by imagining that so wild an idea might be realized, and fancying the manner in which the attack would upset even the well established patience of an Indian.

Middleton was glad to be silent, but the old man who had listened to their words drew a little nigher, and continued the discourse.

"Here is likely to be a marciless and a hellish business!" he said shaking his head in a manner to prove that even his experience was at a loss for a remedy in so trying a dilemma. "Our Pawnee friend is already staked for the torture, and I well know by the eye and the countenance of the Great Sioux, that he is leading on the temper of his people to further enormities."

"Harkee, old trapper," said Paul, writhing in his bonds, to catch a glimpse of the other's melancholy face—"you ar' skilled in Indian tongues, and know somewhat of Indian deviltries. Go you to the council, and tell their chiefs in my name, that is to say in the name of Paul Hover of the State of Kentucky, that provided they will guarantee the safe return of one Ellen Wade into the States, they are welcome to take his scalp, when and in such manner as best suits their amusements; or, if-so-be, they will not trade on these conditions, you may throw in an hour or two of torture, beforehand, in order to sweeten the bargain to their damnable appetites."

"Ah! Lad, it is little that they would hearken to such an offer, knowing as they do, that you are already like a bear in a trap, as little able to fight as to fly. But be not downhearted; for the colour of a white man is sometimes his death warrant, among these far tribes of savages, and sometimes his shield. Though they love us not, cunning often ties their hands. Could the red nations work their will, trees would shortly be growing, again, on the plough'd fields of America, and woods would be whitened with christian bones. No one can doubt that, who knows the quality of the love which a red-skin bears a Pale face; but they have counted our numbers until their memories fail them, and they are not without their policy. Therefore, is our fate unsettled; but I fear me there is small hope left for the Pawnee!"

As the old man concluded, he walk'd slowly towards the subject of his latter observation, taking his post at no great distance from his side. Here he stood, observing such a silence and mien as became him to manifest to a chief so renowned and so situated as his captive associate. But the eye of Hard-Heart was fastened on the distance, and his whole air was that of one whose thoughts were entirely removed from the present scene.

"The Siouxes are in Council on my brother," the trapper at length observed, when he found that he could only attract the other's attention by speaking.

The young partizan turned his head, with a calm smile, as he answered—

"They are counting the scalps over the lodge of Hard-Heart!"

"No doubt, no doubt their tempers begin to mount as they remember the number of Tetons you have struck, and better would it be for you, now, had more of your days been spent in chasing the deer, and fewer on the war-path. Then some childless mother of this tribe, might take you in the place of her lost son, and your time would be fill'd in Peace."

"Does my father think that a warrior can ever die! The Master of Life does not open his hand to take away his gifts, again. When he wants his young men he calls them, and they go. But the red-skin he has once breathed on, lives forever."

"Ay, this is a more comfortable and a more humble faith than that which yonder heartless Teton harbors! There is something in these Loups, which opens my inmost heart to them. They seem to have the courage, ay, and the honesty, too, of the Delawares of the Hills. And this lad,—it is wonderful, it is very wonderful—but the age, and the eye, and the limbs are as if they might have been brothers! Tell me, Pawnee, have you ever, in your traditions heard of a Mighty People, who once lived on the shores of the Salt Lake, hard by the rising sun,—"

"The earth is white, by people of the colour of my father."

"Nay, nay, I speak not, now, of any strollers who have crept into the land to rob the lawful owners of their birthright, but of a people who are, or rather were, what with natur' and what with paint, red as the berry on the bush."

"I have heard the old men say, that there were bands who hid themselves in the woods, under the rising sun, because they dared not come upon the open Prairies, to fight with men."

"Do not your traditions tell you of the greatest, the bravest, and the wisest nation of red-skins that the Wahcondah has ever breathed upon!"

Hard-Heart, raised his head with a loftiness and dignity that even his bonds could not repress, as he answered—

"Has age blinded my father, or does he see so many Siouxes, that he believes there are no longer any Pawnees!"

"Ah! such is mortal vanity and pride!" exclaimed the disappointed old man, in English. "Natur' is as strong in a red-skin, as in the bosom of a man of white gifts. Now would a Delaware conceit himself far mightier, than a Pawnee, just as a Pawnee boasts himself to be of the Princes of the 'arth. And so it was atween the Frenchers of the Canadas, and the red coated English that the King did use to send into the States, when States they were not, but outcrying and petitioning Provinces. They fout, and they fout, and what marvellous boastings did they give forth to the world of their own valor and victories, while both parties forgot to name the humble soldier of the land, who did the real service, but who as he was not privileged then to smoke at the Great Council Fire of his Nation, seldom heard of his deeds, after they were once bravely done."

When the old man had thus given vent to the nearly dormant but far from extinct Military Pride, that had so unconsciously led him into the very error he deprecated, his eye which had begun to quicken and glimmer with some of the ardor of his youth softened, and turned its anxious look on the devoted captive, whose countenance was also restored to its former cold look of abstraction and thought.

"Young warrior," he continued, in a voice that was growing tremulous, "I have never been father, or brother. The Wahcondah made me to live alone. He never tied my heart, to house or field, by the cords with which the men of my race are bound to their lodges; if he had I should not have journeyed so far and seen so much. But I have tarried long among a people, who liv'd in those woods you mention, and much reason did I find to imitate their courage and love their honesty. The Master of Life has made us all, Pawnee, with a feeling for our kind. I never was a father, but well do I know what is the love of one. You are like a lad, I valued, and I had even begun to fancy that some of his blood might be in your veins. But, what matters that! You are a true man, as I know by the way in which you keep your faith, and honesty is a gift too rare to be forgotten. My heart yearns to you, boy, and gladly would I do you good."

The youthful warrior listened to the words which came from the lips of the other with a force and simplicity that established their truth, and he bow'd his head on his naked bosom in testimony of the respect with which he met the proffer. Then lifting his dark eye to the level of the view he seem'd to be, again, considering of things removed from every personal consideration. The trapper, who well knew how high the pride of a warrior would sustain him, in those moments he believed to be his last, awaited the pleasure of his young friend with a meekness and patience that he had acquired by his association with that remarkable race. At length the gaze of the Pawnee began to waver, and then quick, flashing glances were turned, from the countenance of the old man to the air, and from the air, to his deeply marked lineaments, again, as if the spirit which governed their movements was beginning to be troubled.

"Father," the young brave finally answered in a voice of confidence and kindness, "I have heard your words. They have gone in at my ears, and are now within me. The white headed Long-knife has no son, the Hard-Heart of the Pawnees is young, but he is already the oldest of his family. He found the bones of his father on the hunting grounds of the Osages, and he has sent them, to the Prairies of the Good Spirits. No doubt, the great Chief, his father, has seen them, and knows what is part of himself. But the Wahcondah will soon call to us both—you, because you have seen all that is to be seen in this country, and Hard-Heart, because he has need of a warrior who is young. There is not time for the Pawnee to show the Pale Face the duty that a son owes to his Father."

"Old as I am, and miserable and helpless as I now stand to what I once was, I may live to see the sun go down in the Prairie. Does my son expect to do as much?"

"The Tetons are counting the scalps on my lodge," returned the young chief with a smile whose melancholy was singularly illuminated by a gleam of triumph.

"And they find them many. Too many for the safety of its owner, while he is in their revengeful hands. My son is not a woman and he looks on the path he is about to travel with a steady eye. Has he nothing to whisper in the ears of his people, before he starts. These legs are old, but they may yet carry me to the forks of the Loup river."

"Tell them that Hard-Heart has tied a knot in his wampum for every Teton," burst from the lips of the captive, with that vehemence with which sudden passion is known to break through the barriers of artificial restraint. "If he meets one of them all, in the Prairie of the Master of Life, his heart will become Sioux!"

"Ah! that feeling would be a dangerous companion for a man with white gifts to start with on so solemn a journey!" muttered the old man in English. "This is not what the good Moravians said to the Councils of the Delawares, nor what is so often preach'd to the white-skins in the settlements though to the shame of the colour be it said, it is so little heeded. Pawnee, I love you, but being a Christian man, I cannot be the runner to bear such a message."

"If my father is afraid, that the Tetons will hear him, let him whisper it softly, to our old men."

"As for fear, young warrior, it is no more the shame of a Pale face than of a red-skin. The Wahcondah teaches us to love the life he gives; but it is, as men love their hunts, and their dogs and their carybines, and not with the doting that a mother looks upon her infant. The Master of Life will not have to speak aloud twice when he calls my name. I am as ready to answer to it, now, as I shall be to-morrow—or at any time, it may please his mighty will. But what is a warrior without his traditions! Mine forbid me to carry your words."

The chief made a dignified motion of assent, and here there was great danger that those feelings of confidence which had been so singularly awakened would as suddenly subside. But the heart of the old man had been too sensibly touched, through long dormant but still living recollections to break off the communication so rudely. He pondered for a minute, and then bending his look wistfully on his young associate, again, continued—

"Each warrior must be judged by his gifts. I have told my son what I cannot, but let him open his ears to what I can do. An elk shall not measure the Prairie much swifter than these old legs, if the Pawnee will give me a message that a white man may bear."

"Let the Pale face listen," returned the other, after hesitating a single instant longer, under a lingering sensation of his former disappointment. "He will stay here till the Siouxes have done counting the scalps of their dead warriors. He will wait until they have tried to cover the heads of eighteen Tetons with the skin of one Pawnee. Then he will open his eyes wide that he may see the place, where they bury the bones of a warrior."

"All this will I, and may I do, noble boy."

"He will mark the spot that he may know it."

"No fear, no fear that I shall forget the place;" interrupted the other, whose fortitude began to give way under so trying an exhibition of calmness and resignation.

"Then I know that my father, will go to my people. His head is gray, and his words will not be blown away with the smoke. Let him get on my lodge and call the name of Hard-Heart, aloud. No Pawnee will be deaf. Then let my father ask for the colt that has never been ridden, but which is sleeker than the buck and swifter than the elk."

"I understand you, boy, I understand you;" interrupted the attentive old man, "and what you say shall be done, ay, and well done too, or I'm but little skilled in the wishes of a dying Indian."

"And when my young men have given my father, the halter of that colt, he will lead him by a crooked path to the grave of Hard-Heart?"

"Will I! ay, that I will brave youth, though the winter covers these plains in banks of snow, and the sun is hidden as much by day as by night. To the head of the holy spot will I lead the beast, and place him with his eyes looking towards the setting sun."

"And my father will speak to him, and tell him that the master, who has fed him since he was foaled, has now need of him."

"That too will I do; though the Lord he knows that I shall hold discourse with a horse not with any vain conceit that my words will be understood but only to satisfy the cravings of Indian superstition. Hector, my pup, what think *you*, dog, of talking to a horse?"

"Let the gray-head speak to him with the tongue of a Pawnee," interrupted the young victim, perceiving that his companion had used an unknown language for the preceding speech.

"My son's will shall be done. And with these old hands, which I had hoped had nearly done with blood-shed, whether it be of man or beast will I slay the animal on your grave."

"It is good," returned the other, a gleam of satisfaction flitting across his features. "Hard-Heart will ride his horse to the blessed Prairies, and he will come before the Master of Life like a chief!"

The sudden and striking change which instantly occurred in the countenance of the Indian, caused the trapper to look aside, when he perceived, that the conference of the Siouxes had ended, and that Mahtoree, attended by one or two of the principal warriors, was deliberately approaching his intended victims.

Chapter XXVI

"I am not prone to weeping as our sex
Commonly are.—"
—"But I have that honorable
Grief lodged here, which burns worse than
Tears drown."
The Winter's Tale, II.i.108–09, 110–12.

When within twenty feet of the prisoners the Tetons stopped, and their leader made a sign to the old man to draw nigh. The trapper obeyed, quitting the young Pawnee with a significant look, which was received as it was meant, for an additional pledge that he would never forget his promise. So soon as Mahtoree found that the other had stopped within reach of him, he stretch'd forth his arm, and laying a hand upon the shoulder of the attentive old man, he stood regarding him, a minute, with eyes that seem'd willing to penetrate the recesses of his most secret thoughts.

"Is a Pale face always made with two tongues?" he demanded, when he found, that, as usual with the subject of this examination, he was as little intimidated by his present frown, as mov'd by any apprehensions of the future.

"Honesty lies deeper than the skin."

"It is so. Now let my father hear me. Mahtoree has but one tongue, the gray-head, has many. They may be all straight and none of them forked. A Sioux is no more than a Sioux, but a Pale face is every thing! He can talk to the Pawnee, and the Konza and the Omahaw, and he can talk to his own people."

"Ay, there are linguisters in the settlements, that can do still more. But what profits it all. The Master of Life has an ear for every language!"

"The gray-head has done wrong. He has said one thing when he meant another. He has looked before him with his eyes, and behind him with his mind. He has ridden the horse of a Sioux too hard. He has been the friend of the Pawnee, and the enemy of my people."

"Teton, I am your prisoner. Though my words are white, they will not complain. Act your will."

"No; Mahtoree will not make a white hair, red. My father is free. The Prairie is open on every side of him. But before the gray-head turns his back on the Siouxes let him look well at them, that he may tell his own Chief how great is a Dahcotah."

"I am not in a hurry to go on my path. You see a man with a white head, and no woman, Teton; therefore shall I not run myself out of breath to tell the nations of the Prairie what the Siouxes are doing."

"It is good. My Father has smok'd with the chiefs at many Councils," returned Mahtoree, who now thought himself sufficiently sure of the other's favor to go more directly to his object. "Mahtoree will speak with the tongue, of his very dear friend and father. A young pale-face will listen when an old man of that nation opens his mouth. Go. My father will make what a poor Indian says, fit for a white ear."

"Speak aloud," said the trapper, who readily understood the metaphorical manner in which the Teton expressed a desire that he should become an interpreter of his words, into the English language; "speak, my young men, listen. Now Captain, and you, too, friend bee-hunter, prepare yourselves to meet the deviltries of this savage, with the stout hearts of white warriors. If you find yourselves giving way under his threats, just turn your eyes on that noble looking Pawnee, whose time is measured with a hand, as niggardly as that with which a trader in the towns gives forth the fruits of the Lord, inch by inch, in order to satisfy his covetousness. A single look at the boy, will set you both up, in resolution."

"My brother has turned his eyes on the wrong path," interrupted Mahtoree, with a complacency that betrayed how unwilling he was to offend his intended interpreter.

"The Dahcotah will speak to my young men!"

"After he has sung in the ear of the 'flower of the pale faces.' "

"The Lord forgive the desperate villain!" exclaimed the old man in English. "There are none so tender, or so young, or so innocent as to escape his ravenous wishes. But hard words, and cold looks will profit nothing, therefore it will be wise to speak him fair. Let Mahtoree open his mouth."

"Would my father cry out, that the women and children

should hear the wisdom of Chiefs! We will go into the lodge and whisper."

As the Teton ended he pointed significantly towards a tent, vividly emblazoned with the history of one of his own boldest and most commended exploits, and which stood a little apart from the rest, as if to denote it was the residence of some privileged individual of the band. The shield and quiver at its entrance were richer than common, and the high distinction of a fusee, attested the importance of its proprietor. In every other particular, it was rather distinguished by signs of poverty than of wealth. The domestic utensils were fewer in number and simpler in their forms, than those to be seen about the openings of the meanest lodges, nor was there a single one of those high prized articles of civilized life, which were occasionally bought of the traders, in bargains that bore so hard on the ignorant natives. All these had been bestowed, as they had been acquired, by the generous chief on his subordinates to purchase an influence, that might render him the master of their lives and persons, a species of wealth that was certainly more noble in itself, and far dearer to his ambition.

The old man well knew this to be the lodge of Mahtoree, and in obedience to the sign of the chief, he held his way towards it with slow and reluctant steps. But there were others present, who were equally interested in the approaching conference, whose apprehensions were not to be so easily suppressed. The watchful eyes and jealous ears of Middleton had taught him enough to fill his soul with horrible forebodings. With an incredible effort, he succeeded in gaining his feet, and called aloud to the retiring trapper—

"I conjure you, old man, if the love you bore my parents was more than words, or if the love you bear your God is that of a Christian man, utter not a syllable that may wound the ear of that innocent."

Exhausted in spirit and fettered in limbs, he then fell, like an inanimate log to the earth, where he lay like one dead.

Paul had however, caught the clue, and completed the exhortation, in his peculiar manner.

"Harkee, old trapper," he shouted vainly endeavoring at the same time to make a gesture of defiance with his hand, "if you ar' about to play the interpreter speak such words to the ears of that damnable savage, as becomes a white man to use, and a heathen to hear. Tell him from me, that if he does or says the thing that is uncivil, to the girl called Nelly Wade, that I'll curse him with my dying breath; that I'll pray for all good Christians in Kentucky to curse him; sitting and standing; eating and drinking; fighting, praying, or at horse-races; in-doors and out-doors; in summer or winter or in the month of March; in short I'll—ay, it ar' a fact morally true that I'll finally haunt him, if the ghost of a pale-face can contrive to lift itself from a grave made by the hands of a red-skin."

Having thus vented the most terrible denunciation he could devise, and the one, which in the eyes of the honest bee-hunter there seem'd the greatest likelihood of his being able to put in execution, he was obliged to await the fruits of his threat, with that resignation which would be apt to govern a western border man, who in addition to the prospects just named, had the advantage of contemplating them in fetters and bondage. We shall not detain the narrative, to relate the quaint morals with which he next endeavored to cheer the drooping spirits of his more sensitive companion, or the occasional pithy and peculiar benedictions that he pronounced on all the bands of the Dahcotahs, commencing with those whom he accused of stealing, or murdering on the banks of the distant Mississippi, and concluding, in terms of suitable energy, with the Teton tribe. The latter more than once received, from his lips curses as sententious and as complicated as that celebrated anathema of the church, for a knowledge of which most unlettered Protestants are indebted to the pious researches of the worthy Tristram Shandy. But as Middleton recovered from his exhaustion he was fain to appease the boisterous temper of his associate, by admonishing him of the uselessness of such denunciations, and of the possibility of their hastening the very evil he deprecated, by irritating the resentments of a race, who were sufficiently fierce and lawless even, in their most pacific moods.

In the mean time the trapper and the Sioux chief pursued their way to the lodge. The former had watched, with painful interest the expression of Mahtoree's eye, while the words of Middleton and Paul were pursuing their footsteps, but the mien of the Indian was far too much restrained and self-guarded to permit the smallest of his emotions to escape through any of those ordinary outlets, by which the condition of the human volcano is commonly betrayed. His look was fastened on the little habitation they approached, and, for the moment, his thoughts appeared to brood alone on the purposes of this extraordinary visit.

The appearance of the interior of the lodge corresponded with its exterior. It was larger than most of the others, more finished in its form and finer in its materials, but there its superiority ceased. Nothing could be more simple and republican than the form of living that the ambitious and powerful Teton chose to exhibit to the eyes of his people. A choice collection of weapons for the chace, some three or four medals bestowed by the traders and political agents of the Canadas as a homage to, or rather as an acknowledgement of his rank, with a few of the most indispensable articles of personal accommodation, composed its furniture. It abounded in neither venison, nor the wild beef of the Prairies, its crafty owner, having well understood that the liberality of a single individual, would be abundantly rewarded by the daily contributions of a band. Although as pre-eminent in the chase, as in war, a deer or a buffaloe was never seen to enter whole into his lodge. In return, an animal was rarely brought into the encampment, that did not contribute to support the family of Mahtoree. But the policy of the chief seldom permitted more to remain, than sufficed for the wants of the day, perfectly assured that all must suffer, before hunger, the bane of savage life, could lay its fell fangs on so important a victim.

Immediately beneath the favorite bow of the chief, and encircled in a sort of magical ring, of spears, shields, lances and arrows, all of which had in their time done good service, was suspended the mysterious and sacred medicine bag. It was highly wrought in wampum, and profusely ornamented, with beads, and porcupine's quills, after the most cunning devices of Indian ingenuity. The peculiar freedom of Mahtoree's religious creed, has been more than once intimated, and by a singular species of contradiction he appeared to have lavished his attentions on this emblem of a supernatural agency, in a degree that was precisely inverse to his faith. It was merely the manner in which the Sioux imitated the well known expedient of the Pharisees "in order that they might be seen of men."

The tent had not, however, been entered by its owner since his return from the recent expedition. As the reader has already anticipated it had been made the prison of Inez and Ellen. The bride of Middleton was seated on a simple couch of sweet scented herbs, covered with skins. She had already suffered so much, and witnessed so many wild and unlooked for events, within the short space of her captivity, that every additional misfortune fell with a diminished force on her, seemingly, devoted head. Her cheeks were bloodless, her dark, and usually animated eye, was contracted in an expression of settled concern and her form appeared shrinking and sensitive, nearly to extinction. But in the midst of these evidences of natural weakness, there were at times such an air of pious resignation, such gleams of meek but holy hope, lighting her countenance, as might well have rendered it a question whether the hapless captive was most a subject of pity, or of admiration. All the precepts of Father Ignatius were riveted in her faithful memory, and not a few of his pious visions were floating before her imagination. Sustained by so sacred resolutions, the mild, the patient, and the confiding girl was bowing her head to this new stroke of Providence with the same sort of meekness as she would have submitted to any other prescribed penitence for her sins, though nature, at moments, warred powerfully, with so compelled a humility.

On the other hand, Ellen had exhibited far more of the woman, and consequently of the passions of the world. She had wept until her eyes were swollen and red. Her cheeks were flushed and angry, and her whole mien was distinguished by an air of spirit and resentment that was not a little, however, qualified by apprehensions for the future. In short there was that about the eye, and step of the betrothed of Paul, which gave a warranty, that should happier times arrive, and the constancy of the bee-hunter finally meet with its reward, he would possess a partner every way, worthy to cope with his own thoughtless and buoyant temperament.

There was still another, and a third figure in that little knot of females. It was the youngest, the most highly gifted, and, until now, the most favored of the wives of the Teton. Her charms had not been without the most powerful attraction in the eyes of her husband, until they had so unexpectedly opened on the surpassing loveliness of a woman of the Pale faces. From that hapless moment the graces, the attachment, the fidelity of the young Indian had lost their power to please. Still the complexion of Tachechana, though less dazzling than that of her rival, was, for her race, clear and healthy, her hazel eye had the sweetness and playfulness of the antelope's, her voice was soft and joyous as the song of the wren, and her happy laugh was the very melody of the forest. Of all the Sioux girls, Tachechana (or the Fawn) was the lightest-hearted and the most envied. Her father had been a distinguished brave, and her brothers had already left their bones on a distant and dreary war-path. Numberless were the warriors who had sent presents to the lodge of her parents, but none of them were listened to, until a messenger from the great Mahtoree had come. She was his third wife it is true, but she was confessedly the most favored of them all. Their union had existed but two short seasons, and its fruits now lay sleeping at her feet, wrapped in the customary ligatures of skin and bark, which form the swaddlings of an Indian infant.

At the moment when Mahtoree and the trapper arrived at the opening of the lodge, the young Sioux wife, was seated on a simple stool, turning her soft eyes, with looks that varied, like her emotions, with love and wonder from the unconscious child, to those rare beings who had filled her youthful and uninstructed mind with so much admiration and astonishment. Though Inez and Ellen had passed an entire day in her sight, it seemed as if the longings of her curiosity were increasing with each new gaze. She regarded them as beings of an entirely different nature and condition from the females of the Prairie. Even the mystery of their complicated attire had its secret influence on her simple mind, though it was the grace and charm of sex, to which nature has made every people so sensible, that most attracted her admiration. But while her ingenuous disposition freely admitted the superiority of the strangers, over the less brilliant attractions of the Dahcotah maidens, she had seen no reason, to deprecate their advantages. The visit that she was now about to receive was the first which her husband had made to the tent since his return from the recent inroad, and he was ever present to her thoughts, as a successful warrior, who was not ashamed, in the moments of inaction, to admit the softer feelings of a father and a husband.

We have every where endeavored to show, that, while Mahtoree was in all essentials a warrior of the Prairies, he was much in advance of his people, in those acquirements which announce the dawnings of civilization. He had held frequent communion with the traders and troops of the Canadas, and the intercourse had unsettled many of those wild opinions which were his birth-right, without perhaps substituting any others, of a nature sufficiently definite to be profitable. His reasoning was rather subtle than true and his philosophy far more audacious than profound. Like thousands of more enlightened beings who fancy they are able to go through the trials of human existence without any other support than their own resolutions, his morals were accommodating, and his motive, selfish. These several characteristics will be understood always with reference to the situation of the Indian, though little apology is needed for finding resemblances between men who essentially possess the same nature, however it may be modified by circumstances.

Notwithstanding the presence of Inez and Ellen the entrance of the Teton warrior into the lodge of his favorite wife was made with the tread and mien of a master. The step of his moccasin was noiseless, but the rattling of his bracelets and of the silver ornaments of his leggings, sufficed to announce his approach, as he push'd aside the skin covering of the opening of the tent, and stood in the presence of its inmates. A faint cry of pleasure burst from the lips of Tachechana, but the emotion was instantly suppressed in that subdued demeanor which better became a matron of her tribe. Instead of returning the stolen glance of his youthful, and secretly rejoicing wife, Mahtoree mov'd to the couch occupied by his prisoners, and placed himself at his ease, before them in the haughty upright attitude of an Indian chief. The old man had glided past him, and already taken a position suited to the office he had been commanded to fill.

Surprise kept the females silent and nearly breathless. Though accustomed to the sight of savage warriors, in the horrid panoply of their profession, there was something so startling in the entrance, and so audacious in the look of their conqueror, that the eyes of both sunk to the earth under a feeling of terror and embarrassment. Then Inez recovered herself, and addressing the trapper, she demanded with the dignity of an offended gentlewoman, though with her accustomed grace, to what circumstance they owed this extraordinary and unexpected visit. The old man hesitated, but clearing his throat, like one who was about to make an effort to which he was little used, he ventured on the following reply—

"Lady," he said, "a savage is a savage, and you are not to look for the uses and formalities of the settlements on a bleak and windy Prairie. As these Indians would say, fashions and courtesies are things so light, that they would blow away. As for myself, though a man of the forest, I have seen the ways of the great, in my time, and I am not to learn that they differ from the ways of the lowly. I was long a serving man in my youth, not one of your beck and nod runners about a household, but a man that went through the servitude of the forest with his officer, and well do I know, in what manner to approach the wife of a Captain. Now, had I the ordering of this visit, I would first have hemm'd aloud at the door, in order that you might hear that strangers were coming, and then I—"

"The manner is indifferent," interrupted Inez, too anxious to await the prolix explanations of the old man. "Why is the visit made."

"Therein shall the savage speak for himself. The daughters of the Pale faces, wish to know, why the Great Teton has entered his lodge?"

Mahtoree regarded his interrogator with a surprise which show'd how extraordinary he deemed the question; then placing himself in a posture of condescension, after a moment's delay, he answered—

"Sing in the ears of the dark-eye. Tell her that the lodge of Mahtoree is very large, and that it is not full. She shall find room in it; and none shall be greater than she. Tell the light hair, that she too may stay in the lodge of a brave, and eat of his venison. Mahtoree is a great chief. His hand is never shut."

"Teton," returned the trapper, shaking his head in evidence of the strong disapprobation with which he heard this language, "the tongue of a red-skin must be coloured white, before it can make music in the ears of a Pale-face. Should your words be spoken, my daughters would shut their ears, and Mahtoree would seem a trader, to their eyes. Now listen to what comes from a gray-head, and then speak accordingly. My people is a mighty people: The sun rises on their eastern, and sets on their western border. The land is filled with bright-eyed and laughing girls, like these you see, ay. Teton, I tell no lie," observing his auditor to start with an air of distrust; "bright-eyed and pleasant to behold, as these before you."

"Has my father a hundred wives!" interrupted the savage, laying a finger on the shoulder of the trapper, with a look of curious interest in the reply.

"No, Dahcotah; the Master of Life has said to me, 'live alone.' Your lodge shall be the forest, the roof of your wigwam the clouds. But though never bound in the secret faith which, in my nation, ties one man to one woman, often have I seen the workings of that kindness which brings the two together. Go, into the regions of my people. You will see the daughters of the land, fluttering through the Towns, like many coloured and joyful birds in the season of blossoms, you will meet them singing and rejoicing along the great paths of the country and you will hear the woods ringing with their laughter. They are very excellent to behold, and the young men find pleasure in looking at them."

"Hugh!" ejaculated the attentive Mahtoree.

"Ay, well may you put faith in what you hear, for it is no lie. But when a youth has found a maiden to please him, he speaks to her in a voice so soft that none else can hear. He does not say 'my lodge is empty, and there is room for another'; but, 'shall I build, and will the virgin show me near what spring she would dwell?' His voice is sweeter than honey from the locust, and goes into the ear thrilling like the song of a wren. Therefore if my brother wishes his words to be heard, he must speak with a white tongue."

Mahtoree pondered deeply and in a wonder that he did not attempt to conceal. It was reversing all the order of society, and, according to his established opinions, endangering the dignity of a chief for a warrior thus to humble himself before a woman. But, as Inez sat before him, reserved, and imposing in air, utterly unconscious of his object and least of all suspecting the true purport of so extraordinary a visit, the savage felt the influence of a manner, to which he was unaccustomed. Bowing his head, in acknowledgment of his error, he stepp'd a little back, and placing himself in an attitude of easy dignity he began to speak with the confidence of one who had been no less distinguished for eloquence, than for deeds in arms, keeping his eyes riveted on the unconscious bride of Middleton he proceeded in the following words.

"I am a man with a red-skin, but my eyes are dark. They have been open since many snows. They have seen many things. They know a brave from a coward. When a boy I saw nothing but the bison and the deer. I went to the hunts and I saw the cougar and the bear. This made Mahtoree a man. He talk'd with his mother no more, his ears were open to the wisdom of the old men. They told him every thing, they told him of the Big-knives. He went on the war-path. He was then the last; now, he is the first. What Dahcotah dare say he will go before Mahtoree into the hunting grounds of the Pawnees. The Chiefs met him at their doors and they said, my son is without a home. They gave him their lodges, they gave him their riches, and they gave him their daughters. Then Mahtoree became a chief, as his fathers had been. He struck the warriors of all the nations, and he could have chosen wives from the Pawnees, the Omahaws and the Konzas. But he looked at the hunting ground and not at his village. He thought a horse was pleasanter than a Dahcotah girl. But he found a flower on the Prairies, and he pluck'd it, and brought it into his lodge. He forgets that he is the master of a single horse. He gives them all to the stranger, for Mahtoree is not a thief; he will only keep the flower he found on the Prairie. Her feet are very tender. She cannot walk to the door of her father, she will stay in the lodge of a valiant warrior for ever."

When he had finished this extraordinary address, the Teton awaited to have it translated, with the air of a suitor who entertained no very disheartening doubts of his success. The trapper had not lost a syllable of the speech, and he now prepared himself to render it into English, in such a manner as should leave its principal idea even more obscure than in the original. But as his reluctant lips were in the act of parting, Ellen lifted a finger, and with a keen glance from her quick eye at the still attentive Inez, she interrupted him.

"Spare your breath," she said; "all that a savage says is not to be repeated before a Christian Lady."

Inez started, blushed, and bowed with an air of reserve, as she coldly thanked the old man for his intentions and observed that she could now wish to be alone.

"My daughters have no need of ears to understand what a great Dahcotah says," returned the trapper, addressing himself to the expectant Mahtoree. "The look he has given and the signs he has made, are enough. They understand him. They wish to think of his words; for the children of great braves, such as their fathers are, do nothing without much thought."

With this explanation, so flattering to the energy of his eloquence, and so promising to his future hopes, the Teton was every way content. He made the customary ejaculation of assent, and prepared to retire. Saluting the females in the cold, but dignified manner of his people, he drew his robe about him, and moved from the spot where he had stood, with an air of ill-concealed triumph.

But there had been a stricken, though a motionless and unobserved auditor of the foregoing scene. Not a syllable had fallen from the lips of the long and anxiously expected husband, that had not gone directly to the heart of his unoffending wife. In this manner had he wooed her from the lodge of her father, and it was to listen to similar pictures of the renown and deeds of the greatest brave in her tribe, that she had shut her ears to the tender tales of so many of the Sioux youths.

As the Teton turned to leave his lodge, in the manner just mentioned, he found this unexpected and half-forgotten object before him. She stood, in the humble guise and with the shrinking air of an Indian girl, holding the pledge of their former love in her arms, directly in his path. Starting, the chief regained the marble-like indifference of countenance which distinguished in so remarkable a degree the restrained or more artificial expression of his features, and signed to her, with an air of authority, to give place.

"Is not Tachechana the daughter of a chief!" demanded a subdued voice, in which pride struggled with anguish; " were not her brothers, braves!"

"Go. The men are calling their partisan. He has no ears for a woman."

"No," replied the supplicant; "it is not the voice of Tachechana that you hear, but this boy, speaking with the tongue of his mother. He is the son of a chief, and his words will go up to his father's ears. Listen to what he says. When was Mahtoree hungry, and Tachechana had not food for him. When did he go on the path of the Pawnees and find it empty, that my mother did not weep. When did he come back with the marks of their blows, that she did not sing. What Sioux girl has given a brave a son like me. Look at me, well, that you may know me. My eyes are the eagle's. I look at the sun and laugh. In a little time, the Dahcotahs will follow me to the hunts and on the war-path. Why does my father turn his eyes from the woman that gives me milk. Why has he so soon forgotten the daughter of a mighty Sioux."

There was a single instant, as the exulting father suffered his cold eye to wander to the face of his laughing boy, that the stern nature of the Teton seemed touched. But shaking off the grateful sentiment, like one who would gladly be rid of any painful because reproachful emotion, he laid his hand calmly on the arm of his wife, and led her directly in front of Inez. Pointing to the sweet countenance that was beaming on her own, with a look of tenderness and commiseration, he paused, to allow his wife to contemplate a loveliness, which was quite as excellent to her ingenuous mind, as it had proved dangerous to the character of her faithless husband. When he thought abundant time had passed to make the contrast sufficiently striking, he suddenly raised a small mirror that dangled at her breast, an ornament he had himself bestowed, in an hour of fondness, as a compliment to her beauty, and placed her own dark image in its place. Wrapping his robe, again, about him the Teton motioned to the trapper to follow, and stalked haughtily from the lodge, muttering as he went.

"Mahtoree is very wise! What nation has so great a chief as the Dahcotahs."

Tachechana stood frozen into a statue of humility. Her mild, and usually joyous countenance worked, as if the struggle within was about to dissolve the connexion between her soul and that more material part, whose deformity was becoming so loathsome. Inez and Ellen were utterly ignorant of the nature of her interview with her husband, though the quick and sharpened wits of the latter led her to suspect a truth to which the entire innocence of the former furnished no clue. They were both, however, about to tender those sympathies which are so natural to and so graceful in the sex, when their necessity seemed suddenly to cease. The convulsions in the features of the young Sioux disappeared, and her countenance became cold and rigid, like chiselled stone. A single expression of subdued anguish which had made its impression on a brow that had rarely before contracted with sorrow, alone remained. It was never removed, in all the changes of seasons, fortunes and years which in the vicissitudes of a suffering, female, savage life she was subsequently doomed to endure. As in the case of a premature blight, let the plant quicken and revive, as it may, the effects of that withering touch were always present.

Tachechana first stripped her person of every vestige of those rude, but highly prized ornaments, which the liberality of her husband, had been wont to lavish on her, and she tendered them, meekly and without a murmur, as an offering to the superiority of Inez. The bracelets were forced from her wrists, the complicated mazes of beads from her leggings and the broad silver band from her brow. Then she paused long and painfully. But it would seem that the resolution she had once adopted was not to be conquered by the lingering emotions of any affection, however natural. The boy, himself, was next laid at the feet of her supposed rival, and well might the self abased wife of the Teton believe that the burthen of her sacrifice was now full.

While Inez and Ellen stood regarding these several strange movements with eyes of wonder, a low, soft, musical voice was heard saying, in a language that to them was unintelligible—

"A strange tongue will tell my boy the manner to become a man. He will hear sounds that are new, but he will learn them and forget the voice of his mother. It is the will of the Wahcondah, and a Sioux girl should not complain. Speak to him softly, for his ears are very little. When he is big, your words may be louder. Let him not be a girl, for very sad is the life of a woman. Teach him to keep his eyes on the men. Show him how to strike them that do him wrong, and let him never forget to return blow for blow. When he goes to hunt, the 'flower of the Pale faces'," she concluded, using in bitterness the metaphor which had been supplied by the imagination of her truant husband, " will whisper softly in his ears, that the skin of his mother was red, and that she was once the Fawn of the Dahcotahs."

Tachechana pressed a kiss on the lips of her son, and withdrew to the farther side of the lodge. Here she drew her light calicoe robe over her head, and took her seat, in token of humility on the naked earth. All efforts to attract her attention were fruitless. She neither heard remonstrances nor felt the touch. Once or twice her voice rose, in a sort of wailing song, from beneath her quivering mantle, but it never mounted into the wildness of savage music. In this manner she remained unseen for hours, while events were occurring without the lodge which not only materially changed the complexion of her own fortunes, but left a lasting and deep impression on the future movements of the wandering Sioux.

Chapter XXVII

"I'll no swaggerers: I am in good name and fame with the very best:—Shut the door;—There come no swaggerers here: I have not lived all this while, to have swaggering now: —shut the door I pray you."

2 Henry IV, II.iv.75–78.

MAHTOREE encountered at the door of his lodge, Ishmael, Abiram and Esther. The first glance of his eye, at the countenance of the heavy-moulded squatter, served to tell the cunning Teton, that the treacherous truce he had made with these dupes of his superior sagacity was in some danger of a violent termination.

"Look you here, old gray-beard," said Ishmael, seizing the trapper, and whirling him round, as if he had been a top, "that I'm tired of carrying on a discourse, with fingers and thumbs, instead of a tongue, ar' a natural fact; so you'll play linguister, and put my words into Indian, without much caring whether they suit the stomach of a red-skin, or not."

"Say on, friend," calmly, returned the trapper. "They shall be given as plainly as you send them."

"Friend!" repeated the squatter, eyeing the other, for an instant with an expression of indefinable meaning. "But it is no more than a word, and sounds break no bones, and survey no farms. Tell this thieving Sioux, then, that I come to claim the conditions of our solemn bargain, made at the foot of the rock."

When the trapper had rendered his meaning into the Sioux language, Mahtoree demanded with an air of surprise—

"Is my brother cold? buffalo skins are plenty. Is he hungry? let my young men carry venison into his lodges."

The squatter elevated his clenched fist in a menacing manner, and struck it with violence on the palm of his open hand, by way of confirming his determination, as he answered.

"Tell the deceitful liar, I have not come like a beggar to pick his bones, but like a free man asking for his own, and have it I will—and moreover tell him I claim that you, too, miserable sinner as you ar', should be given up to justice.

There's no mistake. My prisoner, my niece, and you. I demand the three at his hands, according to a sworn agreement."

The immovable old man smiled, with an expression of singular intelligence, as he answered—

"Friend squatter, you ask what few men would be willing to grant. You would first cut the tongue from the mouth of the Teton, and then the heart from his bosom!"

"It is little, that Ishmael Bush regards, who or what is damaged in claiming his own. Put you the questions, in straight-going Indian, and when you speak of yourself, make such a sign as a white man will understand, in order that I may know there is no foul-play."

The trapper laughed in his silent fashion, and muttered a few words to himself, before he addressed the chief.

"Let the Dahcotah open his ears very wide," he said, "that big words may have room to enter. His friend the Big-knife comes with an empty hand, and he says that the Teton must fill it."

"Wagh. Mahtoree is a rich chief. He is master of the Prairies."

"He must give the dark-hair!"

The brow of the chief contracted in an ominous frown, that threatened instant destruction to the audacious squatter, but as suddenly recollecting his policy, he craftily replied—

"A girl is too light for the hand of such a brave. I will fill it with buffaloes."

"He says, that he has need of the light-hair, too; who has his blood in her veins."

"She shall be the wife of Mahtoree; then the Long-knife will be the Father of a chief!"

"And, me," continued the trapper, making one of those expressive signs by which the natives communicate, with nearly the same facility as with their tongues, and turning to the squatter, at the same time, in order that the latter might see he dealt fairly by him, "he asks for a miserable and worn out trapper!"

The Dahcotah threw his arm over the shoulder of the old man, with an air of great affection, before he replied to this third and last demand.

"My friend is old," he said, "and cannot travel far. He will stay, with the Tetons, that they may learn wisdom from his words. What Sioux has a tongue, like my Father! No. Let his words be very soft, but let them be very clear. Mahtoree will give skins, and buffaloes. He will give the young men of the Pale-faces wives, but he cannot give away any who live in his own lodge."

Perfectly satisfied, himself, with this laconick reply, the chief was moving towards his expecting counsellors, when, suddenly returning, he interrupted the translation of the trapper, by adding—

"Tell the Great Buffaloe," (a name by which the Tetons had already christened Ishmael), "that Mahtoree has a hand which is always open. See," he added pointing to the hard and wrinkled visage of the attentive Esther, "his wife is too old for so great a chief. Let him put her out of his lodge. Mahtoree loves him as a brother. He *is* his brother. He shall have the youngest wife of the Teton. Tachechana, the pride of the Sioux girls, shall cook his venison, and many braves will look at him with longing minds. Go. A Dahcotah is always generous."

The singular coolness with which the Teton concluded this audacious proposal confounded even the practised trapper. He stared after the retiring form of the Indian with an astonishment he did not care to conceal, nor did he renew his attempt at interpretation, until the person of Mahtoree was blended with the cluster of warriors, who had so long and with so characteristic patience awaited his return.

"The Teton chief has spoken very plainly," the old man continued. "He will not give you the lady, to whom the Lord in Heaven, he knows you have no claim, unless it be such as the wolf has to the lamb. He will not give you, the child you call your niece; and therein, I acknowledge that I am far from certain he has the same justice on his side. Moreover, neighbour squatter, he flatly denies your demand for me, miserable and worthless as I am, nor do I think he has been unwise in so doing, seeing that I should have many reasons against journeying far in your company. But he makes you an offer which it is right and convenient you should know. The Teton says through me, who am no more than a mouth-piece and therein, not answerable for the sin of his words, but he says that as this good woman is getting past the comely age, it is reasonable for you to tire of such a wife. He therefore tells you to turn her out of your lodge, and when it is empty, he will send his own favorite, or rather she that was his favorite, the 'Skipping Fawn' as the Siouxes call her, to fill her place. You see, neighbor, though the red-skin is minded to keep your property, he is willing to give you wherewithal to make yourself some return."

Ishmael listened to these replies, to his several demands, with that species of gathering indignation, with which the dullest tempers mount into the most violent paroxysms of rage. He even affected to laugh at the conceit of exchanging his long tried partner for the more flexible support of the youthful Tachechana, though his voice was hollow and unnatural in the effort. But Esther was far from giving the proposal so facetious a reception. Lifting her voice to its most audible key, she broke forth, after catching her breath like one who had been in some imminent danger of strangulation, as follows—

"Hoity-toity! who set an Indian up for a maker and breaker of the rights of wedded wives! Does he think a woman is a beast of the Prairie that she is to be chased from a village, by dog and gun. Let the bravest squaw of them all come forth and boast of her doings, can she show such a brood as mine! A wicked tyrant is that thieving red-skin, and a bold rogue I warrant me. He would be captain in-doors, as well as out! A honest woman is no better, in his eyes, than one of your broom-stick jumpers. And you, Ishmael Bush, the father of seven sons and so many comely daughters, to open *your* sinful mouth except to curse him! Would ye disgrace colour, and family, and nation, by mixing white blood with red, and would ye be the parent of a race of mules. The Devil has often tempted you, my man, but never before has he set so cunning a snare as this. Go, back among your children, friend, go, and remember that you are not a prowling bear but a Christian man, and thank God, that you ar' a lawful husband."

The clamor of Esther was anticipated by the judicious trapper. He had easily foreseen that her meek temper would overflow at so scandalous a proposal as repudiation, and he, now, profited by the tempest to retire to a place, where he was at least safe from any immediate violence on the part of her less excited, but certainly more dangerous husband. Ishmael, who had made his demands with a stout determination to enforce them, was diverted by the wordy torrent, like many a more obstinate husband, from his purpose, and in order to appease a jealousy, that resembled the fury with which the bear defends her cubs, was fain to retire to a distance from the lodge that was known to contain the unoffending object of the sudden uproar.

"Let your copper-coloured minx come forth, and show her tawney beauty before the face of a woman, who has heard more than one church bell, and seen a power of real quality," cried Esther, flourishing her hand in triumph, as she drove Ishmael and Abiram before her, like two truant boys towards their own encampment. "I warrant me, I warrant me, here is one who would shortly talk her down. Never think to tarry here, my men, never think to shut an eye in a camp, through which the devil walks as openly as if he were a gentleman, and was sure of his welcome. Here, you, Abner, Enoch, Jesse, where ar' ye gotten to. Put to, put to. If that weak-minded, soft-feeling man your father, eats or drinks again in this neighborhood, we shall see him poisoned with the craft of the red-skins. Not that I care, I, who comes into my place when it is once lawfully empty, but, Ishmael, I never thought that you, who have had one woman with a white skin, would find pleasure in looking on a brazen—ay, that she is copper, ar' a fact you cant deny, and I warrant me brazen enough is she too."

Against this ebullition of wounded female pride the experienced husband made no other head, than by an occasional exclamation which he intended to be the precursor of a simple asseveration of his own innocence. The fury of the woman would not be appeased. She listened to nothing but her own voice, and consequently nothing was heard, but her mandates to depart.

The squatter had collected his beasts and loaded his wagons as a measure of precaution, before proceeding to the extremity he contemplated. Esther, consequently found every thing favorable to her wishes. The young men stared at each other, as they witnessed the extraordinary excitement of their mother, but took little interest in an event, which in the course of their experience had found so many parallels. By command of their father, the tents were thrown into the vehicles, as a sort of reprisal for the want of faith in their late ally, and then the train left the spot, in its usual, listless and sluggish order.

As a formidable division of well-armed borderers protected the rear of the retiring party, the Siouxes saw it depart without manifesting the smallest evidence of surprise, or resentment. The savage, like the tiger, rarely makes his attack on an enemy who expects him, and if the warriors of the Tetons meditated any hostility, it was in the still and patient manner with which the feline beasts watch for the incautious moment, in order to ensure the blow. The Councils of Mahtoree, however, on whom so much of the policy of his people depended, lay deep in the depository of his own thoughts. Perhaps he rejoiced at so easy a manner of getting rid of claims so troublesome, perhaps he awaited a fitting time to exhibit his power, or it even might be that matters of so much greater importance were pressing on his mind, that it had not leisure to devote any of its faculties to an event of so much indifference.

But it would seem, that while Ishmael made such a concession to the awakened feelings of Esther, he was far from abandoning his original intentions. His train followed the course of the river for a mile, and then it came to a halt, on the brow of the elevated land, and in a place which afforded the necessary facilities. Here he, again, pitch'd his tents, unharnessed his teams, sent his cattle on the bottom, and in short made all the customary preparations to pass the night with the same coolness and deliberation, as if he had not hurled an irritating defiance into the teeth of his dangerous neighbors.

In the mean time the Tetons proceeded to the more regular business of the hour. A fierce and savage joy had existed in the camp from the instant when it had been announced that their own Chief was returning with the long dreaded and hated Partizan of their enemies. For many hours the crones of the tribe had been going from lodge to lodge, in order to stimulate the tempers of the warriors to such a pass, as might leave but little room for mercy. To one, they spoke of a son whose scalp was drying in the smoke of a Pawnee lodge. To another, they enumerated his own scars, his disgraces and defeats. With a third, they dwelt on his losses of skins and horses, and a fourth was reminded of vengeance, by a significant question concerning some flagrant adventure in which he was known to have been a sufferer.

By these means the men had been so far excited as to have assembled, in the manner already related, though it still remained a matter of doubt how far they intended to carry their revenge. A variety of opinions prevailed on the policy of executing their prisoners, and Mahtoree had suspended the discussions, in order to ascertain how far the measure might propitiate, or retard his own particular views. Hitherto, the consultations had merely been preliminary, with a design that each chief might discover the number of supporters his particular views would be likely to obtain when the important subject should come before a more solemn council of the tribe. The moment for the latter had now arrived, and the preparations were made with a dignity and solemnity suited to the momentous interests of the occasion.

With a refinement in cruelty that none but an Indian would have imagined, the place selected for this grave deliberation was immediately about the post, to which the most important of its subjects, was attached. Middleton and Paul were brought, in their bonds, and laid at the feet of the Pawnee, and then the men began to take their places according to their several claims to distinction. As warrior after warrior approached, he seated himself in the wide circle, with a mien as composed and thoughtful as if his mind were actually in a condition to deal out justice, tempered as it should be, with the heavenly quality of mercy. A place was reserved for three or four of the principal chiefs, and a few of the oldest of the women, as withered, as age, exposure, hardships and lives of savage passions could make them, thrust themselves into the foremost circle, with a temerity to which they were impelled by their insatiable desire for cruelty, and which nothing but their years and their long tried fidelity to the nation would have excused.

All but the chiefs already named were now in their places. These had delayed their appearance, in the vain hope that their own unanimity might smooth the way to that of their respective factions; for, notwithstanding the superior influence of Mahtoree, his power was to be maintained only by constant appeals to the opinions of his inferiors. As these important personages, at length entered the circle in a body, their sullen looks and clouded brows notwithstanding the time thus given to consultation, sufficiently proclaimed the discontent which reigned among them. The eye of Mahtoree was varying in its expression, from sudden gleams, that seemed to kindle with the burning impulses of his soul, to that cold and guarded steadiness which was thought more peculiarly to become a chief in Council. He took his seat, with the studied simplicity of a demagogue, though the keen and flashing glance that he immediately threw around the silent assembly, betrayed the more predominant temper of a tyrant.

When all were present an aged warrior lighted the great pipe of his people, and blew the smoke towards the four quarters of the heavens. So soon as this propitiatory offering was made, he tendered it, to Mahtoree, who in affected humility passed it to a gray-headed chief by his side. After the influence of the soothing weed had been courted by all, a grave silence succeeded, as if each was not only qualified to, but actually did, think more deeply on the matters before them. Then an old Indian arose, and spoke as follows—

"The eagle at the falls of the endless river was in its egg, many snows after my hand had struck a Pawnee. What my tongue says my eyes have seen. Bohrecheena is very old. The hills have stood longer in their places, than he has been in his tribe, and the rivers were full and empty before he was born; but where is the Sioux that knows it, besides himself. What he says they will hear. If any of his words fall to the ground, they will pick them up, and hold them to their ears. If any blow away in the wind, my young men, who are very nimble, will catch them. Now listen. Since water ran and trees grew, the Sioux has found the Pawnee on his war path. As the cougar loves the antelope, the Dahcotah loves his enemy. When the wolf finds the fawn, does he lie down and sleep? When the Panther sees the doe at the spring, does he shut his eyes? You know that he does not. He drinks too; but it is of blood. A Sioux is a leaping panther, a Pawnee a trembling deer. Let my children hear me. They will find my words good. I have spoken."

A deep, guttural exclamation of assent broke from the lips of all the partisans of Mahtoree, as they listened to this sanguinary advice from one, who was certainly among the most aged men of the nation. That deeply seated love of vengeance, which formed so prominent a feature in their character, was gratified by his metaphorical allusions, and the chief himself augured favorably of the success of his own schemes, by the number of supporters who manifested themselves to be in favor of the counsel of his friend. But still unanimity was far from prevailing. A long and decorous pause was suffered to succeed the words of the first speaker, in order that all might duly deliberate on their wisdom, before another chief took on himself the office of refutation. This second orator, though past the prime of his days was far less aged than the one who had preceded him. He felt the disadvantage of this circumstance, and endeavored to counteract it, as far as possible by the excess of his humility.

"I am but an infant," he commenced, looking furtively around him, in order to detect how far his well established character for prudence and courage contradicted his assertion. "I have lived with the women, since my father has been a man. If my head is getting gray, it is not because I am old. Some of the snow which fell on it, while I have been sleeping on the war-paths, has frozen there, and the hot sun near the Osage villages has not been strong enough, to melt it." A low murmur was heard, expressive of admiration of the services to which he thus artfully alluded. The orator modestly waited for the feeling to subside a little, and then he continued with increasing energy, encouraged by their commendations. "But the eyes of a young brave are good. He can see very far. He is a Lynx. Look at me, well. I will turn my back that you may see both sides of me. Now do you know I am your friend, for you look on a part that a Pawnee never yet saw. Now look at my face; not in this seam, for there your eyes can never see into my spirit. It is a hole cut by a Konza. But here is an opening made by the Wahcondah, through which you may look into the soul. What am I? a Dahcotah, within and without. You know it. Therefore hear me. The blood of every creature on the Prairies is red. Who can tell the spot where a Pawnee was struck, from the place where my young men took a bison? It is of the same colour. The Master of Life made them for each other. He made them alike. But will the grass grow green where a Pale-face is killed? My young men must not think *that* Nation so numerous that it will not miss a warrior. They call them over often, and say, 'where are my sons'? If they miss one, they will send into the Prairies to look for him. If they cannot find him, they will tell their runners to ask for him among the Siouxes. My Brethren, the Big-knives are not fools. There is a mighty medecine of their nation, now, among us. Who can tell how loud is his voice, or how long is his arm—"

The speech of the orator, who was beginning to enter into his subject with warmth, was cut short by the impatient Mahtoree, who suddenly arose, and exclaimed in a voice, in which authority was mingled with contempt, and, at the close with a keen tone of irony, also—

"Let my young men, lead the Evil Spirit of the Pale faces to the Council. My brother, shall see his Medecine, face to face."

A death-like and solemn stillness succeeded this extraordinary interruption. It not only involved a deep offence against the sacred courtesy of debate, but the mandate was likely to brave the unknown power of one of those incomprehensible beings, whom few Indians were enlightened enough, at that day, to regard without reverence, or few hardy enough to oppose. The subordinates, however, obeyed; and Obed was led forth from a lodge, mounted on Asinus, with a ceremony and state which was certainly intended for derision, but which, nevertheless, was greatly enhanced by fear. As they entered the ring, Mahtoree, who had foreseen and had endeavored to anticipate the influence of the Doctor by bringing him into contempt, cast an eye around the assembly, in order to gather his success in the various dark visages by which he was encircled.

Truly nature and art had combined to produce such an

effect from the air and appointments of the naturalist as might have made him the subject of wonder in any place. His head had been industriously shaved, after the most approved fashion of Sioux taste. A gallant scalp-lock, which would probably not have been spared had the Doctor himself been consulted in the matter, was all that remained of an exuberant, and at that particular season of the year, far from uncomfortable head of hair. Thick coats of paint had been laid on the naked poll, and certain fanciful designs, in the same material, had even been extended into the neighborhood of the eyes and mouth, lending to the keen expression of the former, a look of twinkling cunning, and to the dogmatism of the latter not a little of the grimness of necromancy. He had been despoiled of his upper garments, and in their stead, his body was sufficiently protected from the cold, by a fantastickally painted robe of dressed deer skin. As if in mockery of his pursuit, sundry toads, frogs, lizards, butterflies, etc. all duly prepared to take their places, at some future day, in his own private cabinet were attached to the solitary lock on his head, to his ears, and to various other conspicuous parts of his person. If, in addition to the effect produced by these quaint auxiliaries to this costume, we add the portentous and troubled gleamings of doubt, which rendered his visage doubly austere and proclaimed the misgivings of the worthy Obed's mind, as he beheld his personal dignity thus prostrated, and, what was of far greater moment in his eyes, himself led forth, as he firmly believed, to be the victim of some heathenish sacrifice, the reader will find no difficulty in giving credit, to the sensation of awe, that was excited by his appearance, in a band already more than half prepared to worship him, as a powerful agent of the Evil Spirit.

Weucha led Asinus directly into the centre of the circle, and leaving them together, (for the legs of the Naturalist were attached to the beast in such a manner that the two animals might be said to be incorporated and to form a new order,) he withdrew to his proper place, gazing at the conjuror as he retired with a wonder and admiration that were natural to the grovelling dulness of his mind.

The astonishment seemed mutual, between the spectators and the subject of this strange exhibition. If the Tetons contemplated the mysterious attributes of the Medecine, with awe and fear, the Doctor gazed on every side of him, with a mixture of quite as many extraordinary emotions, in which the latter sensation, however, formed no inconsiderable ingredient. Every where his eyes, which just at that moment, possessed a secret magnifying quality, seemed to rest on several dark, savage, and obdurate countenances at once, from none of which could he extract a solitary gleam of sympathy or commiseration. At length his wandering gaze fell on the grave and decent features of the trapper, who with Hector at his feet, stood in the edge of the circle, leaning on that rifle, which he had been permitted, as an acknowledged friend to resume, and apparently musing, on the events that were likely to succeed a Council, marked by so many and such striking ceremonies.

"Venerable venator, or hunter, or trapper," said the disconsolate Obed, "I rejoice greatly in meeting thee, again. I fear that the precious time which had been allotted me, in order to complete a mighty labor, is drawing to a premature close, and I would gladly unburthen my mind to one, who if not a pupil of science, has at least some of the knowledge which civilization imparts to its meanest subjects. Doubtless many and earnest enquiries will be made after my fate, by the learned societies of the world, and perhaps expeditions will be sent into these regions to remove any doubts which may arise on so important a subject. I esteem myself happy, that a man who speaks the vernacular is present, to preserve the record of my end. You will say that after a well spent and glorious life, I died a martyr to science, and a victim to mental darkness. As I expect to be particularly calm and abstracted in my last moments, if you add a few details concerning the fortitude and scholastic dignity with which I met my death, it may serve to encourage future aspirants for similar honour, and assuredly give offence to no one. And now, friend trapper, as a duty I owe to human nature, I will conclude by demanding if all hope has deserted me, or if any means still exist, by which so much valuable information may be rescued from the grasp of ignorance, and preserved to the pages of Natural History."

The old man lent an attentive ear to this melancholy appeal, and, apparently, he reflected on every side of the important question, before he would presume to answer.

"I take it, friend physicianer," he, at length, gravely replied, "that the chances of life and death, in your particular case, depend altogether on the will of Providence, as it may be pleased to manifest it, through the accursed windings of Indian cunning. For my own part, I see no great difference in the main end to be gained, inasmuch, as it can matter no one greatly, yourself excepted, whether you live or die."

"Would you account the fall of a corner stone from the foundations of the edifice of learning, a matter of indifference, to contemporaries, or to posterity!" interrupted Obed. "Besides, my aged associate," he reproachfully added, "the interest that a man has in his own existence, is by no means trifling, however it may be eclipsed by his devotion to more general and philanthropic feelings."

"What I would say is this," resumed the trapper, who was far from understanding all the subtle distinctions, with which his more learned companion so often saw fit to embellish his discourse. "There is but one birth and one death to all things, be it hound, or be it deer—be it red-skin, or be it white. Both are in the hands of the Lord; it being as unlawful for man to strive to hasten the one, as impossible to prevent the other. But I will not say that something may not be done to put the last moment aside, for a while at least; and therefore it is a question that any one has a right to put to his own wisdom, how far he will go, and how much pain he will suffer, to lengthen out a time, that may have been too long already. Many a dreary winter and scorching summer has gone by, since I have turned, to the right hand or to the left, to add an hour to a life that has already stretched beyond four-score years. I keep myself as ready to answer to my name as a soldier, at evening roll-call. In my judgment, if your cases, are left to Indian tempers, the policy of the Great Sioux, will lead his people to sacrifice you all, nor do I put much dependance on his seeming love for me; therefore it becomes a question whether you are ready for such a journey, and if, being ready, whether this is not as good a time to start as another. Should my opinion be asked, thus far will I give it in your favor; that is to say, it is my belief your life has been innocent enough touching any great offences that you may have committed, though honesty compels me to add, that I think all you can lay claim to, on the score of activity in deeds, will not amount to any thing worth naming in the great account."

Obed turned a rueful eye on the calm, philosophic countenance of the other, as he answered with so discouraging a statement of his case, clearing his throat as he did so, in order to conceal the desperate concern which began to beset his faculties, with a vestige of that pride which rarely deserts poor human nature, even in the greatest emergencies.

"I believe, venerable hunter," he replied, "considering the question in all its bearings, and assuming that your theory is just, it will be the safest to conclude that I am not prepared to make so hasty a departure, and that measures of precaution should be, forthwith, resorted to."

"Being in that mind," returned the deliberate trapper, "I will act for you as I would for myself, though as time has begun to roll down the hill with you, I will just advise that you look to your case, speedily, for it may so happen that your name will be heard, when quite as little prepared to answer to it, as now."

With this amicable understanding, the old man drew back, again, into the ring, where he stood musing on the course he should now adopt, with the singular mixture of decision and resignation, that proceeded from his habits and his humility, and which united to form a character in which excessive energy and the most meek submission to the will of Providence were oddly enough combined.

Chapter XXVIII

"The witch, in Smithfield, shall be burned to ashes,
And you three shall be strangled on the gallows."
2 Henry VI, II.iii. 7–8.

THE SIOUXES had awaited the issue of the foregoing dialogue with commendable patience. Most of the band were restrained by the secret awe, with which they regarded the mysterious character of Obed, while a few of the more intelligent chiefs gladly profited by the opportunity to arrange their thoughts for the struggle that was plainly foreseen. Mahtoree, influenced by neither of these feelings, was content to show the trapper how much he conceded to his pleasure, and when the old man discontinued the discourse, he received from the chief, a glance, that was intended to remind him of the patience with which he had awaited his movements. A profound and motionless silence succeeded the short interruption. Then Mahtoree arose, evidently prepared to speak. First placing himself in an attitude of dignity he turned a steady and severe look on the whole assembly. The expression of his eye, however, changed as it glanced across the different countenances of his supporters and of his opponents. To the former the look, though stern was not threatening, while it seemed to tell the latter all the hazards they incurred, in daring to brave the resentment of one so powerful.

Still, in the midst of so much hauteur and confidence, the sagacity and cunning of the Teton did not desert him. When he had thrown the gauntlett as it were, to the whole tribe, and sufficiently asserted his claim to superiority, his mien became more affable and his eye less angry. Then it was that he raised his voice, in the midst of a death-like stillness, varying its tones to suit the changing character of his images and of his eloquence.

"What is a Sioux?" the chief sagaciously began. "He is Ruler of the Prairies, and Master of its beasts. The fishes in the 'river of troubled waters,' know him, and come at his call. He is a fox in Council; an eagle in sight; a grizzly bear in combat. A Dahcotah is a man." After waiting for the low murmur of approbation which followed this flattering portrait of his people to subside, the Teton continued. "What is a Pawnee? A thief, who only steals from women; a red-skin, who is not brave; a hunter, that begs for his venison. In Council, he is a squirrel, hopping from place to place; he is an owl, that only goes on the Prairies at night; in battle, he is an elk, whose legs are long. A Pawnee is a woman." Another pause succeeded, during which a yell of delight broke from several mouths, and a demand was made that the taunting words should be translated by the trapper to the unconscious subject of their biting contempt. The old man took his cue from the eye of Mahtoree, and complied. Hard-Heart listened gravely, and then as if apprised that his time to speak had not arrived, he once more bent his look on the vacant air. The orator watched his countenance with an expression that manifested how inextinguishable was the hatred he felt, for the only chief, far and near, whose fame might advantageously be compared with his own. Though disappointed in not having touched the pride of one, whom he regarded as a boy, he proceeded to what he considered as far more important, to quicken the tempers of the men of his own tribe in order that they might be prepared to work his savage purposes. "If the earth was covered with rats, which are good for nothing," he said, "there would be no room for buffaloes, which give food and clothes to an Indian. If the Prairies were covered with Pawnees, there would be no room for the foot of a Dahcotah. A Loup is a rat, a Sioux a heavy buffaloe. Let the buffaloes tread upon the rats, and make room for themselves.

"My Brothers; a little child has spoken to you. He tells you his hair is not gray, but frozen. That the grass will not grow where a pale face has died! Does he know the colour of the blood of a Big-knife? No; I know he does not; he has never seen it. What Dahcotah besides Mahtoree has ever struck a Pale face? Not one. But Mahtoree must be silent. Every Teton will shut his ears when he speaks. The scalps over his lodge were taken by the women. They were taken by Mahtoree and he is a woman. His mouth is shut, he waits for the feasts to sing among the girls."

Notwithstanding the exclamations of regret and resentment

which followed so abasing a declaration, the chief took his seat, as if determined to speak no more. But the murmurs grew louder and more general, and there were threatening symptoms that the Council would dissolve itself, in confusion, and he arose and resumed his speech, by changing his manner to the fierce and hurried enunciation of a warrior bent on revenge.

"Let my young men go look for Tetao;" he cried, "they will find his scalp, drying in Pawnee smoke. Where is the son of Borecheena? His bones are whiter than the faces of his murderers. Is Mahhah asleep in his lodge? You know it is many moons since he started for the blessed Prairies. Would he were here that he might say of what color was the hand that took his scalp!"

In this strain, the artful chief continued for many minutes, calling those warriors by name, who were known to have met their deaths, in battle with the Pawnees, or in some of those lawless frays which so often occurred between the Sioux bands, and a class of white men, who were but little removed from them, in the qualities of civilization. Time was not given to reflect on the merits or rather the demerits of most of the different individuals to whom he alluded, in consequence of the rapid manner in which he ran over their names, but so cunningly did he time his events, and so thrillingly did he make his appeals, aided as they were by the power of his deep-toned and stirring voice, that each of them struck an answering chord in the breast of some one of his auditors.

It was in the midst of one of his highest flights of eloquence, that a man so aged as to walk with the greatest difficulty entered the very centre of the circle, and took his stand directly in front of the speaker. An ear of great acuteness might possibly have detected that the tones of the orator faltered a little as his flashing look first fell on this unexpected object, though the change was so trifling that none but such as thoroughly knew the parties, would have suspected it. The stranger had once been as distinguished for his beauty and proportions, as had been his eagle eye for its irresistible and terrible glance. But his skin was now wrinkled and his features furrowed with so many scars, as to have obtained for him, half a century before, from the French of the Canadas a title which has been borne by so many of the heroes of France, and which had now been adopted into the language of the wild horde of whom we are writing, as the one most expressive of the deeds of their own brave. The murmur of Le Balafré, that ran through the assembly when he appeared, announced not only his name and the high estimation of his character but how extraordinary his visit was considered. As he neither spoke nor moved, however, the sensation created by his appearance soon subsided, and then every eye was again turned upon the speaker, and every ear once more drunk in the intoxication of his maddening appeals.

It would have been easy to have traced the triumph of Mahtoree, in the reflecting countenances of his auditors. It was not long before a look of ferocity and of revenge was to be seen seated on the grim visages of most of the warriors, and each new and crafty allusion to the policy of extinguishing their enemies, was followed by fresh and less restrained bursts of approbation. In the height of this success, the Teton closed his speech, by a rapid appeal to the pride and hardihood of his native band, and suddenly took his seat.

In the midst of the murmurs of applause which succeeded so remarkable an effort of eloquence, a low, feeble and hollow voice was heard rising in the tumult, as if it rolled from the inmost cavities of the human chest, and gathered strength and energy as it issued into the air. A solemn stillness followed the sounds, and then the lips of the aged man were first seen to move.

"The day of Le Balafré, is near its end," were the first words which were distinctly audible. "He is like a buffaloe on whom the hair will grow no longer. He will soon be ready to leave his lodge, to go in search of another, that is far from the villages of the Siouxes. Therefore what he has to say, concerns not him, but those he leaves behind him. His words are like the fruit on the tree, ripe and fit to be given to chiefs."

"Many snows have fallen since Le Balafré has been found on the war path. His blood has been very hot, but it has had time to cool. The Wahcondah gives him dreams of war, no longer; he sees that it is better to live in peace."

"My Brothers, one foot is turned to the Happy hunting grounds, the other will soon follow; and then an old chief will be seen looking for the prints of his Father's moccasins, that he may make no mistake, but be sure to come before the Master of Life by the same path, as so many good Indians have already travelled. But who will follow? Le Balafré has no son. His oldest has ridden too many Pawnee horses; the bones of the youngest, have been gnawed by Konza dogs! Le Balafré has come to look for a young arm on which he may lean, and to find a son, that when he is gone his lodge may not be empty. Tachechana, the skipping fawn of the Tetons, is too weak to prop a warrior who is old. She looks before her, and not backwards. Her mind is in the lodge of her husband."

The enunciation of the veteran warrior had been calm, but distinct, and decided. His declaration was received in silence, and though several of the chiefs who were in the councils of Mahtoree turned their eyes on their leader, none presumed to oppose so aged and so venerated a brave, in a resolution that was strictly in conformity to the usages of the Nation. The Teton, himself, was content to await the result, with seeming composure, though the gleams of ferocity that played about his eye, occasionally betrayed the nature of those feelings, with which he witnessed a procedure that was likely to rob him of that one of all his intended victims, whom he most hated.

In the mean time, Le Balafré moved with a slow and painful step towards the captives. He stopped before the person of Hard-Heart, whose faultless form, unchanging eye, and lofty mien, he contemplated long, with high and evident satisfaction. Then making a gesture of authority, he awaited until his order had been obeyed, and the youth was released from the post and his bonds, by the same blow of the knife. When the young warrior was led nearer to his dimmed and failing sight, the examination was renewed with strictness of scrutiny, and that admiration, which physical excellence is so apt to excite in the breast of a savage.

"It is good," the wary veteran murmured, when he found that all his skill in the requisites of a brave could detect no blemish, "this is a leaping panther! Does my son speak with the tongue of a Teton?"

The intelligence which lighted the eyes of the captive, betrayed how well he understood the question, but still he was far too haughty to communicate his ideas, through the medium of a language that belonged to a hostile people. Some of the surrounding warriors explained to the old chief, that the captive was a Pawnee-Loup.

"My son opened his eyes on the 'waters of the wolves'," said Le Balafré in the language of that nation; "but he will shut them in the bend of the 'river with a troubled stream.' He was born a Pawnee, but he will die a Dahcotah. Look at me. I am a sycamore that once covered many with my shadow. The leaves are fallen and the branches begin to drop. But a single succor is springing from my roots. It is a little vine and it winds itself about a tree that is green. I have long look'd for one, fit to grow by my side. Now have I found him. Le Balafré is no longer without a son; his name will not be forgotten when he is gone! Men of the Tetons, I take this youth, into my lodge."

No one was bold enough to dispute a right, that had so often been exercised, by warriors far inferior to the present speaker, and the adoption was listened to, in grave and respectful silence. Le Balafré, took his intended son by the arm, and leading him into the very centre of the circle, he stepped aside, with an air of triumph, in order that the spectators might approve of his choice. Mahtoree betrayed no evidence of his intentions, but rather seemed to await a moment better suited to the crafty policy of his character. The more experienced and sagacious chiefs distinctly foresaw the utter impossibility of two partisans so renowned, so hostile, and who had so long been rivals in fame, as their prisoner and their native leader, existing amicably in the same tribe. Still the character of Le Balafré was so imposing, and the custom to which he had resorted so sacred, that none dared to lift a voice in opposition to the measure. They watched the result with increasing interest, but with a coldness of demeanor that concealed the nature of their inquietude. From this state of embarrassment, and, as it might readily have proved, of disorganisation, the tribe was unexpectedly relieved by the decision of the one most interested in the success of the aged chief's design.

During the whole of the foregoing scene, it would have

been difficult to have traced a single distinct emotion in the lineaments of the captive. He had heard his release proclaimed with the same indifference as the order to bind him to the stake. But now that the moment had arrived when it became necessary to make his election, he spoke in a way to prove that the fortitude which had bought for him so distinguished a name, had, in no degree, deserted him.

"My father, is very old, but he has not yet look'd upon every thing;" said Hard-Heart, in a voice so clear as to be heard by all in presence. "He has never seen a buffaloe change to a bat. He will never see a Pawnee become a Sioux!"

There was a suddenness and yet a calmness, in the manner of delivering this decision which assured most of the auditors, that it was unalterable. The heart of Le Balafré, however, was yearning towards the youth, and the fondness of age was not so readily repulsed. Reproving the burst of admiration and triumph, to which the boldness of the declaration and the freshened hopes of revenge, had given rise, by turning his gleaming eye around the band, the veteran, again addressed his adopted child as if his purpose was not to be denied.

"It is well," he said. "Such are the words a brave should use, that the warriors may see his heart. The day has been when the voice of Le Balafré was loudest amongst the lodges of the Konzas. But the root of a white hair is wisdom. My child will show the Tetons that he is brave, by striking their enemies. Men of the Dahcotahs this is my son!"

The Pawnee hesitated a moment, and then stepping in front of the chief, he took his hard and wrinkled hand, and laid it, with reverence on his head, as if to acknowledge the extent of his obligation. Then recoiling a step, he raised his person to its greatest elevation, and looked upon the hostile band by whom he was environed, with an air of loftiness and disdain, as he spoke aloud in the language of the Siouxes.

"Hard-Heart has look'd at himself, within and without. He has thought of all that he has done, in the hunts and in the wars. Every where he is the same. There is no change. He is in all things a Pawnee. He has struck so many Tetons, that he could never eat in their lodges. His arrows would fly backwards; the point of his lance would be on the wrong end; their friends would weep at every whoop he gave; their enemies would laugh. Do the Tetons know a Loup? Let them look at him again. His head is painted; his arm is flesh; his heart is rock. When the Tetons see the sun come from the Rocky Mountains and move toward the land of the pale-faces, the mind of Hard-Heart will soften, and his spirit will become Sioux! Until that day, he will live and die a Pawnee."

A yell of delight, in which admiration and ferocity were strangely mingled, interrupted the speaker, and but too clearly announced the character of his fate. The captive awaited a moment, for the commotion to subside, and then turning again to Le Balafré he continued in tones conciliating and kind, as if he felt the propriety of softening his refusal, in a manner not to wound the pride of one who would so gladly be his benefactor.

"Let my father lean heavier on the 'fawn of the Dahcotahs'," he said. "She is weak now, but as her lodge fills with young, she will be stronger. See," he added directing the eyes of the other to the earnest countenance of the attentive trapper, "Hard-Heart is not without a gray-head to show him the path to the blessed Prairies. If he ever has another father, it shall be that just warrior."

Le Balafré turned away in disappointment from the youth, and approached the stranger who had thus anticipated his design. The examination between these two aged men was long, mutual, and curious. It was not easy to detect the real character of the trapper, through the mask which the hardships of so many years had laid upon his features, especially when aided, by his wild and peculiar attire. Some moments elapsed before the Teton spoke, and then it was in doubt whether he addressed one like himself, or some wanderer of that race who, he had heard, were spreading themselves like hungry locusts, throughout the land.

"The head of my brother is very white," he said, "but the eye of Le Balafré is no longer like the eagle's. Of what colour is his skin?"

"The Wahcondah made me like these you see waiting for a Dahcotah judgement; but fair and foul have coloured me darker than the skin of a fox. What of that! Though the bark is ragged and riven, the heart of the tree is sound."

"My brother is a Big-Knife! Let him turn his face toward

the setting sun, and open his eyes. Does he see the salt Lake, beyond the mountains?"

"The time has been, Teton, when few could see the white on the eagle's head farther than I, but the glare of fourscore and seven winters has dimmed my eyes, and, but little can I boast of sight, in my latter days. Does the Sioux think a pale face is a God, that he can look through hills!"

"Then let my brother look at me. I am nigh him, and he can see that I am a foolish red-man. Why cannot his people see every thing, since they crave all."

"I understand you, chief; nor will I gainsay the justice of your words, seeing that they are too much founded in truth. But though born of the race you love so little, my worst enemy, not even a lying Mingo, would dare to say, that I ever laid hands on the goods of another, except such as were taken in manful warfare, or that I ever coveted more ground, than the Lord has intended each man to fill."

"And yet my brother has come among the red-skins to find a son?"

The trapper laid a finger on the naked shoulder of Le Balafré, and looked into his scarred countenance, with a wistful and confidential expression as he answered.

"Ay, but it was only that I might do good to the boy. If you think, Dahcotah, that I adopted the youth in order to prop my age, you do as much injustice to my good will, as you seem to know little of the merciless intentions of your own people. I have made him my son, that he may know that one is left behind him—Peace, Hector, peace: Is this decent, pup, when gray-heads are counselling together, to break in upon their discourse with the whinings of a hound! The dog is old, Teton, and though well taught in respect of behavior, he is getting like ourselves, I fancy, something forgetful of the fashions of his youth"—

Further discourse, between these veterans, was interrupted by a discordant yell, which burst, at that moment, from the lips of the dozen withered crones who have already been mentioned, as having forced themselves into a conspicuous part of the circle. The outcry was excited by a sudden change in the air of Hard-Heart. When the old men turned towards the youth, they saw him standing in the very centre of the ring, with his head erect, his eye fixed on vacancy, one leg advanced, and an arm a little raised, as if all his faculties were absorbed in the act of listening. A smile lighted his countenance, for a single moment, and then the whole man sunk, again, into his former look of dignity and coldness, suddenly recalled to self-possession. The movement had been construed into contempt, and even the tempers of the chiefs began to be excited. Unable to restrain their fury, the women broke into the circle in a body, and commenced their attack by loading the captive with the most bitter revilings. They boasted of the various exploits which their sons had achieved at the expense of the different tribes of the Pawnees. They undervalued his own reputation, and told him to look at Mahtoree, if he had never yet seen a warrior. They accused him of having been suckled by a doe, and of having drunk in cowardice with his mother's milk. In short they lavished upon their unmoved captive a torrent of that vindictive abuse, in which the women of the savages are so well known to excel, but which has been too often described to need a repetition here.

The effect of this outbreaking was inevitable. Le Balafré turned away disappointed, and hid himself in the crowd, while the trapper whose honest features were working with his emotions, pressed nigher to his young friend, as those who are linked to the criminal by ties so strong as to brave the opinions of men, are often seen to stand about the place of execution, to support his dying moments. The excitement soon spread among the inferior warriors, though the chiefs, still forbore to make the signal which committed the victim to their mercy. Mahtoree, who had awaited such a movement among his fellows, with the wary design of concealing his own jealous hatred, soon grew weary of delay, and by a glance of his eye encouraged the tormentors to proceed.

Weucha, who eager for this sanction had long stood watching the countenance of the chief, bounded forward, at the signal, like a blood hound loosened from the leash. Forcing his way into the centre of the hags, who were already proceeding from abuse to violence, he reproved their impatience, and bade them wait, until a warrior had begun to torment, and then they should see their victim shed tears like a woman.

The heartless savage commenced his efforts, by flourishing

his tomahawk about the head of the captive, in such a manner as to give reason to suppose each blow would bury the weapon in the flesh, while, it was so governed as not to touch the skin. To this customary expedient Hard-Heart was perfectly insensible. His eye kept the same, steady, riveted look on air, though the glittering ax described, in its evolutions, a bright circle of light, before his countenance. Frustrated in this attempt, the callous Sioux, laid the cold edge on the naked head of his victim, and began to describe the different manners, in which a prisoner might be flayed. The women kept time to his cruelties with their taunts, and endeavored to force some expression of the longings of nature from the insensible features of the Pawnee. But he evidently reserved himself for the chiefs, and for those moments of extreme anguish, when the loftiness of his spirit might evince itself, in a manner better becoming his high and untarnished reputation.

The eyes of the trapper followed every movement of the tomahawk, with the interest of a real father, until, at length, unable to command his indignation, he exclaimed in the native language of his friend—

"My son has forgotten his cunning. This is a low-minded Indian and one, easily, hurried into folly. I cannot do the thing myself, for my traditions forbid a dying warrior to revile his persecutors, but the gifts of a red-skin are different. Let the Pawnee say the bitter words, and purchase an easy death. I will answer for his success provided he speaks before the grave men, set their wisdom to back the folly of this fool."

The savage Sioux, who heard his words without comprehending their meaning, turned to the speaker and menaced him with death, for his temerity.

"Ay, work your will," said the unflinching old man. "I am as ready now, as I shall be to-morrow. Though it would be a death that an honest man might not wish to die. Look at that noble Pawnee, Teton; and see what a red-skin may become, who fears the Master of Life, and follows his laws. How many of your people has he sent to the distant Prairies;" he continued, in a sort of pious fraud, thinking that while the danger menaced himself there could surely be no sin in extolling the merits of another, "how many howling Siouxes has he struck like a warrior in open combat, while arrows were sailing in the air plentier than flakes of falling snow. Go. Will Weucha, speak the name of one enemy he has ever struck?"

"Hard-Heart!" shouted the Sioux, turning in his fury, and aiming a deadly blow, at the head of his victim. His arm fell into the hollow of the captive's hand. For a single moment the two stood, as if entranced, in that attitude, the one paralyzed by so unexpected a resistance and the other, bending his head, not to meet his death, but in the act of the most intense attention. The women screamed with triumph, for they thought the nerves of the captive had at length failed him. The trapper trembled for the honor of his friend, and Hector, as if conscious of what was passing, raised his nose into the air, and uttered a piteous howl.

But the Pawnee hesitated, only for that moment. Raising the other hand, like lightning, the tomahawk flashed in the air, and Weucha sunk to his feet, brained to its eye. Then cutting a way with the bloody weapon, he darted through the opening left by the frightened women, and seemed to descend the declivity at a single bound.

Had a bolt from heaven fallen in the midst of the Teton band, it would not have occasioned greater consternation, than this act of desperate hardihood. A shrill, plaintive cry burst from the lips of all the women, and there was a moment that even the oldest warriors appeared to have lost their faculties. This stupor endured only for the instant. It was succeeded by a yell of revenge, that burst from a hundred throats, while as many warriors started forward at the cry, bent on the most bloody retribution. But a powerful and authoritative call from Mahtoree arrested every foot. The chief, in whose countenance disappointment and rage were struggling with the affected composure of his station extended an arm towards the river, and the whole mystery was explained.

Hard-Heart, had already cross'd half the bottom, which lay between the acclivity and the water. At this precise moment a band of armed and mounted Pawnees, turned a swell, and galloped to the margin of the stream, into which the plunge of the fugitive was distinctly heard. A few minutes sufficed for his vigorous arm, to conquer the passage, and then, the shout from the opposite shore, told the humbled Tetons the whole extent of the triumph of their adversaries.

Chapter XXIX

"If that shepherd be not in hand-fast, let him fly;
The curses he shall have, the tortures he shall feel,
Will break the back of man, the heart of monster."

The Winter's Tale, IV.iv.768–70.

It will readily be seen that the event just related was attended by an extraordinary sensation among the Siouxes. In leading the hunters of the band, back to the encampment their chief had neglected none of the customary precautions of Indian prudence, in order that his trail might escape the eyes of his enemies. It would seem however that the Pawnees had not only made the dangerous discovery, but had managed, with great art, to draw nigh the place, by the only side on which it was thought unnecessary to guard the approaches with the usual line of sentinels. The latter, who were scattered along the different little eminences, which lay in the rear of the lodges, were among the last to be apprised of the danger.

In such a crisis, there was little time for deliberation. It was by exhibiting the force of his character in scenes of similar difficulty, that Mahtoree had obtained and strengthened his ascendancy among his people, nor did he seem likely to lose it, by the manifestation of any indecision on the present occasion. In the midst of the screams of the young, the shrieks of the women, and the wild howlings of the crones, which were sufficient of themselves to have created a chaos in the thoughts of one less accustomed to act in emergencies, he promptly asserted his authority, issuing his orders with the coolness of a veteran.

While the warriors were arming, the boys were dispatched to the bottom for the horses. The tents were hastily struck by the women, and disposed of on such of the beasts, as were not deemed fit to be trusted in combat. The infants were cast upon the backs of their mothers, and those children who were of a size to march, were driven to the rear, like a herd of less reasoning animals. Though these several movements were made amid outcries and a clamor that likened the place to another Babel, they were executed with incredible alacrity and intelligence.

In the mean time, Mahtoree neglected no duty that belonged to his responsible station. From the elevation on which he stood, he could command a perfect view of the force and evolutions of the hostile party. A grim smile lighted his visage, when he found, that in point of numbers, his own band was greatly the superior. Notwithstanding this advantage, however, there were other points of inequality, which would probably have a tendency to render his success in the approaching conflict, exceedingly doubtful. His people were the inhabitants of a more northern and less hospitable region than their enemies, and were far from being rich in that species of property, horses and arms, which constitutes the most highly prized wealth of a western Indian. The band in view, was mounted to a man, and, as it had come so far to rescue or to revenge their greatest partisan, he had no reason to doubt its being composed entirely of braves. On the other hand, many of his followers were far better in a hunt than in a combat; men who might serve to divert the attention of his foes but from whom he could expect little desperate service. Still, his flashing eye glanced over a body of warriors, on whom he had often relied, and who had never deceived him, and, though, in the precise position in which he found himself, he felt no disposition to precipitate the conflict, he certainly would have had no intention to avoid it, had not the presence of his women and children placed the option altogether in the power of his adversaries.

On the other hand, the Pawnees, so unexpectedly successful in their first and greatest object, manifested no intention to drive matters to an issue. The river was a dangerous barrier to pass, in the face of a determined foe, and it would now have been in perfect accordance with their cautious policy to have retired for a season, in order that their onset might be made in the hours of darkness, and of seeming security. But there was a spirit in their chief, that elevated him, for the moment, above the ordinary expedients of savage warfare. His bosom burned with the desire to wipe out that disgrace of which he had been the subject, and it is possible, that he believed the retiring camp of the Siouxes contained a prize, that begun to have a value in his eyes, far exceeding any that could be found in fifty Teton scalps. Let that be as it might, Hard-Heart had no sooner received the brief congratulations of his band, and communicated to the chiefs such facts as were important to be known, than he prepared himself to act such a part, in the coming conflict, as would at once maintain his well earned reputation, and gratify his secret wishes. A led horse, one that had been long trained in the hunts, had been brought to receive his master, with but little hope however that his services would ever be needed again, in this life. With a delicacy and consideration that proved how much the generous qualities of the youth had touched the feelings of his people, a bow, a lance, and a quiver, were thrown across the animal, which it had been intended to immolate on the grave of the young brave, a species of care, that would have superseded the necessity for the pious duty that the trapper had pledged himself to perform.

Though Hard-Heart was sensible of the kindness of his warriors, and believed that a chief furnished with such appointments, might depart with credit, for the distant hunting grounds of the Master of Life, he seemed equally disposed to think that they might be rendered quite as useful, in the actual state of things. His countenance lighted with stern pleasure, as he tried the elasticity of the bow, and poised the well balanced spear. The glance he bestowed on the shield was more cursory and indifferent, but the exultation with which he threw himself on the back of his favored war-horse was so great, as to break through the forms of Indian reserve. He rode, to and fro, among his scarcely less delighted warriors, managing the animal with a grace and address that no artificial rules can ever supply, at times flourishing his lance, as if to assure himself of his seat, and at others examining critically into the condition of the fusee with which he had also been furnished, with the fondness of one, who was miraculously restored to the possession of treasures, that constituted his pride and his happiness.

At this particular moment, Mahtoree, having completed the necessary arrangements, prepared to make a more decisive movement. The Teton had found no little embarrassment in disposing of his captives. The tents of the squatter were still in sight, and his wary cunning did not fail to apprise him, that it was quite as necessary to guard against an attack from that quarter, as to watch the motions of his more open and more active foes. His first impulse had been to make the tomahawk suffice for the men, and to trust the females under the same protection as the women of his band, but the manner in which so many of his braves continued to regard the imaginary Medecine of the Long-knives, forewarned him of the danger of so hazardous an experiment on the eve of a battle. It might be deemed the omen of defeat. In this dilemma, he motioned to a superannuated warrior, to whom he had confided the charge of the noncombatants, and leading him apart he placed a finger significantly on his shoulder, as he said in a tone, in which authority was tempered by confidence—

"When my young men are striking the Pawnees, give the women knives. Enough; my father is very old; he does not want to hear wisdom from a boy."

The grim old savage, returned a look of ferocious assent, and then the mind of the chief, appeared to be at rest on this important subject. From that moment he bestowed all his care, on the achievement of his revenge and the maintenance of his martial character. Throwing himself on his horse, he made a sign with the air of a Prince, to his followers to imitate his example, interrupting without ceremony the war songs and solemn rites by which many among them were stimulating their spirits to deeds of daring. When all were in order, the whole moved with great steadiness and silence towards the margin of the river.

The hostile bands were, now, separated by the water. The width of the stream was too great to admit of the use of the ordinary Indian missiles, but a few useless shots were exchanged from the fusees of the chiefs, more in bravado, than with any expectation of doing execution. As some time was suffered to elapse, in demonstrations and abortive efforts, we shall leave them, for that period, to return to such of our characters as remained in the hands of the savages.

We have shed much ink in vain, and wasted quires that might possibly have been better employed, if it be necessary, now, to tell the reader that few of the foregoing movements escaped the observation of the experienced trapper. He had been, in common with rest, astonished at the sudden act of Hard-Heart, and there was a single moment when a feeling of regret and mortification got the better of his longings to save the life of the youth. The simple and well-intentioned old man would have felt, at witnessing any failure of firmness on the part of a warrior who had so strongly excited his sympathies, the same species of sorrow that a christian parent would suffer in hanging over the dying moments of an impious child. But, when instead of an impotent and unmanly struggle for existence, he found that his friend had forborne with the customary and dignified submission of an Indian warrior, until an opportunity had offered to escape, and that he had then manifested the spirit and decision of the most gifted brave, his gratification became nearly too powerful to be concealed. In the midst of the wailing and commotion which succeeded the death of Weucha and the escape of the captive, he placed himself nigh the persons of his white associates, with a determination of interfering at every hazard should the fury of the savages take that direction. The appearance of the hostile band spared him however so desperate and probably so fruitless an effort, and left him to pursue his observations, and to mature his plans more at leisure.

He particularly remarked that, while by far the greater part of the women and all the children, together with the effects of the party, were hurried to the rear, probably with an order to secrete themselves in some of the adjacent woods, the tent of Mahtoree himself was left standing, and its contents undisturbed. Two chosen horses, however, stood near by, held by a couple of youths, who were too young to go into the conflict, and yet of an age to understand the management of the beasts. The trapper perceived in this arrangement the reluctance of Mahtoree to trust his newly found 'flowers' beyond the reach of his eye, and at the same time his forethought in providing against a reverse of fortune. Neither had the manner of the Teton in giving his commission to the old savage, nor the fierce pleasure with which the latter had received the bloody charge, escaped his observation. From all these mysterious movements, the old man was aware that a crisis was at hand, and he summoned the utmost knowledge he had acquired, in so long a life, to aid him in the desperate conjecture. While musing on the means to be employed, the Doctor, again, attracted his attention to himself, by a piteous appeal for assistance.

"Venerable trapper, or as I may now say liberator," commenced the dolorous Obed, "It would seem that a fitting time has at length arrived to dissever the unnatural and altogether irregular connexion which exists between my inferior members and the body of Asinus. Perhaps if such a portion of my limbs were released as might leave me master of the remainder, and this favorable opportunity were suitably improved, by making a forced march towards the settlements, all hopes of preserving the treasures of knowledge of which I am the unworthy receptacle, would not be lost. The importance of the results, is surely worth the hazard of the experiment."

"I know not, I know not," returned the deliberate old man. "The vermin and reptiles which you bear about you, were intended by the Lord of the Prairies, and I see no good in sending them into regions that may not suit their natur's. And, moreover you may be of great and particular use as you now sit on the Ass; though it creates no wonder, in my mind, to perceive that you are ignorant of it, seeing that usefulness is altogether a new calling to so bookish a man."

"Of what service can I be, in this painful thraldom, in which the animal functions are in a manner suspended and the spiritual or intellectual, blinded by the secret sympathy that unites mind to matter. There is likely to be blood spilt between yonder adverse hosts of heathens, and, though but little desiring the office, it would be better that I should employ myself in surgical experiments, than in thus wasting the precious moments, mortifying both soul and body."

"It is little that a red-skin would care to have a physicianer at his hurts while the whoop is ringing in his ears. Patience is a virtue in an Indian, and can be no shame to a Christian white-man. Look at these hags of squaws, friend Doctor; I have no judgement in savage tempers if they are not bloody-minded, and ready to work their accursed pleasures on us all. Now, so long as you keep upon the ass and maintain the fierce look, which is far from being your natural gift, fear of so great a Medicine may serve to keep down their courage. I am placed, here, like a general at the opening of the battle, and it has become my duty, to make such use of all my forces, as in my judgement each is best fitted to perform. If I know these niceties, you will be more serviceable for your countenance, just now, than in any more stirring exploits."

"Harkee, old trapper," shouted Paul, whose patience could no longer maintain itself, under the calculating and prolix explanations of the other, "suppose you cut two things I can name, short off. That is to say, your conversation, which is agreeable enough over a well baked buffaloe hump, and these damnable thongs of hide, which, according to my experience, can be pleasant, no where. A single stroke of your knife would be of more service, just now, than the longest speech that was ever made in a Kentucky Court-House."

"Ay Court-Houses are the 'happy hunting grounds' as a red-skin would say, for them that are born with gifts no better than such as lie in the tongue! I was carried into one of the lawless holes myself, once, and it was all about a thing of no more value than the skin of a deer. The Lord forgive them, the Lord forgive them; they knew no better, and they did according to their weak judgements, and therefore the more are they to be pitied. And yet it was a solemn sight to see an aged man, who had always lived in the air, laid neck and heels, by the law, and held up as a spectacle for the women and boys of a wasteful settlement to point their fingers at!"

"If such be your opinions of confinement, honest friend, you had better manifest the same, by putting us at liberty, with as little delay as possible," said Middleton, who like his companion, began to find the tardiness of his often-tried companion, quite as extraordinary as it was disagreeable.

"I should greatly like to do the same; especially in your behalf, Captain, who being a soldier might find not only pleasure but profit, in examining, more at your ease, into the circumventions and cunning of an Indian fight. As to our friend, here, it is of but little matter how much of this affair he examines, or how little, seeing that a bee is not to be overcome, in the same manner as an Indian."

"Old man, this trifling with our misery is inconsiderate, to give it a name no harsher—"

"Ay; your gran'ther was of a hot and hurrying mind, and one must not expect that the young of a Panther will crawl the 'arth like the litter of a porcupine. Now, keep you both silent, and what I say shall have the appearance of being spoken concerning the movements that are going on in the bottom; all of which will serve to put jealousy to sleep, and to shut the eyes of such as rarely close them, on wickedness and cruelty. In the first place, then, you must know, that I have reason to think, yonder treacherous Teton has left an order to put us all to death, so soon as he thinks the deed may be done, secretly and without tumult."

"Great Heaven! will you suffer us to be butchered like unresisting sheep."

"Hist, Captain, hist—a hot temper is none of the best, when cunning is more needed than blows. Ah! the Pawnee is a noble boy! it would do your heart good to see how he draws off from the river in order to invite his enemies to cross, and yet according to my failing sight, they count two warriors to his one! But as I was saying, little good comes of haste and thoughtlessness. The facts are so plain, that any child may see into their wisdom. The savages are of many minds, as to the manner of our treatment. Some fear us for our colour, and would gladly let us go, and other some would show us the mercy that the doe receives from the hungry wolf. When opposition gets fairly into the Councils of a tribe, it is rare that humanity is the gainer. Now see you, these wrinkled and cruel minded squaws—no, you cannot see them as you lie, but nevertheless they are here, ready and willing, like so many raging she-bears to work their will upon us, so soon as the proper time shall come."

"Harkee, old gentleman trapper," interrupted Paul, with a little bitterness in his manner: "Do you tell us these matters for our amusement, or for your own. If for ours, you may keep your breath for the next race you run, as I am tickled nearly to suffocation already with my part of the fun."

"Hist—" said the trapper, cutting with great dexterity and rapidity the thong, which bound one of the arms of Paul to his body and dropping his knife at the same time within reach of the liberated hand. "Hist, boy, hist. That was a lucky moment, the yell from the bottom drew the eyes of these bloodsuckers in another quarter, and so far we are safe. Now make a proper use of your advantages, but be careful that what you do, is done without being seen."

"Thank you for this small favor, old deliberation," muttered the bee-hunter, "though it comes, like a snow in May, somewhat out of season."

"Foolish boy," reproachfully exclaimed the other, who had moved to a little distance from his friends, and appeared to be attentively regarding the movements of the hostile parties; " will you never learn to know the wisdom of patience! And, you too, Captain; though a man, myself, that seldom ruffles his temper by vain feelings, I see that you are silent, because you scorn to ask favors any longer from one you think too slow to grant them. No doubt, ye are both young, and filled with the pride of your strength and manhood, and I dare say you thought it only needful to cut the thongs, to leave you masters of the ground. But he that has seen much, is apt to think much. Had I run like a bustling woman to have given you freedom, these hags of the Siouxes would have seen the same, and then where would you both have found yourselves! Under the tomahawk and the knife, like helpless and outcrying children, though gifted with the size and beards of men. Ask our friend the bee-hunter in what condition he finds himself to struggle with a Teton boy, after so many hours of bondage, much less with a dozen marciless and blood-thirsty squaws!"

"Truly, old trapper," returned Paul, stretching his limbs which were by this time entirely released, and endeavoring to restore the suspended circulation, "you have some judgematical notions in these matters. Now, here am I, Paul Hover, a man who will give in to few, at wrestle or race, nearly as helpless as the day I paid my first visit to the house of old Paul, who is dead and gone, the Lord forgive him any little blunders he may have made, while he tarried in Kentucky. Now there is my foot on the ground, so far as eye-sight has any virtue, and yet it would take no great temptation to make me swear, it didn't touch the earth by six inches! I say, honest friend, since you have done so much have the goodness to keep these damnable squaws, of whom you say so many interesting things, at a little distance 'till I have got the blood of this arm in motion, and am ready to receive them."

The trapper made a sign that he perfectly understood the case, as he walked towards the superannuated savage, who began to manifest an intention of commencing his assigned task, leaving the bee-hunter to recover the use of his limbs as well as he could, and to put Middleton in a similar situation to defend himself.

Mahtoree had not mistaken his man, in selecting the one he did to execute his bloody purpose. He had chosen one of those ruthless savages, more or less of whom are to be found in every tribe, who had purchased a certain share of military reputation, by the exhibition of a hardihood that found its impulses in an innate love of cruelty. Contrary to the high and chivalrous sentiment, which, among the Indians of the Prairies, renders it a deed of even greater merit to bear off the trophy of victory from a fallen foe, than to slay him, he had been remarkable for preferring the pleasure of destroying life, to the glory of striking the dead. While the more self-devoted and ambitious braves were intent on personal honor, he had always been seen established behind some favorable cover, depriving the wounded of hope, by finishing that which a more gallant warrior had begun. In all the cruelties of the tribe he had ever been foremost, and no Sioux was so uniformly found on the side of merciless councils.

He had awaited, with an impatience which his long practised restraint could with difficulty subdue, for the moment to arrive, when he might proceed to execute the wishes of the Great Chief, without whose approbation and powerful protection, he would not have dared to undertake a step, that had so many opposers in the nation. But events had been hastening to an issue, between the hostile parties, and the time had, now, arrived, greatly to his secret and malignant joy, when he was free to act his will.

The trapper found him distributing knives to the ferocious hags, who received the presents, chanting a low monotonous song, that recalled the losses of their people, in various conflicts with the whites, and which extolled the pleasures and glory of revenge. The appearance of such a groupe, was enough of itself to have deterred one, less accustomed to such sights than the old man, from trusting himself within the circle of their wild and repulsive rites.

Each of the crones, as she received the weapon, commenced a slow, and measured, but ungainly, step, around the savage, until the whole were circling him in a sort of magic dance. Their movements were timed, in some degree, by the words of their songs, as were their gestures by the ideas. When they spoke of their own losses, they tossed their long straight locks of gray into the air, or suffered them to fall in confusion upon their withered necks, but as the sweetness of returning blow for blow, was touched upon by any among them, it was answered by a common howl as well as by gestures that were sufficiently expressive of the manner in which they were exciting themselves, to the necessary state of fury.

Into the very centre of this ring of seeming demons, the trapper, now, stalked, with the same calmness and observation, as he would have walked into a village church. No other change was made by his appearance, than a renewal of the threatening gestures, with, if possible, a still less equivocal display of their remorseless intentions. Making a sign for them to cease, the old man demanded—

"Why do the mothers of the Tetons sing with bitter tongues? The Pawnee prisoners are not yet in their village; their young men have not come back loaded with scalps!"

He was answered by a general howl, and a few of the boldest of the furies even ventured to approach him, flourishing their knives within a dangerous proximity of his own steady eye-balls.

"It is a warrior you see, and no runner of the Long-knives whose face grows paler at the sight of a tomahawk;" returned the trapper, without moving a muscle. "Let the Sioux women think. If one white-skin dies, a hundred spring up where he falls."

Still the hags made no other answer, than by increasing their speed in the circle, and, occasionally, raising the threatening expressions of their chaunt, into louder and more intelligible strains. Suddenly, one of the oldest, and the most ferocious of them all broke out of the ring, and skirred away in the direction of her victims, like a rapacious bird, that having wheeled on poised wings, for the time necessary to insure its object, makes the final dart upon its prey. The others followed, a disorderly and screaming flock, fearful of being too late, to reap their portion of the sanguinary pleasure.

"Mighty Medicine of my people!" shouted the old man, in the Teton tongue, "lift your voice, and speak that the Sioux nation may hear!"

Whether Asinus had acquired so much knowledge by his recent experience, as to know the value of his sonorous properties, or the strange spectacle of a dozen hags flitting past him, filling the air with such sounds as were even grating to the ears of an ass, most moved his temper, it is certain that the animal did that which Obed was requested to do, and probably with far greater effect, than if the naturalist, had strove with his mightiest effort to be heard. It was the first time, that the strange beast had spoken, since his arrival in the encampment. Admonished by so terrible a warning, the hags scattered themselves, like vultures frightened from their prey, still screaming, and but half-diverted from their purpose.

In the mean time the sudden appearance and the imminency of the danger, quickened the blood in the veins of Paul and Middleton, more than all their laborious frictions, and physical expedients. The former had actually risen to his feet, and assumed an attitude which perhaps threatened more than the worthy bee-hunter was able to perform, and even the latter had mounted to his knees, and showed a disposition to do good service for his life. The unaccountable release of the captives from their bonds was attributed, by the hags, to the incantations of the Medecine and the mistake was probably of as much service, as the miraculous and timely interposition of Asinus in their favor.

"Now, is the time to come out of our ambushment," exclaimed the old man, hastening to join his friends, "and to make open and manful war. It would have been policy to have kept back the struggle, until the Captain was in better condition to join, but as we have unmasked our battery why we must maintain the ground"—

He was interrupted by feeling a gigantic hand on his shoulder. Turning under a sort of confused impression that necromancy was actually abroad in the place, he found that he was in the hands of a sorcerer—no less dangerous and powerful than Ishmael Bush. The file of the squatter's well-armed sons, that was seen issuing from behind the still standing tent of Mahtoree, explained at once not only the manner in which their rear had been turned, while their attention had been so earnestly bestowed on matters in front, but the utter impossibility of resistance.

Neither Ishmael, nor his sons deemed it necessary to enter into prolix explanations. Middleton and Paul were bound, again, with extraordinary silence and dispatch, and this time not even the aged trapper was exempt from a similar fortune. The tent was struck, the females placed upon the horses, and the whole were on the way towards the squatter's encampment with a celerity that might well have served to keep alive the idea of magic.

During this summary and brief disposition of things, the disappointed Agent of Mahtoree and his callous associates were seen flying across the plain in the direction of the retiring families, and when Ishmael left the spot with his prisoners and his booty, the ground which had so lately been alive with the bustle and life of an extensive Indian encampment was as still and empty as any other spot in those extensive wastes.

Chapter XXX

"Is this proceeding just and honorable?"
2 Henry IV, IV.ii.110.

DURING THE occurrence of these events on the upland plain, the warriors on the bottom had not been idle. We left the adverse bands watching one another on the opposite banks of the stream, each endeavoring to excite its enemy to some act of indiscretion by the most reproachful taunts and revilings. But the Pawnee chief was not slow to discover that his crafty antagonist had no objection to waste the time in so idle, and as they mutually proved, so useless expedients. He changed his plans accordingly, and withdrew from the bank, as has been already explained through the mouth of the trapper, in order to invite the more numerous host of the Siouxes to cross. The challenge was not accepted, and the Loups, were compelled to frame some other method to attain their end.

Instead of any longer throwing away the precious moments, in fruitless endeavors to induce his foe to cross the stream, the young Partisan of the Pawnees led his troop, at a swift gallop, along its margin, in quest of some favorable spot where, by a sudden push, he might throw his own band, without loss, to the opposite shore. The instant, his object was discovered, each mounted Teton received a footman behind him, and Mahtoree was still enabled to concentrate his whole force against the effort. Perceiving that his design was anticipated, and unwilling to blow his horses by a race, that would disqualify them for service, even after they had succeeded in outstripping the more heavily burthened cattle of the Sioux, Hard-Heart drew up, and came to a dead halt on the very margin of the water-course.

As the country was too open for any of the usual devices of savage warfare, and time was so pressing, the chivalrous Pawnee resolved to bring on the result by one of those acts of personal daring for which the Indian braves are so remarkable, and by which they often purchase their highest and dearest renown. The spot he had selected was favorable to such a project. The river, which throughout most of its course was deep and rapid, had expanded there to more than twice its customary width, and the rippling of its waters, proved that it flowed over a shallow bottom. In the centre of the current there was an extensive and naked bed of sand, but a little raised above the level of the stream, and of a colour and consistency that told a practised eye, that it afforded a firm and safe foundation for the foot. To this spot the partisan now turned his wistful gaze, nor was he long in making his decision. First speaking to his warriors and apprising them of his intentions, he dashed into the current, and partly by swimming and more by the use of his horse's feet, he reached the island in safety.

The experience of Hard-Heart had not deceived him. When his snorting steed issued from the water, he found himself on a quivering but damp and compact bed of sand, that was admirably adapted to the exhibition of the finest powers of the animal. The horse seemed conscious of the advantage, and bore his warlike rider, with an elasticity of step and a loftiness of air, that would have done no discredit to the highest trained and most generous charger. The blood of the chief himself, quickened, with the excitement of his situation. He sat the beast, as if conscious that the eyes of two tribes were on his movements, and as nothing could be more acceptable and grateful to his own band than this display of native grace and courage, so nothing could be more taunting and humiliating to their enemies.

The sudden appearance of the Pawnee, on the sands, was announced among the Tetons, by a general yell of savage anger. A rush was made to the shore, followed by a discharge of fifty arrows and a few fusees, and, on the part of several braves, there was a plain manifestation of a desire to plunge into the water, in order to punish the temerity of their insolent foe. But a call and a mandate, from Mahtoree, checked the rising and nearly ungovernable temper of his band. So far from allowing a single foot to be wet, or a repetition of the fruitless efforts of his people to drive away their foe with missiles, the whole of the party was commanded to retire from the shore, while he himself communicated his intentions to one or two of his most favored followers.

When the Pawnees observed the rush of their enemies twenty warriors rode into the stream, but so soon as they perceived that the Tetons had withdrawn, they fell back to a man, leaving their young chief to the support of his own often-tried skill and well established courage. The instructions of Hard-Heart on quitting his band had been worthy of the self-devotion and daring of his character. So long as single warriors came against him, he was to be left to the keeping of the Wahcondah and his own arm, but should the Siouxes attack him in numbers, he was to be sustained, man for man, even to the extent of his whole force. These generous orders were strictly obeyed, and though so many hearts in the troop, panted to share in the glory and danger of their partisan, not a warrior was found among them all who did not know how to conceal his impatience, under the usual mask of Indian self-restraint. They watched the issue with quick and jealous eyes, nor did a single exclamation of surprise escape them, when they saw, as will soon be apparent, that the experiment of their chief was as likely to conduce to peace as to war.

Mahtoree was not long in communicating his plans to his confidants, whom he as quickly dismissed to join their fellows in the rear. The Teton entered a short distance into the stream and halted. Here he raised his hand several times, with the palm outwards, and made several of those other signs which are construed into a pledge of amicable intentions among the inhabitants of those regions. Then, as if to confirm the sincerity of his faith, he cast his fusee to the shore, and entered deeper into the water, where he again came to a stand in order to see in what manner, the Pawnee would receive his pledges of peace.

The crafty Sioux had not made his calculations on the noble and honest nature of his more youthful rival, in vain. Hard-Heart had continued galloping across the sands, during the discharge of missiles and the appearance of a general onset, with the same proud and confident mien, as that with which he had first braved the danger. When he saw the well known person of the Teton partisan enter the river, he waved his hand in triumph, and flourishing his lance, he raised the thrilling war-cry of his people, as a challenge for him to come on. But when he saw the signs of a truce, though deeply practised in the treachery of savage combats, he disdained to show a less manly reliance on himself, than that which his enemy had seen fit to exhibit. Riding to the farthest extremity of the sands he cast his own fusee, from him, and returned to the point whence he had started.

The two chiefs were now armed alike. Each had his spear, his bow, his quiver, his little battle axe, and his knife, and each had also a shield of hides, which might serve as a means of a defense against a surprise from any of these weapons. The Sioux no longer hesitated, but advanced deeper into the stream, and soon landed on a point of the island, which his courteous adversary had left free for that purpose. Had one been there to watch the countenance of Mahtoree, as he crossed the water that separated him from the most formidable and the most hated of all his rivals, he might have fancied that he could trace the gleamings of a secret joy, breaking through the cloud which deep cunning and heartless treachery had drawn before his swarthy visage, and yet, there would have been moments, when he might have believed, that the flashings of the Teton's eye, and the expansion of his nostrils, had their origin in a nobler sentiment and one more worthy of an Indian chief.

The Pawnee awaited the time of his enemy with calmness and dignity. The Teton made a short turn or two, to curb the impatience of his steed, and to recover his seat, after the effort of crossing, and then he rode into the centre of the place, and invited the other, by a courteous gesture to approach. Hard-Heart drew nigh, until he found himself at a distance equally suited to advance or to retreat, and, in his turn, he came to a stand, keeping his glowing eye riveted on that of his enemy. A long and grave pause succeeded this movement, during which these two distinguished braves, who were now for the first time, confronted with arms in their hands, sat regarding each other, like warriors who know how to value the merits of a gallant foe, however hated. But the mien of Mahtoree was far less stern and warlike than that of the partisan of the Loups. Throwing his shield over his shoulder, as if to invite the confidence of the other, he made a gesture of salutation, and was the first to speak.

"Let the Pawnees go upon the hills," he said, "and look

from the morning to the evening sun, from the country of snows to the land of many flowers, and they will see that the earth is very large. Why cannot the red men find room on it, for all their villages!"

"Has the Teton ever known a warrior of the Loups come to his towns to beg a place for his lodge?" returned the young brave, with a look in which pride and contempt were not attempted to be concealed. "When the Pawnees hunt, do they send runners to ask Mahtoree, if there are no Siouxes on the Prairies!"

"When there is hunger in the lodge of a warrior, he looks for the buffaloe, which is given him for food," the Teton continued, struggling to keep down the ire excited by the other's scorn. "The Wahcondah has made more of them, than he has made Indians. He has not said this buffaloe shall be for a Pawnee, and that for a Dahcotah, this beaver for a Konza and that for an Omawhaw. No; he said, there are enough. I love my red children, and I have given them great riches. The swiftest horse shall not go from the village of the Tetons to the village of the Loups in many suns. It is far from the towns of the Pawnees to the river of the Osages. There is room for all that I love. Why, then, should a red-man strike his brother?"

Hard-Heart dropped one end of his lance to the earth, and having also cast his shield across his shoulder, he sat leaning lightly on the weapon, as he answered with a smile of no doubtful expression.

"Are the Tetons weary of the hunts, and of the war-path! do they wish to cook the venison, and not to kill it! Do they intend to let the hair cover their heads, that their enemies shall not know where to find their scalps! Go; a Pawnee warrior will never come among such Sioux squaws for a wife!"

A frightful gleam of ferocity broke out of the restraint of the Dahcotah's countenance as he listened to this biting insult; but he was quick in subduing the tell-tale feeling, in an expression much better suited to his present purpose.

"This is the way a young chief should talk of war," he answered with singular composure. "But Mahtoree has seen the misery of more winters than his brother. When the nights have been long and darkness has been in his lodge, while the young men slept, he has thought of the hardships of his people. He has said to himself, Teton, count the scalps in your smoke. They are all red but two! Does the wolf destroy the wolf, or the rattler strike his brother? You know they do not; therefore Teton, are you wrong, to go on a war-path that leads to the village of a red-skin, with a tomahawk in your hand."

"The Sioux would rob the warrior of his fame! He would say to his young men go, dig roots in the Prairies and find holes to bury your tomahawks in; you are no longer braves!"

"If the tongue of Mahtoree ever says thus," returned the crafty chief, with an appearance of strong indignation, "let his women cut it out, and burn it with the offals of the buffaloe. No," he added, advancing a few feet nigher to the immovable Hard-Heart, as if in the sincerity of confidence, "the red-man can never want an enemy. They are plentier than the leaves on the trees, the birds in the heavens, or the buffaloes on the Prairies. Let my brother open his eyes wide; does he no where see an enemy he would strike?"

"How long is it since the Teton counted the scalps of his warriors that were drying in the smoke of a Pawnee lodge! The hand that took them is here, and ready to make eighteen, twenty."

"Now let not the mind of my brother go on a crooked path. If a red-skin strikes a red-skin, forever, who will be masters of the Prairies, when no warriors are left to say they are mine. Hear the voices of the old men. They tell us, that, in their days, many Indians have come out of the woods, under the rising sun, and that they have filled the Prairies with their complaints of the robberies of the Long-knives. Where a Pale-face comes, a red-man cannot stay. The land is too small. They are always hungry. See, they are here already."

As the Teton spoke he pointed towards the tents of Ishmael, which were in plain sight, and then, he paused to await the effect of his words on the mind of his ingenuous foe. Hard-Heart listened like one, in whom a train of novel ideas had been excited by the reasoning of the other. He mused, for a minute before he demanded—

"What do the wise chiefs of the Sioux say must be done?"

"They think that the moccasin of every pale face, should be followed like the track of the bear. That the Long-knife who comes upon the Prairie, should never go back. That the path shall be open to those who come, and shut to those who go. Yonder are many. They have horses and guns. They are rich, but we are poor. Will the Pawnees meet the Tetons in Council; and when the sun is gone behind the Rocky Mountains, they will say this is for a Loup and this for a Sioux."

"Teton. No. Hard-Heart has never struck the stranger. They come into his lodge and eat, and they go out in safety. A mighty chief is their friend! When my people call the young men to go on the war-path, the moccasin of Hard-Heart is the last. But his village is no sooner hid by the trees, than it is the first. No. Teton. His arm will never be lifted against the stranger."

"Fool; then die, with empty hands!" Mahtoree exclaimed, setting an arrow to his bow, and sending it with a sudden and deadly aim full at the naked bosom of his generous and confiding enemy.

The action of the treacherous Teton was too quick, and too well matured to admit of any of the ordinary means of defense on the part of the Pawnee. His shield was hanging at his shoulder, and even the arrow had been suffered to fall from its place, and lay in the hollow of that hand which grasped his bow. But the quick eye of the brave had time to see the movement, and his ready thoughts did not desert him. Pulling hard and with a jerk upon the rein, his steed reared his forward legs into the air, and as the rider bent his body low, the horse served for a shield against the danger. So true however, was the aim, and so powerful the force by which it was sent, that the arrow entered the neck of the animal, and broke the skin on the opposite side.

Quicker than thought, Hard-Heart sent back an answering arrow. The shield of the Teton was transfixed, but his person was untouched. For a few moments the twang of the bow and the glancing of arrows were incessant, notwithstanding, the combatants were compelled to give so large a portion of their care to the means of defense. The quivers were soon exhausted, and though blood had been drawn, it was not in sufficient quantities to impair the energy of the combat.

A series of masterly and rapid evolutions with the horses now commenced. The wheelings, the charges, the advances and the circuitous retreats, were like the flights of circling swallows. Blows were struck with the lance, the sand was scattered in the air, and the shocks often seemed to be unavoidably fatal, but still each party kept his seat, and still each rein was managed with a steady hand. At length the Teton was driven to the necessity of throwing himself from his horse, in order to escape a thrust that would otherwise have proved fatal. The Pawnee passed his lance through the beast, uttering a shout of triumph as he galloped by. Turning in his tracks, he was about to push the advantage, when his own mettled steed, staggered, and fell under a burthen, that he could no longer sustain. Mahtoree answered his premature cry of victory and rushed upon the entangled youth with knife and tomahawk. The utmost agility of Hard-Heart had not sufficed to extricate himself in season from the fallen beast. He saw that his case was desperate. Feeling for his knife, he took the blade between a finger and thumb, and cast it with admirable coolness at his advancing foe. The keen weapon whirled a few times in the air, and its point meeting the naked breast of the impetuous Sioux, the blade was buried to the buck-horn haft.

Mahtoree laid his hand on the weapon, and seemed to hesitate whether to withdraw it or not. For a moment his countenance darkened with the most inextinguishable hatred and ferocity, and then, as if inwardly admonished how little time he had to lose, he staggered to the edge of the sands, and halted with his feet in the water. The cunning and duplicity which had so long obscured the brighter and nobler traits of his character were lost, in the never dying sentiment of pride, which he had imbibed in the days of his youth and of his comparative innocence.

"Boy of the Loups!" he said, with a smile of grim satisfaction, "the scalp of a mighty Dahcotah shall never dry in Pawnee smoke!"

Drawing the knife from the wound, he hurled it towards his enemy, in disdain. Then, shaking his arm at his successful foe, his swarthy countenance appearing to struggle with volumes of scorn and hatred that he could not utter with the tongue, he cast himself headlong into one of the most rapid, veins of the current, his hand still waving, in triumph, above the fluid even after his body had sunk into the tide, forever. Hard-Heart was by this time free. The silence which had hitherto reigned in the bands, was broken by general and tumultuous shouts. Fifty of the adverse warriors were already in the river, hastening to destroy or to defend the conqueror, and the combat was rather on the eve of its commencement than near its termination. But to all these signs of danger and need, the young victor was insensible. He sprang for the knife, and bounded with the foot of an antelope, along the sands looking for the receding fluid which concealed his prize. A dark, bloody spot, indicated the place, and, armed with the knife, he plunged into the stream, resolute to die in the flood or to return with his trophy.

In the mean time the sands became a scene of bloodshed and violence. Better mounted, and perhaps more ardent the Pawnees had, however, reached the spot in sufficient numbers to force their enemies to retire. The victors pushed their success to the opposite shore, and gained solid ground in the mélée of the fight. Here they were met by all the unmounted Tetons, and in their turn, they were forced to give way.

The combat now became more characteristic and circumspect. As the hot impulses which had driven both parties to mingle in so deadly a struggle began to cool, the chiefs were enabled to exercise their influence, and to temper the assaults with prudence. In consequence of the admonitions of their leaders, the Siouxes sought such covers as the grass afforded, or here and there some bush or slight inequality of the ground, and the charges of the Pawnee warriors necessarily became more wary and of course less fatal.

In this manner the contest continued with a varied success, and without much loss. The Siouxes had succeeded in forcing themselves into a thick growth of rank grass, where the horses of their enemies could not enter, or where when entered they were worse than useless. It became necessary to dislodge the Tetons from this cover or the objects of the combat must be abandoned. Several desperate efforts had been repulsed, and the disheartened Pawnees were beginning to think of a retreat, when the well known war-cry of Hard-Heart was heard at hand, and at the next instant the chief appeared in their centre flourishing the scalp of the Great Sioux, as a banner that would lead to victory.

He was greeted by a shout of delight and followed into the cover with an impetuosity that for the moment drove all before it. But the bloody trophy, in the hand of the partisan served as an incentive to the attacked, as well as to the assailants. Mahtoree had left many a daring brave behind him in his band, and the orator, who in the debates of that day had manifested such pacific thoughts, now exhibited the most generous self-devotion, in order to wrest the memorial of a man he had never loved, from the hands of the avowed enemies of his people.

The result was in favor of numbers. After a severe struggle, in which the finest displays of personal intrepidity were exhibited by all the chiefs, the Pawnees were compelled to retire upon the open bottom, closely pressed by the Siouxes, who failed not to seize each foot of ground ceded by their enemies. Had the Tetons stayed their efforts on the margin of the grass, it is probable that the honor of the day would have been theirs, notwithstanding the irretrievable loss they had sustained in the death of Mahtoree. But the more reckless braves of the band were guilty of an indiscretion, that entirely changed the fortunes of the fight, and suddenly stripped them of their hard earned advantages.

A Pawnee chief had sunk under the numerous wounds he had received, and he fell, a target for a dozen arrows in the very last groupe of his retiring party. Regardless, alike, of inflicting further injury on their foes, and of the temerity of the act, the Sioux braves bounded forward with a whoop, each man burning with the wish to reap the high renown of striking the body of the dead. They were met by Hard-Heart and a chosen knot of warriors, all of whom were just as stoutly bent on saving the honor of their nation, from so foul a stain. The struggle was hand to hand, and blood began to flow more freely. As the Pawnees retired with the body, the Siouxes pressed upon their footsteps, and, at length the whole of the latter broke out of the cover with a common yell, and threatened to bear down all opposition, by sheer physical superiority.

The fate of Hard-Heart and his companions, all of whom

would have died rather than relinquish their object, would have been quickly sealed, but for a powerful and unlooked for interposition in their favor. A shout was heard from a little brake on the left. A volley from the fatal western rifle immediately succeeded. Some five or six Siouxes, leaped forward in the death agony and every arm among them was as suddenly suspended as if the lightning had flashed from the clouds to aid the cause of the Loups. Then came Ishmael and his stout sons, in open view, bearing down upon their late treacherous allies, with looks and voices that proclaimed the character of the succour.

The shock was too much for the fortitude of the Tetons. Several of their bravest chiefs had already fallen, and those that remained were instantly abandoned by the whole of the inferior herd. A few of the most desperate braves still lingered nigh the fatal symbol of their honor, and there nobly met their deaths, under the blows of the re-encouraged Pawnees. A second discharge from the rifles of the squatter and his party, completed the victory.

The Siouxes were now to be seen flying to more distant covers, with the same eagerness and desperation as a few moments before, they had been plunging into the fight. The triumphant Pawnees bounded forward in chase, like so many high-blooded and well trained hounds. On every side were heard the cries of victory, or the yells of revenge. A few of the fugitives endeavored to bear away the bodies of their fallen warriors, but the hot pursuit quickly compelled them to abandon the slain in order to preserve the living. Among all the struggles which were made, on that occasion, to guard the honor of the Siouxes from the stain which their peculiar opinions attached to the possession of the scalp of a fallen brave, but one solitary instance of success occurred.

The opposition of a particular chief to the hostile proceedings in the Councils of that morning has been already seen. But after having raised his voice, in vain, in support of peace, his arm was not backward, in doing its duty in the war. His prowess has been mentioned, and it was chiefly by his courage and example that the Tetons sustained themselves in the heroic manner they did, when the death of Mahtoree was known. This warrior, who, in the figurative language of his people was called, 'the Swooping Eagle,' had been the last to abandon the hopes of victory. When he found that the support of the dreaded rifle had robbed his band of their hard earned advantages, he sullenly retired amid a shower of missiles, to the secret spot where he had hid his horse, in the mazes of the highest grass. Here he found a new and an entirely unexpected competitor ready to dispute with him for the possession of the beast. It was Borecheena, the aged friend of Mahtoree; he whose voice had been given in opposition to his own wiser opinions, transfixed with an arrow, and evidently suffering under the pangs of approaching death.

"I have been on my last war-path," said the grim old warrior, when he found that the real owner of the animal had come to claim his property, "shall a Pawnee carry the white hairs of a Sioux into his village, to be a scorn to his women and children."

The other grasped his hand, answering to the appeal with the stern look of inflexible resolution. With this silent pledge, he assisted the wounded man to mount. So soon as he had led the horse to the margin of the cover, he threw himself also on its back, and securing his companion to his belt, he issued on the open plain, trusting entirely to the well known speed of the beast, for their mutual safety. The Pawnees were not long in catching a view of these new objects, and several turned their steeds to pursue. The race continued for a mile, without a murmur from the sufferer, though in addition to the agony of his body he had the pain of seeing his enemies approach at every leap of their horses.

"Stop," he said, raising a feeble arm to check the speed of his companion. "The eagle of my tribe must spread his wings wider. Let him carry the white hairs of an old warrior into the burnt-wood village."

Few words were necessary, between men who were governed by the same feelings of glory, and who were so well trained in the principles of their romantic honor. The Swooping Eagle, threw himself, from the back of the horse, and assisted the other to alight. The old man raised his tottering frame to its knees and, first casting a glance upward at the countenance of his countryman, as if to bid him adieu, he stretched out his neck to the blow he himself invited. A few strokes of the tomahawk, with a circling gash from the knife, sufficed to sever the head from the less valued trunk. The Teton mounted, again, just in season to escape a flight of arrows, which came from his eager and disappointed pursuers. Flourishing the grim and bloody visage, he darted away from the spot, with a shout of triumph, and was seen scouring the plains as if he were actually borne along on the wings of the powerful bird, from whose qualities he had received his flattering name. The Swooping Eagle reached his village in safety. He was one of the few Siouxes who escaped from the massacre of that fatal day, and for a long time he alone of the saved was able to lift his voice, in the Councils of his nation, with undiminished confidence.

The knife and the lance cut short the retreat of the larger portion of the vanquished. Even the retiring party of the women and children were scattered by the conquerors, and the sun had long sunk behind the rolling outline of the western horizon, before the fell business of that disastrous defeat was entirely ended.

Chapter XXXI

"Which is the merchant here, and which the Jew."
The Merchant of Venice, IV.i.174.

THE DAY dawned, the following morning, on a more tranquil scene. The work of blood had entirely ceased, and as the sun arose its light was shed on a broad expanse of quiet and solitude. The tents of Ishmael were still standing, where they had been last seen; but not another vestige of human existence could be traced in any other part of the waste. Here and there, little flocks of ravenous birds were sailing and screaming above those spots where some heavy-footed Teton had met his death, but every other sign of the recent combat had passed away. The river was to be traced far through the endless meadows by its serpentine and smoking bed, and the little silvery clouds of vapor which hung above the pools and springs were beginning to melt in air, as they felt the quickening warmth, which, pouring from the glowing sky, shed its bland and subtle influence on every object of the vast and unshadowed region. The Prairie was, like the heavens after the passage of the gust, soft, calm and soothing.

It was in the midst of such a scene, that the family of the squatter assembled to make their final decision, concerning the several individuals, who had been thrown into their power, by the fluctuating chances of the incidents related. Every being possessing life and liberty had been afoot, since the first streak of gray had lighted the east, and even the youngest of the erratic brood seemed conscious that the moment had arrived when circumstances were about to transpire that might leave a lasting impression on the wild fortunes of their semi-barbarous condition.

Ishmael moved through his little encampment with the seriousness of one who had been unexpectedly charged with matters of a gravity, exceeding any of the ordinary occurrences of his irregular existence. His sons, however, who had so often found occasions to prove the inexorable severity of their father's character, saw, in his sullen mien and cold eye rather a determination to adhere to his resolutions, which usually were as obstinately enforced as they were harshly conceived, than any evidences of wavering or doubt. Even Esther was sensibly affected by the important matters that pressed so heavily on the interests of her family. While she neglected none of those domestic offices, which would probably have proceeded under any conceivable circumstances, just as the world turns round with earthquakes rending its crust, and volcanoes consuming its vitals, yet her voice was pitched to a lower and more foreboding key than common, and the still frequent chidings of her children were tempered by something like the milder dignity of parental authority.

Abiram, as usual, seemed the one most given to solicitude and doubt. There were certain misgivings in the frequent glances that he turned on the unyielding countenance of Ishmael, which might have betrayed how little of their former confidence and good-understanding existed between them. His looks appeared to be vacillatory between hope and fear. At times his countenance lighted with the gleamings of a sordid joy, as he bent his look on the tent which contained his recovered prisoner, and then, again, the impression seemed unaccountably chased away by the shadows of intense apprehension. When under the influence of the latter feeling, his eye never failed to seek the visage of his dull and impenetrable kinsman. But there he rather found reason for alarm than grounds of encouragement, for the whole character of the squatter's countenance expressed the fearful truth that he had redeemed his dull faculties from the influence of the kidnapper, and that his thoughts were now brooding only on the achievement of his own stubborn intentions.

It was in this state of things that the sons of Ishmael, in obedience to an order from their father, conducted the several subjects of his contemplated decisions from their places of confinement into the open air. No one was exempted from this arrangement. Middleton and Inez, Paul and Ellen, Obed and the trapper were all brought forth, and placed in situations that were deemed suitable to receive the sentence of their arbitrary judge. The younger children gathered around the spot, in momentary but engrossing curiosity, and even Esther quitted her culinary labors and drew nigh to listen.

Hard-Heart, alone, of all his band, was present to witness the novel and far from unimposing spectacle. He stood leaning gravely on his lance, while the smoking steed, that grazed nigh, showed that he had ridden far and hard to be a spectator, on the occasion.

Ishmael had received his new ally with a coldness that showed his entire insensibility to that delicacy, which had induced the young chief to come alone, in order that the presence of his warriors might not create uneasiness, or distrust. He neither courted their assistance, nor dreaded their enmity, and he now proceeded to the business of the hour, with as much composure as if the species of patriarchal power he wielded was universally recognized.

There is something elevating in the possession of authority, however it may be abused. The mind is apt to make some efforts to prove the fitness between its qualities and the condition of its owner, though it may often fail, and render that ridiculous which was only hated before. But the effect on Ishmael Bush was not so disheartening. Grave in exterior, saturnine by temperament, formidable by his physical means and dangerous from his lawless obstinacy, his self-constituted tribunal excited a degree of awe, to which even the intelligent Middleton could not bring himself to be entirely insensible. Little time, however, was given to arrange his thoughts; for the squatter though unaccustomed to haste, having previously made up his mind, was not disposed to waste the moments in delay. When he saw that all were in their places, he cast a dull look over his prisoners, and addressed himself to the Captain as the principal man among the imaginary delinquents.

"I am called upon, this day, to fill the office, which in the settlements you give unto judges who are set apart to decide on matters that arise between man and man. I have but little knowledge of the ways of the courts, though there is a rule that is known unto all, and which teaches that an 'eye must be returned for an eye' and 'a tooth for a tooth.' I am no troubler of County houses, and least of all do I like living on a plantation that the sheriff has surveyed, yet there is a reason in such a law that makes it a safe rule to journey by, and therefore it ar' a solemn fact, that this day shall I abide by it, and give unto all and each, that which is his due and no more."

When Ishmael had delivered his mind thus far, he paused and looked about him as if he would trace the effects in the countenances of his hearers. When his eye met that of Middleton he was answered by the latter—

"If the evil doer is to be punished, and he that has offended none to be left to go at large, you must change situations with me, and become a prisoner instead of a Judge."

"You mean to say that I have done you wrong in taking the lady from her father's house, and leading her so far against her will into these wild districts," returned the unmoved squatter, who manifested as little resentment as he betrayed compunction at the charge. "I shall not put the lie on the back of an evil deed, and deny your words. Since things have come to this pass, between us, I have found time to think the matter over at my leisure, and though none of your swift thinkers, who can see or who pretend to see into the nature of all things, by a turn of the eye, yet am I a man open to reason, and give me my time, one who is not given to deny the truth. Therefore have I mainly concluded that it was a mistake to take a child from its parent, and the Lady shall be returned whence she has been brought, as tenderly and as safely as man can do it."

"Ay, ay," added Esther, "the man is right. Poverty and labor bore hard upon him especially as county officers were getting troublesome, and in a weak moment he did the wicked act; but he has listened to my words, and his mind has got round again into its honest corner. An awful and a dangerous thing it is, to be bringing the daughters of other people into a peaceable and well-governed family!"

"And who will thank you, for the same, after what has been already done!" muttered Abiram, with a grin of disappointed cupidity, in which malignity and terror were disgustingly united. "When the devil has once made out his account, you may look for your receipt in full, only, at his hands."

"Peace!" said Ishmael, stretching his heavy hand towards his kinsman, in a manner that instantly silenced the speaker. "Your voice is like a raven's in my ears. If *you* had never spoken, I should have been spared this shame."

"Since then you are beginning to lose sight of your errors and to see the truth," said Middleton, "do not things by halves, but, by the generosity of your conduct, purchase friends, who may be of use in warding off any future danger from the law—"

"Young man," interrupted the squatter, with a dark frown, "*you*, too, have said enough. If fear of the law had come over me, you would not be here to witness the manner in which Ishmael Bush deals out justice."

"Smother not your good intentions, and remember if you contemplate violence to any among us, that the arm of that law you affect to despise reaches far, and that though its movements are sometimes slow, they are not the less certain."

"Yes, there is too much truth in his words, squatter," said the trapper, whose attentive ears rarely suffered a syllable to be uttered unheeded in his presence. "A busy and a troublesome arm, it often proves to be, here, in this land of America, where as they say, man is left greatly to the following of his own wishes, compared to other countries, and happier, ay, and, more manly, and more honest too, is he for the privilege. Why, do you know, my men, that there are regions where the law is so busy as to say, in this fashion shall you live, in that fashion shall you die, and in such another fashion shall you take leave of the world to be sent before the judgement seat of the Lord! A wicked and a troublesome meddling is that with the business of one, who has not made his creatures to be herded, like oxen and driven from field to field, as their stupid and selfish keepers may judge of their need and wants. A miserable land must that be where they fetter the mind as well as the body, and where the creatures of God, being born children are kept so by the wicked inventions of men who would take upon themselves the office of the great Governor of all!"

During the delivery of this pertinent opinion Ishmael was content to be silent, though the look with which he regarded the speaker manifested any other feeling than that of amity. When the old man was done, he turned to Middleton, and continued the subject which the other had interrupted.

"As to ourselves, young Captain, there has been wrong on both sides. If I have borne hard upon your feelings, in taking away your wife, with an honest intention of giving her back to you when the plans of that devil incarnate were answered, so have you broken into my encampment, aiding and abetting, as they have called many an honester bargain, in destroying my property."

"But what I did, was to liberate—"

"The matter is settled between us," interrupted Ishmael, with the air of one, who, having made up his own opinion on the merits of the question, cared very little for those of other people. "You and your wife are free to go and come, when and how you please. Abner, set the Captain at liberty; and now if you will tarry until I am ready to draw nigher to the settlements you shall both have the benefit of carriage; if not, never say that you did not get a friendly offer."

"Now may the strong oppress me and my sins be visited harshly on my own head if I forget your honesty, however slow it has been in showing itself," cried Middleton, hastening to the side of the weeping Inez, the instant he was released; "and, Friend, I pledge you the honor of a soldier that your own part of this transaction shall be forgotten, whatever I may deem fit to have done, when I reach a place where the arm of Government can make itself felt."

The dull smile with which the squatter answered to this assurance proved how little he valued the pledge that the youth in the first revulsion of his feelings was so free to make.

"Neither fear nor favor, but what I call justice has brought me to this judgement," he said. "Do you that which may seem right in your eyes, and believe that the world is wide enough to hold us both, without our crossing each other's path again. If you ar' content, well; if you ar' not content, seek to ease your feelings in your own fashion. I shall not ask to be let up, when you once put me fairly down. And now, Doctor, have I come to your leaf in my accounts. It is time to foot up the small reckoning that has been running on, for some time atwixt us. With you I entered into open and manly faith; in what manner have you kept it?"

The singular felicity with which Ishmael had contrived to shift the responsibility of all that had passed from his own shoulders to those of his prisoners, backed as it was by circumstances that hardly admitted of a very philosophical examination of any mooted point in Ethics, was sufficiently embarrassing to the several individuals, who were so unexpectedly required to answer for a conduct, which, in their simplicity, they had deemed so meritorious. The life of Obed had been so purely theoretic, that his amazement was not the least embarrassing, at a state of things, which might not have proved so very remarkable had he been a little more practised in the ways of the world. The worthy naturalist was not the first by many, who found himself, at the precise moment when he was expecting praise, suddenly arraigned to answer for the very conduct on which he rested all his claims to commendation. Though not a little scandalized at the unexpected turn of the transaction, he was fain to make the best of circumstances, and to bring forth such matter in justification, as first presented itself to his disordered faculties.

"That there did exist a certain compactum, or agreement, between Obed Batt, M.D. and Ishmael Bush, viator, or erratic husbandman," he said, endeavoring to avoid all offense in the use of terms, "I am not disposed to deny. I will admit that it was therein conditioned or stipulated, that a certain journey should be performed conjointly or in company, until so many days had been numbered. But as the said time has fully expired, I presume it fair to infer, that the bargain may now, be said to be obsolete—"

"Ishmael," interrupted the impatient Esther, "make no words with a man who can break your bones as easily as set them, and let the poisoning devil go! He's a cheat, from box to phial. Give him half the Prairie, and take the other half yourself. He an acclimator! I will engage to get the brats acclimated to a fever and ague bottom in a week and not a word shall be uttered, harder to pronounce than the bark of a cherry-tree, with perhaps a drop or two of western comfort. One thing ar' a fact, Ishmael, I like no fellow-travellers who can give a heavy feel to an honest woman's tongue, ay, and that without caring whether her household is in order, or out of order."

The air of settled gloom which had taken possession of the squatter's countenance, lighted, for an instant, with a look of dull drollery as he answered—

"Different people might judge differently, Eester, of the virtue of the man's art. But sin' it is your wish to let him depart, I will not plough the Prairie to make the walking rough. Friend, you ar' at liberty to go into the settlements and there I would advise you to tarry, as men, like me, who make but few contracts do not relish the custom of breaking them so easily."

"And now, Ishmael," resumed his conquering wife, "in order to keep a quiet family, and to smother all heart-burnings atween us, show yonder red-skin and his daughter," pointing to the aged Le Balafré and the widowed Tachechana, "the way to their village, and let us say to them, God bless you, and farewell, in the same breath."

"They ar' the captives of the Pawnee, according to the rules of Indian warfare, and I cannot meddle with his rights."

"Beware the Devil, my man! He's a cheat and a tempter and none can say they ar' safe with his awful delusions before their eyes! Take the advice of one, who has the honor of your name at heart, and send the tawney Jezebel away."

The squatter laid his broad hand on her shoulder and looking her steadily in the eye, he answered, in tones that were both stern and solemn.

"Woman, we have that before us, which calls our thoughts to other matters than the follies you mean. Remember what is to come, and put your silly jealousy to sleep."

"It is true, it is true," murmured his wife, moving back among her daughters, "God forgive me, that I should forget it!"

"And, now, young man; you who have so often come into my clearing, under the pretence of lining the bee into his hole," resumed Ishmael, after a momentary pause, as if to recover the equilibrium of his mind, " with you there is a heavier account to settle. Not satisfied with rummaging my camp, you have stolen a girl who is akin to my wife, and who I had calculated to make, one day, a daughter of my own."

A stronger sensation was produced by this, than by any of the preceding interrogations. All the young men bent their curious eyes on Paul and Ellen, the former of whom seemed in no small mental confusion, while the latter bent her face on her bosom in shame.

"Harkee, friend Ishmael Bush," returned the Bee-hunter, who found that he was expected to answer to the charge of burglary, as well as to that of abduction. "That I did not give the most civil treatment to your pots and pails I am not going to gainsay. If you will name the price you put upon the articles, it is possible the damage may be quietly settled between us, and all hard feelings forgotten. I was not in a church-going humour when we got upon your rock, and it is more than probable there was quite as much kicking as preaching among your wares, but a hole in the best man's coat can be mended by money. As to the matter of Ellen Wade, here, it may not be got over so easily. Different people have different opinions on the subject of matrimony. Some think it is enough to say yes and no to the questions of the magistrate, or of the parson if one happens to be handy, in order to make a quiet house, but I think that when a young woman's mind is fairly bent on going in a certain direction, it will be quite as prudent to let her body follow. Not that I mean to say, Ellen was not altogether forced to what she did, and therefore she is just as innocent, in this matter, as yonder jack-ass, who was made to carry her, and greatly against his will, too, as I am ready to swear he would say himself, if he could speak as loud as he can bray."

"Nelly," resumed the squatter, who paid very little attention to what Paul considered a highly creditable and ingenious vindication. "Nelly, this is a wide and wicked world on which you have been in such a hurry to cast yourself. You have fed and you have slept, in my camp for a year, and I did hope that you had found the free air of the borders, enough to your mind to wish to remain among us."

"Let the girl have her will," muttered Esther, from the rear, "he who might have persuaded her to stay, is sleeping in the cold and naked Prairie, and little hope is left of changing her humour; besides a woman's mind is a wilful thing and not easily turned from its waywardness as you know yourself, my man, or I should not be here the mother of your sons and daughters."

The squatter seemed reluctant to abandon his views on the abashed girl, so easily, and before he answered to the suggestion of his wife, he turned his usual dull look along the line of the curious countenances of his boys, as if to see whether there was not one among them fit to fill the place of the deceased. Paul was not slow to observe the expression, and hitting nigher than usual on the secret thoughts of the other, he believed he had fallen on an expedient which might remove every difficulty.

"It is quite plain, friend Bush," he said, "that there are two opinions in this matter; yours for your sons, and mine for myself. I see but one amicable way of settling this dispute, which is as follows. Do you make a choice among your boys of any you will, and let us walk off together for the matter of a few miles into the Prairies; the one who stays behind, can never trouble any man's house or his fixen, and the one who comes back may make the best of his way he can, in the good-wishes of the young woman."

"Paul!" exclaimed the reproachful, but smothered voice of Ellen.

"Never fear, Nelly," whispered the literal bee-hunter, whose straight-going mind suggested no other motive of uneasiness on the part of his mistress than concern for himself; "I have taken the measure of them all, and you may trust an eye that has seen to line many a bee into his hole!"

"I am not about to set myself up as a ruler of inclinations," observed the squatter. "If the heart of the child is truly in the settlements, let her declare it; she shall have no let or hindrance from me. Speak, Nelly, and let what you say come from your wishes without fear or favor. Would you leave us to go with this young man into the settled countries, or will you tarry and share the little we have to give, but which to you we give so freely?"

Thus called upon to decide, Ellen could no longer hesitate. The glance of her eye was at first timid and furtive. But as the colour flushed her features and her breathing became quick and excited, it was apparent that the native spirit of the girl was gaining the ascendancy over the bashfulness of sex.

"You took me a fatherless, impoverished, and friendless orphan," she said struggling to command her voice, "when others, who live in what may be called affluence compared to your state, chose to forget me, and may heaven in its goodness bless you for it. The little I have done, will never pay you for that one act of kindness. I like not your manner of life; it is different from the ways of my childhood and it is different from my wishes, still, had you not led this sweet and unoffending lady from her friends, I should never have quitted you, until you yourself had said, 'go, and the blessing of God go with you'!"

"The act was not wise but it is repented of; and so far as it can be done, in safety, it shall be repaired. Now, speak freely; will you tarry, or will you go?"

"I have promised the lady," said Ellen dropping her eyes again to the earth, "not to leave her, and after she has received so much wrong from our hands she may have a right to claim that I keep my word."

"Take the cords from the young man," said Ishmael. When the order was obeyed he motioned for all his sons to advance and he placed them in a row before the eyes of Ellen. "Now let there be no trifling, but open your heart. Here ar' all I have to offer, besides a hearty welcome."

The distressed girl turned her abashed look from the countenance of one of the young men to that of another, until her eye met the troubled and working features of Paul. Then nature got the better of forms. She threw herself into the arms of the bee-hunter, and sufficiently proclaimed her choice by sobbing aloud. Ishmael signed to his sons to fall back, and evidently mortified though perhaps not disappointed by the result, he no longer hesitated.

"Take her," he said, "and deal honestly and kindly by her. The girl has that in her which should make her welcome in any man's house, and I should be loth to hear she ever came to harm. And now I have settled with you all, on terms that I hope you will not find hard, but on the contrary just and manly. I have only another question to ask and that is of the Captain; do you choose to profit by my teams in going into the settlements, or not?"

"I hear that some soldiers of my party are looking for me near the villages of the Pawnees," said Middleton, "and I intend to accompany this chief in order to join my men."

"Then the sooner we part the better. Horses are plenty on the bottom. Go, make your choice and leave us in peace."

"That is impossible while the old man who has been a friend of my family near half-a-century is left a prisoner. What has he done that he too is not released?"

"Ask no questions that may lead to deceitful answers," sullenly returned the squatter; "I have dealings of my own with that trapper, that it may not befit an officer of the States to meddle with. Go, while your road is open."

"The man may be giving you honest counsel, and that which it concerns you all to hearken to," observed the old captive who seemed in no uneasiness at the extraordinary condition in which he found himself. "The Siouxes are a numberless and bloody-minded race and no one can say how long it may be, afore they will be out again on the scent of revenge. Therefore I say to you, go, also; and take especial heed in crossing the bottoms that you get not entangled again in the fires, for the honest hunters often burn the grass, at this season, in order that the buffaloes may find a sweeter and a greener pasturage in the spring."

"I should forget not only my gratitude, but my duty to the laws, were I to leave this prisoner in your hands even by his own consent, without knowing the nature of his crime, in which we may have all been his innocent accessaries."

"Will it satisfy you to know that he merits all he will receive?"

"It will at least change my opinion of his character."

"Look then at this," said Ishmael, placing before the eyes of the Captain the bullet that had been found about the person of the dead Asa; " with this morsel of lead did he lay low as fine a boy as ever gave joy to a parent's eyes!"

"I cannot believe that he has done this deed unless in self-defence, or on some justifiable provocation. That he knew of the death of your son I confess, for he pointed out the brake in which the body lay, but that he has wrongfully taken his life nothing but his own acknowledgment shall persuade me to believe."

"I have lived long," commenced the trapper, who found by the general pause that he was expected to vindicate himself from the heavy imputation, "and much evil have I seen in my day. Many are the prowling bears and leaping panthers that I have met fighting for the morsel which has been thrown in their way, and many are the reasoning men that I have looked on striving against each other unto death, in order that human madness might have its hour. For myself, I hope there is no boasting in saying that though my hand has been needed in putting down wickedness and oppression, it has never struck a blow of which its owner will be ashamed to hear, at a reckoning that shall be far mightier than this."

"If my father, has taken life from one of his tribe," said the young Pawnee, whose quick eye had read the meaning of what was passing, in the bullet and in the countenances of the others, "let him give himself up to the friends of the dead, like a warrior. He is too just to need thongs to lead him to judgment."

"Boy, I hope you do me justice. If I had done the foul deed with which they charge me, I should have manhood enough to come and offer my head to the blow of punishment as all good and honest red-men do the same." Then giving his anxious Indian friend a look to reassure him of his innocence, he turned to the rest of his attentive and interested listeners as he continued in English, "I have a short story to tell, and he that believes it will believe the truth, and he that disbelieves it will only lead himself astray, and perhaps his neighbour too. We were all outlying about your camp, friend squatter, as by this time you may begin to suspect, when we found that it contained a wronged and imprisoned lady, with intentions neither more honest nor dishonest than to set her free, as in nature and justice she had a right to be. Seeing that I was more skilled in scouting than the others, while they lay back in the cover, I was sent upon the plain, on the business of the reconnoitrings. You little thought that one was so nigh who saw into all the circumventions of your hunt, but there was I, sometimes flat behind a bush or a tuft of grass, sometimes rolling down a hill into a bottom, and little did you dream that your motions were watched as the panther watches the drinking deer. Lord, squatter, when I was a man in the pride and strength of my days, I have looked in at the tent door of the enemy, and they sleeping, ay, and dreaming too of being at home and in peace. I wish there was time to give you the partic—"

"Proceed with your explanation," interrupted Middleton.

"Ah! and a bloody and wicked sight it was! There I lay in a low bed of grass, as two of the hunters came nigh each other. Their meeting was not cordial, nor such as men who meet in a desert should give each other, but I thought they would have parted in peace, until I saw one put his rifle to the other's back and do, what I call a treacherous and sinful murder. It was a noble and a manly youth, that boy!—Though the powder burnt his coat he stood the shock for more than a minute, before he fell. Then was he brought to his knees and a desperate and manful fight he made to the brake, like a wounded bear seeking a cover."

"And why, in the name of heavenly justice, did you conceal this!" cried Middleton.

"What! think you, Captain, that a man who has spent more than three-score years in the wilderness has not learned the virtue of discretion. What red-warrior runs to tell the sights he has seen, until a fitting time? I took the Doctor to the place in order to see whether his skill might not come in use, and our friend the bee-hunter, being in company, was knowing to the fact that the bushes held the body."

"Ay; it ar' true," said Paul; "but not knowing what private reasons might make the old trapper wish to hush the matter up, I said as little about the thing as possible; which was just nothing at all."

"And who was the perpetrator of this deed?" demanded Middleton.

"If by perpetrator you mean him who did the act, yonder stands the man, and a shame and a disgrace is it to our race that he is of the blood and family of the dead."

"He lies! he lies!" shrieked Abiram. "I did no murder; I gave but blow for blow."

The voice of Ishmael was deep and even awful, as he answered—

"It is enough. Let the old man go. Boys, put the brother of your mother in his place."

"Touch me not!" cried Abiram. "I'll call on God to curse ye if you touch me!"

The wild and disordered gleam of his eye, at first induced the young men to arrest their steps, but when Abner, older and more resolute than the rest, advanced full upon him with a countenance that bespoke the hostile state of his mind, the affrighted criminal turned, and making an abortive effort to fly, fell with his face to the earth, to all appearance perfectly dead. Amid the low exclamations of horror which succeeded, Ishmael made a gesture which commanded his sons to bear the body into a tent.

"Now," he said, turning to those who were strangers in his camp, "nothing is left to be done, but for each to go his own road. I wish you all well; and to you, Ellen, though you may not prize the gift, I say, God bless you."

Middleton, awe-struck by what he believed a manifest judgment of Heaven, made no further resistance but prepared to depart. The arrangements were brief and soon completed. When they were all ready, they took a short and silent leave of the squatter and his family, and then the whole of the singularly constituted party was seen slowly, and silently following the victorious Pawnee, towards his distant villages.

Chapter XXXII

> "And I beseech you,
> Wrest once the law, to your authority:
> To do a great right, do a little wrong."
> *The Merchant of Venice*, IV.i.214–16.

ISHMAEL AWAITED long and patiently for the motley train of Hard-Heart to disappear. When his scout reported that the last straggler of the Indians, who had joined their chief so soon as he was at such a distance from the encampment as to excite no jealousy by their numbers, had gone behind the most distant swell of the Prairie, he gave forth the order to strike his tents. The cattle were already in the gears, and the moveables were soon transferred to their usual places in the different vehicles. When all these arrangements were completed, the little wagon, which had so long been the tenement of Inez, was drawn before the tent into which the insensible body of the kidnapper had been borne, and preparations were evidently made for the reception of another Prisoner. Then it was, as Abiram appeared, pale, terrified and tottering beneath a load of detected guilt, that the younger members of the family were first apprised that he still belonged to the class of the living. A general and superstitious impression had spread among them, that his crime had been visited by a terrible retribution from heaven, and they now gazed at him as at a being who belonged rather to another world than as a mortal who like themselves had still to endure the last agony, before the great link of human existence could be broken. The criminal himself appeared to be in a state, in which the most sensitive and startling terror was singularly combined with total physical apathy. The truth was, that while his person had been numbed by the shock his susceptibility to apprehension kept his agitated mind in unrelieved distress. When he found himself in the open air, he looked about him, in order to gather, if possible, some evidences of his future fate, from the countenances of those gathered round. Seeing every where grave but composed features, and meeting in no eye any expression that threatened immediate violence, the miserable man began to revive, and, by the time he was seated in the wagon, his artful faculties were beginning to plot the expedients of parrying the just resentment of his kinsmen, or if these should fail him, the means of escaping from a punishment that his forebodings told him would be terrible.

Throughout the whole of these preparations Ishmael rarely spoke. A gesture, or a glance of the eye, served to indicate his pleasure to his sons, and with these simple methods of communication, all parties appeared content. When the signal was made to proceed, the squatter threw his rifle into the hollow of his arm, and his axe across his shoulder, taking the lead as usual. Esther buried herself in the wagon which contained her daughters; the young men took their customary places among the cattle, or nigh the teams, and the whole proceeded at their ordinary, dull, but unremitted gait.

For the first time, in many a day, the squatter turned his back towards the setting sun. The route he held was in the direction of the settled country, and the manner in which he moved, sufficed to tell his children, who had learned to read their father's determinations in his mien, that their journey on the Prairie was shortly to have an end. Still nothing else transpired for hours, that might denote the existence of any sudden, or violent, revolution in the purposes or feelings of Ishmael. During all that time he marched alone, keeping a few hundred rods in front of his teams, seldom giving any sign of extraordinary excitement. Once or twice, indeed, his huge figure was seen standing on the summit of some distant swell, with his head bent towards the earth, as he leaned on his rifle; but then these moments of intense thought were rare, and of short continuance. The train had long thrown its shadows towards the east, before any material alteration was made in the disposition of their march. Water-courses were waded, plains were passed, and rolling ascents risen and descended, without producing the smallest change. Long practised in the difficulties of that peculiar species of travelling, in which he was engaged, the squatter avoided the more impracticable obstacles of their route by a sort of instinct, invariably inclining to the right or left, in season, as the formation of the land, the presence of trees or the signs of rivers forewarned him of the necessity of such movements.

At length the hour arrived when charity to man and beast required a temporary suspension of labor. Ishmael chose the required spot with his customary sagacity. The regular formation of the country, such as it has been described in the earlier pages of our book, had long been interrupted by a more unequal and broken surface. There were it is true in general the same wide and empty wastes, the same rich and extensive bottoms, and that wild and singular combination of swelling fields and of nakedness which gives that region the appearance of an ancient country, incomprehensibly stripped of its people and their dwellings. But these distinguishing features of the rolling Prairies had long been interrupted by irregular hillocks, occasional masses of rock and broad belts of forest.

Ishmael chose a spring that broke out of the base of a rock some forty or fifty feet in elevation as a place well suited to the wants of his herds. The water moistened a small swale that lay beneath the spot, which yielded in return for the fecund gift, a scanty growth of grass. A solitary willow had taken root in the alluvion, and profiting by its exclusive possession of the soil, the tree had sent up its stem far above the crest of the adjacent rock, whose peaked summit had once been shadowed by its branches. But its loveliness had gone with the mysterious principle of life. As if in mockery of the meagre show of verdure that the spot exhibited, it remained a noble and solemn monument of former fertility. The larger, ragged and fantastick branches still obtruded themselves abroad, while the white and hoary trunk stood naked and tempest-riven. Not a leaf, nor a sign of vegetation was to be seen about it. In all things it proclaimed the frailty of existence, and the fulfilment of time.

Here Ishmael after making the customary signal for the train to approach, threw his vast frame upon the earth and seemed to muse on the deep responsibility of his present situation. His sons were not long in arriving, for the cattle no sooner scented the food and water than they quickened their pace, and then succeeded the usual bustle and avocations of a halt.

The impression made by the scene of that morning was not so deep, or lasting, on the children of Ishmael and Esther as to induce them to forget the wants of nature. But while the sons were searching among their stores for something substantial to appease their hunger, and the younger fry were wrangling about their simple dishes, the parents of the unnurtured family were differently employed.

When the squatter saw that all, even to the reviving Abiram were busy in administering to their appetites, he gave his downcast partner a glance of his eye and withdrew towards a distant roll of the land, which bounded the view towards the east. The meeting of the pair, in this naked spot was like an interview held above the grave of their murdered son. Ishmael signed to his wife to take a seat beside him on a fragment of rock, and then followed a space during which neither seemed disposed to speak.

"We have journeyed together long, through good and bad," Ishmael at length commenced; "much have we had to try us, and some bitter cups have we been made to swallow, my woman, but nothing like this has ever before lain in my path."

"It is a heavy cross for a poor, misguided and sinful woman to bear!" returned Esther, bowing her head to her knees, and partly concealing her face in her dress. "A heavy and a burthensome weight is this to be laid upon the shoulders of a sister and a Mother!"

"Ay; therein lies the hardship of the case. I had brought my mind to the punishment of that houseless trapper, with no great strivings, for the man has done me few favors, and God forgive me if I suspected him wrongfully of much evil. This is, however, bringing shame in at one door of my cabin in order to drive it out at the other. But shall a son of mine be murdered and he who did it go at large. The boy would never rest!"

"Oh, Ishmael, we pushed the matter far. Had little been said, who would have been the wiser? our consciences might then have been quiet."

"Eest'er," said the husband turning on her a reproachful but still a dull regard, "the hour has been, my woman, when you thought another hand had done this wickedness?"

"I did, I did; the Lord gave me the feeling as a punishment for my sins; but his mercy was not slow in lifting the veil; I looked into the book, Ishmael, and there I found the words of comfort."

"Have you that book at hand, woman; it may happen to advise in such a dreary business."

Esther fumbled in her pocket, and was not long in producing the fragment of a bible, which had been thumbed and smoke-dried till the print was nearly illegible. It was the only article in the nature of a book that was to be found among the chattels of the squatter, and it had been preserved by his wife as a melancholy relick of more prosperous and possibly of more innocent days. She had long been in the habit of resorting to it under the pressure of such circumstances as were palpably beyond human redress though her spirit and resolution rarely needed support under those that admitted of reparation through any of the ordinary means of reprisal. In this manner Esther had made a sort of convenient ally of the word of God, rarely troubling it for counsel, however, except when her own incompetency to avert an evil was too apparent to be disputed. We shall leave casuists to determine how far she resembled any other believers in this particular, and proceed directly with the matter before us.

"There are many awful passages in these pages, Ishmael," she said, when the volume was opened, and the leaves were slowly turning under her finger, "and some there ar' that teach the rules of punishment."

Her husband made a gesture for her to find one of those brief rules of conduct which have been received among all christian nations as the direct mandates of the Creator, and which have been found so just, that even they who deny their high authority admit their wisdom. Ishmael listened with grave attention, as his companion read all those verses which her memory suggested and which were thought applicable to the situation in which they found themselves. He made her show him the words, which he regarded with a sort of strange reverence. A resolution once taken was usually irrevocable in one who was moved with so much difficulty. He put his hand upon the book and closed the pages himself, as much as to apprise his wife that he was satisfied. Esther, who so well knew his character, trembled at the action, and casting a glance at his steady eye, she said—

"And yet, Ishmael, my blood, and the blood of my children is in his veins! cannot mercy be shown?"

"Woman," he answered sternly, "when we believed that miserable old trapper had done this deed, nothing was said of mercy."

Esther made no reply, but folding her arms upon her breast she sat silent and thoughtful for many minutes. Then she once more turned her anxious gaze upon the countenance of her husband, where she found all passion and care apparently buried in the coldest apathy. Satisfied now that the fate of her brother was sealed, and possibly conscious how well he merited the punishment, that was meditated, she no longer thought of mediation. No more words passed between them. Their eyes met, for an instant and then both arose and walked in profound silence, towards the encampment.

The squatter found his children expecting his return in the usual, listless manner with which they awaited all coming events. The cattle were already herded and the horses in their gears, in readiness to proceed, so soon as he should indicate that such was his pleasure. The children were already in their proper vehicle and, in short, nothing delayed the departure but the absence of the parents of the wild brood.

"Abner," said the Father with the deliberation with which all his proceedings were characterized, "take the brother of your mother from the wagon, and let him stand upon the 'arth."

Abiram issued from his place of concealment, trembling it is true, but far from destitute of hopes as to his final success in appeasing the just resentment of his kinsman. After throwing a glance around him, with the vain wish of finding a single countenance in which he might detect a solitary gleam of sympathy, he endeavoured to smother those apprehensions that were by this time reviving in their original violence by forcing a sort of friendly communication between himself and the squatter.

"The beasts are getting jaded, brother," he said "and as we have made so good a march, already, is it not time to 'camp. To my eye, you may go far, before a better place than this is found to pass the night in."

"'Tis well you like it. Your tarry, here, ar' likely to be long.

My sons, draw nigh, and listen. Abiram White," he added lifting his cap and speaking with a solemnity and steadiness that rendered even his dull mien imposing, "you have slain my first born and according to the laws of God and Man must you die!"

The kidnapper started at this terrible and sudden sentence, with the terror that one would exhibit who unexpectedly found himself in the grasp of a monster from whose power there was no retreat. Although filled with the most serious forebodings of what might be his lot, his courage had not been equal to looking his danger in the face, and with the deceitful consolation with which timid tempers are apt to conceal their desperate condition from themselves, he had rather courted a treacherous relief in his cunning, than prepared himself for the worst.

"Die!" he repeated in a voice that scarcely issued from his chest. "A man is surely safe among his kinsmen!"

"So thought my boy," returned the squatter, motioning for the team that contained his wife and the girls to proceed, as he very coolly examined the priming of his piece. "By the rifle did you destroy my son; it is fit and just that you meet your end by the same weapon."

Abiram stared about him, with a gaze that bespoke an unsettled reason. He even laughed, as if he would not only persuade himself but others that what he heard was some pleasantry intended to try his nerves. But no where did his frightful merriment meet with an answering echo. All around him was solemn and still. The visages of his nephews were excited, but cold towards him, and that of his former confederate frightfully determined. This very steadiness of mien was a thousand times more alarming and hopeless than any violence could have proved. The latter might possibly have touched his spirit, and awakened resistance, but the former threw him entirely on the feeble resources of himself.

"Brother," he said in a hurried, unnatural whisper, "did I hear you?"

"My words are plain, Abiram White; thou hast done murder, and for the same must thou die."

"Esther! Sister, Sister, will you leave me! Oh! Sister, do you hear my call!"

"I hear one speak from the grave," returned the husky tones of Esther, as the wagon passed the spot where the criminal stood. "It is the voice of my first born calling aloud for justice! God have mercy, God have mercy, on your soul!"

The team slowly pursued its route, and the deserted Abiram now found himself deprived of the smallest vestige of hope. Still he could not summon fortitude to meet his death, and had not his limbs refused to aid him, he would yet have attempted to fly. Then by a sudden revolution from hope to utter despair he fell upon his knees and commenced a prayer in which cries for mercy to God and to his kinsman were wildly and blasphemously mingled. The sons of Ishmael turned away in horror at the disgusting spectacle, and even the stern nature of the squatter began to bend before so abject misery.

"May that which you ask of Him, be granted," he said, "but a father can never forget a murdered child."

He was answered by the most humble appeals for time. A week, a day, an hour were each implored, with an earnestness commensurate to the value they receive when a whole life is compressed into their short duration. The squatter was troubled and at length he yielded in part to the petitions of the criminal. His final purpose was not altered, though he changed the means. "Abner," he said, "mount the rock, and look on every hand, that we may be sure none are nigh."

While his nephew was obeying this order, gleams of reviving hope were seen shooting across the quivering features of the kidnapper. The report was favorable, nothing having life, the retiring teams excepted, was to be seen. A messenger was, however, coming from the latter, in great apparent haste. Ishmael awaited its arrival. He received from the hands of one of his wondering and frighted girls a fragment of that book which Esther had preserved with so much care. The squatter beckoned the child away, and placed the leaves in the hands of the criminal.

"Eester has sent you this," he said, "that in your last moments, you may remember God."

"Bless her, bless her; a good and kind sister has she been to me! But time must be given that I may read, time, my brother, time."

"Time shall not be wanting. You shall be your own executioner, and this miserable office shall pass away from my hands."

Ishmael proceeded to put his new resolution in force. The immediate apprehensions of the kidnapper were quieted by an assurance that he might yet live for days, though his punishment was inevitable. A reprieve, to one abject and wretched as Abiram, temporarily, produced the same effects as a pardon. He was even foremost in assisting in the appalling arrangements, and of all the actors, in that solemn tragedy his voice alone was facetious and jocular.

A thin shelf of the rock projected beneath one of the ragged arms of the willow. It was many feet from the ground, and admirably adapted to the purpose, which in fact, its appearance had suggested. On this little platform the criminal was placed, his arms bound at the elbows behind his back beyond the possibility of liberation, with a proper cord leading from his neck to the limb of the tree. The latter was so placed that when suspended the body could find no foothold. The fragment of the bible was placed in his hands, and he was left to seek his consolation as he might from its pages.

"And now, Abiram White," said the squatter when his sons had descended from completing this arrangement, "I give you a last and solemn asking. Death is before you in two shapes. With this rifle can your misery be cut short, or by that cord sooner or later must you meet your end."

"Let me yet live, Oh! Ishmael, you know not how sweet life is, when the last moment draws so nigh!"

" 'Tis done," said the squatter, motioning for his assistants to follow the herds and teams. "And now, miserable man, that it may prove a consolation to your end, I forgive you my wrongs, and leave you to your God."

Ishmael turned, and pursued his way across the plain, at his ordinarily sluggish and ponderous gait. Though his head was bent a little towards the earth, his inactive mind did not prompt him to cast a look behind. Once, indeed, he thought he heard his name called in tones that were a little smothered, but they failed to make him pause.

At the spot where he and Esther had conferred, he reached the boundary of the visible horizon from the rock. Here he stopped and ventured a glance in the direction of the place he had just quitted. The sun was near dipping into the plains beyond, and its last rays lighted the naked branches of the willow. He saw the ragged outline of the whole drawn against the glowing heavens, and he even traced the still upright form of the being he had left to his misery. Turning the roll of the swell he proceeded with the feelings of one, who had been suddenly and violently separated from a recent confederate forever.

Within a mile, the squatter overtook his teams. His sons had found a place suited to the encampment for the night, and merely awaited his approach to confirm their choice. Few words were necessary to express his acquiescence. Every thing passed in a silence more general and remarkable than ever. The chidings of Esther were not heard among her young, or if heard, they were more in the tones of softened admonition, than in her usual, upbraiding, key.

No questions or explanations passed between the husband and his wife. It was only as the latter was about to withdraw among her children for the night that the former saw her taking a furtive look at the pan of his rifle. Ishmael bad his sons seek their rest, announcing his intention to look to the safety of the camp in person. When all was still, he walked out upon the Prairie, with a sort of sensation that he found his breathing among the tents too straightened. The night was well adapted to heighten the feelings which had been created by the events of the day.

The wind had risen with the moon, and it was occasionally sweeping heavily over the plain, in a manner that rendered it easy for the sentinel to fancy strange and unearthly sounds were in the blasts. Yielding to the extraordinary impulses of which he was the subject, he cast a glance around, to see that all were slumbering in security, and then he strayed towards the swell of land already mentioned. Here the squatter found himself at a point that commanded a view to the east and to the west. Light fleecy clouds were driving before the moon, which was cold and watery though there were moments, when its placid rays were shed from clear blue fields seeming to soften objects to its own mild loveliness.

For the first time, in a life of so much wild adventure,

Ishmael felt a keen sense of solitude. The naked Prairies began to assume the forms of illimitable and dreary wastes, and the rushing of the wind sounded like the whisperings of the dead. It was not long before he thought a shriek was borne past him on a blast. It did not sound like a call from earth, but it swept frightfully through the upper air, mingled with the hoarse acompanyment of the wind. The teeth of the squatter were compressed and his huge hand grasped the rifle, as if it would crush the metal. Then came a lull, a fresher blast, and a cry of horror that seemed to have been uttered at the very portals of his ears. A sort of echo burst involuntarily from his own lips, as men will shout under unnatural excitement, and throwing his rifle across his shoulder he proceeded towards the rock with the strides of a giant.

It was not often that the blood of Ishmael moved at the rate with which the fluid circulates in the veins of ordinary men, but, now he felt it ready to gush from every pore in his body. The animal was aroused, in his most latent energies. Ever as he advanced he heard those shrieks, which sometimes seemed ringing among the clouds, and sometimes passed so nigh, as to appear to brush the earth. At length there came a cry in which there could be no delusion, or to which the imagination could lend no horror. It appeared to fill each cranny of the air, as the visible horizon is often charged to fullness by one dazzling flash of the electric fluid. The name of God was distinctly audible, but it was awfully and blasphemously blended with sounds that may not be repeated. The squatter stopped and for a moment, he covered his ears with his hands. When he withdrew the latter, a low and husky voice at his elbow asked in smothered tones,

"Ishmael, my man, heard ye nothing!"

"Hist!" returned the husband, laying a powerful arm on Esther, without manifesting the smallest surprise at the unlooked for presence of his wife. "Hist, woman, if you have the fear of Heaven, be still!"

A profound silence succeeded. Though the wind rose and fell, as before, its rushing was no longer mingled with those fearful cries. The sounds were imposing and solemn, but it was the solemnity and majesty of nature.

"Let us go on!" said Esther. "All is hushed!"

"Woman, what has brought you here!" demanded her husband, whose blood had returned into its former channels, and whose thoughts had already lost a portion of their excitement.

"Ishmael, he murdered our first born; but it is not meet that the son of my mother should lie upon the ground, like the carrion of a dog!"

"Follow," returned the squatter again grasping his rifle, and striding towards the rock. The distance was still considerable, and their approach, as they drew nigh the place of execution, was moderated by awe. Many minutes had passed before they reached a spot, where they might distinguish the outlines of the dusky objects.

"Where have you put the body?" whispered Esther. "See, here are pick and spade, that a brother of mine may sleep, in the bosom of the earth!"

The moon broke from behind a mass of clouds, and the eye of the woman was enabled to follow the finger of Ishmael. It pointed to a human form swinging, in the wind, beneath the ragged and shining arm of the willow. Esther bent her head and veiled her eyes from the sight. But Ishmael drew nigher and long contemplated his work in awe, though not in compunction. The leaves of the sacred book were scattered on the ground, and even a fragment of the shelf had been displaced by the kidnapper in his agony. But all was now in the stillness of death. The grim and convulsed countenance of the victim, was at times brought full into the light of the moon, and again as the wind lulled, the fatal rope drew a dark line across its bright disk. The squatter raised his rifle, with extreme care and fired. The cord was cut, and the body came lumbering to the earth a heavy and insensible mass.

Until now, Esther had not moved nor spoken. But her hand was not slow to assist in the labor of the hour. The grave was soon dug. It was instantly made to receive its miserable tenant. As the lifeless form descended, Esther, who sustained the head, looked up into the face of her husband, with an expression of anguish, and said—

"Ishmael, my man, it is very terrible. I cannot kiss the corpse of my father's child!"

The squatter laid his broad hand on the bosom of the dead, and said,

"Abiram White, we all have need of mercy, from my soul, do I forgive you. May God in Heaven have pity on your sins."

The woman bowed her face, and imprinted her lips long and fervently on the pallid forehead of her brother. After this came the falling clods and all the solemn sounds of filling a grave. Esther lingered on her knees, and Ishmael stood uncovered while the woman muttered a prayer. All was then finished.

On the following morning the teams and herds of the squatter were seen pursuing their course towards the settlements. As they approached the confines of society, the train was blended among a thousand others. Though some of the numerous descendants of this peculiar pair, were reclaimed from their lawless and semi-barbarous lives, the principals of the family, themselves, were never heard of more.

Chapter XXXIII

—"No leave take I; for I will ride,
As far as land will let me, by your side."
Richard II, I.iii.251–52.

THE PASSAGE of the Pawnee to his village was interrupted by no scene of violence. His vengeance had been as complete as it was summary. Not even a solitary scout of the Siouxes was left on the hunting grounds he was obliged to traverse, and of course the journey of Middleton's party was as peaceful as if made in the bosom of the States. The marches were timed to meet the weakness of the females. In short, the victors seemed to have lost every trace of ferocity with their success, and appeared disposed to consult the most trifling of the wants of that engrossing people, who were daily encroaching on their rights, and reducing the red-men of the West, from their state of proud independance to the condition of fugitives and wanderers.

Our limits will not permit a detail of the triumphal entry of the conquerors. The exultation of the tribe was proportioned to its previous despondency. Mothers boasted of the honorable deaths of their sons, wives proclaimed the honor and pointed to the scars of their husbands, and Indian girls rewarded the younger braves with songs of triumph. The trophies of their fallen enemies were exhibited, as conquered standards are displayed in more civilized regions. The deeds of former warriors were recounted by the aged men and declared to be eclipsed by the glory of this victory. While, Hard-Heart, himself, so distinguished for his exploits, from boy-hood to that hour, was unanimously proclaimed and re-proclaimed the worthiest chief and the stoutest brave that the Wahcondah had ever bestowed on his most favored children, the Pawnees of the Loup.

Notwithstanding the comparative security in which Middleton found his recovered treasure, he was not sorry to see his faithful and sturdy artillerists, standing among the throng, as he entered in the wild train, and lifting their voices, in a martial shout to greet his return. The presence of this force, small as it was, removed every shadow of uneasiness from his mind. It made him master of his movements, gave him dignity and importance in the eyes of his new friends, and would enable him to overcome the difficulties of the wide region which still lay between the village of the Pawnees and the nearest fortress of his Countrymen. A lodge was yielded to the exclusive possession of Inez and Ellen, and, even Paul when he saw an armed sentinel in the uniform of the States, pacing before its entrance, was content to stray among the dwellings of the 'redskins' prying with but little reserve into their domestic economy, commenting sometimes jocularly, sometimes gravely and always freely on their different expedients, or endeavoring to make the wondering housewives comprehend his quaint explanations of what he conceived to be the better customs of the whites.

This inquiring and troublesome temper found no imitators among the Indians. The delicacy and reserve of Hard-Heart were communicated to his people. When every attention, that could be suggested by their simple manners and narrow wants, had been fulfilled no intrusive foot presumed to approach the cabins devoted to the service of the strangers. They were left to seek their repose in the manner which most comported with their habits and inclinations. The songs and rejoicings of the tribe, however, ran far into the night, during the deepest hours of which the voice of more than one warrior was heard, recounting from the top of his lodge the deeds of his people and the glory of their triumphs.

Every thing having life, notwithstanding the excesses of the night, was abroad with the appearance of the sun. The expressions of exultation, which had so lately been seen on every countenance, was now changed to one better suited to the feeling of the moment. It was understood by all, that the Pale-faces who had befriended their Chief, were about to take their final leave of the tribe. The soldiers of Middleton in anticipation of his arrival, had bargained with an unsuccessful trader for the use of his boat, which lay in the stream ready to receive its cargo, and nothing remained to complete the arrangements for the long journey.

Middleton did not see this moment arrive, entirely, without distrust. The admiration with which Hard-Heart regarded

Inez, had not escaped his jealous eyes, any more than had the lawless wishes of Mahtoree. He knew the consummate manner in which a savage could conceal his designs, and he felt that it would be a culpable weakness to be unprepared for the worst. Secret instructions were therefore given to his men, while the preparations they made were properly masked behind the show of military parade, with which it was intended to signalise their departure.

The conscience of the young soldier reproached him, when he saw the whole tribe accompanying his party to the margin of the stream with unarmed hands and sorrowful countenances. They gathered in a circle around the strangers and their chief and became not only peaceful but deeply interested observers of what was passing. As it was evident that Hard-Heart intended to speak, the former stopped, and manifested their readiness to listen, the trapper performing the office of an interpreter. Then the chief addressed his people, in the usual, metaphorical language of an Indian. He commenced by alluding to the antiquity and renown of his own nation. He spoke of their successes in the hunts and on the war path; of the manner in which they had always known how to defend their rights and to chastise their enemies. After he had said enough to manifest his respect for the greatness of the Loups, and to satisfy the pride of the listeners, he made a sudden transition to the race of whom the strangers were members. He compared their countless numbers to the flights of migratory birds in the season of blossoms, or in the fall of the year. With a delicacy, that none knew better how to practise than an Indian warrior, he made no direct mention of the rapacious temper, that so many of them had betrayed, in their dealings with the red-men. Feeling, that the sentiment of distrust was strongly engrafted in the tempers of his tribe, he rather endeavored to soothe any just resentment they might entertain, by indirect excuses and apologies. He reminded the listeners that even the Pawnee Loups had been obliged to chase many unworthy individuals from their villages. The Wahcondah sometimes veiled his countenance from a red man. No doubt the Great Spirit of the Pale Faces often looked darkly on his children. Such as were abandoned to the worker of Evil, could never be brave or virtuous, let the color of the skin be what it might. He bade his young men look at the hands of the Big knives. They were not empty, like those of hungry beggars. Neither were they filled with goods like those of knavish traders. They were like themselves warriors and they carried arms, which they knew well how to use. They were worthy to be called brothers!

Then he directed the attention of all to the chief of the strangers. He was a son of their Great White Father. He had not come upon the Prairies to frighten the buffaloes from their pastures, or to seek the game of the Indians. Wicked men had robbed him of one of his wives. No doubt she was the most obedient, the meekest, and the loveliest of them all. They had only to open their eyes to see that his words must be true. Now that the White Chief had found his wife he was about to return to his own people in peace. He would tell them that the Pawnees were just, and there would be a line of wampum between the two nations. Let all his people wish the strangers a safe return to their towns. The warriors of the Loups knew, both, how to receive their enemies, and how to clear the briars from the path of their friends.

The heart of Middleton beat quick, as the young Partisan* alluded to the charms of Inez, and for an instant he cast an impatient glance at his little line of Artillerists; but the chief, from that moment, appeared to forget he had ever seen so fair a being. His feelings, if he had any on the subject, were veiled behind the cold mask of Indian self-denial. He took each warrior by the hand, not even forgetting the meanest soldier, but his cold and collected eye never wandered, for an instant, towards either of the females. Arrangements had been made for their comfort, with a prodigality and care, that had not failed to excite some surprise in his young men, but in no other particular did he shock their manly pride, by betraying any solicitude in behalf of the weaker sex.

The leave-taking was general and imposing. Each male

*The Americans and the Indians have adopted several words, which each believes peculiar to the language of the others. Thus "squaw," "papoose" or child, wigwam &c. &c. though it is doubtful whether they belonged at all to any Indian dialect, are much used by both white and red men in their intercourse. Many words are derived from the French, in this species of Prairie nomaic. Partizan, Brave &c., are part of the number.

Pawnee was sedulous to omit no one of the strange warriors in his attentions, and of course the ceremony occupied some time. The only exception, and that was not general, was in the case of Dr. Battius. Not a few of the young men, it is true were indifferent about lavishing civilities on one of so doubtful a profession, but the worthy naturalist found some consolation in the more matured politeness of the old men, who had inferred, that though not of much use in war, the Medicine of the Big knives, might possibly be made serviceable in peace.

When all of Middleton's party had embarked, the trapper lifted a small bundle, which had lain at his feet, during the previous proceedings, and whistling Hector to his side, he was the last to take his seat. The Artillerists gave the usual cheers which were answered by a shout from the tribe, and then the boat was shoved into the current, and began to glide swiftly down its stream.

A long, and a musing, if not a melancholy, silence succeeded this departure. It was first broken by the trapper, whose regret was not the least visible, in his dejected and sorrowful eye.

"They are a valiant and an honest tribe!" he said; "that will I say boldly in their favor: and second only do I take them to be, to that once mighty but now scattered people, the Delaware of the Hills! Ahs! me; Captain, if you had seen as much good and evil, as I have seen in these nations of red-skins, you would know of how much value, was a brave and simple-minded warrior. I know that some are to be found, who both think and say that an Indian is but little better than the beasts of these naked plains. But it is needful to be honest in one's-self, to be a fitting judge of honesty in others. No doubt, no doubt, they know their enemies, and little do they care to show them, any great confidence, or love."

"It is the way of man," returned the Captain; "and, it is probable they are not wanting in any of his natural qualities."

"No, no, it is little that they want that natur' has had to give. But as little does he know of the temper of a red-skin, who has seen but one Indian, or one tribe, as he knows of the colour of feathers who has only looked upon a crow. Now, friend steersman, just give the boat a sheer towards yonder low, sandy point, and a favor will be granted at a short asking."

"For what?" demanded Middleton, "we are now in the swiftest of the current, and by drawing to the shore we shall lose the force of the stream."

"Your tarry will not be long," returned the old man applying his own hand to the execution of that which he had requested. The oarsmen had seen enough of his influence, with their leader, not to dispute his wishes, and before time was given for further discussion on the subject the bow of the boat had touched the land.

"Captain," resumed the other, untying his little wallet, with great deliberation, and even, in a manner to show, that he found satisfaction in the delay, "I wish to offer you a small matter of trade. No great bargain, mayhap, but still it is the best that one, of whose hand the skill of the rifle has taken leave, and who has become no better than a miserable trapper can offer, before we part."

"Part!" was echoed from every mouth, among those who had so recently shared his dangers, and profited by his care.

"What the devil, old trapper, do you mean to foot it to the settlements, when here is a boat that will float the distance in half the time the Jack Ass the Doctor has given the Pawnee, could trot along the same!"

"Settlements, Boy! It is long sin' I took my leave of the waste and wickedness of the settlements and the village. If I live in a clearing, here it is one of the Lord's making, and I have no hard thoughts, on the matter; but never, again, shall I be seen running wilfully into the danger of immoralities."

"I had not thought of parting," answered Middleton, endeavoring to seek some relief from the uneasiness he felt, by turning his eyes on the sympathizing countenances of his friends, "On the contrary I had hoped and believed that you would have accompanied us below, where, I give you a sacred pledge, nothing shall be wanting to make your days comfortable."

"Yes, lad, yes; you would do your endeavors, but what are the strivings of man against the working of the Devil! Ay, if kind offers and good wishes could have done the thing, I might have been a Congressman or perhaps a Governor, years agone. Your Grand'ther wished the same, and there are them, still living in the Otsego Mountains, as I hope, who would gladly have given me a palace for my dwelling. But what are riches without content! My time must now be short, at any rate, and I hope it is no mighty sin for one, who has acted his part honestly near ninety winters and summers, to wish to pass the few hours that remain in comfort. If you think that I have done wrong in coming thus far to quit you, again, Captain, I will own the reason of the act, without shame or backwardness. Though I have seen so much of the wilderness it is not to be gainsayed, that my feelings as well as my skin are white. Now, it would not be a fitting spectacle that yonder Pawnee Loups should look upon the weakness of an old warrior, if weakness he should happen to show in parting forever from those he has reason to love, though he may not set his heart so strongly on them, as to wish to go into the settlements in their company."

"Harkee, old trapper," said Paul, clearing his throat with a desperate effort, as if determined to give his voice a clear exit. "I have just one bargain to make, since you talk of trading, which is neither more nor less than this. I offer you as my side of the business, one half of my shanty, nor do I much care if it be the biggest half; the sweetest and the purest honey that can be made of the wild-locust; always enough to eat, with now and then a mouthful of venison or, for that matter a morsel of buffaloe's hump, seeing that I intend to push my acquaintance with the animal, and as good and as tidy cooking as can come from the hands of one like Ellen Wade, here, who will shortly be Nelly some-body-else, and altogether such general treatment as a decent man might be supposed to pay to his best friend or, for that matter to his own father: in return for the same you ar' to give us, at odd moments, some of your ancient traditions, perhaps a little wholesome advice on occasions, in small quantities at a time, and as much of your agreeable company as you please."

"It is well, it is well, boy," returned the old man fumbling at his wallet, "honestly offered and not unthankfully declined. But it cannot be; no, it can never be."

"Venerable venator," said Doctor Battius, "there are obligations which every man owes to society and to human nature. It is time that you should return to your countrymen to deliver up some of those stores of experimental knowledge, that you have doubtless obtained by so long a sojourn in the wilds, which, however, they may be corrupted by preconceived opinions, will prove acceptable bequests to those whom as you say, you must shortly leave forever."

"Friend, Physicianer," returned the trapper, looking the other steadily in the face, "as it would be no easy matter to judge of the temper of a rattler by considering the fashions of the moose, so it would be hard to speak of the usefulness of one man by thinking too much of the deeds of another. You have your gifts, like others I suppose, and little do I wish to disturb them. But as to me, the Lord has made me for a doer and not a talker, and, therefore, do I consider it no harm to shut my ears to your invitation."

"It is enough," interrupted Middleton. "I have seen and heard so much of this extraordinary man as to know that persuasions will not change his purpose. First we will hear your request, my friend, and then we will consider what may be best done for your advantage here."

"It is a small matter, Captain," returned the old man, succeeding at length in opening his bundle. "A small and trifling matter is it to what I once used to offer in the way of bargain; but then it is the best I have, and, therein, not to be despised. Here are the skins of four beavers that I took, it might be a month afore we met, and here is another from a raccoon, that is of no great matter to-be-sure, but which may serve to make weight atween us."

"And what do you propose to do with them?"

"I offer them in lawful barter. Them knaves, the Siouxes, the Lord forgive me for ever believing it was the Konzas, have stolen the best of my traps, and driven me altogether to make-shift inventions, which might foretell a dreary winter for me, should my time stretch into another season. I wish you therefore to take the skins, and to offer them to some of the trappers you will not fail to meet below in exchange for a few traps, and to send the same into the Pawnee village in my name. Be careful to have my mark painted on them. A letter N, with a hound's ear, and the lock of a rifle. There is no red-skin who will then dispute my right. For all which trouble I have little more to offer than my thanks, unless my friend the Bee-hunter, here, will accept of the raccoon and take on himself the special charge of the whole matter."

"If I do may I be—" the mouth of Paul was stopped by the hand of Ellen, and he was obliged to swallow the rest of the sentence, which he did with a species of emotion that bore no slight resemblance to the process of strangulation.

"Well, well," returned the old man meekly; "I hope there is no heavy offence in the offer. I know that the skin of a raccoon is of small price, but then it was no mighty labor that I asked in return."

"You entirely mistake the meaning of our friend," interrupted Middleton, who observed that the bee-hunter was looking in every direction but the right one, and that he was utterly unable to make his own vindication. "He did not mean to say that he declined the charge, but merely that he refused all compensation. It is unnecessary, however, to say more of this, it shall be my office to see that the debt we owe is properly discharged and that all your necessities shall be anticipated."

"Anan!" said the old man, looking up enquiringly into the other's face as if to ask an explanation.

"It shall all be as you wish. Lay the skins with my baggage. We will bargain for you as for ourselves."

"Thankee, thankee, Captain. Your Grand'ther was of a free and generous mind. So much so, in truth, that those just people the Delawares called him the 'open hand.' I wish now, I was as I used to be, in order that I might send in the Lady a few delicate martens for her tippets and over-coats, just to show you that I know how to give courtesy for courtesy. But do not expect the same, for I am too old to give a promise! It will all be just as the Lord shall see fit. I can offer *you* nothing else, for I haven't lived so long in the wilderness not to know the scrupulous ways of Gentlemen."

"Harkee, old trapper," cried the Bee hunter striking his own hand into the open palm which the other had extended, with a report but little below the crack of a rifle. "I have just two things to say. Firstly, that the Captain has told you my meaning better than I can myself, and secondly, that if you want a skin either for your private use, or to send abroad, I have it at your service, and that is the skin of one Paul Hover."

The old man returned the grasp he received, and opened his mouth to the utmost in his extraordinary, silent, laugh.

"You couldn't have given such a squeeze, boy, when the Teton squaws were about you with the knives! Ah! you are in your prime, and in your vigor and happiness, if honesty lies in your path." Then the expression of his rugged features, suddenly changed to a look of seriousness and thought. "Come hither, lad," he said, leading the bee-hunter by a button to the land, and speaking apart in a tone of admonition and confidence. "Much has passed atween us, on the pleasures and respectableness of a life in the woods, or on the borders. I do not, now, mean to say that all you have heard is not true; but different tempers call for different employments. You have taken to your bosom, there, a good and kind child, and it has become your duty to consider her as well as yourself, in setting forth in life. You are a little given to skirting the settlements, but to my poor judgement the girl would be more like a flourishing flower in the sun of a clearing, than in the winds of a Prairie. Therefore forget any thing you may have heard from me, which is nevertheless true, and strive to turn your mind on the ways of the inner country."

Paul could only answer with a squeeze of the hand, that would have brought tears from the eyes of most men, but which produced no other effect on the indurated muscles of the other, than to make him laugh and nod, as if he received the same as a pledge that the bee-hunter would remember his advice. The trapper then turned away from his rough but warm hearted companion, and having called Hector from the boat, he seemed anxious still to utter a few words more.

"Captain," he, at length, resumed, "I know that when a poor man talks of credit, he deals in a delicate word, according to the fashions of the world, and when an old man talks of life, he speaks of that which he may never see. Nevertheless, there is one thing I will say, and that is not so much on my own behalf, as on that of another person. Here is Hector, a good and faithful pup, that has long outlived the time of a dog, and like his master he looks more to comfort now than to any deeds in running. But the creatur' has his feelings as well as a christian. He has consorted latterly with his kinsman, there, in such a sort, as to find great pleasure in his company, and, I will acknowledge that it touches my feelings a little to part the pair so soon. If you will set a value on your hound, I will endeavor to send it to you in the spring, more especially should them same traps come safe to hand, or if you dislike parting with the animal, altogether, I will just ask you for his loan through the winter. I think I can see my pup will not last beyond that time, for I have judgment in these matters, since many is the friend, both hound and red-skin, that I have seen depart in my day, though the Lord has not yet seen fit to order his angels to sound forth my name."

"Take him, take him," cried Middleton. "Take all, or any thing!"

The old man whistled the younger dog to the land, and then he proceeded to the final adieus. Little was said on either side. The trapper took each person solemnly by the hand, and uttered something friendly and kind to all. Middleton was perfectly speechless and was driven to affect busying himself among the baggage, Paul whistled with all his might, and even, Obed, took his leave with an effort that bore the appearance of desperate philosophical resolution. When he had made the circuit of the whole the old man, with his own hands, shoved the boat into the current, wishing God to speed them. Not a word was spoken nor a stroke of the oar given, until the travellers had floated past a knoll that hid the trapper from their view. He was last seen standing on the low point, leaning on his rifle, with Hector crouched at his feet, and the younger dog frisking along the sands, in the playfulness of youth and vigor.

Chapter XXXIV

—"Methought, I heard a voice—"
Macbeth, II.ii.32.

THE WATER-COURSES were at their height, and the boat went down the swift current like a bird. The passage proved prosperous and speedy. In less than a third of the time that would have been necessary for the same journey by land, it was accomplished by the favor of those rapid rivers. Issuing from one stream into another, as the veins of the human body communicate with the larger channels of life, they soon entered the grand artery of the western waters and landed safely, at the very door of the father of Inez.

The joy of Don Augustin, and the embarrassment of the worthy Father Ignatius may be imagined. The former wept and returned thanks to Heaven, the latter returned thanks, and did not weep. The mild provincials were too happy to raise any questions on the character of so joyful a restoration, and, by a sort of general consent it soon came to be an admitted opinion that the bride of Middleton had been kidnapped by a villain and that she was restored to her friends by human agency. There were as respects this belief, certainly a few sceptics, but then they enjoyed their doubts in private, with that species of sublimated and solitary gratification that a miser finds in gazing at his growing, but useless, hoards.

In order to give the worthy priest something to employ his mind, Middleton made him the instrument of uniting Paul and Ellen. The former consented to the ceremony, because he found that all his friends laid great stress on the matter, but shortly after he led his bride into the plains of Kentucky, under the pretence of paying certain customary visits to sundry members of the family of Hover. While there, he took occasion to have the marriage properly solemnized, by a justice of the peace of his acquaintance, in whose ability to forge the nuptial chain he had much more faith than in that of all the gownsmen within the Pale of Rome. Ellen who appeared conscious that some extraordinary preventives might prove necessary to keep one of so erratic a temper, as her partner, within the proper matrimonial boundaries, raised no objections to these double knots, and all parties were content.

The local importance Middleton had acquired by his union with the daughter of so affluent a proprietor as Don Augustin, united to his personal merit, attracted the attention of the Government. He was soon employed in various situations of responsibility and confidence, which both served to elevate his character in the public estimation and to afford the means of patronage. The bee-hunter was among the first of those to whom he saw fit to extend his favor. It was far from difficult to find situations suited to the abilities of Paul in the state of society that existed three and twenty years ago in those regions. The efforts of Middleton and Inez in behalf of her husband were warmly and sagaciously seconded by Ellen, and they succeeded, in process of time, in working a great and beneficial change in his character. He soon became a landholder, then a prosperous cultivator of the soil, and shortly after a town-officer. By that progressive change in fortune, which in the republicks is often seen to be so singularly accompanied by a corresponding improvement in knowledge and self-respect, he went on, from step to step, until his wife enjoyed the maternal delight of seeing her children placed far beyond the danger of returning to that state from which both their parents had issued. Paul is, actually, at this moment, a member of the lower branch of the Legislature of the State where he has long resided, and he is even notorious for making speeches, that have a tendency to put that deliberative body in good humour, and which as they are based on great practical knowledge suited to the condition of the country, possess a merit that is much wanted in many more subtle and fine spun theories that are daily heard in similar assemblies, to issue from the lips of certain instinctive politicians. But all these happy fruits were the results of much care, and of a long period of time. Middleton, who fills, with a credit better suited to the difference in their educations, a seat in a far higher branch of Legislative Authority, is the source from which we have derived most of the intelligence necessary to compose our legend. In addition to what he has related of Paul, and of his own continued happiness, he has added a short narrative of what took place in a subsequent visit to the

Prairies, with which, as we conceive it a suitable termination to what has gone before, we shall judge it wise to conclude our labors.

In the autumn of the year that succeeded the season in which the preceding events occurred, the young man, still in the military service, found himself on the waters of the Missouri, at a point not far remote from the Pawnee towns. Released from any immediate calls of duty, and strongly urged to the measure by Paul, who was in his company, he determined to take horse and cross the country, to visit the Partisan and to inquire into the fate of his friend the trapper. As his train was suited to his functions and rank, the journey was effected, with the privations and hardships that are the accompanyments of all travelling in a wild, but, without any of those dangers and alarms that marked his former passage through the same regions. When within a proper distance, he dispatched an Indian runner belonging to a friendly tribe, to announce the approach of himself and party, continuing his route at a deliberate pace, in order that the intelligence might as was customary precede his arrival. To the surprise of the travellers their message was unanswered. Hour succeeded hour, and mile after mile was passed without bringing either the signs of an honorable reception or the more simple assurances of a friendly welcome. At length the cavalcade, at whose head rode Middleton and Paul, descended from the elevated plain, on which they had long been journeying, to a luxuriant bottom, that brought them to the level of the village of the Loups. The sun was beginning to fall, and a sheet of golden light was spread over the placid plain, lending to its even surface, those glorious tints and hues that, the human imagination is apt to conceive, form the embellishment of still more imposing scenes. The verdure of the year yet remained and herds of horses and mules were grazing peacefully in the vast natural pasture, under the keeping of vigilant Pawnee boys. Paul pointed out, among them, the well known form of Asinus, sleek, fat and luxuriating in the fulness of content, as he stood with reclining ears and closed eye-lids, seemingly musing on the exquisite nature of his present indolent enjoyment.

The route of the party led them at no great distance from one of those watchful youths, who was charged with a trust heavy as the principal wealth of his tribe. He heard the trampling of the horses and cast his eye aside, but instead of manifesting curiosity or alarm, his look instantly returned, whence it had been withdrawn, to the spot where the village was known to stand.

"There is something remarkable in all this," muttered Middleton, half offended at what he conceived to be not only a slight to his rank, but offensive to himself, personally; "yonder boy has heard of our approach, or he would not fail to notify his tribe; and yet he scarcely deigns to favor us with a glance. Look to your arms, men, it may be necessary to let these savages feel our strength!"

"Therein, Captain, I think you're in an error," returned Paul. "If honesty is to be met on the Prairies at all, you will find it in our old friend, Hard-Heart; neither is an Indian to be judged of by the rules of a white—see, we are not altogether slighted for here comes a party at last to meet us, though it is a little pitiful as to show and numbers."

Paul was right in both particulars. A groupe of horsemen were, at length, seen wheeling round a little copse and advancing across the plain directly towards them. The advance of this party was slow and dignified. As it drew nigh the Partisan of the Loups was seen at its head, followed by a dozen younger warriors of his tribe. They were all unarmed, nor did they even wear any of those ornaments or feathers, which are considered testimonials of respect to the guest an Indian receives, as well as evidence of his own importance.

The meeting was friendly though a little restrained on both sides. Middleton, jealous of his own consideration no less than of the authority of his government, suspected some undue influence on the part of the agents of the Canadas, and, as he was determined to maintain the authority of which he was the representative, he felt himself constrained to manifest an hauteur that he was far from feeling. It was not so easy to penetrate the motives of the Pawnees. Calm, dignified and yet far from repulsive, they set an example of courtesy blended with reserve, that many a diplomatist of the most polished court might have strove in vain to imitate.

In this manner the two parties continued their course to the town. Middleton had time, during the remainder of the ride, to revolve in his mind, all the probable reasons which his ingenuity could suggest for this strange reception. Although he was accompanied by a regular interpreter, the chiefs made their salutations in a manner that dispensed with his services. Twenty times, the Captain turned his glance on his former friend endeavoring to read the expression of his rigid features. But every effort and all conjectures proved equally futile. The eye of Hard-Heart was fixed, composed, and a little anxious, but as to every other emotion, impenetrable. He neither spoke himself, nor seemed willing to invite discourse in his visiters. It was therefore necessary for Middleton to adopt the patient manners of his companions, and to await the issue for the explanation.

When they entered the town, the whole of its inhabitants were seen collected in an open space where they were arranged with the customary deference to age and rank. The whole formed a large circle, in the centre of which were perhaps a dozen of the principal chiefs. Hard-Heart waved his hand as he approached, and, as the mass of bodies opened, he rode through, followed by his companions. Then they dismounted, and as the beasts were led apart, the strangers found themselves environed by a thousand, grave, composed but solicitous faces.

Middleton gazed about him, in growing concern, for no cry, no song, no shout, welcomed him among a people, from whom he had so lately parted with regret. His uneasiness, not to say apprehensions, was shared by all his followers. Determination and stern resolution began to assume the place of anxiety in every eye, as each man silently felt for his arms, and assured himself that his several weapons were in a state for service. But there was no answering symptom of hostility on the part of their hosts. Hard-Heart beckoned for Middleton and Paul to follow, leading the way towards the cluster of forms that occupied the centre of the circle. Here the visiters found a solution of all the movements which had given them so much reason for apprehension.

The trapper was placed on a rude seat, which had been made, with studied care to support his frame, in an upright and easy attitude. The first glance of the eye told his former friends that the old man was, at length, called upon to pay the last tribute of nature. His eye was glazed, and apparently as devoid of sight, as of expression. His features were a little more sunken and strongly marked, than formerly, but there all change so far as exterior was concerned, might be said to have ceased. His approaching end was not to be ascribed to any positive malady but had been a gradual and mild decay of the physical powers. Life it is true still lingered in his system, but it was as if at times, entirely ready to depart, and then it would appear to reanimate the sinking form as if reluctant to give up the possession of a tenement that had never been corrupted by vice or undermined by disease. It would have been no violent fancy to have imagined, that the spirit fluttered about the placid lips of the old woodsman, reluctant to depart from a shell that had so long given it an honest and an honourable shelter.

His body was placed so as to let the light of the setting sun, fall full upon the solemn features. His head was bare, the long, thin, locks of gray, fluttering lightly in the evening breeze. His rifle lay upon his knee, and the other accoutrements of the chase were placed at his side, within reach of his hand. Between his feet lay the figure of a hound, with its head crouching to the earth as if it slumbered, and so perfectly easy and natural was its position, that a second glance was necessary to tell Middleton he saw only the skin of Hector stuffed by Indian tenderness and ingenuity, in a manner to represent the living animal. His own dog was playing at a distance, with the child of Tachechana and Mahtoree. The mother herself, stood at hand holding in her arms a second offspring that might boast of a parentage no less honorable than that which belonged to a son of Hard-Heart. Le Balafré was seated nigh the dying trapper, with every mark about his person that the hour of his own departure, also, was not far distant. The rest of those immediately in the centre, were aged men, who had apparently drawn near, in order to observe the manner in which a just and fearless warrior would depart on the greatest of his journeys.

The old man was reaping the rewards of a life so remarkable for temperance and activity, in a tranquil and placid death. His vigor had in a manner endured, to the very last. Decay when it did occur, was rapid, but free from pain. He had hunted with the tribe in the spring, and even throughout most of the summer, when his limbs suddenly refused to perform their customary offices. A sympathysing weakness took possession of all his faculties, and the Pawnees believed that they were going to lose, in this unexpected manner, a sage and counsellor whom they had begun both to love and to respect. But, as we have already said, the immortal occupant seemed unwilling to desert its tenement. The lamp of life often flickered, without becoming extinguished. On the morning of the day on which Middleton arrived, there was a general reviving of the powers of the whole man. His tongue was again heard in wholesome maxims, and his eye, from time to time, recognised the persons of his friends. It merely proved to be a brief and final intercourse with the world on the part of one who had already been considered, as to mental communion, to have taken his leave of it forever.

When he had placed his guests in front of the dying man, Hard-Heart after a pause that proceeded as much from sorrow as decorum, leaned a little forward, and demanded—"Does my Father hear the words of his son?"

"Speak," returned the trapper, in tones that issued from his chest, but which were rendered awfully distinct by the stillness that reigned in the place. "I am about to depart from the village of the Loups, and, shortly shall be beyond the reach of your voice."

"Let the wise chief have no cares for his journey!" continued Hard-Heart, with an earnest solicitude that led him to forget, for the moment, that others were waiting to address his adopted parent. "A hundred Loups shall clear his path from briars."

"Pawnee, I die, as I have lived, a christian man," resumed the trapper with a force of voice, that had the same startling effect on his hearers as is produced by the trumpet, when its blast rises suddenly and freely on the air, after its obstructed sounds have been heard struggling in the distance. "As I came into life, so will I leave it. Horses and arms are not needed to stand in the Presence of the Great Spirit of my people! He knows my colour, and according to my gifts will he judge my deeds."

"My father will tell my young men, how many Mingoes he

has struck, and what acts of valour and justice he has done, that they may know how to imitate him."

"A boastful tongue is not heard in the heaven of a white man!" solemnly returned the old man. "What I have done, he has seen. His eyes are always open. That which has been well done will he remember. Wherein I have been wrong, will he not forget to chastise, though he will do the same in mercy. No, my son; a pale-face may not sing his own praises, and hope to have them acceptable before his God!"

A little disappointed, the young partisan stepped modestly back, making way for the recent comers to approach. Middleton took one of the meagre hands of the trapper, and struggling to command his voice, he succeeded in announcing his presence. The old man listened like one, whose thoughts were dwelling on a very different subject, but when the other had succeeded in making him understand that he was present, an expression of joyful recognition passed over his faded features.

"I hope you have not so soon forgotten those whom you so materially served!" Middleton concluded. "It would pain me to think my hold on your memory was so light."

"Little that I have ever seen is forgotten," returned the trapper, "I am at the close of many weary days, but there is not one among them all that I could wish to overlook. I remember you, with the whole of your companions; ay, and your gran'ther, that went before you. I am glad that you have come back upon these plains, for I had need of one, who speaks the English, since little faith can be put in the traders of these regions. Will you do a favor, to an old and dying man?"

"Name it," said Middleton. "It shall be done."

"It is a far journey to send such trifles," resumed the old man, who spoke at short intervals, as strength and breath permitted. "A far and weary journey is the same! But kindnesses and friendships are things not to be forgotten. There is a settlement among the Otsego hills."

"I know the place," interrupted Middleton, observing that he spoke with increasing difficulty. "Proceed to tell me what you would have done."

"Take this rifle, and pouch, and horn, and send them to the

person whose name is graven on the plates of the stock. A trader cut the letters with his knife, for it is long that I have intended to send him such a token of my love."

"It shall be so. Is there more that you could wish?"

"Little else have I to bestow. My traps I give to my Indian son; for honestly and kindly has he kept his faith. Let him stand before me."

Middleton explained to the chief what the trapper had said and relinquished his own place to the other.

"Pawnee," continued the old man, always changing his language to suit the person he addressed, and not unfrequently according to the ideas he expressed, "it is a custom of my people for the Father to leave his blessing with the son, before he shuts his eyes forever. This blessing I give to you. Take it, for the prayers of a Christian man will never make the path of a just warrior to the blessed Prairies, either longer, or more tangled. May the God of a white man look on your deeds with friendly eyes, and may you never commit an act that shall cause him to darken his face. I know not whether we shall ever meet again. There are many traditions concerning the place of good Spirits. It is not for one like me, old and experienced though I am, to set up my opinions against a nation's. You believe in the blessed Prairies, and I have faith in the sayings of my fathers. If both are true, our parting will be final; but if it should prove that the same meaning is hid under different words, we shall yet stand together, Pawnee, before the face of your Wahcondah who will then be no other than my God. There is much to be said in favor of both religions, for each seems suited to its own people, and no doubt it was so intended. I fear I have not altogether followed the gifts of my colour, inasmuch as I find it a little painful to give up forever the use of the rifle, and the comforts of the chase. But then the fault has been my own, seeing that it could not have been His. Ay, Hector," he continued leaning forward a little and feeling for the ears of the hound, "our parting has come at last, dog, and it will be a long hunt. You have been an honest, and a bold and a faithful hound. Pawnee, you cannot slay the pup on my grave, for where a christian dog falls there he lies forever, but you can be kind to him, after I am gone, for the love you bear his Master?"

"The words of my father, are in my ears," returned the young Partisan, making a grave and respectful gesture of assent.

"Do you hear what the chief has promised, dog?" demanded the trapper making an effort to attract the notice of the insensible effigy of his hound. Receiving no answering look, nor hearing any friendly whine, the old man felt for the mouth and endeavored to force his hand between the cold lips. The truth then flashed upon him, although he was far from perceiving the whole extent of the deception. Falling back in his seat, he hung his head like one who felt a severe and unexpected shock. Profiting by this momentary forgetfulness, two young Indians removed the skin, with the same delicacy of feeling that had induced them to attempt the pious fraud.

"The dog is dead!" muttered the trapper, after a pause of many minutes, "a hound has his time as well as a man; and well has he filled his days! Captain," he added making an effort to wave his hand for Middleton. "I am glad you have come, for, though kind, and well meaning according to the gifts of their colour, these Indians are not the sort of men to lay the head of a white man in his grave. I have been thinking too, of this dog at my feet: it will not do to set forth the opinion that a christian can expect to meet his hound, again, still there can be little harm in placing what is left of so faithful a servant nigh the bones of his master?"

"It shall be done as you desire."

"I'm glad you think with me in this matter. In order then to save labor, lay the pup at my feet—or for that matter put him, side by side. A hunter need never be ashamed to be found in company with his dog!"

"I charge myself with your wish."

The old man made a long and, apparently, a musing pause. At times he raised his eyes, wistfully, as if he would again address Middleton, but some innate feeling appeared ever to suppress his words. The other, who observed his hesitation, enquired in a way most likely to encourage him to proceed, whether there was aught else that he could wish to have done.

"I am without kith or kin in the wide world!" the trapper answered. "When I am gone there will be an end of my race.

We have never been chiefs; but honest and useful in our way, I hope it cannot be denied we have always proved ourselves. My father lies buried near the sea, and the bones of his son will whiten on the Prairies."

"Name the spot and your remains shall be placed by the side of your father," interrupted Middleton.

"Not so, not so, Captain. Let me sleep where I have lived, beyond the din of the settlements! Still I see no need why the grave of an honest man should be hid, like a red-skin in his ambushment. I paid a man in the settlements to make and put a graven stone at the head of my father's resting-place. It was of the value of twelve beaver-skins; and cunningly and curiously was it carved! Then it told to all comers that the body of such a christian lay beneath, and it spoke of his manner of life, of his years and of his honesty. When we had done with the Frenchers in the old war, I made a journey to the spot, in order to see that all was rightly performed, and glad I am to say the workman had not forgotten his faith."

"And such a stone you would have at your grave?"

"I! no, no, I have no son, but Hard-Heart, and it is little that an Indian knows of white fashions and usages. Besides I am his debtor, already, seeing it is so little I have done since I have lived in his tribe. The rifle might bring the value of such a thing—but then I know it will give the boy pleasure to hang the piece in his hall, for many is the deer and the bird that he has seen it destroy. No, no, the gun must be sent to him whose name is graven on the lock."

"But there is one who would gladly prove his affection in the way you wish. He who owes you not only his own deliverance from so many dangers, but who inherits a heavy debt of gratitude from his ancestors. The stone shall be put at the head of your grave."

The old man extended his meagre hand, and gave the other a squeeze of thanks.

"I thought you might be willing to do it, but I was backward in asking the favour," he said, "seeing that you are not of my kin. Put no boastful words on the same; but just the name, the age, and the time of the death, with something from the holy book. No more, no more. My name will then not be altogether lost on 'arth; I need no more."

Middleton intimated his assent, and then followed a pause that was only interrupted by distant and broken sentences from the dying man. He appeared now to have closed his accounts with the world, and to wait merely for the final summons to quit it. Middleton and Hard-Heart placed themselves on the opposite sides of his seat, and watched with melancholy solicitude, the variations of his countenance. For two hours there was no very sensible alteration. The expression of his faded and time-worn features was that of a calm and dignified repose. From time to time, he spoke, uttering some brief sentence in the way of advice, or asking some simple question concerning those in whose fortunes he still took a friendly interest. During the whole of that solemn and anxious period each individual of the tribe kept his place, in the most self-restrained patience. When the old man spoke, all bent their heads to listen; and when his words were uttered they seemed to ponder on their wisdom and usefulness.

As the flame drew nigher to the socket, his voice was hushed, and there were moments when his attendants doubted whether he still belonged to the living. Middleton, who watched each wavering expression of his weather-beaten visage with the interest of a keen observer of human nature softened by the tenderness of personal regard, fancied that he could read the workings of the old man's soul, in the strong lineaments of his countenance. Perhaps what the enlightened soldier took for the delusion of mistaken opinion did actually occur, for who has returned from that unknown world to explain by what forms and in what manner he was introduced into its awful precincts. Without pretending to explain what must ever be a mystery to the quick, we shall simply relate facts as they occurred.

The trapper had remained nearly motionless for an hour. His eyes, alone, had occasionally opened and shut. When opened his gaze seemed fastened on the clouds which hung around the western horizon, reflecting the bright colours and giving form and loveliness to the glorious tints of an American sunset. The hour—the calm beauty of the season—the occasion all conspired to fill the spectators with solemn awe. Suddenly, while musing on the remarkable position in which he was placed, Middleton felt the hand which he held, grasp his own, with incredible power, and the old man, supported on either side by his friends, rose upright to his feet. For a moment, he looked about him, as if to invite all in presence to listen, (the lingering remnant of human frailty) and then, with a fine military elevation of the head, and with a voice that might be heard in every part of that numerous assembly he pronounced the word—

"Here!"

A movement so entirely unexpected, and the air of grandeur and humility which were so strikingly united in the mien of the trapper, together with the clear and uncommon force of his utterance, produced a short period of confusion in the faculties of all present. When Middleton and Hard-Heart, each of whom involuntarily extended a hand to support the form of the old man, turned to him again, they found that the subject of their interest, was removed forever beyond the necessity of their care. They mournfully placed the body in its seat, and Le Balafré arose to announce the termination of the scene, to the tribe. The voice of the old Indian, seemed a sort of echo from that invisible world to which the spirit of the honest trapper had just departed.

"A valiant, a just, and a wise warrior has gone on the path which will lead him to the blessed grounds of his people!" he said. "When the voice of the Wahcondah called him, he was ready to answer. Go: my children; remember the just chiefs of the Pale-faces, and clear your own tracks from briars."

The grave was made beneath the shade of some noble oaks. It has been carefully watched to the present hour by the Pawnees of the Loup, and is often shown, to the traveller and the trader, as a spot where a just white-man sleeps. In due time the stone was placed at its head, with the simple inscription, which the trapper had himself requested. The only liberty taken by Middleton, was to add, *"May no wanton hand ever disturb his remains."*

Chronology

1789 Born James Cooper to William Cooper and Elizabeth Fenimore Cooper, both of Quaker ancestry, September 15 in Burlington, N. J., the twelfth of thirteen children. Four brothers (Richard, b. 1775, Isaac, b. 1781, William, b. 1785, and Samuel, b. 1787) and two sisters (Hannah, b. 1777, and Anne, b. 1784) survive childhood.

1790–91 Family moves to Lake Otsego, in upper New York State, where father has acquired a large tract of land formerly owned by Col. George Croghan and has established the wilderness settlement to be known as Cooperstown.

1791–1800 Otsego is made a county, and Cooper's father, a Federalist squire with firm convictions about the relationship between property and political power, begins term as first judge of the Court of Common Pleas for Otsego County, and is elected to Congress in 1795 and 1799. Cooper attends public school in Cooperstown (except for the winters of 1796–97 and 1798–99, when he is enrolled in school in Burlington, N. J.). Reported to have been venturesome, athletic, and an enthusiastic reader. Sister Hannah says her brothers are "very wild" and "show plainly that they have been bred in the Woods." Hannah dies when she falls from a horse September 10, 1800. (Cooper later wrote that she was "a sort of second mother to me. From her I received many of my earliest lessons. . . . A lapse of forty years has not removed the pain with which I allude to the subject at all.")

1801–02 Becomes a boarding student in the home of father's friend, Rev. Thomas Ellison, rector of St. Peter's Church, Albany, N.Y., where he is drilled in Latin and forced to memorize long passages of Virgil. After Ellison dies in April 1802, goes to New Haven to be tutored for Yale College.

1803 Matriculates at Yale in February. (One of his professors, Benjamin Silliman, recalled twenty-five years later that the young Cooper was a "fine sparkling beautiful boy of alluring person and interesting manners.") Career at Yale marred by inattention to studies and a series of pranks (family tradition says that he tied a donkey in a professor's chair and stuffed a rag impregnated with gunpowder into the keyhole of another student's door and set it afire). Dismissed from Yale in junior year, returns to Cooperstown, and continues education with tutor, the Reverend William Neill, who regards him as rather wayward, disinclined to study, and addicted to novel-reading.

1806–07 To prepare for a naval career, serves as sailor-before-the-mast on the merchant vessel *Stirling*. Sails October 1806 to the Isle of Wight, London, Spain, then London again before returning home September 1807. On this voyage meets Edward R. Meyers, an apprentice seaman (whose biography he would write in 1843).

1808–09 Receives midshipman's warrant January 1, 1808. Serves in the bomb ketch *Vesuvius* from March to July. Stationed at Fort Oswego, a frontier outpost on Lake Ontario, August 22, 1808, to October 1809 to apprehend smugglers during the 1808 embargo. In November, requests transfer to the sloop *Wasp 18*, anchored in New York, under Lieutenant James Lawrence, and is assigned task of recruiting sailors. Meets fellow recruiter William Branford Shubrick (later Rear Admiral), who becomes his most intimate friend. Judge Cooper dies December 22 of pneumonia (contracted after being struck from behind by a political opponent). Cooper willed $50,000 as his share of the legacy and a remainder interest with his brothers and sister in the $750,000 estate.

1810 Meets Susan Augusta De Lancey, eighteen, daughter of a prominent Westchester County family that had supported the Loyalist cause during the war. "I loved her like a man," Cooper writes to his brother Richard, "and told her of it like a sailor." Requests a year's furlough to settle affairs following father's death, and a year later resigns from the navy.

1811–13 On New Year's Day, 1811, marries Susan De Lancey at her home in Mamaroneck, N.Y.; in April begins farming in a small way in New Rochelle. First child, Elizabeth, born September 27. Buys a farm, which he names Fenimore, on the western shore of Lake Otsego about a mile from

Cooperstown, hoping to establish residence there permanently. Oldest brother, Richard, dies March 6, 1813. Second daughter, Susan Augusta, born April 17, 1813. Elizabeth dies July 13th, 1813, soon after the move to Fenimore.

1814 Family lives in small frame house while permanent stone manor house is built. Cooper, a gentleman farmer and one of the founders of the county agricultural society, is active in the militia and the local Episcopal church.

1815–17 Two more daughters are born: Caroline Martha, June 26, 1815, and Anne Charlotte, May 14, 1817. Family moves back to Westchester County, autumn, 1817, because Mrs. Cooper wishes to be near her family and also because Cooper faces increasing financial difficulties caused by the depression following the War of 1812, claims against estate, and personal debts.

1818 Builds home on De Lancey land, Scarsdale, N.Y., and names farm Angevine. Attempts to retrieve family fortune in speculative ventures. Becomes active in local Clintonian Republican politics. Two brothers die: William, to whom he was most attached, and Isaac, who had been most like his father. Mother, who has been living in the family residence, Otsego Hall, dies in December.

1819 With associate Charles Thomas Dering, invests in Sag Harbor whaler *The Union*, April 15 (Cooper owns the ship and two-thirds of the outfit); frequently sails on it. June 15, daughter Maria Frances is born. Appointed quartermaster, with rank of colonel, in New York State militia, July 1819. Last remaining brother, Samuel, dies.

1820 Writes first novel, *Precaution*, an imitation of a class of popular British novels, reportedly on challenge from wife. Its publication in November brings him into New York City literary and artistic circles. Begins to frequent the bookshop of Charles Wiley, and to write reviews for Wiley's *Literary and Scientific Repository*, meeting friends—among them Fitz-Greene Halleck and William Dunlap—in a back room he later christens "The Den."

1821 First son, Fenimore, born October 23. Second novel, *The Spy*, published December 22, is an immediate and resounding success. Translated into French and published in Paris.

1822 Quarrels with De Lancey family, and moves with wife and children from Westchester County to New York City, to be near publishers and to improve daughters' opportunities for schooling. Founds the Bread and Cheese, a lunch club often referred to as "the Cooper Club," whose informal membership would include merchants, painters, poets, journalists, and army and navy officers. Though his earnings are improved, Cooper's financial difficulties are not fully resolved.

1823 3500 copies of *The Pioneers* sold on the morning of publication (February 1). English edition published by Murray is the first of Cooper's works not to be pirated. Becomes interested in journalism; writes account of a horse race for the New York *Patriot*. April, becomes a member of the American Philosophical Society. Moves to 3 Beach Street, New York City, in May. In July, the house at Fenimore burns to the ground. Son Fenimore dies August 5. In autumn, household goods inventoried (but not sold) by Sheriff of New York. Has "bilious attack" from which he continues to suffer for several years.

1824 Publishes first sea romance, *The Pilot*, in January, an attempt in part to show the nautical inaccuracies in Sir Walter Scott's *The Pirate*. Paul Fenimore Cooper born February 5. Writes account of the celebration at Castle Garden in honor of General Lafayette for the New York *American*. Moves family in May to 345 Greenwich Street, New York City. In August, receives honorary M.A. from Columbia College. Accompanies four English noblemen (including Edward Stanley, Earl of Derby and future prime minister of England) on a sight-seeing trip to Saratoga, Ballston, Lake George, Ticonderoga, and Lake Champlain. In a cavern in Glen Falls with Stanley, decides to write *The Last of the Mohicans*. ("I must place one of my old Indians here.")

1825 Publishes *Lionel Lincoln*, the first of his commercial failures. Forms close friendship with Samuel F. B. Morse, artist (and future inventor of the telegraph).

1826 *The Last of the Mohicans*, published in February, receives enthusiastic press and becomes the best known of his novels on both sides of the Atlantic. Formally adds Fenimore to his name in fulfillment of pledge to his mother. Receives silver medal in May from the Corporation of the City of New York. Attends a farewell banquet in his honor given by the Bread and Cheese. In June, the family (including sixteen-year-old nephew William) sails for Europe for Cooper's health, the children's education, and, as Cooper confesses, "perhaps . . . a little pleasure concealed in the bottom of the cup"; European residence will extend to seven years. Carries with him unfinished manuscript of *The Prairie* and a nominal commission as U.S. Consul for Lyons, France. Following a brief visit to England, family settles in Paris, July 22, and after a few weeks in the Hotel Montmorency, moves to the Hotel Jumilhac, 12 Rue St. Maur, in the Faubourg St. Germain, where Cooper is courted by Parisian society. "The people," he writes to a friend, "seem to think it marvelous that an American can write." Visits Lafayette, who becomes his closest European friend, at his home, La Grange. November, Sir Walter Scott visits to enlist his help to change the American copyright laws and secure revenue from his American imprints.

1827 Publishes *The Prairie* (April, London; May, Philadelphia). Works on *The Red Rover* and, at Lafayette's suggestion, begins work on *Notions of the Americans*, intended to describe American institutions and the American character and to correct misconceptions about the United States current in England. Translations of works into French are paid for and published by Goddelin. June 1 to November 16, family lives in a thirty-room walled-in villa in St. Ouèn, on the Seine, four miles from Paris. Health improves in the country air. *The Red Rover* published November in Paris and London, and January in Philadelphia.

1828–29 February, visits London with wife, son Paul, and nephew William to finish *Notions* and see it through the press and is astonished by the warmth of his reception in literary and political, mainly Whig, circles. Finishes the book May 17. Returns to Paris June 9, via Holland and Belgium. July 28, family settles in Berne, Switzerland, where Cooper works on *The Wept of Wish-ton-Wish* and makes notes on his Swiss travels. Takes excursions to many parts of the country. Resigns as Consul of Lyons September 8, and leaves for Italy in October. Resides at Palazzo Ricasoli in Florence, November 25 to May 11, 1829. (Later writes of Italy: ". . . it is the only region of the earth that I truly love.") Mingles widely in Florentine society and comes to know members of the Bonaparte family. Among American expatriates, is especially attracted to young American sculptor Horatio Greenough, from whom he commissions a work. (". . . of all the arts that of statuary is perhaps the one we most want, since it is more openly and visibly connected with the taste of the people.") February, sets out alone to Paris to arrange for the printing of *The Wept of Wish-ton-Wish*, but after negotiations in Marseilles, the work is set and printed in Florence. *Notions of the Americans* published in England June 1828, and in America two months later. In July 1829, family travels from Leghorn to Naples in a chartered felucca, and in August settles in a chateau called "Tasso's house" in Sorrento, where Cooper writes most of *The Water-Witch*. December, family settles in Rome for a stay of several months. Goes riding on the campagna. ("Rome is only to be seen at leisure, and I think, it is only to be seen well, on horseback.")

1830 Reads Jefferson's letters and writes to a friend: "Have we not had a false idea of that man? I own he begins to appear to me, to be the greatest man, we ever had." Coopers leave Rome in mid-April, travel slowly north, pausing ten days in Venice, and arrive late in May in Dresden, where Cooper supervises the printing of *The Water-Witch*. August, returns to Paris (". . . the revolution which was consummated in Paris . . . induced me to come post haste . . ."). Through Lafayette, a prime mover in the events of the July revolution, follows closely the course of the new monarchy of Louis Philippe, to whom he is presented. Interests himself also in revolutionary movements in Belgium, Italy, and particularly Poland, whose struggle with Russia he actively supports.

1831 Decides to stay at least another year in Europe so daughters can finish their education, and in April takes large, unfurnished flat at 59 St. Dominique in the Faubourg St. Germain. Undertakes to revise and write new prefaces to his previously published works for Colburn and Bentley, who pay him £50 per title. Receives additional money from European translations of his works. No longer encumbered by debts, expects to earn $20,000 during the year. September, tours Belgium and the Rhine with wife, Paul, and Frances. Sends nephew William, who has been ill, to Le Havre in the hope that sea air may cure him. William dies of consumption October 1. *The Bravo*, first novel in a European trilogy chronicling the decline of feudalism and the rise of popular institutions, published October 15. At Lafayette's urging, enters the "Finance Controversy" (provoked by an article in the *Revue Brittanique* on the French national budget that claims monarchy is less expensive than the American republic) by writing a "Letter to General Lafayette," dated November 25 (published in English by Baudry in December, and in French translation in the *Revue des Deux Mondes* in January), citing official records to prove the republic is less expensive.

1832 Letter becomes focus of debate in the January session of the Chamber of Deputies, and further exchanges of letters are published. Cooper suspects, incorrectly, that the American minister to France, William C. Rives, has taken a view contrary to his. Goes less into society; spends much time with Samuel Morse after he comes to Paris in September, visiting galleries, viewing and discussing art. Writes to William Dunlap: "I have cut all Kings & Princes, go to no great Officers and jog on this way from the beginning to the end of the month." Considers visiting America to decide whether family should ever return permanently. Feels "heart-sick" about unfavorable American criticism of his political actions in Europe and of *The Bravo*. Cholera epidemic breaks out in Paris in April. Morse returns to America in July. *The Heidenmauer*, second volume in European trilogy, published (London, July; Philadelphia, Sept.). Between July and October the Coopers travel in Belgium, the Rhineland, and Switzerland for Mrs. Cooper's health and a long-deferred vacation. On return to Paris, works on *The Headsman*. Arranges for Bentley's publication of William Dunlap's *History of the American Theatre*. Becomes increasingly restive as European attacks on his republicanism are published in America together with adverse reviews of his books. Resents what he calls "this slavish dependence on foreign opinion" and determines to abandon writing after *The Headsman*.

1833 June 15, goes to London to supervise the printing of *The Headsman*, last volume of the European trilogy (published London, Sept.; Philadelphia, Oct.). Soon after returning to Paris at the end of July, family leaves for America, stopping en route for a few weeks in England. Arrives in New York November 5, and moves family temporarily into a house on Bleecker Street rented for them by Samuel Morse. Sensing a chill in homecoming reception, Cooper declines testimonial dinner in his honor proposed by the Bread and Cheese. Enters speculative cotton market with James de Peyster Ogden and makes tour of Washington, Baltimore, and Philadelphia in December for business reasons and to observe firsthand the effects of five years of Jacksonian democracy. Concludes that country has changed but not improved and that there is "a vast expansion of mediocrity." Writes a friend that " were it not for my family, I should return to Europe, and pass the remainder of my life there."

1834 Spring, family moves to townhouse at 4 St. Marks Place. Publication, in June, of *A Letter to His Countrymen* (arguing that American "practice of deferring to foreign opinion is dangerous to the institutions of the country") increases unpopularity and provokes widespread attacks in the Whig press. After seventeen years' absence, revisits Cooperstown in June; October, purchases the family seat, Otsego Hall, and sets about renovating it for possible permanent occupancy. "My pen is used up—or rather it is thrown away," he writes a correspondent. "This is not a country for literature, at least not yet." Resumes the writing of *The Monikins*, allegorical satire on England, France, and America begun in Paris in 1832. Writes the first of a series of political articles in December—dealing mainly with the payment of the French debt, the differences between American constitutional government and the French system, and the functions of the three branches of government in America—for the New York *Evening Post* under the pseudonym "A.B.C."

1835 Sends manuscript chapter of *The Bravo* to Princess Victoria (later Queen of England) when asked for autograph.

The Monikins, published July, fails with critics and public. Family spends summer in Cooperstown, winter in New York City.

1836 Family leaves house at St. Marks Place in May and moves the remainder of their furniture to Cooperstown. Cooper goes to Philadelphia in July to see *Sketches of Switzerland* through the press (a practice he will continue with many of his future works). Part I published May, Part II, October.

1837 Becomes involved in a misunderstanding with townspeople over public use of Three Mile Point, a picnic ground on Lake Otsego owned by the Cooper family for which Cooper is trustee. After users damage the property, Cooper publishes No Trespass Notice, offending those who assumed the Point was public property. Local excitement subsides after Cooper sends two letters to the *Freeman's Journal* explaining the situation. Some county newspaper editors disregard explanation and publish articles attacking him. When offending newspapers refuse to retract statements, Cooper sues for libel. (Before these suits come to trial, publishes *Home as Found*, a novel of social criticism, in which a fictionalized version of the incident caricatures a newspaper editor. Major New York Whig editors now join in the quarrel against Cooper, justifying their attacks by maintaining that he put himself into the book and has thus made himself a legitimate target. Cooper begins suits against them. Though eventually winning most of these suits, it is at the cost of much time, energy, and popularity. Awarded $400 in damages in May 1839, writes to a correspondent, "We shall bring the press, again, under the subjection of the law. When one considers the characters, talents, motives and consistency of those who control it, as a body, he is lost in wonder that any community should have so long submitted to a tyranny so low and vulgar. When it is rebuked thoroughly, it may again become useful.") Travel books drawn from his European letters and journals are published under the general title *Gleanings in Europe*. (*France*: London, Jan., Phila., Mar.; *England*: London, May, Phila., Sept.; and *Italy*, published as *Excursions in Italy* in London, Feb. 28, 1838, Phila., May 1838.)

1838 Publishes *The American Democrat* (Cooperstown, Apr.), *Chronicles of Cooperstown, Homeward Bound* (London, May; Phila., August) and its sequel *Home as Found* (Nov.). Attacked in Whig press for his condescending portrayal of American manners. Meanwhile, works on *History of the Navy of the United States of America*, a project contemplated for more than a decade. December, goes with wife and four daughters to Philadelphia to research and see the work through the press. Stays until May 1839.

1839 Begins friendship with historian George Bancroft. *History of the Navy*, published May, sells well until it is attacked in the press by partisans of Commodore Oliver Hazard Perry for its account of the controversial Battle of Lake Erie. Defends account in letters to the *Freeman's Journal* and sues his critics (particularly William A. Duer). Suits for libel continue to occupy much of his time for the next several years. Writes *The Pathfinder* and goes to Philadelphia in December to see it through the press.

1840 *The Pathfinder* published (London, Feb.; Phila., March). It is well received, and Balzac writes an admiring tribute to Cooper's work. Goes again to Philadelphia to see *Mercedes of Castile* (his "Columbus book") through the press in October, taking a cruise during this time with old friend Commodore Shubrick on the *Macedonian*. The work is published November in Philadelphia, and a month later in London.

1841 Continues to purchase old family property. June, tries once again, unsuccessfully, to interest publishers in a "sea story all ships and no men." August, delivers the commencement address at Geneva College, where son Paul is a student, on the thesis "Public Opinion is a Despot in a Democracy." Travels to Philadelphia in June, and again in August to see works through the press. *The Deerslayer* and a short version of *The History of the Navy* published in September.

1842 Addresses a series of letters to "Brother Jonathan" (begun Dec. 1841), defending *Homeward Bound* and *Home as Found* as fictions. ("When a work *professes* to be fiction, the reader is bound to consider all those parts fiction, which cannot be proved otherwise.") Wins judgments in court in libel suits against William Leete Stone of the *Commercial Advertiser* (for the William A. Duer articles on the Battle of Lake Erie) and against Thurlow Weed and Horace Greeley (for articles on Three Mile Point). Large audience attends the Duer-Stone trial and Cooper speaks eloquently for himself. Publishes *The Two Admirals* (May) and *The Wing-and-Wing* (*Jack O'Lantern* in England, Nov.). Persuaded by editor Rufus Wilmot Griswold to write for *Graham's Magazine*, agrees to do a series of brief biographies of naval officers, for the first time receiving pay for serial publication (sketches appear between 1842–45, beginning with "Richard Somers," October).

1843 Becomes engrossed with the *Somers* mutiny case and the proceedings against Capt. Alexander Slidell Mackenzie, on whose orders one midshipman and two crew members, presumed mutineers, had been executed at sea, the midshipman being the son of the Secretary of War in Tyler's cabinet. Writes eighty-page review of the case (published as an annex to the *Proceedings* of the naval court martial in 1844). *Autobiography of a Pocket Handkerchief* (or *Le Mouchoir*) serialized in *Graham's* January through April. After thirty-six years hears from old shipmate, Edward (Ned) Meyers, and brings him for five-month stay in Cooperstown. Writes Ned's biography, using his own words as much as possible. Journeys with John Pendleton Kennedy and William Gilmore Simms to Philadelphia. Publishes *The Battle of Lake Erie* (June), *Wyandotté* (London, Aug.; Phila., Sept.), *Ned Myers, or a Life Before the Mast* (Nov.). Income from writings begins to diminish seriously because of cheap reprints from abroad and difficult economic conditions at home.

1844 Writes in January to William Gilmore Simms, "We serve a hard master, my dear Sir, in writing for America." *Afloat and Ashore* published by Cooper himself in America and by Bentley in London, June. Second part, entitled *Miles Wallingford*, published October (Sept. in England, with title *Lucy Hardinge*). Begins work on the anti-rent (or Littlepage) trilogy, tracing the history of four generations of a landed New York family which culminates in conflict between tenants and landlords.

1845 First two volumes of the trilogy, *Satanstoe* (June) and *The Chainbearer* (Nov.), published and criticized on the grounds that Cooper is too partial to the interests of landed proprietors. John Pendleton Kennedy family visits Otsego in August. Attends Annual Diocesan Convention of the Protestant Episcopal Church in September, to consider the charge against Bishop Benjamin Tredwell Onderdonk of "immorality and impurity." Convinced of the truth of the charges, speaks at the convention, offering a solution to the tangled procedural system, but without success.

1846 Final volume of the anti-rent trilogy, *The Redskins* (*Ravensnest* in England), published July. *The Lives of Distinguished Naval Officers*, originally serialized in *Graham's*, published in two volumes in Philadelphia, March and May. *Jack Tier* serialized in *Graham's* and Bentley's *Miscellany*, November 1846–March 1848, under title "The Islets of the Gulf" (published March 1848; English title, *Captain Spike*).

1847 Begins a series of trips in June to Michigan in connection with unfortunate land investments and is impressed with the unspoiled country. August, publishes *The Crater*. ("It is a remarkable book, and ought to make a noise.") October, goes again to Detroit on business.

1848 Enters debate concerning the circumstances of General Nathaniel Woodhull's death during the American Revolution, writing several letters to the *Home Journal*, February–June. Writes letters on the new French republic in March and April for the Albany *Argus*. June and October, travels to Michigan. Publishes *The Oak Openings; or the Bee Hunter*, set in frontier Michigan, in August.

1849 Writes a long appreciative letter to Louis Legrand Nobel about Thomas Cole: "As an artist, I consider Mr. Cole one of the very first geniuses of the age." Daughter Caroline Martha marries Henry Frederick Phinney in Cooperstown, February 8. Though Cooper has quarreled with members of the groom's family and is unhappy about the match, he writes his daughter: ". . . your happiness will be the first consideration . . . Under no circumstances must there be coldness, alienation, or indifference. You are my dearly beloved child . . ." Publishes *The Sea Lions*, April, which does well in America but fails in England. The success of the collected edition of Washington Irving's writings encourages G. P. Putnam to begin issuing a uniform edition of Cooper, extending only to eleven volumes. Spends most of the time from October through April at the Globe Hotel, New York City, mainly to be close to the publishing center. Works on *The Ways of the Hour* and renews old acquaintances.

1850 Last novel, *The Ways of the Hour*, published in April. Cooper's only play, *Upside Down, or, Philosophy in Petticoats*, a satire on socialism, is performed June 18–21 at Burton's Chambers Street Theatre, New York, featuring actor-producer William E. Burton. Works on a projected third volume of his *History of the Navy*. July, travels to Niagara and Michigan with wife and daughter Charlotte. Goes to New York City in November to consult Dr. John Wakefield Francis about health problems: sharp pains in heels, with other symptoms, such as numbness of hands and feet. Daughter Maria Francis marries cousin Richard Cooper, December 10, in Cooperstown.

1851 Works on a history of greater New York, *The Towns of Manhattan* (unfinished, though he dictates a chapter in August after he is too ill to hold a pen). Writes to friend that he has lost twenty-two pounds. Continues to suffer from ailments, and in March goes to New York on business, and also to consult doctor. Consents to receive sacraments of the Protestant Episcopal Church. With great effort, travels the short distance to Christ Church, July 27, to be confirmed by Bishop De Lancey (his wife's brother). Sends introduction and eight chapters of *The Towns of Manhattan* to Putnam in July. Handwriting fails, and he dictates letters and work in progress to wife and daughters. Condition worsens, though he feels little pain. Dies at 1:30 P.M., September 14, 1851, in Otsego Hall. Buried in the family plot in Cooperstown.

Note on the Texts

This volume contains the first three of James Fenimore Cooper's five Leatherstocking Tales: *The Pioneers* (1823), *The Last of the Mohicans* (1826), and *The Prairie* (1827). A companion volume contains *The Pathfinder* (1840) and *The Deerslayer* (1841). The texts reprinted here are those established for *The Writings of James Fenimore Cooper* under the general editorship of James Franklin Beard, with James P. Elliott as textual editor, and published by the State University of New York Press, Albany (hereafter referred to as the SUNY edition): *The Pioneers* (1980), *The Last of the Mohicans* (1983), and *The Prairie* (page proofs). These texts were prepared according to the standards established by—and they have received the official approval of—the Center for Editions of American Authors (or its successor, the Center for Scholarly Editions) of the Modern Language Association of America (see *The Center for Scholarly Editions: An Introductory Statement*, 1977). The aim of the SUNY edition is to establish a text which as nearly as possible represents the author's final intentions. In selecting their copy-text, the editors give priority to the holograph manuscript, in whole or part, when it exists; when it does not survive, preference goes next to proofs corrected in the author's hand, or, if these do not exist, to the editions Cooper is known to have supervised or revised. Though circumstances beyond his control frequently defeated his intentions, Cooper was a painstaking reviser who corrected compositorial errors, rewrote sentences and phrases, altered punctuation and spelling (his own punctuation and spelling were not always consistent), sharpened diction, and in particular resisted the attempts of editors, compositors, and amanuenses to normalize dialect expression (e.g. " 'arth" to "earth," "ag'in" to "again," "Injin" to "Indian").

The Pioneers, Cooper's third novel, was written during a critical period in his life when, having lost his properties and finding himself burdened with debt, he was thrown upon his writing to support his wife and four children. The novel was begun in November or December 1821 at the family farm at Scarsdale in Westchester County. As with *The Last of the Mohicans* and *The Prairie*, the writing was subject to other demands on Cooper's time, and took approximately a year to complete. After a delay caused by the yellow fever epidemic in New York, *The Pioneers* was published on February 1, 1823, by Charles Wiley, with Edward B. Clayton listed as printer, in an edition of 3500 copies that was exhausted on the day of publication.

In the absence of a manuscript or proofs, the copy-text for this edition is the text of the earliest known copy (owned by James F. Beard) of the Wiley-Clayton edition, an unusually corrupt text that Cooper immediately set about amending. The result was three revised texts of *The Pioneers* in the winter of 1823: one consisted of excerpts from three chapters, published in the New York *Commercial Advertiser* on January 18 and 25; the second was the first British edition, published by John Murray on February 26; and the last was the second New York edition, printed by Seymour and Clayton and published by Charles Wiley, which was available about the same time as the first. Early in 1831 the London firm of Colburn and Bentley, anxious to share the British copyright, offered to pay the novelist fifty pounds per volume for revised texts of several of his early novels for their Standard Novels Edition. Cooper asked Bentley to provide him with a copy of the Carey & Lea reprint, "cut open and rebound with a leaf of writing paper between each two pages." On these pages he wrote the revisions to be incorporated into the text reset by Bentley's compositors, rewriting passages and phrases and altering diction and word order, and supplying a new introduction and sixteen explanatory footnotes. This edition appeared on March 31, 1832, in a printing of 1000 copies. Finally, in 1850, Cooper reviewed the text for Putnam's Author's Revised Edition, preserving the introduction and notes to the 1832 edition but adding two paragraphs to the introduction, reworking the style of the later chapters, and otherwise undertaking only minimal revisions. Since no holograph manuscript or proof sheets are known to exist, the task of the SUNY editors, Lance Schachterle and Kenneth M. Andersen, Jr., was to sift through the many variants among the authorized texts and determine which of those were Cooper's intended emendations, and which were editorial intervention or typographical errors. The intended emendations were then inserted into the copy-text.

The writing of *The Last of the Mohicans* occupied Cooper during most of 1825. He was then living in New York City and enjoying the success inaugurated by *The Spy* (1821), reinforced by the reception of *The Pioneers* and *The Pilot* (1824), and marred only by the commercial failure of *Lionel Lincoln* (1825). Because his publisher (Charles Wiley) was ill and on the verge of bankruptcy, Cooper made overtures to the Philadelphia firm of Carey & Lea, and in January 1826, following Wiley's death, agreed to their proposal to issue a first edition of 5,000 copies and to pay him $5,000. The novel was published on February 6, 1826; the first English edition of 1250 copies, set from advance sheets forwarded to London as they came off the press in Philadelphia, was published by John Miller on March 18.

The textual history of *The Last of the Mohicans* is in many respects similar to that of *The Pioneers*. In the absence of the manuscript, or any author-corrected proof (it is almost certain that Cooper destroyed the manuscripts of his early novels before his departure for Europe in 1826), the earliest version of the text of the first American edition serves as copy-text. As he did for *The Pioneers*, Cooper requested an interleaved copy of the Carey & Lea edition, and on these pages wrote his revisions of *The Last of the Mohicans* for the Colburn and Bentley Standard Novels series, adding a new introduction and notes. His revisions were far less numerous than for *The Pioneers*, and over half the substantive variations were, in the opinion of the SUNY textual editors, James A. Sappenfield and E. N. Feltskog, deletions made in order to accelerate the pace of the narrative. The third and final authorial edition of the novel was Putnam's Author's Revised Edition in 1850, for which Cooper made few revisions, except in the introduction, where sentences are recast and two paragraphs deleted and one added. Again, as was the case for *The Pioneers*, the SUNY editors had to examine the many variants among the authorized editions and determine which were made by Cooper.

When the Cooper family sailed for Europe on June 1, 1826, the novelist carried with him the unfinished manuscript of *The Prairie*. He completed the writing in Paris, and the novel was published by Colburn (later Colburn and Bentley) in London on April 21, 1827; by Hector Bossange (in English) in Paris on April 25; and by Carey, Lea & Carey in Philadelphia on May 17.

The problem of establishing a copy-text for *The Prairie* is considerably more complicated than for the earlier Leatherstocking Tales. A portion of the holograph manuscript has survived; moreover, there exists an amanuensis copy of one third of the complete manuscript (in part overlapping the holograph), which was made by William Cooper, the author's nephew. William Cooper misread or failed to decipher his uncle's hand on occasion and introduced new errors into the copy. Cooper, preparing copy for the printer, corrected some of his nephew's alterations, but, apparently unaware of the extent to which his original text had been corrupted, allowed most of them to stand. In addition, *The Prairie* is the earliest of Cooper's works for which any of the corrected proofs survive. The proof sheets of the Bossange edition (set from the corrected amanuensis copy), which were forwarded as printer's copy to both the American and English publishers of *The Prairie*, reflect Cooper's direct intervention by corrections introduced into proof and standing type. Among the three 1827 editions of *The Prairie*, the Bossange edition is the only one that can be considered authorial, for, as James P. Elliott, the editor of the SUNY text, concluded, "it is the only one that directly represents Cooper's final efforts to embody his intentions." The copy-text for the SUNY edition is pre-publication material whenever appropriate, emended with Cooper's revisions from the Bossange edition; when such material does not exist, the copy-text is the Bossange edition itself.

Four years after the initial publication of *The Prairie*, Cooper revised the text and wrote a new introduction and notes for the Colburn and Bentley Standard Novels edition, again using an interleaved copy of the Carey, Lea & Carey edition to do this work, which was published on June 30, 1832. It may be regarded as the second of the authorial editions. Cooper made more insertions than deletions and paid particular attention to punctuation, reflecting his concern for the rhetorical emphasis, the sound of his prose—an emphasis that has been retained, as far as feasible, in the SUNY edition. In 1850, when *The Prairie* was added to Putnam's Author's Revised Edition, Cooper's revisions were again minor, as with earlier novels he had prepared for this series. He was primarily concerned with altering the introduction "to adapt it," as he explained, "to these later times." This version provides a third authorial text.

The standards for American English continue to fluctuate and in some ways were conspicuously different in earlier periods from what they are now. In nineteenth-century writings, for example, a word might be spelled in more than one way, even in the same work, and such variations might be carried into print. Commas were sometimes used expressively to suggest the movements of voice, and capitals were sometimes meant to give significances to a work beyond those it might have in its uncapitalized form. Since modernization would remove such effects, this volume preserves the spelling, punctuation, capitalization, and wording of the SUNY edition, which strives to be as faithful to Cooper's usage as surviving evidence permits.

This volume offers the reader the results of the most detailed scholarly effort thus far made to establish the texts of *The Pioneers*, *The Last of the Mohicans*, and *The Prairie*. The present edition is concerned only with representing the *texts* of these editions; it does not attempt to reproduce features of the typographic design—such as the display capitalization of chapter openings. Epigraphs from Shakespeare have been keyed by the SUNY editors to *The Riverside Shakespeare*, ed. G. Blakemore Evans (Boston: Houghton Mifflin, 1974); other epigraphs are keyed to unspecified "standard editions," "first editions," or "early American editions" available to Cooper at the time he wrote the Tales. The texts in this volume follow exactly the SUNY *The Pioneers* (first printing), *The Last of the Mohicans* (first printing), and *The Prairie* (page proofs), except for the following errors: 229.10, reminder; 379.3, ii;

477.6, considdered; 509.4, 47–48; 566.8, he he; 677.5, 293–294; 717.14, sort; 727.5, *Midsummer*; 802.3, *About*; 802.3, 4.; 821.37, a effort; 829.21, moments;. (These errors in the SUNY edition will be corrected in future printings.)

Notes

In the notes below, the numbers refer to page and line of this volume (the line count includes chapter headings). No note is made for material included in a standard desk-reference book. Notes at the foot of the page are Cooper's own. For additional textual and explanatory notes, see the relevant volumes in the SUNY edition.

THE PIONEERS

10.1 one . . . machines] Probably the cast-iron plough perfected by Jethro Wood (1774–1834) of Cayuga County, New York.

10.20 The author . . . said] In his introduction to the 1831 revised edition of *The Last of the Mohicans*, published in London by Henry Colburn and Richard Bentley.

11.3 Country.] The following paragraphs were added here to the 1832 Introduction when it was reprinted in the 1851 Putnam edition:

"It may be well to say here, a little more explicitly, that there was no intention to describe with particular accuracy any real characters in this book. It has often been said, and in published statements, that the heroine of this book was drawn after a sister of the writer, who was killed by a fall from a horse now near half a century since. So ingenious is conjecture, that a personal resemblance has been discovered between the fictitious character and the deceased relative! It is scarcely possible to describe two females of the same class in life, who would be less alike, personally, than Elizabeth Temple and the sister of the author who met with the deplorable fate mentioned. In a word, they were as unlike in this respect, as in history, character, and fortunes.

"Circumstances rendered this sister singularly dear to the author. After a lapse of half a century, he is writing this paragraph with a pain that would induce him to cancel it, were it not still more painful to have it believed that one whom he regarded with a reverence that surpassed the love of a brother, was converted by him into the heroine of a work of modern fiction."

25.2–3 Sir William] Sir William Johnson (1715–74), for many years Superintendent of Indian Affairs for the British government, a landed proprietor, a military leader, and a figure of great influence over the Indians of the Six Nations.

25.12 a broad joe] A Portuguese gold coin, minted in the eighteenth century and worth eight or nine dollars, which was circulated among French soldiers during the Revolution. Also called a "Johannes."

52.32 Wethersfield meeting-house] The First Protestant Episcopal Church in Wethersfield, Connecticut, built by dissidents who split from the Congregational Church in 1797.

58.21–22 the window . . . palace] Aladdin, in commanding the genie to raise a palace for himself and his bride facing the palace of his father-in-law, the Sultan, stipulated that one of the twenty-four heavily jeweled casement windows in the upper hall be left uncompleted. The Sultan, lamenting that the palace fell short of perfection, offered to finish it, but nearly bankrupted himself in the process. To conclude this staged drama, Aladdin magnanimously ordered the genie to finish the window and make restitution to the Sultan.

59.24 lobskous] A cracker hash consisting of salt meat, baked or stewed with preserved vegetables and hardtack.

60.6 Rodney's victory] Vice-Admiral George Brydges Rodney (1719–92), later Lord Rodney, defeated the French squadron commanded by the Comte de Grasse in an engagement off the Iles des Saintes, just south of Guadeloupe, on April 12, 1782. De Grasse's flagship was damaged beyond repair and de Grasse taken prisoner.

63.10 the boatswain's colt] A rope knotted at one end and used by the boatswain's mate on those who were slow in carrying out orders.

67.17 Brandywine] On September 11, 1777, the American forces under Washington were defeated by Major General Sir William Howe's army advancing on Philadelphia.

67.39 King's . . . evil] The King's touch was formerly thought to be able to cure scrofula, known as "the King's evil."

70.39 Denman's Midwifery] *An Introduction to the Practice of Midwifery* (London, 1782; New York, 1802), in two volumes, by Thomas Denman, M.D. (1733–1815), the standard treatise in its field on both sides of the Atlantic.

79.28 lubber-holes] In larger square-rigged ships, a hole in a top platform next to the lower masthead through which a man could crawl instead of climbing over the outer edge of the top when going aloft.

80.1–2 Captain . . . Foody-rong] Presumably the *Foudroyant*, a French ship captured by the British in 1758. From 1775 to 1783 it was under the command of Captain John Jervis, later Earl St. Vincent (1735–1823), who in the battle off the Iles des Saintes (see note 60.6) received a splinter in his right temple.

93.1 Sallick law] The Salic Law or Lex Salica is an early Teutonic legal code dating from the sixth century that denies daughters the right to inherit.

101.7–8 "Titty-ree too . . . aa-ve-ny"] The Latin text of the first two lines of Virgil's first eclogue are as follows: "Tityre, tu patulae recubans sub tegmine fagi / silvestrem tenui musam meditaris avena." Translated: "Thou, Tityrus, recumbant under the shade of a spreading beech / Playest on the shepherds pipe a woodland song."

111.1–2 Dutch . . . sloop] A long-boat was the largest boat formerly carried by merchant vessels; it was equipped with mast, sails, and oars and was used for transporting stores, water, or cargo between ship and shore.

120.10–11 Radcliffe-highway] Ratcliffe High Way, as it was known in the eighteenth century, ran from east to west through the area north of the docks at Wapping. Called St. George Street in the nineteenth century, it is currently known as The Highway.

120.29–30 Royal . . . Paris] The "Billy de Paris" is probably the three-decker *Ville de Paris*, the pride of the French fleet and the Comte de Grasse's flagship in the engagement off the Iles des Saintes (see note 60.6). The "Royal Billy" is possibly the British *Prince William*, which took part in the same engagement. Formerly a Spanish ship, it was captured by the British and named for the future William IV, who was then serving as a midshipman.

125.11–12 "The Lord . . . him."] Habakkuk 2:20.

132.31 'Bay . . . O?'] A sea song in four stanzas, attributed to Andrew Cherry (1762–1812), recounting the destruction of a ship in a storm in the Bay of Biscay and the subsequent rescue of its crew.

135.24 old Crumhorn] A wild and barren promontory in the town of Maryland, Otsego County.

135.26 Garman Flats] German Flats, a town three miles south of the town of Herkimer, in Herkimer County, whose alluvial flats along the Mohawk were early settled by Germans.

138.40 Miquon] Delaware name for William Penn, meaning quill or feather pen.

139.4 Mingo."*] The only footnote that appeared in the first edition, 1823.

142.4 Gipsy hat] A bonnet with large side flaps.

145.2–4 "And . . . Barley-Mow."] A drinking song in which the size of the drinking measure is doubled at each verse; it was customarily sung when the mowing and stacking of the barley were finished.

150.26–27 'filius nullius.'] Literally, a son of nothing; hence, a bastard.

151.5–6 'Far. Av.'] Presumably Elnathan Todd's own coinage, combining the Latin "far," one of whose meanings is "coarse meal," with "avena," meaning "oats" and, specifically, "common oats," to produce "far avenae."

154.36 Shirley's] William Shirley (1694–1771), British governor of Massachusetts, who as a major general in 1755 was commander of the Niagara expedition. Natty is making a distinction between the rangers like himself and the foot soldiers under Shirley, whose military competence was later called into question.

155.30 the morning . . . Dieskau] Baron Ludwig August Dieskau (1701–67), a German officer commanding a force of Canadians and Iroquois serving the French, encountered and nearly overcame the forces of Sir William Johnson near Fort Lyman on September 8, 1755. Johnson's forces rallied behind improvised breastworks and turned the day. Dieskau, thrice wounded, was captured.

158.28–29 a Pumfretman] Probably a resident of Pomfret, a town in Windham County, Connecticut, sixteen miles northeast of Willimantic, though there was also a smaller Pomfret in Windsor County, Vermont.

160.10 Roshambow] Jean Baptiste Donatien de Vimeur, Comte de Rochambeau (1725–1807), who commanded the French forces in the siege that brought about Cornwallis's surrender at Yorktown on October 19, 1781.

172.33 slushed] To "slush down" meant to grease the standing rigging.

173.12–13 Cape . . . Finish-there] In other words, from Cape de la Hague, on the Cotentin Peninsula west of Cherbourg, to Cape Finisterre, the westernmost point of the Spanish mainland.

174.2–3 Boadishey frigate] Boadicea, the queen of the Iceni in eastern Britain, led a revolt against the Romans but was finally defeated in 61 A.D. and took her own life. The H.M.S. *Boadicea*, a frigate of thirty-eight guns, would have been commissioned after Ben retired from the sea. It took part in the Battle of Grand Port, in 1810.

175.3 Pico] A mountainous island in the Azores.

176.34 Tor-bay] Inlet of the English Channel in south Devon between the promontories of Hope's Nose and Berry Head, with good anchorage for ocean-going ships.

178.12 Della-cruscan humour] The Florentine Accademia della Crusca, founded in 1582, devoted itself in large part to stabilizing the Italian literary language. By Cooper's time, "della Cruscan" had come to signify stylistic pedantry or affectation.

225.5–22 "The Eastern . . . &c.] Verses to be sung to the tune of "Yankee Doodle."

295.32–33 when . . . 'Sopus] On October 16, 1777, British troops under General John Vaughan entered the undefended town of Kingston, or Esopus, on the Hudson and set it afire. The town was reduced to ashes.

335.22 Mohawk Flats] Also German Flats; see note 135.26.

384.10 a ship's cousin] An expression of contempt, possibly inspired by "ship's husband," the term for an agent who attends to the business of a ship in port.

386.26–27 Port . . . us] Ben evidently is alluding to the attack by the French commander, the Chevalier de Suffren, on Commodore George Johnstone's squadron of five small ships of the line in La Praya Bay at the island of Santiago in the Portuguese Cape Verde Islands on April 16, 1781.

THE LAST OF THE MOHICANS

469.1 Preface] Written for the 1826 edition.

473.1 Introduction] Added in 1831.

476.28–477.10 These . . . fit.] Added in 1850.

483.7 General Webb] Brigadier General Daniel Webb, commander of the royal forces at Fort Edward (originally Fort Lyman), unable to relieve the garrison under Lt. Colonel George Monro at Fort William Henry, ultimately ordered Monro to surrender to Montcalm.

483.18 Fort du Quesne] Built on the present site of Pittsburgh in 1754, it was named for the French governor, Ange de Menneville, Marquis de Duquesne.

486.28 snows] Two-masted vessels.

486.33–36 'He . . . shouting.'] Job 39:21, 25.

493.5 Canterbury gallop] A moderate gallop.

496.33–39 'Tis . . . England.'] This revised edition of the Bay Psalm Book, published in Boston in 1744, is a pocket-sized volume which includes, as an annex, "An Introduction to the Singing of Psalm Tunes," by the Reverend Mr. Tufts, and "A Table of Tunes" that includes all of the traditional settings that David Gamut will employ.

497.5 "Standish,"] One of the traditional hymns contained in "A Table of Tunes." See note 496.33–39.

497.12–19 "How . . . unto."] Psalms 133:1–2 (second metre), "A Song of Degrees of David."

512.5 Major Effingham] See *The Pioneers*.

524.30 Glenn's] The present Glen Falls, N.Y. In 1824, Cooper accompanied a party of English noblemen that included Edward Geoffrey Smith Stanley, the fourteenth Earl of Derby (1799–1869), on a visit to the site. Stanley suggested that the cavern and falls were "the very scene for a romance." In February 1826, Cooper wrote his English friend John Miller: "He [Stanley] and I, were, together, in the caverns at Glen Falls, and it was there I determined to write the book, promising him a Copy."

526.25–28 "First . . . too!"] Psalms 135:8–9.

533.14 his*] This footnote was also in the 1826 edition.

534.11 a little spruce] Spruce beer, or "sprouts beer," is obtained from the young sprouts of the black spruce. Aside from its pleasant flavor, it was regarded as useful as an anti-scorbutic.

566.6 "Isle of Wight"] Another traditional hymn in "A Table of Tunes." See note 496.33–39.

582.21 Sir William Johnson] See note 25.2–3.

587.8 'city of cannon'] Quebec.

605.24 'Northampton.'] In "A Table of Tunes." See note 496.33–39.

616.6 the Albany Patteroon] Stephen Van Rensselaer (1742–69), Patroon of the Manor of Rensselaerswyck, a vast landed estate on the Hudson River.

627.7–34 "Qui . . . remplir."] "Who goes there?" / "France." / "Where do you come from— where are you going at such an early hour?" / "I come from reconnoitering, and I am going to bed." / "Are you an officer of the king?" / "To be sure, comrade; do you take me for a provincial! I am a captain of infantry—I have here with me the daughters of the fort commander. Aha! You have heard tell of them! I took them prisoners near the other fort, and I am conducting them to the general." / "Faith, ladies; I am grieved for you; but—the fortune of war! You will find our general a brave man, and very polite with the ladies." / "That is the character of military men. Adieu, my friend; I could wish you a pleasanter duty to perform."

628.3 "Vive . . . &c.] The refrain of an old French marching song, "Vive la Compagnie."

635.29–40 "Qui . . . feu!"] "Who goes there?" / "It is I." / "Fool! who? I?" / "Friend of France." / "For me you have more the air of an *enemy* of France; stop! or, to be sure, I will make you a friend of the devil! No! fire; comrades; fire!"

637.5 "Point . . . coquins!"] "Give no quarter to the rascals!"

639.2 Mount Defiance] A height (formerly called Rattlesnake Hill) overlooking Fort Ticonderoga that served as an observation post and a vantage point for firing on the French below.

645.3 Woolwich Warren] The Royal Arsenal (called the "Warren" until 1805) located near the royal dockyard at Woolwich, England.

646.31–38 "Monsieur . . . avec eux.] "Sir, I take a great deal of pleasure in—bah! where is that interpreter?" / "I believe, sir, that he won't be necessary. I speak a little French." / "Ah, I am much relieved. I detest those rascals; one never knows what footing one is on with them."

648.3 Salique laws] See note 93.1.

651.24–30 the knights . . . chivalry!] Munro is alluding to Montcalm's rank as Chevalier of the Military Order of St. Louis and contrasting it unfavorably to the Scots Most Ancient and Most Noble Order of the Epistle, whose Latin motto is: "No one provokes me with impunity."

656.4 Monsieur Vauban] Sébastien le Prestre de Vauban (1633–1707), the favorite architect of Louis XIV and dominant military engineer of the second half of the seventeenth century, when he built or rebuilt 120 fortresses. His designs featured defense in depth, overlapping fields of fire, and multiple sally ports for sorties; his successful and deeply influential siegecraft relied on the methodical digging of trenches and saps and the careful use of artillery.

657.28–29 "En . . . peu."] "Fall back, my children—he feels warm; withdraw a little."

663.4–21 "Qui . . . jamais!"] "Who goes there?" / "Frenchman." / "The password?" / "Victory." / "That's good. You're going out very early, sir." / "It's necessary to be vigilant, my child." / "In truth, he is vigilant. I believe we have a corporal who never sleeps."

666.17–18 one horrid scene] Following the siege and surrender of Fort Oswego in August 1756, Montcalm allegedly permitted his Indian allies to plunder the garrison, massacre several soldiers on the parade, and scalp all of the wounded in the hospital.

668.39 'Southwell.'] Used for the line at 669.21 from Psalms 2:1, in "A Table of Tunes." See note 496.33–39.

704.2 Jarmans . . . Mohawk] See note 135.26.

717.14 the Scaroon] The party crosses the Scroon River (in present-day Scroon County) at a point fifteen or twenty miles northwest of Ticonderoga.

729.15 non-composser] In law, one who is *non compos mentis*, not of sound mind.

811.3 "Tamenund"] Also known as Tamanund and Tammany; appears in the recorded accounts of the first settlers of Pennsylvania, and by the time he is last reported has achieved among the Delawares a reputation for justice and piety approximating sainthood.

830.7–8 "my . . . earth!] The Tortoise, or Turtle, tribe, one of the leading clan-societies among the Delaware, claimed superiority over lesser clans because, according to one of Cooper's chief sources, the Rev. John G. E. Heckewelder, "their *relation*, the great Tortoise, a fabled monster, the Atlas of their mythology, bears according to their traditions this great *island* on his back."

830.19 Great Unâmis."*] Footnote in 1826 edition.

850.27–28 children . . . Shechemites] See Genesis 34.

THE PRAIRIE

884.34 westward.] In 1849, while revising for the Putnam edition, Cooper inserted the following sentence: "Since the original publication of this book, however, the boundaries of the republic have been carried to the Pacific, and 'the settler,' preceded by the 'trapper,' has already established himself on the shores of that vast sea."

885.7–11 The reader . . . just.] This paragraph was dropped in 1844 and the following two paragraphs were put in its place:

"Recent events have brought the Grand Prairies into familiar notice, and we now read of journeys across them as, half a century since, we perused the narratives of emigrants to Ohio and Louisiana. It is a singular commentary on the times that places for railroads across these vast plains are in active discussion, and that men have ceased to regard the project as chimerical.

"This book closes the career of Leather-stocking. Pressed upon by time, he had ceased to be the hunter and the warrior, and has become a warrior of the great West. The sound of the axe has driven him from his beloved forests to seek a refuge, by a species of desperate resignation, on the denuded plains that stretch to the Rocky Mountains. Here he passes the few closing years of his life, dying as he had lived, a philosopher of the wilderness, with few of the failings, none of the vices, and all the nature and truth of his position."

887.29–30 European master] Napoleon.

888.40 ninety second] Boone went to Missouri when he was sixty-five, and died at the age of eighty-six.

894.16 the Pawnee Loups] The Skidi Pawnees of the Loup Fork of the Platte River were the most important and most fiercely independent group among the Pawnee tribes occupying what is now eastern Nebraska. Their relations with the Grand Pawnees were hostile and the latter did not regard the Skidi Pawnees as part of their nation.

957.26 *fortiter in re*] Literally, with firmness in action.

972.33–34 accursed Huron"] See Chapter XXXII of *The Last of the Mohicans*.

983.21 chevaux de frieze] A barrier of sharpened wooden stakes, used as a defense against cavalry attack.

990.22 belluae] Beasts.

993.29–31 ursus horridus . . . feræ] The scientific designation for the grizzly bear is *ursus horridus*; "canis latrans" is Doctor Bat's coinage for "barking dog"; and "genus feræ" is simply "genus wild."

994.8 phalangacrura] Literally, phalanx-legged.

1009.28 Lewis] Captain Meriwether Lewis (1774–1809) and Lt. William Clark (1770–1838), leading a company of some forty soldiers and civilians, set out in March 1804 with a commission from President Jefferson to explore a northern route to the Pacific. The expedition spent months ascending the Missouri; in 1805, when the action of *The Prairie* occurs, they were still on the east side of the Rockies.

1017.1–2 I am neither . . . Obed] Obed was the father of Jesse, who was the father of David. One of David's sons was Absalom, another was Solomon, who was the grandfather of Asa.

1020.3–4 *orders* . . . feræ] That is, flocks or herds, beasts, and wild animals.

1062.26 felo de se] Literally, a felon on himself; a suicide.

1073.20 the Kentucky hunters] Probably "Hunters of Kentucky," words by Samuel Woodworth and music credited to William Blondell, celebrating the victory of the Kentuckians at the Battle of New Orleans. Woodworth possibly was reworking a traditional song about the Kentucky riflemen; his version was extremely popular and became a campaign song for Andrew Jackson.

1089.1–2 Alston or Greenough] American artists who made their reputations abroad, Washington Allston (1779–1843) as a painter of Biblical and historical scenes in England and Horatio Greenough (1805–52) as a sculptor in the neo-classical mode in Italy. The latter was a protégé of both Allston and Cooper. The novelist gave Greenough one of his earliest commissions, helped to secure others, and, in the sculptor's words, "saved me from despair after my second return to Italy."

1110.34 a companion . . . sing] David Gamut in *The Last of the Mohicans*.

1141.35–36 drove . . . island] See Chapter VI of *The Last of the Mohicans*.

1161.3–4 Columbus . . . end] At a banquet in Columbus's honor given by the Grand Cardinal of Spain, a jealous courtier asked the navigator if, in the event he had not discovered the Indies, other men might not have been equally capable of doing so. According to Washington Irving's account, in his *Life and Voyages of Columbus*, "Columbus made no immediate reply, but, taking an egg, invited the company to make it stand on one end. Everyone attempted it, but in vain, whereupon he struck it upon the table so as to break the end, and left it standing on the broken part; illustrating, in this simple manner, that when he had once shown the way to the New World, nothing was easier than to follow it."

1202.27–29 celebrated . . . Shandy.] In Chapter 11, Book III, of Laurence Sterne's *The Life and Opinions of Tristram Shandy, Gentleman* (1760–67), Dr. Slop, at the insistence of Tristram's father, reads aloud "a form of excommunication of the Church of Rome," consisting mainly of a series of curses.

1203.40–1204.1 well known . . . Pharisees] Matthew 6:5.

1231.5 Le Balafré] "The scarred one."

1246.21–28 The Lord . . . at!"] See *The Pioneers.*

1313.1 person . . . graven] Oliver Effingham, of *The Pioneers.*

LIBRARY OF CONGRESS CATALOGING IN PUBLICATION DATA

Cooper, James Fenimore, 1789–1851.
The Leatherstocking tales.

(The Library of America; 26–27)
Edited by Blake Nevius.
Contents: v.1. The pioneers, or The sources of the Susquehanna. The last of the Mohicans. The prairie.—v.2. The Pathfinder, or The inland sea. The Deerslayer, or The first war-path.
1. United States—History—Colonial period, ca. 1600–1775—Fiction. I. Nevius, Blake, 1916– II. Title: The Leatherstocking tales. III. Title: The pioneers. IV. Title: The last of the Mohicans. V. Title: The prairie. VI. Title: The Pathfinder. VII. Title: The Deerslayer. VIII. Series: The Library of America.
PS1402 1985 813'.2 84–25060
ISBN 0–940450–20–8 (v.1)
ISBN 0–940450–21–6 (v.2)

This book is set in 10 point Linotron Galliard, a face designed for photocomposition by Matthew Carter and based on the sixteenth-century face Granjon. The paper is Olin Nyalite and conforms to guidelines adopted by the Committee on Book Longevity of the Council on Library Resources. The binding material is Brillianta, a 100% rayon cloth made by Van Heek-Scholco Textielfabrieken, Holland. Composition by Haddon Craftsmen, Inc. and The Clarinda Company. Printing and binding by R. R. Donnelley & Sons Company. Designed by Bruce Campbell.